ROOK & WARD
ON
SEXUAL OFFENCES
LAW AND PRACTICE

First Supplement to the Fourth Edition

ROOK & WARD
ON
SEXUAL OFFENCES
LAW AND PRACTICE

First Supplement to the

Fourth Edition

H.H. Judge Peter Rook QC, M.A. (Cantab.),
a Judge at the old Bailey
and Robert Ward, C.B.E., M.A., LL.B. (Cantab.),
LL.M. (U.B.C.), of the Middle Temple, Barrister,
Formerly Fellow of Gonville and Caius College, Cambridge

SWEET & MAXWELL  THOMSON REUTERS

First edition   *1990 by Peter Rook and Robert Ward*
Second edition   *1997 by Peter Rook and Robert Ward*
Third edition   *2004 by Peter Rook and Robert Ward*
Fourth edition   *2010 by Peter Rook and Robert Ward*

This edition published in 2014 by
Thomson Reuters (Legal) Limited (Registered in England & Wales,
Company No 1679046. Registered Office and address for service:
100 Avenue Road, Swiss Cottage,
London NW3 3PF) trading as Sweet & Maxwell

For further information on our products and services, visit
http://www.sweetandmaxwell.co.uk

Typeset by Interactive Sciences Ltd., Gloucester
Printed and bound in Great Britain by
CPI Group (UK) Ltd, Croydon, CR0 4YY

ISBN: 978 0 414 02883 8

No natural forests were destroyed to make this product;
only farmed timber was used and replanted.

A CIP catalogue record for this book is available
from the British Library.

HOW TO USE THIS SUPPLEMENT

This is the First Supplement to the Fourth Edition of *Rook and Ward on Sexual Offences Law & Practice* and has been compiled according to the structure of the main work.

At the beginning of each chapter of this Supplement the mini table of contents from the main work has been included.

Where a heading in this table of contents has been marked with a square pointer (■), this indicates that there is material that is new to the work in the Supplement to which the reader should refer.

Within each chapter, updating information is referenced to the relevant paragraph in the main work. New paragraphs which have been introduced in this Supplement have been identified as, e.g. 25.19A. This enables references contained within these paragraphs to be identified in the tables included in this Supplement.

Foreword

By the Rt Hon. Lord Justice Fulford,
Lord Justice of Appeal

This considerably expanded version of an already first-rate guide for practitioners, academics and others who have a serious interest in this complex field could not have arrived at a more welcome time. The new Definitive Guideline from the Sentencing Council comes into force on April 1, 2014, and there has been a significant body of jurisprudence from the Court of Appeal since the last edition on a wide range of issues such as grooming, trafficking, consent, delay and abuse of process. This is a fast-moving area of the criminal law, and it is critical that there is awareness of the many developments, coupled with a real understanding of their significance. This book shines a penetrating—indeed brilliant—light on this rapidly evolving landscape.

Sexual offences threaten to dominate the work of many Crown Courts in England and Wales, and it is not unusual for between 30–50 per cent of the daily lists to be taken up by trials of this kind. This increase in sexual cases has coincided with a growing awareness that much work still needs to be done to ensure that members of the public who participate in these often difficult trials—but most particularly those who are potentially vulnerable—are treated with real sensitivity and understanding. The courts must ensure that victims and other individuals whose position may be precarious (including some defendants and jurors) are not traumatised by their involvement in these trials. For instance, a considerable amount of work has been undertaken over the last few years to ensure that there is a sea change in the approach to cross-examination, eradicating the confrontational posturing and the aggressive style of questioning that has too frequently been evident in the past. These changes to, and the new focus on, the treatment of victims and others are addressed in this book in sections as wide-ranging as anonymity, reporting restrictions and the up-to-date approach that should be taken to cross-examination.

The medical chapters also deserve particular mention. The developments in the approach to the examination of victims and the problems that have accompanied the changes to diagnostic criteria are mapped with care and lucidity. This is an area of high importance to all practitioners. However, it is invidious to highlight individual parts of a text that is comprehensive and uniformly of a very high standard.

This book, which is the fruit of great learning, has been written by two individuals who between them have a depth of knowledge and unparalleled hands-on experience which has enabled them to provide the reader with a real understanding of an area of the criminal law which has become something of a refinement of complication. It is difficult to see how anyone involved in these cases will be able to manage to discharge their function properly without this text lying somewhere close at hand. I commend it without reservation.

Preface to Supplement to the Fourth Edition

In light of the wide range of significant developments affecting the prosecution of sex cases since our fourth edition was published in December 2010, this Supplement represents a comprehensive update of virtually all the chapters in that edition, including the medical and DNA chapters. It follows that this Supplement does not confine itself to the significant changes in substantive law, but also covers the many evidential, procedural and medical developments.

We wish to put these developments in context. Those more familiar with the criminal justice system even as recently as half a generation ago would be struck today by the seismic changes that have taken place in the nature of the cases brought before the criminal courts, with far more sex case prosecutions being brought and coming to trial. An analysis by Professor Cheryl Thomas of jury verdicts in all cases between 2006 and 2008 found that sexual offences made up 17 per cent of all charges against all defendants and amounted to the single largest proportion of jury verdicts (31 per cent).[1] The pace of change has not slackened during the last five years.

This may not indicate an increase in the nature and scale of sexual offending, except where modern technology is involved; rather, it is the product of a much greater understanding of sexual abuse and greater disclosure. We have addressed this greater awareness in this Supplement.

By way of example, it would have been difficult to live in the United Kingdom during the last two years without appreciating the discovery of new phenomena in respect of sexual offending.

First, there have been revelations of abuse carried out many years ago by a wide range of celebrities and others in positions of authority. Many of these cases carry with them the possibility of collusive conduct by those who must have been aware of what was happening, and the certainty that the families of at least some of those who had been abused felt powerless take matters further at the time. We cover this in our discussion in Ch.26 of the issues that arise in historic sex cases.

Secondly, there have been high profile cases involving the sexual exploitation of vulnerable girls by gangs in various cities. On occasions these cases have not reflected well on the police and social services at the time, who failed to react adequately to powerful indications of abuse. It is clear from these cases that the authorities now have a better understanding that highly sexualised behaviour by young girls may be an indication that they are in the process of being groomed and abused. In Ch.1 we deal with the issue of consent in the context of grooming.

Quite apart from these examples of the changing landscape, a number of high profile cases have led to the way the criminal justice system treats vulnerable witnesses being subjected to public scrutiny.

[1] Professor Cheryl Thomas, *Are juries fair?* Ministry of Justice Research series 1/10, p.28, available at *http://www.justice.gov.uk/downloads/publications/research-and-analysis/moj-research/are-juries-fair-research.pdf* [accessed December 31, 2013].

These developments underline the paramount need for those within the criminal justice system who deal with sex cases to keep abreast of all significant developments in this sensitive and complex area. In cases of this sort, particularly where there may be highly vulnerable witnesses and significant evidential problems, a general knowledge of the criminal law is wholly insufficient. We welcome the recognition of this by the senior judiciary and the Crown Prosecution Service. We also commend the excellent work undertaken by the Criminal Bar Association and others in the training DVD *A Question of Practice* (discussed in Ch.18). We would welcome an across-the-board accreditation system for all those who practice in this area.

Sexual offences – the new Definitive Guideline

The greater awareness of sexual offending extends to an increased understanding of the impact of abuse upon victims. It is against this background that the Sentencing Council has conducted a timely review of the *Sexual Offences Act 2003: Definitive Guideline*, which had been in place since April 2007 and which, following a thorough consultation process, the Council has replaced with a new guideline.

The new *Definitive Guideline* is to be welcomed. It is important that sentencing guidelines adapt to long term changes associated with the particular criminal behaviour to which they relate. This is particularly so in relation to the sensitive and complex area of sexual offending. The long, but wholly justified, gestation period whilst important research was undertaken has helped achieve a guideline which addresses core aspects of harm and culpability whilst being sufficiently flexible to accommodate future developments and increased understanding.

From April 1, 2014, the new guideline will apply to all sentencing of adult sex offenders, whenever the offences were committed. The old guideline applies to cases sentenced up until then.[2] The new guideline will apply to historic cases following the guidance given by the then Lord Chief Justice in *R. v H (J).*[3]

The timing of the publication has enabled us not only to include the new guideline in this Supplement, but also to provide an analysis and identify where there is a change in approach. In Ch.1 we explain the structure of the new guideline. We have also included the relevant parts of the guideline in the chapters dealing with specific offences. In Ch.27, where we deal with all changes to the sentencing regime, including the demise of imprisonment for public protection and the new extended sentence, we have undertaken an analysis of the significant changes introduced by the new guideline.

Underpinning the guideline is a greater awareness of the long-term harmful effects of sexual violence and abuse, particularly the long-term psychological impact on the lives of the victims and their families.

---

[2] *Boakye and others* [2012] EWCA Crim 838.
[3] [2012] EWCA Crim 2753. The guidance is summarised in Annex B to the guideline, which is reproduced in full in Appendix A to this Supplement.

The Council has adopted the decision-making process for sentencing that it developed for the *Assault: Definitive Guideline*. It is a step-by-step process with nine steps to be followed for each offence. An emphasis is placed on harm and culpability, and the structure for determining these varies according to the offence concerned so that the guideline is tailored to the particular offending behaviour.

The new guideline focuses on the extent of the harm to the victim rather than on the nature of the particular physical activity. It uses a number of models for addressing harm and culpability, each different from the model used in the previous guideline. The model used for the majority of offences, including rape and sexual assault, has a lowest level (a baseline) where inherent harm and culpability are assumed. One or more from an exhaustive list of factors can move the offence to a higher category of harm or culpability with a higher starting point. Factors raising harm and culpability have in certain instances been revised. For instance, the term "abuse of trust" is used rather than the previous "abuse of position of trust" as it is capable of applying even where the offender is not in a formal position of responsibility towards the victim.

Significantly, the new guideline moves away from the language of "ostensible consent" so that the focus in relation to children aged between 13 and 15 is placed not on the behaviour of the victim but on the behaviour and culpability of the offender. Accordingly, harm is determined by the nature of the sexual activity involved, so avoiding the need to consider the child's behaviour or their understanding of their "relationship" with the offender. The guideline places more emphasis on how the offender has persuaded the child to engage in the activity and obtain their apparent consent. Following on from the consideration given to "remote offending" in *Prince*,[4] the guideline confirms that the approach to sentencing and the starting points and ranges apply equally where the offender commits the offence remotely over the internet.

The new guideline contains some important guidance on the weight that should be attributed to good character, including how the use of previous good character/exemplary conduct, including celebrity status,[5] to facilitate an offence may constitute an aggravating factor.

We have been greatly assisted by Tim Moloney QC with his work on the sentencing chapters. We wish to thank William Hotham for his valuable work on notification orders in Ch.28. We are delighted that HH Judge Martin Picton, the current Course Director of the Judicial College's seminar on serious sexual offences, has joined our writing team. In the light of important new case law on the drafting of Sexual Offences Prevention Orders (SOPOs), HH Judge Picton has completely revised Ch.29. His lucid treatment of the subject is very welcome in the light of the drafting difficulties these orders can cause, as illustrated by the number of times the Court of Appeal has had to consider them even after the helpful guidance provided in *Smith*.[6] As HH Judge Picton explains, while the

---

[4] [2013] EWCA Crim 1768.
[5] See *Att Gen's Ref (No.38 of 2013) (R. v Stuart Hall)* [2013] EWCA Crim 1450.
[6] [2011] EWCA Crim 1772.

Anti-Social Behaviour, Crime and Policy Bill is expected shortly to combine SOPOs and Foreign Travel Orders into Sexual Harm Prevention Orders (SHPOs), this is unlikely materially to affect the case law.

Non-consensual offences

The new guideline is only one reason why a supplement to our fourth edition was necessary, if not overdue. We have also undertaken a close examination of important case law since that edition was published in December 2010 in which the courts have (i) given a wide interpretation to the definition of consent in s.74 of the Sexual Offences Act 2003,[7] (ii) stressed the all-importance of context when the issue of consent is considered, and (iii) illuminated how evidence of grooming may be relevant to consent.[8]

Furthermore, in *Assange v Swedish Prosecution Authority*,[9] the Divisional Court, when ruling upon an extradition request, has clarified that deceptions falling short of deceptions falling within s.76 of the 2003 Act may entitle a jury to conclude there was no genuine consent. In addition the Court of Appeal has taken a restrictive view of s.76,[10] illustrated the operation of the s.75 evidential presumptions[11] and shed further light on the extent to which a defendant's mental disorder may be relevant to whether he had a reasonable belief that the complainant was consenting.[12]

Other sexual offences

We have sought to explain all significant developments in the law relating to other sexual offences, including those relating to indecent images of children. These developments have included further guidance from the Court of Appeal as to the framing of indictments which relate to numerous incidents extending over a long period in order to ensure that the indictment properly reflects the offending;[13] and the need to avoid duplicity when an offence is defined to include alternative elements such as causing or inciting.[14] We have also given detailed consideration to the development of the law in respect of the application of art.26 of the Council of Europe Trafficking Convention to the prosecution of those who may themselves have been the victims of trafficking. The culpability of any victim of trafficking may be significantly diminished, and in some cases effectively extinguished, not merely because of age but also because there was no realistic alternative available to the exploited victim.[15] We are grateful to Peter Carter QC of Red Lion Chambers for his comments on Ch.10.

---

[7] *Assange v Swedish Prosecution Authority* [2011] EWHC 2489 (Admin); *R(F) v DPP* [2013] EWHC 945 (admin); *Justine McNally v The Queen* [2013] EWCA Crim 1051.
[8] *C v R* [2012] EWCA Crim 2034; *Robinson* [2011] EWCA Crim 916.
[9] Above, fn.8.
[10] *R. v B* [2013] EWCA Crim 823.
[11] *Ciccarelli* [2011] EWCA Crim 2665.
[12] *B v The Queen* [2013] EWCA Crim 3.
[13] *Hartley* [2011] EWCA Crim 1299.
[14] *Grout* [2011] EWCA Crim 299.
[15] *L and others v R.* [2013] EWCA Crim 991; *R. v N and Le* [2012] EWCA Crim 189.

Evidence

Difficult evidential issues often arise in sex cases. As more cases reach the Court of Appeal, there have been many decisions illustrating the operation of the provisions on bad character, hearsay and previous sexual history (s.41 of the Youth Justice and Criminal Evidence Act 1999). Two judgments of Hughes L.J. (as he then was) are of particular importance. First, *R. v D, P and U*[16] provides valuable guidance as to the approach to be taken in determining the admissibility under gateway (d)[17] of bad character evidence in the form of the possession of indecent photographs where a defendant is charged with a contact offence. Secondly, *Riat*[18] is in our view required reading not only because of its clear exposition of the statutory framework governing hearsay evidence, but also because it provides three instructive examples of the application of the law in sex cases.

An examination of recent Court of Appeal judgments makes clear to us that issues of cross-admissibility are sometimes not properly addressed by counsel and the judge in advance speeches. This has led to some strong comment, including expressions of surprise and disappointment from the Court of Appeal: see in particular Chs 16.75 and 16.76A.

Inevitably, issues concerning the posting of entries upon social networking sites have been considered by the Court of Appeal, which has held that a sexual entry may constitute sexual behaviour that engages s.41 of the YJCEA 1999.[19]

We would like to thank David Claxton of Red Lion Chambers for his excellent work updating our chapter on expert evidence (Ch.20).

Reporting restrictions in sex cases

We explain in Ch.17 the important new case law on reporting restrictions.[20] These include the clarification of the limits of the complainant anonymity provisions: although judges may express concern as to the consequences of the publication of material, and give guidance as to the application of the provisions, ultimately it is the responsibility of reporters and editors not to publish material that might lead to the identification of the complainant.

Vulnerable witnesses

We are very grateful to Alexandra Ward who, in updating Ch.18, not only sets out all significant developments in an area where the criminal justice system is under scrutiny, but also includes useful guidance and Court of Appeal authority of the last three years which is designed to assist practitioners to develop appropriate and necessary skills when questioning vulnerable witnesses.

---

[16] [2011] EWCA Crim 1474.
[17] Criminal Justice Act 2003, s.101(1)(d).
[18] [2012] EWCA 1509.
[19] *Ben-Rejab* [2011] EWCA Crim 1136; *R. v D* [2011] EWCA Crim 2305.
[20] *R. (Press Association) v Cambridge Crown Court* [2012] EWCA Crim 2434.

Historic cases

Today, sex case prosecutions relating to events that occurred many years ago are more common than ever before. Indeed, developments in the context of the prosecution of historic cases would in themselves have justified a Supplement. In the wake of high profile police investigations such as Operation Yewtree, we analyse these important developments in Ch.26. In doing so we give close consideration to highly significant Court of Appeal decisions which, against the background of contradictory guidance, have finally clarified the approach to be taken to applications for a stay due to delay[21] and to the sentencing of historic cases.[22]

Medical chapters

We are grateful to our three medical contributors for covering the developments of the last three years in their particular chapters. Dr Fiona Mason, Consultant Forensic Psychiatrist at St Andrews, Northampton, has updated her pioneering work on the psychological impact of the trauma of sexual assault upon victims (Ch.23), whilst Dr Beata Cybulska, the Clinical Director of "The Bridge" Sexual Assault Referral Centre, University Hospitals Foundation Trust, Bristol and Dr Catherine White OBE, Clinical Director of the Sexual Assault Referral Centre, St. Mary's Hospital, Manchester, chart with their customary lucidity developments in respect of the medical examination of adult victims (Ch.21) and child victims (Ch.22) respectively. Dr White also refers to cases in which the Court of Appeal has allowed appeals against conviction where fresh evidence relating to changes in diagnostic criteria for child sexual abuse meant that the convictions could not be regarded as safe.[23]

Other important developments

We are fortunate to have a number of other very valuable contributions.

HH Judge Johannah Cutts QC, now the Resident judge at Reading Crown Court, has found time to cover all significant developments in respect of disclosure, including the recently published *Protocol and Good Practice Model: Disclosure of information in cases of alleged child abuse and linked criminal and care directions hearings* which represents an overdue grant of a long standing wish.

Gillian Jones and Naomi Parsons, both of Red Lion Chambers, have ensured that coverage of issues particular to the trial of sex cases in the youth courts are brought up-to-date.

Similarly, HH Judge David McFarland, the Recorder of Belfast, has provided his expertise in respect of developments in Northern Ireland (Ch.32).

We welcome the lucid contribution of Victoria Oakes in updating Graham Cooke's much admired chapter on *DNA, Law and Statistics* (Ch.24). We wish to

---

[21] *R. v F (S)* [2011] EWCA Crim 1844.
[22] *R. v H (J)* [2012] EWCA Crim 2753.
[23] *S, B, C & R v R.* [2012] EWCA Crim 1433.

express our enormous gratitude to Graham Cooke for his work in our previous editions.

All chapters have been updated with the exception of Dr Ruth Mann's relating to the assessment and treatment of sex offenders after sentencing (Ch.30).

We would like to give special thanks to Professor David Ormerod QC, Law Commissioner, who was always ready to discuss, assist and shed light should a particular legal problem arise. William Hotham played several important roles: as well as providing valuable drafting input on notification (Ch.28) and the mentally disordered (Ch.6) and assembling the appendices, he was always available to undertake any necessary research.

HH Judge Peter Rook QC,   Robert Ward CBE,
The Old Bailey   *Cambridge*

January 26, 2014

CONTENTS

TABLE OF CASES

TABLE OF STATUTES

xli

clarified that deceptions falling short of s.76 deceptions may entitle a jury to conclude that there was no genuine consent.[2]

However, in contrast to the width of s.74, cases continue to show that s.75 evidential presumptions hardly ever arise,[3] although a case has at last come before the Court of Appeal in which the trial judge was held to have been right to hold that s.75 applied.[4] The Court of Appeal, recognising that the provisions on deception in s.76 effectively extend the definition of rape, has again taken a restrictive view when interpreting that section.[5]

The Court of Appeal has also, to some extent, clarified the extent to which a defendant's mental disorder may be relevant to whether he had a reasonable belief that the complainant was consenting.[6]

There has been significant change to the sentencing regime. The Sentencing Council has conducted a timely review of the *Sexual Offences Act 2003: Definitive Guideline*, which had been in place since April 30, 2007, and has replaced it with a new guideline. This guideline represents a new approach to sentencing in sexual cases in that it places particular emphasis on the harm caused to the victim. It sets out a step-by-step decision-making process along the lines of the Council's *Assault: Definitive Guideline*.

As for the sentencing of offenders who are "dangerous" within the meaning of the Criminal Justice Act 2003 ("CJA 2003"), the demise of the sentence of imprisonment for public protection ("IPP") brought about by the Legal Aid, Sentencing and Punishment of Offenders Act 2012 has limited the options of a court concerned to protect the public to discretionary life imprisonment,[7] the new extended sentence or a determinate sentence accompanied by appropriate ancillary orders. These sentences are considered below.

SENTENCING

Definitive Guideline

1.20   Following a thorough consultation process,[8] the Sentencing Council has issued a new Definitive Guideline in accordance with the Coroners and Justice Act 2009 ("2009 Act"). The content of the new guideline is set out in the relevant chapters of this Supplement (with the guideline reproduced in Appendix A). It applies to offenders aged 18 and older sentenced on or after April 1, 2014.[9] Section 125(1) of the 2009 Act provides that when sentencing offences committed on or after April 6, 2010:

"Every court—

---

[2] *Assange v Swedish Prosecution Authority* [2011] EWHC 2489 (Admin); *R. (F) v DPP* [2013] EWHC 945 (Admin); *Justine McNally v The Queen* [2013] EWCA Crim 1051.

[3] *Kapezi* [2013] EWCA Crim 560; *Lewis Mba* [2012] EWCA Crim 2773.

[4] *Ciccarelli* [2011] EWCA Crim 2665.

[5] *R. v B* [2013] EWCA Crim 823.

[6] *B v The Queen* [2013] EWCA Crim 3.

[7] For explanation of the effect of the Legal Aid, Sentencing and Punishment of Offenders Act 2012 on sentencing options, see *Red Saunders and others v R.* [2013] EWCA Crim 1027, discussed in para.1.42C, below.

[8] *Sexual Offences Guideline Consultation*, December 2012.

[9] Although the new guideline was published in December 2013, the previous guideline (published on April 30, 2007) continues to apply to all sexual offences sentenced before April 1, 2014: cf. *Boakye and others* [2012] EWCA Crim 838. From that date the new guideline applies to all such offences, whenever committed. In respect of historic cases, sentence will be imposed at the date of the sentencing hearing on the basis of the legislative provisions then current, and by measured reference to the new sentencing guidelines: see *H(J)* [2011] EWCA Crim 2753, and para.26.72, below.

CHAPTER 1

RAPE

INTRODUCTION

The Court of Appeal has now had an opportunity to consider all of the key definitions in the Sexual Offences Act 2003, following the Act's commencement on May 1, 2004. Many of the key decisions had been reported before publication of the fourth edition of this work (the "main work") in December 2010 and so were included in that edition. However, the last three years have seen important case law giving a wide interpretation to the definition of consent in s.74 of the Act. The decisions have underlined that context is all-important, illuminated how evidence of "grooming" may be relevant to the issue of consent,[1] and

1.01

---

[1] *C v R.* [2012] EWCA Crim 2034; *Robinson* [2011] EWCA Crim 916.

TABLE OF STATUTORY INSTRUMENTS

(a) must, in sentencing an offender, follow any sentencing guideline which is relevant to the offender's case, and

(b) must, in exercising any other function relating to the sentencing of offenders, follow any sentencing guidelines which are relevant to the exercise of the function,

unless the court is satisfied that it would be contrary to the interests of justice to do so."[10]

The Council felt that the time had been reached for a review of the existing guideline issued by the Sentencing Guidelines Council in 2007. It was over eight years since the commencement of the 2003 Act[11] and the Council considered that the guideline required amendment to reflect developments since then. In particular, a clearer picture was available of the way in which the offences under the Act are being used by the courts. In addition, there were areas where the nature of offending had changed, e.g. the increased use of technology to facilitate the sexual exploitation and grooming of children, and there was also better understanding of offenders' behaviour when targeting children. Furthermore, the Council was conscious of the need for judges and magistrates involved in this complex area of sentencing to have relevant and up-to-date guidance against the background of an increased volume of cases coming before the courts.[12]

In its consultation the Council sought views on (i) the main factors that reflect harm caused to the victim by an offence and the culpability of the offender, which lead the court to decide the starting-point sentence for the offence, (ii) the additional factors that should influence sentence, and (iii) the approach and structure of the guidance and how this should be tailored to different offences.

A key issue to emerge from research commissioned by the Council was a strong desire on the part of victims for the criminal justice system, and in particular the sentencing process, to demonstrate an accurate understanding of the overarching and long-term harmful effects of sexual violence and abuse, and how this impacts on the life of the victim and their family.[13]

---

[10] See the commentary to *Karam (Mawawe Ibrahim)* [2013] Crim. L.R. 12, 998-1000, for a criticism by the late Dr David Thomas QC of the Court of Appeal's failure to have regard to s.125(3) of the Act, which qualifies the obligation to "follow" the guidelines and makes it clear that the obligation relates to offence range rather than category range. Dr Thomas argues that "the effect of s.125(3) when read as a whole is to preserve the critical discretion of the judge to achieve a just sentence, based upon the detailed facts of the case rather than the increasingly mechanistic application of quasi-statutory guidelines". We disagree. Judges should ordinarily sentence within the category range they have identified. The guidelines which are designed to promote consistency pursuant to s.120(11) reflect s.125(3) by expressly providing in step 2 the power to move outside the category range where there are powerful aggravating or mitigating factors.

[11] May 1, 2004.

[12] A total of 6,932 people were sentenced for sexual offences in 2011. This includes 1,468 people sentenced for offences concerning indecent images of children which, whilst not covered under the 2003 Act, are covered by the new Definitive Guideline. See the Joint Statistical Bulletin published by the Ministry of Justice, the Home Office and the Office of National Statistics, *An Overview of Sexual Offending in England and Wales*, January 10, 2013, which is available at *https://www.gov.uk/government/publications/an-overview-of-sexual-offending-in-england-and-wales* [accessed December 31, 2013].

[13] See *Sexual Offences Guideline Consultation*, Section Two, p.10.

The structure of the new Definitive Guideline: The nine steps

1.20A   The Council has adopted the decision-making process for sentencing that it developed for *Assault: Definitive Guideline*. It is a step-by-step process with nine steps to be followed for each offence. An emphasis is placed on harm and culpability, and the structure for determining these varies according to the offence concerned so that the guideline is tailored to the particular offending behaviour. The nine steps are:

STEP ONE: Determining the offence category based on the principal factual elements of the case which demonstrate the harm caused, or likely to be caused, and the culpability of the offender in carrying out the offence. The offence category reflects the severity of the offence and sets out the starting point and range of sentences within which the offender is sentenced. A case of particular gravity, reflected by multiple features of culpability or harm in step one, could merit upward adjustment from the starting point before further adjustment for aggravating or mitigating features.

STEP TWO: Determining a provisional sentence using the recommended starting-point. Based on the offence category identified at step one, the court should then consider the weight to be given to any relevant aggravating and mitigating factors in order to move upwards and downwards from the starting point. Starting points apply to all offenders in all cases irrespective of plea or previous convictions. Where an offender has recent and/or relevant previous convictions these must be treated as an aggravating factor. Previous good character/exemplary conduct is different from having no previous convictions. The more serious the offence, the less weight should normally be attributed to this factor. Where previous good character/exemplary conduct has been used to facilitate the offence, this mitigation should not normally be allowed and such conduct may constitute an aggravating factor.

STEP THREE   The court should consider whether there are any factors which indicate a reduction in sentence, such as assistance to the prosecution. The court should take into account ss.73 and 74 of the Serious Organised Crime and Police Act 2005 (assistance by defendants: reduction or review of sentence) and any other rule of law by virtue of which an offender may receive a discounted sentence in consequence of assistance given (or offered) to the prosecutor or investigator.

STEP FOUR: Reduction for guilty pleas. The court should take account of any potential reduction for a guilty plea in accordance with s.144 of the Criminal Justice Act 2003 and the Guilty Plea guideline.

STEP FIVE: Dangerousness. The court should consider whether, having regard to the criteria contained in Ch.5 of Pt 12 of the Criminal Justice Act 2003, it would be appropriate to award a life sentence (s.224A or s.225 of that Act) or an extended sentence (s.226A). When sentencing offenders to a life sentence under these provisions, the notional determinate sentence should be used as the basis for the setting of a minimum term.

STEP SIX: Totality principle. If sentencing an offender for more than one offence, or where the offender is already serving a sentence, consider whether the total sentence is just and proportionate to the offending behaviour.

STEP SEVEN: Ancillary orders. The court must also consider what other requirements or provisions may automatically apply.

STEP EIGHT: Reasons. Section 174 of the Criminal Justice Act 2003 imposes a duty to give reasons for, and explain the effect of, the sentence.

STEP NINE: Consideration of time spent on bail. The court must consider whether to give credit for time spent on bail in accordance with s.240A of the Criminal Justice Act 2003.

STEP ONE

Category of offence—Harm

The new guideline's approach to determining the offence category directs the **1.20B** sentencing court, as a first step, to consider the main factual elements of the offence in terms of the harm to the victim. This approach differs from the SGC's Definitive Guideline in that gravity is not to be evaluated by considering just the physical nature of the offence. The Sentencing Council was concerned that simply labelling sentence levels in terms of the activity concerned does not fully reflect the seriousness or complexity of the offence. The guideline recognises that all rape is extremely harmful to the victim by assuming there is *always* a baseline of harm. This is reflected in offence category 3, which covers offences in which harm factors identified in categories 1 or 2 are not present. This is designed to indicate to the sentencer that once an offender has been found guilty of rape, they do not need to identify additional factors for the offence to be deemed harmful or serious. The Council felt that the violation of the victim through the act of rape is harm

• **Prolonged detention/sustained incident**

The Council has separated prolonged detention from abduction in recognition that it is a different and distinct factor. This factor reflects the fact that a prolonged or sustained incident may increase the psychological harm to the victim where there is a fear of escalation and the psychological trauma of not knowing when and if they may escape from the offender. The feature in the SGC guideline of repeated rape in the course of one attack is not included. It follows that where there is vaginal and anal rape in the course of one attack, this should in the Council's view be treated as two offences of rape.

• **Violence or threats of violence (beyond that which is inherent in the offence)**

This reflects the fact that not all rapes are accompanied by violence and that fear of violence can be as harmful as violence itself.

• **Forced/uninvited entry into victim's home**

This factor covers not only an offender who breaks into the victim's home, but also an ex-partner who enters the victim's home uninvited. In addition at step two the Council have retained the location of the offence as an aggravating factor, so that if the sentencer feels that the damage to the victim is increased by virtue of the fact it occurred in their home, this can be taken into account as that stage.

• **Victim is particularly vulnerable due to personal circumstances**

This factor elevates to category 2 a rape committed against someone who had been subject to habitual sexual abuse and is also broad enough to include many other factors relating to the victim's personal circumstances that make them particularly vulnerable, for example, a background of emotional or physical abuse or vulnerability through age or disability.

Culpability

1.20C   Having identified the offence category as set out above, the court should then determine whether any culpability A factors are present in order to ascertain the sentencing starting point. The Council took the view that the use of "lower culpability" would not be appropriate in a rape case as an offender who carries out a rape necessarily demonstrates a high degree of culpability. The Council therefore listed factors which may take the rape beyond the culpability inherent in the act of rape itself. The culpability factors in relation to rape are as follows:

STEP FOUR:

sequence of assistance given (or offered) to the prosecutor or investigator.

Reduction for guilty pleas. The court should take account of any potential reduction for a guilty plea in accordance with s.144 of the Criminal Justice Act 2003 and the Guilty Plea guideline.

STEP FIVE:

Dangerousness. The court should consider whether, having regard to the criteria contained in Ch.5 of Pt 12 of the Criminal Justice Act 2003, it would be appropriate to award a life sentence (s.224A or s.225 of that Act) or an extended sentence (s.226A). When sentencing offenders to a life sentence under these provisions, the notional determinate sentence should be used as the basis for the setting of a minimum term.

STEP SIX:

Totality principle. If sentencing an offender for more than one offence, or where the offender is already serving a sentence, consider whether the total sentence is just and proportionate to the offending behaviour.

STEP SEVEN:

Ancillary orders. The court must also consider what other requirements or provisions may automatically apply.

STEP EIGHT:

Reasons. Section 174 of the Criminal Justice Act 2003 imposes a duty to give reasons for, and explain the effect of, the sentence.

STEP NINE:

Consideration of time spent on bail. The court must consider whether to give credit for time spent on bail in accordance with s.240A of the Criminal Justice Act 2003.

STEP ONE

Category of offence—Harm

The new guideline's approach to determining the offence category directs the   1.20B
sentencing court, as a first step, to consider the main factual elements of the
offence in terms of the harm to the victim. This approach differs from the SGC's
Definitive Guideline in that gravity is not to be evaluated by considering just the
physical nature of the offence. The Sentencing Council was concerned that simply
labelling sentence levels in terms of the activity concerned does not fully reflect
the seriousness or complexity of the offence. The guideline recognises that all rape
is extremely harmful to the victim by assuming there is *always* a baseline of harm.
This is reflected in offence category 3, which covers offences in which harm
factors identified in categories 1 or 2 are not present. This is designed to indicate
to the sentencer that once an offender has been found guilty of rape, they do not
need to identify additional factors for the offence to be deemed harmful or serious.
The Council felt that the violation of the victim through the act of rape is harm

in itself and that it would be unhelpful to articulate this as "lesser harm" as these offences are inherently harmful. However, the Council recognised that the level of harm caused by rape can vary and categories 1 and 2 build upon the baseline of harm assumed in category 3. The offence categories for rape specified in the guideline are as follows:

Harm	
Category 1	• The extreme nature of one or more category 2 factors or the extreme impact caused by a combination of category 2 factors **may** elevate to category 1
Category 2	• Severe psychological or physical harm • Pregnancy or STI as a consequence of offence • Additional degradation/humiliation • Abduction • Prolonged detention/sustained incident • Violence or threats of violence (beyond that which is inherent in the offence) • Forced/uninvited entry into victim's home • Victim is particularly vulnerable due to personal circumstances* *for children under 13 please refer to the guideline on page 27 of the Definitive Guideline
Category 3	Factor(s) in categories 1 and 2 not present

Category 1

The new guideline adopts a different approach from the previous SGC guideline, which placed repeated rape of the same victim over a course of time *or* rape involving multiple victims in the category with the highest starting sentence. The Sentencing Council took the view that the guideline is concerned with sentence levels for a single offence. If there are multiple rapes or victims, these should be charged as separate instances of rape with the overall sentence subject to the principle of totality.

• The extreme nature of one or more category 2 factors may elevate to category 1

In contrast with other guidelines issued by the Council, category 1 does not rely on new factors to increase the severity of sentence but instead permits a combination of category 2 factors to elevate a case. The Council believes that many of the factors set out in category 2, when combined, will increase the psychological and/or physical harm to the victim. This approach relies on the sentencer, in full possession of all the facts of the case, being best placed to determine when either the extreme nature of a factor, or a combination of the factors in category 2, justifies the elevation of the case to category 1.

Category 2

● **Severe psychological or physical harm**

The Council was sensitive to the fact that individuals will have different psychological responses and that assumptions should not be made about the severity of rape based solely upon the resilience or lack of resilience of a victim.[14] It therefore included severe psychological harm in the consultation draft guideline as an aggravating factor at step two. Some respondents to the consultation argued that where there is either severe psychological or physical harm this should be reflected at step one. The Council did not wish to propagate the myth that a lack of physical harm makes rape less serious and so in the published guideline it moved severe psychological harm to step one, to allow sentencers to reflect the severe nature of the harm in selecting the offence category.

● **Pregnancy or STI as a consequence of offence**

The Council treats these as principal factual elements which, where present, may exacerbate still further the long-term harm experienced by the victim. It has not kept the specific reference in the SGC's guideline to "ejaculation" on the basis that harm to the victim occurs at the point penetration takes place, whether or not the offender subsequently ejaculates. However, "ejaculation" is included as an aggravating factor at step two, enabling the starting point to be increased where this has occurred. This does not mean mitigation is available if there is an absence of ejaculation. In order to deal with any concerns about double counting where "STI/pregnancy as a consequence" is present at step one, the step two factor is worded as: "ejaculation (where not taken into account at step one)".

● **Additional degradation/humiliation**

This factor relates to cases where the offender has subjected the victim to further acts of degradation and humiliation not inherent in all rape cases. Examples given are: urinating or ejaculating over the victim, leaving the victim naked in a public place, or forcing the victim to dress up or strip for the offender.

● **Abduction**

This factor reflects the increased psychological harm that being detained or abducted would have on the victim. It includes preventing the victim from leaving their home during an attack.

---

[14] In this respect the Council cite Dr Fiona Mason in *Psychological effects of rape and serious sexual assault*, Ch.23 in the main work.

• Prolonged detention/sustained incident

The Council has separated prolonged detention from abduction in recognition that it is a different and distinct factor. This factor reflects the fact that a prolonged or sustained incident may increase the psychological harm to the victim where there is a fear of escalation and the psychological trauma of not knowing when and if they may escape from the offender. The feature in the SGC guideline of repeated rape in the course of one attack is not included. It follows that where there is vaginal and anal rape in the course of one attack, this should in the Council's view be treated as two offences of rape.

• Violence or threats of violence (beyond that which is inherent in the offence)

This reflects the fact that not all rapes are accompanied by violence and that fear of violence can be as harmful as violence itself.

• Forced/uninvited entry into victim's home

This factor covers not only an offender who breaks into the victim's home, but also an ex-partner who enters the victim's home uninvited. In addition at step two the Council have retained the location of the offence as an aggravating factor, so that if the sentencer feels that the damage to the victim is increased by virtue of the fact it occurred in their home, this can be taken into account as that stage.

• Victim is particularly vulnerable due to personal circumstances

This factor elevates to category 2 a rape committed against someone who had been subject to habitual sexual abuse and is also broad enough to include many other factors relating to the victim's personal circumstances that make them particularly vulnerable, for example, a background of emotional or physical abuse or vulnerability through age or disability.

Culpability

1.20C Having identified the offence category as set out above, the court should then determine whether any culpability A factors are present in order to ascertain the sentencing starting point. The Council took the view that the use of "lower culpability" would not be appropriate in a rape case as an offender who carries out a rape necessarily demonstrates a high degree of culpability. The Council therefore listed factors which may take the rape beyond the culpability inherent in the act of rape itself. The culpability factors in relation to rape are as follows:

Culpability
A
• Significant degree of planning • Offender acts together with others to commit the offence • Use of alcohol/drugs on victim to facilitate the offence • Abuse of trust • Previous violence against victim • Offence committed in course of burglary • Recording of the offence • Commercial exploitation and/or motivation • Offence racially or religiously aggravated • Offence motivated by, or demonstrating, hostility to the victim based on his or her sexual orientation (or presumed sexual orientation) or transgender identity (or presumed transgender identity) • Offence motivated by, or demonstrating, hostility to the victim based on his or her disability (or presumed disability)
B
Factor(s) in category A not present

Culpability A

• Significant degree of planning

Research showed that the public saw this factor as increasing the culpability of the offender. The SGC guideline states that the planning of an offence indicates a higher level of culpability than an opportunistic or impulsive offence.

• Offender acts together with others to commit the offence

This area is the subject of recent and continuing research, especially in relation to the exploitation of children, particularly young teenagers, by groups. There were a number of high profile cases of this type in 2012 and 2013. The Sentencing Council cites the emerging findings of the Children's Commissioner for England[15]:

> " . . . that children are being victimised through gang and group associated sexual exploitation from the age of 10 upwards, and are both female and male (although predominantly female). They come from a full range of ethnic backgrounds represented in England, and some are disabled. The abuse is taking place across England in urban, rural and metropolitan areas. Children are being sexually

---

[15] *Emerging findings from the inquiry into gangs and groups* (Children's Commissioner, July 2012).

exploited by groups and gangs made up of people who are both the same, and different, ages, ethnicities and social backgrounds from those that characterise them as victims."

Committing rape as a member of a group of course raises culpability not only in relation to child victims. The factor in essence identifies situations where two or more offenders act together, irrespective of the nature or formal structure of the grouping. It has also been included in other guidelines, e.g. dealing with assault, and reflects the enhanced fear and intimidation created by the presence of more than one offender.

● **Use of alcohol/drugs on the victim to facilitate the offence**

This factor reflects the increased culpability of someone who, in a common scenario, deliberately gets a victim drunk, stupefied or intoxicated, or administers some form of drug in order to render them incapable of consenting to sexual activity. This reflects an element of deliberation and planning which is always an aggravating feature. For a recent example of an Attorney General's Reference in respect of sentence for the rape of two women where the offender used alcohol to render his victims unconscious, see *R. v M(H)*.[16]

● **Abuse of trust**

An offender's culpability is increased if they are in a position of responsibility towards the victim.[17] However, the term "abuse of trust" is wider than "abuse of position of trust", and includes circumstances where the offender may not hold a formal position in relation to the victim but they have abused the trust engendered by their status and/or standing.

● **Previous violence against the victim**

The Council believes it important that the culpability factors are not just weighted towards rape by someone unknown to the victim but also recognise the reality that rape is more often committed by someone known to them (although this factor could also apply to "stranger rape").

● **Offence committed in course of burglary**

This is a factor that Lord Judge C.J. identified in *Att Gen's Ref (Nos 73, 75 and 03 of 2010) (R. v Anigbugu)*.[18]

---

[16] [2013] EWCA Crim 1642. Offender contacted his two female victims via a social networking site, took each of them to a hotel room, gave them alcohol to the extent that they were rendered unconscious and then took sexual advantage of them. He filmed his offending against one victim and photographed the other while she was naked and unconscious. It followed that, not only were there two separate victims, but there were aggravating features in the use of alcohol and the photographing. The Court of Appeal increased the total sentence from 6 to 9 years' imprisonment.

[17] A number of examples are given in *Billam* [1986] 1 W.L.R. 349.

[18] [2011] EWCA Crim 633.

● **Recording of the offence**

The Sentencing Council believed that creating a permanent record of the attack, thereby subjecting the victim to re-victimisation, should be reflected at step one. It noted that this activity has become more prevalent since the SGC guideline was published. In *Att Gen's Ref (Nos 73, 75 and 03 of 2010) (R. v Anigbugu)*, above, Lord Judge C.J. said[19]:

> "A pernicious new habit has developed by which criminals take photographs of their victims—often just to show off to their friends; often just to add something to the humiliation which the victim is already suffering; and sometimes . . . either as a form of pressure to discourage any complaint . . . but also possibly for the purposes of blackmail. Anyone can understand what a powerful lever may be given to the criminal by his possession of photographs taken of the victim when, as in these cases, she has been subjected to degrading treatment. . . . We make it clear that from now onwards the taking of photographs should always be treated as an aggravating feature of any case and in particular of any sexual cases. Photography in these circumstances usually constitutes a very serious aggravating feature of the case."

To this should be added the filming and later editing by the offender of his sexual abuse of the victim for the purposes of his own further sexual gratification.[20]

● **Commercial exploitation and/or motivation**

● **Offence racially or religiously aggravated**

● **Offence motivated by, or demonstrating, hostility to the victim based on his or her sexual orientation (or presumed sexual orientation) or transgender identity (or presumed transgender identity)**

● **Offence motivated by, or demonstrating, hostility to the victim based on his or her disability (or presumed disability)**

These are factors found in the *Assault: Definitive Guideline*. The Sentencing Council considered that if the offender demonstrates motivation on one of these grounds, that increases his culpability and should therefore be reflected at step one.

Culpability B

Culpability B has no factors listed. This is to reflect the fact that the act of rape inherently involves a high level of culpability. It is not a lower culpability category but reflects the absence of any of the additional factors found in culpability A and indicates a baseline of culpability that exists whenever rape is committed.

---

[19] [2011] EWCA Crim 633, at [7]. See also *R. v M(H)*, above, fn.16, where both victims were photographed.

[20] *Red Saunders and others v R.* [2013] EWCA Crim 1027.

STEP TWO

Starting point and category range

1.20D Once it has determined the offence category, the second step is for the court to use the corresponding starting point specified in the guideline in order to reach a sentence within the category range. The starting point applies to all offenders irrespective of plea or previous convictions. Having determined the starting point, step two allows further adjustment for aggravating or mitigating factors (for which see below). A case of particular gravity, reflected by multiple features of culpability or harm, could merit upward adjustment from the starting point before further adjustment for aggravating or mitigating factors.

In relation to rape, having considered the application of the SGC guideline based on *Millberry*,[21] the Sentencing Council decided to keep the starting points of 5 and 8 years' imprisonment with a clearer articulation of the culpability of the offender. This means that where any of the culpability A factors are present, the starting point is likely to be 7 and 10 years, not 5 and 8, before any further adjustment for aggravating or mitigating features.

The highest category, with a starting point of 15 years' imprisonment, can now be used for single rapes of particular severity, so providing the opportunity for a full reflection of harm in these cases. In the SGC guideline, a starting point of 15 years was reserved for multiple rapes. The Council took the view that multiple rapes should be charged and sentenced separately and the totality principle applied as to whether those sentences should be concurrent or consecutive.

The starting points and category ranges for rape are as follows:

	A	B
Category 1	**Starting point** 15 years' custody	**Starting point** 12 years' custody
	Category range 13–19 years' custody	**Category range** 10–15 years' custody
Category 2	**Starting point** 10 years' custody	**Starting point** 8 years' custody
	Category range 9–13 years' custody	**Category range** 7–9 years' custody

---

[21] [2002] EWCA Crim 2891.

Category 3	Starting point	Starting point
	7 years' custody	5 years' custody
	Category range	Category range
	6–9 years' custody	4–7 years' custody

Aggravating and mitigating factors

After identifying the starting point and category range, the court should consider **1.20E** whether the presence of aggravating or mitigating factors should result in an upward or downward adjustment from the starting point or the imposition of a sentence outside the category range. In particular, relevant recent convictions are likely to result in an upward adjustment. The list of aggravating and mitigating factors for rape is not exhaustive and any factors not considered at step one, but which the sentencer considers relevant to either the harm to the victim or the culpability of the offender, can be taken into account. It is a matter for the sentencer whether such a factor should be taken into account and, if so, how much weight should be given to it. It is envisaged that in exceptional cases the impact of these factors may lead the sentencer to go outside the category range identified for category 1. The list of factors is as follows:

Aggravating factors
Statutory aggravating factors
• Previous convictions, having regard to a) the nature of the offence to which the conviction relates and its relevance to the current offence; and b) the time that has elapsed since the conviction
• Offence committed whilst on bail
Other aggravating factors
• Specific targeting of a particularly vulnerable victim
• Ejaculation (where not taken into account at step one)
• Blackmail or other threats made (where not taken into account at step one)
• Location of offence
• Timing of offence
• Use of weapon or other item to frighten or injure
• Victim compelled to leave their home (including victims of domestic violence)
• Failure to comply with current court orders
• Offence committed whilst on licence
• Exploiting contact arrangements with a child to commit an offence

- Presence of others, especially children
- Any steps taken to prevent the victim reporting an incident, obtaining assistance and/or from assisting or supporting the prosecution
- Attempts to dispose of or conceal evidence
- Commission of offence whilst under the influence of alcohol or drugs

Mitigating factors

- No previous convictions **or** no relevant/recent convictions
- Remorse
- Previous good character and/or exemplary conduct*
- Age and/or lack of maturity where it affects the responsibility of the offender
- Mental disorder or learning disability, particularly where linked to the commission of the offence

* Previous good character/exemplary conduct is different from having no previous convictions. The more serious the offence, the less the weight which should normally be attributed to this factor. Where previous good character/exemplary conduct has been used to facilitate the offence, this mitigation should not normally be allowed and such conduct may constitute an aggravating factor.

In the context of this offence, previous good character/exemplary conduct should not normally be given any significant weight and will not normally justify a reduction in what would otherwise be the appropriate sentence.

Aggravating factors

1.20F

- **Previous convictions**

- **Offence committed whilst on bail**

There is a statutory requirement for sentencers to take these factors into account when assessing the seriousness of an offence. As with other guidelines, the Council recommends that these factors are considered at step two, only after the starting point has been established. Previous convictions for sexual offences will be regarded as particularly aggravating, as will an offence committed on bail for an offence against the same victim.

- **Ejaculation (where not taken into account at step one)**

This does not mean mitigation is available if there is an absence of ejaculation. In order to deal with any concerns about double counting where "STI/pregnancy as a consequence" is present at step one, the step two factor is worded as: "ejaculation (where not taken into account at step one)".

● **Blackmail or other threats made (where not taken into account at step one)**

This reflects the fact that not all rapes are accompanied by actual violence and that threats which induce a fear of violence or cause inner torment can be as harmful as violence itself.

● **Location of offence**

● **Timing of offence**

The Council has deliberately framed these factors in a non-prescriptive way to allow the sentencer to decide whether in the circumstances of the individual case before them the offence is aggravated by its location or timing. This adopts the approach set out in the *Assault: Definitive Guideline* with which judges are already familiar.

● **Use of weapon or other item to frighten or injure**

The Council believed that this means of controlling the victim should be reflected as an aggravating factor.

● **Victim compelled to leave their home (including victims of domestic violence)**

The Council concluded that a particularly aggravating feature is the physical removal of the victim from what should be their place of safety. Compulsion to leave home might apply not only to an offence within a domestic relationship but also where, following a stranger attack in the home, the victim feels unable to return there. It should be noted that the factors at step two are non-exhaustive, enabling a court to take into account the wider circumstances in the context of a specific case, such as whether the victim wants to leave their home but feel compelled to stay for financial reasons.

● **Failure to comply with current court orders**

● **Offence committed whilst on licence**

● **Exploiting contact arrangements with a child to commit an offence**

● **Presence of others, especially children**

These are all factors found in other guidelines and have their roots in the SGC guideline on domestic violence. The Council believes that it is important to include aggravating features that pertain to a rape that has occurred within a relationship, particularly because such rapes are far more prevalent than "stranger rape".

- Any steps taken to prevent the victim reporting an incident, obtaining assistance and/or from assisting or supporting the prosecution

- Attempts to dispose of or conceal evidence

These factors are intended to reflect the serious aggravation created where offenders attempt to intimidate victims into remaining silent. This is a very frequent occurrence. Steps taken to prevent reporting cover a wide range of scenarios and could, in the case of rape, include threats of physical harm, or to circulate photographs taken during the offence, if a report is made.

- Commission of offence whilst under the influence of alcohol or drugs

This factor has been included as intoxication generally aggravates offences, and in the context of rape may mean the offender has lost self control, thereby demonstrating a degree of recklessness and made himself insensible to the effect upon his victim.

Mitigating factors

1.20G   The mere presence of a mitigating factor does not lead to an automatic reduction in the sentence because the precise weight to be attached, if any, will depend on the individual circumstances of the case.

- No previous convictions or no relevant/recent convictions

The following caveat is applied to all offences:

> "*Previous good character/exemplary conduct is different from having no previous convictions. The more serious the offence, the less the weight which should normally be attributed to this factor. Where previous good character/exemplary conduct has been used to facilitate the offence, this mitigation should not normally be allowed and such conduct may constitute an aggravating factor."

In addition further wording is added to all offences carrying a maximum of life or 14 years, including rape:

> "In the context of this offence, good character/exemplary conduct should not normally be given any significant weight and will not normally justify a substantial reduction in what would otherwise be the appropriate sentence."[22]

The difficulties raised by previous and/or subsequent good character in historic cases were highlighted by Lord Judge C.J. in *R. v H*[23]:

---

[22] See the principle set out in *Millberry* [2002] EWCA Crim 2891: " . . . the defendant's good character, although it should not be ignored, does not justify a substantial reduction of what would otherwise be the appropriate sentence."
[23] [2011] EWCA Crim 2753, at [47(e)].

"The passing of the years may demonstrate aggravating features if, for example, the defendant has continued to commit sexual crime or he represents a continuing risk to the public. On the other hand, mitigation may be found in an unblemished life over the years since the offences were committed, particularly if accompanied by evidence of positive good character."

● Remorse

A number of respondents to the Sentencing Council's consultation queried the inclusion of "remorse" on the basis that it could be easily faked and "switched on" by manipulative offenders. These comments confirmed the Council's experience that the consideration of remorse is nuanced, and all the circumstances of the case will be considered by the sentencer in deciding whether any expressed remorse is in fact genuine.

● Age and/or lack of maturity where it affects the responsibility of the offender

This is a standard factor in Sentencing Council guidelines. It is intended to deal with those offenders who are just over the age of 18 or those over 18 who are not as mature as others in their peer group. The age factor can also be applied to offenders who are very elderly at the time of sentence, where the offender is sentenced decades after their offences have taken place. In *Millberry*[24] the Court of Appeal said:

"In addition, the court is always entitled to show a limited degree of mercy to an offender who is of advanced years, because of the impact that a sentence of imprisonment can have on an offender of that age."

In *Att Gen's Ref (No.38 of 2013) (R. v Stuart Hall)*[25] a sentence of 15 months' imprisonment for 14 historic indecent assaults was held to be unduly lenient and increased to 30 months. Even though the offender was 83 years old and not in good health, the original sentence did not reflect the criminality of the offences.

● Mental disorder or learning disability, where linked to the commission of the offence

The research commissioned by the Sentencing Council indicated this was the only mitigating factor on which there was broad agreement. It was felt to influence the nature but not the duration of the custodial sentence suggested, with an emphasis on treatment or care under supervision.[26] The Court of Appeal in *R. v M*,[27] whilst concluding that a defendant's belief in consent arising from a condition such as delusional psychotic illness or personality disorder must be judged by objective standards of reasonableness, observed

---

[24] [2002] EWCA Crim 2891.
[25] [2013] EWCA Crim 1450.
[26] Natcen research, see Sentencing Offences Guideline Consultation, December 2012, p.24.
[27] [2013] EWCA Crim 3, at [40] per Hughes L.J. (as he then was).

that a defendant's mental condition, and its impact on his behaviour, is of course extremely relevant to sentence. If punishment is appropriate, a non-custodial sentence may result when otherwise there would be a substantial sentence of imprisonment, whether or not a hospital order is needed by the time of trial. In other cases it may significantly mitigate the punishment required. In yet others, it may result in a substantial custodial sentence in recognition of the danger the defendant poses.

STEPS THREE TO NINE

1.20H The remaining steps are as follows. The court should consider any factors which would indicate a reduction in sentence, e.g. assistance to the prosecution (ss.73 and 74 of the Serious Organised Crime and Police Act 2005) and a guilty plea (s.144 of the CJA 2003 and Guilty Plea guideline). It should then consider dangerousness, i.e. whether it would be appropriate to award a life sentence (s.224A or s.225 of the CJA 2003) or an extended sentence (s.226A). Following that, the court should consider whether the total sentence is just and proportionate to the offending behaviour. It should then consider whether to make a compensation order and/or other ancillary order (e.g. a sex offender prevention order, a disqualification order preventing the offender working with children, or a restraining order) and inform the offender of any notification requirements that apply. Finally, it should fulfil its duty to give reasons for, and explain the effect of, the sentence awarded (s.174 of the CJA 2003), and take into account any time spent on remand (s.240A of the CJA 2003).

Sentences passed under the SGC Definitive Guideline

1.20I Sentences passed under the previous guideline need to be treated with some care in light of the changes made in the new guideline. In any event, cases are fact-specific. However, we have included in this Supplement some sentencing appeals that we regard as significant in that the principles have not changed, or are unlikely to have done. We have also included those appeals which have been adopted by the Sentencing Council in the new guideline.[28]

The Criminal Justice Act 2003 "dangerousness provisions"

1.26 Under step five the court should consider whether, having regard to the criteria contained in c.5 of Pt 12 of the CJA 2003, it would be appropriate to award a life sentence (s.224A or s.225(2)) or an extended sentence (s.226A). When sentencing offenders to a life sentence under these provisions, the notional determinate sentence should be used as the basis for the setting of a minimum term.

Section 227 of the CJA 2003, which provided for extended sentences of imprisonment, was replaced by a new s.226A and s.226B inserted by the Legal

---

[28] Notably *Att Gen's Refs (Nos 73, 75 and 03 of 2010) (R. v Anigbugu)* [2011] EWCA Crim 633.

elderly victims, mostly living alone, had been subjected to serious sexual assaults over a period of over 10 years, concurrent life sentences with minimum terms of 27 years were passed on a man in his fifties.

In *David Oakes and others v R.*[36] the Court of Appeal considered whether a whole life order was appropriate in cases involving very grave crimes. It noted that among the cases in which such orders had been imposed, none could be found in the context of sexual crime where one or more of the victims had not been murdered. Lord Judge C.J. observed[37]:

> "It is regrettably possible to envisage, and there have been cases, where dreadful sexual assaults have been followed by murderous violence. The whole life order is reserved for the most exceptional cases. Without suggesting that the court is prohibited from making a whole life order unless the defendant is convicted of at least one murder, such an order will, inevitably be a very rare event indeed."

In one of the conjoined appeals (*Michael Roberts*) the Court agreed with the submission that the whole life order should be reserved for cases where the criminal had gone even further than the appellant. Roberts, then aged 45, had been convicted at Southwark Crown Court of a series of rapes which had multiple aggravating features. There were three rape victims. A fourth victim was 84 when she was severely assaulted, although there was no evidence of sexual assault. All four victims were women, no longer young, and living alone, who were attacked in their homes during the course of burglaries. The rapes involved a high level of violence, including terrible facial injuries to the first victim. Each was subjected to an ordeal which would have been likely to have blighted the remainder of their lives. The offences, together with some of the appellant's earlier convictions, confirmed that he was cruel and ruthless and a real and continuing danger to vulnerable people. The Court of Appeal quashed the whole life order and substituted a minimum term of 25 years. In so doing, Lord Judge C.J. observed that the court was not to be taken as implying anything less than that the appellant was highly dangerous, and on the evidence before them at that time, it seemed highly improbable that he would, after the expiry of 25 or 30 or more years, or indeed ever, be safe for release.

Life imprisonment

"Discretionary" life sentence under s.225(1) and (2) of the Criminal Justice Act 2003

A sentence of life imprisonment may be imposed under s.225(1) and (2) of the CJA 2003 if the court is of the opinion that there is "a significant risk to members of

1.42A

---

[36] [2012] EWCA Crim 2435. See *Vinter v UK*, Application Nos 66069/09, 130/10 and 3896/10 [2014] Crim. L.R. 81, where the Grand Chamber of the European Court of Human Rights held that a whole-life term, in the absence of a statutory review mechanism and given the lack of clarity of the Secretary of State's powers, was a violation of art.3 because it was irreducible. This goes against the position in England and Wales as confirmed by the Court of Appeal in *Oakes*, where it was understood that a whole-life tariff could be imposed for murders of exceptional seriousness.

[37] At [102].

the public occasioned by the commission by [the offender] of further specified offences" and concludes that "the seriousness of the offence, or of the offence and one or more offences associated with it, is such as to justify the imposition of a sentence of imprisonment for life". In *Red Saunders and others v R.*[38] Lord Judge C.J., giving the judgment of the court, explained that the sentence of life imprisonment under s.225 continues in force after the changes made to the CJA 2003 by the Legal Aid, Sentencing and Punishment of Offenders Act 2012, and has been frequently described as the discretionary life sentence, although once the statutory conditions in s.225(1) and (2) are established it "must" be imposed. His Lordship said[39]: "In that broad sense, therefore, this sentence is also statutory, but it may only be imposed if justified by reference to the seriousness of the offence and the protection of the public in accordance with s.225(1) and (2)".

Life imprisonment remains the sentence of last resort. In *Wilkinson*[40] the Court of Appeal said:

> "In our judgment it is clear that as a matter of principle the discretionary life sentence under section 225 should continue to be reserved for offences of the utmost gravity. Without being prescriptive, we suggest that the sentence should come into contemplation when the judgment of the court is that the seriousness is such that the life sentence would have . . . a 'denunciatory' value, reflective of public abhorrence of the offence, and where, because of its seriousness, the notional determinate sentence would be very long, measured in very many years."

Impact of the abolition of IPP

1.42B   The abolition of IPP by the Legal Aid, Sentencing and Punishment of Offenders Act 2012 with effect from December 3, 2012[41] may lead to more sentences of life imprisonment being passed under s.225 where the sentencer concludes that an extended sentence under the new s.226A of the CJA 2003 would not afford sufficient public protection. In the past, in the overwhelming majority of cases, the relatively minor distinctions between life imprisonment and IPP were irrelevant, and so IPP was normally sufficient to address the protection of the public from a dangerous offender who would, if made subject to the order, continue to be detained until the Parole Board was satisfied he no longer represented a risk to the public.

Now, where a dangerous offender is convicted of rape, the sentencing options will be a sentence of life imprisonment imposed under s.225(1) and (2) of the CJA 2003, an extended sentence imposed under s.226A of the CJA 2003, inserted in place of s.227 by the Legal Aid, Sentencing and Punishment of Offenders Act 2012 ("LASPO"),[42] or a determinate sentence.

---

[38] [2013] EWCA Crim 1027.
[39] At [9].
[40] [2009] EWCA Crim 1925, at [19] per Lord Judge C.J.
[41] There is an exception which will become increasingly rare where a defendant was convicted before December 3, 2012 but was not sentenced before that date.
[42] The new LASPO extended sentence is explained in para.27.60C, below.

In *Red Saunders* Lord Judge C.J. explained the impact of the removal of IPP as a   **1.42C**
sentencing option as follows[43]:

> "The new statutory life sentence[44] has not replaced the IPP. Many offenders who
> represent a danger to the public may not 'qualify' for the statutory life sentence. Yet,
> for some offenders, the imperative of public protection continues undiminished, and
> is not wholly met by the 'new' extended sentence. Very long term public protection
> must therefore be provided by the imposition of a discretionary life sentence. That is
> consequent on s.225(1) and (2) which, in the context of the discretionary life sentence
> for serious offences continue, as we have explained, in full force."

His Lordship noted that under the new LASPO extended sentence the offender
will not be released during the custodial term until at least the two-thirds point of
it has been reached. Where the custodial term is 10 years or more, or the offences
for which the sentence was imposed included one in Sch.15B to the CJA 2003, he
will not be released until the Parole Board has directed his release on the ground
that his continued incarceration is no longer necessary for public protection.
Under the old form of extended sentence, release was automatic half way through
the custodial term. In relation to public protection as it arises under the new
extended sentence, having assessed the appropriate custodial term, the extension
period during which the offender would be subject to licence is limited, in the
context of a specified sexual offence, to 8 years. Further, in relation to some of the
specified sexual offences, the maximum available term is 10 years', or 14 years'
imprisonment, and that term may not be exceeded. His Lordship said that it is
therefore clear that in relation to the offender who will continue to represent a
significant risk to the safety of the public for an indefinite period, the new
extended sentence cannot be treated as a direct replacement for the old IPP. He
continued[45]:

> "Accordingly, in cases in which, prior to the enactment of LASPO, the court would
> have been driven to the conclusion that an IPP was required for public protection (on
> the basis on a judgment made on the particular facts rather than one to which the
> court was driven by some of the more troublesome assumptions required by the
> legislation in its original form) the discretionary life sentence will arise for considera-
> tion, and where appropriate, if the necessary level of public protection cannot be
> achieved by the new extended sentence, ordered. The 'denunciatory' ingredient
> identified to distinguish between the circumstances in which the discretionary life
> sentence rather than the IPP should be imposed is no longer apposite. By that we mean
> that although the 'denunciatory' element of the sentencing decision may continue to
> justify the discretionary life sentence, its absence does not preclude such an order. As
> every judge appreciates, however, the life sentence remains the sentence of last
> resort."

In *Red Saunders* the Court of Appeal took the view that a life sentence was
correctly imposed even though the option of an IPP or an extended sentence had
been available to the judge. The Lord Chief Justice noted the appalling nature of

---

[43] Above, fn.38 at [15].
[44] Under s.224A of the CJA 2003, inserted by s.122 of the Legal Aid, Sentencing and Punishment
of Offenders Act 2012: see para.1.42E, below.
[45] At [18].

the offences. He observed that the evidence underlined that, for an indefinite period, the appellant would represent a very high risk to children. There was no getting away from the stark, profoundly disturbing facts.

The appellant had been sentenced to life imprisonment with a minimum term of 8 years for the rape of a child under 13, contrary to s.5 of the 2003 Act. He was given concurrent sentences for various other sexual offences. There were two child victims. The appellant, a photography student, was aged 23. In 2005, when he was only 16, he was convicted of a sexual assault upon a 5-year-old girl. He had admitted downloading sexual images of children since he was 12. The probation officer described him as having an entrenched pattern of sexual offending against children.

In the autumn of 2011, the appellant answered an advertisement on the internet for a baby sitter for G, a little girl then aged six. He provided the parents with a bogus employment history and bogus references. He said, again untruthfully, that he would provide the relevant criminal records check when it was available. To the parents and prospective employers, he appeared plausible, even charming; he seemed to interact with the child in a natural way. This was all a front, for he had always intended to abuse G whilst the parents were out, and indeed, he wrote a script in advance describing what he planned to do. Following his script, he introduced G to a so-called game. As he lay on the bed, fully clothed, but with an obviously erect penis, he made her sit astride him and tried to persuade her to open her legs, but the girl was reluctant. This was charged as sexual assault upon a child under 13 contrary to s.7 of the 2003 Act. There was a further sexual assault when they were both on the floor and he tried to lift the child's skirt. All this he filmed using his photographic skills. He later edited the footage giving it various crude titles. He increased the speed of the film so as to give the impression that he was having intercourse with her.

The appellant then obtained similar employment with another family who had a daughter D, aged seven. Again he wrote himself a script. The offences occurred on two consecutive days in April 2012. He invited D to perform various games and he filmed her. He made her wear a blindfold. He put various phallic objects in her mouth asking her to guess the taste. He then covered his erect penis in chocolate and twice put it in the child's mouth. This was charged as oral rape of a child under 13 contrary to s.5 of the 2003 Act. At one stage he got the child to sit astride him, bouncing her up and down on his exposed erect penis. Later he professionally edited the film footage of the abuse, giving it such titles as "Pedo Productions". When police searched his house, they found the films and 4,000 indecent images of children, some at level 4 or 5 on the Copine scale. When the appellant was asked in interview about the indecent images, he said that he considered the children to be willing participants. He told the writer of the pre-sentence report that, after a time, viewing was not enough and he wanted to be part of it.

Police also found a diary in which the appellant set out in disturbing detail how to abduct, sexually abuse, kill and dispose of a child. He wrote of selecting a girl at a particular primary school and that whoever discovered the material had discovered his heart's intent. When asked about this, he said that these writings were just fantasy and that he would never have carried them out. The author of the pre-sentence report did not accept that his expressions of remorse were genuine. He was plainly dangerous.

In his sentencing remarks the judge observed that these were truly grave sexual offences and concluded that the public would consider this offence warranted a sentence of denunciatory value and accordingly imposed a sentence of life imprisonment on the s.5 count. If sentence had been passed one month later, after the coming into force of the relevant provisions of the Legal Aid, Sentencing and Punishment of Offenders Act 2012 and the abolition of IPP, it would no longer have been apposite to identify a "denunciatory" ingredient to distinguish between the circumstances in which discretionary life should be imposed rather than IPP. However, as the Court of Appeal agreed with the judge's decision, even if the judge had not found the "denunciatory" element, its absence would not have precluded the imposition of a life sentence.

The second form of discretionary life sentence

In *Red Saunders and others v R.*[46] Lord Judge C.J. concluded that the jurisdiction   1.42D
to impose a life sentence in an appropriate case (where the maximum sentence for the particular offence is life) has survived the enactment of the CJA 2003 and the changes to the sentencing regime affected by the Legal Aid, Sentencing and Punishment of Offenders Act 2012. He pointed out that if it had been intended to abolish that jurisdiction, the appropriate legislative change could readily have been made by the provisions restricting the life sentence (other than the mandatory sentence) to the statutory sentence or the discretionary life sentence under s.225(1) and (2) of the CJA 2003. Neither that Act nor the Legal Aid, Sentencing and Punishment of Offenders Act 2012 imposed any limit on the power of the court to impose a sentence of life imprisonment in such cases. However, the occasions when this second form of discretionary life sentence is likely to be imposed will be rare. In the vast majority of cases, offenders who represent a danger to the public requiring long term public protection will be sentenced in accordance with s.225(1) and (2) of the CJA 2003.

There will, though, be some very grave sexual offences committed before the implementation of s.225 of the CJA 2003 where a discretionary life sentence will be appropriate, provided the case was sufficiently grave and the offender might remain a serious danger to the public for a period which could not be reliably estimated at sentence time.[47] For sentencing dangerous offenders for offences committed before April 2005, see para.26.72 et seq. In *R. v D*[48] the Court of

---

[46] Above, fn.38.
[47] See the criteria in *Hodgson* (1968) 52 Cr. App. R. 113 (referred to below); *Whittaker* [1997] 1 Cr. App. R.(S.) 261. For recent examples, see *DP* [2013] EWCA Crim 1143 and *Robertshaw* [2013] EWCA Crim 635.
[48] [2012] EWCA Crim 2370.

Appeal upheld a sentence of discretionary life imprisonment passed in August 2011 in respect of a rape committed approximately 30 years earlier. The appellant had pleaded guilty to the rape of his grandmother in 1982 when she was 64 and the appellant was 16. The appellant was tried for her rape in 1983 but was found not guilty. His grandmother died in 1992. In 2002 the appellant was arrested on suspicion of rape of his step-daughter. The appellant absconded and left the country. Subsequent investigation of the rape of his grandmother resulted in the production of a DNA profile which was found to match that of the appellant. He was surrendered to the UK and in 2008 pleaded guilty to the rape of his step-daughter. His acquittal of the rape of his grandmother was quashed under s.76 of the CJA 2003. The appellant subsequently pleaded guilty to that rape and was sentenced to life imprisonment with a minimum term of 3-and-a-half years. The sentencing judge considered that if the appellant had been adult at the time of the offence in 1982 and there was no mitigation, the appropriate determinate sentence would have been 11 years. However, taking account of the aggravating and mitigating circumstances, in particular the fact that the appellant was 16 when the offence was committed, the judge said that the determinate sentence would have been 7 years.[49]

Leave to appeal was granted so that the Court of Appeal could consider whether the conditions laid down in *Hodgson*,[50] which must be satisfied before a discretionary sentence may be imposed, were satisfied in this case. The Court of Appeal in *Hodgson* said that a life sentence would be justified where the offence or offences were in themselves grave enough to require a very long sentence, where it appeared from the nature of the offences and from the defendant's history that he was a person of unstable character likely to commit such offences in the future, and where if such offences were committed the consequences to others might be especially injurious.

On appeal it was submitted that the first condition was not satisfied, as the offence was committed when the appellant was 16 and it could not be said to be grave enough to require a very long sentence of imprisonment. The Court rejected this argument, taking into account the statements of Lord Judge C.J. in *Att Gen's Refs (Nos 3, 73, and 75 of 2010) (R. v Anigbugu)*[51] on how seriously the courts regard offences of rape committed against a lone woman in her home at night after forced entry into the house, and the guidance given by his Lordship on the length

---

[49] It appears that the sentencing judge was not referred to *Att Gen's Refs (Nos 3, 73 and 75 of 2010) (R. v Anigbugu)* [2011] EWCA Crim 633, where it was said that in a case where rape was committed after or in the course of burglary in the home, the starting point would rarely be less than 12 years' imprisonment and the presence of aggravating features would increase the starting point to 15 years' imprisonment and beyond. The Court of Appeal took the view that if this authority had been drawn to the attention of the judge, it was possible that the determinate sentence might have been higher.

[50] (1968) 52 Cr. App. R. 113. These conditions had been considered and confirmed in subsequent cases, in particular *Att Gen's Ref (No.32 of 1996) (Whitaker)* [1997] 1 Cr. App. R.(S.) 261 and *Chapman* [2000] 1 Cr. App. R.(S.) 377.

[51] [2011] EWCA Crim 633.

of the determinate sentence that such offences will attract. The Court concluded that it was impossible to argue that the offence committed in 1982 was not "grave enough to require a very long sentence".

The "new automatic life sentence"—statutory life under s.224A of the Criminal Justice Act 2003 following conviction for a second listed offence

Under s.224A of the CJA 2003, inserted by s.122 of the Legal Aid, Sentencing and Punishment of Offenders Act 2012, a sentence of imprisonment for life "must" be imposed following conviction for a second listed offence, unless particular circumstances would make it unjust. It follows that there is a discretionary power in the court to disapply what would otherwise be a provision requiring an obligatory sentence. In contrast to the original automatic life sentence under s.9 of the Powers of Criminal Courts (Sentencing) Act 2000, the sentencer does not have to find "exceptional circumstances".   **1.42E**

To qualify for an automatic life sentence, the offender must be aged 18 or over and must be convicted of an offence listed in Pt 1 of new Sch.15B to the CJA 2003.[52] The offence must have been committed on or after December 3, 2012. The Schedule lists a large number of offences, some of which are not punishable with life imprisonment in normal circumstances. It includes numerous offences contrary to the 2003 Act.

The "sentence condition" and the "previous offence condition" which must be met before s.224A is engaged will ensure that this new "automatic" life sentence is of limited application, although those who commit a second rape and/or second child sex offence could, in certain circumstances, qualify. For the "sentence condition" to be satisfied, the sentencer must conclude that a sentence of 10 years' imprisonment or more is appropriate after taking into account all relevant considerations, including the offender's plea, and disregarding any extension period which might be imposed as part of an extended sentence. For the "previous offence condition" to be satisfied, the offender at the time the latest offence was committed must have been convicted of an offence in Sch.15B[53] (not just in Pt 1 of that Schedule) *and* that a "relevant life sentence" or a "relevant sentence of imprisonment or detention for a determinate period" had been imposed on the offender for the previous offence. A determinate sentence of imprisonment or detention is "relevant" for this purpose if it was for a period of 10 years or more. An extended sentence is relevant if the custodial sentence was 5 years or more. A life sentence or other indeterminate sentence will be relevant if the minimum sentence, disregarding any time spent in custody on remand, was at least 5 years.

---

[52] Added to the CJA 2003 by the Legal Aid, Sentencing and Punishment of Offenders Act 2012, s.122 and Sch.18, and set out at para.27.60D, below.
[53] Pt 2 of Sch.15B includes various offences under the Sexual Offences Act 1956, including rape.

"Historic" cases

1.48   In *R. v H*[54] the Court of Appeal considered sentencing issues in the context of crimes brought to justice many years after they were committed, sometimes described as "historic" or "cold" cases. Although Lord Judge C.J., delivering the judgment of the Court, gave sentencing guidance of general application, he specifically considered a number of "historic" sex cases of which three involved sentencing decisions following convictions for rape.

His Lordship stated that sentence will be imposed at the date of the sentencing hearing on the basis of the legislative provisions then current, and by measured reference to any definitive sentencing guidelines relevant to the situation revealed by established facts. Although sentence must be limited to the maximum sentence at the date when the offence was committed, it is wholly unrealistic to attempt an assessment of sentence by seeking to identify at the time of sentencing what the sentence for the individual offence was likely to have been if the offence had come to light at or shortly after the date when it was committed.

The limitation to the then maximum sentence does not affect the full offence of rape. The maximum sentence was discretionary life under the Sexual Offences Act 1956. However, the maximum sentence for attempted rape was 7 years' imprisonment until 1985, when it was increased to life. As the *Definitive Guideline* frequently recommends sentences significantly higher than those that would have been passed 20 or even 10 years ago, the appropriate sentence for "historic" cases of rape may be very much higher than if the matter had been dealt with at the time. For a graphic example, see *R. v D*,[55] where a discretionary life sentence was upheld in respect of a rape committed in the 1980s.

For more detailed discussion of sentencing historic cases, see para.26.72.

INDICTMENT

1.49A   In *Stocker*[56] the appellant was convicted of rape, contrary to s.1(1) of the Sexual Offences Act 1956. The offence was committed in 2008 and so the relevant statutory provision had been wrongly identified: it should have been s.1(1) of the 2003 Act. The question for the Court of Appeal was whether this was a purely technical defect or whether the count was fundamentally flawed because it breached r.14(2) of the Criminal Procedure Rules by failing to identify accurately the legislation contravened. From the beginning to the end of the process, the charge was, in substance, one of rape under the 2003 Act. The error could have been cured easily by an amendment at any time. The Court of Appeal did not accept that an error in the date of the statute on these facts was so fundamental as to render the proceedings a nullity, or that the draftsman of r.14(2) would have

---

[54] [2011] EWCA Crim 2753, discussed more fully in para.26.72, below.
[55] [2012] EWCA Crim 2370. See para.1.42D, above.
[56] [2013] EWCA Crim 1993.

intended such an outcome for a breach of this kind. Nothing had occurred during the trial to render the indictment a nullity or the conviction unsafe.

ALTERNATIVE VERDICTS

It was held in *Beaney*[57] that on a charge of attempted rape, where the jury are not   **1.50**
sure that the defendant intended penile penetration, but are sure he intended sexual touching, they may bring in an alternative verdict of attempted sexual assault.

Beaney was followed in *Ferriter*,[58] which involved an appeal against conviction for attempted rape. The appellant spent a night drinking in a bar where the complainant was the barmaid. When he was the last customer, he walked behind the bar and struggled with the complainant. Both ended up on the floor. The complainant escaped and the appellant stole spirits and cash from the till. He was charged with theft and with attempted rape or sexual assault in the alternative, based on the complainant's evidence that he had tried during the struggle to pull her trousers down more than once. The appellant, who pleaded guilty to the thefts, denied this and claimed he just wanted to take money from the tills. The trial judge refused to accede to a submission of no case on the charge of attempted rape. It was submitted on appeal on behalf of the appellant that a) there had been insufficient evidence to leave to the jury that he had gone beyond mere preparation, and b) even assuming that he had gone beyond mere preparation, there had been insufficient evidence to leave to the jury to justify the inference that his intent had not been to assault the complainant sexually, but to commit the specific offence of rape.

The Court of Appeal allowed the appeal. It took the view that there was not the slightest doubt that that the appellant's acts went well beyond mere preparation and into trying to commit a sexual offence. However, although there was ample evidence on which a jury could conclude that the appellant's intent was sexual molestation, there was no evidence which pointed to an intent to commit rape rather than some other sexual offence. The Court observed that the defendant's activities were more explicit than in *Beaney* in that the defendant had molested the complainant and was in the act of removing her trousers. The Court accordingly quashed the conviction for attempted rape and substituted a conviction for sexual assault.

PARTIES TO THE OFFENCE

Boys under the age of 14

In three recent cases the Court of Appeal considered presumptions based on age   **1.61**
in historic cases of rape. However anachronistic the presumptions may be, they

---

[57] [2010] EWCA Crim 2551.
[58] [2012] EWCA Crim 2211.

apply to allegations of offences committed up until the time when they were abolished. Until September 20, 1993, there was an irrebuttable presumption at common law that a boy under the age of 14 was incapable of penetrative sexual intercourse and it followed that he could not be guilty of committing rape (or buggery) as a principal. Similarly, until September 30, 1998, there was a rebuttable presumption that a child aged 10 or over but under 14 at the date of the act alleged was doli incapax and it was necessary for the prosecution to prove to the criminal standard that the defendant knew the act to be seriously wrong.

In *Fethney*[59] the Court of Appeal observed that neither presumption had been abolished retrospectively. If the act of penetration alleged had been committed before September 20, 1993, but could not be shown to have been committed before the appellant's fourteenth birthday, he could not be convicted of the offence. With respect to doli incapax, a failure to direct as to the doctrine in this case rendered convictions unsafe relating to conduct committed before September 30, 1998, when the appellant was aged between 10 and 14.

In *J.OC*[60] a lawyer in the Criminal Appeals Office noticed that one of 14 counts was a rape upon the appellant's 5-year-old sister, alleged to have taken place when the appellant was aged 10 or 11. In light of the irrebuttable presumption, the conviction on that count had to be quashed.

A similar situation arose in *Bevan*,[61] where the Court of Appeal had no choice but to quash a conviction for rape alleged to have been committed by the appellant when he may have been aged under 14, thereby engaging the irrebuttable presumption of penetrative incapacity. However, the Court held that other convictions which did not involve penile penetration were safe. Although the jury should have been directed that the rebuttable presumption applied, a number of features of the evidence led the court to conclude that there was no prospect that the jury would not have been convinced that the appellant had known his actions were seriously wrong. The decision therefore shows that, when there is a failure to direct as to the rebuttable presumption, the Court of Appeal will look at the circumstances to see if it was inevitable that the presumption would have been rebutted.

"PENETRATES THE VAGINA, ANUS OR MOUTH"

Specimen counts

1.67   Specimen counts are frequently used in trials of sexual offences. They are appropriate where a complainant cannot particularise any specific incident and merely alleges a pattern of similar conduct, and there is no room for the jury to

---

[59] [2010] EWCA Crim 3906.
[60] [2012] EWCA 2458.
[61] [2011] EWCA Crim 654.

focus on one incident rather than another because no single occasion is sufficiently distinct. However, care must be taken to identify cases in which separate particularised incidents are wrapped up in one count within a pattern of conduct, where it may be necessary for the judge to give a *Brown*[62] direction along the lines that the jury have to be unanimous about the same incident. In most cases where a specimen count is relied on, it is enough for the judge to tell the jury that they may convict if they are sure that the offence has been committed at least once. *Williams v R.*[63] is a classic example of the use of specimen counts in a sex case, and the submissions that arise at the close of evidence when the defence ask for a direction in accordance with *Brown*.[64] The appellant was convicted on one count of oral rape and one count of vaginal rape. These were specimen counts because the victim alleged that she had been orally and vaginally raped several times during the night she spent in the appellant's home. The allegations covered a single night, the same parties, the same place, and the same defence was put forward in relation to the activity in each count. In relation to the allegation of oral rape, it was agreed the activity took place and the issue was consent. In relation to the allegation of vaginal rape, the issue was whether there had been any vaginal sexual intercourse. The trial judge explained to the jury that the prosecution had selected one example of each allegation instead of loading up the indictment with counts that charged numerous offences of the same kind. He directed them that they could only convict the defendant if they were sure that he committed the particular offence charged in that particular count, whether or not they were sure that he also committed other offences.

On appeal, it was submitted on behalf of the appellant that this was a misdirection and that the judge should specifically have directed the jury that they could not convict upon any specimen count unless they were all agreed as to which offending incident they were sure the appellant committed. His failure to direct them meant the jury might have been divided as to which course of conduct they were sure the appellant committed. For example, they might have been divided as to whether the complainant's account in relation to matters later in the evening after admittedly taking crack cocaine and alcohol was accurate. Some jury members might have been sure that she had been raped vaginally or orally at some point, but not agreed as to precisely when. Relying on *Brown*,[65] it was argued that the judge's direction left it open to some members of the jury to convict of rape,

---

[62] [1984] 79 Cr. App. R. 115.

[63] [2012] EWCA Crim 2516.

[64] Whilst this is clearly correct on the basis that this case was put to the jury with separate specimen counts for oral and vaginal rape, *R. v K* [2009] 1 Cr. App. R. 331 remains good law where one act of penetration, either anal or vaginal, is alleged. The Court of Appeal held in that case that a trial judge's direction to the jury in respect of a count alleging a single episode involving the penetration of the six-year-old complainant's vagina or anus could not be criticised. The judge had directed the jury that they could convict the defendant if they were sure he had penetrated either the vagina or the anus. It did not matter if they disagreed as to which was penetrated as long as they were sure that one of them was penetrated. See para.1.67 of the main work.

[65] [1984] 79 Cr. App. R. 115.

being sure of an account of one incident, with others only being sure in relation to a different incident later on that night.

The Court of Appeal pointed out that *Brown* was concerned with the situation that arises where a count contains a number of different ingredients, representing alternative ways in which an offence may be committed. In those circumstances, the judge must direct the jury that where a number of matters are specified in the count as together constituting an ingredient in the offence, and any one of them was capable of doing so, any individual matter must be proved to the satisfaction of the whole jury. It would not, where an indictment alleges different types of activity, be sufficient for six members of the jury to find one activity proved and another six members to find a different activity proved. As was observed in *Keeton*[66]:

> " . . . it is only in cases where truly alternative bases for a finding of guilt are being put forward by the Crown and where there is a risk that the jury might feel it is permissible for some of them to be satisfied by one basis and others by another, that the *Brown* direction need be given. It is not appropriate to complicate what are essentially straightforward cases with a *Brown* direction."

As this was not a case where the counts specified a number of different ingredients, the Court of Appeal concluded that a *Brown* direction was not necessary, and the judge's direction was sufficient. There was no disparity as to time, place, particulars or nature of the act required to prove a count. The separate allegations of oral and vaginal rape stood or fell together within each count. At no stage was the case conducted on the basis that some jurors might be satisfied in relation to one episode, with some being satisfied in relation to another.

The situation in *Williams* should be contrasted with that in *Hobson*,[67] where the complainants gave evidence identifying specific occasions alleged to be part of a pattern of conduct, and there was evidence which could have caused a reasonable jury to acquit on the specimen charge but convict on the particularised occasion, or vice versa. In those circumstances it was possible that the jury was not at one in relation to any specific occasion. Where this occurs, an obvious solution is for the prosecution to apply to amend the indictment in order to add the particular incident or incidents as separate counts. However, if the specific occasions are not particularised on the indictment, it will be incumbent on the judge to tell the jury that they can only convict if they are sure the offence has been committed on the same occasion, either an occasion in the course of the unspecified pattern of offending or one of the particular occasions identified in the evidence. The nature of the incidents alleged in *Hobson* was such that the jury could, on the evidence, have been satisfied about the course of conduct but not about the specific occasions, or vice versa. In such circumstances, it could not be said that the verdicts were safe.

---

[66] [1995] 2 Cr. App. R. 241, at p.259G.
[67] [2013] EWCA Crim 819. See commentary at [2014] Crim. L.R. 83, and the guidance given by Hughes L.J. (as he then was) in *Hartley* [2011] EWCA Crim 1299.

ABSENCE OF CONSENT

MEANING OF "CONSENT"

What are the boundaries of "free agreement?"

Context is all-important when considering whether an apparent consent was in **1.94** fact a genuine consent. An instructive case is *Robinson*,[68] where the Court of Appeal held that a jury was entitled to find that a 12-year-old girl's immaturity, coupled with evidence of her acquiescence rather than enthusiastic consent, particularly in the context of what could be perceived as grooming, meant that there was no proper consent. The case is a good illustration of the appropriate way to approach consent where there is evidence of grooming.

The appellant was charged with rape and other sexual offences allegedly committed against the daughter of his former partner in the 1990s. The appellant had formed a relationship with the complainant's mother following the breakdown of her marriage. He formed a particularly close relationship with the complainant, ZK. She would visit him at his flat and play computer games when she was 11 or 12. She referred to a particular occasion when she got into bed with the appellant and her mother and he touched her legs under the cover. He would kiss and stroke her leg when they were in the car together. He showed her pornographic films on television when she was at his flat. Gradually this developed into a fuller sexual relationship and they had sexual intercourse, first when she was 12, and thereafter the relationship continued for some three years. The appellant denied that anything untoward had occurred or that there was anything inappropriate in the relationship.

The trial judge rejected an application that there was insufficient evidence for the rape charges to be left to the jury because the evidence suggested that the complainant had been a willing participant. In his ruling, the judge referred to passages in the complainant's ABE interview. The complainant had said that she did not initiate sexual intercourse. During the act she felt detached from it. When asked whether she had said "no" to having sex with the appellant, she said:

> "I remember sort of half-heartedly saying no, and then—especially to things I didn't want to do, or at first just being very like 'no, I don't think so'. And it was, I remember, it was being him definitely persuading me a lot, but not, maybe not really forcibly, just like 'oh, come on, what are you worried about?' and almost talking me through it, like 'why are you so nervous? Why don't you want me to do this?'"

There were passages in the ABE interview that clearly demonstrated that the child was infatuated with the appellant, that she thought he had fallen in love with her, and that she wanted to be with him, at least at various stages during the period of their relationship.

---

[68] [2011] EWCA Crim 916.

The trial judge observed that the interviewing officers had not in terms asked the complainant whether she had consented. Whilst she was being cross-examined, he asked her about the first occasion of sexual intercourse when she was 12. She answered:

> "I did not ask the defendant not to, I did not move to stop him. He reassured me it was okay. I did not make it plain to him I did not want to. There was no occasion when I said that I didn't want him to do it, at least not before I met T [a boyfriend with whom she started a relationship when aged 15]."

The judge said that it would be open to the jury on these facts to infer that the complainant did not genuinely consent, or, put the other way, that what happened was mere submission on her part, having been comprehensively groomed the appellant:

> "The defendant spent a great deal of time with her, he played with her, watched films with her, and enjoyed her company, and indeed continually praised her, said how pretty she was and clever she was, and indeed how much he loved her. They held hands, he sat her on his lap, stroked her hair and so on. Clear evidence of grooming."

On appeal, counsel for the appellant submitted that there was no evidence of submission of the kind falling within the situations described by Roche L.J. in *Malone*,[69] referred to in para.1.138 of the main work. He accepted that the fact that the complainant was a 12-year-old at the time of the first act of sexual intercourse was potentially relevant when considering whether there was true consent. However, here the judge had found on the evidence that she was a mature 12-year-old, who plainly understood the nature of the sexual act and was capable of making up her own mind, and so the only proper inference was that she had full capacity. She never expressed any lack of enthusiasm for sex and did not at any stage say she was an unwilling participant.

Counsel for the appellant criticised the judge for putting some weight in his ruling on his finding that the girl may have been groomed by the appellant. He submitted that this was not necessarily pertinent to the question of consent at all. He asked rhetorically whether, if she positively asserted that she had consented, the issue of consent could have been left to the jury because she was being groomed.

Elias L.J., giving the judgment of the Court of Appeal, said that some 12-year-olds plainly do not have the capacity to consent, and whilst the complainant did not fall into that category, there was evidence on which a jury was entitled to find that her immaturity, coupled with the evidence of acquiescence rather than enthusiastic consent, particularly in the context of what could be perceived as grooming, meant there was no proper consent. Dismissing the appeal, he stated that the trial judge had taken the only sensible view that could be taken. In the course of his judgment, Elias L.J. made some significant observations about grooming, which are likely to be helpful in respect of young complainants older

---

[69] [1998] 2 Cr. App. R. 447.

than the complainant in *Robinson*, where grooming involves providing alcohol and drugs to a targeted victim[70]:

"Grooming is not a term of art, but it suggests cynical and manipulative behaviour designed to achieve a particular sexual objective. Not all relationships with underage children can fairly be characterised as involving grooming, although many will. But even where they can, the fact of grooming plainly does not necessarily vitiate consent. Many a seducer achieves his objectives with the liberal and cynical employment of gifts, insincere compliments and false promises. But such manipulative and deceitful methods could not be relied upon to establish a lack of consent whenever the seduction was successful. The situation will often be no different where the complainant is under age. But where the exploitation is of a girl who is of an age where she does not, or may not, have the capacity to understand the full significance of what she is doing, and in particular, where, as here, there was evidence of acquiescence or acceptance rather than positive consent, we think that, as the judge found, it would be open to the jury to conclude that the complainant, perhaps out of embarrassment or some other reason, had in reality unwillingly gone along with the acts which she did not in fact wish to engage in."

C v R.[71] provides a further strong example of the importance of context when considering evidence of apparent consent. The appellant was charged with 18 offences relating to the sexual abuse of his step-daughter over a period of about 20 years, from when she was 5 until she was 25. His defence was there had been no sexual activity of any kind between them before she was 16, and that thereafter there was a sexual relationship between them in which all the sexual activity was entirely consensual. There was a substantial body of evidence available in respect of the later counts (relating to the period after the complainant reached 16) which tended to show apparent consent. This included photographs of the complainant posing naked and, by her smile and demeanour, appearing to indicate that she was willing for the appellant to take these photographs of her. A video film was available which showed her apparently performing oral sex on the appellant. There were intimate text messages using pet names and uninhibited sexually explicit language. The appellant's counsel submitted there was evidence that during the later period the appellant did not oblige her to participate in sexual activity if she was reluctant. The trial judge directed the jury that they could only proceed to consider their verdicts on the later counts if they were sure of earlier sexual abuse.

1.94A

The convictions were upheld on appeal. The Court of Appeal, in a judgment delivered by Lord Judge C.J., held that the reality of the case could not be understood without reference to the long years of the complainant's childhood during which she was the victim of repeated sexual abuse by the appellant. The appellant was domineering, aggressive and controlling. The evidence of prolonged grooming and potential corruption of the complainant when she was a child provided the context in which the evidence of her apparent consent after she had grown up should be examined and assessed. Properly analysed, the evidence of

---

[70] At [22].
[71] [2012] EWCA Crim 2034.

apparent consent did not undermine the credibility of the complainant's evidence that she had never consented. Once the jury were satisfied that the sexual activity of the type alleged had occurred when the complainant was a child, and that it impacted on and reflected the appellant's dominance and control over the complainant, it was open to them to conclude that the evidence of apparent consent when the complainant was no longer a child was indeed apparent, not real, and that the appellant was well aware that in reality she was not consenting.

The relevant time for the purposes of determining consent

1.94B   The Court of Appeal has yet to tackle the problem of a pre-arranged sober agreement to have sex followed by the complainant losing unconsciousness. Would this be an exception to the normal rule that the relevant time for the purposes of determining consent is the time of the sexual activity? The Supreme Court of Canada in *HM Queen v JA and Attorney General of Canada and Women's Legal Education and Action Fund*[72] had to resolve the issue of whether a person can lawfully perform sexual acts on an unconscious person if the person consented to those acts in advance of being rendered unconscious. In that case, the complainant had consciously agreed to engage in a sexual practice involving transitory unconsciousness (erotic asphyxiation), and lost consciousness before JA inserted a dildo into her anus. The Supreme Court decided that Parliament had defined consent in a way that required the complainant be conscious throughout the sexual activity in question; the definition did not extend to advance consent to sexual acts committed while the complainant was unconscious. The legislation required ongoing, conscious consent to ensure that women and men are not the victims of sexual exploitation, and that individuals engaging in sexual activity are capable of asking their partners to stop at any point.

There are significant differences between the definitions of consent in the Canadian Criminal Code, where it is limited by stipulated circumstances, and in s.74 of the 2003 Act. However, under both, consent for this purpose is actual subjective consent in the mind of the complainant at the time of the sexual activity in question.[73] We therefore consider it likely that the courts in this jurisdiction would interpret the meaning of consent in the same way as the Canadian Supreme Court. This would be in line with the approach taken by Baroness Hale in *R. v C*,[74] admittedly in the different context of the potentially fluctuating capacity of mentally disordered complainants, where she stated: " . . . one consents to this act of sex with this person at this time and in this place". The necessity for the prosecution to prove that the defendant did not reasonably believe that the complainant was consenting will ensure that no injustice arises.

---

[72] [2011] 2 S.C.R. 440.
[73] *Criminal Code*, s.273; *Ewanchuk* [1999] 1 S.C.R. 330.
[74] [2009] UKHL 42 at [27].

Deceptions falling short of deceptions as to the nature or purpose of the act: does s.76 limit the definition of consent in s.74?

It is now clear that s.76 goes no further than establishing that lesser deceptions, i.e. those falling outside the ambit of the section, do not automatically vitiate consent. Jo Miles had argued[75] that that the basic definition of consent in s.74 must be read subject to s.76, which identifies two cases in which it will be conclusively presumed that the complainant was not consenting and the defendant did not reasonably believe she was consenting: (a) deception as to the nature or purpose of the act, and (b) deception by impersonating a person known to the complainant. Miles contended that other mistakes "but for" which the complainant would not have consented, will not vitiate consent for the purposes of s.74. In the main work we doubted the correctness of this argument for the following reasons: **1.99**

    (i) The Miles' interpretation exaggerates the scope of s.76, which in many ways simply replicates the scope of the common law.

    (ii) The whole purpose of s.74 is to focus upon the autonomy of the complainant. It is for the jury to decide on all the relevant evidence whether a particular complainant "agreed by choice and had the freedom and capacity to make that choice". Choice is crucial to the issue of consent.

    (iii) The presumptions were designed to buttress s.74, not to limit it.

    (iv) The presumptions are concerned with proof of the absence of consent rather than with its definition.

The position has now been clarified in *Assange v Swedish Prosecution Authority*.[76] The Divisional Court, in considering an appeal against extradition, had to consider whether the conduct alleged to amount to the Swedish offence of sexual molestation was an offence under the law of England and Wales. The essence of the offence as described in the European arrest warrant was that the appellant knew that the complainant would consent to sexual intercourse only if he used a condom throughout but, nevertheless, went on to have unprotected sexual intercourse with her. **1.99A**

    It was submitted by the appellant that the conduct described in the warrant was not an offence under the law of England and Wales, in that a consent to sexual

---

[75] *Sexual offences: consent, capacity and children*, Archbold News, Issue 10, Dec 5, 2008.

[76] [2011] EWHC 2849 (Admin). See also Jonathan Rogers, *The effect of "deception" in the Sexual Offences Act 2003*, Archbold Review, Issue 4, May 14, 2013, where it is argued that *Assange* is wrongly decided and an alternative interpretation of the legislation should be preferred. Rogers argues that it is a mistake to conflate concerns about sexual health and/or pregnancy with sexual autonomy. He expresses the hope that *Assange* will not be followed and that liability for non-consensual offences will arise only where the sexual autonomy of the victim has been compromised. In fact *Assange* has been followed: see *McNally* [2013] EWCA Crim 1051 and *R(F) v DPP* [2013] EWHC 945 (Admin), discussed below. It is quite clear that s.74 is being given a wide interpretation unrestricted by s.76.

intercourse on condition that the appellant wore a condom remained a consent to sexual intercourse, even if he had not used a condom or had removed or damaged the condom he had used. The appellant relied heavily upon *R. v B*,[77] in which the Court of Appeal held that deception as to HIV status was not a deception as to the nature or purpose of the act of sexual intercourse, and accordingly the conclusive presumption in s.76 did not apply: the act remained a consensual act. Furthermore, the Court in *R. v B* had gone on to hold that the fact that B had not disclosed he was HIV positive was not in any way relevant to the issue of consent to sexual intercourse under s.74. It was submitted that the present case was analogous, as the complainant had consented to sexual intercourse and it did not matter that she had consented only on the basis that the appellant would use a condom, as that did not change the nature of the act. It was accepted on the appellant's behalf that this contention might not be one that contemporary society would readily understand or consider justifiable, but Parliament had enacted the law in those terms and the duty of the courts was to apply the law.

The Divisional Court, in deciding that the extradition requirement of dual criminality was satisfied, rejected the appellant's submissions based on *R. v B*. It noted that in *Jheeta*[78] the Court of Appeal had made it clear that in most cases, the absence of consent and of a reasonable belief in consent would be proved without reference to the presumptions set out in ss.75 and 76. In the Divisional Court's view, s.76 had no application to this case. The section should be given a stringent construction because it provides for a conclusive presumption. The question of consent, and the issue of the materiality of the use of a condom, fell to be determined by reference to s.74. It would be open to a jury to hold that, if the complainant had made clear that she would consent to sexual intercourse only if the appellant used a condom, then there would be no consent if, without her consent, he did not use a condom, or removed or tore it. Thus his conduct would amount to an offence under the 2003 Act, whatever the position may have been prior to the Act.

In short, if a deception is not within s.76 (i.e. it is not a deception as to the nature or purpose of the act or a case of impersonation), that does not preclude reliance upon s.74. Section 76 simply establishes a conclusive presumption in the very limited circumstances to which it applies. In *Assange*, the Divisional Court rejected the argument that if the deception was not a deception within s.76, then it could not be taken into account for the purposes of s.74. Sir John Thomas P., as he then was, stated[79]:

> "It would, in our view, have been extraordinary if Parliament had legislated in terms that, if conduct that was not deceptive could be taken into account for the purposes of s.74, conduct that was deceptive could not be."

---

[77] [2007] 1 Cr. App. R. 29, discussed in para.1.99 of the main work.
[78] [2007] 2 Cr. App. R. 34, discussed in para.1.99 of the main work.
[79] At [88].

His Lordship observed that there was nothing in *R. v B* to suggest such a construction. That decision went no further than deciding that failure to disclose HIV infection is not of itself relevant to consent under s.74. It did not permit the appellant to contend that if he deceived the complainant as to whether he was using a condom or one that he had not damaged, that that was irrelevant to the issue of consent to sexual intercourse or his belief in consent.

Assange clarifies the relevance of deceptions, falling short of s.76 deceptions, to the question of consent. This has led to academic criticism suggesting that the line between frauds that can vitiate consent and those that cannot is "murky and uncertain".[80] It is a matter for the jury to determine whether the particular deception meant that the complainant was not agreeing by choice. Two subsequent cases illustrate this process in action.

In *R. (F) v DPP*[81] the claimant challenged a decision not to prosecute her former   **1.99B**
partner for rape and/or sexual assault where the allegation was that consent was forthcoming on the basis that ejaculation would take place outside the body. There was evidence that the former partner, the intervener in the proceedings, knew and understood that the claimant was consenting only on the basis that he withdrew before ejaculation, and that he deliberately ignored the basis of her consent as a manifestation of his control over her. Lord Judge C.J., giving the judgment of the Divisional Court, observed[82]:

> "What *Assange* underlines is that 'choice' is crucial to the issue of 'consent' . . . The evidence relating to 'choice' and the 'freedom' to make any particular choice must be approached in a broad common sense way. If before penetration began the intervener had made up his mind that he would penetrate and ejaculate within the claimant's vagina, or even, because 'penetration is a continuing act from entry to withdrawal' (see s.79(2) of the 2003 Act) he decided that he would not withdraw at all, just because he deemed the claimant subservient to his control, she was deprived of choice relating to the crucial feature on which her original consent to sexual intercourse was based. Accordingly her consent was negated. Contrary to her wishes, and knowing that she would not have consented, and did not consent to penetration or the continuation of penetration if she had any inkling of his intention, he deliberately ejaculated within her vagina. In law, this combination of circumstances falls within the statutory definition of rape."

---

[80] See Professor J.R. Spencer, *Sex by deception*, *Archbold Review*, Issue 9, Nov 14, 2013, pp.6–9, where it is pointed out that the 2003 Act, in repealing the offence of procuring a woman by false representations to have unlawful sexual intercourse in any part of the world, has left a gap in the criminal law governing sexual misconduct.

[81] [2013] EWHC 945 (Admin). Jonathan Rogers, in *Further developments under the Sexual Offences Act*, *Archbold Review*, Issue 7, August 7, 2013, pp.7–9, whilst acknowledging that the alleged facts in *F* make the case hard to distinguish from *Assange*, argues that liability for non-consensual sexual offences should only arise where the victim has not been willing to be used for the sexual gratification of another in a way that shows regard to his or her sexual preferences. He contends that in both *Assange* and *F*, the sexual intercourse itself was in accordance with the complainants' own sexual preference. This criticism ignores the width of s.74 as described in the main work and above.

[82] At [26].

1.99C In *Justine McNally v R.*[83] the appellant and the complainant were both young teenage girls. They met on the internet through a social networking game. The appellant led the complainant to believe she was a boy called "Scott Hill" from Glasgow. Arrangements were made for them to meet in London once the complainant was 16. Over four visits it was alleged that various forms of penetration took place. On the fourth visit, the appellant was confronted by the complainant's mother, and the complainant learnt the appellant's true gender. It was the prosecution case that the complainant had only consented because she believed she was engaging in sex with a boy called Scott. The Court of Appeal, in a judgment delivered by Leveson L.J., rejected the appellant's argument that deception as to gender cannot vitiate consent. The Court accepted that some deceptions (such as, for example, in relation to wealth) will obviously not be sufficient to vitiate consent. The Court adopted the approach set out by Lord Judge C.J. in *R. (F) v DPP* that the evidence as to "choice" and the "freedom" to make any particular choice must be approached in a broad common sense way. While, in a physical sense, the acts of assault by penetration of the vagina are the same whether perpetrated by a male or a female, the sexual nature of the acts is, on any common sense view, different where the complainant is deliberately deceived by a defendant into believing that the latter is a male. Leveson L.J. concluded[84]:

> "Assuming the facts to be proved as alleged, [the complainant] chose to have sexual encounters with a boy and her preference (her freedom to choose whether or not to have a sexual encounter with a girl) was removed by the appellant's deception."

Consent and rape where the parties are married or have a long-standing relationship

1.102 Where the parties are in a long-standing relationship, Pill J.'s direction in *Mohammed Zafar*[85] remains useful provided it is appropriately updated. In the Crown Court Bench Book 2010[86] the statement "The fact that such consent is given reluctantly or out of a sense of duty to her partner, is still a consent" has been qualified with the words:

---

[83] [2013] EWCA Crim 1051. This decision is criticised by Jonathan Rogers in his article in the *Archbold Review*, op. cit. fn.82, on the basis that *McNally* was a s.76 case and s.74 did not arise. The thrust of the argument is that if the core "agreement" to the acts is present, then s.74 says nothing about any deception making any difference. Where a competent person has freely agreed to the sexual activity which takes place, then, if any type of misunderstanding is to make any difference at all, it should be the result of intentional deception by the defendant. This type of misunderstanding, on the face of the statute, is the exclusive province of s.76. A difference in gender, as in *McNally*, should only make a difference to the "nature of the act" under s.76(2) of the Act. If s.76 applied, the prosecution would have had to prove that the appellant intentionally induced the complainant's mistake, which was not a pre-condition under s.74. This argument again ignores the wide ambit of s.74, which focuses on a jury's decision whether the particular complainant agreed to the particular sexual activity alleged. Sections 74 and 76 are not mutually exclusive.

[84] At [26].

[85] Unreported, June 18, 1993, CA (No.92/2762, W2).

[86] p.376.

"However, a woman is entitled to say 'no' even to her husband or long-term partner. There is a critical difference between free agreement, on the one hand, and mere submission under coercion, physical or mental, on the other."

This full direction will not be required in every case where there has been a prior relationship, particularly where the prosecution and defence cases are diametrically opposed and the complainant alleges violence. A good example is *Doyle*,[87] where the Court of Appeal upheld a conviction for a violent rape of an ex-girlfriend. In the summing up, the judge had distinguished between consent as defined in s.74 and "mere submission to something she did not want". It was submitted on appeal that the judge should have assisted the jury on how to approach the issue of consent in the context of a consensual sexual relationship and that he failed to give any further explanation as to the distinction between submission and consent freely given. The Court of Appeal concluded that the judge had directed the jury appropriately in the context of the case. There would be circumstances in which a jury would require assistance with the distinction between a reluctant but free exercise of choice, especially in a long-term loving relationship, and unwilling submission due to fear of worse circumstances. Here, the judge had drawn clear distinctions between the complainant's and the appellant's accounts and there was no possibility that he might have given the jury the wrong impression or that they had convicted the appellant on the basis of a misunderstanding between consent and submission.

Consent and "Capacity" Under the Sexual Offences Act 2003

Current position at the common law

In the main work, we considered the position should the issue arise as to whether   1.114
a complainant had the capacity to consent in a prosecution for rape, as opposed to one of the specific offences to protect the mentally disordered. We took the view that the criminal courts are likely to follow an approach consistent with the speech of Baroness Hale in *R. v C* and the Mental Capacity Act 2005. There has been some consideration in the Court of Protection of Baroness Hale's remarks in respect of capacity issues. Roderic Wood J. in *D County Council v LS*[88] attempted to build a bridge between conflicting viewpoints, holding that the approach in *R. v C* applied to questions of capacity, or lack of it, to make decisions on the issue of sexual relations (and indeed of marriage) in both the civil and criminal arena. In Roderic Wood J.'s judgment this approach was wholly consistent with the statutory requirements of s.3 of the Mental Capacity Act 2005. In *D Borough Council v AB*[89] Mostyn J. had to decide what legal test should be applied in determining whether a 41-year-old with an IQ assessed at 48 had the mental capacity to consent to sexual relations. The learned judge considered Baroness Hale's observations in *R. v C*, the old common law decisions and Roderic Wood J.'s judgment in *D County Council v LS*. However, he preferred the approach set

[87] [2010] EWCA Crim 119.
[88] [2010] EWHC 1544 (Fam).
[89] [2011] EWHC 101 (CoP).

out by Munby J. (as he then was) in *X City Council v MB, NA and MAB*[90] that the capacity test involves a consideration of whether there is "sufficiently rudimentary knowledge of what the act comprises and of its sexual character".

We continue to believe that appropriate test for incapacity by reason of mental disorder in a criminal case is as we set out in the main work: a person does not have the capacity to make a choice to agree to a sexual act by reason of mental disorder where (i) they do not understand the nature and character of the act (particularly its sexual character), or (ii) they do not understand the information relevant to that choice or whilst they understand the information, they are not able to use it and weigh in the balance to arrive at a choice.

CONSENT AND "CAPACITY" UNDER THE SEXUAL OFFENCES ACT 2003

Lack of capacity through voluntary consumption of alcohol and/or drugs[91]

1.122   When directing a jury on capacity in the context of voluntary intoxication, a judge is under no obligation to use the express words that "a drunken consent is still a consent". Indeed, in *Chedwyn Evans*[92] Lord Judge C.J. observed that on occasions when the words "drunken consent" are used or the issue is put in that way, it causes umbrage and indeed distress. In that case, the Court of Appeal took the view that the trial judge had amply encapsulated the concept of the drunken consent amounting to consent without using those express words. He had referred to two ways in which drink and/or drugs can affect an individual who is intoxicated:

> "First it can remove inhibitions and a person may do things which she would not do or be less likely to do if sober. Secondly, she may consume so much alcohol and/or drugs that it affects her state of awareness. So you need to reach a conclusion upon

---

[90] [2006] EWHC 168.

[91] See Clare Gunby, Anna Carline, and Caryl Beynon, *Alcohol-related Rape Cases: Barristers' Perspectives on the Sexual Offences Act 2003 and its Impact on Practice*, J. Crim. L. 2010, 74(6), 579–600, a study in which 14 barristers were interviewed about the "law-in-action reality" of rape cases involving alcohol intoxication. The conclusion reports that advocates were reluctant to see additional legislative changes being brought into the area of voluntary intoxication and rape, as legal reform was not a cure-all solution. Education and awareness at societal level were deemed paramount in order to allow the legislation to have its best impact. Barristers felt the best way to tackle the issue of rape following voluntary intoxication was to promote societal messages that dispel rape myths, which highlight the importance of acting ethically when drinking, of acceptable behaviour and social responsibility on the part of men as well as women. Barristers felt that such messages should be built into the educational programme and this was the critical factor in developing a society that could negotiate sexual consent and openly discuss sexual issues, expectations and intentions. In practice, attitudinal change may be difficult to foster, particularly because attitudes around consumption of alcohol are embedded within complex social beliefs that link alcohol use with sex. The authors call for greater public education and awareness of the provisions of the 2003 Act to help enlighten the lay public in their understanding of sexual offences and to make clear what is acceptable and unacceptable sexual behaviour.

[92] [2012] EWCA Crim 2559. See also *Kamki* [2013] EWCA Crim 2335.

what was the complainant's state of intoxication as you find it to be. Was she just disinhibited, or had what she had taken removed her capacity to exercise a choice?"

The judge went on to explain:

"A woman clearly does not have the capacity to make a choice if she is completely unconscious through the effects of drink and drugs, but there are various stages of consciousness, from being wide awake to dim awareness of reality. In a state of dim and drunken awareness you may, or may not, be in a condition to make choices. So you will need to consider the evidence of the complainant's state and decide these two questions: was she in a condition in which she was capable of making any choice one way or another? If you are sure that she was not, then she did not consent. If, on the other hand, you conclude she chose to agree to sexual intercourse, or may have done, then you must find the defendant not guilty."

On appropriate evidence the prosecution is entitled to put its case in respect of **1.122A** absence of consent on an alternative basis alleging (i) lack of capacity and, in any event, (ii) absence of consent, i.e. no agreement by choice. However, it is important for the trial judge not to leave lack of capacity as a route to a guilty verdict where the prosecution has not put its case on that basis and where the defence have not had an opportunity to cross-examine the complainant on the issue of capacity or to make submissions to the jury on the issue. In *Shehu*[93] the Court of Appeal dismissed an appeal against conviction of rape and assault by penetration in circumstances where the judge had made reference to the issue of capacity in his summing up, notwithstanding that the prosecution case was simply that the complainant had not consented, and it had not advanced its case on the basis of lack of capacity to consent. The judge provided a route to verdict referring to the issue of capacity when it was not a live issue in the case. Whilst the Court of Appeal felt that, looking at the summing up as a whole, the direction had not left the issue of capacity to the jury, clearly it would have been wiser not to risk leaving an alternative route to conviction on a basis which had not been a live issue during the trial.

EVIDENTIAL PRESUMPTIONS AS TO CONSENT

Section 75 of the Sexual Offences Act 2003

The presumptions in s.75 arise very rarely in practice.[94] Normally there will be **1.139** sufficient evidence from the defendant or some other source to raise the issue of consent and/or reasonable belief as to consent, and the appropriate direction to the jury will be on the basis of s.74. Furthermore, a s.75 presumption must *not* be

---

[93] [2011] All E.R.(D.) 79.
[94] It is the authors' experience that many barristers feel that s.75 arises in circumstances where it clearly does not. For the proper application of s.75, see *Gavin White* [2010] EWCA Crim 1929 and para.1.139 of the main work.

elevated into an irrebuttable presumption: see *Kapezi*,[95] where the trial judge corrected his earlier direction to the jury in appropriate terms. In *Shanji Zhang*[96] the Court of Appeal upheld a rape conviction even though the trial judge had mistakenly referred to the evidential presumptions in his summing up, on the basis that the jury could have been in no doubt as to what they had to decide. To similar effect is *Lewis Mba*[97] where a conviction was upheld following a hybrid s.74/s.75 direction. This should not be interpreted as an endorsement of such directions; rather, it was an acceptable direction on the special facts of that case.

In most cases, the defendant will be in a position to point to sufficient evidence to raise an issue as to whether the complainant consented and/or whether the defendant reasonably believed that the complainant was consenting. However, in practical terms, the existence of s.75 may well mean that the defendant is obliged to enter the witness box to provide an explanation, if sufficient evidence has not been established in cross-examination of the prosecution witnesses.

Ciccarelli[98] provides a good example of a s.75 presumption arising as there was insufficient evidence that the appellant's belief that the complainant was consenting was reasonable. It was alleged that he had sexually assaulted a young woman who was fast asleep or unconscious through drink and/or drugs. There had been no previous relationship between the parties, not even a short sexual relationship of any kind. It was accepted that the complainant had not consented. There was only one issue in the case, which was whether the appellant might have reasonably believed that she was consenting. At the end of the evidence, including the appellant's, the trial judge concluded that no sufficient evidence had been adduced in accordance with s.75(1) on which the appellant could argue that he had reasonably believed the complainant was consenting. The judge indicated that she would give appropriate directions to the jury. Following her ruling, the appellant pleaded guilty.

On appeal, the Court of Appeal held that the trial judge's approach had been entirely correct. Lord Judge C.J. stated[99] that the basis of the appellant's submission was that it was enough for him to give the evidence he gave that he believed the complainant was consenting. Thereafter, whether or not the belief was reasonable was a matter for the jury. In other words, his asserted belief was sufficient to raise an issue. However, the trial judge had carried out a careful evaluation of the evidence and, on the facts of the case, her conclusion was entirely justified. These were two strangers and, before he touched the complainant sexually, the appellant made no attempt to awaken her. The reasonableness of his asserted belief was based on the single advance she had made to him (according to his account) at an earlier stage in the evening when she was awake, in a different

[95] [2013] EWCA Crim 560.
[96] [2007] EWCA Crim 2018.
[97] [2012] EWCA Crim 2773.
[98] [2011] EWCA Crim 2665.
[99] At [19]–[20].

place, before she was taken to the flat he shared with his girlfriend and put to bed in the spare room to sleep off her drunken stupor. There must be some evidence that the belief was reasonable. The evidence here did not raise an issue for the consideration of the jury.

CONCLUSIVE PRESUMPTIONS AS TO CONSENT

Deception as to the "nature or the purpose of the act"

As the conclusive presumptions in s.76 of the 2003 Act provide an alternative route for a jury to convict a defendant, they require careful scrutiny. The presumption in s.76(2)(a) is relevant only in the comparatively rare case where the defendant has deliberately deceived the complainant about the nature or purpose of the relevant sexual act. The ambit of the provision is limited to the "act" to which the deception relates, and to deceptions as to the "nature or purpose" of the act as opposed to its quality. Beyond this very limited type of case, and assuming that none of the evidential presumptions in s.75 applies, the issue of consent in rape must be addressed by reference to the definition of consent in s.74 and the provision as to reasonable belief in consent in s.1(2).   1.181

Restrictive interpretation of "purpose"

In *R. v B*[100] the Court of Appeal considered the application of s.76 and confirmed the restrictive interpretation of the "purpose" of the act adopted in the leading case of *Jheeta*.[101] The facts are instructive. The appellant was convicted on seven counts of causing his girlfriend to engage in sexual activity without consent, contrary to s.4(1) of the 2003 Act. He established a fake Facebook account and under a pseudonym ("G") established an online relationship with his girlfriend. She had no idea that G was in reality the appellant. Using the pseudonym he persuaded her to share sexual photos with him, and then blackmailed her into performing more sexual acts. She confided in the appellant as to what had happened. He told her he had dealt with the matter by killing G. The appellant then established another fake online account purporting to be a friend of G. Through that account he contacted his girlfriend online and blackmailed her into providing yet more sexually explicit photographs of herself.   1.181A

At trial the appellant admitted setting up the accounts and persuading his girlfriend to engage in the sexual activity, but claimed that he believed she was consenting. The Crown sought to rely upon the conclusive presumption in s.76 on the basis that the appellant had intentionally deceived the complainant as to the

---

[100] [2013] EWCA Crim 823.
[101] [2007] EWCA Crim 1699.

purpose of the relevant acts (it was not contended that she was deceived as to the *nature* of the acts). The trial judge agreed that a s.76 issue arose for the jury to consider. He decided he would leave to the jury the issue of whether the complainant had been deceived as to the purpose of the acts and that he would direct them that if they found deceit proved, the conclusive presumption applied. The complainant was not asked at trial what she understood the purpose or the motive of the person at the end of the webcam to be. The Court of Appeal quashed the convictions and ordered a re-trial. Hallett L.J. stated[102]:

> "Reliance upon section 76 in this case, on these facts and this evidence, was misplaced. The prosecution needed to look no further than the provisions of section 74. It provides that 'a person consents if he agrees by choice and has the freedom and capacity to make that choice'. If the complainant only complied because she was being blackmailed, the prosecution might argue forcefully she did not agree by choice."

In *R. v B* there was no deception as to the "nature" of the acts: the complainant knew that they were sexual acts of vaginal and anal penetration. There was, undoubtedly, a deception as to the identity of the person who was intentionally causing her to engage in sexual activity. Could there have been a deception as to identity within the meaning of s.76? The obstacle to that argument has been identified by Professor Ormerod. The conclusive presumption in s.76 has to be restrictively interpreted as it effectively widens the definition of rape. Parliament has provided that a fraud as to identity will trigger the application of s.76 only where a defendant impersonates someone "known personally to the complainant". The identities used in this case were not the true identities of anyone known personally to the complainant.

Arguably, there was in *R. v B* a deception as to motivation, in that it is likely that the girlfriend thought she was being intentionally caused to engage in the sexual acts for someone's sexual gratification, whereas the true motivation was to test her fidelity or to humiliate her. Clearly, the deception as to identity was inextricably linked to the appellant's motivation or purpose. However, on these facts, the Court of Appeal suggested that if the complainant had assumed that the motive of the other person was sexual gratification, she would not have been misled as to the purpose. The Court of Appeal distinguished *Devonald*,[103] and preferred *Jheeta* to the extent that there is a conflict between the two decisions.

For s.76 to be triggered, the complainant must be deceived as to the nature or purpose of the "relevant act". Professor David Ormerod, in a commentary on *R. v B*,[104] has criticised the drafting of s.77 which defines the "relevant act" for the purposes of the s.4 offence as the defendant intentionally causing the complainant to engage in sexual activity. Professor Ormerod describes the question that the Act

---

[102] At [24].
[103] [2008] EWCA Crim 257. For further criticism of *Devonald*, see para.1.192 in the main work and the article by Jonathan Rogers, above, fn.81.
[104] Currently in an unpublished paper on the Judicial College website.

forces us to ask as rather odd: "Has the defendant deceived the complainant as to the nature or purpose of him intentionally causing her to engage in sexual activity?"

Finally, where s.76 does apply, the judge must give the jury clear directions as to the limited extent of the meaning of the word "purpose" and identify the relevant evidence going to that issue.

Deception as to HIV status

R. v B,[105] discussed in the main work, needs to be considered in the context of the   1.206
decision of the Divisional Court in *Assange v Swedish Prosecution Authority*.[106] The Court in that case rejected the argument that, if a deception does not fall within s.76, it cannot be taken into account for the purposes of s.74 of the Act. Sir John Thomas P, as he then was, observed that all the court had said in *R. v B*[107] was that:

> " . . . as a matter of law, the fact that the defendant may not have disclosed his HIV status is not a matter which could in any way be relevant to the issue of consent under section 74 in relation to sexual activity in this case."

Sir John continued[108]:

> "*R v B* goes no further than deciding that failure to disclose HIV infection is not of itself relevant to consent under s.74. *R v B* does not permit Mr Assange to contend that, if he deceived AA as to whether he was using a condom or one that he had not damaged, that was irrelevant to the issue of AA's consent to sexual intercourse as a matter of the law of England and Wales or his belief in her consent. On each of those issues, it is clear that it is the prosecution case she did not consent and he had no or no reasonable belief in that consent. Those are issues to which s.74 and not s.76 is relevant; there is nothing in *R v B* which compels any other conclusion. Furthermore it does not matter whether the sexual contact is described as molestation, assault or, since it involved penile penetration, rape. The dual criminality issue is the absence of consent and the absence of a reasonable belief in consent. Those issues are the same regardless of the description of the conduct."

It remains to be seen whether the decision in *Assange* will have any impact upon the situation where there is an established sexual relationship between the parties, and the defendant does not reveal to his partner that he has just been diagnosed as HIV positive. Whilst the effect of the decision would be that the failure to reveal his HIV status would not be relevant in itself to consent, there may be circumstances in which the failure to disclose would, when considered with other evidence, be relevant to the issue of consent.

---

[105] [2006] EWCA Crim 2945.
[106] [2011] EWHC 2849 (Admin), at [88] et seq.
[107] At [21].
[108] At [90].

PERMISSIBLE JUDICIAL COMMENT IN RAPE CASES

1.223 This is an area where there have been significant developments in the six years since *Doody*.[109] Judicial comment to prevent false assumptions has become a regular feature in sex cases and is positively encouraged by the Judicial College and the Crown Court Bench Book.[110] Any comment must be balanced, as its purpose is to warn the jury against the unfairness of approaching the evidence with *any* pre-formed assumptions. For instance, in *R. v GJB*[111] the trial judge gave a direction examining possible reasons why the complainant did not make disclosure for several years, but failed to strike a balance by putting the defence case before the jury in the same context. Similarly, in *R. v CE*,[112] the judge directed the jury that it was a common misconception that victims of sexual abuse are eager to complain to the police about what has been done to them. That made it sound as if there are no victims of sexual abuse who are eager to complain to the police, which would, as the Court of Appeal pointed out, be significantly to overstate the position. It is essential that the direction does not implant in the jury's mind any contrary assumption.[113]

It is important that directions are tailored to the facts of the particular case, that they are confined to matters which are well-established and that the judge does not exceed legitimate comment. *MM v R.*[114] is an illustration of a rape case where the trial judge went further than was legitimate. The judge gave appropriate directions cautioning the jury against stereotyping, pointing out that the image of rape as an attack by a stranger is a myth. However, he continued:

> "Rapes occur in a whole variety of situations. Evidence shows us that in over 90% of allegations that come before the court, the two principal people involved know each other and have often on occasions known each [other] for a long time and very well. It is sadly not unheard of that those that love each other can rape each other. Those in relationships can attack each other. It is nothing, it is human nature."

The Court of Appeal accepted that the judge exceeded legitimate comment in respect of his reference to the proportion of cases. However, apart from this reference, about which there was no evidence before the jury and no source known to the Court of Appeal, the judge's remarks were unexceptional. The effect of the judge's words read as a whole was simply to caution the jury against stereotyping, and the Court did not consider the mention of the proportion deprived his direction of balance.

---

[109] [2008] EWCA Crim 2394.

[110] See Crown Court Bench Book: March 2010, Appendix E, Directing the jury. See Ch.17 at E.06. For a useful update, see the Crown Court Bench Book, First supplement, October 2011. For an article written by counsel experienced in these cases supporting these directions, see Felicity Gerry and Catarina Sjolin, *Rape Trauma Direction, Counsel Magazine*, April 2011, p.27.

[111] [2011] EWCA Crim 867.

[112] [2012] EWCA Crim 1324. The Court of Appeal held that, although the wording as not ideal, it did not so far depart from what is acceptable as to render the conviction unsafe.

[113] This is stressed in the Crown Court Bench Book, First Supplement, above, fn.110.

[114] [2011] EWCA Crim 1291, at [39].

It has become common practice for judges to provide juries with written directions on matters of law. We suggest that there is no reason why directions designed to prevent false assumptions should not also be provided in written form,[115] and it should become routine in more complex cases. The use of expressive and emotive language should, of course, be avoided.[116]

The Court of Appeal indicated in *Miller*[117] that, although such directions have been given for some years, it would have been better if the judge had discussed them as part of the routine analysis of the directions to be contained in the summing up, which should take place before counsel's speeches in almost every case and certainly every case of this type. In *Miller* the appellant was convicted on five counts of rape of a child under 13, contrary to s.5 of the 2003 Act. The trial judge had given directions on late reporting and the reaction of children to abuse in the context of the family. On appeal, it was submitted that judicial comment designed to question stereotypical assumptions about the behaviour of rape case complainants offended the common law principle that judicial notice can only be taken of facts of particular notoriety or common knowledge. This submission was given short shrift. The countering of generalisations was the intent of such judicial observations.

Expert evidence inadmissible if matter can properly be covered by balanced judicial direction even if outwith a jury's experience—a gloss on the rule in *Turner*[118]

Even before the recent case of *R. v ER*[119] it had become clear that the way forward   1.230A
in this difficult area was the use of balanced judicial direction to prevent false assumptions. The trial judge in *ER* allowed a psychotherapist (a specialist in counselling in child abuse cases) to give evidence in respect of complainant behaviour and reasons for delay in such cases. *ER* was a historical sex abuse case. The appellant was convicted of serious sexual assaults committed against his sister-in-law in the 1970s when she was aged between 11 and 13. Hughes L.J., as he then was, giving the judgment of the Court, stated that the psychotherapist's evidence should not have been called. The remedy was a neutral judicial warning. Expert evidence carries the danger that it invests the warning with special weight. It may lack any consideration of the appellant's contrary assertion. Expert evidence may divert attention away from critical witnesses. Hughes L.J. put a new

---

[115] See the research of Professor Cheryl Thomas that reveals juries' strong preference for written directions: lecture delivered for the Judicial College, Warwick University, 2013.

[116] See *Joseph* [2010] EWCA Crim 2445, where the Court of Appeal upheld the conviction but noted that through some of his comments the judge had expressed some judicial hostility in strong terms. This was a strong case where the points of criticism of the summing up did not undermine the safety of the conviction.

[117] [2010] EWCA Crim 1578, at [26] per Leveson L.J. See also *R. v CE* [2012] EWCA Crim 1324, at [27]; *MM v R.* [2011] EWCA Crim 1291, at [39], where the Court of Appeal noted that perhaps if the matter had been raised in discussions with counsel before speeches, the error would have been avoided.

[118] [1975] Q.B. 874, discussed in the main work, para.20.03.

[119] [2010] EWCA Crim 2522. For further analysis of *R. v ER*, see para.20.19 in the main work.

gloss on the general rule in *Turner*: unless this kind of expert evidence is directed to something which is quite outside both the experience of the jury and the ability of the judge to explain common understanding and common patterns of behaviour, it should not be adduced.

MENTAL ELEMENT

ABSENCE OF REASONABLE BELIEF IN CONSENT

The defendant's characteristics

Is a psychological condition that affects the defendant's ability to determine whether the complainant was consenting relevant to the reasonableness of his belief in consent?

1.243   Under s.1(2) of the 2003 Act, a defendant's belief in consent will not assist him to avoid conviction unless it was reasonable having regard to all the circumstances. The Act does not state that the belief must be one that would have been held by a reasonable man. Rather, under s.1(1)(c) the prosecution must prove that the defendant himself did not reasonably believe the complainant was consenting. The Act does not provide any assistance as to which of a defendant's personal characteristics are relevant to the issue of whether his belief was reasonable. In the main work, in the absence of any authority, we suggested that a delusional belief in consent can never be reasonable. The reasonableness of an asserted belief should be determined independently of any psychosis or delusional thinking. Any other approach would be doing violence to the English language. The issue as to what personal characteristics are relevant when considering the reasonableness of a person's belief that another person was consenting was left unresolved until the Court of Appeal's judgment in *B v The Queen*[120] in January 2013, discussed below.

1.243A   The issue was identified by the Court of Appeal in *R. v MM*,[121] in which the appellant was convicted of raping his ex-girlfriend three days after she had broken off the relationship. At his first trial, defence psychiatric medical experts concluded that he had possibly been suffering from bi-polar affective disorder at the relevant time. The trial judge indicated that it was his intention to direct the jury that the appellant's psychiatric condition was not relevant to whether his belief in the complainant's consent to sexual intercourse was reasonable. The judge then discharged the jury to enable the defence to consider the appellant's best interests. At the appellant's re-trial, one expert concluded that the appellant's mental condition meant that he did not understand the complainant's signals that she did not consent to sex. The same expert's opinion was that the appellant was

[120] [2013] EWCA Crim 3.
[121] [2011] EWCA Crim 1291.

not guilty by virtue of insanity. However, the appellant's counsel informed the judge that he was not instructed to adduce any psychiatric evidence as the appellant wished to rely on the defence of consent. The appellant was convicted.

The Court of Appeal decided the appeal without having to interpret s.1(2). It held that the appellant had not been prevented from adducing evidence at trial and had chosen not to do so. A close analysis of the psychiatric evidence revealed that it would inevitably have resulted in a finding that he knew the complainant was not consenting.

As to whether the appellant's mental disorder was relevant to the issue of whether he had a reasonable belief in consent, Pitchford L.J. (giving the judgment of the Court) stated[122]:

> "There is, we recognise, an interesting argument to be addressed as to whether there is a material difference between (1) an honest belief held by a defendant which may have been reasonable in the circumstances and (2) a belief which a reasonable man, placed in the defendant's circumstances, may have held. A statutory reasonable man test was held by the Privy Council in *Attorney General for Jersey v Holley*[123] to be stricter than the 'looser' concept of an honest belief which was reasonable in the circumstances ... In the latter case it is arguable that the circumstances may include a mental illness which materially affected the defendant's ability to interpret the complainant's lack of consent. This, however, is not the time to engage in that argument since, on the facts of this case, a permissive construction of the section would not have availed the defendant."

R. v MM left the stage open for the issue to be considered by the Court of Appeal   **1.243B**
in *B v The Queen*[124] which has, to some extent, whether a mental disorder that might affect a defendant's ability to understand the true nature of a situation may be a relevant characteristic. The Court held that delusional thinking, psychotic or otherwise, can never be considered to be reasonable. Such a permissive construction would fly in the face of the legislative intention to reverse the decision of *DPP v Morgan*.[125] The 2003 Act represented a deliberate departure from the model of criminal offences where a defendant was judged only by his subjective state of mind. It deliberately does not make a genuine belief in consent a complete defence to rape. There was a conscious departure from the former law which may well have been because it is not unreasonable to require a person to take care to establish that a sexual event was consensual; the cost to him was very slight whilst the cost to a victim of forced sexual activity was very high indeed.[126]

---

[122] At [54].
[123] [2005] A.C. 580. See [17]–[25] per Lord Nicholls.
[124] [2013] EWCA Crim 3.
[125] [1976] A.C. 182.
[126] The then Government's view expressed by Lord Falconer during the debate as the Bill was passing through Parliament. See *B v The Queen*, above, fn.103 at [28], [37]. See also the analysis of the distinction between self-defence and sexual cases by Professor Ormerod in *Smith & Hogan* (13th ed., 2011, at p.744), cited in *B v The Queen* (at [37]): "The generosity of the law, extending to accepting a defendant's genuine but unreasonable mistakes in, for example matters of self defence, need not be replicated in sexual cases because the conduct in question calls for a qualitatively different degree of vigilance on his part."

The Court of Appeal concluded that, unless and until the state of mind of a defendant amounts to insanity in law, then under the rule enacted in s.1(2) of the 2003 Act, beliefs in consent arising from conditions such as delusional psychotic illness or personality disorders must be judged by objective standards of reasonableness and not by taking into account a mental disorder which induced a belief which could not reasonably arise without it. Once a belief could be judged reasonable only by a process which labelled a plainly irrational belief as reasonable, it cannot be open to a jury to conclude that it was reasonable without straying outside the Act.

Point left open: autism, Asperger's syndrome

1.243C   The Court in *B v The Queen* did, however, acknowledge that there may be cases in which the personality and abilities of the defendant may be relevant to whether his positive belief in consent was reasonable. Cases could arise in which the reasonableness of such a belief depends on the reading by the defendant of subtle social signals, and in which his impaired ability to do so is relevant to the reasonableness of his belief. The Court did not attempt exhaustively to foresee what circumstances might arise in which a belief might be held which is not in any sense irrational, even though most people would not have held it.

The Court illustrated the difficulty in identifying the dividing line in such cases. It gave as a possible example the case of a defendant of less than ordinary intelligence or with a demonstrated inability to recognise behavioural cues. However, the Court indicated that whether such a defendant's belief ought properly to be characterised as unreasonable must await a decision on the facts of a particular case. The Court felt that it is possible that beliefs generated by such factors may not properly be described as irrational and might be judged by a jury not to be unreasonable on the particular facts. This has left open the possible relevance of conditions such as autism spectrum disorder and Asperger's syndrome, which might lead to an impaired or distorted perception of a complainant's behaviour.

Tipu Sultan[127] is an example of a rape case under the old law in which, had it been tried under the 2003 Act, there would have been a strong argument, following the steer in *B v The Queen*, that the appellant's psychological condition at the relevant time was a relevant factor for the jury to consider when deciding if his belief may have been reasonable. Evidence that the appellant was suffering from Asperger's syndrome, which might have affected his ability to determine another's intentions, beliefs or desires in ambiguous situations, would have been a relevant factor for a jury to consider. In that case, the appellant was convicted in 2005 of the rape of his estranged wife. His conviction was quashed in the light of a fresh diagnosis in 2007 that he had had Asperger's syndrome at the time. The original diagnosis had been delusional jealousy, which would be irrelevant following *R. v MM*. On appeal, it was successfully argued that the appellant, as a

[127] [2008] EWCA Crim 6.

sufferer from Asperger's syndrome, would have been liable to misunderstand in real time the signs and even straightforward indications of those with whom he came into contact. Clearly, this was relevant and admissible at a time when the test was the purely subjective one of honest belief in consent.

It is instructive to consider the facts of *B v The Queen* as it provides an example   1.243D
where evidence of a psychiatric condition was not relevant to whether a defendant's belief was reasonable. The appellant was convicted of two rapes upon his partner following a deterioration in his behaviour which, with hindsight, would suggest his illness was developing. They had been in a relationship since 2004 and had a child. The prosecution case was that the complainant had objected and she had simply submitted in the face of his insistence. The defence was consent. The appellant did not give evidence and so there was no direct evidence that he believed that his partner was consenting. However, the appellant had told the police in interview that he never had intercourse with her without her consent.

A consultant psychiatrist gave evidence that the appellant was a paranoid schizophrenic harbouring a number of delusional beliefs. The psychiatrist stated that when ill, the appellant lacked insight into his condition. The acts of intercourse might have been motivated by delusional beliefs that he had sexual healing powers. They might also have been motivated by delusional beliefs that the complainant was having improper contact with men at work. The appellant might have believed that although she was saying no to sexual intercourse, it would still be good for her, and so he might have continued notwithstanding her response. Any such delusional beliefs did not, however, extend to a belief that she was consenting; his illness was not relevant to his understanding whether she was consenting to sexual intercourse or saying no. However, the consultant psychiatrist did give evidence that at the time the appellant had an impaired ability to interpret events normally. His ability to read signals and see things as others did had been impaired by illness.

The trial judge ruled that the psychiatric evidence was only relevant to the genuineness of the appellant's belief. It should be left out of the equation when considering reasonableness. A delusional belief in consent or a belief in consent as a result of his mental illness could not be a reasonable belief. He directed the jury that, as a matter of public policy, the law does not permit defendants suffering from mental illness to avoid the consequences of their crimes by relying upon the explanation: "I only did it because I was mentally ill."

The Court of Appeal, in dismissing the appeal, decided that the issue had not arisen on the facts as the psychiatrist's opinion was that the appellant's illness did not affect his ability to understand whether or not his partner was saying "no". The fact that defence counsel had skilfully elicited the evidence that the appellant had an impaired ability to interpret events normally did not alter the position. The Court added that, if they were wrong about that, and the appellant's delusional beliefs could have led him to believe that his partner consented when she did not, they took the clear view that such delusional beliefs cannot in law render reasonable a belief that his partner was consenting when in fact she was not. A delusional belief in consent, if entertained, would be by definition irrational and thus *un*reasonable and not reasonable. If such delusional beliefs were capable of being described as reasonable, then the more irrational the belief of a defendant, the better would be its prospects of being held reasonable. The Court said that the possible condition of the defendant in *R. v MM* might afford an example. It seemed that he may have been suffering from a bi-polar affective disorder which disinhibited him and made him grossly impulsive. He apparently believed he was entitled to have intercourse with his former girlfriend despite her objections because those objections were, to him, invalid.

CAN SELF-INDUCED INTOXICATION EVER BE A DEFENCE TO RAPE?

1.251   In *Grewal*[128] the Court of Appeal approved the two-stage test under s.1(1)(c) as set out in the main work.[129] Essentially there are two questions:

(i) May the defendant have genuinely believed that the complainant was consenting? Here, the jury are entitled to take into account any evidence of intoxication. If the jury are sure that the defendant did not have such a belief, the prosecution have proved the mental element. If the defendant may have had such a belief, the jury need to consider question

(ii) Was the defendant's belief reasonable in all the circumstances? Here intoxication is irrelevant. The reasonableness of the defendant's belief must be evaluated as if he had been sober. Of course, this does not preclude a jury finding that a drunken man may have had a reasonable belief provided that the belief was reasonable.

MENTAL ELEMENT OF CONSPIRACY TO RAPE

1.259   In *G and F v R.*[130] the Court of Appeal quashed convictions for conspiracy to rape as the actions of the appellants in exchanging text messages were as consistent with nothing more than fantasy in the appellants' minds about raping a young boy from which each gained sexual pleasure as they were with an intent to carry out the plan. The prosecution sought to distinguish the similar case of *Hedgcock, Dyer and Mayers*[131] where Laws L.J. stated that, in the highly unusual circumstances of that case, the jury could only conclude that the participants in the "chat room" conversations actually intended to carry out the agreement to rape if there was some extraneous evidence favouring that interpretation. The conclusion reached by the Court of Appeal was that the internet conversations only carried the matter so far and the other "objective circumstances" if anything pointed the other way. In *G and F* the prosecution case was that the text messages were evidence of an agreement to rape a six-year-old boy. The messages referred to one of the

---

[128] [2010] EWCA Crim 2448, at [30] per Elias L.J.
[129] For an example of such a direction, see Crown Court Bench Book 2010, p.374.
[130] [2012] EWCA Crim 1756.
[131] [2007] EWCA Crim 3486, discussed in the main work.

appellants being "best friends with his Mum" and the possibility of drugging the boy. The prosecution contended that, unlike in *Hedgcock*, a particular boy was the target of the rape plan, and F had access to the boy through his relationship with the boy's mother. Furthermore, again unlike in *Hedgcock*, no visual pornographic material was exchanged between the two defendants. However, the Court of Appeal came to the same conclusion as in *Hedgcock*. No reasonable jury, taking the prosecution case at its highest, could infer that the appellants intended to carry out the agreement. The evidence was equivocal. It was particularly striking that these men never met at any stage, either before or after the text exchange, nor did they even suggest meeting to discuss the plan further. Nor was there any evidence that they took any steps to advance the plan beyond suggesting "Friday night". No place or time or practical details were identified. Nothing at all happened after the exchange of text messages.

ENCOURAGING OR ASSISTING RAPE

In *R. v S and H*[132] the Court of Appeal attempted to resolve a number of problems **1.260** of construction and application of the offence under s.46 of the Serious Crime Act 2007 in the context of supplying Class A or Class B drugs. Section 46 should only be used if it might be that it was the defendant's belief at the time of doing the act that one or more offences would be committed, but he had no belief as to which. The prosecution has to identify which offences the defendant's act was capable of encouraging and assisting and upon which it wishes to rely. Assuming the acts are X, Y and Z (it could be two or more of them), there should be a separate s.46 count for each of X, Y and Z. It is clear that s.46 should be used sparingly, and, in many cases in the context of sexual offences, there may be clear evidence as to which offence the defendant believed would be committed. However, there may be circumstances where a number of different sexual offences could have been anticipated.

---

[132] [2011] EWCA Crim 2872 [2011] Crim. L.R. 449 (for valuable commentary). See also *Sadique (Omar)* [2013] EWCA Crim 1150; [2014] Crim. L.R. 61.

CHAPTER 2

SEXUAL ASSAULTS AND SEXUAL ACTIVITY WITHOUT CONSENT

ASSAULT BY PENETRATION

MODE OF TRIAL AND PUNISHMENT

From December 3, 2012, when ss.122–128 of the Legal Aid, Sentencing and **2.07** Punishment of Offenders Act 2012 were brought into force[1]:

- The offence of assault by penetration is a serious specified offence for the purposes of ss.224 and 225(2) of the Criminal Justice Act 2003 ("CJA 2003") (life sentence for serious offences).
- For offences committed on or after that date, the offence of assault by penetration is listed in Pt 1 of Sch.15B to that Act for the purposes of s.224A of the Act (life sentence for second listed offence).
- For convictions on or after that date (irrespective of the date of commission of the offence), the offence is a specified offence for the purposes of s.226A of the CJA 2003 (extended sentence for certain violent or sexual offences).

BAIL

Section 25 of the Criminal Justice and Public Order Act 1994 was amended on **2.08** December 3, 2012,[2] so that a person charged with, or convicted of, an offence to which the section applies shall be granted bail by a constable only if the constable

---

[1] By the Legal Aid, Sentencing and Punishment of Offenders Act 2012 (Commencement No.4 and Saving Provisions) Order 2012 (SI 2012/2906).
[2] By the Legal Aid, Sentencing and Punishment of Offenders Act 2012, s.90 and Sch.11 para.33, which was brought into force by the Legal Aid, Sentencing and Punishment of Offenders Act 2012 (Commencement No.4 and Saving Provisions) Order 2012, last note.

is "of the opinion", rather than "satisfied" (as before), that there are exceptional circumstances which justify it.

Form of Indictment

2.11   The fundamental principle set out in *Canavan* is still frequently overlooked by the courts. The leading recent example is *Hartley*,[3] in which the appellant was convicted on two counts alleging that he had sexual intercourse with a neighbour's daughter. He was sentenced to 8 years' imprisonment on each count. The complainant's evidence was that the abuse fell into two periods: a few months in the summer of 1980, when she was 11, and a further period of months in 1981, when she was 12. During both periods, sexual intercourse took place two or three times a week. The first count in the indictment related to the period in 1980 and the second to the period in 1981. Neither count related to an identifiable, specific occasion. When the judge came to approach sentence, the appellant's counsel reminded him that the appellant had been convicted of only two offences. The judge rejected this submission, saying that he had to take into account the whole period of time involved and the entirety of the appellant's relationship with the complainant. On appeal, the Crown accepted that *Canavan* was clear authority that an offender can be sentenced only for that of which he has been convicted, but nonetheless sought, unsuccessfully, to uphold the sentence on two alternative bases.

First, relying on an exception identified in *Canavan* itself, it argued that the appellant had assented to the two counts being treated as representative of a longer course of conduct, and to a guilty verdict being taken as a verdict of guilt of that entire course of conduct. The Court of Appeal accepted that this is in principle a permissible approach. Further, the Crown had from the outset presented the case as one of specimen or representative counts and the Court had little doubt that the judge had left it to the jury on the same basis. However, this approach will work only if the defendant explicitly assents to it, and that had not happened here. One might add that it will be rare for such explicit assent to be given, as there will generally be no advantage to the defendant in giving it; it would certainly be unsafe for a prosecutor to rely on assent being forthcoming or, if given at the outset, being maintained as the case unfolds.[4]

Alternatively, the Crown argued that the counts as framed in this case fell within r.14.2(2) of the Criminal Procedure Rules, which, as explained in the main work, permits more than one incident of the same offence to be charged in a single count if the incidents taken together amount to a course of conduct having regard to the

---

[3] [2011] EWCA Crim 1299. See also *R. v A.(N.) (Att Gen's Ref (No.1 of 2011))*, *The Times*, April 11, 2011, in which the defendant was convicted of 16 counts of rape of his wife, but the court sentenced on the basis that he had raped her once or twice a week over a period of two years.

[4] Though see *R. v BDG* [2012] EWCA Crim 1283, in which the four counts were preferred as specimens, on the basis that the assaults had happened so often that the complainant could not remember them all, and defence counsel expressly invited the judge to sentence on the basis that they had occurred on 9 or 10 occasions. The resulting sentence was upheld on the basis of the exception identified in *Hartley*.

time, place or purpose of their commission. The Court rejected this argument too, on the basis that the two counts in this case did not charge a course of conduct but rather single offences. It said that to fall within r.14.2(2), a count must make it clear that what is charged is a course of conduct and indeed the period over which the conduct persisted. Whilst such a count may be of assistance in some cases of sexual misbehaviour persisted in over a period, the Court drew attention to the necessity that the result is not a verdict which is impossible to interpret. Further, in the often encountered case of allegations of a course of conduct over a long period where it is a possible conclusion that there was but a single incident, it will normally be appropriate to include not only a course of conduct count but also a single count in relation to the same period, so that the basis of any verdict can be clear.

The Court went on to consider whether any general assistance might be given as to the framing of indictments in cases of this sort[5]:

> "This is not a new problem. We accept that it is a very common situation and we accept that *Canavan* does create significant difficulties for courts and thus also for prosecutors. That is particularly so in cases of sexual offending because a great many of them are of allegations of a course of conduct involving multiple but unidentified instances; probably rather more are of that kind than are of single incidents.
>
> We do not think that it is possible to attempt any general statement of how indictments ought to be framed in the very wide range of cases that come before the courts. Everything in reality depends on the facts of the individual case, on what is alleged and on what issue is raised by the defendant. We have been reminded that there exist two new potential procedures. One we have already referred to, the Criminal Procedure Rules and we add nothing to what we have said about those. There is also now in existence the Domestic Violence (Crime and Victims) Act 2004 which in sections 17 to 19 does provide in some cases for an order to be made for representative counts to remain on the indictment and in the event of conviction for guilt of outstanding instances to be determined by the judge without the jury . . . [B]ut we draw attention to the fact that [those provisions] are limited in application. There are strict conditions for when they can be employed and in particular they can be employed only where otherwise the indictment would be of such a size as to be impracticable for the jury to cope with. It seems to us much more likely that in general terms the problem of which this case is an example can normally be dealt with by the framing of an indictment which does not contain an enormous number of counts but does contain sufficient to enable the judge to pass sentence on a basis which sufficiently represents what really happened. More than that we do not attempt to say, beyond perhaps this. Where specific incidents are capable of identification, however exiguously, for example 'the time the vase broke', or 'the time we went by train to Brighton', then ordinarily we would expect the indictment to contain a count referable and identifiably referable to that event so that the jury can determine it. That of course is subject to not, if there are hundreds of them, overloading the indictment with more counts than the jury can be expected to determine. Generally it is necessary for those who are framing indictments to pay attention to any issues flagged up by what the defendant has said either in interview with the police or later in a defence statement. Ordinarily we would suggest where there is simply a complaint of a course of conduct over a period of months, often years, more than a single count for each period is usually appropriate, although one per year may well suffice if the alleged period is

---

[5] At [21]–[22] per the Vice President, Hughes L.J.

extended. But the overall principle is simply that regard must be had in an intelligent way to the possible views of the case at which a jury might arrive and to the position of the judge in due course should there be convictions. If thought is given to those questions we have little doubt that it will normally be possible to frame an indictment in a manner which enables the sentencing to be realistic and complies with the strict rules of law as set out in *R v Canavan*."

2.11A   Despite these clear words, indictments are still being preferred that fail to particularise the allegations so as properly to reflect what the complainant says happened, with the result that on conviction the principle in *Canavan* prevents the court imposing a sentence that fully reflects the extent of the offending. A recent example of a "woefully defective"[6] indictment is *Hobson*,[7] where the appellant was alleged to have indecently assaulted the complainants K and N, two sisters, in the same way on a large number of occasions over a period of years, but the indictment contained just one specimen count in relation to each complainant. In evidence, the complainants differentiated between various particular incidents by giving details such as the location of the offence, the occasion of it, and who else was there. Nobody suggested amending the indictment to reflect this evidence. It was held on appeal that it had been incumbent on the judge, in those circumstances, to direct the jury that they had to be agreed about a particular occasion before they could convict, and it was not sufficient that some jurors were satisfied in relation to one occasion and others in relation to another. The Court of Appeal said:

> "16. Given that the complainants each alleged repeated conduct over many years, specimen counts were in principle appropriate. Moreover, there was no request by the defence with respect to any of the specimen counts for the particulars to be identified with greater precision. Nonetheless, when giving evidence both K and N spoke with some particularity about particular occasions. Relating to count 1. K described incidents when the defendant came up to her bedroom to read her a story when she was going to bed and would touch her vagina under her clothing. She said that this happened on many occasions. She also said that it happened on a number of occasions in his garden shed. She then identified in much greater detail a specific incident which she said had occurred when she and the adults were all sitting on a patio and she was on the appellant's knee. She said that the applicant requested that her parents get a blanket for her. Someone got a blanket to cover her and the defendant then abused her under the blanket by touching her vagina in the presence of the other adults. The judge recounted her evidence and then directed the jury as follows . . .
>
> > 'All you have to decide is this. Are you sure he touched her at least once? Forget about dates, do not worry about legal definitions, are you satisfied that he touched her outside her vagina but on her vagina at least once during those years?'
>
> 17. Later . . . he repeated this injunction in the following way:
>
> > 'You can then go through each of the individual indictment counts and say in respect of each, are we sure using all the relevant evidence are we sure he did this to that girl at least once?'
>
> 18. The complaint is that this does not tell the jury that they have to be unanimous about the same incident. They were not told that they should be unanimous about the patio incident for example, or else be sure that on at least one unspecified occasion the offence was committed. We agree that the direction does not tell the jury that they

---

[6] James Richardson QC in *Criminal Law Week*, Issue 28, July 22, 2013, p.1.
[7] [2013] EWCA Crim 819.

must approach matters in that way. The question is whether that renders the summing up defective and casts doubt upon the safety of the verdicts.

19. The appellant submits that it does. The failure to issue such a direction leaves open the possibility that some members of the jury could believe that one of the incidents occurred, such as the patio occasion, and other members could believe that a different incident occurred, such as touching in the bedroom at bed-time, but the jury may not be agreed about the same occasion.

20. The position with N was essentially the same. In her evidence with respect to count 4 she gave evidence that the defendant regularly touched her over her clothing. She also recounted in some detail a specific occasion in his garden shed when he assaulted her in that way when he was teaching her to play the guitar; and a separate occasion in the bedroom when her sister was there and he was reading a story to them both.

21. Again the judge told the jury that it was enough that the jury were sure that he had assaulted her by touching her over her clothing at least once. The appellant makes the same point as with respect to K: the jury could have convicted without being unanimous with respect to the same incident. Without a direction to the effect that they had to be sure about the same incident, it was possible that the jury were not in fact in agreement, in which case the verdict is unsafe.

Discussion

22. In *R v Rackham* [1997] 2 Cr. App. R. 222 the defence asked for identification of the various specific incidents on which the Crown relied in a specimen count of sexual misconduct. The judge refused to order this and this court held that he was wrong not to do so. The defendant should be allowed to know with such particularity as the circumstances admit what case he has to meet. Furthermore, it is incumbent on the judge to relate the evidence to the particular counts: *R v Farrugia*, *The Times*, January 18 1988.

23. No doubt in most cases where a specimen count is relied on, it is enough for the judge to tell the jury, as the judge did in this case, that they may convict if they are sure that the offence has been committed at least once. Where the complainant cannot particularise any specific incident and merely alleges a pattern of similar conduct, the question for the jury will be whether they are sure that the account of the complainant is reliable. There will be no room for the jury to focus on one incident rather than another because no single occasion is sufficiently distinct, and it would be meaningless and unhelpful to tell the jury that they had to be sure in relation to the same incident.

24. However, where the complainant gives evidence identifying specific occasions alleged to be part of a pattern of conduct and there is evidence before the jury which could cause a reasonable jury to acquit on the specimen charge but convict on the particularised occasion or vice versa, then it is possible that the jury is not at one on any specific occasion. Where that is the case, an obvious solution is for the prosecution to apply to amend the indictment and add the particular incident or incidents as separate counts on the indictment. But if these specific occasions are not particularised in the indictment, it will be incumbent on the judge to tell the jury that they can only convict if they are sure that the offence has been committed on the same occasion, either on an occasion in the course of the unspecified pattern of offending, or on one of the particular occasions identified in the evidence.

25. Mr Mullarkey, counsel for the prosecution, contended that this would be unduly onerous. We do not agree; it simply requires that a specimen offence should be directed to a pattern of conduct which cannot be particularised in any specific way. It is an elementary principle that the jury should be sure about each element of the

offence and that is not the case if it is open to a reasonable jury to convict on the basis of different incidents or occasions. Absent such a direction, it will not be possible to say that the jury were unanimous with respect to the same occasion. Take this appeal, if the specific occasion relating to occasion on the patio had been the subject of a separate count to an occasion in the bedroom, it plainly would not have been possible to convict on either count where only half the jury were sure that the bedroom incident had occurred as alleged and the other half had only been sure of the patio incident. There can be no magic about the fact that these incidents are wrapped up together in the context of a specimen count: it cannot lead to a different conclusion . . .

28. It follows that, in our view, the critical question is whether the evidence before the jury was such that there was a realistic possibility that a reasonable jury could have reached its verdict in respect of a specimen count by focusing on different occasions. If so, the summing up would be defective and the convictions would be unsafe without a direction that the jury had to be sure with respect to the same occasion.

29. In answering that question in this case, we bear in mind that the defendant did not give evidence; and we note too that the defence did not at the time raise with the judge the need to distinguish between any particular incidents or occasions. Nevertheless, in our view the nature of the incidents here was such that the members of the jury could on the evidence have been satisfied about the course of conduct but not the specific occasion, or vice versa. The distinctive feature of the patio incident was that it allegedly occurred in the presence of K's parents. Some members of the jury may have thought that it distinctly unlikely that the defendant would have acted in such a risky manner. Others may have felt that the detail had the ring of truth. Similarly, with respect to N's account of the offence occurring in the presence of her sister (who does not appear to have confirmed this in her evidence). Also, in her case there was some evidence, albeit slender, from a defence witness that children were not allowed into the hut where the first incident was alleged to have occurred. Moreover, the fact that the jury found the defendant not guilty of other specimen counts suggests that they must have had some doubts about the reliability of the evidence of the complainants. In these circumstances it cannot be said that the verdicts are safe and therefore they must be quashed."

The judge in *Hobson* had sentenced the appellant on the basis that he had repeatedly assaulted the complainants over many years. The Court of Appeal quashed the convictions and so did not need to consider sentence, but it took the opportunity to emphasise that the judge should have passed sentence in accordance with *Canavan*, i.e. on the basis that the appellant had been guilty of a single offence against each complainant. If, in fact, he had been guilty of a prolonged course of abuse of the sisters, as they had stated in evidence, then that outcome would, of course, have been a travesty of justice. It would be hard to find a clearer illustration of the need for prosecutors to draft indictments with great care in cases of prolonged alleged abuse and to consider applying to amend them in the course of the trial so as to particularise the allegations if the evidence justifies that course.

Sentencing

2.14   The Sentencing Council has issued a new guideline applicable to sex offenders aged 18 or over who are sentenced on or after April 1, 2014: see para.1.20 et seq., above. In its consultation on the draft guideline,[8] the Council noted that the types of penetration and offending behaviours that may be involved in assault by penetration are wider than in relation to rape, and range from acts as severe as the highest category rape (for example, a violent sexual attack involving penetration of the victim with an object intended or likely to cause significant injury to the victim), to an activity that, whilst involving severe sexual violation of a victim, is more akin to a serious sexual assault (e.g. momentary penetration with fingers). The Council noted that research had found a general view among the public and victims that assault by penetration is akin to rape and should be sentenced accordingly. Participants described penetration by objects such as bottles or knives as a particularly aggravated form of rape, potentially more serious and more physically damaging than penetration with a penis. The Council agreed that there is a high degree of crossover between the two offences. However, because the range of potential types of offending is wider for assault by penetration, the Council favoured treating the two offences separately in the guideline.

Under the previous guideline, issued by the Sentencing Guidelines Council in 2007 and covered in the main work, a lower sentence would be given for penetration with a body part, such as a finger or tongue, where no other physical harm was sustained. A higher sentence would be given for penetration with an object (the larger or more dangerous the object, the higher the sentence would be) or penetration combined with abduction, detention, abuse of trust or more than one offender acting together. The Sentencing Council agreed with the conclusions of public research that stated:

> "Generally where penetration of genitals had occurred, the public and victims/ survivors felt this was akin to rape regardless of what had been used to penetrate due to the level of violation inherent."[9]

The Council therefore proposed that such assaults should generally be treated in very similar terms to rape in terms of the harm caused. Indeed, there are only two differences in the harm factors specified in relation to the two offences. First, the factor relating to pregnancy or an STI occurring as a consequence of the offence is included in the guideline for rape, but not for assault by penetration, because that offence does not involve penile penetration and so these risks do not arise. Secondly, "penetration using large or dangerous object(s)" is included as a harm factor in relation to assault by penetration because, whilst it acknowledged that psychological harm results whatever the means of penetration, the Council was of the view that where a large or dangerous object is used, this increases the physical consequences of the attack and also the psychological harm, and so should increase the starting point for sentence.

---

[8] *Sexual Offences Guideline: Consultation* (December 6, 2012). The consultation closed on March 14, 2013.

[9] *Attitudes to sentencing sexual offences*: Sentencing Council Research series 01/12 (*www.sentencing-council.org.uk* [accessed June 18, 2013]).

New sentencing guideline

Step One—Harm and culpability

2.14A   Under the new guideline, the sentencing court is to go through a series of steps in order to determine the appropriate sentence. Step one involves determining the offence category by reference to the degree of harm caused and then the culpability level for the offence. In relation to the offence of assault by penetration, the harm and culpability factors are as follows:

HARM		CULPABILITY	
Category 1	• The extreme nature of one or more category 2 factors or the extreme impact caused by a combination of category 2 factors **may** elevate to category 1	**A** • Significant degree of planning • Offender acts together with others to commit the offence • Use of alcohol/drugs on victim to facilitate the offence	
Category 2	• Severe psychological or physical harm • Penetration using large or dangerous object(s) • Additional degradation/humiliation • Abduction • Prolonged detention/sustained incident • Violence or threats of violence (beyond that which is inherent in the offence) • Forced/uninvited entry into victim's home • Victim is particularly vulnerable due to personal circumstances* *for children under 13 please refer to the guideline on page 27 of the Definitive Guideline	• Abuse of trust • Previous violence against victim • Offence committed in course of burglary • Recording of the offence • Commercial exploitation and/or motivation • Offence racially or religiously aggravated • Offence motivated by, or demonstrating, hostility to the victim based on his or her sexual orientation (or presumed sexual orientation)	
		B	
		Factor(s) in category A not present	

Step Two—Starting point and category range

Having determined the offence category and culpability level, the court should then use the corresponding starting point specified in the guideline in order to reach a sentence within the category range. The starting point applies to all offenders irrespective of plea or previous convictions. Once the starting point has been determined, step two allows further adjustment for aggravating or mitigating features, set out below. A case of particular gravity, reflected by multiple features of culpability or harm, could merit upward adjustment from the starting point before further adjustment for aggravating or mitigating features. Where there is a sufficient prospect of rehabilitation, a community order with a sex offender treatment programme requirement under s.202 of the CJA 2003 can be a proper alternative to a short or moderate length custodial sentence. The starting points and category ranges for assault by penetration are as follows: **2.14B**

	A	B
Category 1	**Starting point** 15 years' custody **Category range** 13–19 years' custody	**Starting point** 12 years' custody **Category range** 10–15 years' custody
Category 2	**Starting point** 8 years' custody **Category range** 5–13 years' custody	**Starting point** 6 years' custody **Category range** 4–9 years' custody
Category 3	**Starting point** 4 years' custody **Category range** 2–6 years' custody	**Starting point** 2 years' custody **Category range** High level community order–4 years' custody

As noted above, the Sentencing Council considered that the violation incurred by reason of penetration is equally severe whatever the means used, whether it be the penis, another body part or an object. Accordingly, the Council saw no justification for any difference in sentencing between rape and assault by penetration for the most serious offences, i.e. those in category 1, and the same starting points therefore apply. In categories 2 and 3, the ranges are broader than those in the rape guideline to accommodate the broader range of offending that can be encompassed by this offence. For example, a category 2 assault by penetration could include an assault where the victim has been detained in their home by a partner for a prolonged period and there has been very brief penetration with a finger. However, it could also include a scenario where an ex-partner has broken into the victim's home and carried out a violent assault and penetrated the victim with his fist. As for category 3, the starting points are higher than those in the SGC guideline for offences where any of the culpability A factors are present (4 years' imprisonment as opposed to 2 years'). In the SGC guideline this category was focused solely on the type of penetration, e.g. by fingers, toes or tongue. The Council's aim was to move away from a focus on the physical acts involved and instead to reflect the harm caused to the victim by the penetration, irrespective of the way in which it is carried out. Category 3 therefore reflects a baseline of harm without the need for the presence of any other factors. It is evident from the Council's comments on categories 2 and 3 that brief penetration with fingers, toes or tongues, where no harm is caused to the victim (not simply no *physical* harm, as under the SGC guideline), will continue to attract a sentence towards the lower end of the range.[10]

Aggravating and mitigating factors

2.14C   After identifying the starting point and category range, the court should consider whether the presence of aggravating or mitigating factors should result in an upward or downward adjustment from the starting point or the imposition of a sentence outside the category range. In particular, relevant recent convictions are likely to result in an upward adjustment. When sentencing appropriate category 3 offences, the court should also consider whether the custody threshold has been passed; if so, whether a custodial sentence is unavoidable; and if it is, whether that sentence can be suspended. The non-exhaustive list of aggravating and mitigating factors for assault by penetration is as follows:

Aggravating factors
Statutory aggravating factors
• Previous convictions, having regard to a) the nature of the offence to which the conviction relates and its relevance to the current offence; and b) the time that has elapsed since the conviction   • Offence committed whilst on bail
Other aggravating factors
• Specific targeting of a particularly vulnerable victim   • Ejaculation (where not taken into account at step one)

---

[10] For the approach to such cases under the SGC guideline, see, e.g. *Bukhtor Singh* [2012] EWCA Crim 1274, discussed in para.2.14G, below; *Park* [2008] EWCA Crim 1806, discussed in para.3.65 of the main work.

- Blackmail or other threats made (where not taken into account at step one)
- Location of offence
- Timing of offence
- Use of weapon or other item to frighten or injure
- Victim compelled to leave their home (including victims of domestic violence)
- Failure to comply with current court orders
- Offence committed whilst on licence
- Exploiting contact arrangements with a child to commit an offence
- Presence of others, especially children
- Any steps taken to prevent the victim reporting an incident, obtaining assistance and/or from assisting or supporting the prosecution
- Attempts to dispose of or conceal evidence
- Commission of offence whilst under the influence of alcohol or drugs

Mitigating factors

- No previous convictions **or** no relevant/recent convictions
- Remorse
- Previous good character and/or exemplary conduct*
- Age and/or lack of maturity where it affects the responsibility of the offender
- Mental disorder or learning disability, particularly where linked to the commission of the offence

* Previous good character/exemplary conduct is different from having no previous convictions. The more serious the offence, the less the weight which should normally be attributed to this factor. Where previous good character/exemplary conduct has been used to facilitate the offence, this mitigation should not normally be allowed and such conduct may constitute an aggravating factor.

In the context of this offence, previous good character/exemplary conduct should not normally be given any significant weight and will not normally justify a reduction in what would otherwise be the appropriate sentence.

Steps Three to Nine

The remaining steps cover the following points. At step three the court should **2.14D** consider any factors which would indicate a reduction in sentence, e.g. assistance to the prosecution. At step four it should consider any reduction for a guilty plea. At step five the court should consider dangerousness, i.e. whether it would be appropriate to award a life sentence (s.224A or s.225(2) of the CJA 2003) or an extended sentence (s.226A). Step six requires the court to consider whether the total sentence is just and proportionate to the offending behaviour. At step seven it should consider whether to make an ancillary order (e.g. a compensation order, a sexual offences prevention order ("SOPO") or a restraining order). Step eight requires the court to fulfil its duty under s.174 of the CJA 2003 to give reasons for, and explain the effect of, the sentence. Finally, at step nine the court should consider whether to give credit for time spent on bail in accordance with s.240A of that Act.

Sentencing examples

2.14E   The following decisions all pre-date the new guideline, but are useful illustrations of the approach taken by the Court of Appeal to different factual scenarios.

2.14F   *Duffy*[11] concerned an appeal against a sentence of 6 years' imprisonment imposed following a plea of guilty to assault by penetration. The complainant (31) had been at home in bed, asleep, when she became aware of the appellant (23) standing by her, kissing her face and neck. He had then inserted his fingers into her vagina before leaving the house. The appellant was able to offer no explanation for his behaviour. He said he had consumed about 14 alcoholic drinks, that the complainant lived next-door-but-one to his parents, and that a good friend of his had previously lived in the house and occupied the complainant's bedroom. The previous occupants had had an open door policy and the appellant had once been found sleeping in that bedroom in a drunken state. The judge took account of the fact that the appellant was effectively of good character and was well thought of by everyone who knew him, and gave credit for the guilty plea. However, he indicated that the offence was almost as serious as rape and that the examples in the SGC guideline indicated that, after a trial, the sentence would have been 8 or more years' imprisonment. The Court of Appeal allowed the appeal, stating that the offence had been serious and disturbing but should not have been equated with rape. The guideline for "ordinary" digital penetration gave a range of between 1 and 4 years. In those circumstances, a starting point of 8 years had been too high. Equally, however, there were aggravating features of the case which meant that something beyond the bare guideline bracket for digital penetration was appropriate. Taking account of the guilty plea, the Court substituted a sentence of 4 years' imprisonment for the original term.

2.14G   In *Singh (Bukhtor)*[12] a taxi driver appealed against a sentence of 7 years' imprisonment imposed following his conviction for assault by penetration committed against a passenger. In the early hours of the morning the appellant had driven the complainant to an abandoned petrol station where he exposed and fondled her breasts, put his hands in her underwear and digitally penetrated her vagina. The defence at trial was consent, but following conviction a pre-sentence report found that the appellant accepted the verdict and expressed remorse. The

---

[11] [2011] EWCA Crim 544.
[12] [2012] EWCA Crim 1274.

sentencing judge held that the case fell on the cusp of levels 1 and 2 of the SGC guideline, and that the major factor was the appellant's abuse of his position of trust as a taxi driver. The Court of Appeal allowed the appeal, holding that the judge had been justified in placing the offence at the lower end of level 1. There was an element of abduction, although that was in large part embraced within the concept of abuse of trust. In any event, the sentence should be tailored to the particular features of the offence; a different result should not be reached whether one started at the lower end of level 1 or put the case at level 2 with a significant aggravating feature such as breach of trust. But for the abuse of trust, the sentence would have been significantly lower, but it was important that those using taxis felt safe, and such offences damaged the interests of taxi drivers as a community. The Court added that the appellant's proposition that non-penile penetration should be sentenced less severely was in principle "self-evident", not least because there was no risk of impregnation or infection. Moreover, the SGC guideline emphasised that brief penetration with fingers, toes or tongue could result in a significantly lower sentence, where no physical harm was done.[13] In the circumstances a starting point of 7–8 years would not have been out of line. But taking into account the limited and fleeting act of digital penetration, the lack of premeditation, the element of remorse and the appellant's essentially good character, the Court reduced the sentence from 7 to 5 years.

In *Scully*[14] the applicant (38) was convicted of assault by vaginal penetration of the   **2.14H**
complainant. He was acquitted of attempted rape and assault by anal penetration. The defence at trial was consent. The appellant and the complainant had been travelling in the same railway carriage. In passing sentence, the judge indicated he was satisfied that the applicant had realised that the complainant, who had vomited, had been drinking and had missed her stop. He told the other passengers that he would take care of her and ensure she got home. All those present, including the complainant, had trusted him. He helped her off the train. Outside there were taxis and no waiting passengers, but the applicant charmed and reassured the complainant and led her away from the station to a secluded area where he attacked her, forced her to the ground and inserted his fingers into her vagina. Despite her befuddled state, she had resisted and struggled as best she could. She had suffered multiple injuries, the majority being scratches. She had bruising and reddening to one of her eyes suggesting a powerful blow to her face and there was an injury to her neck. The complainant remembered that the applicant restricted her breathing, leading her to black out. The judge was satisfied that the complainant had not removed her own underwear, which were left at the scene along with her shoes and some of her other belongings. The attack ended when the complainant bit the applicant's fingers so deeply that he had rolled away in agony, when she managed to run for help. The judge noted the complainant had been traumatised by the incident, and took into account that the applicant was a

---

[13] For the approach taken to penetration of this sort in the new guideline, see para.2.14B, above.
[14] [2013] EWCA Crim 2288.

family man of good character and a high-flying civil servant who had destroyed his future. The judge observed this offence did not fall into the highest category of offending in the SGC guideline, but equally in his view the lowest category did not adequately reflect the criminality of the conduct. He sentenced the applicant to 5 years' and 4 months' imprisonment. The applicant submitted to the Court of Appeal that the judge had made a number of unjustifiable findings of fact and had erred in finding that the lowest sentencing range suggested in the guideline (1–4 years) was insufficient to meet the gravity of the offence. The Court of Appeal rejected these arguments. The judge's factual conclusions were entirely justified on the basis of the evidence called by the prosecution. This was a premeditated attack in the sense that the applicant deliberately left the train before his stop in order to abuse the complainant, who was clearly unable to look after herself. This was a particularly grave instance of the violent exploitation of a clearly inebriated young woman, in a deserted location to which she was led. She was scratched, punched in the face and strangled to the point at which she lost consciousness. The complainant has set out clearly and credibly in her victim impact statement that she would never recover from what occurred and she was subjected to material physical harm. Accordingly, the judge had been entitled to conclude that this case came above the lowest category in the guideline. The applicant had acted as a "good Samaritan" and thereby breached the trust the complainant put in him and he led her to a place where he was able to restrain and attack her. The Court recognised that he had lost his good character and an excellent job, and that the consequences for him and his family would be considerable, but the gravity of the crime made it unarguable that the sentence was manifestly excessive.

Consent

Consent and public policy

2.24   There is growing interest in this area of the law, driven by what is widely regarded as the pernicious impact of the decision in *Brown*. Thus H.H. Judge Peter Murphy has argued that, as the 2003 Act makes absence of consent an element of the offences of assault by penetration and sexual assault, a defendant charged with one of those offences must be allowed to run a consent defence[15] even in circumstances where the general principle established in *Donovan* and applied by the House of Lords in *Brown* would otherwise apply.[16] This interesting argument is, with respect, flawed, since it was equally true of the repealed, pre-2003 Act offence of indecent assault that absence of consent had to be proved in order to secure a conviction, and it remains true of the subsisting offences under the Offences against the Person Act 1861 of which assault is a constituent element. Yet that has not prevented the principle in *Donovan* applying to those offences. In

[15] Though as absence of consent is an element of the offence, its presence is not a "defence", properly so-called.

[16] *Flogging Live Complainants and Dead Horses: We May No Longer Need to Be in Bondage To Brown* [2011] Crim. L.R. 758.

truth, regardless of the context, where the elements of an offence, whether statutory or common law, require absence of consent, it is clearly established that the defendant may rely only upon a consent which the courts recognise as capable of being legally effective. Putting it another way, the courts have determined what may and may not amount to an effective consent, and the law that they have developed applies regardless of the nature and origins of the offence in question.

As explained in the main work, where A inflicts actual bodily harm on a willing **2.24A** B, in circumstances not falling within one of the recognised exceptions, A may be convicted of a non-consensual offence despite B's apparent consent. But can B himself be convicted as an accessory to the offence, or of encouraging or assisting it?

It seems he can, applying the reasoning of the majority of the Supreme Court in *Gnango*.[17] In that case the majority held (Lord Kerr dissenting) that where D1 and D2 voluntarily enter into a fight against each other, each intending to kill or cause grievous bodily harm to the other and each foreseeing that the other has a reciprocal intention, and where D1 mistakenly kills a third party (V) in the course of the fight, then not only D1 but also D2 is guilty of murdering V. The significance of the decision for present purposes is that in the course of its reasoning the majority held that there is no general statutory or common law bar to a defendant being convicted as an accessory to a crime of which he was the actual or intended victim. The exception is the general rule,[18] illustrated by the decision in *Tyrrell*, that where legislation creates an offence that is intended to protect a class of persons, a member of that class cannot be convicted as an accessory to such an offence committed in respect of him.

How should the Supreme Court's reasoning be applied where the victim is a participant in a sado-masochistic encounter? The decision of the House of Lords in *Brown* establishes that his consent to the infliction on himself of actual bodily harm cannot provide a defence to a criminal charge brought against the person who inflicted the injury. As the rule in *Tyrrell* is not relevant in this context, the effect of the reasoning of the majority in *Gnango* is that, not only does the sadist have no defence to a charge, but also the masochist is party to the offence committed against himself. It is worth noting that in *Gnango* the view of the majority was that by voluntarily entering into the gun fight, D2 encouraged or assisted D1 to kill or seriously injure him. This proposition is, with respect, wholly artificial, given that D2's whole purpose was to avoid being killed and instead to kill D1, and the decision may be criticised for that reason. However, the circumstances in that case are clearly distinguishable in this respect from a sado-masochistic encounter, where the victim will certainly be encouraging and perhaps also assisting the infliction of injury upon himself.

---

[17] [2011] UKSC 59.
[18] Identified by Professor Glanville Williams in his article "Victims and other exempt parties in crime" (1990) 10 Legal Studies at p.245.

Time will tell whether the CPS regards *Gnango* as shifting the boundaries in this area so as to justify the prosecution of the masochist in cases such as *Brown* (in which the defendants were all convicted of inflicting harm). But this seems an unlikely development given the lack of any compelling public interest in such prosecutions and the criticism to which *Brown* is already subject. There is currently no guidance on the CPS website that bears upon the issue.

2.27 In *Entertainment – The Painful Process of Rethinking Consent*,[19] Simon Cooper and Mark James consider the application of the law of consent to the ever more significant phenomenon of the infliction of pain or injury for the purposes of entertainment. They go on to advocate a new approach to the categorisation of consensual activities for the purposes of the criminal law, whereby consent would operate in relation to activities that involve the intentional infliction of harm, or carry a significant risk of unintended injury, in circumstances which are tolerated by society, but not otherwise. The authors suggest that this approach would relax the rigid and narrow categories of activity that currently prevail, allowing an activity to move between categories depending upon society's attitude towards it at a given time, and better enabling participants to determine in advance whether or not an activity is lawful. The argument is attractively put, but seems to underestimate the uncertainty that would be injected into the law by abolishing the existing categories and replacing them with the authors' more open-textured approach.

2.27A Rather more attractive, in this respect at least, is Julia Tolmie's argument in *Consent to Harmful Assaults: The Case for Moving Away from Category Based Decision Making*.[20] In Tolmie's view the current approach to the operation of consent results in arbitrary and piecemeal decision-making that does not properly reflect considerations of free will and of harm arising from the facts of the particular case. She advocates instead the approach adopted by the New Zealand Court of Appeal in *Lee*,[21] under which consent is presumptively available as a defence in respect of the intentional or reckless infliction of grievous bodily harm, but the presumption can be displaced in respect of certain dangerous categories of activity with limited social utility or which society will not tolerate. For Tolmie, this approach has the advantage that, in deciding whether the presumption is displaced, the court is able and required to engage directly with considerations of harm, victim vulnerability and social utility arising from the facts of the particular case, rather than (as under the current law in England and Wales) assessing these considerations in relation to the generic category of behaviour to which it belongs. But she acknowledges that applying this approach to activities involving the intentional or reckless infliction of actual, as opposed to grievous bodily harm would create uncertainty as to the lawfulness of an unworkably broad array of social interactions: for example, every ear piercing would be susceptible to

---

[19] [2012] Crim. L.R. 188.
[20] [2012] Crim. L.R. 656.
[21] (2006) 22 C.R.N.Z. 568.

prosecution so that the public policy factors for and against allowing consent to operate in the particular case could be examined on the facts. To avoid this, she proposes to confine her approach, as in *Lee* itself, to cases in which grievous bodily harm is intended or risked. This would certainly avoid much of the uncertainty that would flow from an all-embracing approach such as the one advocated by Cooper and James, above. But for that very reason it generates problems of its own, since the effect of restricting the approach to grievous bodily harm would to be create a stark and unsatisfactory difference in the way in which the law treats the intentional or reckless infliction of different degrees of harm. Cases of actual bodily harm would continue to be subject to the piecemeal decision-making of the current law, but cases of grievous bodily harm would benefit from a more sophisticated and fact-responsive analysis of the sort reflected in *Lee*. This could produce some strange results. Thus, a sadist who inflicted upon a willing masochist actual bodily harm of the sort considered in *Brown* would, if prosecuted, remain unable to rely upon the masochist's consent. But if he went further and inflicted grievous bodily harm, then on Tolmie's approach, he would be able to invite the court to consider whether, given considerations of free will and, possibly, societal tolerance, he should be able to rely on consent notwithstanding the seriousness of the harm that he inflicted.

SEXUAL ASSAULT

MODE OF TRIAL AND PUNISHMENT

For convictions on or after December 3, 2012, when s.124 of the Legal Aid,   **2.50**
Sentencing and Punishment of Offenders Act 2012 was brought into force,[22] sexual assault is a specified offence for the purposes of s.226A of the CJA 2003 (extended sentence for certain violent or sexual offences), irrespective of the date of commission of the offence.

ALTERNATIVE VERDICT

A defendant indicted for sexual assault may be convicted in the alternative of   **2.53**
battery if the "sexual" element of the offence is not established. On the face of it this is surprising, since under s.6(3) of the Criminal Law Act 1967 a jury may bring in an alternative verdict only in relation to "another offence falling within the jurisdiction of the court of trial", and battery, which used to be triable either way, was turned into a summary offence by s.39 of the Criminal Justice Act 1988.[23]

---

[22] By the Legal Aid, Sentencing and Punishment of Offenders Act 2012 (Commencement No.4 and Saving Provisions) Order 2012 (SI 2012/2906).

[23] Thus in *Mearns* [1991] 1 Q.B. 82 it was held that an alternative verdict of guilty of common assault was not available on an indictment charging assault occasioning actual bodily harm. *Mearns* was followed in *Burt* (1996) 161 J.P. 77; *Brownless*, Unreported, May 9, 2000; *Clifford, The Times*, December 5, 2003.

However, s.40 of the 1988 Act, as construed in *Lynsey*,[24] makes provision for a count charging battery to be included on an indictment if it is founded on the same facts or evidence as a count charging an indictable offence. As a result, a count of battery, preferably expressed as "assault by beating",[25] may be included as an alternative count on any indictment charging sexual assault. Moreover, by virtue of subsequent changes to the Criminal Law Act 1967, an alternative verdict of guilty of assault by beating may now be brought in if the prosecutor *could* have included a count charging that offence on the indictment in accordance with s.40 of the 1988 Act, even if that was not in fact done.[26] The net result is that a verdict of assault by beating may now be brought in whenever sexual assault is indicted. However, the Crown Court may only deal with the offender for the assault in a manner in which a magistrates' court could have dealt with him. On a summary charge, the magistrates have no jurisdiction to find the defendant guilty of a lesser offence.[27]

Sentencing

2.54   The Sentencing Council has issued a new guideline applicable to sex offenders aged 18 or over who are sentenced on or after April 1, 2014: see para.1.20 et seq. above. The previous guideline, issued in 2007 by the Sentencing Guidelines Council and covered in the main work, categorises the offence of sexual assault purely by reference to the type of touching involved, e.g. "contact between either the clothed genitalia of offender and naked genitalia of victim or naked genitalia of offender and clothed genitalia of victim". The Sentencing Council said in its consultation on the draft guideline[28] that this focus on the activity in question was too narrow and could make it difficult for sentences to reflect fully the harm caused to the victim, in particular the fear and intimidation that they may have suffered. The new guideline is accordingly intended to reflect the emotional and physical harm that can be caused by this offence.

New sentencing guideline

Step One—Harm and culpability

2.54A   Under the new guideline, the sentencing court is to go through a series of steps in order to determine the appropriate sentence. Step one involves determining the offence category by reference to the degree of harm caused and then the

---

[24] [1995] 2 Cr. App. R. 667.
[25] To distinguish it from common assault: *DPP v Taylor* [1992] Q.B. 645, at 651 per Mann L.J.
[26] Criminal Law Act 1967, s.6(3A), (3B), inserted by the Domestic Violence, Crime and Victims Act 2004, s.11, which was introduced to overturn *Mearns*, above.
[27] *Lawrence v Lawrence* [1968] 2 Q.B. 93.
[28] *Sexual Offences Guideline: Consultation* (December 6, 2012).

culpability level for the offence. In relation to the offence of sexual assault the harm and culpability factors are as follows:

HARM		CULPABILITY	
Category 1	• Severe psychological or physical harm • Abduction • Violence or threats of violence • Forced/uninvited entry into victim's home	A	
			• Significant degree of planning • Offender acts together with others to commit the offence • Use of alcohol/drugs on victim to facilitate the offence • Abuse of trust
Category 2	• Touching of naked genitalia or naked breasts • Prolonged detention/ sustained incident • Additional degradation/ humiliation • Victim is particularly vulnerable due to personal circumstances* *for children under 13 please refer to the guideline on page 27		• Previous violence against victim • Offence committed in course of burglary • Recording of offence • Commercial exploitation and/or motivation • Offence racially or religiously aggravated • Offence motivated by, or demonstrating, hostility to the victim based on his or her sexual orientation (or presumed sexual orientation) or transgender identity (or presumed transgender identity)
Category 3	Factor(s) in categories 1 and 2 not present		• Offence motivated by, or demonstrating, hostility to the victim based on his or her disability (or presumed disability)
		B	
		Factor(s) in category A not present	

The factors identified in category 1 are placed in category 2 in the guidelines for rape and assault by penetration. This is because the Sentencing Council considered that category 1 sexual assaults will never be as severe as category 1 rapes or assaults by penetration, as reflected by the lower statutory maximum (10 years' imprisonment rather than life). For example, a rape during the course of a forced entry into a home would warrant a starting point of 10 years and is placed in category 2. For sexual assault, forced entry into the home has to be placed in category 1 in order to enable a sentence to be passed that reflects the severity of this aggravation.

The factor "violence or threats of violence" is included in category 1 because the Council thought that fear of escalation of an attack is likely to increase the psychological harm to the victim, to the extent that it should affect the starting point. For example, an offender may seek to control the victim using threatening language, and especially violent sexual language, to force compliance.

The first factor in category 2 was expressed in the consultation draft of the guideline simply as "touching of genitalia". The Sentencing Council said that, whilst the type of physical touching should not be the only determinant of harm, the degree of violation inherent in the touching of genitalia is such that an offence with that feature should always fall within category 2 (i.e. should never fall within category 3). The previous SGC guideline drew a distinction between clothed and unclothed genitalia, but the Council did not believe that a clear distinction can always be drawn between the two in terms of harm caused. For example, where the victim is followed home at night by a stranger who, on a quiet street, grabs the victim between the legs, touches their clothed genitalia and pulls them to the ground, the degree of psychological harm caused by the isolation and the fear of escalation should bring the offence within category 2, irrespective of the fact the victim's genitalia are touched over their clothing. Accordingly, the draft guideline did not distinguish between clothed and naked genitalia. This produced mixed responses: some respondents felt that assaults over clothing are less harmful, a lesser violation and show a lower level of intent to harm, and that category 2 should cover only offences involving naked genitalia. Others favoured drawing no distinction. In light of the need for clarity, the Council decided to amend the factor to "touching of naked genitalia or naked breasts". As a result, touching of clothed genitalia or breasts, without more, will fall within category 3. The Council did however express the hope that when the context of the offence makes touching of clothed genitalia or breasts more threatening, this will be captured by the other factors in the harm categories, as in the example given above of the victim followed home at night.

Finally, as with rape and assault by penetration, category 3 does not list any factors in order to reflect the fact that there is an inherent degree of harm caused by any sexual assault.

Step Two—Starting point and category range

2.54B   Having determined the offence category and culpability level, the court should then use the corresponding starting point specified in the guideline in order to reach a sentence within the category range. The starting point applies to all offenders irrespective of plea or previous convictions. Once the starting point has been determined, step two allows further adjustment for aggravating or mitigating features, set out below. A case of particular gravity, reflected by multiple features of culpability or harm, could merit upward adjustment from the starting point before further adjustment for aggravating or mitigating features. Where there is a sufficient prospect of rehabilitation, a community order with a sex offender treatment programme requirement under s.202 of the CJA 2003 can be a proper alternative to a short or moderate length custodial sentence. The proposed starting points and category ranges for sexual assault are as follows:

	A	B
Category 1	**Starting point** 4 years' custody **Category range** 3–7 years' custody	**Starting point** 2 years 6 months' custody **Category range** 2–4 years' custody
Category 2	**Starting point** 2 years' custody **Category range** 1–4 years' custody	**Starting point** 1 year's custody **Category range** High level community order–2 years' custody
Category 3	**Starting point** 26 weeks' custody **Category range** High level community order–1 year's custody	**Starting point** High level community order **Category range** Medium level community order–26 weeks' custody

The starting points and ranges for offences with level "A" culpability factors are slightly higher than under the SGC guideline. This reflects the inclusion in the new guideline of a broader range of such factors, as a result of the Sentencing Council's view that sentencing should reflect more than just the physical activity that has taken place.

In its consultation, the Council said that it had included community orders at the bottom of the range of available sentences for sexual assaults in categories 2B and 3 in order to reflect the very wide range of offending behaviour that can come before the courts. Whilst all cases are serious, the aims of preventing reoffending and rehabilitating the offender may be better achieved by imposing a community sentence rather than a short custodial sentence which is likely to leave the offender's behaviour unaddressed. The Council gave as an example an offender with no previous convictions who approaches a woman at a crowded bus stop and grabs her breast over her clothing. This would be a very distressing experience for the victim, and the sentencer would want to impose a sentence that prevents the offender from assaulting other women in a similar way. For this type of case, the Council thought the judge may wish to impose a community order for a period of up to 2 years with a requirement to attend a sex offender treatment programme where the offender's behaviour can be challenged and addressed.

Aggravating and mitigating factors

2.54C After identifying the starting point and category range, the court should consider whether the presence of aggravating or mitigating factors should result in an upward or downward adjustment from the starting point or the imposition of a sentence outside the category range. In particular, relevant recent convictions are likely to result in an upward adjustment. When sentencing appropriate category 2 or 3 offences, the court should also consider whether the custody threshold has been passed; if so, whether a custodial sentence is unavoidable; and if it is, whether that sentence can be suspended. The non-exhaustive list of aggravating and mitigating factors for sexual assault is as follows:

Aggravating factors
Statutory aggravating factors
• Previous convictions, having regard to a) the nature of the offence to which the conviction relates and its relevance to the current offence; and b) the time that has elapsed since the conviction
• Offence committed whilst on bail
Other aggravating factors
• Specific targeting of a particularly vulnerable victim
• Blackmail or other threats made (where not taken into account at step one)
• Location of offence
• Timing of offence
• Use of weapon or other item to frighten or injure
• Victim compelled to leave their home (including victims of domestic violence)
• Failure to comply with current court orders
• Offence committed whilst on licence
• Exploiting contact arrangements with a child to commit an offence
• Presence of others, especially children
• Any steps taken to prevent the victim reporting an incident, obtaining assistance and/or from assisting or supporting the prosecution
• Attempts to dispose of or conceal evidence
• Commission of offence whilst under the influence of alcohol or drugs

Mitigating factors
• No previous convictions or no relevant/recent convictions
• Remorse
• Previous good character and/or exemplary conduct*
• Age and/or lack of maturity where it affects the responsibility of the offender
• Mental disorder or learning disability, particularly where linked to the commission of the offence

* Previous good character/exemplary conduct is different from having no previous convictions. The more serious the offence, the less the weight which should normally be attributed to this factor. Where previous good character/exemplary conduct has been used to facilitate the offence, this mitigation should not normally be allowed and such conduct may constitute an aggravating factor.

Steps Three to Nine

The remaining steps cover the following points. At step three the court should **2.54D** consider any factors which would indicate a reduction in sentence, e.g. assistance to the prosecution. At step four it should consider any reduction for a guilty plea. At step five the court should consider dangerousness, i.e. whether it would be appropriate to award an extended sentence (s.226A of the CJA 2003). Step six requires the court to consider whether the total sentence is just and proportionate to the offending behaviour. At step seven it should consider whether to make an ancillary order (e.g. a compensation order, a SOPO or a restraining order). Step eight requires the court to fulfil its duty under s.174 of the CJA 2003 to give reasons for, and explain the effect of, the sentence. Finally, at step nine the court should consider whether to give credit for time spent on bail in accordance with s.240A of that Act.

Sentencing examples

The following decisions pre-date the new guideline but are useful illustrations of **2.54E** the approach taken by the Court of Appeal to particular factual scenarios.

In *John Joseph*[29] the appellant (46) appealed against a sentence of 12 months' **2.54F** imprisonment imposed following his conviction of sexual assault. The complainant was a young woman who managed an interior design shop. She was working alone in the shop one day when the appellant came in with his son on the pretext that he wanted to buy some flooring. When the complainant needed to go downstairs, he followed her while his son waited on the ground floor. When they were alone the appellant grabbed the complainant's arms, pushed her back and attempted to kiss her. The assault ended when someone else came down the stairs. At that point the appellant grabbed the complainant's hand and pushed a small

[29] [2013] EWCA Crim 2345.

note into it which contained his phone number. He then walked off casually. The complainant was shocked and very disturbed by what had happened. She was afraid that if the appellant came back he would try and take it further than kissing. She called her manager and told him what had happened. He said that if she saw the appellant again she should warn him that she would call the police. She did not call the police because she felt it was not serious enough to raise a complaint or that they would not be able to do anything. After about three weeks the appellant returned to the shop, the complainant asked him to leave her alone and he left. On a subsequent visit he made what she interpreted as a threatening comment and she reported the matter to the police. The appellant was arrested and, when interviewed, he denied the offence. He had been convicted in 2003 of two offences of indecent exposure and one offence of harassment, after he repeatedly exposed himself to a schoolgirl who lived next door to him over a period of several months. In sentencing, the judge said that she considered the offence so serious that a community order was not appropriate. That appears to have been a reference to the element of the SGC guideline that applied in the case of "contact between part of the offender's body (other than the genitalia) with part of the victim's body (other than the genitalia)". The starting point suggested in the guideline in the case of a victim aged 13 or over was a community order, attracting a range limited to an appropriate non-custodial sentence. However, earlier in her sentencing remarks the judge appeared to say that the guideline suggested a range of between 4 weeks and 18 months' imprisonment in the present case, a range that applied only where the victim was under the age of 13. Accordingly there appeared to be some confusion as to which part of the SGC guideline the judge considered applicable. In any event, the judge said that she considered the case to be outside the guideline because it had so many unusual features. She considered it passed the custody threshold and that the very least sentence she could impose was one of 12 months' imprisonment, given four aggravating factors: first, the appellant used his son to remain upstairs while he attacked his victim; second, he produced in evidence a fabricated tape of an alleged conversation he had with the complainant to support his case; third, the victim suffered harassment after the sexual assault itself; and fourth, there was the matter of the appellant's previous convictions. The Court of Appeal allowed the appeal. It shared the judge's view of the seriousness of the offence, which was a calculated course of conduct against a vulnerable woman, working on her own in a shop, whom the appellant targeted. The judge had been entitled to have regard to three of the aggravating factors to which she referred, but not the second, namely the way that the appellant conducted his defence at trial, which did not aggravate the offence. The judge had also been entitled to form the view that an immediate custodial sentence was required. However, the Court concluded that the appropriate term of imprisonment was one of 6 months.

2.54G   In *MacLeod*[30] the appellant (31) appealed against a sentence of 3 years'

----

[30] [2012] EWCA Crim 1916.

imprisonment imposed after he pleaded guilty to sexual assault on a 17-year-old boy. He had pushed the complainant into a toilet cubicle as he was leaving some public toilets. He placed one hand under the complainant's waistband and made contact with his penis and genitalia. The complainant managed to get hold of the appellant's hand and remove it. The appellant then pulled down his own trousers and underwear and started to masturbate. He repeatedly said to the complainant that if he performed oral sex on him he would let him leave, but the complainant repeatedly declined. Eventually the appellant gave up and the complainant was able to push past him and walk out. The complainant, a diabetic, became unwell and was taken to hospital, where he remained for a number of hours. The pre-sentence report identified a high risk of offending in a similar way and noted that the appellant's life revolved around the consumption of alcohol. He had been convicted in 2001 of lewd and libidinous practice, for which a two-year probation order was imposed, and he had been cautioned in 2011 for sexual activity in a public lavatory. The SGC guideline range suggested a starting point of 12 months' imprisonment and a range of 26 weeks to 2 years for "contact with genitalia of victim by offender using part of his body other than the genitalia". The judge sentenced outside this range because of the element of false imprisonment, the fact that the offence had been committed in a public place and the significant effect that it had had on the complainant. The Court of Appeal allowed the appeal. The offence was aggravated by the detention of the complainant, the persistence shown by the appellant and the significant emotional and psychological impact of the offence on the complainant. However, the appellant realised that he had a serious alcohol problem and was remorseful about the offence. He had signed up for a sexual offender treatment programme. The judge clearly had deterrence in mind to protect those who used public conveniences. He had been entitled to go outside the guideline in the light of his findings, but he strayed too far outside. The effect of the sentence was to place the offence at the top end of the most serious category of offence, involving "contact between naked genitalia of offender and naked genitalia of the victim", where the range was 2–5 years' imprisonment, with a starting point of 3 years. The appropriate starting point in this case was 3 years. With credit for the plea, the appropriate sentence was 2 years' imprisonment.

Syed (Aliuddin Jawad)[31] concerned an appeal against a sentence of 15 months' imprisonment imposed following a conviction for sexual assault committed on a young woman on a bus at night in central London. The appellant (27 and of previous good character) had sat next to the complainant on the top deck, although there were other empty seats. He put his hand on her thigh over her jeans and, using some pressure, moved it closer to the inside of her thigh, touching the side of her vagina. The complainant pushed past him, got off the bus and boarded another. The appellant followed her. When she got off the second bus, he followed her onto a third. The complainant, who had become afraid for her safety, telephoned a friend and met her by arrangement at a bus stop, at which point the

2.54H

---

[31] [2012] EWCA Crim 1699.

appellant stopped following her. The incident lasted around an hour. The complainant was so frightened by it that she became afraid to use public transport. The appellant denied everything but was convicted after a trial. In imposing the 15-month sentence, the judge said that the offence was aggravated by the fact that the appellant had targeted and followed the complainant, and took the view that there had to be a significant deterrent element. The Court of Appeal dismissed the appeal. It held that the appellant's conduct involved "contact with genitalia of victim by offender using part of his body other than the genitalia" within the SGC guideline. While the touching had been over, rather than under, the complainant's clothing, it had been done deliberately, with pressure, and with the intention of making clear that it was sexual in nature. In principle, a starting point of 12 months' imprisonment was not wrong. Although the judge had gone 3 months above that point, he had nonetheless kept well within the indicated range of 26 weeks to 2 years. While the assault itself was relatively brief, the whole episode was far from fleeting, and the seriously aggravating features were the targeting of the complainant, and the appellant's stalking of her over a substantial period, despite her obvious and increasingly desperate attempts to shake him off. Had she not managed to contact her friend, there was little doubt that the stalking would have continued. Nor could the judge be criticised for mentioning the requirement of general deterrence. A young woman travelling on public transport had become the unwilling object of a young male sexual predator and had been put in fear for a prolonged period. There had to be a clear message that such offending would not be tolerated and was likely to be dealt with in an exemplary way. Against the appellant's previous good character had to be set his continued denials and lack of remorse. Weighing all those matters in the balance, there was no proper basis upon which the sentence could be interfered with as being either wrong in principle or manifestly excessive.

2.54I   In *Pitchei (Mashain)*[32] the appellant appealed against an extended sentence of 9 years, comprising 4 years' imprisonment and an extended licence period of 5 years, imposed following his plea of guilty to sexual assault. The complainant was making her way home after an evening out with friends. She was extremely drunk and got into the front seat of the appellant's car thinking it was a taxi as it was parked at the rear of a line of taxis. The appellant drove around for a short time before parking in a dark area. He grabbed the complainant's wrist and prevented her from leaving the car before sexually assaulting her. She eventually managed to get out of the car to attract the attention of a real taxi-driver who stopped to help her. The appellant initially denied the allegations, only pleading guilty at the plea and case management hearing. He was aged 45 at the date of the hearing and had no other relevant convictions other than a caution for harassment. The judge identified the aggravating features as the degree of planning and the premeditation involved in the appellant pretending to be a taxi-driver in order to lure a victim into the car; his targeting late at night of vulnerable females who were drunk and

---

[32] [2013] EWCA Crim 2108.

who might mistake his car for a taxi; his driving the complainant to a dark area where he assaulted her in extremely frightening circumstances; and his preventing her from leaving the car for some time. The judge considered that the appropriate sentence after trial was 6 years but gave full credit of one-third for the guilty plea, so the appropriate determinate sentence was 4 years. The judge was also satisfied that there was a significant risk to members of the public, particularly lone females, of serious harm from the appellant committing further specified offences so that the criteria of dangerousness under the CJA 2003 were met, and he passed an extended sentence. The Court of Appeal held that the judge had been entitled to treat the offence as having the aggravating features identified. However, the level of force was minimal and during the time when the complainant was in the appellant's car, there was no attempt to undress her or degrade her in any way. A sentence of 6 years after a trial was too long and contrary to the SGC guideline for the offence, even taking into account the aggravating features. The appropriate sentence after a trial was 4 years' imprisonment, which after giving credit for the guilty plea would have been reduced to 32 months' imprisonment, and a sentence of that length was substituted.

CAUSING A PERSON TO ENGAGE IN SEXUAL ACTIVITY WITHOUT CONSENT

MODE OF TRIAL AND PUNISHMENT

From December 3, 2012, when ss.122–128 of the Legal Aid, Sentencing and **2.82** Punishment of Offenders Act 2012 were brought into force[33]:
- An offence under s.4 that carries a maximum of life imprisonment (i.e. an offence involving penetration) is a serious specified offence for the purposes of ss.224 and 225(2) of the CJA 2003 (life sentence for serious offences).
- For offences committed on or after that date, an offence under s.4 that carries a maximum of life imprisonment is listed in Pt 1 of Sch.15B to that Act for the purposes of s.224A of the Act (life sentence for second listed offence).
- For convictions on or after that date (irrespective of the date of commission of the offence), an offence under s.4 that carries a maximum of life imprisonment is a specified offence for the purposes of s.226A of the CJA 2003 (extended sentence for certain violent or sexual offences).

---

[33] By the Legal Aid, Sentencing and Punishment of Offenders Act 2012 (Commencement No.4 and Saving Provisions) Order 2012 (SI 2012/2906).

Bail

2.83 Section 25 of the Criminal Justice and Public Order Act 1994 was amended on December 3, 2012,[34] so that a person charged with or convicted of an offence to which the section applies shall be granted bail by a constable only if the constable is "of the opinion", rather than "satisfied" (as before), that there are exceptional circumstances which justify it.

Sentencing

2.85 The Sentencing Council has issued a new guideline applicable to sex offenders aged 18 or over who are sentenced on or after April 1, 2014: see para.1.20 et seq., above. The Council proposed in its consultation on the draft guideline[35] that s.4 offences should be sentenced according to the approach and sentence levels specified for the offence of assault by penetration, given the closeness of the range of behaviours covered by the two offences. This is the approach followed in the published guideline and reference should accordingly be made to the discussion, above, of the guideline for assault by penetration.

New sentencing guideline

Step One—Harm and culpability

2.85A Under the new guideline, the sentencing court is to go through a series of steps in order to determine the appropriate sentence. Step one involves determining the offence category by reference to the degree of harm caused and then the culpability level for the offence. In relation to offences under s.4, the harm and culpability factors are as follows:

HARM		CULPABILITY	
Category 1	• The extreme nature of one or more category 2 factors or the extreme impact caused by a combination of category 2 factors **may** elevate to category 1	A	
		• Significant degree of planning • Offender acts together with others to commit the offence • Use of alcohol/drugs on victim to facilitate the offence	
Category 2	• Severe psychological or physical harm	• Abuse of trust	
	• Penetration using large or dangerous object(s)	• Previous violence against victim	

[34] By the Legal Aid, Sentencing and Punishment of Offenders Act 2012, s.90 and Sch.11 para.33, which was brought into force by the Legal Aid, Sentencing and Punishment of Offenders Act 2012 (Commencement No.4 and Saving Provisions) Order 2012, last note.
[35] *Sexual Offences Guideline: Consultation* (December 6, 2012).

	• Pregnancy or STI as consequence of the offence • Additional degra-dation/humiliation • Abduction • Prolonged detention/ sustained incident • Violence or threats of violence • Forced/uninvited entry into victim's home • Victim is particularly vulnerable due to personal circumstances* *for children under 13 please refer to the guideline on page 27	• Offence committed in course of burglary • Recording of the offence • Commercial exploitation and/or motivation • Offence racially or religiously aggravated • Offence motivated by, or demon-strating, hostility to the victim based on his or her sexual orientation (or presumed sexual orientation) or transgender identity (or presumed transgender identity) • Offence motivated by, or demon-strating, hostility to the victim based on his or her disability (or presumed disability) **B** Factor(s) in category A not present
Category 3	Factor(s) in categories 1 and 2 not present	

Step Two—Starting point and category range

Having determined the offence category and culpability level, the court should **2.85B** then use the corresponding starting point specified in the guideline in order to reach a sentence within the category range. The starting point applies to all offenders irrespective of plea or previous convictions. Once the starting point has been determined, step two allows further adjustment for aggravating or mitigating features, set out below. A case of particular gravity, reflected by multiple features of culpability or harm, could merit upward adjustment from the starting point before further adjustment for aggravating or mitigating features. Where there is a sufficient prospect of rehabilitation, a community order with a sex offender treatment programme requirement under s.202 of the CJA 2003 can be a proper alternative to a short or moderate length custodial sentence. The starting points and category ranges for offences under s.4 are as follows:

Where offence involved penetration

	A	B
Category 1	**Starting point** 15 years' custody	**Starting point** 12 years' custody
	Category range 13–19 years' custody	**Category range** 10–15 years' custody
Category 2	**Starting point** 8 years' custody	**Starting point** 6 years' custody
	Category range 5–13 years' custody	**Category range** 4–9 years' custody
Category 3	**Starting point** 4 years' custody	**Starting point** 2 years' custody
	Category range 2–6 years' custody	**Category range** High level community order–4 years' custody

Where offence did not involve penetration

	A	B
Category 1	**Starting point** 4 years' custody	**Starting point** 2 years 6 months' custody
	Category range 3–7 years' custody	**Category range** 2–4 years' custody
Category 2	**Starting point** 2 years' custody	**Starting point** 1 year's custody
	Category range 1–4 years' custody	**Category range** High level community order–2 years' custody

	A	B
Category 3	**Starting point** 26 weeks' custody **Category range** High level community order–1 year's custody	**Starting point** High level community order **Category range** Medium level community order–26 weeks' custody

Aggravating and mitigating factors

After identifying the starting point and category range, the court should consider **2.85C** whether the presence of aggravating or mitigating factors should result in an upward or downward adjustment from the starting point or the imposition of a sentence outside the category range. In particular, relevant recent convictions are likely to result in an upward adjustment. When sentencing appropriate category 2 or 3 offences, the court should also consider whether the custody threshold has been passed; if so, whether a custodial sentence is unavoidable; and if it is, whether that sentence can be suspended. The non-exhaustive list of aggravating and mitigating factors for offences under s.4 is as follows:

Aggravating factors
Statutory aggravating factors
• Previous convictions, having regard to a) the nature of the offence to which the conviction relates and its relevance to the current offence; and b) the time that has elapsed since the conviction • Offence committed whilst on bail
Other aggravating factors
• Specific targeting of a particularly vulnerable victim • Ejaculation (where not taken into account at step one) • Blackmail or other threats made (where not taken into account at step one) • Location of offence • Timing of offence • Use of weapon or other item to frighten or injure • Victim compelled to leave their home (including victims of domestic violence) • Failure to comply with current court orders • Offence committed whilst on licence • Exploiting contact arrangements with a child to commit an offence

- Presence of others, especially children
- Any steps taken to prevent the victim reporting an incident, obtaining assistance and/or from assisting or supporting the prosecution
- Attempts to dispose of or conceal evidence
- Commission of offence whilst under the influence of alcohol or drugs

Mitigating factors

- No previous convictions **or** no relevant/recent convictions
- Remorse
- Previous good character and/or exemplary conduct*
- Age and/or lack of maturity where it affects the responsibility of the offender
- Mental disorder or learning disability, particularly where linked to the commission of the offence

* Previous good character/exemplary conduct is different from having no previous convictions. The more serious the offence, the less the weight which should normally be attributed to this factor. Where previous good character/exemplary conduct has been used to facilitate the offence, this mitigation should not normally be allowed and such conduct may constitute an aggravating factor.

In the context of this offence, previous good character/exemplary conduct should not normally be given any significant weight and will not normally justify a reduction in what would otherwise be the appropriate sentence.

Steps Three to Nine

2.85D   The remaining steps cover the following points. At step three the court should consider any factors which would indicate a reduction in sentence, e.g. assistance to the prosecution. At step four it should consider any reduction for a guilty plea. At step five the court should consider dangerousness, i.e. whether it would be appropriate to award a life sentence (s.224A or s.225(2) of the CJA 2003) or an extended sentence (s.226A). Step six requires the court to consider whether the total sentence is just and proportionate to the offending behaviour. At step seven it should consider whether to make an ancillary order (e.g. a compensation order, a SOPO or a restraining order). Step eight requires the court to fulfil its duty under s.174 of the CJA 2003 to give reasons for, and explain the effect of, the sentence. Finally, at step nine the court should consider whether to give credit for time spent on bail in accordance with s.240A of that Act.

Sentencing examples

2.85E   The following decisions pre-date the new guideline but are useful illustrations of the approach taken by the Court of Appeal to particular factual scenarios.

In *Ayeva*[36] the appellant appealed against a sentence of 3-and-a-half years' imprisonment imposed after he pleaded guilty to causing a person to engage in sexual activity without consent. He had approached the 19-year-old complainant outside a public library and sought to engage her in conversation. She attempted to evade him by walking away down an alleyway. He grabbed her from behind and bent her arm behind her back, forcing her to take hold of his erect penis and masturbate him. The complainant managed to escape and ran back to the library, where she vomited. The appellant had previously been cautioned for an offence of battery near the same library, when he had approached another woman and grabbed her arm. A pre-sentence report stated that he minimised his behaviour and posed a medium to high risk of harm to others, namely lone adult women. After the attack the complainant had to take sleeping tablets, was reluctant to socialise, had been signed off work with stress and had left college because of her fear of meeting people whom she felt she could not trust. The judge, referring to the SGC guideline, said that the appropriate sentencing range was 2–5 years' imprisonment. The Court of Appeal held that this was the wrong range. The appropriate sentencing guideline was "contact between naked genitalia of offender and another part of victim's body", with a suggested starting point of 12 months' custody and a range from 26 weeks to 2 years. However, the aggravating features took the case significantly beyond that range: the appellant had persisted in his unwelcome conduct over a significant period of time; the complainant had made it clear that his attention was not welcome; not only was it a touching of the penis but a masturbation of it to the extent that he ejaculated, although the complainant had been unaware of that at the time; and the effect of what he did was immediately significant as the complainant was sick, but she also suffered longer term effects as outlined in her victim impact statement. The guidelines were not tram lines, and the appropriate sentence after trial would have been in the region of 30 months' imprisonment. Making allowance for the late guilty plea, the proper sentence in this case was 2 years and 3 months' imprisonment. 2.85F

In *Orchard*[37] the appellant appealed against a sentence of 2 years' imprisonment imposed following his conviction for offences of causing a person to engage in sexual activity without consent and sexual assault. The appellant and the complainant were patients in a psychiatric hospital. He suffered from bipolar affective disorder and she had a history of depression. The appellant asked the complainant to meet him in a room where he forced her to hold his penis and kissed her breasts. When she tried to leave he initially barred her way, and when she did leave he warned her not to tell anyone. He insisted that the sexual contact had been consensual. The pre-sentence report described the complainant as being particularly vulnerable and having self-harmed following the incident. The appellant had previous convictions, including for threatening and abusive behaviour amounting to harassment. The judge acknowledged that the appellant had his 2.85G

---

[36] [2009] EWCA Crim 2640.
[37] [2010] EWCA Crim 1538.

own problems, but stated that he had taken advantage of the complainant and that the impact on her would be very severe. The appellant contended that the sentence was excessive as it was at the top end of the sentencing range and the judge had failed to take sufficient account of the fact that he was a psychiatric patient at the material time. The Court of Appeal agreed that the sentence was excessive. It said that the appellant's bipolar affective disorder could not explain or excuse the offences nor lessen their impact on the complainant. The circumstances surrounding the offences, their nature and the effect on her clearly merited a custodial sentence. The appellant's attempts to bar the complainant's exit and warning her not to tell anyone about what had happened was consistent with the observation in the pre-sentence report that he had a propensity for using threats to meet his needs. That was also borne out by his previous convictions. However, the sentence of 2 years' imprisonment was at the top of the sentencing range (which was the same range as in *Ayeva*), and the Court reduced it to 18 months' imprisonment on each count to run concurrently.

" . . . to Engage in an Activity"

2.90 In *Grout*,[38] decided under s.8 of the 2003 Act, the Court of Appeal said:

"We are prepared to accept, for the purposes of this appeal, that 'activity' on the part of the child could embrace 'the activity' of conversation or sending text or MSN messages, depending on the circumstances."

2.91 For an example of a s.4 offence committed by causing another person to engage in sexual activity with an animal, see *H and R v R*.[39]

Consent

2.95 Professor John Spencer has called for the enactment of offences of obtaining sexual activity by threats and obtaining sexual activity by false pretences, on the basis that s.4 is an "imperfect instrument" for penalising such conduct as it applies only where the threat or pretence is such as to nullify consent.[40]

Mental Element

2.96 In *Grout*,[41] decided under s.8 of the 2003 Act, the Court of Appeal said:

"The causing or inciting must be intentional, i.e. deliberate; recklessness or less will not do."

---

[38] [2011] EWCA Crim 299, at [29].
[39] [2008] EWCA Crim 1202.
[40] *Sex by Deception*, *Archbold Review*, Issue 9, November 14, 2013, pp.6–9.
[41] [2011] EWCA Crim 299, at [26], citing *Heard*; [2007] EWCA Crim 125, at [22] per Hughes L.J.

CHAPTER 3

OFFENCES AGAINST CHILDREN UNDER 13

INTRODUCTION

CPS charging guidance

The CPS has issued two sets of guidance relating to the prosecution of child   **3.10**
sexual offences: the general guidance in *Rape and Sexual Offences*[1] and the
important new *Guidelines on Prosecuting Cases of Child Sexual Abuse*, issued on
October 17, 2013.[2] The new *Guidelines* are considered in para.4.01, below. As for
the prosecution of children, this is dealt with in the guidance on *Rape and Sexual
Offences*, which contains two relevant sections (in Chs 2 and 11), and also in the
separate guidance on *Youth Offenders*.[3] These two pieces of guidance overlap to a
substantial degree and it is worth setting out the key elements verbatim. Chapter
2 of *Rape and Sexual Offences* provides:

> **"Code for Crown Prosecutors—Child defendant (under 18)**
>
> See CPS Legal Guidance on Youth Offenders including sections on:
> - Principles guiding the decision to prosecute
> - Sexual Offences and Child Abuse by Young Offenders
> - Rape and other offences against children under 13 (sections 5 to 8 Sexual
>   Offences Act 2003)
> - Child sex offences committed by children or young persons
> - Familial sexual offences committed by young people
>
> See also Rape and Sexual Offences: Chapter 11.
>
> The overriding public concern is to protect children. It was not Parliament's intention
> to punish children unnecessarily or for the criminal law to intervene where it is wholly
> inappropriate. During the passage of the bill, Lord Falconer said:

---

[1] http://www.cps.gov.uk/legal/p_to_r/rape_and_sexual_offences/ [accessed December 27, 2013].

[2] The Guidelines are set out in Appendix I to this Supplement and are also available at http://www.cps.gov.uk/legal/a_to_c/child_sexual_abuse/ [accessed December 27, 2013].

[3] http://www.cps.gov.uk/legal/v_to_z/youth_offenders/ [accessed December 27, 2013].

"Our overriding concern is to protect children, not to punish them unnecessarily. Where sexual relationships between minors are not abusive, prosecuting either or both children is highly unlikely to be in the public interest. Nor would it be in the best interests of the child . . . "

There are two important points to note:

(1) The Directors Guidance on Charging (fourth edition: January 2011) states that offences under the Sexual Offences Act 2003 committed by or upon persons under the age of 18 years must always be referred to the CPS for a charging decision, whether admitted or not.

(2) Youth Offender Specialists should review all files involving youth offenders and take all major decisions in relation to those cases, in particular, whether or not a prosecution should take place.

In addition:

- Chief Crown Prosecutors must be notified of any case where at least one of the complainants and at least one of the suspects are under the age of 13. This includes cases which are diverted from prosecution, whether on evidential or public interest grounds.

- All such cases must be reviewed by a prosecutor who is both a rape specialist and a youth specialist. All advocates conducting these cases must have a rape specialism and should also have a youth specialism.

Where a sexual offence committed by a child passes the evidential stage of the Full Code Test, it is essential that when considering the public interest, prosecutors have as much information as possible from sources including the police, Youth Offending Teams (YOTs), and any professionals assisting those agencies, about the defendants background and the circumstances surrounding the alleged offence, as well as any information known about the victim. Failure to do so may lead to judicial review of any decision: *R v Chief Constable of Kent ex parte L and R v DPP ex parte B* [1991] 93 Cr App R 416.

Views expressed by the victim, and where appropriate the victim's family, should be taken into account in accordance with the Code.

Furthermore prosecutors must consider the interests of the youth when deciding whether it is in the public interest to prosecute (paragraph 4.12 (d) of the Code for Crown Prosecutors).

In reaching the decision to prosecute a youth for a sexual offence, prosecutors should ensure that they not only apply the Code in conjunction with any relevant CPS policy on youth offenders and the Sexual Offences Act, but that they record that they have done so in their review of the case.

Factors: whether or not to prosecute young defendants

In deciding whether or not to prosecute, prosecutors should have careful regard to the factors below. The weight to be attached to a particular factor will vary depending on the circumstances of each case. The factors are:

- The age and understanding of the offender. This may include whether the offender has been subjected to any exploitation, coercion, threat, deception, grooming or manipulation by another which has led him or her to commit the offence;

- The relevant ages and levels of maturity of the parties, i.e. the same or no significant disparity in age;

- Whether the complainant entered into sexual activity willingly, i.e. did the complainant understand the nature of his or her actions and that she/he was able to communicate his or her willingness freely;

- Parity between the parties in regard to sexual, physical, emotional and educational development;
- The relationship between the parties, its nature and duration and whether this represents a genuine transitory phase of adolescent development;
- Whether there is any element of exploitation, coercion, threat, deception, grooming, seduction, manipulation or breach of trust in the relationship;
- Whether the child under 13 freely consented (even though in law this is not a defence) or a genuine mistake as to her/ his age was in fact made;
- The nature of the activity e.g. penetrative or non-penetrative activity;
- The sexual and emotional maturity of the parties and any emotional or physical effects resulting from the conduct; and
- The likely impact of any prosecution on the parties."

Chapter 11 of *Rape and Sexual Offences* provides as follows: 3.10A

"Youths

This guidance expands on, and should be read in conjunction with other specific sections elsewhere in this Sexual Offences guidance. Also note the Notification requirements. Any decision to prosecute or not to prosecute should be free of discrimination on the grounds of sexual orientation and gender.

If an allegation of any sexual abuse committed by a youth offender has been fully investigated and there is sufficient evidence to justify instituting proceedings, the balance of the public interest must always be carefully considered before any prosecution is commenced. Positive action may need to be taken at an early stage of offending of this type. Although a reprimand or final warning may provide an acceptable alternative in some cases, in reaching any decision, the police and the CPS will have to take into account fully the view of other agencies involved in the case, in particular the Social Services. The consequences for the victim of the decision whether or not to prosecute, and any views expressed by the victim or the victim's family should also be taken into account.

In child abuse cases, it will be important to have the views of the Social Services on file if at all possible, as well as any background or history of similar conduct, information about the relationship between the two and the effect a prosecution might have on the victim.

Any case referred to the CPS for advice, or in which a prosecution does proceed, must be dealt with as quickly as possible to minimise the delay before the case comes to court.

Irrespective of whether the evidence is sufficient to found a criminal prosecution, The Social Services will consider taking civil action, such as care proceedings, to protect the child. The police and the CPS may well be asked to disclose evidence to assist in this process. Great care should be taken to follow the guidance set out in the section on disclosure to third parties

Chief Crown Prosecutors must be notified of any case where at least one of the complainants and at least one of the suspects are under the age of 13. This includes cases which are diverted from prosecution, whether on evidential or public interest grounds.

All such cases must be reviewed by a prosecutor who is both a rape specialist and a youth specialist. All advocates conducting these cases must have a rape specialism and should also have a youth specialism.

When reviewing a case, in which a youth under 18 is alleged to have committed an offence contrary to sections 5 to 8, prosecutors should obtain and consider:

- the views of local authority Childrens and Young Peoples Service;

- any risk assessment or report conducted by the local authority or youth offending service in respect of sexually harmful behaviour (such as AIM (Assessment, Intervention and Moving On);
- background information and history of the parties;
- the views of the families of all parties.
- Careful regard should be paid to the following factors:
- the relative ages of the parties;
- the existence of and nature of any relationship;
- the sexual and emotional maturity of the parties and any emotional or physical effects as a result of the conduct;
- whether the child under 13 in fact freely consented (even though in law this is not a defence) or a genuine mistake as to age was in fact made;
- whether any element of seduction, breach of any duty of responsibility to the child or other exploitation is disclosed by the evidence;
- the impact of a prosecution on each child involved.

If the sexual act or activity was in fact genuinely consensual and the youth and the child under 13 concerned are fairly close in age and development, a prosecution is unlikely to be appropriate. Action falling short of prosecution may be appropriate. In such cases, the parents and/or welfare agencies may be able to deal with the situation informally. There is a fine line between sexual experimentation and offending and in general, children under the age of 13 should not be criminalised for sexual behaviour in the absence of coercion, exploitation or abuse of trust.

However, if a very young child has been seduced by a youth, or a baby-sitter in a position of responsibility has taken advantage of a child under 13 in his/her care, prosecution is likely to be in the public interest. Where a child under 13 has not given ostensible consent to the activity, then a prosecution contrary to sections 5 to 8 is likely to be the appropriate course of action. Where the Full Code Test is satisfied in a case in which a youth is suspected of committing a sexual offence involving a child under the age of 13, the appropriate charge will be an offence contrary to sections 5 to 8 Sexual Offences Act 2003, depending on the act, and not the lesser offence contrary to section 13 Sexual Offences Act 2003.

. . .

See Code for Crown Prosecutors considerations and Code for Crown prosecutors– child defendant (under 18) in Sexual Offences elsewhere in this guidance.

It should be noted that where both parties to sexual activity are under 16, then they may both have committed a criminal offence. However, the overriding purpose of the legislation is to protect children and it was not Parliament's intention to punish children unnecessarily or for the criminal law to intervene where it was wholly inappropriate. Consensual sexual activity between, for example, a 14 or 15 year-old and a teenage partner would not normally require criminal proceedings in the absence of aggravating features. The relevant considerations include:

- the respective ages of the parties;
- the existence and nature of any relationship [and] their level of maturity;
- whether any duty of care existed;
- whether there was a serious element of exploitation."

3.10B   Finally, the guidance on *Youth Offenders* provides:

"Sexual Offences and Child Abuse by Young Offenders

This guidance expands on, and should be read in conjunction with other specific sections elsewhere in Legal Guidance, such as Sexual Offences. Also note the Notification requirements. Any decision to prosecute or not to prosecute should be free of discrimination on the grounds of sexual orientation and gender.

If an allegation of any sexual abuse committed by a youth offender has been fully investigated and there is sufficient evidence to justify instituting proceedings, the balance of the public interest must always be carefully considered before any prosecution is commenced. Positive action may need to be taken at an early stage of offending of this type. Although a youth caution or youth conditional caution may provide an acceptable alternative in some cases, in reaching any decision, the police and the CPS will have to take into account fully the view of other agencies involved in the case, in particular the Social Services. The consequences for the victim of the decision whether or not to prosecute, and any views expressed by the victim or the victims family should also be taken into account.

In child abuse cases, it will be important to have the views of the Social Services on file if at all possible, as well as any background or history of similar conduct, information about the relationship between the two and the effect a prosecution might have on the victim.

Any case referred to the CPS for advice, or in which a prosecution does proceed, must be dealt with as quickly as possible to minimise the delay before the case comes to court.

Irrespective of whether the evidence is sufficient to found a criminal prosecution, The Social Services will consider taking civil action, such as care proceedings, to protect the child. The police and the CPS may well be asked to disclose evidence to assist in this process. Great care should be taken to follow the guidance set out in the section on disclosure to third parties Refer to Disclosure of Material to Third Parties.

Rape and other offences against children under 13 (sections 5 to 8 Sexual Offences Act 2003)

CCPs or DCCPs must be notified of any such case where there are both defendants and victims under the age of 13. This includes cases which are diverted from prosecution, whether on evidential or public interest grounds.

All such cases must be reviewed by a prosecutor who is both a rape specialist and a youth specialist. All advocates conducting these cases must have a rape specialism and should also have a youth specialism.

Where the Full Code Test is satisfied in a case in which a youth is suspected of committing a sexual offence involving a child under the age of 13, the appropriate charge will be an offence contrary to sections 5 to 8 Sexual Offences Act 2003, depending on the act, and not the lesser offence contrary to section 13 Sexual Offences Act 2003.

Rape of a child under 13 (section 5), assault of a child under 13 by penetration (section 6) and causing or inciting a child under 13 to engage in sexual activity that involves penetration (section 8) are indictable only offences with a maximum sentence of life imprisonment. The offences of sexual assault of a child under 13 (section 7), causing or inciting a child under 13 to engage in sexual activity where there has been no penetration (section 8) are punishable on indictment with imprisonment for a term not exceeding 14 years. They are all grave crimes for the purposes of section 24 Magistrates Courts Act 1980 and section 91 Powers of Criminal Courts (Sentencing) Act 2000.

A mistaken belief that the child under 13 was 16 or over and consented to intercourse is not a defence to an allegation of rape of a child under 13, assault of a child under 13 by penetration, sexual assault of a child under 13 or causing or inciting a child under 13 to engage in sexual activity contrary to sections 5 to 8 Sexual Offences Act 2003 respectively.

When reviewing a case, in which a youth under 18 is alleged to have committed an offence contrary to sections 5 to 8, prosecutors should obtain and consider:

- the views of local authority Children's and Young Peoples Service;
- any risk assessment or report conducted by the local authority or youth offending service in respect of sexually harmful behaviour (such as AIM (Assessment, Intervention and Moving On);
- background information and history of the parties;
- the views of the families of all parties.

Careful regard should be paid to the following factors:
- the relative ages of both parties;
- the existence of and nature of any relationship;
- the sexual and emotional maturity of both parties and any emotional or physical effects as a result of the conduct;
- whether the child under 13 in fact freely consented (even though in law this is not a defence) or a genuine mistake as to her age was in fact made;
- whether any element of seduction, breach of any duty of responsibility to the girl or other exploitation is disclosed by the evidence;
- the impact of a prosecution on each child involved.

If the sexual act or activity was in fact genuinely consensual and the youth and the child under 13 concerned are fairly close in age and development, a prosecution is unlikely to be appropriate. Action falling short of prosecution may be appropriate. In such cases, the parents and/or welfare agencies may be able to deal with the situation informally.

However, if a very young child has been seduced by a youth, or a baby-sitter in a position of responsibility has taken advantage of a child under 13 in his/her care, prosecution is likely to be in the public interest. Where a child under 13 has not given ostensible consent to the activity, then a prosecution contrary to sections 5 to 8 is likely to be the appropriate course of action.

There is a fine line between sexual experimentation and offending and in general, children under the age of 13 should not be criminalised for sexual behaviour in the absence of coercion, exploitation or abuse of trust.

Refer to guidance.

Child sex offences committed by children or young persons

Section 13 of the 2003 Act makes it an offence for a youth under 18 to have sexual activity with a child under 16, cause or incite a child under 16 to engage in sexual activity, engage in sexual activity in the presence of a child under or cause a child under 16 to watch a sexual act. These offences are punishable on indictment with imprisonment for a term not exceeding 5 years. They are grave crimes for the purposes of section 24 Magistrates Courts Act 1980 and section 91 Powers of Criminal Courts (Sentencing) Act 2000. Section 13(2) (a) purports to restrict the maximum penalty on summary conviction to a maximum of 6 months imprisonment, although this should be read in the light of section 101(2) Powers of Criminal Courts (Sentencing) Act 2000 to allow a Detention and Training Order of up to 24 months.

An offence is not committed if the child is over 13 but is under 16 and the youth has a reasonable belief that the child is 16 or over.

It should be noted that where both parties to sexual activity are under 16, then they may both have committed a criminal offence. However, the overriding purpose of the legislation is to protect children and it was not Parliaments intention to punish children unnecessarily or for the criminal law to intervene where it was wholly in appropriate. Consensual sexual activity between, for example, a 14 or 15 year-old and a teenage partner would not normally require criminal proceedings in the absence of aggravating features. The relevant considerations include:
- the respective ages of the parties;

- the existence and nature of any relationship
- their level of maturity;
- whether any duty of care existed;
- whether there was a serious element of exploitation.

Refer also to Sexual Offences."

Despite the apparent good sense of the CPS guidance set out above, the concern **3.11** we expressed in the main work about the possibility of young children being inappropriately prosecuted for committing sexual offences against other young children was borne out by *E, S and R, R. (on the application of) v DPP*,[4] in which the court quashed what has been characterised as the "perturbing and perplexing"[5] decision of the CPS to treat a 12-year-old victim of sexual exploitation, who was persuaded by a paedophile to abuse her own siblings, as herself a paedophile and worthy of prosecution. The case arose out of the discovery by officers of the Child Exploitation and Online Protection Centre of an internet video showing E (aged 12) engaging in sexual activities with her younger sisters, S (3) and R (2). The local authority convened a multi-agency strategy group to co-ordinate the response to the concerns raised by the video, consisting of representatives from the local authority, the NSPCC, the local safeguarding children board, the youth offending team, the child and adolescent mental health service, the children's school and the police. The police informed the group that they intended to arrest and interview E under caution with a view to her being prosecuted. The remainder of the group were unanimous in considering that this proposed course of action was not in the best interests of either E or her sisters. Under police interview E stated that she had been groomed over the internet by an adult male and had been persuaded by him to do to her sisters the things recorded on the video. The police passed the papers to the CPS.

Meanwhile, the strategy group produced a report analysing the best interests of the children, the key elements of which were:

- Neither E nor her sisters S and R could be therapeutically supported while the prosecution was pursued.
- The likely delay in getting such support to the children as a result of the prosecution was both "great" and "harmful to their eventual recovery".
- In relation to E, therapeutic work was "essential" and would help to quantify and minimise any potential future risk she might pose, including to S and R.
- The parents were critical agents in the support and recovery of the children, and the loss of their cooperation would "seriously jeopardise" both the children's ability to recover from their experiences and potentially the family's ability to remain intact.
- Although the parents had worked in partnership with the agencies to protect and support all their children, it was "very difficult" to imagine

[4] [2011] EWHC 1465 (Admin).
[5] [2012] Crim. L.R. 42 (commentary by Laura Hoyano).

how they would construe criminal proceedings against E as anything other than hostile.

The CPS prosecutor who considered the papers was a specialist in cases of child abuse and sexual offences. Her decision letter stated that she had carefully considered the interests and welfare of E and the strategy group's report, in particular the reference in it to the likelihood of E's parents regarding a prosecution with hostility, but she nonetheless concluded that the public interest favoured E's prosecution. E was accordingly charged with sexually assaulting S, assaulting R by penetration, making an indecent photograph of both S and R (in the form of the video) and distributing that indecent photograph. She appeared before the Youth Court, which committed her for trial. At that point the girls' mother sought a judicial review of the decision to prosecute.

The Administrative Court began its judgment by noting that the version of the Code for Crown Prosecutors then current required prosecutors to comply with the Human Rights Act and the guidance issued on behalf of the DPP and, in cases involving persons under the age of 18, to have regard to the obligations arising under the UN Convention on the Rights of the Child.[6] The UN Convention provides that in all actions concerning children undertaken by (inter alia) public institutions and administrative authorities, the best interests of the child shall be "a primary consideration" and that States shall take all appropriate measures to promote the physical and psychological recovery and social reintegration of a child victim of any form of exploitation or abuse.[7] The Court also referred to the provisions of the Code dealing with the public interest in prosecution and the relevance to this of the views of the victim and, in appropriate cases, of their family[8] and the relevant legal guidance issued by the DPP, namely *Young Offenders*,[9] the guidance on the *Sexual Offences Act 2003* (see now the guidance on *Rape and Sexual Offences*),[10] and *Safeguarding Children as Victims and Witnesses* (updated in November 2009).[11] The Court summarised the key elements of these various documents as:

- The interests of any child involved are a primary consideration.
- Crown Prosecutors must consider what is in the best interests and welfare of the defendant.
- Crown Prosecutors must consider what is in the best interests and welfare of the victim.
- Specifically, Crown Prosecutors must consider the consequences for the victim of a decision to prosecute, the effect a prosecution might have on the victim and, in particular, whether a prosecution is likely to have an adverse impact on the victim's physical or mental health.

[6] paras 2.6 and 8.2 (for the latter see now para.4.12(d) of the current Code).
[7] para.3.1 and art.39.
[8] paras 4.17–19 (for which see now para.4.12(c) of the current Code).
[9] Under the heading *Sexual Offences and Child Abuse by Young Offenders*, set out in para.3.10B, above.
[10] Relevant sections set out in paras 3.10–10A, above.
[11] *http://www.cps.gov.uk/legal/v_to_z/safeguarding_children_as_victims_and_witnesses/* [accessed December 27, 2013], under the heading *Public interest stage*.

- Crown Prosecutors must take into account any views expressed by the victim or, where the victim is a child, any views expressed by the victim's family, including the views of the victim about the effect of a prosecution on her physical or mental health.
- Crown Prosecutors must take into account "fully" the views of other agencies and "in particular" of social services.

The Court gave short shrift to the claimant mother's argument that the DPP's guidance was unlawful as being inconsistent with the UK's obligations under international law, especially the UN Convention on the Rights of the Child, in that it failed, except in relation to child victims of trafficking, to address the "special status" of the child who is both defendant and victim. The DPP's guidance provided a "comprehensive, appropriate and lawful framework" for prosecutorial decision-making, which paid particular attention to the position of children in the criminal justice system, whether as defendants or victims, and focused as a central theme on their welfare. The Court declined to decide whether the various international instruments cited to it were binding as a matter of domestic law or because the DPP had incorporated them in his guidance. But even assuming they were, it did not follow that the DPP's policy was thereby invalidated. If a decision in a particular case failed to give effect to the obligations imposed on the UK by those instruments, it might be amenable to challenge. But the Court rejected the proposition that the legality of the DPP's "carefully crafted and clearly formu-lated" policy depended upon the amount of detail which he chose to apply in exegesis of such obligations. It also rejected the argument that the failure to seek the mother's views as to how a prosecution would impact on S and R itself breached the requirement, in both the Code and the guidance, for the best interests of the victims to be placed "foremost" when reaching a decision as to whether or not to prosecute. The Court emphasised that neither the Code nor the guidance imposed any obligation to seek out the victim's views, but rather to have regard to any views that were expressed. Moreover, neither required priority to be given to the interests of the victim; on the contrary, they required a proper balancing of the interests of the defendant, the victim and the public at large.

However, the Court went on to find "irrefutable substance" in the claimant's argument that the Crown Prosecutor had failed properly to apply the DPP's guidance. It referred to the key elements of the report of the multi-agency strategy group, cited above, and said that the Crown Prosecutor's decision letter was striking not so much for what it said as for what it did *not* say: the only references to S and R were to their ages and vulnerability at the time of the offences and it contained no reference to what the strategy report said about their need for therapy and the fact that delay would be harmful to their eventual recovery; there was no reference to their interests having been considered; and there was no reference to what the report said about E's need for therapy and the adverse consequences of her for delay. In short, the decision letter did not engage with what the report had said "in plain and concerning terms" about the adverse effects on the welfare of all three children of the decision to prosecute E. Whilst decisions by prosecutors are to be read in a broad and common sense way, and on the assumption that the decision-maker knew how she should perform her functions and which matters she should take into account, in this case the errors were patent on the face of the decision letter and as a result the decision had to be quashed.

Victims' Right to Review

3.11A   In *Killick*[12] the Court of Appeal said that "as a decision not to prosecute is in reality a final decision for a victim, there must be a right to seek a review of such a decision". It also ruled that reversing a decision could be compatible with a suspect's rights. In response to this judgment, the then DPP, Keir Starmer QC, in June 2013 launched a new policy enshrining a victim's right to request a review of any decision taken by the CPS not to charge a suspect or to stop a prosecution. Mr Starmer said[13]:

> "The new Victims' Right to Review (VRR) policy[14] is one of the most significant victim initiatives ever launched by the CPS. It provides victims with a straight-forward opportunity to ask the CPS to look again at a decision to not start, or to stop, a prosecution. It not only demonstrates how attitudes to victims have changed; it also clearly shows how the CPS has changed.
>   The criminal justice system historically treated victims as bystanders and accordingly gave them little say in their cases. The decisions of prosecutors were rarely reversed because it was considered vital that decisions, even when later shown to be questionable, were final and could be relied upon. This approach was intended to inspire confidence, but in reality it had the opposite effect. Refusing to admit mistakes can seriously undermine public trust in the criminal justice system.
>   It is now recognised by the criminal justice system that the interests of justice and the rights of the victim can outweigh the suspect's right to certainty. This is already reflected in the Code for Crown Prosecutors, but more needs to be done to correct this historic imbalance and ensure that the people affected by our decisions can hold us to account. Victims' Right to Review is a major step in the right direction. It recognises that victims are active participants in the criminal justice process, with both interests to protect and rights to enforce."

Any victim of crime, which includes bereaved family members or other representatives, can now ask the CPS to look again at a case following a decision not to charge, to discontinue proceedings or to offer no evidence. Those entitled to an enhanced service under the Victims' Code will also be offered a discussion with a prosecutor about the outcome of the review. Mr Starmer said:

> "These reviews will be an entirely fresh examination of all the evidence and circumstances of a case. If a charge is justified and there are no legal barriers to prosecution, the mistake will be put right. Making fair decisions and delivering justice is the priority."

---

[12] [2011] EWCA Crim 1608.

[13] See *http://www.cps.gov.uk/news/latest_news/victims_right_to_review/* [accessed December 27, 2013].

[14] The policy is available at *http://www.cps.gov.uk/victims_witnesses/victims_right_to_review/index.html* [accessed December 27, 2013].

In cases where a defendant has been formally acquitted at the Crown Court after a decision to offer no evidence, it will not normally be possible to reinstate proceedings. Prosecutors will, wherever possible, consult with victims before taking such decisions and in these cases, although it is not possible to reverse the decision, the review will determine if the right decision was made and, if not, whether any lessons could be learned.

Child Sexual Abuse Review Panel

The VRR scheme does not apply to cases where the police have decided to take no   **3.11B**
further action and a file of evidence has not been submitted to the CPS. However, in parallel with the launch of the VRR scheme, in June 2013, the Association of Chief Police Officers and the CPS established a Child Sexual Abuse Review Panel to review cases in which the police or CPS decided to take no action on an allegation of child sexual abuse and the complainant is not satisfied that the allegations were dealt with properly at the time. The role of the Panel is to consider whether the approach originally taken was wrong and to advise whether the allegations should be reinvestigated by the police or the prosecution decision reviewed by the CPS. The Panel will only consider cases in which the child abuse is alleged to have occurred before the introduction of the VRR scheme, on the basis that later cases will be dealt with under that scheme. The Panel consists of five experts: a Chief Crown Prosecutor, an ACPO rank police officer, a specialist prosecutor, an experienced child abuse police investigator, and an independent representative, who will come from either the NSPCC or the Office of the Children's Commissioner for England. The Panel's Terms of Reference can be found   at   *http://www.acpo.police.uk/documents/crime/2013/201306-cba-csa-review-panel.pdf* [accessed December 27, 2013].

Article 8 ECHR

As a coda to *R. v G*, discussed in the main work, the European Court of Human   **3.19**
Rights subsequently declared inadmissible an application by the convicted defendant in which he rehearsed the argument based upon art.8 that had been rejected by a majority of the House of Lords.[15] The Court held, also by a majority, that the applicant's prosecution for the conduct at issue in this case constituted an interference with his "private life" within the meaning of art.8(1). However, in determining whether such an interference was "necessary in a democratic society" within the meaning of art.8(2), it took into account that Member States enjoy a wide margin of appreciation as regards the means of ensuring adequate protection against rape, especially where, as in this case, the public interest at stake was the need to protect the complainant and other children in her position against premature sexual activity, exploitation and abuse. The authorities could not be said to have exceeded that margin of appreciation by creating the s.5 offence, nor by

---

[15] [2011] E.H.H.R. 1308 (Application No.37334/08).

deciding to prosecute the applicant for it, particularly given that the possible sentences covered a broad range from absolute discharge to detention for life, and that the applicant's mitigating circumstances were fully taken into account by the Court of Appeal.

3.19A Several months before the Strasbourg decision, *R. v G* was cited in *E, S and R, R. (on the application of) v DPP*, discussed above (para.3.11 et seq.). One argument advanced by the mother of the three girls for quashing the decision to prosecute E was that it failed to have proper regard to the girls' rights under arts 3 and 8 of the ECHR. The Court declined to decide the point on the basis that it had already determined to quash the decision on another ground. However, it noted that the decision and reasoning in *R. v G* "present formidable obstacles" to the success of any art.8 challenge to a decision to prosecute.

3.19B For an exploration of the relationship between art.8 and the prosecutorial decision-making process, focussing on the House of Lords decision in *R. v G* (and written before the Strasbourg decision in that case), see Dr Bharat Malkani, *Article 8 of the European Convention on Human Rights, and the Decision to Prosecute* [2011] Crim. L.R. 943.

RAPE OF A CHILD UNDER 13

Definition

3.21 Since the main work was published, the CPS's legal guidance has been simplified to say: "In cases where a defendant admits sexual activity with a child under 13 but states that the victim consented, the proper course is to invite the court to hold a *Newton* hearing. On no account should a section 1 rape count be added as an alternative."[16]

Conspiracy

3.21A In *R. v G and F*[17] the appellants were convicted of conspiracy to rape a male child under 13 in circumstances where they had communicated only by text message. They did not meet at any stage, either before or after the text exchange, nor did they suggest meeting to discuss the plan. There was no evidence that they had taken any steps to advance the plan. No place or time or other details were identified. They were arrested some three years after the text exchange. They were silent in interview. At trial, the judge rejected a half-time submission of no case to

---

[16] Rape and Sexual Offences, *http://www.cps.gov.uk/legal/p_to_r/rape_and_sexual_offences/soa_2003_and_soa_1956/£a14* [accessed December 27, 2013].
[17] [2012] EWCA Crim 1756; see also *Hedgecock, Dyer and Mayers* [2007] EWCA Crim 3486, discussed in para.1.259 of the main work.

answer. The convictions were quashed on appeal. The Court of Appeal said that on the submission of no case to answer, the vital question in this case was whether a jury could be sure that both the appellants intended to carry out the agreement to rape a male child under 13. The Court's view was that no reasonable jury, taking the prosecution evidence at its highest, could infer that the appellants did so intend. The evidence was all equivocal and was as consistent with fantasy as with an intent to carry out the plan. The appellants' silence in interview and their failure to mention it was all a fantasy could be taken into account, but it was of little weight given the other facts, or rather lack of them.

MODE OF TRIAL AND PUNISHMENT

From December 3, 2012, when ss.122–128 of the Legal Aid, Sentencing and **3.23** Punishment of Offenders Act 2012 were brought into force[18]:

- An offence under s.5 is a serious specified offence for the purposes of ss.224 and 225(2) of the Criminal Justice Act 2003 ("CJA 2003") (life sentence for serious offences).
- For offences committed on or after that date, an offence under s.5 is listed in Pt 1 of Sch.15B to that Act for the purposes of s.224A of the Act (life sentence for second listed offence).
- For convictions on or after that date (irrespective of the date of commission of the offence), an offence under s.5 is a specified offence for the purposes of s.226A of the CJA 2003 (extended sentence for certain violent or sexual offences).

BAIL

Section 25 of the Criminal Justice and Public Order Act 1994 was amended on **3.24** December 3, 2012,[19] so that a person charged with or convicted of an offence to which the section applies shall be granted bail by a constable only if the constable is "of the opinion", rather than "satisfied" (as before), that there are exceptional circumstances which justify it.

SENTENCING

The Sentencing Council has issued a new guideline applicable to sex offenders **3.26** aged 18 or over who are sentenced on or after April 1, 2014: see para.1.20 et seq., above. In its consultation on the draft guideline,[20] the Council noted that the previous guideline, issued in 2007 by the Sentencing Guidelines Council, covered together the under-13 offences and the equivalent offences for victims aged over 13; for example, there was a single guideline covering both rape (s.1) and rape of

[18] By the Legal Aid, Sentencing and Punishment of Offenders Act 2012 (Commencement No.4 and Saving Provisions) Order 2012 (SI 2012/2906).
[19] By the Legal Aid, Sentencing and Punishment of Offenders Act 2012, s.90 and Sch.11 para.33, which was brought into force by the Legal Aid, Sentencing and Punishment of Offenders Act 2012 (Commencement No.4 and Saving Provisions) Order 2012, last note.
[20] *Sexual Offences Guideline: Consultation* (December 6, 2012).

a child under 13 (s.5). The Council proposed instead to issue separate guidelines for the under-13 offences and for offences against victims aged 13 and over, in recognition that "there are issues and sensitivities unique to offences against children under 13 that require a separate guideline to ensure clarity for sentencers as to the factors to be taken into account and to provide a transparent process for others concerned with these cases".[21] This is the approach taken in the published guideline.

In publishing the guideline, the Sentencing Council noted (in Annex A) that s.5 offences may involve a range of factual circumstances that will influence the type and length of sentence awarded. The guideline seeks to deal with the most common of these factual circumstances, which can range from "forced non-consensual activity to instances where an adult offender has exploited or groomed a child to the extent that the child maintains consent and may even regard themselves as in a genuine relationship with the offender because they have become habituated to the activity, right through to cases where an offender who is just over 18 but who lacks maturity themselves has formed an illegal and inappropriate but non-exploitative relationship with the child". The Council felt it important that cases where a child under 13 has been groomed into acquiescence are treated equally for sentencing purposes with cases of forced non-consensual activity, given evidence that younger children are increasingly at risk of sexual exploitation. As for the exceptional case of a truly non-exploitative relationship, the Council considered that such cases should be sentenced outside the guideline. In order to give sentencers the confidence to do so, it included in the guideline the following, highly important narrative:

When dealing with the statutory offence of rape of a child under 13, the court may be faced with a wide range of offending behaviour.

Sentencers should have particular regard to the fact that these offences are not only committed through force or fear of force but may include exploitative behaviour towards a child which should be considered to indicate high culpability.

Offences may be of such severity, for example involving a campaign of rape, that sentences of 20 years and above may be appropriate.

This guideline is designed to deal with the majority of offending behaviour which deserves a significant custodial sentence; the starting points and ranges reflect the fact that such offending merits such an approach. There may also be exceptional cases, where a lengthy community order with a requirement to participate in a sex offender treatment programme may be the best way of changing the offender's behaviour and of protecting the public by preventing any repetition of the offence. This guideline may not be appropriate where the sentencer is satisfied that on the available evidence, and in the absence of exploitation, a young or particularly immature defendant genuinely believed, on reasonable grounds, that the victim was aged 16 or over and that they were engaging in lawful sexual activity.

Sentencers are reminded that if sentencing outside the guideline they must be satisfied that it would be contrary to the interests of justice to follow the guideline.

---

[21] *Sexual Offences Guideline: Consultation* (December 6, 2012), p.36.

New sentencing guideline

Step One—Harm and culpability

Under the new guideline, the sentencing court is to go through a series of steps
in order to determine the appropriate sentence. Step one involves determining the
offence category by reference to the degree of harm caused and then the
culpability level for the offence. In relation to the s.5 offence of rape of a child the
harm and culpability factors are as follows: **3.26A**

HARM		CULPABILITY	
Category 1	• The extreme nature of one or more category 2 factors or the extreme impact caused by a combination of category 2 factors **may** elevate to category 1	**A**	
Category 2	• Severe psychological or physical harm		• Significant degree of planning
	• Pregnancy or STI as a consequence of offence		• Offender acts together with others to commit the offence
	• Additional degradation/humiliation		• Use of alcohol/drugs on victim to facilitate the offence
	• Abduction		• Grooming behaviour used against victim
	• Prolonged detention/sustained incident		• Abuse of trust
	• Violence or threats of violence		• Previous violence against victim
	• Forced/uninvited entry into victim's home		• Offence committed in course of burglary
	• Child is particularly vulnerable due to extreme youth and/or personal circumstances		• Sexual images of victim recorded, retained, solicited or shared
Category 3	Factor(s) in categories 1 and 2 not present		• Deliberate isolation of victim
			• Commercial exploitation and/or motivation
			• Offence racially or religiously aggravated
			• Offence motivated by, or demonstrating, hostility to the victim based on his or her sexual orientation (or presumed sexual orientation) or transgender identity (or presumed transgender identity)
			• Offence motivated by, or demonstrating, hostility to the victim based on his or her disability (or presumed disability)

B
Factor(s) in categories 1 and 2 not present

As noted above, the offence of rape of a child under 13 can cover a very wide range of offending behaviours, including exploitative behaviour used to obtain the victim's acquiescence. For this reason, the culpability factors in this guideline are wider than those in the guideline for rape.

Categories 1 and 2 contain a list of factors indicating additional harm; these are the same factors as those in the rape guideline. Category 3 has no factors listed, in order to reflect the fact that any rape of a child under the age of 13 involves inherent serious harm, without the presence of any other factors.

In its consultation on the draft guideline, the Sentencing Council elaborated its reasons for adopting some of the culpability factors. In relation to "use of alcohol/drugs on victim to facilitate the offence" it noted that in addition to the use of alcohol to incapacitate the victim, offenders may use access to alcohol and/or drugs as part of the grooming process in order to gain the trust or friendship of a child by allowing them to behave in a way that would not be permitted by their parents or other responsible adults. "Grooming behaviour used against victim" is included as a factor to cover a wide variety of sexual exploitation, of which the use of alcohol and gifts are examples. As for "abuse of trust", in relation to children under 13 trust may arise not only from a position of formal responsibility but also from a relationship with the child, e.g. as babysitter or family friend who has been trusted to look after the child on a day out.

Step Two—Starting point and category range

3.26B Having determined the offence category and culpability level, the court should then use the corresponding starting point specified in the guideline in order to reach a sentence within the category range. The starting point applies to all offenders irrespective of plea or previous convictions. Once the starting point has been determined, step two allows further adjustment for aggravating or mitigating features, set out below. A case of particular gravity, reflected by multiple features of culpability or harm, could merit upward adjustment from the starting point before further adjustment for aggravating or mitigating features.

The starting points and category ranges for rape of a child under 13 are set out in the table below. They are higher than the starting points and ranges in the rape guideline, in order to reflect the increased harm and culpability that exists when an adult offender decides to engage in penetrative sexual activity with a child under the age of 13. The Sentencing Council recognised that the wide range of offending behaviour with which a sentencer may be faced means there is a need for flexibility in the sentencing regime.

	A	B
Category 1	Starting point 16 years' custody Category range 13–19 years' custody	Starting point 13 years' custody Category range 11–17 years' custody
Category 2	Starting point 13 years' custody Category range 11–17 years' custody	Starting point 10 years' custody Category range 8–13 years' custody
Category 3	Starting point 10 years' custody Category range 8–13 years' custody	Starting point 8 years' custody Category range 6–11 years' custody

The SGC guideline suggested higher starting points and ranges for victims under the age of 13, except in the highest category, where the starting point was 15 years' custody whatever the age of the victim. The reason given for this was that when a rape has factors placing it in the highest category, the age of the victim becomes secondary to the extreme nature of those other factors. The Sentencing Council, in its consultation, said that it appreciated the logic of this approach but felt that there should be a differential in the level of sentence to reflect the inherent vulnerability of a young victim and the harm done to them by the commission of this offence. It therefore raised the starting point in the highest category to 16 years' custody for victims under the age of 13, as compared to 15 years' custody for victims over the age of 13. The highest sentence level in the SGC guideline was reserved for multiple rapes, but the new guideline moves away from that by making the 16-year starting point available for single rapes.

Aggravating and mitigating factors

After identifying the starting point and category range, the court should consider whether the presence of aggravating or mitigating factors should result in an upward or downward adjustment from the starting point or the imposition of a sentence outside the category range. In particular, relevant recent convictions are likely to result in an upward adjustment. The non-exhaustive list of aggravating and mitigating factors for the s.5 offence is as follows:

3.26C

Aggravating factors
Statutory aggravating factors
• Previous convictions, having regard to a) the nature of the offence to which the conviction relates and its relevance to the current offence; and b) the time that has elapsed since the conviction
• Offence committed whilst on bail
Other aggravating factors
• Specific targeting of a particularly vulnerable child
• Ejaculation (where not taken into account at step one)
• Blackmail or other threats made (where not taken into account at step one)
• Location of offence
• Timing of offence
• Use of weapon or other item to frighten or injure
• Victim compelled to leave their home, school, etc
• Failure to comply with current court orders
• Offence committed whilst on licence
• Exploiting contact arrangements with a child to commit an offence
• Presence of others, especially other children
• Any steps taken to prevent the victim reporting an incident, obtaining assistance and/or from assisting or supporting the prosecution
• Attempts to dispose of or conceal evidence
• Commission of offence whilst offender under the influence of alcohol or drugs
• Victim encouraged to recruit others

Mitigating factors
• No previous convictions **or** no relevant/recent convictions
• Remorse
• Previous good character and/or exemplary conduct*
• Age and/or lack of maturity where it affects the responsibility of the offender
• Mental disorder or learning disability, particularly where linked to the commission of the offence

> * Previous good character/exemplary conduct is different from having no previous convictions. The more serious the offence, the less the weight which should normally be attributed to this factor. Where previous good character/exemplary conduct has been used to facilitate the offence, this mitigation should not normally be allowed and such conduct may constitute an aggravating factor.
>
> In the context of this offence, previous good character/exemplary conduct should not normally be given any significant weight and will not normally justify a reduction in what would otherwise be the appropriate sentence.

The Council noted that the caveat, stating that it may be more appropriate to treat previous good character/exemplary conduct as an aggravating factor rather than as mitigation where it has been used to facilitate the offence, is especially pertinent to some historic child sex offences that have come before the courts recently, where status and "good character" have been one of the main reasons the offender has been able to evade justice for such a significant amount of time (cf. the well-known cases of the broadcasters Jimmy Savile and Stuart Hall).

Steps Three to Nine

The remaining steps cover the following points. At step three the court should consider any factors which would indicate a reduction in sentence, e.g. assistance to the prosecution. At step four it should consider any reduction for a guilty plea. At step five the court should consider dangerousness, i.e. whether it would be appropriate to award a life sentence (s.224A or s.225(2) of the CJA 2003) or an extended sentence (s.226A). Step six requires the court to consider whether the total sentence is just and proportionate to the offending behaviour. At step seven it should consider whether to make an ancillary order (e.g. a compensation order, a sexual offences prevention order ("SOPO") or a restraining order). Step eight requires the court to fulfil its duty under s.174 of the CJA 2003 to give reasons for, and explain the effect of, the sentence. Finally, at step nine the court should consider whether to give credit for time spent on bail in accordance with s.240A of that Act. **3.26D**

Approach to sentencing where child ostensibly consented and/or offender believed child to be 16 or over

In *Att Gen's Refs (Nos 74 and 83 of 2007) (Fenn and Foster)*,[22] discussed in the main work, the Court of Appeal held that the value of "ostensible consent" as mitigation of a s.5 offence will depend on the extent to which it was true consent as opposed to consent obtained opportunistically or by coercion or exploitation; and that the value as mitigation of a mistaken belief that the complainant was 16 or over will depend on whether the belief was a reasonable one reached after due consideration, on the basis that the older the offender, the less relevant such a mistake will be. **3.28**

[22] [2007] EWCA Crim 2550.

3.28A   These points were again considered in *Att Gen's Refs (Nos 11 and 12 of 2012) (Channer and Monteiro)*,[23] where Pitchford L.J., giving the judgment of the Court of Appeal, sounded a cautionary note about the use in this context of the terms "ostensible consent" and "willingness". His Lordship summarised as follows the considerations relevant to sentence where the offender claims that the victim consented and/or that he believed her to be 16 or over[24]:

> "(1) Careful analysis of the circumstances of a section 5 offence is always required and a *Newton* hearing may be necessary when the claim is made that the victim was consenting in fact and/or that the offender believed the victim to be significantly older than her chronological age. The prosecutor bears a burden of responsibility to ensure that factual concessions to a basis of plea or mitigation of the offence are made only when justified and that, if made, the precise import of the concession is understood by the offender and the court (see further paragraph (3) below);
>
> (2) There is a strong element of deterrence in sentencing for sexual offences committed against young children, whether they are sexually experienced and 'willing' or not. They are, by reason of their young age, vulnerable to exploitation and require protection, sometimes from themselves. It can be assumed that, whatever the circumstances, there is likely to be considerable long-term harm caused by such offences;
>
> (3) Exploitative sexual behaviour towards a child under 13 without consideration for the vulnerability of that child may be just as serious as submission obtained by the use of force or the threat of force. 'Ostensible consent' and 'willingness' are terms which, in the context of offences against the young in particular, are susceptible to misunderstanding and, even if accurately used, are liable to obscure the true nature of the encounter between the offender and the victim (see *Fenn and Foster* at para.11);
>
> (4) The culpability of the offender is measured in part by his own understanding of the harm he was causing or was likely to cause. The guideline does not, however, recognise as a mitigating factor a belief by the offender that the victim was aged 13-15 years. There is a good reason for this. Such an offender knew that the victim was not in law consenting. Nevertheless, the younger the victim, the more serious is the harm likely to result and the greater is likely to be the culpability of the offender. We repeat the advice of the court in *Corran* at para.8 that the respective ages of the offender and the victim is an important factor in the assessment of seriousness;
>
> (5) The starting point for consideration of the appropriate sentence for a section 5 offence is the table at page 25 of the guideline,[25] and not the table at page 53 which applies to offences contrary to section 9. If the judge decides to sentence outside the guideline range that decision should be justified and explained."

In that case the offenders, who were aged 20 at the time of the offences, had pleaded guilty to raping a child under 13 on the same occasion and sentenced to

---

[23] [2012] EWCA Crim 1119. See also the controversial decision in *Charles and others* [2011] EWCA Crim 2153, where the Court of Appeal did not refer to *Fenn and Foster* but took its lead from the pre-guideline case of *Corran* [2005] EWCA Crim 192, discussed in the main work at para.3.32. For criticism, see Kim Stevenson, *It is what "girls of indifferent character" do . . . Complications concerning the legal age of consent in the light of R. v C (2011)*, J. Crim. L. 2012, 76(2), 130–9.

[24] At [34].

[25] i.e. the guideline issued by the Sentencing Guidelines Council in 2007, discussed in the main work, which has been replaced by the guideline issued in 2014 by the Sentencing Council, discussed above.

40 months' detention. The victim had been aged 11 at the time but the offenders claimed they thought she was much older and that she had been a "willing participant". The judge concluded that the offenders could reasonably have believed the victim to be 14, but no older. He found the offences aggravated by the fact that there was more than one offender each committing an offence in the presence of the other; they gave implicit approval to the filming of the incident by other young males, and they used the victim for casual sex not caring what her age was. In mitigation, the judge cited the "willingness" of the victim, the guilty pleas at the first opportunity, some remorse and the absence of previous convictions for sexual offences. He said that the case was not an exceptional one which required him to depart from the guideline, which specified a starting point of 13 years' custody and a range of 11–17 years. However, taking into account that the offence "was consensual in the sense that [the victim] was a willing participant" and that the offenders reasonably believed her to be 14, he took a starting point of 5 years' detention which, after a discount of one-third for the guilty pleas, produced sentences of 40 months.

The Attorney General referred the sentences to the Court of Appeal. The Court, having considered the SGC guideline and *Fenn and Foster*, and expounded the principles set out above, found that the sentences were unduly lenient. While the judge had identified the factual basis for sentence in an exemplary manner, he had reached the wrong conclusion as to the seriousness of the offences. Pitchford L.J. emphasised the following facts[26]:

> "(1) These offenders could not have thought that the complainant was older than 14 years of age. It follows that no significant mitigation was available to them on the basis of a mistaken belief in the girl's age. They knew that the girl was incapable of consenting in law to the activity in which they required her to engage.
> (2) They did not care how old she was. They did not make any enquiry of the girl. The circumstances were such that they must have realised that she was a child and, therefore, vulnerable.
> (3) There was a substantial disparity between their ages and the complainant's actual age; there was a significant disparity between their ages and the complainant's age as they might reasonably have believed it to be. We use these descriptions in order to emphasise the gulf in maturity between an 11 or 14 year old victim and the 20 year old offenders. Nonetheless these offenders were still young men.
> (4) The only mitigating feature available to the offenders was the complainant's willingness to engage in sexual activity. As explained in *Fenn and Foster*, however, such 'willingness' is of little value in mitigation where the offence amounts to the exploitation of a young child. The circumstances here were that two adults jointly took advantage of a child in degrading circumstances.
> (5) The group nature of the activity (which should not be double-counted) and the recording of the event constituted serious aggravating features of an already exploitative offence.
> (6) The harm done by the offenders will be long-lasting, perhaps permanent."

He went on:

> "The primary sentencing objective in these circumstances was punishment and deterrence. The aggravating factors identified by the judge serve only to identify the

[26] Above, fn.23 at [38]–[39].

nature of the evil against which the Act and the sentencing guideline seek to achieve the protection of children. In our judgment, the starting point for these offences of rape should not have fallen below 11 years custody and may have been somewhat higher. We are conscious that this must result in a substantial increase in sentence even after giving full credit for guilty pleas. We agree with the judge that there is no reason to distinguish between these offenders. In each case we quash the sentences imposed and substitute sentences of 7 years detention in a young offender institution."

3.28B   Both *Fenn and Foster* and *Channer and Monteiro* were decided by reference to the guideline issued in 2007 by the Sentencing Guidelines Council, which has been replaced by the one issued by the Sentencing Council in 2014. As noted above, recognition of the scope of the s.5 offence led the Sentencing Council to include in the new guideline a narrative acknowledging that there is a wide range of activity that may potentially come before the courts, and that there may be:

> " . . . exceptional cases, where a lengthy community order with a requirement to participate in a sex offender treatment programme may be the best way of changing the offender's behaviour and of protecting the public by preventing any repetition of the offence, for example where the sentencer is satisfied that on the available evidence, and in the absence of exploitation, a young or particularly immature defendant genuinely believed, on reasonable grounds, that the victim was aged 16 or over and that they were engaging in lawful sexual activity."

This narrative was well received by respondents to the consultation draft, though a number of judges requested the inclusion of the mitigating factor from the SGC guideline "reasonable belief (by a young offender) that the victim was aged 16 or over". The Council declined this request, saying that it had considered the point with great care prior to the consultation and deliberately omitted this as a mitigating factor. Instead, it had taken the narrative approach and identified very limited factual circumstances in which a sentencer might be warranted in imposing a sentence lower than the bottom end of the category range. The Council said it remained of the view that including a mitigating factor would not be as effective as the narrative. Further, mitigation is normally used to move down the sentencing range, not to move significantly outside it; and the mitigating factors were intended to capture the most frequent factors relevant to the offence, whereas the cases about which the judges were concerned are unusual and fact-specific.

The sentence in the narrative cited above broadly reflects the approach taken in *Fenn and Foster* and *Channer and Monteiro*, in that it acknowledges that an offence may attract a sentence beneath the category range where the offender genuinely and reasonably believed the victim to be 16 or over and consenting, and there was no element of exploitation. However, it leaves unaddressed the question whether an offence may be mitigated to any degree where there was a genuine and reasonable belief in consent, and an absence of exploitation, but the offender knew or believed the victim to be under 16; or where the offender believed the victim to be 16 or over but had exploited her in order to secure her apparent consent to sexual activity. For this reason, we suggest that when cases of this sort arise, sentencing courts may still be assisted by the fuller consideration given to the issues in *Fenn and Foster* and *Channer and Monteiro*.

The new guideline also departs from the SGC guideline by dropping the language of "ostensible consent". As we have seen, Pitchford L.J. said in *Channer and Monteiro* that "'[o]stensible consent' and 'willingness' are terms which, in the context of offences against the young in particular, are susceptible to misunderstanding and, even if accurately used, are liable to obscure the true nature of the encounter between the offender and the victim". The Sentencing Council agreed with this comment and decided to move away from this language so that the focus of the new guideline is not the behaviour of the victim but the behaviour and culpability of the offender. This approach is to be welcomed and was well received by respondents to the Council's consultation draft.

Sentencing examples

These decisions all pre-date the new definitive guideline but are useful examples of the approach taken by the Court of Appeal to different factual scenarios. **3.37**

In *Waite*[27] the appellant (18) pleaded guilty to three counts of rape of a child **3.37A** contrary to s.5 and was sentenced to 6 years' detention in a young offender institution. Following an exchange of text messages with the victim (12), she visited him at his home knowing what was going to happen and, in her words, just agreed to what took place. The appellant penetrated the victim three times over a period of 40 minutes, without using a condom and ejaculating over her leg. He asked her afterwards not to tell anyone. Her parents found out a year later and the appellant was arrested. The victim later described herself as emotionally scarred and began to self-harm, and her family relationships were adversely affected. On appeal against sentence, the Court of Appeal said that while rape of a child under 13 is always serious, even where there has been some degree of consent, the judge had attached disproportionate significance to the fact that there were three offences, given that they occurred over a relatively short period. There was also potent mitigation in the appellant's early guilty plea, frankness with the police, age, emotional immaturity and lack of previous convictions, the fact that he had mistakenly believed the victim was 15, and the "degree of consensuality" present in the offence (however, as to these last points see the discussion at para.3.28 et seq., above). The SGC guideline indicated a range of 8–13 years' custody, but the judge had made too much of the number of rapes and not enough of the significant mitigation. The appropriate starting point, given the appellant's age, would have been 6 years, and so the Court substituted 4 years' detention.

In *Hudd*[28] the appellant appealed against concurrent sentences of 10 years' **3.37B** imprisonment imposed after his conviction under s.5. He was aged 23 or 24 when the offences took place and had no previous convictions for sexual offences. The victim was approaching her thirteenth birthday. The appellant befriended her and

[27] [2014] 1 Cr. App. R.(S.) 35(8).
[28] [2012] EWCA Crim 846.

had sexual intercourse with her five times over the course of one week. He did not use contraception. He later introduced her to a friend (R) who also had sexual intercourse with her on two occasions several months later. R received concurrent sentences of 5 years' imprisonment because by the date of his offences the victim was over the age of 13. The appellant submitted that the judge had taken insufficient account of the victim's proximity to her thirteenth birthday, and there was a large disparity between the sentences imposed upon him and R for similar offences. The appeal was allowed. The Court of Appeal said that the judge had taken account of the sentencing guideline and identified the aggravated and mitigating features, but there was force in the appellant's argument that the judge could legitimately have attached more weight to the peculiar circumstance that victim was within a few weeks or days of her thirteenth birthday at the time of the statutory rapes. The significance of the age 13 was demonstrated by the fact that R received sentences of 5 years for each of his two offences, committed when the victim was aged 13-and-a-half. There were striking similarities between the circumstances of the appellant's and R's offences. They were both men with no previous convictions for sexual offences. They both had positive reports and references. Their offending had occurred over a short period of time. The critical distinguishing factor was that in the appellant's case the offences occurred before the victim's thirteenth birthday, and in R's case, some months after that. In addition, R had committed two offences whereas H had committed five, which would have merited a different sentence. However, having regard to the similarities between the two sets of offences, and the two offenders, the disparity was such that it was exceptionally possible for the Court to intervene and to substitute sentences of 8 years for the sentences of 10 years. However, offences of the instant type were rightly regarded as very serious and nothing in the judgment should be taken as undermining the importance of that principle.

PARTIES TO THE OFFENCE

3.44   In the main work we expressed the view that if the child who is raped encourages the offence, they are in principle liable to conviction as an accessory. We considered the decision in *Tyrrell*[29] to be distinguishable in this context, since the offence in that case was created to protect girls against men and there was no indication in the statute of an intention to criminalise the girls themselves, whereas any male person over the age of criminal responsibility may be convicted of the s.5 offence, and if a male child may commit the offence as principal, it is difficult to conclude that they cannot do so as accessory, even where the offence is committed against them. Further, it cannot have been Parliament's intention that *Tyrrell* should apply in a gender-divisive way so as to protect from accessoryship penetrated female but not penetrated male children. On that reasoning, there

---

[29] [1894] 1 Q.B. 710; and see *DPP v Whitehouse* [1977] Q.B. 868.

appeared to be no logical objection based upon *Tyrrell* to convicting a child as an accessory to a s.5 offence of which they were the victim.

Of relevance to this point is a passage in the reasoning of the majority of the Supreme Court in the decision in *Gnango*.[30] In that case, the majority held (Lord Kerr dissenting) that where D1 and D2 voluntarily enter into a fight against each other, each intending to kill or cause grievous bodily harm to the other and each foreseeing that the other has a reciprocal intention, and where D1 mistakenly kills a third party (V) in the course of the fight, then not only D1 but also D2 is guilty of murdering V. The significance of the decision for present purposes is that in the course of its reasoning the majority considered the decision in *Tyrrell*, which it said was an illustration of a general rule[31] that where legislation creates an offence that is intended to protect a class of persons, a member of that class cannot be convicted as an accessory to such an offence committed in respect of him. Defined in this broad way, the rule in *Tyrrell* would, contrary to the argument in the main work, operate to prevent the victim of a s.5 offence (or another under-13 sex offence) from being prosecuted as an accessory to the offence, since the s.5 offence was undoubtedly designed to protect the class of persons comprising children under 13, albeit that a child under that age can commit the offence as principal or indeed as accessory where they are not the victim.

As a practical matter the point has been put beyond argument by *Att Gen's Ref (No.53 of 2013) (R. v Wilson)*,[31a] in which the offender pleaded guilty and was sentenced to 8 months' imprisonment for an offence of sexual activity with a child, a girl aged 13, contrary to s.9 of the 2003 Act. The girl was sexually experienced and prosecuting counsel described her in the course of the sentencing hearing as "predatory", a term picked up by the judge in his sentencing remarks. On a reference by the Attorney General under s.36 of the Criminal Justice Act 1988, the Court of Appeal held that the sentence was plainly unduly lenient. In doing so, it accepted the Attorney General's submission that the fact that the victim had initiated what had happened was an aggravating, rather than a mitigating, factor. Lord Thomas C.J. said[31b]:

> "It has been clear since at least the Offences Against the Person Act 1861, and subsequent nineteenth century legislation, that the purpose of Parliament in passing legislation to make it a crime punishable with imprisonment to have sexual relations with those under 16 was to protect those under 16. Indeed the Criminal Law Amendments Act 1885 makes it expressly clear that that was the purpose of the legislation. That can be seen from the preamble to the Act and was made clear by this court in *R. v Tyrrell* [1894] 1 QB 710.
>
> That long-standing principle is well-known. The reduction of punishment on the basis that the person who needed protection encouraged the commission of an offence is therefore simply wrong. We agree with the submission of the Attorney General that an underage person who encourages sexual relations with her needs more protection, not less. Accepting that as the basis for sentencing for the reasons we have explained,

---

[30] [2011] UKSC 59 at [17]–[19], [47]–[53].
[31] Identified by Professor Glanville Williams in his article "Victims and other exempt parties in crime" (1990) 10 Legal Studies at p.245.
[31a] [2013] EWCA Crim 2544.
[31b] At [19]–[20].

the fact that the offender took advantage of what he asserted the victim did aggravated the offence."

If a child who initiates sexual relations is more in need of the law's protection than other child victims, it must follow that there can be little or no public interest in prosecuting such a child in relation to sexual offences committed against her. Accordingly, whatever the precise ambit of the rule in *Tyrrell*, it is almost inconceivable that the public interest would ever require the prosecution of a child in relation to a s.5 offence of which she was herself the victim.

ASSAULT OF A CHILD UNDER 13 BY PENETRATION

Mode of Trial and Punishment

3.56 From December 3, 2012, when ss.122–128 of the Legal Aid, Sentencing and Punishment of Offenders Act 2012 were brought into force[32]:

- An offence under s.6 is a serious specified offence for the purposes of ss.224 and 225(2) of the CJA 2003 (life sentence for serious offences).
- For offences committed on or after that date, an offence under s.6 is listed in Pt 1 of Sch.15B to that Act for the purposes of s.224A of the Act (life sentence for second listed offence).
- For convictions on or after that date (irrespective of the date of commission of the offence), an offence under s.6 is a specified offence for the purposes of s.226A of the CJA 2003 (extended sentence for certain violent or sexual offences).

Bail

3.57 Section 25 of the Criminal Justice and Public Order Act 1994 was amended on December 3, 2012,[33] so that a person charged with or convicted of an offence to which the section applies shall be granted bail by a constable only if the constable is "of the opinion", rather than "satisfied" (as before), that there are exceptional circumstances which justify it.

Sentencing

3.59 The Sentencing Council has issued a new guideline applicable to sex offenders

---

[32] By the Legal Aid, Sentencing and Punishment of Offenders Act 2012 (Commencement No.4 and Saving Provisions) Order 2012 (SI 2012/2906).

[33] By the Legal Aid, Sentencing and Punishment of Offenders Act 2012, s.90 and Sch.11 para.33, which was brought into force by the Legal Aid, Sentencing and Punishment of Offenders Act 2012 (Commencement No.4 and Saving Provisions) Order 2012, last note.

aged 18 or over who are sentenced on or after April 1, 2014: see para.1.20 et seq., above. In its consultation on the draft guideline,[34] the Council noted that the previous guideline, issued in 2007 by the Sentencing Guidelines Council, covered together the under-13 offences and the equivalent offences for victims aged 13 and over; for example, there was a single guideline covering assault by penetration (s.2) and assault of a child under 13 by penetration (s.6). The Sentencing Council proposed instead to issue separate guidelines for the under-13 offences and for offences against victims of 13 and over, in recognition that "there are issues and sensitivities unique to offences against children under 13 that require a separate guideline to ensure clarity for sentencers as to the factors to be taken into account and to provide a transparent process for others concerned with these cases".[35] This is the approach that in due course it took in the new guideline.

The guideline for assault by penetration of a child under 13, like that for rape of a child under 13, follows the format of the guideline for the offence against victims aged 13 and over, but with the addition of factors that relate more specifically to "grooming", since the under-13 offences may involve a child being coerced and groomed into sexual activity. The starting points and category ranges for the under-13 offence are higher than those for the offence against victims aged 13 and over; but the guideline also acknowledges that the potential range of offending behaviours is such that there may be exceptional cases where a greater degree of flexibility is required. On this aspect see the discussion, above, of the guideline for rape of a child under 13.

New sentencing guideline

Step One—Harm and culpability

Under the new guideline, the sentencing court is to go through a series of steps in order to determine the appropriate sentence. Step one involves determining the offence category by reference to the degree of harm caused and then the culpability level for the offence. In relation to the s.6 offence of assault by penetration of a child under 13, the harm and culpability factors are as follows: 3.59A

---

[34] *Sexual Offences Guideline: Consultation* (December 6, 2012).
[35] *Sexual Offences Guideline: Consultation* (December 6, 2012), p.36.

HARM		CULPABILITY
Category 1	• The extreme nature of one or more category 2 factors or the extreme impact caused by a combination of category 2 factors **may** elevate to category 1	**A** • Significant degree of planning • Offender acts together with others to commit the offence • Use of alcohol/drugs on victim to facilitate the offence • Grooming behaviour used against victim • Abuse of trust • Previous violence against victim • Offence committed in course of burglary • Sexual images of victim recorded, retained, solicited or shared • Deliberate isolation of victim • Commercial exploitation and/or motivation • Offence racially or religiously aggravated • Offence motivated by, or demonstrating, hostility to the victim based on his or her sexual orientation (or presumed sexual orientation) or transgender identity (or presumed transgender identity) • Offence motivated by, or demonstrating, hostility to the victim based on his or her disability (or presumed disability)
Category 2	• Severe psychological or physical harm • Penetration using large or dangerous object(s) • Additional degradation/humiliation • Abduction • Prolonged detention/sustained incident • Violence or threats of violence • Forced/uninvited entry into victim's home • Child is particularly vulnerable due to extreme youth and/or personal circumstances	
Category 3	Factor(s) in categories 1 and 2 not present	
		B
		Factor(s) in categories 1 and 2 not present

Categories 1 and 2 contain a list of factors indicating additional harm but category 3 has no listed factors, in order to reflect the fact that any assault by penetration of a child under the age of 13 involves inherent serious harm.

Step Two—Starting point and category range

3.59B   Having determined the offence category and culpability level, the court should then use the corresponding starting point specified in the guideline in order to reach a sentence within the category range. The starting point applies to all offenders irrespective of plea or previous convictions. Once the starting point has been determined, step two allows further adjustment for aggravating or mitigating features, set out below. A case of particular gravity, reflected by multiple features of culpability or harm, could merit upward adjustment from the starting point before further adjustment for aggravating or mitigating features. The starting points and category ranges for offences under s.6 are as follows:

	A	B
Category 1	**Starting point** 16 years' custody **Category range** 13–19 years' custody	**Starting point** 13 years' custody **Category range** 11–17 years' custody
Category 2	**Starting point** 11 years' custody **Category range** 7–15 years' custody	**Starting point** 8 years' custody **Category range** 5–13 years' custody
Category 3	**Starting point** 6 years' custody **Category range** 4–9 years' custody	**Starting point** 4 years' custody **Category range** 2–6 years' custody

Aggravating and mitigating factors

After identifying the starting point and category range, the court should consider whether the presence of aggravating or mitigating factors should result in an upward or downward adjustment from the starting point or the imposition of a sentence outside the category range. In particular, relevant recent convictions are likely to result in an upward adjustment. The non-exhaustive list of factors relevant to offences under s.6 is as follows:

3.59C

Aggravating factors
Statutory aggravating factors
• Previous convictions, having regard to a) the nature of the offence to which the conviction relates and its relevance to the current offence; and b) the time that has elapsed since the conviction

• Offence committed whilst on bail

Other aggravating factors
• Specific targeting of a particularly vulnerable victim
• Blackmail or other threats made (where not taken into account at step one)
• Location of offence
• Timing of offence
• Use of weapon or other item to frighten or injure
• Victim compelled to leave their home, school etc
• Failure to comply with current court orders
• Offence committed whilst on licence
• Exploiting contact arrangements with a child to commit an offence
• Presence of others, especially other children
• Any steps taken to prevent the victim reporting an incident, obtaining assistance and/or from assisting or supporting the prosecution
• Attempts to dispose of or conceal evidence
• Commission of offence whilst under the influence of alcohol or drugs
• Victim encouraged to recruit others

Mitigating factors
• No previous convictions **or** no relevant/recent convictions
• Remorse
• Previous good character and/or exemplary conduct*
• Age and/or lack of maturity where it affects the responsibility of the offender
• Mental disorder or learning disability, particularly where linked to the commission of the offence

* Previous good character/exemplary conduct is different from having no previous convictions. The more serious the offence, the less the weight which should normally be attributed to this factor. Where previous good character/exemplary conduct has been used to facilitate the offence, this mitigation should not normally be allowed and such conduct may constitute an aggravating factor.
In the context of this offence, previous good character/exemplary conduct should not normally be given any significant weight and will not normally justify a reduction in what would otherwise be the appropriate sentence.

"Victim compelled to leave their home, school, etc" is included in order to reflect the fact that where a child has to move from their home, place of care or school as a result of the offence it can create even longer term harm, as they will have had their education disrupted or been uprooted from friendship and support networks.

Steps Three to Nine

The remaining steps cover the following points. At step three the court should **3.59D** consider any factors which would indicate a reduction in sentence, e.g. assistance to the prosecution. At step four it should consider any reduction for a guilty plea. At step five the court should consider dangerousness, i.e. whether it would be appropriate to award a life sentence (s.224A or s.225(2) of the CJA 2003) or an extended sentence (s.226A). Step six requires the court to consider whether the total sentence is just and proportionate to the offending behaviour. At step seven it should consider whether to make an ancillary order (e.g. a compensation order, a SOPO or a restraining order). Step eight requires the court to fulfil its duty under s.174 of the CJA 2003 to give reasons for, and explain the effect of, the sentence. Finally, at step nine the court should consider whether to give credit for time spent on bail in accordance with s.240A of that Act.

On the relevance to sentence of the offender's belief that the victim consented **3.63** and/or that she was older than her true age, see para.3.28 et seq., above.

SEXUAL ASSAULT OF A CHILD UNDER 13

MODE OF TRIAL AND PUNISHMENT

From December 3, 2012, when ss.122–128 of the Legal Aid, Sentencing and **3.76** Punishment of Offenders Act 2012 were brought into force[36]:
- For offences committed on or after that date, an offence under s.7 is listed in Pt 1 of Sch.15B to the CJA 2003 for the purposes of s.224A of that Act (life sentence for second listed offence).
- For convictions on or after that date (irrespective of the date of commission of the offence), an offence under s.7 is a specified offence for the purposes of s.226A of that Act (extended sentence for certain violent or sexual offences).

SENTENCING

The Sentencing Council has issued a new guideline applicable to sex offenders **3.79** aged 18 or over who are sentenced on or after April 1, 2014: see para.1.20 et seq.,

[36] By the Legal Aid, Sentencing and Punishment of Offenders Act 2012 (Commencement No.4 and Saving Provisions) Order 2012 (SI 2012/2906).

above. In its consultation on the draft guideline,[37] the Council noted that the previous guideline, issued by the Sentencing Guidelines Council in 2007, covered together the under-13 offences and the equivalent offences for victims aged 13 and over; for example, there was a single guideline covering sexual assault (s.3) and sexual assault of a child under 13 (s.7). The Sentencing Council proposed instead to issue separate guidelines for the under-13 offences and for offences against victims aged 13 and over, in recognition that "there are issues and sensitivities unique to offences against children under 13 that require a separate guideline to ensure clarity for sentencers as to the factors to be taken into account and to provide a transparent process for others concerned with these cases".[38] This is the approach that in due course it took in the new guideline.

The guideline for sexual assault of a child under 13, like those for rape and assault by penetration of a child under 13, follows the format of the guideline for the offence against victims aged 13 and over, but with the addition of factors that relate more specifically to "grooming", since the under-13 offences may involve a child being coerced and groomed into sexual activity. The starting points and category ranges for the under-13 offence are higher than for the offence against victims aged 13 and over; but the guideline also acknowledges that the potential range of offending behaviours is such that there may be exceptional cases where a greater degree of flexibility is required. On this aspect see the discussion, above, of the guideline for rape of a child under 13.

New sentencing guideline

Step One—Harm and culpability

3.79A Under the new guideline, the sentencing court is to go through a series of steps in order to determine the appropriate sentence. Step one involves determining the offence category by reference to the degree of harm caused and then the culpability level for the offence. In relation to the s.7 offence of sexual assault of a child under 13, the harm and culpability factors are as follows:

HARM		CULPABILITY	
Category 1	• Severe psychological or physical harm	A	
	• Abduction	• Significant degree of planning	
	• Violence or threats of violence	• Offender acts together with others to commit the offence	
	• Forced/uninvited entry into victim's home	• Use of alcohol/drugs on victim to facilitate the offence	

---

[37] *Sexual Offences Guideline: Consultation* (December 6, 2012).
[38] *Sexual Offences Guideline: Consultation* (December 6, 2012), p.36.

Category 2	• Touching of naked genitalia or naked breast area • Prolonged detention/ sustained incident • Additional degrad- ation/humiliation • Child is particularly vulnerable due to extreme youth and/or personal circumstances	• Grooming behaviour used against victim • Abuse of trust • Previous violence against victim • Offence committed in course of burglary • Sexual images of victim recorded, retained, solicited or shared • Deliberate isolation of victim • Commercial exploitation and/or motivation • Offence racially or religiously aggravated • Offence motivated by, or demon- strating, hostility to the victim based on his or her sexual orientation (or presumed sexual orientation) or transgender identity (or presumed transgender identity) • Offence motivated by, or demonstrating, hostility to the victim based on his or her disability (or presumed disability)
Category 3	Factor(s) in categories 1 and 2 not present	
		B
		Factor(s) in category A not present

Categories 1 and 2 contain a list of factors indicating additional harm but category 3 has no listed factors, in order to reflect the fact that any sexual assault of a child under the age of 13 involves inherent serious harm.

Step Two—Starting point and category range

Having determined the offence category and culpability level, the court should **3.79B** then use the corresponding starting points specified in the guideline in order to reach a sentence within the category range. The starting point applies to all offenders irrespective of plea or previous convictions. Once the starting point has been determined, step two allows further adjustment for aggravating or mitigating features, set out below. A case of particular gravity, reflected by multiple features of culpability or harm, could merit upward adjustment from the starting point before further adjustment for aggravating or mitigating features. Where there is a sufficient prospect of rehabilitation, a community order with a sex offender treatment programme requirement under s.202 of the CJA 2003 can be a proper alternative to a short or moderate length custodial sentence.

The starting points and category ranges for offences under s.7 are as follows:

	A	B
Category 1	**Starting point** 6 years' custody **Category range** 4–9 years' custody	**Starting point** 4 years' custody **Category range** 3–7 years' custody
Category 2	**Starting point** 4 years' custody **Category range** 3–7 years' custody	**Starting point** 2 years' custody **Category range** 1–4 years' custody
Category 3	**Starting point** 1 year's custody **Category range** 26 weeks'–2 years' custody	**Starting point** 26 weeks' custody **Category range** High level community order–1 year's custody

Aggravating and mitigating factors

3.79C After identifying the starting point and category range, the court should consider whether the presence of aggravating or mitigating factors should result in an upward or downward adjustment from the starting point or the imposition of a sentence outside the category range. In particular, relevant recent convictions are likely to result in an upward adjustment. The non-exhaustive list of factors relevant to offences under s.7 is as follows:

Aggravating factors
Statutory aggravating factors
• Previous convictions, having regard to a) the nature of the offence to which the conviction relates and its relevance to the current offence; and b) the time that has elapsed since the conviction • Offence committed whilst on bail
Other aggravating factors
• Specific targeting of a particularly vulnerable child • Blackmail or other threats made (where not taken into account at step one)

- Location of offence

- Timing of offence

- Use of weapon or other item to frighten or injure

- Victim compelled to leave their home, school, etc

- Failure to comply with current court orders

- Offence committed whilst on licence

- Exploiting contact arrangements with a child to commit an offence

- Presence of others, especially other children

- Any steps taken to prevent the victim reporting an incident, obtaining assistance and/or from assisting or supporting the prosecution

- Attempts to dispose of or conceal evidence

- Commission of offence whilst under the influence of alcohol or drugs

- Victim encouraged to recruit others

Mitigating factors

- No previous convictions **or** no relevant/recent convictions

- Remorse

- Previous good character and/or exemplary conduct*

- Age and/or lack of maturity where it affects the responsibility of the offender

- Mental disorder or learning disability, particularly where linked to the commission of the offence

* Previous good character/exemplary conduct is different from having no previous convictions. The more serious the offence, the less the weight which should normally be attributed to this factor. Where previous good character/exemplary conduct has been used to facilitate the offence, this mitigation should not normally be allowed and such conduct may constitute an aggravating factor.

In the context of this offence, previous good character/exemplary conduct should not normally be given any significant weight and will not normally justify a reduction in what would otherwise be the appropriate sentence.

"Victim compelled to leave their home, school, etc" is included in order to reflect the fact that where a child has to move from their home, place of care or school as a result of the offence it can create even longer term harm, as they will have had their education disrupted or been uprooted from friendship and support networks.

125

Steps Three to Nine

3.79D The remaining steps cover the following points. At step three the court should consider any factors which would indicate a reduction in sentence, e.g. assistance to the prosecution. At step four it should consider any reduction for a guilty plea. At step five the court should consider dangerousness, i.e. whether it would be appropriate to award a life sentence (s.224A of the CJA 2003) or an extended sentence (s.226A). Step six requires the court to consider whether the total sentence is just and proportionate to the offending behaviour. At step seven it should consider whether to make an ancillary order (e.g. a compensation order, a SOPO or a restraining order). Step eight requires the court to fulfil its duty under s.174 of the CJA 2003 to give reasons for, and explain the effect of, the sentence. Finally, at step nine the court should consider whether to give credit for time spent on bail in accordance with s.240A of that Act.

Sentencing examples

3.82 The following decisions pre-date the new definitive guideline but are useful examples, additional to those in the main work, of the approach taken by the Court of Appeal to particular factual scenarios.

3.82A In *Prior*[39] the appellant (75) appealed against a sentence of 4-and-a-half years' imprisonment for a single offence of sexual assault on a child under the age of 13, imposed after he pleaded guilty on the day of trial. The victim, an 8-year-old boy, had been riding his bicycle near a gate at Bushey Park. His mother and sister were behind him but he was out of his mother's sight. The appellant touched the victim in the groin area through his clothes. He asked the victim where has mother was. The victim replied "just over there". The appellant then touched the victim again in the groin area and walked off. The victim told his mother and the police were called. They found at the appellant's home a notebook containing magazine and newspaper cuttings of children naked and clothed. He denied the offence in interview and up to the day of his trial. Three years before he had committed an identical offence against an 11-year-old boy, also in Bushey Park. He committed another such offence shortly afterwards at the same place and was given a community order of 3 years, which included a requirement to complete a Sex Offender Course. The appellant ignored the order and so was returned to court and resentenced to 6 months' imprisonment. In the instant case, the pre-sentence report recorded that the appellant described the incident as trivial and continued to deny any intent sexually to assault the victim. There was no remorse and no insight at all into his offending. The author assessed the risk of re-offending at medium but that there was a high risk of harm to children. It was common ground before the judge that the offence involved "contact with genitalia of victim by offender using part of his body other than the genitalia" within the SGC

---

[39] [2012] EWCA Crim 1418.

sentencing guideline. The suggested sentence was between 1 and 4 years' imprisonment for a man of good character after a contested trial, with a starting point of 2 years. The judge was concerned to reflect the seriously aggravating features of the previous offending and the apparent lack of concern about it. His conclusion was that the starting point after a trial would have been 6 or 7 years, which he reduced to 4-and-a-half years to reflect the appellant's age and his late plea. The Court of Appeal agreed that the offence fell within the category of the guideline cited above. In its judgment this offence, viewed in isolation, would fall towards the lower end of the range. The difficult question was the extent to which the seriously aggravating feature of two identical previous convictions moved the sentence through the range and perhaps beyond it, when considered with the mitigating factors which could properly be prayed in aid. The Court concluded that the judge's suggested starting point of 6–7 years was too high. That said, the judge had been generous in discounting by as much as he did for the appellant's age and plea. The plea in itself would not justify more than 10 per cent discount. Taking those matters into account, a starting point of 3 years would have been appropriate in this case resulting, after a modest discount for plea, in a sentence of 2 years and 9 months' imprisonment, and the Court so ordered.

In *Reynolds*[40] the appellant appealed against an extended sentence comprising a custodial term of 6 years and an extended licence period of 6 years, imposed after he pleaded guilty to sexual assault of a child under 13 and breach of a SOPO. The appellant had approached a 5-year-old girl in a shop and led her to an area that was not covered by surveillance cameras; he had put his hand in her knickers and touched her vagina. He had previous convictions for attempted voyeurism and outraging public decency and the SOPO had restricted indefinitely his contact with any person under 16. In passing sentence, the recorder assessed the appellant as being a dangerous offender but gave full credit for his guilty pleas. He considered each offence to be punishable in its own right and passed sentences of 4-and-a-half years' imprisonment for the sexual assault and 18 months for the breach of the SOPO. He also made the appellant subject to an extended 6-year licence period. The Court of Appeal held that the sentence was manifestly excessive. Although the assault had been short, its spontaneous nature and the appellant's readiness to act in such a way in a busy shop were a disturbing indication of his attitude towards young children. He was not a first-time offender and was the subject of a SOPO. The guilty pleas were mitigating factors; however, they had not been entered at the earliest opportunity. The SGC guideline indicated a starting point of 2 years' imprisonment and a range of 1–4 years for a first-time offence of sexual assault on a child under 13 where there was contact between the victim's genitalia and a part of the offender's body. While the recorder had been entitled to regard the SOPO breach as a distinct offence, rather than an aggravating feature of the sexual assault, it would have been preferable to have taken the breach into account when determining the length of the notional

3.82B

---

[40] [2011] EWCA Crim 2336.

determinate sentence for the assault, and then to have passed a concurrent sentence for the breach. The overall criminality of the appellant's offending, having regard to his guilty pleas and the breach of the SOPO, merited a notional determinate sentence of 4-and-a-half years' imprisonment and an extended licence period of 6 years for the sexual assault, with a concurrent 18 month sentence for the breach.

CAUSING OR INCITING A CHILD UNDER 13 TO ENGAGE IN SEXUAL ACTIVITY

Definition

3.92   The last two sentences in para.3.92 of the main work, stating that s.8 creates four offences (causing penetrative sexual activity; inciting penetrative sexual activity; causing non-penetrative sexual activity; and inciting non-penetrative sexual activity) and that a count in an indictment should specify which of these offences is being charged, were cited with approval in *Grout*.[41] In that case the appellant was convicted on a count (count 1) charging that between specified dates he had "intentionally caused or incited [H] a child under the aged of 13, namely 12 years, to engage in sexual activity, namely taking part in a webcam conversation when you asked [H] to show you her bra and asked her if she would take off clothing". The Court of Appeal quashed the conviction on this count, saying[42]:

> "On any view count 1 alleges at least four different offences. These are: (1) intentionally *causing* H to engage in sexual activity in taking part in a webcam conversation when the defendant asked H to show her bra; (2) intentionally *inciting* H to engage in sexual activity in taking part in a webcam conversation when the defendant asked H to show her bra; (3) intentionally *causing* H to engage in sexual activity in taking part in a webcam conversation and asking her to take off clothing; and (4) intentionally *inciting* H to engage in sexual activity in taking part in a webcam conversation and asking her to take off clothing. It might be thought that the count also contains allegations of (a) intentionally causing and (b) intentionally inciting H to engage in 'sexual activity' in the form of a webcam conversation in the circumstances alleged. Technically speaking, the count was bad because it contained within it allegations regarding a multiplicity of offences, which depended on proof of different facts and different actions, and a different state of mind by the defendant (an intention to cause and an intention to incite) for each allegation. More importantly and practically, this jumble of offences in one count created difficulties for both judge and jury.
>
> The count should have been broken down. In essence there were two prosecution allegations that mattered in this case. The first allegation was that the appellant had intentionally *caused* H to engage in 'sexual activity' by asking her to show her bra on the webcam, which, all were agreed, she had actually done by showing her bra strap.

---

[41] [2011] EWCA Crim 299, at [27].
[42] At [32]–[37] per Aitkens L.J.

The two key questions in relation to that allegation were whether, in the circumstances, the action of showing the bra strap amounted to 'sexual activity' and whether the appellant had 'intentionally caused' H to engage in such 'sexual activity'.

The second relevant allegation was that the appellant had intentionally *incited* H to engage in 'sexual activity' by asking her if she would take off clothing. Whether that activity was meant to be on the webcam or otherwise is not clear. H did not, of course, take off clothing. The key questions in relation to that allegation would be whether, in the circumstances, 'taking off clothing' amounted to 'sexual activity' by H and whether the appellant had 'intentionally incited' H to engage in that 'sexual activity'.

In our view the judge erred in not making this analysis of count 1 at the beginning of the trial. He should have directed the prosecution to decide what specific offences it wished to allege. Then, for the benefit of the jury, if not to ensure that there was no 'duplicity' or even 'quadruplicity' or 'sextuplicity' in the count, he should have directed that there be separate counts for each specific alleged offence. If this analysis had been undertaken, it would have become immediately clear that there was no evidence at all to support an allegation that the appellant had intentionally caused H to engage in 'sexual activity' in the form of taking off clothing. H had not done so at any stage, so the appellant could not have 'intentionally caused' her to do so. In addition, in our view, the evidence in support of an allegation that the appellant had 'intentionally incited' H actually to take off clothing, i.e. deliberately encouraged her to do so by a text or MSN message which asked her if she would do that, was either non-existent or so vague that no jury could have safely convicted of that offence. We note that nowhere in the summing up did the judge refer to any MSN or text exchange in which the appellant even asked H the question 'would you take off clothing'.

Therefore, if a careful analysis of count 1 had been undertaken at the outset of the trial, the judge would have had to conclude that two out of the four parts of it should not go before the jury, viz. those alleging that the appellant had intentionally caused or had intentionally incited H to engage in 'sexual activity' by taking off clothing. Those allegations, should have been withdrawn on the simple ground that there was insufficient evidence on which a jury, properly directed, could convict of those offences. Moreover, it is clear that the offence of 'intentionally inciting' H to show her bra was itself duplication, because the evidence was that she had actually shown her bra strap, so that the offence of 'intentionally causing' H to do so was sufficient to cover those facts.

We have concluded that this failure in itself makes the conviction unsafe because the jury were asked to consider, within the one count, two possible offences which they should not have been asked to consider. We do not know on what basis the jury did, in fact, convict the appellant."

MODE OF TRIAL AND PUNISHMENT

From December 3, 2012, when ss.122–128 of the Legal Aid, Sentencing and   3.96
Punishment of Offenders Act 2012 were brought into force[43]:

- An offence under s.8 is a serious specified offence for the purposes of ss.224 and 225(2) of the CJA 2003 (life sentence for serious offences).

- For offences committed on or after that date, an offence under s.8 is listed in Pt 1 of Sch.15B to that Act for the purposes of s.224A of the Act (life sentence for second listed offence).

---

[43] By the Legal Aid, Sentencing and Punishment of Offenders Act 2012 (Commencement No.4 and Saving Provisions) Order 2012 (SI 2012/2906).

- For convictions on or after that date (irrespective of the date of commission of the offence), an offence under s.8 is a specified offence for the purposes of s.226A of the CJA 2003 (extended sentence for certain violent or sexual offences).

BAIL

3.97   Section 25 of the Criminal Justice and Public Order Act 1994 was amended on December 3, 2012,[44] so that a person charged with or convicted of an offence to which the section applies shall be granted bail by a constable only if the constable is "of the opinion", rather than "satisfied" (as before), that there are exceptional circumstances which justify it.

SENTENCING

3.98   The Sentencing Council has issued a new guideline applicable to sex offenders aged 18 or over who are sentenced on or after April 1, 2014: see para.1.20 et seq., above. In its consultation on the draft guideline,[45] the Council noted that the previous guideline, issued by the Sentencing Guidelines Council in 2007, covered together the under-13 offences and the equivalent offences for victims aged 13 and over; for example, there was a single guideline covering causing a person to engage in sexual activity without consent (s.4) and causing or inciting a child under 13 to engage in sexual activity (s.8). The Sentencing Council proposed instead to issue separate guidelines for the under-13 offences and for offences against victims aged 13 and over, in recognition that "there are issues and sensitivities unique to offences against children under 13 that require a separate guideline to ensure clarity for sentencers as to the factors to be taken into account and to provide a transparent process for others concerned with these cases".[46] This is the approach that in due course it took in the new guideline.

The guideline for causing or inciting a child under 13 to engage in sexual activity, like that for the other under-13 offences, follows the format of the guideline for the offence against victims aged 13 and over, but with the addition of factors that relate more specifically to "grooming", since the under-13 offences may involve a child being coerced and groomed into sexual activity. The starting points and category ranges for the under-13 offence are higher than for the offence against victims aged 13 and over; but the guideline also acknowledges that the potential range of offending behaviours is such that there may be exceptional cases where a greater degree of flexibility is required. On this aspect see further the discussion, above, of the guideline for rape of a child under 13.

---

[44] By the Legal Aid, Sentencing and Punishment of Offenders Act 2012, s.90 and Sch.11 para.33, which was brought into force by the Legal Aid, Sentencing and Punishment of Offenders Act 2012 (Commencement No.4 and Saving Provisions) Order 2012, last note.
[45] *Sexual Offences Guideline: Consultation* (December 6, 2012).
[46] *Sexual Offences Guideline: Consultation* (December 6, 2012), p.36.

New sentencing guideline

Step One—Harm and culpability

Under the new guideline, the sentencing court is to go through a series of steps **3.98A** in order to determine the appropriate sentence. Step one involves determining the offence category by reference to the degree of harm caused and then the culpability level for the offence. In relation to the s.8 offence of causing or inciting a child under 13 to engage in sexual activity, the offence categories are as follows:

HARM		CULPABILITY	
Category 1	• The extreme nature of one or more category 2 factors or the extreme impact caused by a combination of category 2 factors **may** elevate to category 1	**A**	
		• Significant degree of planning	
		• Offender acts together with others to commit the offence	
		• Use of alcohol/drugs on victim to facilitate the offence	
Category 2	• Severe psychological or physical harm	• Grooming behaviour used against victim	
	• Penetration of vagina or anus (using body or object) by, or of, victim	• Abuse of trust	
		• Previous violence against victim	
	• Penile penetration of mouth by, or of, victim	• Offence committed in course of burglary	
	• Additional degradation/humiliation	• Sexual images of victim recorded, retained, solicited or shared	
	• Abduction	• Deliberate isolation of victim	
	• Prolonged detention/sustained incident	• Commercial exploitation and/or motivation	
	• Violence or threats of violence	• Offence racially or religiously aggravated	
	• Forced/uninvited entry into victim's home	• Offence motivated by, or demonstrating hostility to the victim based on his or her sexual orientation (or presumed sexual orientation) or transgender identity (or presumed transgender identity)	
	• Child is particularly vulnerable due to extreme youth and/or personal circumstances		

Category 3	Factor(s) in categories 1 and 2 not present	• Offence motivated by, or demonstrating, hostility to the victim based on his or her disability (or presumed disability)

B
Factor(s) in category A not present

Category 3 has no factors listed, to reflect the fact that any offence of causing or inciting a child under 13 to engage in sexual activity involves inherent serious harm.

Step Two—Starting point and category range

3.98B Having determined the offence category and culpability level, the court should then use the corresponding starting point specified in the guideline in order to reach a sentence within the category range. The starting point applies to all offenders irrespective of plea or previous convictions. Once the starting point has been determined, step two allows further adjustment for aggravating or mitigating features, set out below. A case of particular gravity, reflected by multiple features of culpability or harm, could merit upward adjustment from the starting point before further adjustment for aggravating or mitigating features. The starting points and category ranges for offences under s.8 are:

	A	**B**
Category 1	**Starting point** 13 years' custody	**Starting point** 11 years' custody
	Category range 11–17 years' custody	**Category range** 10–15 years' custody
Category 2	**Starting point** 8 years' custody	**Starting point** 6 years' custody
	Category range 5–10 years' custody	**Category range** 3–9 years' custody
Category 3	**Starting point** 5 years' custody	**Starting point** 2 years' custody
	Category range 3–8 years' custody	**Category range** 1–4 years' custody

Aggravating and mitigating factors

After identifying the starting point and category range, the court should consider 3.98C
whether the presence of aggravating or mitigating factors should result in an
upward or downward adjustment from the starting point or the imposition of a
sentence outside the category range. In particular, relevant recent convictions are
likely to result in an upward adjustment. The non-exhaustive list of factors
relevant to offences under s.8 is as follows:

Aggravating factors
Statutory aggravating factors
• Previous convictions, having regard to a) the nature of the offence to which the conviction relates and its relevance to the current offence; and b) the time that has elapsed since the conviction • Offence committed whilst on bail
Other aggravating factors
• Specific targeting of a particularly vulnerable child • Ejaculation (where not taken into account at step one) • Blackmail or other threats made (where not taken into account at step one) • Pregnancy or STI as a consequence of offence • Location of offence • Timing of offence • Use of weapon or other item to frighten or injure • Victim compelled to leave their home, school, etc • Failure to comply with current court orders • Offence committed whilst on licence • Exploiting contact arrangements with a child to commit an offence • Presence of others, especially other children • Any steps taken to prevent the victim reporting an incident, obtaining assistance and/or from assisting or supporting the prosecution • Attempts to dispose of or conceal evidence • Commission of offence whilst offender under the influence of alcohol or drugs • Victim encouraged to recruit others

Mitigating factors
• No previous convictions **or** no relevant/recent convictions

- Remorse

- Previous good character and/or exemplary conduct*

- Age and/or lack of maturity where it affects the responsibility of the offender

- Mental disorder or learning disability, particularly where linked to the commission of the offence

- Sexual activity was incited but no activity took place because the offender voluntarily desisted or intervened to prevent it

---

* Previous good character/exemplary conduct is different from having no previous convictions. The more serious the offence, the less the weight which should normally be attributed to this factor. Where previous good character/exemplary conduct has been used to facilitate the offence, this mitigation should not normally be allowed and such conduct may constitute an aggravating factor.

In the context of this offence, previous good character/exemplary conduct should not normally be given any significant weight and will not normally justify a reduction in what would otherwise be the appropriate sentence.

"Victim compelled to leave their home, school, etc" is included in order to reflect the fact that where a child has to move from their home, place of care or school as a result of the offence it can create even longer term harm, as they will have had their education disrupted or been uprooted from friendship and support networks.

Steps Three to Nine

3.98D   The remaining steps cover the following points. At step three the court should consider any factors which would indicate a reduction in sentence, e.g. assistance to the prosecution. At step four it should consider any reduction for a guilty plea. At step five the court should consider dangerousness, i.e. whether it would be appropriate to award a life sentence (s.224A or s.225(2) of the CJA 2003) or an extended sentence (s.226A). Step six requires the court to consider whether the total sentence is just and proportionate to the offending behaviour. At step seven it should consider whether to make an ancillary order (e.g. a compensation order, a SOPO or a restraining order). Step eight requires the court to fulfil its duty under s.174 of the CJA 2003 to give reasons for, and explain the effect of, the sentence. Finally, at step nine the court should consider whether to give credit for time spent on bail in accordance with s.240A of that Act.

Sentencing examples

3.100   There are a number of cases pre-dating the new definitive guideline that nonetheless provide helpful examples of the approach taken by the Court of Appeal to sentencing cases of "cyber sex" committed against children.

The first is *Butcher*,[47] referred to in para.3.100 of the main work, in which the **3.100A** applicant (34 and of previous good character) pleaded guilty to inter alia an offence under s.8 committed in relation to a 12-year-old girl and was sentenced to 3 years' imprisonment on that count and a total sentence of 6 years. Over a period of 3 months the applicant had used an internet chat room to exchange messages with the victim. He asked her various sexually explicit questions and attempted to persuade her to meet him for sex. He asked her to show her breasts via the web cam and she did so. She told the applicant that she was 13 years old. He discussed purchasing a vibrator for her and performing a sex act upon her using a vibrator. He told her he was 29 years old and asked her if that was too old. On appeal against sentence, the Court of Appeal noted that the suggested ranges in the SGC guideline for the s.8 offence all presupposed physical contact between the offender and the victim. The only element which approximated in any way to the facts of the applicant's offences was that for "contact between naked genitalia of offender and naked genitalia of victim, or causing two or more victims to engage in such activity with each other, or causing victim to masturbate him/herself", where the starting point, where the victim was a child under 13, was 5 years' custody with a sentencing range of 4–8 years. Where, as here, there had been no contact and the offending amounted to no more than incitement, there had to be a significant reduction in that starting point and sentencing range. Previous decisions of the Court indicated that in cases in which the child victim was incited to expose her private parts and did so and/or the perpetrator exposed his private parts, a starting point of some 3 years, following conviction, was appropriate for an offender of previous good character, before taking account of aggravating and mitigating factors. There were a number of aggravating features in the present case: the use of the internet in breach of a prohibited activity requirement and when the applicant was subject to a suspended sentence; the deliberate targeting of a young victim; the persistence of the contact with her; the nature of the activities incited which, had he succeeded in inciting her, would inevitably have occasioned her some harm; the likelihood that had he been able to persuade the victim to meet him, there would have been at least an attempt at sexual activity; and the applicant's previous conviction for making and possessing indecent photographs of children. In the Court's judgment, the s.8 offence would have merited, following a conviction, a sentence of 4-and-a-half years' imprisonment. Allowing the maximum discount to which the applicant was entitled, following his guilty plea, the appropriate sentence was 3 years (as the judge had imposed). The Court ordered the sentence for the remaining offence to run consecutively to that sentence.

Butcher was followed in *Att Gen's Ref (No.24 of 2011)*,[48] where the Attorney **3.100B** General referred to the Court of Appeal as unduly lenient a sentence of 4 months' imprisonment, suspended for 2 years, which had been imposed on the offender

---

[47] [2009] EWCA Crim 1458.
[48] [2011] EWCA Crim 1960, Hughes L.J. (as he then was) presiding.

following his plea of guilty to a number of offences of viewing child pornography on the internet and one offence under s.10 of the 2003 Act of inciting a girl aged 13 to engage in sexual activity. The offender (22) was found to have viewed 639 indecent images of children, at various levels, on his computer. As for the chat line offence, he had made contact with the victim and had five or six conversations with her over a period of about 21 days. The exchanges advanced to the point where the victim masturbated in front of the camera, at times using some kind of household instrument. The offender's messages to her encouraged her in such activity, even if she was a volunteer and had done it before. In allowing the Reference the Court noted that the SGC guideline was addressed to contact sexual offences rather than to offences of "cyber sex". It endorsed the approach recommended in *Butcher* of looking at the nearest applicable guideline for general assistance, but no more, and remembering that offences of "cyber sex", serious as they are, are, in ordinary terms at least, likely to be less serious than physical contact offences. There were a number of reasons for that. The obvious ones included the greater freedom of activity for any child when connected only electronically, the reduced opportunities for coercion or influence, and the absence of health risks or pregnancy. The nearest analogy to the present case in the SGC guideline for s.10 of the 2003 Act was the entry for "contact between naked genitalia of offender or victim and clothed genitalia of victim or offender or contact with naked genitalia of victim by offender using part of his or her body other than the genitalia or an object", which set a bracket of 6 months to 2 years. There had to be a reduction from that range to account for the absence of contact. The judge had been right to suspend the offender's sentence so that he could take part in a sex offender treatment programme, but the sentence was unduly lenient in respect of its length. Had the offender contested the case, the appropriate sentence would have been in the order of 18 months' imprisonment. Given his guilty plea, the Court substituted a sentence of 12 months.

3.100C   In *Att Gen's Ref (No.35 of 2013)*[49] the Attorney General referred to the Court of Appeal as unduly lenient sentences totalling 16 months' imprisonment imposed on the offender following his guilty pleas to 15 counts of inciting, or attempting to incite, children to engage in sexual activity and two counts of making indecent photographs of children. The offender (32) had posed as a teenage boy or girl on the social media site Facebook, befriended boys aged between 9 and 13, and incited them to perform sexual activities such as masturbation in front of a web camera so that he could see them. Those offences were the subject of the first 14 counts. Count 15 charged attempting to incite a child to engage in sexual activity: the offender admitted having befriended up to 220 children and seeking to engage them in sexual activity. He had also made 11 indecent images of children at level 1 and 3 at level 3; the subjects were boys of a similar age to the victims of the incitement offences. The offender made full admissions in interview. Whilst on bail, he incited a further eight children to sexual activity. Those offences were

---

[49] [2013] EWCA Crim 1757.

taken into consideration. The sentencing judge took a starting point of two years' imprisonment and then gave a discount for the guilty pleas. The Solicitor General submitted that, absent a guideline specifically tailored to offences of this sort, the Court should refer to the SGC guideline for s.8 which gives the sentencing range for non-consensual sexual offences committed against victims under 13. The Court allowed the Reference. The SGC guideline addressed contact sexual offences rather than "cyber sex" offences and so, applying *Butcher* and *Att Gen's Ref (No.24 of 2011)*, it was possible to derive general assistance, but no more, from the nearest applicable guideline. The Court noted the observation of Hughes L.J. in *Att Gen's Ref (No.24 of 2011)* that offences of cyber sex, serious as they are, are, in ordinary terms at least, likely to be less serious than physical contact offences. So it may be, but the Court did not construe those words "as intending in any way to dilute the seriousness on their own facts of offences such as these". Also, whilst offences of cyber sex are in one sense less serious than physical contact offences, they are arguably more difficult to prevent; and contact offences could be readily envisaged which are less serious than some cyber sex offences, particularly where, as in this case, those offences are in number. Further, the long-term effect on a child confronting personal exposure to a stranger is likely to be severe, though inevitably only time will tell. The starting point under the s.8 guideline would be 5 years and the range 4–8 years. However, the guideline was predicated on "one victim on one occasion" offences. In this case an appropriate starting point would have been 6 years which, with an appropriate discount, resulted in a sentence of 4 years.

These decisions confront the fact that the SGC guidelines focused exclusively on physical contact. The new guideline deliberately contemplates a wider range of possible harm and as such is fully apt to cover cyber sex as well as contact offending. However, it is worth noting that the new guideline for ss.9 and 10 (sexual activity with a child and causing or inciting a child to engage in sexual activity) includes the statement: "This guideline also applies to offences committed remotely/online". It is perhaps unfortunate that the Sentencing Council did not include a similar statement in the s.8 guideline, and we hope that its absence does not mislead sentencing courts into thinking that the guideline does not contemplate cyber offending. **3.100D**

Finally, mention should be made of *Att Gen's Ref (No.28 of 2010)* (also known as *Charnley*),[50] in which the Attorney General referred as unduly lenient a total sentence of 5 years' imprisonment imposed on the offender (C) following his pleas of guilty to 23 counts relating to the horrific sexual abuse of vulnerable children aged 2-17 in many different countries. Counts 1-19 charged him with making indecent photographs of a child, counts 20-22 with causing or inciting a child under 13 to engage in sexual activity not involving penetration, and count 23 with causing or inciting a child under 13 to engage in sexual activity involving **3.100E**

---

[50] [2010] EWCA Crim 1996.

penetration.[51] Over a period of 18 months C had made, downloaded and retained 110,000 still images and 356 films depicting indecent acts with children. The children lived in dire circumstances and C had exploited their vulnerability. He had paid adults to sexually abuse them and, using his computer, he had directed, watched and filmed the activities in real time, issuing instructions about the abuse that he wanted to see. That abuse involved children being tied up and penetrated, vaginally, anally and orally. The judge sentenced C, who was of previous good character, to a total of 4 years' imprisonment on counts 1-19, 3 years' imprisonment on counts 20-22 and 5 years' imprisonment on count 23. Those terms were to run concurrently. The Court of Appeal allowed the Reference on the ground that the judge had made two major errors. First, he had made no reference to the aggravating features. The offences were planned, they involved acts of penetration, there were multiple victims and there were sustained and repeated assaults on vulnerable children. The overall sentence imposed was wholly inadequate and did not begin to meet the gravity of the offences or reflect the fact that the victims were young, vulnerable children. The fact that the victims were on the other side of the world and that the offences were enabled by modern communications was no mitigation, indeed, it was an aggravating factor. Secondly, the judge had erred in ordering the sentences to run concurrently. They were separate offences committed against separate children, and each merited severe punishment. Offenders such as C needed to be deterred and their victims needed protection. Nothing in the previous authorities or in the SGC guidelines grappled with offending like C's. In respect of counts 1–19 the starting point after a trial would have been around 7 years' imprisonment. Given the guilty plea, the 4-year sentence imposed would not be altered. On counts 20–22 the starting point after a trial would again have been around 7 years' imprisonment. The 3-year sentence was too low and would be replaced with a consecutive 4-year term. The starting point on count 23, after a trial, would have been around 13 years' imprisonment, with a range of 11–17 years. Allowing for the guilty plea, the appropriate sentence was one of 8 years' imprisonment, to be served consecutively to the 4-year sentence on counts 1–19 and concurrently with the 4-year sentence on counts 20–22. Those were the very minimum sentences that could be imposed. There was no room for any deduction for double jeopardy or personal mitigation. The total sentence imposed was therefore one of 12 years' imprisonment.

"Causes or Incites Another Person . . . "

3.105   In *Grout*[52] the Court of Appeal said that the essence of the offence of "incitement" in s.8 is "the intentional seeking to bring about something by encouragement or persuasion".

---

[51] The charges are so described in the official transcript. However, if C was indeed charged with "causing or inciting" then the indictment was duplicitous: see para.3.92, above.
[52] [2011] EWCA Crim 299, at [26].

" . . . To Engage in an Activity"

In *Grout*[53] the Court of Appeal said: 3.111

"We are prepared to accept, for the purposes of this appeal, that 'activity' on the part of the child could embrace 'the activity' of conversation or sending text or MSN messages, depending on the circumstances."

"The Activity is Sexual"

The point made in the main work, that s.8 requires sexual activity on the part of 3.112
the child, B, that is caused or incited by A, and not sexual activity on the part of
A, is supported by *Grout*[54] in which the Court of Appeal said:

"The . . . offences created by section 8 are directed towards a defendant who intentionally causes or incites *the child*, that is (B) himself or herself, to engage in 'sexual activity'. The offence is not concerned with whether the defendant engages in sexual activity."

Mental Element

In *Grout*[55] the Court of Appeal said that for the purposes of s.8: 3.115

"The causing or inciting must be intentional, i.e. deliberate; recklessness or less will not do."

---

[53] [2011] EWCA Crim 299, at [29].
[54] [2011] EWCA Crim 299, at [28].
[55] [2011] EWCA Crim 299, at [26], citing *Heard*; [2007] EWCA Crim 125, at [22] per Hughes L.J.

CHAPTER 4

CHILD SEX OFFENCES

INTRODUCTION

Following a three-month public consultation exercise, on October 17, 2013, the 4.01 CPS issued important new *Guidelines on Prosecuting Cases of Child Sexual Abuse*. The *Guidelines*, reproduced in Appendix I to this Supplement,[1] set out a new approach to be taken to prosecuting cases of child sexual abuse, with the key emphasis placed on the credibility of the allegation rather than on that of the child complainant. This was explained as follows by the then DPP, Keir Starmer QC, when introducing the *Guidelines*[2]:

"In the past five years our approach to prosecuting sexual offences has matured and developed—but this change marks the most fundamental attitude shift across the Criminal Justice System for a generation. For too long, child sexual abuse cases have been plagued by myths about how 'real' victims behave which simply do not withstand scrutiny. The days of the model victim are over. From now on these cases will be investigated and prosecuted differently, whatever the vulnerabilities of the victim.

The final guidelines ... confirm that the now accepted approach is that the prosecution must focus on the overall credibility of an allegation rather than the perceived weakness of the person making it ...

In order that we challenge those past assumptions, I have produced a list of common myths and stereotypes around this type of offending so that we can actively challenge them in court.

The list of common myths and stereotypes covers:
- The victim invited sex by the way they dressed or acted
- The victim used alcohol or drugs and was therefore sexually available

[1] They are also available at *http://www.cps.gov.uk/legal/a_to_c/child_sexual_abuse/* [accessed December 28, 2013].

[2] *http://www.cps.gov.uk/news/latest_news/csa_guidelines_and_tpp/index.html* [accessed December 28, 2013].

- The victim didn't scream, fight or protest so they must have been consenting
- The victim didn't complain immediately, so it can't have been a sexual assault
- The victim is in a relationship with the alleged offender and is therefore a willing sexual partner
- A victim should remember events consistently
- Children can consent to their own sexual exploitation
- [Child sexual exploitation] is only a problem in certain ethnic/cultural communities
- Only girls and young women are victims of [child sexual abuse]
- Children from BME backgrounds are not abused
- There will be physical evidence of abuse"

The *Guidelines* also highlight the ways that offenders may manipulate and blackmail child victims into keeping quiet about their abuse, including through threats to publish indecent images or by implicating the victims in other offending. In addition, they refer to the control that offenders can exert over their victims in some ethnic communities where emphasis is placed on notions of "honour" and "shame". Mr Starmer said:

> "We know that child sexual abuse is not limited to any one type of community and that has been addressed. But prosecutors need to be aware of the additional barriers that some victims might face in coming forward and reporting abuse, such as fearing the shame that making an allegation of sexual abuse might bring upon their family. We know that offenders do all they can to deter their victims from making a complaint and we must be alive to the very nasty manipulation that can be used."

SEXUAL ACTIVITY WITH A CHILD

DEFINITION

4.18 In *Rae*,[3] Pitchford L.J., giving the judgment of the Court of Appeal, said that in the case of children under 13, there may be a dilemma as to whether to charge the defendant under s.8 (causing a child under 13 to engage in sexual activity) or s.9, and that s.9 is often charged where the child was or may have been ostensibly consenting and s.8 where there was manifestly no consent. To the extent that this is indeed prosecutorial practice, we suggest it is wrong, and that in the case of child victims under the age of 13 it will always be appropriate to charge under ss.5–8: see the final sentence of para.4.18 of the main work. *Rae* is an unfortunate example of a charge being brought under s.9, rather than s.8, where the victim was 12 at the relevant time. The judge then highlighted the error by determining sentence by reference to the guideline for s.8, rather than s.9. The Court of Appeal held that he had been wrong to do so, but that he had been entitled to regard the absence of "ostensible consent" as an aggravating factor, although it was not

---

[3] [2013] EWCA Crim 2056, at [11]–[13].

specified as such in the s.9 guideline. The net result was that the Court reduced the sentence from 10 to 7 years' imprisonment, i.e. a sentence at the top end of the range specified in the s.9 guideline.

In *Rae*[4] Pitchford L.J. also noted what he said was the suggestion in para.4.18 of the main work that, where a defendant admits conduct in relation to a child under 13 but there is an issue as to consent, it may be appropriate to include in the indictment an alternative charge under s.9, i.e. alternative to one under ss.5–8. We regret that a lack of clarity in the drafting of para.4.18 may have misled his Lordship. We intend to suggest in that paragraph that where a defendant is alleged to have engaged in sexual activity with a child aged 13–16, and there is an issue as to consent, it may be appropriate to charge him both with a non-consensual offence, i.e. under ss.1–4, and in the alternative under s.9, so that the jury can determine the issue as to consent. See *Blore*[5] for an example of this being done (where an alternative charge under s.9 was added in response to evidence suggestive of consent that emerged during the course of a trial for rape). We will make this point explicit in the fifth edition.

However, where a defendant is alleged to have engaged in sexual activity with a child under 13, but states that the child consented, it will *not* be appropriate to bring a charge under s.9 as an alternative to one under ss.5–8. This is because absence of consent is not an element of s.9 any more than it is of ss.5–8, and so adding an alternative charge under s.9 to the indictment would do nothing to resolve the issue of consent. Rather, in any case involving a complainant under 13, one of the under-13 offences should be charged and any issue as to consent (so far as relevant to sentence, as to which see para.3.28 et seq., above), should be resolved in a *Newton* hearing.

MODE OF TRIAL AND PUNISHMENT

From December 3, 2012, when ss.122–128 of the Legal Aid, Sentencing and   **4.20**
Punishment of Offenders Act 2012 were brought into force[6]:

- For offences committed on or after that date, an offence under s.9 is listed in Pt 1 of Sch.15B to the Criminal Justice Act 2003 ("CJA 2003") for the purposes of s.224A of that Act (life sentence for second listed offence).
- For convictions on or after that date (irrespective of the date of commission of the offence), an offence under s.9 is a specified offence for the purposes of s.226A of that Act (extended sentence for certain violent or sexual offences).

SENTENCING

The Sentencing Council has issued a new guideline applicable to sex offenders   **4.22**
aged 18 or over who are sentenced on or after April 1, 2014: see para.1.20 et seq.,

---

[4] At [13].
[5] [2013] EWCA Crim 2301.
[6] By the Legal Aid, Sentencing and Punishment of Offenders Act 2012 (Commencement No.4 and Saving Provisions) Order 2012 (SI 2012/2906).

above. In its consultation on the draft guideline,[7] the Council noted that the offence of sexual activity with a child (and the other child sex offences) will normally be charged where the victim is aged 13–15 and maintains that they agreed to the sexual activity. Where a victim is over 13, lack of consent must be proved to obtain a rape conviction, and where a victim over the age of 13 maintains that they consented to the sexual activity, a rape prosecution is unlikely to be successful. However, the offence of sexual activity with a child can be charged instead, as it requires proof only that the offender engaged in the sexual activity, irrespective of whether the child maintains that they agreed to it. Charging this offence will allow the court to look at issues such as whether the child had been manipulated, groomed or exploited. The previous guideline, issued in 2007 by the Sentencing Guidelines Council, referred to this offence and the others discussed in this chapter as "ostensible consent offences".[8] In *Att Gen's Refs (Nos 11 and 12 of 2012) (R. v Channer and another)*,[9] Pitchford L.J. said:

> "'Ostensible consent' and 'willingness' are terms which, in the context of offences against the young in particular, are susceptible to misunderstanding and, even if accurately used, are liable to obscure the true nature of the encounter between the offender and the victim."

As noted in para.3.28 et seq., above, the Sentencing Council decided to move away from this language so that the focus of the new guideline is not the behaviour of the victim but the behaviour and culpability of the offender. This approach is to be welcomed, and was well received by respondents to the Council's consultation draft.

New sentencing guideline

Step One—Harm and culpability

4.22A A single guideline covers the offences of sexual activity with a child (s.9 of the 2003 Act) and causing or inciting a child to engage in sexual activity (s.10). For the avoidance of doubt, the guideline for these offences contains a prominent note that it "also applies to offences committed remotely/online". The guideline requires the sentencing court to go through a series of steps in order to determine the appropriate sentence. Step one involves determining the offence category by reference to the degree of harm caused and then the culpability level for the offence.

Harm

4.22B The Sentencing Council in general sought to avoid identifying harm by reference to the nature of the sexual activity in question, on the basis that this approach fails

---

[7] *Sexual Offences Guideline: Consultation* (December 6, 2012).
[8] Sentencing Guidelines Council, *Sexual Offences Act 2003: Definitive Guideline*, pp.48–58.
[9] [2012] EWCA Crim 1119, at [34].

fully to reflect the seriousness or complexity of the offending. For offences under ss.9 and 10, however, the Council decided that harm should be determined by reference to the relevant sexual activity on the ground that, in relation to these offences, the child may not see him/herself as a victim and may not be conscious that harm has been done to them. They may see the offender as their "boyfriend" and may be unable or reluctant to articulate or recognise that they have suffered any psychological or emotional harm. The guideline therefore correlates harm to the nature of the sexual activity, on the basis that penetrative sexual activity will generally be more harmful and corrupting to the child than non-penetrative activity. The offence categories for these offences are accordingly as follows:

HARM	
Category 1	• Penetration of vagina or anus (using body or object) • Penile penetration of mouth In either case by, or of, the victim
Category 2	• Touching, or exposure, of naked genitalia or naked breasts by, or of, the victim
Category 3	Other sexual activity

Category 1 involves penetration on the ground that the consequences of this type of sexual activity are the most harmful to victims. The law already recognises the increased severity if penetration occurs, as the offence is then triable only in the Crown Court.[10] As for category 2, the Council proposed in its consultation that this should refer only to masturbation, as its analysis of case law showed that masturbation and penetrative activity are involved in the majority of cases that come before the courts for sentence. It was also keen to move away from the complex formulation of physical contact found in the SGC guideline, for example, "contact between naked genitalia of offender and naked genitalia or another part of victim's body, particularly face or mouth". Although the Council did not mention this, the concentration in the SGC guideline on physical contact had also made it difficult for the courts to identify the appropriate sentence for s.10 offences committed over the internet, where the offender incited the child to perform some sexual act such as masturbating or exposing themselves, and no physical contact between the parties was even possible.[11] The growing incidence of "cyber offending" of this sort was highlighted in responses to the consultation, as was the fact that, as drafted, the guideline placed touching of naked genitalia in category 3, which would have had the effect of lowering the sentences awarded for such activity. As a result, the Council revised category 2 by replacing "masturbation by or of the victim" with "touching, or exposure, of naked genitalia or naked

---

[10] s.9(2) of the 2003 Act.
[11] See *Butcher* [2009] EWCA Crim 1458 and *Att Gen's Ref (No.24 of 2011)* [2011] EWCA Crim 1960, discussed in para.3.100 et seq., above; *Brocklebank* [2013] EWCA Crim 1813, discussed in para.4.50A, below.

breasts by, or of, the victim". It said that the new wording captures a range of contact and remote offending that is serious but was not catered for in the original proposal, including the situation where a victim has been blackmailed via webcam into stripping. The Council said it was "confident the guideline can cope with both online and face to face offending".

Culpability

4.22C   The culpability factors specified in the guideline for offences under ss.9 and 10 are as follows:

CULPABILITY
A
• Significant degree of planning
• Offender acts together with others to commit the offence
• Use of alcohol/drugs on victim to facilitate the offence
• Grooming behaviour used against victim
• Abuse of trust
• Use of threats (including blackmail)
• Sexual images of victim recorded, retained, solicited or shared
• Specific targeting of a particularly vulnerable child
• Offender lied about age
• Significant disparity in age
• Commercial exploitation and/or motivation
• Offence racially or religiously aggravated
• Offence motivated by, or demonstrating, hostility to the victim based on his or her sexual orientation (or presumed sexual orientation) or transgender identity (or presumed transgender identity)
• Offence motivated by, or demonstrating, hostility to the victim based on his or her disability (or presumed disability)
B
Factor(s) in category A not present

In its consultation, the Sentencing Council elaborated its reasons for adopting some of the culpability A factors:

- "Use of alcohol/drugs on victim to facilitate the offence" is included because, in addition to the use of alcohol to incapacitate the victim, offenders may use access to alcohol and/or drugs as part of the grooming process in order to gain the child's trust or friendship by allowing them to behave in a way that would not be permitted by their parents or other responsible adults.

- "Abuse of trust" is used rather than "abuse of position of trust" because in relation to children trust may arise not only from a position of formal responsibility but also from the offender's relationship with the child, e.g. as a family friend who has been trusted to look after the child on a day out.
- "Use of threats (including blackmail)" will cover the case where the offender threatens to tell others about the activity as a way of controlling the victim.
- "Sexual images of victim recorded, retained, solicited or shared" is wider than "recording of the offence", found in the rape and assault guidelines. The reason is that, in committing an offence of sexual activity with a child, the offender may persuade the victim to take naked pictures of him/herself, in which case the images will be recorded by the victim rather than the offender. The words "sexual images solicited" were included on the basis that an offender is culpable if he solicits such images from his victim, regardless of whether the victim is robust enough to turn down the request.
- "Specific targeting of a particularly vulnerable child" caters for the case where, for example, an offender targets a child who is in care or whose home life is chaotic or dysfunctional, knowing they are likely to be more susceptible to the attention of an adult who befriends them and professes to care for them.
- "Offender lied about age" is included to cover those cases, especially when contact has been made over the internet, where an offender misleads the victim about his age so that the victim believes they are in contact with a peer.
- Finally, the Council felt it important to acknowledge "significant disparity in age" as a culpability factor, though as the offence may be committed only by offenders over the age of 18, it thought there will be very few instances where the disparity in age is not significant. The implication of this comment is, of course, that the Council believes there will be very few cases which do *not* fall within culpability A.

As with other guidelines, no factors are listed under culpability B. The Sentencing Council envisaged the type of offender who would fall into this category as one who is in an unlawful and inappropriate relationship with their victim, but where there is no significant disparity in age and there are no signs of exploitation.

Step Two—Starting point and category range

Having determined the offence category and culpability level, the court should **4.22D** then use the corresponding starting point specified in the guideline in order to reach a sentence within the category range. The starting point applies to all offenders irrespective of plea or previous convictions. Once the starting point has been determined, step two allows further adjustment for aggravating or mitigating features, set out below. A case of particular gravity, reflected by multiple features of culpability or harm, could merit upward adjustment from the starting point before further adjustment for aggravating or mitigating features. Where there is a sufficient prospect of rehabilitation, a community order with a sex offender treatment programme requirement under s.202 of the CJA 2003 may be a proper alternative to a short or moderate length custodial sentence. The starting points and category ranges for offences under ss.9 and 10 of the Act are as follows:

	A	B
Category 1	**Starting point** 5 years' custody **Category range** 4–10 years' custody	**Starting point** 1 year's custody **Category range** High level community order–2 years' custody
Category 2	**Starting point** 3 years' custody **Category range** 2–6 years' custody	**Starting point** 26 weeks' custody **Category range** High level community order–1 year's custody
Category 3	**Starting point** 26 weeks' custody **Category range** High level community order–3 years' custody	**Starting point** Medium level community order **Category range** Low level community order–High level community order

In its consultation, the Sentencing Council said these starting points and category ranges are influenced more by culpability than harm, and that sentence levels are substantially lower where the offence does not involve the exploitation or grooming of the victim than when it does. For culpability B, a non-custodial option will be open to the sentencer as part of the available range. The sentencer must assess the facts in the case before them and be able to pass a sentence that will not only punish the offender but also protect the public by addressing the offender's behaviour and thinking, such that they do not reoffend. In some cases the sentencer may decide that the best way to do this is through a lengthy community order with punitive elements and a requirement to engage in a sexual offender treatment programme. Where, however, there has been penetrative sexual activity, there is always a custodial starting point, as there is where there is evidence of exploitation or grooming. Additionally, for the top category, the SGC guideline's 4-year starting point and 3–7 year range is increased to a 5-year starting point with a range of 4–10 years. The Council believed this increase was representative of sentences already being passed by the courts and was needed in order to address what can be very serious offending.

Aggravating and mitigating factors

After identifying the starting point and category range, the court should consider **4.22E** whether the presence of aggravating or mitigating factors should result in an upward or downward adjustment from the starting point or the imposition of a sentence outside the category range. In particular, relevant recent convictions are likely to result in an upward adjustment. When sentencing appropriate category 2 or 3 offences, the court should also consider whether the custody threshold has been passed; if so, whether a custodial sentence is unavoidable; and if it is, whether that sentence can be suspended. The non-exhaustive list of aggravating and mitigating factors for offences under ss.9 and 10 is as follows:

Aggravating factors
Statutory aggravating factors
• Previous convictions, having regard to a) the nature of the offence to which the conviction relates and its relevance to the current offence; and b) the time that has elapsed since the conviction
• Offence committed whilst on bail
Other aggravating factors
• Severe psychological or physical harm
• Ejaculation
• Pregnancy or STI as a consequence of offence
• Location of offence
• Timing of offence
• Victim compelled to leave their home, school, etc.
• Failure to comply with current court orders
• Offence committed whilst on licence
• Exploiting contact arrangements with a child to commit an offence
• Presence of others, especially other children
• Any steps taken to prevent the victim reporting an incident, obtaining assistance and/or from assisting or supporting the prosecution
• Attempts to dispose of or conceal evidence

- Failure of offender to respond to previous warnings
- Commission of offence whilst under the influence of alcohol or drugs
- Victim encouraged to recruit others
- Period over which offence committed

Mitigating factors

- No previous convictions **or** no relevant/recent convictions
- Remorse
- Previous good character and/or exemplary conduct*
- Age and/or lack of maturity where it affects the responsibility of the offender
- Mental disorder or learning disability, particularly where linked to the commission of the offence
- Sexual activity was incited but no activity took place because the offender voluntarily desisted or intervened to prevent it

---

* Previous good character/exemplary conduct is different from having no previous convictions. The more serious the offence, the less the weight which should normally be attributed to this factor. Where previous good character/exemplary conduct has been used to facilitate the offence, this mitigation should not normally be allowed and such conduct may constitute an aggravating factor.

In the context of this offence, previous good character/exemplary conduct should not normally be given any significant weight and will not normally justify a reduction in what would otherwise be the appropriate sentence.

It is notable that "pregnancy or STI as a consequence of offence" is included as an aggravating factor at step two, whereas for other offences it is at step one. This is because, for offences under ss.9 and 10, penetrative sexual activity places the offender in the highest category of harm. If pregnancy or STI resulted from the penetrative activity, and was placed at step one, there would be no opportunity for the sentencer to aggravate the sentence to take it into account as an additional factor. Including pregnancy or STI at step two allows the sentencer to move upwards from the starting point from the highest category by treating pregnancy or STI as an aggravating factor.

As for the mitigating factors, the consultation draft included "determination and/or demonstration of steps taken to address sexual behaviour", as the Council thought it appropriate to give the offender some credit for recognising and trying to address their behaviour and to prevent future offending. This factor does not appear in the published guideline, though it does appear in the guidelines for certain other offences (cf. the child sex offences in ss.11, 12 and 15 of the Act and the abuse of trust offences in ss.16–19).

Steps Three to Nine

The remaining steps cover the following points. At step three the court should **4.22F**
consider any factors which would indicate a reduction in sentence, e.g. assistance
to the prosecution. At step four it should consider any reduction for a guilty plea.
At step five the court should consider dangerousness, i.e. whether it would be
appropriate to award a life sentence (s.224A of the CJA 2003) or an extended
sentence (s.226A). Step six requires the court to consider whether the total
sentence is just and proportionate to the offending behaviour. At step seven it
should consider whether to make an ancillary order (e.g. a compensation order, a
sexual offences prevention order or a restraining order). Step eight requires the
court to fulfil its duty under s.174 of the CJA 2003 to give reasons for, and explain
the effect of, the sentence. Finally, at step nine the court should consider whether
to give credit for time spent on bail in accordance with s.240A of that Act.

Sentencing examples

The following decisions pre-date the new definitive guideline but are useful **4.25**
examples of the approach taken by the Court of Appeal to different factual scenarios.

In *Rae*[12] the Court of Appeal held that a sentencing judge may take into account **4.25A**
the absence of "ostensible consent" as an aggravating factor for the purposes of the
SGC guideline; see further on this subject para.3.28 et seq., above.

In *R. v P*[13] the appellant (54 and of good character) appealed against a total **4.25B**
sentence of 7 years' imprisonment following his conviction for three offences
under s.9. He had employed the 15-year-old victim as a stablehand. They had
sexual intercourse on three occasions over a three-week period. The sentencing
judge observed that the SGC guideline's starting point was 4 years' imprisonment,
but that as the victim was 15 it would be right to adopt a starting point of 3 years
for a single offence. He referred to the age difference between the appellant and
the victim and to the abuse of trust and imposed sentences of 7 years'
imprisonment on each count to run concurrently. The Court of Appeal held that
the sentence was too high: it was not far short of the sentence recommended for
an offence of rape with aggravating features. The case had some serious features:
there was a significant difference in age and an element of breach of trust.
However, it did not involve a significant element of manipulation or grooming.
The offences took place over a comparatively short period of time and with the
victim's consent. Balancing all those features, the appropriate sentence was 4
years' imprisonment on each count to be served concurrently.

[12] [2013] EWCA Crim 2056, at [20].
[13] [2012] EWCA Crim 1337.

4.25C In the much-discussed case of *Att Gen's Ref (No.53 of 2013) (R. v Wilson)*,[13a] the Attorney General referred to the Court of Appeal as unduly lenient a 12-month sentence of imprisonment suspended for 2 years imposed on the offender for offences of sexual activity with a child, making indecent photographs of a child and possessing extreme pornographic images. The offender (40) was approached in the street by the victim (13). She asked for cigarettes and he bought her some. She told him she was 16 and asked if she could use his home phone. They kissed at his house but he rejected her advances. They kept in touch and the victim went to his home on another occasion where she undressed and masturbated him. He said that he told her to stop, but she had attempted to lower herself onto his penis. He pushed her away and she left. When the offender was arrested, his computer was found to contain indecent images of children which had been viewed around the time of the offence and extreme pornographic images of adults performing sex acts with animals. He pleaded guilty to the offences. During the sentencing hearing, prosecuting counsel described the victim as "predatory". The judge sentenced the offender to 8 months' imprisonment for the offence under s.9, a consecutive term of 4 months for the indecent photographs and a concurrent term of 4 months for the extreme images. He said that a term of imprisonment would normally be appropriate on such facts, but in all the circumstances, including that the victim was predatory and had encouraged the offender, he suspended the sentence for 2 years. The Attorney General submitted that the fact that the victim had initiated what had happened was an aggravating, not a mitigating factor. The Court agreed, and allowed the reference. Lord Thomas C.J. said[13b]:

> "It has been clear since at least the Offences Against the Person Act 1861, and subsequent nineteenth century legislation, that the purpose of Parliament in passing legislation to make it a crime punishable with imprisonment to have sexual relations with those under 16 was to protect those under 16. Indeed the Criminal Law Amendments Act 1885 makes it expressly clear that that was the purpose of the legislation. That can be seen from the preamble to the Act and was made clear by this court in *R. v Tyrrell* [1894] 1 QB 710.
>
> That long-standing principle is well-known. The reduction of punishment on the basis that the person who needed protection encouraged the commission of an offence is therefore simply wrong. We agree with the submission of the Attorney General that an underage person who encourages sexual relations with her needs more protection, not less. Accepting that as the basis for sentencing for the reasons we have explained, the fact that the offender took advantage of what he asserted the victim did aggravated the offence."

The Court said that the Crown had made a fundamental error in describing the victim as predatory for the first time prior to sentencing. That word had not featured in the papers. There were several aggravating features: the offender must have known that she was under 16 and vulnerable; he preyed on her vulnerability; there was a significant age gap; and he had viewed indecent images of children around the time of the offence. The sentence was unduly lenient and the Court

---

[13a] [2013] EWCA Crim 2544.
[13b] At [19]–[20].

substituted a sentence of 2 years' imprisonment for the 8-month sentence imposed for the s.9 offence, with the other 4-month sentences to run concurrently.

Wilson makes clear that a s.9 offence will be aggravated where the victim initiates the sexual activity and the offender takes advantage of them. At the same time, the new guideline treats the offender's culpability as increased where he grooms the victim, as where he softens them up in some way before initiating sexual activity himself. The logic of treating the seriousness of a s.9 offence as increased both where the offender initiates the activity and where the victim initiates it is not immediately apparent and is likely to require further guidance from the Court of Appeal. See further on this point Lyndon Harris, *Children initiating sexual offences as aggravating features*, C.L. & J. 2014, 178(5), 55–56.

Complainants just under 16

In *R. v J*[14] the appellant (38) had consensual sexual intercourse on one occasion 4.28 with the complainant, his next-door-neighbour, who was aged 15 years and 10 months. They had known each other for eight years. A year or so earlier, the complainant had developed feelings for the appellant; at first he did not agree to have sex with her because of her age; however, they continued to meet secretly in his van, where talking progressed to hugging and kissing and eventually to intercourse. The appellant pleaded guilty to an offence under s.9 and was sentenced to 3 years' imprisonment. On his appeal, the Court of Appeal held that this sentence was too high. In assessing seriousness, an important consideration was that the complainant had been almost 16 and was a mature 15-year-old. Additional mitigating factors were that she had pursued the appellant and he had, for a long time, resisted her advances; it was a single act; and he was of previous good character. On the other hand, there was a considerable disparity in age between them, and the appellant had continued to meet the complainant surreptitiously when he knew she wanted a sexual relationship and when he had been warned about his behaviour by the police, who had been alerted by her parents. In all the circumstances, the Court substituted a sentence of 6 months' imprisonment.

PARTIES TO THE OFFENCE

In the main work we expressed the view that if the child victim of a s.9 offence 4.33 encourages its commission, they are in principle liable to conviction as an accessory. We considered the decision in *Tyrrell*[15] to be distinguishable in this context, since the offence in that case was created to protect girls against men and there was no indication in the statute of an intention to criminalise the girls themselves; and while the s.9 offence was clearly created to protect children under

[14] [2012] EWCA Crim 3025.
[15] [1894] 1 Q.B. 710; and see *DPP v Whitehouse* [1977] Q.B. 868.

16 from sexual touching by adults, the effect of s.13 is that such children can themselves be prosecuted for the sexual touching of other children falling within the scope of s.9. If a child over the age of criminal responsibility may commit the s.13 offence as principal, it is difficult to conclude that they cannot do so as accessory; and if they may be an accessory to a s.13 offence committed against another child, there seems to be no reason of principle why they cannot also be an accessory to such an offence committed against them. Finally, we argued that it surely cannot have been Parliament's intention that *Tyrrell* should apply to the offence under s.9 but not the one under s.13, so that a child may be an accessory where their abuser is under 18 but not where he is an adult. We therefore suggested that the better view is that *Tyrrell* has no application to either offence and that a child may be convicted as accessory to an offence of sexual touching of which they were the victim, regardless of the age of their abuser.

Of relevance to this point is a passage in the reasoning of the majority of the Supreme Court in the decision in *Gnango*.[16] In that case, the majority held (Lord Kerr dissenting) that where D1 and D2 voluntarily enter into a fight against each other, each intending to kill or cause grievous bodily harm to the other and each foreseeing that the other has a reciprocal intention, and where D1 mistakenly kills a third party (V) in the course of the fight, then not only D1 but also D2 is guilty of murdering V. The significance of the decision for present purposes is that in the course of its reasoning the majority considered the decision in *Tyrrell*, which it said was an illustration of a general rule[17] that where legislation creates an offence that is intended to protect a class of persons, a member of that class cannot be convicted as an accessory to such an offence committed in respect of him. Defined in this broad way, the rule in *Tyrrell* would, contrary to the argument in the main work, operate to prevent the victim of a s.9 offence (or any other under-16 sexual offence, including one under s.13) from being prosecuted as an accessory to the offence, since the offence was undoubtedly designed to protect the class of persons comprising children under 16, albeit that a child under that age can commit the offence as principal or indeed as accessory where they are not the victim.

As a practical matter the point has been put beyond argument by *Att Gen's Ref (No.53 of 2013) (R. v Wilson)*,[17a] discussed in para.4.25C, above, in which Lord Thomas C.J. said[17b]:

> "It has been clear since at least the Offences Against the Person Act 1861, and subsequent nineteenth century legislation, that the purpose of Parliament in passing legislation to make it a crime punishable with imprisonment to have sexual relations with those under 16 was to protect those under 16. Indeed the Criminal Law Amendments Act 1885 makes it expressly clear that that was the purpose of the legislation. That can be seen from the preamble to the Act and was made clear by this court in *R. v Tyrrell* [1894] 1 QB 710.

---

[16] [2011] UKSC 59 at [17]–[19], [47]–[53].

[17] Identified by Professor Glanville Williams in his article "Victims and other exempt parties in crime" (1990) 10 Legal Studies at p.245.

[17a] [2013] EWCA Crim 2544.

[17b] At [19]–[20].

That long-standing principle is well-known. The reduction of punishment on the basis that the person who needed protection encouraged the commission of an offence is therefore simply wrong. We agree with the submission of the Attorney General that an underage person who encourages sexual relations with her needs more protection, not less. Accepting that as the basis for sentencing for the reasons we have explained, the fact that the offender took advantage of what he asserted the victim did aggravated the offence."

If a child who initiates sexual relations is more in need of the law's protection than other child victims, it must follow that there can be little or no public interest in prosecuting such a child in relation to sexual offences committed against her. Accordingly, whatever the precise ambit of the rule in *Tyrrell*, it is almost inconceivable that the public interest would ever require the prosecution of a child in relation to a s.9 offence of which she was herself the victim.

CAUSING OR INCITING A CHILD TO ENGAGE IN SEXUAL ACTIVITY

MODE OF TRIAL AND PUNISHMENT

From December 3, 2012, when ss.122–128 of the Legal Aid, Sentencing and Punishment of Offenders Act 2012 were brought into force[18]:   **4.48**

- For offences committed on or after that date, an offence under s.10 is listed in Pt 1 of Sch.15B to the CJA 2003 for the purposes of s.224A of that Act (life sentence for second listed offence).
- For convictions on or after that date (irrespective of the date of commission of the offence), an offence under s.10 is a specified offence for the purposes of s.226A of that Act (extended sentence for certain violent or sexual offences).

SENTENCING

The Sentencing Council has issued a new guideline applicable to sex offenders   **4.50** aged 18 or over who are sentenced on or after April 1, 2014: see para.1.20 et seq., above. A single guideline covers offences under both s.9 and s.10 of the 2003 Act and is considered at para.4.22 et seq., above.

A welcome feature of the new guideline is that it has been designed to assist the   **4.50A** courts in sentencing "cyber sex" offences, i.e. offences under s.10 committed

---

[18] By the Legal Aid, Sentencing and Punishment of Offenders Act 2012 (Commencement No.4 and Saving Provisions) Order 2012 (SI 2012/2906).

remotely over the internet, as well as offences involving physical contact. A good illustration of the lack of assistance given in this regard by the previous guideline, issued in 2007 by the Sentencing Guidelines Council, is *Brocklebank*[19] in which the appellant (27) was sentenced to 2 years' imprisonment after pleading guilty to three offences under s.10. He appealed on the ground that the sentence was manifestly excessive in light of the basis of plea accepted by the prosecution and the fact of his early plea. Over a period of six months the appellant exchanged messages with three 14-year-old girls using Blackberry messenger. He pretended to be a 16-year-old boy and his BlackBerry profile picture was consistent with that disguise. He exchanged up to a hundred messages a day with the girls. In some he asked the girls to play a game called "bets", similar to truth or dare, with either truths being told or forfeits being taken. In the list of forfeits and truths that he sent each of the girls was a forfeit inviting the girl to send a picture of herself topless. One of them responded by sending a picture of herself wearing just jeans and a bra. The other girls received the same request, but neither sent a picture. The appellant discussed the possibility of meeting up with the girls, but the basis of plea was that this was all talk on his part and he would never have gone through with it.

The appellant had a considerable criminal record, mainly for dishonesty, and had served custodial sentences before. But there were also offences involving children: in 2005 he was sentenced to 30 months' imprisonment for child abduction involving a young boy and in 2009 a SOPO was made against him on a civil complaint to the magistrates' court. He breached that order in 2011. The sexual assault on that same occasion involved a girl who was working with him as a telephone canvasser for a double glazing company. His job involved recruiting young girls for telesales. He told this particular girl that there was an office culture of completing dares if a booking was secured, and following that through, he undid her bra and touched her indecently. The sentence imposed for that offence was 20 months' imprisonment with 8 months consecutive for the breach of the SOPO. He was released from that sentence very shortly before the s.10 offences were committed.

The pre-sentence report expressed serious concern about the appellant's commission of these offences so soon after his release from custody and recommended a custodial sentence sufficient to allow him time to address his treatment needs. He was described in the report as an "egocentric individual" who had little understanding of victim perspectives. He had not completed any meaningful sex offender treatment and was described as being capable of sophisticated controlling behaviour.

In passing sentence, the judge described the appellant as a sexual pest who fed on young girls to gratify himself. He had tricked his way into the lives of the three

---

[19] [2013] EWCA Crim 1813. See also *Shayne Prince* [2013] EWCA Crim 1768 and the cases discussed at para.3.100 et seq., above.

14-year-old girls to obtain sexual gratification for himself. He had a history of displaying an unhealthy sexual interest in much younger females. However, there was mitigation in the fact that he had stopped short of making contact with the girls in person and in his guilty plea. The judge considered the SGC guideline, but said—understandably, in the view of the Court of Appeal—that he derived little or no assistance from it, as it applied to a first offender who had committed a single offence whereas the appellant had a criminal record and his offences involved a number of children. Making due allowance for the available mitigation, the judge concluded that the sentence must be 2 years' imprisonment.

On appeal, the appellant submitted that the judge's starting point must have been significantly above 2 years to have afforded credit for the guilty plea, and that was too high given the appellant had had no contact with the girls and had not pushed for any. Dealing with credit for plea, the Court of Appeal was quite satisfied that proper credit must have been allowed, although the judge had not specified what it was. It observed that this was a case where full credit may not have been appropriate in any event, because the messages were captured on a phone traced to the appellant, and there was no dispute that he was responsible for them, so to that extent there was an overwhelming case. As to length of sentence, the appellant's counsel drew attention to three earlier decisions of the Court involving inciting sexual behaviour by messaging without any physical contact,[20] in each of which a sentence of 9 months' was upheld or substituted. However, the Court noted considerable factual differences between those cases and this one, such that the appellant could derive little assistance from any of them. In particular, in none of those cases was there the gravely aggravating feature present in this case, that the appellant committed the offences against a background of convictions for serious sexual offences and within a very short time of release from such a sentence. Also, in two of the three cases the defendant was a man of previous good character, and in the third, the sentence of 9 months had to be confined to that length as part of a longer total sentence. In concluding, the Court said:

> "In our view, the judge was correct to identify that a stern sentence was called for here. It is right to say that this case, like the other cases to which reference was made, does not fit easily into the Sentencing Council [sic] guideline for causing or inciting a child to engage in sexual activity. That guideline only envisages contact of a direct physical nature, whereas it is quite clear, in our view, that there is serious culpability present in a situation such as this, where there are multiple victims and the invitation is to indulge in sexually inappropriate behaviour. That is certainly how the parents of any 14-year-old girl would view such offending, we are quite sure."

Taking all these matters into account, the Court was not persuaded that the sentence of 2 years was manifestly excessive, and it dismissed the appeal.

---

[20] *Price* [2008] EWCA Crim 1974; *Moorhouse* [2011] EWCA Crim 170; *Evans* [2012] EWCA Crim 2183.

ENGAGING IN SEXUAL ACTIVITY IN THE PRESENCE OF A CHILD

Mode of Trial and Punishment

4.65 From December 3, 2012, when ss.122–128 of the Legal Aid, Sentencing and Punishment of Offenders Act 2012 were brought into force[21]:

- For offences committed on or after that date, an offence under s.11 is listed in Pt 1 of Sch.15B to the CJA 2003 for the purposes of s.224A of that Act (life sentence for second listed offence).

- For convictions on or after that date (irrespective of the date of commission of the offence), an offence under s.11 is a specified offence for the purposes of s.226A of that Act (extended sentence for certain violent or sexual offences).

Sentencing

4.67 The Sentencing Council has issued a new guideline applicable to sex offenders aged 18 or over who are sentenced on or after April 1, 2014: see para.1.20 et seq., above. In its consultation on the draft guideline,[22] the Council said that it proposed to deal in one guideline with the offences of engaging in sexual activity in the presence of a child (s.11 of the 2003 Act) and causing a child to watch a sexual act (s.12), as the offences involve common offending behaviours, are equally harmful and share a statutory maximum of 10 years' imprisonment. The previous guideline, issued in 2007 by the Sentencing Guidelines Council, treated the two offences separately, but the Sentencing Council considered that there is now increased understanding of the ways in which children can be groomed and that the activities covered by both of these offences can be deployed by offenders to normalise and desensitise children to sexual activity. It duly followed its proposed approach in the new guideline as published.

New sentencing guideline

Step One—Harm and culpability

4.67A The guideline requires the sentencing court to go through a series of steps in order to determine the appropriate sentence. Step one involves determining the offence category by reference to the degree of harm caused and then the culpability level for the offence.

---

[21] By the Legal Aid, Sentencing and Punishment of Offenders Act 2012 (Commencement No.4 and Saving Provisions) Order 2012 (SI 2012/2906).
[22] *Sexual Offences Guideline: Consultation* (December 6, 2012).

Harm

Severity of harm is determined in this guideline by the type of sexual activity **4.67B** viewed by the victim. The SGC guideline gave the highest starting point to images of consensual penetration and live sexual activity. However, the Sentencing Council believed that certain images of sexual activity should attract the highest starting point because of the depravity portrayed in them and their distorting effect on the child's view of such activity. The harm factors for these offences are therefore as follows:

HARM	
Category 1	• Causing victim to view extreme pornography • Causing victim to view indecent/prohibited images of children • Engaging in, or causing a victim to view live, sexual activity involving sadism/violence/sexual activity with an animal/a child
Category 2	Engaging in, or causing a victim to view images of or view live, sexual activity involving: • penetration of vagina or anus (using body or object) • penile penetration of the mouth • masturbation
Category 3	Factor(s) in categories 1 and 2 not present

Category 1 covers offences where the child is exposed to extreme pornography, defined in s.63(7) of the Criminal Justice and Immigration Act 2008 as an image which "portrays, in an explicit and realistic way ... (a) an act which threatens a person's life, (b) an act which results, or is likely to result, in serious injury to a person's anus, breasts or genitals, (c) an act which involves sexual interference with a human corpse, or (d) a person performing an act of intercourse or oral sex with an animal (whether dead or alive)". The offence of extreme pornography had not been created when the SGC guideline was drafted and the Sentencing Council believed that its existence needed to be reflected in sentencing guidance for offences under ss.11 and 12. As for category 2, this deals with penetrative sexual activity and masturbation. Causing a victim to view penetrative activity was the highest category of harm in the SGC guideline. As will be seen below, the Sentencing Council has retained similar sentence levels for causing a child to view this type of activity, but it did feel the level of imagery covered by category 1 deserved even higher sentence starting points and ranges.

Culpability

As for culpability, the Sentencing Council noted that offenders can expose a child **4.67C** to sexual imagery in order to desensitise them and so facilitate further sexual offending by the offender or others. It therefore considered that the culpability factors for offences under ss.11 and 12 of the 2003 Act should focus on whether there is evidence of such grooming or manipulation of the child. As a result, an offender's culpability will increase where, alongside the sexual gratification they gain by exposing the child to the sexual activity or imagery, the offender deliberately tries to corrupt and desensitise the child. The culpability factors for these offences are:

CULPABILITY
A
• Significant degree of planning • Offender acts together with others in order to commit the offence • Use of alcohol/drugs on victim to facilitate the offence • Grooming behaviour used against victim • Abuse of trust • Use of threats (including blackmail) • Specific targeting of a particularly vulnerable child • Significant disparity in age • Commercial exploitation and/or motivation • Offence racially or religiously aggravated • Offence motivated by, or demonstrating, hostility to the victim based on his or her sexual orientation (or presumed sexual orientation) or transgender identity (or presumed transgender identity) • Offence motivated by, or demonstrating, hostility to the victim based on his or her disability (or presumed disability)
B
Factor(s) in category A not present

For discussion of the culpability A factors, see para.4.22 et seq., above. No factors are listed under culpability B, but the sentence starting points and ranges reflect the inherently abusive and corrupting behaviour that will always be present when an offender exposes a child to sexual imagery for the offender's sexual gratification.

Step Two—Starting point and category range

4.67D Having determined the offence category and culpability level, the court should then use the corresponding starting point specified in the guideline in order to reach a sentence within the category range. The starting point applies to all offenders irrespective of plea or previous convictions. Once the starting point has been determined, step two allows further adjustment for aggravating or mitigating features, set out below. A case of particular gravity, reflected by multiple features of culpability or harm, could merit upward adjustment from the starting point before further adjustment for aggravating or mitigating features. Where there is a sufficient prospect of rehabilitation, a community order with a sex offender treatment programme requirement under s.202 of the CJA 2003 may be a proper alternative to a short or moderate length custodial sentence. The starting points and category ranges for offences under ss.11 and 12 of the Act are as follows:

	A	B
Category 1	**Starting point** 4 years' custody **Category range** 3–6 years' custody	**Starting point** 2 years' custody **Category range** 1–3 years' custody
Category 2	**Starting point** 2 years' custody **Category range** 1–3 years' custody	**Starting point** 1 year's custody **Category range** High level community order–18 months' custody
Category 3	**Starting point** 26 weeks' custody **Category range** High level community order–1 year's custody	**Starting point** Medium level community order **Category range** Low level community order–Medium level community order

As noted above, there is a significant difference between the new guideline and the SGC guideline. The maximum sentences recommended in the latter were 2 years' imprisonment with a range of 1–4 years' imprisonment for sexual activity in the presence of a child involving consensual penetration, and 18 months' imprisonment with a range of 12 months to 2 years' imprisonment for causing or inciting a child to watch a live sexual act. Both of these types of activity are now likely to be encompassed in category 2, though with sentence levels similar to those under the SGC guideline. As explained above, the Council has placed in category 1 activity that it regarded as more harmful to the child, for example, where the child is forced to watch pornography that involves sadism or is shown indecent images of children, for the sexual gratification of the offender. The Council considered that the harm done to the child is increased in such cases by the extreme nature of the imagery and that, where it is combined with manipulative and coercive behaviour on the part of the offender, it should attract a custodial sentence higher than that suggested in the SGC guideline.

Aggravating and mitigating factors

4.67E   After identifying the starting point and category range, the court should consider whether the presence of aggravating or mitigating factors should result in an upward or downward adjustment from the starting point or the imposition of a sentence outside the category range. In particular, relevant recent convictions are likely to result in an upward adjustment. When sentencing appropriate category 2 or 3 offences, the court should also consider whether the custody threshold has been passed; if so, whether a custodial sentence is unavoidable; and if it is, whether that sentence can be suspended. The non-exhaustive list of aggravating and mitigating factors for offences under ss.11 and 12 is as follows:

Aggravating factors
Statutory aggravating factors
• Previous convictions, having regard to a) the nature of the offence to which the conviction relates and its relevance to the current offence; and b) the time that has elapsed since the conviction
• Offence committed whilst on bail
Other aggravating factors
• Location of offence
• Timing of offence
• Victim compelled to leave their home, school, etc
• Failure to comply with current court orders
• Offence committed whilst on licence
• Exploiting contact arrangements with a child to commit an offence
• Presence of others, especially other children
• Any steps taken to prevent the victim reporting an incident, obtaining assistance and/or from assisting or supporting the prosecution
• Attempts to dispose of or conceal evidence
• Failure of offender to respond to previous warnings
• Commission of offence whilst offender under the influence of alcohol or drugs
• Victim encouraged to recruit others

Mitigating factors
• No previous convictions **or** no relevant/recent convictions
• Remorse
• Previous good character and/or exemplary conduct*
• Age and/or lack of maturity where it affects the responsibility of the offender
• Mental disorder or learning disability, particularly where linked to the commission of the offence
• Demonstration of steps taken to address offending behaviour

---

* Previous good character/exemplary conduct is different from having no previous convictions. The more serious the offence, the less the weight which should normally be attributed to this factor. Where previous good character/exemplary conduct has been used to facilitate the offence, this mitigation should not normally be allowed and such conduct may constitute an aggravating factor.

For an example of possible additional aggravating factors, see *Buckingham*,[23] decided under the SGC guideline, where the court treated the offences as aggravated by the fact that they were part of a course of conduct lasting two or three days and involved extensive humiliation of the complainant.

Steps Three to Nine

The remaining steps cover the following points. At step three the court should **4.67F** consider any factors which would indicate a reduction in sentence, e.g. assistance to the prosecution. At step four it should consider any reduction for a guilty plea. At step five the court should consider dangerousness, i.e. whether it would be appropriate to award a life sentence (s.224A of the CJA 2003) or an extended sentence (s.226A). Step six requires the court to consider whether the total sentence is just and proportionate to the offending behaviour. At step seven it should consider whether to make an ancillary order (e.g. a compensation order, a SOPO or a restraining order). Step eight requires the court to fulfil its duty under s.174 of the CJA 2003 to give reasons for, and explain the effect of, the sentence. Finally, at step nine the court should consider whether to give credit for time spent on bail in accordance with s.240A of that Act.

Sentencing example

Brown[24] pre-dates the new definitive guideline but is a useful example of the **4.69** approach taken by the Court of Appeal to a particular factual scenario. The appellant appealed against a sentence of 15 months' imprisonment imposed after

[23] [2013] EWCA Crim 1874.
[24] [2010] EWCA Crim 1203.

he pleaded guilty to two counts of attempting to commit the s.11 offence. An undercover police officer had posed as a 14-year-old girl on a social networking site on the internet. The appellant contacted her, told her he was 35 years old and on two occasions asked her to watch his web camera. On each occasion, he appeared naked and masturbated in front of the camera. The appellant argued that the sentence was manifestly excessive given that the SGC guideline starting point was 18 months, he had pleaded guilty and his offences were attempts. The Court of Appeal dismissed the appeal. The SGC guideline was based on conviction after a trial on one count, whereas in the instant case there were two almost identical offences, committed within three weeks of each other. Accordingly, the judge had been entitled to take a higher starting point. While it was true that the viewer of the webcam had been an adult and therefore attempts rather than full offences had been committed, from the appellant's perspective and experience the offences were complete because he did not know that there was no 14-year-old watching him. The judge had therefore been correct to say that the fact that the offences were attempts made little difference to the sentence. He had also explicitly taken into account the guilty plea, and the sentence could not be said to be manifestly excessive.

CAUSING A CHILD TO WATCH A SEXUAL ACT

MODE OF TRIAL AND PUNISHMENT

4.84   From December 3, 2012, when ss.122–128 of the Legal Aid, Sentencing and Punishment of Offenders Act 2012 were brought into force[25]:

- For offences committed on or after that date, an offence under s.12 is listed in Pt 1 of Sch.15B to the Criminal Justice Act 2003 for the purposes of s.224A of that Act (life sentence for second listed offence).
- For convictions on or after that date (irrespective of the date of commission of the offence), an offence under s.12 is a specified offence for the purposes of s.226A of that Act (extended sentence for certain violent or sexual offences).

SENTENCING

4.86   The Sentencing Council has issued a new guideline applicable to sex offenders aged 18 or over who are sentenced on or after April 1, 2014: see para.1.20 et seq., above. A single guideline covers both offences under s.12 of the Act and offences under s.11 of engaging in sexual activity in the presence of a child, and is considered at para.4.67 et seq., above.

---

[25] By the Legal Aid, Sentencing and Punishment of Offenders Act 2012 (Commencement No.4 and Saving Provisions) Order 2012 (SI 2012/2906).

Attempt

R. v K[26] concerned an appeal against conviction on one count of attempting to   **4.90A**
commit the s.12 offence. The appellant worked as a security guard in a residential
tower block. He spoke to some children aged 13, 11 and 6 outside the entrance to
the block and, according to the evidence of the 11-year-old, asked the 6-year-old
if he would like to look at pornographic DVDs. The appellant's account was
instead that it was the 6-year-old who asked if he could view girls on the internet.
The judge directed the jury that they were entitled to draw an inference from the
evidence that the appellant had a laptop in the concierge area of the block. He went
on to direct them that in order to convict they had to be sure that the invitation
had been made, and if they were sure of that, they then had to decide whether the
invitation was mere preparation or an attempt. When the jury sought clarification,
the judge directed them to the effect that if they were sure that the invitation had
been issued and that there was a laptop in the concierge area that the appellant
would use to show pornography, then they would have to consider whether the
appellant's actions were more than merely preparatory. The ensuing conviction
was quashed by the Court of Appeal on the ground that the invitation and the
presence of a laptop were not in themselves sufficient to constitute an attempt.

The editors of *Blackstone's* consider the decision in *R. v K* likely to stimulate
debate, since "if the child had accepted the invitation, all that would have
remained for the full offence to be committed would be for the child to accompany
the accused to the concierge area and then for the accused to show the
pornography".[27] The decision does indeed seem borderline, given that by issuing
the invitation to the child the appellant was taking perhaps the critical step towards
committing the full offence. On the other hand, even if the child had accepted the
invitation, the appellant would have committed the full offence only when he had
accompanied the child to the concierge area and showed him pornography on the
laptop. For that reason, it is understandable that the Court of Appeal held that the
appellant had not gone beyond mere preparation, though clearly the preparation
could be said to have been at an advanced stage. The editors of *Blackstone's* say the
decision should be contrasted with *R. v R*,[28] discussed in para.4.19 et seq. of the
main work, in which a man who asked a prostitute to find a girl of 12 or 13 for sex
was convicted of attempting the offence under s.14 of the 2003 Act of arranging
the commission of a child sexual offence. Why did the request in that case amount
to an attempt, but the invitation in this one did not? The answer is that in *R. v R*
the appellant had done all he needed to do to commit the full offence, since if the
prostitute had responded positively to his request then the arrangement required
by s.14 would have been made, with no need for any further action on the
appellant's part. By contrast, the appellant in *R. v K* would have committed the
full offence only if he had taken further steps after issuing the invitation.

---

[26] [2009] EWCA Crim 1931.
[27] Commentary in 2009 update to Blackstone's Criminal Practice, s.B3.86.
[28] [2008] EWCA Crim 619.

CHILD SEX OFFENCES COMMITTED BY CHILDREN OR YOUNG PERSONS

MODE OF TRIAL AND PUNISHMENT

4.104   For convictions on or after December 3, 2012,[29] an offence under s.13 as read with ss.9–12 is a specified offence for the purposes of s.226B of the CJA 2003 (extended sentence for certain violent or sexual offences: persons under 18), irrespective of the date of commission of the offence.

SENTENCING

4.105   The Sentencing Council has issued a new guideline applicable to sex offenders aged 18 or over who are sentenced on or after April 1, 2014: see para.1.20 et seq., above. In its consultation on the draft guideline,[30] the Council noted that the principal aim of the youth justice system is to prevent offending by children and young persons[31] and the court is obliged to have regard to the welfare of the offender.[32] The previous guideline issued in 2007 by the Sentencing Guidelines Council contained four separate but similar guidelines for young offenders convicted under s.13 read with ss.9–12. The Sentencing Council proposed instead to mirror the structure of the adult guidelines by adopting two guidelines: one for s.13 read with ss.9–10 and the other for s.13 read with ss.11–12. The proposed guidelines reflected both the lower statutory maximum for offences under s.13 and the different options available when sentencing youths.

However, respondents to the consultation expressed mixed views about the desirability of this approach and several argued against inclusion of the proposed guidelines. Some were concerned that replicating the adult guidelines for those under 18 would lead to wrong sentences or the need to ignore certain factors, and thought separate guidelines would be preferable in order to avoid treating children and young people who offend sexually as mini-adults. A number of respondents suggested that the issues should be covered in the review of the youth sentencing guidelines that the Council is due to commence in autumn 2014. Part of the Council's rationale for including the proposed guidelines was that offences under s.13 were covered in the SGC guideline and omitting them might create a sentencing "gap". However, respondents did not feel that this was a significant risk, given that sexual offences constitute a very small proportion of offences which come before the youth court.

---

[29] When s.124 of the Legal Aid, Sentencing and Punishment of Offenders Act 2012 was brought into force by the Legal Aid, Sentencing and Punishment of Offenders Act 2012 (Commencement No.4 and Saving Provisions) Order 2012 (SI 2012/2906).

[30] *Sexual Offences Guideline: Consultation* (December 6, 2012).

[31] s.37 of the Crime and Disorder Act 1998.

[32] s.44 of the Children and Young Persons Act 1933.

In the event, the Council was persuaded that to include guidelines for offences under s.13 was at this stage more likely to cause difficulties than be of assistance. It appreciated that child sex offences committed by young offenders can be very different in nature to those committed by adults, not least because of the use of social media. It was also concerned that producing guidelines for a very narrow range of serious youth offending now, without considering the wider approach that should be adopted to the sentencing of those under 18, could cause problems when it came to review youth sentencing generally. Accordingly, the Council decided not to include the proposed guidelines. But in order to minimise the risk of sentencers continuing to follow the SGC guideline, or of creating a sentencing "gap", it included the following narrative guidance instead:

> "When sentencing offenders under 18, a court must in particular:
> * follow the definitive guideline **Overarching Principles—Sentencing Youths**;
> and have regard to:
> * the principal aim of the youth justice system (to prevent offending by children and young people); and
> * the welfare of the young offender."

Sentencing example

R. v W (Christopher John)[33] pre-dates the new definitive guideline but is a useful   **4.105A** example of the approach taken by the Court of Appeal to a particular factual scenario. The appellant appealed against a sentence of 14 months' detention imposed following his plea of guilty to 17 offences of making indecent photographs of a child, three offences of inciting a child to engage in sexual activity, and one of engaging in sexual activity in the presence of a child. The appellant, when aged between 15 and 17, had made contact over the internet with 100 young girls from various parts of the world. He enticed them to take their clothes off and pose for him, exposing their genitals for the camera. He also persuaded some of them to masturbate. He recorded the sessions. Of a total of 57 images, 38 were at level 1 and 19 were at level 2. As to the offences of inciting a child to engage in sexual activity, he had caused 15-year-old girls to masturbate; that was similar conduct to that alleged in the other counts, but the charges were aimed at the interaction of the two parties as opposed to the making of indecent photographs. As to the offence of engaging in sexual activity in the presence of a child, the appellant had masturbated so that the 15-year-old girl at the other end of the link could see him doing so. He pleaded guilty at the first opportunity. The Court of Appeal allowed the appeal. A court imposing a sentence on a youth had to have regard to his welfare, maturity, sexual development and intelligence. An important factor was the age gap between the child and the offender; here, it seemed to have been a maximum of approximately two years. While in one sense the appellant's conduct was persistent predatory behaviour, these were not contact offences; the behaviour was ostensibly consensual and there was no coercion. There were certain

---

[33] [2012] EWCA Crim 1447.

aggravating features: a vast number of girls had been induced to pose for the camera; the offences had been committed for the appellant's sexual gratification; the conduct continued for a protracted period; and while there was no evidence of the girls being adversely affected, there was the potential for psychological harm if any appreciated that their image was being used for sexual gratification. The judge had correctly had the protection of vulnerable young girls very much in mind and had been entitled to depart from the SGC guideline; the convergence of the aggravating features and the scale of the offending called for a custodial sentence. However, the judge failed to give sufficient weight to the appellant's age when he committed the offences, to the time that had elapsed and to the appellant's increased maturity since his arrest in 2010. The judge's starting point of 20 months was too high; the appropriate starting point was 12 months. Accordingly, given the early pleas, an appropriate sentence would have been 8 months. Further, given the appellant's age and immaturity at the time, the sentence should have been suspended. The Court accordingly quashed the appellant's sentence and substituted one of 8 months' detention, suspended for 2 years, with a 2-year supervision order and a requirement that the appellant undertake one-to-one sexual-offending work.

ARRANGING OR FACILITATING COMMISSION OF A CHILD SEX OFFENCE

Mode of Trial and Punishment

4.112 From December 3, 2012, when ss.122–128 of the Legal Aid, Sentencing and Punishment of Offenders Act 2012 were brought into force[34]:

- For offences committed on or after that date, an offence under s.14 is listed in Pt 1 of Sch.15B to the CJA 2003 for the purposes of s.224A of that Act (life sentence for second listed offence).

- For convictions on or after that date (irrespective of the date of commission of the offence), an offence under s.14 is a specified offence for the purposes of s.226A of that Act (extended sentence for certain violent or sexual offences).

Sentencing

4.114 The Sentencing Council has issued a new guideline applicable to sex offenders aged 18 or over who are sentenced on or after April 1, 2014: see para.1.20 et seq., above. By a curious omission, the Sentencing Council's draft guideline contained

[34] By the Legal Aid, Sentencing and Punishment of Offenders Act 2012 (Commencement No.4 and Saving Provisions) Order 2012 (SI 2012/2906).

no guidance on sentencing offences under s.14. This was, however, put right in the published guideline, which states:

> "Sentencers should refer to the guideline for the applicable, substantive offence of arranging or facilitating under sections 9 to 12. The level of harm should be determined by reference to the type of activity arranged or facilitated. Sentences commensurate with the applicable starting point and range will ordinarily be appropriate. For offences involving substantial commercial exploitation and/or an international element, it may, in the interests of justice, be appropriate to increase a sentence to a point in excess of the category range. In exceptional cases, such as where a vulnerable offender performed a limited role, having been coerced or exploited by others, sentences below the starting point and range may be appropriate."

Sentencing example

Bayliss[35] pre-dates the new definitive guideline but is a useful example of the approach taken by the Court of Appeal to a particular factual scenario. The appellant appealed against a total sentence of 3 years' imprisonment imposed following his early guilty plea to offences of attempting to facilitate the commission of a child sex offence, possession of indecent images of children and making an indecent photograph of a child. A covert police investigator had posed as the mother in an "open family" in which inter-familial sexual activity took place. The appellant had extensive exchanges with her in an internet chat room about what he wanted to do, and how far he was prepared to go, with her 10-year-old son. He met her twice and on both occasions said that he wanted sexual activity with the boy but was unsure about progressing to penetration. Arrangements were made for him to meet the boy and he was told to bring condoms, which he had with him, along with lubricant, when he was arrested. The appellant's case was that he would not have had penile penetration with the child. At a *Newton* hearing, the judge concluded that the appellant had intended to touch the boy sexually and to have oral sex with him, but had not intended to have anal sex, though that remained a possibility if he had become carried away. In sentencing, the judge bore in mind that no actual child had been involved, but focused on the harm that had been intended. He noted the appellant's previous good character and his early guilty plea, but reduced the credit to one quarter because of the outcome of the *Newton* hearing. He imposed a three-year custodial term for attempting to facilitate the commission of a child sex offence, with concurrent sentences of 6 months' imprisonment for the other offences. The appellant submitted that the judge's starting point for the facilitation offence was too high, given that there had been no victim, and that it had been wrong to reduce credit as a result of the *Newton* hearing when the issues had been largely decided in his favour. The Court of Appeal allowed the appeal in part. The judge had seemingly taken 4 years as his starting point, which he had then reduced by one quarter to reach a sentence of 3 years' imprisonment. In the absence of a victim and so of actual harm, a 3-year starting point was appropriate. After a reduction of one quarter, the Court

4.115

---

[35] [2012] EWCA Crim 269.

substituted a term of two-and-a-quarter years' imprisonment. As for the *Newton* hearing, that had not been resolved entirely in the appellant's favour and so the reduction in credit to one quarter was not excessive.

MEETING A CHILD FOLLOWING SEXUAL GROOMING ETC.

MODE OF TRIAL AND PUNISHMENT

4.136 From December 3, 2012, when ss.122–128 of the Legal Aid, Sentencing and Punishment of Offenders Act 2012 were brought into force[36]:

- For offences committed on or after that date, an offence under s.15 is listed in Pt 1 of Sch.15B to the CJA 2003 for the purposes of s.224A of that Act (life sentence for second listed offence).
- For convictions on or after that date (irrespective of the date of commission of the offence), an offence under s.15 is a specified offence for the purposes of s.226A of that Act (extended sentence for certain violent or sexual offences).

SENTENCING

4.138 The Sentencing Council has issued a new guideline applicable to sex offenders aged 18 or over who are sentenced on or after April 1, 2014: see para.1.20 et seq., above. In its consultation on the draft guideline,[37] the Council noted that the s.15 offence is often referred to as "grooming", a term that can also be used to describe a wide range of manipulative behaviour used by offenders to condition victims in order to obtain their apparent acquiescence to sexual activity, e.g. "on-street grooming" or "internet grooming". The Council emphasised the importance of distinguishing this wider grooming activity from the more limited range of conduct covered by the s.15 offence.

New sentencing guideline

Step One—Harm and culpability

4.138A The guideline requires the sentencing court to go through a series of steps in order to determine the appropriate sentence. Step one involves determining the offence category by reference to the degree of harm caused and then the culpability level for the offence. The Sentencing Council noted that the s.15 offence differs from

---

[36] By the Legal Aid, Sentencing and Punishment of Offenders Act 2012 (Commencement No.4 and Saving Provisions) Order 2012 (SI 2012/2906).
[37] *Sexual Offences Guideline: Consultation* (December 6, 2012).

the other child sex offences in that it is essentially preparatory, i.e. it is committed by persons who are preparing to commit another child sex offence. The offence is designed to enable early intervention, and harm and culpability may not have been fully realised at the time of intervention, so it is difficult to articulate them in the same way as for other sexual offences. For this reason, the guideline describes the offence categories for this offence as follows:

Category 1	Raised harm **and** raised culpability
Category 2	Raised harm **or** raised culpability
Category 3	Grooming **without** raised harm or culpability factors present

The previous guideline issued in 2007 by the Sentencing Guidelines Council had just two categories of offence, the highest reserved for cases where the offender's intent was to commit rape or an assault by penetration and the second applying where their intent was to coerce the child into another form of sexual activity. The new guideline articulates both harm and culpability in more detail than the SGC guideline. It provides that the court should determine the harm caused or intended and culpability by reference only to the factors listed below. Where an offence does not fall squarely into an offence category, individual factors may require a degree of weighting before the sentencer makes an overall assessment of which category is appropriate.

Raised harm

The factors listed as raising harm in relation to the s.15 offence are: 4.138B

| **Factors indicating raised harm** |
| • Continued contact despite victim's attempts to terminate contact |
| • Sexual images exchanged |
| • Victim exposed to extreme sexual content for example, extreme pornography |
| • Child is particularly vulnerable due to personal circumstances |

In its consultation, the Sentencing Council said that "continued contact despite victim's attempts to terminate contact" is included because persistent contact of that sort is likely to induce a sense of menace in the victim and therefore increase the psychological harm to them. As for "sexual images exchanged", in other guidelines this is expressed as the culpability factor "sexual images of victim recorded, retained, solicited or shared". It is included as a feature of harm for the s.15 offence because of the damage caused by the victim's knowledge that the offender holds images which may be circulated and over which the victim has no control. "Victim exposed to extreme sexual content for example, extreme pornography" is included to reflect the fact that that such exposure will have a harmful and corrupting effect on the child. "Child is particularly vulnerable due to personal circumstances" (which appeared in the consultation draft as "vulnerable victim targeted") is intended to cover vulnerability over and above the fact that the victim is a child, e.g. where they are living in care, particularly residential care, are excluded from mainstream school or are misusing drugs and alcohol.

Raised culpability

4.138C The following factors are listed as increasing culpability for the s.15 offence:

Factors indicating raised culpability
• Offender acts together with others to commit the offence
• Communication indicates penetrative sexual activity is intended
• Offender lied about age/persona
• Use of threats (including blackmail), gifts or bribes
• Abuse of trust
• Specific targeting of a particularly vulnerable child
• Abduction/detention
• Commercial exploitation and/or motivation
• Offence racially or religiously aggravated
• Offence motivated by, or demonstrating, hostility to the victim based on his or her sexual orientation (or presumed sexual orientation) or transgender identity (or presumed transgender identity)
• Offence motivated by, or demonstrating, hostility to the victim based on his or her disability (or presumed disability)

In its consultation, the Sentencing Council said it included "offender lied about age/persona" because this additional deception increases the offender's culpability. The Council accepted that not all offenders will disguise their identity and that some will exploit the fact that, for example, a young girl may be looking for an older, "grown up" boyfriend. Most importantly, it made clear that it did not intend an offender who was honest about their age and persona to be able to use this as mitigation.

Step Two—Starting point and category range

4.138D Having determined the offence category and culpability level, the court should then use the corresponding starting point specified in the guideline in order to reach a sentence within the category range. The starting point applies to all offenders irrespective of plea or previous convictions. Once the starting point has been determined, step two allows further adjustment for aggravating or mitigating features, set out below. A case of particular gravity, reflected by multiple features of culpability or harm, could merit upward adjustment from the starting point before further adjustment for aggravating or mitigating features. The starting points and category ranges for the s.15 offence are as follows:

Category 1	**Starting point**
	4 years' custody
	Category range
	3–7 years' custody
Category 2	**Starting point**
	2 years' custody
	Category range
	1–4 years' custody
Category 3	**Starting point**
	18 months' custody
	Category range
	1 year–2 years 6 months' custody

Category 1 has the same starting point and range as the top range under the SGC guideline. However, that guideline had higher starting points and ranges for offences committed against those under the age of 13. The Sentencing Council felt this was inappropriate and proposed in its consultation that where there is raised harm and raised culpability, regardless of the child's age, the highest sentence level and range should be available. The majority of respondents strongly supported removing the age distinction in this way. Accordingly, under the new guideline, the higher SGC starting point is available regardless of the age of the victim where raised harm and raised culpability are present.

Aggravating and mitigating factors

After identifying the starting point and category range, the court should consider whether the presence of aggravating or mitigating factors should result in an upward or downward adjustment from the starting point or the imposition of a sentence outside the category range. In particular, relevant recent convictions are likely to result in an upward adjustment. The non-exhaustive list of aggravating and mitigating factors for offences under s.15 of the Act is as follows:

4.138E

Aggravating factors
Statutory aggravating factors
<ul><li>Previous convictions, having regard to a) the nature of the offence to which the conviction relates and its relevance to the current offence; and b) the time that has elapsed since the conviction</li><li>Offence committed whilst on bail</li></ul>
Other aggravating factors
<ul><li>Failure to comply with current court orders</li><li>Offence committed whilst on licence</li><li>Any steps taken to prevent the victim reporting an incident, obtaining assistance and/or from assisting or supporting the prosecution</li><li>Attempts to dispose of or conceal evidence</li><li>Victim encouraged to recruit others</li></ul>

Mitigating factors
<ul><li>No previous convictions **or** no relevant/recent convictions</li><li>Remorse</li><li>Previous good character and/or exemplary conduct*</li><li>Age and/or lack of maturity where it affects the responsibility of the offender</li><li>Mental disorder or learning disability, particularly where linked to the commission of the offence</li><li>Demonstration of steps taken to address offending behaviour</li></ul>

* Previous good character/exemplary conduct is different from having no previous convictions. The more serious the offence, the less the weight which should normally be attributed to this factor. Where previous good character/exemplary conduct has been used to facilitate the offence, this mitigation should not normally be allowed and such conduct may constitute an aggravating factor.

Steps Three to Nine

4.138F   The remaining steps cover the following points. At step three the court should consider any factors which would indicate a reduction in sentence, e.g. assistance to the prosecution. At step four it should consider any reduction for a guilty plea. At step five the court should consider dangerousness, i.e. whether it would be appropriate to award a life sentence (s.224A of the CJA 2003) or an extended sentence (s.226A). Step six requires the court to consider whether the total sentence is just and proportionate to the offending behaviour. At step seven it should consider whether to make an ancillary order (e.g. a compensation order, a SOPO or a restraining order). Step eight requires the court to fulfil its duty under s.174 of the CJA 2003 to give reasons for, and explain the effect of, the sentence. Finally, at step nine the court should consider whether to give credit for time spent on bail in accordance with s.240A of that Act.

ABUSE OF POSITION OF TRUST

ABUSE OF POSITION OF TRUST: SEXUAL ACTIVITY WITH A CHILD

MODE OF TRIAL AND PUNISHMENT

For convictions on or after December 3, 2012,[1] an offence under s.16 is a specified **5.09** offence for the purposes of s.226A of the Criminal Justice Act 2003 ("CJA 2003") (extended sentence for certain violent or sexual offences), irrespective of the date of commission of the offence.

SENTENCING

The Sentencing Council has issued a new guideline applicable to sex offenders **5.11** aged 18 or over who are sentenced on or after April 1, 2014: see para.1.20 et seq., above. In its consultation on the draft guideline,[2] the Council proposed to follow the approach of the Sentencing Guidelines Council by covering the offences in ss.16 and 17 of the 2003 Act in the same guideline, on the ground that harm and culpability are equally weighted in these offences and they have the same statutory maximum. This is the course it duly followed in the published guideline. For

[1] When s.124 of the Legal Aid, Sentencing and Punishment of Offenders Act 2012 was brought into force by the Legal Aid, Sentencing and Punishment of Offenders Act 2012 (Commencement No.4 and Saving Provisions) Order 2012 (SI 2012/2906).

[2] *Sexual Offences Guideline: Consultation* (December 6, 2012).

clarity, there is a text box at the start of the guideline stating "This guideline also applies to offences committed remotely/online".

New sentencing guideline

Step One—Harm and culpability

5.11A   Under the new guideline, the sentencing court is to go through a series of steps in order to determine the appropriate sentence. Step one involves determining the offence category by reference to the degree of harm caused and then the culpability level for the offence. The Sentencing Council adopted in this guideline the approach to harm taken in the guideline for the s.9 offence (sexual activity with a child), discussed at para.4.22. As with that offence, the victim may believe him/herself to be in a relationship with the adult in the position of trust and may not be aware of the harm that is being done to them. Harm is therefore attributed based upon the sexual activity that has taken place. The harm and culpability factors for offences under ss.16 and 17 are as follows:

HARM		CULPABILITY
Category 1	• Penetration of vagina or anus (using body or object) • Penile penetration of mouth in either case by, or of, the victim	**A** • Significant degree of planning • Offender acts together with others to commit the offence • Use of alcohol/drugs on victim to facilitate the offence • Grooming behaviour used against victim • Use of threats (including blackmail) • Sexual images of victim recorded, retained, solicited or shared • Specific targeting of a particularly vulnerable child • Commercial exploitation and/or motivation • Offence racially or religiously aggravated • Offence motivated by, or demonstrating, hostility to the victim based on his or her sexual orientation (or presumed sexual orientation) or transgender identity (or presumed transgender identity)
Category 2	• Touching, or exposure, of naked genitalia or naked breasts by, or of, the victim	
Category 3	• Factor(s) in categories 1 and 2 not present	

• Offence motivated by, or demonstrating, hostility to the victim based on his or her disability (or presumed disability)
B
Factor(s) in category A not present

This list omits some of the culpability factors in the s.9 guideline. "Abuse of trust" is omitted because such abuse is an essential feature of these offences.[3] "Offender lied about age" is dropped as deception about age is unlikely to be a principal factor in abuse of trust cases. Finally, "significant disparity in age" is omitted as the Sentencing Council felt that the offender's age is not as significant a culpability factor as the position of trust the offender holds in relation to the child.

Step Two—Starting point and category range

Having determined the offence category and culpability level, the court should **5.11B** then use the corresponding starting point specified in the guideline in order to reach a sentence within the category range. The starting point applies to all offenders irrespective of plea or previous convictions. Once the starting point has been determined, step two allows further adjustment for aggravating or mitigating features, set out below. A case of particular gravity, reflected by multiple features of culpability or harm, could merit upward adjustment from the starting point before further adjustment for aggravating or mitigating features. Where there is a sufficient prospect of rehabilitation, a community order with a sex offender treatment programme requirement under s.202 of the CJA 2003 may be a proper alternative to a short or moderate length custodial sentence. The starting points and category ranges for offences under ss.16 and 17 of the Act are as follows:

	A	B
Category 1	**Starting point** 18 months' custody	**Starting point** 1 year's custody
	Category range 1–2 years' custody	**Category range** 26 weeks'–18 months' custody

[3] cf. *Cornwall* [2012] EWCA Crim 1227, discussed in para.5.12, below, in which the Court of Appeal criticised the sentencing judge for taking into account abuse of trust as an aggravating factor when it "is not an aggravating factor but is what makes otherwise lawful activity unlawful" (at [19]).

	A	B
Category 2	**Starting point** 1 year's custody **Category range** 26 weeks'–18 months' custody	**Starting point** 26 weeks' custody **Category range** High level community order–1 year's custody
Category 3	**Starting point** 26 weeks' custody **Category range** High level community order–1 year's custody	**Starting point** Medium level community order **Category range** Low level community order–High level community order

Although factors used to determine the offence categories in this guideline are similar to those used in the guideline for the s.9 offence, the starting points and ranges are lower in order to reflect the fact that the statutory maximum for an offence under s.16 or s.17 is 5 years, as opposed to 14 years under s.9.

Aggravating and mitigating factors

5.11C   After identifying the starting point and category range, the court should consider whether the presence of aggravating or mitigating factors should result in an upward or downward adjustment from the starting point or the imposition of a sentence outside the category range. In particular, relevant recent convictions are likely to result in an upward adjustment. When sentencing appropriate category 2 or 3 offences, the court should also consider whether the custody threshold has been passed; if so, whether a custodial sentence is unavoidable; and if it is, whether that sentence can be suspended. The non-exhaustive list of aggravating and mitigating factors for offences under ss.16 and 17 is as follows:

Aggravating factors
Statutory aggravating factors
• Previous convictions, having regard to a) the nature of the offence to which the conviction relates and its relevance to the current offence; and b) the time that has elapsed since the conviction
• Offence committed whilst on bail

Other aggravating factors

- Ejaculation
- Pregnancy or STI as a consequence of offence
- Location of offence
- Timing of offence
- Victim compelled to leave their home, school, etc
- Failure to comply with current court orders
- Offence committed whilst on licence
- Presence of others, especially other children
- Any steps taken to prevent the victim reporting an incident, obtaining assistance and/or from assisting or supporting the prosecution
- Attempts to dispose of or conceal evidence
- Failure of offender to respond to previous warnings
- Commission of offence whilst under the influence of alcohol or drugs
- Victim encouraged to recruit others

Mitigating factors

- No previous convictions or no relevant/recent convictions
- Remorse
- Previous good character and/or exemplary conduct*
- Age and/or lack of maturity where it affects the responsibility of the offender
- Mental disorder or learning disability, particularly where linked to the commission of the offence
- Sexual activity was incited but no activity took place because the offender voluntarily desisted or intervened to prevent it
- Demonstration of steps taken to address offending behaviour

* Previous good character/exemplary conduct is different from having no previous convictions. The more serious the offence, the less the weight which should normally be attributed to this factor. Where previous good character/exemplary conduct has been used to facilitate the offence, this mitigation should not normally be allowed and such conduct may constitute an aggravating factor.

As appears from its consultation, the Sentencing Council included "victim compelled to leave their home, school etc" as an aggravating factor because of the type of offender likely to be charged with this offence. Where, for example, the victim has had to change schools because the offender was their teacher, the long-term effect of the disruption to their education should be reflected in an upward movement from the starting point. "Failure of offender to respond to previous warnings" is included to cover situations where, for example, a teacher has been warned by the school about becoming too close to a pupil and has then proceeded to engage in sexual activity with that pupil.

Steps Three to Nine

5.11D   The remaining steps cover the following points. At step three the court should consider any factors which would indicate a reduction in sentence, e.g. assistance to the prosecution. At step four it should consider any reduction for a guilty plea. At step five the court should consider dangerousness, i.e. whether it would be appropriate to award an extended sentence (s.226A of the CJA 2003). Step six requires the court to consider whether the total sentence is just and proportionate to the offending behaviour. At step seven it should consider whether to make an ancillary order (e.g. a compensation order, a sexual offences prevention order ("SOPO") or a restraining order). Step eight requires the court to fulfil its duty under s.174 of the CJA 2003 to give reasons for, and explain the effect of, the sentence. Finally, at step nine the court should consider whether to give credit for time spent on bail in accordance with s.240A of that Act.

Sentencing examples

5.12   In *Cornwall*,[4] which was decided before the new guideline came into effect, the appellant schoolteacher (26) pleaded guilty to three offences of causing or inciting a child to engage in sexual activity, contrary to s.17(1).[5] A pupil (16) at the appellant's school, who was not taught by him, contacted him on Facebook. Over an eight-month period he sent her text messages that became increasingly explicit, describing the sexual activity he wanted to indulge in with her and asking her to send pictures of herself. She sent picture of herself in a bikini and topless. Two months after contact with the first pupil ceased, the offender contacted another pupil (14) on Facebook. Using that means and text messages he described the sexual activity he wanted to engage in with her and suggested they meet. She told a friend about the messages and the friend told the school. In sentencing, the judge treated the offences as falling in category 1 of the guideline issued by the Sentencing Guidelines Council. He sentenced the appellant to 16 months' imprisonment concurrent on each count, with a SOPO and an order under s.28 of the Criminal Justice and Courts Services Act 2000 disqualifying him from working with children. On appeal against sentence, the Court of Appeal noted that the judge had treated the offences as aggravated by the prolonged nature of the offending, the fact that there was more than one victim and the abuse of trust.

---

[4] [2012] EWCA Crim 1227.

[5] The reference to the charges is taken from the official transcript. However, if the appellant was indeed charged with "causing or inciting" then the indictment was duplicitous, as "causing" and "inciting" should be regarded for the purposes of s.17 as constituting two separate offences: see para.5.40 of the main work.

However, in the Court's view the judge had misjudged the appellant's activity. The offences were offences of inciting only, and no sexual activity actually took place. One of the girls had instigated the contact. The judge should not have rejected the appellant's loss of career as a mitigating factor. This resulted in the judge pitching the offences at a level which was much higher in terms of seriousness than was justified by the facts of the case. In the Court's judgment, the appropriate sentence after trial would have been no more than 6 months. Giving the appellant credit for his early guilty plea, the Court substituted a sentence of 4 months concurrent on each count. It also set aside the SOPO as the appellant would never again be in a position of trust working with children, as the disqualification from working with children meant that he would be placed on the barred list by the Independent Safeguarding Authority (now the Disclosure and Barring Service).

The decision in *Cornwall* appears somewhat generous. The appellant's loss of his career undoubtedly deserved to be treated as mitigation. However, the fact that the offences involved only incitement and no actual sexual activity appears to have been purely fortuitous. The new guideline treats the absence of sexual activity as a mitigating factor only where the offender voluntarily desisted or intervened to prevent the activity taking place (and not, say, where the only reason the activity did not take place was the reluctance of the victim or the arrival of a third party). Finally, although the Court treated as a mitigating factor the fact that one of the victims initiated contact, it appears from the transcript that contact was initially in non-sexual terms and it was the appellant who introduced the sexual element. Further, the initiation of sexual contact by the victim does not appear in the list of mitigating factors in the new sentencing guideline for ss.16 and 17. Indeed, whilst the listed factors are not exhaustive, the decision in *Att Gen's Ref (No.53 of 2013) (R. v Wilson)*[5a] indicates that where an offender takes advantage of sexual advances made by the victim this may well operate as an aggravating, rather than a mitigating factor.

PARTIES TO THE OFFENCE

We considered in the main work whether, if the victim of an offence under s.16 **5.15** encourages the offence, they are liable to conviction as an accessory. We noted the argument for applying here the principle in *Tyrrell*,[6] in which it was held that a young girl could not be convicted as accessory to an offence of having unlawful carnal knowledge with a girl under 16 committed against herself, as the offence was created to protect girls against men and there was no indication in the statute of an intention to criminalise the girls themselves. The abuse of trust offences were clearly created to protect children under 18 from sexual exploitation by adults with whom they are in a relationship of trust, and there is no provision in the Act which would criminalise children who engage in sexual activity with such an adult. However, given our earlier conclusion that *Tyrrell* did not apply to the

---

[5a] [2013] EWCA Crim 2544, concerning the offence of sexual activity with a child (s.9 of the 2003 Act) and discussed in para.4.25C, above; see also para.5.15, below.
[6] [1894] 1 Q.B. 710; and see *DPP v Whitehouse* [1977] Q.B. 868.

under-13 and child sex offences in the 2003 Act, we suggested that, in order to avoid some potentially strange results, it should be taken to have no application to the abuse of trust offences either.

Of relevance to this point is a passage in the reasoning of the Supreme Court in the decision in *Gnango*.[7] In that case, the majority held (Lord Kerr dissenting) that where D1 and D2 voluntarily enter into a fight against each other, each intending to kill or cause grievous bodily harm to the other and each foreseeing that the other has a reciprocal intention, and where D1 mistakenly kills a third party (V) in the course of the fight, then not only D1 but also D2 is guilty of murdering V. The significance of the decision for present purposes is that in the course of its reasoning the majority considered the decision in *Tyrrell*, which it said was an illustration of a general rule[8] that where legislation creates an offence that is intended to protect a class of persons, a member of that class cannot be convicted as an accessory to such an offence committed in respect of him. Defined in this broad way, the rule in *Tyrrell* would certainly operate to prevent the victim of an abuse of trust offence from being prosecuted as an accessory to the offence, since these offences are clearly intended to protect the class of persons comprising children, and a child cannot be convicted of the offences as principal.

As a practical matter the point has been put beyond argument by *Att Gen's Ref (No.53 of 2013) (R. v Wilson)*,[8a] in which the defendant pleaded guilty and was sentenced to 8 months' imprisonment for an offence of sexual activity with a child, a girl aged 13, contrary to s.9 of the 2003 Act. The girl was sexually experienced and prosecuting counsel described her in the course of the sentencing hearing as "predatory", a term picked up by the judge in his sentencing remarks. On a reference by the Attorney General under s.36 of the Criminal Justice Act 1988, the Court of Appeal held that the sentence was plainly unduly lenient. In doing so, it accepted the Attorney General's submission that the fact that the victim had initiated what had happened was an aggravating, rather than a mitigating, factor. Lord Thomas C.J. said[8b]:

> "It has been clear since at least the Offences Against the Person Act 1861, and subsequent nineteenth century legislation, that the purpose of Parliament in passing legislation to make it a crime punishable with imprisonment to have sexual relations with those under 16 was to protect those under 16. Indeed the Criminal Law Amendments Act 1885 makes it expressly clear that that was the purpose of the legislation. That can be seen from the preamble to the Act and was made clear by this court in *R. v Tyrrell* [1894] 1 QB 710.
>
> That long-standing principle is well-known. The reduction of punishment on the basis that the person who needed protection encouraged the commission of an offence is therefore simply wrong. We agree with the submission of the Attorney General that an underage person who encourages sexual relations with her needs more protection, not less. Accepting that as the basis for sentencing for the reasons we have explained,

---

[7] [2011] UKSC 59 at [17]–[19], [47]–[53].

[8] Identified by Professor Glanville Williams in his article "Victims and other exempt parties in crime" (1990) 10 Legal Studies at p.245.

[8a] [2013] EWCA Crim 2544.

[8b] At [19]–[20].

the fact that the offender took advantage of what he asserted the victim did aggravated the offence."

If a child who initiates sexual relations is more in need of the law's protection than other child victims, it is almost inconceivable that the public interest would ever require the prosecution of a child in relation to an abuse of trust offence of which she was herself the victim.

"POSITION OF TRUST"

The amendment referred to in fn.29 of the main work came into effect in England **5.21** on April 1, 2011 by virtue of the Children and Young Persons Act 2008 (Commencement No.3, Saving and Transitional Provisions) Order 2010 (SI 2010/2981).

Section 21(12) of the 2003 Act was amended with effect from April 6, 2013 by the **5.24** Family Procedure (Modification of Enactments) Order 2011 (SI 2011/1045), art.15, so as to add to the listed positions of trust that in which A is appointed to be the children's guardian of B under r.59 of the Family Procedure (Adoption) Rules 2005 (SI 2005/2795) or r.16.3(1)(ii) or r.16.4 of the Family Procedure Rules 2010 (SI 2010/2955).

The position of the NSPCC, and of the Child Protection in Sport Unit established **5.26** on a partnership basis by the NSPCC and Sport England, Sport Northern Ireland and Sport Wales, is that sports coaches should be brought within the scope of the abuse of trust offences.[9]

ABUSE OF POSITION OF TRUST: CAUSING OR INCITING A CHILD TO ENGAGE IN SEXUAL ACTIVITY

MODE OF TRIAL AND PUNISHMENT

For convictions on or after December 3, 2012,[10] an offence under s.17 is a specified **5.41** offence for the purposes of s.226A of the CJA 2003 (extended sentence for certain violent or sexual offences), irrespective of the date of commission of the offence.

SENTENCING

The Sentencing Council has issued a new guideline applicable to the sex offenders **5.42** aged 18 or over who are sentenced on or after April 1, 2014: see para.1.20 et seq.,

[9] *http://www.wru.co.uk/downloads/Abuse_of_positions_of_trust_within_sport_wdf81074.pdf* [accessed December 23, 2013].

[10] When s.124 of the Legal Aid, Sentencing and Punishment of Offenders Act 2012 was brought into force by the Legal Aid, Sentencing and Punishment of Offenders Act 2012 (Commencement No.4 and Saving Provisions) Order 2012 (SI 2012/2906).

above. A single guideline covers the offences under ss.16 and 17 of the 2003 Act and is considered at para.5.11 et seq., above.

ABUSE OF POSITION OF TRUST: ENGAGING IN SEXUAL ACTIVITY IN THE PRESENCE OF A CHILD

MODE OF TRIAL AND PUNISHMENT

5.61   For convictions on or after December 3, 2012,[11] an offence under s.18 is a specified offence for the purposes of s.226A of the CJA 2003 (extended sentence for certain violent or sexual offences), irrespective of the date of commission of the offence.

SENTENCING

5.62   The Sentencing Council has issued a new guideline applicable to sex offenders aged 18 or over who are sentenced on or after April 1, 2014: see para.1.20 et seq., above. In its consultation on the draft guideline,[12] the Council noted that the offences in ss.18 and 19 of the 2003 Act mirror those in ss.11 and 12 of the Act, and accordingly proposed to cover them in the same way in a single guideline. This is the course it duly followed.

New sentencing guideline

Step One—Harm and culpability

5.62A   Under the new guideline, the sentencing court is to go through a series of steps in order to determine the appropriate sentence. Step one involves determining the offence category by reference to the degree of harm caused and then the culpability level for the offence. In this guideline, the Sentencing Council adopted the approach to harm and culpability that it took in the guideline for offences under ss.11 and 12 of the Act, discussed at para.4.67, above. The harm and culpability factors for offences under ss.18 and 19 are accordingly as follows:

---

[11] When s.124 of the Legal Aid, Sentencing and Punishment of Offenders Act 2012 was brought into force by the the Legal Aid, Sentencing and Punishment of Offenders Act 2012 (Commencement No.4 and Saving Provisions) Order 2012 (SI 2012/2906).

[12] *Sexual Offences Guideline: Consultation* (December 6, 2012).

HARM		CULPABILITY	
Category 1	• Causing victim to view extreme pornography • Causing victim to view indecent/prohibited images of children • Engaging in, or causing a victim to view live, sexual activity involving sadism/violence/sexual activity with an animal/ a child	**A**	
		• Significant degree of planning • Offender acts together with others to commit the offence • Use of alcohol/drugs on victim to facilitate the offence • Grooming behaviour used against victim • Use of threats (including blackmail)	
Category 2	Engaging in, or causing a victim to view images of or view live, sexual activity involving: • penetration of vagina or anus (using body or object) • penile penetration of mouth • masturbation	• Specific targeting of a particularly vulnerable child • Commercial exploitation and/or motivation • Offence racially or religiously aggravated • Offence motivated by, or demonstrating, hostility to the victim based on his or her sexual orientation (or presumed sexual orientation) or transgender identity (or presumed transgender identity)	
Category 3	Factor(s) in categories 1 and 2 not present	• Offence motivated by, or demonstrating, hostility to the victim based on his or her disability (or presumed disability)	
		B	
		Factor(s) in category A not present	

Step Two—Starting point and category range

Having determined the offence category and culpability level, the court should **5.62B** then use the corresponding starting point specified in the guideline in order to reach a sentence within the category range. The starting point applies to all offenders irrespective of plea or previous convictions. Once the starting point has been determined, step two allows further adjustment for aggravating or mitigating features, set out below. A case of particular gravity, reflected by multiple features of culpability or harm, could merit upward adjustment from the starting point before further adjustment for aggravating or mitigating features. Where there is a sufficient prospect of rehabilitation, a community order with a sex offender treatment programme requirement under s.202 of the CJA 2003 may be a proper alternative to a short or moderate length custodial sentence. The starting points and category ranges for offences under ss.18 and 19 of the Act are as follows:

	A	B
Category 1	**Starting point** 18 months' custody **Category range** 1–2 years' custody	**Starting point** 1 year's custody **Category range** 26 weeks'–18 months' custody
Category 2	**Starting Point** 1 year's custody **Category range** 26 weeks'–18 months' custody	**Starting Point** 26 weeks' custody **Category range** High level community order–1 year's custody
Category 3	**Starting Point** 26 weeks' custody **Category range** High level community order–1 year's custody	**Starting Point** Medium level community order **Category range** Low level community order–High level community order

Although this guideline uses very similar factors to determine the offence categories as the guideline for offences under ss.11 and 12, the starting points and ranges are lower in order to reflect the fact that the statutory maximum under ss.18 and 19 is 5 years, as opposed to 10 years under ss.11 and 12.

In the previous guideline, issued in 2007 by the Sentencing Guidelines Council, the starting point and ranges for an offender who had consensual intercourse in the presence of the victim, contrary to s.18, were higher (at 2 years and 1–4 years) than for an offender who had penetrative intercourse with the victim, contrary to s.16 (18 months and 1 year to 2 years 6 months). The Sentencing Council accepted in its consultation that both forms of activity should have a custodial starting point but saw no justification for the difference between the two scenarios, and accordingly the starting point and ranges in the new guideline are the same in both cases.

Aggravating and mitigating factors

5.62C After identifying the starting point and category range, the court should consider whether the presence of aggravating or mitigating factors should result in an upward or downward adjustment from the starting point or the imposition of a sentence outside the category range. In particular, relevant recent convictions are likely to result in an upward adjustment. When sentencing appropriate category 2 or 3 offences, the court should also consider whether the custody threshold has been passed; if so, whether a custodial sentence is unavoidable; and if it is, whether that sentence can be suspended. The non-exhaustive list of aggravating and mitigating factors for offences under ss.18 and 19 is as follows:

Aggravating factors
Statutory aggravating factors
• Previous convictions, having regard to a) the nature of the offence to which the conviction relates and its relevance to the current offence; and b) the time that has elapsed since the conviction
• Offence committed whilst on bail
Other aggravating factors
• Location of offence
• Timing of offence
• Victim compelled to leave their home, school, etc
• Failure to comply with current court orders
• Offence committed whilst on licence
• Presence of others, especially other children
• Any steps taken to prevent the victim reporting an incident, obtaining assistance and/or from assisting or supporting the prosecution
• Attempts to dispose of or conceal evidence
• Failure of offender to respond to previous warnings
• Commission of offence whilst under the influence of alcohol or drugs
• Victim encouraged to recruit others

Mitigating factors
• No previous convictions or no relevant/recent convictions
• Remorse
• Previous good character and/or exemplary conduct*
• Age and/or lack of maturity where it affects the responsibility of the offender
• Mental disorder or learning disability, particularly where linked to the commission of the offence
• Demonstration of steps taken to address offending behaviour

> * Previous good character/exemplary conduct is different from having no previous convictions. The more serious the offence, the less the weight which should normally be attributed to this factor. Where previous good character/exemplary conduct has been used to facilitate the offence, this mitigation should not normally be allowed and such conduct may constitute an aggravating factor.

The non-statutory aggravating factors are the same as in the guideline for ss.16 and 17, discussed at para.5.11 et seq., above, except that "ejaculation" and "pregnancy or STI as a consequence of offence" are omitted as they are irrelevant to offences under ss.18 and 19, which involve causing a child to view, rather than to engage in, sexual activity.

Steps Three to Nine

5.62D The remaining steps cover the following points. At step three the court should consider any factors which would indicate a reduction in sentence, e.g. assistance to the prosecution. At step four it should consider any reduction for a guilty plea. At step five the court should consider dangerousness, i.e. whether it would be appropriate to award an extended sentence (s.226A of the CJA 2003). Step six requires the court to consider whether the total sentence is just and proportionate to the offending behaviour. At step seven it should consider whether to make an ancillary order (e.g. a compensation order, a SOPO or a restraining order). Step eight requires the court to fulfil its duty under s.174 of the CJA 2003 to give reasons for, and explain the effect of, the sentence. Finally, at step nine the court should consider whether to give credit for time spent on bail in accordance with s.240A of that Act.

ABUSE OF POSITION OF TRUST: CAUSING A CHILD TO WATCH A SEXUAL ACT

MODE OF TRIAL AND PUNISHMENT

5.80 For convictions on or after December 3, 2012,[13] an offence under s.19 is a specified offence for the purposes of s.226A of the CJA 2003 (extended sentence for certain violent or sexual offences), irrespective of the date of commission of the offence.

SENTENCING

5.81 The Sentencing Council has issued a new guideline applicable to sex offenders aged 18 or over who are sentenced on or after April 1, 2014: see para.1.20 et seq., above. A single guideline covers the offences under ss.18 and 19 of the 2003 Act and is considered at para.5.62 et seq., above.

---

[13] When s.124 of the Legal Aid, Sentencing and Punishment of Offenders Act 2012 was brought into force by the Legal Aid, Sentencing and Punishment of Offenders Act 2012 (Commencement No.4 and Saving Provisions) Order 2012 (SI 2012/2906).

CHAPTER 6

FAMILIAL SEXUAL OFFENCES*

INTRODUCTION

Sex with an adult relative

Whether the criminalisation of consensual sexual intercourse between siblings is **6.07**
compatible with art.8 of the ECHR was considered in *Stubing v Germany*.[1] The
complainant (S) was estranged from his natural family between the ages of 3 and
24. When reunited, S and his sister (K), of whose existence he was previously
unaware, lived together for several years and had consensual sexual intercourse,
producing four children. S was convicted three times of incest under the German
Criminal Code and jailed. K, who was found to be only partially liable for her
actions on account of a serious personality disorder and mild learning disabilities,
was not sentenced. S contended that his convictions had violated his art.8 right to
respect for his family life by preventing him from participating in the upbringing
of his children and interfering with his sex life. The European Court of Human
Rights dismissed the complaint, holding that although S's conviction of incest
interfered with his right to respect for his private life, which included his sex life,
the interference was in accordance with the law and pursued a legitimate aim
within the meaning of art.8(2), namely the protection of morals and of the rights
of others. As to whether it was necessary in a democratic society, the Court noted
the broad consensus in the contracting States that sexual relationships between
siblings are accepted neither by the legal order nor by society as a whole, from
which it followed that the domestic authorities enjoy a wide margin of appreciation
in determining how to confront sexual relationships between consenting family

---

* The authors are indebted to William Hotham, Barrister, of Six Pump Court, for his enormous
assistance in updating this chapter.
[1] [2013] 1 F.C.R. 107.

members. The Federal Constitutional Court, having analysed the arguments put forward in favour of and against criminal liability, and relying on an expert opinion, had concluded that the imposition of criminal liability was justified by "a combination of objectives, including the protection of the family, self-determination and public health, set against the background of a common conviction that incest should be subject to criminal liability". The Court found these aims "not unreasonable" and also relevant to S's case, and accordingly concluded that his conviction corresponded to a pressing social need such that the German courts had acted within their margin of appreciation in convicting him.

The decision relates to siblings and will not necessarily be determinative of an art.8 challenge by someone convicted under s.64 or s.65 of the 2003 Act for having or consenting to sex with a more distant adult relative.

SEXUAL ACTIVITY WITH A CHILD FAMILY MEMBER

MODE OF TRIAL AND PUNISHMENT

6.11　From December 3, 2012, when ss.122–128 of the Legal Aid, Sentencing and Punishment of Offenders Act 2012 were brought into force[2]:
- For offences committed on or after that date, an offence under s.25 is listed in Pt 1 of Sch.15B to the Criminal Justice Act 2003 ("CJA 2003") for the purposes of s.224A of that Act (life sentence for second listed offence).
- For convictions on or after that date (irrespective of the date of commission of the offence), an offence under s.25 is a specified offence for the purposes of s.226A of that Act (extended sentence for certain violent or sexual offences).

SENTENCING

6.13　New sentencing guideline

The Sentencing Council has issued a new guideline applicable to sex offenders aged 18 or over who are sentenced on or after April 1, 2014: see para.1.20 et seq., above. Under the new guideline, the sentencing court is to go through a series of steps in order to determine the appropriate sentence.

Step One—Harm and culpability

6.13A　Step one involves determining the offence category by reference to the degree of harm caused and then the culpability level for the offence. For offences under ss.25 and 26 of the 2003 Act, the court should determine which categories of harm and culpability the offence falls into by reference only to the tables below. As these

---

[2] By the Legal Aid, Sentencing and Punishment of Offenders Act 2012 (Commencement No.4 and Saving Provisions) Order 2012 (SI 2012/2906).

offences involve those who have a family relationship with the victim, the court should assume that the greater the abuse of trust within the relationship, the more grave the offence. The harm and culpability factors in relation to ss.25 and 26 are as follows:

HARM		CULPABILITY	
Category 1	• Penetration of vagina or anus (using body or object) • Penile penetration of mouth in either case by, or of, the victim	**A** • Significant degree of planning • Offender acts together with others to commit the offence • Use of alcohol/drugs on victim to facilitate the offence • Grooming behaviour used against victim • Use of threats (including blackmail) • Sexual images of victim recorded, retained, solicited or shared • Specific targeting of a particularly vulnerable child • Significant disparity in age • Commercial exploitation and/or motivation • Offence racially or religiously aggravated • Offence motivated by, or demonstrating, hostility to the victim based on his or her sexual orientation (or presumed sexual orientation) or transgender identity (or presumed transgender identity) • Offence motivated by, or demonstrating, hostility to the victim based on his or her disability (or presumed disability)	
Category 2	• Touching of naked genitalia or naked breasts by, or of, the victim		
Category 3	• Other sexual activity		
		B	
		Factor(s) in category A not present	

Step Two—Starting point and category range

Having determined the offence category and culpability level, the court should then use the corresponding starting point specified in the guideline in order to   6.13B reach a sentence within the category range. The starting point applies to all offenders irrespective of plea or previous convictions. Once the starting point has been determined, step two allows further adjustment for aggravating or mitigating features, as set out below. A case of particular gravity, reflected by multiple features of culpability or harm, could merit upward adjustment from the starting point before further adjustment for aggravating or mitigating features. Where there is a sufficient prospect of rehabilitation, a community order with a sex offender treatment programme requirement under s.202 of the CJA 2003 can be a proper alternative to a short or moderate length custodial sentence. The starting points and category ranges for offences under ss.25 and 26 are as follows:

	A	B
Category 1	**Starting point** 6 years' custody **Category range** 4–10 years' custody	**Starting point** 3 years 6 months' custody **Category range** 2 years 6 months'–5 years' custody
Category 2	**Starting point** 4 years' custody **Category range** 2–6 years' custody	**Starting point** 18 months' custody **Category range** 26 weeks'–2 years 6 months' custody
Category 3	**Starting point** 1 year's custody **Category range** High level community order–3 years' custody	**Starting point** Medium level community order **Category range** Low level community order–High level community order

Aggravating and mitigating factors

6.13C   After identifying the starting point and category range, the court should consider whether the presence of aggravating or mitigating factors should result in an upward or downward adjustment from the starting point or the imposition of a sentence outside the category range. In particular, relevant recent convictions are likely to result in an upward adjustment. When sentencing appropriate category 3 offences, the court should also consider whether the custody threshold has been passed; if so, whether a custodial sentence is unavoidable; and if it is, whether that sentence can be suspended. The non-exhaustive list of aggravating and mitigating factors for offences under ss.25 and 26 is as follows:

Aggravating factors
Statutory aggravating factors
• Previous convictions, having regard to a) the nature of the offence to which the conviction relates and its relevance to the current offence; and b) the time that has elapsed since the conviction • Offence committed whilst on bail
Other aggravating factors
• Severe psychological or physical harm • Ejaculation • Pregnancy or STI as a consequence of offence • Location of offence • Timing of offence • Victim compelled to leave their home, school, etc • Failure to comply with current court orders • Offence committed whilst on licence • Exploiting contact arrangements with a child to commit an offence • Presence of others, especially other children • Any steps taken to prevent the victim reporting an incident, obtaining assistance and/or from assisting or supporting the prosecution • Attempts to dispose of or conceal evidence • Failure of offender to respond to previous warnings • Commission of offence whilst under the influence of alcohol or drugs • Victim encouraged to recruit others • Period over which offence committed

Mitigating factors
• No previous convictions or no relevant/recent convictions • Remorse • Previous good character and/or exemplary conduct*

- Age and/or lack of maturity where it affects the responsibility of the offender
- Mental disorder or learning disability, particularly where linked to the commission of the offence
- Sexual activity was incited but no activity took place because the offender voluntarily desisted or intervened to prevent it

---

* Previous good character/exemplary conduct is different from having no previous convictions. The more serious the offence, the less the weight which should normally be attributed to this factor. Where previous good character/exemplary conduct has been used to facilitate the offence, this mitigation should not normally be allowed and such conduct may constitute an aggravating factor.

In the context of this offence, previous good character/exemplary conduct should not normally be given any significant weight and will not normally justify a reduction in what would otherwise be the appropriate sentence.

Steps Three to Nine

6.13D The remaining steps cover the following points. At step three the court should consider any factors which would indicate a reduction in sentence, e.g. assistance to the prosecution. At step four it should consider any reduction for a guilty plea. At step five the court should consider dangerousness, i.e. whether it would be appropriate to award a life sentence (s.224A of the CJA 2003) or an extended sentence (s.226A). Step six requires the court to consider whether the total sentence is just and proportionate to the offending behaviour. At step seven it should consider whether to make an ancillary order (e.g. a compensation order, a sexual offences prevention order ("SOPO") or a restraining order). Step eight requires the court to fulfil its duty under s.174 of the CJA 2003 to give reasons for, and explain the effect of, the sentence. Finally, at step nine the court should consider whether to give credit for time spent on bail in accordance with s.240A of that Act.

Offenders under 18

6.17 The definitive guideline does not apply to offences committed by offenders under the age of 18. Broader work on youth guidelines will commence in August 2014. In the meantime, the guideline states that sentencers must in particular follow the definitive guideline *Overarching Principles – Sentencing Youths*, and have regard to the principal aim of the youth justice system (to prevent offending by children and young people) and the welfare of the young offender.

Sentencing examples

6.18 The following examples predate the new definitive guideline but are useful examples of the approach taken by the Court of Appeal under the previous guideline to different factual scenarios.

Offender against daughter

In *Att Gen's Ref (No.124 of 2010)*,[3] the offender (F) pleaded guilty to one count 6.18A
of sexual activity with a child family member contrary to s.25 of the 2003 Act
committed against his 17-year-old daughter. He had kissed, fondled the breasts
and digitally penetrated the vagina of his daughter. It was F's birthday and he and
the victim had been drinking at his house. He surrendered to the police and made
full admissions in interview. Nothing like this incident had occurred before. The
probation report opined that F sought to suggest that the victim was complicit in
the offence, but that he did show an awareness of the impact on the victim and a
genuine willingness to try and understand his offending behaviour. F was assessed
as a high risk of re-offending but a low risk of harm to the general public. He had
two previous convictions which tended to demonstrate problems with alcohol but
no offences of a sexual nature. F was sentenced to 40 weeks' imprisonment
suspended for 2 years with a 2-year supervision order. On a reference, it was
argued on behalf of the Attorney General that the offence was aggravated by an
abuse of trust and authority and the close familial relationship. The Court said one
must be very careful in classifying these as aggravating features, because the
offence itself is one that necessarily involves a close familial relationship and
therefore, normally, a breach of trust. However it accepted that this case involved
the closest possible familial relationship, namely father and daughter. The offence
was aggravated by the fact that F was drinking with his 17-year-old daughter who
was also, to his knowledge, drinking heavily. Further, the victim expressed
unwillingness to become involved in F's activity and his failure to heed this was
also an aggravating factor. As to mitigation, the offender made full admissions to
the police at the earliest opportunity and followed that with the earliest possible
indication of an intention to plead guilty. He had shown remorse and the victim
was only two or three days off being 18 years old. The Court said that the relevant
category in the sentencing guideline was the first, involving penetration of the
vagina with another body part, albeit not penile penetration, which had a starting
point of 5 years and a sentencing range of 4–8 years. It said that in view of the
mitigating circumstances and in particular the fact that the victim was very nearly
18, the proper starting point was at the lower end, namely 4 years. With a
deduction of a third to represent the very early plea and remorse, the sentence
came down to 2 years 8 months. Given that F had not been sentenced to custody
and had already completed a number of the requirements under the order that was
made, the right sentence was one of 2 years' imprisonment.

Compare *R. v H*,[4] in which the offender (67) pleaded guilty to 15 sexual offences 6.18B
comprising two offences of rape, one of assault by penetration (s.2 of the 2003
Act), five of sexual activity with a child family member (s.25), four of inciting a
child family member to engage in sexual activity (s.26) and two of causing a child

---

[3] [2011] EWCA Crim 337.
[4] [2012] EWCA Crim 1521.

under 13 to engage in sexual activity (s.4). He was sentenced to 16 years' imprisonment comprising 12 years for the two rape counts, 4 years consecutive for one offence of causing a child under 13 to engage in sexual activity and concurrent terms of different lengths for the remaining offences. All the offences except the rapes were specimen offences. The case involved the systematic sexual abuse of the offender's two young daughters over a five-year period. H started abusing E when she was 11, beginning with simulated intercourse, followed by raping her without protection when she was 13, painfully inserting a vibrator insider her, and causing her to masturbate him on several occasions. He also caused G to masturbate him when she was aged 11. His offending culminated in a final act of forcefully raping E when she was aged 16. The judge stated that he had considered the sentencing guidelines and given H full credit for his guilty pleas, and that he had borne in mind H's age, his lack of previous convictions, his remorse and also the contents of a psychiatric report which indicated that H had suffered from an adjustment disorder with emotional disturbance, albeit he had responded well to treatment. H argued that the judge had adopted too high a starting point and taken insufficient account of his mitigation, remorse, previous good character, the lengthy period after his interview before sentence, the impact of imprisonment on a person of his age, and in particular the principle of totality. His appeal was allowed. In relation to the offences against E, the sentencing guideline indicated a starting point of 15 years with a sentencing range of 13–19 years for the repeated rape of the same victim, and a starting point of 10 years with a sentencing range of 8–13 years for a rape accompanied by an abuse of trust for a victim aged 13 or over but under 16. However, that was before any additional aggravating features: here, there was repeated serious sexual abuse. Whichever way the case was put, the judge was right to categorise the case as extremely serious, and the facts in relation to E were all capable of justifying a sentence of 18 years before any discount for a guilty plea. While the sentence imposed was at the high end of the range, it was not by itself appealable. As to the offences against G, the starting point for masturbation involving a child under 13 was 5 years with a sentencing range of 4–8 years. G was 11 at the time of the incidents and there were a number of them. In isolation, a sentence of 6 years before a discount for a guilty plea was justified. The question was whether the sentences should have been ordered to run consecutively and in full. The principle of totality was that a total sentence should be passed that reflected all of the offending behaviour, and was justified and proportionate. In light of the mitigation as a whole, including H's age, the sentence was manifestly excessive and the appropriate total sentence was 12 years' imprisonment.

Offender against step-daughter aged 17

6.18C   In *R. v P*[5] the appellant (P) pleaded guilty to three counts of sexual activity with a child family member (s.25). P had been the victim's (C's) stepfather since she

---

[5] [2011] EWCA Crim 1925.

was 10 years old and sexual intercourse had begun when she was 17. The counts against P were specimen counts to cover the course of conduct until C was 18, although the sexual activity continued after that. P entered a basis of plea, accepted by the prosecution, in which he denied that he had manipulated or groomed C and stated that it was C who had indicated that she wanted the relationship to become intimate. A pre-sentence report stated that P was minimising his conduct, described the likelihood of re-offending as between medium and low and indicated that if reoffending happened it would most likely occur in a similar context. The judge sentenced P to 12 months' imprisonment on each count concurrently. P argued that the sentence should have been suspended, particularly as he was suffering from health problems. The Court of Appeal upheld the decision of the judge at first instance not to suspend the sentence. It said that ordinarily an immediate custodial sentence was appropriate in such a case, citing *Att Gen's Ref (No.50 of 2008)*.[6] The sentence awarded was entirely appropriate given the seriousness of the offending, the grave breach of trust and P's efforts to minimise his behaviour. The judge had not been obliged to suspend the sentence, and it would have been remarkable had he done so.

Offender against step-daughter aged 16

In *R v A*[7] the appellant (X) pleaded guilty to an offence of sexual activity with a   6.18D
child family member (s.25) and was sentenced to 3 years' imprisonment. X had purportedly had a consensual sexual relationship, and fathered a child, with his step-daughter (C) during an eight-month period when she was aged 16 and 17. X used to be married to C's mother. C was conceived in another relationship when X and her mother split up for a while, but they were reconciled when C was a baby and she was brought up to have a normal father/daughter relationship with X until the age of six when she was taken into care. Thereafter, she had no contact with him until she got in touch when she was 16 and moved into his one-bedroom flat. X pleaded guilty at the earliest opportunity and was treated by the sentencing judge as being a person of good character who was entitled to substantial credit. However, he found that X had taken advantage of C's immaturity and vulnerability, repeatedly having unprotected sexual intercourse and deliberately bringing about pregnancy. He also found that the 35-year age difference was an aggravating feature. X submitted that the sentence was manifestly excessive in that the judge had not given enough credit for his frank admissions, his guilty plea, his good character, and the harmoniousness of the situation. He also complained that the judge had not taken account of the limited period during which he was C's stepfather. The appeal was allowed. The Court of Appeal said that the sentencing guideline suggested a sentencing range of 1–4 years' custody for a case of penile penetration. The judge's starting point must have been towards the top of the range, which was not justified in the absence of the aggravating features of

---

[6] [2009] EWCA Crim 289, referred to in the main work.
[7] [2012] EWCA Crim 1824.

coercion or grooming. A custodial sentence was inevitable to mark X's breach of trust and the advantage he took of C's immaturity, but in view of the early plea and the frank admissions, the right sentence was one of 2 years' imprisonment.

Offender against stepdaughter aged 13–17/18

6.18E   In *R. v B*[8] the appellant (B) pleaded guilty to six counts of sexual activity with a child family member (s.25) and received a sentence of imprisonment for public protection with a minimum term of 3 years. The victim (V) was B's step-daughter. The offending began when she was 13 and lasted until she was 17 or 18. All of the sexual activity was purportedly consensual. When V was 13, B began to press himself against her and to fondle her breasts. He then progressed to digitally penetrating her vagina. When she was 14, the offending escalated to full sexual intercourse, which occurred at least twice a week. In her victim impact statement, V's mother stated that the offending had totally destroyed the family; V had nightmares and they had had to move house as V could not bring herself to enter certain rooms; she described V as having become a recluse and was worried for her future well-being. The pre-sentence report referred to B's distorted thinking skills, to his avoiding full responsibility for the offending and placing the weight of responsibility on V, and to his lack of recognition of the seriousness of the offences and the breach of trust involved; it stated that he posed a high risk of harm to children within the community. On appeal against sentence, B argued that the sentencing judge had erred in finding him dangerous; alternatively, if that assessment was correct, the future risk that he represented could be met by an extended sentence in conjunction with a SOPO. The Court of Appeal allowed the appeal. The judge had been entitled to conclude that B was dangerous. First, V had been young and vulnerable when the offending began. Second, the abuse had taken place over a lengthy period of time and the offending developed into a consistent and established pattern whereby B was having sexual intercourse with V at least twice a week in return for which he gave her money and gifts. Third, the judge took into account B's poor attitude towards his offending. Fourth, the pre-sentence report provided ample support for a finding of dangerousness. Fifth, the judge had the benefit of presiding over a 10-day trial. Sixth, the victim impact statements made abundantly clear the serious degree of harm that not only V but also her mother had suffered as a result of B's offending. However, applying *Att Gen's Ref (No.55 of 2008)*,[9] the appropriate sentence was an extended sentence with a custodial term of 6 years and an extended licence period of 4 years.

Abuse of trust

6.18F   Abuse of trust is not specified in the guideline either as a factor in "culpability A" or as an aggravating factor. This reflects the view of the Sentencing Council,

---

[8] [2012] EWCA Crim 1417.
[9] [2008] EWCA Crim 2790.

expressed in its consultation on the draft guideline, that abuse of trust is an "inherent feature" of the offences in ss.25 and 26. A similar approach was evident in *Att Gen's Ref (No.124 of 2010)*,[10] in which the Court of Appeal said that one must be very careful before treating a s.25 offence as aggravated by abuse of trust and authority, because the offence necessarily involves a close familial relationship and therefore, normally, a breach of trust. We respectfully agree, and suggest that a s.25 offence may properly be regarded as aggravated by abuse of trust only if there is an element of such abuse which goes clearly beyond the abuse of trust inherent in the offence.

PARTIES TO THE OFFENCE

The principle in *Tyrrell*

In the main work we expressed the view that there is no reason of principle why 6.32 a child who has reached the age of criminal responsibility should not, in appropriate circumstances, be convicted as an accessory to an offence under s.25 committed against them. We considered the decision in *Tyrrell*[11] to have no application in this context, since the offence in that case was created to protect girls against men and there was no indication in the statute of an intention to criminalise the girls themselves. By contrast, a child over the age of criminal responsibility may commit the s.25 offence as a principal, and it is therefore difficult to conclude that they cannot do so as accessory, even where the offence is committed against them. However, of relevance to this point is a passage in the reasoning of the majority of the Supreme Court in the decision in *Gnango*.[12] In that case, the majority held (Lord Kerr dissenting) that where D1 and D2 voluntarily enter into a fight against each other, each intending to kill or cause grievous bodily harm to the other and each foreseeing that the other has a reciprocal intention, and where D1 mistakenly kills a third party (V) in the course of the fight, then not only D1 but also D2 is guilty of murdering V. The significance of the decision for present purposes is that in the course of its reasoning the majority considered the decision in *Tyrrell*, which it said was an illustration of a general rule[13] that where legislation creates an offence that is intended to protect a class of persons, a member of that class cannot be convicted as an accessory to such an offence committed in respect of him. Defined in this broad way, the rule in *Tyrrell* would, contrary to the argument in the main work, operate to prevent the victim of a s.25 offence from being prosecuted as an accessory to the offence, since s.25 was undoubtedly designed to protect children under 18, albeit a child under that age can commit the offence as principal or indeed as accessory where they are not the victim.

[10] Above, fn.3.
[11] [1894] 1 Q.B. 710; and see *DPP v Whitehouse* [1977] Q.B. 868.
[12] [2011] UKSC 59 at [17]–[19], [47]–[53].
[13] Identified by Professor Glanville Williams in his article "Victims and other exempt parties in crime" (1990) 10 Legal Studies at p.245.

As a practical matter the point has been put beyond argument by *Att Gen's Ref (No.53 of 2013) (R. v Wilson)*,[13a] in which the defendant pleaded guilty and was sentenced to 8 months' imprisonment for an offence of sexual activity with a child, a girl aged 13, contrary to s.9 of the 2003 Act. The girl was sexually experienced and prosecuting counsel described her in the course of the sentencing hearing as "predatory", a term picked up by the judge in his sentencing remarks. On a reference by the Attorney General under s.36 of the Criminal Justice Act 1988, the Court of Appeal held that the sentence was plainly unduly lenient. In doing so, it accepted the Attorney General's submission that the fact that the victim had initiated what had happened was an aggravating, rather than a mitigating factor. Lord Thomas C.J. said[13b]:

> "It has been clear since at least the Offences Against the Person Act 1861, and subsequent nineteenth century legislation, that the purpose of Parliament in passing legislation to make it a crime punishable with imprisonment to have sexual relations with those under 16 was to protect those under 16. Indeed the Criminal Law Amendments Act 1885 makes it expressly clear that that was the purpose of the legislation. That can be seen from the preamble to the Act and was made clear by this court in *R. v Tyrrell* [1894] 1 QB 710.
> That long-standing principle is well-known. The reduction of punishment on the basis that the person who needed protection encouraged the commission of an offence is therefore simply wrong. We agree with the submission of the Attorney General that an underage person who encourages sexual relations with her needs more protection, not less. Accepting that as the basis for sentencing for the reasons we have explained, the fact that the offender took advantage of what he asserted the victim did aggravated the offence."

If a child who initiates sexual relations is more in need of the law's protection than other child victims, it is almost inconceivable that the public interest would ever require the prosecution of a child in relation to a s.25 offence of which she was herself the victim.

INCITING A CHILD FAMILY MEMBER TO ENGAGE IN SEXUAL ACTIVITY

Mode of Trial and Punishment

6.48   From December 3, 2012, when ss.122–128 of the Legal Aid, Sentencing and Punishment of Offenders Act 2012 were brought into force[14]:

- For offences committed on or after that date, an offence under s.26 is listed in Pt 1 of Sch.15B to the CJA 2003 for the purposes of s.224A of that Act (life sentence for second listed offence).

[13a] [2013] EWCA Crim 2544.
[13b] At [19]–[20].
[14] By the Legal Aid, Sentencing and Punishment of Offenders Act 2012 (Commencement No.4 and Saving Provisions) Order 2012 (SI 2012/2906).

- For convictions on or after that date (irrespective of the date of commission of the offence), an offence under s.26 is a specified offence for the purposes of s.226A of that Act (extended sentence for certain violent or sexual offences).

SENTENCING

The Sentencing Council has issued a new guideline applicable to sex offenders **6.49** aged 18 or over who are sentenced on or after April 1, 2014: see para.1.20 et seq., above. A single guideline covers offences under ss.25 and 26 of the 2003 Act and is discussed at para.6.13, above.

SEX WITH AN ADULT RELATIVE: PENETRATION

MODE OF TRIAL AND PUNISHMENT

For convictions on or after December 3, 2012,[15] an offence under s.64 is a specified **6.61** offence for the purposes of s.226A of the CJA 2003 (extended sentence for certain violent or sexual offences), irrespective of the date of commission of the offence.

SENTENCING

New sentencing guideline 6.63

The Sentencing Council has issued a new guideline applicable to sex offenders aged 18 or over who are sentenced on or after April 1, 2014: see para.1.20 et seq., above. Under the new guideline, the sentencing court is to go through a series of steps in order to determine the appropriate sentence.

Step One—Harm and culpability

Step one involves determining the offence category by reference to the degree of **6.63A** harm caused and then the culpability level for the offence. For offences under ss.64 and 65 of the 2003 Act, the court should determine the offence category using the tables below, which turn upon whether the harm caused or intended by the offence or the culpability of the offender, or both, are raised. Where an offence does not fall squarely into a category, individual factors may require a degree of weighting before making an overall assessment and determining the appropriate offence category. The categories and harm and culpability factors are as follows:

[15] When s.124 of the Legal Aid, Sentencing and Punishment of Offenders Act 2012 was brought into force by the Legal Aid, Sentencing and Punishment of Offenders Act 2012 (Commencement No.4 and Saving Provisions) Order 2012 (SI 2012/2906).

Category 1	Raised harm **and** raised culpability
Category 2	Raised harm **or** raised culpability
Category 3	Sex with an adult relative **without** raised harm or culpability factors present

Factors indicating raised harm
• Victim is particularly vulnerable due to personal circumstances • Child conceived

Factors indicating raised culpability
• Grooming behaviour used against victim • Use of threats (including blackmail)

Step Two—Starting point and category range

6.63B   Having determined the offence category and culpability level, the court should then use the corresponding starting point specified in the guideline in order to reach a sentence within the category range. The starting point applies to all offenders irrespective of plea or previous convictions. Once the starting point has been determined, step two allows further adjustment for aggravating or mitigating features, as set out below. A case of particular gravity, reflected by multiple features of culpability or harm, could merit upward adjustment from the starting point before further adjustment for aggravating or mitigating features. Where there is a sufficient prospect of rehabilitation, a community order with a sex offender treatment programme requirement under s.202 of the CJA 2003 can be a proper alternative to a short or moderate length custodial sentence. The starting points and category ranges for offences under ss.64 and 65 are as follows:

Category 1	**Starting point** 1 year's custody
	Category range 26 weeks'–2 years' custody
Category 2	**Starting point** High level community order
	Category range Medium level community order–1 year's custody

Category 3	Starting point
	Medium level community order
	Category range
	Band A fine–High level community order

Aggravating and mitigating factors

After identifying the starting point and category range, the court should consider **6.63C** whether the presence of aggravating or mitigating factors should result in an upward or downward adjustment from the starting point or the imposition of a sentence outside the category range. In particular, relevant recent convictions are likely to result in an upward adjustment. When sentencing appropriate category 2 offences, the court should also consider whether the custody threshold has been passed; if so, whether a custodial sentence is unavoidable; and if it is, whether that sentence can be suspended. When sentencing category 3 offences, the court should consider whether the community order threshold has been passed. The non-exhaustive list of aggravating and mitigating factors for offences under ss.64 and 65 is as follows:

Aggravating factors
Statutory aggravating factors
• Previous convictions, having regard to a) the nature of the offence to which the conviction relates and its relevance to the current offence; and b) the time that has elapsed since the conviction
• Offence committed whilst on bail
Other aggravating factors
• Failure to comply with current court orders
• Offence committed whilst on licence
• Failure of offender to respond to previous warnings
• Any steps taken to prevent reporting an incident, obtaining assistance and/or from assisting or supporting the prosecution
• Attempts to dispose of or conceal evidence

Mitigating factors
• No previous convictions **or** no relevant/recent convictions
• Remorse

- Previous good character and/or exemplary conduct*

- Age and/or lack of maturity where it affects the responsibility of the offender

- Mental disorder or learning disability, particularly where linked to the commission of the offence

- Demonstration of steps taken to address offending behaviour

---

* Previous good character/exemplary conduct is different from having no previous convictions. The more serious the offence, the less the weight which should normally be attributed to this factor. Where previous good character/exemplary conduct has been used to facilitate the offence, this mitigation should not normally be allowed and such conduct may constitute an aggravating factor.

Steps Three to Nine

6.63D   The remaining steps cover the following points. At step three the court should consider any factors which would indicate a reduction in sentence, e.g. assistance to the prosecution. At step four it should consider any reduction for a guilty plea. At step five the court should consider dangerousness, i.e. whether it would be appropriate to award an extended sentence (s.226A of the CJA 2003). Step six requires the court to consider whether the total sentence is just and proportionate to the offending behaviour. At step seven it should consider whether to make an ancillary order (e.g. a compensation order, a SOPO or a restraining order). Step eight requires the court to fulfil its duty under s.174 of the CJA 2003 to give reasons for, and explain the effect of, the sentence. Finally, at step nine the court should consider whether to give credit for time spent on bail in accordance with s.240A of that Act.

Sentencing example

6.64A   The decision in *R. v B*[16] predates the new definitive guideline but is a useful example of the approach taken by the Court of Appeal under the previous guideline to a particular factual scenario. In that case the appellant (B), aged 72, pleaded guilty to six counts of indecent assault, two counts of sexual assault and four counts of penetrative sex with an adult relative. He appealed against his sentence of imprisonment for public protection with a minimum term of 4 years together with a concurrent determinate sentence of 5 years' imprisonment. The offences had been committed against his granddaughter (K); they began when she was 10 and ended when she was a young adult. They progressed from touching K's chest area to touching all parts of her body, including the vagina. B also inserted his finger into her vagina and there were four acts of oral sex. In imposing a sentence of imprisonment for public protection, the judge had regard to the pre-sentence report which stated that B showed "a distorted level of internal controls and moral

---

[16] [2012] EWCA Crim 328.

understanding of appropriate behaviour" and that he posed a high risk of serious harm. The Court of Appeal allowed an appeal against sentence. While the judge had approached a difficult sentencing exercise with care, the draconian sanction of imprisonment for public protection was not necessary and appropriate protection could be afforded by the imposition of an extended sentence, with a custodial term of 8 years and an extended period of 2 years.

SEX WITH AN ADULT RELATIVE: CONSENTING TO PENETRATION

MODE OF TRIAL AND PUNISHMENT

For convictions on or after December 3, 2012,[17] an offence under s.65 is a specified   6.77
offence for the purposes of s.226A of the CJA 2003 (extended sentence for certain violent or sexual offences), irrespective of the date of commission of the offence.

SENTENCING

The Sentencing Council has issued a new guideline applicable to sex offenders   6.78
aged 18 or over who are sentenced on or after April 1, 2014: see para.1.20 et seq., above. A single guideline covers offences under ss.64 and 65 of the 2003 Act and is discussed at para.6.63, above.

---

[17] When s.124 of the Legal Aid, Sentencing and Punishment of Offenders Act 2012 was brought into force by the Legal Aid, Sentencing and Punishment of Offenders Act 2012 (Commencement No.4 and Saving Provisions) Order 2012 (SI 2012/2906).

CHAPTER 7

SEXUAL OFFENCES AGAINST THOSE WITH A MENTAL DISORDER*

A. OFFENCES AGAINST PERSONS WITH A MENTAL DISORDER IMPEDING CHOICE

SEXUAL ACTIVITY WITH A PERSON WITH A MENTAL DISORDER IMPEDING CHOICE

MODE OF TRIAL AND PUNISHMENT

An offence contrary to s.30 of the 2003 Act involving penetration is a serious   7.44

---

* The authors are indebted to Alexandra Ward, Barrister, of 9–12 Bell Yard, who was the principal drafter of the update of this chapter.

specified offence for the purposes of ss.224 and 225(2) (life sentences for serious offences) of the Criminal Justice Act 2003 ("CJA 2003"). From December 3, 2012, when ss.122–128 of the Legal Aid, Sentencing and Punishment of Offenders Act 2012 were brought into force[1]:

- For offences committed on or after that date, an offence under s.30 involving penetration is listed in Pt 1 of Sch.15B to the CJA 2003 for the purposes of s.224A of that Act (life sentence for second listed offence).
- For convictions on or after that date (irrespective of the date of commission of the offence), an offence under s.30 is a specified offence for the purposes of s.226A of the CJA 2003 (extended sentence for certain violent or sexual offences).

BAIL

7.46   Section 25 of the Criminal Justice and Public Order Act 1994 was amended with effect from December 3, 2012,[2] so that a person charged with or convicted of an offence to which the section applies shall be granted bail by a constable only if the constable is "of the opinion", rather than "satisfied" (as before), that there are exceptional circumstances which justify it.

SENTENCING

7.47   The Sentencing Council has issued a new guideline applicable to sex offenders aged 18 or over who are sentenced on or after April 1, 2014: see para.1.20 et seq., above. The previous guideline, issued by the Sentencing Guidelines Council in 2007, dealt with offences of mental disorder impeding choice (ss.30–33 of the 2003 Act) and engaging a victim in sexual activity through inducement, threat or deception (ss.34–37) in a single guideline. In its consultation on the draft guideline,[3] the Sentencing Council said it thought these offences should be covered by separate guidelines. Where a victim is unable to refuse, then in practical, if not legal, terms this is likely to have a similar impact to lack of consent in cases where the victim does not have a mental disorder and the Council therefore proposed that the guideline for offences where there is a mental disorder impeding choice should follow a similar structure to the guidelines for rape, assault by penetration and sexual assault (ss.1–3). However, the mental disorder offence of inducement, threat or deception will often involve offender behaviours that are more akin to grooming and exploitation as set out in the guideline for sexual activity with a child (s.9). This may lead to the appearance of a victim having "agreed" to the activity, but the reality is that any apparent agreement will have been obtained by exploitation. This approach was generally welcomed by

---

[1] By the Legal Aid, Sentencing and Punishment of Offenders Act 2012 (Commencement No.4 and Saving Provisions) Order 2012 (SI 2012/2906).

[2] By the Legal Aid, Sentencing and Punishment of Offenders Act 2012, s.90 and Sch.11 para.33, which was brought into force by the Legal Aid, Sentencing and Punishment of Offenders Act 2012 (Commencement No.4 and Saving Provisions) Order 2012, above, fn.1.

[3] *Sexual Offences Guideline: Consultation* (December 6, 2012).

respondents to the consultation and the Council duly followed it in the published guideline.

New sentencing guideline

Step One—Harm and culpability

A single guideline covers the offences in ss.30 and 31 of the 2003 Act (sexual activity with a person with a mental disorder impeding choice and causing or inciting such a person to engage in sexual activity). The sentencing court is to go through a series of steps in order to determine the appropriate sentence. Step one involves determining the offence category by reference to the degree of harm caused and then the culpability level for the offence. The court should determine which categories of harm and culpability the offence falls into by reference only to the tables below: **7.47A**

HARM		CULPABILITY	
Category 1	• The extreme nature of one or more category 2 factors or the extreme impact caused by a combination of category 2 factors **may** elevate to category 1	**A**	
Category 2	• Severe psychological or physical harm • Pregnancy or STI as a consequence of offence • Additional degradation/ humiliation • Abduction • Prolonged detention/ sustained incident • Violence or threats of violence • Forced/uninvited entry into victim's home or residence	• Significant degree of planning • Offender acts together with others to commit the offence • Use of alcohol/drugs on victim to facilitate the offence • Grooming behaviour used against victim • Abuse of trust • Previous violence against victim • Offence committed in course of burglary • Sexual images of victim recorded, retained, solicited or shared • Deliberate isolation of victim • Commercial exploitation and/or motivation • Offence racially or religiously aggravated • Offence motivated by, or demonstrating, hostility to the victim based on his or her sexual orientation (or presumed sexual orientation) or transgender identity (or presumed transgender identity)	
Category 3	Factor(s) in categories 1 and 2 not present		

• Offence motivated by, or demonstrating, hostility to the victim based on the victim's disability (or presumed disability)

B
Factor(s) in category A not present

Step Two—Starting point and category range

7.47B   Having determined the offence category and culpability level, the court should then use the corresponding starting point specified in the guideline in order to reach a sentence within the category range. The starting point applies to all offenders irrespective of plea or previous convictions. Once the starting point has been determined, step two allows further adjustment for aggravating or mitigating features, set out below. A case of particular gravity, reflected by multiple features of culpability or harm, could merit upward adjustment from the starting point before further adjustment for aggravating or mitigating features. Where there is a sufficient prospect of rehabilitation, a community order with a sex offender treatment programme requirement under s.202 of the CJA 2003 may be a proper alternative to a short or moderate length custodial sentence. The starting points and category ranges for offences under ss.30 and 31 of the Act differ according to whether the offence involves penetrative or non-penetrative activity, and are as follows:

Where offence involved penetration		
	A	B
Category 1	**Starting point** 16 years' custody	**Starting point** 13 years' custody
	Category range 13–19 years' custody	**Category range** 11–17 years' custody
Category 2	**Starting point** 13 years' custody	**Starting point** 10 years' custody
	Category range 11–17 years' custody	**Category range** 8–13 years' custody
Category 3	**Starting point** 10 years' custody	**Starting point** 8 years' custody
	Category range 8–13 years' custody	**Category range** 6–11 years' custody

Where offence did not involve penetration		
	A	**B**
Category 1	**Starting point** 6 years' custody **Category range** 4–9 years' custody	**Starting point** 4 years' custody **Category range** 3–7 years' custody
Category 2	**Starting point** 4 years' custody **Category range** 3–7 years' custody	**Starting point** 2 years' custody **Category range** 1–4 years' custody
Category 3	**Starting point** 1 year's custody **Category range** 26 weeks'–2 years' custody	**Starting point** 26 weeks' custody **Category range** High level community order–1 year's custody

Aggravating and mitigating factors

After identifying the starting point and category range, the court should consider **7.47C** whether the presence of aggravating or mitigating factors should result in an upward or downward adjustment from the starting point or the imposition of a sentence outside the category range. In particular, relevant recent convictions are likely to result in an upward adjustment. In appropriate cases, the court should also consider whether the custody threshold has been passed; if so, whether a custodial sentence is unavoidable; and if it is, whether that sentence can be suspended. The non-exhaustive list of aggravating and mitigating factors for offences under ss.30 and 31 is as follows:

Aggravating factors
Statutory aggravating factors
• Previous convictions, having regard to a) the nature of the offence to which the conviction relates and its relevance to the current offence; and b) the time that has elapsed since the conviction
• Offence committed whilst on bail

Other aggravating factors

- Ejaculation (where not taken into account at step one)

- Blackmail or other threats made (where not taken into account at step one)

- Location of offence

- Timing of offence

- Use of weapon or other item to frighten or injure

- Victim compelled to leave their home or institution (including victims of domestic violence)

- Failure to comply with current court orders

- Offence committed whilst on licence

- Presence of others, especially children

- Any steps taken to prevent the victim reporting an incident, obtaining assistance and/or from assisting or supporting the prosecution

- Attempts to dispose of or conceal evidence

- Commission of offence whilst under the influence of alcohol or drugs

---

Mitigating factors

- No previous convictions **or** no relevant/recent convictions

- Remorse

- Previous good character and/or exemplary conduct*

- Age and/or lack of maturity where it affects the responsibility of the offender

- Mental disorder or learning disability, particularly where linked to the commission of the offence

- Sexual activity was incited but no activity took place because the offender voluntarily desisted or intervened to prevent it

---

* Previous good character/exemplary conduct is different from having no previous convictions. The more serious the offence, the less the weight which should normally be attributed to this factor. Where previous good character/exemplary conduct has been used to facilitate the offence, this mitigation should not normally be allowed and such conduct may constitute an aggravating factor.

Steps Three to Nine

7.47D   The remaining steps cover the following points. At step three the court should consider any factors which would indicate a reduction in sentence, e.g. assistance to the prosecution. At step four it should consider any reduction for a guilty plea. At step five the court should consider dangerousness, i.e. whether it would be appropriate to award a life sentence (s.224A or s.225(2) of the CJA 2003) or an extended sentence (s.226A). Step six requires the court to consider whether the total sentence is just and proportionate to the offending behaviour. At step seven it should consider whether to make an ancillary order (e.g. a compensation order, a sexual offences prevention order ("SOPO") or a restraining order). Step eight requires the court to fulfil its duty under s.174 of the CJA 2003 to give reasons for, and explain the effect of, the sentence. Finally, at step nine the court should consider whether to give credit for time spent on bail in accordance with s.240A of that Act.

Sentencing examples

There remain few reported examples of sentencing for offences under this Part of **7.48** the 2003 Act. In 2011, 22 people were sentenced for offences contrary to ss.30–33, no one was sentenced for offences contrary to ss.34–37 and eight people were sentenced for offences contrary to ss.38–41.[4] The following decisions all pre-date the new guideline, but provide useful illustrations of the approach of the Court of Appeal to particular factual scenarios.

In *Att Gen's Ref (No.35 of 2010) (Edward M)*,[5] the Attorney General referred to **7.48A** the Court of Appeal as unduly lenient a sentence of 6 years' imprisonment imposed on the offender following his plea of guilty, after the jury was sworn, to nine counts of sexual activity with a person with a mental disorder impeding choice, contrary to s.30 of the 2003 Act. The offender was 67 and of positive good character. Over a period of about a year he had sexually exploited and abused the victim (30), the daughter of his partner of nine years, who suffered from significant learning disabilities and did not have the capacity to resist sexual advances. The offender was well aware of her disability. The activity which he induced her to engage in included sexual intercourse, anal sex, digital penetration of the vagina, masturbation and oral sex. The victim stated that the sexual activity made her feel sick; she felt deeply unhappy and wanted to commit suicide; there were times when she would injure herself to take away the emotional pain; her real concern was that the offender should be with her mother, not with her. The Court held that the sentence was unduly lenient. The offender had committed sexual offences of considerable seriousness, treating the victim as a "sex toy". She was vulnerable and would not and could not refuse to participate in whatever sexual activity he wished to indulge in. This was a very serious breach of trust. The offender knew perfectly well that the victim was not making a choice when she agreed to allow him to touch her sexually. The victim had been suffering from an acute sense of concern about the fact that she had become the object of his sexual attention. On the other hand, the offender was a man of mature years and there was mitigation in his previous positive good character. It was clear that his

---

[4] *Sexual Offences Guideline: Consultation* (December 6, 2012).
[5] [2010] EWCA Crim 2555.

relationship with the victim's mother began as a genuine relationship and there was no thought in his mind at that early stage of any kind of sexual relationship with the victim. During those years, his relationship with her was a decent one and he helped her in the context of her disabilities. The lateness of his plea meant that the offender was not entitled to a full discount. In all the circumstances, the Court increased his sentence to one of 9 years' imprisonment.

7.48B In *Adcock*[6] the appellant (62) pleaded guilty to three offences under s.30 and received a sentence of 4 years' imprisonment. The victim (56) was a resident in a care home. A severe stroke had left her with significant cognitive difficulties and unable to care for herself. The appellant's wife also resided in the home and he visited her almost daily. He pleaded guilty on the basis that he had fondled the victim's breasts on three or four occasions, that he had rubbed and inserted his finger into her vagina on two occasions, and that at all times the victim had initiated the contact. The judge commented that the offences involved significant depravity on the appellant's part and that he posed a significant, if not high, risk of causing serious harm in the future to vulnerable females. The appellant was of previous good character, devoted to his wife and daughters, with an exemplary employment record and standing in the community. The appellant argued that his sentence was manifestly excessive and that this was a case of ostensible consent, where his criminality arose out of his lack of judgment in acquiescing in the victim's requests. The Court of Appeal held the sentence manifestly excessive. It had to reflect the basis of plea and there was force in the submission that the appellant had made as to his criminality. The judge's conclusion about the risk that he posed was not justified on the evidence. Nevertheless, the appellant had known that the victim was vulnerable and had committed more than one offence. The appropriate sentence, after a trial, would have been 4 years' imprisonment. Having regard to the guilty plea, the Court reduced the sentence to 3 years' imprisonment. It should be noted that the new sentencing guideline discourages the idea that in such cases there may be ostensible consent and instead treats the victim's inability to refuse as making the s.30 offence akin to the non-consensual offences. Consequently, if a victim who is unable to refuse engages in behaviour that might be regarded as encouraging of the sexual activity, this is unlikely in future to be regarded as a substantial or significant mitigating factor. Indeed, the decision in *Att Gen's Ref (No.53 of 2013) (R. v Wilson)*[6a] indicates that where an offender takes advantage of sexual advances made by the victim this may well operate as an aggravating, rather than a mitigating factor.

7.48C In *Johnson*[7] the appellant (76) pleaded guilty to nine counts under s.30 and six counts under s.31 of causing or inciting a person with a mental disorder to engage in sexual activity. He was sentenced to 6 years' imprisonment. The appellant

---

[6] [2010] EWCA Crim 700.

[6a] [2013] EWCA Crim 2544, concerning the offence of sexual activity with a child (s.9 of the 2003 Act) and discussed in para.4.25C, above.

[7] [2010] EWCA Crim 2082.

volunteered as a driver for a local authority and took a woman (42) who suffered from autism and learning difficulties for trips. In respect of the victim's capacity, a doctor concluded that her "autistic traits would make it obvious to another individual that she was vulnerable and had significant problems of comprehension, personal autonomy and will". The appellant made full admissions in interview during which he described a sexual relationship, which had evolved from sexual touching to penetration. The Court of Appeal accepted that the relationship was one of genuine affection for both parties. The Court held that the sentencing judge had passed a sentence in accordance with the sentencing guidelines but had given insufficient weight to the mitigating factors of the appellant's age and the affectionate motivation behind the offending. It accordingly reduced the sentence to one of 5 years' imprisonment.

Harrigan[8] is illustrative of the difficulty of applying guidelines when the **7.48D** circumstances of the offending could fall within different categories of offence. The Court of Appeal in that case upheld a sentence of 5 years' imprisonment for trespass with intent to commit a sexual offence under s.63 of the 2003 Act. The appellant, through his employment with a local council, was responsible for the transport of elderly people to and from day-care centres. His victim, an 83-year-old woman with mobility problems and advanced Alzheimer's disease, was a regular passenger. She lacked capacity to consent to any form of sexual relationship. She believed that her husband, who had died 30 years previously, was still alive and that they continued to have sexual intercourse. The victim's carer attended her home to find her sitting on the sofa naked from the waist down; the appellant was found in the toilet, panicky, breathless and pulling up his trousers. He claimed to be a friend of the victim, kissed her on the cheek and left; the concerned carer reported the matter to the police. Much to her distress the victim had to be moved into a care home for several weeks whilst her home was forensically examined, and she would no longer attend the day-care centre because of embarrassment. As a result of plea discussions prior to trial, the prosecution did not proceed with an allegation under s.30 of the 2003 Act and the appellant fell to be sentenced for the s.63 offence. The basis of plea was that there had been genital contact but no penetration. The judge expressly departed from the sentencing guideline for s.63 (starting point of 2 years' imprisonment with a range of 1–4 years' imprisonment) and for non-penetrative offences committed by care workers (range of up to 2 years' imprisonment). The Court of Appeal agreed with the judge's approach because the offence involved "a gross breach of trust, committed in the home of a vulnerable, elderly lady". The Court also cited "the significant consequences for [the victim's] already significantly impaired way of life". As the Court acknowledged, this was a difficult sentencing exercise. However, it appears that the sentence upheld was in accordance with the guideline for the s.30 offence, rather than for the offence to which he had pleaded guilty. The starting point for

---

[8] [2011] EWCA Crim 683.

non-penetrative activity contrary to s.30 of the 2003 Act (after trial) under the SGC guideline was 5 years' imprisonment with a range of 4–8 years.

"Unable to Refuse"

7.62   There has been some consideration in the Court of Protection of Baroness Hale's remarks in *R. v C* in respect of capacity issues. Roderic Wood J. in *D County Council v LS*[9] attempted to build a bridge between conflicting viewpoints, holding that the approach in *R. v C* applied to questions of capacity, or lack of it, to make decisions on the issue of sexual relations (and indeed of marriage) in both the civil and criminal arena. In Roderic Wood J.'s judgment this approach was wholly consistent with the statutory requirements of s.3 of the Mental Capacity Act 2005. In *D Borough Council v AB*[10] Mostyn J. had to decide what legal test should be applied in determining whether a 41-year-old with an IQ assessed at 48 had the mental capacity to consent to sexual relations. The learned judge considered Baroness Hale's observations in *R. v C*, the old common law decisions and Roderic Wood J.'s judgment in *D County Council v LS*. However, he preferred the approach set out by Munby J. (as he then was) in *X City Council v MB, NA and MAB*[11] that the capacity test involves a consideration of whether there is "sufficiently rudimentary knowledge of what the act comprises and of its sexual character". See also Robert Sandland's article, *Sex and Capacity: The Management of Monsters?*[12]

CAUSING OR INCITING A PERSON, WITH A MENTAL DISORDER IMPEDING CHOICE, TO ENGAGE IN SEXUAL ACTIVITY

Mode of Trial and Punishment

7.77   An offence contrary to s.31 of the 2003 Act involving penetration is a serious specified offence for the purposes of ss.224 and 225(2) (life sentence for serious offences) of the CJA 2003. From December 3, 2012, when ss.122–128 of the Legal Aid, Sentencing and Punishment of Offenders Act 2012 were brought into force[13]:

- For offences committed on or after that date, an offence under s.31 involving penetration is listed in Pt 1 of Sch.15B to the CJA 2003 for the purposes of s.224A of that Act (life sentence for second listed offence).

---

[9] [2010] EWHC 1544 (Fam).
[10] [2011] EWHC 101 (CoP).
[11] [2006] EWHC 168.
[12] [2013] 76(6) M.L.R. 981–1009.
[13] By the Legal Aid, Sentencing and Punishment of Offenders Act 2012 (Commencement No.4 and Saving Provisions) Order 2012 (SI 2012/2906).

- For convictions on or after that date (irrespective of the date of commission of the offence), an offence under s.31 is a specified offence for the purposes of s.226A of the CJA 2003 (extended sentence for certain violent or sexual offences).

BAIL

Section 25 of the Criminal Justice and Public Order Act 1994 was amended with effect from December 3, 2012,[14] so that a person charged with or convicted of an offence to which the section applies shall be granted bail by a constable only if the constable is "of the opinion", rather than "satisfied" (as before), that there are exceptional circumstances which justify it.   7.79

SENTENCING

The Sentencing Council has issued a new guideline applicable to sex offenders aged 18 or over who are sentenced on or after April 1, 2014: see para.1.20 et seq., above. A single guideline covers offences under both s.30 and s.31 of the 2003 Act and is considered at para.7.47 et seq., above.   7.80

"UNABLE TO REFUSE"

See the discussion in para.7.62, above.   7.84

ENGAGING IN SEXUAL ACTIVITY IN THE PRESENCE OF A PERSON WITH A MENTAL DISORDER IMPEDING CHOICE

MODE OF TRIAL AND PUNISHMENT

For convictions on or after December 3, 2012, when s.124 of the Legal Aid, Sentencing and Punishment of Offenders Act 2012 was brought into force,[15] an offence under s.32 is a specified offence for the purposes of s.226A of the CJA 2003 (extended sentence for certain violent or sexual offences), irrespective of the date of commission of the offence.   7.89

SENTENCING

The Sentencing Council has issued a new guideline applicable to sex offenders aged 18 or over who are sentenced on or after April 1, 2014: see para.1.20 et seq.,   7.91

---

[14] By the Legal Aid, Sentencing and Punishment of Offenders Act 2012, s.90 and Sch.11 para.33, which was brought into force by the Legal Aid, Sentencing and Punishment of Offenders Act 2012 (Commencement No.4 and Saving Provisions) Order 2012, last note.

[15] By the Legal Aid, Sentencing and Punishment of Offenders Act 2012 (Commencement No.4 and Saving Provisions) Order 2012 (SI 2012/2906).

above. The previous guideline, issued by the Sentencing Guidelines Council in 2007, dealt with offences of mental disorder impeding choice (ss.30–33 of the 2003 Act) and engaging a victim in sexual activity through inducement, threat or deception (ss.34–37) in a single guideline. In its consultation on the draft guideline,[16] the Sentencing Council said it thought these offences should be covered by separate guidelines. Where a victim is unable to refuse, then in practical, if not legal, terms this is likely to have a similar impact to lack of consent in cases where the victim does not have a mental disorder and the Council therefore proposed that the guideline for offences where there is a mental disorder impeding choice should follow a similar structure to the guidelines for rape, assault by penetration and sexual assault (ss.1–3). However, the mental disorder offence of inducement, threat or deception will often involve offender behaviours that are more akin to grooming and exploitation as set out in the guideline for sexual activity with a child (s.9). This may lead to the appearance of a victim having "agreed" to the activity, but the reality is that any apparent agreement will have been obtained by exploitation. This approach was generally welcomed by respondents to the consultation and the Council duly followed it in the published guideline.

New sentencing guideline

Step One—Harm and culpability

7.91A A single guideline covers the offences in ss.32 and 33 of the 2003 Act (engaging in sexual activity in the presence of a person with mental disorder impeding choice, and causing such a person to watch a sexual act). These offences replicate the offence behaviours covered by ss.11 and 12 of the Act (engaging in sexual activity in the presence of a child and causing or inciting a child to watch a sexual act), and the Sentencing Council's approach was to use the guideline for offences under those sections as a template for the offence categories and sentence levels for ss.32 and 33. As a result, harm is predicated on the extreme nature of the activity which the victim has had to view and the culpability factors focus on exploitative and manipulative behaviour on the part of the offender.

Under the new guideline, the sentencing court is to go through a series of steps in order to determine the appropriate sentence. Step one involves determining the offence category by reference to the degree of harm caused and then the culpability level for the offence. The court should determine which categories of harm and culpability the offence falls into by reference only to the tables below:

---

[16] *Sexual Offences Guideline: Consultation* (December 6, 2012).

HARM		CULPABILITY	
Category 1	• Causing victim to view extreme pornography • Causing victim to view indecent/prohibited images of children • Engaging in, or causing a victim to view live, sexual activity involving sadism/violence/sexual activity with an animal/ a child	**A**	
			• Significant degree of planning • Offender acts together with others in order to commit the offence • Use of alcohol/drugs on victim to facilitate the offence • Grooming behaviour used against victim • Abuse of trust • Use of threats (including blackmail) • Commercial exploitation and/or motivation • Offence racially or religiously aggravated • Offence motivated by, or demonstrating, hostility to the victim based on his or her sexual orientation (or presumed sexual orientation) or transgender identity (or presumed transgender identity) • Offence motivated by, or demonstrating, hostility to the victim based on his or her disability (or presumed disability)
Category 2	Engaging in, or causing a victim to view images of or view live, sexual activity involving: • penetration of vagina or anus (using body or object) • penile penetration of mouth • masturbation		
Category 3	Factor(s) in categories 1 and 2 not present		
		B	
		Factor(s) in category A not present	

Step Two—Starting point and category range

7.91B

Having determined the offence category and culpability level, the court should then use the corresponding starting point specified in the guideline in order to reach a sentence within the category range. The starting point applies to all offenders irrespective of plea or previous convictions. Once the starting point has been determined, step two allows further adjustment for aggravating or mitigating features, set out below. A case of particular gravity, reflected by multiple features of culpability or harm, could merit upward adjustment from the starting point before further adjustment for aggravating or mitigating features. Where there is a sufficient prospect of rehabilitation, a community order with a sex offender treatment programme requirement under s.202 of the CJA 2003 may be a proper alternative to a short or moderate length custodial sentence. The starting points and category ranges are as follows:

	A	B
Category 1	**Starting point** 4 years' custody **Category range** 3–6 years' custody	**Starting point** 2 years' custody **Category range** 1–3 years' custody
Category 2	**Starting point** 2 years' custody **Category range** 1–3 years' custody	**Starting point** 1 year's custody **Category range** High level community order–18 months' custody
Category 3	**Starting point** 26 weeks' custody **Category range** High level community order–1 year's custody	**Starting point** Medium level community order **Category range** Low level community order–Medium level community order

Aggravating and mitigating factors

7.91C   After identifying the starting point and category range, the court should consider whether the presence of aggravating or mitigating factors should result in an upward or downward adjustment from the starting point or the imposition of a sentence outside the category range. In particular, relevant recent convictions are likely to result in an upward adjustment. When sentencing appropriate category 2 or 3 offences, the court should also consider whether the custody threshold has been passed; if so, whether a custodial sentence is unavoidable; and if it is, whether that sentence can be suspended. The non-exhaustive list of aggravating and mitigating factors for offences under ss.32 and 33 is as follows:

Aggravating factors
Statutory aggravating factors
• Previous convictions, having regard to a) the nature of the offence to which the conviction relates and its relevance to the current offence; and b) the time that has elapsed since the conviction

- Offence committed whilst on bail

Other aggravating factors

- Location of offence
- Timing of offence
- Failure to comply with current court orders
- Offence committed whilst on licence
- Any steps taken to prevent the victim reporting an incident, obtaining assistance and/or from assisting or supporting the prosecution
- Attempts to dispose of or conceal evidence
- Commission of offence whilst under the influence of alcohol or drugs

Mitigating factors

- No previous convictions or no relevant/recent convictions
- Remorse
- Previous good character and/or exemplary conduct*
- Age and/or lack of maturity where it affects the responsibility of the offender
- Mental disorder or learning disability, particularly where linked to the commission of the offence
- Demonstration of steps taken to address offending behaviour

* Previous good character/exemplary conduct is different from having no previous convictions. The more serious the offence, the less the weight which should normally be attributed to this factor. Where previous good character/exemplary conduct has been used to facilitate the offence, this mitigation should not normally be allowed and such conduct may constitute an aggravating factor.

Steps Three to Nine

The remaining steps cover the following points. At step three the court should   **7.91D** consider any factors which would indicate a reduction in sentence, e.g. assistance to the prosecution. At step four it should consider any reduction for a guilty plea. At step five the court should consider dangerousness, i.e. whether it would be appropriate to award an extended sentence (s.226A of the CJA 2003). Step six requires the court to consider whether the total sentence is just and proportionate to the offending behaviour. At step seven it should consider whether to make an ancillary order (e.g. a compensation order, a SOPO or a restraining order). Step eight requires the court to fulfil its duty under s.174 of the CJA 2003 to give reasons for, and explain the effect of, the sentence. Finally, at step nine the court should consider whether to give credit for time spent on bail in accordance with s.240A of that Act.

"Unable to Refuse"

7.96   See the discussion in para.7.62, above.

CAUSING A PERSON, WITH A MENTAL DISORDER IMPEDING CHOICE, TO WATCH A SEXUAL ACT

Mode of Trial and Punishment

7.102   For convictions on or after December 3, 2012, when s.124 of the Legal Aid, Sentencing and Punishment of Offenders Act 2012 was brought into force,[17] an offence under s.33 is a specified offence for the purposes of s.226A of the CJA 2003 (extended sentence for certain violent or sexual offences), irrespective of the date of commission of the offence.

Sentencing

7.104   The Sentencing Council has issued a new guideline applicable to sex offenders aged 18 or over who are sentenced on or after April 1, 2014: see para.1.20 et seq., above. A single guideline covers offences under both s.32 and s.33 of the 2003 Act and is considered at para.7.91 et seq., above.

"Unable to Refuse"

7.109   See the discussion in para.7.62, above.

B. INDUCEMENTS ETC. TO PERSONS WITH A MENTAL DISORDER

INDUCEMENT, THREAT OR DECEPTION TO PROCURE SEXUAL ACTIVITY WITH A PERSON WITH A MENTAL DISORDER

Mode of Trial and Punishment

7.117   An offence contrary to s.34 of the 2003 Act involving penetration is a serious specified offence for the purposes of ss.224 and 225(2) (life sentence for serious

---

[17] By the Legal Aid, Sentencing and Punishment of Offenders Act 2012 (Commencement No.4 and Saving Provisions) Order 2012 (SI 2012/2906).

offences) of the CJA 2003. From December 3, 2012, when ss.122 and 124 of the Legal Aid, Sentencing and Punishment of Offenders Act 2012 were brought into force[18]:

- For offences committed on or after that date, an offence under s.34 involving penetration is listed in Pt 1 of Sch.15B to the CJA 2003 for the purposes of s.224A of that Act (life sentence for second listed offence).
- For convictions on or after that date (irrespective of the date of commission of the offence), an offence under s.34 is a specified offence for the purposes of s.226A of the CJA 2003 (extended sentence for certain violent or sexual offences).

SENTENCING

The Sentencing Council has issued a new guideline applicable to sex offenders   **7.119**
aged 18 or over who are sentenced on or after April 1, 2014: see para.1.20 et seq., above. A single guideline covers the offences in ss.34 and 35 of the 2003 Act (inducement, threat or deception to procure sexual activity with a person with a mental disorder, and causing such a person to engage in sexual activity by inducement, threat or deception). The guideline is modelled on the one for the offences in ss.9 and 10 of the Act of engaging in sexual activity with a child. In its consultation,[19] the Council explained that this is because the offences share a statutory maximum (14 years) and, in relation to all of them, the victim may appear to have acquiesced in sexual activity but only due to exploitation or manipulation by the offender. In the guideline for ss.9 and 10, harm is linked to the sexual activity that has been engaged in (with penetrative sexual activity treated as the highest level of harm) whilst culpability concentrates on the exploitation and manipulation employed by the offender in order to procure the sexual activity. The same approach is taken in the guideline for ss.34 and 35, which also adopts the sentence starting points and ranges used in the guideline for ss.9 and 10. Like that guideline, the one for ss.34 and 35 contains at its head the statement "This guideline also applies to offences committed remotely/online".

New sentencing guideline

Step One—Harm and culpability

The sentencing court is to go through a series of steps in order to determine the   **7.119A**
appropriate sentence. Step one involves determining the offence category by reference to the degree of harm caused and then the culpability level for the offence. The court should determine which categories of harm and culpability the offence falls into by reference only to the tables below:

---

[18] By the Legal Aid, Sentencing and Punishment of Offenders Act 2012 (Commencement No.4 and Saving Provisions) Order 2012 (SI 2012/2906).
[19] *Sexual Offences Guideline: Consultation* (December 6, 2012).

HARM		CULPABILITY	
Category 1	• Penetration of vagina or anus (using body or object) • Penile penetration of mouth in either case by, or of, the victim	**A** • Significant degree of planning • Offender acts together with others to commit the offence • Use of alcohol/drugs on victim to facilitate the offence • Abuse of trust • Sexual images of victim recorded, retained, solicited or shared • Commercial exploitation and/or motivation • Offence racially or religiously aggravated • Offence motivated by, or demon-strating, hostility to the victim based on his or her sexual orientation (or presumed sexual orientation) or transgender identity (or presumed transgender identity) • Offence motivated by, or demon-strating, hostility to the victim based on his or her disability (or presumed disability)	
Category 2	• Touching, or exposure, of naked genitalia or naked breasts by, or of, the victim		
Category 3	• Other sexual activity		
		B	
		Factor(s) in category A not present	

Step Two—Starting point and category range

7.119B Having determined the offence category and culpability level, the court should then use the corresponding starting point specified in the guideline in order to reach a sentence within the category range. The starting point applies to all offenders irrespective of plea or previous convictions. Once the starting point has been determined, step two allows further adjustment for aggravating or mitigating features, set out below. A case of particular gravity, reflected by multiple features of culpability or harm, could merit upward adjustment from the starting point before further adjustment for aggravating or mitigating features. Where there is a sufficient prospect of rehabilitation, a community order with a sex offender treatment programme requirement under s.202 of the CJA 2003 may be a proper alternative to a short or moderate length custodial sentence. The starting points and category ranges for offences under ss.34 and 35 are as follows:

	A	B
Category 1	**Starting point** 5 years' custody **Category range** 4–10 years' custody	**Starting point** 1 year's custody **Category range** High level community order–2 years' custody
Category 2	**Starting point** 3 years' custody **Category range** 2–6 years' custody	**Starting point** 26 weeks' custody **Category range** High level community order–1 year's custody
Category 3	**Starting point** 26 weeks' custody **Category range** High level community order–3 years' custody	**Starting point** Medium level community order **Category range** Low level community order–High level community order

Aggravating and mitigating factors

After identifying the starting point and category range, the court should consider   **7.119C**
whether the presence of aggravating or mitigating factors should result in an
upward or downward adjustment from the starting point or the imposition of a
sentence outside the category range. In particular, relevant recent convictions are
likely to result in an upward adjustment. When sentencing appropriate category 2
or 3 offences, the court should also consider whether the custody threshold has
been passed; if so, whether a custodial sentence is unavoidable; and if it is, whether
that sentence can be suspended. The non-exhaustive list of aggravating and
mitigating factors for offences under ss.34 and 35 is as follows:

Aggravating factors
Statutory aggravating factors
• Previous convictions, having regard to a) the nature of the offence to which the conviction relates and its relevance to the current offence; and b) the time that has elapsed since the conviction

• Offence committed whilst on bail

Other aggravating factors

• Severe psychological or physical harm
• Ejaculation
• Pregnancy or STI as a consequence of offence
• Location of offence
• Timing of offence
• Victim compelled to leave their home or institution (including victims of domestic violence)
• Failure to comply with current court orders
• Offence committed whilst on licence
• Any steps taken to prevent the victim reporting an incident, obtaining assistance and/or from assisting or supporting the prosecution
• Attempts to dispose of or conceal evidence
• Commission of offence whilst under the influence of alcohol or drugs

Mitigating factors
• No previous convictions **or** no relevant/recent convictions
• Remorse
• Previous good character and/or exemplary conduct*
• Age and/or lack of maturity where it affects the responsibility of the offender
• Mental disorder or learning disability, particularly where linked to the commission of the offence

* Previous good character/exemplary conduct is different from having no previous convictions. The more serious the offence, the less the weight which should normally be attributed to this factor. Where previous good character/exemplary conduct has been used to facilitate the offence, this mitigation should not normally be allowed and such conduct may constitute an aggravating factor.
In the context of this offence, previous good character/exemplary conduct should not normally be given any significant weight and will not normally justify a reduction in what would otherwise be the appropriate sentence.

Steps Three to Nine

7.119D The remaining steps cover the following points. At step three the court should consider any factors which would indicate a reduction in sentence, e.g. assistance to the prosecution. At step four it should consider any reduction for a guilty plea. At step five the court should consider dangerousness, i.e. whether it would be appropriate to award a life sentence (s.224A or s.225(2) of the CJA 2003) or an extended sentence (s.226A). Step six requires the court to consider whether the total sentence is just and proportionate to the offending behaviour. At step seven it should consider whether to make an ancillary order (e.g. a compensation order, a SOPO or a restraining order). Step eight requires the court to fulfil its duty under s.174 of the CJA 2003 to give reasons for, and explain the effect of, the sentence. Finally, at step nine the court should consider whether to give credit for time spent on bail in accordance with s.240A of that Act.

CAUSING A PERSON WITH A MENTAL DISORDER TO ENGAGE IN OR AGREE TO ENGAGE IN SEXUAL ACTIVITY BY INDUCEMENT, THREAT OR DECEPTION

MODE OF TRIAL AND PUNISHMENT

An offence contrary to s.35 of the 2003 Act involving penetration is a serious specified offence for the purposes of ss.224 and 225(2) (life sentence for serious offences) of the CJA 2003. From December 3, 2012, when ss.122 and 124 of the Legal Aid, Sentencing and Punishment of Offenders Act 2012 were brought into force[20]:   **7.129**

- For offences committed on or after that date, an offence under s.35 involving penetration is listed in Pt 1 of Sch.15B to the CJA 2003 for the purposes of s.224A of that Act (life sentence for second listed offence).
- For convictions on or after that date (irrespective of the date of commission of the offence), an offence under s.35 is a specified offence for the purposes of s.226A of the CJA 2003 (extended sentence for certain violent or sexual offences).

SENTENCING

The Sentencing Council has issued a new guideline applicable to sex offenders aged 18 or over who are sentenced on or after April 1, 2014: see para.1.20 et seq., above. A single guideline covers offences under both s.34 and s.35 of the 2003 Act and is considered at para.7.119 et seq., above.   **7.131**

---

[20] By the Legal Aid, Sentencing and Punishment of Offenders Act 2012 (Commencement No.4 and Saving Provisions) Order 2012 (SI 2012/2906).

ENGAGING IN SEXUAL ACTIVITY IN THE PRESENCE, PROCURED BY INDUCEMENT, THREAT OR DECEPTION, OF A PERSON WITH A MENTAL DISORDER

Mode of Trial and Punishment

7.140   For convictions on or after December 3, 2012, when s.124 of the Legal Aid, Sentencing and Punishment of Offenders Act 2012 was brought into force,[21] an offence under s.36 is a specified offence for the purposes of s.226A of the CJA 2003 (extended sentence for certain violent or sexual offences), irrespective of the date of commission of the offence.

Sentencing

7.142   The Sentencing Council has issued a new guideline applicable to sex offenders aged 18 or over who are sentenced on or after April 1, 2014: see para.1.20 et seq., above. A single guideline covers the offences in ss.36 and 37 of the 2003 Act (engaging in sexual activity in the presence, procured by inducement, threat or deception, of a person with a mental disorder, and causing such a person to watch a sexual act by inducement, threat or deception).

New sentencing guideline

Step One—Harm and culpability

7.142A   The sentencing court is to go through a series of steps in order to determine the appropriate sentence. Step one involves determining the offence category by reference to the degree of harm caused and then the culpability level for the offence. The court should determine which categories of harm and culpability the offence falls into by reference only to the tables below:

HARM		CULPABILITY	
Category 1	• Causing victim to view extreme pornography	A	
	• Causing victim to view indecent/prohibited images of children		• Significant degree of planning
			• Offender acts together with others in order to commit the offence
	• Engaging in, or causing a victim to view live, sexual activity involving sadism/violence/sexual		• Use of alcohol/drugs on victim to facilitate the offence
			• Abuse of trust

---

[21] By the Legal Aid, Sentencing and Punishment of Offenders Act 2012 (Commencement No.4 and Saving Provisions) Order 2012 (SI 2012/2906).

	activity with an animal/a child	• Commercial exploitation and/or motivation
Category 2	Engaging in, or causing a victim to view images of or view live, sexual activity involving: • penetration of vagina or anus (using body or object) • penile penetration of mouth • masturbation	• Offence racially or religiously aggravated • Offence motivated by, or demonstrating, hostility to the victim based on his or her sexual orientation (or presumed sexual orientation) or transgender identity (or presumed transgender identity) • Offence motivated by, or demonstrating, hostility to the victim based on his or her disability (or presumed disability)
Category 3	Factor(s) in categories 1 and 2 not present	**B**
		Factor(s) in category A not present

Step Two—Starting point and category range

Having determined the offence category and culpability level, the court should **7.142B** then use the corresponding starting point specified in the guideline in order to reach a sentence within the category range. The starting point applies to all offenders irrespective of plea or previous convictions. Once the starting point has been determined, step two allows further adjustment for aggravating or mitigating features, set out below. A case of particular gravity, reflected by multiple features of culpability or harm, could merit upward adjustment from the starting point before further adjustment for aggravating or mitigating features. Where there is a sufficient prospect of rehabilitation, a community order with a sex offender treatment programme requirement under s.202 of the CJA 2003 may be a proper alternative to a short or moderate length custodial sentence. The starting points and category ranges for offences under ss.36 and 37 are as follows:

	A	B
Category 1	**Starting point** 4 years' custody **Category range** 3–6 years' custody	**Starting point** 2 years' custody **Category range** 1–3 years' custody

	A	B
Category 2	**Starting point** 2 years' custody	**Starting point** 1 year's custody
	Category range 1–3 years' custody	**Category range** High level community order–18 months' custody
Category 3	**Starting point** 26 weeks' custody	**Starting point** Medium level community order
	Category range High level community order–1 year's custody	**Category range** Low level community order–Medium level community order

Aggravating and mitigating factors

7.142C After identifying the starting point and category range, the court should consider whether the presence of aggravating or mitigating factors should result in an upward or downward adjustment from the starting point or the imposition of a sentence outside the category range. In particular, relevant recent convictions are likely to result in an upward adjustment. When sentencing appropriate category 2 or 3 offences, the court should also consider whether the custody threshold has been passed; if so, whether a custodial sentence is unavoidable; and if it is, whether that sentence can be suspended. The non-exhaustive list of aggravating and mitigating factors for offences under ss.36 and 37 is as follows:

Aggravating factors
Statutory aggravating factors
• Previous convictions, having regard to a) the nature of the offence to which the conviction relates and its relevance to the current offence; and b) the time that has elapsed since the conviction
• Offence committed whilst on bail
Other aggravating factors
• Location of offence
• Timing of offence
• Failure to comply with current court orders
• Offence committed whilst on licence

- Any steps taken to prevent the victim reporting an incident, obtaining assistance and/or from assisting or supporting the prosecution

- Attempts to dispose of or conceal evidence

- Commission of offence whilst under the influence of alcohol or drugs

---

Mitigating factors

- No previous convictions **or** no relevant/recent convictions

- Remorse

- Previous good character and/or exemplary conduct*

- Age and/or lack of maturity where it affects the responsibility of the offender

- Mental disorder or learning disability, particularly where linked to the commission of the offence

- Demonstration of steps taken to address offending behaviour

---

* Previous good character/exemplary conduct is different from having no previous convictions. The more serious the offence, the less the weight which should normally be attributed to this factor. Where previous good character/exemplary conduct has been used to facilitate the offence, this mitigation should not normally be allowed and such conduct may constitute an aggravating factor.

Steps Three to Nine

The remaining steps cover the following points. At step three the court should 7.142D consider any factors which would indicate a reduction in sentence, e.g. assistance to the prosecution. At step four it should consider any reduction for a guilty plea. At step five the court should consider dangerousness, i.e. whether it would be appropriate to award an extended sentence (s.226A of the CJA 2003). Step six requires the court to consider whether the total sentence is just and proportionate to the offending behaviour. At step seven it should consider whether to make an ancillary order (e.g. a compensation order, a SOPO or a restraining order). Step eight requires the court to fulfil its duty under s.174 of the CJA 2003 to give reasons for, and explain the effect of, the sentence. Finally, at step nine the court should consider whether to give credit for time spent on bail in accordance with s.240A of that Act.

CAUSING A PERSON WITH A MENTAL DISORDER TO WATCH A SEXUAL ACT BY INDUCEMENT, THREAT OR DECEPTION.

Mode of Trial and Punishment

For convictions on or after December 3, 2012, when s.124 of the Legal Aid, 7.153 Sentencing and Punishment of Offenders Act 2012 was brought into force,[22] an

---

[22] By the Legal Aid, Sentencing and Punishment of Offenders Act 2012 (Commencement No.4 and Saving Provisions) Order 2012 (SI 2012/2906).

offence under s.37 is a specified offence for the purposes of s.226A of the CJA 2003 (extended sentence for certain violent or sexual offences), irrespective of the date of commission of the offence.

Sentencing

7.155   The Sentencing Council has issued a new guideline applicable to sex offenders aged 18 or over who are sentenced on or after April 1, 2014: see para.1.20 et seq., above. A single guideline covers offences under both s.36 and s.37 of the 2003 Act and is considered at para.7.142 et seq., above.

C. OFFENCES RELATING TO CARE WORKERS

CARE WORKERS: SEXUAL ACTIVITY WITH A PERSON WITH A MENTAL DISORDER

Mode of Trial and Punishment

7.168   For convictions on or after December 3, 2012, when s.124 of the Legal Aid, Sentencing and Punishment of Offenders Act 2012 was brought into force,[23] an offence under s.38 is a specified offence for the purposes of s.226A of the CJA 2003 (extended sentence for certain violent or sexual offences), irrespective of the date of commission of the offence.

Sentencing

7.171   The Sentencing Council has issued a new guideline applicable to sex offenders aged 18 or over who are sentenced on or after April 1, 2014: see para 1.20 et seq., above. A single guideline covers the offences in ss.38 and 39 of the 2003 Act (care workers: sexual activity with a person with a mental disorder and care workers: causing or inciting sexual activity by a person with a mental disorder). The guideline contains at its head the statement "This guideline also applies to offences committed remotely/online".

New sentencing guideline

Step One—Harm and culpability

7.171A   The sentencing court is to go through a series of steps in order to determine the appropriate sentence. Step one involves determining the offence category by

---

[23] By the Legal Aid, Sentencing and Punishment of Offenders Act 2012 (Commencement No.4 and Saving Provisions) Order 2012 (SI 2012/2906).

reference to the degree of harm caused and then the culpability level for the offence. The court should determine which categories of harm and culpability the offence falls into by reference only to the tables below. The approach taken by the Sentencing Council is to identify the type of sexual activity which took place as determinative of the harm caused; this is because victims of these types of offences may be reluctant to articulate harm or may regard themselves as in a genuine relationship with the offender:

HARM		CULPABILITY	
Category 1	• Penetration of vagina or anus (using body or object) • Penile penetration of mouth in either case by, or of, the victim	**A** • Significant degree of planning • Offender acts together with others to commit the offence • Use of alcohol/drugs on victim to facilitate the offence	
Category 2	• Touching, or exposure, of naked genitalia or naked breasts by, or of, the victim	• Grooming behaviour used against victim • Use of threats (including blackmail)	
Category 3	Factor(s) in categories 1 and 2 not present	• Sexual images of victim recorded, retained solicited or shared • Commercial exploitation and/or motivation • Offence racially or religiously aggravated • Offence motivated by, or demonstrating, hostility to the victim based on his or her sexual orientation (or presumed sexual orientation) or transgender identity (or presumed transgender identity) • Offence motivated by, or demonstrating, hostility to the victim based on his or her disability (or presumed disability)	
		B	
		Factor(s) in category A not present	

Step Two—Starting point and category range

Having determined the offence category and culpability level, the court should then use the corresponding starting point specified in the guideline in order to   7.171B reach a sentence within the category range. The starting point applies to all offenders irrespective of plea or previous convictions. Once the starting point has been determined, step two allows further adjustment for aggravating or mitigating features, set out below. A case of particular gravity, reflected by multiple features of culpability or harm, could merit upward adjustment from the starting point before further adjustment for aggravating or mitigating features. Where there is a sufficient prospect of rehabilitation, a community order with a sex offender treatment programme requirement under s.202 of the CJA 2003 may be a proper alternative to a short or moderate length custodial sentence. The starting points and category ranges for offences under ss.38 and 39 are as follows:

	A	B
Category 1	Starting point 5 years' custody Category range 4–10 years' custody	Starting point 18 months' custody Category range 1–2 years' custody
Category 2	Starting point 3 year's custody Category range 2–6 years' custody	Starting point 26 weeks' custody Category range Medium level community order–1 year's custody
Category 3	Starting point 26 weeks' custody Category range High level community order–3 years' custody	Starting point Medium level community order Category range Low level community order–High level community order

The starting points and ranges in the draft guideline for ss.38 and 39 were based on those in the previous guideline issued by the Sentencing Guidelines Council in 2007. Accordingly, the starting point for the highest category of offence was 3 years and the top of the range was 5 years. However, the Sentencing Council was persuaded by representations made by those who work with vulnerable adults that, taking into consideration the statutory maximum of 14 years, sentencing levels should be raised when there is evidence of exploitation or grooming. Accordingly, in the published guideline the starting point in the highest category is 5 years with a range of 4–10 years. This is in line with the sentencing levels available for exploitation cases under s.9 of the Act, and allows higher sentences to be imposed where vulnerable adults are groomed and exploited by care workers, whom they trust as they would a family member.

Aggravating and mitigating factors

After identifying the starting point and category range, the court should consider whether the presence of aggravating or mitigating factors should result in an upward or downward adjustment from the starting point or the imposition of a sentence outside the category range. In particular, relevant recent convictions are likely to result in an upward adjustment. When sentencing appropriate category 2 or 3 offences, the court should also consider whether the custody threshold has been passed; if so, whether a custodial sentence is unavoidable; and if it is, whether that sentence can be suspended. The non-exhaustive list of aggravating and mitigating factors for offences under ss.38 and 39 is as follows: 7.171C

Aggravating factors
Statutory aggravating factors
• Previous convictions, having regard to a) the nature of the offence to which the conviction relates and its relevance to the current offence; and b) the time that has elapsed since the conviction
• Offence committed whilst on bail
Other aggravating factors
• Ejaculation
• Pregnancy or STI as a consequence of offence
• Location of offence
• Timing of offence
• Victim compelled to leave their home or institution (including victims of domestic violence)
• Failure to comply with current court orders
• Offence committed whilst on licence
• Any steps taken to prevent the victim reporting an incident, obtaining assistance and/or from assisting or supporting the prosecution
• Attempts to dispose of or conceal evidence
• Failure of offender to respond to previous warnings
• Commission of offence whilst under the influence of alcohol or drugs

Mitigating factors
• No previous convictions **or** no relevant/recent convictions
• Remorse
• Previous good character and/or exemplary conduct*
• Age and/or lack of maturity where it affects the responsibility of the offender
• Mental disorder or learning disability, particularly where linked to the commission of the offence
• Sexual activity was incited but no activity took place because the offender voluntarily desisted or intervened to prevent it

* Previous good character/exemplary conduct is different from having no previous convictions. The more serious the offence, the less the weight which should normally be attributed to this factor. Where previous good character/exemplary conduct has been used to facilitate the offence, this mitigation should not normally be allowed and such conduct may constitute an aggravating factor.

In the context of this offence, previous good character/exemplary conduct should not normally be given any significant weight and will not normally justify a reduction in what would otherwise be the appropriate sentence.

Steps Three to Nine

7.171D   The remaining steps cover the following points. At step three the court should consider any factors which would indicate a reduction in sentence, e.g. assistance to the prosecution. At step four it should consider any reduction for a guilty plea. At step five the court should consider dangerousness, i.e. whether it would be appropriate to award an extended sentence (s.226A of the CJA 2003). Step six requires the court to consider whether the total sentence is just and proportionate to the offending behaviour. At step seven it should consider whether to make an ancillary order (e.g. a compensation order, a SOPO or a restraining order). Step eight requires the court to fulfil its duty under s.174 of the CJA 2003 to give reasons for, and explain the effect of, the sentence. Finally, at step nine the court should consider whether to give credit for time spent on bail in accordance with s.240A of that Act.

7.173   There remain few reported sentencing decisions in this area. The two included here both pre-date the new guideline but nonetheless remain of interest as showing the approach of the Court of Appeal to particular factual scenarios.

7.173A   In *Philip Calver*[24] the appellant was sentenced to 16 months' imprisonment after pleading guilty to a single offence under s.38. He had been employed as a support worker for the victim, who was a 25-year-old female with the mental age of a five-

[24] Unreported, December 5, 2012.

year-old. He had taken her to a woodland area, removed her top and kissed her mouth and breasts. The appellant was of previous good character. The Court of Appeal held that the judge's starting point of 24 months had been too high and the correct starting point was 15 months, which, when reduced by virtue of the guilty plea, resulted in a sentence of 10 months' imprisonment.

In *Bennett*, one of the conjoined appeals in *Riat and others*,[25] the appellant was sentenced to 2 years' imprisonment following his conviction of one offence under s.38. He was a community psychiatric nurse and the Crown case was that he had had an ongoing sexual relationship with a patient for some months. The complainant (47) was, despite her mental disorder, capable of consenting. She gave a long, garrulous, and by no means always consistent account of a continuing sexual relationship between them. When the appellant was interviewed by the police, he at first denied any such relationship. However, it gradually became apparent that this first response was untruthful, and eventually he was confronted with a number of affectionate messages and cards which he had sent her, including a Valentine's card and a second card in which he had thanked her for "the great sex". At this, he broke down and gave the police a detailed account of a sexual relationship in which they had, he said, had intercourse on a number of occasions. Subsequently he faced disciplinary proceedings in his job. The Crown charged two offences, count one intended to be representative of vaginal intercourse and count two to reflect a specific occasion on which the complainant had said that the defendant penetrated her with his fingers without her consent. At trial the appellant did not deny having a continuing affectionate and sexual relationship with the patient but he contended that there had never been any successful penetration. The jury convicted him on count one but acquitted him on count two. In passing sentence, the judge observed that it was the greatest pity that the appellant had forfeited the mitigation which would have been afforded had he stood by the admissions which he had made. There were a number of impressive testimonials to his character, and his career of 15 years or more was ruined. Also, there was no element of offending against a woman who could not properly consent. But the sentence of 2 years was somewhat low in the range suggested in the SGC guideline for offences of this kind. There was the plainest breach of trust, and considerable actual and potential harm to a woman of fragile psyche. Accordingly, there was no basis for saying that the sentence was either manifestly excessive or wrong in principle. 7.173B

"INVOLVED IN B'S CARE"

Section 42 of the 2003 Act[26] defines when a person is involved in the care of another for the purposes of ss.38–41. It provides: 7.175

[25] [2012] EWCA 1509.
[26] As amended by SI 2007/961, art.3 and Sch. para.33, and SI 2010/813, art.13(4).

"(1) For the purposes of sections 38 to 41, a person (A) is involved in the care of another person (B) in a way that falls within this section if any of subsections (2) to (4) applies.

(2) This subsection applies if—

(a) B is accommodated and cared for in a care home, community home, voluntary home or children's home, and

(b) A has functions to perform in the home in the course of employment which have brought him or are likely to bring him into regular face to face contact with B.

(3) This subsection applies if B is a patient for whom services are provided—

(a) by a National Health Service body or an independent medical agency;

(b) in an independent hospital; or

(c) in Wales, in an independent clinic,

and A has functions to perform for the body or agency or in the hospital or clinic in the course of employment which have brought A or are likely to bring A into regular face to face contact with B.

(4) This subsection applies if A—

(a) is, whether or not in the course of employment, a provider of care, assistance or services to B in connection with B's mental disorder, and

(b) as such, has had or is likely to have regular face to face contact with B.

(5) In this section—

'care home' means an establishment which is a care home for the purposes of the Care Standards Act 2000;

'children's home' has the meaning given by section 1 of that Act;

'community home' has the meaning given by section 53 of the Children Act 1989;

'employment' means any employment, whether paid or unpaid and whether under a contract of service or apprenticeship, under a contract for service, or otherwise than under a contract;

'independent clinic' has the meaning given by section 2 of the Care Standards Act 2000;

'independent hospital'—

(a) in England, means—

(i) a hospital as defined by section 275 of the National Health Service Act 2006 that is not a health service hospital as defined by that section; or

(ii) any other establishment in which any of the services listed in section 22(6) are provided and which is not a health service hospital as so defined; and

(b) in Wales, has the meaning given by section 2 of the Care Standards Act 2000;

'independent medical agency' means an undertaking (not being an independent hospital, or in Wales an independent clinic) which consists of or includes the provision of services by medical practitioners;

'National Health Service body' means—

(a) a Local Health Board,

(b) a National Health Service trust,

(c) a Primary Care Trust, or

(d) a Special Health Authority;

'voluntary home' has the meaning given by section 60(3) of the Children Act 1989.

(6) In subsection (5), in the definition of 'independent medical agency', 'undertaking' includes any business or profession and—

(a) in relation to a public or local authority, includes the exercise of any functions of that authority; and

(b) in relation to any other body of persons, whether corporate or unincorporate, includes any of the activities of that body."

CARE WORKERS: CAUSING OR INCITING SEXUAL ACTIVITY

MODE OF TRIAL AND PUNISHMENT

For convictions on or after December 3, 2012, when s.124 of the Legal Aid, Sentencing and Punishment of Offenders Act 2012 was brought into force,[27] an offence under s.39 is a specified offence for the purposes of s.226A of the CJA 2003 (extended sentence for certain violent or sexual offences), irrespective of the date of commission of the offence. 7.189

SENTENCING

The Sentencing Council has issued a new guideline applicable to sex offenders aged 18 or over who are sentenced on or after April 1, 2014: see para.1.20 et seq., above. A single guideline covers offences under both s.38 and s.39 of the 2003 Act and is considered at para.7.171 et seq., above. 7.191

CARE WORKERS: SEXUAL ACTIVITY IN THE PRESENCE OF A PERSON WITH A MENTAL DISORDER

MODE OF TRIAL AND PUNISHMENT

For convictions on or after December 3, 2012, when s.124 of the Legal Aid, Sentencing and Punishment of Offenders Act 2012 was brought into force,[28] an offence under s.40 is a specified offence for the purposes of s.226A of the CJA 2003 (extended sentence for certain violent or sexual offences), irrespective of the date of commission of the offence. 7.201

SENTENCING

The Sentencing Council has issued a new guideline applicable to sex offenders aged 18 or over who are sentenced on or after April 1, 2014: see para.1.20 et seq., above. A single guideline covers the offences in ss.40 and 41 of the 2003 Act (care workers: sexual activity in the presence of a person with a mental disorder and care workers: causing a person with a mental disorder to watch a sexual act). 7.203

---

[27] By the Legal Aid, Sentencing and Punishment of Offenders Act 2012 (Commencement No.4 and Saving Provisions) Order 2012 (SI 2012/2906).

[28] By the Legal Aid, Sentencing and Punishment of Offenders Act 2012 (Commencement No.4 and Saving Provisions) Order 2012 (SI 2012/2906).

New sentencing guideline

Step One—Harm and culpability

7.203A   The sentencing court is to go through a series of steps in order to determine the appropriate sentence. Step one involves determining the offence category by reference to the degree of harm caused and then the culpability level for the offence. The court should determine which categories of harm and culpability the offence falls into by reference only to the tables below. The approach taken by the Sentencing Council is to identify the type of sexual activity which took place as determinative of the harm caused; this is because victims of these types of offences may be reluctant to articulate harm or may regard themselves as in a genuine relationship with the offender:

HARM	
Category 1	• Causing victim to view extreme pornography • Causing victim to view indecent/prohibited images of children • Engaging in, or causing a victim to view live, sexual activity involving sadism/violence/sexual activity with an animal/a child
Category 2	Engaging in, or causing a victim to view images of or view live, sexual activity involving: • penetration of vagina or anus (using body or object) • penile penetration of mouth • masturbation
Category 3	Factor(s) in categories 1 and 2 not present

CULPABILITY
A • Significant degree of planning • Offender acts together with others to commit the offence • Use of alcohol/drugs on victim to facilitate the offence • Grooming behaviour used against victim • Use of threats (including blackmail) • Commercial exploitation and/or motivation • Offence racially or religiously aggravated • Offence motivated by, or demonstrating, hostility to the victim based on his or her sexual orientation (or presumed sexual orientation) or transgender identity (or presumed transgender identity) • Offence motivated by, or demonstrating, hostility to the victim based on his or her disability (or presumed disability)
B
Factor(s) in category A not present

Step Two—Starting point and category range

Having determined the offence category and culpability level, the court should   **7.203B**
then use the corresponding starting point specified in the guideline in order to
reach a sentence within the category range. The starting point applies to all
offenders irrespective of plea or previous convictions. Once the starting point has
been determined, step two allows further adjustment for aggravating or mitigating
features, set out below. A case of particular gravity, reflected by multiple features
of culpability or harm, could merit upward adjustment from the starting point
before further adjustment for aggravating or mitigating features. Where there is a
sufficient prospect of rehabilitation, a community order with a sex offender
treatment programme requirement under s.202 of the CJA 2003 may be a proper
alternative to a short or moderate length custodial sentence. The starting points
and category ranges for offences under ss.40 and 41 are as follows:

	A	**B**
Category 1	**Starting point** 18 months' custody **Category range** 1–2 years' custody	**Starting point** 1 year's custody **Category range** 26 weeks'–18 months' custody
Category 2	**Starting Point** 1 year's custody **Category range** 26 weeks'–18 months' custody	**Starting point** 26 weeks' custody **Category range** High level community order–1 year's custody
Category 3	**Starting Point** 26 weeks' custody **Category range** High level community order–1 year's custody	**Starting point** Medium level community order **Category range** Low level community order–High level community order

Aggravating and mitigating factors

After identifying the starting point and category range, the court should consider   **7.203C**
whether the presence of aggravating or mitigating factors should result in an
upward or downward adjustment from the starting point or the imposition of a
sentence outside the category range. In particular, relevant recent convictions are
likely to result in an upward adjustment. When sentencing appropriate category 2

or 3 offences, the court should also consider whether the custody threshold has been passed; if so, whether a custodial sentence is unavoidable; and if it is, whether that sentence can be suspended. The non-exhaustive list of aggravating and mitigating factors for offences under ss.40 and 41 is as follows:

Aggravating factors
Statutory aggravating factors
<ul><li>Previous convictions, having regard to a) the nature of the offence to which the conviction relates and its relevance to the current offence; and b) the time that has elapsed since the conviction</li><li>Offence committed whilst on bail</li></ul>
Other aggravating factors
<ul><li>Location of offence</li><li>Timing of offence</li><li>Failure to comply with current court orders</li><li>Offence committed whilst on licence</li><li>Any steps taken to prevent the victim reporting an incident, obtaining assistance and/or from assisting or supporting the prosecution</li><li>Attempts to dispose of or conceal evidence</li><li>Failure of offender to respond to previous warnings</li><li>Commission of offence whilst under the influence of alcohol or drugs</li></ul>

Mitigating factors
<ul><li>No previous convictions **or** no relevant/recent convictions</li><li>Remorse</li><li>Previous good character and/or exemplary conduct*</li><li>Age and/or lack of maturity where it affects the responsibility of the offender</li><li>Mental disorder or learning disability, particularly where linked to the commission of the offence</li><li>Demonstration of steps taken to address offending behaviour</li></ul>

> * Previous good character/exemplary conduct is different from having no previous convictions. The more serious the offence, the less the weight which should normally be attributed to this factor. Where previous good character/exemplary conduct has been used to facilitate the offence, this mitigation should not normally be allowed and such conduct may constitute an aggravating factor.

Steps Three to Nine

The remaining steps cover the following points. At step three the court should 7.203D
consider any factors which would indicate a reduction in sentence, e.g. assistance
to the prosecution. At step four it should consider any reduction for a guilty plea.
At step five the court should consider dangerousness, i.e. whether it would be
appropriate to award an extended sentence (s.226A of the CJA 2003). Step six
requires the court to consider whether the total sentence is just and proportionate
to the offending behaviour. At step seven it should consider whether to make an
ancillary order (e.g. a compensation order, a SOPO or a restraining order). Step
eight requires the court to fulfil its duty under s.174 of the CJA 2003 to give
reasons for, and explain the effect of, the sentence. Finally, at step nine the court
should consider whether to give credit for time spent on bail in accordance with
s.240A of that Act.

CARE WORKERS: CAUSING A PERSON WITH A MENTAL DISORDER TO WATCH A SEXUAL ACT

MODE OF TRIAL AND PUNISHMENT

For convictions on or after December 3, 2012, when s.124 of the Legal Aid, 7.215
Sentencing and Punishment of Offenders Act 2012 was brought into force,[29] an
offence under s.41 is a specified offence for the purposes of s.226A of the CJA
2003 (extended sentence for certain violent or sexual offences), irrespective of the
date of commission of the offence.

SENTENCING

The Sentencing Council has issued a new guideline applicable to sex offenders 7.217
aged 18 or over who are sentenced on or after April 1, 2014: see para.1.20 et seq.,
above. A single guideline covers offences under both s.40 and s.41 of the 2003 Act
and is considered at para.7.203 et seq., above.

---

[29] By the Legal Aid, Sentencing and Punishment of Offenders Act 2012 (Commencement No.4 and
Saving Provisions) Order 2012 (SI 2012/2906).

CHAPTER 8

INDECENT PHOTOGRAPHS OF CHILDREN

TAKING (ETC.) AN INDECENT PHOTOGRAPH OR PSEUDO-PHOTOGRAPH OF A CHILD

MODE OF TRIAL AND PUNISHMENT

From December 3, 2012, when ss.122–128 of the Legal Aid, Sentencing and **8.04** Punishment of Offenders Act 2012 were brought into force[1]:

---

[1] By the Legal Aid, Sentencing and Punishment of Offenders Act 2012 (Commencement No.4 and Saving Provisions) Order 2012 (SI 2012/2906).

- For offences committed on or after that date, an offence under s.1 of the Protection of Children Act 1978 ("1978 Act") is listed in Pt 1 of Sch.15B to the Criminal Justice Act ("CJA 2003") for the purposes of s.224A of that Act (life sentence for second listed offence);
- For convictions on or after that date (irrespective of the date of commission of the offence), an offence under s.1 is a specified offence for the purposes of s.226A of that Act (extended sentence for certain violent or sexual offences).

Restriction on prosecution

8.05   In *R. v DM*[2] a Crown Prosecutor considered the case before charge and decided that the evidential and public interest tests for prosecution were met, but on the relevant form he wrote "not relevant" against the issue of the DPP's consent. This error was corrected some months later when another Crown Prosecutor gave consent before the PCMH, which was the first hearing of substance in the case. On appeal against conviction, the appellant argued that these timings demonstrated that no proper consideration had been given to whether it was appropriate to prosecute him, that the later consent was no more than a rubber stamp, and that the consent requirement did not provide an effective safeguard against inappropriate prosecution. The Court of Appeal rejected this argument and upheld the conviction on the basis that the first Crown Prosecutor had undertaken a proper scrutiny before deciding to prosecute and, whilst as a matter of good practice he should have given consent when deciding to charge, his failure to do so was rectified when consent was later given by the second Crown Prosecutor before the appellant was asked to answer the charge. The case differs somewhat from *Jackson*,[3] referred to in the main work, where the Crown Prosecutor did not give consent in writing but had the need for it in mind when settling the indictment. Here, the first Crown Prosecutor wholly overlooked the need for consent, but the later consent was held to be effective for the purposes of s.1(3). This may be regarded as somewhat generous to the prosecution, since s.1(3) provides that proceedings for an offence under the 1978 Act "shall not be instituted" except by or with the DPP's consent. The proceedings in this case were clearly instituted without consent, and although consent was purportedly given before the first hearing of substance, there is no provision in the Act that permits consent to be given retrospectively.

SENTENCING

8.11   The Sentencing Council has issued a new guideline applicable to sex offenders aged 18 or over who are sentenced on or after April 1, 2014: see para.1.20 et seq.,

---

[2] [2011] EWCA Crim 2752.
[3] [1997] Crim. L.R. 293.

above. In its consultation on the draft guideline,[4] the Sentencing Council said that due to advances in technology, this area of offending, i.e. the making, etc. of indecent images of children, has changed since the offences were created and even since the Sentencing Guidelines Council issued the previous guideline in 2007. The ease with which images, including moving images, can be shared and downloaded has increased the ability of offenders to share or trade in such images; and advances in electronic storage capacity have also meant that offenders can retain a much larger volume of images than previously. These developments, amongst others, have shaped the way such offences are committed. Judicial understanding of the way in which offenders behave has also developed.

The new guideline for offences relating to indecent images of children applies to offences under both s.1 of the 1978 Act and s.160 of the Criminal Justice Act 1988. It takes a different approach to the guidelines for other sexual offences since the harm and culpability model used for those offences is not readily applicable here, often because there is no identified victim before the court because the victim in the image has not been identified or located. However, harm and culpability remain the focus of the guideline, albeit expressed in a different way. Where the victim has not been identified the court will consider the nature and level of harm caused by the indecent images. The victim who has been abused to create the images is subjected to further harm due to the images being recorded and viewed. There is also further harm due to the fact that viewing creates a market and demand for such images and so leads to further abuse. In this connection the Council cited with approval the following passage in *Beaney*[5]:

> "The serious psychological injury which they [the children in the picture] would be at risk of being subjected to arises not merely from what they are being forced to do but also from their knowledge that what they are being forced to do would be viewed by others. It is not difficult to imagine the humiliation and lack of self-worth they are likely to feel. It is not simply the fact that without a market for these images the trade would not flourish. If people . . . continue to download and view images of this kind . . . the offences which they commit can properly be said to contribute to the psychological harm which the children in those images would suffer by virtue of the children's awareness that there were people . . . watching them forced to pose and behave in this way."

New sentencing guideline

Step One—Harm and culpability

Under the new guideline, the sentencing court is to go through a series of steps in order to determine the appropriate sentence. Step one involves determining the offence category by reference to the degree of harm caused and then the culpability level for the offence. The court's first task is to determine the offence category, which in other guidelines is done by reference to the degree of harm

8.11A

---

[4] *Sexual Offences Guideline: Consultation* (December 6, 2012).
[5] [2004] EWCA Crim 449, at [9] per Keith J.

caused. However, in this context the Sentencing Council chose to determine the offence category by identifying the role of the offender (broadly reflecting culpability) and then by considering the severity of the image (broadly representing harm).

Role of the offender

8.11B   The Council identified three categories of role: possession, distribution and production/taking.

- **Possession**: An offender falls within this category if they possess images but there is no evidence of distributing, possession with a view to distributing, or involvement in the production of the image. For this purpose "making" an image by downloading should be distinguished from the category "production/taking", discussed below. If "making" is charged in relation to simple downloading, then for sentencing purposes it should be treated as possession. This resolves an anomaly that existed under the previous SGC guideline, which drew a distinction between the deliberate saving of an image and mere viewing of it and treated mere viewing without storage as a mitigating factor. However, indecent photographs which the user browses on the Internet but does not deliberately save are nonetheless saved in the Internet browser cache as an automated function of the browser software. Where such images are recovered, the offender will commonly be charged with "making" the image rather than "possession" of it. This is because the file data that is saved along with the offending image by the browser software will provide evidence of when the image was created, i.e. made. Ironically, given the disparity in maximum sentences between the making and possession offences, under the SGC guideline an offender would stand to receive a stiffer sentence for making an image recovered in this way from his browser than if he possessed the same image in a stored format. The new guideline resolves this by ensuring that both cases should be sentenced as possession.
- **Distribution**: This category includes both actual distribution and possession of images with a view to distributing them, showing them or sharing them with others (see s.1(1)(c) of the 1978 Act).
- **Production/taking**: This category includes involvement in the actual taking or making of an image at source, i.e. involvement in its production, and is the highest category for sentencing purposes.

Severity of the image

8.11C   As explained in the main work, the SGC guideline identified five levels of prohibited image based on those set out in the judgment in *Oliver, Hartrey and Baldwin.*[6] The levels were:

---

[6] [2003] 1 Cr. App. R. 28.

Level 1   Images depicting erotic posing with no sexual activity;
Level 2   Non-penetrative sexual activity between children, or solo masturbation by a child;
Level 3   Non-penetrative sexual activity between adults and children;
Level 4   Penetrative sexual activity involving a child or children or both children and adults; and
Level 5   Sadism or penetration of, or by, an animal.

In consulting on the draft guideline, the Sentencing Council acknowledged that classification of images can be difficult and resource intensive for investigating and prosecuting authorities, and that the images before the court may give only a partial indication of the abuse suffered by the victim and of the offender's behaviour. However, the court can only sentence on the basis of what is before it, and the Council believed that, despite the limitations around using image level, the severity of the sexual offence depicted in the image can be an initial guide to the harm that will have been suffered by the victim. It did, however, set out in the new guideline to simplify the levels as follows:

Category A: "Images involving penetrative sexual activity" and "images involving sexual activity with an animal or sadism". The Council thought that any image showing a child involved in penetrative sexual activity should be placed in the highest category. In line with the other child sexual offences covered in the new guideline, it envisaged that this would involve penetration of the vagina or anus (using body or object) and penile penetration of the mouth, in either case by, or of, the victim. No distinction is made for this purpose between penetrative activity between an adult and a child and penetrative activity between children. Category A also includes images involving sexual activity with an animal or sadism. In the SGC guideline, "penetrative activity and sadism" and "penetration of, or by, an animal" were expressed as different levels of image (4 and 5 respectively), but they attracted the same sentence starting points and ranges, and the Council therefore placed both of them in category A in the new guideline. The Council also changed the wording "penetration of, or by, an animal" to "sexual activity with an animal" to ensure that it covers images involving non-penetrative activity such as a photograph showing an animal licking a child's sexual organs, which on a strict interpretation of the SGC guideline fell outside not only level 5 but also any level other than, conceivably, level 1.

Category B: "Images involving non-penetrative sexual activity". This category combines the SGC's levels 2 and 3. The SGC guideline made a distinction between non-penetrative sexual activity between children (or a child on their own) and non-penetrative sexual activity between an adult and a child. However, the Sentencing Council considered that even if the image does not contain an adult, this does not mean that an adult was not involved in making it or otherwise exploiting the victim in order to generate the image. In addition, the continuing victimisation of the child that flows from the image being recorded and viewed will be great even if there is no adult in the picture. Taking into account the law enforcement resources needed to classify images, the Council believed that a distinction between images involving just children and those involving adults and children is not required for sentencing purposes, as both create similar levels of harm and culpability. Accordingly, all non-penetrative sexual activity is dealt with in Category B, and so has the same starting point and category ranges.

Category C: "Other indecent images not falling within categories A or B". In its consultation draft, the Council defined this category as "images of erotic posing". The term "erotic posing" was used in the SGC guideline, but the Council thought it capable of misleading as there may be cases where an image that is not posed or "erotic" is still indecent, e.g. a picture of a naked child not engaged in sexual activity but with a focus on the child's genitals. The majority of respondents to the consultation agreed, the general view being that the term "erotic posing" was outdated and also inappropriate in that it indicated that responsibility for the nature of the posing lay with the victim rather than the offender. The Council accordingly dropped the term in the published guideline in favour of a neutral formulation referring to "other indecent images".

Responses to the consultation showed almost universal support for the Council's simplifying approach. The new levels are labelled A, B and C, rather than numbered, because the general scheme of the new guideline is that offences in category 1 attract the highest starting points and ranges, whereas under the SGC grading system based on *Oliver* category 1 images attracted the lowest starting point and range. That being so, the Council thought it would be confusing to retain numerical classification in relation to offences involving indecent images and that such offences should instead be categorised using the labels A, B and C.

Mixed levels of images

8.11D   Most offenders have collections containing images at a mix of levels and this can cause difficulties for sentencers. The Council has resolved this by providing that for "mixed collections", the appropriate starting point and range should initially be determined by the highest category of image level present in the collection. If, however, those images are unrepresentative of the offender's conduct, a lower category may be appropriate. However, a lower category will not be appropriate if the offender has produced or taken images of a higher category.

An important difference from the SGC guideline is that the quantity of material is no longer used to determine the offence category. The SGC guideline determined sentence starting points and ranges for different levels of images by reference to whether there were a "small number" or a "large number" of images. These terms were not defined and this caused difficulties for judges in assessing what "small" or "large" meant in this context. The Council formed the view that the best indicator of the offender's culpability is what he has done with the images, rather than their number. For example, an offender who has produced even a small number of images attracts a higher starting point than one who is in possession of the same number. However, as a large volume of images may provide an additional indicator of increased culpability in some cases, it is included in the guideline as an aggravating feature, allowing the court to move up from the starting point as and when appropriate.

In light of these points, the offence categories are as follows:

	Possession	Distribution*	Production**
Category A	Possession of images involving penetrative sexual activity Possession of images involving sexual activity with an animal or sadism	Sharing images involving penetrative sexual activity Sharing images involving sexual activity with an animal or sadism	Creating images involving penetrative sexual activity Creating images involving sexual activity with an animal or sadism
Category B	Possession of images involving non-penetrative sexual activity	Sharing of images involving non-penetrative sexual activity	Creating images involving non-penetrative sexual activity
Category C	Possession of other indecent images not falling within categories A or B	Sharing of other indecent images not falling within categories A or B	Creating other indecent images not falling within categories A or B

*Distribution includes possession with a view to distributing or sharing images.

**Production includes the taking or making of any image at source i.e. the original image.

Making an image by simple downloading should be treated as possession for the purposes of sentencing.

In most cases the intrinsic character of the most serious of the offending images will initially determine the appropriate category. If, however, the most serious images are unrepresentative of the offender's conduct a lower category may be appropriate. A lower category will not, however, be appropriate if the offender has produced or taken (i.e. photographed) images of a higher category.

Step Two—Starting point and category range

Having determined the offence category and culpability level, the court should   8.11E
then use the corresponding starting points specified in the guideline in order to reach a sentence within the category range. The starting point applies to all offenders irrespective of plea or previous convictions. Once the starting point has been determined, step two allows further adjustment for aggravating or mitigating features, set out below. A case of particular gravity, reflected by multiple features of culpability or harm, could merit upward adjustment from the starting point before further adjustment for aggravating or mitigating features. Where there is a

sufficient prospect of rehabilitation, a community order with a sex offender treatment programme requirement under s.202 of the CJA 2003 may be a proper alternative to a short or moderate length custodial sentence.

For the highest category of images (category A) a custodial option is recommended as a starting point in all cases whether the offender has been charged with possession, distribution or production. Where an offender has been involved in taking or making an image at source and this involves penetration, sadism or an animal, the recommended range goes towards the very top end of the 10-year statutory maximum and a starting point of 6 years' custody with a range of 4–9 years is recommended.

Category B images also attract a custodial starting point. The Council has moved away from the very short custodial sentences recommended in the SGC guideline under which, for example, 4 weeks was available in two of the categories. The Council said in its consultation that it did not believe that such short sentences are appropriate because of the very limited work the prison authorities can do in such a period to address the behaviour of the offender. A non-custodial starting point is recommended for possession and distribution of category C images and for possession of category B images. The Council added that there may be cases where the sentencer considers that a lengthy community order with a sexual offences treatment programme will be more appropriate than a very short custodial sentence, on the basis that the offender's thinking and behaviour will be better addressed through treatment and the degree of risk they pose to the community can be closely monitored. It added that a sexual offences prevention order ("SOPO") can provide a useful additional safeguard to a community order. However, it also deliberately included a custodial option as part of the sentencing range in every category to ensure that it is available to sentencers in appropriate cases. This is a change from the SGC guideline, under which possession of the lowest level of images attracted only a non-custodial option.

The sentence starting points and ranges are:

	Possession	**Distribution**	**Production**
Category A	**Starting point** 1 year's custody **Category range** 26 weeks–3 years' custody	**Starting point** 3 years' custody **Category range** 2–5 years' custody	**Starting point** 6 years' custody **Category range** 4–9 years' custody

	Possession	Distribution	Production
Category B	**Starting point** 26 weeks' custody **Category range** High level community order–18 months' custody	**Starting point** 1 year's custody **Category range** 26 weeks–2 years' custody	**Starting point** 2 years' custody **Category range** 1–4 years' custody
Category C	**Starting point** High level community order **Category range** Medium level community order–26 weeks' custody	**Starting point** 13 weeks' custody **Category range** High level community order–26 weeks' custody	**Starting point** 18 months' custody **Category range** 1–3 years' custody

Aggravating and mitigating factors

After identifying the starting point and category range, the court should consider   **8.11F** whether the presence of aggravating or mitigating factors should result in an upward or downward adjustment from the starting point or the imposition of a sentence outside the category range. In particular, relevant recent convictions are likely to result in an upward adjustment. When sentencing appropriate category 2 or 3 offences, the court should also consider whether the custody threshold has been passed; if so, whether a custodial sentence is unavoidable; and if it is, whether that sentence can be suspended. The list of aggravating and mitigating factors is non-exhaustive: the Council stated in its consultation that its intention was to set out factors that are likely to be relatively common to offences relating to indecent images of children to ensure that they are considered equally by all courts. The factors are:

Aggravating factors

Statutory aggravating factors

- Previous convictions, having regard to a) the nature of the offence to which the conviction relates and its relevance to the current offence; and b) the time that has elapsed since the conviction
- Offence committed whilst on bail

Other aggravating factors

- Failure to comply with current court orders
- Offence committed whilst on licence
- Age and/or vulnerability of the child depicted*
- Discernable pain or distress suffered by child depicted
- Period over which images were possessed, distributed or produced
- High volume of images possessed, distributed or produced
- Placing images where there is the potential for a high volume of viewers
- Collection includes moving images
- Attempts to dispose of or conceal evidence
- Abuse of trust
- Child depicted known to the offender
- Active involvement in a network or process that facilitates or commissions the creation or sharing of indecent images of children
- Commercial exploitation and/or motivation
- Deliberate or systematic searching for images portraying young children, category A images or the portrayal of familial sexual abuse
- Large number of different victims
- Child depicted intoxicated or drugged

*Age and/or vulnerability of the child should be given significant weight. In cases where the actual age of the victim is difficult to determine sentencers should consider the development of the child (infant, pre-pubescent, post-pubescent)

Mitigating factors

- No previous convictions **or** no relevant/recent convictions
- Remorse
- Previous good character and/or exemplary conduct*
- Age and/or lack of maturity where it affects the responsibility of the offender

- Mental disorder or learning disability, particularly where linked to the commission of the offence
- Demonstration of steps taken to address offending behaviour

---

* Previous good character/exemplary conduct is different from having no previous convictions. The more serious the offence, the less the weight which should normally be attributed to this factor. Where previous good character/exemplary conduct has been used to facilitate the offence, this mitigation should not normally be allowed and such conduct may constitute an aggravating factor.

The Sentencing Council's consultation on the draft guideline explained its reasons for including the various aggravating factors: **8.11G**

- It thought "age and/or vulnerability of the child depicted" should be given significant weight. In cases where the victim's actual age is difficult to determine, sentencers should consider their development (infant, pre-pubescent, post-pubescent). The SGC guideline included a suggestion that starting points should be higher where the subject of the photograph was under the age of 13. The Council recognised the difficulty for sentencers in ascribing an age to an unidentified victim and said it did not believe there should be a strict cut-off in age terms when assessing the harm caused to the victim, and that an assessment of the child's developmental stage will assist the sentencer more.
- "Discernable pain or distress suffered by child depicted" appeared in the consultation draft as "visible physical pain suffered by the child depicted". The Council intended this factor to cover the increased harm demonstrated where the victim is visibly responding to physical pain. But it expanded the factor in the published guideline by replacing "visible physical pain" with "discernable pain or distress", in response to comments that this factor should apply equally where distress as opposed to pain is suffered and where the pain or distress is audible rather than visible.
- "Period over which the images were possessed, made or distributed" is included as it enables a more comprehensive picture to be formed of the offender's behaviour and may be relevant to risk. Where an offender has been involved with such images over a long period, sentencers may wish to take this into consideration in determining whether to give any weight to a claim of previous good character.
- "High volume of images possessed, distributed or produced" allows the sentencer to take into account the volume of images where this is a significant consideration. There will be cases when a high volume of images is a very significant aggravating factor especially where the material is being distributed or produced.
- "Placing images where there is the potential for a high volume of viewers" is intended to deal with the increased harm to the victim where an offender puts images in a place where, potentially, a large number of people could

access them. It is intended to reflect the emotional distress caused to the victim by the potential for large numbers of unknown individuals to view them in a vulnerable state.

- "Collection includes moving images" is included because the Council felt that one moving image lasting, for example, 20 minutes does not equate directly with one still image as more than one abusive incident may take place during that period and potentially hundreds of still images may be taken from one 20-minute film.
- "Attempts to dispose of or conceal evidence" is designed to address issues arising from the increasingly sophisticated efforts of offenders to prevent images being discovered. It will cover activity ranging from the mis-labelling of files to give the impression that the content is lawful to advanced encryption techniques.
- "Abuse of trust" and "child depicted known to the offender" are aggravating factors because both indicate the close proximity of the offender to the commission of the abuse. In very many cases the victim will not have been identified, but where the evidence establishes the offender's knowledge of the child or abuse of trust it will demonstrate increased culpability due to the targeting or manipulation of the victim.
- "Active involvement in a network or process that facilitates or commissions the creation or sharing of indecent images of children" is included as this demonstrates a higher level of culpability on the part of the offender.
- As for "deliberate or systematic searching for images portraying young children, category A images or the portrayal of familial sexual abuse", where such searches are uncovered by forensic examination they can reveal that the offender has been searching for higher levels of image than those recovered. Whilst the offender can only be sentenced for the images recovered, such searches can assist the court in assessing culpability.
- The factors "commercial exploitation and/or motivation", "large number of different victims" and "child depicted intoxicated or drugged" were all added in response to comments made on the consultation draft. The consultation draft included as an aggravating factor "systematic storage of collection", on the basis that such storage may increase culpability by demonstrating the deliberate thought and effort invested by the offender in collecting indecent images. However, responses to the consultation queried how systematic storage can amount to an aggravating factor if it does not involve hiding or concealment. The Council accepted that hiding or concealment is the greater aggravation and so retained "attempts to dispose or conceal evidence" but removed the reference to systematic storage.

Steps Three to Nine

8.11H   The remaining steps cover the following points. At step three the court should consider any factors which would indicate a reduction in sentence, e.g. assistance to the prosecution. At step four it should consider any reduction for a guilty plea. At step five the court should consider dangerousness, i.e. whether it would be appropriate to award an extended sentence (s.226A of the CJA 2003). Step six requires the court to consider whether the total sentence is just and proportionate to the offending behaviour. At step seven it should consider whether to make an ancillary order (e.g. a compensation order, a SOPO or a restraining order). Step eight requires the court to fulfil its duty under s.174 of the CJA 2003 to give reasons for, and explain the effect of, the sentence. Finally, at step nine the court should consider whether to give credit for time spent on bail in accordance with s.240A of that Act.

Sentencing examples

Officer[7] pre-dates the new guideline but remains of interest. The appellant **8.19** appealed against sentences imposed, following guilty pleas, of 3 years' imprisonment for two offences of making indecent photographs of children and 3 years' imprisonment concurrent for possessing an extreme pornographic image. He had previously been convicted of nine offences, including seven for sexual assault on a girl under 13, and had been sentenced to 54 months' imprisonment. Since those convictions he had completed the Sex Offender Treatment Programme, the Thames Valley Sex Offender Groupwork Programme and a further Sex Treatment (South East Consortium) Impaired Development Programme, which was directed at relapse prevention. Shortly after the expiration of his licence period he was caught with level 4 images and videos on his computer. The appellant submitted that the judge had wholly ignored the SGC guideline in passing the sentence. His appeal was allowed in part, because the sentence of 3 years' imprisonment for possessing an extreme pornographic image had exceeded the statutory maximum and was therefore quashed and, in light of the appellant's guilty plea, a sentence of 16 months' imprisonment was substituted. As to the indecent photograph offences, the judge had not ignored the guideline. He had adverted to it, but had correctly decided that it was of limited value on the facts of this case. The judge had been bound to move outside the guideline for five reasons: the very serious nature of the previous convictions, which had been predatory offences in breach of trust on very young girls; the fact that since his conviction the appellant had undergone a comprehensive programme of treatment, but, according to a probation officer, there was a knowledge gap for professionals as to how he met his sexual needs and the content of his fantasies; his lack of candour as to the reason for requiring a laptop computer; the fact that the instant offences occurred so soon after the expiry of his licence period from his previous sentence; and the fact that the instant offences were a repeat of the escalation that had previously been seen from adult pornography to child pornography, which had led to the earlier offences. There was every reason to think that the appellant would, if unchecked, progress once more to the same type

---

[7] [2012] EWCA Crim 1685.

of offending. There were no countervailing factors to suggest that such escalation would not occur. The Court therefore endorsed the judge's approach and upheld the sentence for making indecent photographs of children.

Parties to the Offence

8.23 In the main work we expressed the view that if the child who is photographed encourages the offence, they are in principle liable to conviction as an accessory, though it is highly unlikely that a prosecution in those circumstances would be considered to be in the public interest. We considered that the decision in *Tyrrell*[8] was distinguishable in this context, since the offence in that case was created to protect girls against men and there was no indication in the statute of an intention to criminalise the girls themselves, whereas anyone over the age of criminal responsibility may be convicted under the 1978 Act, and if a child may commit the offence as principal, it is difficult to conclude that they cannot do so as accessory, even where the offence is committed against them. On that basis there appears to be no logical objection based upon *Tyrrell* to convicting a child as an accessory to a 1978 Act offence of which they were the victim.

Of relevance to this point is a passage in the reasoning of the majority of the Supreme Court in the decision in *Gnango*.[9] In that case, the majority held (Lord Kerr dissenting) that where D1 and D2 voluntarily enter into a fight against each other, each intending to kill or cause grievous bodily harm to the other and each foreseeing that the other has a reciprocal intention, and where D1 mistakenly kills a third party (V) in the course of the fight, then not only D1 but also D2 is guilty of murdering V. The significance of the decision for present purposes is that in the course of its reasoning the majority considered the decision in *Tyrrell*, which it said was an illustration of a general rule[10] that where legislation creates an offence that is intended to protect a class of persons, a member of that class cannot be convicted as an accessory to such an offence committed in respect of him. Defined in this broad way, the rule in *Tyrrell* would, contrary to the argument in the main work, operate to prevent the victim of a 1978 Act offence from being prosecuted as an accessory to the offence, since the Act is undoubtedly designed to protect the class of persons comprising children under 18, albeit that a child under that age can commit the offence as principal or indeed as accessory where they are not the victim.

As a practical matter the point has been put beyond argument by *Att Gen's Ref (No.53 of 2013) (R. v Wilson)*,[10a] in which the defendant pleaded guilty and was sentenced to 8 months' imprisonment for an offence of sexual activity with a child, a girl aged 13, contrary to s.9 of the 2003 Act. The girl was sexually experienced and prosecuting counsel described her in the course of the sentencing

---

[8] [1894] 1 Q.B. 710; and see *DPP v Whitehouse* [1977] Q.B. 868.

[9] [2011] UKSC 59 at [17]–[19], [47]–[53].

[10] Identified by Professor Glanville Williams in his article "Victims and other exempt parties in crime" (1990) 10 *Legal Studies* at p.245.

[10a] [2013] EWCA Crim 2544.

hearing as "predatory", a term picked up by the judge in his sentencing remarks. On a reference by the Attorney General under s.36 of the Criminal Justice Act 1988, the Court of Appeal held that the sentence was plainly unduly lenient. In doing so, it accepted the Attorney General's submission that the fact that the victim had initiated what had happened was an aggravating, rather than a mitigating factor. Lord Thomas C.J. said[10b]:

> "It has been clear since at least the Offences Against the Person Act 1861, and subsequent nineteenth century legislation, that the purpose of Parliament in passing legislation to make it a crime punishable with imprisonment to have sexual relations with those under 16 was to protect those under 16. Indeed the Criminal Law Amendments Act 1885 makes it expressly clear that that was the purpose of the legislation. That can be seen from the preamble to the Act and was made clear by this court in *R. v Tyrrell* [1894] 1 QB 710.
>
> That long-standing principle is well-known. The reduction of punishment on the basis that the person who needed protection encouraged the commission of an offence is therefore simply wrong. We agree with the submission of the Attorney General that an underage person who encourages sexual relations with her needs more protection, not less. Accepting that as the basis for sentencing for the reasons we have explained, the fact that the offender took advantage of what he asserted the victim did aggravated the offence."

If a child who initiates sexual relations is more in need of the law's protection than other child victims, it must follow that there can be little or no public interest in prosecuting such a child in relation to sexual offences committed against her. Accordingly, whatever the precise ambit of the rule in *Tyrrell*, it is almost inconceivable that the public interest would ever require the prosecution of a child in relation to a 1978 Act offence of which she was herself the victim.

Officers of corporations

Of relevance to the discussion in the main work is *Chargot (t/a Contract Services)*   **8.25** *& others*[11] which concerned proceedings under ss.2(1) and 3(1) of the Health and Safety at Work Act 1974. Section 37 of that Act makes provision for the liability of a director, manager, secretary or other officer of a body corporate in terms almost identical to s.3 of the 1978 Act. The House of Lords held in that case that no fixed rule could be laid down as to what the prosecution must identify and prove in order to establish that a company officer's state of mind had been such as amounted to consent, connivance or neglect within the meaning of s.37 of the 1974 Act. Where the officer's place of activity was remote from the workplace or what was done there was not under his immediate direction and control, it might require the reading of quite detailed evidence, of which fair notice might have to be given. Where the officer was in day-to-day contact with what was done at the workplace, very little more than establishing that the body corporate had committed an offence might be necessary. The question will always be whether the officer in question should have been put on enquiry so as to take steps to

---

[10b] At [19]–[20].
[11] [2008] UKHL 73.

determine whether or not the appropriate safety features had been in place. The state of mind that connivance and neglect contemplated was one that could also be established by inference. Where it was shown that the body corporate failed to achieve or prevent the result contemplated by ss.2(1) and 3(1), it would be a relatively short step for the inference to be drawn that there had been connivance or neglect on the part of the officer, if the circumstances under which the risk had arisen had been under his direction or control. The more remote his area of responsibility was in those circumstances, the harder it would be to draw that inference.

Section 1(1)(a)—"To Make"

8.41   Further to fn.22 in the main work, for an analysis of the law as it applies to "sexting", i.e. the taking and sending of indecent self-portraits by mobile telephone, and whether, in the case of children, treating recipients as sex offenders risks unfairly stigmatising consensual sexual activity, see Felicity Gerry, "Sexting and the Criminal Law" (2010) C.L. & J. 174 (51/52), 786.

Section 1(1)(b)—"distribute or show"

8.45   It is, we suggest, an offence under s.1(1)(b) for a person in the UK to upload indecent images of children to a website to which other computer users have access, even if the website is hosted by a remote server in another jurisdiction. This proposition derives strong support from *Sheppard and Whittle*,[12] in which it was held that a person who, in the UK, had produced racially inflammatory material and posted it on a website hosted by a remote server in the USA could be tried in the UK under s.19 of the Public Order Act 1986 because a substantial measure of his activities had taken place here, in accordance with the test laid down in *Smith (Wallace Duncan) (No.4)*.[13] In that case the appellants appealed against convictions for possessing, publishing and distributing racially inflammatory material contrary to s.19 of the 1986 Act. W had written material which cast doubt on the existence of the holocaust and contained derogatory remarks about a number of racial groups. S had edited the material and uploaded it to a website which he had set up for the purpose of disseminating it. The website was hosted by a remote server located in California. Once posted on the site, the material was available to be viewed and downloaded in a number of countries including the UK. Some of the material was distributed in the UK in print form through the post. At trial, the prosecution relied upon evidence from a police officer who had visited the site and downloaded the documents. The judge, applying *Smith (Wallace Duncan) (No.4)*, decided that the court had jurisdiction because a substantial measure of S and W's activities had taken place in the UK. The appellants submitted that the judge should not have applied the "substantial measure" test

---

[12] [2010] EWCA Crim 65.
[13] [2004] EWCA Crim 631.

as offences concerning publication on the internet could only be heard in the jurisdiction where the web server was located. The Court of Appeal dismissed that contention. In considering whether there was any basis for not applying the "substantial measure" test, the starting point was the terms of the 1986 Act. Section 42 provided that the Act's provisions extended to England and Wales save for some limited exceptions which mainly related to Scotland and Northern Ireland. The section did not assist in taking the case outside the jurisdiction principle in *Smith*. It was not a restriction of jurisdiction to England and Wales, rather, it set out the limitations as to its extent within England and Wales and was not determinative of the jurisdiction of the court. Further, the "substantial measure" test not only accorded with the purpose of the relevant provisions of the Act, it also reflected the practicalities of the instant case, where almost everything related to the UK, which was where the material was generated, edited, uploaded and controlled. The material was aimed primarily at the British public. The only foreign element was that the website was hosted by a server in California, but the use of the server was merely a stage in the transmission of the material. There was accordingly abundant evidence to satisfy the "substantial measure" test.

To what extent does this analysis apply to offences under the 1978 Act? The jurisdictional point reads across exactly, since s.9 of the 1978 Act, which describes the Act's extent, is materially identical in its terms to s.42 of the 1986 Act. As to the "substantial measure" test, this would seem equally applicable in the context of the 1978 Act. Whether the test is satisfied in any given case will of course depend upon the evidence, but if it is established that the defendant uploaded and controlled the indecent material in this jurisdiction, whether or not he generated or edited it, we suggest the test will be satisfied, and this is regardless of the material aimed at.

EXCEPTIONS FOR CONSENT WITHIN MARRIAGE OR OTHER RELATIONSHIP

The defence in s.1A, which applies where the photograph or pseudo-photograph   8.54
was taken when the child was 16 or 17 and shows the child alone or with the defendant, and at the time of the alleged offence the child and the defendant were married or cohabiting, has been extended to cases in which at that time the child and the defendant were in a civil partnership.[14] From the date on which the Marriage (Same Sex Couples) Act 2013 comes into force, on a day to be appointed, the reference to marriage in s.1A is to be read as including a reference to marriage of a same sex couple.[15]

In *R. v DM*[16] it was held that the s.1A defence should not be interpreted as   8.56
applying where the defendant and a child engaged in lawful and consensual sexual intercourse as a "one night stand" immediately before the photographs in

---

[14] Civil Partnership Act 2004, s.261(1) and Sch.27 para.60, which came into force on December 5, 2005.
[15] Marriage (Same Sex Couples) Act 2013, s.11 and Sch.3, Pt 1 para.1.
[16] [2011] EWCA Crim 2752.

question were taken. The complainant (17) and the appellant (23) had drunk alcohol and smoked cannabis together before having sex. Immediately afterwards, the appellant took intimate photographs of the complainant with his mobile phone. He was charged under s.1(1)(a) of the 1978 Act with making indecent photographs of a child. At the close of the evidence, the Recorder rejected an argument that, in order to give effect to the appellant's rights under art.8 (private and family life) and art.10 (freedom of expression) of the European Convention on Human Rights, the s.1A defence should be interpreted as applying to a brief sexual relationship or "one night stand" of the sort that had occurred in this case. The appellant was convicted and argued on appeal that the Recorder had erred in interpreting the defence as he had. Sexual relations between the complainant and the appellant had, he said, been consensual and therefore lawful. There was no evidence of an intention to distribute the photographs; indeed, such evidence as there was indicated than the appellant would probably have deleted them in order that his girlfriend did not see them. The limitation of the s.1A defence to 16- and 17-year-olds who were married or "living together as partners in an enduring family relationship" was arbitrary, unjustified and disproportionate, since it meant that an unmarried, non-cohabiting 16- or 17-year-old has the capacity in law to consent to intercourse but not to the taking of photographs during intercourse, whereas a married or cohabiting 16- or 17-year-old has both. The appellant argued that the taking of an image with consent, following lawful consensual sexual relations, cannot require the imposition of criminal liability so as to protect children from sexual exploitation, particularly in the light of the existence of the offences in s.1(1)(b)–(d) of the Act, in relation to which no defence of consent arises. An argument that the taking of such a photograph must be subject to criminal liability so as to prevent future pornographic use is speculative. Accordingly, arts 8 and 10 were engaged; the interference with the appellant's rights was not necessary in a democratic society for any of the legitimate aims listed in art 8(2) or 10(2); and the Act's failure to make allowance for the private lives of 16- and 17-year-olds who are sexually active whilst living with their parents was accordingly a violation of those rights.

The Court of Appeal rejected what it called this "bold submission". It noted the UK's obligations under international law (art.34 of the UN Convention on the Rights of the Child and art.3 of the EU Framework Decision 2004/68/JHA) to take measures to protect children from exploitation through pornography. It also noted the decision in *Smethurst*,[17] decided when the 1978 Act protected children under 16, that s.1(1)(a) of the Act was compatible with arts 8 and 10. In the course of its decision, the Court of Appeal in that case had rejected an argument that s.1(1)(a) should apply only where the photographs were intended for indecent purposes, on the basis that "once the photographs come into existence, the harm may be done [as the] person in possession may circulate them". The Court went on to consider the obligation placed on it by s.3 of the Human Rights Act 1998, so far as possible to read and give effect to legislation compatibly with Convention

[17] [2002] 1 Cr. App. R. 6.

rights. But it concluded that s.1A was drafted so as to provide effective protection for children whilst balancing Convention rights, and without the prohibition on the taking of indecent photographs there could be no effective protection. The Act did no more than was necessary to accomplish that objective. Parliament had identified circumstances in which the taking of such a photograph should *not* be criminalised, and without limiting those circumstances as it had (i.e. to married and cohabiting couples) there could not be the same degree of certainty about the genuine nature of the commitment in a relationship, which can easily be terminated and may be very short term. A defence which included a brief sexual relationship would diminish the protection provided and risk introducing issues as to the circumstances in which the photograph was taken and the motivation for taking it. In short, the limitation was necessary for the prevention of crime and the protection of morals, in particular the protection of children from being exploited, and struck the balance between keeping to a minimum the interference by the State in the private lives of individuals and maintaining the maximum protection of children from sexual abuse and exploitation.

This decision prompted James Turner QC to lambast:

> " . . . the absurdity of a law that says a man may have sexual intercourse with a 17-year-old girl, but commits an offence if he takes a photograph of her in a state of undress even though she gives her wholehearted consent. If 16- and 17-year-olds need protection from persons who may wish to take photographs of them when undressed, they surely must be in much more urgent need of protection from predators who would like to take them to bed."[18]

Whatever the force of this comment, it is not so much a criticism of *R. v DM* as an argument for raising the age of consent, which is perhaps unlikely to gain much traction. Ashworth and Collins put the matter a little differently by asking "whether Parliament was being inconsistent when, given that the age of consent to sexual activity is 16, it raised the age of consent to being photographed in an indecent pose to 18".[19] In this respect the authors note that Parliament was not compelled by the UK's international obligations to increase the age limit for consent to 18, and that in English law 16 has long been the age of consent to sexual activity. Why, therefore, is a higher age of consent necessary in relation to indecent photographs? Why is it necessary to protect children from exploitation in the form of sexual activity until they are 16, but in the form of indecent photography until they are 18? These are good questions, to which there is no ready answer; but whatever their merit, *R. v DM* has settled the law until such time as Parliament sees fit to reconsider it.

FORENSIC EVIDENCE

For a discussion of ACPO's *Good Practice Guide for Computer-Based Electronic*   **8.78**
Evidence, and the issues which may arise when digital evidence is adduced in court, see Colin Smith, "Is Digital Evidence Really Forensic?", *Counsel* magazine,

---

[18] *Criminal Law Week*, Issue 34, 2012, p.2.
[19] [2012] Crim. L.R. 789 and 790-1.

January 2012, pp.27–28. More generally, see Micheál O'Floinn and David Ormerod, "Social Networking Material as Criminal Evidence" [2012] Crim. L.R. 486.

Recovery of encrypted images

8.85A   Suppose the police suspect an individual of holding indecent images of children on a computer or other digital storage medium, but are unable to gain access to the contents of the relevant files because they are protected by a password or some form of encryption? In those circumstances, they may be able to compel the individual to disclose the password or encryption key by service of a notice under s.49 of the Regulation of Investigatory Powers Act 2000.

Section 49 enables a properly authorised person, who may be a police officer, to serve a notice on an individual or body requiring them to disclose "protected information" in an intelligible form. Protected information is defined as any electronic data which, without the key to the data, cannot, or cannot readily, be accessed, or cannot, or cannot readily, be put into an intelligible form. Section 49 applies inter alia where the police have come into possession of protected information in the exercise of a statutory power to seize, detain, inspect, search or otherwise to interfere with documents or other property, e.g. on the execution of a search warrant issued under the Police and Criminal Evidence Act 1984. In those circumstances an officer with the "appropriate permission" (as defined in Sch.2 to the Act) may serve a s.49 notice requiring disclosure of protected information if he believes, on reasonable grounds:

- that a key to the protected information is in the possession of the person on whom the notice is served;
- that the imposition of a disclosure requirement in respect of the protected information is necessary in the interests of national security, for the purpose of preventing or detecting crime, in the interests of the economic well-being of the United Kingdom, or for the purpose of securing the effective exercise or proper performance by a public authority of any statutory power or duty;
- that imposing a disclosure requirement is proportionate to what is sought to be achieved by doing so; and
- that it is not reasonably practicable to obtain the protected information in an intelligible form in any other way.

A notice under s.49:

- must be given in writing or in a manner that produces a record of its having been given;
- must describe the protected information to which it relates;
- must specify the grounds on which the notice is given;
- must specify the office, rank or position held by the person giving it;
- must specify the office, rank or position of the person who granted permission for the notice to be given;
- must specify the time by which the notice is to be complied with;

- must set out the disclosure that is required by the notice and the form and manner in which it is to be made; and
- must allow a period for compliance which is reasonable in all the circumstances.

Section 50 of the Act explains the effect of serving a notice. Where the recipient has, when the notice is served, possession of the protected information and a means of accessing it and of disclosing it in an intelligible form, the effect of the notice is that they may use any key in their possession (such as a password, code, algorithm or encryption key) to access the information or to put it into intelligible form and they must disclose the information in accordance with the terms of the notice. Provision is made for a person who is required to disclose information in an intelligible form to instead disclose a relevant key if they so choose. Where the recipient of the notice does not have possession of the protected information, or of a key needed to access it, or the notice contains a direction (pursuant to s.51, below) that a key must be disclosed, the recipient must disclose any key to the information that is in their possession. The person giving the notice may allow the recipient access to the protected information in order to enable them to produce plain text rather than disclose a key. The recipient need only provide those keys which suffice to access the information and render it intelligible, and may choose which keys to provide to achieve that end. Where they no longer possess a key to the information, they must disclose all information in their possession that would facilitate the discovery of the key.

Section 51 sets out extra tests that are to be satisfied if a notice requires disclosure of a key rather than of protected information in an intelligible form. Such a notice may be given only if a direction to this effect has been given by the person giving permission for the notice to be served. A direction for the disclosure of a key must be authorised expressly by a person of the rank of chief officer of police or equivalent. A person may only give such a direction if he believes that there are special circumstances to the case making this necessary; and that giving such a direction is proportionate to what is sought to be achieved by doing so. In deciding whether it is proportionate to require that a key be disclosed, consideration must be given to the other sorts of information protected by the key in question and any potential adverse impact on a business that might result from requiring that a key be disclosed. Any direction to disclose a key given by the police must be notified, within seven days, to the Chief Surveillance Commissioner.

Section 53 makes it an offence knowingly to fail to comply with the disclosure requirements contained in a s.49 notice. It is a defence for a person to show that it was not practicable to comply with the disclosure requirement placed upon him by the time he was required to do so, but that he did what was required as soon as was reasonably practicable. There is no maximum penalty on conviction on indictment, but on summary conviction the maximum is a fine of £5,000.

The service of a s.49 notice may be capable of interfering with the recipient's **8.85B** privilege against self-incrimination. This issue arose for consideration in *Greater*

Manchester Police v Andrews,[20] in which the respondent was arrested on suspicion of committing offences under s.1(1)(a) of the 1978 Act by making indecent images of children. His laptop was seized together with two pen drives. The laptop contained indecent images of children and the police wished to know what was on the pen drives, but they were unable to access the files contained in them. The respondent declined to provide any information as to the passwords and software applications that he had used to protect the files. The police therefore applied to a circuit judge for permission to serve on the respondent an order under s.49 of the Regulation of Investigatory Powers Act 2000 requiring him to disclose encryption keys to the pen drives. The judge refused permission on the ground that requiring the respondent to reveal the keys would be incompatible with his privilege against self-incrimination, since if by complying with the notice he revealed his knowledge of the keys, this would itself be an incriminating fact which had no existence independent of the recipient's will.[21] The Administrative Court allowed an appeal against this ruling, holding that an application for permission to serve a notice under s.49 engages the privilege against self-incrimination only to a very limited extent, and that in this case the interference with the privilege was entirely proportionate (within the meaning of s.49(2)(c) of the Act) to what the police were seeking to achieve, namely the protection of the public from crime. In reaching this decision the Court noted that at any trial following service of the notice, the judge would be empowered to exclude evidence of material discovered on the pen drives, of the keys or other means of access to the drives, and of the respondent's knowledge of those keys or means of access, as in the judge's discretion seemed appropriate in order to preserve the respondent's privilege against self-incrimination.

Perverting the course of justice by deleting indecent images

8.85C   In *T v R.*[22] the appellant was charged with doing an act tending and intended to pervert the course of public justice on evidence that she had deleted files with titles indicative of child pornography from a memory stick belonging to her husband. The husband had been convicted some years before of downloading indecent images of children from the internet and was still a registered sex offender. The appellant's daughter had asked the appellant for a memory stick on which to download homework from her laptop. The appellant told her to look for one in a drawer. The appellant maintained that, when her daughter plugged the memory stick into her laptop, she had seen one file the title of which was something like "16 Sex". She had deleted it thinking it was adult pornography, so that her daughter would not see it. A computer expert later recovered from the

[20] [2011] EWHC 1966 (Admin).
[21] cf. *Saunders v U.K.* (1996) 23 E.H.R.R. 313, where the European Court of Human Rights said (at 358) "[T]he right not to incriminate oneself . . . does not extend to the use in criminal proceedings of material which may be obtained from the accused through compulsory powers but which have an existence independent of the will of the suspect, such as, inter alia, documents acquired pursuant to a warrant, breath, blood and urine samples and bodily tissue for the purpose of DNA testing."
[22] [2011] EWCA Crim 729.

memory stick three deleted files with titles indicative of child pornography, though the files did not contain any such material. The prosecution case was that the appellant had deleted these files with the intention of preventing a potential criminal investigation of her husband. The appellant was convicted and appealed on two grounds. First, the computer expert had been able to retrieve the names and contents of the deleted files, so there was no evidence that the appellant's deletion of the files tended to pervert the course of justice. Secondly, given the inoffensive content of the files, there was insufficient evidence that their deletion did tend to pervert the course of justice. The appeal was rejected. The Court of Appeal said that for the offence to be proved it must be established both that the defendant intended to pervert the course of justice and that the act in question tended to do so. In this case there was clear evidence that the appellant intended to pervert the course of justice by deleting the files, in order, as she must be taken to have thought, to render them unavailable to the police. The jury must be assumed to have found that she lied about the names of the files on the memory stick. Those lies, and the deletion of the files, were sufficient to justify the jury's finding of intent. As for the requirement that the act tended to pervert the course of justice, the Court said that it is not necessary to establish that the act did in fact affect the course of justice; it is sufficient that it created a serious risk that the course of justice would be affected. The course of justice includes the investigation by the police of a possible crime. An act that makes such an investigation more difficult, or which may mislead it, may tend to pervert the course of justice. Further, it is irrelevant that the act may be prejudicial to a potential defendant rather than to the police or the prosecuting authorities. For that reason, it was irrelevant that the files in this case, despite their titles, did not in fact contain child pornography. For similar reasons, the fact that the files were in the event recovered by a computer expert did not mean that their deletion could not be effective; in fact, if there had been sufficient use of the memory stick before the expert examined it, the files would have been overwritten and irrecoverable. For these reasons, the appellant had been rightly convicted.

POSSESSION OF AN INDECENT PHOTOGRAPH OR PSEUDO-PHOTOGRAPH OF A CHILD

Restriction on prosecution

See para.8.05, above.   8.88

SENTENCING

The Sentencing Council has issued a new guideline applicable to sex offenders   8.91
aged 18 or over who are sentenced on or after April 1, 2014: see para.1.20 et seq.,

above. A single guideline covers offences relating to indecent images of children and is discussed in para.8.11 et seq., above.

Parties to the Offence

8.92 As to whether the child depicted in the photograph or another child may be convicted as an accessory to the s.160 offence, see para.8.23 et seq., above.

Officers of corporations

8.93 See para.8.25, above.

"Possession"

8.98 In *MacLennan v HM Advocate*[23] the appellant was convicted of possessing indecent photographs or pseudo-photographs of a child contrary to s.52A(1) of the Civic Government (Scotland) Act 1982. The evidence related to images held on a laptop computer at his home. There were others in the house at the relevant time and the defence case was that one of them had been responsible for the images. The judge gave the jury no direction as to the meaning of "possession". The High Court of Justiciary quashed the conviction on the ground that the trial judge's omission to give the jury guidance as to the legal concept of possession, including the elements of knowledge and control, amounted to a miscarriage of justice. It said[24]:

> "Even if there had been no other occupant of the house who might have had access to the computer, we consider that the jury required guidance on the legal concept of possession, including basic directions about the elements of knowledge and control: cf. the observations of Dyson L.J. in *R v Porter*. Such directions were required a fortiori in this case, where there were several people who might have had access to the computer, and where the accused disclaimed responsibility and raised questions about the responsibility of another."

We respectfully agree with these comments, and suggest that the right course is for the judge to direct the jury on the meaning of "possession" in any case in which the defendant raises, or the evidence is capable of raising, an issue as to whether he had the necessary knowledge and control of the images in question.

8.98A The decision in *Porter* was followed in *Leonard*,[25] which concerned deleted indecent images of children found in a temporary internet file on the appellant's computer. The files would have been accessible only to someone with specialist computer skills or specialist software, and there was no evidence that the appellant had either. The judge directed the jury on the meaning of "possession" but did not directly address the issue of the retrievability of the images. After some

---

[23] [2012] HCJAC 94.
[24] [2012] HCJAC 94, at [19].
[25] [2012] EWCA Crim 277.

deliberation the jury sent her a note asking "If an image is stored on a computer but the user cannot actually retrieve it, could the image, in law, be said to be in a person's possession?" In the light of *Porter*, the appellant's counsel urged the judge to answer this question with a simple "No", but she instead directed the jury that there was no proof the appellant was a computer expert, indeed the evidence was to the contrary; and the images were not irretrievable, but in order to retrieve them special equipment was needed and no such equipment had been found. The Court of Appeal quashed the ensuing conviction on the basis that there was no sufficient evidence that the appellant was capable of retrieving the images so as to be in law in possession of them on the relevant date (which appears to have been the date on which the images were found). It said the jury should have been directed that for the appellant to be convicted, the prosecution had to prove that he was capable of retrieving the images or in a position to retrieve them; and, as the appellant's counsel had argued, the jury's question to the judge should have been answered with a simple "No". Indeed, though the Court did not say this, it seems clear that the evidence relating to retrievability was such that it would have been in order for the judge to withdraw the case from the jury at the close of the prosecution case.

The Court in *Porter* said that the problem addressed in that case, of whether **8.101** deleted files remain in the "possession" of the individual concerned, would not arise if he was charged with possession during the period from the time when he viewed the images[26] until he deleted them. In the main work we noted a practical difficulty with this approach, in that although deleted images may be retrievable from the unallocated disc space of the computer hard disc drive (if they have not been overwritten), the file data in the form of the dates of file creation, last modification and last access are not retained. Accordingly, in the absence of other evidence, it will not be possible for the prosecution to say when an image was created and when it was deleted. Such other evidence did however exist in *Miller*.[27] That case was tried before the decision in *Porter* and so the judge did not have the benefit of the analysis of the law declared in that case and did not direct the jury accordingly. The defendant was convicted, but after *Porter* was decided the Criminal Cases Review Commission referred his conviction to the Court of Appeal. The Court noted that no evidence had been adduced at trial that the defendant had access to the kind of specialist software which could enable him to access and control deleted material in the unallocated disc space of the computer's hard disc drive, and accordingly, following *Porter*, on the date the computer was seized he could not be said to have been in possession of the images. However, in order to rebut possible innocent explanations for the presence of the images raised by the defendant, and his denial that the computer had ever been connected to the internet, the prosecution had led evidence showing that in March 2001 someone using the name D Miller had installed Windows 98 on the computer; that someone

---

[26] Or, as suggested in *Miller* [2010] EWCA Crim 2883 at [25], the time when he assumed control of the computer.
[27] Last note.

using the initials DM had re-installed Windows 98 in February 2002; that the defendant's email address, using his own name, was in use on the computer in January and February 2002; that in those same months the computer had been used to visit a large number of child pornography websites; and that in the same period a number of internet searches had been made on the computer using key words which were plainly used in order to find images of child pornography. This evidence was adduced at trial in order to prove the knowledge necessary for possession, and the Court of Appeal said that the jury's verdict meant they must have accepted it, i.e. they must have found that the defendant and not somebody else had searched for child pornography and accessed it many times in January and February 2002. On those facts, unlike in *Porter*, there was clear evidence linking the defendant to the images beyond the simple fact of their presence on his computer. The potential fly in the ointment was that the indictment charged the defendant with possession "on or before 20th November 2002", the date on which the computer was seized, and the Court of Appeal said the inclusion of the words "or before" was conventional drafting and had not been intended and was not apt to focus attention on the period January–February 2002. However, the Court solved this conundrum by accepting the argument of counsel for the Crown that as a matter of general law the date referred to in an indictment is not a material averment. Accordingly, it was not necessary for the Crown to prove that the defendant had the images in his possession on the date of seizure of the computer, and it was sufficient to prove that he had them in his possession *at some time*, as was the case here. By these means the Court of Appeal was able to avoid having to quash a well-merited conviction because of a defect in the drafting of the indictment. However, in a future case in which there is evidence of possession relating to a period prior to the date of seizure of the computer, the appropriate course would be to specify that period in the indictment. An even better option, in cases such as *Miller* where there is evidence of internet browsing, is to charge the defendant with making, rather than possessing, indecent images: see para.8.41 of the main work. If it can be proved who deleted the images, then if all else fails it may be possible to charge that person with doing an act tending and intended to pervert the course of justice: see *T v R.*,[28] discussed in para.8.85C, above.

Exception for Consent within Marriage or other Relationship

8.102   The defence in s.160A, which applies where the photograph or pseudo-photograph was taken when the child was 16 or 17 and shows the child alone or with the defendant, and at the time the defendant possessed or obtained it he and the child were married or cohabiting, has been extended to cases in which at that time the defendant and the child were in a civil partnership.[29] From the date on

[28] [2011] EWCA Crim 729.
[29] Civil Partnership Act 2004, s.261(1) and Sch.27 para.127, which came into force on December 5, 2005.

which the Marriage (Same Sex Couples) Act 2013 comes into force, on a day to be appointed, the reference to marriage in s.160A is to be read as including a reference to marriage of a same sex couple.[30]

---

[30] Marriage (Same Sex Couples) Act 2013, s.11 and Sch.3, Pt 1 para.1.

CHAPTER 9

CHILD ABDUCTION

MODE OF TRIAL AND PUNISHMENT

The Criminal Practice Directions 2013[1] have replaced the Consolidated Criminal   **9.08**
Practice Direction 2002,[2] but with a saving for section III.21 of that Direction
dealing with classification of Crown Court business and allocation to Crown Court
centres. Accordingly, an offence under s.2(1) of the Police and Criminal Evidence
Act 1984 continues to fall within Class 3 by virtue of that provision.

SENTENCING

Two further sentencing examples are worthy of mention. In *Oakes*[3] the offender   **9.11**
was a man of 44 with drink-related convictions, though none for sexual or violent
offences. On the occasion in question, heavily intoxicated, he approached an
11-year-old boy who was waiting outside his school and said "Walk up here with
us". He then put his arms around the back of the boy's neck and said "Fucking
walk up here with us". They walked to the entrance to an alleyway where the
offender tried to kiss and cuddle the boy, who was pinned against the wall. He
succeeded in kissing the boy twice on the cheek. The boy was frightened. A
teacher shouted at the offender to stop and the boy managed to slip away. The
offender pleaded guilty to an offence under s.2(1)(b) of the 1984 Act and was
sentenced to 32 months' imprisonment and made subject to an indefinite sexual
offences prevention order and a restraining order in relation to the boy, his mother,
and the school. The sentence was upheld on appeal, the Court of Appeal

[1] [2013] EWCA Crim 1631.
[2] [2002] 1 W.L.R. 2870; (2002) 2 Cr. App. R. 35.
[3] [2011] 2 Cr. App. R.(S.) 588(102).

commenting that the incident was short but was only stopped because of the teacher's intervention. Whilst both a psychiatrist and a probation officer were of the opinion that the offender was not a danger to children, the judge had been entitled to infer that his motivation had been sexual. There was no mitigation in the fact that the offender had been drunk, and the sentence was plainly within the appropriate range.

9.11A   In *Wakeman*[4] the offender was an educated man of previous good character who had become an alcoholic. He was sitting on a park bench with another man when two three-year-old girls passed nearby, pushing their buggies. The girls had been taken to the park by their mothers. The appellant took hold of the girls' hands and walked with them a distance of 20–30 metres, leaving the buggies by the bench. When confronted by the mothers he said he was going to show the girls a teddy bear in the window of a house overlooking the park. It was not in dispute at trial that such a bear existed and could be seen from an area not far from where the mothers confronted the offender. There was no evidence of any ulterior motive. The offender was convicted on two counts under s.2(1)(a) of the 1984 Act. The judge took the view that the offences were of the utmost severity and crossed the custody threshold, and he sentenced the offender to 9 months' imprisonment concurrent on each count. The Court of Appeal disagreed that the custody threshold was crossed. The judge should, it said, have sentenced on the basis that the offender did not intend to remove the girls from the control of their mothers and that his only intention was to show them the teddy bear. His intention and motive were highly relevant to sentence and, in the Court's view, a non-custodial sentence should have been passed. As the offender had already served the equivalent of a 6-month sentence, it quashed the sentence of 9 months' imprisonment and substituted a conditional discharge for 1 year.

9.11B   These sentencing examples, and the others referred to in the main work, relate to offences committed by a stranger, possibly with a sexual purpose, rather than those committed in a familial setting by a parent following the breakdown of the parental relationship. For sentencing in that very different context, see *Kayani*.[5]

Parties to the Offence

9.14   We considered in the main work whether a child over the age of criminal responsibility but under the age of 16 could be convicted as an accessory to an offence of child abduction of which they are the victim. We suggested that the case could be made that there is no scope here to apply the principle in *Tyrrell*,[6] in which it was held that a young girl could not be convicted as accessory to an offence of having unlawful carnal knowledge with a girl under 16 committed against herself, as the offence was created to protect girls against men and there

---

[4] [2011] EWCA Crim 1649.
[5] [2011] EWCA Crim 2871.
[6] [1894] 1 Q.B. 710; and see *DPP v Whitehouse* [1977] Q.B. 868.

was no indication in the statute of an intention to criminalise the girls themselves. We suggested that the distinction from the present context rests on the fact that children over the age of criminal responsibility may commit an offence of child abduction as principal, so it is difficult to argue that Parliament did not intend to criminalise them; and if that is so, there is logically no basis for ruling out the possibility of them incurring secondary liability.

Of relevance to this point is a passage in the reasoning of the majority of the Supreme Court in the decision in *Gnango*.[7] In that case, the majority held (Lord Kerr dissenting) that where D1 and D2 voluntarily enter into a fight against each other, each intending to kill or cause grievous bodily harm to the other and each foreseeing that the other has a reciprocal intention, and where D1 mistakenly kills a third party (V) in the course of the fight, then not only D1 but also D2 is guilty of murdering V. The significance of the decision for present purposes is that in the course of its reasoning the majority considered the decision in *Tyrrell*, which it said was an illustration of a general rule[8] that where legislation creates an offence that is intended to protect a class of persons, a member of that class cannot be convicted as an accessory to such an offence committed in respect of him. Defined in this broad way, the rule in *Tyrrell* would indeed operate to prevent a victim of child abduction from being prosecuted as an accessory to the offence, since the abduction offence is undoubtedly intended to protect children under 16, though a child over the age of criminal responsibility can commit it as principal or indeed as accessory where they are not the victim.

As a practical matter the point has been put beyond argument by *Att Gen's Ref (No.53 of 2013) (R. v Wilson)*,[8a] in which the defendant pleaded guilty and was sentenced to eight months' imprisonment for an offence of sexual activity with a child, a girl aged 13, contrary to s.9 of the 2003 Act. The girl was sexually experienced and prosecuting counsel described her in the course of the sentencing hearing as "predatory", a term picked up by the judge in his sentencing remarks. On a reference by the Attorney General under s.36 of the Criminal Justice Act 1988, the Court of Appeal held that the sentence was plainly unduly lenient. In doing so, it accepted the Attorney General's submission that the fact that the victim had initiated what had happened was an aggravating, rather than a mitigating factor. Lord Thomas C.J. said[8b]:

> "It has been clear since at least the Offences Against the Person Act 1861, and subsequent nineteenth century legislation, that the purpose of Parliament in passing legislation to make it a crime punishable with imprisonment to have sexual relations with those under 16 was to protect those under 16. Indeed the Criminal Law Amendments Act 1885 makes it expressly clear that that was the purpose of the legislation. That can be seen from the preamble to the Act and was made clear by this court in *R. v Tyrrell* [1894] 1 QB 710.

---

[7] [2011] UKSC 59 at [17]–[19], [47]–[53].
[8] Identified by Professor Glanville Williams in his article "Victims and other exempt parties in crime" (1990) 10 Legal Studies at p.245.
[8a] [2013] EWCA Crim 2544.
[8b] At [19]–[20].

That long-standing principle is well-known. The reduction of punishment on the basis that the person who needed protection encouraged the commission of an offence is therefore simply wrong. We agree with the submission of the Attorney General that an underage person who encourages sexual relations with her needs more protection, not less. Accepting that as the basis for sentencing for the reasons we have explained, the fact that the offender took advantage of what he asserted the victim did aggravated the offence."

If a child who initiates sexual relations is more in need of the law's protection than other child victims, it must follow that there can be little or no public interest in prosecuting such a child in relation to sexual offences committed against her. Accordingly, whatever the precise ambit of the rule in *Tyrrell*, it is almost inconceivable that the public interest would ever require the prosecution of a child in relation to an abduction offence of which she was herself the victim.

"WITHOUT LAWFUL AUTHORITY OR REASONABLE EXCUSE"

9.17 In *R. v S(C)*[9] the Court of Appeal held that the defence of necessity is not available to a parent or guardian charged under s.1 of the 1984 Act with removing a child from the jurisdiction. However, the s.1 offence, unlike the offence of child abduction in s.2, can be committed without proof of absence of lawful authority or reasonable excuse, s.1 instead being subject to an exception based on consent. The better view, we suggest, is that the term "reasonable excuse" in s.2 is capable of covering those circumstances in which a defendant could otherwise run a defence of necessity.

Reasonable excuse

9.18 In *Wakeman*,[10] the facts of which are set out in para.9.11, above, the sole issue for the jury was whether the appellant had had a reasonable excuse for taking the girls out of the control of their mothers in the light of his evidence about why he took hold of their hands and walked with them, namely in order to show them a teddy bear in the window of a house overlooking the park. The jury convicted.

"TAKES OR DETAINS"

9.23 A useful authority on the meaning of "detains" in s.2(1) of the 1984 Act is *Mortimore*.[11] The appellant (21) was convicted under s.2(1)(b) of detaining SR (15) so as to keep her out of the lawful control of her mother. The background to the offence was that on a number of previous occasions SR had been found with the appellant after being reported missing by her mother. The appellant had

---

[9] [2012] EWCA Crim 389.
[10] [2011] EWCA Crim 1649.
[11] [2013] EWCA Crim 1639.

previously pleaded guilty to an offence of taking or detaining SR contrary to s.2(1)(b). On that occasion he had admitted SR into his home, where he lived with his family. When the police came to the address he told them SR was not there, but she was found hiding under a bed in an upstairs room. On the occasion which formed the basis of the charge, SR had left home one morning to go to school but instead went to the appellant's house. When she was reported missing, the police went to the appellant's home. They found him sitting on his bed wearing boxer shorts and a T-shirt. SR was lying fully-clothed in the same bed under a duvet. The appellant was arrested and made no comment either then or in interview. At trial he did not give evidence and put forward no defence but simply challenged the prosecution to prove its case. The jury convicted.

The appellant appealed against conviction on a number of grounds, one of which was that there was no evidence upon which the jury could have found that he "detained" SR within the meaning of the 1984 Act. It was accepted for the purposes of this submission that SR had been in the appellant's company for some four-and-a-quarter hours. The Court of Appeal noted that, under s.3(c) of the Act, a person shall be regarded as detaining a child if he "induces the child to remain with him". The judge had accepted that the prosecution was required to prove that the appellant had, by his positive act, induced SR to remain at his home. Such an inducement could, the judge found, be by the provision of shelter, company or hospitality. It was also necessary for the prosecution to prove that the appellant's inducement was a cause of SR's continued presence in his house. These were matters, the judge said, for the jury to resolve and he directed them as follows:

> "A person shall be regarded as detaining a child if he causes her to be detained or induces the child to remain with him . . . The word 'detained' does not mean that the prosecution need to prove that it was against [SR's] will. It did does not matter so far as the offence is committed whether SR wanted to be there, consented to being in the defendant's company, although such things would be relevant to what sentence may be appropriate in due course. . . . On the facts of this case the defendant has, say the prosecution, caused her to be detained by allowing her to be there from, on one view of the evidence, 8 o'clock in the morning until 2.15 in the afternoon. He has, say the prosecution, permitted her to be there, provided hospitality to her, at least in form of shelter, allowing her to be in his house, in his bedroom, on his bed. He need not be, I direct you . . . the only cause of her being there, just one cause. The prosecution say that she would not have been there or been there for that length of time without some action on his part and that to suggest that his was in the circumstances of this case an entirely passive role, in her being in his room on this afternoon and morning would be absurd."

The Court of Appeal held that this direction as to the necessary constituents of the offence was correct. It accepted that there had been no direct evidence of inducement. The question for the jury was whether, as a matter of objective fact, the appellant had by his inducement to SR caused her to remain with him so as to keep her out of the lawful control of her mother. It was an inference plainly available to them that SR could not and would not have remained away from her home or school were it not for the appellant's preparedness to offer her shelter at his home. On that basis the Court upheld the conviction.

"REMOVE FROM ... LAWFUL CONTROL"

9.26 In *Wakeman*[12] the facts of which are set out in para.9.11 above, the Court of Appeal held that defence counsel at trial had been entitled on the facts of the case to concede that there was a "removal from lawful control", in the sense established in *Leather* that the children were deflected by the defendant's actions from what they would, with parental consent, have been doing.

MENTAL ELEMENT

9.28 The decision of the Divisional Court in *Foster v DPP,*[13] that the *mens rea* of the child abduction offence in s.2 of the 1984 Act is "an intentional or reckless taking or detention of a child under the age of 16, the effect or objective consequence of which is to remove or to keep that child within the meaning of section 2(1)(a) or (b)" was cited with approval by the Court of Appeal in *R. v X*[14] and *Wakeman.*[15]

9.30 Confirmation that even an unreasonable belief that the child was 16 or over will provide a defence under s.2(3)(b) is provided by *Heys and Murtagh,*[16] in which the Court of Appeal said[17]:

> "It is entirely clear ... that this statutory defence does not require proof of a reasonable belief; only a honestly held subjective belief."

In that case, prosecution counsel had wrongly stated in his opening speech that a reasonable belief was required. He corrected himself in closing. The judge did not mention the error in summing up, but did mention various objective factors which logically would be at least as relevant to a question of reasonable belief as to a question of honest belief. The Court accepted that the reasonableness of an asserted belief is material to the question whether it is honestly held (citing *Williams*[18] and *Beckford*[19]). But it concluded that in this case, in the absence of a clear statement by the judge that honesty and not reasonableness was the test, there had been a "lively chance" that the jury had taken the judge's direction to express a requirement of reasonable belief, and for that reason the convictions were unsafe.

[12] Above, fn.10.
[13] [2004] EWHC 2955 (Admin); [2005] 1 W.L.R. 1402.
[14] [2010] EWCA Crim 2367, para 18.
[15] Above, fn.10 at [16].
[16] [2011] EWCA Crim 2112.
[17] At [6].
[18] (1984) 78 Cr. App. R. 276.
[19] [1988] A.C. 130.

CHAPTER 10

PROSTITUTION: EXPLOITATION AND TRAFFICKING

A. ABUSE OF CHILDREN THROUGH PROSTITUTION AND PORNOGRAPHY

PAYING FOR SEXUAL SERVICES OF A CHILD

MODE OF TRIAL AND PUNISHMENT

For convictions on or after December 3, 2012,[1] an offence under s.47 committed   **10.07**
against a person under the age of 16 is a specified offence for the purposes of
s.226A of the Criminal Justice Act 2003 ("CJA 2003") (extended sentence for
certain violent or sexual offences), irrespective of the date of commission of the
offence.

In 2007 the Council of Europe adopted the *Convention on the Protection of Children*   **10.08**
against Sexual Exploitation and Sexual Abuse.[2] Following its fifth ratification, the

---

[1] When s.124 of the Legal Aid, Sentencing and Punishment of Offenders Act 2012 was brought into
force by the Legal Aid, Sentencing and Punishment of Offenders Act 201212 (Commencement No.4
and Saving Provisions) Order 2012 (SI 2012/2906).

[2] CETS No.201.

Convention entered into force on July 1, 2010. The UK signed the Convention on May 5, 2008 but has yet to ratify it. The Convention was the first international treaty to address all forms of sexual violence against children including child prostitution, child pornography, grooming and corruption of children through exposure to sexual content and activities. Its trademark is the "4 Ps" approach:

- Prevent and combat sexual exploitation and abuse of children,
- Protect the rights of child victims,
- Prosecute the perpetrators, and
- Promote appropriate policies and national and international co-operation against this phenomenon.

The Convention covers the following main topics: preventive and protective measures; assistance to child victims and their families; intervention programmes or measures for child sex offenders; criminal offences; child-friendly procedures for investigation and prosecution; recording and storing of data on convicted sex offenders; international co-operation; and a monitoring mechanism based on a body, the Committee of the Parties, composed of representatives of the parties to the Convention.

10.08A   The EU's 2004 *Framework Decision on combating the sexual exploitation of children and child pornography*[3] laid down a set of common minimum rules for EU States. In particular, it established common provisions on criminalisation, sanctions, aggravating circumstances, assistance to victims and jurisdiction. In order to enhance the level of protection for children from sexual exploitation, in March 2010 the Commission submitted a proposal for a new Directive on sexual abuse, sexual exploitation of children, and child pornography to replace the 2004 Framework Decision. The UK opted-in to the proposal in June 2010. The European Parliament and the Council reached an agreement on the text of the Directive in June 2011 and it came into force in December 2011.[4] Member States had until December 2013 to implement the Directive, which contains provisions on the prosecution of offenders, the protection of victims, and crime prevention. It was expected to have little, if any, impact on domestic criminal law, which the Government regarded as already compliant with the Directive. Crispin Blunt MP, the Parliamentary Under-Secretary of State for Justice, said in the Commons[5]:

> "As a leader in this field, we already comply with much of what is required by the directive, but by opting in, we have shown our support for the European Union's work in this area and we ensure that other member states will also have high standards in this field. The effect on our justice system will be minimal and we are developing co-operation mechanisms with other member states in seeking to ensure that all

---

[3] Council Framework Decision 2004/68/JHA of December 22, 2003 on combating the sexual exploitation of children and child pornography.

[4] Directive 2011/93/EU of the European Parliament and of the Council of December 13, 2011 on combating the sexual abuse and sexual exploitation of children and child pornography, and replacing Council Framework Decision 2004/68/JHA.

[5] HC (2010-11), European Committee B, April 26, 2011, col.18.

member states have common minimum standards of protection for children from sexual exploitation across Europe. We will seek to transpose by administrative measures, but some secondary legislation may be required."

For transposing regulations, see the Special Measures for Child Witnesses (Sexual Offences) Regulations 2013,[6] discussed at para.18.15, below, and the Working with Children (Exchange of Criminal Conviction Information) (England and Wales and Northern Ireland) Regulations 2013.[7] The latter place an obligation upon the chief officer of a police force to comply with the information-sharing requirements of art.10(3) of the Directive; require the Secretary of State to identify a chief officer to implement those requirements; and allow that chief officer to obtain on request relevant information relating to disqualification from working with children from the Disclosure and Barring Service.

Finally, the CPS's guidance to prosecutors on the 2003 Act referred to in the main work has been archived.[8]   **10.08B**

SENTENCING

The Sentencing Council has issued a new guideline applicable to sex offenders   **10.10**
aged 18 or over who are sentenced on or after April 1, 2014: see para.1.20 et seq., above. The previous guideline, issued in 2007 by the Sentencing Guidelines Council, was drafted on the basis that where the victim is under 16, the offender will be charged under ss.5–8 or s.9 of the 2003 Act (i.e. with an under-13 offence or an offence of sexual activity with a child). In its consultation on the draft guideline,[9] the Sentencing Council noted that since 2006, s.47 had been sentenced on 13 occasions with 4 of these cases involving a child under 16. Given the low volume of cases, the Council proposed that when sentencing for a s.47 offence committed in relation to a victim under the age of 16, the sentencer should follow the guidelines for offences under ss.5–8 or s.9 (as appropriate), with the sentence being increased to reflect the element of commercial exploitation. This approach, which was universally supported in responses to the consultation, has the result that the new guideline in relation to s.47 should be used only where the victim was aged 16 or 17.

An issue that was not directly covered in the consultation but upon which the Sentencing Council received some of the strongest representations was the language used in relation to the exploitation offences, including those in s.47. See further on this at para.10.22, below.

---

[6] SI 2013/2971.
[7] SI 2013/2945.
[8] It can be found at *http://webarchive.nationalarchives.gov.uk/20121210165327/http://www.cps.gov.uk/legal/s_to_u/sexual_offences_act/* [accessed December 30, 2013].
[9] *Sexual Offences Guideline: Consultation* (December 6, 2012).

New sentencing guideline

Step One—Harm and culpability

10.10A   Under the new guideline, the sentencing court is to go through a series of steps in order to determine the appropriate sentence. Step one involves determining the offence category by reference to the degree of harm caused and then the culpability level for the offence. As with offences of sexual activity with a child contrary to s.9 of the Act (for which see para.4.22 et seq., above), the guideline correlates harm to the sexual activity that has taken place. The harm and culpability factors for offences under s.47 are accordingly as follows:

HARM		CULPABILITY
Category 1	• Penetration of vagina or anus (using body or object) by, or of, victim	**A**
	• Penile penetration of mouth by, or of, victim	• Abduction/detention
	• Violence or threats of violence	• Sexual images of victim recorded, retained, solicited or shared
	• Victim subjected to unsafe/degrading sexual activity (beyond that which is inherent in the offence)	• Offender acts together with others to commit the offence
		• Use of alcohol/drugs on victim
		• Abuse of trust
		• Previous violence against victim
Category 2	• Touching of naked genitalia or naked breasts by, or of, the victim	• Sexual images of victim recorded, retained, solicited or shared
Category 3	• Other sexual activity	• Blackmail or other threats made (including to expose victim to the authorities, family/friends or others)
		• Offender aware that he has a sexually transmitted disease
		• Offender aware victim has been trafficked
		B
		Factor(s) in category A not present

In its consultation, the Sentencing Council said in relation to category 1 that, even where the victim is over the age of consent, being subjected to an activity that involves violence, or is unsafe or particularly degrading, will constitute high harm, as it will expose the victim to increased risk. However, the consultation placed penetrative activity within category 2. The Council acknowledged that in other guidelines relating to sexual activity with children, such activity is placed in the highest category of harm. However, those guidelines apply where the victim is under the age of consent, whereas the s.47 guideline applies only to victims aged 16 and 17. Ordinarily it is lawful to engage in penetrative activity with someone aged 16 or 17; it is the fact that the offender is paying for sexual services that makes this an offence. In consequence, the Council considered that the fact of penetration should not of itself place the offence in the highest category of harm. A number of respondents took issue with this approach, arguing that penetrative activity should be within category 1 regardless of age because the element of commercial exploitation outweighs the issue of the age of consent. The Council conceded the force of this argument and in the published guideline placed penetrative activity within category 1.

As regards culpability, the Council said that "abduction/detention" is included within level A because any limitation of the victim's freedom will increase the culpability inherent in a s.47 offence, whether the offender was involved in the abduction or detention or simply knew of it. "Offender aware that he has a sexually transmitted disease" reflects the increased culpability where the offender deliberately exposes the victim to the risk of contracting such a disease. "Offender aware victim has been trafficked" is included as there may be an overlap between the trafficking of a child and their sexual exploitation for commercial purposes, and if the offender is aware of the trafficking this will increase their culpability.

Step Two—Starting point and category range

Having determined the offence category and culpability level, the court should **10.10B** then use the corresponding starting point specified in the guideline in order to reach a sentence within the category range. The starting point applies to all offenders irrespective of plea or previous convictions. Once the starting point has been determined, step two allows further adjustment for aggravating or mitigating features, set out below. A case of particular gravity, reflected by multiple features of culpability or harm, could merit upward adjustment from the starting point before further adjustment for aggravating or mitigating features. Where there is a sufficient prospect of rehabilitation, a community order with a sex offender treatment programme requirement under s.202 of the CJA 2003 may be a proper alternative to a short or moderate length custodial sentence. The starting points and category ranges for offences under s.47 applicable where the victim is aged 16 or 17 are as follows:

	A	B
Category 1	**Starting point** 4 years' custody **Category range** 2–5 years' custody	**Starting point** 2 years' custody **Category range** 1–4 years' custody
Category 2	**Starting point** 3 years' custody **Category range** 1–4 years' custody	**Starting point** 1 year's custody **Category range** 26 weeks'–2 years' custody
Category 3	**Starting point** 1 year's custody **Category range** 26 weeks'–2 years' custody	**Starting point** 26 weeks' custody **Category range** High level community order–1 year's custody

Aggravating and mitigating factors

10.10C   After identifying the starting point and category range, the court should consider whether the presence of aggravating or mitigating factors should result in an upward or downward adjustment from the starting point or the imposition of a sentence outside the category range. In particular, relevant recent convictions are likely to result in an upward adjustment. When sentencing appropriate category 3 offences, the court should also consider whether the custody threshold has been passed; if so, whether a custodial sentence is unavoidable; and if it is, whether that sentence can be suspended. The non-exhaustive list of aggravating and mitigating factors for offences under s.47 is as follows:

Aggravating factors
Statutory aggravating factors
• Previous convictions, having regard to a) the nature of the offence to which the conviction relates and its relevance to the current offence; and b) the time that has elapsed since the conviction • Offence committed whilst on bail

Other aggravating factors
• Ejaculation
• Failure to comply with current court orders
• Offence committed whilst on licence
• Any steps taken to prevent the victim reporting an incident, obtaining assistance and/or from assisting or supporting the prosecution
• Attempts to dispose of or conceal evidence

Mitigating factors
• No previous convictions **or** no relevant/recent convictions
• Remorse
• Previous good character and/or exemplary conduct*
• Age and/or lack of maturity where it affects the responsibility of the offender
• Mental disorder or learning disability, particularly where linked to the commission of the offence
• Demonstration of steps taken to address offending behaviour

* Previous good character/exemplary conduct is different from having no previous convictions. The more serious the offence, the less the weight which should normally be attributed to this factor. Where previous good character/exemplary conduct has been used to facilitate the offence, this mitigation should not normally be allowed and such conduct may constitute an aggravating factor.

Steps Three to Nine

The remaining steps cover the following points. At step three the court should **10.10D** consider any factors which would indicate a reduction in sentence, e.g. assistance to the prosecution. At step four it should consider any reduction for a guilty plea. At step five the court should consider dangerousness, i.e. whether it would be appropriate to award an extended sentence (s.226A of the CJA 2003). Step six requires the court to consider whether the total sentence is just and proportionate to the offending behaviour. At step seven it should consider whether to make an ancillary order (e.g. a sexual offences prevention order ("SOPO") or a restraining order). Step eight requires the court to fulfil its duty under s.174 of the CJA 2003 to give reasons for, and explain the effect of, the sentence. Finally, at step nine the court should consider whether to give credit for time spent on bail in accordance with s.240A of that Act.

PARTIES TO THE OFFENCE

As to whether the child victim of a s.47 offence is liable to conviction as an **10.11** accessory to the offence, see the discussion in para.3.44 et seq., above.

CAUSING OR INCITING CHILD PROSTITUTION OR PORNOGRAPHY

Definition

10.19   The CPS's guidance to prosecutors on the 2003 Act referred to in the main work has been archived.[10]

Mode of Trial and Punishment

10.21   From December 3, 2012, when ss.122–128 of the Legal Aid, Sentencing and Punishment of Offenders Act 2012 were brought into force[11]:
- For offences committed on or after that date, an offence under s.48 is listed in Pt 1 of Sch.15B to the CJA 2003 for the purposes of s.224A of that Act (life sentence for second listed offence).
- For convictions on or after that date (irrespective of the date of commission of the offence), an offence under s.48 is a specified offence for the purposes of s.226A of that Act (extended sentence for certain violent or sexual offences).

Sentencing

10.22   The Sentencing Council has issued a new guideline applicable to sex offenders aged 18 or over who are sentenced on or after April 1, 2014: see para.1.20 et seq., above. In its consultation on the draft guideline,[12] the Sentencing Council noted that the offences in ss.48–50 of the 2003 Act are aimed at the commercial sexual exploitation of children. They have similarities with the offences in ss.8 and 10 of the Act (causing or inciting a child under 13/under 16 to engage in sexual activity), a key difference being that the definition of "child" extends here to all those under 18, i.e. it includes 16 and 17-year-olds. The Council noted that, perhaps because there are alternative charges for victims under 16, cases under ss.48–50 are rare: between 2006 and 2010 only 46 such cases were sentenced. It proposed to cover the offences in one guideline, given the commonality in the harm caused and in the culpability of the offender and the fact that the offences share a statutory maximum. It duly followed this approach in the published guideline.

An issue not directly covered in the consultation but upon which the Sentencing Council received some of the strongest representations was the language used in relation to the exploitation offences. In particular, the very strong

---

[10] It can be found at *http://webarchive.nationalarchives.gov.uk/20121210165327/http://www.cps.gov.uk/legal/s_to_u/sexual_offences_act/* [accessed December 30, 2013].

[11] By the Legal Aid, Sentencing and Punishment of Offenders Act 2012 (Commencement No.4 and Saving Provisions) Order 2012 (SI 2012/2906).

[12] *Sexual Offences Guideline: Consultation* (December 6, 2012).

view of a substantial number of respondents was that using the terms "child prostitution" and "child pornography" was wholly inappropriate as they do not reflect the fact that the underlying criminal activity is child abuse. The Council noted that this wording is taken directly from the legislation, but that in drafting the guideline it had been alive to the sensitivity of the language and so had referred where possible to "victims" rather than "child prostitutes". It also included the following statement on the title page of these offences: "The terms 'child prostitute', 'child prostitution' and 'child involved in pornography' are used in this guideline in accordance with the statutory language contained in the Sexual Offences Act 2003". The aim is to make it clear that the terminology is not intended to stigmatise but is a reflection of the statutory language. The Council also committed to revise and update the guideline if and when statutory changes are made to the titles of these offences.

New sentencing guideline

Step One—Harm and culpability

Under the new guideline, the sentencing court is to go through a series of steps in order to determine the appropriate sentence. Step one involves determining the offence category by reference to the degree of harm caused and then the culpability level for the offence. The harm and culpability factors for offences under ss.48–50 are as follows:

10.22A

HARM		CULPABILITY	
Category 1	• Victims involved in penetrative sexual activity • Abduction/detention • Violence or threats of violence • Sustained and systematic psychological abuse • Victim(s) participated in unsafe/degrading sexual activity beyond that which is inherent in the offence • Victim(s) passed around by the offender to other "customers" and/or moved to other brothels	A • Directing or organising child prostitution or pornography on significant commercial basis • Expectation of significant financial or other gain • Expectation of significant financial or other gain • Abuse of trust • Exploitation of victim(s) known to be trafficked • Significant involvement in limiting the freedom of the victim(s) • Grooming of a victim to enter prostitution or pornography including through cultivation of a dependency on drugs or alcohol	

Category 2	• Factor(s) in category 1 not present	B
		• Close involvement with inciting, controlling, arranging or facilitating child prostitution or pornography (where offender's involvement is not as a result of coercion)
		C
		• Performs limited function under direction • Close involvement but engaged by coercion/intimidation/exploitation

Many of the harm factors for these offences are adapted from the offences of sexual exploitation of adults (ss.52–53 of the 2003 Act) and are discussed in para.10.70 et seq., below. In its consultation document, the Sentencing Council gave its reasons for including certain harm factors in category 1:

- "Victim involved in penetrative sexual activity" is included because, although the offender may have had no direct sexual contact with the victim, where penetrative activity takes place the offender's actions will have exposed the victim to a very high degree of harm.
- As to "victim(s) participated in unsafe/degrading sexual activity beyond that which is inherent in the offence", the Council said that any sexual activity that commercially exploits a child is degrading and that this harm factor is intended to cover situations where there is additional degradation.
- In relation to "victim(s) passed around by the offender to other 'customers' and/or moved to other brothels", the Council thought that such "trading" of victims and exposure to other offenders significantly increases the harm caused to the victim. One respondent to the consultation opposed the inclusion of this factor on the basis that it identifies behaviours which imply trafficking, which may in turn encourage the CPS to charge offenders under ss.48–50 instead of with the human trafficking offences, so perpetuating the under-use of those offences. The Sentencing Council decided to retain the factor, saying that these offences are in practice sometimes used as alternative charges to trafficking, and the guideline is drafted with the intention that, whichever offence is charged, where there is evidence of a child being passed between offenders or trafficked, the increased harm should be reflected in the sentence starting point.

As for the culpability factors, the Council said in its consultation that culpability

A covers offenders with a high degree of influence and control:

- "Directing or organising child prostitution or pornography on significant commercial basis" and "expectation of significant financial or other gain" will apply to individuals who orchestrate activity for substantial commercial gain. The previous guideline, issued in 2007 by the Sentencing Guidelines Council, included organised commercial exploitation in the highest category of offence, but the new guideline widens this to cover situations where the activity may not be formally organised. As with the adult offences, the Council wished to move away from placing a monetary value on "significant financial or other gain" and so whether gain is "significant" will depend on the facts of the case.
- "Abuse of trust" will be particularly relevant to an offender involved in the exploitation of children and where present it will demonstrate the highest level of culpability.
- As for "exploitation of victim(s) known to be trafficked", the Council said that where an offender knows that a child has been trafficked this demonstrates the highest level of culpability due to the increased isolation and vulnerability of such children, whether they are trafficked into the UK from abroad or within the country.
- The final culpability A factor, "grooming of a victim to enter prostitution or pornography including through cultivation of a dependency on drugs or alcohol" was included in the published guideline as a result of a response to the consultation.

As regards culpability C, the Council said that the specified factors are intended to cover the offender who plays a peripheral role or who is engaged because they are exploited or coerced themselves. Nonetheless, as these offences concern the commercial sexual exploitation of children, even where the offender performs a limited role, a high level of culpability will exist which is reflected in the sentencing starting points and ranges.

Step Two—Starting point and category range

Having determined the offence category and culpability level, the court should **10.22B** then use the corresponding starting point specified in the guideline in order to reach a sentence within the category range. The guideline specifies different starting points and ranges for victims under 13, those aged 13–15 and those aged 16–17. The starting point applies to all offenders irrespective of plea or previous convictions. Once the starting point has been determined, step two allows further adjustment for aggravating or mitigating features, set out below. A case of particular gravity, reflected by multiple features of culpability or harm, could merit upward adjustment from the starting point before further adjustment for aggravating or mitigating features. Where there is a sufficient prospect of rehabilitation, a community order with a sex offender treatment programme requirement under s.202 of the CJA 2003 may be a proper alternative to a short or moderate length custodial sentence. The starting points and category ranges for offences under ss.48–50 are as follows:

		A	B	C
Category 1	**U13**	**Starting point** 10 years' custody	**Starting point** 8 years' custody	**Starting point** 5 years' custody
		Category range 8–13 years' custody	**Category range** 6–11 years' custody	**Category range** 2–6 years' custody
	13–15	**Starting point** 8 years' custody	**Starting point** 5 years' custody	**Starting point** 2 years' 6 months' custody
		Category range 6–11 years' custody	**Category range** 4–8 years' custody	**Category range** 1–4 years' custody
	16–17	**Starting point** 4 years' custody	**Starting point** 2 years' custody	**Starting point** 1 years' custody
		Category range 3–7 years' custody	**Category range** 1–4 years' custody	**Category range** 26 weeks'–2 years' custody
Category 2	**U13**	**Starting point** 8 years' custody	**Starting point** 6 years' custody	**Starting point** 2 years' custody
		Category range 6–11 years' custody	**Category range** 4–9 years' custody	**Category range** 1–4 years' custody
	13–15	**Starting point** 6 years' custody	**Starting point** 3 years' custody	**Starting point** 1 years' custody
		Category range 4–9 years' custody	**Category range** 2–5 year's custody	**Category range** 26 weeks'–2 years' custody
	16–17	**Starting point** 3 years' custody	**Starting point** 1 years' custody	**Starting point** 26 weeks' custody
		Category range 2–5 years' custody	**Category range** 26 weeks'–2 years' custody	**Category range** High level community order– 1 year's custody

Aggravating and mitigating factors

After identifying the starting point and category range, the court should consider **10.22C** whether the presence of aggravating or mitigating factors should result in an upward or downward adjustment from the starting point or the imposition of a sentence outside the category range. In particular, relevant recent convictions are likely to result in an upward adjustment. When sentencing appropriate category 2 offences, the court should also consider whether the custody threshold has been passed; if so, whether a custodial sentence is unavoidable; and if it is, whether that sentence can be suspended. The non-exhaustive list of aggravating and mitigating factors for offences under ss.48–50 is:

Aggravating factors
Statutory aggravating factors
• Previous convictions, having regard to a) the nature of the offence to which the conviction relates and its relevance to the current offence; and b) the time that has elapsed since the conviction
• Offence committed whilst on bail
Other aggravating factors
• Failure to comply with current court orders
• Offence committed whilst on licence
• Deliberate isolation of victim(s)
• Vulnerability of victim(s)
• Threats made to expose victim(s) to the authorities (e.g, immigration or police), family/friends or others
• Harm threatened against the family/friends of victim(s)
• Passport/identity documents removed
• Victim(s) prevented from seeking medical treatment
• Victim(s) prevented from attending school
• Food withheld
• Earnings withheld/kept by offender or evidence of excessive wage reduction or debt bondage, inflated travel or living expenses etc
• Any steps taken to prevent the victim reporting an incident, obtaining assistance and/or from assisting or supporting the prosecution
• Attempts to dispose of or conceal evidence
• Timescale over which the operation has been run

Mitigating factors
• No previous convictions **or** no relevant/recent convictions
• Remorse
• Previous good character and/or exemplary conduct*
• Age and/or lack of maturity where it affects the responsibility of the offender
• Mental disorder or learning disability, particularly where linked to the commission of the offence

* Previous good character/exemplary conduct is different from having no previous convictions. The more serious the offence, the less the weight which should normally be attributed to this factor. Where previous good character/exemplary conduct has been used to facilitate the offence, this mitigation should not normally be allowed and such conduct may constitute an aggravating factor.

In the context of this offence, previous good character/exemplary conduct should not normally be given any significant weight and will not normally justify a reduction in what would otherwise be the appropriate sentence.

A number of these factors are replicated from the guideline relating to the adult sexual exploitation offences in ss.52 and 53 of the Act and are discussed in para.10.70 et seq., below. In its consultation, the Sentencing Council said that "deliberate isolation of victim(s)" from family and friends will aggravate the offence as it removes the victim from any support network or the possibility of seeking assistance. "Vulnerability of victim(s)" is intended to deal with additional vulnerability over and above the age of the child, which is already factored into the sentencing starting points and ranges. For example, children who are in care or who have been subject to sexual abuse may be particularly vulnerable and targeted by offenders for this very reason.

Steps Three to Nine

10.22D   The remaining steps cover the following points. At step three the court should consider any factors which would indicate a reduction in sentence, e.g. assistance to the prosecution. At step four it should consider any reduction for a guilty plea. At step five the court should consider dangerousness, i.e. whether it would be appropriate to award a life sentence (s.224A of the CJA 2003) or an extended sentence (s.226A). Step six requires the court to consider whether the total sentence is just and proportionate to the offending behaviour. At step seven it should consider whether to make an ancillary order (e.g. a SOPO or a restraining order). Step eight requires the court to fulfil its duty under s.174 of the CJA 2003 to give reasons for, and explain the effect of, the sentence. Finally, at step nine the court should consider whether to give credit for time spent on bail in accordance with s.240A of that Act.

Sentencing example

Dunkova,[13] discussed in para.10.119B below, pre-dates the new definitive guideline   **10.22E**
but is a useful example of the approach taken by the Court of Appeal to a
particular factual scenario.

CONTROLLING A CHILD PROSTITUTE OR A CHILD INVOLVED IN PORNOGRAPHY

DEFINITION

The CPS's guidance to prosecutors on the 2003 Act referred to in the main work   **10.33**
has been archived.[14]

MODE OF TRIAL AND PUNISHMENT

From December 3, 2012, when ss.122–128 of the Legal Aid, Sentencing and   **10.34**
Punishment of Offenders Act 2012 were brought into force[15]:
- For offences committed on or after that date, an offence under s.49 is listed
  in Pt 1 of Sch.15B to the CJA 2003 for the purposes of s.224A of that Act
  (life sentence for second listed offence).
- For convictions on or after that date (irrespective of the date of commission of the offence), an offence under s.49 is a specified offence for the
  purposes of s.226A of that Act (extended sentence for certain violent or
  sexual offences).

SENTENCING

The Sentencing Council has issued a new guideline applicable to sex offenders   **10.36**
aged 18 or over who are sentenced on or after April 1, 2014: see para.1.20 et seq.,
above. A single guideline covers offences under ss.48–50 of the 2003 Act and is
discussed at para.10.22 et seq., above.

Sentencing example

Dunkova,[16] discussed in para.10.119B below, pre-dates the new definitive guideline   **10.36A**
but is a useful example of the approach taken by the Court of Appeal to a
particular factual scenario.

---

[13] [2010] EWCA Crim 1318.
[14] It can be found at *http://webarchive.nationalarchives.gov.uk/20121210165327/http://www.cps. gov.uk/legal/s_to_u/sexual_offences_act/* [accessed December 30, 2013].
[15] By the Legal Aid, Sentencing and Punishment of Offenders Act 2012 (Commencement No.4 and Saving Provisions) Order 2012 (SI 2012/2906).
[16] [2010] EWCA Crim 1318.

Parties to the Offence

10.37 As to whether the child victim of a s.49 offence is liable to conviction as an accessory to the offence, see the discussion in para.3.44 et seq., above.

ARRANGING OR FACILITATING CHILD PROSTITUTION OR PORNOGRAPHY

Definition

10.48 The CPS's guidance to prosecutors on the 2003 Act referred to in the main work has been archived.[17]

Mode of Trial and Punishment

10.49 From December 3, 2012, when ss.122–128 of the Legal Aid, Sentencing and Punishment of Offenders Act 2012 were brought into force[18]:
- For offences committed on or after that date, an offence under s.50 is listed in Pt 1 of Sch.15B to the CJA 2003 for the purposes of s.224A of that Act (life sentence for second listed offence).
- For convictions on or after that date (irrespective of the date of commission of the offence), an offence under s.50 is a specified offence for the purposes of s.226A of that Act (extended sentence for certain violent or sexual offences).

Sentencing

10.50 The Sentencing Council has issued a new guideline applicable to sex offenders aged 18 or over who are sentenced on or after April 1, 2014: see para.1.20 et seq., above. A single guideline covers offences under ss.48–50 of the 2003 Act and is discussed at para.10.22 et seq., above.

Parties to the Offence

10.51 As to whether the child victim of a s.50 offence is liable to conviction as an accessory to the offence, see the discussion in para.3.44 et seq., above.

---

[17] See *http://webarchive.nationalarchives.gov.uk/20121210165327/http://www.cps.gov.uk/legal/s_to_u/sexual_offences_act/* [accessed December 30, 2013].

[18] By the Legal Aid, Sentencing and Punishment of Offenders Act 2012 (Commencement No.4 and Saving Provisions) Order 2012 (SI 2012/2906).

B. SEXUAL EXPLOITATION OF ADULTS

CAUSING OR INCITING PROSTITUTION FOR GAIN

MODE OF TRIAL AND PUNISHMENT

For convictions on or after December 3, 2012,[19] an offence under s.52 is a specified **10.69** offence for the purposes of s.226A of the CJA 2003 (extended sentence for certain violent or sexual offences), irrespective of the date of commission of the offence.

SENTENCING

The Sentencing Council has issued a new guideline applicable to sex offenders **10.70** aged 18 or over who are sentenced on or after April 1, 2014: see para.1.20 et seq., above. In its consultation,[20] the Sentencing Council proposed to deal with the offences of causing or inciting prostitution (s.52) and controlling prostitution (s.53) in the same guideline, as they have the same statutory maximum (7 years' imprisonment) and raise similar issues in relation to harm and culpability. It duly followed this approach in the published guideline.

An issue not directly covered in the consultation but upon which the Sentencing Council received some of the strongest representations was the language used in relation to the exploitation offences. These representations focused on the offences of child exploitation in ss.47–50, but some respondents also expressed concern about the use in relation to the adult offences of the term "prostitute", which they regarded as loaded and pejorative. The suggested alternatives included "women in prostitution", "victim" and "those involved in prostitution". The Council considered carefully whether to adopt the last of these terms but felt that it could reduce clarity by making the language of the guideline wider than that of the Act. It also considered whether to use the term "victim", but noted some would take issue with the use of this term in relation to adults involved in prostitution. As an alternative, the Council decided, where possible and where clarity would not be affected, not to use the term "prostitute" with the result that, e.g. "prostitute forced or coerced into seeing many customers" in the draft guideline became "individual(s) forced or coerced into seeing many customers" in the guideline as published. The Council also included in the title

---

[19] When s.124 of the Legal Aid, Sentencing and Punishment of Offenders Act 2012 was brought into force by the Legal Aid, Sentencing and Punishment of Offenders Act 2012 (Commencement No.4 and Saving Provisions) Order 2012 (SI 2012/2906).

[20] *Sexual Offences Guideline: Consultation* (December 6, 2012).

pages of the adult exploitation offences the statement: "The terms 'prostitute' and 'prostitution' are used in this guideline in accordance with the statutory language contained in the Sexual Offences Act 2003". The aim is to make it clear that the terminology is not intended to stigmatise but follows the language used in the Act. The Council also committed to revise and update the guideline if and when statutory changes are made to the titles of these offences. These various measures indicate a curious defensiveness on the part of the Council in relation to the use of what are, after all, statutory terms. They are also unlikely to satisfy those who object to the use of the terms.

New sentencing guideline

Step One—Harm

10.70A   Under the new guideline, the sentencing court is to go through a series of steps in order to determine the appropriate sentence. Step one involves determining the offence category by reference to the degree of harm caused and then the culpability level for the offence. The harm factors for the offences in ss.52 and 53 are:

HARM	
Category 1	• Abduction/detention
	• Violence or threats of violence
	• Sustained and systematic psychological abuse
	• Individual(s) forced or coerced to participate in unsafe/degrading sexual activity
	• Individual(s) forced or coerced into seeing many "customers"
	• Individual(s) forced/coerced/deceived into prostitution
Category 2	• Factor(s) in category 1 not present

In its consultation on the draft guideline, the Sentencing Council explained its reasons for including the harm factors in category 1 as follows:
- "Abduction/detention" increases the harm suffered by the prostitute because they will be isolated from others and less able to seek help.
- As for "violence or threats of violence", the Council acknowledged that control and coercion can be exercised without the use of violence, and a lack of violence will not reduce the seriousness of the offence. But it also recognised that female prostitutes are often at risk of violent crime in the course of their work, in the form of both physical and sexual attacks, including rape, by violent clients or pimps, and the use of such violence should place the offence in the higher category.

- The same is true of "sustained and systematic psychological abuse", as psychological abuse may be a powerful weapon in controlling and exploiting prostitutes and can be as coercive and damaging as physical violence.
- "Individual(s) coerced or forced to participate in unsafe/degrading sexual activity" reflects the situation in which the offender coerces or forces a prostitute to have unprotected sex knowing that some clients will pay a premium for such activity. This increases the harm to the prostitute through exposing them to the risk of sexually transmitted infections and pregnancy. A prostitute may also be coerced or forced by the offender to undertake sexual activity with clients that the prostitute finds degrading. The harm results from the prostitute's lack of choice or control over the activity engaged in and the risk or humiliation they are exposed to as a consequence of the activity.
- "Individual(s) forced or coerced into seeing many 'customers'" again may increase the harm done to the prostitute as they will be coerced or forced into working in a way that they may not wish, over which they have little control and which increases their exposure to risk of physical and psychological harm.
- "Individual(s) forced/coerced/deceived into prostitution" reflects the fact that an offence under s.52 or s.53 will sometimes be charged instead of trafficking and so there may be instances where an individual is forced or deceived into entering into prostitution, e.g. they have willingly travelled to this country with the promise of a legitimate job and are then deceived into prostitution upon arrival. By this stage they may be isolated and unable financially to support themselves and the harm to them is increased because of the lack of control they have over the choices made.

Culpability

This guideline contains three levels of culpability, rather than two as in most 10.70B others. The Sentencing Council explained in its consultation that this approach was intended to reflect the wide range of culpability found in these offences. In particular, the element of "control" in s.53 is satisfied by the intentional control of *any* of the activities of another person relating to prostitution, and as a result may range from an offender with links to organised crime controlling a network of prostitutes, through to a former prostitute, who has been exploited, looking after the diary of another prostitute and involved in this work as a means of moving away from having to see clients. The previous guideline, issued in 2007 by the Sentencing Guidelines Council, dealt with the wide range of culpability by including "using employment as a route out of prostitution" and "coercion" as mitigating factors. The Sentencing Council thought it clearer and more transparent to set out the differing levels of culpability as part of step one. The three categories are as follows:

CULPABILITY
A
• Causing, inciting or controlling prostitution on significant commercial basis • Expectation of significant financial or other gain • Abuse of trust • Exploitation of those known to be trafficked • Significant involvement in limiting the freedom of prostitute(s) • Grooming of individual(s) to enter prostitution including through cultivation of a dependency on drugs or alcohol
B
• Close involvement with prostitute(s) e.g. control of finances, choice of clients, working conditions, etc (where offender's involvement is not as a result of coercion)
C
• Performs limited function under direction • Close involvement but engaged by coercion/intimidation/ exploitation

Culpability A includes factors which show a very high degree of culpability:

- "Causing, inciting or controlling prostitution on significant commercial basis" is intended to cover offenders who deliberately engage in a role causing harm to a large number of people.
- As for "expectation of significant financial or other gain", the SGC guideline referred to "substantial gain", on which it placed a monetary value of £5,000. The Sentencing Council decided not to place a value on "significant gain", as what will qualify as "significant" is dependent on the circumstances of the offence and will change over time.
- "Abuse of trust" will increase an offender's culpability even in the absence of commercial scale or significant financial gain because of the manipulation involved.
- "Exploitation of those known to be trafficked" is included because human trafficking for sexual exploitation fuels the market for prostitution in the UK, is a lucrative business and is often linked with other organised criminal activity such as immigration crime, violence, drug abuse and money laundering. Women may be vulnerable to exploitation because of their immigration status, economic situation or, more often, because they are subjected to abuse, coercion and violence.
- "Significant involvement in limiting the freedom of prostitute(s)" will increase an offender's culpability because it is an extreme example of control over the prostitute.
- "Grooming of individual(s) to enter prostitution including through cultivation of a dependency on drugs or alcohol" was introduced as a result of a response to the consultation.

As to culpability B, the Council said that this will apply to cases where the offender has a close degree of control of the prostitute, and is, for example, exerting influence and making decisions on their behalf, e.g. controlling which clients they see. An offender will fall in this category if there is an absence of evidence that they were in any way coerced into involvement. The category could apply if the offender controls more than one prostitute, though if their activity is on a significant commercial scale it would, as noted above, fall within culpability A.

The Council said that culpability C applies to the offender who plays a relatively peripheral role, e.g. (in relation to the s.53 offence) by taking bookings on behalf of a prostitute or driving the prostitute around. This category may also apply if an offender has close involvement but are themselves exploited, intimidated or coerced.

Step Two—Starting point and category range

Having determined the offence category and culpability level, the court should   **10.70C** then use the corresponding starting point specified in the guideline in order to reach a sentence within the category range. The starting point applies to all offenders irrespective of plea or previous convictions. Once the starting point has been determined, step two allows further adjustment for aggravating or mitigating features, set out below. A case of particular gravity, reflected by multiple features of culpability or harm, could merit upward adjustment from the starting point before further adjustment for aggravating or mitigating features. Where there is a sufficient prospect of rehabilitation, a community order with a sex offender treatment programme requirement under s.202 of the CJA 2003 can be a proper alternative to a short or moderate length custodial sentence.

In all category 1 cases where there is evidence of increased harm, a custodial starting point and range is recommended, in some cases near the statutory maximum. In category 2 cases there is a custodial starting point and range for offenders who demonstrate the highest level of culpability. Where the offender is shown to have been exploited themselves or has very limited involvement, and there are none of the category 1 harm factors present, a community order may be the most suitable disposal because it will deal with the underlying reasons why the offender has become involved and seek to avoid them re-offending. The starting points and category ranges for offences under ss.52 and 53 are as follows:

	A	B	C
Category 1	**Starting point** 4 years' custody **Category range** 3–6 years' custody	**Starting point** 2 years 6 months' custody **Category range** 2–4 years' custody	**Starting point** 1 year's custody **Category range** 26 weeks'–2 years' custody
Category 2	**Starting point** 2 years' 6 months' custody **Category range** 2–5 years' custody	**Starting point** 1 year's custody **Category range** High level community order –2 years' custody	**Starting point** Medium level community Order **Category range** Low level community order –High level community order

Aggravating and mitigating factors

10.70D   After identifying the starting point and category range, the court should consider whether the presence of aggravating or mitigating factors should result in an upward or downward adjustment from the starting point or the imposition of a sentence outside the category range. In particular, relevant recent convictions are likely to result in an upward adjustment. When sentencing appropriate category 2 offences, the court should also consider whether the custody threshold has been passed; if so, whether a custodial sentence is unavoidable; and if it is, whether that sentence can be suspended. The non-exhaustive list of aggravating and mitigating factors for offences under ss.52 and 53 is:

Aggravating factors
Statutory aggravating factors
• Previous convictions, having regard to a) the nature of the offence to which the conviction relates and its relevance to the current offence; and b) the time that has elapsed since the conviction • Offence committed whilst on bail
Other aggravating factors
• Failure to comply with current court orders • Offence committed whilst on licence • Deliberate isolation of prostitute(s)

- Threats made to expose prostitute(s) to the authorities (eg immigration or police), family/friends or others

- Harm threatened against the family/friends of prostitute(s)

- Passport/identity documents removed

- Prostitute(s) prevented from seeking medical treatment

- Food withheld

- Earnings withheld/kept by offender or evidence of excessive wage reduction or debt bondage, inflated travel or living expenses or unreasonable interest rates

- Any steps taken to prevent the reporting of an incident, obtaining assistance and/or from assisting or supporting the prosecution

- Attempts to dispose of or conceal evidence

- Prostitute(s) forced or coerced into pornography

- Timescale over which operation has been run

Mitigating factors

- No previous convictions or no relevant/recent convictions

- Remorse

- Previous good character and/or exemplary conduct*

- Age and/or lack of maturity where it affects the responsibility of the offender

- Mental disorder or learning disability, particularly where linked to the commission of the offence

- Demonstration of steps taken to address offending behaviour

---

* Previous good character/exemplary conduct is different from having no previous convictions. The more serious the offence, the less the weight which should normally be attributed to this factor. Where previous good character/exemplary conduct has been used to facilitate the offence, this mitigation should not normally be allowed and such conduct may constitute an aggravating factor.

The Sentencing Council explained in its consultation its reasons for including many of the aggravating factors:

- "Deliberate isolation of prostitute(s)" will aggravate the offence as it means that the offender can exert a greater degree of control over them. This will be particularly relevant if the prostitute is from another country and so has been cut off from all social and family ties.

- "Threats made to expose prostitute(s) to the authorities (eg immigration or police), family/friends or others" is included as such threats are frequently used to control and coerce individuals involved in prostitution and are particularly effective where the prostitute has been brought into the country illegally and fears deportation. It was expanded in the light of responses to the consultation to cover threats or exposure to family/friends.

- "Harm threatened against the family/friends of prostitute(s)" covers another means by which an offender may control their victim. The victim's feelings of helplessness and fear are likely to increase where they know the offender has influence over or access to their family which could result in harm befalling family members.
- "Passport/identity documents removed" is included as this is a direct way of limiting the physical movement and freedom of the prostitute thereby placing them under the offender's control.
- "Prostitute(s) prevented from seeking medical treatment" demonstrates a high level of control that impacts on the welfare and physical wellbeing of the individual.
- "Food withheld" and "earnings withheld/kept by offender or evidence of excessive wage reduction or debt bondage, inflated travel or living expenses or unreasonable interest rates" are further specific examples of how control can be exercised over prostitutes.

The Council of Circuit Judges submitted in response to the consultation that many of the aggravating factors are simply means of committing the s.53 offence and so raised the risk of "double counting", with the result that almost every s.53 offence will be aggravated. The Sentencing Council rejected this point, saying that the controlling behaviours identified in the guideline are particularly severe examples which should be reflected in sentence, and that sentencing judges would be able to weigh up the facts to avoid any risk of double counting.

The draft guideline also contained the aggravating factor "use of drugs/alcohol or other substance to secure prostitute's compliance", in order to reflect the strong link between drug use and street prostitution. The Council said that where the offender has either assisted the prostitute to develop a dependency or exploited a pre-existing dependency in order to control and manipulate them, this will aggravate the offence. As a result of responses to the consultation, the reference to drugs and alcohol was moved to step one, where it appears in the harm factors as "grooming of individual(s) to enter prostitution including through cultivation of a dependency on drugs or alcohol".

Steps Three to Nine

10.70E   The remaining steps cover the following points. At step three the court should consider any factors which would indicate a reduction in sentence, e.g. assistance to the prosecution. At step four it should consider any reduction for a guilty plea. At step five the court should consider dangerousness, i.e. whether it would be appropriate to award an extended sentence (s.226A of the CJA 2003). Step six requires the court to consider whether the total sentence is just and proportionate to the offending behaviour. At step seven it should consider whether to make an ancillary order (e.g. a SOPO or a restraining order). Step eight requires the court to fulfil its duty under s.174 of the CJA 2003 to give reasons for, and explain the effect of, the sentence. Finally, at step nine the court should consider whether to give credit for time spent on bail in accordance with s.240A of that Act.

CONTROLLING PROSTITUTION FOR GAIN

MODE OF TRIAL AND PUNISHMENT

For convictions on or after December 3, 2012,[21] an offence under s.53 is a specified **10.81** offence for the purposes of s.226A of the CJA 2003 (extended sentence for certain violent or sexual offences), irrespective of the date of commission of the offence.

Erratum: the reference in the penultimate line in the main work to "s.52" should be to "s.53".

SENTENCING

The Sentencing Council has issued a new guideline applicable to sex offenders **10.83** aged 18 or over who are sentenced on or after April 1, 2014: see para.1.20 et seq., above. A single guideline covers offences under ss.52 and 53 of the 2003 Act and is discussed at para.10.70 et seq., above.

Sentencing examples

Carroll[22] pre-dates the new definitive guideline but is a useful example of the **10.83A** approach taken by the Court of Appeal to a particular factual scenario. The applicant sought leave to appeal against a total sentence of 7 years' imprisonment imposed following his pleas of guilty to offences of conspiracy to control prostitution and conspiracy to launder money. The applicant had pleaded guilty shortly before trial and was sentenced to 5 years' imprisonment for conspiracy to control prostitution and 2 years to run consecutively for conspiracy to money launder. Together with his wife and daughter, the applicant had operated a large-scale and highly lucrative prostitution business in Ireland. Following their arrest in 2006 and release on bail, he and his wife moved to Wales where they continued to operate the business. The proceeds were used for property investments in the UK and abroad. The prostitutes were mainly foreign nationals and included young women who had been trafficked and tricked into prostitution. Although it was not the Crown's case that the applicant had been involved in people trafficking, he was alleged to have been aware in general terms of the pressure and threats of violence experienced by some of the prostitutes. He had no previous

[21] When s.124 of the Legal Aid, Sentencing and Punishment of Offenders Act 2012 was brought into force by the Legal Aid, Sentencing and Punishment of Offenders Act 2012 (Commencement No.4 and Saving Provisions) Order 2012 (SI 2012/2906).
[22] [2010] EWCA Crim 2463.

convictions. He pleaded guilty on the basis that he had not coerced anyone into prostitution or used violence and, although the judge referred to him having chosen to ignore the behaviour of others involved in the business, he was sentenced on that basis. The applicant contended that the imposition of consecutive sentences was wrong in the circumstances and that the judge had failed to have regard to the principle of totality. The application was refused. The judge had properly directed himself on the approach to be taken in determining whether the sentences should be concurrent or consecutive. There would be cases where a money laundering charge might well not add to the overall criminality disclosed in the substantive offences. However, in this case the business involved relatively sophisticated channelling and disposition of the proceeds from the criminal activities and the judge was entitled to conclude that the money laundering added significantly to the overall culpability of the exercise. It was a mechanism which enabled the profits from the unlawful trade in Ireland to be moved to another jurisdiction, and the imposition of a consecutive sentence was correct in principle. The judge had also been well aware of the need to ensure that the total sentence reflected the applicant's mitigation, in particular his late plea of guilty and previous good character, as well as his criminality. However, there were a number of seriously aggravating features: first, the sheer size of the enterprise and the vast illegal profits made from it; secondly, the fact that having been arrested in Ireland and released on bail, the applicant moved to Wales and continued precisely the same activity; thirdly, although the applicant had not coerced anyone into prostitution or used violence, there was evidence that others had and he had taken no steps to find out the true position. At best, he had closed his eyes to the obvious risk of force being used. It was an extremely serious conspiracy over many months in which vulnerable women were exploited to provide the applicant with large sums of money which he laundered and removed from the jurisdiction. The total sentence imposed was not manifestly excessive.

10.83B   See also *Nualpenyai*,[23] discussed in para.10.119A, below.

PAYING FOR SEXUAL SERVICES OF A PROSTITUTE SUBJECTED TO FORCE ETC

Sentencing

10.100   The offence is not as yet the subject of a sentencing guideline issued by the Sentencing Council or a guideline judgment handed down by the Court of Appeal.

---

[23] [2010] EWCA Crim 692.

"Exploitative Conduct"

The Home Office circular referred to in fn.124 of the main work is Home Office **10.104**
circular 006/2010, titled *Provisions in the Policing and Crime Act 2009 that relate to
prostitution (sections 14 to 21)* and published on 29 March, 2010.[24]

C. TRAFFICKING FOR THE PURPOSES OF SEXUAL EXPLOITATION

INTRODUCTION

EU Directive on Trafficking in Human Beings

In March 2010, the European Commission issued a proposal for a new anti-   **10.108**
trafficking Directive, which would build on the Convention on Action against
Trafficking in Human Beings:

> "The new Directive covers action on different fronts:
>
> **CRIMINAL LAW PROVISIONS**, including a common definition of the crime,
> aggravating circumstances and higher penalties, as well as non-punishment of the
> victims for unlawful activities such the use of false documents in which they have been
> involved for being subjected to by traffickers.
>
> **PROSECUTION OF OFFENDERS**, including extraterritorial jurisdiction (the
> possibility to prosecute EU nationals for crimes committed in other countries), use of
> investigative tools typical for organised crime cases such as phone tapping and tracing
> proceeds of crime.
>
> **VICTIMS' RIGHTS IN CRIMINAL PROCEEDINGS**, including specific
> treatment for particularly vulnerable victims aimed at preventing secondary victim-
> isation (no visual contact with the defendant, no questioning on private life, no
> unnecessary repetition of the testimony, etc.), police protection of victims, legal
> counselling also aimed to enable victims to claim compensation; special protective
> measures are envisaged for children such as holding interviews in a friendly envi-
> ronment.
>
> **VICTIMS' SUPPORT**, including national mechanisms for early identification and
> assistance to victims, based on cooperation between law enforcement and civil society
> organisations, providing victims with shelters, medical and psychological assistance,
> information, interpretation services. A victim shall be treated as such as soon as there
> is an indication that she/he has been trafficked, and will be provided with assistance
> before, during and after criminal proceedings.
>
> **PREVENTION**, including measures aimed at discouraging the demand that fosters
> trafficking, i.e. employers hiring trafficked persons and clients buying sexual services
> from victims of trafficking, training for officials likely to come into contact with
> victims, and of potential victims to warn them about the risks of falling prey to
> traffickers.
>
> **MONITORING**, providing for the establishment of National Rapporteurs or
> equivalent mechanisms, which should be independent bodies, in charge of monitoring

[24] See   *https://www.gov.uk/government/publications/provisions-in-the-policing-and-crime-act-2009
-that-relate-to-prostitution-sections-14-to-21* [accessed December 30, 2013].

the implementation of the measures foreseen by the Framework Decision. Such bodies should have further tasks including giving advice and addressing recommendations to governments."[25]

10.108A   In August 2010, Her Majesty's Government indicated that the UK would not at that stage be opting in to the proposed Human Trafficking Directive, on the grounds that most of what it provided for was already in place in the UK. According to a Home Office spokesman:

> "While the draft directive will help improve the way other EU states combat trafficking, it will make very little difference to the way the UK tackles the problem as there are no further operational co-operation measures which we will benefit from.
>
> Opting in now would also require us to make mandatory the provisions which are currently discretionary in UK law. These steps would reduce the scope for professional discretion and flexibility and might divert already limited resources.
>
> The government will review the UK's position once the directive has been agreed, and will continue to work constructively with European partners on matters of mutual interest.
>
> By not opting in now but reviewing our position when the directive is agreed, we can choose to benefit from being part of a directive that is helpful, but avoid being bound by measures that are against our interests."[26]

10.108B   The final text of the Directive was adopted by the Council of Ministers on March 21, 2011 and was subsequently issued as *Directive 2011/36/EU of the European Parliament and of the Council of 5 April 2011 on preventing and combating trafficking in human beings and protecting its victims, and replacing Council Framework Decision 2002/629/JHA*. On March 22, 2011, the day after the Directive's adoption, the Government announced that, subject to parliamentary scrutiny, the UK would after all be opting in to the measure. Home Office minister Damian Green MP said:

> "In June [2010], the Government took the decision not to opt in at the outset to the proposal for a directive to combat human trafficking but undertook to review the position when there was a finalised text. We have now carefully considered the finalised text. The main risk associated with the text has now been overcome: by waiting to apply to opt in, we have a text that has been finalised and we have avoided being bound by measures that are against the UK's interests.
>
> The new text still does not contain any measures that would significantly change the way the UK fights trafficking. However, the UK has always been a world leader in fighting trafficking and has a strong international reputation in this field. Applying to opt in to the directive would continue to send a powerful message to traffickers that

---

[25] Europa press release MEMO/10/108, *Proposal for a Directive on preventing and combating trafficking in human beings and protecting victims, repealing Framework Decision 2002/629/JHA*, March 29, 2010. For the full text of the proposal, see European Commission, COM(2010)95 final, 2010/0065 (COD), *Proposal for a Directive of the European Parliament and of the Council on preventing and combating trafficking in human beings, and protecting victims, repealing Framework Decision 2002/629/JHA*, March 29, 2010.

[26] Home Office press release, *Home Office defends position on human trafficking*, August 31, 2010.

the UK is not a soft touch, and that we are supportive of international efforts to tackle this crime."[27]

The minister indicated that compliance with the Directive would require primary legislation; in particular, to comply with art.10(1) it would be necessary to enlarge the territorial extent of the trafficking offences in the 2003 Act and the Asylum and Immigration (Treatment of Claimants, etc.) Act 2004 so as to cover trafficking by a UK national where the country of arrival, entry, travel or departure was not the UK. The Government used the Protection of Freedoms Bill to legislate for these changes, introducing new clauses for this purpose during Lords Committee Stage. Home Office minister Lord Henley said:

10.108C

> "The first new clause relates to trafficking offences for the purpose of sexual exploitation. Under Sections 57 to 59 of the Sexual Offences Act 2003, it is already an offence to traffic a person into, within or out of the United Kingdom for the purposes of sexual exploitation. In the interests of clarity, Amendment 152B proceeds by consolidating these existing trafficking offences into new Section 59A and also adding the necessary additional provisions to ensure extra-territorial application of the offences where a UK national commits a trafficking offence anywhere in the world . . . These provisions will apply to England and Wales only. We have been advised by the Scottish Government that, following the enactment of provisions in the Criminal Justice and Licensing (Scotland) Act 2010, the criminal law in Scotland already satisfies the criminal law requirements of the directive. The Northern Ireland Administration intend to bring forward separate legislation in the Northern Ireland Assembly to achieve a similar effect.
>
> The Government are committed to implementing the rest of the EU directive on human trafficking. These amendments deal with those points of the directive that require primary legislation. The rest we will implement through secondary legislation or by other appropriate means."[28]

The clause inserting s.59A into the 2003 Act was passed without a division and was enacted as s.109 of the Protection of Freedoms Act 2012, which came into force on April 6, 2013. Section 59A is discussed at para.10.114J et seq., below.

During the Lords Committee debate on the amendment, Lord McColl of Dulwich asked the minister to outline in more detail the matters on which the Government would be introducing secondary legislation and other measures in order to achieve compliance. In a written response, Lord Henley indicated that the Government considered secondary legislation might be required in relation to the following matters:

10.108D

> "Article 9 (investigation and prosecution), where we are already compliant in practice to enable access to 'effective investigative tools' but where we may need to transpose into legislation.
>
> Article 11 (assistance and support for victims), where we already comply in practice through the National Referral Mechanism and victim care model introduced in July 2011 as part of the Government's Human Trafficking Strategy but are considering whether more is required.

---

[27] *Hansard*, HC Vol.525, col.52 WS (March 22, 2011).
[28] *Hansard*, HL Vol.734, cols 61–62 GC (January 12, 2012).

Article 12(4), to ensure that victims of human trafficking are *automatically* eligible for special measures during court proceedings. Under the current regime in the Youth Justice and Criminal Evidence Act 1999, children and victims of sex offences are automatically eligible. Victims of human trafficking who are not children or victims of sex offences are only eligible 'if the court is satisfied that the quality of evidence given by the witness is likely to be diminished by reason of fear or distress on the part of the witness in connection with testifying in the proceedings'. We are considering whether this is adequate implementation.

Also on Article 12, in relation to police investigations, we are exploring whether we need to make changes to CPS guidance or introduce Court Rules or secondary legislation to fully implement these obligations.

Article 15 (protection of child victims etc): Victims are not party to prosecutions, so will not require a representative in this context. Currently, the provision of a supporter (representative) for child witnesses during investigations is already included in best practice guidance but not enshrined in legislation and we may seek to address this."[29]

10.108E   The UK duly opted in to the Directive in July 2011, and the Directive came into effect on April 6, 2013.[30] The Government, having considered what secondary legislation was needed in order to achieve compliance, made the Trafficking People for Exploitation Regulations 2013,[31] which came into force on the same date. Regulations 3 and 4 apply where there is a police investigation into a human trafficking offence, and set out measures aimed at the protection of complainants. The measures in reg.3 apply in relation to all complainants and reg.4 contains specific measures in relation to child complainants. The two regulations provide as follows:

"Protection of complainants in criminal investigations

3. Without prejudice to the rights of the accused, and in accordance with an individualised assessment of the personal circumstances of the complainant, the relevant chief officer of police shall ensure that the complainant receives specific treatment aimed at preventing secondary victimisation by avoiding, as far as possible, during an investigation of a human trafficking offence—
  (a) unnecessary repetition of interviews;
  (b) visual contact between the complainant and the accused, using appropriate means including communication technologies;
  (c) unnecessary questioning concerning the complainant's private life.

Protection of child complainants in criminal investigations

4. (1) This regulation applies where the complainant is under the age of 18 and without prejudice to regulation 3.
  (2) Without prejudice to the rights of the accused, during an investigation of a human trafficking offence, the relevant chief officer of police shall ensure that—

---

[29] Letter from Lord Henley to Lord McColl of Dulwich re *Protection of Freedoms Bill: Human Trafficking*, February 1, 2012, DEP2012-0194.

[30] *Directive 2011/36/EU of the European Parliament and of the Council of 5 April 2011 on preventing and combating trafficking in human beings and protecting its victims, and replacing Council Framework Decision 2002/629/JHA.*

[31] SI 2013/554.

(a) interviews with the complainant take place without unjustified delay after the facts have been reported;

(b) interviews with the complainant take place, where necessary, in premises designed or adapted for the purpose;

(c) interviews with the complainant are carried out, where necessary, by or through professionals trained for the purpose;

(d) if possible and where appropriate, the same persons conduct all the interviews with the complainant;

(e) the number of interviews with the complainant is as limited as possible and interviews are carried out only where strictly necessary for the purposes of the investigation;

(f) the complainant may be accompanied by an adult of the complainant's choice, unless a reasoned decision has been made to the contrary in respect of that adult."

Regulation 5 and the Schedule to the Regulations amend the Youth Justice and Criminal Evidence Act 1999, in particular to ensure that the complainant in respect of every human trafficking offence is eligible for special measures under that Act when giving evidence in criminal proceedings. Regulation 6 requires the Secretary of State to review the operation and effect of the Regulations and publish a report within five years after they come into force and every five years after that. Following a review, it will fall to the Secretary of State to consider whether the Regulations should remain as they are, or be revoked or be amended.

Human Trafficking: The Government's Strategy

On July 19, 2011 the Government published *Human Trafficking: The Government's* **10.108F** *Strategy*. The immigration minister, Damian Green MP, said[32]:

> "Victim care arrangements remain central to the Government's approach to combating trafficking. Adult victim care arrangements will be strengthened, with support offered by a greater range of specialist care providers. This will ensure that victims have access to the care they need, tailored to their particular circumstances and in line with our international commitments. We will also ensure that children remain a focus of our efforts as we look to combat those traffickers who exploit vulnerable children.
>
> A renewed focus on preventing human trafficking is required. The UK is already a world leader in the fight against trafficking but we recognise more can be done with international partners to reduce the threat from overseas. The strategy recognises the importance of working with source and transit countries to target and disrupt the work of traffickers and prevent more vulnerable men, women and children from becoming trafficking victims. A key aspect of our approach will be better intelligence gathering and sharing and, from 2013 the National Crime Agency will play a vital role in spearheading our fight against organised criminal groups who are engaged in human trafficking.
>
> The strategy also sets out our aim to better co-ordinate our border and policing law enforcement efforts to prevent traffickers from entering the UK. We will use intelligence to target those convicted or suspected of trafficking at the border as well

---

[32] *Hansard*, HC Vol.531, col.107WS (July 19, 2011).

as developing risk-based indicators to facilitate the systematic targeting of high risk passengers.

We will also ensure we monitor intelligence in relation to key events such as the Olympics and Paralympics to respond quickly and appropriately to any potential increased risk of trafficking."

The key objectives set out in Annex A to the *Strategy* include working with the private sector to strengthen the overall approach to trafficking, working to implement the Human Trafficking Directive by April 2013, raising the quality of decision-making under the National Rapporteur Mechanism, working more closely with other countries and the airline industry, improving UKBA guidance and procedures and (in conjunction with CEOP) tackling the issue of trafficked children who go missing from local authority care. In addition, the Government undertook in the *Strategy* to review by December 31, 2011 whether current legislation supported the effective prosecution of traffickers. An internal review was conducted between September and December 2011 of the effectiveness of existing human trafficking legislation in relation to the range of other activities underway to deter and disrupt traffickers. The *Report on the Internal Review of Human Trafficking Legislation* (May 2012) identified three areas in which legislation in England and Wales could be strengthened. The first and second involved expanding the territorial extent of the trafficking offences in the 2003 Act and the Asylum and Immigration (Treatment of Claimants, etc) Act 2004. As explained above, Parliament had already taken this step by amending the Protection of Freedoms Bill in order to comply with the Human Trafficking Directive. The third area related to the regime for unduly lenient sentences, under which the Attorney General could refer sentences for trafficking offences to the Court of Appeal only where the trafficking was for sexual exploitation. The Government announced an intention to correct this anomaly by extending the regime to sentences for trafficking for non-sexual exploitation, a change which falls outside the scope of this book.

Article 26 of the Council of Europe Trafficking Convention

10.114 The application of art.26 of the Council of Europe Convention was again considered by the Court of Appeal in *R. v N and Le*.[33] The decision concerned two unconnected cases in which the defendants (aged 16 and 17 respectively) had been sentenced to detention after pleading guilty to being concerned in the production of cannabis, the class B controlled drug. Le obtained and N sought permission to appeal against conviction and both sought leave to appeal against sentence on the ground, inter alia, that they had been victims of child trafficking for labour exploitation and the prosecution ought therefore to have been

---

[33] [2012] EWCA Crim 189. These cases are now the subject of an application to the European Court of Human Rights. See also *Dao* [2012] EWCA Crim 1717, citing both *LM* and *R. v N and Le* in approving terms and expressing a strong disinclination to accept the proposition that a threat of false imprisonment suffices for the defence of duress, without an accompanying threat of death or serious injury.

discontinued or stayed as an abuse of process, pursuant to the UK's obligation under art.26. The Court said that art.26 does not provide trafficked victims with blanket immunity from prosecution or preclude the imposition of penalties upon them in a broad general way, but provides for the possibility of not imposing penalties where the victims were compelled to participate in criminal activities and the defence of duress was unavailable to them. It referred with approval to *LM and others* and went on[34]:

> "Summarising the essential principles, the implementation of the United Kingdom's Convention obligation is normally achieved by the proper exercise of the long established prosecutorial discretion which enables the Crown Prosecution Service, however strong the evidence may be, to decide that it would be inappropriate to proceed or to continue with the prosecution of a defendant who is unable to advance duress as a defence but who falls within the protective ambit of Article 26. This requires a judgment to be made by the CPS in the individual case in the light of all the available evidence. That responsibility is vested not in the court but in the prosecuting authority. The court may intervene in an individual case if its process is abused by using the 'ultimate sanction' of a stay of the proceedings. The burden of showing that the process is being or has been abused on the basis of the improper exercise of the prosecutorial discretion rests on the defendant. The limitations on this jurisdiction are clearly underlined in *R v LM*. The fact that it arises for consideration in the context of the proper implementation of the United Kingdom's Convention obligation does not involve the creation of new principles. Rather, well established principles apply in the specific context of the Article 26 obligation, no more, and no less. Apart from the specific jurisdiction to stay proceedings where the process is abused, the court may also, if it thinks appropriate in the exercise of its sentencing responsibilities implement the Article 26 obligation in the language of the article itself, by dealing with the defendant in a way which does not constitute punishment, by ordering an absolute or a conditional discharge."

In N's case, the Court said that there had been no evidence before the Crown Court, or for that matter the CPS or indeed the defence, which suggested that N had been trafficked into the UK or fell within the protective ambit of art.26. Rather, the effect of the evidence was that he was a volunteer, "smuggled" into this country to make a better life for himself and that he had a home with a family member to which he could have gone and where he would have been welcome.[35] He was very young, and in a vulnerable position as an illegal immigrant, and in his short time working in the cannabis factory he had been exploited by others. All that provided real mitigation, but in the light of the facts as they appeared to be, and on the basis of the CPS's Guidance to Prosecutors then current, the decision to prosecute rather than to conduct further investigations did not involve any misapplication of the prosecutorial discretion sufficient to justify the conclusion that N's prosecution constituted an abuse of process on the basis of a breach of art.26. The position was unaffected by the substantial quantity of fresh evidence adduced on the appeal:

[34] At [21].
[35] Laura Hoyano has pointed out that the Court's emphasis on the fact that N was "smuggled" rather than "trafficked" into the UK was misplaced, as the Trafficking Convention is not restricted to cases of cross-border migration but applies also to exploitation of willingly smuggled immigrants: see [2012] Crim. L.R. 964.

"None of the pre-sentence evidence, and none of the fresh material, begins to suggest bad faith or improper motivation on the part of any investigating police officer or the CPS, or even deliberate, or neglectful, or innocent concealment of relevant material from the court either when the original decision was made that [N] should be prosecuted or indeed subsequently. This fresh material does not lead us to conclude that the CPS blinded itself or allowed itself to be blinded to significant facts emerging since N's conviction (or for that matter the sentence) . . . "[36]

The Court reached a similar conclusion in Le's case.

10.114A   Laura Hoyano has criticised the decision's "anaemic" approach to art.26, which (she argues) serves to undermine efforts by anti-trafficking agencies and charities to encourage reporting, since the threat of prosecution, regardless of the likely sentence, gives the trafficker an additional weapon with which to entrap his victim into silent compliance.[37] For this reason she welcomes the provision in art.8 of the Human Trafficking Directive (discussed above) that Member States "are *entitled not to prosecute* or impose penalties on victims of trafficking for their involvement in criminal activities which they have been compelled to commit as a direct result" of the prohibited acts (emphasis added). This marks a step forward from the somewhat ambiguous provision in art.26 of the Council of Europe Convention, which requires signatories to "provide for the *possibility of not imposing penalties* on victims for their involvement in unlawful activities to the extent that they have been compelled to do so". The specific reference in the Directive to the non-prosecution of victims, as well as their non-punishment, seems, says Hoyano, to have been a response to criticism of the narrowness of art.26, and she expresses the hope "that the CPS and the British courts will take account of this . . . evinced intention" when construing and applying art.8.

It is indeed clear from *R. v N and Le* that the content and application of the CPS's guidance to prosecutors will be key to the UK's ability to comply with its obligations in this respect. The point is forcefully made in relation to art.26 in a passage in the judgment in which, noting that it had examined "a vast bundle of post-conviction evidence, much of which is, on analysis repetitive [and] numerous publications", the Court concluded that:

"[I]n future the only publication likely to be relevant to an inquiry into an alleged abuse of process in the context of Convention obligations is the CPS Guidance in force at the time when the relevant decisions were made. It should normally be assumed that the contemporaneous CPS Guidance will have taken account of all the relevant material to be found in all the guidance offered by different authorities with responsibilities in this area, and indeed that it will be updated in the light of any new information. Unless it is to be argued that the CPS Guidance itself is inadequate and open to question because it has failed to keep itself regularly updated in the light of developing knowledge, for the purposes of the court considering an abuse of process

---

[36] Above, fn.33 at [87].
[37] See [2012] Crim. L.R. 960 et seq.; and see Michelle Brewer, *The Prosecution of Child Victims of Trafficking*, Archbold Review, Issue 4, May 17, 2013.

for which the prosecutorial authority is responsible, it is the CPS Guidance which should be the starting point, and in the overwhelming majority of cases, the finishing point for any argument of alleged non-compliance with Article 26."[38]

The Court added that it had not been assisted in determining the case by the substantial body of expert evidence adduced before it, and expressed great reservations about the value of expert evidence which is said to bear upon the abuse of process issue. It concluded:

"[I]n making its decisions in future, save to the extent that its own Guidance may make provision for it, we do not anticipate that the CPS would normally be required to seek evidence of the expert nature deployed in these appeals."[39]

CPS guidance

As one would expect, the CPS has revised its guidance to prosecutors to reflect the impact of art.8. Its Legal Guidance on Human Trafficking and Smuggling[40] should, following *R. v Le and N*, be the key document in the great majority of cases in which art.8 falls to be considered. It currently provides as follows in relation to the victims of trafficking: **10.114B**

"**Defendants who might be Trafficked Victims**

Prosecution of Defendants (children and adults) charged with offences who might be Trafficked Victims

The UK is bound by the Council of Europe Treaty ratified by Parliament on 17 December 2008 and which places specific and positive obligations upon EU States to prevent and combat trafficking and protect the rights of victims. It provides for the possibility of not imposing penalties on victims for their involvement in unlawful activities to the extent that they have been compelled to do so. This is replaced with effect from 6 April 2013 by Article 8 of the EU Directive 2011/36/EU on human trafficking which provides for the non-prosecution or non-application of penalties on victims of trafficking in human beings for their involvement in criminal activities which they have been compelled to commit as a direct consequence of being subjected to any of the acts of trafficking referred to above.

Adults and children arrested by the police and charged with committing criminal offences might be the victims of trafficking. This most frequently arises when they have been trafficked here to commit criminal offences (some of the offences most frequently committed appear below):
- Causing or inciting / controlling prostitution for gain: Sections 52 and 53 Sexual Offences Act 2003;
- Keeping a brothel: Section 33 or 33a Sexual Offences Act 1956;
- Theft (in organised "pickpocketing" gangs), under section 1 Theft Act 1968;

---

[38] Above, fn.33 at [86(b)].
[39] Above, fn.33 at [86(b)].
[40] *http://www.cps.gov.uk/legal/h_to_k/human_trafficking_and_smuggling/* [accessed December 30, 2013]. We understand that the guidance is being further reviewed and may change again.

- Cultivation of cannabis plants, under section 6 Misuse of Drugs Act 1971.

But trafficked victims may also be apprehended by law enforcement where they are escaping from their trafficking situation, the most obvious being immigration offences:

- using a false instrument under section 3 of the Forgery and Counterfeiting Act 1981;
- possession of a forged passport or documents under section 5 of the Forgery and Counterfeiting Act 1981;
- possession of a false identity document under section 6 Identity Documents Act 2010;
- failure to have a travel document at a leave or asylum interview under section 2 Asylum and Immigration (Treatment of Claimants) Act 2004.

When reviewing any such cases, prosecutors must be alert to the possibility that the suspect may be a victim of trafficking and take the following steps:

- Advise the senior investigating officer to make enquiries and obtain information about the circumstances in which the suspect was apprehended and whether there is a credible suspicion or realistic possibility that the suspect has been trafficked (this should be done by contacting the UK Human Trafficking Centre (UKHTC));
- The police should be advised to consider referring the suspect through the national referral mechanism (NRM) to the competent authority for victim identification and referral to appropriate support. In the case of children, this can be done by the Local Authority. Referral forms can be found here: referral form.
- Where the suspect is assessed as being under 18 and has been arrested in connection with offences of cannabis cultivation, police should be referred to ACPO Child Protection: Position on Children and Young People Recovered in Cannabis Farms Prosecutors should also consider information from other sources that a suspect might be the victim of trafficking, for example from a non-government organisation (NGO) which supports trafficked victims. That information may be in the form of medical reports (for example, psychiatrist reports) claiming post traumatic stress as a result of their trafficking experience;
- Re-review the case in light of any fresh information or evidence obtained;
- If new evidence or information obtained supports the fact that the suspect has been trafficked and committed the offence whilst they were coerced, consider whether it is in the public interest to continue prosecution. Where there is clear evidence that the suspect has a credible defence of duress, the case should be discontinued on evidential grounds (but see separate section on Children).

In complying with the judgment in *R v O* [2008] EWCA Crim 2835, it is the duty of the prosecutor to be pro-active in causing enquiries to be made about the suspect and the circumstances in which they were apprehended. In giving their judgment the Court highlighted a number of important issues in cases such as this:

- It required that both Prosecutors and Defence lawyers are 'to make proper enquiries' in criminal prosecutions involving individuals who may be victims of trafficking, in line with the findings of the Parliamentary Joint Committee on Human Rights report on Human Trafficking, that there must be coordinated law enforcement in protecting the rights of victims of trafficking;
- CPS legal guidance on the prosecution of trafficked victims was recognised; the court advised that this is published more widely to ensure others are aware of it;
- The court, defence and prosecution were criticised for failing to recognise that *O* was a minor.

- In the case of *O*, guidance on the prosecution of trafficked victims was not followed. The importance of following the guidance was further re-enforced by *LM, MB, DG, Betti Tabot and Yutunde Tijani v The Queen* [2010] EWCA Crim 2327.

In the case of *R v N and Le* [2012] EWCA Crim 189 there were recognised links with trafficking, Article 4 of the ECHR and the need for investigation (*Rantsev v Cyprus and Russia* [2010]. There was also reference to *R v SK* [2011] where the victim was subject to enforced control. However, the appeals against conviction in respect of both appellants were dismissed; the evidence did not lead to the conclusion that the convictions were unsafe on the basis that the prosecution constituted an abuse of process. Further guidance was offered from *R v LM, MB* which advised that criminal courts do not decide whether someone should be prosecuted or not; they decide whether an offence has been committed. A stay of proceedings on the grounds of abuse is in limited circumstances available if an exercise of judgment has not been properly carried out and may well have resulted in a decision not to prosecute. However in both cases, sentences were varied.

Some trafficked victim's experiences are likely to be outside the knowledge and experience of prosecutors. For example young female victims may be subject to cultural and religious practices such as witchcraft and juju rituals inherent in their culture which binds them to their traffickers through fear of repercussions.

Other trafficked victims may be held captive, physically and sexually assaulted and violated, or they may be less abused physically but are psychologically coerced and are dependent on those who are victimising them.

Prosecutors should therefore have regard to these wider factors when considering whether the circumstances of the person's situation might support a defence of duress in law. In *Lynch v DPP for Northern Ireland* [1975] A.C. 653, HL (Archbold 2011 17-120), Lord Simon said:

'. . . such well grounded fear, produced by threats,' of death or grievous bodily harm or unjustified imprisonment if a certain act is not done, as overbears the wish not to perform the act, and is effective, at the time of the act, in constraining him to perform it.'

The following are also factors which prosecutors might consider:
- When considering duress was the defendant driven to do what he did because he genuinely believed that if he didn't, he or a member of his family would be killed or seriously injured?
- Might a reasonable person with the defendant's belief and in his situation have been driven to do what he did?
- Was there opportunity for the defendant to escape from the threats without harm to himself, for example by going to the police?
- Did the defendant put himself into a position in which he was likely to be subject to threats made to persuade him to commit an offence of the seriousness of the charge, eg getting involved in a criminal gang likely to subject him to threats to commit criminal offences?

Even where the circumstances do not meet the requirements for the defence of duress, prosecutors must consider whether the public interest is best served in continuing the prosecution in respect of the criminal offence. The following factors are relevant when deciding where the public interest lies:
- is there a credible suspicion that the suspect might be a trafficked victim?
- the role that the suspect has in the criminal offence?
- was the criminal offence committed as a direct consequence of their trafficked situation?
- were violence, threats or coercion used on the trafficked victim to procure the commission of the offence?
- was the victim in a vulnerable situation or put in considerable fear?

Guidance has been issued to police and UK Border Agency (UKBA) on identification of victims and the indicators that might suggest that someone is a trafficked victim. However, all decisions in the case remain the responsibility of the prosecutor.

Children

Children are particularly vulnerable to trafficking and exploitation. Recent experience has highlighted the following offences as those most likely to be committed by trafficked children:

- Cultivation of cannabis plants, under section 6 Misuse of Drugs Act 1971;
- Theft (in organised "pickpocketing" gangs), under section 1 Theft Act 1968.

Prosecutors should be alert to the possibility that in such circumstances, a young offender may be a victim of trafficking and have committed the offences by being exploited by their traffickers or others controlling them. Child trafficking is first and foremost a child protection issue and they are likely to be in need of protection and safeguarding. In these circumstances, prosecutors should take the steps outlined above to make pro-active enquiries about the circumstances in which the child was apprehended.

The Protocol to Prevent, Suppress and Punish Trafficking in Persons, Especially Women and Children (Palermo Protocol) makes it clear that for child victims, consent is irrelevant; therefore there is no requirement to show the means of trafficking (that is the threat, coercion, or deception).

When considering the evidential factors set out in the previous section, in particular the reasonableness of the defendant's belief in the likely harm which might be caused to them or to their family and the likelihood of taking up opportunities to escape the threats, proper allowance should be made for the age, vulnerability and lack of maturity of the young person.

Children who have been trafficked may be reluctant to disclose the circumstances of their exploitation or arrival into the UK for fear of reprisals by the trafficker or owner, or out of misplaced loyalty to them. Experience has shown that inconsistencies in accounts given are often a feature of victims of trafficking and should not necessarily be regarded as diminishing the credibility of their claim to be a victim of trafficking.

The child may have been coached by their trafficker to not disclose their true identity or circumstances to the authorities. In some cases, they may have been coached with a false version of events and warned not to disclose any detail beyond this as it will lead to their deportation.

In a similar way to adults, children may have been subject to more psychological coercion or threats, such as threatening to report them to the authorities; threats of violence towards members of the child's family; keeping them socially isolated; telling them that they/their family owes large sums of money and that they must work to pay this off; or through juju or witchcraft practices.

Police should work with local authorities to ensure early identification of trafficked victims before entering any suspected cannabis farm, in line with the "Safeguarding Children Who May Have Been Trafficked" guidance. Police and prosecutors should also be alert to the fact that an appropriate adult in interview could be the trafficker or a person allied to the trafficker.

Any child who might be a trafficked victim should be afforded the protection of our child care legislation if there are concerns that they have been working under duress or if their well being has been threatened. Prosecutors are also alerted to the DCSF Guidance Safeguarding Children and Young People from Sexual Exploitation (June 2009).

In these circumstances, the youth may well then become a victim or witness for a prosecution against those who have exploited them. The younger a child is the more careful investigators and prosecutors have to be in deciding whether it is right to ask them to become involved in a criminal trial.

Prosecutors are reminded of the principles contained within the CPS policy statement on Children and Young People and in particular, our commitment to always consider the welfare of children in criminal cases.

Age disputes

Young people may have no identifying information on them, their documents may be false or they may have been told to lie about their age to evade attention from the authorities. Some victims may claim to be adults when they are in fact under 18 years of age.

Where it is not clear whether the young person is a child (i.e. under 18 years of age) then in line with the United Nations Convention of the Rights of the Child, the benefit of the doubt should be given and the young person should be treated as a child. This is re-enforced in the Council of Europe Convention on Action against Trafficking in Human Beings.

Where there is uncertainty about a suspected victim's age, Children's Services will be responsible for assessing their age. The Local Authority in whose area the victim has been recovered will have responsibility for the care of the child as required by the Children Act 1989.

Where a person is brought before any court and it appears that they are a child or young person, it is the responsibility of the court to make due enquiry as to their age. Under section 99 Children and Young Persons Act 1933 and section 150 Magistrates' Courts Act 1980 the age presumed or declared by the court is then regarded to be their true age.

For further reference on age assessment refer to *R (on the application of A) v London Borough of Croydon* [2009]; *R (M) v London Borough of Lambeth* [2009]. This case concerned the duty imposed on local authorities in providing services under the Children's Act 1989 in instances where the local authorities disputed age and assessed them as adults."

L and others v R.

The CPS's guidance is not, however, the last word on the subject. Most recently, **10.114C** in the conjoined appeals of *L and others v R.*,[41] the Court of Appeal provided guidance as to how courts should approach the interests of those who are or may be victims of human trafficking, in particular children, who become enmeshed in criminal activities in consequence, after criminal proceedings against them have begun. In a judgment delivered by Lord Judge C.J., the Court considered the decisions in *LM and others* and *R. v N and Le* and also the Human Trafficking Directive, discussed above. It had the benefit of written submissions not only from the appellants and the prosecution but also from the Children's Commissioner for England and the Equality and Human Rights Commission. In addition, it was provided with "a multiplicity of reports and papers, protocols and conventions in which, using different language to the same effect, the evils of trafficking . . . are simultaneously highlighted and condemned".[42] The court annexed a list of these documents to its judgment, but commented that in reality "despite lengthy

---

[41] [2013] EWCA Crim 991.
[42] At [10].

repetition, the principles to be applied are not complicated, and we shall endeavour to encapsulate them in this judgment. Henceforth it will rarely be necessary for them, or even a substantial proportion of them, to be copied and repeated in proceedings where these and similar issues arise."[43]

The Court went on to provide the following guidance as to how a court should approach issues relating to the defendant's age, or whether they are a victim of trafficking, or whether the alleged offending was an aspect of their exploitation[44]:

> " . . . when there is evidence that victims of trafficking have been involved in criminal activities, the investigation and the decision whether there should be a prosecution, and, if so, any subsequent proceedings require to be approached with the greatest sensitivity. The reasoning is not always spelled out, and perhaps we should do so now. The criminality, or putting it another way, the culpability, of any victim of trafficking may be significantly diminished, and in some cases effectively extinguished, not merely because of age (always a relevant factor in the case of a child defendant) but because no realistic alternative was available to the exploited victim but to comply with the dominant force of another individual, or group of individuals.
>
> In the context of a prosecution of a defendant aged under 18 years of age, the best interests of the victim are not and cannot be the only relevant consideration, but they represent a primary consideration. These defendants are not safeguarded from prosecution or punishment for offences which were unconnected with the fact that they were being or have been trafficked, although we do not overlook that the fact that they have been trafficked may sometimes provide substantial mitigation. What, however, is required in the context of the prosecutorial decision to proceed is a level of protection from prosecution or punishment for trafficked victims who have been compelled to commit criminal offences. These arrangements should follow the "basic principles" of our legal system. In this jurisdiction that protection is provided by the exercise by the 'abuse of process' jurisdiction.
>
> It was submitted, particularly, on behalf of L and T, that the courts' obligation to safeguard a trafficked victim's rights was independent of any review of the prosecutor's decision to bring or continue a prosecution . . . It was argued that the court should afford the protection required by the Directive and Convention by exercising what was described as a 'primary role'. The submission was based on the Supreme Court's consideration of the need to ensure that confiscation orders are proportionate in order to safeguard a defendant's rights under A1P1 of the ECHR in *R v Waya* [2012] UKSC 51, [2013] 1 AC 294:
>
>> 'But the safeguard of the defendant's Convention right under A1P1 not to be the object of a disproportionate order does not, and must not, depend on prosecutorial discretion, nor on the very limited jurisdiction of the High Court to review the exercise of such discretion by way of judicial review' [19].
>
> *Waya* is not analogous. In that case the Supreme Court was seeking to ensure that the order of the court adequately protected the rights of a defendant against whom an order of confiscation was sought. The court is the primary decision-maker as to whether a confiscation order should be made. In contrast, the prosecution is and remains responsible for deciding whether to prosecute or not. In any case, where it is necessary to do so, whether issues of trafficking or other questions arise, the court reviews the decision to prosecute through the exercise of the jurisdiction to stay. The court protects the rights of a victim of trafficking by overseeing the decision of the prosecutor and refusing to countenance any prosecution which fails to acknowledge

---

[43] At [10].
[44] At [13]–[18].

and address the victim's subservient situation, and the international obligations to which the United Kingdom is a party. The role of the court replicates its role in relation to *agents provocateurs*. It stands between the prosecution and the victim of trafficking where the crimes are committed as an aspect of the victim's exploitation (see *R v Loosely A-G's Ref. (No.3 of 2000)* [2001] UKHL, [2002] 1 Cr. App. R. 29).

It may be that the submissions advanced in erroneous reliance on *Waya* stem from a fear that the court will do no more than review the prosecutor's decision on traditional *Wednesbury* grounds and decline to interfere, even though its own conclusion would be that the offences were a manifestation of the exploitation of a victim of trafficking. For the reasons we have already given, no such danger exists. In the context of an abuse of process argument on behalf of an alleged victim of trafficking, the court will reach its own decision on the basis of the material advanced in support of and against the continuation of the prosecution. Where a court considers issues relevant to age, trafficking and exploitation, the prosecution will be stayed if the court disagrees with the decision to prosecute. The fears that the exercise of the jurisdiction to stay will be inadequate are groundless.

If issues relating to the age of the victim arise, and questions whether the defendant is or was a victim of trafficking, or whether the alleged offences were an aspect of the victim's exploitation, have reached the Crown Court, or a magistrates court, they must be resolved by the exercise of the jurisdiction to stay a prosecution. In accordance with the process endorsed in *M(L)* (15-19) and *N;L* (86) that remains the correct procedure for determining such issues even after the EU Directive 2011/36/EU became directly effective. This provides sufficient vindication for the rights enshrined in the EU Directive as well as the Anti-Trafficking Convention, and indeed in Articles 4, 6 and 8 of the European Convention of Human Rights . . . "

Turning to issues of evidence, the Court said that resolving an issue as to the age of the defendant[45]:

" . . . requires much more than superficial observation of the defendant in court or in the dock to enable the judge to make an appropriate age assessment. The facial features of the defendant may provide a clue or two, but experience has shown that this is very soft evidence indeed and liable to mislead. What we do know is that young people mature at different ages, and that their early life experiences can sometimes leave them with a misleading appearance. We also appreciate that young people from an ethnic group with which the court is unfamiliar may seem older, or indeed younger, than those from ethnic groups with which the court has greater experience. Therefore when an age issue arises, the court must be provided with all the relevant evidence which bears on it. Although the court may adjourn proceedings for further investigations to be conducted, these have to be undertaken by one or other or both sides, or by the relevant social services. The court is not vested with any jurisdiction, and is not provided with the resources to conduct its own investigations into the age of a potential defendant until after the investigation has completed its course, and the individual in question is brought before the court.

In this context we repeat the observations of this court in *R v Steed* [1990] 12 Cr. App. R.(S.) 230, where the question of the appellant's age was significant to the different methods of the disposal of the case on sentence, and therefore went to the legality of the sentence,

'It may often be right, indeed might usually be right, for the matter to be adjourned, if there is any real doubt about it, so that it may be more satisfactorily determined'.

---

[45] At [22]–[25].

More recently, this approach was underlined in *R v O* [2008] EWCA Crim 2835 where the court emphasised that:

'(W)here there is doubt about the age of a defendant who is a possible victim of trafficking, proper enquiries must be made, indeed statute so required.'

The Children's Commissioner invites us to consider the impact of Article 10(3) of the Anti-Trafficking Convention which provides:

'When the age of the victim is uncertain and there are reasons to believe that the victim is a child, he or she shall presume to be a child and shall be accorded special protection measures pending verification of his/her age'.

The explanatory report to the Anti-Trafficking Convention also refers to a requirement that the parties should 'presume that a victim is a child if there are reasons for believing that to be so and if there is uncertainty about their age'. In our judgment Article 10(3) addresses evidential issues. Where there are reasons to believe that the defendant is a child, then he should be treated as a child. In other words it is not possible for the court to brush aside evidence which suggest that the defendant may be a child. The issue must be addressed head on. If at the end of an examination of the available evidence, the question remains in doubt, the presumption applies and the defendant must be treated as a child. There is therefore no relevant difference between the approach required by Article 10(3) of the Anti-Trafficking Convention and the Guidance provided by the Director of Public Prosecutions."

10.114D As to the issue of whether the defendant is a victim of trafficking, the Court said[46]:

"The National Referral Mechanism (NRM) was set up on 1 April 2009 to give effect in the United Kingdom to Article 10 of the Council of Europe Anti-Trafficking Convention. Enough is now known about people who are trafficked into and within the United Kingdom for all those involved in the criminal justice process to recognise the need to consider at an early stage whether the defendant (child or adult) is in fact a victim of trafficking. The NRM establishes a three stage process for this purpose:

i) An initial referral of a potential victim of trafficking by a first responder[47] to a competent authority. At present there are two competent authorities. They are UKBA and the United Kingdom Human Trafficking Centre (UKHTC), a multi disciplinary organisation led by SOCA (The Serious and Organised Crime Agency). In the present appeals we are concerned only with UKBA because the potentially trafficked individuals were subject to immigration control. We note that where the potential victim of trafficking is a child his consent is not necessary before the referral is made, but where he is an adult consent is required.

ii) An UKBA official decides whether the person referred might have been a victim of trafficking. This is known as a 'reasonable grounds' decision, for which UKBA have a target of five days. We are told that the average time is nine days. If and when a favourable reasonable grounds decision has been made the first responder is notified, and, in effect that decision allows for a period of forty five days[48] during which the final stage of the NRM process continues, leading to

iii) consideration by UKBA whether the evidence is sufficient to confirm conclusively that the individual has been trafficked.

We were informed that the median time now taken for this third stage to be concluded is not short of three months. The delay is unfortunate, but any decision on the

---

[46] At [26]–[28].

[47] First responders for this purpose include UKBA, the UK Human Trafficking Centre, local authorities, UK police forces, NSPCC/CTAC, Barnados and the Salvation Army.

[48] This is a "reflection and recovery" period during which the individual can access services such as those provided by children's services, the Poppy Project, the Salvation Army and Migrant Help.

trafficking question adverse to the defendant in whose favour a reasonable grounds decision has already been made, but before the third stage in the process has been completed is liable to be flawed.

Neither the appellants nor the interveners accept that the conclusive decision of UKBA (or whichever department becomes a competent authority for these purposes) is determinative of the question whether or not an individual has been trafficked. They, of course, are concerned with the impact of a decision adverse to the individual. We are asked to note that the number of concluded decisions in favour of victims of trafficking is relatively low, and it seems unlikely that a prosecutor will challenge or seem to disregard a concluded decision that an individual has been trafficked, but that possibility may arise. Whether the concluded decision of the competent authority is favourable or adverse to the individual it will have been made by an authority vested with the responsibility for investigating these issues, and although the court is not bound by the decision, unless there is evidence to contradict it, or significant evidence that was not considered, it is likely that the criminal courts will abide by it.

The Court concluded[49]:

"In the final analysis all the relevant evidence bearing on the issue of age, trafficking, exploitation and culpability must be addressed. The Crown is under an obligation to disclose all the material bearing on this issue which is available to it. The defendant is not so obliged, but if any such material exists, it would be remarkably foolish for the investigating authority to be deprived of it. Without any obligation to refer the case to any of the different organisations or experts specialising in this field for their assessments or observations, the court may adjourn as appropriate, for further information on the subject, and indeed may require the assistance of various authorities, such as UKBA, which deal in these issues. However that may be, the ultimate responsibility cannot be abdicated by the court.

What these appeals have revealed is that the issue of age in cases involving trafficked victims tends to attract less focus from those who act for the defendant rather than the Crown Prosecution Service which, on the whole appears to pursue the issues relating to age assessment with a measure of determination. Our view is that the professions are less well informed about the importance of these issues in the context of those who are or may be trafficked youngsters than perhaps they should be. Their importance is obvious and underlined by the outcome in each of the present appeals.

We suggest that where any issue arises, it should be addressed head on at the first appearance before the court, and that the documentation accompanying the defendant to court should record his date of birth, whether as asserted by him, or as best known to the prosecution, or indeed both. Alternatively, the issues should be raised at the plea and case management hearing and appropriate adaptations should be made to the relevant forms to ensure that potential problems on this question are not over-looked.

Indeed it is clear that abundant guidance is available to the various public bodies who may be involved with young people who have been subjected to trafficking, all consistent with our general approach. In particular, such guidance is provided to the Crown Prosecution Service, the Police, and to Social Workers. There is significant co-operation and sharing of information throughout the United Kingdom. Thus, for example, we have read the Guidance provided by the Association of Chief Police Officers to officers investigating offences involving the commercial cultivation of cannabis where children are found on the relevant premises. The availability of detailed informed guidance reinforces the seriousness with which the issue of trafficking is being taken by the many different authorities into whose responsibility child victims of trafficking may come, long before the court processes begin. No doubt

---

[49] At [29]–[33].

it will be at the heart of the fresh guidance to be issued by the Director of Public Prosecutions.

As we have already explained the distinct question for decision once it is found that the defendant is a victim of trafficking is the extent to which the offences with which he is charged, or of which he has been found guilty are integral to or consequent on the exploitation of which he was the victim. We cannot be prescriptive. In some cases the facts will indeed show that he was under levels of compulsion which mean that in reality culpability was extinguished. If so when such cases are prosecuted, an abuse of process submission is likely to succeed. That is the test we have applied in these appeals. In other cases, more likely in the case of a defendant who is no longer a child, culpability may be diminished but nevertheless be significant. For these individuals prosecution may well be appropriate, with due allowance to be made in the sentencing decision for their diminished culpability. In yet other cases, the fact that the defendant was a victim of trafficking will provide no more than a colourable excuse for criminality which is unconnected to and does not arise from their victimisation. In such cases an abuse of process submission would fail."

The Court went on to apply these principles to the four appeals before it, all of which it allowed on the basis that there was evidence that the appellant was a victim of trafficking whose criminal activities were part and parcel of the circumstances of their trafficking. In each case, the Court said that if that evidence had been available at an earlier stage, either the appellant would not have been prosecuted or an abuse of process argument would have been likely to succeed.

TRAFFICKING PEOPLE FOR SEXUAL EXPLOITATION

Introduction

10.114E   From April 6, 2013, a new s.59A was introduced into the 2003 Act[50] to replace the existing ss.57–59. Those provisions made it an offence to arrange or facilitate the trafficking of a person into, within or out of the UK for purposes of sexual exploitation. The new s.59A creates a single, integrated offence to replace the existing offences, whilst adding the provisions necessary to be able to prosecute a UK national regardless of where the arrangement or facilitation of the trafficking takes place and regardless of where in the world the trafficking occurs or is intended to occur. This addition was necessary as a result of the UK opting in, in 2011, to the EU Human Trafficking Directive, discussed in para.10.108 et seq., above, which Member States were required to implement by April 2013.

The new offence incorporates the amendments made to ss.57–59 by the UK Borders Act 2007 (discussed below), i.e. the expansion of the s.57 offence to cover arranging or facilitating entry into, as well as arrival in, the UK for the purposes of sexual exploitation, and the extension of the offences in ss.57–59 to acts of trafficking into (etc.) the UK wherever in the world they are done. The novel

---

[50] By s.109(1), (2) of the Protection of Freedoms Act 2012, brought into force by the Protection of Freedoms Act 2012 (Commencement No.5 and Saving and Transitional Provision) Order 2013 (SI 2013/470).

feature of the new s.59A is that it further extends the offences to catch a UK national who arranges or facilitates the trafficking of a person for sexual exploitation into (etc.) any country and not only the UK. Otherwise, the new provision is modelled on ss.57–59 and reference should accordingly be made to the main work in interpreting it.

In summary, s.59A makes it an offence for a person (A) intentionally to arrange or facilitate the arrival in or entry into, travel within or departure from the UK or any other country of another person (B) for the purposes of sexual exploitation. Section 59A(2) provides that the arranging or facilitating is done with a view to the sexual exploitation of B if A intends to do anything to or in respect of B, or believes that any other person is likely to do something to or in respect of B, after B's arrival in, entry into or departure from the UK or other country which, if done, will involve the commission of a relevant offence. Section 59A(3) makes equivalent provision for the meaning of sexual exploitation where B is trafficked within the UK or other country, but here the exploitation may take place during or after the journey. Section 59A(4) provides that a UK national commits an offence under s.59A regardless of where in the world the arranging or facilitating takes place or regardless of which country is the country of arrival, entry, travel or departure. Section 59A(5) provides that a non-UK national commits the offence if any part of the arranging or facilitating takes place in the UK or if the UK is the country of arrival, entry, travel or departure.

NEW OFFENCE

The new s.59A provides as follows: 10.114F

"59A Trafficking people for sexual exploitation

(1) A person ("A") commits an offence if A intentionally arranges or facili-
    tates—
    (a) the arrival in, or entry into, the United Kingdom or another country of
        another person ("B"),
    (b) the travel of B within the United Kingdom or another country, or
    (c) the departure of B from the United Kingdom or another country,
    with a view to the sexual exploitation of B.

(2) For the purposes of subsection (1)(a) and (c) A's arranging or facilitating is with
    a view to the sexual exploitation of B if, and only if—
    (a) A intends to do anything to or in respect of B, after B's arrival, entry or
        (as the case may be) departure but in any part of the world, which if done
        will involve the commission of a relevant offence, or
    (b) A believes that another person is likely to do something to or in respect of
        B, after B's arrival, entry or (as the case may be) departure but in any part
        of the world, which if done will involve the commission of a relevant
        offence.

(3) For the purposes of subsection (1)(b) A's arranging or facilitating is with a view
    to the sexual exploitation of B if, and only if—
    (a) A intends to do anything to or in respect of B, during or after the journey
        and in any part of the world, which if done will involve the commission of
        a relevant offence, or

(b) A believes that another person is likely to do something to or in respect of B, during or after the journey and in any part of the world, which if done will involve the commission of a relevant offence.

(4) A person who is a UK national commits an offence under this section regardless of—

(a) where the arranging or facilitating takes place, or

(b) which country is the country of arrival, entry, travel or (as the case may be) departure.

(5) A person who is not a UK national commits an offence under this section if—

(a) any part of the arranging or facilitating takes place in the United Kingdom, or

(b) the United Kingdom is the country of arrival, entry, travel or (as the case may be) departure.

(6) A person guilty of an offence under this section is liable—

(a) on summary conviction, to imprisonment for a term not exceeding 12 months or a fine not exceeding the statutory maximum or both;

(b) on conviction on indictment, to imprisonment for a term not exceeding 14 years.

(7) In relation to an offence committed before the commencement of section 154(1) of the Criminal Justice Act 2003, the reference in subsection (6)(a) to 12 months is to be read as a reference to 6 months."

The following consequential amendments are made by s.109(1), (3)–(5) of the 2012 Act:

"(3) For subsection (1) of section 60 (sections 57 to 59: interpretation) substitute—

"(1) In section 59A—

"country" includes any territory or other part of the world;

"relevant offence" means—

(a) any offence under the law of England and Wales which is an offence under this Part or under section 1(1)(a) of the Protection of Children Act 1978, or

(b) anything done outside England and Wales which is not an offence within paragraph (a) but would be if done in England and Wales;

"UK national" means—

(a) a British citizen,

(b) a person who is a British subject by virtue of Part 4 of the British Nationality Act 1981 and who has the right of abode in the United Kingdom, or

(c) a person who is a British overseas territories citizen by virtue of a connection with Gibraltar."

(4) Omit section 60(2) (sections 57 to 59: jurisdiction).

(5) Accordingly, the title of section 60 becomes "Section 59A: interpretation.""

Mode of Trial and Punishment

10.114G By s.59A(6), a person found guilty under s.59A is liable on summary conviction to a term of imprisonment not exceeding 12 months or a fine not exceeding the statutory maximum, or both. On conviction on indictment, a person is liable to a term of imprisonment not exceeding 14 years.

SENTENCING

The Sentencing Council has issued a new guideline applicable to sex offenders **10.114H** aged 18 or over who are sentenced on or after April 1, 2014: see para.1.20 et seq., above. The Council's consultation on the draft of the new guideline[51] preceded the introduction of s.59A and so dealt with the offences in ss.57–59 of the 2003 Act, which it covered together, as the harm to the victims and the culpability of the offender are the same. The new guideline post-dates the commencement of s.59A and so covers that provision alone. The guideline is, however, identical to the one initially proposed for ss.57–59, and we draw below on the Council's comments in its consultation in explaining it.

New sentencing guideline

Step One—Harm

Under the new guideline, the sentencing court is to go through a series of steps **10.114I** in order to determine the appropriate sentence. Step one involves determining the offence category by reference to the degree of harm caused and then the culpability level for the offence. In these respects the guideline for s.59A takes the same general approach as the guideline for the offences in ss.52 and 53 of the 2003 Act, in recognition that the offences share common factors relating to the sexual exploitation of the victim. As such, the harm factors for offences under s.59A are:

HARM	
Category 1	• Abduction/detention
	• Violence or threats of violence
	• Sustained and systematic psychological abuse
	• Victim(s) under 18
	• Victim(s) forced or coerced to participate in unsafe/degrading sexual activity
	• Victim(s) forced/coerced into prostitution
	• Victim(s) tricked/deceived as to purpose of visit
Category 2	• Factor(s) in category 1 not present

Some of the category 1 factors appear in the guideline for ss.52 and 53 and are discussed in para.10.70 et seq., above. As for the others, the Council explained in its consultation that "abduction/detention" is included because the harm caused by the offence is increased by reason of the fear and loss of control the victim will have experienced. "Victim(s) under 18" is included because harm is increased by

---

[51] *Sexual Offences Guideline: Consultation* (December 6, 2012).

virtue of the corrupting effect on a young victim's emotional development. As for "victim(s) forced/coerced into prostitution" and "victim(s) tricked/deceived as to purpose of visit", these are included because the use of force or deception increases the harm to the victim flowing from the offence.

In responding to the consultation, the CPS suggested extending the factor "victim tricked/deceived as to purpose of visit" to cover instances where the victim knew they were coming to the UK to work as a prostitute but on arrival were tricked and exploited as to the nature and conditions of the work. The Council thought this might over-complicate the factor at step one, but noted that it is open to prosecutors to rely on deception of this sort as an aggravating factor at step two, given that the list of aggravating factors is non-exhaustive.

Culpability

10.114J   This guideline, like the one for ss.52 and 53, contains three levels of culpability rather than the usual two. The Sentencing Council explained that this reflects the fact that the court may be faced with offenders who have played various roles, from directing and organising a trafficking chain to limited involvement through pressure, exploitation or coercion. The previous guideline, issued in 2007 by the Sentencing Guidelines Council, determined the category level for offences under ss.57–59 as involvement at any level in any stage of the trafficking operation where the victim was coerced (starting point 6 years' custody, range 4–9 years) and where there was no coercion (starting point 2 years' custody, range 1–4 years). The new guideline moves away from this categorisation in order better to reflect the offender's culpability and to recognise that there may be harm even where coercion is not obvious. The categories of culpability are accordingly as follows:

CULPABILITY
A
• Directing or organising trafficking on significant commercial basis
• Expectation of significant financial or other gain
• Significant influence over others in trafficking organisation/hierarchy
• Abuse of trust
B
• Operational or management function within hierarchy
• Involves others in operation whether by coercion/ intimidation/ exploitation or reward (and offender's involvement is not as a result of coercion)

C
• Performs limited function under direction
• Close involvement but engaged by coercion/ intimidation/ exploitation

Culpability A is intended to deal with those offenders with the highest levels of culpability. In its consultation, the Sentencing Council said that the factor which appears in the published guideline as "directing or organising trafficking on significant commercial basis" would encompass an offender who was at the top of an organised trafficking chain. Such offenders have high levels of influence and control and therefore their lack of interaction with individual victims should not decrease their culpability. It is the power and influence they exert in directing the operation that are significant.

As for culpability B, the Council said that this will apply to an offender who has more than a peripheral role and is responsible for engaging others in the trafficking operation or has a degree of oversight or control over the trafficking activity.

Culpability C is intended to apply to offenders who play a peripheral role and have not directed, controlled or managed any activity, along with those whose involvement is as a result of their own exploitation or trafficked status.

Step Two—Starting point and category range

Having determined the offence category and culpability level, the court should **10.114K** then use the corresponding starting point specified in the guideline in order to reach a sentence within the category range. The starting point applies to all offenders irrespective of plea or previous convictions. Once the starting point has been determined, step two allows further adjustment for aggravating or mitigating features, set out below. A case of particular gravity, reflected by multiple features of culpability or harm, could merit upward adjustment from the starting point before further adjustment for aggravating or mitigating features. Where there is a sufficient prospect of rehabilitation, a community order with a sex offender treatment programme requirement under s.202 of the CJA 2003 can be a proper alternative to a short or moderate length custodial sentence.

The new guideline has a starting point in the top category of 8 years' custody with a range of 6–12 years, whereas under the previous SGC guideline the starting point was 6 years' custody and the range 4–9 years. In its consultation, the Council proposed a range of 6–10 years, an increase that it said reflected sentencing practice, since in the period 2007–11 around 30 per cent of offenders received a sentence of more than 6 years' custody and 6 per cent received one of over 9 years. However, the Council acceded to requests by a number of respondents to extend the top of the range to 12 years to reflect the very high harm associated with trafficking and the particular harms and culpability levels that could be evidenced at the top end of offending.

Also, the SGC guideline did not distinguish between types of offender, which meant that an offender who was head of a trafficking operation where victims had been coerced and an offender who had been coerced or exploited themselves and involved in a very limited way would be faced with the same starting point of 6 years' custody. The Council believed that there should be a greater acknowledgment of differences in types of offender and therefore favoured a wider range of sentence starting points and ranges than under the SGC guideline.

The starting points and category ranges for offences under ss.59A are accordingly as follows:

	A	B	C
Category 1	**Starting point** 8 years' custody	**Starting point** 6 years' custody	**Starting point** 18 months' custody
	Category range 6–12 years' custody	**Category range** 4–8 years' custody	**Category range** 26 weeks'–2 years' custody
Category 2	**Starting point** 6 years' custody	**Starting point** 4 years' custody	**Starting point** 26 weeks' custody
	Category range 4–8 years' custody	**Category range** 2–6 years' custody	**Category range** High level community order –18 months' custody

Aggravating and mitigating factors

10.114L   After identifying the starting point and category range, the court should consider whether the presence of aggravating or mitigating factors should result in an upward or downward adjustment from the starting point or the imposition of a sentence outside the category range. In particular, relevant recent convictions are likely to result in an upward adjustment. When sentencing appropriate category 2 offences, the court should also consider whether the custody threshold has been passed; if so, whether a custodial sentence is unavoidable; and if it is, whether that sentence can be suspended. The non-exhaustive list of aggravating and mitigating factors for offences under s.59A is:

Aggravating factors

Statutory aggravating factors

- Previous convictions, having regard to a) the nature of the offence to which the conviction relates and its relevance to the current offence; and b) the time that has elapsed since the conviction
- Offence committed whilst on bail

Other aggravating factors

- Failure to comply with current court orders
- Offence committed whilst on licence
- Deliberate isolation of victim(s)
- Children of victim(s) left in home country due to trafficking
- Threats made to expose victim(s) to the authorities (eg immigration or police), family/friends or others
- Harm threatened against the family/friends of victim
- Exploitation of victim(s) from particularly vulnerable backgrounds
- Victim(s) previously trafficked/sold/passed around
- Passport/identity documents removed
- Victim(s) prevented from seeking medical treatment
- Food withheld
- Use of drugs/alcohol or other substance to secure victim's compliance
- Earnings of victim(s) withheld/kept by offender or evidence of excessive wage reduction, debt bondage, inflated travel or living expenses, unreasonable interest rates
- Any steps taken to prevent the victim reporting an incident, obtaining assistance and/or from assisting or supporting the prosecution
- Attempts to dispose of or conceal evidence
- Timescale over which operation has been run

Mitigating factors

- No previous convictions **or** no relevant/recent convictions
- Remorse
- Previous good character and/or exemplary conduct*
- Age and/or lack of maturity where it affects the responsibility of the offender
- Mental disorder or learning disability, particularly where linked to the commission of the offence

---

* Previous good character/exemplary conduct is different from having no previous convictions. The more serious the offence, the less the weight which should normally be attributed to this factor. Where previous good character/exemplary conduct has been used to facilitate the offence, this mitigation should not normally be allowed and such conduct may constitute an aggravating factor.

In the context of this offence, previous good character/exemplary conduct should not normally be given any significant weight and will not normally justify a reduction in what would otherwise be the appropriate sentence.

The Sentencing Council explained in its consultation the reasons for the inclusion of many of the aggravating factors:

- In relation to "deliberate isolation of victim(s)" the Council recognised that a degree of isolation will be an inevitable consequence of the victim being in a different country or area of the UK, but felt that the seriousness of the offence is increased where the victim is then denied access to any form of communication with family/friends or is deliberately separated from people they have travelled with.

- "Children of victim(s) left in home country due to trafficking" is included as this situation is likely to cause considerable further anguish to the victim and additional harm to the children left behind. Where the motivation for travelling is improved prospects for the victim's family, this may make them susceptible to being trafficked and the harmful consequences for such victims are also greater.

- "Harm threatened against the family/friends of victim" is included since this means of controlling the victim is likely to increase their feelings of helplessness and fear.

- As for "exploitation of victim(s) from particularly vulnerable backgrounds", the Council said that all victims of trafficking are likely to be vulnerable in some way, but the exploitation of particularly vulnerable groups, e.g. children in care or from dysfunctional backgrounds, increases the severity of the offence.

- "Victim(s) previously trafficked/sold/passed around" increases the seriousness of the offence as there is continuing damage and harm to the victim.

- Finally, "passport/identity documents removed", "victim(s) prevented from seeking medical treatment", "food withheld", "use of drugs/alcohol or other substance to secure victim's compliance" and "earnings of victim(s) withheld/kept by offender or evidence of excessive wage reduction, debt bondage, inflated travel or living expenses, unreasonable interest rates" are included as they are all common means by which offenders exert control over their victims.

As for the mitigating factors, the Council said that where offenders have previously been exploited or trafficked themselves, this should be dealt with by placing them in the lowest category of offending rather than by treating previous exploitation as mitigation, and this is the approach followed in the guideline (see the discussion of culpability, above).

Steps Three to Nine

The remaining steps cover the following points. At step three the court should **10.114M** consider any factors which would indicate a reduction in sentence, e.g. assistance to the prosecution. At step four it should consider any reduction for a guilty plea. At step five the court should consider dangerousness, i.e. whether it would be appropriate to award an extended sentence (s.226A of the CJA 2003). Step six requires the court to consider whether the total sentence is just and proportionate to the offending behaviour. At step seven it should consider whether to make an ancillary order (e.g. a SOPO or a restraining order). Step eight requires the court to fulfil its duty under s.174 of the CJA 2003 to give reasons for, and explain the effect of, the sentence. Finally, at step nine the court should consider whether to give credit for time spent on bail in accordance with s.240A of that Act.

TRAFFICKING INTO THE UK FOR SEXUAL EXPLOITATION

N.B. The offence in s.57 of the Sexual Offences Act 2003 has been repealed and replaced by s.59A of that Act: see above.

DEFINITION

Section 57(1) of the 2003 Act was amended by the UK Borders Act 2007, s.31(3), **10.115** which inserted the words ", or the entry into," after "the arrival in". The purpose of the amendment was to extend the s.57 offence to cover acts of facilitation done after B had arrived at a UK port or airport with a designated immigration area but before they had been granted entry by an immigration officer, i.e. in the secure areas of our major ports and airports.[52] In the Committee debate on the Bill relating to a similar amendment made to the Immigration Act offence of helping an asylum seeker to enter the UK, the Parliamentary Under-Secretary of State for the Home Department, Joan Ryan MP, said:

> "A person is said to have arrived in the United Kingdom upon disembarkation. That is distinct from his or her entry into the United Kingdom, which takes place at border control. At some ports there can be a considerable distance between. I am thinking that, after stepping off the plane at Heathrow, it can be some time and distance before one gets to the point where one meets the immigration officer and has one's passport checked. That physical and legal gap is exploited by facilitators, who use the opportunity to carry out acts such as the destruction or disposal of false passports. Even though such acts are often captured on CCTV or witnessed by surveillance

[52] For the distinction between arrival and entry, see *Nailie* [1993] A.C. 674, decided under s.25 of the Immigration Act 1971 (facilitating illegal entry); *Javaherifard* [2005] EWCA Crim 3231 (which makes clear that "entry" in the context of immigration law is an ordinary word and will take place on arrival in the UK elsewhere than at a port or airport with a designated immigration area).

officers, they cannot currently be taken into account as evidence of facilitation because they have occurred after a person has disembarked or arrived."[53]

The amendment was brought into force on January 31, 2008.[54]

MODE OF TRIAL AND PUNISHMENT

10.116 For convictions on or after December 3, 2012,[55] an offence under s.57 is a specified offence for the purposes of s.226A of the CJA 2003 (extended sentence for certain violent or sexual offences), irrespective of the date of commission of the offence.

SENTENCING

Sentencing examples

10.119 The following decisions pre-date the new definitive guideline but are useful examples of the approach taken by the Court of Appeal to different factual scenarios.

10.119A In *Nualpenyai*[56] the appellant appealed against a sentence of 6-and-a-half years' imprisonment imposed for offences of trafficking for sexual exploitation and controlling prostitution for gain. She had run brothels in the UK. The victims were two young women from Thailand who had arranged with the appellant to travel to the UK to work as prostitutes. They had been aware that they would owe the appellant money, but were only told on arrival in the UK that they were to pay her sums of £25,000 and £30,000. She took their passports as security for the supposed debts. The victims were made to work almost continuously and were encouraged to have unprotected sex with clients. The appellant pleaded guilty to two counts of trafficking for sexual exploitation, for each of which she was sentenced to 6-and-a-half years' imprisonment, and two counts of controlling prostitution for gain, for each of which she was sentenced to 2 years, all the sentences to run concurrently. The appellant had pleaded guilty when the case was listed for trial. She argued that the total sentence was outside the parameters set by the SGC guideline and that she had received insufficient credit for her guilty pleas and other matters of personal mitigation, including her previous good character and the fact that she would be separated from her young child. Her appeal was allowed. The judge had been right to pass concurrent sentences to reflect the overall seriousness of the offences. The judge had said that on

---

[53] *Hansard*, Public Bill Committee, cols 394–395 (March 15, 2007).

[54] UK Borders Act 2007 (Commencement No.1 and Transitional Provisions) Order 2008 (SI 2008/99).

[55] When s.124 of the Legal Aid, Sentencing and Punishment of Offenders Act 2012 was brought into force by the Legal Aid, Sentencing and Punishment of Offenders Act 2012 (Commencement No.4 and Saving Provisions) Order 2012 (SI 2012/2906).

[56] [2010] EWCA Crim 692.

conviction after trial the sentence would have been 8 years. The reduction to 6-and-a-half years in view of the guilty pleas and mitigation was quite generous in the circumstances and no further reduction was required. The sentencing guidelines for both types of offence drew a distinction between cases where there was coercion and cases where there was not. There was no evidence that the victims had been coerced into travelling to the UK to work as prostitutes. However, they had been to an extent deceived as to the kind of life they would have, and there had been mental coercion of both of them. They had been in vulnerable positions and had had little real choice, and the removal of their passports was clearly designed to keep them under the appellant's control. The element of coercion was primarily relevant to the offences of controlling prostitution for gain, for which lower penalties were appropriate. On the other hand, it was a significant feature of the trafficking offences that, in arranging for them to travel to the UK, the appellant had intended to exploit the victims. Although it was difficult to fit such a case into the sentencing guideline, and the offences had involved the exploitation and coercion of two young women, the starting point of 8 years was too high. An appropriate starting point would have been between 6 and 6-and-a-half years, and giving appropriate credit for the guilty pleas and mitigation, sentences of 5 years on the trafficking counts were substituted for the original sentences, with the other sentences left unchanged.

In *Dunkova*[57] the appellant appealed against a sentence of 16 years' imprisonment **10.119B** imposed following her conviction on various counts of child prostitution. The appellant, who was herself a prostitute, had brought a 15-year-old girl (P) to the UK from Slovakia and, in league with her brother and husband, forced her to work as a prostitute. P gave all her earnings to the appellant, who gave them to her husband. He inflicted violence on P and, with the appellant's brother, threatened to kill her should she run away. The appellant was convicted on two counts of trafficking for sexual exploitation, one of causing child prostitution and one of controlling a child prostitute. She was given consecutive sentences of 8 years' imprisonment for the trafficking and 8 for the controlling. Her brother and husband were each sentenced to 17 years' imprisonment. The appellant submitted that her sentence failed to reflect the essential disparity between her and the other two defendants' involvement. Her appeal was allowed. Although the appellant's role had been substantial from start to finish, it had been subordinate to that of the two males. Whilst she had fetched P from Slovakia and supervised her, they had organised the transit and threatened and falsely imprisoned P. She had essentially minded P on their behalf. The justice of the case could be met by quashing the appellant's two sentences of 8 years' imprisonment and substituting 7 years, giving a total sentence of 14 years' imprisonment.

In *Att Gen's Ref (No.44 of 2010)*[58] the Attorney General referred as unduly lenient **10.119C** the sentences imposed on the offenders (O and M) following their conviction of

[57] [2010] EWCA Crim 1318.
[58] [2010] EWCA Crim 2341.

trafficking for sexual exploitation and controlling prostitution. They had been involved in trafficking the 19-year-old victim from her native Romania to the UK in order for her to work as a prostitute. O had told the victim that the offenders would find her legitimate employment in a restaurant. Once in the UK, they made her work as a prostitute and controlled her so that they could make money from her activities. O was of good character. M had no relevant previous convictions and had played a secondary role in the offences. O was sentenced to 30 months' imprisonment for trafficking and 24 months concurrent for controlling prostitution. M was sentenced to 24 months' imprisonment for trafficking and 18 months concurrent for controlling prostitution. The Reference was allowed. The Court of Appeal referred to the relevant SGC guideline. In the case of both offenders, the relevant category in the trafficking guideline was the second, "involvement at any level in any stage of the trafficking operation where there was no coercion of the victim", with a starting point of 2 years' imprisonment and a sentencing range of 1–4 years. The aggravating factors listed in the guideline include deception, which was apt to include deception of the sort practised here, i.e. where a vulnerable 19-year-old from a rural area in Romania was persuaded to come to the UK on the pretext of obtaining well paid work. Looking at the trafficking count on its own, the proper sentence for O would have been in the region of 3 years and for M in the region of 2 years. As for controlling prostitution, this case fell within the first category in the guideline, "evidence of physical and/or mental coercion", with a starting point of 3 years and a sentencing range of 2–5 years. This case was aggravated by the threat made by the offenders to disclose the victim's activity to her friends or relatives. Further, in the Court's view it was an aggravating feature that the victim was corrupted into becoming a prostitute, something which would not have occurred but for her being brought to this country. If count 2 had stood on its own, O would have merited a sentence of at least 3 years. The sentences imposed by the judge failed to reflect the totality of the offending, bringing the victim into this country by deception and then controlling through coercion her work as a prostitute and corrupting her in the process. The Court therefore quashed the sentences imposed in respect of the trafficking offences and, taking into account double jeopardy, increased it in O's case to 4 years and in M's case to 3 years, with the sentence for controlling prostitution left unaltered.

10.119D In *Brusch and Horvat*[59] the appellants each appealed against total sentences of 10 years' imprisonment imposed following their pleas of guilty to trafficking women for sexual exploitation. B and H, who were Czech citizens, had trafficked two women (Z and G) from the Czech Republic. Z was 19, suffered from a serious illness, had a drug problem and had left her parental home after a disagreement. She was clearly vulnerable. G was 37, a drug addict, and had worked as a prostitute in the past. B's role was to get the women abroad, and he persuaded them to go with him to the Republic of Ireland to take part in bogus marriages.

---

[59] [2011] EWCA Crim 1554.

Once there they met H, whose role was to enforce their sexual exploitation. They were coerced into having sex with a number of men. From Ireland all four travelled to the UK where Z and G were again coerced into having sex with a number of men. They were threatened with violence and their phones were removed. The offending came to an end only when they managed to escape. In a personal impact statement, Z said she had been hospitalised for three weeks following her escape. Her internal organs had been damaged, she suffered from nightmares, was frightened to have a relationship with a man and felt dirty and degraded. G described herself as having been mentally tortured and brutalised into submission. Both B and H had previous convictions in the Czech Republic. In sentencing, the judge had considered the SGC guideline and identified the previous convictions as an aggravating factor. B and H submitted there was nothing to take the case outside the guideline range of 4–9 years' imprisonment, and nothing to warrant the sentence being much above the 6-year starting point. Their appeals were allowed. In considering the guideline it was important to bear in mind that each appellant had previous convictions, though not for offences of the instant kind, and that each had been involved in dealing with more than one woman. The offences were not single offences. What happened in Ireland aggravated the offences, showing a continued course of conduct which lengthened and intensified the ordeal to which the victims had been subjected in the UK. It was important to remember that there were two victims and a significant degree of coercion. Z and G were vulnerable women who had been detained, kept isolated, degraded and forced to engage in sexual intercourse. However, given that the maximum sentence for each offence was 14 years' imprisonment, the 10-year sentence was too high. The sentences were therefore quashed and replaced with total sentences of 8 years' imprisonment.

PARTIES TO THE OFFENCE

By virtue of s.60(2), (3) of the 2003 Act, as enacted, s.57 applied to anything done **10.122** in the UK, and to anything done outside it by a body incorporated under the law of a part of the UK or by:
- a British citizen,
- a British overseas territories citizen,
- a British National (Overseas),
- a British Overseas citizen,
- a person who is a British subject under the British Nationality Act 1981, or
- a British protected person within the meaning given by s.50(1) of that Act.

The UK Borders Act 2007, s.31(4), substituted for these provisions a new s.60(2), by which s.57 applied simply to anything done whether inside or outside the UK. The effect of this amendment was that the s.57 offence could be committed by something done outside the UK by anyone, and not only someone falling within the statuses listed above. The purpose of the amendment was to remove the limitations on the territorial application of the ss.57–59 offences so that they covered facilitating a person's trafficking into, within or out of the UK for the purposes of sexual exploitation, regardless of where the facilitation took place and irrespective of the nationality of the facilitator. In the Committee debate on the Bill relating to a similar amendment made to the Immigration Act offence of assisting unlawful immigration and helping an asylum seeker to enter the UK, the Parliamentary Under-Secretary of State for the Home Department, Joan Ryan MP, referred to:

> " . . . the challenge that we face from those who seek to profit from the misery of those seeking to migrate illegally. As we have heard, people smugglers do not respect international boundaries or immigration laws and they will seek to exploit any gaps and vulnerabilities. The clause seeks to amend the existing facilitation offences to ensure that those who carry out acts of facilitation, whether those acts are committed within or outside the UK, can be prosecuted, irrespective of their nationality. Currently, these offences cover only acts of facilitation committed within the United Kingdom. Unless a perpetrator overseas is a British national or a body incorporated in the UK, they are not encompassed within the scope of the offences. We know that people carry out acts of facilitation outside the UK, for example by planning a route, making transportation arrangements, purchasing tickets and false documents or assisting people in deceiving carriers at check-in. Many are responsible for multiple attempts on the border, and it is simply unacceptable that those who engage in such activity abroad can be held accountable for their actions only if they are British nationals. That is why we have acted to remedy that unfairness. The purpose of the clause, then, is to extend the scope of the offences by removing the existing limitations on their extraterritorial applications so that they cover acts of facilitation directed at the United Kingdom wherever in the world they are committed and regardless of the nationality of the perpetrator. That will ensure that immigration officers are fully able to tackle individuals who exploit vulnerable people."[60]

The amendment was brought into force on January 31, 2008.[61]

"ARRANGES OR FACILITATES"

10.123   We suggest in the main work that the provision of food or water will only "facilitate" B's arrival in the UK if B would not have made the journey or would not have survived without it, and that no offence would be committed if its provision merely facilitated B's arrival in a better state of health than would otherwise have been the case. The proposition that providing food or water to B may, in appropriate circumstances, properly be regarded simply as serving his human needs rather than facilitating his entry into the UK derives some support from the following dictum of Ouseley J., giving the judgment of the Court of Appeal in *Javaherifard*[62] (which concerned the offence of facilitating a breach of immigration law contrary to s.25 of the Immigration Act 1971):

---

[60] *Hansard*, Public Bill Committee, cols 394–395 (March 15, 2007).

[61] UK Borders Act 2007 (Commencement No.1 and Transitional Provisions) Order 2008 (SI 2008/99).

[62] [2005] EWCA Crim 3231, at [50].

"If someone provides food, money or accommodation to an illegal entrant, knowing or having reasonable cause for believing[63] that such acts facilitate him being in the country *as an illegal entrant*, he would be guilty of an offence and we see no reason why that should not be so. If food, money or accommodation is supplied to someone known to the provider to be an illegal immigrant, but is not supplied with the knowledge that it will assist his presence *as an illegal entrant* but instead is supplied knowing that it will assist him simply as a human being e.g. to avoid degradation or destitution, there would be no offence."

The better view is that it is possible to facilitate a person's arrival or entry in the UK by an act which occurs close to but after the person's actual arrival or entry, if the act is necessary for the arrival or entry to be effective and is closely related to it in place and time. The Court of Appeal so held in *Javaherifard*,[64] which concerned the offence of facilitating a breach of immigration law (contrary to s.25 of the Immigration Act 1971). The Court referred with approval to *Singh and Meeuwsen*,[65] in which the appellants had assisted some illegal entrants to get away from a trailer, in which they had been concealed, after it left the port area. They had not been involved in bringing the trailer into the UK. The Court of Appeal rejected the argument that they could not be guilty of an offence of facilitating entry on the ground that the individuals had already entered by the time they were released. The court reasoned that those who wish to enter illegally have no wish to be discovered as soon as they disembark, and effective plans for their illegal entry would involve plans for their getting away from the port, undiscovered, as soon as possible. No doubt the courts would apply same analysis in relation to the offences under ss.57–59, and now s.59A, of the 2003 Act.

10.123A

TRAFFICKING WITHIN THE UK FOR SEXUAL EXPLOITATION

N.B. The offence in s.58 of the Sexual Offences Act 2003 has been repealed and replaced by s.59A of that Act: see above.

Mode of Trial and Punishment

For convictions on or after December 3, 2012,[66] an offence under s.58 is a specified offence for the purposes of s.226A of the CJA 2003 (extended sentence for certain violent or sexual offences), irrespective of the date of commission of the offence.

10.129

---

[63] It should be noted that the offences in ss.57–59A of the 2003 Act require an intention to facilitate; it is not sufficient to know or have reasonable cause to believe that the act in question will facilitate.

[64] Above, fn.62 at [25]–[29].

[65] [1972] 1 W.L.R. 1600.

[66] When s.124 of the Legal Aid, Sentencing and Punishment of Offenders Act 2012 was brought into force by the Legal Aid, Sentencing and Punishment of Offenders Act 2012 (Commencement No.4 and Saving Provisions) Order 2012 (SI 2012/2906).

Parties to the Offence

10.131 By virtue of s.60(2), (3) of the 2003 Act, as enacted, s.58 applied to anything done in the UK, and to anything done outside it by a body incorporated under the law of a part of the UK or by:

- a British citizen,
- a British overseas territories citizen,
- a British National (Overseas),
- a British Overseas citizen,
- a person who is a British subject under the British Nationality Act 1981, or
- a British protected person within the meaning given by section 50(1) of that Act.

The UK Borders Act 2007, s.31(4), substituted for these provisions a new s.60(2), by which s.58 applied simply to anything done whether inside or outside the UK. The effect of this amendment was that the s.58 offence could be committed by something done outside the UK by anyone, and not only someone falling within the statuses listed above. The purpose of the amendment was to remove the limitations on the territorial application of the ss.57–59 offences so that they covered facilitating a person's trafficking into, within or out of the UK for the purposes of sexual exploitation, regardless of where the facilitation took place and irrespective of the nationality of the facilitator: see further para.10.122, above. The amendment was brought into force on January 31, 2008.[67]

TRAFFICKING OUT OF THE UK FOR SEXUAL EXPLOITATION

N.B. The offence in s.59 of the Sexual Offences Act 2003 has been repealed and replaced by s.59A of that Act: see above.

Mode of Trial and Punishment

10.138 For convictions on or after December 3, 2012,[68] an offence under s.59 is a specified offence for the purposes of s.226A of the CJA 2003 (extended sentence for certain violent or sexual offences), irrespective of the date of commission of the offence.

---

[67] UK Borders Act 2007 (Commencement No.1 and Transitional Provisions) Order 2008 (SI 2008/99).

[68] When s.124 of the Legal Aid, Sentencing and Punishment of Offenders Act 2012 was brought into force by the Legal Aid, Sentencing and Punishment of Offenders Act 2012 (Commencement No.4 and Saving Provisions) Order 2012 (SI 2012/2906).

Parties to the Offence

By virtue of s.60(2), (3) of the 2003 Act, as enacted, s.59 applied to anything done   **10.139**
in the UK, and to anything done outside it by a body incorporated under the law
of a part of the UK or by:
- a British citizen,
- a British overseas territories citizen,
- a British National (Overseas),
- a British Overseas citizen,
- a person who is a British subject under the British Nationality Act 1981,
  or
- a British protected person within the meaning given by s.50(1) of that
  Act.

The UK Borders Act 2007, s.31(4), substituted for these provisions a new s.60(2),
by which s.59 applied simply to anything done whether inside or outside the UK.
The effect of this amendment was that the s.59 offence could be committed by
something done outside the UK by anyone, and not only someone falling within
the statuses listed above. The purpose of the amendment was to remove the
limitations on the territorial application of the ss.57–59 offences so that they
covered facilitating a person's trafficking into, within or out of the UK for the
purposes of sexual exploitation, regardless of where the facilitation took place and
irrespective of the nationality of the facilitator: see further para.10.122 above. The
amendment was brought into force on January 31, 2008.[69]

---

[69] UK Borders Act 2007 (Commencement No.1 and Transitional Provisions) Order 2008 (SI
2008/99).

CHAPTER 11

OFF-STREET PROSTITUTION AND RELATED
OFFENCES

INTRODUCTION

The Coalition Government is yet to announce any proposal to reform or amend **11.08** the law relating to prostitution. It has, though, published *A Review of Effective Practice in Responding to Prostitution* (October 2011),[1] which is aimed at local authorities and community safety partnerships and encourages them "to develop a response to prostitution that aims to improve the outcomes for the community and particularly those involved in prostitution." In relation to the policing response to off-street prostitution, it provides:

> "7.9. While the approach to policing off-street prostitution may be different from that for street prostitution, it is important that an effective response is developed. In this respect a number of areas focus on the premises where sexual services are sold and that present a nuisance, or where exploitation, trafficking or the involvement of children is suspected. This highlights the need for areas to develop a definition of exploitation and a way of identifying and responding to it, including ensuring that support is in place for victims identified.
>
> 7.10. As with street prostitution, it is important that the approach to policing off-street prostitution is developed in partnership with specialist services and takes account of other services that may be being delivered to those involved. In some areas those involved in off-street prostitution raised concerns about accessing services because they perceived them to be associated with the police or were concerned that disclosing information about their involvement in prostitution (or in some cases their

---

[1] See *https://www.gov.uk/government/uploads/system/uploads/attachment_data/file/97778/respond ing-to-prostitution.pdf* [accessed December 19, 2013].

343

immigration status) would be passed to the police. This highlights the importance of the police building trust so as not to disrupt the provision of other services."

11.08A In addition, the Association of Chief Police Officers has published the *ACPO Strategy & Supporting Operational Guidance for Policing Prostitution and Sexual Exploitation* (November 2011),[2] the purpose of the which is to provide a framework for the policing of this area of the law. Deputy Chief Constable Simon Byrne of Greater Manchester Police writes in the Foreword:

> "The policing of prostitution continues to present difficult challenges for those involved. This is understandable but needs to be addressed. It is understandable because society as a whole has an equivocal attitude towards prostitution and those involved. Some regard prostitution as a moral rather than criminal issue, some as an anti-social behaviour problem, some as a crime of abuse and exploitation, others as an issue of social care and welfare, and some may even regard it simply as a career choice.
>
> . . .
>
> [It] is the purpose of this strategy to assist forces in making the difficult operational choices relating to prostitution and sexual exploitation in a world of other competing priorities. There are many factors at play, which can be summarised under two main headings. The first is the continual association between on-street prostitution and addiction to illegal drugs, often heroin and crack cocaine. This not only motivates those already engaged in prostitution, but also acts as an incentive to both women and men to become sex workers in the vain search for, what some may perceive as, easy money. The second is the off-street prostitution linked to organised crime—a lucrative business for those in charge.
>
> This strategy also addresses the issue of the sexual exploitation of children and young people since this can involve, or lead to, commercial sexual exploitation. In the case of children and young people the emphasis is always on safeguarding the young person and on the proactive disruption and prosecution of their abusers.
>
> This strategy emphatically recognises that anyone abused and exploited through prostitution needs help and support to access health, welfare and exit services, in order to leave it behind and start a new life. It also, however, recognises that communities as well as individuals can be victimised and need help too. At the same time those who abuse and exploit must be rigorously investigated and prosecuted. This strategy, therefore, promotes a holistic approach to the policing of prostitution that keeps in balance the three essential elements of individual, community, and the investigation and prosecution of those who exploit and abuse. It is not possible to effectively choose between these three facets of effective policing; they must operate simultaneously and sustainably.
>
> In addition to recommending this approach, this strategy also recommends an approach based throughout on partnership with local authorities, other statutory agencies and nongovernmental organisations. It takes account of the National Threat Assessment and the link to drugs and organised crime. Again to put the matter simply, the policing of prostitution will at best only achieve short-term results unless there is effective partnership at the local and strategic level to support victimised individuals and communities with appropriate legislation and enforcement resources.

[2] See   *http://www.acpo.police.uk/documents/crime/2011/20111102%20CBA%20Policing%20Prosti tution%20and%20%20Sexual%20Exploitation%20Strategy_Website_October%202011.pdf*   [accessed December 8, 2013].

The main ethos that will run through this strategy is the need to reduce harm and increase public confidence, utilising approaches that consider risk, threat and harm to all."

In December 2011, the Home Office launched a national "Ugly Mugs" pilot scheme run by the UK Network of Sex Work Projects ("UKNSWP") to help protect sex workers from violent and abusive individuals. The Home Office provided £108,000 to fund a 12-month pilot which included establishing a national online network to bring together and support locally-run "Ugly Mug" schemes. These local "Ugly Mug" or "dodgy punter" schemes have been running for some years and, according to the UKNSWP, have proved very useful in passing on warnings to sex workers about dangerous people, as well as helping to increase the reporting, detection and conviction of crimes. The scheme was still operating in October 2013. Details can be found on the UKNSWP website.[3] **11.08B**

Finally, in March 2012 the Greater London Authority published a report on the policing of off-street sex work and sex trafficking in London, entitled *Silence on Violence–improving the safety of women*.[4] The report was written by London Assembly Member Andrew Boff at the request of the Mayor of London after a number of questions were raised on the topic during Mayor's Question Time. Mr Boff found evidence that sex workers were reporting fewer crimes to police and that raids had increased in some parts of London. He made a number of recommendations, among them that sex workers should be included in the formulation of police strategies that affect them, and that crimes of violence against sex workers should be labelled as hate crimes and prioritised for prosecution. **11.08D**

The Canadian experience: *Canada (Attorney General) v Bedford*

It is worth noting that in the recent case *Canada (Attorney General) v Bedford*,[5] Canada's Supreme Court struck down as unconstitutional the criminal prohibitions on bawdy-houses, living on the avails of prostitution and public communication for purposes of prostitution, on the ground that they violated the safety of prostitutes contrary to s.7 of the Charter of Fundamental Rights and Freedoms (which provides that the State cannot deny a person's right to life, liberty or security of the person except in accordance with the principles of fundamental justice). The unanimous (9–0) decision was suspended for one year to allow time for the Canadian Parliament to devise another way to regulate the sex trade if it chooses to do so. **11.08E**

The case was brought by one current and two former prostitutes who argued that sex workers would be safer if they were allowed to screen clients, or "johns",

---

[3] *https://uknswp.org/um/* [accessed December 19, 2013].
[4] See *http://glaconservatives.co.uk/wp-content/uploads/downloads/2012/03/Report-on-the-Safety-of-Sex-Workers-Silence-on-Violence.pdf* [accessed December 8, 2013].
[5] [2013] SCC 72.

and operate in brothels with bodyguards if they chose. The safety of prostitutes became a high-profile issue in Canada following the conviction in 2007 of serial killer Robert Pickton, who preyed on prostitutes and other women in Vancouver's Downtown Eastside. Against that background the Supreme Court found the prohibitions overly broad or grossly out of proportion to the law's goals. Beverley McLachlin C.J. said that a law that banned what she called "safe havens" for prostitutes exposed them to risks from predators. She said many prostitutes had no choice but to work in the sex trade, and the law should not make their work more dangerous[6]:

> "The prohibitions at issue do not merely impose conditions on how prostitutes operate. They go a critical step further, by imposing *dangerous* conditions on prostitution; they prevent people engaged in a risky—but legal—activity from taking steps to protect themselves from the risks."

In relation to the prohibition on bawdy-houses, McLachlin C.J. said[7]:

> "It is not an offence to sell sex for money. The bawdy-house provisions, however, make it an offence to do so in any 'place' that is 'kept or occupied' or 'resorted to' for the purpose of prostitution . . .
>
> The practical effect . . . is to confine lawful prostitution to two categories: street prostitution and out-calls . . . In-calls, where the john comes to the prostitute's residence, are prohibited. Out-calls, where the prostitute goes out and meets the client at a designated location, such as the client's home, are allowed. Working on the street is also permitted, though the practice of street prostitution is significantly limited by the prohibition on communicating in public . . .
>
> The application judge found, on a balance of probabilities, that the safest form of prostitution is working independently from a fixed location . . . She concluded that indoor work is far less dangerous than street prostitution—a finding that the evidence amply supports. She also concluded that out-call work is not as safe as in-call work, particularly under the current regime where prostitutes are precluded by virtue of the living on the avails provision from hiring a driver or security guard. Since the bawdy-house provision makes the safety-enhancing method of in-call prostitution illegal, the application judge concluded that the bawdy-house prohibition materially increased the risk prostitutes face under the present regime. I agree.
>
> First, the prohibition prevents prostitutes from working in a fixed indoor location, which would be safer than working on the streets or meeting clients at different locations, especially given the current prohibition on hiring drivers or security guards. This, in turn, prevents prostitutes from having a regular clientele and from setting up indoor safeguards like receptionists, assistants, bodyguards and audio room monitoring, which would reduce risks . . . Second, it interferes with provision of health checks and preventive health measures. Finally—a point developed in argument before us—the bawdy-house prohibition prevents resort to safe houses, to which prostitutes working on the street can take clients. In Vancouver, for example, 'Grandma's House' was established to support street workers in the Downtown Eastside, at about the same time as fears were growing that a serial killer was prowling the streets—fears which materialized in the notorious Robert Pickton. Street prostitutes—who the application judge found are largely the most vulnerable class of prostitutes, and who face an alarming amount of violence—were able to bring clients to Grandma's House. However, charges were laid under [the bawdy-house provision] and although the charges were eventually stayed . . . Grandma's House was shut

---

[6] At [60].
[7] At [61]–[65].

down . . . For some prostitutes, particularly those who are destitute, safe houses such as Grandma's House may be critical. For these people, the ability to work in brothels or hire security, even if those activities were lawful, may be illusory.

I conclude, therefore, that the bawdy-house provision negatively impacts the security of the person of prostitutes and engages s.7 of the *Charter*."

As to the purpose of the prohibition, McLachlin C.J. held that it was not directed at the mischief of prostitution per se but rather at the harm to the community in which prostitution is carried on in a notorious and habitual manner. The harm imposed by the prohibition, as set out above, was grossly disproportionate to this purpose and accordingly the relevant provisions were unconstitutional. In so holding, McLachlin C.J. dismissed the Federal Government's argument that it is the prostitute's choice to engage in prostitution, rather than the laws that govern the activity, that puts the prostitute at risk[8]:

"First, while some prostitutes may fit the description of persons who freely choose (or at one time chose) to engage in the risky economic activity of prostitution, many prostitutes have no meaningful choice but to do so . . .

Second, even accepting that there are those who freely choose to engage in prostitution, it must be remembered that prostitution—the exchange of sex for money—is not illegal. The causal question is whether the impugned laws make this lawful activity more dangerous. An analogy could be drawn to a law preventing a cyclist from wearing a helmet. That the cyclist chooses to ride her bike does not diminish the causal role of the law in making that activity riskier. The challenged laws relating to prostitution are no different.

. . . It makes no difference that the conduct of pimps and johns is the immediate source of the harms suffered by prostitutes. The impugned laws deprive people engaged in a risky, but legal, activity of the means to protect themselves against those risks. The violence of a john does not diminish the role of the state in making a prostitute more vulnerable to that violence."

This is not, however, the end of the story. In explaining why the Court suspended the effect of its decision for a year, McLachlin C.J. said[9]:

"Parliament is [not] precluded from imposing limits on where and how prostitution may be conducted. Prohibitions on keeping a bawdy-house, living on the avails of prostitution and communication related to prostitution are intertwined. They impact on each other. Greater latitude in one measure—for example, permitting prostitutes to obtain the assistance of security personnel—might impact on the constitutionality of another measure—for example, forbidding the nuisances associated with keeping a bawdy-house. The regulation of prostitution is a complex and delicate matter. It will be for Parliament, should it choose to do so, to devise a new approach, reflecting different elements of the existing regime."

The question arises whether the arguments accepted by the Canadian Supreme Court in *Bedford* could be run successfully in this jurisdiction. We suggest not. It is true that the language of s.7 of the Canadian Charter, guaranteeing a person's right to "security of the person", is mirrored in the right to "liberty and security of person" conferred by art.5 of the ECHR. However, the better view is that the focus of art.5 is the protection of liberty in its classic sense of personal freedom,   11.08F

[8] At [86]–[89].
[9] At [165].

and that "liberty and security of person" are best considered as one concept, with "security" meaning freedom from arrest or detention rather than "safety".[10] It nonetheless remains to be seen whether the issues in *Bedford* will be given an airing before a UK court.

KEEPING A BROTHEL USED FOR PROSTITUTION

Sentencing

11.32 The Sentencing Council has issued a new guideline applicable to sex offenders aged 18 or over who are sentenced on or after April 1, 2014: see para.1.20 et seq., above. As with other offences covered by the guideline, when sentencing for an offence under s.33A, the court is to go through a series of steps in order to determine the appropriate sentence.

Step One—Harm

11.32A Step one involves determining the offence category by reference to the degree of harm caused and then the culpability level for the offence. The harm factors for offences under s.33A are:

HARM	
Category 1	• Under 18 year olds working in brothel
	• Abduction/detention
	• Violence or threats of violence
	• Sustained and systematic psychological abuse
	• Those working in brothel forced or coerced to participate in unsafe/degrading sexual activity
	• Those working in brothel forced or coerced into seeing many "customers"
	• Those working in brothel forced/coerced/deceived into prostitution
	• Established evidence of community impact
Category 2	• Factor(s) in category 1 not present

In its consultation on the draft guideline,[11] the Sentencing Council said that it had focused on factors that increase the harm to prostitutes working within the

---

[10] See, e.g. *Guide on Article 5 – Right to Liberty and Security: Article 5 of the Convention* (Council of Europe/European Court of Human Rights, 2012), available at *www.echr.coe.int* [accessed December 23, 2013], para.17: "The key purpose of Article 5 is to prevent arbitrary or unjustified deprivations of liberty."

[11] *Sexual Offences Guideline: Consultation* (December 6, 2012).

brothel. This focus is not, however, exclusive, as the harm factors for category 1 include "established evidence of community impact". The Council included this factor to take account of cases where the brothel has an impact on the local area; for example, it is located near a school and there are clients going in and out frequently, or it is in a residential area and the presence of clients is intimidating for residents at night. Many of the other harm factors also appear in the guideline for the offences of causing or inciting prostitution for gain (s.52 of the 2003 Act) and controlling prostitution for gain (s.53) and are discussed at para.10.70, above.

Culpability

In its consultation, the Sentencing Council said that the main focus of the s.33A **11.32B** offence is the role played by the offender and the level of deliberate exploitation and corruption of those working in the brothel. As the offence penalises those who keep, manage or act or assist in the management of a brothel, it covers a wide range of involvement and of culpability. The culpability factors therefore seek to distinguish between those who have genuine power and influence in relation to the brothel and those who have a minor role or are coerced or exploited themselves. The factors are:

CULPABILITY
A
• Keeping brothel on significant commercial basis • Involvement in keeping a number of brothels • Expectation of significant financial or other gain • Abuse of trust • Exploitation of those known to be trafficked • Significant involvement in limiting freedom of those working in brothel • Grooming of a person to work in the brothel including through cultivation of a dependency on drugs or alcohol
B
• Keeping/managing premises • Close involvement with those working in brothel e.g. control of finances, choice of clients, working conditions, etc. (where offender's involvement is not as a result of coercion)
C
• Performs limited function under direction • Close involvement but engaged by coercion/intimidation/exploitation

A number of these factors appear in the guideline for ss.52 and 53 of the 2003 Act and are discussed at para.10.70, above. In its consultation document, the Sentencing Council said that "keeping brothel on significant commercial basis" and "involvement in keeping a number of brothels" are at culpability A to reflect the fact that the offender will be directing and involving a large number of people in the operation of brothels. "Keeping/managing premises" is at culpability B to reflect the level of culpability of those that undertake a management role with a degree of day-to-day responsibility for the running of the brothel. "Close involvement with those working in brothel e.g. control of finances, choice of clients, working conditions, etc (where offender's involvement is not as a result of coercion)" is intended to reflect situations where the offender has a degree of control and autonomy in the running of the brothel. As for culpability C, the factors "performs limited function under direction" and "close involvement but engaged by coercion/intimidation/exploitation" would apply in this context to "maids" who may help look after the other women in the brothel or have a limited role such as answering the door and letting in clients, and to those helping run the brothel but who are doing so due to coercion or exploitation.

Step Two—Starting point and category range

11.32C Having determined the offence category and culpability level, the court should then use the corresponding starting point specified in the guideline in order to reach a sentence within the category range. The starting point applies to all offenders irrespective of plea or previous convictions. Once the starting point has been determined, step two allows further adjustment for aggravating or mitigating features, set out below. A case of particular gravity, reflected by multiple features of culpability or harm, could merit upward adjustment from the starting point before further adjustment for aggravating or mitigating features. Where there is a sufficient prospect of rehabilitation, a community order with a sex offender treatment programme requirement under s.202 of the Criminal Justice Act 2003 ("CJA 2003") may be a proper alternative to a short or moderate length custodial sentence. The starting points and category ranges for offences under s.33A are as follows:

	A	B	C
Category 1	**Starting point** 5 years' custody	**Starting point** 3 years' custody	**Starting point** 1 year's custody
	Category range 3–6 years' custody	**Category range** 2–5 years' custody	**Category range** High level community order –18 months' custody

	A	B	C
Category 2	**Starting point** 3 years' custody	**Starting point** 12 months' custody	**Starting point** Medium level community order
	Category range 2–5 years' custody	**Category range** 26 weeks'–2 years' custody	**Category range** Low level community order –High level community order

At the top level, the starting point and range are higher than in the previous guideline, issued in 2007 by the Sentencing Guidelines Council, which had at its top level a starting point of 2 years' custody with a range of 1–4 years. The highest category under that guideline was for an offence where the offender was the keeper of the brothel and had made profits in the region of £5,000 and upwards. The top category in the new guideline has a starting point of 5 years' custody with a range of 3–6 years. In its consultation document, the Sentencing Council said this category will apply where, e.g. the offender has been involved in serious exploitation or the brothel used child prostitutes, and in addition there is a degree of larger scale management of the brothel and either an abuse of trust or an element of limiting the freedom of the prostitute. At the other end of the offending scale, where the offender has had minimal involvement and there are no signs of exploitation of prostitutes working in the brothel, a community order is proposed. Such a disposal would be designed to address the reasons the offender has become involved in the brothel.

Aggravating and mitigating factors

The court should next consider whether the presence of aggravating or mitigating **11.32D** factors should result in an upward or downward adjustment from the starting point or the imposition of a sentence outside the category range. In particular, relevant recent convictions are likely to result in an upward adjustment. When sentencing appropriate category 1 offences, the court should also consider whether the custody threshold has been passed; if so, whether a custodial sentence is unavoidable; and if it is, whether that sentence can be suspended. The non-exhaustive list of aggravating and mitigating factors for offences under s.33A is:

Aggravating factors
Statutory aggravating factors
• Previous convictions, having regard to a) the nature of the offence to which the conviction relates and its relevance to the current offence; and b) the time that has elapsed since the conviction

• Offence committed whilst on bail

Other aggravating factors

• Failure to comply with current court orders
• Offence committed whilst on licence
• Deliberate isolation of those working in brothel
• Threats made to expose those working in brothel to the authorities (eg immigration or police), family/friends or others
• Harm threatened against the family/friends of those working in brothel
• Passport/identity documents removed
• Those working in brothel prevented from seeking medical treatment
• Food withheld
• Those working in brothel passed around by offender and moved to other brothels
• Earnings of those working in brothel withheld/kept by offender or evidence of excessive wage reduction or debt bondage, inflated travel or living expenses or unreasonable interest rates
• Any steps taken to prevent those working in brothel reporting an incident, obtaining assistance and/or from assisting or supporting the prosecution
• Attempts to dispose of or conceal evidence
• Those working in brothel forced or coerced into pornography
• Timescale over which operation has been run

Mitigating factors

• No previous convictions **or** no relevant/recent convictions
• Remorse
• Previous good character and/or exemplary conduct*
• Age and/or lack of maturity where it affects the responsibility of the offender
• Mental disorder or learning disability, particularly where linked to the commission of the offence
• Demonstration of steps taken to address offending behaviour

* Previous good character/exemplary conduct is different from having no previous convictions. The more serious the offence, the less the weight which should normally be attributed to this factor. Where previous good character/exemplary conduct has been used to facilitate the offence, this mitigation should not normally be allowed and such conduct may constitute an aggravating factor.

A number of these factors appear in the guideline for ss.52 and 53 of the 2003 Act and are discussed at para.10.70, above.

Steps Three to Eight

The remaining steps cover the following points. At step three the court should **11.32E** consider any factors which would indicate a reduction in sentence, e.g. assistance to the prosecution. At step four it should consider any reduction for a guilty plea. Step five requires the court to consider whether the total sentence is just and proportionate to the offending behaviour. At step six it should consider whether to make an ancillary order (e.g. a confiscation order, a Serious Crime Prevention Order or a restraining order). Step seven requires the court to fulfil its duty under s.174 of the CJA 2003 to give reasons for, and explain the effect of, the sentence. Finally, at step eight the court should consider whether to give credit for time spent on bail in accordance with s.240A of that Act.

KEEPING A DISORDERLY HOUSE

Charge based on the Provision of Sexual Services

The recent decision in *Court and Gu*[12] emphatically bears out the suggestion in the **11.73** main work that the offence of keeping a disorderly house is not apt to penalise the provision of "ordinary" sexual services. The appellants in that case rented two properties in which sexual services were provided. They placed two "commonplace, unremarkable and non-descript" advertisements in the personal services section of the local newspaper. When police officers called the mobile phone numbers given in the advertisements, they were offered sexual services. When the properties were searched a scantily dressed woman was found in one and a large number of condoms in both. In one property a vibrator was found, but no other devices or instruments. No customers were found at either property and no customers and no women offering services were observed going to or from the properties. The case proceeded on the basis that only one woman was ever offering sexual services at any one time and that only one customer at a time was ever present at either property, and that the sexual services on offer did not go further than normal sexual intercourse. No complaint had been received and no concern expressed by people living in either neighbourhood. The appellants were first charged with acting or assisting in the management of a brothel, contrary to s.33A of the 2003 Act. However, the prosecution concluded that they could not establish that the premises were a brothel for the purposes of that provision. The appropriate charge should have been that, as tenants, the appellants knowingly

---

[12] [2012] EWCA Crim 133. For an approving consideration of the decision, see Dermot Keating, *An Orderly House?* C.L. & J., Vol.176, pp.233–4, April 21, 2012.

permitted the premises to be used for the purposes of habitual prostitution, contrary to s.36 of the Sexual Offences Act 1956. But that is a summary offence and the usual 6-month limitation period had expired. For that reason, the indictment was amended to charge the appellants with keeping a disorderly house. They were convicted by the jury but the convictions were quashed on appeal. Lord Judge C.J., giving the judgment of the Court, said[13]:

"The Sexual Offences Act 2003 is vast and, taking into account a number of provisions from earlier Sexual Offences Acts which were not repealed, apparently comprehensive legislation identifying the vast number of different activities which constitute sexual crime. Counsel reminded us that there are now 35 different statutory provisions which relate to what can loosely be described as the sex trade. Comprehensive as it appears to be, the statute did not abolish the common law offence of keeping a disorderly house.

In the context of such detailed statutory provisions relating to sexual crime in its many different manifestations, an ancient common law offence should not normally be expanded beyond well-established parameters by judicial decision. The reality is that on the evidence available in this case the conviction of the appellants represented a significant widening of the ambit of the ancient offence.

Our attention was focused on *R v Tan and others* [1983] QB 1053. Tan and others were accused of keeping a disorderly house. The difference between the facts of that case and the present are encapsulated in the advertisements, of which one example in *Tan* read:

'Humiliation enthusiast, my favourite past time is humiliating and disciplining mature male submissives, in strict bondage, lovely tan coloured mistress invites humble applicants, T.V., C.P., B.D. and rubber wear . . . '

Services of this kind were indeed provided. According to the judgment, they were 'of a particularly revolting and perverted kind . . . with the aid of a mass of equipment, some manual (such as whips and chains), some mechanical and some electrical, clients were subjected at their own wish and with their full consent, to a variety of forms of humiliation, flagellation, bondage and torture . . . '

In one of the earlier cases referred to in the judgment, *R v Berg and others* [1927] 20 Cr. App. R 38, the activities in the disorderly house involved exhibitions of a perverted nature, and in *R v Quinn and others* [1962] 2 QB 245 the premises were used for the performance of acts which were 'seriously indecent and, in some respects, revolting', and the public was invited to resort to the premises for indulging in 'perverted and revolting practices'.

In *R v Tan* itself the court indicated that before a defendant could be convicted the jury had to be satisfied that the services provided were open to members of the public who wished to partake of them, and were 'of such a character and conducted in such a manner (whether by advertisement or otherwise) that their provision amounts to an outrage of public decency, or is otherwise calculated to injure the public interest to such an extent as to call for condemnation and punishment'. The entire judgment proceeds on the basis that the provision of what was described as 'straightforward sexual intercourse' would not be sufficient to constitute this offence.

The researches of counsel have not found anything in the old books which suggest any case where, on facts remotely similar to those present in this case, there has ever been a prosecution, let alone a conviction for the offence of keeping a disorderly house.

We have reached the unhesitating conclusion that the circumstances described here, taken at their highest, were not capable of falling within the scope of the common law

---

[13] At [8]–[15].

offence. The criminality which should have been alleged was that the appellants allowed the premises of which they were tenants to be used for prostitution. That however cannot be an appropriate basis for upholding the use of the common law charge."

CHAPTER 12

STREET-BASED PROSTITUTION

INTRODUCTION

Where next?

The Coalition Government is yet to announce any proposal to reform or amend **12.20**
the law relating to prostitution. It has, though, published *A Review of Effective
Practice in Responding to Prostitution* (October 2011).[1] The Review is aimed at local
authorities and community safety partnerships and encourages them "to develop
a response to prostitution that aims to improve the outcomes for the community
and particularly those involved in prostitution". In relation to the policing
response to street prostitution, it provides, somewhat blandly:

> "7.7. The policing of street prostitution needs to take account of those buying sex, as
> well as those selling sex. In a number of areas visited the focus of enforcement was
> primarily on those seeking to buy sexual services on the street. Any approach that
> focuses on those selling sex needs to take account of the need to ensure access to
> services as an initial response.
> 7.8. A number of areas support the enforcement of offences related to soliciting by
> running a programme aimed at getting men engaging in kerb crawling to reflect on
> their conduct and cease offending. A number of areas noted that this course was run
> on a self-funding basis as it was paid for by attendees (having consented to do so as
> a condition of the sentence set by the court)."

At about the same time, the Association of Chief Police Officers published the **12.20A**
ACPO Strategy & Supporting Operational Guidance for Policing Prostitution and

---

[1] See *https://www.gov.uk/government/uploads/system/uploads/attachment_data/file/97778/respond
ing-to-prostitution.pdf* [accessed December 19, 2013].

Sexual Exploitation (November 2011),[2] the purpose of which is to provide a framework for the policing of this area of the law. The Foreword, by Deputy Chief Constable Simon Byrne of Greater Manchester Police, can be found at para.11.08, above.

12.20B   In December 2011, the Home Office launched a national "Ugly Mugs" pilot scheme run by the UK Network of Sex Work Projects ("UKNSWP") to help protect sex workers from violent and abusive individuals. The Home Office provided £108,000 to fund a 12-month pilot which includes establishing a national online network to bring together and support locally-run "Ugly Mug" schemes. These local "Ugly Mug" or "dodgy punter" schemes have been running for some years and, according to the UKNSWP, have proved very useful in passing on warnings to sex workers about dangerous people, as well as helping to increase the reporting, detection and conviction of crimes. The scheme was still operating in October 2013. Details can be found on the UKNSWP website.[3]

The Canadian experience: *Canada (Attorney General) v Bedford*

12.20D   It is worth noting that in *Canada (Attorney General) v Bedford*,[4] Canada's Supreme Court recently struck down as unconstitutional the criminal prohibitions on bawdy-houses, living on the avails of prostitution and public communication for purposes of prostitution, on the ground that they violated the safety of prostitutes contrary to s.7 of the Charter of Fundamental Rights and Freedoms (which provides that the State cannot deny a person's right to life, liberty or security of the person except in accordance with the principles of fundamental justice). The unanimous (9–0) decision was suspended for one year to allow time for the Canadian Parliament to devise another way to regulate the sex trade if it chooses to do so.

    The case was brought by one current and two former prostitutes who argued that sex workers would be safer if they were allowed to screen clients, or "johns", and operate in brothels with bodyguards if they chose. The safety of prostitutes became a high-profile issue in Canada following the conviction in 2007 of serial killer Robert Pickton, who preyed on prostitutes and other women in Vancouver's Downtown Eastside. Against that background the Supreme Court found the prohibitions overly broad or grossly out of proportion to the law's goals. Beverley McLachlin C.J. said that a law that banned what she called "safe havens" for prostitutes exposed them to risks from predators. She said many prostitutes had no choice but to work in the sex trade, and the law should not make their work more dangerous[5]:

---

[2] See *http://www.acpo.police.uk/documents/crime/2011/20111102%20CBA%20Policing%20Prostitution%20and%20%20Sexual%20Exploitation%20Strategy_Website_October%202011.pdf* [accessed December 20, 2013].

[3] *https://uknswp.org/um/* [accessed December 19, 2013].

[4] [2013] SCC 72.

[5] At [60].

"The prohibitions at issue do not merely impose conditions on how prostitutes operate. They go a critical step further, by imposing *dangerous* conditions on prostitution; they prevent people engaged in a risky—but legal—activity from taking steps to protect themselves from the risks."

In relation to the prohibition on communicating for the purpose of prostitution, McLachlin C.J. said[6]:

"The application judge found that face-to-face communication is an 'essential tool' in enhancing street prostitutes' safety ... Such communication, which the law prohibits, allows prostitutes to screen prospective clients for intoxication or propensity to violence, which can reduce the risks they face ... The application judge also found that the communicating law has had the effect of displacing prostitutes from familiar areas, where they may be supported by friends and regular customers, to more isolated areas, thereby making them more vulnerable ... By prohibiting communicating in public for the purpose of prostitution, the law prevents prostitutes from screening clients and setting terms for the use of condoms or safe houses. In these ways, it significantly increases the risks they face."

The purpose of the prohibition was not to eliminate street prostitution for its own sake, but to take prostitution "off the streets and out of public view" in order to prevent the nuisances that street prostitution can cause. McLachlin C.J. held that the harm imposed by the prohibition was grossly disproportionate to this purpose and that the prohibition was therefore unconstitutional. In so holding, McLachlin C.J. dismissed the Federal Government's argument that it is the prostitute's choice to engage in prostitution, rather than the laws that govern the activity, that puts the prostitute at risk[7]:

"First, while some prostitutes may fit the description of persons who freely choose (or at one time chose) to engage in the risky economic activity of prostitution, many prostitutes have no meaningful choice but to do so ... As the application judge found, street prostitutes, with some exceptions, are a particularly marginalized population ... Whether because of financial desperation, drug addictions, mental illness, or compulsion from pimps, they often have little choice but to sell their bodies for money. Realistically, while they may retain some minimal power of choice—what the Attorney General of Canada called 'constrained choice' ... these are not people who can be said to be truly 'choosing' a risky line of business ...

Second, even accepting that there are those who freely choose to engage in prostitution, it must be remembered that prostitution—the exchange of sex for money—is not illegal. The causal question is whether the impugned laws make this lawful activity more dangerous.

... It makes no difference that the conduct of pimps and johns is the immediate source of the harms suffered by prostitutes. The impugned laws deprive people engaged in a risky, but legal, activity of the means to protect themselves against those risks. The violence of a john does not diminish the role of the state in making a prostitute more vulnerable to that violence."

This is not, however, the end of the story. In explaining why the Court suspended the effect of its decision for a year, McLachlin C.J. said[8]:

---

[6] At [68]–[71].
[7] At [86]–[89].
[8] At [165].

"Parliament is [not] precluded from imposing limits on where and how prostitution may be conducted. Prohibitions on keeping a bawdy-house, living on the avails of prostitution and communication related to prostitution are intertwined. They impact on each other. Greater latitude in one measure—for example, permitting prostitutes to obtain the assistance of security personnel—might impact on the constitutionality of another measure—for example, forbidding the nuisances associated with keeping a bawdy-house. The regulation of prostitution is a complex and delicate matter. It will be for Parliament, should it choose to do so, to devise a new approach, reflecting different elements of the existing regime."

12.20E   The question arises whether the arguments accepted by the Canadian Supreme Court in *Bedford* could be run successfully in this jurisdiction. We suggest not. It is true that the language of s.7 of the Canadian Charter, guaranteeing a person's right to "security of the person", is mirrored in the right to "liberty and security of person" conferred by art.5 of the ECHR. However, the better view is that the focus of art.5 is the protection of liberty in its classic sense of personal freedom, and that "liberty and security of person" are best considered as one concept, with "security" meaning freedom from arrest or detention rather than "safety".[9] It nonetheless remains to be seen whether the issues in *Bedford* will be given an airing before a UK court.

LOITERING OR SOLICITING FOR THE PURPOSE OF PROSTITUTION

MODE OF TRIAL AND PUNISHMENT

12.24   Section 18(2) of the Policing and Crime Act 2009 amends the Rehabilitation of Offenders Act 1974 so that the rehabilitation period applicable to a rehabilitation order under s.1(2A) of the Street Offences Act 1959 is six months from the date of conviction for the offence in respect of which the order is made. On a date to be appointed, s.18(2) will be repealed by the Legal Aid, Sentencing and Punishment of Offenders Act 2012 and replaced by a further amendment of the 1974 Act by which the rehabilitation period will begin on the date of conviction and end on the day provided for by or under the rehabilitation order as the last day on which the order is to have effect.[10]

PARTIES TO THE OFFENCE

12.26   Home Office circular 20/2000 is no longer available on the Home Office website. However, the guidance contained in it to the effect that children under 18 who are

---

[9] See, e.g. *Guide on Article 5—Right to Liberty and Security: Article 5 of the Convention* (Council of Europe/European Court of Human Rights, 2012), available at *www.echr.coe.int* [accessed December 23, 2013], para.17: "The key purpose of Article 5 is to prevent arbitrary or unjustified deprivations of liberty."

[10] Legal Aid, Sentencing and Punishment of Offenders Act 2012, ss.139, 141 and Sch.25, Pt 2.

engaged in prostitution should be treated as victims and prosecuted only as a last resort, is replicated in Home Office circular 006/2010, titled *Provisions in the Policing and Crime Act 2009 that relate to prostitution (sections 14 to 21)* and published on March 29, 2010.[11] This Circular, which is referred to (under a slightly different title) in fn.3 of the main work, provides in paras 53–55:

"Under 18s found loitering and soliciting

The offence of loitering or soliciting under the Street Offences Act 1959 is applicable to those under 18. However, when a child who is being sexually exploited in street prostitution comes to the attention of the police, the police must treat securing the welfare of the child as their priority and should only consider criminal sanctions as a last resort when all other options have been exhausted.

This approach is in accordance with guidance issued by the Department for Children, Schools and Families 'Safeguarding Children from Sexual Exploitation' (June 2009) which states that:

"the criminal law is rarely an effective or appropriate response to children and young people under the age of 18 found loitering or soliciting for the purposes of prostitution and that the responsibility for the sexual exploitation of children or young people lies with the abuser: either the person who pays for sex, in some way, or the person who grooms the child and/or organises the exploitation".

Action taken in relation to a child who is sexually exploited in prostitution should comply with the UK's obligations under the United Nations Convention on the Rights of the Child (1990), particularly Articles 34–36 which relate to child sexual exploitation and sexual abuse ... In short, any steps taken, whether relating to criminal proceedings or not, should be designed to protect the child from continuing sexual exploitation and abuse."

THE CAUTIONING SYSTEM

Home Office circular 20/2000, referred to in fn.68 in the main work, is no longer available on the Home Office website. However, the guidance contained in it relating to cautioning for offences of prostitution is replicated in Home Office circular 006/2010, titled *Provisions in the Policing and Crime Act 2009 that relate to prostitution (sections 14 to 21)* and published on March 29, 2010.[12] This Circular, which is referred to (under a slightly different title) in fn.68 of the main work, provides: **12.45**

"Current practice, as established by the 1959 Home Office Circular, is to use a non-statutory 'prostitutes' caution' to demonstrate that a person is involved in prostitution and offenders are not prosecuted until at least 2 cautions have been given. It is expected that prostitutes' cautions will continue to be used to demonstrate 'persistence' under the amended legislation [*sc.* s.1(1) of the Street Offences Act 1959].

Two officers would need to witness the activity and administer the caution. Details of these 'prostitutes' cautions' are recorded at the local police station. However there are two respects in which prostitutes' cautions differ from ordinary police cautions:

* The behaviour leading to a caution may not itself be evidence of a criminal offence for which the prostitute could be prosecuted.

---

[11] See   https://www.gov.uk/government/publications/provisions-in-the-policing-and-crime-act-2009-that-relate-to-prostitution-sections-14-to-21 [accessed December 20, 2013].

[12] Last note.

* There is no requirement for a woman to admit guilt before she may be given a 'prostitutes caution', unlike an ordinary police caution. The caution is not a formal pre-requisite of conviction but it has become the way in which evidence is adduced to prove that an individual charged for the first time is a 'common prostitute.' It is expected that 'prostitutes' cautions' will continue to be used to adduce evidence of persistence."

ADVERTISING BY OR ON BEHALF OF PROSTITUTES

12.47   In recent years there has been a significant decline in the placement of cards in phone boxes to advertise sexual services, as sex workers have increasingly favoured the use instead of the internet, including social media such as Facebook and Twitter. As a result, the offence in s.46 of the Criminal Justice and Police Act 2001 now has an increasingly archaic flavour. The statistics show a recent decline in the number of convictions for this offence[13]:

    2007–2008: 330
    2008–2009: 349
    2009–2010: 457
    2010–2011: 331
    2011–2012: 149

There is little or no policing interest in online advertising of sexual services, primarily since, unlike advertising in a public place which may offend passers-by, advertising through social media is perceived as essentially victimless and thus commands no law enforcement priority. However, some concern has been expressed about the phenomenon and in particular the risk that on-line advertising of sexual services may be too readily accessed by children.[14]

ANTI-SOCIAL BEHAVIOUR ORDERS

12.65   In May 2013, the Coalition Government introduced into Parliament the Anti-Social Behaviour, Crime and Policing Bill, which contains (in Pt 1) measures to reform the existing "toolkit" for dealing with anti-social behaviour. In particular, the Bill will abolish the anti-social behaviour order ("ASBO"), both on application and as an ancillary order to a criminal conviction (commonly referred to as a "CRASBO"). The Bill will replace the CRASBO with the Criminal Behaviour

---

[13] http://www.cps.gov.uk/data/violence_against_women/prostitution_key_findings_11_12/prostitution_table_4_advertising_prostitution_offences_0708_1112.csv [accessed December 20, 2013].

[14] See http://www.telegraph.co.uk/technology/facebook/9836358/Prostitutes-advertising-on-Facebook-and-Twitter.html [accessed December 20, 2013] and http://www.dailymail.co.uk/femail/article-2296576/How-Twitter-Facebook-expose-children-websites-prostitutes-Vice-girl-ads-illegal-phone-boxes-social-media.html [accessed December 20, 2013].

Order ("CBO"), whilst a new form of injunctive relief called the Injunction to Prevent Nuisance and Annoyance ("IPNA") will replace the ASBO on application. At the time of writing (December 18, 2013), the Bill is at Report stage in the House of Lords.

The Bill provides (cl.1) that a court may grant an IPNA against a person aged 10 or over ("the respondent") if it is satisfied, on the balance of probabilities, that the respondent has engaged or threatens to engage in conduct capable of causing nuisance or annoyance to any person ("anti-social behaviour"), and the court considers it just and convenient to grant the injunction for the purpose of preventing the respondent from engaging in such behaviour. An IPNA may prohibit the respondent from doing anything described in the injunction and/or require the respondent to do anything so described. Prohibitions and requirements in an injunction must, so far as practicable, avoid (a) any conflict with the respondent's religious beliefs; (b) any interference with the times, if any, at which the respondent normally works or attends school or any other educational establishment; and (c) any conflict with the requirements of any other court order or injunction to which the respondent may be subject. An injunction must specify the period for which it has effect or state that it has effect until further order. In the case of an injunction granted against a respondent under the age of 18, a period must be specified and it must be no more than 12 months. An injunction may be granted by a youth court, in the case of a respondent aged under 18, and by the High Court or the county court in any other case.

As for the CBO, the Bill provides (cl.21) that where a person is convicted of an offence the court may make such an order, on the application of the prosecution, if it is satisfied that the offender has engaged in behaviour that caused or was likely to cause harassment, alarm or distress to any person, and it considers that making the order will help in preventing the offender from engaging in such behaviour. A CBO may prohibit the offender from doing anything described in the order and/ or require the offender to do anything so described. A CBO may only be made in addition to a sentence imposed in respect of the offence or an order discharging the offender conditionally. The prosecution must find out the views of the local youth offending team before applying for a CBO to be made against an offender under the age of 18. Prohibitions and requirements in a CBO must, so far as practicable, avoid (a) any conflict with the offender's religious beliefs; (b) any interference with the times, if any, at which the offender normally works or attends school or any other educational establishment; and (c) any conflict with the requirements of any other court order or injunction to which the offender may be subject.

As a matter of law there is no reason why, should the Bill pass into law, the IPNA **12.65A** and CBO should be used any less than the ASBO and CRASBO are currently used to deal with anti-social behaviour on the part of prostitutes or their would-be clients. The proposed new orders have generated significant concern on the part of civil liberties organisations. Liberty has described the IPNA as:

"a super-punitive ASBO which will be easier to obtain for even more broadly defined behaviour. It is likely therefore that it will be used even more than the current ASBO and the damaging ramifications of this policy even more widely felt."[15]

The organisation JUSTICE has taken a leading role in urging changes to the Bill, arguing in particular for:

- a requirement that an application for an IPNA or CBO must meet the criminal standard of proof;
- the replacement of the "nuisance or annoyance" test for an IPNA with the current "harassment, alarm or distress" test applicable to ASBOs; and
- a requirement that the court must consider the imposition and terms of an IPNA or CBO to be necessary and proportionate.[16]

So far the Government has resisted all pressure and it seems unlikely to change tack at this late stage in the Parliamentary process.

12.66 For an example of an ASBO being made against a user of the services of prostitutes, see *http://swns.com/news/pensioner-69-asbo-caught-hookers-times-night-30924/* [accessed December 20, 2013].

---

[15] *Liberty's Response to the Home Office's Proposals on More Effective Responses to Anti-Social Behaviour* (London: Liberty, 2011), p.15.

[16] See *http://www.justice.org.uk/data/files/JUSTICE_briefing_ASB_Crime_and_Policing_Bill _to_the_JCHR_and_PBC.pdf* [accessed December 20, 2013].

CHAPTER 13

PREPARATORY OFFENCES

ADMINISTERING A SUBSTANCE WITH INTENT TO STUPEFY OR OVERPOWER

MODE OF TRIAL AND PUNISHMENT

For convictions on or after December 3, 2012,[1] the s.61 offence is a specified **13.09**
offence for the purposes of s.226A of the Criminal Justice Act 2003 ("CJA 2003")
(extended sentence for certain violent or sexual offences), irrespective of the date
of commission of the offence.

SENTENCING

The Sentencing Council has issued a new guideline applicable to sex offenders **13.11**
aged 18 or over who are sentenced on or after April 1, 2014: see para.1.20 et seq.,
above. The guideline for offences under s.61 of the 2003 Act adopts the same harm
and culpability factors as those for offences of exposure (s.66) and voyeurism
(s.67), which are discussed in Ch.14, below.

New sentencing guideline

Step One—Harm and culpability

Under the new guideline, the sentencing court is to go through a series of steps **13.11A**
in order to determine the appropriate sentence. Step one involves determining the

---

[1] When s.124 of the Legal Aid, Sentencing and Punishment of Offenders Act 2012 was brought into
force by the Legal Aid, Sentencing and Punishment of Offenders Act 2012 (Commencement No.4 and
Saving Provisions) Order 2012 (SI 2012/2906).

offence category. The categories are defined by reference to whether the harm to the victim and the culpability of the offender are raised. As this offence is a preparatory one, harm and culpability are unlikely to have been fully realised at the time of commission. Accordingly, the Sentencing Council found it difficult to articulate harm and culpability in the same way as for other sexual offences[2] and so specified the offence categories for offences under s.61 as follows:

Category 1	Raised harm **and** raised culpability
Category 2	Raised harm **or** raised culpability
Category 3	Administering a substance with intent **without** raised harm or culpability factors present

The previous guideline issued in 2007 by the Sentencing Guidelines Council distinguished between s.61 offences by reference to the nature of the offence that was to be committed; for example, an intention to carry out a rape or assault by penetration would result in the offender being placed in the highest category. The Sentencing Council considered that, whilst this is an important factor, there are others which should also be taken into consideration as indicating raised harm:

Factors indicating raised harm
• Severe psychological or physical harm
• Prolonged detention /sustained incident
• Additional degradation/humiliation

The Council specified the following factors as raising culpability under s.61:

Factors indicating raised culpability
• Significant degree of planning
• Specific targeting of a particularly vulnerable victim
• Intended sexual offence carries a statutory maximum of life
• Abuse of trust
• Recording of offence
• Offender acts together with others to commit the offence
• Commercial exploitation and/or motivation
• Offence racially or religiously aggravated

---

[2] See *Sexual Offences Guideline: Consultation* (December 6, 2012).

> - Offence motivated by, or demonstrating, hostility to the victim based on his or her sexual orientation (or presumed sexual orientation) or transgender identity (or presumed transgender identity)
>
> - Offence motivated by, or demonstrating, hostility to the victim based on his or her disability (or presumed disability)

The guideline provides that the sentencing court should determine culpability and harm caused or intended by reference *only* to these factors. Where an offence does not fall squarely into a category, individual factors may require a degree of weighting before making an overall assessment and determining the appropriate offence category. The guideline also states that where no substantive sexual offence has been committed, the main consideration for the court will be the offender's conduct as a whole including, but not exclusively, their intention. This statement was included in the published guideline on the request of the senior judges following the decision in *Watson*,[3] discussed in para.13.12A, below, in order to provide guidance to sentencers when dealing with offenders who, after committing the preparatory offence in s.61, have *not* then gone on to commit a sexual offence.

Step Two—Starting point and category range

Having determined the offence category by considering these harm and culpability factors, the court should then use the corresponding starting point specified in the guideline in order to reach a sentence within the category range. The starting point applies to all offenders irrespective of plea or previous convictions. Once the starting point has been determined, step two allows further adjustment for aggravating or mitigating features, set out below. A case of particular gravity, reflected by multiple features of culpability or harm, could merit upward adjustment from the starting point before further adjustment for aggravating or mitigating features. The starting points and category ranges for offences under s.61 are as follows:

13.11B

Category 1	**Starting point**
	6 years' custody
	Category range
	4–9 years' custody
Category 2	**Starting point**
	4 years' custody
	Category range
	3–7 years' custody

---

[3] Unreported, October 17, 2013, CA.

Category 3	Starting point
	2 years' custody
	Category range
	1–5 years' custody

Aggravating and mitigating factors

13.11C   After identifying the starting point and category range, the court should consider whether the presence of aggravating or mitigating factors should result in an upward or downward adjustment from the starting point or the imposition of a sentence outside the category range. In particular, relevant recent convictions are likely to result in an upward adjustment. The non-exhaustive list of aggravating and mitigating factors for offences under s.61 is:

Aggravating factors
Statutory aggravating factors
•   Previous convictions, having regard to a) the nature of the offence to which the conviction relates and its relevance to the current offence; and b) the time that has elapsed since the conviction •   Offence committed whilst on bail
Other aggravating factors
•   Location of offence •   Timing of offence •   Any steps taken to prevent reporting an incident, obtaining assistance and/or from assisting or supporting the prosecution •   Attempts to dispose of or conceal evidence •   Failure to comply with current court orders •   Offence committed whilst on licence

Mitigating factors
•   No previous convictions **or** no relevant/recent convictions •   Remorse •   Previous good character and/or exemplary conduct* •   Age and/or lack of maturity where it affects the responsibility of the offender

- Mental disorder or learning disability, particularly where linked to the commission of the offence
- Demonstration of steps taken to address offending behaviour

---

* Previous good character/exemplary conduct is different from having no previous convictions. The more serious the offence, the less the weight which should normally be attributed to this factor. Where previous good character/exemplary conduct has been used to facilitate the offence, this mitigation should not normally be allowed and such conduct may constitute an aggravating factor.

Steps Three to Nine

The remaining steps cover the following points. At step three the court should   13.11D
consider any factors which would indicate a reduction in sentence, e.g. assistance
to the prosecution. At step four it should consider any reduction for a guilty plea.
At step five the court should consider dangerousness, i.e. whether it would be
appropriate to award an extended sentence (s.226A of the CJA 2003). Step six
requires the court to consider whether the total sentence is just and proportionate
to the offending behaviour. At step seven it should consider whether to make an
ancillary order (e.g. a sexual offences prevention order ("SOPO") or a restraining
order). Step eight requires the court to fulfil its duty under s.174 of the CJA 2003
to give reasons for, and explain the effect of, the sentence. Finally, at step nine the
court should consider whether to give credit for time spent on bail in accordance
with s.240A of that Act.

Sentencing examples

The following decisions pre-date the new guideline but are useful illustrations of   13.12
the approach taken by the Court of Appeal to different factual scenarios.

In *Watson*[4] the appellant (38 and effectively of good character) was convicted of   13.12A
administering a substance with intent, contrary to s.61 of the 2003 Act, and
acquitted of rape. He was sentenced to 8 years' imprisonment. The appellant and
the complainant had been together for eight years and had had a child together,
but the complainant had ended the relationship. The appellant was desperate to
continue it. One day he persuaded the complainant to drink from an opened can
of Red Bull which he had laced with ecstasy. She became nauseous and he helped
put her on her bed. She lay there unable to move her limbs and struggling to
speak. He had sexual intercourse with her to ejaculation. She then became so ill
that she suffered a seizure and an ambulance was called. The appellant did not tell
the paramedics or hospital staff about the ecstasy he had administered, but this

---

[4] Unreported, October 17, 2013, CA.

was revealed by medical tests. In prepared statements the appellant claimed the intercourse was consensual and denied administering the drug. In sentencing, the judge observed that the appellant had turned to foul means to rekindle his relationship with the complainant, giving her ecstasy to enable him to have sexual intercourse with her without resistance. She observed that in convicting the appellant under s.61 the jury must have disbelieved his denial of having administered the ecstasy, but that in acquitting him of rape they must have concluded that he may have reasonably believed the complainant was consenting. However, on the evidence the judge was sure that the complainant had not consented but was unable to convey that or resist because of the effects of the drug. There were many aggravating features. The appellant had planned the offence, determined to achieve his aim of having intercourse with the complainant. This was a gross breach of trust, committed in her own home by the mother of his child. On appeal against sentence, the Court of Appeal agreed that there were serious aspects to the case and that the judge had been entitled to make the findings she did, including that the jury must have concluded that the appellant may reasonably have believed the complainant was consenting to sexual inter-course. The judge had faced a difficult sentencing exercise since the s.61 offence may be committed where the offender's intention is to engage in consensual sexual activity, but the guideline issued by the Sentencing Guidelines Council did not contemplate a case in which no sexual offence was intended. In such circum-stances, the Court considered the vital considerations to be the culpability involved in and the harm caused by the offender's overall conduct. In this case, the exceptional facts did not fit neatly into either category in the SGC guideline, both of which assumed that a sexual offence was intended. In the event, the judge took the view that the case fell within the higher category as the appellant's intention was to have sexual intercourse rather than some lesser sexual activity. In the Court's view, the guideline was of limited assistance in this case since its focus is upon a completed sexual offence. The judge had placed the case in the higher category on the basis that the category was reserved for penetrative sex, but a significant allowance should have been made for the fact that, on the basis of the jury verdicts, no non-consensual activity was intended and that it was not unreasonable for the appellant to have believed the complainant was consenting. In the circumstances, the Court considered that the sentence of 8 years was manifestly excessive and it substituted one of 4-and-a-half years.

13.12B   As noted above, as the result of a request made to the Sentencing Council by the senior judges following *Watson*, the new guideline for s.61 states that where no substantive sexual offence has been committed, the main consideration for the court will be the offender's conduct as a whole including, but not exclusively, their intention. This statement was included in order to provide guidance to sentencers when dealing with offenders such as the one in *Watson* who, after committing the preparatory offence in s.61, do *not* then go on to commit a sexual offence. A similar statement appears in the guideline for s.63.

In *Penfold*[5] the appellant was convicted of sexual assault and administering a **13.12C** substance with intent, contrary to s.3 and s.61 of the 2003 Act respectively. He met the victim, an elderly, disabled woman, while working as an aerial and satellite installer in her home. He visited her after completing the work and stayed for some time. After he had left, the complainant realised she had been drugged and, while unconscious, sexually interfered with. Although the appellant had no previous convictions for sexual offences, the judge concluded that he had met the dangerousness criteria and that it would be a long time before the public could be safe from his activities. She therefore imposed an indeterminate sentence of imprisonment for public protection. For the offence of administering a substance with intent, the judge concluded that there would have been a starting point of 4 years with a range of 3–7 years. Her sentence would have been 7 years to reflect the nature and gravity of the appellant's intentions. As for the sexual assault, the sentence would have been 5 years' imprisonment. The judge concluded that the determinate sentence would have been 12 years, and the minimum term to be specified was therefore 6 years. On appeal, the Court of Appeal held that the judge had been entitled to conclude as she did because of the appellant's extraordinary behaviour. The psychological harm suffered by the complainant was serious and it was reasonable to apprehend a significant risk that some other vulnerable person might similarly be targeted. The judge was entitled to conclude, on the evidence, that it would be a long time before the public would be safe from the appellant. In relation to the notional determinate term, the court had to bear in mind the statutory maximum sentences laid down by Parliament in respect of the offences committed by the appellant, and the fact that they formed a continuum of wrongdoing on the same occasion. Against that background, it would have been more appropriate to treat the determinate sentences as being concurrent with one another. Therefore, the minimum term specified was too long. For the sexual assault, the appropriate determinate sentence would have been 9 years. The notional term of 7 years selected by the judge in respect of administering the drugs could not be criticised. The resulting sentence should have been 54 months, representing a reduction of 18 months.

COMMITTING AN OFFENCE WITH INTENT TO COMMIT A SEXUAL OFFENCE

MODE OF TRIAL AND PUNISHMENT

From December 3, 2012, when ss.122–128 of the Legal Aid, Sentencing and **13.26** Punishment of Offenders Act 2012 were brought into force[6]:

---

[5] [2012] EWCA Crim 1222.
[6] By the Legal Aid, Sentencing and Punishment of Offenders Act 2012 (Commencement No.4 and Saving Provisions) Order 2012 (SI 2012/2906).

- For offences committed on or after that date, an offence under s.62 is listed in Pt 1 of Sch.15B to the CJA 2003 for the purposes of s.224A of that Act (life sentence for second listed offence).
- For convictions on or after that date (irrespective of the date of commission of the offence), an offence under s.62 is a specified offence for the purposes of s.226A of that Act (extended sentence for certain violent or sexual offences).

SENTENCING

13.29   The Sentencing Council has issued a new guideline applicable to sex offenders aged 18 or over who are sentenced on or after April 1, 2014: see para.1.20 et seq., above. The previous guideline, issued in 2007 by the Sentencing Guidelines Council, took the approach that the starting point and sentencing range for offences under s.62 should be commensurate with that for the preliminary offence actually committed, but with an enhancement to reflect the intention to commit a sexual offence, which should vary depending on the nature and the seriousness of the intended offence. It suggested 2 years as a suitable enhancement where the intent was to commit rape or an assault by penetration. The Council followed this approach in the new guideline, which provides:

> "The starting point and sentence range should be commensurate with that for the preliminary offence actually committed, but with an enhancement to reflect the intention to commit a sexual offence.
>
> The enhancement will need to be varied depending on the nature and seriousness of the intended sexual offence, but 2 years is suggested as a suitable enhancement where the intent was to commit rape or assault by penetration."

TRESPASS WITH INTENT TO COMMIT A SEXUAL OFFENCE

MODE OF TRIAL AND PUNISHMENT

13.38   For convictions on or after December 3, 2012,[7] the s.63 offence is a specified offence for the purposes of s.226A of the CJA 2003 (extended sentence for certain violent or sexual offences), irrespective of the date of commission of the offence.

SENTENCING

13.40   The Sentencing Council has issued a new guideline applicable to sex offenders aged 18 or over who are sentenced on or after April 1, 2014: see para.1.20 et seq.,

---

[7] When s.124 of the Legal Aid, Sentencing and Punishment of Offenders Act 2012 was brought into force by the Legal Aid, Sentencing and Punishment of Offenders Act 2012 (Commencement No.4 and Saving Provisions) Order 2012 (SI 2012/2906).

above. The guideline for offences under s.63 of the 2003 Act adopts a similar approach to the guideline for s.61, discussed in para.13.11 et seq., above.

New sentencing guideline

Step One – Harm and culpability

Under the new guideline, the sentencing court is to go through a series of steps **13.40A** in order to determine the appropriate sentence. Step one involves determining the offence category. The categories are defined by reference to whether the harm to the victim and the culpability of the offender are raised. As this offence is a preparatory one, harm and culpability are unlikely to have been fully realised at the time of commission. Accordingly, the Sentencing Council found it difficult to articulate harm and culpability in the same way as for other sexual offences[8] and so specified the offence categories for offences under s.63 as follows:

Category 1	Raised harm **and** raised culpability
Category 2	Raised harm **or** raised culpability
Category 3	Trespass with intent to commit a sexual offence **without** raised harm or culpability factors present

The previous guideline issued in 2007 by the Sentencing Guidelines Council distinguished between s.63 offences by reference to the nature of the offence that was to be committed; for example, an intention to carry out a rape or assault by penetration would result in the offender being placed in the highest category. In its consultation document, the Sentencing Council considered that, whilst this is an important factor, there are other factors which should also be taken into consideration as indicating greater harm, namely:

| Factors indicating raised harm |
| • Prolonged detention/sustained incident |
| • Additional degradation/humiliation |
| • Offence committed in victim's home |

As regards "offence committed in victim's home", the Sentencing Council noted that while the s.63 offence requires trespass, the trespass may be on any premises and does not require forced entry but rather entry without consent. But it thought that, where the trespass does involve forced entry into the victim's home, this may increase the psychological harm done to the victim and so should indicate raised harm. The harm factor "forced entry into victim's home" was therefore included in the consultation draft. However, in responding to the consultation, the Criminal

[8] See *Sexual Offences Guideline: Consultation* (December 6, 2012).

Bar Association pointed out that harm may equally be raised where the entry into the victim's home is *unforced*. In acknowledgment of this, the Council amended the factor in the published guideline to "offence committed in victim's home".

13.40B   As for culpability, the Council specified the following factors as increasing culpability under s.63:

Factors indicating raised culpability
• Significant degree of planning
• Specific targeting of a particularly vulnerable victim
• Intended sexual offence attracts a statutory maximum of life imprisonment
• Possession of weapon or other item to frighten or injure
• Abuse of trust
• Offender acts together with others to commit the offence
• Commercial exploitation and/or motivation
• Offence racially or religiously aggravated
• Offence motivated by, or demonstrating, hostility to the victim based on his or her sexual orientation (or presumed sexual orientation) or transgender identity (or presumed transgender identity)
• Offence motivated by, or demonstrating, hostility to the victim based on his or her disability (or presumed disability)

The guideline provides that the sentencing court should determine culpability and harm caused or intended by reference only to these factors. Where an offence does not fall squarely into a category, individual factors may require a degree of weighting before making an overall assessment and determining the appropriate offence category. The guideline also states that where no substantive sexual offence has been committed, the main consideration for the court will be the offender's conduct as a whole including, but not exclusively, their intention. This statement was included in the published guideline on the request of the senior judges following the decision in *Watson*,[9] discussed in para.13.12A, above, in order to provide guidance to sentencers when dealing with offenders who, after committing the preparatory offence in s.63, have not then gone on to commit a sexual offence.

Step Two—Starting point and category range

13.40C   Having determined the offence category by considering these harm and culpability factors, the court should then use the corresponding starting point specified in the guideline in order to reach a sentence within the category range. The starting

___

[9] Unreported, October 17, 2013, CA.

point applies to all offenders irrespective of plea or previous convictions. Once the starting point has been determined, step two allows further adjustment for aggravating or mitigating features, set out below. A case of particular gravity, reflected by multiple features of culpability or harm, could merit upward adjustment from the starting point before further adjustment for aggravating or mitigating features. The starting points and category ranges for offences under s.63 are as follows:

Category 1	**Starting point** 6 years' custody **Category range** 4–9 years' custody
Category 2	**Starting point** 4 years' custody **Category range** 3–7 years' custody
Category 3	**Starting point** 2 years' custody **Category range** 1–5 years' custody

Aggravating and mitigating factors

After identifying the starting point and category range, the court should consider **13.40D** whether the presence of aggravating or mitigating factors should result in an upward or downward adjustment from the starting point or the imposition of a sentence outside the category range. In particular, relevant recent convictions are likely to result in an upward adjustment. The non-exhaustive list of aggravating and mitigating factors for offences under s.63 is:

Aggravating factors
Statutory aggravating factors
• Previous convictions, having regard to a) the nature of the offence to which the conviction relates and its relevance to the current offence; and b) the time that has elapsed since the conviction
• Offence committed whilst on bail

Other aggravating factors
• Location of offence
• Timing of offence
• Any steps taken to prevent reporting an incident, obtaining assistance and/or from assisting or supporting the prosecution
• Attempts to dispose of or conceal evidence
• Failure to comply with current court orders
• Offence committed whilst on licence

Mitigating factors
• No previous convictions **or** no relevant/recent convictions
• Remorse
• Previous good character and/or exemplary conduct*
• Age and/or lack of maturity where it affects the responsibility of the offender
• Mental disorder or learning disability, particularly where linked to the commission of the offence
• Demonstration of steps taken to address offending behaviour

* Previous good character/exemplary conduct is different from having no previous convictions. The more serious the offence, the less the weight which should normally be attributed to this factor. Where previous good character/exemplary conduct has been used to facilitate the offence, this mitigation should not normally be allowed and such conduct may constitute an aggravating factor.

Steps Three to Nine

13.40E The remaining steps cover the following points. At step three the court should consider any factors which would indicate a reduction in sentence, e.g. assistance to the prosecution. At step four it should consider any reduction for a guilty plea. At step five the court should consider dangerousness, i.e. whether it would be appropriate to award an extended sentence (s.226A of the CJA 2003). Step six requires the court to consider whether the total sentence is just and proportionate to the offending behaviour. At step seven it should consider whether to make an ancillary order (e.g. a SOPO or a restraining order). Step eight requires the court to fulfil its duty under s.174 of the CJA 2003 to give reasons for, and explain the effect of, the sentence. Finally, at step nine the court should consider whether to give credit for time spent on bail in accordance with s.240A of that Act.

Sentencing where offender goes on to commit the intended offence

A person who commits a s.63 offence by trespassing in someone's home intending **13.40F** to commit a sexual offence, and who does commit a sexual offence there, may be charged both under s.63 and with the relevant sexual offence. In such cases, it will be important to avoid effectively penalising the offender twice for the same conduct. Accordingly, if the sentencer enhances the sentence for the sexual offence to reflect the element of trespass, by treating the trespass as an aggravating factor, the better course will be to impose no separate sentence for the s.63 offence[10] or a concurrent sentence which avoids double-counting and respects the totality principle.[11]

---

[10] cf. *Barclay* [2012] EWCA Crim 2375.
[11] cf. *Taylor* [2012] EWCA Crim 1326.

CHAPTER 14

OFFENCES AGAINST PUBLIC DECENCY

INTRODUCTION

See *Hardy*[1] for a recent case of exposure of the penis charged as outraging public **14.03** decency. It appears from the transcript that a charge of exposure contrary to s.66 of the 2003 Act would have been inappropriate, as there was no evidence that the defendant intended someone to see his penis and be caused alarm or distress. It is however noteworthy that the Court of Appeal disposed of the appeal against sentence in that case by reference to the sentencing guideline for the s.66 offence, which it said "mirrored" the criminality of the appellant's offence.

Outraging public decency

The Law Commission's consultation on proposed reforms to the common law **14.10** offences of public nuisance and outraging public decency, referred to in the main work, ran from March 31–June 21, 2010. No date has yet been set for the Commission's final report and recommendations.[2]

OUTRAGING PUBLIC DECENCY

MODE OF TRIAL AND PUNISHMENT

The Consolidated Criminal Practice Direction 2002,[3] section III.21, deals with the **14.26** classification of Crown Court business and allocation to Crown Court centres.

---

[1] [2013] EWCA Crim 2125.
[2] http://lawcommission.justice.gov.uk/areas/public-nuisance-and-outraging-public%20-decency.htm [accessed December 28, 2013].
[3] [2002] 1 W.L.R. 2870; (2002) 2 Cr. App. R. 35.

Offences of outraging public decency fall within Class 3 in that provision. Although the 2002 Direction has been replaced by the Criminal Practice Directions 2013,[4] the new Directions contain a saving for section III.21 which accordingly continues to apply.

Sentencing

14.29 In *Vaiculevicius*[5] the applicant (30) sought leave to appeal a sentence of 6 months' imprisonment imposed after he pleaded guilty to outraging public decency in relation to an incident when he and a woman, both heavily intoxicated, had consensual sexual intercourse in a public park on a Sunday afternoon. They made no attempt to conceal their activity and were visible to others in the park, including young children who were playing there. They had removed their lower clothing. They stopped only when spoken to by police officers. The applicant admitted the offence in interview and said that he was disgusted by his own behaviour. Before the Court of Appeal, the applicant argued that this sentence was wrong in principle or manifestly excessive given that the other persons were some distance away in the park, that his genitals and those of the woman were not deliberately exposed to view and that the offence did not involve any element of exhibitionism or even knowledge that others might see the sexual activity. The Court of Appeal noted that the applicant had previous convictions for a total of 30 offences, mainly involving dishonesty and none involving any form of sexual activity. A feature of his record was a repeated disregard for court orders. The Court also noted that the sentence for the offence of outraging public decency is at large and there is no sentencing guideline directly applicable to it, though it was relevant to consider the guidelines for the offences of exposure (s.66 of the 2003 Act) and sexual activity in a public lavatory (s.71). The s.66 offence involves the intentional exposure of the genitals with the intention that someone will see them and thereby be caused alarm or distress and is punishable on indictment with a maximum of 2 years' imprisonment. The sentencing guideline then current indicated that a first offence, without aggravating features, should result in an appropriate non-custodial sentence, whilst the repeat offender should receive a sentence in the range of 4–26 weeks' custody, with a starting point of 12 weeks. The s.71 offence is triable only summarily and carries a maximum sentence of 6 months' imprisonment. The sentencing guideline indicated a non-custodial sentence. The applicant placed particular reliance upon the guideline for the s.66 offence, though he acknowledged that it did not provide a perfect analogy to his case. The Court of Appeal accepted that there were no reported cases involving broadly similar facts, though, as the learned judge had said in the court below, such guidance as can be obtained confirms that "[t]he courts take this type of activity rather seriously". The Court said it could well understand why the judge came to that conclusion, and referred to the decision in *Cosco*,[6] but the reality was that

---

[4] [2013] EWCA Crim 1631.
[5] [2013] EWCA Crim 185.
[6] [2005] EWCA Crim 207, referred to in para.14.30 of the main work.

there was only very limited guidance to be obtained as to the appropriate sentence from either guidelines or reported decisions of the courts. It went on to identify the following aggravating features in this case: (i) the offence was committed in public, with a complete disregard for the shock or distress that it was likely to cause anyone who witnessed it; (ii) young children were present nearby, and whether or not the applicant realised this, it was readily foreseeable that such children would be playing in the park on a Sunday afternoon; (iii) the applicant's intoxication; and (iv) his previous convictions, albeit they were for different types of offence, and the fact that he had very recently been released from prison. For all these reasons, notwithstanding that this was the first offence of this sort that the applicant had committed, the learned judge had been entitled to view the case as serious. The Court rejected the submission that a sentence of immediate imprisonment was wrong in principle: the judge had been entitled to conclude that this offence passed the custody threshold and that only an immediate sentence of imprisonment would suffice. However, the judge had taken a starting point of nine months before giving full credit for the prompt guilty plea. The Court was persuaded that the resulting sentence of 6 months' imprisonment was manifestly excessive. Having regard to all relevant factors, including the guilty plea, the appropriate sentence here would have been 3 months' imprisonment, and accordingly the Court quashed the sentence imposed below and substituted a term of that length.

In *Carton*[7] the appellant (C) appealed against a sentence of 14 months' imprison-   **14.29A** ment imposed after he pleaded guilty to five offences of outraging public decency relating to incidents in which he had used his mobile phone to take photographs or videos up women's skirts. Upon his arrest his mobile phone was found to have 48 clips of various women on it. The women had been unaware of C's actions. He admitted the offences. A pre-sentence report considered that he posed a low risk of re-offending and a medium risk to women, and recommended a community order with a supervision requirement and attendance on a sex offender programme. The sentencing judge concluded that C should be sentenced upon the totality of his offending. He took a 20-month starting point and reduced it to 14 months to take account of C's early plea and mitigation. He also imposed an anti-social behaviour order prohibiting C from having in his possession in a public place a mobile phone with a video or photographic function. C submitted that the starting point was too high. The appeal was allowed. The Court of Appeal said that the judge had been required to sentence C for a very large number of offences of a kind that could not be regarded as commonplace. The sentencing guideline for voyeurism dealt with offences that were rather more serious than the instant offence, although the guideline for the basic offence of spying through a hole in a changing room wall was of some assistance. For a single offence of that kind, the guideline then in force suggested a community sentence. C's offending behaviour had persisted for some months but there was no evidence to suggest that he

---

[7] [2012] EWCA Crim 3199.

showed any of his films to anyone else. He had already taken steps to reduce his ability to re-offend by obtaining a mobile phone that did not have a camera and ceasing to be connected to the internet. However, it was also important not to minimise the effect of this type of offending. Those who became aware of what C had done were understandably shocked and distressed. But the interests of the public, and women in particular, would be best served by requiring C to undergo therapy to assist him in changing his attitude and urges. The recommendation in the pre-sentence report was realistic and was more likely to lead to C's rehabilitation than a custodial sentence. C had already spent 2-and-a-half months in custody, which would serve as both punishment and a reminder of what awaited him if he offended in that way again. The Court quashed C's sentence and replaced it with a community order for 3 years, comprising a supervision requirement and a requirement to attend a community sex offence group work programme. The ASBO was not altered.

"Outrage to Public Decency"

14.39   In November 2012, in a 6–5 vote, San Francisco's Board of Supervisors approved a proposal making it illegal to expose one's genitals in a public place.[8] Infractions attract a $100 fine on the first two occasions and $500 thereafter. Supervisor Scott Wiener, who introduced the proposal, said after the vote: "San Francisco . . . is a place of freedom, expression and acceptance. But freedom, expression and acceptance does not mean anything goes under any circumstances. Our public spaces are for everyone and as a result it's appropriate to have some minimal standards of behavior." However, the ban is not absolute: it includes an exception applicable during festivals and on certain beaches.

14.39A   In relation to fn.79 in the main work, see *Gough v DPP*,[9] discussed in para.14.134 et seq., below, in which the Administrative Court upheld the conviction of pro-nudity campaigner Stephen Gough of disorderly behaviour contrary to s.5 of the Public Order Act 1986 after he had walked naked through Halifax town centre.

14.40   In *Jacob*[10] the Ontario Court of Appeal quashed the conviction of engaging in an indecent act, contrary to s.173 of the Criminal Code, of a woman who had gone topless in public. On a very hot and humid day, the appellant had strolled along several urban streets and sat on the porch of a house with no top on. She was seen by a number of people and complaints were made to the police. When arrested, she said that men were permitted to appear in public with their chests uncovered and she had a constitutional right to do likewise. In quashing her conviction, Osborne J.A. said:

---

[8] *http://www.theatlanticwire.com/national/2012/11/san-franciscos-naked-days-are-over/59209/* [accessed December 28, 2103].
[9] [2013] EWHC 3267 Admin.
[10] 142 DLR (4th) 411; 112 CCC (3d) 1.

"There was nothing degrading or dehumanizing in what the appellant did. The scope of her activity was limited and was entirely non-commercial. No one who was offended was forced to continue looking at her. I cannot conclude that what the appellant did exceeded the community standard of tolerance when all of the relevant circumstances are taken into account. It follows that what the appellant did ... did not constitute an indecent act."

The fact that Jacob's acts had no commercial motivation was clearly integral to the decision. Thus in *Gowan*,[11] a known sex worker, under the impression that after *Jacob* it was lawful to expose her breasts, was convicted of engaging in an indecent act after she had solicited clients at an intersection, motioned to her breasts and called out "Do you want to fuck?".

With reference to the discussion in the main work of the decisions in *Balaszy* and **14.40A** *Hecker*, note the case of Liam Warriner, an anti-monarchist Sydney bartender who pleaded guilty to public nuisance and was fined $750 after "mooning" the Queen, with an Australian flag between his buttock cheeks, during her visit to Queensland in October 2011.[12] It was suggested in mitigation that if Warriner had carried out his actions in front of the New South Wales team bus prior to a State of Origin match (i.e. one of the annual best-of-three rugby league matches played between Queensland and New South Wales), it would not have raised an eyebrow.

In *R. (On the application of Green) v City of Westminster Magistrates' Court*[13] the **14.41** claimant, a member of the organisation Christian Voice, sought to bring a private prosecution for blasphemous libel in relation to the theatrical work *Jerry Springer: the Opera* which had been performed in various theatres and a recording of a live performance of which had been broadcast by the BBC. The claimant sought magistrates' court summonses against the producer of the stage play and the Director General of the BBC. The District Judge refused to issue the summonses, inter alia because the prosecution was prevented by s.2(4) of the Theatres Act 1968. The Administrative Court refused the claimant's application for judicial review of the District Judge's decision. In doing so, it held in relation to the Theatres Act 1968 that a "play" is defined by s.18 of that Act in terms which mean, in effect, a live performance and that the District Judge had been correct to hold that s.2(4) of the Act prevented the prosecution which the claimant sought to bring at least so far as the live performances were concerned. It went on to hold that the Theatres Act did not apply to the broadcast by the BBC because it was not within the definition of a "play", in that it was not a live performance given to the viewer by persons present and performing. However, the Broadcasting Act 1990, Sch.15 para.6, contains provisions applicable to broadcasts which are couched in terms identical to those of s.2(4) as it applies to plays. Although the

---

[11] March 3, 1998; Doc. Ottawa 97-20544 (Ontario Court of Justice, Provincial Division).
[12] *http://www.guardian.co.uk/world/2012/feb/14/man-who-mooned-queen-fined* [accessed December 28, 2013].
[13] [2007] EWHC 2785 (Admin).

District Judge had not been referred to that Act, her reasoning in relation to the Theatres Act applied equally to it, and accordingly she had been right to refuse to issue the summonses.

The "Two Person" Rule

14.43   In *R. v F*[14] the defendant faced trial on one count of outraging public decency. Before the trial commenced, the prosecution and the defence agreed to invite the judge to make a ruling in relation to the application to the case of the "two person" rule, i.e. the requirement that the defendant's act was capable of being seen by two or more persons who were actually present. As presented to the judge, the question was whether, on the assumption that the sole prosecution witness gave evidence in accordance with her witness statement, the case would get past a half-time submission. In other words, the contents of the witness statement were effectively treated as the agreed facts. The statement described an incident in which the defendant, over a period of about 10 minutes, masturbated in his car which was parked adjacent to local playing fields on which children were playing football, but that he covered himself up and ceased to masturbate whenever anybody came into view. The judge, applying the law as most recently expounded in *Hamilton*, ruled that on those facts the "two person" rule was not satisfied:

> " . . . it is perfectly plain from the evidence of [the witness], which is the only evidence which the Crown have, that when people other than herself were seen to be present by her, on each occasion that that occurred the defendant stopped indulging in the act and covered himself with a sheet of paper that was clearly placed on the seat next to him for that purpose. And it seems plain to me that although these people were present, they were not capable of seeing the act in which he was indulging because on each of the occasions that they were observed to be present by [the witness], he ceased the act in which he was engaged and covered himself up. So . . . the evidence available, therefore, does not in my view satisfy the requirement that at least two people are present and capable of seeing the nature of the act and being affected by it."

On an appeal against this ruling, the Court of Appeal held that the judge's conclusion was not one which no reasonable judge could have reached, albeit there was "an element of unreality to the suggestion that nobody else could have seen the defendant masturbating". For the Court to seek to go behind the agreed facts and to say that there must have been a possibility of other people seeing the defendant masturbating would be impermissible speculation. However, their Lordships also said that they themselves would not, in the particular circumstances of this case, have necessarily "gone down the route taken by the judge", given that the question of whether or not people passing by might have seen what the defendant was doing was quintessentially a question for the jury. This is a clear indication that the Court thought the matter should have gone to trial. We

---

[14] [2010] EWCA Crim 2243, applying *Hamilton* [2007] EWCA Crim 2062.

respectfully disagree. The evidence that the sole prosecution witness was expected to give was incapable of satisfying the "two person" rule and indeed was inconsistent with the requirements of that rule. Whilst it is conceivable that in the course of giving oral evidence she might have been less definitive as to the effectiveness of the defendant's actions in covering himself up when people passed by, that can only be a matter of speculation and as such, in our view, could not in itself justify allowing the case to proceed.

EXPOSURE

Mode of Trial and Punishment

For convictions on or after December 3, 2012,[15] an offence under s.66 is a specified **14.58** offence for the purposes of s.226A of the CJA 2003 (extended sentence for certain violent or sexual offences), irrespective of the date of commission of the offence.

Sentencing

The Sentencing Council has issued a new guideline applicable to sex offenders **14.58** aged 18 or over who are sentenced on or after April 1, 2014: see para.1.20 et seq., above. The guideline for exposure adopts the same approach as the guideline for voyeurism (s.67, discussed in para.14.71 et seq., below), i.e. the categorisation of the offence, and so the starting points and sentencing ranges, depend upon whether there are factors indicating raised harm and/or raised culpability.

New sentencing guideline

Step One—Harm and culpability

Under the new guideline, the sentencing court is to go through a series of steps **14.58A** in order to determine the appropriate sentence. Step one involves determining the offence category. The categories are defined by reference to whether the harm to the victim and the culpability of the offender are raised. The court should determine harm and culpability by reference only to the factors set out in the

---

[15] When s.124 of the Legal Aid, Sentencing and Punishment of Offenders Act 2012 was brought into force by the Legal Aid, Sentencing and Punishment of Offenders Act 2012 (Commencement No.4 and Saving Provisions) Order 2012 (SI 2012/2906).

guideline (below). Where an offence does not fall squarely into a category, individual factors may require a degree of weighting before making an overall assessment and determining the appropriate offence category. The offence categories for offences under s.66 are as follows:

Category 1	Raised harm **and** raised culpability
Category 2	Raised harm **or** raised culpability
Category 3	Exposure **without** raised harm or culpability factors present

The guideline identifies the following factors as raising the harm caused by the offence:

| **Factors indicating raised harm** |
| • Victim followed/pursued |
| • Offender masturbated |

In its consultation on the draft guideline,[16] the Sentencing Council said that following or pursuit increases the harm to the victim as it will increase the sense of fear and menace they experience. This is no doubt true, but there are other forms of offender behaviour which could also increase the victim's sense of fear or menace, e.g. where an offender moves towards or confronts the victim with their genitalia exposed,[17] or where they expose their genitalia in circumstances in which the victim has difficulty in escaping, e.g. by sitting in the aisle seat on a bus when the victim is in the window seat and so is effectively trapped in place.[18] The focus in the new guideline on following or pursuit seems to indicate that such scenarios do not indicate raised harm. We doubt, however, that the courts will regard themselves as disabled from enhancing a sentence in such cases by regarding such offender behaviour as aggravating the offence (aggravating factors are considered below). As for "offender masturbated", the Council said that where the offender masturbates in front of the victim in addition to exposing their genitalia, this is likely to increase the shock and disgust felt by the victim.

14.58B   As for culpability, the Sentencing Council identified the following factors as raising culpability for the offence:

---

[16] *Sexual Offences Guideline: Consultation* (December 6, 2012).

[17] See, e.g. *Jones* [2013] EWCA Crim 145, in which the offender walked towards complainant in an alleyway at night with his penis exposed, leaving her disgusted, angry and shaken; and *Ashford* [2013] EWCA Crim 720, in which the offender exposed his penis to a 17-year-old girl at a bus stop, manipulating it as he did so. She turned away in shock and the offender moved to stand directly in front of her, then sat next to her on the seat at the bus stop. She realised he was wearing a mask or stocking to conceal his mouth and nose. She was terrified.

[18] cf. *Mailer* [2006] EWCA Crim 665, cited in the main work.

Factors indicating raised harm
• Specific or previous targeting of a particularly vulnerable victim
• Abuse of trust
• Use of threats (including blackmail)
• Offence racially or religiously aggravated
• Offence motivated by, or demonstrating, hostility to the victim based on his or her sexual orientation (or presumed sexual orientation) or transgender identity (or presumed transgender identity)
• Offence motivated by, or demonstrating, hostility to the victim based on his or her disability (or presumed disability)

In the Council's consultation draft the first of these factors appeared as "vulnerable victim targeted". It was included on the basis that the offender's culpability will be increased where they have deliberately sought out someone who may be less able to deal with, or more affected by, their actions because of, for example, youth, old age or disability. Some respondents to the consultation suggested adding as a further factor "multiple offences against the same victim". However, the Council noted that the s.66 offence is normally committed against strangers and so, rather than adopting this suggestion, it decided to cover the point by amending the factor "vulnerable victim targeted" to "specific or previous targeting of a vulnerable victim". As for "abuse of trust", the Council thought that culpability is increased, as with other offences, where the offender has exploited a position of trust in order to commit an offence. "Use of threats (including blackmail)" is included because, whilst the offence of exposure is inherently upsetting, the Council thought that an offender increases his culpability if he uses deliberately or explicitly threatening language to further intimidate or frighten the victim.

Step Two—Starting point and category range

Having determined the offence category by considering these harm and culpability factors, the court should then use the corresponding starting point specified in the guideline in order to reach a sentence within the category range. The starting point applies to all offenders irrespective of plea or previous convictions. Once the starting point has been determined, step two allows further adjustment for aggravating or mitigating features, set out below. A case of particular gravity, reflected by multiple features of culpability or harm, could merit upward adjustment from the starting point before further adjustment for aggravating or mitigating features. Where there is a sufficient prospect of rehabilitation, a community order with a sex offender treatment programme requirement under s.202 of the CJA 2003 can be a proper alternative to a short or moderate length custodial sentence. The starting points and category ranges for offences under s.66 are as follows:

14.58C

Category 1	Starting point
	26 weeks' custody
	Category range
	12 weeks'–1 year's custody
Category 2	Starting point
	High level community order
	Category range
	Medium level community order– 26 weeks' custody
Category 3	Starting point
	Medium level community order
	Category range
	Band A fine– High level community order

The previous guideline, issued in 2007 by the Sentencing Guidelines Council, had two categories, "basic offence" and "repeat offender", with the latter carrying a 12-week custodial starting point and a 4–26 week range. In its consultation the Sentencing Council noted that in 2011, 6.8 per cent of offenders were sentenced above the ranges. The Council considered that there are some offences for which a sentence longer than 26 weeks may need to be available as an option, for example where there are vulnerable victims or there is targeting of children. It therefore increased the highest starting point (for category 1 offences) to a 26-week custodial starting point with a range of 12 weeks to 1 year.

Aggravating and mitigating factors

14.58D   After identifying the starting point and category range, the court should consider whether the presence of aggravating or mitigating factors should result in an upward or downward adjustment from the starting point or the imposition of a sentence outside the category range. In particular, relevant recent convictions are likely to result in an upward adjustment. When sentencing a category 2 offence, the court should also consider whether the custody threshold has been passed; if so, whether a custodial sentence is unavoidable; and if so, whether that sentence can be suspended. When sentencing a category 3 offence, the court should also consider whether the community order threshold has been passed. The non-exhaustive list of aggravating and mitigating factors for offences under s.66 is as follows:

Aggravating factors
Statutory aggravating factors
• Previous convictions, having regard to a) the nature of the offence to which the conviction relates and its relevance to the current offence; and b) the time that has elapsed since the conviction
• Offence committed whilst on bail
Other aggravating factors
• Location of the offence
• Timing of the offence
• Any steps taken to prevent the victim reporting an incident, obtaining assistance and/or from assisting or supporting the prosecution
• Failure to comply with current court orders
• Offence committed whilst on licence
• Commission of offence whilst under the influence of alcohol or drugs
• Presence of others, especially children

Mitigating factors
• No previous convictions **or** no relevant/recent convictions
• Remorse
• Previous good character and/or exemplary conduct*
• Age and/or lack of maturity where it affects the responsibility of the offender
• Mental disorder or learning disability, particularly where linked to the commission of the offence
• Demonstration of steps taken to address offending behaviour

* Previous good character/exemplary conduct is different from having no previous convictions. The more serious the offence, the less the weight which should normally be attributed to this factor. Where previous good character/exemplary conduct has been used to facilitate the offence, this mitigation should not normally be allowed and such conduct may constitute an aggravating factor.

Steps Three to Nine

The remaining steps cover the following points. At step three the court should **14.58E** consider any factors which would indicate a reduction in sentence, e.g. assistance to the prosecution. At step four it should consider any reduction for a guilty plea. At step five the court should consider dangerousness, i.e. whether it would be appropriate to award an extended sentence (s.226A of the CJA 2003). Step six requires the court to consider whether the total sentence is just and proportionate to the offending behaviour. At step seven it should consider whether to make an ancillary order (e.g. a SOPO or a restraining order). Step eight requires the court to fulfil its duty under s.174 of the CJA 2003 to give reasons for, and explain the effect of, the sentence. Finally, at step nine the court should consider whether to give credit for time spent on bail in accordance with s.240A of that Act.

Sentencing examples

14.59   *Mead*[19] was decided by reference to the SGC guideline but, we suggest, the analysis and outcome would be very similar under the new one. The appellant (29) was convicted of one offence of exposure contrary to s.66 and was sentenced to 9 months' imprisonment. The offence was committed in broad daylight one Saturday morning on a public path adjacent to a riding school. The complainant was a young woman who was having a riding lesson in a yard facing the path. As she rode round the yard she noticed the appellant on the path standing facing her. She could see that he had his penis out. At first she thought he was urinating and turned away. As she passed him on a later circuit of the yard she saw that he had his hand on his penis and was masturbating. She told her riding instructor, and as the instructor went over to the fence the appellant walked off. In a witness statement made on the day, the complainant said that she felt very frightened about what had happened not only because of what the appellant had done, but also because she feared he might follow her. The riding instructor said in her witness statement that there were children in the arena next to the yard and adjacent to the path. When arrested, the appellant insisted that all he had done was stop to relieve himself. That was his defence at trial. The appellant had a record of offences of violence, robbery and possession of a Class A drug with intent to supply. He had previously served substantial custodial sentences. He had no previous convictions for exposure but there were convictions for two previous sexual offences. In 1999, aged 14, he was made the subject of a supervision order for an offence of indecent assault on a female. In 2002, aged 18, he was sentenced to 4 months' detention for another offence of indecent assault on a female. The judge considered the SGC guideline, under which the starting point for a repeat offender was 12 weeks' custody with a range of 4–26 weeks. He took the view that, although the appellant was not a repeat offender as such, the previous convictions for indecent assault gave cause for concern and in effect put him into the same or an analogous category. The judge also noted that it was an aggravating factor under the SGC guideline if the victim was a child. He took the view that although the victim of this offence was an adult, there had been a considerable risk of children seeing what the appellant was doing, and that in itself amounted to an aggravating factor.

[19] [2013] EWCA Crim 1806.

On appeal against sentence, counsel for the appellant challenged the judge's finding that there was a risk of the offence being observed by children. He also submitted that the judge paid insufficient heed to the guideline, and that there was no justification for passing a sentence which was 50 per cent higher than the upper limit of the range. On the issue of risk to children, the Court of Appeal noted that the judge had the opportunity to make his own assessment having heard the evidence at trial. However, it appeared to be the case that, although there were children having a riding lesson in a nearby paddock, they were a considerable distance away, perhaps 100m or so. Moreover, it is only because the complainant was in an elevated position on horseback that she could see what the appellant was doing, as the lower part of the fence, behind which he was standing, was made of solid wood. In those circumstances, the judge may have been unduly concerned about the children being able to see what the appellant was doing. But the offence nonetheless took place on a public path on a Saturday morning, where there could very easily have been children or others passing by at the time. There was greater force in counsel's second submission. Unpleasant as the offence was, it did not have the features encountered in more serious offences of this kind. The appellant did not expose himself to a child, or at least not directly. The offence was a single episode, albeit prolonged. Even for a repeat offender, the top of the sentencing range suggested in the guideline was only 6 months. The Court concluded that a sentence above the range was not called for on the facts of this case and it therefore substituted a sentence of 4 months' imprisonment for the 9 months awarded by the judge.

"EXPOSES"

A case that contrasts neatly with *Hunt v DPP*, discussed in the main work, is **14.62** *Mohammed Rakib*.[20] The complainant (17) was walking along a footpath one morning when she heard music coming from an area of bushes nearby. She turned and saw a man standing in the bushes with his trousers and boxer shorts round his ankles, masturbating his naked erect penis with his left hand. She turned away and continued walking but did not report the incident to the police. Some weeks later, at about the same time of day, she was again walking along the footpath when she heard music and turned to see the same man, standing in the same location as before. She looked him in the face before walking off. On this occasion she did not look towards his genitals but, from the motion of his left arm, which she did see, she said he was "doing the same thing" and that his arm was making motions as if he were masturbating. On this occasion she complained to the police and the appellant was subsequently arrested and charged with two offences of exposure contrary to s.66 of the 2003 Act. He was convicted by a jury and appealed on two grounds which essentially turned on the same point. First, it was submitted on his

[20] [2011] EWCA Crim 870.

behalf that the judge had erred in rejecting the submission at the close of the prosecution case that the count relating to the second incident should be withdrawn from the jury because, as the complainant did not suggest that she actually saw the appellant's penis on that occasion, the jury could not safely conclude that it had been exposed merely because the complainant said that his left arm was moving in the same way as on the first occasion as if he was masturbating. The appellant could, it was submitted, have been masturbating under his clothing without exposing his private parts, or could simply have been engaged in some preparatory acts without any exposure having taken place. Secondly, the judge had been wrong to direct the jury that they were entitled to take into account that there had been exposure of the penis during the first incident when deciding whether they were sure that there had been exposure during the second. The Court of Appeal rejected both grounds. As to the first, it was clearly implicit in the jury's verdict in relation to the first incident that they were satisfied on the basis of the complainant's evidence that on that occasion the appellant was masturbating his exposed penis, with music playing, with the intent that someone should be attracted to see him and with the intent that alarm or distress should be caused thereby. This was patently relevant to whether he was exposing himself on the second occasion. Given the similarity of the arm movements that the complainant saw, and the similar circumstances in which she saw them, it was clearly open to the jury to be satisfied that, on the second occasion as on the first, the appellant was masturbating his naked penis. Simply because there might possibly have been another, innocent interpretation did not mean that the matter had to be withdrawn from the jury, and it would have been inappropriate for the judge to withdraw it, since whether the appellant was exposing himself was a matter for the jury to consider on all the evidence. As for the second ground, the judge had taken an unimpeachable approach in directing the jury to the effect that they could and should take into account any exposure they found to have taken place on the first occasion when considering whether exposure had also taken place on the second. He had directed them to the effect that the incidents were so similar that they were entitled to find that it would be beyond coincidence if the appellant was not doing on the second occasion what he was doing on the first, i.e. masturbating his naked penis. The direction, taken overall, was at the very least adequate, and no further or more complex direction was required.

14.62A   The decision is not vulnerable to the criticism made in the main work of *Hunt*, where no evidence was given that anyone had seen or could have seen the appellant's exposed penis, which makes it exceedingly difficult to see how his penis could be found to have been "exposed". In *Rakib*, by contrast, the complainant had seen the appellant's exposed penis on the first occasion and she would undoubtedly have been able to see it on the second, if it had then been exposed and if she had looked towards it. The question was rather whether, given the fact of exposure on the first occasion and the similarity of circumstances between the two incidents, the fact of exposure could also be inferred on the second. We suggest the Court of Appeal's decision on that point is impeccable.

VOYEURISM

MODE OF TRIAL AND PUNISHMENT

For convictions on or after December 3, 2012,[21] an offence under s.67 is a specified **14.69** offence for the purposes of s.226A of the CJA 2003 (extended sentence for certain violent or sexual offences), irrespective of the date of commission of the offence.

Fitness to plead

The issue of fitness to plead arose in *R. v B*,[22] where the appellant was charged **14.69A** with two counts of voyeurism contrary to s.67(1) after two incidents at a sports centre in which he was alleged to have looked under partitions into cubicles in which two young boys were changing. It became clear at an early stage that the appellant suffered from a learning disability and autistic spectrum disorder so that there would be an issue as to whether he was fit to be tried. Psychiatric reports were obtained, and when the matter came before the Crown Court, the judge considered the reports and ruled that the appellant was unfit to plead and stand trial by reason of disability, pursuant to s.4(5) and (6) of the Criminal Procedure (Insanity) Act 1964 ("1964 Act"). In the light of that ruling, s.4A(2) of the 1964 Act required the jury to decide whether they were satisfied that the appellant had committed "the act . . . charged against him as the offence". The judge invited submissions as to what matters the jury should consider in order to reach a decision on this point. The prosecution submitted that they had only to decide whether the appellant had observed each of the two boys doing a private act. The defence submission was that, given the serious consequences for the appellant, this was not sufficient and that the jury had also to decide whether he had observed the boys "for the purpose of sexual gratification". The judge ruled in favour of the prosecution, and the jury decided that the appellant had observed one the boys as alleged. On appeal, it was argued that the judge's ruling had been in error and that where the charge is voyeurism contrary to s.67(1) of the 2003 Act, the jury can be satisfied that the appellant did "the act . . . charged against him as the offence" for the purposes of s.4A(2) of the 1964 Act only if they are satisfied that he acted for the purpose of sexual gratification, since this purpose forms part of the "act"

---

[21] When s.124 of the Legal Aid, Sentencing and Punishment of Offenders Act 2012 was brought into force by the Legal Aid, Sentencing and Punishment of Offenders Act 2012 (Commencement No.4 and Saving Provisions) Order 2012 (SI 2012/2906).

[22] [2012] EWCA Crim 770.

charged and cannot be divorced from it as being an independent mental element. The Court of Appeal accepted this argument.

14.69B It began by considering *Antoine*,[23] in which the House of Lords considered *obiter* the question whether a jury that has to determine, pursuant to s.4A(2) of the 1964 Act, whether the accused did the act charged against him as the offence need only be satisfied as to the *actus reus* of the offence or whether it must also be satisfied as to *mens rea*. Lord Hutton, in the only reasoned speech with which the other members of the House agreed, said that the jury need only be satisfied as to the *actus reus*.[24] In doing so, he said that the purpose of s.4A(2) is[25]:

> " . . . to strike a fair balance between the need to protect a defendant who has, in fact, done nothing wrong and is unfit to plead at his trial and the need to protect the public from a defendant who has committed an injurious act which would constitute a crime if done with the requisite *mens rea* . . . "

Lord Hutton considered that the provision strikes this balance by distinguishing between "a person who has not carried out the *actus reus* of the crime charged against him and a person who has carried out an act (or made an omission) which would constitute a crime if done (or made) with the requisite *mens rea*". The Court in *R. v B* said that in the light of this analysis, the problem in any given case lies in discerning what elements of the offence with which the person is charged constitutes the "injurious act" (in the words of Lord Hutton) and what constitutes the mental element.

Turning to the case before it, the Court said that as a preliminary, despite the widespread use in other cases of the Latin tag "*actus reus*" in order to isolate and define what, for a particular offence, constitutes the "act" charged, for the purposes of s.4A(2) of the 1964 Act, it preferred not to do so. The statute uses ordinary English words and their meaning is a matter of interpretation; substituting imprecise terms in a foreign language did not facilitate the resolution of the problem. Secondly, it seemed to the Court that in s.67(1) of the 2003 Act the link between deliberate observation and the purpose of sexual gratification of the observer is central to the offence. It accepted that enquiring into someone's purpose for doing something is to enquire into their state of mind when they did it. However, a person's state of mind is just as much a fact as the "outward act" of deliberate observation and, in this case at least, the creation of the state of mind must be the result of a positive thought process by the observer. For the offence of voyeurism, these two actions, the one aimed at the outside world and the other going on in the consciousness of the observer, have to go together; the deliberate observation must be done simultaneously with the specific, albeit subjective, purpose of obtaining sexual gratification. That being so, then in the case of an offence of voyeurism under s.67(1) of the 2003 Act, the "act . . . charged as the

---

[23] [2001] 1 A.C. 340.
[24] Approving *Att Gen's Ref (No.3 of 1998)* [2000] Q.B. 401 (CA).
[25] Above, fn.23 at [376A].

offence" for the purposes of s.4A(2) is the act of deliberate observation of another doing a private act where the observer's specific purpose is the obtaining of sexual gratification. That omnibus activity is the "injurious act". Although the activity has two components, deliberate observation and the purpose of obtaining sexual gratification, they are indissoluble and together comprise the relevant "act". The other element in the offence, namely the observer's knowledge that the person observed does not consent to being observed for the purpose of the observer's sexual gratification, is not directly linked to the outward component of the "act". It refers to the state of mind that the observer must have, but it is not the reason for the observation, and so is not part of the "act . . . charged" for the purposes of s.4A(2).

The Court considered this conclusion to be consistent with the social purpose of s.4A of the 1964 Act, since if all that a jury had to determine was whether a person deliberately observed another doing a private act, then the consequence would be that the defendant would have to be dealt with in accordance with s.5 of the 1964 Act and so could be subject to a hospital order, with or without a restriction order; he would have to register as a sex offender (s.80(1)(c) of the 2003 Act); and he could be made the subject of a SOPO. In the Court's view, although a person observing another doing a private act can be regarded as an unpleasant nuisance, there is not the same pressing social need to protect the public from him as there would be if it were proved that the observation was done for the specific purpose of his sexual gratification. It followed that the judge's ruling that the jury need determine only whether the appellant deliberately observed each of the two boys doing a private act was wrong as a matter of law, as was his direction to the jury to the same effect. Accordingly, the determination of the jury on what had been count two was unsafe and the appeal had to be allowed.

This is an unsatisfactory decision. The essence of Lord Hutton's analysis in **14.69C** *Antoine* was that "the act" for the purposes of s.4A(2) of the 1964 Act means the *actus reus* of the offence charged and not the *mens rea*. It is true that towards the end of his speech Lord Hutton noted that a number of learned authors have commented that it is difficult in some cases to distinguish precisely between the *actus reus* and the *mens rea* and that the *actus reus* can include a mental element.[26] He concluded that nevertheless, *actus reus* and *mens rea* are useful terms. He also said that:

> "[W]here a person is unfit to be tried in the normal way because of his mental state, it would be unrealistic and contradictory that in carrying out the determination under s.4A(2) the jury should have to consider what intention that person had in his mind at the time of the alleged offence. I consider that . . . by using the word "act" and not the word "offence" in [s.4A(2)] Parliament made it clear that the jury was not to consider the mental ingredients of the offence."

[26] Above, fn.23 at [376C].

Accordingly, there is nothing in Lord Hutton's speech to suggest that an element which is part of the *mens rea* of the offence needs to be proved for the purposes of s.4A(2), indeed to the contrary. The element of the s.67(1) offence that requires the defendant's observation of the complainant to be for the purpose of his, i.e. the defendant's, sexual gratification must surely be a matter of *mens rea*, since it is part of the defendant's state of mind that must be proved for the offence to be established, and is separate from any element of deliberation that may be required as part of the act of observation itself. The purpose of sexual gratification cannot be said to be part of the *actus reus* merely because, as the Court said, its existence is an objective fact or because it is the result of "positive thought processes" by the observer. The Court sought to sidestep these difficulties by avoiding the terms "*actus reus*" and "*mens rea*" and by focussing rather on the question what was the "injurious act" that had to be proved, picking up a passing reference to that term in Lord Hutton's speech. This sleight of hand enabled it to reach the opposite conclusion to the one to which that speech ought to have driven it.

This might not matter if its conclusion was the right one, but we doubt that it was. First, it produced the "unrealistic and contradictory" situation which Lord Hutton sought to avoid through his comments in *Antoine*, whereby the jury were required to consider the appellant's state of mind at the time of the alleged offence despite the fact that his mental state made him unfit to be tried. It would surely also have been unfair to the appellant for the jury to be asked to determine his purpose in observing the boys, since this would put him at risk of an adverse finding when the jury's decision on the point would have to be reached without the evidence of the person best placed to enlighten them, i.e. the appellant. Secondly, the "injurious act" in s.67(1) is the act of observing another person doing a private act and, from the perspective of the person being observed, the injury is done by the observation itself, regardless of the purpose with which it is done. It is true, as the Court said, that a finding that the appellant did "the act" charged would have put him at risk of a hospital order and a SOPO and would have involved his registration as a sex offender. But it would also have enabled the court to make a supervision and treatment order. The result achieved by the court was that none of these options was available to it and the appellant was acquitted, so that he did not have the opportunity to benefit from any of the orders which might have been made. The Court, acknowledging the possibility of public concern about the outcome of the appeal, emphasised that, even on the limited directions of the judge, the jury were not satisfied that the appellant deliberately observed one of the two boys; that there was no finding that the appellant observed the other boy for the purpose of sexual gratification; that neither the authors of the psychiatric reports nor the judge considered the appellant to be in any way a sexual predator, indeed the judge went out of his way to say the opposite; and that the appellant had and continued to have a good character. But the fact remains that the appellant was found to have observed a young boy under the partition of a changing cubicle, and the Court's conclusion precluded the imposition of any treatment or restriction that might have prevented him doing the same again. For these reasons, the decision is to be regretted.

SENTENCING

The Sentencing Council has issued a new guideline applicable to sex offenders   **14.71**
aged 18 or over who are sentenced on or after April 1, 2014: see para.1.20 et seq.,
above. The guideline for offences of voyeurism adopts the same approach as the
guideline for exposure (s.66, discussed in para.14.58 et seq., above), i.e. the
categorisation of the offence, and so the starting points and sentencing ranges,
depend upon whether there are factors indicating raised harm and/or raised
culpability.

New sentencing guideline

Step One—Harm and culpability

Under the new guideline, the sentencing court is to go through a series of steps   **14.71A**
in order to determine the appropriate sentence. Step one involves determining the
offence category. The categories are defined by reference to whether the harm to
the victim and the culpability of the offender are raised. The court should
determine harm and culpability by reference only to the factors set out in the
guideline (below). Where an offence does not fall squarely into a category,
individual factors may require a degree of weighting before making an overall
assessment and determining the appropriate offence category. The offence
categories for offences under s.67 are as follows:

Category 1	Raised harm **and** raised culpability
Category 2	Raised harm **or** raised culpability
Category 3	Voyeurism **without** raised harm or culpability factors present

The guideline identifies the following factors as raising the harm caused by the
offence:

| **Factors indicating raised harm** |
| • Image(s) available to be viewed by others |
| • Victim observed or recorded in their own home or residence |

In its consultation on the draft guideline,[27] the Sentencing Council said that it
included "image(s) available to be viewed by others" because where a permanent
record of the image has been made, the victim will be subject to ongoing
humiliation and anxiety about others viewing and accessing the image, thereby
increasing the harm caused by the offence. As for "victim observed or recorded in
their own home or residence", this factor is designed to deal with the increased

---

[27] *Sexual Offences Guideline: Consultation* (December 6, 2012).

harm caused by the victim no longer feeling safe in their own home and having the knowledge of intrusion.

14.71B   As for culpability, the Sentencing Council identified the following factors as raising culpability for the offence:

Factors indicating raised culpability
• Significant degree of planning
• Image(s) recorded
• Abuse of trust
• Specific or previous targeting of a particularly vulnerable victim
• Commercial exploitation and/or motivation
• Offence racially or religiously aggravated
• Offence motivated by, or demonstrating, hostility to the victim based on his or her sexual orientation (or presumed sexual orientation) or transgender identity (or presumed transgender identity)
• Offence motivated by, or demonstrating, hostility to the victim based on his or her disability (or presumed disability)

In its consultation, the Sentencing Council said it included "image(s) recorded" to reflect the increased culpability of an offender who records (rather than simply views) images of the victim. "Abuse of trust" is included to reflect the increased culpability of an offender who has abused their position in order to observe or record people, e.g. a manager of a leisure centre who sets up recording equipment in the female changing rooms, or a stepfather who sets up recording equipment in the home to spy on a stepchild. As for "significant degree of planning", this reflects the increased culpability of the offender who has put forethought into how to observe their victim(s) and who may also have been involved in setting up recording equipment.

Step Two—Starting point and category range

14.71C   Having determined the offence category by considering these harm and culpability factors, the court should then use the corresponding starting point specified in the guideline in order to reach a sentence within the category range. The starting point applies to all offenders irrespective of plea or previous convictions. Once the starting point has been determined, step two allows further adjustment for aggravating or mitigating features, set out below. A case of particular gravity, reflected by multiple features of culpability or harm, could merit upward adjustment from the starting point before further adjustment for aggravating or mitigating features. Where there is a sufficient prospect of rehabilitation, a community order with a sex offender treatment programme requirement under s.202 of the CJA 2003 can be a proper alternative to a short or moderate length custodial sentence. The starting points and category ranges for offences under s.67 are as follows:

Category 1	**Starting point** 26 weeks' custody **Category range** 12 weeks'–18 months' custody
Category 2	**Starting point** High level community order **Category range** Medium level community order–26 weeks' custody
Category 3	**Starting point** Medium level community order **Category range** Band A fine– High level community order

The proposed sentence levels are very similar to those for offences of exposure under s.66 of the 2003 Act, for which see para.14.58 et seq., above. However, the top of the range for category 1 is higher than for that offence, as the Council said in its consultation that it felt a higher sanction should be available where an offence of voyeurism has involved the aggravating factors of recording and/or distribution of images.

Aggravating and mitigating factors

After identifying the starting point and category range, the court should consider   **14.71D** whether the presence of aggravating or mitigating factors should result in an upward or downward adjustment from the starting point or the imposition of a sentence outside the category range. In particular, relevant recent convictions are likely to result in an upward adjustment. When sentencing a category 2 offence, the court should also consider whether the custody threshold has been passed; if so, whether a custodial sentence is unavoidable; and if so, whether that sentence can be suspended. When sentencing a category 3 offence, the court should also consider whether the community order threshold has been passed. The non-exhaustive list of aggravating and mitigating factors for offences under s.67 is as follows:

Aggravating factors

Statutory aggravating factors

- Previous convictions, having regard to a) the nature of the offence to which the conviction relates and its relevance to the current offence; and b) the time that has elapsed since the conviction
- Offence committed whilst on bail

Other aggravating factors

- Location of offence
- Timing of offence
- Failure to comply with current court orders
- Offence committed whilst on licence
- Distribution of images, whether or not for gain
- Placing images where there is the potential for a high volume of viewers
- Period over which victim observed
- Period over which images were made or distributed
- Any steps taken to prevent victim reporting an incident, obtaining assistance and/or from assisting or supporting the prosecution
- Attempts to dispose of or conceal evidence

Mitigating factors

- No previous convictions **or** no relevant/recent convictions
- Remorse
- Previous good character and/or exemplary conduct*
- Age and/or lack of maturity where it affects the responsibility of the offender
- Mental disorder or learning disability, particularly where linked to the commission of the offence
- Demonstration of steps taken to address offending behaviour

---

* Previous good character/exemplary conduct is different from having no previous convictions. The more serious the offence, the less the weight which should normally be attributed to this factor. Where previous good character/exemplary conduct has been used to facilitate the offence, this mitigation should not normally be allowed and such conduct may constitute an aggravating factor.

In its consultation, the Sentencing Council said that "placing images where there is the potential for a high volume of viewers" does not rely on establishing how many people actually saw the images but is based on the potential for them to be viewed, e.g. where the offender places them on a website or a social networking site which has a high volume of access. Although the guideline refers here to "images" rather than "image(s)", we suggest that placing even one image where there is potential for a high volume of viewers should trigger this aggravating factor. "Period over which images were made or distributed" covers the case where there is a pattern of offending on the part of the offender. Some respondents to the consultation submitted that the factor "observed in own home" in the consultation draft was too narrowly drawn and should be expanded to cover other private settings similar to a home. In light of these representations, the Council amended this factor to "victim observed or recorded in their home or residence" in order to cover situations where, for example, the victim resides at a care home or other institution.

Steps Three to Nine

The remaining steps cover the following points. At step three the court should   **14.71E**
consider any factors which would indicate a reduction in sentence, e.g. assistance to the prosecution. At step four it should consider any reduction for a guilty plea. At step five the court should consider dangerousness, i.e. whether it would be appropriate to award an extended sentence (s.226A of the CJA 2003). Step six requires the court to consider whether the total sentence is just and proportionate to the offending behaviour. At step seven it should consider whether to make an ancillary order (e.g. a SOPO or a restraining order). Step eight requires the court to fulfil its duty under s.174 of the CJA 2003 to give reasons for, and explain the effect of, the sentence. Finally, at step nine the court should consider whether to give credit for time spent on bail in accordance with s.240A of that Act.

Sentencing examples

The case of *Sturgess*[28] pre-dates the new guideline but remains useful as an   **14.72**
illustration of the approach taken by the Court of Appeal to a particularly offensive case of voyeurism. The applicant (S) sought leave to appeal against a total sentence of 2-and-half years' imprisonment imposed after his conviction for voyeurism, taking indecent photographs of a child and abstracting electricity. He had installed hidden cameras in the living room, bathroom and bedrooms of holiday accommodation owned by him. Police found a CCTV monitor in his bedroom showing a live feed from the holiday accommodation, and a video tape containing images of holidaymakers undressing, showering and having sexual intercourse. The images included footage of two girls aged 17 and one aged 14. The holidaymakers had been unaware that they were being filmed. S was sentenced to 6 months' imprisonment for voyeurism and 2 years for taking indecent photographs of a child, to run consecutively. The judge accepted that S had not specifically targeted underage girls. S submitted that the sentence imposed in relation to photographing the children was manifestly excessive. The Court of Appeal refused the

---

[28] [2010] EWCA Crim 2550.

application. S had installed covert CCTV cameras in most, if not all, of the rooms of his holiday let. He had done so in order to spy on the families who were his paying guests, videotaping women getting undressed, bathing and showering and undertaking sexual activity with their partners. The offences took place over an extensive period of about 12 months and clearly constituted one of the more serious cases of voyeurism. The offences were a gross intrusion into the privacy of the victims. They rightly felt devastated about S spying on them. Looking at the totality of the sentence, and taking into account the extreme gravity of the voyeurism and the additional aggravating offence of photographing young girls, a total sentence of 2-and-a-half years was not manifestly excessive.

"Observes"

14.77   In *R. v B*,[29] when considering the elements of the s.67(1) offence, the Court of Appeal said:

> "The verb 'observes' is not further defined in the SOA but we think it must connote a deliberate decision on the part of the defendant to look at someone doing a 'private act', as opposed to an accidental perception of someone doing a 'private act'. 'Observes' must also exclude a careless and, we think, reckless perception."

This is surely correct and chimes with the approach taken in *Heard*,[30] discussed in para.2.75 of the main work, where the Court of Appeal held that for the purposes of the offence of sexual assault (s.3 of the 2003 Act), the required touching must be deliberate and that a reckless, careless or accidental touching will not suffice. Strictly speaking this is, of course, an aspect of *mens rea* rather than *actus reus*, though as noted above,[31] the Court in *R. v B* may have been led to blur the distinction by the context in which it was analysing the matter.

"Doing a Private Act"

14.78   In *R. v B*,[32] when considering the requirement in s.68(1) of the 2003 Act that, for the purposes of s.67, a person is doing a private act if they are in a place which, in the circumstances, would reasonably be expected to provide privacy, the Court of Appeal said: "Whether a particular place is such would appear to be an objective test". With respect, this must be so, given that the expectation of privacy must be a reasonable one, i.e. an expectation which a reasonable person could hold, as opposed to one which was in fact held by the person concerned, which would constitute a subjective test. As the Court said in *Bassett*,[33] the question whether the complainant had a reasonable expectation of privacy is one for the jury (or magistrates) in each case.

---

[29] [2012] EWCA Crim 770, at [59]; the case is discussed in para.14.69 et seq., above.
[30] [2007] EWCA Crim 125.
[31] para.14.69E.
[32] Above, fn.29 at [59].
[33] [2008] EWCA Crim 1174 discussed in the main work, para.14.81.

MENTAL ELEMENT

In *R. v B*[34] the Court of Appeal said that it is clear from the use of the words "he" and "his" in s.67(1)(b) that the s.67(1) offence requires the defendant's purpose in observing the complainant's private act to be his own sexual gratification, and not that of someone else. This is surely correct, though it is Parliament's use of the words "obtaining" in s.67(1)(a) and "his" in s.67(1)(b), both preceding the words "sexual gratification", that most clearly indicate this interpretation. By way of contrast, the offence in s.67(2) requires the defendant to have acted for the purpose of enabling another person to obtain sexual gratification, and the offence in s.67(3) requires him to have acted for the purpose of either obtaining or enabling another person to obtain such gratification. **14.86**

The Court of Appeal in *R. v B* went on to say[35] that the word "purpose" in s.67(1)(a) must refer to the defendant's subjective thought process and that it is irrelevant whether he actually obtained any sexual gratification, although proof that he did would be evidence of his purpose. **14.86A**

Lastly, the Court said[36] that the requirement in s.67(1)(b) that the defendant "knows that the other person does not consent to being observed for his sexual gratification" involves proof of a specific state of mind on the part of the defendant, i.e. actual knowledge that the other person does not consent to being observed by the defendant for the purpose of the defendant obtaining sexual gratification from that observation. As noted in para.11.45 of the main work, there is some authority that "knowledge" in a criminal statute includes deliberately shutting one's eyes to the truth, but the better view appears to be that this is a matter of evidence and that, as indicated by the Court of Appeal in *R. v B*, nothing short of actual knowledge will suffice. **14.86B**

INTERCOURSE WITH AN ANIMAL

DEFINITION

For a consideration of the conceptual basis of the s.69 offence, see Imogen Jones, *A beastly provision: why the offence of "intercourse with an animal" must be butchered*, 75 J. Crim. L. 528. The author asks whether the way in which the offence is constructed is defensible given that arguments based on the concepts of autonomy, consent and rights are irrelevant in the context of the use of animals by humans. She also argues that limiting the offence to penile penetration draws an illogical line that excludes other harmful and sexually deviant behaviour from the ambit of **14.87**

[34] Above, fn.29 at [60].
[35] Above, fn.29 at [60].
[36] Above, fn.29 at [61].

the offence. The author concludes that Parliament should reconsider the offence in order to achieve a more consistent, principled and rationally defensible approach to the criminalisation of sexual acts involving animals.

14.88   For a critical discussion of the s.63 offence, see Erika Rackley and Clare McGlynn, *Prosecuting the Possession of Extreme Pornography: a Misunderstood and Misused Law* [2013] Crim. L.R. 400. The authors note[37] that the vast majority of cases prosecuted under s.63 of the Criminal Justice and Immigration Act 2008 relate to images of bestiality (89 per cent in 2011), though the conviction rate under s.63 appears to be very low (in the order of 5.7 per cent).[38]

Sentencing

14.91   The Sentencing Council has issued a new guideline applicable to sex offenders aged 18 or over who are sentenced on or after April 1, 2014: see para.1.20 et seq., above. The guideline does not, however, cover the offences in ss.69–71 of the 2003 Act. In its consultation on the draft guideline,[39] the Sentencing Council explained:

> "Given that these are very low volume offences with low maximum sentences available, the Council has taken the view that sentencing guidance is not needed for these offences."

Clearly, in the absence of any guidance as to the sentencing of these offences, there is a risk that sentencing courts will adopt inconsistent approaches. To mitigate this risk we suggest that, although the new guideline has formally replaced the one issued by the Sentencing Guidelines Council in 2007, it will nonetheless be appropriate for a court to consult that guideline when sentencing an offence under s.69 and to take into account the earlier cases discussed in the main work, i.e. *Higson*[40] and *Tierney*.[41]

SEXUAL PENETRATION OF A CORPSE

Sentencing

14.108   The Sentencing Council has issued a new guideline applicable to sex offenders aged 18 or over who are sentenced on or after April 1, 2014: see para.1.20 et seq., above. The guideline does not, however, cover the offences in ss.69–71 of the 2003

---

[37] At 405.
[38] For CPS legal guidance in relation to s.63, see *http://www.cps.gov.uk/legal/d_to_g/extreme_pornography/* [accessed December 28, 2013].
[39] *Sexual Offences Guideline: Consultation* (December 6, 2012).
[40] *The Times*, January 21, 1984. See also *R. v P (Pamela Jean)* (1992) 13 Cr. App. R.(S.) 369; *Williams* [1974] Crim. L.R. 558.
[41] (1990) 12 Cr. App. R.(S.) 216.

Act. In its consultation on the draft guideline,[42] the Sentencing Council explained:

"Given that these are very low volume offences with low maximum sentences available, the Council has taken the view that sentencing guidance is not needed for these offences."

Clearly, in the absence of any guidance as to the sentencing of these offences, there is a risk that sentencing courts will adopt inconsistent approaches. To mitigate this risk we suggest that, although the new guideline has formally replaced the one issued by the Sentencing Guidelines Council in 2007, it will nonetheless be appropriate for a court to consult that guideline when sentencing an offence under s.70.

SEXUAL ACTIVITY IN A PUBLIC LAVATORY

SENTENCING

The Sentencing Council has issued a new guideline applicable to sex offenders   14.116
aged 18 or over who are sentenced on or after April 1, 2014: see para.1.20 et seq., above. The guideline does not, however, cover the offences in ss.69–71 of the 2003 Act. In its consultation on the draft guideline,[43] the Sentencing Council explained:

"Given that these are very low volume offences with low maximum sentences available, the Council has taken the view that sentencing guidance is not needed for these offences."

This is not, however, the whole story, as sentencing guidance for the s.71 offence remains in effect in the Magistrates' Court Sentencing Guidelines.[44] That guidance is taken from the previous sexual offences guideline, issued by the Sentencing Guidelines Council in 2007. Whilst the Magistrates' Court Sentencing Guidelines have been updated to reflect the replacement of the SGC guideline by the new one,[45] the update leaves in place the guidance relating to the offence under s.71. Accordingly, in a magistrates' court, the sentencing starting point and range for a first time offender pleading not guilty, where there are no aggravating or mitigating factors, is a Band C fine. Where there are aggravating factors, the starting point is a low level community order and the range a Band C fine to a medium level community order. For a repeat offender, the starting point is a low level community order and the range a Band C fine to a medium level community order. Two factors are identified as indicating higher culpability: intimidating

[42] *Sexual Offences Guideline: Consultation* (December 6, 2012).
[43] *Sexual Offences Guideline: Consultation* (December 6, 2012).
[44] p.92. The Guidelines are available at *http://sentencingcouncil.judiciary.gov.uk/docs/MCSG_Update9_October_2012.pdf* [accessed January 4, 2014].
[45] See   *http://sentencingcouncil.judiciary.gov.uk/docs/Final_MCSG_Update_10_-_December_2013_(web).pdf* [accessed January 4, 2014].

behaviour/threats of violence to member(s) of the public and blatant behaviour. The presence of aggravating factors may suggest that a sentence above the range is appropriate.

As for the Crown Court, in the absence of any sentencing guidance there is a risk that courts will adopt inconsistent approaches when sentencing an offence under s.71. To mitigate this risk we suggest that, although the new guideline has formally replaced the one issued by the Sentencing Guidelines Council in 2007, it will nonetheless be appropriate for a court to consult that guideline, and also the Magistrates' Courts Sentencing Guidelines, when sentencing such an offence.

INSULTING OR DISORDERLY BEHAVIOUR UNDER SECTION 5 OF THE PUBLIC ORDER ACT 1986

Definition

14.129   Section 5 of the 1986 Act is amended by s.57 of the Crime and Courts Act 2013 so that it is no longer a criminal offence to use "insulting" words or behaviour within the sight of a person likely to be caused harassment, alarm or distress thereby. This amendment comes into force on a day to be appointed, and at that point the potential for the s.5 offence to be used to penalise indecent acts in public will effectively cease.

"Insulting or Disorderly Behaviour"

14.132   *Gough v DPP*[46] concerned the well-known pro-nudity campaigner Stephen Gough, who for some 10 years[47]:

> " ... has walked naked through the highways and byways of the United Kingdom, from John o' Groats to Land's End. He has made it clear that arrests, prosecutions and convictions will not deter him from nude walking in the future."

In March 2013, Mr Gough was convicted at the Calderdale Magistrates' Court in Halifax of contravening s.5(1) of the 1986 Act by walking naked through Halifax town centre. He appealed unsuccessfully against the conviction by way of case stated. Although the facts of the case are some way from the central subject matter of this book, the decision of the Administrative Court throws an interesting light on the scope for prosecuting authorities to use s.5 of the 1986 Act to penalise public displays of nudity, whatever their motivation.

The facts found by the judge (which were not in dispute) were that the appellant was released from Halifax Police Station at approximately 11.30am on October 25, 2012, through the main public entrance. He was wearing only walking boots, socks, a hat, a rucksack and a compass on a lanyard around his neck. He was

---

[46] [2013] EWHC 3267 Admin.
[47] At [1] per Sir Brian Leveson P.

otherwise naked and his genitalia were on plain view. He then walked through Halifax town centre for approximately 15 minutes. He received a mixed reaction. Two women gave evidence to the effect that they were "alarmed and distressed" and "disgusted" at seeing him naked. One of the women was with a number of children at least one of whom, 12 years old, she reported as "shocked and disgusted". The district judge found, based on the evidence, that the appellant's conduct had caused alarm or distress.

The appellant said in interview that he did not think that what he was doing was indecent, the human body was not indecent, and he did not know what the problem was. He had heard some of the comments directed to him; those who made such comments were entitled to their opinion. He said "It's their belief that the human body is dirty". The judge found that the appellant foresaw that his actions would cause alarm or distress and was at least aware that his behaviour may have been threatening, abusive, insulting or disorderly. The appellant said that he would continue to walk naked and that his aim was to be accepted as are others who campaign for human rights. Being nude allowed him to express what he fundamentally was: this was not indecent.

The judge decided, based upon authority[48] that the words "insulting" and, by extrapolation, "threatening", "abusive" and "disorderly" in the 1986 Act are not to be narrowly construed. He concluded that "insulting" meant disrespectful or scornfully abusive and "threatening" behaviour was behaviour that was hostile, had a deliberately frightening quality or manner or which caused someone to feel vulnerable or at risk. "Abusive" meant extremely offensive and insulting and "disorderly" behaviour was behaviour that involved or contributed to a breakdown of peaceful and law abiding behaviour. A degree of passivity could amount to insulting behaviour and the judge was satisfied that: 14.132A

"Mr Gough's behaviour in walking naked was insulting and was also threatening in that it caused [one of the witnesses] to feel at risk. This behaviour could also be described as abusive and disorderly as it contributed to a breakdown of peaceful and law-abiding behaviour as evidenced by the reactions of the public to Mr Gough's public display of nudity."

The judge went on to conclude that the appellant foresaw this consequence of his voluntary decision to walk naked through Halifax town centre and was at least aware that his behaviour may have been threatening, abusive, insulting or disorderly. Thus the mental element required for the s.5 offence was proved.

In his defence, the appellant argued that his conduct had been reasonable, within the meaning of s.5(3)(c) of the 1986 Act, given that his right to express himself was guaranteed by art.10 of the ECHR. The judge accepted that art.10 was engaged here on the basis that being naked in public was a form of expression. However, he held that there was a pressing social need for the restriction of the appellant's right to be naked in the context of this case and that the restriction imposed as a consequence of s.5 corresponded to that social need; as a summary

[48] *Vigon v DPP* [1998] Crim. L.R. 289 and *Hammond v DPP* [2004] EWHC 69 Admin.

harassment, alarm or distress as a result and no basis for inferring that anyone within earshot had been likely to experience such a reaction.

OTHER RELEVANT OFFENCES

14.139   Section 231(1)(d) of the Public Health Act 1936 was repealed on January 27, 2010, by the Local Government and Public Involvement in Health Act 2007.[52]

---

[52] s.135 and Sch.6 para.2(c): for commencement, see SI 2010/112.

CHAPTER 15

EVIDENCE: GENERAL

INTRODUCTION

This chapter does not attempt a comprehensive analysis of the developments in **15.01** the law governing the admissibility of hearsay evidence since the publication of our fourth edition. We have instead selected the cases that we consider most likely to be of assistance to those involved in trials of sexual offences. There have been significant developments in the law governing the admissibility of hearsay evidence during the last three years that will be of relevance to such trials, particularly where the prosecution seeks to rely upon the untested statement of an absent complainant or previous consistent or inconsistent statements made by a complainant who is available to give evidence. We commend the case of *Riat and others*[1] beyond all others as providing not only a clear exposition of the statutory framework governing hearsay evidence, with a step-by-step approach to its application, but also three instructive examples illustrating the application of the law.

JOINDER AND SEVERANCE

SEVERANCE

Cross-admissibility is not an essential pre-condition for court to refuse severance

For developments in cross-admissibility, see paras 16.63–16.75, below. **15.10**

[1] [2012] EWCA 1509.

HEARSAY EVIDENCE

INCONSISTENT STATEMENTS: SECTION 119 OF THE CRIMINAL JUSTICE ACT 2003

Inconsistent statements become evidence of the truth

15.23   By virtue of s.119 of the Criminal Justice Act 2003 ("CJA 2003"), a previous inconsistent statement is capable of being evidence of the truth of any matter stated if the witness admits making the statement or the witness is proved to have made a previous statement related to the subject matter of the indictment. Thus:

(i) If the witness is silent, s.119 does not apply.

(ii) If the witness adopts his earlier statement or could reasonably be understood to be endorsing it, then s.119 does not apply.[2]

(iii) If the witness admits making the previous statement but does not repeat it at trial, or denies its contents, and the statement is proved to be "inconsistent" with his present testimony,[3] then the statement is potentially admissible under s.119.[4] It may also be admissible in the interest of justice under s.114(1)(d) of the Act, for which see para.15.33, below. See, however, *Coates*,[5] discussed in para.15.26 of the main work.

(iv) If the witness is hostile and the statement is proved to be inconsistent, then s.119 applies: see para.15.24 of the main work. There is no bar to calling a witness, expecting them to resile from what they said before, and then applying to make them hostile.[6]

ADMISSIBILTY OF A COMPLAINANT'S STATEMENT WHEN COMPLAINANT ABSENT

No rule that there cannot be a conviction for rape without oral evidence from the complainant

15.28   There is no over-arching rule, either in domestic law or under the ECHR, that hearsay evidence which is "sole or decisive" is automatically inadmissible. The Supreme Court held in *Horncastle*[7] that there is nothing in English law to prevent a conviction being based solely or decisively on hearsay, provided appropriate safeguards are in place and due caution is adopted. The CJA 2003 provides a code

---

[2] *R. v M* [2011] EWCA Crim 1458.

[3] *Chinn* [2012] EWCA Crim 50, where s.119 was held not to apply where there was no suggestion that the witness was making an inconsistent statement. However, a claim to have no recollection may lead to a clear inference of inconsistency: see *Bennett* [2008] EWCA Crim 248.

[4] *R. v B* [2008] EWCA Crim 365.

[5] [2007] EWCA Crim 1471.

[6] *Osborne* [2010] EWCA Crim 1981.

[7] [2010] UKSC 14.

for admissibility which, approached properly, secures a fair trial. In *Al Khawaja and Tahery v UK*[8] the European Court of Human Rights, in a Grand Chamber decision, had held that a conviction based solely or decisively on untested hearsay evidence can be compatible with art.6(3)(d) where the accused has not caused the witness's absence, the absence is for a good reason and there are sufficient safeguards in place. In so far as the decision of the Grand Chamber may be inconsistent with the approach of the Supreme Court, courts must, absent wholly exceptional circumstances, follow faithfully the decision of the latter.[9]

Correct approach where hearsay evidence is the sole or decisive evidence against the defendant

The importance of the evidence to the case against the defendant is central to the   15.28A
various decisions that have to be considered. A number of cases have stressed that, notwithstanding the decision of the Grand Chamber in *Al Khawaja*, the admissibility of evidence which is the sole or decisive evidence against the accused must be approached with great care. Notably, the Court of Appeal took the opportunity in *Riat and others*[10] to consider the correct approach in English law to cases involving the admission of hearsay evidence after the Supreme Court decision in *Horncastle*, read, as Lord Phillips explained that it must be, together with the judgment of the Court of Appeal[11] in the same case. We commend *Riat* as the clearest resumé of the law as it now stands. It is of particular importance to sex cases, as three of the conjoined appeals (*Riat, Clare* and *Bennett)* involved sexual allegations based upon hearsay evidence. We consider these appeals below. In *Riat* the Court of Appeal cited *Ibrahim*,[12] another case involving allegations of sexual offences, as a good illustration of the working of the statutory framework governing the admission of hearsay. For this reason we also set out the facts of *Ibrahim* below.

The Supreme Court in *Horncastle* did not lay down any general rule that hearsay evidence has to be demonstrated to be reliable before it can be admitted, or before it can be left to the jury. Nor does hearsay evidence have to be independently verified, as that would be to re-introduce the abolished rules for corroboration.

Hughes L.J. (as he then was) explained in *Riat* that in working through the statutory framework in a hearsay case, the court is concerned at several stages with both (i) the extent of risk of unreliability, and (ii) the extent to which the reliability of the evidence can safely be tested and assessed. It is clear that hearsay evidence must not be "nodded through". A focused decision must be made as to whether

---

[8] [2009] 49 EHRR 1.
[9] *Ibrahim* [2012] EWCA Crim 837; *R. (RJM) v Secretary of State for Work and Pensions (Equality and Human Rights Commissioner Intervening)* [2008] UKHL 63, at [64] per Lord Neuburger.
[10] [2012] EWCA Crim 1509.
[11] [2009] EWCA Crim 964.
[12] [2012] EWCA Crim 837.

it is to be admitted or not. His Lordship set out the statutory framework for hearsay evidence under the CJA 2003 in terms of six successive steps:

(i) Is there a specific statutory justification (or "gateway") permitting the admission of hearsay evidence (ss.116–118)? The general principle under s.116 is that the necessity to resort to second-hand evidence must be demonstrated under one or other of the statutory exceptions.

(ii) What material is there which can help to test or assess the hearsay (s.124)? The court should always consider the vital linked questions of the apparent reliability of the evidence and the practicality of the jury testing and assessing its reliability. In the Court of Appeal's view, the judge will often not be able to make the decision as to whether the hearsay evidence should be admitted unless he considers first, as well as the importance of the evidence and its apparent strengths and weaknesses, what material is available to help test and assess it.

(iii) Is there a specific "interests of justice" test at the admissibility stage?

(iv) If there is no other justification or gateway, should the evidence nonetheless be considered for admission on the ground that admission is, despite the difficulties, in the interests of justice (s.114(1)(d))? Section 114(1)(d) contains a general residual power to admit hearsay evidence which does not otherwise pass a statutory gateway, if the judge is satisfied that it is in the interests of justice for it to be admitted. If this gateway is invoked, the judge is specifically directed to have regard to the (non-exhaustive) considerations set out in s.114(2). As the Court emphasised in *R. v D(E)*,[13] s.114(1)(d) cannot be used routinely to avoid the statutory conditions for the admission of evidence which properly falls to be considered under ss.116–118.

(v) Even if prima facie admissible, ought the evidence to be ruled inadmissible under s.78 of the Police and Criminal Evidence Act 1984 and/or s.126 of the CJA 2003? The non-exhaustive considerations listed in s.114(2) are useful *aides memoires* for any judge considering the admissibility of hearsay evidence, whether under that subsection or under s.78 of the 1984 Act or otherwise. Section 126 provides a freestanding jurisdiction to refuse to admit hearsay evidence. If the evidence is tendered by the Crown, it stands in parallel to the general jurisdiction under s.78 of the 1984 Act, but it goes further than s.78 because it applies also to evidence tendered by a defendant, which might be targeted either at refuting Crown evidence or at inculpating a co-accused.

(vi) If the evidence is admitted, then should the case subsequently be stopped under s.125? That provision is an important safeguard against unfairness. In a non-hearsay case, the jury must be left to assess the evidence. It is not for the judge to do so. Under the rule in *Galbraith*,[14]

[13] [2010] EWCA Crim 1213.
[14] [1981] 1 W.L.R. 1039.

the judge's power to stop the case upon a submission that of no case to answer is limited to doing so if the necessary minimum evidence does not exist upon which a jury, properly directed, could convict the defendant. It is essential to understand that the rule is different for hearsay cases. There, the judge is required by s.125 to look to see whether the hearsay evidence is so unconvincing that any conviction would be unsafe. That means looking at its strengths and weaknesses, at the tools available to the jury for testing it, and at its importance to the case as a whole.

Ibrahim: Where the untested hearsay evidence is critical

In *Ibrahim*[15] the appellant was convicted of three rapes. The allegations of rape   **15.28B** and of a separate wounding were contained in statements made by a complainant, a drug addict who was working at the time as a street prostitute and who had subsequently died. The trial judge, pursuant to s.116 of the CJA 2003, allowed the prosecution to admit three statements that the complainant had made to the police. The Court of Appeal identified four questions that had to be answered:

   (i) Was there proper justification for admitting the untested hearsay? Here the conditions in s.116(1) and (2)(a) were met, subject to the issue of counterbalancing measures.

   (ii) How important were the three untested hearsay statements in relation to the prosecution's case? Did they amount to the "central corpus of evidence"[16] without which the case could not proceed? In *Ibrahim* the Court of Appeal had no doubt the statements were central.

   (iii) How demonstrably reliable were those statements? As a drug user, the complainant in *Ibrahim* belonged to a category of potentially very unreliable witnesses. She had made a false allegation of rape and then withdrawn it. She had been prepared to make this false allegation in a statement under s.9 of the 1967 Act. Further, there had been a 2-and-a-half year delay in making the key statement. The Court concluded that on the central issue of whether the defendant had non-consensual sexual intercourse with her, it could not be shown that the complainant's statements were reliable.

   (iv) Were the counterbalancing safeguards inherent in the common law, the CJA 2003 and s.78 of the 1984 Act properly applied in this case? The Court concluded that they were not, observing that the trial judge had not invited the jury to scrutinise the hearsay evidence with care nor drawn their attention to the specific risks of relying upon the evidence, such as the discrepancies between the complainant's statements.

The Court of Appeal held that the hearsay statements were so flawed, so central to the case, and so difficult to assess, that it was unfair for them to be left to the

---

[15] [2012] EWCA Crim 837.

[16] This phrase was used by Professor John Spencer in an article in *Archbold Review*, February 16, 2012, p.7.

jury. The Court rejected the prosecution submission that the question of the reliability and credibility of the complainant's evidence should have been left to the jury. Aitkens L.J., analysing the effect of the judgments of the Court of Appeal and Supreme Court in *Horncastle*, concluded that it is a pre-condition of the admission of untested hearsay evidence that it is shown to be "potentially safely reliable" before it is admitted. A trial judge should rule on this issue either at the admission stage or after the close of the prosecution case pursuant to s.125 of the CJA 2003. Hughes L.J. explained in the later case of *Riat* that the critical word is "potentially"[17]:

> "The job of the judge is not to look for independent complete verification. It is to ensure that the hearsay can *safely* be held to be reliable. That means looking . . . at its strengths and weaknesses, at the tools available to the jury for testing it, and at its importance to the case as a whole."

Riat: Hearsay statement by a complaint who has subsequently died

15.28C   The appellant was a karate instructor in his forties who was charged with 10 sexual offences committed against one of his pupils when she was aged 13 or 14. She had died before the trial, so the statutory gateway under s.116(2)(a) was passed, and the prosecution successfully applied to adduce her several detailed statements and video-interviews as hearsay evidence. The issue in the case was whether there was any sexual relationship at all between the defendant and his pupil. The prosecution case was that there had been an active sexual relationship lasting about 14 months. The jury convicted the appellant of the eight offences in relation to which consent was not an issue but acquitted of the two non-consensual counts of rape. On appeal, it was submitted that the hearsay evidence was central to the case and was not reliable because the complainant could be shown to have lied on some occasions. The Court of Appeal held that the evidence had been rightly admitted for the following reasons:

> (i) The central allegation had its origins in frequent spontaneous state-ments which were separately proved and which were made in circum-stances redolent of truth. Several of the complainant's friends gave evidence that she made no secret to them, contemporaneously, of her relationship with her instructor. The first time the relationship came to the attention of anyone in any authority strongly suggested reliability and was not sensibly explainable away as either bragging or fantasy. The complainant had made a visit to the school nurse and had confided her fear that she might be pregnant, telling the nurse in detail about her relationship with her karate instructor. When the nurse said she would have to report the matter, the complainant immediately asserted that that the man in question was not her instructor after all, but a boy of 18 about whom she gave no information apart from a first name. The complainant then attempted suicide and was accommodated, when recovering, in a

---

[17] [2012] EWCA Crim 1509, at [33].

supervised psychiatric rehabilitation unit for young people. There she told her head of house that the man in question was the appellant and not the 18-year-old.

(ii) Two of the complainant's friends gave evidence of the relationship independent of the complainant.

(iii) When resident at the supervised unit, the complainant had asked permission to contact the appellant.

(iv) Although there could be no questioning of the complainant, the jury was able to see her since her evidence had been video-recorded.

(v) There was a great deal of material by which the evidence of the complainant could be tested and assessed.

The complainant's hearsay evidence was strongly supported and did not stand as a bare, untestable allegation. It could be safely assessed by the jury. The jury acquitted of the two counts of non-consensual activity, which did depend wholly upon the unsupported evidence of the complainant, which showed that it applied itself realistically and responsibly to the assessment of her evidence. The overwhelming likelihood, on the evidence as a whole, was that the consensual, but abusive, relationship had indeed existed, and that the complainant had done her best from time to time to avoid getting the appellant into trouble.

Clare: **Hearsay statement by a young child**

The appellant had been convicted of a single offence of sexual assault upon a child   **15.28D** aged three-and-a-half. On a summer's day he was a visitor at the home of the child's family. He had been drinking for some of the day. There was a tent in the garden and in the early evening he was in it with the little girl. The child told her mother that the appellant had licked her private parts. By the time the mother had decided what to do and had called the police, the appellant had left without saying anything by way of farewell. The child was never a potential witness.

The medical evidence was neutral. The appellant was arrested the same evening and interviewed the next day. In the course of his arrest he told one of the officers not to look at him as if he were a paedophile, before the officers had said anything to suggest they were enquiring into indecency with a child. In interview, the appellant said that it was possible that his DNA would be found on the girl's knickers and gave an unlikely explanation suggesting that his face had been pressed up against her groin when he had been attempting to swat a wasp and remove a sticky sweet from her knickers. In the event, there was no scientific evidence of matchable DNA on the knickers. There was both a full female profile and a contribution from a male.

The prosecution applied to adduce the child's complaint to her mother under the "interests of justice" gateway in s.114(1)(d). The judge worked his way carefully through the s.114(2) factors. He concluded, and the Court of Appeal agreed, that the case depended substantially on the girl's statement, which was admitted.

On appeal it was submitted on behalf of the appellant that no assessment had been undertaken of the ability of the little girl to be interviewed under ABE conditions. The Court of Appeal agreed that, if that had not been done when it should have been done, it might have been a material consideration when confronting the 1984 Act s.78 question of fairness in relation to the admission of evidence. But the Court was quite satisfied that the judge had correctly concluded that the police had approached the question responsibly and reached a proper answer. On any view, the child was near the bottom of the age range in which an ABE interview might be achievable. Her strong reaction to any examination or enquiry was a powerful reason not to trouble her further, and more enquiry of her risked being abusive.

If the girl's one-line statement to her mother had stood alone, it would have been wrong to admit it. Children of three-and-a-half vary a good deal. The jury could have had no opportunity to assess her, nor could she have been asked any questions. However, the girl's statement did not stand alone. It was powerfully supported by (i) the appellant leaving the house without a word, (ii) his remark to the officer about paedophiles, and (iii) the remarkable story about the wasp and the sweet. There was sufficient support for the girl's statement to her mother, which was also spontaneous, unprompted and made originally not by way of complaint but simply by way of request for cream.

Bennett: Hearsay statement by patient with mental disorder who was too ill to give evidence[18]

15.28E   The appellant, a community psychiatric nurse, was convicted of sexual activity with a person with mental disorder. The prosecution case was that he had had an ongoing sexual relationship with his patient for some months. There was no doubt that the complainant was, despite her mental disorder, capable of consenting. She had given very long interviews to the police which had been video-recorded and were available to the jury. By the time of trial she was plainly too ill to give oral evidence, and that was not in dispute. Accordingly, the trial judge, on the application of the prosecution, admitted the complainant's recorded interviews as hearsay under the s.116(2)(b) gateway (person unfit to be a witness because of bodily or mental condition). In the interviews, the complainant gave a long, garrulous and by no means always consistent account of a continuing sexual relationship. When interviewed, the appellant initially denied any kind of affectionate or sexual relationship with the patient. Later, he broke down and gave a detailed account of their sexual relationship. At trial, the appellant, whilst accepting a sexual relationship, denied any penetration.

The Court of Appeal was satisfied that the judge had been correct to admit the evidence of the interviews with the patient. The case could be proved against the appellant without the complainant's evidence, by relying on messages and cards which he had sent her, his initial lies to the police and then his explicit confessions.

---

[18] See also para.7.33 in the main work.

Furthermore, there was ample material which enabled the reliability of the complainant to be tested. She was internally inconsistent. She could be shown to have asserted that she suffered from serious medical conditions when her doctor gave evidence that she did not. She had subsequently made another complaint against a second erstwhile boyfriend, whose virtues she had in the interviews repeatedly contrasted with what she said were the appellant's demerits; there was a clear basis for concern that she was prone first to profess great affection and then rapidly to turn to wounded resentment. She had made non-sexual complaints against neighbours and could be shown to have threatened to set fire to some property. It is impossible that any juror could have thought her wholly reliable.

Frightened witnesses: Admission through gateway s.116(2)(e)

It happens not infrequently in sex cases that a complainant refuses to give evidence   **15.28F** or to continue to give evidence. When such a situation arises, it will usually be necessary for the judge to tell the witness that, as a witness in a court of law, he or she is under an obligation to answer questions and does not have a choice in the matter. The situation requires a blend of sensitivity and fairness which may involve giving the witness time to reflect. If the witness maintains their refusal, the judge is entitled to reinforce their direction by pointing out that they have the power to punish the witness. Whether or not there is evidence to suggest that the refusal is attributable to fear, a court may grant legal representation to such a witness, who has come to court as a result of a summons or warrant but is steadfastly refusing to give evidence. The court-appointed lawyer will not be able to discuss the witness's evidence with them, but will be able to explain the implications of failing to give evidence, which may amount to a contempt of court. We are firmly of the view that the court-appointed lawyer should have appropriate experience of sex cases in order that they are in a position to give proper advice in these highly sensitive cases.

In *Shabir*[19] Aitkens L.J., drawing upon the decisions of the Supreme Court and   **15.28G** Court of Appeal in *Horncastle*, and of the Court of Appeal in *Ibrahim* and *Riat*, gave a very clear exposition of the law governing the admissibility of hearsay evidence when reliance is placed upon s.116(2)(e). We set out below the 12 steps that he identified, with references to recent cases.

The 12 steps

When it is sought to admit a hearsay statement through the gateway of s.116(2)(e),   **15.28H** because it is said that the witness will not give oral evidence at the trial "through fear", the framework is as follows[20]:
    (1) The "default" position is that hearsay evidence is not admissible.

---

[19] [2012] EWCA Crim 2564.
[20] At [64]–[65] per Aitkens L.J.

(2) It is a pre-condition to the admission of a hearsay statement that the witness concerned is identified: s.116(1)(b).

(3) The necessity to resort to second-hand evidence must be clearly demonstrated. The more central the evidence, the greater the scrutiny that has to be undertaken.

(4) Although "fear" is to be widely construed in accordance with s.116(3) and, specifically, fear of a witness does not have to be attributed to the defendant, a court has to be satisfied to a criminal standard that the proposed witness will not give evidence (either at all or in connection with the subject matter of the relevant statement) "through fear". Thus a causative link between the fear and the failure or refusal to give evidence must be proved.

(5) How it is proved that a witness will not give evidence "through fear" depends upon the background together with the history and the circumstances of the particular case. Every effort must be made to get the witness to court to test the issue of his "fear". The witness alleging "fear" may be cross-examined by the defence (if needs be in a voir dire), if necessary using "special measures" to assist the witness. However, Aitkens L.J. acknowledged that whilst that procedure may be possible, in certain cases it may not be appropriate. Subsequent cases have illustrated this.

For instance, in *Adeojo*[21] a voir dire was held in which the witness indicted he would refuse to answer questions from the defence, but no questions were put to the witness on the issue of the genuineness of his fear either by defence counsel or the judge. The judge subsequently concluded that there was an abundance of material which satisfied him that the witness was genuinely in fear for himself and his family. He considered s.78 of the 1984 Act by examining the s.114(2) factors and concluded that it was in the interests of justice to admit the statement. He gave an appropriate warning to the jury in his summing up. The Court of Appeal concluded that the verdicts of the jury were safe.

In *Jabbar*[22] the appellant's counsel sought to criticise the trial judge for not explaining to the witness, who was available for a voir dire, that it was the witness's public duty to give evidence. It was contended that might have produced a change of heart. Treacy L.J. stated:

> "Although Riat encourages the court to take all possible steps to enable a fearful witness to give evidence, notwithstanding his or her apprehension, it has to be recognised that the factual situation will vary from case to case, as will the steps a judge should take in any given circumstances. Given the judge's finding that Tahir's fears were genuine and that he attended court, explained his position after meeting prosecuting counsel and had been cross-examined as to credibility, we do not find any failure in the way Tahir

---

[21] [2013] EWCA Crim 41.
[22] [2013] EWCA Crim 801.

was handled which could avail the appellant on his challenge to the
admissibility of the evidence."

Further, in *Fagan*[23] the Court of Appeal stated that, whilst it would have
been wise to ensure the witness was brought to court, nevertheless, in the
circumstances of that case the failure to do so was nowhere near fatal to
the judge's conclusion that the witness was in a state of extreme fear.

(6) If testing by the defence is properly refused (after consideration) then "it
is incumbent on the judge to take responsibility vigorously to test the
evidence of fear and to investigate all the possibilities of the witness
giving oral evidence in the proceedings". The manner in which that
should be done will depend on the circumstances of the case and upon
the witness and will necessarily involve discussions with counsel as to the
approach and questions to be asked. For example, if a court cannot hear
from a witness, a tape recording or video of an interview on the question
of his "fear" should, if possible, be made available. The critical thing is
that "every effort is made to get the witness to court."

In *Clarke*[24] it was alleged that the victim had given the name of his
attacker "off the record" to a police officer. In evidence the victim denied
that he had told the officer the identity of the attacker but in all other
respects he was co-operative. The trial judge accepted that the victim was
plainly in fear and ruled that in was in the interests of justice that the
officer should give evidence of the hearsay "off the record" statement.
Hallett L.J. observed that it is clear from the wording of s.116(2)(e),
which applies where a person does not give or "does not continue to
give" evidence, that the provision may apply where a witness is available.
In that case there was sufficient evidence to justify the finding that the
witness was in genuine and substantial fear of the appellant. This came
not only from the circumstances of the attack upon him, but also from
the evidence of the appellant's background.

(7) In relation to the gateway of s.116(2)(e), leave to admit the statement will
only be given if the conditions for passing through a specific "secondary
gateway" are satisfied. These are set out in s.116(4). Overall, a court will
only admit a statement under s.116(2)(e) if it considers that it is "in the
interests of justice" to do so. In that respect, the court has to have specific
regard to the matters set out in s.116(4)(a)–(c).

(8) When a court considers s.116(4)(c), it should take all possible steps to
enable a fearful witness to give evidence notwithstanding his apprehen-
sion. "A degree of (properly supported) fortitude can legitimately be
expected in the fight against crime". A court must therefore have regard
to whether (in an appropriate case) a witness would give evidence if a
direction for "special measures" were to be made under s.19 of the Youth
Justice and Criminal Evidence Act 1999.

[23] [2012] EWCA Crim 2248.
[24] [2012] EWCA Crim 2354.

(9) In this regard it is important that, before the court has ruled on the application to admit under s.116(2)(e), no indication, let alone assurance, is given to a potential witness that his evidence will or may be read if he says he is afraid, because that can only give rise to an expectation that this will, indeed, happen. Aitken L.J., following the lead of Thomas L.J. (as he then was) in *Horncastle* who had enunciated a general prohibition on such assurances, went so far as to indicate that if that does happen, then the statement will have been admitted on an improper basis; the impact of the evidence will be diminished and that may have further consequences, e.g. an application to the judge under s.125 at the end of the prosecution case to stop the case. However, the subsequent case of *Abdulle*[25] illustrates that these outcomes are necessarily fact-dependent. In that case, a young witness was given an assurance before a second ABE interview that he would not have to testify. This was held not to be fatal to the interview's admissibility under s.114(1)(d). The judge had made express reference to all the points in *Horncastle* and had explained his reasoning in a very full ruling at the outset of the trial. The judge had carefully considered the whole issue of reliability. He had found that it was understandable in the circumstances that the assurance had been given. In summing-up, he had highlighted the potential disadvantage to the defence in not being able to cross-examine the witness and had stressed the need for caution. Overall, he had exercised his discretion in a proper manner and his ruling could not be criticised.

(10) When a judge considers the "interests of justice" test under s.116(4), although he or she is not obliged to consider all the factors set out in s.114(2)(a)–(i), those factors may be a convenient check list for them to consider.

(11) Once the judge has concluded that the specific gateways in s.116(4) have been satisfied, the court must consider the vital linked questions of (a) the apparent reliability of the evidence sought to be adduced as hearsay and (b) the practicality of the jury testing and assessing its reliability. In this regard, s.124 (which permits a wide range of material going to the credibility of the witness to be adduced as evidence) is vital.

(12) In many cases, a judge will not be able to make a decision as to whether to admit an item of hearsay evidence unless he has considered not only the importance of the evidence and its apparent strengths and weaknesses, but also what material is available to help test and assess it, in particular what evidence could be admitted as to the credibility of the witness and the hearsay evidence under s.124. The judge is entitled to expect that "very full" enquiries as to witness credibility will have been made if it is the prosecution that wishes to put in the hearsay evidence, and if it is the defence, they too must undertake proper checks.

---

[25] [2013] EWCA Crim 1069.

(iii) *Statement admitted in the interests of justice under s.114(1)(d) of the Criminal Justice Act 2003*

It is necessary to approach s.114(1)(d) with caution, particularly where a party is seeking to adduce hearsay evidence from a witness who is not being called, but whose absence is not within the reasons listed in s.116. What is the situation where the witness is called but has no recollection of making an earlier disclosure or of the events described in it? This is not an uncommon feature of cases where there are allegations of long-term abuse. A complainant may have little or no recollection of a contemporaneous report to a police officer or a social worker. Earlier disclosures may be relevant to rebut allegations of fabrication (see para.15.52 et seq.). It may also be in the interests of justice for the jury to hear a contemporaneous account by a witness given during the grooming process. **15.33**

MH v R.[26] provides some assistance as to how to approach earlier disclosures unconfirmed by a complainant in evidence. In that case, it was held that unconfirmed disclosures made by a small child were admissible in the interests of justice under s.114(1)(d). The respondent's counsel sought to counter the suggestion that such admitting evidence would infringe the prohibition against "self-corroboration". He submitted that there was a material difference between an adult, or an older child, making repeated allegations of sexual misconduct (with the risk that mere repetition may provide spurious self-support) and a child aged three who did not possess the sophistication required to manipulate such opportunities to his own advantage, consciously or sub-consciously. The child's repeated and unsolicited references, in an unchallenging domestic context, to the appellant's conduct towards him provided cogent evidence of the child's truthfulness and reliability. It was in the interests of justice for such evidence to be considered by the jury both for its capacity to demonstrate the truth of the witness's evidence and, on account of its inherent reliability, because it was evidence of the appellant's conduct. The Court of Appeal, whilst acknowledging that the trial judge had not been asked to exercise his discretion under s.114(1)(d) and so had not addressed these issues, concluded that there would have been no prospect of successfully resisting the prosecution's wish to adduce the evidence. The circumstances were overwhelmingly in favour of the admission of the hearsay evidence in the interests of justice, whether or not it was capable of admission under s.120(2) to rebut a suggestion of fabrication. **15.33A**

---

[26] [2012] EWCA Crim 2725. See also *R. v SJ* [2009] EWCA Crim 1869, considered in para.15.33 of the main work, where the victim of sexual assault was a child aged 30 months who was not competent to give an ABE interview. There was a strong circumstantial case against the appellant. The child's responses to questions asked by her mother and on one occasion by a social worker were held to have been properly admitted under s.114(1)(d). The Court in *MH v R.* derived from *R. v SJ* the proposition that, whilst care must be exercised, there may be circumstances in which the interests of justice demand the admission of hearsay evidence, even if it is of critical importance to the main issue in case.

Consistent Statements—Evidence of Earlier Complaints by the
Complainant

15.36   As noted in the main work, the scope for admission of previous consistent
        statements and the use of such evidence as evidence of the truth represents a major
        shift from the common law position. In *Chinn*[27] the Court of Appeal shed light
        upon the correct use of s.120(3) (previous statements relied upon to refresh
        memory), (4) (confirmation by the witness of truth of statement), (5) (identifica-
        tion by witness of truth of statement) and (6) (witness cannot be expected to recall
        earlier statement).

15.42   As explained in the main work, the jury should be warned about the lack of
        independence of evidence of previous complaint.[28] The importance of giving the
        warning is underlined by the fact that under s.120 such evidence is now evidence
        of the truth of the complaint. However, whilst the direction should be routinely
        given, an omission to give it will not necessarily be fatal to a conviction;[29] it is after
        all self-evident that complaint evidence does not come from an independent
        source. The Court of Appeal has also indicated that there may be cases where an
        independence warning is not necessary at all. *R. v H*[30] concerned the historic
        abuse by the appellant of his three stepsons. Two of them had reported the abuse
        to their mother. The Court held that the failure to give an independence direction
        in relation to this complaint did not render the appellant's convictions unsafe. The
        trial judge had not been asked by defence (or Crown) counsel to give such a
        direction. Much had to be allowed for the feel of the case which the judge and
        counsel would have had. The defence case was that the boys were fabricating. In
        circumstances where it was the defence rather than, or as much as, the prosecution
        which was relying on the evidence of complaint, there was a danger in
        overcomplicating matters. It was clear from the trial as a whole and the judge's fair
        and helpful directions that the jury had to decide whether the truth was to be
        found in the complainants' allegations or in the defence, but that the burden lay
        on the prosecution. The judge emphasised that the reliability of the complainants
        was the critical question. In the circumstances, the Court inclined to the
        conclusion that had been no misdirection at all. In any event, the case was
        distinguishable from *R. v AA*, above, where a single and prompt complaint to a
        friend following a single act of what was either rape or consensual intercourse was
        of special significance. By contrast, the allegations in *R. v H* were of an ongoing
        course of conduct, both before and after the complaint, and the appellant relied on
        the evidence of the complaint for his own purposes as being part of the fabrication
        of which he complained.

---

[27] [2012] EWCA Crim 501.
[28] See *R. v AA* [2007] EWCA Crim 1779.
[29] *Amrani* [2011] EWCA Crim 1517; *R. v A* [2011] EWCA Crim 1943.
[30] [2011] EWCA Crim 2344.

A previous complaint about relevant conduct is not admissible under s.120(4) and **15.42A** (7) of the Act unless the complainant confirms that they described such conduct to the reporting witness, and that the description was true. This is a result of s.120(4)(b), which provides that a previous statement by the witness is admissible as evidence of any matter stated of which oral evidence by him would be admissible, if "while giving evidence the witness indicates that to his belief that he made the statement, and that to the best of his belief it states the truth". For this reason, a previous complaint was not admissible in *MH v R*.[31] In that case, a father was convicted of various sexual offences committed against his very young son. The child gave evidence, but was not asked to confirm that he had described the appellant's conduct to his mother or that the description he had given her was true. The Court of Appeal observed that, despite the warnings in *R. v AA*[32] and *Athwal and others*,[33] "complaints" continue to be admitted as if the former common law still applied.

Section 112 of the Coroners and Justice Act 2009[34] repealed s.120(7)(d) of the CJA **15.46** 2003, which contained a requirement that the complaint be made as soon as could reasonably be expected after the alleged conduct. Accordingly, the law now allows for multiple complaints to be admitted whenever they were made.

Evidence to rebut a suggestion that oral evidence has been fabricated

The evidence of early disclosures in *MH v R*.,[35] although not admissible under **15.52** s.120(4) and (7), was potentially admissible on two other bases. First, the fact that the disclosure was made tended to disprove the accusation of coaching and so was relevant evidence. However, that would not make the disclosure admissible as proof of its content. Secondly, it was admissible under s.120(2) to rebut the accusation of fabrication, and as such was admissible as proof of its contents and not merely as evidence going to the issue of consistency.[36]

CORROBORATION AND WARNINGS ABOUT RELIANCE ON A COMPLAINANT'S EVIDENCE

In cases which depend upon the credibility of the complainant, there will **15.69** frequently be evidence of (i) contemporary lies, (ii) late disclosure, (iii) significant inconsistencies between accounts, and (iv) particularly in cases where sexual abuse is alleged over a substantial period, allegations raised for the first time when the

---

[31] Above, fn.26.
[32] Above, fn.28.
[33] [2009] EWCA 789.
[34] Which came into force on February 1, 2010.
[35] Above, fn.26.
[36] *Athwal and others* [2009] EWCA Crim 789; *R. v T* [2008] EWCA Crim 484, at [18] per David Clarke J.

complainant gives evidence at trial. Where any of these issues are of significance to the complainant's reliability and credibility, the trial judge should properly expose them in his summing up. It does not, however, follow that in such cases a *Makanjuola* warning is necessary. The critical issue is that the jury is reminded of the lies, inconsistencies and late disclosures and any explanations for them, so that the jury can properly evaluate the evidence.

The Decision in *Makanjuola and Easton*

15.71   In *Udaykamaur Joshi*[37] the Court of Appeal for Northern Ireland, in a judgment by Lord Morgan C.J., considered the application of the principles set out by Lord Taylor C.J. in *Makanjuola*[38] when considering an appeal against conviction on two counts of buggery and one of indecent assault committed against a "minor" in 1979. It was alleged that the appellant had committed the offences whilst he had been employed as a professional at a cricket club of which the complainant's father was a member. The principal ground advanced on behalf of the appellant was that the trial judge had failed to give a warning to the jury that they should exercise caution before acting on the evidence of the complainant. At trial, the appellant had raised the issue of the need to give the jury such a warning in advance of speeches. The submission, which was opposed by the prosecution, was that the jury should be told that it would be unwise to convict on the unsupported evidence of the complainant. Lord Morgan went through the process of identifying those factors which point towards the need for a *Makanjoula* warning of some kind and then examining how they were dealt with by the judge. The complainant had admitted that on two occasions he had lied about the allegations. First, he had lied in the account he gave a year after the incident when he had said that he had resisted the appellant and had fought him off with a shoe. In evidence he said that he had been ashamed to admit that he had not tried to resist the appellant. This was also his explanation for late disclosure. Secondly, the complainant had told his therapist that the appellant had leant over him and clasped his arm in order to get him into the appellant's bedroom. In evidence he explained that he had gone into his bedroom quietly as he did not want his grandmother to be wakened and the events of the previous week to be discovered. Lord Morgan stated[39]:

> " . . . it is clear from Lord Taylor's guidance that the nature of any warning that a judge decides to give in relation to a witness should be woven into the review of the evidence and the language used should reflect the strength of the warning considered appropriate by the judge."

Having regard to the nature of the lies admitted and the explanations provided (which were all covered by the judge in her summing up), the Court did not consider that the judge could be criticised for taking the view that this was not one

[37] [2012] NICA 56.
[38] [1995] 1 W.L.R. 1348.
[39] Above, fn.37 at [32].

of those cases where the lies called for the need for supporting material before relying on the evidence of the complainant. There were a number of inconsistencies in the complainant's evidence, most notably between his accounts to his therapist and his evidence. The complainant's explanation in evidence was that in some cases it was too painful to give a full account, in other cases the issues were irrelevant and on some occasions he merely gave a summary because the purpose of the therapy was not to investigate the detail of the attacks. All these inconsistencies were put before the jury by the trial judge on the basis that they were material to the issue of who the jury should believe. The Court concluded that the appellant's case was fully explored by the judge who had properly dealt with the issues in the complainant's case which touched on his reliability and credibility. It was a paradigm case for a decision by the jury. There was no basis upon which to interfere with the jury's decision and the Court was not left with any sense of unease about the verdict.

EVIDENCE OF DEFENDANT'S SPOUSE OR CIVIL PARTNER

It was held in *R. v BA*[40] that the decision whether an offence is one in respect of **15.81** which the defendant's spouse or civil partner can be compelled to give evidence under s.80(3)(a) of the 1984 Act, on the ground that it involves "an assault on, or injury or threat of injury to" the spouse or a child under 16, has to be taken by reference to the legal nature of the charged offence and not the factual circumstances surrounding the offence.

Erratum: the decision referred to in the main work is *R. v L.*[41] For a critique of **15.86** this decision, see Janice Brabyn, *A Criminal Defendant's Spouse as a Prosecution Witness* [2007] Crim. L.R. 613.

---

[40] [2012] EWCA Crim 1529.
[41] [2008] EWCA Crim 973.

CHAPTER 16

EVIDENCE OF BAD CHARACTER

THE CRIMINAL JUSTICE ACT 2003

A supplement is not the place to develop an academic treatise on the law of **16.01** evidence and we therefore propose to limit ourselves to the most important cases in this area. The last few years have seen a number of appeals to the Court of Appeal in respect of sexual offences in which bad character issues have been involved. We have included these if either they have clarified how a certain category of bad character evidence should be treated, as in *D, P and U*,[1] or they provide instructive examples of how bad character evidence should be approached in sex cases. In addition, some appeals relating to other criminal offences have shed valuable light on the proper approach to this area of evidence.

The admissibility of evidence of homosexual disposition has received recent attention from the Court of Appeal,[2] which has emphasised the vast difference between an interest in consensual sex with an adult male partner and an interest in paedophile sex with boys. A mutually agreed sexual relationship between adults, without more, does not show a propensity to commit sexual offences against children. Normally such evidence will not be relevant and admissible. However, there may be cases where a defendant makes his sexual disposition an issue in the case such that the gateway in s.101(1)(f) of the 2003 ("CJA 2003") applies. In these

---

[1] [2011] EWCA Crim 1474.
[2] *Laws-Chapman* [2013] EWCA 1851, discussed in para.16.26G, below.

circumstances, the jury should be given a powerful warning as to the limits of the relevance of such evidence.[3]

Bad character evidence is, of course, highly relevant to issues of (a) joinder and severance, (b) cross-admissibility, and (c) the risk of collusion and/or contamination. A number of Court of Appeal decisions have underlined the need for the judge and counsel to address these issues before closing speeches.[4] We have formed the view that, in more complicated cases, it may assist the jury if they are provided with a written direction on these issues.

Finally, in *Dizaei*[5] the Court of Appeal explained the relevance of possible satellite litigation to applications to adduce evidence of the bad character of a non-defendant.

Notice Requirements

16.02   The relevant notice requirements are now contained in the Criminal Procedure Rules ("CPR") 2013. In *Dalby*[6] the Court of Appeal described the late bad character application advanced at trial in oral form as "unfortunate". The Court underlined the importance of following the practice set out in the CPR. Applications should be made in proper form and on time so that there is an adequate opportunity for them to be considered.

Proving The Details of a Previous Sexual Offence

16.06   Where evidence of bad character is admitted, and is challenged, there may be circumstances in which the judge has to give the jury both a full good character direction and a full bad character direction, depending upon the jury's factual finding. In *Olu*[7] the judge admitted evidence of the appellant's acceptance of a caution for possession of a flick knife, which contained an admission that the offence had occurred, as evidence of propensity to possess a knife in a public place. The admission was challenged in evidence by the appellant. Apart from the caution, the appellant was a young man of good character. The Court of Appeal held that the jury should have been directed that, if they were not sure that the appellant had committed the caution offence, they should treat him as a person of good character.

The Definition of "Bad Character"

16.11   A harassment warning, like a penalty notice, does not involve an admission of culpability and so will not, on its own, ordinarily be capable of constituting bad

---

[3] *R. v IJ* [2011] EWCA Crim 2734, discussed in para.16.26H, below.
[4] *R. v AT* [2013] EWCA Crim 1850.
[5] [2013] EWCA Crim 88 at [36]–[38] per Lord Judge C.J.
[6] [2012] EWCA Crim 701.
[7] [2010] EWCA Crim 2975. Not only was the application late, but it involved a harassment notice based upon the complaint of a witness whose identity remained anonymous. The harassment warning did not involve an admission of culpability, but there was underlying material capable of constituting bad character evidence.

character evidence.[8] However, the underlying material may be capable of doing so.

THE GATEWAYS

Section 101(1)(c)—"important explanatory evidence"

In *R. v D, P and U*[9] the Court of Appeal observed that gateway (c) is open to **16.23** misuse. It is designed to deal with the situation in which a jury cannot properly understand the case without hearing evidence which amounts to or includes evidence of bad character. In that case, the Court held that the possession of child pornography could not amount to important explanatory evidence in respect of an allegation of physical child abuse, as the jury could properly understand the allegations without that evidence. The trial judge in *D* had been correct not to admit the evidence under gateway (c).

In *Lee*[10] Hughes L.J., as he then was, took the opportunity further to underline the **16.23A** importance of reading gateway (c) with s.102 of the Act, and for counsel and the judge to focus upon the exact basis upon which evidence has been admitted. To say that evidence fills out the picture is not the same as saying the rest of the picture is either impossible or difficult to see without it. In *Lee* the appellant appealed against a single conviction for indecent assault committed on a friend of his step-daughter, S. He was acquitted of other charges. The trial judge had allowed the prosecution to adduce under gateway (c) evidence of two occurrences which S alleged had taken place after the incidents which gave rise to the charges. First, the appellant had placed a camcorder in the bathroom to allow him to watch S bathing. Secondly, after she had left home, S returned to babysit for her younger brother and discovered on the family computer indecent photographs of pubescent children, which it was suggested the appellant had uploaded. The trial judge ruled that evidence of these two occurrences amounted to important explanatory evidence on the grounds (i) that it explained how events progressed and it was the trigger behind S's decision to leave the house at the age of 16, (ii) that to exclude it would leave a lacuna as to what happened, and (iii) that S's reaction to the appellant's behaviour was an important part of the evidence and was necessary to enable the jury to understand why events moved on in the way that they did and, in particular, to address the delay in allegations being made over a number of years. The Court of Appeal acknowledged that these observations may well have been true. However, s.102 of the Act states that evidence will be important explanatory evidence if, first, without it the court or jury would find it impossible or difficult properly to understand other evidence in the case and, second, its value for understanding the case as a whole is substantial. The first condition was not met in this case: S's evidence was perfectly comprehensible without her evidence about

---

[8] *Dalby*, above, fn.6.
[9] Above, fn.1.
[10] [2012] EWCA Crim 316.

the camcorder and computer incidents. The computer evidence of the appellant taking an unhealthy interest in pubescent children was potentially admissible through gateway (d): see *D, P and U*, discussed below. However, the judge had not been invited to rule on that basis, and had not given the jury the appropriate direction as to how to approach evidence of propensity. In those circumstances, it was impossible to exclude the possibility that some members of the jury may have relied on the two additional pieces of evidence when arriving at a verdict on the single count on which the appellant was convicted, and so that conviction was simply not safe.

Section 101(1)(d)—evidence "relevant to an important matter in issue between the defendant and the prosecution"

16.26   It is vital to appreciate that admissibility under gateway (d) is not confined to propensity. Indeed that gateway does not use the expression "propensity", which appears in s.103(1), which makes it clear that propensity is included amongst the issues between the prosecution and the defence.[11]

Possession of indecent photographs

16.26A   Where a young male complainant alleges as part of his account that the defendant used to show him pictures of child pornography, evidence of the existence of indecent photographs of children including boys on the defendant's computer may be admissible independently of the bad character provisions to support the complainant's evidence of being shown pornography.[12] In such circumstances, the evidence is not bad character evidence by virtue of s.98(a) of the CJA 2003 in that it has to do with the alleged facts of the offence.

16.26B   Not infrequently in a case of alleged child sexual abuse there will be evidence that the defendant had viewed and/or made indecent photographs of children. Where the defendant denies any sexual contact with the complainant(s), it is likely that the prosecution will seek to adduce evidence of the indecent photographs as bad character evidence under s.101(1) of the CJA 2003. In *R. v D, P and U*[13] the Court of Appeal, dealing with three conjoined appeals, held that if a defendant is charged with the sexual abuse of a child, evidence of his possession of indecent photographs of children is capable of being admitted by way of bad character evidence under gateway (d) on the ground that evidence of a sexual interest in children is relevant to an important matter in issue between the defendant and the prosecution. Hughes L.J., as he then was, giving the judgment of the Court, did however stress that such evidence is not automatically admissible. An exercise of judgment is required, and there may be a sufficient difference between what has been viewed and what is alleged to have been done for there to be no plausible link.

---

[11] *R. v D, P and U* [2011] EWCA Crim 1474, at [5].
[12] See the appeal of *P*, one of the conjoined appeals in *R. v D, P and U*, last note.
[13] Last note.

Further, the conclusion that the evidence is capable of admission under gateway (d) is only the first part of the exercise for the court. It must also direct its attention to whether it is unfair to admit the evidence, and in some cases it might be particularly so where the probative value of the evidence is marginal.

The Court of Appeal in *R. v D, P and U* observed that evidence that a defendant collects or views child pornography is by itself evidence of the commission of a criminal offence. That offence is not itself one involving sexual assault or abuse or indeed any sexual activity which is prohibited. It is obvious that it does not necessarily follow that a person who enjoys viewing such pictures will act out in real life the kind of activity which is depicted in them by abusing children. Accordingly, evidence of the possession of such photographs is not evidence that the defendant has demonstrated a practice of committing offences of sexual abuse or assault. However, the critical question is whether the evidence is relevant to demonstrate that the defendant exhibited a sexual interest in children. The Court of Appeal held that such evidence can indeed be relevant. A sexual interest in small children or pubescent girls is a relatively unusual character trait. The case against a defendant charged with the sexual abuse of children is that in addition to this character trait, he has translated the interest into active abuse of a child. The evidence of his interest tends to prove the first part of the case. In such cases it is important that juries should be reminded that they cannot proceed directly from possession of photographs to active sexual abuse. The relevance of the indecent photographs is limited to demonstrating a sexual interest in children. The extra step does not necessarily follow. They must ask themselves whether this further step is proved so that they are sure.

The Court also recommended that judges should consider including a warning to juries, in a case where there is such a risk, not to allow any revulsion at the use of child pornography to overcome their duty as jurors to examine carefully the question whether the evidence shows that the interest has been translated beyond actual viewing and into active abuse. It is a sensible practice to avoid the jury seeing the photographs so as to avoid the risk of the effects of distaste. It is likely that in most cases a suitable description of the general contents of the photographs, which should be as neutral and dispassionate as possible, can be agreed and presented to the jury. The Court suggested that it is better for such a description to be linked to the photographs actually found, rather than to generalised descriptions of categories such as the Copine scale. When dealing with the appeal of *D*, the Court pointed out that the evidence of both the internet searches for child pornography and the product of those searches would have been admissible, and the judge had been wrong to exclude the bulk of the photographic evidence.

The Court in *R. v D, P and U* observed that in *R. v A*[14] the trial judge had limited the bad character evidence to photographs, films and the like demonstrating a particular interest in incestuous relationships, so the Court of Appeal did not have to decide whether the collection of child pornography falling short of a

---

[14] [2009] EWCA Crim 513.

particular interest in incest would also be admissible. However, the tenor of the trial judge's decision as approved by the Court plainly demonstrates that it could. The judge had said that:

> "[A] reasonable jury would be entitled to consider the complainant's independent complaint and assess it in the light of the complainant's subsequent computer misuse, and conclude that the proposition that the complainant should make her complaints against an innocent man who just happened later in life to develop peculiar sexual preoccupations consistent with the complainant's complaint is profoundly unlikely."

Hughes L.J. noted that this brief expression of principle was approved by the Court of Appeal and would apply *mutatis mutandis* to a demonstrated sexual interest in young children.

Generalised history as opposed to unusual form of sexual interest

16.26C   The line of cases dealing with child pornography is to be contrasted with cases where the evidence sought to be adduced shows nothing more than a generalised history of exceeding sexual boundaries. In *Clements*[15] the appellant had been charged with two sexual assaults upon adults. He had a previous conviction for consensual sexual behaviour, apparently amounting to kissing, involving a 14-year-old girl. The Court of Appeal held that the previous conviction should not have been admitted. Whilst it could be said to demonstrate an inability to recognise, or perhaps a willingness to disregard, the normal boundaries of sexual propriety, the dividing line between consensual and non-consensual behaviour in sexual matters is very significant and the circumstances of the previous offence and the offences for which the appellant was being tried were very different. In the Court's view, the previous conviction was not probative of a propensity on the part of the appellant to commit sexual assaults of the kind under consideration, and to the extent that it could be said to be probative of a general inability to recognise the normal boundaries of sexual propensity its probative force was, at best, weak. On the other hand, the prejudicial effect of admitting the conviction was likely to be very significant. Furthermore, in that case the previous incident did not show any unusual form of sexual interest which was relevant to the charges before the court.

16.26D   *Clements* should be compared with *R. v P*,[16] in which the applicant (56) was convicted of 13 counts of sexual assault upon his god-daughter when she was aged 10. He was caught on CCTV with his hand up her skirt. When interviewed, she disclosed extensive abuse by him over a number of years. It was the applicant's case that the complainant was fabricating or mistaken. At trial the judge had admitted as bad character evidence emails sent by the applicant to three other young girls in which he had pretended to be 16. He had told one of the girls that he looked good and another that he loved her. In a renewed application for leave to appeal,

---

[15] [2009] EWCA Crim 2726.
[16] [2013] EWCA Crim 913.

it was submitted that the admissibility of online communication with other children depended upon the prosecution being able to show that the applicant had an unusual sexual interest in children. The prosecution had been able to go no further than to show he had an "odd" but non-sexual relationship with children and so the emails should not have been admitted. The Court of Appeal refused the application for leave and accepted the prosecution's submission that the evidence of the emails supported the complainant's account that the applicant had an unhealthy interest in girls. The computer contact between him and the three girls was capable of showing a propensity to get close to and have non-innocent relationships with girls. It was not necessary to show a propensity to commit offences such as those charged. The Court also held that, although the trial judge had not made specific reference to s.101(3) of the CJA 2003, he had been entitled to conclude that the prejudice caused by admission of the evidence was not such as to require its exclusion.

Evidence of homosexual disposition

In cases involving allegations of sexual offences against male children, is evidence   **16.26E** that the defendant is not purely heterosexual, has bisexual interests or has had consensual sexual relations with other men relevant and admissible?

This is a difficult area. In addressing such questions it is always vitally important   **16.26F** to identify what matters are in issue in the particular case and whether the bad character evidence that the prosecution seeks to adduce is truly relevant to those issues and complies with the bad character regime criteria. The fact that the defendant has had consensual sexual relations with males over the present-day age of consent on other occasions is not germane to the question whether he has committed violent paedophile offences. Problems have arisen when the prosecution has sought to argue (i) that the defendant's homosexual disposition is relevant because it shows an unusual sexual interest, or (ii) that the defendant's apparent heterosexuality demonstrated by his marriage or by other acts consistent with heterosexuality risks giving the jury a false impression. Given the potential pitfalls and the obvious scope for significant prejudice, even in 2014, both lines of reasoning need to be scrutinised with great care before such evidence is admitted. Three recent cases are highly instructive. What they make clear is that, in the event of such evidence being relevant and admissible, a powerful direction is called for to prevent juries adopting an illegitimate line of reasoning.[17]

Laws-Chapman[18] is a strong example of a case in which the bad character evidence   **16.26G** did not have any real relevance to the matters in issue and its admission would inevitably have been highly prejudicial. The issue on appeal was whether, in the

---

[17] *R. v IJ* [2011] EWCA Crim 2734 at [29] and [44] per Pitchford L.J. See para.16.26H, below; and see *R. v B (Peter)* [2012] EWCA Crim 1659, discussed in para.16.26I, below.
[18] [2013] EWCA Crim 1851. The decision was strongly criticised by James Richardson QC in *Criminal Law Week*, Issue 46, December 16, 2013, pp.2–4.

context of two historic sexual offences alleged to have been committed in 1978,[19] which involved an allegation of violent paedophile behaviour against the will of the victim (who was aged 12 or 13 at the time), the trial judge had been right to admit in evidence a single conviction for buggery in 1985, involving a 17-year-old, where the buggery may well have been consensual and when the court had no details relating to the latter offending apart from the identity of the victim and the location of the offence.

The applicant denied the entirety of the sexual allegations made by the complainant. In interview, when asked whether he had ever touched any boys inappropriately, he answered "No, definitely no". When the allegations were put in more detail he stated, "I should never think I would want to do that sort of thing" and "When you're a married man why the hell do you want to do a thing like that?" The defence case was that the principal witness was mistaken in his identification. The applicant did not give evidence.

The judge allowed the prosecution's application to admit the 1985 conviction on the basis that it provided evidence from which the jury could properly conclude that the applicant had a sexual interest in boys and was inclined towards buggery. He concluded that the fact that it was an isolated conviction would not preclude the jury properly concluding that the applicant had the relevant propensity. The judge also considered that the assertion by the defence that the complainant had mistakenly identified the applicant, and that the more likely candidate was an identified individual who had convictions for child sex abuse, meant that the application was properly made out under gateway (g) on the basis of an attack on the character of another. The judge also suggested that the evidence served to contradict the impression created in interview by the applicant that he would never have acted as alleged towards the victim in the present case and "was not that way inclined."

In summing up, the judge directed the jury that the principal reason why they had heard about the offence was because the prosecution said that it contradicted the impression the jury might think the applicant gave during interview, when he had suggested he was not the sort of person to do something like that. He continued:

> "The Crown say, on the contrary, his conviction demonstrates that he was someone with a particular side to his character, which included having a sexual interest in boys and being inclined to act pursuant to that interest, even to the extent of buggery . . . "

The judge then left the 1985 conviction for the jury's consideration in two further issues: if the applicant did have that side to his character, it potentially made it more likely that he committed the 1978 offences, and it was also relevant to whether the identified man with convictions for child sexual abuse was the perpetrator rather than the applicant.

---

[19] Gross indecency with a child under 14, contrary to s.1(1) of the Indecency with Children Act 1960, and buggery of a person under the age of 21, contrary to s.12 of the Sexual Offences Act 1956.

The Court of Appeal observed that the 1978 allegations being tried by the jury were that the applicant committed violent, paedophile offences against the will of a 12 or 13-year-old victim, and none of those features formed part of the 1985 incident. Fulford L.J., giving the judgment of the Court, explained why the judge's directions involved flawed reasoning:

"During the course of oral submissions—in order to explore the relevance of the 1985 conviction—these overall circumstances were notionally transposed into a heterosexual context, and the Crown accepted that it is inconceivable that an attempt would be made to introduce the fact that a male defendant, at some stage in his past, had had lawful, consensual sexual intercourse with a female—however great the age difference between them—in support of a prosecution for violent and paedophile offences, committed against an unwilling young victim. Lawful and consensual sexual activity would simply be irrelevant in this context, regardless of whether the offender is a homosexual or heterosexual. Put otherwise, mutually agreed sexual relations between individuals over the age of consent do not, certainly without more, tend to prove that the older participant is a paedophile, who has a propensity to commit violent crimes against children."

The Court added that the applicant's assertion in interview that he had never had sexual intercourse with a man was irrelevant and could have been excluded from the interview transcripts put before the jury. Further, the 1985 conviction was of no legitimate use to the jury when assessing whether the other identified man, as opposed to the applicant, was the perpetrator.

The argument against admission was particularly strong in the case of *Laws-* **16.26H** *Chapman*. The issues are not always so clear-cut, as for example in *R. v IJ*,[20] where the Court of Appeal held that controversial evidence of a consensual homosexual affair had been properly admitted and no improper prejudice had resulted. The evidence had relevance in the light of the way the case had been run and the appellant's own evidence. The Court of Appeal acknowledged the need for an adequate direction containing powerful words to the jury designed to prevent them from using the evidence for an inadmissible or prejudicial purpose.

The appellant in that case had been convicted of sexual offences against two boys (his own son when aged between five and seven and his wife's son over a period of over 12 years between the ages of 4 and 17). During the course of the appellant's interview with the police, he was asked about his sexuality. He told them that in about 1998 or 1999 he was using homosexual internet chatrooms. This had lasted in all for some two years. As a result, he had arranged a sexual encounter with a 20-year-old man with whom he had an "affair" for "some time". As a result, he left the family home for about a year.

The defence case at trial was that there never had been inappropriate physical contact between the appellant and the two boys. The prosecution sought the admission of the unexpurgated contents of the interview. It was submitted that these were relevant to the issue whether the appellant was a man who, despite being married with children, had a sexual interest in males. It was relevant that,

[20] [2011] EWCA Crim 2734.

at the time covered by the indictment, when his step-son was aged 16 to 19, he admitted having an affair with a man aged 20. It was further submitted that the jury should hear the evidence in case they were otherwise left with a mistaken impression that the appellant was by reason of his long-term marriage exclusively heterosexual. The appellant's counsel opposed the admission of the unexpurgated interview on the grounds that it was irrelevant, or of marginal relevance, and plainly prejudicial.

The trial judge made it clear that the evidence could not go to propensity, but he ruled that it was highly relevant to prevent the jury from forming a false impression of the appellant's family life and the background against which the complaints were made. The jury ought to know that the appellant was a man with dual sexual interests, particularly as the last counts related to when the complainant was a young adult, and the appellant was having a consensual relationship with an adult at the time. Otherwise they would be likely to deal with the matter on a false basis.

The evidential picture changed after the judge's ruling. When the appellant gave evidence, contrary to the summary of his interview, he suggested that both his sons knew that he was bisexual before one of them made the complaint to the police. An argument was put forward on the appellant's behalf that it was that knowledge which became the cause of or a contributory factor leading to malicious complaints. In cross-examination, prosecution counsel challenged the appellant's assertion that he became interested in a homosexual affair only because he thought his wife was having an affair. He suggested that the appellant was in fact a closet homosexual and must have known for some years about his attraction towards the male sex.

On appeal, it was argued that this cross-examination demonstrated the extent of the prejudice which was risked by the admission of this evidence before the jury. Secondly, the suggestion that the appellant had not been entirely truthful about his homosexual activity, subject to a *Lucas* direction, could go to his credibility. The judge had added:

> "The most important thing to remember is that the fact of the defendant's homosexual activity does not affect his credibility as a witness and does not show he has a propensity to commit the offences against him.
>
> He admits to consensual homosexual activity with a 20 year old man, that is sexual activity to which they both consented. That does not show that he had a sexual interest in boys, or unwanted or forced sexual activity with boys or young men. Not every heterosexual man has an interest in young girls. Not every homosexual man has an interest in boys."

The Court of Appeal accepted that evidence of a consensual sexual relationship with a 20-year-old was not reprehensible behaviour and so the bad character regime did not apply. It followed that the issue was whether it amounted to relevant evidence under the common law. The Court followed the same line of reasoning as in *Manister*[21] in holding that a sexual attraction by one male for another is still sufficiently unusual to make that disposition relevant to the

---

[21] [2005] EWCA Crim 2844.

question whether the appellant had an innocent or a sexual association with his own male children. Nevertheless, the evidence should not have been admitted if its prejudicial effect would outweigh its probative value. The Court accepted that the probative value of the evidence in this case was modest. However, it did not conclude that the judge's decision was wrong. At the time when he decided to admit the evidence, he had been correct to conclude that it was relevant. But the Court did not agree that at that time the evidence was admissible in order to counteract any false impression which the appellant attempted to give merely by asserting in the course of his interview that he had been married for a period of 15 years.

As can happen, by the time of the summing-up the evidence was different from that anticipated at the time of the earlier ruling. By that stage, it *was* the prosecution case that the appellant had attempted to give a false picture to the jury about his committed family life, only interrupted, on his own account, by his wife's infidelity. Secondly, the prosecution said that he had attempted to turn the fact of his own sexuality into an argument that it was for this reason that false complaints had been made against him. The Court of Appeal concluded that once the evidence had been admitted, prosecution counsel was not prevented from challenging the appellant upon the terms in which he dealt with it in his own evidence-in-chief. By mounting such a challenge, prosecuting counsel was in no sense bringing about prejudice to the appellant which outweighed the relevance of the evidence.

The judge had also added that it was a matter for the jury to make a judgment whether the appellant had told the truth about the reason for his homosexual interest. If they concluded he had lied, that lie was relevant to the question whether he had given truthful evidence generally. The Court of Appeal acknowledged that a risk of prejudice must have been present without adequate directions from the judge. However, the powerful direction quoted above, which was designed to prevent the jury from using the evidence for an inadmissible or prejudicial purpose, would have drawn the sting save for the strictly limited purposes which the judge identified.

A similar point arose in *Bullas*[22] where the applicant, a trainer with St. John's **16.26I** Ambulance, was convicted of offences involving sexual abuse of five young boys who attended training sessions. The applicant denied the offences in interview, stating that he knew the complainants but nothing had occurred. He denied being homosexual and said the thought of the acts made him sick. At trial the prosecution adduced evidence from CW to the effect that when he was 17 he had a consensual relationship with the applicant when he was 21. One of the complainants also gave evidence that he had been with the applicant to a gay bar. The Court of Appeal rejected the argument that evidence tending to show that the applicant had a homosexual disposition was irrelevant as the applicant himself had put his sexual disposition in issue. The jury was entitled to hear evidence to

---

[22] [2012] EWCA Crim 1659.

contradict the applicant's denial in interview and at trial that he had any homosexual disposition and that he engaged in any homosexual acts with young boys, as the complainants had alleged. The position would be no different with a heterosexual male who, for example, sought to bolster his defence that he had not engaged in sexual intercourse with an under-age girl by asserting falsely that he had chosen to live a wholly celibate life, or because of some physical or psychological disability he was incapable of having such sexual relations with any female.

The Court of Appeal did however grant leave[23] on the ground that the trial judge should have given a direction on the lines of the strong direction approved by the Court in *R. v IJ*.[24] The Court identified a risk of prejudice only if the jury would be likely to draw an inference that evidence of homosexual disposition tended to show, by reason of that fact alone, that a defendant has a disposition to abuse young boys. The Court accepted that homosexuals have suffered historic prejudice where perhaps illogical inferences have been drawn. Kenneth Parker J. said:

> "The question arises whether in 2012 there remains a real risk that such illogical and discriminatory inferences would be drawn."

The Court accepted that in the light of *R. v IJ* it appeared that it was at least arguable that to avoid a risk of unfair prejudice, a more extensive direction should have been given.

The Court that heard the full appeal[25] concurred with Kenneth Parker J.'s encapsulation of the issue. The Court considered that there may be circumstances such as in *R. v IJ* when, to avoid prejudice arising from the admission of the evidence, it will be necessary to provide the jury with an explanation of the use to which the evidence can be put and to warn them against using it for a purpose which is unfairly prejudicial or not logically open to them. However, the Court considered that there was no risk of unfair prejudice in *Bullas*. It regarded the possibility that the jury might have jumped to the conclusion that the appellant was guilty of sexual abuse of children solely upon their finding that he was a homosexual who had been in a close and loving relationship with CW as highly improbable. There had been no scope for misunderstanding. The jury well knew, because they were so directed, that the evidence of CW was admitted to rebut the assertion as to the appellant's sexual preference which the prosecution said was false. The trial judge had made the distinction between inferences which might be drawn from a proved lie on an important issue in the case and propensity to commit sexual offences against young boys. The evidence of CW was only mentioned in connection with the lies issue, and the judge explicitly identified the need to concentrate not on the question whether the appellant was homosexual, but on the issue whether he had committed offences against the complainants.

---

[23] At the time of writing it is not clear whether the appeal was pursued and/or whether it was successful.

[24] Above, fn.20 at [44] per Pitchford L.J.

[25] [2012] EWCA Crim 2451.

Section 101(1)(f)—evidence to correct a false impression given by the defendant

In *R. v D, P and U*[26] the Court of Appeal observed that in their Lordships' **16.46** experience, gateway (f) is "too often invoked". First, a defendant who has on proper analysis done no more than deny the offence is not by doing so giving a false impression to the court for the purposes of gateway (f). If that were true, virtually every defendant would be within the gateway. Gateway (f) and s.105 of the CJA 2003 are in broad terms concerned with attempts to mislead the court in a way which goes beyond denying the offence, even if the offence subsequently be proved. The Court held that the judge in *D* had been wrong to admit evidence of the appellant's internet searches for child pornography on the basis that the appellant's denial that he had an interest in teenage girls and his claim that his relationship with his niece was honourable had created a false impression which needed to be corrected.

Furthermore, the false impression must be one which is given *to the court*: see s.105(1)(a). It may be given via a police interview, but only if that interview is given in evidence: see s.105(2)(b). If, however, the defendant withdraws the impression or dissociates himself from it, gateway (f) ceases to apply: see s.105(3). In *P*, the trial judge had ignored the effect of s.105(1)(a) and (3) in that she had been invited on the appellant's behalf to edit the passage in the interview where the appellant had stated that he preferred females. This would have withdrawn any false impression. The judge overlooked the fact that a defendant is entitled to disassociate himself from what he said earlier in interview.

The Court also said that if evidence is admissible only under gateway (f) and not also under gateway (d), considerable care is required in summing up because the jury must be warned that the evidence is not capable of being used as evidence of propensity.

See also cases on the relevance of homosexual sexual disposition, discussed in para.16.26H et seq., above.

Section 101(1)(g)—the defendant has made an attack on another person's character

In *R. v D, P, and U*[27] the issue arose as to whether the judge had properly admitted **16.50** the evidence of child pornography in the trial of *D* as the appellant had made an attack upon another's character. The appellant had asserted to the police, and maintained at trial, that far from abusing his niece, he had to discourage her when she made inappropriate approaches to him. The Court of Appeal was satisfied that gateway (g) had been opened. The judge did not direct the jury on this gateway but, as he had explained the potential relevance of the evidence under gateway (d), that omission was of no assistance to the appellant.

---

[26] [2011] EWCA Crim 1474, at [21] per Hughes L.J.
[27] Last note.

16.54 *Benabbou*[28] is a recent example of a case where, although the evidence of a previous offence of rape was technically admissible, the Court of Appeal held that it should not have been admitted in evidence as its admission must have been highly prejudicial to the fairness of the proceedings. Reliance was placed upon s.101(3) of the CJA 2003. In *Benabbou* the appellant was tried in respect of offences of sexual assault and assault by penetration. The allegations related to wholly separate episodes and different complainants. The first alleged offence was said to have occurred after an impromptu party at a flat where the complainant was sleeping. The second allegation related to events at a flat after the appellant had played "truth or dare" with the complainant and her partner. His defence to the first allegation was that nothing had happened between him and the complainant and he was the victim of a false identification. His defence to the second was that nothing had happened between himself and the complainant and the allegation was being made by the complainant and her partner because they had stolen £100 in cash and his mobile phone.

At trial, the prosecution applied successfully to adduce evidence that in 2002 the appellant had been convicted of rape, in order to demonstrate a propensity on his part to commit offences of the kind with which he was now charged. The victim on that occasion, described as a drunk lesbian female, was stopped in the street by two offenders, one being the appellant. She was pulled into a car and driven to a house where she was raped in turn by the two offenders whilst a third person held her down.

The defence had submitted that the rape conviction should not be admitted. It was a single offence committed some eight years before the two offences now being tried. The circumstances of the rape were markedly different. On the earlier occasion the appellant had not been acting alone but as one of three offenders. The victim had been a complete stranger. She had been encountered in the street and taken in a vehicle to a place in which she had been raped not once but twice and with the co-operation of a third party. The only truly common feature was that the earlier rape constituted an assault of a sexual nature.

The prosecution contended that there were similarities between the earlier rape and the alleged offences in that each was an opportunistic offence committed at night in relation to a young woman who was vulnerable because she was either drunk or asleep.

The judge concluded that there was sufficient similarity between the earlier rape and the current offences, in particular the assault by penetration, to render evidence of it admissible. Maddison J., giving the judgment of the Court of Appeal, stated that, though the rape bore some similarities to the current offences, they were limited and there were also dissimilarities. It followed that the probative value of the earlier rape in establishing propensity was limited. Although it was technically admissible under gateway (d), the admission of the evidence must have

---

[28] [2012] EWCA Crim 3088.

had a highly prejudicial effect upon the fairness of the trial. The circumstances of the offence, involving as it did participation in a multiple rape of a vulnerable stranger picked up in a street, was in the Court's view such as potentially to distract the jury from considering and indeed blind them to the issues in the case.

The Court of Appeal's conclusion in *Benabbou* was, as Maddison J. pointed out, very much a decision on the particular facts of that case involving questions of fact and degree. As Rose L.J. stated in *Hanson*, circumstances demonstrating probative force are not confined to those showing striking similarity. The decision is, however, a reminder of the potential prejudice of admitting evidence of a previous offence of a more serious nature than the allegations at the trial.

Section 101(4) of the Act provides that when a court is determining whether to **16.54A** exclude evidence of bad character under s.101(3) it must have regard in particular to the length of time between the events said to constitute the bad character evidence and the offences with which the defendant is charged. In *Imiela*[29] the Court of Appeal upheld convictions of rape, indecent assault and buggery which were alleged to have occurred on Christmas Day 1987. In March 2003 the applicant was convicted of a number of offences of rape which had occurred in 2001 or 2002. As a consequence of his conviction of these rapes, the applicant's DNA was obtained and retained upon a police database. Some years went by, and after a cold case review it was discovered that the DNA in the semen taken from the 1987 complainant's vagina and anus matched the applicant's DNA. The match probability was one in a billion. When in 2010 the applicant was first interviewed under caution about this matter, after comprehensive disclosure, he declined to answer any questions put to him. In the applicant's defence statement, he admitted for the first time that he had engaged in vaginal and oral intercourse with the complainant, but claimed it was consensual. In the same statement he denied that anal intercourse had taken place.

At trial, the prosecution applied under s.101(1)(d) to adduce evidence of the applicant's 2003 convictions for rape on the basis that it showed he had a propensity to commit such crimes. The prosecution also alleged that the circumstances of the offences leading to the rape convictions bore strong similarities to those surrounding the alleged attack upon the 1987 complainant. The evidence was relevant to the issue of consent. The prosecution also submitted that it was relevant to rebut the suggestion that the buggery had not taken place.

The applicant's counsel sought leave to appeal from the full Court of Appeal on the basis of the time that had elapsed between 1987 (the time of the allegation) and 2001 or 2002 (the time of the rape convictions). The Court held that the evidence of the later convictions was properly admitted, and the admission of the convictions would not have had such an adverse effect upon the fairness of the trial that they ought to have been excluded. In particular, the Court acknowledged that

[29] [2013] EWCA Crim 2171.

the intervening years amounted to a significant period, but observed that the applicant had been in prison serving sentences for serious offences for some of that time, which drew some of the sting in the point made by the applicant that a long time had lapsed between the relevant offences. There could not be any criticism of the summing-up whatsoever. The trial judge had given directions about the probative value of the convictions and the caution with which the jury should proceed in relation to those convictions in trenchant terms.

In written grounds of appeal, reliance had been placed upon the fact that the evidence relating to the convictions for rape in 2003 was presented to the jury by adducing witness statements of the complainants in those cases. The judge declined a defence request that the witnesses should be brought to court for cross-examination. The Court of Appeal gave this point short shrift. In the applicant's trial in 2003 there was no dispute but that each of the complainants had been raped. The defence was mistaken identity. The Court was unable to see why the complainants from the 2003 case were necessary live witnesses to describe events about which essentially there was no dispute.

CROSS-ADMISSIBILITY AND BAD CHARACTER

Cross-admissibility and the danger of collusion and/or unconscious influence

16.75   In *N(H) v R.*[30] the Court of Appeal considered the necessity for the jury to exclude collusion or innocent contamination as an explanation for the similarity of complaints in any case where the evidence of the complainants is treated as cross-admissible, before they can assess the force of the argument that they are unlikely to be the product of coincidence. The Court concluded that, save in an obvious case, in which the evidence has plainly excluded the risk of collusion and innocent contamination and no point is taken on behalf of the defendant, a direction to the jury will be required. Where, however, the evidence is not treated as cross--admissible, the need to provide the jury with guidance upon the risk of collusion and/or contamination will depend upon the particular circumstances of the case.

16.75A   Where there is no evidence from which a jury could reasonably conclude that innocent contamination could be an explanation for the complaints, there is no necessity for a warning, as there is no duty upon a judge to address the jury about hypothetical possibilities. In *N(H) v R.* the Court examined in detail the evidence given at trial and the conduct of the defence. The appeal did not concern allegations of historic abuse which, in consequence of possible repetition in the household, or by other innocent means, could have become the learned memory of the complainants. The case put to the complainants was that S's evidence was lies, driven not by a wish to tell the truth but by misplaced loyalty to her mother,

---

[30] [2011] EWCA Crim 730.

and the evidence of L and A was solely motivated by dishonest support for S. It was a case where, as the lines were drawn between the prosecution and the defence, there was no room for innocent contamination. Furthermore, this was not a case where there was a risk of collusion between the witnesses which may have become obscured by the passage of time. The appellant's counsel was unable to demonstrate to the Court a route by which the jury could have sensibly concluded that, while the witnesses had not deliberately put their heads together, they may have learned the complaints they made shortly afterwards.

To similar effect is *R. v K*,[31] a case concerning allegations of abuse dating back to **16.75B** the 1970s by two brothers who were neighbours of the appellant. In that case the battleground was drawn between honest attempted recollection by mature adults of incidents many years past in their teenage years and deliberate dishonesty, said to be at the behest of an ex-partner. The judge had directed the jury to consider each allegation separately without directing them on cross-admissibility. The Court of Appeal held that issue of innocent collusion or contamination did not arise and so there was no merit in the argument that the judge had failed properly to direct the jury of the risk surrounding possible contamination.

In *R. v AT*,[32] which involved allegations made by two sisters against their father, **16.75C** the Court of Appeal analysed how the case had been put and concluded that innocent contamination was not, realistically, a feature arising in the case; accordingly, no direction on innocent contamination had been necessary. Again, *Coull*[33] is an example of a sex case with multiple complainants where close analysis of the evidence revealed that the appellant had never suggested deliberate or innocent contamination. The judge's directions on cross-admissibility had dealt with the possibility of contamination and had focused upon the critical issue whether the complaints made by the women were truly independent of each other.

In many cases involving family or friends, it is inevitable that the complainants will **16.75D** have had the opportunity to discuss their respective allegations and they may have done so. However, the fact that complainants are close and know each other well does not mean that their complaints are not independent of each other. As Davis L.J. put it in *R. v AT*[34]:

> "It is not the position in sex abuse cases that where two (or more) siblings have had the opportunity to discuss matters (and, indeed, have discussed matters) between themselves, then necessarily their evidence never can be pooled or treated as supportive, the one of the other".

---

[31] [2008] EWCA Crim 3301; [2009] Crim. L.R. 517.
[32] [2013] EWCA Crim 1850.
[33] [2012] EWCA Crim 2893.
[34] Above, fn.32 at [91].

16.75E   In *R. v PR*[35] the appellant had been convicted on 24 counts relating to sexual offences (indecent assault and incest) committed against his two daughters. The judge had given a conventional direction on cross-admissibility explaining the extent to which the evidence of one complainant could support the evidence of the other. He asked the jury to bear in mind that the mere fact that some discussion had taken place or might have taken place between the sisters, or that they might have heard of the nature of the other's complaint, did not automatically mean that the complaints could not be regarded as independent of the other. On appeal, it was submitted on behalf of the appellant that it was not open to the jury in this particular case to find that the complaints were independent, and that the direction on cross-admissibility should not have been given at all. The Court of Appeal rejected this argument, stating that it did not accept that the family context and the fact there had been discussions between the daughters, and between them and their mother, precluded a finding that the complaints were independent of each other. The judge's findings accorded with common sense. It was for the jury to decide whether the discussions that took place amounted to or may have amounted to collusion.

Cross-admissibility—need for counsel and trial judge to consider the issue before summing up

16.76A   An examination of recent Court of Appeal judgments in sex cases involving multiple allegations and/or defendants reveals that in a number of cases the issue of cross-admissibility was not properly addressed before speeches. In *R. v SW*[36] the Court of Appeal expressed surprise and disappointment that the prosecution considered that the rape allegations ought to be tried with the balance of the indictment when the gulf between the rape and the other allegations was very wide in terms of harm, of culpability and of intervening period. Rafferty L.J., giving the judgment of the Court, indicated that each member of the Court would unhesitatingly have ordered severance of the rape counts. The trial judge had been confronted with an apparent agreement between counsel. There had been no detailed discussion of the issue of cross-admissibility, and the judge had given a direction on cross-admissibility in its widest possible form without giving the jury particular guidance as to how to treat the evidence of various complainants on the various counts. Furthermore, he had not stressed the great gulf in seriousness between the first three counts (the rape allegations) and the remaining counts. The Court of Appeal concluded that the verdicts were unsafe, as the judge's directions did not give the jury proper assistance on the all-important issue of cross-admissibility.

16.76B   There may be cases where, because of the strong similarity between the allegations made by separate complainants, there is a significant risk that the jury will treat the

---

[35] [2010] EWCA Crim 2741.
[36] [2011] EWCA Crim 2463.

allegations as cross-admissible even in the face of a direction to give each count separate consideration. Although, at first blush, a direction to give separate consideration would seem in these circumstances to be overly favourable to the defence, there may be a risk that otherwise the jury will treat the allegations as cross-admissible without the protection of a direction as to the appropriate approach. It will depend upon the circumstances whether such a direction should be given.[37]

In *R. v AT*[38] the Court of Appeal stated that it was unsatisfactory that the **16.76C** relatively brief discussion between judge and counsel before speeches meant that there could not have been proper consideration of the appropriate directions to be given on matters such as (in particular) cross-admissibility. The two complainants, who were sisters, had made allegations of sexual abuse against their father, the applicant. The abuse was alleged to have occurred between 1975 and 1983 when J was aged between 6 and 13 and V between 7 and 12. Each alleged that during this period their father would frequently summon them to his bedroom when his wife was away. It was alleged that he would require each of them to take her clothes off and masturbate him to ejaculation. These allegations were covered by specimen counts, counts 1 and 4, alleging indecency with a child contrary to s.1(1) of the Indecency with Children Act 1960. The judge gave a separate treatment direction, but his invitation to "deal with counts one and four first" was suggestive of a cross-admissibility approach. Furthermore, the prosecution had adopted a similar stance in their closing speech. The Court decided, given such circumstances, that it would be appropriate for them to approach matters on the footing that the jury would have pooled the evidence of J and V, at least in considering counts 1 and 4. It is plain that the Court considered the similarities between the complainants' allegations meant that they were cross-admissible, and the applicant's counsel did not argue otherwise. In a sense, the lack of an express cross-admissibility direction potentially told against the prosecution and not the defence. However, the fact that the jury may have pooled the complainants' evidence inexorably led to the issue of collusion/contamination. On that point, the trial judge's closing remarks in the summing up had encapsulated the central issue in the case, i.e. whether J and V may have discussed matters by way of deliberate collusion so as to fabricate the allegations. Whilst conventionally, the direction might have come earlier the summing up, but it was not necessarily diminished by reason of being placed at the very end, and the convictions were accordingly held to be safe.

Where there is more than one complainant, and the complainants' evidence is not **16.76D** cross-admissible, there is no rule of law that the judge must direct the jury that the evidence of one complainant cannot be treated as proof of an allegation against the

---

[37] *R. v H* [2011] EWCA Crim 2344.
[38] [2013] EWCA Crim 1850, discussed in para.16.75C, above. See also *Suleiman (Omar Mohammed)* [2012] EWCA Crim 1569 (not a sex case) in which the Court of Appeal expressed regret that there was no discussion before speeches as to the judge's directions on the admissibility of bad character evidence.

defendant made by another complainant.[39] The supposed need for such a direction had represented the approach adopted in *R. v D*[40] in the early days of the cross-admissibility jurisprudence. However, the principles and subsequent authorities were reviewed fully by the Court of Appeal in *R. v H,*[41] where the Court of Appeal observed that the suggested direction in *R. v D* has not fared well as a ground of appeal. No complaint could be made about the giving of such a direction, but it is not required as a rule of law. Everything depends on the directions and facts of a particular case, and the danger that the jury might seek to use the evidence of one complainant as evidence of a defendant's guilt on counts concerned only with another complainant.

Cross-admissibility—whether statistical assessment of unlikelihood of coincidence required

16.76E   *Nicholson*[42] is a classic case in which a direction on cross-admissibility based upon the unlikelihood of coincidence was appropriate. In that case a pre-condition for such a direction was expert evidence as to the unlikelihood of a number of victims suffering from false memory. However, it is not the law that statistical value must be placed upon the unlikelihood of coincidence before such a direction is appropriate, although any evidence capable of narrowing a range of relevant possibilities is likely to be admissible.

The facts are instructive. The appellant was a nurse who was convicted of three counts of sexual assault upon three patients in his care whilst they were coming round from a general anaesthetic. At trial, there had been an issue as to whether the three complainants were suffering from false memories as a side effect of anaesthesia. Expert evidence was called and it was agreed that such false memories are very rare.

On appeal, an argument was mounted based on *Norris*[43] that, since proof that one complainant was not suffering from false memories did not make it statistically less likely that that the next complainant was, the rarity of false memory in recovering patients, and the unlikelihood of coincidence of false memory in these four patients, should have been treated as inadmissible by the judge to support (i) the proposition that any of the patients were not subject to false memory, or (ii) the proposition that all four were not subject to it. The Court of Appeal held that *Norris* only supported the second proposition, and the defence argument defied experience. Coincidence may be unlikely in a variety of circumstances. One was that the four independent complainants were suffering from the rare phenomenon of false memory of sexual assault. The jury was just as entitled, when considering

[39] *R. v F* [2005] EWCA Crim 3217, at [22] per Scott Baker L.J.
[40] [2004] 1 Cr. App. R.(S.) 19.
[41] [2011] EWCA Crim 2344, at [31] per Rix L.J.; see also the judgment of Spencer J. in the recent case of *Sanderson* [2013] EWCA Crim 2037, an application for leave to appeal in which the Court of Appeal took the view that such a direction could not have been usefully given without causing confusion and potentially undermining the force of the defence case.
[42] [2012] EWCA Crim 1568.
[43] [2009] EWCA Crim 2697.

the evidence of any of the complainants, to have regard to the unlikelihood of a cluster of false memories as they would have been entitled, if the appellant's assertion had been that they had been lying, to have regard to the unlikelihood of the coincidence that they were all liars.

Before the jury could be entitled to have regard to the unlikelihood of a cluster of victims of false memory, there would have to be, as there was in this case, expert evidence that the coincidence was indeed unlikely, because the jury would not have experience of that matter. What the jury could not do was, on the basis of coincidence, leap to the conclusion that all four complainants were giving true accounts rather than false memories. What was required was an examination of the evidence relevant to each count separately and a separate conclusion upon the reliability of each complainant's memory. In reaching that conclusion upon the evidence relevant to each count, the jury was entitled to have in mind the rarity of false memory and, if they so concluded, the unlikelihood of the coincidence. It followed that the judge had not been wrong to direct the jury that when assessing the evidence of each complainant, they could have regard to the evidence of the other complainants (and a similar incident admitted as bad character evidence), when deciding whether a complainant was suffering from a false memory, on the basis that they could consider the unlikelihood of coincidence that four women should each have had false memories of sexual interference in the same hospital in similar circumstances in the relevant period. The judge had made it clear to the jury that that, while the evidence of one complainant might be treated as supportive of another, they were not entitled to lump the evidence together to reach a blanket conclusion on all the counts. Following the judge's direction, there was no prospect that the jury might have fallen into the trap of reasoning improperly so as to reach the conclusion that the rarity of the coincidence disproved the defence on all three counts, without examining the evidence on each count separately.

NON-DEFENDANT'S BAD CHARACTER

Notwithstanding the assumption contained in s.109 of the CJA 2003 as to the **16.77** truth of the evidence for the purposes of determining admissibility, in many cases it will be inappropriate to ask a witness questions about mere allegations, as opposed to convictions or cautions, as the s.100 criteria will not be established. In *Dizaei*[44] the question arose as to whether, in the context of the bad character of a non-defendant, there is an exclusionary discretion to avoid satellite litigation. Lord Judge C.J., giving the judgment of the Court, made it clear that if the judge is satisfied that the pre-conditions of admissibility are satisfied, there is no such discretion.[45] However, the assumption in s.109 is not determinative of the admissibility question. It provides the context in which the admissibility decision falls to be made. The bare fact of an allegation (even if assumed to be true) is not

---

[44] [2013] EWCA Crim 88.
[45] At [35].

necessarily conclusive of the question whether it constitutes evidence of substantial probative value or evidence of substantial importance in the context of the case as a whole (the s.100 criteria). If evidence sought to be introduced at trial about the bad character of a witness requires investigation of a nature which may be liable to distract the attention of the jury from the crucial issue, which is whether the case against the defendant has been proved, that may be a relevant consideration bearing on the assessment of the probative value of the evidence and its importance in the overall context of the case. When the court is assessing the probative value of evidence of the bad character of a witness in accordance with the s.100 criteria, among the factors relevant to the admissibility judgment, it should reflect on whether the admission of the evidence might make it more difficult for the jury to understand the remainder of the evidence, and whether its understanding of the case as a whole might be diminished. In such cases the conclusion may be that the evidence is not of substantial probative value in establishing the propensity or lack of credit worthiness of the witness, or that the evidence is not of substantial importance in the context of the case as a whole, or both. If so, the pre-conditions to admissibility will not be established.

CHAPTER 17

ANONYMITY IN SEX CASES AND REPORTING RESTRICTIONS RELATING TO CHILDREN AND YOUNG PERSONS

INTRODUCTION

For anonymity of defendants in sex cases, see para.17.25, below. **17.04**

Section 4(2) of the Contempt of Court Act 1981 has no role to play in protecting **17.06**
the identities of complainants of sexual offences. Section 4(2) provides:

> "In any [legal proceedings held in public] the court may, where it appears necessary
> for avoiding a substantial risk of prejudice to the administration of justice in those
> proceedings, or in any other proceedings pending or imminent, order that the
> publication of any report of the proceedings, or any part of the proceedings, be
> postponed for such period as the court thinks necessary for that purpose."

In *R. (Press Association) v Cambridge Crown Court*[1] the trial judge, in response to
expressions of concern by prosecuting counsel at the sentencing hearing that
reporting of the defendant's name would compromise the complainant's anonymity, initially purported to make an order under s.4(2) imposing an indefinite
prohibition on the publication of "anything relating to the name of the defendant
which could lead to the identification of the complainant". Shortly afterwards, he
was persuaded by a representative of the local press that s.4(2) did not apply and
he purported instead to make an order in similar terms under s.1(2) of the Sexual
Offences (Amendment) Act 1992 ("1992 Act"), as to which see para.17.12,
below.

    On appeal by the Press Association against both orders, the Court of Appeal
held that orders under s.4(2) are intended to avoid "a substantial risk of prejudice"
to the proceedings in which they are made, or to linked or related proceedings,
such as a subsequent trial involving the same defendants or witnesses. Examples
of the use of the power in s.4(2) can be found in prohibitions against the

---

[1] [2012] EWCA Crim 2434.

451

publication of evidence or argument before the judge in the absence of the jury and, after a successful appeal against conviction, when a new trial is ordered, to avoid prejudice to any retrial. In the *Cambridge* case, at the time of the making of the order the defendant had been tried, convicted and sentenced in public, with no order restricting publication of his identity, and there were no pending proceedings which might be prejudiced by the publication of his name. Further, as its wording suggests, s.4(2) is aimed at the postponement of publication rather than a permanent ban. An order prohibiting publication for an indefinite period carries with it the natural inference that publication has not simply been postponed, but permanently banned. Accordingly, s.4(2) was, as the judge had swiftly recognised, inapt for the making of the initial order.

It follows that an order may be made under s.4(2) protecting a defendant's identity only where it is necessary temporarily to prevent publication of his identity in order to avoid prejudice to the trial or other pending proceedings. Such an order cannot be made simply in order to protect the identity of a complainant.

17.06A   The Court added for completeness a reference to s.11 of the Contempt of Court Act 1981, which provides:

> "In any case where a court (having the power to do so) allows a name or other matter to be withheld from the public in proceedings before the court, the court may give such directions prohibiting the publication of that name or matter in connection with the proceedings as appear to the court to be necessary for the purpose for which it was so withheld."

The Court said that this section plainly could not have been relied on as the foundation for the initial order, as it does not arise for consideration unless the court, having the power to do so, withholds the name or other matter from the public in the proceedings before it (citing *R. v Arundel Justices Ex p. Westminster Press Limited*[2] and in *Re Trinity Mirror Plc*[3]). It followed that an order such as that made in the *Cambridge* case can only be made on the basis of s.11 if the name of the defendant has been withheld throughout the proceedings.

ANONYMITY OF COMPLAINANTS IN SEX CASES

The Sexual Offences (Amendment) Act 1992

17.10   It is important to note that there is no anonymity protection for the victim of a sexual offence once they are deceased. This no doubt reflects the primary purpose of according anonymity, namely to spare the victim the indignity and potential harm of being identified as such and so avoid the risk that this could deter them

---

[2] [1985] 1 W.L.R. 708.
[3] [2008] Q.B. 770.

from coming forward. It might be argued that neither rationale applies once the victim is deceased. However, it is conceivable that in at least some circumstances knowledge that they would forfeit their anonymity on death could deter individuals from coming forward, most obviously if they have reason to believe that they may not have long to live. Further, making anonymity permanent would not cause significant additional prejudice to the public interest in open justice. We would favour this modest adjustment to the law should the opportunity arise to make it.

As noted in para.17.02, above, in *R. (Press Association) v Cambridge Crown Court*,[4] **17.12** the trial judge, in response to expressions of concern by prosecuting counsel at the sentencing hearing that reporting of the defendant's name would compromise the complainant's anonymity, purported to make an order under s.1(2) of the 1992 Act imposing an indefinite prohibition on the publication of "anything relating to the name of the defendant which could lead to the identification of the complainant". On appeal by the Press Association, the Court of Appeal held that s.1(2) confers no power to make such an order:

"Section 1 confers lifelong anonymity on complainants in cases which involve sexual offences to which the 1992 Act applies. What however cannot be found in the Act is the conferring of any express power on the court to make an order restricting publication of the defendant's name in order to protect or enforce a complainant's right to anonymity. There are, as it seems to us, a number of difficulties in reading any such power into the 1992 Act. First, the absence of an express power to make such an order is telling. All the more so, given that the only express power to make an order impacting on the complainant's right to anonymity under s.1 is conferred by s.3, which provides that the judge may give a direction which lifts the anonymity of the complainant in a number of carefully defined situations where the interests of justice so require. Second, on the face of it there is no need for any such power. The complainant enjoys the protection provided by s.1, and a contravention of the complainant's right to anonymity involves the commission of a criminal offence. Third, the absence of a judicial power to restrict publication provides a clear demarcation of responsibility. Decisions about what should or should not be published in a newspaper, or for that matter in the media generally, are left to editors and reporters. As we have explained, if s.1 is contravened, they face criminal prosecution. The court lacked the necessary jurisdiction. It was for the press to decide how appropriately to report the case so as to ensure the anonymity of the complainant: it was not for the court to instruct the press how to do so by making an order which in effect imposed a blanket prohibition against publication of the defendant's name."

However, the Court went on to dismiss a submission by the Press Association that for the judge to give any guidance to the press risked usurpation of the editor's discretion about what and how to publish:

"The judge is entitled to express concerns as to the possible consequences of publication, and indeed to engage in a discussion with representatives of the press present in court about these issues, whether on his own initiative, or in a response to a request from them. The judge is in charge of the court, and if he thinks it appropriate to offer comment, we anticipate that a responsible editor would carefully

[4] [2012] EWCA Crim 2434.

consider it before deciding what should be published. The essential point is that whatever discussions may take place, the judicial observations cannot constitute an order binding on the editor or the reporter."

17.16　In *R. (Press Association) v Cambridge Crown Court*[5] it was submitted that r.16.1 of the Criminal Procedure Rules confers a general power to vary, as well as to remove, the protection conferred by s.1 of the 1992 Act. The submission turned on the language of r.16.1, which states that Pt 16 of the Rules, dealing with reporting restrictions, applies "where the court can . . . vary or remove a reporting . . . restriction that is imposed by legislation". The Court of Appeal rejected the submission on the ground that r.16.1 cannot be read as providing the court with a power not conferred on it by primary legislation.

17.17　In *R. (Press Association) v Cambridge Crown Court*[6] the Court of Appeal said that s.1 of the 1992 Act:

" . . . encompasses publication of prohibited material by anyone by whatever means publication occurs, and extends to bloggers and twitterers [sic] or any other commentators."

The Court also noted that the sentence for breaches of s.1 is confined to a financial penalty, and commented:

"Whether this is always a sufficient punishment for those who deliberately breach the anonymity of the victim of sexual crime appears to us to require urgent reconsideration."

There would indeed seem to be a case, in the internet age, for courts to have the power to impose a custodial sentence for particularly egregious breaches of s.1, and it is to be hoped that the Government will find scope in the legislative programme to create such a power.

17.17A　In relation to offences by companies, see *Chargot (t/a Contract Services) & others*,[7] discussed at para.8.25, above.

ANONYMITY AND THE DEFENDANT

17.18　In *R. (Press Association) v Cambridge Crown Court*[8] the Court of Appeal suggested that there are two limited circumstances in which the Crown Court has power to order at the outset of proceedings that the defendant should not be named: where this is required in order to counter a significant threat to the interests of justice, and where the court is satisfied that there is a real and immediate risk to the life or safety of the defendant or his family. It is clear from the narrow terms used by

[5] [2012] EWCA Crim 2434.
[6] [2012] EWCA Crim 2434.
[7] [2008] UKHL 73.
[8] [2012] EWCA Crim 2434, at [18].

the court that the power to accord anonymity to a defendant on these grounds is unlikely ever to be in play where the sole concern is to protect an alleged victim of a sexual offence committed by the defendant from the indignity and humiliation of being named.

In a Commons debate on the Coalition Government's commitment to extend   **17.25** anonymity to rape defendants, held on July 8, 2010, the Justice Minister, Crispin Blunt MP, said that the Government had asked the director of analytical services in the Ministry of Justice to produce "an independent assessment of the current research and statistics on defendant anonymity in rape cases". He indicated that the report would be published in the final week of July 2010 and would cover all the available research and statistics.[9] The report, *Providing anonymity to those accused of rape: an assessment of evidence*, was eventually published in November 2010.[10] It brought together and summarised available evidence relevant to the debate about extending anonymity to rape defendants, drawing on official statistics and findings from primary research studies conducted in the UK and, in some cases, North America, as well as other evidence reviews. The report's headline conclusion was that there was insufficient reliable empirical evidence on which to base an informed decision as to the value of anonymity for rape defendants.

Announcing the report's publication, Mr Blunt said that the Government was dropping its plans to introduce anonymity for such defendants as there was insufficient evidence to support them:

> "The assessment has found insufficient reliable empirical evidence on which to base an informed decision on the value of providing anonymity to rape defendants. Evidence is lacking in a number of key areas, in particular, whether the inability to publicise a person's identity will prevent further witnesses to a known offence from coming forward, or further unknown offences by the same person from coming to light.
>
> The coalition Government made it clear from the outset that they would proceed with defendant anonymity in rape cases only if the evidence justifying it was clear and sound, and in the absence of any such finding they have reached the conclusion that the proposal does not stand on its merits. It will not, therefore, be proceeded with further."[11]

The Government has not sought to re-introduce its proposals. It seems highly unlikely to do so in light of the recent, much-reported cases involving sexual offences committed or allegedly committed over many years by well-known public figures, including the broadcasters Jimmy Savile and Stuart Hall, in which significant numbers of victims came forward after publicity was given to other

---

[9] *Hansard*, HC Vol.513, col.559 (July 8, 2010).

[10] Ministry of Justice Research Series 20/10, available at *http://www.justice.gov.uk/downloads/ publications/research-and-analysis/moj-research/anonymity-rape-research-report.pdf* [accessed December 1, 2013]. For a discussion of the report, see Philip N.S. Rumsey and Rachel Anne Fenton, *Rape, defendant anonymity and evidence-based policy making*, M.L.R. 2013, 76(1), 109–133.

[11] *Hansard*, HL Vol.722, cols 27–28 WS (November 12, 2010).

allegations.[12] Defendant anonymity in sex cases does, however, still have proponents in positions of authority, such as Maura McGowan QC, then Chairman of the Bar Council, who in early 2013 said in a radio interview that defendants should have the same anonymity as complainants as charges of sexual offences carry "such stigma".[13] Her comments provoked immediate and strong rebuttals,[14] indicating that the subject remains contentious. See further on this subject Clare McGlynn, *Rape, Defendant Anonymity and Human Rights: Adopting a "Wider Perspective"* [2011] Crim. L.R. 199, and David Wolchover and Anthony Heaton-Armstrong, *Rape Defendant Anonymity*, 176 C.L. & J. 5 and 24.

17.26   There has been heated debate during the last year or so about the varying approaches of different police forces to the naming of persons arrested on suspicion of child sexual offences. The controversy has stemmed from the police investigation of historic allegations against well-known public figures, including the broadcasters Jimmy Savile, Stuart Hall and Rolf Harris, which have provoked intense media interest. As noted in the main work, ACPO guidance has for some time been that persons should be anonymous before charge. However, this guidance has frequently been honoured more in the breach than in the observance. In light of the varying approaches taken by different police forces, the Home Secretary wrote to the College of Policing in May 2013 stating her belief that there should be a right to anonymity on arrest, save in highly unusual circumstances where the public interest requires an arrested person to be named, but no right to anonymity on charge. She invited the College to work up new guidance to make the position clear.[15] There had already been media reports that ACPO was considering issuing new guidance, effectively re-iterating its current position that UK police forces should not confirm the names of arrested individuals to the media.[16] The draft guidance reportedly states that "save in exceptional and clearly

---

[12] The Metropolitan Police are investigating alleged sexual abuse, predominantly of children, by Savile (who died in 2011) and others under Operation Yewtree. The investigation started in October 2012 and, after a period of assessment, became a full criminal investigation involving inquiries into living people as well as Savile. In December 2012 the Metropolitan Police stated that there had been 589 alleged victims, 450 of whom alleged abuse by Savile. Stuart Hall, having initially issued a full-throated denial, pleaded guilty in April 2013 to sexually abusing 13 girls aged between 9 and 17 in the period 1967–1986. He was subsequently charged with further historic sexual offences.

[13] *http://www.bbc.co.uk/news/uk-21487266* [accessed December 1, 2013]. See also *http://www.guardian.co.uk/media/2013/apr/21/press-intrusion-name-suspects* [accessed December 1, 2013], quoting to similar effect the Conservative MP Robert Buckland and Frances Crook, Chief Executive of the Howard League for Penal Reform.

[14] See, e.g. *http://www.northumbria-pcc.gov.uk/node/160* (by Vera Baird, formerly Solicitor General and now Police and Crime Commissioner for Northumbria) [accessed December 1, 2013]; *http://www.politics.co.uk/comment-analysis/2013/02/19/comment-anonymity-for-rape-defendants-is-a-tired-argument-th* (by Holly Dustin, Director of the End Violence Against Women Coalition) [accessed December 1, 2013].

[15] See *http://www.bbc.co.uk/news/uk-22548065* [accessed December 1, 2013]. The Attorney General, by contrast, is reported to have said that, whilst the police should not be subject to "fishing expeditions" by the media, where the name of an arrested person becomes known, it would be right for them to confirm it: *The Times*, June 5, 2013, p.20. Clearly, there is scope for disagreement as to when a name "becomes known" for this purpose.

[16] See, e.g. *http://www.pressgazette.co.uk/acpo-mulls-nationwide-no-names-guidance-media-inquiries-those-arrested-police* [accessed December 1, 2013].

identified circumstances, the names or identifying details of those who are arrested or suspected of a crime should not be released by police forces to the press or the public". Exceptional circumstances are said to include a threat to life, the prevention or detection of crime, or a matter of significant public interest and confidence. However, the draft guidance makes clear that all suspects should be named when they are charged with an offence. We welcome this ACPO initiative as a response to the current debate, though one cannot be optimistic that the new guidance will put a stop to leaks or their widespread reporting, including on social networking sites.

Separately, the Law Commission has been consulting on proposals to refine the law of contempt in which it calls for "greater certainty and consistency" in the way that police forces release information about those arrested.[17] Contrary to the line favoured by the Home Secretary and ACPO, it proposed that suspects should generally be identified following a media request. It said:

> "We propose that the Home Office request that the Association of Chief Police Officers issue guidance, for dissemination to police forces, which would encourage the police to adopt consistent decision-making about whether to release information about arrestees following a request from the media to identify the arrestee. We consider that such policy should establish that, generally, the names of arrestees will be released, but that appropriate safeguards will need to be put in place to ensure that some names are withheld, for example, where it would lead to the unlawful identification of a complainant, where the arrestee is a youth or where an ongoing investigation may be hampered."

However, in responding to the consultation on behalf of the senior judiciary, Treacey L.J. and Tugendhat J. reflected the orthodox line by expressing a preference for withholding the identification of those arrested save in exceptional circumstances.[18] They commented[19]:

> "If there were a policy that the police should consistently publish the fact that a person has been arrested, in many cases that information would attract substantial publicity, causing irremediable damage to the person's reputation."

The two judges adopted the following extract from Sir Brian Leveson's *Report on the Culture, Practice and Ethics of the Press*[20]:

> "[T]he current guidance in this area needs to be strengthened. For example, I think that it should be made abundantly clear that save in exceptional and clearly identified circumstances (for example, where there may be an immediate risk to the public), the names or identifying details of those who are arrested or suspected of a crime should not be released to the press nor the public."

---

[17] *Contempt of Court*, Law Commission Consultation Paper No.209 (TSO, 2012), para.2.20. See http://lawcommission.justice.gov.uk/docs/cp209_contempt_of_court.pdf [accessed December 1, 2013].

[18] *Contempt of Court: A Judicial response to Law Commission Consultation Paper No.209* (March 4, 2013). See http://www.judiciary.gov.uk/Resources/JCO/Documents/Consultations/sen-judiciary-response-to-law-comm-on-contempt-court.pdf [accessed December 1, 2013].

[19] At para.5.

[20] *Leveson Inquiry: Culture, Practice and Ethics of the Press* (TSO, 2013) at G, Ch.3, para.2.39. The report can be downloaded at http://www.official-documents.gov.uk/document/hc1213/hc07/0780/0780.asp [accessed December 1, 2013].

REPORTING RESTRICTIONS RELATING TO CHILDREN AND YOUNG PERSONS

Restrictions on Identification of Child or Young Person by Media: The Current Law

Children "concerned in" proceedings: s.39 of the Children and Young Persons Act 1933

17.30   As noted in the main work, s.39 has been extended from newspaper reports to television and sound broadcast services and digital sound programme services, and to reports or matters included in them.[21] However, in *MXB v East Sussex Hospitals MHS Trust*,[22] Tugendhat J. said there was force in the argument that s.39 does not prohibit the making of a report by other means. We suggest this argument is indeed correct, and in particular that internet reports are within the scope of the section only if they are carried on streamed television or radio broadcasts or, perhaps, in a newspaper's on-line coverage, but not, for example, if they appear on social media sites such as Facebook and Twitter. The *MXB* case involved the settlement of a damages claim where there was a perceived risk that the funds paid out under the settlement would be misused to the detriment of the complainant. Tugendhat J. therefore felt able to impose reporting restrictions to protect the claimant's identity under r.39.2(4) of the Civil Procedure Rules,[23] which states:

> "The court may order that the identity of any party or witness must not be disclosed if it considers non-disclosure necessary in order to protect the interests of that party or witness."

There is, however, no similar provision in the Criminal Procedure Rules.

The Court of Appeal in *R. v Jolleys (Robert), Ex p. Press Association*[24] noted Tugendhat J.'s comments in the *MXB* case and said that orders under s.39 should be restricted to the language of the section, the proper construction of which can be considered as and when the need arises. Leveson L.J., giving the judgment of the Court, went on[25]:

> "[W]e recognise the responsible attitude adopted by the Press Association which makes it clear that it will abide by the spirit as well as the letter of section 39 and would not draw a distinction between publication in news stories or online through the mechanism of micro-blogging sites such as Twitter.[26] Any further developments in this area of the law must be for Parliament."

---

[21] Children and Young Persons Act 1963, s.57(4); Broadcasting Act 1990, ss.201, 203 and Sch.20 para.3(2).

[22] [2012] EWHC 3279 (QB).

[23] *http://www.justice.gov.uk/courts/procedure-rules/civil/rules* [accessed December 1, 2013].

[24] [2013] EWCA Crim 1135.

[25] At [19].

[26] This sentence presumably reflects submissions made to the Court by the Press Association, although this is not clear from the judgment.

The responsible attitude of the Press Association is to be commended, but it may not be shared by others who are in a position to identify child complainants, witnesses or defendants on line.

In this connection it is notable that s.45 of the Youth Justice and Criminal Evidence Act 1999 ("YJCEA 1999"),[27] which when brought into force will replace s.39, applies to "any publication". This term is defined by s.63(1) of the YJCEA 1999 to include "any speech, writing, relevant programme or other communication in whatever form, which is addressed to the public at large or any section of the public". This definition is, we suggest, fully adequate cover publication on the internet, including on social media sites, and for that reason we hope s.45 is brought into force as quickly as possible.

Factors relevant to the decision whether to make or discharge an order under s.39

In the main work, we suggest that in any post-Human Rights Act case in which   **17.32**
the application of s.39 is in issue, the court's decision is likely to turn on the balance between the child's rights under art.8 of the ECHR and the freedom of the media to report proceedings under art.10. We remain of this view, but it is worth noting that in *R. (on the application of Y) v Aylesbury Crown Court, CPS, Newsquest Media Group Limited* [28] the Administrative Court said that, having regard to the mandatory requirement in s.44 of the Children and Young Persons Act 1933 ("1933 Act") for the court to have regard to the welfare of the child when deciding a s.39 application, it is probably unnecessary to consider art.8. Section 44 provides:

> "Every court in dealing with a child or young person who is brought before it, either as an offender or otherwise, shall have regard to the welfare of the child or young person, and shall in a proper case take steps for removing him from undesirable surroundings, and for securing that proper provision is made for his education and training."

In *R. (on the application of Y) v Aylesbury Crown Court, CPS, Newsquest Media*   **17.33**
Group Limited[29] the Administrative Court said that the onus lies on the party contending for a s.39 order to satisfy the court that there is a good reason to impose it, and that it would seem to follow that, if a court is considering whether to discharge or vary an order already made, then the party who obtained the order, if they wish to maintain it, must satisfy the court that there remains a good reason not to discharge or vary it.

For guidance on the principles involved in the application of s.39 of the 1933 Act,   **17.33A**
see para.4.2 of *Reporting Restrictions in the Criminal Courts*, published jointly by the Judicial Studies Board, the Newspaper Society, the Society of Editors and Times

---

[27] See para.17.53 of the main work.
[28] [2012] EWHC 1140 (Admin), at [41].
[29] Last note, citing *Lee* (1993) 96 Cr. App. R. 188.

Newspapers Ltd in October 2009.[30] In his Foreword to the document, the then Lord Chief Justice, Sir Igor (now Lord) Judge, said that it was designed as a "practical guide which would provide rapid answers to immediate problems in a form to which both the judiciary and the magistracy and the media could refer with equal confidence for authoritative guidance".

17.33B   The CPS has also issued guidance to prosecutors on the approach to be taken to reporting restrictions under ss.39 and 49 (Youth Courts) of the 1933 Act, which contains a useful summary of the relevant legal principles.[31]

17.34   In *R. v Winchester CC Ex p. B*[32] Simon Brown L.J. (as he then was) identified the following principles to be applied when the court is deciding whether to impose or lift restrictions under s.39 in relation to a defendant. These principles were cited with approval in *R. (A) v St Albans Crown Court Ex p. T*[33] and, most recently, in *R. (on the application of Y) v Aylesbury Crown Court, CPS, Newsquest Media Group Limited*[34]:

"i) In deciding whether to impose or thereafter to lift reporting restrictions, the court will consider whether there are good reasons for naming the defendant;

ii) In reaching that decision, the court will give considerable weight to the age of the offender and to the potential damage to any young person of public identification as a criminal before the offender has the benefit or burden of adulthood;

iii) By virtue of section 44 of the 1933 Act, the court must 'have regard to the welfare of the child or young person';

iv) The prospect of being named in court with the accompanying disgrace is a powerful deterrent and the naming of a defendant in the context of his punishment serves as a deterrent to others. These deterrents are proper objectives for the court to seek;

v) There is a strong public interest in open justice and in the public knowing as much as possible about what has happened in court, including the identity of those who have committed crime;

vi) The weight to be attributed to the different factors may shift at different stages of the proceedings and, in particular, after the defendant has been found, or pleads, guilty and is sentenced. It may then be appropriate to place greater weight on the interest of the public in knowing the identity of those who have committed crimes, particularly serious and detestable crimes;

vii) The fact that an appeal has been made may be a material consideration."

---

[30] *http://www.judiciary.gov.uk/Resources/JCO/Documents/Guidance/crown_court_reporting_restrictions_021009.pdf* [accessed December 1, 2013]. Paragraph 4.2 was quoted extensively and described as "helpful" in *R. (on the application of Y) v Aylesbury Crown Court, CPS, Newsquest Media Group Limited*, above, fn.28 at [29]–[31].

[31] *Reporting Restrictions – Children and Young People as Victims, Witnesses and defendants, http://www.cps.gov.uk/legal/p_to_r/reporting_restrictions/* [accessed December 1, 2013]. This guidance replaced an earlier version referred to as "very useful" in *R. (on the application of Y) v Aylesbury Crown Court, CPS, Newsquest Media Group Limited*, above, fn.28 at [12].

[32] [2000] 1 Cr. App. R. 11.

[33] [2002] EWHC 1129 (Admin), at [20].

[34] [2012] EWHC 1140 (Admin), at [26].

In *Aylesbury*[35] the Administrative Court went on describe the way in which a court   17.34A
should approach an application by a defendant to restrict publication under
s.39:

> "The defendant will have to satisfy the court that there is a good reason to impose it.
> This is probably an evaluative exercise and would not involve the application of any
> burden or standard of proof (unless perhaps there is a factual dispute) . . .
>
> In most cases the good reason upon which the defendant child or young person will
> rely is his or her welfare. Section 44 of the Children and Young Persons Act 1933
> requires the court to have regard to his or her welfare when deciding a section 39
> application. Having regard to the mandatory requirement of section 44, it is probably
> unnecessary to consider Article 8.
>
> Because the defendant is a child or young person and not an adult, his or her future
> progress may well be assisted by restricting publication. Publication could well have a
> significant effect on the prospects and opportunities of the young person, and,
> therefore, on the likelihood of effective integration into society. Identifying a
> defendant in the media may constitute an additional and disproportionate punishment
> on the child or young person. In rare cases (and not in this case) the child or young
> person may be at serious personal risk if identified.
>
> In reaching the decision upon an application by a defendant to restrict publication
> under section 39, the court must, in addition to having regard to the welfare of the
> child, have regard to the public interest and to Article 10 of the ECHR.
>
> Amongst the possible public interests is the public interest in knowing the outcome
> of proceedings in court and the public interest in the valuable deterrent effect that the
> identification of those guilty of at least serious crimes may have on others.
>
> In so far as Article 10 is concerned . . . any order restricting publication must be
> necessary, proportionate and there must be a pressing social need for it.
>
> The court must thus balance the welfare of the child or young person which is likely
> to favour a restriction on publication with the public interest and the requirements of
> Article 10 which are likely to favour no restriction on publication. Prior to conviction
> the welfare of the child or young person is likely to take precedence over the public
> interest. After conviction, the age of the defendant and the seriousness of the crime of
> which he or she has been convicted will be particularly relevant.
>
> What the court should do is to identify the factors which would favour restriction
> on publication and the factors which would favour no restriction. The court may also
> decide, as the judge did in this case, to permit the publication of some details but not
> all.
>
> If having conducted the balancing exercise between the welfare of the child or
> young person, on the one hand, and the public interest and the requirements of Article
> 10 on the other, the factors favouring a restriction on publication and the factors
> favouring publication are very evenly balanced, then it seems to us . . . that a court
> should make an order restricting publication."

In that case, the claimant, a youth of 16, pleaded guilty to a single count of arson
and was sentenced to an 8 months' detention and training order. His adult
co-defendant also pleaded guilty. The prosecution offered no evidence in relation
to other alleged arsons which, if proved, would have shown, on the prosecution's
case, a serious campaign of "revenge arson" against a number of individuals. The
claimant's identity was protected by an order made earlier under s.39. Following
sentence, the publishers of the local newspaper and the police applied to the trial
judge to lift the s.39 order. The trial judge acceded to the application in part, by

---

[35] [2012] EWHC 1140 (Admin), at [39]–[48].

461

varying the order so as to permit the publication of the claimant's name and address but not a photograph or other description of him. The judge gave two reasons for his decision: the claimant's identity was already known to local people, and the limited publication of his name and address together with the fact that he had pleaded guilty to one arson and sentenced accordingly would give him, on his release, some protection from those who thought him to have been involved in more arsons.

On the claimant's application to quash this decision, the Administrative Court said that neither of the judge's reasons was satisfactory. The fact that the defendant's identity was already known to some people in the locality was not a good reason for letting a very large number of others know about it. Secondly, it was doubtful on the facts of the case whether it was permissible to allow publication in order, in some way, to help the claimant, particularly whilst at the same time letting many people know not only his name but also his address. In any event the judge did not, as he should have done, apply the relevant principles (as set out above) and so the Court quashed his decision and proceeded to consider the matter itself. The publishers and the police had contended that it was in the public interest to publish the claimant's name and address for the following reasons:

    i) it would deter others from committing such a grave offence;

    ii) it would be an additional necessary punishment for him;

    iii) the naming not just of one offender but of both offenders would demonstrate to the community that the police had done all that they could do in the face of a serious problem of gang-related arson and intimidation and so would restore the confidence of the community in the criminal justice system; and

    iv) the naming of not just one offender but of both offenders would encourage victims of arson attacks and other individuals, who were frightened of the repercussions of coming forward, to feel confident about coming forward and give information about some 100 other arsons.

The Court said that these were reasons for identifying the claimant which a court would be entitled to take into account, and that if the claimant had been convicted of an offence or offences which showed that he was a party to a serious campaign of revenge arson, a restriction on publication would not have been appropriate. However, he had pleaded guilty to one count of simple arson committed when he was 16. That being so, on the facts of the case the public interest in publication did not take precedence over the claimant's welfare.

The procedure to be followed in making an order under s.39

17.35 *Reporting Restrictions in the Criminal Courts*, referred to in para.17.33, above, states in para.4.2:

    "If a reporting restriction is imposed, the judge must make it clear in court that a formal order has been made. The order should use the words of section 39 and identify the child or children involved with clarity. A written copy should be drawn up as soon as possible after the order has been made orally. Copies must be available for inspection and communicated to those not present when the order was made (e.g. by inclusion in the daily list). Court staff should assist media inquiries in relation to the order."

Reporting restrictions are dealt with in r.16 of the Criminal Procedure Rules,[36] which determine the way in which a criminal case is managed as it progresses through the criminal courts in England and Wales. Rule 16.2 provides:

(1) When exercising a power to which this Part applies, as well as furthering the overriding objective, in accordance with rule 1.3, the court must have regard to the importance of—
   (a) dealing with criminal cases in public; and
   (b) allowing a public hearing to be reported to the public.
(2) The court may determine an application or appeal under this Part—
   (a) at a hearing, in public or in private; or
   (b) without a hearing.
(3) But the court must not exercise a power to which this Part applies unless each party and any other person directly affected—
   (a) is present; or
   (b) has had an opportunity—
     (i) to attend, or
     (ii) to make representations.

In *R. v Jolleys (Robert), Ex p. Press Association*[37] the Court of Appeal made it clear that if the press are not given an opportunity to make representations before an order is made under s.39, in accordance with r.16.2(3)(b)(ii), this will be a serious procedural defect that could lead to the overturning of the order. Leveson L.J., giving the judgment of the Court, said[38]:

"The requirements of open justice demand that judges are fully mindful of the underlying principles which this judgment has sought to elucidate. In most cases, the application of the law is obvious and nobody will contend to the contrary. The fact that an order has been or may be made under section 39 of the Act and is so identified in the court list is more than enough notice to the press should any reporter wish to make representations or challenge a subsisting order.

Where, however, there is the slightest doubt, or any novel approach is suggested, it should be identified in good time and notice provided as required by the Criminal Procedure Rules so that the press can also consider the matter in good time. Even then, judges cannot expect local reporters to be in a position to instruct lawyers or argue the principles in depth, and in any event counsel should be required to research and develop the arguments to assist the court in a balanced way. That is not in any way to limit the right of reporters or their lawyers to advance argument on their own behalf."

The Law Commission has been consulting on proposals to refine the law of **17.35A** contempt, including the introduction in England and Wales of a system similar to

---

[36] See *http://www.legislation.gov.uk/uksi/2013/1554/article/n16/made* [accessed December 1, 2013].
[37] [2013] EWCA Crim 1135.
[38] At [16], [20]–[21].

the one already operating in Scotland, whereby information about orders under s.4(2) of the Contempt of Court Act 1981 (postponement of reporting of proceedings) are posted online with a facility to register for electronic alerts of any new orders.[39] The Commission suggests that if such a system were successful, there may be merit in expanding it to cover orders made under s.82 of the Criminal Justice Act 2003 (restricting publicity where there is to be a retrial of a previously acquitted person) and also orders under s.39 of the 1933 Act. In responding to the consultation on behalf of the senior judiciary, Treacey L.J. and Tugendhat J. favoured the introduction of such a system, but not its extension to orders under s.39[40]:

> "[W]e would favour a scheme for making accessible on a central database the existence of s.4(2) and reporting restriction orders. We do not consider that this need include those relating to children under the Children and Young Persons Act 1933 s.39, where the need for restraint in reporting will be obvious."

With respect, this comment rather misses the point that unless the media or others are made aware of the existence of a s.39 order, they may not appreciate the need to show restraint. Further, whilst the risk of reporting in breach of such an order may in practice be low, it is not obviously lower than in relation to the other orders referred to by the Commission. We hope that if the proposed system can be introduced, it will be applied to orders under s.39.

Challenging the making or discharge of an order under s.39

17.36   In *R. (on the application of Y) v Aylesbury Crown Court, CPS, Newsquest Media Group Limited*[41] the Administrative Court said that, although doubts had been expressed on the point in the past, it seemed clear that it had jurisdiction to entertain an application for judicial review of a judge's order varying an order under s.39. Section 29(3) of the Supreme Court Act 1981 precludes judicial review "in matters relating to trail on indictment", and one might think this would include decisions as to the exercise of the discretion conferred by s.39. The point must remain open to argument, but there is now a substantial body of case law in which the Administrative Court has regarded itself as having jurisdiction.

Can an order under s.39 expressly prohibit the identification of a defendant?

17.38   *Reporting Restrictions in the Criminal Courts*, referred to in para.17.33, above, states in para.4.2 that:

---

[39] *Contempt of Court*, Law Commission Consultation Paper No.209 (TSO, 2012), paras 2.104–5. See http://lawcommission.justice.gov.uk/docs/cp209_contempt_of_court.pdf [accessed December 1, 2013].

[40] *Contempt of Court: A Judicial response to Law Commission Consultation Paper No.209* (March 4, 2013), para.26. See http://www.judiciary.gov.uk/Resources/JCO/Documents/Consultations/sen-judiciary-response-to-law-comm-on-contempt-court.pdf [accessed December 1, 2013].

[41] Above, fn.33 at [21].

"[T]here is no power [under s.39] to prohibit the publication of the names of adults involved in the proceedings or other children or young persons not involved in the proceedings as witnesses, defendants or victims. The court may, however, give guidance to the media if it considers that the naming of an adult defendant would be likely to identify a child. Such guidance is not binding. The media may, for instance, be able to name a defendant without infringing the order, if the relationship of the victim to the defendant is omitted or the nature of the offence is blurred (e.g. 'a sexual offence' rather than incest). Media codes have been aligned to assist this. See 5.5 below on jigsaw identification."

Paragraph 5.5 provides:

"Jigsaw identification refers to the phenomenon whereby the identity of a person protected by a reporting restriction order may be inadvertently disclosed as a result of different media reports, none of which breach the terms of any order or statutory provision, but which taken together enable the protected person to be identified. In most cases this is not an issue but particular difficulties arise in relation to sex offences within the same family. For example, where one report refers to an unnamed defendant convicted of raping his daughter and another refers to the name of the defendant, the daughter will be identifiable to the public in breach of the automatic prohibition protecting victims of sexual offences.

In recognition of these potential difficulties the newspapers and broadcasters have aligned their respective codes so that the media adopt a common approach when reporting sexual offences. Typically the media will name the defendant but not name the victim (this would breach the statutory prohibition) or give any details of his or her relationship with the defendant. It is routine for in-house lawyers to check what information is already in the public domain before advising on whether a report of court proceedings is likely to breach any legal requirement, so, even in non-sex cases, in practice the media often end up adopting a common approach."

Is there any means of protecting the identity of a child who is not a complainant, defendant or witness?

If there was any doubt on the point, the Court of Appeal in *R. v Jolleys (Robert), Ex p. Press Association*[42] has definitively settled that an order may not be made under s.39 to protect the identity of a child who may be adversely affected by proceedings but who is not concerned in them in one of the ways specified in the section. Leveson L.J., giving the judgment of the Court of Appeal, said of s.39[43]:

    17.42

"The phrase 'concerned in the proceedings' is defined and limited by the words that follow 'the person by or against, or in respect of whom proceedings are taken, or as being a witness therein'. It does not extend to children or young persons simply on the basis that they may be concerned in the more general sense of being affected thereby."

However, there may be circumstances in which a child who is not a complainant, defendant or witness may nonetheless fall within the scope of s.39. This appears from *R. (on the application of A) v Lowestoft Magistrates' Court*,[44] where A was

---

[42] [2013] EWCA Crim 1135.
[43] At [13], citing the authorities referred to in fn.60 of the main work.
[44] [2013] EWHC 659 (Admin).

charged with being found drunk in a public place while having the charge of a child apparently under the age of seven years, contrary to s.2(1) of the Licensing Act 1902. The Administrative Court held that the proceedings were taken "in respect of" the child referred to in the charge, who was therefore "concerned in the proceedings" for the purposes of s.39. Kenneth Parker J., giving the leading judgment, said[45]:

> "In a strictly formal sense, it might be argued that the only two parties to criminal proceedings are the prosecution and the defendant, and that criminal proceedings are not taken 'in respect of' any other person. However, it is plain that the legislature in enacting section 39 sought to capture, in wide language, at least the central participants in proceedings, whether civil or criminal, who would for that very reason be likely to be the focus of any report of the proceedings; and a narrow interpretation of section 39 would tend to defeat the main objective of protecting, where appropriate, the identity of a child or young person in that position. It is notable that section 39 extends in terms to a child or young person as a witness in proceedings, even if in a particular case the child or young person may have a relatively insignificant part in the proceedings. A broad interpretation of section 39 would now also be supported by article 8 of the European Convention of Human Rights ('ECHR') and the jurisprudence emphasising the best interests of children as a primary consideration, to which I shall turn later. Where in any event someone is prosecuted on a charge of violently or sexually assaulting a child or young person, or of inflicting cruelty on a child, it has never been seriously doubted that the putative victim of such conduct is a person 'in respect of whom' the criminal proceedings are brought.
>
> A here stood charged with 'being drunk in a public place while having the charge of a child under the age of 7 years', contrary to section 2(1) of the Licensing Act 1902. Under section 2(1) it is unnecessary to show that the defendant positively inflicted physical or psychological harm on the young child, or even that the defendant in the particular circumstances was likely to do so. In that strict sense the child might not be considered a victim as in the case of a violent or sexual assault, or of child cruelty. However, whatever the original intent of section 2(1), I am prepared to give it an interpretation that would best promote public policy in modern conditions, namely, that it is intended, among other things, to promote the welfare of small children who could be at risk of physical or psychological harm, because the person responsible for that welfare is intoxicated. Accordingly, the child that is specifically referred to in any charge under section 2(1) is in a real sense a subject of the criminal proceedings, and these proceedings on any sensible construction of section 39 of the CYP Act 1933 are taken 'in respect of', and thus 'concern', that child."

17.46   For other authorities in which an order restricting publication has been made under the High Court's inherent jurisdiction, see *A (A Minor)*,[46] *A Council v M & Ors (Judgment 3: Reporting Restrictions)*[47] and *Z v News Group Newspapers Ltd.*[48] The first of these decisions concerned care proceedings but the others related wholly or in part to sexual offences, and there is value in explaining briefly the issues that arose and how they were addressed.

---

[45] At [8]–[9].
[46] [2011] EWHC 1764 (Fam).
[47] [2012] EWHC 2038 (Fam).
[48] [2013] EWHC 1150 and 1371 (Fam).

A Council v M & Ors (Judgment 3: Reporting Restrictions) concerned a mother, M,   **17.46A**
who had adopted three children, A, B and C, from different countries. M then
purchased donor sperm and made A impregnate herself in order that she might
have a child which M could bring up as her own. A became pregnant and
miscarried at the age of 14. She became pregnant at the age of 16 and gave birth
to a baby boy. M's behaviour in hospital gave serious concern to the midwives who
alerted social services. Care proceedings were commenced. At the time of the care
proceedings there were criminal proceedings pending. B was still residing with M
but C was in alternative long-term foster care. A and her son, D, were living
together in foster care. This judgment concerned the reporting restrictions in
respect of the proceedings. Peter Jackson J. considered the decision in *Re S (A*
Child) (Identification: Restriction on Publication),[49] which he noted had led to the
conclusion that it will be "highly exceptional, though not beyond contemplation"
for the art.8 rights of individuals to prevail over the art.10 rights of the public so
as to restrict the reporting of criminal proceedings. He said[50]:

> "The resolution of this conflict of legitimate interests can only be achieved by close
> attention to the circumstances that actually exist in the individual case. As Sir Mark
> Potter has said,[51] the approach must be hard-headed and even, from the point of view
> of this jurisdiction, hard-hearted.
>
> Rights arising under art.8 on the one hand and art.10 on the other are different in
> quality. Article 8 rights are by their nature of crucial importance to a few, while art.10
> rights are typically of general importance to many. The decided cases, together with
> s.12(4) HRA, act as a strong reminder that the rights of the many should not be
> undervalued and incrementally eroded in response to a series of hard cases of
> individual misfortune.
>
> On the other hand, there is no hierarchy of rights in this context and there are cases
> where individual rights must prevail. In highly exceptional cases this can even include
> making inroads into the fundamental right to report criminal proceedings, but only
> where that is absolutely necessary."

On the facts before him, Jackson J. found that the children were in exceptionally
unusual circumstances and were highly vulnerable to exploitation and that their
identification would "at best be harmful and at worst disastrous". The reporting
restrictions sought, by contrast, were not absolute. Accordingly, reporting of the
care proceedings and the criminal proceedings would be allowed, subject to the
restriction that nothing must be published which might compromise the identity
of the children. The order would last until 2029, at which time D would be 18
years old.

In *Z v News Group Newspapers Ltd* the applicant was the father of five of eight   **17.46B**
children whose mother was being tried in the Crown Court for serious benefit
fraud. The charges arose from claims made by her in relation to supposed multiple
complex disabilities and needs of the children. An order for reporting restrictions
made earlier in the criminal proceedings under s.39 of the 1933 Act had been

---

[49] [2004] UKHL 47; [2005] 1 A.C. 593; discussed in para.17.44 in the main work.
[50] At [82]–[84].
[51] *A Local Authority v W* [2005] EWHC 1564 (Fam) at [72].

successfully challenged by News Group Newspapers Ltd ("NGN") on the basis
that s.39 applies only to children concerned in the proceedings as defendants,
victims or witnesses (but see further on this: para.17.42, above). In this case,
although the children's medical and other conditions would be the subject of
"lengthy and detailed analysis", they were not "caught" by the Act. Accordingly,
the father of the five younger children applied to the High Court for an injunction.
In determining the application, Cobb J. noted that the inherent jurisdiction
enabled the court to conduct the exercise of balancing the competing ECHR rights
under arts 8 and 10. He considered *Re S* and s.12(4) of the Human Rights Act
1998, the relevant press code of practice and the applicable case law. He expressly
adopted the analysis of Peter Jackson J. in *A Council v M & Ors* on the need for
close attention to be paid to the circumstances of each case; the need to remember
that art.8 rights concern "a few", whereas art.10 rights are typically of importance
to "the many" whose rights should not be eroded by "hard cases of individual
misfortune"; but that, equally, no hierarchy of rights exist, such that in highly
exceptional cases inroads can be made into the fundamental right to report
criminal proceedings. In applying these principles to reporting the criminal
process, he bore in mind the importance to democratic society of reporting such
trials; the need to guard against the "instinctive desire to extend a protective wing
to shield the children of parents who are accused of criminal activity"; that press
freedom should only be displaced in exceptional circumstances and that the
burden of proof lay with the applicant. NGN advanced a public interest argument
and the applicant contended that the circumstances were exceptional and that any
identification of the children would cause them serious detriment. At the
particular stage that the trial had reached, Cobb J. found that the balance was
"exquisitely finely poised" but that the applicant had discharged the heavy burden
of proof required for the making of the reporting restriction. He set out four
specific reasons for imposing the restriction:

- The central role of the children in the case which would involve
  "constant" references to their private lives and upbringing.
- The trial was about to focus on detailed examination of the children's
  medical records which would constitute a serious intrusion into their
  private lives and was therefore a powerful art.8 consideration.
- When considering the art.8 rights of the children the court must have
  regard to their "unusual stated vulnerabilities".
- In terms of proportionality: (i) the order would be a considerable
  interference with art.10, (ii) although there was a "hierarchy" amongst the
  children in respect of the need for protection, it was necessary and
  proportionate to protect the art.8 rights of the most vulnerable to preclude
  the identification of all the family, and (iii) the balancing exercise he had
  conducted pertained to the particular point reached in the criminal
  trial.

Cobb J. then considered the impact that a conviction might have upon the
balancing exercise he had conducted, observing that in such circumstances, there
should probably not be "reporting restraint". Accordingly, whilst making the

injunction, he invited the parties to make further representations before him at the point at which the trial judge started summing up, in order that he could make a further decision in time for the verdict.

On the matter being restored, it was accepted that no party sought a variation of the reporting restriction if the mother were to be acquitted, but NGN sought a variation in the event of conviction. Cobb J. gave a short judgment focussing on whether or not art.10 should prevail in such circumstances. After hearing argument, the learned judge reminded himself of the need to guard against an assumption that reporting would be "sensational" and of the duty on the press (of which they hardly needed reminding in the current climate) to maintain the highest professional standards. Having acknowledged the exceptional nature of the case and, whilst regretting that the consequence of naming the defendant would identify the children (who were wholly innocent), he concluded that the "marginal re-weighting of factors in the event of a conviction would tilt the balance in favour of freedom of expression". However, while the balance had tipped in favour of allowing reporting, it did not eradicate the art.8 rights of the children. Accordingly, "intense focus" was required to strike the right balance, leading Cobb J. to vary the order but to impose restrictions including precluding the publication of photographs, disclosure of the forenames of the children and applicant father and of the children's medical conditions/disabilities. He concluded by noting that, in the event of a conviction leading to the variation of the reporting restriction, it would be the mother's responsibility alone for having caused the "misery, shame and disadvantage, which is the inevitable cause of her offending".

H.H. Judge Denyer QC has commented that, in the light of previous authority emphasising the importance of the general principle of open justice and the need for exceptional circumstances before it is departed from, including the speech of Lord Steyn in *Re S*, Cobb J.'s decision to grant an injunction in this case "comes as a bit of a surprise".[52] Judge Denyer continues:

> "Of course, cases turn on their own facts. Given the particular circumstances and that the health of the children was a central issue, there is some force in the argument that the position was analogous to that dealt with by s.39. In other words, it may truly be regarded as 'exceptional'. It is to be hoped that it is not perceived as a green light for the more general granting of injunctions restraining press freedom."

It is certainly to be hoped that injunctions of this sort continue to be granted only rarely and where circumstances give rise to a pressing need to protect art.8 rights. But the carefully reasoned decision of Cobb J. in *Z v News Group Newspapers Ltd* seems to us to fall the right side of a line that is inevitably very difficult to draw in practice.

HM Courts Service combined with the Tribunals Service in 2011 to form HM **17.48** Courts and Tribunals Service. The Practice Direction referred to in the main work has been replaced by *Practice Direction 12I – Applications for Reporting Restriction*

---

[52] *Restrictions on reporting the name of a defendant*, *Archbold News*, Issue 8, September 11, 2013, pp.3–5.

Orders, which can be found on the HMCTS website.[53] The Practice Note referred to in the main work remains in force and is referred to in the Practice Direction (at 4.1).[54]

17.49   For the power of the Crown Court to order the anonymity of a defendant, see para.17.18, above.

RESTRICTIONS ON IDENTIFICATION OF PERSONS UNDER 18 BY MEDIA: THE YOUTH JUSTICE AND CRIMINAL EVIDENCE ACT 1999

Restrictions on reporting alleged offences involving persons under 18

17.52   By virtue of amendments made by the Armed Forces Act 2006,[55] s.44(13)(c) reads:

> "(c) any reference to a person subject to service law is to—
>> (i) a person subject to service law within the meaning of the Armed Forces Act 2006, or
>> (ii) a civilian subject to service discipline within the meaning of that Act."

For transitional provisions as to the meaning of "person subject to service law" in s.44(1), (9), see the Armed Forces Act 2006 (Transitional Provisions etc) Order 2009 (SI 2009/1059), para.44(1).

Power to restrict reporting of criminal proceedings involving persons under 18

17.55   For modifications of s.45 in relation to courts-martial and standing civilian courts, see the Youth Justice and Criminal Evidence Act 1999 (Application to Courts-Martial) Order 2006 (SI 2006/2886) and (Application to Standing Civilian Courts) Order 2006 (SI 2006/2888).

Breach of restrictions or direction

17.57   *Erratum*: The reference in the second bullet of the main work to para.16.43 should be to para.17.54.

---

[53] *http://www.justice.gov.uk/courts/procedure-rules/family/practice_directions/pd_part_12i* [accessed December 1, 2013].
[54] See *http://www.justice.gov.uk/downloads/publications/corporate-reports/ospt/practice_note_reporting_restrictions_july.doc* [accessed December 1, 2013].
[55] Section 378 and Sch.16 para.158, which came into force on October 9, 2009 by virtue of the Armed Forces Act 2006 (Commencement No.5) Order 2009 (SI 2009/1167), para.4.

CHAPTER 18

VULNERABLE WITNESSES "SPECIAL MEASURES" AND RELATED MATTERS

by Alexandra Ward, Barrister

INTRODUCTION

Following a series of high profile cases, there has recently been much debate as to **18.01** how child and other witnesses of sexual offences should give their evidence. The debate has focused upon the cross-examination of vulnerable witnesses and the piloting of pre-recorded cross-examination, a special measure provided by s.28 of the Youth Justice and Criminal Evidence Act 1999 ("YJCEA 1999"), which is not yet in force.

The debate has been informed by a growing understanding of the difficulties that such witnesses may have in giving best evidence. *The Bercow report: A Review of Services for Children and Young People (0–19) with Speech, Language and Communication Needs*[1] found that 7 per cent of five-year-old children entering school in England have significant difficulties with speech or language; those with good speech sounds and poor language skills are most at risk of being missed; and approximately 50 per cent in some socio-economically disadvantaged populations have speech and language skills that are significantly lower than those of other children of the same age. In addition, 10 per cent of children in Britain aged 5–16 have a clinically recognisable mental disorder and rates of childhood autism are thought to be around 1 per cent (higher than previous estimates).[2] Also of concern

---

[1] Department for Children, Schools and Families (2008), p.13. The report is available at *http://webarchive.nationalarchives.gov.uk/20130401151715/https://www.education.gov.uk/publications/eOrderingDownload/Bercow-Report.pdf* [accessed November 27, 2013].
[2] See materials cited in *European Commission Communication on the Rights of the Child 2011–2014: Contribution by the Bar Council of England & Wales*, para.8. The Contribution is available at *http://ec.europa.eu/justice/news/consulting_public/0009/contributions/unregistered_organisations/127_bar_council_england_wales_sept10.pdf* [accessed November 27, 2013].

is the finding that chronic childhood trauma interferes with neurobiological development and questions reminding child victims of the trauma may cause them to "freeze" and shut down their ability to respond.[3]

There is now widespread recognition that cross-examination of very young children is a specialist skill; there is a plethora of useful guidance and Court of Appeal authority to assist the advocate.[4] Every practitioner in this area must be aware of relevant developments. Leading the field in this respect are professional organisations such as the Criminal Bar Association ("CBA") and the Advocacy Training Council, and senior members of the Judiciary. In January 2012, the Judiciary issued a Bench Checklist for young witness cases.[5] The Court of Appeal has made clear that the "traditional" approach of the advocate putting their case in stark terms may be neither necessary nor appropriate in relation to a vulnerable witness. It may instead be proper for an advocate to explain to the jury prior to the complainant's evidence that the allegation is denied and to set out the fundamental aspects of the defence (i.e. the complainant is lying and seeking attention). It is recognised that advocates will need to adjust their style of cross-examination for such witnesses. As His Honour Judge Peter Collier QC states on the training video *A Question of Practice*, produced by the CBA and others:

> "Many advocates have quite a journey to make to achieve changes in habits of questioning that have been learned over many years and often have become deeply entrenched but which are not appropriate for the examination of children and vulnerable witnesses."

The decision in *Wills*[6] has confirmed that it is the responsibility of the trial judge to ensure that the defence advocate cross-examines a vulnerable witness in a manner that enables the witness to give their best evidence. Trial judges must ensure that the tenor, tone, language and duration of the questioning is developmentally appropriate to the particular child; prevent questioning that is irrelevant, repetitive, oppressive or intimidating; and be alert to possible difficulties in understanding. Ground rules as to how questioning will proceed should be settled at a pre-trial hearing or at the beginning of the trial. Counsel who persistently flout the ground rules, as in *Wills*, can place the trial judge in a difficult position, as frequent intervention from the Bench disrupts the flow of the evidence and risks confusing witness and jury alike.

---

[3] See materials cited in *European Commission Communication on the Rights of the Child 2011–2014: Contribution by the Bar Council of England & Wales*, para.8. The Contribution is available at *http://ec.europa.eu/justice/news/consulting_public/0009/contributions/unregistered_organisations/127_bar_council_england_wales_sept10.pdf* [accessed November 27, 2013].

[4] See *Barker* [2010] EWCA Crim 4; *Wills* [2011] EWCA Crim 1938; *R. v E* [2011] EWCA Crim 3028; Lord Judge C.J., *Toulmin Lecture in Law & Psychiatry* (King's College London, March 20, 2013, accessible at *http://www.judiciary.gov.uk/media/speeches/2013/lcj-speech-toulmin-lecture* [accessed November 27, 2013]); Criminal Bar Association, Advocate's Gateway Toolkits; Advocacy Training Council, CPS and NSPCC training video *A Question of Practice* (2013), accessible at *http://www.theadvocatesgateway.org/* [accessed November 27, 2013].

[5] *http://www.judiciary.gov.uk/publications-and-reports/guidance/2012/jc-bench-checklist-young-wit-cases* [accessed September 21, 2013].

[6] [2011] EWCA Crim 1938.

In its report *Raising the Bar: the Handling of Vulnerable Witnesses, Victims and Defendants in Court*,[7] the Advocacy Training Council endorsed the "ticketing" of advocates as a pre-requisite to prosecuting or defending cases involving such witnesses. The Crown Prosecution Service will only instruct advocates whom it has approved to prosecute sexual offences; to obtain approval, an advocate must fulfil certain criteria and have attended a recognised training course such as that provided by the CBA. The call for compulsory training for all advocates (prosecution and defence) appearing in cases involving sexual offences and vulnerable witnesses is gathering momentum. The time may therefore have come to require all advocates appearing in cases that involve young witnesses to attend a training course in this highly specialised area of practice. General guidance for advocates is set out at para.18.123 et seq., below.

Finally, the Coroners and Justice Act 2009 ("2009 Act") has made significant amendments to the YJCEA 1999 which came into force on June 27, 2011.[8] In particular, the 2009 Act extended automatic eligibility for special measures and protection from cross-examination by a defendant in person from those aged under 17 to those aged under 18.

Earlier provision and the Pigot report

Speaking Up for Justice

The third edition of *Achieving Best Evidence: Guidance on Interviewing Victims and*   18.08
Witnesses, and Guidance on using Special Measures[9] ("the ABE guidance") was published in March 2011 and supersedes the previous version.[10] In addition, *Vulnerable and Intimidated Witnesses – A Police Service Guide* (2011)[11] sets out good practice for police officers and staff who are the first point of contact for vulnerable and intimidated victims and witnesses. Also useful is ACPO's *Advice on the Structure of Visually Recorded Witness Interviews* (August 2010),[12] which provides guidance to police on how to interview victims and witnesses effectively. Practitioners and investigators will recognise the necessity for such guidance in light of the problems often encountered with the sound, visual quality and length of visually recorded interviews.

---

[7] Final Report of the Advocacy Training Council Working Group on Vulnerable Witness Handling (Advocacy Training Council, 2011), accessible at *http://www.advocacytrainingcouncil.org/images/word/raisingthebar.pdf* [accessed November 27, 2013].

[8] See Coroners and Justice Act 2009 (Commencement No.7) Order 2011 (SI 2011/1452).

[9] *http://www.cps.gov.uk/publications/docs/best_evidence_in_criminal_proceedings.pdf* [accessed November 27, 2013].

[10] Ministry of Justice Circular 2011/03.

[11] Available at *http://www.justice.gov.uk/downloads/victims-and-witnesses/vulnerable-witnesses/vulnerable-intimidated-witnesses.pdf* [accessed November 27, 2013].

[12] *http://www.acpo.police.uk/documents/crime/2011/20110418%20CBA%20Advice%20on%20-the%20Structure%20of%20Visually%20Recorded%20Witness%20interviewsAug2010.pdf* [accessed November 27 2012].

Measuring Up?

18.10   In *Young Witnesses in Criminal Proceedings: A Progress Report on Measuring Up?*
(2009),[13] Joyce Plotnikoff and Richard Woolfson provide an update on the
position as regards the treatment of child witnesses. They record that progress has
been made in some areas and note the coming into force of provisions of the 2009
Act and the steps taken by the CPS, Association of Chief Police Officers and HM
Courts and Tribunals Service in reviewing and improving guidance on how to
approach young witnesses throughout the court process. They conclude, however,
that action is still needed in relation to how young witnesses are treated at court.
In this area, ensuring appropriate questioning and avoiding long delays at court
remain key priorities, particularly in light of the increasing number of children
giving evidence in proceedings. Whilst there are no official figures for the number
of children who gave evidence, around 48,000 were called to court in 2008/9,
compared to around 30,000 in 2006/7, an increase of 60 per cent.

The *Equal Treatment Bench Book* (updated in 2013) includes advice on dealing
with witnesses with specific learning difficulties where only some areas of
functioning are affected.[14] It provides assistance for judges in recognising learning
difficulties and identifying the consequential effect on court proceedings.

VULNERABLE WITNESSES AND "SPECIAL MEASURES"

The Legislation

18.12   In addition to the provisions of the YJCEA 1999 discussed in the main work, s.31
of the Children and Young Persons Act 1933 requires arrangements to be made to
prevent the association of young persons with adult defendants, unless they are a
relative and/or jointly charged. The terms of s.31 apply to any child witness,
although provision is usually in place through witness services to ensure that
young witnesses do not come into contact with adult defendants. In *R.(T) v
Secretary of State for Justice*[15] the Ministry of Justice was held to have breached
s.31 when a 13-year-old boy (with severe impairment of mental functioning,
autism and attention deficit hyperactivity disorder) was detained, following his
arrest for breach of bail, in the same area as adult defendants at a magistrates'
court. The cell block for young persons was unavailable due to refurbishment. The
young person was detained where he could see the custody desk, had transitory

---

[13] Nuffield Foundation, June 2011, available at *http://www.nuffieldfoundation.org/sites/default/files/
files/Young%20witnesses%20in%20criminal%20proceedings_a%20progress%20report%20on%20Mea
suring%20up_v_FINAL.pdf* [accessed November 27, 2013].
[14] Available at *http://www.judiciary.gov.uk/publications-and-reports/judicial-college/2013/equal-
treatment-bench-book* [accessed November 27, 2013].
[15] [2013] EWHC 1119 (Admin).

contact with at least two adult prisoners in the corridor and could hear other prisoners shouting at him.

ELIGIBILITY

Section 17(5) of the YJCEA 1999 came into force on June 27, 2011.[16]   **18.14**

Child witnesses

Eligibility under s.16(1)(a) of the YJCEA 1999 was extended to those under 18 on   **18.15**
June 27, 2011.[17]

The Special Measures for Child Witnesses (Sexual Offences) Regulations   **18.15A**
2013,[18] which came into force on December 18, 2013, amend s.33 of the YJCEA
1999 so that a complainant of a "relevant offence" whose age is uncertain will be
presumed to be under the age of 18 if there are reasons to believe they are under
that age. For this purpose a "relevant offence" includes a sexual offence (as defined
in s.62 of the YJCEA 1999), an offence under s.1 of the Protection of Children Act
1978 and an offence under s.160 of the Criminal Justice Act 1988. The effect is
that the complainant of such an offence will be eligible for "special measures"
under s.16 of the Act. Previously the presumption applied only to a complainant
of a human trafficking offence (an offence under s.59A of the 2003 Act or s.4 of
the Asylum and Immigration (Treatment of Claimants, etc) Act 2004). The
Regulations are made as part of the implementation in England and Wales of
*Directive 2011/93/EU of the European Parliament and of the Council of 13 December
2011 on combating the sexual abuse and sexual exploitation of children and child
pornography, and replacing Council Framework Decision 2004/68/JHA.*

Qualifying witnesses

The definition of "qualifying witness" was extended as from June 27, 2011, to   **18.16**
those who have attained the age of 18 at the time of the hearing but were aged 17
or under at the date of the recording.[19] For changes to legislation in respect of
child witnesses in need of special protection, see paras 18.42 et seq., below.

Adult witnesses

Section 17

Witnesses to alleged specified offences involving knives, firearms or offensive   **18.19**
weapons are eligible by virtue of the YJCEA 1999, s.17(5) and Sch.1A, which
came into force on June 27, 2011.[20]

---

[16] See the Coroners and Justice Act 2009 (Commencement No.7) Order 2011 (SI 2011/1452).
[17] See the Coroners and Justice Act 2009 (Commencement No.7) Order 2011 (SI 2011/1452).
[18] SI 2013/2971.
[19] SI 2013/2971.
[20] SI 2013/2971.

Special Measures and the Defendant

18.21   Professor Jenny McEwan considered fair trial issues relating to vulnerable
defendants in a recent article in the Criminal Law Review.[21] The difficulty in
recognising a defendant's vulnerability may arise at the police station but could go
unnoticed. Professor McEwan notes that a key problem is identifying whether a
defendant is vulnerable, particularly in magistrates' courts, where defendants are
often unrepresented and required to progress the case on the first occasion. Even
if they have the benefit of being represented by an experienced duty solicitor, in
the short time available it will be almost impossible for the representative to
identify that their client may have difficulty participating effectively in the
proceedings. As one might sadly anticipate, children with communication difficulties and low IQs are over-represented in the court system, yet the fact that such
difficulties are familiar does not mean that the courts should do nothing to address
them.[22] In the Crown Court, judges at early hearings (i.e. preliminary hearings or
plea and case management hearings) should be alive to any vulnerability of the
defendant. With the exception, in certain limited circumstances, of live-link,
statutory special measures remain unavailable to child or vulnerable defendants.
As Professor McEwan notes, the courts recognise that flexibility may be required
in respect of some defendants and r.3.8(4)(b) of the Criminal Procedure Rules
2012 requires the Court to "take every reasonable step . . . to facilitate the
participation of . . . the defendant". For useful guidance from the Advocacy
Training Council in relation to the effective participation of young defendants in
their own trial, see the Advocate's Gateway Toolkit 8.[23]

In addition, the Criminal Practice Directions[24] provide (in CPD General
Matters 3G) detailed direction as to how vulnerable defendants should be treated.
Matters for consideration include whether a vulnerable defendant should be part
of what would otherwise be a joint trial; whether a court familiarisation visit is
necessary; ensuring, subject to security considerations, that a child can sit with
their family or supporter throughout the proceedings as opposed to being seated
in the dock; and timetabling the trial so that it is conducted at a pace at which the
defendant can follow and maintain concentration. In the Crown Court, robes and
wigs should not be worn without good reason, security guards should not be in
uniform and consideration should be given to restricting the members of the
public and press who are permitted access to the courtroom (it may, for example,
be preferable for the press to report from another room to which proceedings are
live-streamed by video). Any adaptations for a vulnerable defendant should be
explained to the jury so as to not prejudice the defendant.

---

[21] *Vulnerable defendants and the fairness of trials* [2013] Crim. L.R. (2) 100–113.
[22] See *R. (on the application of AS) v Great Yarmouth Youth Court* [2011] EWHC 2059 (Admin);
[2012] Crim. L.R. 478.
[23] Available to download at *http://www.theadvocatesgateway.org/toolkits* [accessed November 27,
2013].
[24] [2013] EWCA Crim 1631.

Professor McEwan cites in her article an example of a jury disapproving of the behaviour of a young defendant with a short attention span who would talk throughout the proceedings to the social worker seated next to them. The judge should be alert to the defendant's behaviour and either increase the number of breaks or explain to the jury why the defendant is seated in the well of the court together with the reason why frequent communication with their social worker is permitted. We discuss below the questioning of vulnerable witnesses and the same approach should be adopted when questioning vulnerable defendants. Prosecutors should be no more tempted to try to "catch-out" a vulnerable defendant by asking confusing questions which are likely to obtain unreliable answers than defence counsel should be tempted to try to trick a vulnerable complainant. The training video *A Question of Practice* prepared by the CBA and others illustrates this point very well.[25]

Practitioners should also refer to the excellent information pack, *Mental health and learning disabilities in the criminal courts: Information for magistrates, district judges and court staff*, prepared by Polly McConnell and Jenny Talbot on behalf of the Prison Reform Trust and Rethink Mental Illness.[26] The pack addresses the difficulty in identifying a vulnerable defendant and reinforces how alienating an appearance in a criminal court can be for someone with a mental health condition or learning disability. It gives practical advice as to how the courts might obtain assistance from other agencies at various stages of the process. An overview is also provided of fitness to plead, bail, sentencing and mental health disposals.

Limited provision for defendants: live-link and intermediaries

Section 33BA of the YJCEA 1999 is not yet in force. The courts (including the   **18.26** magistrates' courts and the Youth Court) have a common law power to appoint an intermediary to assist a defendant. In *R. (on the application of AS) v Great Yarmouth Youth Court*[27] Mitting J. held that "[t]here was a right, which might in certain circumstances amount to a duty, to appoint a registered intermediary to assist the defendant to follow the proceedings and give evidence if without assistance he would not be able to have a fair trial". In their article, "A day late and a dollar short: in search of an intermediary scheme for vulnerable defendants in England and Wales",[28] Penny Cooper and David Wurtzel compare the position of a defendant who needs an intermediary in order to understand and be understood with a non-English speaking defendant who requires an interpreter. They develop the powerful argument that the absence of an interpreter for a non-English speaking defendant would constitute a violation of the defendant's right to a fair hearing under art.6 of the ECHR, and that the absence of an intermediary for a vulnerable defendant would constitute the same violation.

---

[25] Available at *http://www.theadvocatesgateway.org/* [accessed November 27, 2013].
[26] Available at *http://www.mhldcc.org.uk* [accessed November 27, 2013].
[27] Above, fn.22.
[28] [2013] Crim. L.R. 1, 4–22.

The issue of intermediaries for defendants was considered by the Court of Appeal, Lord Judge C.J. presiding, in *Cox*.[29] The appellant suffered from complex psychiatric difficulties and at a special measures hearing the trial judge, relying upon his common law powers in accordance with *R. (on the application of C) v Sevenoaks Youth Court*,[30] made a direction for an intermediary to assist the appellant at trial. Unfortunately an intermediary could not be identified for whom funding was available. The judge refused to stay the prosecution on the basis that absent an intermediary the appellant could not have a fair trial. He applied the test set out in *R. (TP) v West London Youth Court*,[31] namely "Taking into account the steps that can be taken in the [youth] court will the claimant be able effectively to participate in his trial?" The judge answered this question in the affirmative as there would be regular breaks (every 20 minutes), evidence would be adduced by simply phrased questions, witnesses would be asked to express their answers in short sentences, and the video of the appellant's police interview under caution would be played to enable the jury to become accustomed to his patterns of speech. Also, an admission would be made as to the appellant's complex learning difficulties and the extent of his understanding. Throughout the trial the judge kept matters under review and revisited his ruling prior to closing speeches. In upholding the conviction, the Court held that ultimately the judge retains overall responsibility for the fairness of a trial. Even if the presence of an intermediary is desirable, where one is not available the judge must make an informed assessment of whether the absence of an intermediary would make the proposed trial unfair or whether fairness can be safeguarded by modifications to the trial process. It will be most unusual for a defendant who is fit to plead to be found to be so disadvantaged by his condition that a properly brought prosecution would be stayed.

In outlining the history of the case, the Court of Appeal in *Cox* referred to funding difficulties in respect of intermediaries for defendants; the judgment is silent, however, on whether the unavailability of an intermediary in this case was ultimately due to a lack of funding or the particular communication needs of the appellant. It is understood that that the Legal Services Commission will fund an intermediary's initial conference with a defendant/solicitor, whilst HM Courts and Tribunals Service will fund the intermediary's attendance at trial. The rates are £36.00 per hour for preparation/attendance and £16.00 per hour travel time.[32] If a lack of funding was the problem in *Cox*, this is most regrettable; it seems clear that the presence of an intermediary would have enabled the Court to be assured that the appellant was able to participate effectively in his trial. Instead, the money that may have been saved by not paying for an intermediary was no doubt spent several times over in the form of court delays and the abuse of process application.

---

[29] [2012] EWCA Crim 549.
[30] [2009] EWHC 3088 (Admin), discussed at para.18.25 of the main work.
[31] [2005] EWHC 2583 (Admin).
[32] Cooper & Wurtzel, "A day late and a dollar short" [2013] Crim. L.R. 1, 4–22.

The process of finding a defendant intermediary carries its own problems. Until February 2011, defence solicitors had access to a Ministry of Justice service which matched the skills of Registered Intermediaries with a defendant's needs, as long as their use of the service did not impact upon the provision of Registered Intermediaries for vulnerable witnesses. The inevitable has occurred and due to increased demand for witness intermediaries the MoJ has withdrawn the service "because there is no longer spare capacity to fulfil requests for defendants".[33]

AVAILABILITY

Availability of special measures: pre-recorded cross-examination

The Government has brought s.28 of the YJCEA 1999 into force for the purpose   18.34
of a six-month pilot scheme being run from December 30, 2013, in the Crown Court at Kingston-upon-Thames, Leeds and Liverpool, under which the cross-examination and re-examination of witnesses under the age of 16 and vulnerable adult witnesses is to be pre-recorded for later admission in court.[34] The Ministry of Justice said the scheme will allow children and vulnerable adults to "escape being grilled in court, in front of an audience, by recording their cross-examination away from the highly charged court environment".[35] If the pilot is a success, the MoJ plans to roll out the scheme across England and Wales.

We welcome this development, given the trauma that may be suffered by a child or vulnerable witness who has to give evidence about alleged events several months, or longer, after they have been reported to the police and they have given their account in an ABE interview. In cases involving several defendants there can be considerable delay before trial. However, even if pre-recorded cross-examination becomes the norm, safeguards will have to be included to ensure that further questions may be asked if they are justified. The judge will need to know in advance the questions to be asked and be able to give proper consideration to their appropriateness. We also consider that the witness will need to be available during the trial as their pre-recorded evidence is played, because the jury may have their own questions to ask. Pre-recorded cross-examination will put pressure upon the courts to ensure that the trial judge is available during the recording of the cross-examination; this will require early allocation. Cases will also have to be fixed rather than placed in the warned list, in order to ensure the availability of the same advocate. Crucially, the prosecution will need to comply with disclosure obligations (and consider third party disclosure) at a much earlier stage than is current practice. The defence must have all the material required to conduct the cross-examination in order to ensure a fair trial. We also suggest that cases involving pre-

---

[33] Email to Penny Cooper from the MoJ, April 24, 2012, cited in Cooper & Wurtzel, "A day late and a dollar short" [2013] Crim. L.R. 1, 4–22. The organisations Communicourt and Triangle may be in a position to assist defence solicitors.
[34] SI 2013/3236.
[35] http://www.gov.uk/government/news/victims-to-be-spared-from-harrowing-court-cases   [accessed November 27, 2013).

recorded cross-examination will justify the allocation of a reviewing lawyer and assigned caseworker by the Crown Prosecution Service, although this will involve additional resources.

18.35   For a collection of essays advocating the use of pre-recorded cross-examination by reference to experience in different jurisdictions, see *Children and Cross-Examination: Time to Change the Rules?*[36] On the same theme is the article, "Pre-recording children's evidence: the Western Australian experience".[37] The pre-recording of children's evidence has been the norm in Western Australia (which operates an adversarial system) since the early 1990s. After studying its advantages and disadvantages, the authors conclude:

> "In Western Australia, both the judiciary and advocates believe that pre-recording children's entire evidence carries significant advantages, not only in the reduction of children's stress and improvement in their recovery prospects but also the improved quality of their evidence and advantages to the trial process itself. These include the ability to edit the recording of pre-judicial material, to shorten the time juries spend watching the child's evidence, and the advantages to both counsel of knowing the strength and content of the complainant's evidence before trial, raising the prospect of cutting weaker cases from the court waiting list, whether by a guilty plea or prosecutorial withdrawal.
>
> Most importantly Western Australian defence counsel do not believe that pre-recording disadvantages the defence or threatens the defendant's right to a fair trial. In fact, many consider it to have, in one Western Australian judge's words, 'distinct advantages to defence counsel'."

18.37   Professor J.R. Spencer's continued support for "full Pigot" and pre-recorded evidence from children is expressed in his recent article, *Child Witnesses and Cross-examination at Trial: Must it Continue?*[38] He has the support of Lord Judge, recently retired as Lord Chief Justice, who in delivering the Bar Council's annual law reform lecture, *The Evidence of Child Victims: the Next Stage*, on November 21, 2013, said that the requirement for the physical presence of a child witness or victim in the court building should be seen as an "antediluvian hangover from laughable far off days of the quill pen and the ink well".[39] See also *Child Q, England's Youngest Witness*,[40] about a case of child abuse where the three-year-old victim gave evidence, in which prosecution counsel Caroline Wigin is supportive of pre-recorded cross-examination. The child, when aged two, was caused life-threatening injuries by being kicked in the stomach by his mother's cohabitee. There was a delay of one year before the ABE interview and thereafter a further delay of eight months before trial. It was inevitably traumatic for the child to relive the experience many months later. Pre-recorded cross-examination could have

---

[36] Professors John R Spencer QC and Michael E Lamb (eds), *Children and Cross-Examination: Time to Change the Rules?* (Oxford: Hart Publishing, 2012).

[37] E Henderson, K Hanna and E Davies, "Pre-recording children's evidence: the Western Australian experience" [2012] Crim. L.R. 3.

[38] *Archbold Review*, Issue 3, April 3, 2011, pp.7–9.

[39] The lecture is available at *http://www.barcouncil.org.uk/media/241783/annual_law_reform_lec ture_rt_hon_the_lord_judge_speech_2013.pdf* [accessed November 27, 2013].

[40] Caroline Wigin, *Counsel Magazine*, July 2012, pp.24–5.

taken place much earlier around a table with the judge, counsel and the intermediary present; as it was, the first occasion on which the defence were able to put their case was on the live-link video.

THE "PRIMARY RULE" FOR CHILD WITNESSES: VIDEO-RECORDED EVIDENCE-IN-CHIEF AND LIVE-LINK

The classification of child witnesses in need of "special protection" has been **18.42** abolished by amendments made to the YJCEA 1999 by the 2009 Act[41] (see para.18.49 et seq. of the main work). The presumption that child witnesses give their evidence-in-chief by video-recorded statement and any further evidence by live-link applies now to all child witnesses. An option is preserved whereby the witness can inform the court that they wish the rule to be disapplied.[42] The Court may then direct alternative special measures. For example, the witness may wish to give their evidence-in-chief by live-link rather than pre-recorded interview, or from behind a screen in court, or dispensing with a screen altogether. However, the court must be satisfied that the alternative special measures would not diminish the quality of the witness's evidence and would be likely to maximise the quality of that evidence so far as practicable.[43]

TYPES OF SPECIAL MEASURES

Section 22A of the YJCEA 1999, inserted by s.101 of the 2009 Act as from June **18.56** 27, 2011,[44] provides that adult complainants in trials for sexual offences in the Crown Court (but not in magistrates' courts) may give evidence-in-chief by way of video-recorded statement under s.27 of the YJCEA 1999, unless this would not be in the interests of justice or would not maximise the quality of the complainant's evidence.

LIVE-LINK

The amendments made by s.102 of the 2009 Act came into force on June 27, **18.63** 2011.[45] When making a special measures direction for a witness supporter, the judge must consider the wishes of the witness.[46] For example, whilst a young child might be reassured by the presence of an older supporter, a teenager may feel uncomfortable giving evidence about personal sexual matters in the presence of

---

[41] 2009 Act, s.100, amending s.21 of the YJCEA 1999 as from June 27, 2011: see the Coroners and Justice Act 2009 (Commencement No.7) Order 2011 (SI 2011/1452).
[42] 2009 Act, s.100(4)(ba).
[43] 2009 Act, s.100(5).
[44] See the Coroners and Justice Act 2009 (Commencement No.7) Order 2011 (SI 2011/1452).
[45] See the Coroners and Justice Act 2009 (Commencement No.7) Order 2011 (SI 2011/1452).
[46] Criminal Practice Directions, CPD Evidence 29B.1.

such a person. Also, it should not be assumed that the witness would prefer the support of an individual of the same gender.

Until recently, the supporter was required to be someone completely independent of the witness or their family, as well as without knowledge of or personal involvement in the case.[47] The new Criminal Practice Directions have loosened this requirement[48]:

> "An increased degree of flexibility is appropriate as to who can act as supporter. This can be anyone known to and trusted by the witness who is not a party to the proceedings and has no detailed knowledge of the evidence in the case. The supporter may be a member of the Witness Service but need not be an usher or court official. Someone else may be appropriate."

In practice, if the supporter is not an usher, they will often be a representative of the Witness Service. A supporter from the Witness Service does not assume the responsibilities of the usher in the live-link room, and as such the usher should continue to be available to assist the witness and the supporter and to ensure that the judge's requirements are properly complied with in the room.[49]

It is important to be flexible and to understand the needs of a vulnerable witness; the usual way of eliciting evidence may not in fact enable that particular witness to give their best evidence. In his article, "Time to Change the Rules",[50] David Wurtzel cites an example where a five-year-old (aged four at the date of the incident) was to give evidence. The intermediary had identified that the child's communication was most effective when she was face-to-face with the person asking her questions. Before trial the child had practiced communicating through the live-link, but her communication was less effective and she found it more difficult to concentrate. It is no surprise that children (and indeed adults) may find answering questions to a screen disengaging. The suggestion at the "ground rules" meeting was that the advocates join the witness in the live-link room. This was permitted by the judge and had the advantage of visual aids being in the same room as the advocate and the witness. Counsel noted that the proximity between him and the witness made it easier for him to adjust his tone and pace when appropriate.

Video-Recorded Evidence-In-Chief

18.66 Section 27 of the YJCEA 1999 was amended by s.103 of the 2009 Act as from June 27, 2011,[51] so as to reduce the restrictions on witnesses giving additional evidence-in-chief following the playing of their video-recorded statement. In particular, the previous requirement under s.27(7)(a) of a material change of circumstances since the time of the recording has been removed.

---

[47] Consolidated Criminal Practice Direction 2011, para.III.29.2.
[48] Criminal Practice Directions, CPD Evidence 29B.2.
[49] Criminal Practice Directions, CPD Evidence 29B.3.
[50] *Counsel Magazine*, November 2012, pp.32–34.
[51] See the Coroners and Justice Act 2009 (Commencement No.7) Order 2011 (SI 2011/1452).

In *Davies*[52] the appellant was convicted of six counts of indecent assault (contrary   **18.67**
to s.14 of the Sexual Offences Act 1956) which took place over a period of two-
and-a-half years between 1985 and 1988 when the complainant was aged 8–11
years old. At trial, the defence objected to the ABE interview being played as the
complainant's evidence-in-chief because it potentially deprived them of the ability
to cross-examine on any differences between the account provided by the
complainant in her ABE interview and what she might say if she gave live evidence
before the jury. The appeal was allowed on other grounds, but Roderick Evans J.,
delivering the judgment of the Court of Appeal, said that when a witness is eligible
for special measures under s.19(2) of the YJEA 1999, it is for the judge to
determine whether any of the available special measures would be likely to improve
the quality of the witness's evidence by considering all the circumstances of the
case, including the views of the witness and whether the special measure requested
would inhibit the effective testing of the evidence by the defendant. The
speculative possibility that a witness might say something when giving evidence
that is different to the account given during the ABE interview is not, in itself, an
adequate reason for the ABE interview not to stand as the witness's evidence-
in-chief. Laura Hoyano has remarked that, had this ground of appeal succeeded,
the legislation would have been eviscerated.[53]

In *R. v M(A)*[54] the Court of Appeal underlined the importance of securing   **18.70**
agreement or a judicial ruling on edits in advance of trial, and held that the parties
are entitled to rely upon edited passages not being admitted into evidence. In that
case the trial judge, in response to a question from the jury, adduced evidence of
recent complaint which, somewhat surprisingly, had been edited by agreement
from the complainant's ABE interview. The witness was then recalled. The Court
of Appeal allowed an appeal against conviction on the ground that the appellant
had been caused unfair prejudice. An agreement as to edits was generally binding,
though not absolute, and whilst it was important to answer questions from the jury
accurately and without in any way misleading them, it should be remembered that
the trial process was adversarial, not inquisitorial. The Court said it was of crucial
importance that there had been no criticism in this case of how the defence had
conducted their case, and in particular they had not sought to ambush the
prosecution with their line of questioning, such as would have entitled the
prosecution to revisit the agreement over editing.

Replaying the video

Rawlings and Broadbent,[55] discussed in the main work, was affirmed in *R. v W*[56]   **18.79**
in which Rix L.J., giving the judgment of the Court of Appeal, said that if the

---

[52] [2011] EWCA Crim 1177.
[53] See commentary at [2011] Crim. L.R. 732.
[54] [2012] EWCA Crim. 899; [2013] 1 Cr. App. R. 245.
[55] [1995] 2 Cr. App. R. 222.
[56] [2011] EWCA Crim 1142.

video evidence is replayed or the jury are reminded of passages from the transcript it is incumbent upon the judge to warn them not to give disproportionate weight to the evidence because it is repeated after all of the evidence has been given. The judge should also remind the jury of cross-examination, re-examination and any relevant defence evidence.

Jury access to video transcripts

18.84   The question whether the jury should be provided with the transcripts of the ABE interview was considered most recently in *Sardar*.[57] In that case the Court of Appeal, applying *Popescu*,[58] overturned a rape conviction where the transcript was provided to the jury and remained with them during cross-examination, defence closing submissions and their retirement. The judge did not warn the jury as to the dangers of giving the transcript undue weight. The Court of Appeal held that the fact that the defence consented to the jury being provided with the transcript and that the jury had a transcript of the defendant's police interview under caution did not justify the provision of the ABE transcript. The danger was that the jury would have paid disproportionate attention to what was written in the ABE transcript rather than concentrate on "their impression of the witness and their assessment of that witness as she gives her evidence, both in the form of a video recording and during cross-examination".

In his article, "Showing Video Transcripts to the Jury",[59] Judge Roderick Denyer QC summarises the correct approach as follows:

- Transcripts should only be provided to the jury if there is good reason, they should not be provided as a matter of routine.
- The judge should direct the jury, when they are provided with the transcript, that they should concentrate on the recording rather than the transcript so that they are able to observe the demeanour of the witness.
- Save in "very exceptional circumstances" the transcript should be taken back from the jury when the recording has finished being played.
- If the judge considers that the jury should keep the transcript through cross-examination he should explain to the jury the reason for his or her decision.
- The transcript should only remain with the jury after the witness has given evidence if the judge rules that there is "a very good reason".
- It would only be in exceptional circumstances that a jury would retire with the transcript.
- Where a jury has kept a transcript during their retirement, the judge should direct them as to the limited use they may make of it (i.e. to assist them to understand the witness's evidence-in-chief) and must warn them against over reliance on the document. In such circumstances any cross-examination must be summed up in detail.

---

[57] [2012] EWCA Crim 134.
[58] [2010] EWCA Crim 1230.
[59] 176 C.L. & J., 235.

INTERMEDIARIES

As noted in para.18.26C, above, the Register of Intermediaries maintained by the   18.89
Ministry of Justice is now available only to the prosecution.

Killick[60] is a case in which conscientious pre-trial preparation and a flexible   18.89A
approach on the part of the court enabled witnesses who, according to the trial
judge, would not have given evidence half a generation ago, to give their accounts
to the jury. The accused, who was himself physically disabled, was convicted of
sexual assaults committed against three disabled victims. In her article about the
case in *Counsel* magazine,[61] Elizabeth Smaller describes how the complainants
suffered with cerebral palsy and severe speech difficulties, which made it
impossible for them to give evidence in the conventional way. They were unable
to move, dress or feed themselves and every action required assistance (they all
had personal assistants). The main issue at trial was the witnesses' severe speech
difficulties and how their answers could be given in a manner intelligible to the
jury. One witness ("A") could speak but his answers were intelligible only to those
who were very experienced in speaking with him. The other two complainants
relied upon Voice Output Communication Aids, or "VOCA". One operated his
VOCA by hand (a painfully slow process), the other through a pressure pad on his
wheelchair at the back of his head; the vocabulary was limited to 900 pre-
programmed words. Early special measures meetings were held with each
complainant. They all wanted to give evidence in court from behind a screen and
to be given sufficient time to give their evidence. The vocabulary on the VOCAs
was prepared ahead of trial, but preparations were also made to add further words
if necessary. A registered intermediary explained to the jury how VOCAs operate
and that the mechanical voice meant that it would be impossible for the jury to
judge the complainants from their inflections or choice of words. During the
course of A's evidence it became apparent that the quality of his evidence would
be maximised if his personal assistant acted as his intermediary; this provided
greater flexibility than the use of a registered intermediary and so enabled the time
A spent giving evidence to be kept to a minimum.

The judge and parties in *Killick* are to be commended for doing everything
possible to ensure that the complainants were able to give their best evidence. All
those involved understood the need to adapt their questioning of the complainants
and the court timetable to accommodate the complainants' requirements. Also, the
evidence given by the intermediary before the complainants were called no doubt
demystified the disability they suffered, so ensuring that the jury were best placed
to focus on assessing the evidence.

A further example of intermediaries playing a key role in trial preparation is the   18.89B
case of Child Q, discussed in para.18.37, above. When assessing the child's

---

[60] [2011] EWCA Crim 1608. For the complex pre-trial history of this case, see para.26.50B,
below.
[61] Elizabeth Smaller, Junior Counsel for the Prosecution, January 2012.

competence to give evidence, the trial judge had the benefit of the intermediary's initial assessment, the ABE interview (at which the intermediary was present), an intermediary report following the ABE interview and a further report considering the impact of the delay awaiting trial. The intermediary also assisted at the "ground rules" meeting with respect to how questions should be asked and Child Q's likely period of concentration.[62] In yet another case, following a recommendation from the intermediary, both trial counsel joined the witness in the live-link room throughout cross-examination and re-examination.[63]

VULNERABLE WITNESSES: PRACTICAL CONSIDERATIONS

18.105   Guidance for interviewers is found in the latest edition of *Achieving Best Evidence in Criminal Proceedings: Guidance on Interviewing Victims and Witnesses and Guidance on Using Special Measures*[64] ("the ABE guidance") and ACPO's *Advice on the Structure of Visually Recorded Witness Interviews*.[65] The impact of a witness's evidence may be reduced when their ABE interview is relied upon as evidence-in-chief. In respect of an adult witness, consideration should always be given as to whether they would be prepared to provide a witness statement and give their evidence-in-chief live before the jury, with screens if appropriate. This will of course be a matter for the individual witness, but simply because a witness meets the eligibility criteria for a particular special measure does not mean that the advocate should be inflexible as to how they present their case.

We understand that new digital video-recording equipment is being installed in certain ABE suites, which should improve the quality of recordings. Officers interviewing vulnerable witnesses must ensure that the camera is in the best position to maximise the impact of the evidence. The camera is often positioned at ceiling height in the corner of the room. As the sensitive nature of the subject matter often means that the witness looks down when speaking, this can result in the jury seeing only the top of the witness's head throughout the entire interview. This is disengaging and the impact of the evidence can be lost. Also, the camera lens is all too often focused some distance from the witness, leaving a jury in a large courtroom unable to see the witness's facial expressions and demeanour. It is not a question of putting the camera physically close to the witness, but of zooming in to the witness's face so that the jury are afforded the best possible view. The assistant interviewer who watches the interview from a separate room should be aware of such matters and intervene if the witness cannot be seen properly on

---

[62] Caroline Wigin, "Child Q, England's Youngest Witness", *Counsel Magazine*, July 2012, pp.24–25.

[63] cf. David Wurtzel, "Time to Change the Rules", para.18.63, above.

[64] Above, fn.9. See also Dr. Kevin Smith, "Recorded Evidence", *Counsel Magazine*, November 2011, pp.30–33.

[65] Above, fn.12.

the screen. Best practice is for the camera to show the witness's head, face and upper body clearly.

The ABE guidance also suggests brevity in respect of neutral topics and at the rapport stage. If extensive rapport is needed, this can be dealt with prior to the recorded interview. Moreover, there is no requirement for interviewers to summarise throughout the interview everything the witness says. Continued repetition by the interviewing officer may discourage the witness from giving their best evidence and the evidence is likely to have less impact in front of the jury.

The case of *R. v MH*[66] involved a four-year-old giving evidence at a trial held 15 months after the recording of his ABE interview. The appellant was critical of the interview, which did not strictly comply with the ABE guidance in three respects: the child had not been asked about truth and lies; the allegation followed a leading question ("Can you remember what happened to your winky?"); and the child had been praised at the end of the interview as "a very good boy". The appeal was dismissed. The Court of Appeal said that the leading question did not suggest what the boy's answer should be and could have prompted a comment which accorded with the appellant's case. In fact the boy's response, "Daddy sucked it", was "immediate, unguarded, direct and clear". It was not essential for a child of such an age to be confronted with the concepts of truth and lies, and that the praise at the end of the interview was insignificant.

ROLE OF THE TRIBUNAL

A seminar organised by the Nuffield Foundation on the subject of *Questioning*   18.107
young witnesses and incorporating good practice into advocacy training[67] and attended by, amongst others, members of the judiciary, the Bar Council, CPS, ACPO and the CBA, led to a proposal for the MoJ to consider promoting a statutory provision incorporating the current position on developmentally appropriate questioning, similar to that applying in New Zealand. Section 85(1) of the New Zealand Evidence Act 2006 provides:

> "Unacceptable questions: the judge may disallow, or direct that a witness is not obliged to answer, any question that the judge considers improper, unfair, misleading, needlessly repetitive, or expressed in language that is too complicated for the witness to understand".

Precisely how such a provision might be drafted and work in practice in England and Wales is a matter for debate. It is, however, clear that judicial prevention of inappropriate questioning is essential to ensure fairness to the young or vulnerable witness.

---

[66] [2012] EWCA Crim 2725; [2013] Crim. L.R. 10, 849–853 (with commentary by Laura Hoyano).
[67] See   *http://ec.europa.eu/justice/news/consulting_public/0009/contributions/unregistered_organisa tions/127_bar_council_england_wales_sept10.pdf* [accessed November 27, 2013] and *http://www.nuf fieldfoundation.org/sites/default/files/files/Young%20witnesses%20in%20criminal%20proceedings_ a%20progress%20report%20on%20Measuring%20up_v_FINAL.pdf* [accessed November 27, 2013].

The role of the court is to ensure a fair trial. An advocate cannot complain that their client has been denied such a trial if they are prevented from cross-examining in a way that is liable to elicit false evidence from a confused witness. Where necessary, the court should impose limitations on cross-examination to protect the witness and enable them to give their best evidence. Such limitations, properly applied, will not prevent the defence advocate from eliciting necessary evidence, but will require them to use a less confrontational style of questioning than the "traditional" approach. It is the responsibility of the trial judge to ensure that if restrictions are imposed on the conduct of cross-examination, the advocate keeps within them. In this respect an illuminating decision is *Wills*.[68] The appellant and his co-defendant, who was separately represented, were both charged with and acquitted of one count of sexual activity with a child. The appellant was convicted of a further 13 serious sexual offences committed against young girls. It therefore appears that the jury could not be sure that the offence alleged against both men occurred. The trial judge imposed strict limitations on how the eight young witnesses could be questioned; in particular counsel were not to challenge the witnesses or put to them their inconsistent statements. Counsel representing the appellant observed the limitations, using short questions which he did not tag with a comment. By contrast, counsel for the co-defendant paid the judge's directions only passing regard. The judge found it necessary to intervene throughout the cross-examination because counsel for the co-defendant asked long questions and made inappropriate comment in order to prompt an answer. In summing-up, the judge directed the jury that it was necessary to tailor the style of cross-examination of vulnerable witnesses to their age and maturity and that the different styles of the two advocates did not reflect the strengths or weaknesses of either case.

The appellant appealed against conviction, arguing that the fact that his counsel observed the limitations set by the judge when cross-examining, whilst counsel for his co-defendant adopted a less constrained and more traditional approach, rendered the trial so unfair that the judge ought to have discharged the jury. The Court of Appeal rejected this argument. Whilst the cross-examination by counsel for the co-defendant failed to comply with the proper limitations imposed by the judge, and to that extent differed from the cross-examination by the appellant's counsel, the Court did not consider that this led to any unfairness in the way in which the trial was conducted from the point of view of the appellant. Any unfairness was properly dealt with by the form of direction given by the judge. However, the Court went on to make the following observations[69]:

> "First, we consider that in cases where it is necessary and appropriate to have limitations on the way in which the advocate conducts cross-examination, there is a duty on the judge to ensure that those limitations are complied with. This is important to ensure that vulnerable witnesses are able to give the best evidence of which they are capable. Where appropriate the judge, in fairness to defendants, should explain the limitations to the jury and the reasons for them. It is also important that defendants do not perceive, whatever the true position, that the cross-examination by their

[68] [2011] EWCA Crim 1938.
[69] At [36]–[39].

advocate was less effective than that of another advocate in eliciting evidence to defend them on allegations such as those raised in the present case.

This means that the limitations must be clearly defined. One way of achieving this, as suggested in the Advocacy Training Counsel's report,[70] is for a practice note or protocol to be drafted for use by advocates and the trial judge containing the relevant matters set out in paragraph 15 of part 5 of that Report.

Secondly, we observe that if there is some lapse by counsel in failing to comply with the limitations on cross-examination, it is important that the judge gives a relevant direction to the jury when that occurs, both for the benefit of the jury and any other defendant. To leave that direction until the summing up will in many cases mean that it is much less effective than a direction given at the time.

Thirdly, this case highlights that, for vulnerable witnesses, the traditional style of cross-examination where comment is made on inconsistencies during cross-examination must be replaced by a system where those inconsistencies can be drawn to the jury at or about the time when the evidence is being given and not, in long or complex cases, for that comment to have to await the closing speeches at the end of the trial. One solution would be for important inconsistencies to be pointed out, after the vulnerable witness has finished giving evidence, either by the advocate or by the judge, after the necessary discussion with the advocates."

Wills should provide judges with the confidence that in appropriate cases the restriction of questioning by advocates will not render a trial unfair. Important inconsistencies can be pointed out after the vulnerable witness has finished giving evidence, either by the advocate or by the judge, following the necessary discussion between them. The jury should be directed as to the approach the advocate will take in cross-examination when the witness gives their evidence (as would be the case with a direction in respect of special measures). Moreover, if a trial judge sets rules in respect of questioning, it is their responsibility to ensure that advocates comply with those rules, which will ensure the fairness of the trial to all parties by enabling a vulnerable witness to give the best evidence of which they are capable. See also in this regard the informative training materials and guidance issued by the CBA and the Advocacy Training Council.[71]

PRE-TRIAL PREPARATION: PRACTICALITIES

The CPS and police should jointly approach the issue of special measures in   **18.109**
relation to witnesses from an early stage. It is particularly important that police officers clearly communicate information concerning special measures to witnesses, taking care not to raise their expectations and not making promises, which may turn out to be misleading given that it is for the court to decide what, if any, special measures are necessary. Similarly, the ABE guidance notes that early identification of a vulnerable or intimidated witness by the police and discussion

---

[70] Final Report of the Advocacy Training Council Working Group on Vulnerable Witness Handling, *Raising the Bar: The Handling of Vulnerable Witnesses, Victims and Defendants in Court* (Advocacy Training Council, 2011), accessible at *http://www.advocacytrainingcouncil.org/images/word/raisingth ebar.pdf* [accessed November 27, 2013]; see further para.18.01 et seq., above, and para.18.123 et seq., below.

[71] See Advocate's Gateway Toolkits and the training video *A Question of Practice*, available at *http://www.theadvocatesgateway.org/* [accessed November 27, 2013].

with the CPS prosecutor will enable the prosecutor to make informed decisions about special measures at an early stage, e.g. in relation to the appointment of an intermediary. Early identification can also assist the police to record the witness's statement in a format designed to achieve best evidence. As a result of the amendments made to the YJCEA 1999 by the 2009 Act, explained earlier in this chapter, there is now greater flexibility in respect of special measures and so all options should be explained to the witness. The prosecution may well be able to play an adult complainant's ABE interview as their evidence-in-chief, but the prosecutor should ask themselves whether that particular interview maximises the quality of the evidence. If the recording is of poor quality or the interview was not conducted particularly well by the interviewer, the evidence may be more effective given direct to the jury, either from a live-link room or from behind a screen. The witness should not of course be placed under any pressure, but all options should be explored.

PRE-TRIAL THERAPY FOR WITNESSES

18.113   In a recent case, a victim of indecent assault, Mrs Frances Andrade, committed suicide days after giving evidence against her abusers. Her family were critical of the advice given to her to delay therapy until after the trial.[72] We reiterate that there is no bar to a complainant receiving therapy before they give evidence and that in our view, the witness's well-being should be the priority.

LIVE-LINK ROOM

18.121   The position of the camera in the live-link room when a witness is giving evidence is as important as its position when recording the ABE interview, for which see para.18.105A, above. The camera should be focused on the witness so as to pick up facial expressions and demeanour thereby ensuring that the impact of their evidence is not lost.

QUESTIONING BY ADVOCATES

18.123   The guidance given by the Court of Appeal in *Barker* was approved in *Wills*.[73]
         In many cases it will be perfectly possible for a defence advocate to contradict the evidence of a child or vulnerable witness by reference to other evidence rather than by "putting their case" directly to the witness. Other evidence may be found in first complaints or in records held by social services or education departments. Even if external evidence is not available, the advocate may still be able to outline to the jury the basis of their defence and the elements of dispute with the witness before the witness gives evidence, to avoid putting to the witness that they have lied.

[72] See *http://www.theguardian.com/uk/2013/feb/10/frances-andrade-killed-herself-lying* [accessed November 27, 2013].
[73] Above, fn.68.

As noted in the discussion of *Wills* in para.18.107, above, it may be necessary and appropriate for the trial judge to control the style of cross-examination. Any restrictions, and the means by which an advocate intends to challenge the witness's account without putting their case directly to the witness, should be agreed in advance between the advocate and judge. One way of achieving this is for a practice note or protocol to be drafted for use by advocates and the judge at trial, as suggested in the Advocacy Training Council's report, *Raising the Bar: The Handling of Vulnerable Witnesses, Victims and Defendants in Court*.[74] The practice note should describe the nature of the witness's vulnerability and any particular developmental issues to be taken into account when questioning or for trial management purposes, and an agreed outline for the formulation of appropriate questions.[75]

The case of *R. v M and W*[76] involved two 10-year-old defendants alleged to have   18.123A
raped an 8-year-old girl. Somewhat surprisingly, there was no intermediary to assist either the witness or the defendants. The Court of Appeal reaffirmed that vulnerable witnesses should not be asked "questions which contain a statement of the answer which is sought". As David Wurtzel points out, this is the definition of a leading question, which indicates the changes many defence advocates will have to make to their "usual" style of cross-examination.[77]

In *R. v E*[78] the appellant was convicted of child cruelty by punching his five-year-   18.123B
old step-daughter, C. The jury were made aware throughout the trial that he denied punching C. The trial judge prevented defence counsel from putting this assertion directly to C, but specifically directed the jury to make allowances for the difficulties faced by the defence when questioning her.[79] The appellant appealed on the basis that his counsel had been unduly restricted in his cross-examination. In dismissing the appeal, the Court of Appeal stated[80]:

> "The real complaint here, in our view, is that the defence was deprived of the opportunity to confront C in what we might venture to call 'the traditional way'. It is common, in the trial of an adult, to hear, once the nursery slopes of cross-examination have been skied, the assertion: 'You were never punched, hit, kicked as you have suggested, were you?' It was precisely that the judge was anxious to avoid and, in our view, rightly. It would have risked confusion in the mind of the witness whose evidence was bound to take centre stage, and it is difficult to see how it could have been helpful.

[74] Final Report of the Advocacy Training Council Working Group on Vulnerable Witness Handling, *Raising the Bar: The Handling of Vulnerable Witnesses, Victims and Defendants in Court* (Advocacy Training Council, 2011), available at http://www.advocacytrainingcouncil.org/images/word/raisingthebar.pdf [accessed November 27, 2013].
[75] For an overview of the Advocacy Training Council guidance and the Judicial College Checklist, see Adrian Keene, *Towards a Principled Approach to the Cross-Examination of Vulnerable Witnesses* [2012] Crim. L.R. (6) (407–420).
[76] [2010] EWCA Crim 1926.
[77] "Advocacy Focus", *Counsel Magazine*, January 2011, pp.40–42.
[78] [2011] EWCA Crim 3028.
[79] For the appropriateness of such directions, see Adrian Keane, "Towards a Principled Approach to the Cross-Examination of Vulnerable Witnesses" [2012] Crim. L.R. 407.
[80] Above, fn.78 at [28].

Putting the same thing a different way, we struggle to understand how the defendant's right to a fair trial was in any way compromised simply because [his counsel] was not allowed to ask: 'S did not punch you in the tummy, did he?'"

Laura Hoyano has described the combination in *R. v E* of the judge's efforts and defence counsel's cross-examination of C as a textbook case of how to put a defence case to a very young witness.[81] The Court of Appeal also commented: "it is difficult to see that the Appellant could with greater skill have been represented or his interests better served". Defence counsel showed real skill in putting the defence's alternative hypotheses to account for C's injuries with courtesy and gentleness. Tag questions were occasionally used, and with the advantage of being able to analyse the transcript after the conclusion of the trial process, it is possible to see how such questions might have been avoided. With the benefit of pre-recorded examination-in-chief for child witnesses, it is possible for an advocate to plan their cross-examination in some detail and there is an advantage in these types of cases in writing out questions in full before they are asked. By so doing, it is possible to avoid tag questions.

18.124   In addition to those set out in the main work, the points that advocates should bear in mind when questioning vulnerable witnesses include:
- adapt questions to child's developmental stage, enabling *this* child's "best evidence",
- follow a logical sequence,
- allow full opportunity to answer,
- do not ask children to give their address aloud unless for a specific reason,
- never assume that the witness (particularly if a teenager) will tell you that they do not understand the question,
- avoid intimidating or distracting body language, and
- keep tenor, tone and language appropriate to *this* child.

COMPETENCE TO GIVE EVIDENCE

COMPETENCE

18.128   In *R. v F*[82] the Court of Appeal stressed the importance of a trial judge, when determining competence, having the benefit of a full assessment by an intermediary to assist them to understand the witness's capability (with the benefit of special measures). The complainant in that case was profoundly deaf and suffered mild learning difficulties. Two intermediaries assessed her as able to give evidence. The prosecution proposed to rely upon her ABE interview as evidence-in-chief. An

---

[81] See commentary in [2012] Crim. L.R. 563.
[82] [2013] EWCA Crim 424.

intermediary and British sign language ("BSL") interpreter would be present. The judge watched a short extract of the ABE interview and prosecution counsel then asked the complainant a series of questions, including asking her to point to different parts of her body. As a result, it became apparent that the BSL interpreter would have to point to a part of the body to ask the question, so in part leading the witness. The BSL interpreter could not use finger-spelling to see whether the complainant could understand the name of the body part because he was unprepared for that type of questioning. The intermediary's suggestion of drawings or pictures was not taken up. The prosecutor asked no more questions. The judge then asked questions dealing with the concept of time and abstract matters, topics which had not been covered in the intermediaries' assessments. Thereafter it appears that, outside of court, the complainant was shown anatomical drawings and indicated animatedly that she could point to places where she could recall being touched. The judge nonetheless gave a terminating ruling that the complainant was not competent to give evidence, on the basis that there were difficulties asking her about body parts in a non-leading way and she had difficulty dealing with abstract concepts and concepts of time.

The prosecution successfully appealed the ruling under s.58 of the Criminal Justice Act 2003. The Court of Appeal reviewed the ABE interview and transcript and concluded that with "time and patience", and the assistance of a BSL interpreter, the complainant was able to give a comprehensible account of the alleged offences. The difficulties in this case arose out of the questioner's inability to ask questions appropriately for this particular witness, as opposed to the witness's lack of comprehension. The competence hearing did not fully and fairly explore the complainant's ability to communicate. There was "a lack of preparation and a lack of ability to respond flexibly to the difficulties which arose". The Court recognised that the questioning of vulnerable witnesses requires "not only training, flexibility and sensitivity but time and patience". It approved the guidance in *Barker* and drew attention to the further guidance offered in the Crown Court Bench Book and the Advocacy Training Council's report *Raising the Bar: the Handling of Vulnerable Witnesses, Victims and Defendants in Court*.[83] As noted in para.18.123, this report includes the recommendation that the advocates and the trial judge agree a practice direction and protocol as to the limits of cross-examination.

In allowing the prosecution appeal, the Court of Appeal held that whilst the judge had identified the correct test, she had substituted the issue of the interpreter's difficulties for the test of whether the witness could understand questions and give intelligible answers. With the right assistance from a BSL interpreter, the witness could understand and be understood. Clearly the judge remains under a continuing duty to keep the issue of competence under review and the Court of Appeal reiterated that careful consideration should be given

---

[83] Above, fn.70.

before deciding that a competence hearing is required at the beginning of a case.

18.132   *R. v MH*[84] involved a four-year-old giving evidence at a trial for sexual abuse 15 months after the recording of the ABE interview. The reason for the delay was to allow the forensic examination of the appellant's computer. The Court of Appeal confirmed that delay of itself will not necessarily render a very young witness incompetent to give evidence, but the passage of time may affect the child's ability to give intelligible answers about the incident. It follows that where a child is, despite the passage of time, able to give intelligible answers they will be competent. The trial judge should, of course, direct the jury to consider any disadvantage to the defendant because of the delay.

---

[84] [2012] EWCA Crim 2725, also reported at [2013] Crim. L.R. 10, 849–853, with commentary by Laura Hoyano.

CHAPTER 19

RESTRICTIONS ON EVIDENCE OR QUESTIONS ABOUT THE COMPLAINANT'S SEXUAL HISTORY

INTRODUCTION

A clear understanding of the restrictions set out in s.41 of the Youth Justice and **19.01** Criminal Evidence Act 1999, as explained in *R. v A (No.2)*, is critical to the smooth running of trials of sexual offences. The courts are frequently faced with wholly unmeritorious applications and appeals, even over 10 years after the provision was implemented.[1] Many applications will have great difficulty in surmounting the credibility restriction in s.41(4) (evidence may not be adduced nor question asked if the purpose would be to impugn the complainant's credibility as a witness) and the test set out in s.41(2)(b) (court must be satisfied that refusal of leave might render unsafe a conclusion of the jury on a relevant issue in the case). A close scrutiny of applications is essential in order to tease out the real issues. *R. v DB*,[2] discussed below, is an excellent recent example of a case in which the Court of Appeal subjected complicated matters founding the s.41 applications at trial to rigorous examination, concluding that s.41(4) applied and the s.41(2)(b) test, in the Court's view, did not begin to be satisfied.

The wide use of social networking sites has led to s.41 issues arising in respect of entries posted by complainants both before and after the time of the allegation. Recent Court of Appeal judgments on this issue are highly instructive.[3]

---

[1] See *R. v KJC* [2012] EWCA Crim 1669, where it was suggested that the complainant was drawing on what she had alleged against another over three years before; *Sunny Islam* [2012] EWCA Crim 3106.

[2] [2012] EWCA Crim 1235.

[3] *Ben-Rejab* [2011] EWCA Crim 1136; *R. v D* [2011] EWCA Crim 2305.

SECTIONS 41 TO 43 OF THE YOUTH JUSTICE AND CRIMINAL EVIDENCE ACT 1999

Scope and Application of Section 41

"any sexual behaviour"

Posting entries on social networking sites

19.26 The words "any sexual behaviour or experience" in s.42(1)(c) are extremely wide in their ambit and have been given a wide meaning by the Court of Appeal. Words alone can amount to sexual behaviour.[4] The behaviour or experience need not necessarily involve another person. In *Ben-Rejab*[5] the Court of Appeal took the view that the expression is plainly wide enough to embrace the activity of viewing pornography or engaging in sexually-charged messaging over a live internet connection. It followed that it included answering questions in a sexually explicit quiz. The Court had little difficulty in rejecting the submission that activity by the complainant (C) in entering such quizzes and posting this fact on a publicly available website page amounted to relevant and admissible evidence.

The appellant in that case was charged with two rapes, sexual assault by penetration and sexual assault of C. It was alleged that C had been subjected to a sexual ordeal by the appellant and two others in October 2008 after meeting the appellant at a nightclub. C was a Facebook user who regularly made entries on her own page and uploaded photographs to it. In February 2010 she made a victim impact statement in which she described how she had become a changed person as a result of the ordeal. She did not socialise any more. She rarely went to town because of fear of seeing the appellant and his associates. She had not been clubbing since the incident happened. She had flash-backs and panic attacks. She had undergone counselling and had been prescribed anti-depressants and sleeping tablets. Her entries on Facebook tended to demonstrate that her victim impact statement was untrue or exaggerated. The trial judge gave leave for C to be cross-examined about this suggested inconsistency. She maintained that she had been changed by the experience but conceded she had been out socialising on a number of occasions, contrary to the impression she had given in her victim impact statement.

However, the appellant's counsel wished to go further and ask C about other entries she had posted on her Facebook page. On December 18, 2008 she posted:

"[C] is having sex! Click here to see more or try it yourself!"

On or about February 9, 2009 the following further entries appeared:

---

[4] cf. *Grout* [2011] EWCA Crim 299, relating to the meaning of "sexual activity" in s.8 of the 2003 Act.

[5] [2011] EWCA Crim 1136.

"[C] just took the Best Places to have Sex Around the House quiz. See your match score!"

"[C] took How good are you in bed? Quiz and the result is Incredible Lover. Click to compare your results or try other quizzes."

"[C] took Whats your sex style? Quiz and the result is YOU ARE FIERCE. Click here to compare your results or try other quizzes."

On January 12, 2010 the following entries appeared:

"[C] Answered some questions on some weird questionnaire where you get fined for ceetain [sic] sexual encounters!!! Lol xxxx"

"[C] My fine is ... wait for it ... £660.60!!!! oops! Apparently I'v [sic] been a naughty girl!!!!"

The judge refused leave to ask C about these Facebook entries. He took the view that questions concerning these entries would inevitably be about C's sexual behaviour on other occasions and so were caught by s.41. The purpose of the questions was, the judge concluded, to undermine C's credibility as a witness. It followed that, even if one of the gateways in s.41(3) was satisfied, the purpose of the questions prohibited their admission. In the alternative, if s.41(3) or the rebuttal gateway in s.41(5) applied, it could not be said, as required by s.41(2)(b), that a refusal of leave might have the result of rendering unsafe a conclusion of the jury on any relevant issue.

On appeal, the Court of Appeal rejected the appellant's submission that C's participation in the quizzes was not sexual behaviour. Pitchford L.J. posed the question: What motive can there have been when engaging in the activity of answering sexually explicit questions unless it was to obtain sexual pleasure from it? It was certainly the purpose for which the judge concluded the defence sought to ask these questions. The questions had no purpose unless the jury was being invited to conclude that C was the sort of person who would engage in consensual foursome sexual activity and was not the sort of person who had recently been the victim of rape. Furthermore, the Court stated that even if it was wrong about that, since the proposed questions all related to activity which took place two months or so after the time of the allegation, they would have been of minimal value to the jury's task.

It follows that sexually provocative postings on Facebook may amount to "sexual behaviour" and will engage the s.41 regime. Applications to adduce such material are likely to fall foul of the credibility restriction in s.41(4). In any event, whether s.41 is engaged or not, where there is no direct connection to the allegation, such postings are likely to be of little or no relevance to the issues in the case.

R. v D[6] is an excellent illustration of the difficulties likely to be encountered by   **19.26A**
those wishing to adduce evidence of a complainant's social network postings. On an application for leave to appeal against his conviction of rape, the applicant wished to apply for the introduction of fresh evidence under s.23 of the Criminal

[6] [2011] EWCA Crim 2305.

Appeal Act 1968. The "fresh" material consisted of 57 pages of Facebook printouts taken from the 13-year-old complainant's profile. Apart from one which was posted a day or so before the alleged rape, all the other postings post-dated the event and the trial. They contained pictures of the complainant posing provocatively, boasting about how much she drank and her interest in having sexual intercourse. Mackay J. commented:

> "The complex mixture of motives which impels people, especially young people, to post messages on such sites includes, the court suspects, the desire to attract attention, admiration from peers and to provoke the interest of others in the person posting the material. We suspect the objective truth and the dissemination of factual evidence comes low on the list. In this instance the complainant's postings can be summarised as her saying outrageous or provocative things or claiming daring behaviour on her part. There are many entries, for example, boasting about how much she drank and the great hangovers she suffered as a result. In addition, there are claims of interest in sexual matters. These come later in the postings and are to be found at the time of trial. By the following August she was posting photographs of herself and of herself with other girls. All the pictures are of the girls clothed, but provocatively so, no doubt in a way perceived by her and by them sexually attractive. Choosing our words with care, they are images not dissimilar in content and presentation to what can be seen travelling many an underground escalator, albeit the model in question here is a girl in her early teens rather than a grown woman. None of these postings lays claim to direct sexual activity on the part of the complainant, though three or four of them indicate that she thinks quite a lot about her sexuality and indeed about having sexual intercourse."

The Court of Appeal had to consider whether, had the material been available at trial, it would have been admissible, and whether its introduction would have required an application under s.41. The applicant's counsel submitted that no application under s.41 was necessary and the jury might have taken a different view about the complainant had they known that such thoughts as these were in her mind and such boasts or claims about her activity were being made, if not to the world at large, at least to the world that visits Facebook. The Court reacted in a similar way as in *Ben-Rejab*. First, the so-called "fresh evidence" was of a non-existent value and not relevant to the issues the jury had to decide. The complainant had never been put forward as a "complete innocent". Secondly, if the Court's leave was required under s.41, there were immovable barriers to the introduction of the evidence. No gateway had been opened. The evidence would have fallen foul of the credibility restriction in s.41(4).

19.26B In an instructive analysis of social networking sites as criminal evidence, Michael O'Floinn and Professor David Ormerod observe that the most likely admissibility route for evidence of sexual behaviour in a posting on a social networking site is as rebuttal evidence under s.41(5).[7] This could arise where a complainant has given evidence suggesting that she is monogamous, sexually modest or, in the words of Mackay J. in *R. v D*, a "complete innocent". O'Floinn and Ormerod refer to a case reported to them in which a complainant had given evidence that "she

---

[7] *Social networking material as criminal evidence* [2012] Crim. L.R. 501.

did not go in for one night stands" and "did not go prepared with condoms". In such circumstances, reference to a specific instance or instances of previous or subsequent sexual behaviour in a Facebook posting which rebut this assertion might be admissible under the rebuttal gateway.

PROCEDURE

Part 36 of the Criminal Procedure Rules 2013 set out the procedure in the same terms as Pt 36 of the Criminal Procedure Rules 2010. The mandatory requirement that the application must be in writing is still frequently overlooked.[8] Courts should ensure that there is strict compliance.[9]   **19.42**

THE FOUR GATEWAYS AND TWO RESTRICTIONS

THE THIRD GATEWAY—SECTION 41(3)(C)—CONSENT AND SIMILARITY

Mere similarity is not sufficient to open this gateway. The behaviour of the complainant must be so similar to the allegation that the similarity cannot reasonably be explained as a coincidence. Furthermore, the similarity must be relevant similarity. In *R. v MM*[10] the Court of Appeal held that the trial judge had been right to reject the argument that the complainant's sexual behaviour on two earlier occasions opened this gateway. At the appellant's trial for rape, it was an admitted fact that the complainant and the appellant had engaged in full sexual relations, including anal intercourse, before the complainant ended the relationship. The complainant's evidence was that she was simply not prepared to engage in sexual activity in the circumstances in which the appellant was demanding it. The "parallels" to which the appellant referred were (i) the complainant's willingness to engage in fellatio in a public place (oral sex performed by the complainant upon the appellant in a cinema), and (ii) her willingness to engage in sexual intercourse in her own bedroom (anal and vaginal sexual intercourse with the appellant in the complainant's bedroom after sending her younger brother out of the house). The incidents took place four months and three months respectively before the time of the allegation. The material feature of the alleged sexual behaviour of the complainant at the time of the alleged rape was not the fact of intercourse of any particular type, which was not in issue, but the circumstances in which it occurred, namely at 07.00 in a bedroom adjoining the complainant's mother's bedroom and with her sister, brother and friend moving about outside the room. In its environmental circumstances this behaviour was not so similar that it might support a conclusion that coincidence could be excluded, nor was it probative on the issue of consent. Nor was there any sufficient chronological nexus   **19.73**

---

[8] *Ogbodo* [2011] EWCA Crim 564.
[9] *McKendrick* [2004] EWCA Crim 1393.
[10] [2011] EWCA Crim 1291.

between the events to render the previous behaviour in any sense probative of the issue the jury had to resolve.

Relevance to the issue of consent of the complainant's previous (and subsequent) sexual behaviour with the defendant

19.91   In *Ogbodo*[11] the Court of Appeal held that the trial judge had made the correct distinction between the admissibility of alleged previous sexual behaviour of the complainant with the applicant and her alleged previous sexual behaviour with third parties. The prosecution case was that the applicant lured the complainant to a flat on the false pretence of there being some emergency but the real purpose was to rape. Once at the flat, he locked her in and detained her against her will. The applicant held a knife to her throat and threatened to burn her eyes out with a burning cigarette if she did not comply. He then forcibly chewed her nipples and anally raped her twice. He also orally raped her after he had anally raped her.

The defence case was that all the sexual activity was consensual. They had met that day for the purpose of having sex. They had previously engaged in sex on over 30 occasions and had known each other for a number of years. The judge allowed the applicant's counsel to explore the question of previous sexual relations between the complainant and the appellant, but refused an application in relation to allegations about the complainant's sexual behaviour with other persons. There was no suggestion that anyone other than the applicant and the complainant was present at the time of the incident that the jury had to consider. Previous group sex was, on the face of it, irrelevant. The Court of Appeal held that the judge had not unduly limited the complainant's cross-examination.

19.91A   It is not to be thought that, merely because there has been a previous sexual relationship between the complainant and the defendant, the date of the last act of sexual intercourse between them is necessarily admissible. In *R. v S*[12] the appellant had been convicted of a single count of rape of his wife. It was alleged that on 15 December 2008 he had gone to his wife's flat and committed a particularly violent rape. It was argued on appeal that the trial judge had wrongly refused leave under s.41 to cross-examine the complainant about consensual sex with the appellant that had occurred just days before the alleged rape, on December 6, 2008. It was conceded by the appellant's counsel that this evidence did not fall within the provisions of s.41(3)(c) if literally interpreted. However, it was argued that the judge should have adopted the permissive construction of the section which the House of Lords approved in the speech of Lord Steyn in *R v A (No.2)*, i.e. he should have admitted the evidence on the basis that it was so relevant to the issue of consent that to exclude it would endanger the fairness of the trial.[13] It was submitted that, without the knowledge that the complainant and appellant had sexual intercourse together on December 6, the jury may have been under the

[11] Above, fn.8.
[12] [2010] EWCA Crim 1579.
[13] [2002] 1 A.C. 45, at [46].

mistaken impression that there had been no sexual intercourse for a period of six months during which the complainant said in interview she had been very unhappy.

In the Court of Appeal's view it was perfectly clear to the jury that unhappiness had caused the separation but that in November there had been a resumption of normal co-habitation between husband and wife at their new flat. It was also clear that the complainant was describing a sexually active relationship which was, nevertheless, a source of unhappiness for her. Furthermore there was no logical connection between the last act of consensual intercourse between husband and wife and the event of the alleged rape.

As for the responsibility of trial judges, in accordance with the speech of Lord Steyn in *R. v A (No.2)*, to admit evidence that is so relevant to the issue of consent that to exclude it would endanger the fairness of the trial, the judgment of fairness is fact-sensitive and will depend upon the detail of the issues which arise in the case. In the view of the Court of Appeal in *R. v S*, it was of no particular moment in the jury's assessment of the issue of consent in that case whether the last act of intercourse occurred on December 6 or a few days or a week or more earlier. What mattered to the jury was the nature of the relationship after December when, it was common ground, the deterioration became terminal. The question was whether the admitted contact between the parties can only have confirmed to the appellant that the complainant meant what she said, and clearly the jury found that she did.

THE FOURTH GATEWAY—SECTION 41(5)—THE REBUTTAL GATEWAY

For discussion of rebuttal evidence arising from postings on social networking sites, see para.19.26B, above.   **19.102**

THE COURT'S OVERRIDING DUTY UNDER SECTION 41(2)(B)

A careful analysis is required of the evidence sought to be adduced under s.41.   **19.112**
This is likely to involve considering whether the evidence is relevant to an issue in the case falling to be proved by the prosecution or defence, whether a gateway has truly been opened, whether the evidence simply goes to credit and so is outlawed by s.41(4), and whether the s.41(2)(b) test is satisfied.

By virtue of s.41(2)(b), the court may not give leave even if it is satisfied that a   **19.112A**
gateway is open under s.41(3) or (5), unless it also satisfied that a refusal of leave may have the result of rendering unsafe a conclusion of the jury or (as the case may be) the court on any relevant issue in the case. The application of the provision is illustrated by *R. v DB*,[14] in which the appellant was convicted at a re-trial of six counts of rape and two counts of assault by penetration of his daughter over a

---

[14] [2012] EWCA Crim 1235.

period of over a year when she was aged 13 or 14. At trial the appellant categorically denied all the sexual abuse offences.

The complainant had undergone two abortions. She said that the appellant was the "father" of the terminated pregnancies. She ran away on August 22 alleging she had been raped on that day, and she was taken into police protection five days later. She was examined medically on August 27 and at the time she said that she had only had intercourse with her father. She repeated this in her ABE interview the following day; indeed, she said that, but for her father, she still would have been a virgin. In fact, endocervical swabs identified the presence of male DNA which was not the appellant's. The medical assessment was that it would have been deposited some three or four days before the examination. It was found to belong to a 41-year-old Asian man referred to by the court as X.

Later, the complainant admitted that she had had intercourse with her boyfriend on three occasions when her father was away on holiday. This was before the last occasion on which she was raped. Notwithstanding the evidence about the DNA, she denied ever having intercourse with the Asian male X.

The prosecution conceded that the appellant ought to be allowed to cross-examine the complainant with respect to her boyfriend. This was because it was evidence of sexual intercourse occurring during the period of the abortions and the complainant had been secretive about the relationship, so the prosecution accepted it was potentially relevant to the appellant's contention that he was not the father.

However, the trial judge rejected an application under s.41 in relation to X. The basis of the application was that the appellant had lied about her relationship with X. It was submitted that this was potentially relevant to the question whether she was lying about having intercourse with her father, and also the evidence provided a potential motive for her leaving home. She might have wanted to leave home in order to have a sexual relationship with X rather than, as claimed, to escape the clutches of a father who had just raped her. Section 41(4) was not engaged as the primary reason for seeking to adduce the evidence was to demonstrate her motive in leaving the house.

The judge expressly adopted the prosecution's reasoning. The evidence in respect of X concerned sexual activity which had occurred outside the relevant period when the alleged sexual involvement with the appellant had occurred. It cast no light on what might have happened during that period; it was wholly collateral to any issue in the case. The aim was to show that the complainant had lied about having a relationship with anyone other than her father. That went to credit and was outlawed by s.41(4). In any event, there was already evidence before the jury that she had lied about having sex only with her father, because she had admitted in evidence having sex with her boyfriend. It followed that the refusal would not render unsafe a conclusion of the jury on any relevant issue in the case.

The Court of Appeal accepted that, to the extent that the existence of a relationship with X might have provided a motive for the complainant to leave home other than the reason she gave, it would not be an entirely collateral issue because of its relevance to the last allegation of rape. However, even in relation to that count, the judge had been right for a number of reasons to reject the application in relation to X:

  (i) Section 42(1)(a) defines a "relevant issue in the case" as "any issue falling to be proved by the prosecution or defence in the trial of the accused". It was highly questionable whether an issue of motive can be said to constitute an issue in the case as so defined. Elias L.J. accepted that the concept of "an issue in the case" will sometimes have to be stretched in order to ensure that a trial is art.6 compliant.[15] Too rigid a construction of the subsection might, in some cases, exclude evidence of motive which it would be unfair to exclude. However, the Court did not believe this was such a case. Even if it were the case that the complainant had wanted to leave home in order to continue her relationship with X, that did not explain why she would make sexual abuse allegations against her father. The allegations of physical abuse established at the first trial would have been sufficient to provide cover for her actions. It was pure speculation to suppose she would need to have fabricated such an extravagant claim in order to create a false reason to leave the house.

  (ii) Section 41(2)(b) did not begin to be satisfied in this case. The Court of Appeal could not see how the failure to leave the jury the possibility of this particular motive could have led them to reach an unsafe conclusion on any relevant issue in the case. In any event, a range of other possible explanations, unconnected with any alleged rape, as to why the complainant wanted to leave the house that morning had been deployed in evidence. Furthermore, given the weakness and essentially wholly peripheral nature of this allegation, the only reason left for wanting to adduce this evidence would be to challenge the credit of the complainant, and that would be unambiguously barred by s.41(4).

The Court of Appeal also rejected the submission that the identity of X should have been revealed, since then he could have been interviewed and he may have admitted to a longstanding relationship with the complainant, which could have explained how it was that she became pregnant. The Court said that this submission faced insurmountable practical difficulties and was based on wholly speculative contentions. Further, there was no evidence to suggest that the relationship with X had existed for that lengthy period of time.

THE TWO RESTRICTIONS

The credibility restriction—section 41(4)

See the analysis of *R. v DB* in para.19.112A et seq., above.   **19.114**

---

[15] Citing (at [45]) the observations of Keene L.J. in *R. v RT, R. v MH* [2001] EWCA Crim 1877, for which see the main work, para.19.62.

Evidence that the Complainant Has Made False Complaints

19.126 There must be a complaint. An analysis of the four alleged false complaints in *Lefeuvre*[16] revealed there had either been no complaint of sexual assault, or nothing to suggest it was a false complaint, or no complaint had been made. The Court of Appeal held that the judge had been correct to refuse to allow the defence to cross-examine the complainant about each of these matters.

Proper evidential foundation, not strong factual foundation

19.131 In the leading case *R. v RT; R. v MH*,[17] it was held that false statements in the past by a complainant about sexual assaults are not about sexual behaviour and so are not caught by s.41. More recently, guidance was given in *R. v AM*[18] as to the need for an evidential foundation for an allegation of false complaint. Both cases are discussed in the main work.[19] Recent decisions illustrate the principles in operation. Judges need to evaluate the evidence so as to decide (i) whether there was an earlier complaint and, if so, (ii) whether there is a proper evidential foundation that it was false, i.e. the jury could have been satisfied on the evidence that it was untrue (not that there was a strong factual foundation). Suggestions of false complaint must not be used as a device to avoid the s.41 restrictions on evidence about sexual behaviour.[20] In *R. v K*[21] the Court of Appeal, when dismissing the appellant's appeal against conviction of rape of his 16-year-old step-daughter, emphasised that for a complaint to be relevant, there has to be evidence to demonstrate both that there was a complaint and that it was false. It had been argued on appeal that when aged 14 the complainant had made a false allegation of rape against a boy at school, in a 999 call in which she stated that the boy "basically forced her to do it". She made a statement the following day saying that the sexual intercourse had been consensual and that she had gone along with it as she had not wished to hurt the boy's feelings. At trial, the judge accepted that the complainant had never made an allegation of rape, false or otherwise, and the evidence in relation to that incident was irrelevant. The Court of Appeal agreed.

19.131A In *R. v MC*[22] it was held that where it is contended on appeal that there was a proper evidential foundation for the conclusion that a complaint was false, the appellant has to show that the judge reached a conclusion that was not reasonably open to him in his evaluation of materials relied upon in support of the s.41 application.

---

[16] [2011] EWCA Crim 1253.
[17] [2001] EWCA Crim 1877.
[18] [2009] EWCA Crim 618.
[19] paras 19.128 and 19.131 et seq.
[20] [2012] EWCA Crim 1669.
[21] *Knight* [2013] EWCA Crim 2486.
[22] [2012] EWCA Crim 213.

What amounts to a false complaint? In *Guled Yusuf*[23] the Court of Appeal made clear that earlier cases that made reference to "false statements" were not giving some formal meaning to the word "statement". In that case, the trial judge had refused to allow cross-examination about a previous allegation of rape on the basis that the complainant had not made a statement. No formal statement had been taken, there was no ABE interview, and no withdrawal statement. The Court of Appeal held that the complainant had made statements to various officers and presumably to the doctor who examined her. Hooper L.J. explained: **19.131B**

> "Whatever the precise words used by her, she was rightly understood by the officers to be making an allegation of rape which they then investigated and recorded as "no crime". The defence, in our view, had a proper evidential basis for asserting that she made a statement and that it was untrue, and the judge was wrong to prevent the appellant's advocate from cross-examining the complainant about these matters."

There has been a tendency for the courts and counsel to overlook the fact that, if there is an application to cross-examine a complainant on the basis that she has made a previous (or subsequent) false complaint of a sexual offence, this engages s.100 of the CJA 2003, which regulates the admissibility of evidence of bad character against non-defendants.[24] In *Guled Yusuf* the trial judge failed to make reference to s.100 in her ruling, although the defence case statement referred to such an application. Hooper L.J. observed: **19.131C**

> "There can be no doubt, in our view, that the [Crime Record Information System] report[25] provided ample evidence of misconduct, or of a disposition towards misconduct, and thus of bad character on the part of [the complainant] . . . namely setting in motion a substantial investigation and identifying three suspects and then declining to co-operate by producing the knickers; by not telling the officer that the blood on her clothing and from her vagina was, was likely to be, menstrual; and by not attending scheduled ABE interviews and by making herself scarce, so that police resources were wasted."

The Court of Appeal took the view that if the trial judge had considered the provisions of s.100(1)(b), she would have found that there was sufficient material to pass the s.100 threshold of "substantive probative value".

---

[23] [2010] EWCA Crim 359.
[24] Discussed in para.16.77 et seq. of the main work and above.
[25] The Court of Appeal pointed out that the CRIS report was a business record and so prima facie admissible as to the truth of its contents under s.117 of the CJA 2003.

EXPERT EVIDENCE IN SEX CASES*

EXPERT EVIDENCE

In 2011 the Law Commission reported on the admissibility of expert evidence in **20.04** criminal trials in England and Wales.[1] It criticised the laissez-faire approach that had developed at common law to the admission of expert opinion evidence without sufficient regard to whether it was sufficiently reliable to be considered by a jury. In the Commission's view, this problem was exacerbated by two factors. First, expert evidence is often technical and complex, and jurors lack the experience to assess its reliability properly. Secondly, there is no clear legal test to safeguard the reliability of expert evidence. The Commission recommended the introduction of a new reliability-based test of admissibility for expert evidence in criminal proceedings, with a view to excluding unreliable evidence. It published a draft Bill alongside the report, but there are no current signs that the Commission's recommendations will be taken forward in full. See also the Forensic Science Regulator's recently published consultation paper on validation.[2]

THE DUTIES OF AN EXPERT

For r.33.3 of the Criminal Procedure Rules 2010, see now r.33.3 of the Criminal **20.09** Procedure Rules 2013. The two provisions are identical in all material respects.

---

* The authors are indebted to David Claxton, Barrister, of Red Lion Chambers, who was the principal drafter of the update of this chapter.

[1] *Expert Evidence in Criminal Proceedings in England and Wales*, March 22, 2011 (Law Com 325).

[2] Forensic Science Regulator, *Guidance: Validation Consultation Draft*, August 2013, available at *https://www.gov.uk/government/uploads/system/uploads/attachment_data/file/229944/fsr-validation-guidance-consulation-2013.pdf* [accessed November 24, 2013].

General Considerations

20.13 *R. v T*,[3] which concerned the admissibility of the expression of conclusions by an
expert from the Forensic Science Service, established a wider principle concerning
the presentation of expert evidence. The appellant had been convicted of murder.
Part of the case against him rested on a comparison of a shoe-print found at the
crime scene with shoes seized from the appellant. The conventional approach to
such analyses is to look at the pattern on the sole, the alignment of the sole-
pattern, general wear and specific damage. It is usual practice to express the
findings that result from such analysis using a linguistic scale. The specific
conclusion of this expert ("moderately strong support") was underpinned by a
mathematical formula which used likelihood-ratios, i.e. a statistical methodology.
This was also the standard practice of the Forensic Science Service. In allowing
the appeal, giving the judgment of the Court of Appeal, Thomas L.J. (as he then
was) held that statistical formulae should not be used, given the state of the data
in relation to shoe-markings. The state of the underlying data was insufficient and
inadequately precise to support propositions which purported to be based on a
scientific approach. Arguably, the *ratio* of this case would apply to any field in
which the raw data used to perform a comparative analysis is limited in scale or
precision.

Expert evidence of the effects of sexual assault on victims

20.13 *R. v ER* was followed in *C v R.*,[4] which concerned sexual offences allegedly
committed some years before against the appellant's daughter (D) and his step-
son. At trial, evidence was adduced from a school art therapist and a counsellor
with the aim of establishing the circumstances in which D originally complained
and how the complaints came to light. During the course of their evidence, the
witnesses were asked their opinions on the truth of D's evidence. The judge
directed the jury that they could use that evidence as evidence supporting the
truth of the allegations. C was convicted of buggery and indecency with a child,
4 counts of anal rape and 15 counts of rape. On appeal, the Court of Appeal
quashed the convictions and ordered a retrial. It said that evidence given by
experts which tended to convey to the jury the expert's opinion of the truth or
otherwise of the complaint was clearly inadmissible. *R. v ER* established that the
truth and reliability of the evidence was a matter for the jury, not for the expert.
The judge had misdirected the jury by explicitly inviting them to use the experts'
opinion as to the truth of the allegations in reaching their conclusion. There was
a real risk that the jury founded their conclusion in part upon the views of the
experts and, as such, it was not possible to conclude that the verdicts were safe in
respect of D. Further, that evidence might have influenced the jury in their

---

[3] [2010] EWCA Crim 2439.
[4] [2012] EWCA Crim 1478.

decision in relation to C's step-son. Accordingly, the convictions in relation to both complainants had to be quashed.

EXPERT EVIDENCE AS TO MEMORY

In *R. v H*[5] the appellant was convicted of 22 offences relating to the sexual abuse **20.30** of his three step-sons. One of the step-sons, D, was between five and eight years' old during the period when the abuse was said to have occurred. One of the arguments advanced in support of an appeal against the convictions, addressed under the heading *Early Childhood Memory*, related to the evidence of D, whose earliest recollection took him back to the age of three or four years' old. It was submitted that the judge ought to have warned the jury about the dangers and unreliability of purported memories of early childhood. The Court was referred to expert evidence on the unreliability of detailed early childhood memories proffered from Professor Conway, which was to the effect that there is childhood amnesia until about the age of six or seven, before which childhood memory is disjointed and patchy, so that detailed recollection should be regarded as unreliable. Rix L.J., giving the judgment of the Court, stated[6]:

> "[S]uch evidence has come to be regarded as unsatisfactory in itself: see *R. v Jonathan CWS; R. v Malcolm W* [2006] EWCA Crim 1404, [2007] 2 All ER 974; *R v E* [2009] EWCA Crim 1370. At most this controversial evidence, now sceptically regarded, could in any event relate only to counts 1 and 2 on the indictment ... Moreover, D did not purport to remember early matters in any suspicious detail. [Counsel for the appellant] suggested that the jury should have been warned that even an honest and apparently credible witness, speaking of his extreme childhood, may be mistaken and then led astray by false recollection: as though this was the constant experience of the courts, as a sort of analogy to a *Turnbull* identification direction ... We disagree. The difficulties of recollection of our early childhood are familiar to us all: although perhaps it is only those who have suffered abuse at an early age who can really understand the extent to which the abuse may be known even if the details of the surrounding circumstances are not. In any event the judge did warn the jury, in more traditional terms, of the problem of delay, the danger of prejudice to a defendant, and that this must be in the jury's mind when deciding whether the prosecution had made them sure of the defendant's guilt. He also cautioned them that the passage of time 'may play tricks on memories'; and asked them to 'Look at all of the evidence fairly and apply your collective knowledge of life in deciding where the truth lies'. In our judgment these were entirely satisfactory directions."

In *Anderson*[7] the expert opinion of Professor Conway was used as the basis of an **20.30A** appeal against a conviction from 16 years earlier. The appellant was a former schoolteacher and the complainant of sexual abuse was one of his former pupils. Giving the judgment of the Court of Appeal, Hallett L.J. stated[8]:

---

[5] [2011] EWCA Crim 2344.
[6] At [40]–[41].
[7] [2012] EWCA Crim 1785.
[8] At [9].

"His [Professor Conway's] reports are controversial. Only once to our knowledge, in an 'unusual' case, has this court accepted his evidence (see *R. v JH and R. v TG* [2006] 1 Cr. App. R. 10). However, the court was unaware at that time of significant criticisms of Professor Conway's methodology which have led to the courts declining to receive his evidence (see *R. v S* [2006] EWCA Crim 1404, *R. v E* [2009] EWCA Crim 1370 and *R. v H* [2011] EWCA Crim 2344). In the light of those decisions, we have our doubts as to whether *JH and TG*, which was restricted very much to a specific set of facts, would be decided the same way today. Professor Conway may wish to consider amending his CV in which, we note, he mentions only *R v JH* and *R v TG*."

Hallett L.J. added[9] that "[i]t is also highly unlikely, given the state of medical opinion, that this court will receive the evidence of the kind put forward by Professor Conway in the near future."

[9] At [18].

CHAPTER 21

MEDICAL ASPECTS OF SEXUAL ASSAULT

by Dr Beata Cybulska

SEXUAL ASSAULT STATISTICS

Based on aggregated data from the Crime Survey for England and Wales in   **21.03**
2009/10, 2010/11 and 2011/12, 2.5 per cent of females and 0.4 per cent of males
said that they had been a victim of a sexual offence (including attempts) in the
previous 12 months.[1] This equates to around 473,000 adult victims of sexual
offences (around 404,000 females and 72,000 males) on average per year. Their
experiences span the full spectrum of sexual offences. Around 90 per cent of
victims of the most serious sexual offences knew the perpetrator, compared with
less than half for other sexual offences.

In 2011/12, the police recorded 53,700 sexual offences in England and Wales.[2]
Of those, 71 per cent were the most serious sexual offences of rape and sexual
assault. There were 4,155 offences initially recorded as sexual offences that the
police later decided were not crimes. The "no crime" rate for sexual offences was
7.2 per cent, compared with a "no crime" rate for overall police recorded crime

[1] *An overview of sexual offending in England and Wales* (Home Office and Ministry of Justice, January
2013), available at *https://www.gov.uk/government/publications/an-overview-of-sexual-offending-in-eng
land-and-wales* [accessed January 2, 2014].
[2] *An overview of sexual offending in England and Wales* (Home Office and Ministry of Justice, January
2013), available at *https://www.gov.uk/government/publications/an-overview-of-sexual-offending-in-eng
land-and-wales* [accessed January 2, 2014].

of 3.4 per cent. The "no crime" rate for rape was 10.8 per cent. The 7 per cent increase in recorded sexual offences between 2008/09 and 2010/11 is attributed to greater encouragement by the police for victims to come forward and improvements in police recording, rather than an increase in the level of victimisation.

In 2011, 2,873 defendants were prosecuted for rape, on a principal offence basis, at the magistrates' courts, with 2,807 committed to the Crown Court for trial and 1,153 convicted, giving a prosecution to conviction ratio in 2011 of 40 per cent, which represents a 34 per cent rise over the previous year.[3] In 2011/12, 8,334 defendants were prosecuted for sexual offences excluding rape and the proportion of successful outcomes was 75.7 per cent, with a rise of just under 3 per cent in guilty pleas to 63 per cent.

21.04   A commonly held rape myth is that most victims of rape will try to fight off their attacker, whereas in reality most victims will show little physical resistance to an attack.[4] There is often an incorrect assumption that if there is no injury, torn clothing, struggle or cry for help, an assault was not committed. Other rape myths involve blaming victims for bringing it on themselves through their allegedly provocative behaviour or clothing complicated by an inaccurate assumption as to how a victim should respond to being raped.[5] Published literature on the subject highlights the negative attitudes of potential jury members towards rape and the need to educate the public about the reality of rape.[6] For the permissibility of judicial comment designed to prevent a jury being influenced by rape myths, see para.1.221 et seq. of the main work.

PSYCHOLOGICAL CONSEQUENCES OF RAPE

21.06   Recent literature on the psychological response to sexual assault[7] highlights the impact of neurophysiological mechanisms on the reaction to a threat, in contrast to the reaction to a perceived threat. When imagining our response, we use our higher brain function and think rationally and logically; yet when the experience actually occurs, our higher brain functions are likely to be impaired (as a result of the threat we are experiencing) and we respond instinctively.

Most people faced with a threat of sexual assault do not actively defend themselves. The perception of threat, not the actual threat, typically governs individual responses during the assault. Most will be fearful, disorientated and

---

[3] *Violence against Women and Girls Crime Report 2011-2012,* available at *http://www.cps.gov.uk/publications/docs/cps_vawg_report_2012.pdf* [accessed January 2, 2014].

[4] F. Mason and Z. Lodrick. *Psychological consequences of sexual assault.* Best Practice & Research Clinical Obstetrics & Gynaecology, Feb, 2013: 27(1): 27–37.

[5] *Do Rape Myths Affect Juror Decision Making? A systematic review of the literature,* A BPP School of Health/Professional Development Working Paper, November 2012, available at *http://www.bpp.com/carbon-content-1.0-SNAPSHOT/resources/ECMDocument?contentName=Rape_myths_Dec_2012* [accessed January 2, 2014].

[6] *Do Rape Myths Affect Juror Decision Making? A systematic review of the literature,* A BPP School of Health/Professional Development Working Paper, November 2012, available at *http://www.bpp.com/carbon-content-1.0-SNAPSHOT/resources/ECMDocument?contentName=Rape_myths_Dec_2012* [accessed January 2, 2014].

[7] See Mason and Lodrick, above, fn.4.

helpless. Others may cut off, dissociating from reality. Some women may submit to sexual intercourse from fear of what might happen if they were to resist. The response may range from "fight, flight, freeze" to "friend" and "flop". The survival strategy will depend on what seems most likely to ensure survival, what may have worked in the past and what did not work previously. This explains why some resist the attacker and some are passive. Submission is not an indication of consent.

The effect of such a threat on brain function can be to impair severely recollection of the assault. Memories of the traumatic event are often initially fragmented. Victims questioned soon after the assault focus on perceptions such as feeling, smelling and hearing. With time, and especially with sleep, the higher brain structures will potentially process memory that has been encoded and recall may increase over time. With further questioning, more sleep, and talking the assault through, more of the details of the assault will become accessible and the victim's account may change and become more detailed. An understanding of the above is crucial in police investigations and in prosecutions for sexual assault, as well as on the part of members of the public who may be called upon for jury service.

In the last few years the Crown Prosecution Service has made progress in ensuring   **21.08** that vulnerable and intimidated witnesses are not denied access to treatment such as emotional support and counselling before trial. The CPS guidance produced on the subject for therapists and lawyers makes it clear that the best interests of the witness are paramount in deciding what therapeutic help is given and when.[8]

INITIAL DISCLOSURE AND MANAGEMENT

Delayed disclosure has been misunderstood in the past and has affected conviction   **21.10** rates, which dropped from 73 per cent in cases reported within the first 24 hours post-event to 38 per cent in cases reported between 24 hours and three months later.[9] One of the reasons for delayed disclosure may be the complainant's fear of being disbelieved or blamed, or having their behaviour exposed and scrutinised. Many victims feel shame, disbelief and denial, which prevents them from coming forward early. Others need time to process what has happened to them, as not all will immediately see their experience as rape. There may also be other factors contributing to delayed disclosure, such as the victim having childcare responsibilities, transport difficulties, or sharing a home with the perpetrator.

Those with post-traumatic stress disorder may avoid engaging with the investigative and criminal processes, which may result in re-traumatisation. It requires well-trained, sensitive and skilled healthcare professionals and specialist police officers and prosecutors to facilitate the necessary support and meet the

---

[8] *Provision of therapy for vulnerable or intimidated adult witnesses prior to a criminal trial—Practice guidance*, available at *http://www.cps.gov.uk/publications/prosecution/pretrialadult.html* [accessed January 2, 2014].
[9] See Mason and Lodrick, above, fn.4.

demands of the judicial system whilst also addressing the victims' best interests.

Some Sexual Assault Referral Centres ("SARCs") offer a non-police referral option to those complainants of sexual assault who do not want to report the incident to the police immediately, or at all. This allows a full forensic medical examination ("FME") to gather evidence, gives an opportunity to offer immediate medical aftercare and allows the complainant time to consider all their options.

Sexual Assault Referral Centres

21.11   A revised service guide for developing sexual assault centres has been published by the Home Office, the Department of Health, and the Association of Chief Police Officers, setting minimum standards for SARCs.[10]

Over the last few years more SARCs have been set up throughout the UK. Baroness Stern's review (2010) into how rape complaints are handled by public authorities in England and Wales welcomed the Government's commitment to have one SARC in every police force area by 2011.[11] Baroness Stern noted that funding arrangements for SARCs varied across the country and did not wish to be prescriptive about how they should be set up and run. She made it clear that there is a greater chance of success when there is strong partnership and shared commitment between the National Health Service ("NHS"), the police and local government. In her review, Baroness Stern strongly supported the transfer from the police to the NHS of sexual offences forensic examination work, and of the funding and commissioning of such services. The transition process has already started under the Health and Social Care Act 2012, and is due to become law in 2015. The commissioning of sexual assault services, including SARCs, will be the responsibility of the NHS Commissioning Board, aiming to provide "a 24/7, one-stop shop" for victims, offering services that include: FMEs, medical aftercare including emergency contraception, and post-exposure prophylaxis against sexually transmitted infections ("STIs") including human immunodeficiency virus ("HIV") infection. Referral for psychological support, including pre-trial counselling is also recommended.[12] As children comprise about 30 per cent of all cases, care and support for sexually abused children will be integrated with care pathways to local paediatric services and community mental health services.

---

[10] *Revised National Service Guide—A Resource for Developing Sexual Assault Referral Centres* (Home Office, Department of Health and ACPO, October 2009), available at *http://www.reading.gov.uk/documents%5Ccommunity-living%5Ccommunity-safety/13618/ResourceforDevelopingSexualAssaultReferralCentres.pdf* [accessed January 2, 2014].

[11] *The Stern Review—A Report by Baroness Vivien Stern CBE of an Independent Review into how Rape Complainants are Handled by Public Authorities in England and Wales* (Home Office, 2010), available at *http://webarchive.nationalarchives.gov.uk/20110608160754/http://www.equalities.gov.uk/PDF/Stern_Review_acc_FINAL.pdf* [accessed January 2, 2014].

[12] *Securing Excellence in Commissioning for Offender Health* (NHS Commissioning Board, February 2013), available at *http://www.england.nhs.uk/wp-content/uploads/2013/03/offender-commissioning.pdf* [accessed January 2, 2014].

INVESTIGATION AND PROSECUTION OF RAPE

The Stern review[13] highlighted the need to focus less on conviction rates and more   21.13
on treating the victim with dignity and respect:

> "[P]rosecuting and convicting in rape cases . . . is important, and necessary. But in
> dealing with rape there is a range of priorities that needs to be balanced. Support and
> care for victims should be a higher priority. The obligations the State has to those who
> have suffered a violent crime, and a crime that strikes at the whole concept of human
> dignity and bodily integrity, are much wider than working for the conviction of a
> perpetrator."

In addition the review encouraged the Government to consider the introduction
of a right for victims to have their own lawyer in court, alongside the prosecutor
and the defendant's representative, in order to protect their interests.

FORENSIC MEDICAL EXAMINATION

No major changes have been made in relation to FMEs since publication of the   21.16
main work. The recent emphasis has been on improving standards of forensic
healthcare professionals.[14] Some SARCs started training nurses to carry out
FMEs of complainants of sexual assault. The Faculty of Forensic and Legal
Medicine ("FFLM") has produced the document *Quality Standards in Forensic
Medicine* for general forensic and sexual assault medicine.[15] The FFLM has also
published quality standards for Nurse Sexual Offences Examiners,[16] emphasising
the need for appropriate recruitment from related specialities, e.g. sexual health or
genitourinary medicine, induction, training, supervision and mentoring. Training
is focused on the core competencies of the Society of Apothecaries' Diploma in
Forensic and Medical Aspects of Sexual Assault.[17] The FFLM has also published
updates of forensic pro-formas,[18] body diagrams,[19] a guide to establishing the
urgency of sexual offences examination,[20] and recommendations on collecting hair
samples for toxicology.[21]

---

[13] Above, fn.11, p.11.

[14] *FFLM Quality Standards in Forensic Medicine* (updated September 2013), available at *http://
/fflm.ac.uk/librarydetail/4000113* [accessed January 2, 2014].

[15] *FFLM Quality Standards in Forensic Medicine* (updated September 2013), available at *http://
/fflm.ac.uk/librarydetail/4000113* [accessed January 2, 2014].

[16] *Quality Standards for Nurses—Sexual Offence Medicine (SOM)* (August 1, 2013), available at
http://fflm.ac.uk/library/ [accessed January 2, 2014].

[17] See   *http://www.apothecaries.org/examination/diploma-in-the-forensic-and-clinical-aspects-of-se/*
[accessed January 2, 2014].

[18] *Pro forma: Forensic Medical Examination Forms* (July 11, 2013), available at *http://fflm.ac.uk/
library/* [accessed January 2, 2014].

[19] *Pro forma—Body diagrams* (May 31, 2013), available at *http://fflm.ac.uk/library/* [accessed
January 2, 2014].

[20] *Guide to establishing urgency of sexual assault examinations* (May 31, 2013), available at *http://
/fflm.ac.uk/library/* [accessed January 2, 2014].

[21] *Recommendations—Collecting Hair Samples for Toxicology* (July 1, 2013), available at *http://
/fflm.ac.uk/library/* [accessed January 2, 2014].

Forensic Samples

21.23   The FFLM has been regularly updating its *Recommendations for the Collection of Forensic Specimens from Complainants and Suspects* and its Forensic Medical Examination Forms 1–4, which list summary information about the assault and the forensic samples taken.[22]

Injuries in Vaginal Penetration

21.31   A review of literature on genital injuries in sexual assault showed a variation in the prevalence of injuries, ranging from 5 per cent on visual inspection to 87 per cent when magnification using a colposcope was used,[23] calling for a multidimensional definition of genital injury pattern and measurement strategies for injury severity and skin colour, in order to to improve health care, forensic and criminal justice outcomes.

A more recent study looking at female genital injuries from consensual and non-consensual vaginal intercourse showed that most complainants of rape (95 per cent) will not sustain any genital injury, although women are three times more likely to sustain a genital injury from an assault than from consensual intercourse.[24]

Injuries in complainants of sexual assault, and in particular genito-anal injuries, require an assessment from the point of view of the risk of blood-borne STIs like Hepatitis B and HIV.[25] Understanding genital injury rates, type of injury, site and healing will assist the clinician in interpreting findings in the context of the allegations made.[26]

In a study carried out in Belfast on injury and related factors in female complainants of sexual assault, half of the study subjects were under 20 years of age and 80 per cent of those sustained associated body injury.[27] Genital injury was more frequent in acquaintance assault and in victims not using hormonal contraception.

Consensual sexual intercourse has been shown to cause genital injury, suggesting that genital injuries alone do not corroborate an allegation of rape.[28] These

[22] *Recommendations for the Collection of Forensic Specimens from Complainants and Suspects* (July 2013), available at *http://fflm.ac.uk/library/* [accessed January 2, 2014].

[23] M. Sawyer Sommers, *Defining patterns of genital injury from sexual assault—a review*, Trauma Violence Abuse, July 2007; 8(3): 270–280.

[24] I. McLean, S.A. Roberts. C. White, S. Paul, *Female genital injuries resulting from consensual and non-consensual vaginal intercourse*, Forensic Sci Int, Jan 30, 2011; Forensic Sci Int, 204(1–3): 27–33.

[25] P. Benn et al., *UK guideline for the use of post-exposure prophylaxis for HIV following sexual exposure*, Int J STD AIDS 2011; 22: 695–708: B. Cybulska et al., *UK National Guidelines on the Management of Adult and Adolescent Complainants of Sexual Assault 2011*, available at *http://www.bashh.org/documents/4450.pdf* [accessed January 2, 2014]; J.E. Draughon, *Sexual Assault Injuries and Increased Risk of HIV Transmission*, Adv Emerg Nurs J., Jan–Mar 2012; 34(1): 82–87.

[26] C. White, *Genital Injuries in Adults*, Best Practice & Research Clinical Obstetrics & Gynaecology, February 2013; Vol.27(1): 113–130 Medicine.

[27] W. Maguire, E. Goodall, T. Moore, *Injury in adult female sexual assault complainants and related factors*, Eur J Obstet Gynecol Reprod Biol, 2009; 142: 149–153.

[28] B.S. Astrup et al., *Nature, frequency and duration of genital lesions after consensual sexual intercourse*, Forensic Sci Int, 2011; 219: 50–56.

injuries must be documented and may assist in the investigation of rape at a later stage.

Another study found that post-menopausal women were more likely to sustain genital injury in a sexual assault than pre-menopausal women. There was no significant difference between the two groups in relation to sustained extra-genital injuries, except for the size of bruises which were larger in post-menopausal women.[29]

EXTRA-GENITAL INJURIES

A Swedish study showed that women assaulted by an intimate partner were more   **21.45**
likely to have extra-genital injuries than those assaulted by a stranger or an acquaintance. A previous history of sexual assault was more common in this group, as was the seeking of medical care within 72 hours. Being under the influence of alcohol during the assault was less frequent in this group.[30]

DRUG-FACILITATED SEXUAL ASSAULT

Alcohol and drugs are commonly associated with sexual assault. Early-evidence   **21.52**
samples should be taken for toxicology and DNA testing purposes, with care being taken to address all possible types of sexual assault. Prevention should focus on education about drug facilitated sexual assault (DFSA).[31] Medical, scientific and legal aspects of DFSA are explored by a review paper from Ireland in an attempt to clear confusion around this topic.[32]

ASPECTS OF MEDICAL AFTERCARE

The Intrauterine Device (IUD) is the most reliable form of emergency contra-   **21.55**
ception and should be discussed and offered to those complainants of sexual assault at highest risk.[33] If it is not possible to insert an IUD immediately, referral pathways should be in place.

The majority of complainants of sexual assault prefer to take oral forms of emergency contraception such as Levonelle or EllaOne (Ullipristol). The latter is a new oral emergency contraception, which is offered to those under 16 years of

---

[29] L. Morgan, A. Dill, J. Welch, *Sexual assault of postmenopausal women: a retrospective review*, BJOG, 2011; 118: 832–843.

[30] S.A. Möller et al., *Patterns of Injury and Reported Violence Depending on Relationship to Assailant in Female Swedish Sexual Assault Victims*, J Interpers Violence, November 2012, Vol.27, No.16; 3131–3148: 21.45.

[31] B. Butler, J. Welch, *Drug-facilitated sexual assault*, CMAJ, March 3, 2009; Vol.180(5): 493–494.

[32] D. McBrierty, A. Wilkinson, W. Tormey, *A review of drug-facilitated sexual assault evidence: an Irish prespective*, J Forensic Leg Med, May 2013; 20(4): 189–97.

[33] *Emergency contraception* (Faculty of Family Planning and Reproductive Health Care, Clinical Effectiveness Unit, FFPRHC Guidance; April 2006), J Fam Plan Reprod Health Care 2006; 32: 121–128.

age and for up to five days after unprotected sexual exposure.[34] The complainant should be offered a pregnancy test prior to taking emergency contraception to reduce the chance they are already pregnant with their partner's child.[35] A pregnancy test should be considered three weeks after oral emergency contraception in the absence of inter-menstrual bleeding.[36]

Pregnancy as a result of sexual assault

21.57   Those women who become pregnant following sexual assault and wish to terminate the pregnancy should be advised about the forensic and evidential significance of the products of conception. The collection of such samples must be arranged by appointment. A chain of evidence of the custody of the samples must be managed in line with the Human Tissue Act 2004 and appropriate guidelines.[37]

HIV infection

21.60   The guidelines issued by the British Association of Sexual Health and HIV ("BASHH") on post-sexual exposure prophylaxis against HIV infection ("PEPSE") recognise sexual assault as one of the risk factors for HIV transmission. The HIV PEPSE should be offered routinely to complainants of sexual assault in high prevalence areas. Recommendation and subsequent uptake will be lower in most UK settings unless the perpetrator is from a high prevalence group or perceived to be so.[38]

VULNERABLE RAPE VICTIMS

21.67   A new University of Bristol study investigated the high "drop out" rate in rape cases and the lower likelihood of conviction, particularly among those with mental health problems.[39] Although domestic violence cases were most likely to be seen as crimes, historical cases were more likely to result in a conviction. The study highlighted victim vulnerability as the main factor undermining credibility, leading to a large "drop out" in rape cases, and called for a more victim-focused approach in responses to rape cases.

---

[34] *EllaOne—a new emergency contraceptive*, MIMS 2009 available at *http://www.mims.co.uk* [accessed September 7, 2013].

[35] R. Jina et al., *Report of the FIGO Working Group on Sexual Violence/HIV: Guidelines for the management of female survivors of sexual assault*, I.J. of Gynae and Obst, 2010; 10: 85–92.

[36] See above, fn.26.

[37] *Guidelines for handling medicolegal specimens and preserving evidence* (Royal College of Pathologists, 2008), currently under review but still available at *http://www.rcpath.org/publications-media/publications/archived-withdrawn-documents.htm* [accessed January 2, 2014].

[38] P. Benn, M. Fisher, R. Kulasegaram, *UK guideline for the use of post-exposure prophylaxis for HIV following sexual exposure*, I J of STD & AIDS, 2011; 22: 695–708.

[39] Prof M. Hester OBE, *From Report to Court: Rape cases and the criminal justice system in the North East* (Centre for Gender and Violence Research, School for Policy Studies, University of Bristol, July 2013), available at *http://www.nr-foundation.org.uk/wp-content/uploads/2013/07/From-Report-to-Court-final-5-july-13.pdf* [accessed January 2, 2014].

The World Health Organisation ("WHO") has recognised violence against 21.69
women, violence by intimate partners and sexual violence against women as major
public health problems and violations of women's human rights.[40] A WHO multi-
country study found that between 15 and 71 per cent of women aged 15–49
reported physical and/or sexual violence by an intimate partner at some point in
their lives. Domestic violence may result in physical, mental, sexual, reproductive
and other health and other health problems, including an increased vulnerability
to HIV. Risk factors for being a perpetrator include low education, past exposure
to child mistreatment or witnessing violence in the family, harmful use of alcohol,
attitudes accepting of violence and gender inequality. Risk factors for being a
victim of domestic violence include low education, witnessing violence between
parents, exposure to abuse during childhood and attitudes accepting violence and
gender inequality.

On September 18, 2012, the Home Office announced changes to the Govern- 21.69A
ment's definition of domestic abuse, the effect which is that young people aged
16–17, including boys, are now recognised as capable of being victims of domestic
abuse and that coercive control is included as a form of abuse.[41] The definition
now covers:

> " . . . any incident or pattern of incidents of controlling, coercive, threatening
> behaviour, violence or abuse between those aged 16 or over who are, or have been,
> intimate partners or family members regardless of gender or sexuality. The abuse can
> encompass, but is not limited to:
> - psychological
> - physical
> - sexual
> - financial
> - emotional"

The NHS has acknowledged that domestic violence is chronically under-reported,
causes physical and mental injuries to sufferers, and is the leading cause of
morbidity for women aged 19–44.[42]

INDEPENDENT SEXUAL VIOLENCE ADVISER

The Stern review[43] noted widespread praise of the role of Independent Sexual 21.70
Violence Advisor ("ISVA"), which it described (using the Home Office definition)
as:

---

[40] *Intimate partner violence during pregnancy* (WHO, 2011), available at: *http://whqlibdoc.who.int/hq/2011/WHO_RHR_11.35_eng.pdf* [accessed January 2, 2014].
[41] *Domestic Violence* (Home Office, September 2012), available at *https://www.gov.uk/domestic-violence-and-abuse* [accessed January 2, 2014].
[42] *Domestic Violence London: A Resource for Health Professionals* (NHS, 2013), available at *http://www.domesticviolencelondon.nhs.uk/1-what-isdomestic-violence-/22-teen-dating-abuse.html* [accessed January 2, 2014].
[43] Above, fn.11, p.11.

"[a] pro-active service to victims of sexual violence through risk assessment and safety planning; enabling victims to access those statutory and other services they need; and ensuring victims are kept informed and supported as their case progresses through the criminal justice system."

The review recommended that ISVAs be seen as an intrinsic part of the way rape complainants are dealt with, as the service that enables the rest to operate effectively and a crucial part of the way the State fulfils its obligations to victims of violence, and that funding for ISVAs should be available in all areas where the demand makes a post viable.

MEDICAL WITNESS IN COURT

21.71   The General Medical Council has published guidance as to the duties and responsibilities of a doctor appearing in legal proceedings as a witness of fact or as a medical expert.[44] They include working within the limits of competence and knowledge when giving evidence and co-operating with formal inquiries and complaints procedures whilst protecting confidentiality.

---

[44] *Acting as a witness in legal proceedings* (GMC, March 25, 2013), available at *http://www.gmc-uk.org/Acting_as_a_witness.pdf_51448308.pdf* [accessed January 2, 2014].

CHAPTER 22

MEDICAL EVIDENCE: CHILDREN

by Dr Catherine White OBE*

INTRODUCTION

Brain plasticity

There is increasing scientific evidence to support the concepts of both brain **22.01**
plasticity and the structural changes that can occur in the child's developing brain
if exposed to a sustained adverse environment, such as living with and observing
on-going violence.[1] This is important to understand for a number of reasons,
including that such children will be at increased risk of both being victims to
violence and perpetrating it, and also that they may not respond in a way that an
observer might expect.[2]

Child sexual exploitation

Child sexual exploitation is a phenomenon that has doubtless been a problem for **22.01A**
many years but has recently become more widely recognised.[3] The sexual

* Clinical Director of the Sexual Assault Referral Centre, St Mary's Hospital, Manchester. Author
of *Sexual Assault, A Forensic Physician's Practice Guide* (Manchester, St Mary's Sexual Assault Referral
Centre, 2010).

[1] *Early Intervention: The Next Steps*, An Independent Report to Her Majesty's Government,
Graham Allen MP, at *http://www.dwp.gov.uk/docs/early-intervention-next-steps.pdf* [accessed December 7, 2013].

[2] Richard J. Davidson and Bruce S. McEwen, *Social influences on neuroplasticity: stress and
interventions to promote well-being*, 689–695, Vol.15, No.5, May 2012, Nature Neuroscience.

[3] See, e.g. *Puppet on a string: The urgent need to cut children free from sexual exploitation* (Barnardo's,
2011), available at *http://s3.amazonaws.com/rcpp/assets/attachments/1179_ctf_puppetonastring_report_
final_original.pdf* [accessed December 7, 2013]; and three reports published by the Office of the
Children's Commissioner for England in November 2013, *"If only someone had listened": Office of the*

exploitation of children and young people under-18 has been defined as that which:

> " . . . involves exploitative situations, contexts and relationships where young people (or a third person or persons) receive 'something' (e.g. food, accommodation, drugs, alcohol, cigarettes, affection, gifts, money) as a result of them performing, and/or another or others performing on them, sexual activities. Child sexual exploitation can occur through the use of technology without the child's immediate recognition; for example being persuaded to post sexual images on the Internet/mobile phones without immediate payment or gain. In all cases, those exploiting the child/young person have power over them by virtue of their age, gender, intellect, physical strength and/or economic or other resources. Violence, coercion and intimidation are common, involvement in exploitative relationships being characterised in the main by the child or young person's limited availability of choice resulting from their social/economic and/or emotional vulnerability".[4]

22.01B One of the difficulties with some cases of child sexual exploitation is that the vulnerability of these children that makes them a target for predators can also mean that they are seen as "poor" witnesses by the criminal justice system. In June 2013, the Director of Public Prosecutions produced *Interim Guidelines on Prosecuting Cases of Child Sexual Abuse*,[5] which covers some of these issues, including assessing the credibility of child abuse allegations and the credibility or reliability of a child or young person.

22.01C In 2012, the Office of the Children's Commissioner for England ("OCC") began an enquiry into child sexual exploitation in gangs and groups. The report of this enquiry (*"If only someone had listened"*)[6] outlines a list of vulnerabilities which may be present in children prior to abuse and a further list of signs and behaviours generally seen in children who are already being sexually exploited. Prosecutors should consider whether the victim whose evidence they are considering demonstrates any of these factors. Whilst the absence of any of these characteristics does not mean that an allegation is unlikely to be true, their presence may assist the prosecutor in forming an overall view in the case. The OCC list is as follows:

Children's Commissioner's Inquiry into Child Sexual Exploitation in Gangs and Groups Final Report; "It's wrong... but you get used to it" A qualitative study of gang-associated sexual violence towards, and exploitation of, young people in England; and *"Sex without consent, I suppose that is rape": How young people in England understand sexual consent*, available at *http://www.childrenscommissioner.gov.uk* [accessed December 7, 2013].

[4] *Tackling Child Sexual Exploitation: National Action Plan Progress Report*, Department for Education, London (2012).

[5] Available at *http://www.cps.gov.uk/consultations/csa_consultation.html£a13* [accessed December 7, 2013].

[6] Above, fn.3.

Child Sexual Exploitation	
Typical vulnerabilities in children prior to abuse:	**The following signs and behaviour are generally seen in children who are already being sexually exploited:**
• Living in a chaotic or dysfunctional household (including parental substance use, domestic violence, parental mental health issues, parental criminality); • History of abuse (including familial child sexual abuse, risk of forced marriage, risk of "honour"–based violence, physical and emotional abuse and neglect); • Recent bereavement or loss; • Gang association either through relatives, peers or intimate relationships (in cases of gang associated CSE only); • Attending school with young people who are sexually exploited; • Learning disabilities; • Unsure about their sexual orientation or unable to disclose sexual orientation to their families; • Friends with young people who are sexually exploited; • Homeless; • Lacking friends from the same age group; • Living in a gang neighbourhood; • Living in residential care; • Living in hostel, bed and breakfast accommodation or a foyer; • Low self-esteem or self-confidence; • Young carer.	• Missing from home or care; • Physical injuries; • Drug or alcohol misuse; • Involvement in offending; • Repeat sexually-transmitted infections, pregnancy and terminations; • Absent from school; • Change in physical appearance; • Evidence of sexual bullying and/or vulnerability through the internet and/or social networking sites; • Estranged from their family; • Receipt of gifts from unknown sources; • Recruiting others into exploitative situations; • Poor mental health; • Self-harm; • Thoughts of or attempts at suicide

THE MEDICAL RESPONSE TO AN ALLEGATION OR SUSPICION OF CHILD SEXUAL ABUSE

WHO SHOULD DO THE MEDICAL EXAMINATION?

Forensic physician qualifications

22.04 For the FFLM's *Interim Quality Standards in Forensic Medicine*, see now the *Quality Standards in Forensic Medicine: General Forensic (GFM) and Sexual Offence Medicine (SOM)*, updated to September 2013.[7] In July 2013 the FFLM also published *Quality Standards for Nurses: Sexual Offences Medicine*.[8]

Peer Review

22.05 There would appear to be growing acceptance of the value of peer review in relation to reviewing photo documentation of the anogenital aspect of the examination of a child suspected to have been the victim of sexual abuse. In broad terms the following applies to peer review:

Purpose

- To provide a proactive culture of learning where clinicians and SARC staff can review cases, discuss procedures, process and evidence base underpinning diagnosis and in doing so provide a supportive environment to debrief cases with peers undertaking similar work.

Objectives

- To provide time for discussion of cases in a relaxed, non-threatening environment.
- To provide support through the sharing experience of others.
- To review cases seen to ensure appropriate evidence based management.
- To view photo documentation accompanying the case presentation.
- To provide opportunity for emotional support.
- To provide training for clinicians and SARC staff.

22.05A There has been some unease within the legal community regarding the application of the law of disclosure to the process of peer review and its conclusions. With that in mind, the FFLM is currently producing guidelines on the subject. Charlotte Triggs, Senior Policy Advisor in the CPS Strategy and Policy Directorate, has expressed the following view in a letter to the author:

---

[7] Available at *http://fflm.ac.uk/librarydetail/4000113* [accessed December 7, 2013].
[8] Available at *http://fflm.ac.uk/upload/documents/1384794533.pdf* [accessed December 7, 2013].

"I am familiar with the concept of peer review as practised at St Mary's. I agree that it is best carried out during the life of a case.

CPS interest in any peer review arises in relation to the disclosure of unused material. The disclosure provisions require that any material held by the prosecution which weakens its case or strengthens that of the defendant, if not relied upon as part of its formal case, should be disclosed to the defence.

Notes of the peer review would not be material held by the prosecution but would meet the definition of 3rd party material.

Where material is held by a 3rd party such as a SARC investigators and the prosecution may need to make enquiries of the 3rd party with a view to inspecting the material and determining whether the relevant test for disclosure is met and whether any material should be retained, recorded and in due course disclosed to the defence.

If peer review revealed a dispute or difference of opinion over the findings and/or opinion of the forensic physician who carried out the examination, this could potentially weaken the prosecution case or strengthen that of the defendant. It is this type of information that, if it was in the possession of the investigators or the prosecution, we would need to consider disclosing to the defence.

In those circumstances it might assist with the smooth running of cases and assist the prosecution with its duty of disclosure if any dispute and/or difference of opinion in the course of peer review involving a case in the criminal justice system could be routinely revealed to the police and passed to the prosecution for consideration."

WHEN SHOULD AN EXAMINATION BE DONE?

The decision as to when to undertake a forensic examination is a complex one and   22.07
requires evaluation of numerous factors. Using guidance originally devised by St Mary's SARC Manchester, in May 2013 the FFLM published a *Guide to establishing urgency of sexual offence examination*,[9] which comprises two flowcharts, one for pre-pubertal children and the other for post-pubertal children and adults. This guidance aims to encourage decision-makers (primarily the clinician but in discussion with others such as police and social services) to consider the therapeutic and forensic aspects of the case as well as issues such as safeguarding risks.

The Forensic Committee of the FFLM continues to update every six months the   22.08
document *Recommendations for the collection of forensic specimens from complainants and suspects*.[10] Previously these recommendations were held on a secure part of the FFLM website, but they have now been made accessible to the public.

INTERPRETATION OF ANOGENITAL FINDINGS

The Royal College of Paediatrics and Child Health ("RCPCH"), in collaboration   22.31
with the FFLM, in March 2008 published *The Physical Signs of Child Sexual*

---

[9] Available at *http://fflm.ac.uk/librarydetail/4000132* [accessed December 2, 2013].
[10] Available at *http://fflm.ac.uk/librarydetail/4000068* [accessed December 7, 2013].

Abuse.[11] This is often referred to as *"The Purple Book"*. A full update is currently being undertaken and a second edition is due to be published in Autumn 2014. This will include new sections on healing, thermal injuries and accidental/non-intentional injuries. An *Interim statement* was published in July 2011[12] and reports the findings of the first phase of the update. It is based on a review of the literature from 2003 to 2009 and addresses comments made during the consultation with potential users in 2009.

The *Interim statement* addresses key information of relevance and importance to the interpretation of physical signs. Typographical and other minor changes which do not affect the meaning are not included. The *Interim statement* includes an updated evidence review, for example the chapter on genital signs of sexual abuse in girls updates on Genital lacerations/tears and Healing/healed genital injuries. It also includes an update on Good Practice, and an agreed statement on Female Genital Mutilation.

22.31A   As a result of the publication of *The Physical Signs of Child Sexual Abuse*, it has become clear that diagnostic criteria for such abuse have changed over the years. This has resulted in a number of appeals seeking to rely upon fresh evidence to challenge convictions.[13] The most notable of these is *S, B, C and R v R.*,[14] in which the Court of Appeal determined four conjoined appeals against conviction all of which turned upon fresh medical evidence. The fresh evidence was given by two experts, Dr Mary Pillai for the appellants and Dr Jean Price for the Crown, though the source of their instructions was in fact immaterial as they were agreed on all relevant points. The appeals of S, B and C were allowed, but R's was dismissed.

The Court referred at the outset to the principles to be applied where fresh evidence is adduced on appeal. Thus it is for the Court of Appeal to evaluate the importance of the fresh evidence in the context of the remainder of the evidence in the case, the question being whether, in light of the fresh evidence, the conviction is safe, not what effect the fresh evidence would have had on the mind of the jury.[15] Further, when assessing the impact of fresh evidence, the Court should assume that the jury was faithful to the directions of law.[16] In these appeals the impact of the fresh evidence was the main issue, there being, in at least three of the cases, no issue as to the truth, reliability or accuracy of that evidence. In the cases of S, B and C, the fresh evidence gave rise to no factual issues and was accepted as correct. Insofar as the evidence given at trial was significantly inconsistent with it, that evidence was conceded to have been incorrect. In the case of C, and possibly also of S and B, it was arguable that errors in the medical

---

[11] *The Physical Signs of Child Sexual Abuse*, RCPCH, March, 2008.

[12] Available at *http://www.rcpch.ac.uk/csa* [accessed December 7, 2013].

[13] It is, of course, open to the Crown in such cases to adduce fresh evidence in response.

[14] [2012] EWCA Crim 1433. See also *R. v PF* [2009] EWCA Crim 1086.

[15] [2012] EWCA Crim 1433. See also *R. v PF* [2009] EWCA Crim 1086, at [3], citing *Pendleton*; [2002] 1 Cr. App. R. 34; *Hakala* [2002] EWCA Crim 730; *Dial and another v State of Trinidad and Tobago* [2005] 1 WLR 1660; *Noye* [2011] EWCA Crim 650.

[16] *Christou* [1996] 2 Cr. App. R. 360, per Lord Taylor L.C.J.

examination and interpretation arose from incorrect or inadequate practice even by the standards of the time. It was agreed that in all the appeals the fresh evidence rendered neutral the medical evidence.

Of use in some of the appeals was the ability to review the medical evidence in the form of photo documentation of the anogenital examination. In October 2012 the FFLM, together with the RCPCH, updated their *Guidelines on Paediatric Forensic Examinations in relation to Possible Child Sexual Abuse.*[17] This version updates the original statement and versions from 1988, 2002, 2007 and 2009. The amendments are summarised as follows:

- It is essential that high quality photo–documentation be obtained during a paediatric forensic examination. If it is not obtained the practitioner must document in their notes the reason for this.
- A single doctor can conduct a paediatric forensic examination provided they have all the necessary skills.
- The examining doctor must ensure that they are familiar with evidence-based guidance regarding the interpretation of the signs.

It is worth summarising the cases in some detail (we do so in the order in which they were considered by the Court of Appeal).

B's case

B had been convicted in 1994 of offences of buggery, indecency with a child and **22.31B** indecent assault committed against A, his partner's daughter. In an ABE interview, A said that B used to put his willy up her poo hole and had asked her to lick his willy. The examining police surgeon, Dr Bassindale, gave evidence that she found nothing abnormal about A's vaginal area. In the anal area between half past 5 and 8 o'clock the skin was smooth and shiny. Between 7 and 8 o'clock on top of the smooth area was a thick, more prominent fold which was scar tissue. Just after 6 o'clock there was a smaller, pale, raised area. These findings were consistent with chronic repeated anal intercourse. The smooth area was not a congenital variation. She had never seen findings so striking: "I remember this child's bottom but cannot now remember her face". The Crown also relied upon a complaint made by A to her mother and evidence from the mother that B had told her he had a previous conviction for a sexual offence. B declined to answer questions in interview and his case at trial was a simple denial. A defence medical expert, Dr Clarke, gave evidence that the smooth area of skin observed by Dr Bassindale was known to occur naturally and could be a congenital variation. He accepted that the more prominent fold could be the result of substantial injury. His resting position was to disagree with Dr Bassindale's findings and to consider them to be within normal variations, but he did not exclude the possibility of buggery.

The fresh evidence on appeal took the form of two reports produced in 2010 by Dr Bassindale, in which she retracted salient features of her evidence, and reports by Dr Price and Dr Pillai. It was agreed that the evidence given at trial by Dr

---

[17] Available at *http://fflm.ac.uk/upload/documents/1352802061.pdf* [accessed December 2, 2013].

Bassindale was incorrect and that the opinion shared by the two consultants as to good practice was correct and was supported by post-trial developments in medical knowledge. Dr Price considered that Dr Bassindale had carried out an appropriate examination and that the issue was whether what she saw was, or was not, scar tissue. If it were, then, absent a history of major trauma to the anus, it would in 1993 have been diagnostic of anal abuse. But in 2008, under the RCPCH guidance, it was only supportive of anal penetration: the guidance states that "good evidence suggests that anal scars are associated with anal abuse". However, no photographs had been taken during Dr Bassindale's examination and so it was impossible to say whether A had experienced anal penetration or whether the clinical findings were normal variants. Dr Pillai agreed with Dr Price.

B submitted that the jury had heard medical evidence given in striking terms that the state of A's anus was consistent with chronic penetrative abuse, and it was impossible to say that they without that evidence they would still have convicted. The Court agreed, finding that in the light of Dr Price's evidence it could not be confident of the safety of the buggery conviction. Although the jury had heard the evidence of Dr Clarke, whose opinion found an echo in that of Dr Price, nevertheless Dr Bassindale's evidence was unlikely to have been less than compelling. Further, in the light of that evidence it would not be surprising if the jury had deduced that A was reliable and truthful and applied those conclusions to the remaining counts. It followed that the Court could not be certain that, without the evidence of Dr Bassindale, the jury would still have convicted and, for that reason, it quashed the convictions on all counts.

C's case

22.31C   C was convicted in 2005 of rape, attempted rape and two counts of indecent assault on S, his daughter. The Crown relied upon evidence from S; an account by C's step-daughter, T, of similar behaviour with her; evidence from a fellow prisoner, N, that C had admitted sexually abusing S on at least one occasion; and evidence from a consultant community paediatrician, Dr Rees, who had examined S. The examination had been video recorded. Dr Rees's evidence was that the posterior part of S's hymen, which would normally have been thick, curved and intact, was worn away. The rubbing away was typical of abuse on more than one occasion caused by digital penetration or the insertion of a penis or penis-sized object. S appeared to have suffered repeated abuse. The defence case was that the allegations were fabricated, S and T were in collusion, and N was a liar.

The fresh evidence on appeal took the form of reports from Dr Pillai and Dr Price. Having reviewed the video recording of Dr Rees's examination, her report and the transcript of her evidence, the consultants agreed that her evidence was reflective of past practices where attenuation of the posterior rim of the hymen was suggested as an indicator of sexual abuse. In current practice, "attenuation" should describe only the position when examination of the hymen prior to alleged abuse establishes the presence of a greater amount of tissue. There had been no such previous examination of S such as to afford a comparison. The 2008 RCPCH guidance describes "attenuation" and "rubbing/tearing away" as "not helpful" terms. The consultants also agreed that increased knowledge since 2005 had undermined the bases upon which Dr Rees explained her conclusions. It is now known that a girl's oestrogen levels affect the thickness of the hymen, and that the amount of hymenal tissue can vary widely and can overlap between abused and non-abused girls, as can the size of the hymenal orifice, which in S's case Dr Rees had described as "dilated". A complete cleft or notch in the posterior rim of the hymen, as suggested by Dr Rees's diagram, would be very supportive of penile penetration. However, Dr Rees did not describe it as such when giving evidence. The video recording did not show a hymen consistent with the diagram, rather it revealed a distant rim of hymen throughout the posterior 180 degrees. The opening was not dilated but normal. The edge of the hymen was slightly irregular but had no deep or superficial notches. It did not meet the vestibule wall at 6 to 7 o'clock as described by Dr Rees. The 2008 RCPCH guidance indicates that a narrow hymen or slight irregularities are non-specific findings. Not only were a number of statements made by Dr Rees in evidence no longer accurate from a scientific standpoint, but also several were not supported by her examination.

The Court held that Dr Rees's evidence was highly likely substantially to have influenced the jury, to C's disadvantage. So far as it could tell, Dr Rees was firm in her findings and conclusions and not susceptible to challenge in cross-examination. More importantly, she was not challenged by a medical expert called for the defence. Dr Rees was a highly experienced paediatrician. The Crown, understandably, emphasised her qualifications and the significant number of examinations of this type which she had undertaken. The evidence of T and N was capable of supporting the case for the Crown, but Dr Rees was "the sharpest strongest arrow in the Crown's quiver". The Court rejected the Crown's submission that the fresh evidence went only to the safety of the two counts that pleaded penetration. Once the credibility of S was so firmly bolstered by an independent expert, importing the apparent certainty of science into an area often clouded in uncertainty, the advantage to the Crown remained when the jury considered each count. The Court was not confident that the convictions were safe and accordingly quashed them all.

S's case

S was convicted in 2002 of rape, attempted rape and 10 counts of indecency with **22.31D** a child committed against his partner's daughters, E and K, between 1992 and 2001, when the girls were respectively 4–13 and 2–11 years old. One count alleged that he had involved the girls' cousin, B, an adult with the mental age of a child, in the sexual abuse of E. The Crown's case was that the evidence of E and K was supported by their similar accounts, the evidence of SB, the similarity between their evidence and that of their mother relating to the propensity of one of S's testicles to "go up inside" during sexual intercourse, and the findings of the examining doctor, Dr Galbraith. Dr Galbraith had found damage to E's vagina consistent with repeated penetration with something larger than a tampon. K had suffered similar injuries. S denied the allegations and pointed out that K had not alleged penetration. He also had a report by Dr Primavesi, which was a mixed blessing in that its conclusions about K were capable of supporting the case for the Crown, whereas its conclusions as to E were capable of supporting that for S. K was the complainant in one count alleging penetration. That count was withdrawn from the jury, probably at the conclusion of the case for the Crown (though this could not be established with confidence). This was almost certainly because K did not in evidence speak of penetration or even attempted penetration. Consequently, the Crown argued, once the count was withdrawn Dr Primavesi was available to be called for S.

For the purposes of the appeal, Dr Price reviewed the evidence and/or reports of Dr Galbraith and of Dr Primavesi. Her conclusions, with which Dr Pillai agreed, were as follows:

- E was examined in the supine, frog leg position. This revealed early oestrogenisation of the inner labia, the labia minora being fairly prominent. The hymenal orifice appeared triangular and asymmetric in outline and it was difficult to establish its actual size due to thickening in the posterior and lateral part of the hymen.

- E was unable to tolerate Dr Galbraith's use of a cotton wool swab further to define the outline of the hymen. Dr Galbraith reported "anal examination in the left lateral position revealed no abnormality and no sign of injury". She concluded "both these girls showed evidence of hymenal damage, which in my opinion would be consistent with repeated episodes of penetrative injury".

- Dr Primavesi commented: "the findings of the hymen were thickening and distortion between 2 to 6 o'clock. These are not generally accepted signs of child sexual abuse." If the implication is that the thickening and distortion were due to oedema from acute trauma, then a follow up examination should have been performed to look for evidence of hymenal resolution. The hymenal diameter was not measured (a hymenal diameter of greater than 1cm is considered suggestive of sexual abuse in a prepubertal child) and the reflex anal dilatation test was not performed (also suggestive of anal penetration if positive). He concluded "in my opinion, examination of E did not show definitive findings of child sexual abuse".

- The 2008 RCPCH guidance does not describe thickening of the hymen in the finding of abused children, it states rather that as puberty approaches, the hymen thickens, may assume a fimbriated appearance and hymenal elasticity increases. Neither distortion nor asymmetry of the hymen is referred to as a sign of sexual abuse.

- Thickening and distortion must however be considered in the light of both the examination technique and positions in which the child was placed. Whether the thickening was to do with oestrogenisation could have been clarified had E been examined in a different position and/or a follow up examination carried out.

- That E's hymenal orifice was described as "appearing triangular and asymmetric in outline" may simply indicate that she was not relaxed.
- Dr Galbraith found "it was difficult to establish the actual size of the hymenal orifice due to this thickening in the posterior and lateral part of the hymen". Measurement of the hymenal orifice is no longer recommended. The 1997 guidance recommended the supine "frog leg" position. By 2008 both supine and prone positions were recommended, and as to E, might have produced very different clinical findings.

In Dr Price's opinion it was difficult to argue that the clinical findings described by Dr Galbraith, viewed in the light of current practice, provided clear indicators that penetration of E occurred, resulting in damage to her hymen.

As for K, scar tissue on her anus at both 6 and 12 o'clock could be indicative of penetration. However Dr Price also found the examination of K questionable, given that she too was not examined in the knee-chest position. That did not negate the possibility that some sexual activity, including vaginal and anal penetration, did occur. Medical literature includes a wealth of reference to the majority of examinations for suspected child sexual abuse revealing normal or non-specific findings. Indeed the key message within RCPCH 2008 is "normal/ non-specific findings have been reported in up to 99 per cent of children referred for evaluation of sexual abuse".

The Crown submitted that the fresh evidence was relevant only to S's conviction on the single count of vaginal rape of E. Even in respect of that count, the significance of the evidence of Dr Galbraith and the fresh evidence of Dr Price was greatly diminished by the directed acquittal on the count of penetration relating to K. The flaw, as the Crown described it, in Dr Galbraith's evidence, which referred to injuries to K's vagina consistent with repeated penetration when K herself did not speak of penetration, was squarely before the jury. That the jury went on to convict S of the vaginal rape of E was explicable only on the basis that it found E an honest and reliable witness. Further, in the absence of any specific explanation to the contrary, the inference should be drawn that S did not call Dr Primavesi because it was unnecessary for him to do so, the medical evidence in respect of E already being discredited as a consequence of the directed acquittal relating to K.

The Court rejected these submissions. As to Dr Primavesi, the decision not to call him, once he became available, was a tactical one and the Court was not surprised that he was not called: his conclusions about K were capable of supporting the Crown's case, and so to call him would have risked putting back into the spotlight matters more effectively dealt with by relying on the directed acquittal. As to Dr Galbraith's evidence, this went to the heart of the appeal. That a professional witness of experience gave evidence at trial supportive, putting it at its lowest, of the evidence of E would almost certainly have weighed heavily in the jury's consideration. If nothing else, it introduced or might well have appeared to introduce dispassion. Further, to view it as going only to the safety of the conviction on the count of the vaginal rape of E would be to adopt an approach too narrow in the circumstances of the case. The medical evidence at trial "shone like a beacon", and the Court could not be confident that all the convictions were safe.

R's case

22.31E   R had been convicted in 2003 of rape of M, his sister. The Crown relied upon evidence from M and from Dr Han, who had examined M's genitalia with the police surgeon, Dr Lockhat. Dr Han's opinion was that the clinical findings relating to the hymen supported the allegation of penetration, but that it was difficult to assess whether this was penile. R denied the allegation both in interview and at trial.

Dr Han's evidence was read and included the following:

> " . . . there was no bruising bleeding laceration. There is some white discharge in the genital area . . . The hymenal opening was not seen initially but with labial traction and labial separation the hymenal opening was 15mm in diameter. The hymen was thin, there was a cleft at 7 o'clock position. The hymen was not oestrogenised. Hymen margin was blunt from 7 o'clock to 12 o'clock and sharp from 12 o'clock to 6 o'clock. Posterior fourchette was intact. I also examined her in the knee-chest position and the clinical findings were the same."

Her clinical finding was of a cleft in the hymen at 7 o'clock when the examination was conducted with M supine. The examination was then conducted with M in the knee-chest position and the finding was the same. Dr Lockhat described the hymen as "intact" but said there was a "little healed tear at . . . 7 o'clock".

In their evidence on appeal, Dr Pillai and Dr Price pointed out that Dr Han described M's hymenal orifice as 15mm but did not describe how this measurement was achieved. Visual estimates are notoriously inaccurate and measurements will vary depending on the examination position used and the state of relaxation of the child. The 2008 RCPCH guidance in regard to pubertal girls is that there is insufficient evidence to determine the significance of the hymenal diameter, so that no significance would now be attached to the described measurement. As for the notch in the hymen, whether or not this was evidence consistent with penetration depended upon its depth. It could only with certainty be regarded as such if it were more than 50 per cent full thickness. Had it been of such a depth, Dr Han might have been expected to say so in terms. Dr Han herself accepted that she did not measure it and did not say, as normally she would were it the case that it was of such a depth. That it was still apparent in the knee-chest position might make it more likely to be of significance. However, it was impossible to say with certainty what interpretation might be put on the findings described.

The findings of Dr Pillai and Dr Price, and the 2008 guidance, prompted Dr Han to alter her conclusion that her clinical findings supported the allegation. The parties agreed that if Dr Han's description of the hymen was unreliable, then the effect of the medical evidence was neutral.

The Court nonetheless held that the central evidence at trial was that of M. Dr Han's evidence did no more than support M to the extent that Dr Han was of the view that there had been penetration. Her evidence was not presented as conclusive of penile rape but at most as supportive of penetration, penile, digital or with an object. The effect of the revised evidence of Dr Han and the opinion of the two consultants was as follows:

> "The clinical findings may not be conclusive of penetration but neither do they exclude it.
>
> That the notch in the hymen was persistent in the knee chest position would support the opinion that it was a healed traumatic injury."

Nothing in the fresh evidence undermined the evidence of M. On the contrary, it was agreed that there was evidence of a healed traumatic injury. In those circumstances, the fresh evidence did not undermine the safety of R's conviction.

CHAPTER 23

PSYCHOLOGICAL EFFECTS OF RAPE AND SERIOUS SEXUAL ASSAULT

by Dr Fiona Mason MB BS FRCPsych DFP*

INTRODUCTION

This chapter outlines pertinent additions to the literature relating to the **23.01** psychological effects of rape and serious sexual assault.

Sexual violence is a global problem. Aggregated data (2009/10, 2010/11 and **23.02** 2011/12) from the Crime Survey for England and Wales ("CSEW"), which surveyed those between the ages of 16 and 59, showed that on average, 2.5 per cent of females and 0.4 per cent of males said that they had been a victim of a sexual offence (including attempts) in the previous 12 months. This equates to around 473,000 adult victims of sexual offences (around 404,000 females and 72,000 males) on average per year.[1] Data from the 2011/12 CSEW[2] indicates that:

- Women were more likely than men to have experienced domestic or sexual violence. For example, 3 per cent of women had experienced some form of sexual assault (including attempts) in the last year compared with 0.3 per cent of men.

- Less than 1 per cent of both women and men reported having experienced serious sexual assault.

---

* Consultant Forensic Psychiatrist.

[1] An overview of sexual offending in England and Wales (2013), for which see *https://www.gov.uk/government/publications/an-overview-of-sexual-offending-in-england-and-wales* [accessed January 2, 2014].

[2] 2011/12 Crime Survey for England and Wales, for which see *http://ons.gov.uk/ons/rel/crime-stats/crime-statistics/focus-on-violent-crime/index.html* [accessed January 2, 2014].

- Women aged between 16 and 34 were more likely than any other age group, male or female, to be victims of sexual assaults in the preceding year.
- In the previous year 7.3 per cent of women and 5 per cent of men reported having experienced domestic abuse, equivalent to an estimated 1.2 million female victims and 800,000 male victims. It is noted that this abuse includes both sexual and non-sexual abuse.

By contrast, in 2011/12 the police recorded a total of 53,665 offences across England and Wales. The most serious offences of rape (16,041 offences) and sexual assault (22,053 offences) accounted for 71 per cent of sexual offences recorded by the police. A further 6,300 of the most serious sexual offences related to sexual activity with minors. This differs markedly from victims responding to the CSEW; only 13 per cent of victims of serious sexual assault from the 2011/12 CSEW told police about the incident. It is estimated that 0.5 per cent of females report being a victim of the most serious offences of rape and sexual assault by penetration in the previous 12 months, equivalent to around 85,000 victims on average a year. Among males, less than 0.1 per cent (around 12,000) report being a victim of the same type of offences in the previous 12 months.

A recent US study[3] notes that rape affects one in seven women in the USA. The authors investigated the prevalence of reporting rape among a national sample of 3001 women, and examined concerns, barriers and predictors about reporting. Results demonstrated that the overall prevalence of reporting (15.8 per cent) had not significantly increased since the 1990s. Differences were found between rape types, with those involving drug or alcohol incapacitation or facilitation being less likely to be reported than forcible rapes. The authors advocate the need to conduct further research into identification of barriers to reporting that will inform recommendations.

23.03   Recent years have seen a plethora of new victim-focused guidance, for police,[4] CPS prosecutors,[5] Sexual Offence Examiners/Practitioners, Sexual Assault Referral Centres[6] and other professionals who come into contact with rape complainants,[7] but implementation remains patchy. Recent developments, however, indicate a cultural shift; there have been changes in the way rape is dealt with by the police, prosecutors and judiciary and the number of convictions is slowly rising, with official figures showing an increase from 1,778 in 2006/7 to 2,021 in

[3] K.B. Wolitzky-Taylor, H.S. Resnick, J.L. McCauley, A.B. Amstadter, D.G. Kilpatrick and K.J. Ruggiero, *Is reporting of rape on the rise? A comparison of women with reported versus unreported rape experiences in the national women's study-replication*, Journal of Interpersonal Violence, Vol./is. 26/4 (807-832) (2011).

[4] *An assessment of the viability of the dedicated team approach to rape investigation* (Association of Chief Police Officers, 2008); *Guidance on investigating and prosecuting rape* (Association of Chief Police Officers and Crown Prosecution Service, 2009).

[5] *Policy for prosecuting cases of rape* (Crown Prosecution Service, 2009).

[6] *Revised national service guide: a resource* (Department of Health, Home Office and Association of Chief Police Officers, 2009).

[7] *Responding to violence against women and children—the role of the NHS. The report of the violence against women taskforce* (Department of Health, 2010).

2008/9.[8] More recently, there has been a focus on the arrest and prosecution of high profile offenders, particularly in relation to historic child sexual abuse cases.

MYTHS AND STEREOTYPES

Myths and stereotypes about rape persist in society, despite available data outlining the reality. Myths can have a significant impact on those affected by rape, as well as on those involved in the judicial system, and it is important to tackle such myths and barriers.   **23.04**

Research indicates that rape myths differ with time and within different societies and cultural settings. Awareness is needed if such myths are to be challenged. Further research has been undertaken in relation to these.

A joint publication by the Ministry of Justice, Home Office and the Office for National statistics, *An Overview of Sexual Offending in England and Wales*,[9] reported that around 90 per cent of victims of the most serious sexual offences in the previous year knew the perpetrator, compared with less than half for other sexual offences. This contradicts the commonly held beliefs that rapes are most frequently perpetrated by strangers.

A number of studies utilise data from surveys of US college students to examine attitudes and beliefs among a "normal" population. A meta-analysis of the correlates of rape myth acceptance ("RMA") was published in 2010.[10] Continuing the results of 37 studies, the findings indicated that men displayed a significantly higher endorsement of RMA than women. Such acceptance was also strongly associated with hostile attitudes and behaviours toward women, thus supporting the feminist premise that sexism perpetuates RMA. It was also found to be correlated with other "isms", such as racism, heterosexism, classism, and ageism. A study published in 2013 highlighted that RMA was positively correlated with psychopathy.[11] Myths transferring responsibility to victims were related to Factor 1 psychopathy (i.e. callous and manipulative traits). The myth that "rape is trivial" was associated with both Factor 1 and Factor 2 (i.e. impulsive and antisocial behaviour), suggesting it bears relation to a wider tendency to excuse aggressive behaviour.

A 2012 study examined the antecedents of RMA, in which 237 students were surveyed. Knowledge, social norms regarding sexual behaviour, future time perspective and RMA were examined.[12] The majority of the sample was female.

---

[8] The Stern Review, *A report by Baroness Vivien Stern CBE of an independent review into how rape complaints are handled by public authorities in England and Wales* (Government Equalities Office and Home Office, 2010).

[9] An overview of sexual offending in England and Wales (2013), above, fn.1.

[10] E. Suarez and T.M. Gadalla, *Stop blaming the victim: A meta-analysis on rape myths*, Journal of Interpersonal Violence, Vol./is. 25/11 (2010–2035) (2010).

[11] E.R. Mouilso and K.S. Calhoun, *The role of rape myth acceptance and psychopathy in sexual assault perpetration*, Journal of Aggression, Maltreatment and Trauma, Vol./is. 22/2 (159–174) (2013).

[12] T. Aronowitz, C.A. Lambert and S. Davidoff, *The Role of Rape Myth Acceptance in the Social Norms Regarding Sexual Behaviour Among College Students*, Journal of Community Health Nursing, Vol./is. 29/3 (173–182) (2012).

Forty-one per cent believed that a woman who was raped while drunk was responsible. Limited sexual knowledge was associated with high levels of RMA among men.

Compared with the US, in Europe there are relatively few studies concerning this issue. A preliminary study in Italy[13] comprised surveys of 210 participants who were asked to express their opinions on two scenarios of sexual assault (a forced rape and an acquaintance rape). Only 48 per cent of the participants thought that acquaintance rape should be tried in a criminal court.

Issues of vulnerability are also subject to misinterpretation. Women with, for example, a history of childhood sexual abuse, mental health problems or learning disability, are more likely to be targeted by sex offenders and be the subject of repeat victimisation.[14] Yet multiple reports of rape or sexual assault by an individual are still, on occasion, used to suggest that they are lying, attention-seeking or a serial false complainant.

Men who are raped, and men who rape men, are often assumed to be homosexual. On the contrary, both the perpetrators and victims of male rape are frequently heterosexual.[15] The impact of such ignorance is profound, leaving male victims with feelings of shame, confusion and a sense of isolation.

PSYCHOLOGICAL REACTIONS FOLLOWING SEXUAL ASSAULT

23.13   A recent study by Hester et al.[16] (2012) found that:

"[V]ictim/survivors stressed the long term psychological impact of being the victim of a sexual offence. The offence may have caused injury and alarm at the time it occurred and the survivor may have experienced numerous episodes of sexual abuse or violence. Survivors identified post-traumatic stress disorder, depression, anxiety, inability to sleep and other effects such as physical disability, as the long term effects they directly attributed to the offence. These had the secondary effect of reducing their ability to work or study, to forge new relationships or maintain positive relationships with family and friends, or their ability to care for others, such as their children. Suicide attempts were also reported."

The same study found that whilst the public acknowledged that sexual offences were harmful to the victim, they had:

" . . . monolithic views of the type of harm the offence may have to victims, relating it to the immediate details and aftermath—the fear and distress the victim would feel,

---

[13] I. Sarmiento, *Rape stereotypes and labelling: Awareness of victimization and trauma*, Psychological Reports, Vol./is. 108/1 (141–148) (2011).

[14] C.C. Classen, O. Palesh and R. Aggarwal, *Sexual revictimisation: A review of the empirical literature*, Trauma, Violence & Abuse, Vol.6, No.2, 103–129 (2005); N.N. Sarkar and R. Sarkar, *Sexual assault on woman: Its impact on her life and living in society*, Sexual & Relationship Therapy, 20(4), 407–419 (2005); J. Read, J. van Os, A. Morrison and C. Ross, *Childhood trauma, psychosis and schizophrenia: A literature review with theoretical and clinical implications*, Acta Psychiatrica Scandinavia, 112 pp.330–350 (2005).

[15] N. Abdullah-Kahn, *Male rape: The emergence of a social and legal issue* (Hampshire: Palgrave MacMillan, 2008); A.N. Groth, H.J. Birnbaum, *Men who rape: the psychology of the offender* (New York: Plenum Press, 1979).

[16] M. Hester, *Attitudes to Sentencing Sexual Offences*, Sentencing Council Research Series 01/12 (2012).

the injuries sustained due to violence—rather than the long term harm that victim/survivors described and ensuing effect on their day to day life. However, public perception tended to focus on any immediate harm (such as physical injury) or broader harm to society (such as increased fear of crime) rather than the long term impact that victim/survivors themselves described."[17]

Mason and Lodrick outlined the psychological reactions to serious sexual assault and rape, including development of post-traumatic stress disorder, in their article published in 2013.[18] Other publications of relevance have addressed a variety of related issues as summarised below.

Many studies have documented associations between sexual victimisation, post-traumatic stress disorder ("PTSD") symptoms and alcohol use. A study published in 2012[19] evaluated the effect of sexual victimisation on the longitudinal trajectory of PTSD symptoms and binge drinking among adolescent girls, a population already known to have high rates of sexual victimisation and alcohol use. Interviews were conducted with 1,808 participants regarding PTSD symptoms, binge drinking and sexual victimisation experiences over approximately three years. Multilevel modelling revealed decreases in PTSD symptoms over the course of the study; however, compared with non-victims, adolescents who were sexually victimised reported greater PTSD symptoms at initial interview and maintained higher levels of PTSD symptoms over the course of the study after controlling for age. Sexual victimisation reported during the study also predicted an acute increase in PTSD symptoms at that occasion. Binge drinking increased significantly over the course of the study, however, sexual victimisation did not predict initial binge drinking or increases over time. Sexual victimisation reported during the study was associated with acute increases in binge drinking at that occasion, although this effect diminished when participants reporting substance-involved rape were excluded. Sexual victimisation was associated with immediate and long-lasting elevations in PTSD symptoms, but not with initial or lasting elevations in binge drinking over time, suggesting that adolescent victims have yet to develop problematic patterns of alcohol use to cope with sexual victimisation. However, sexual victimisation was associated with acute increases in PTSD symptoms and binge drinking, suggesting a need for binge drinking interventions to reduce alcohol-related sexual victimisation. **23.13A**

Issues of behaviour during rape were addressed in a 2012 article which reported two studies that examined qualitatively the behaviour of female rape victims **23.13B**

---

[17] M. Hester, *Attitudes to Sentencing Sexual Offences*, Sentencing Council Research Series 01/12 (2012).

[18] F. Mason and Z. Lodrick, *Psychological Consequences of Sexual Assault*, Best Practice and Research: Clinical Obstetrics and Gynaecology, Vol./is.27/1 (27–37) (2013).

[19] K. Walsh, C.K. Danielson, J. McCauley, R.R. Hanson, D.W. Smith, H.S. Resnick, B.E. Saunders and D.G. Kilpatrick, *Longitudinal trajectories of posttraumatic stress disorder symptoms and binge drinking among adolescent girls: The role of sexual victimization*, Journal of Adolescent Health, Vol./is. 50/1 (54–59) (2012).

during sexual assaults.[20] The first study was an analysis of 78 stranger sexual assaults, committed in the UK, by male offenders. The second study was an analysis of 89 allegations of stranger rape, again from the UK, perpetrated by multiple male suspects. Information about victim behaviour was extracted from victims' accounts given to the police. More than 100 different victim behaviours were identified in each study, and more than 80 behaviours were common across studies. Myth-congruent behaviours were present in the sample, however, the behaviours displayed by victims were complex and diverse. Indirect and face-saving communications were used by victims and they discussed their ordeal in terms of expectations regarding victim behaviour and rape stereotypes. The implications of the findings for training legal professionals, educating jurors and counselling victims were discussed.

23.13C   Many factors will affect an individual's initial response to trauma and subsequent psychological responses. Issues of resilience have previously been considered, however a more recent study identified that high levels of distress were evident in nearly all participants (119 female sexual assault survivors) at one month post-assault. The results of the study suggested that theoretical models of post-trauma response positing resilience as the modal outcome may not generalise to all cases of sexual assault.[21]

23.13D   As reported previously, women who have been sexually abused in childhood are at significantly higher risk of revictimisation in adolescence and adulthood. Revictimisation is associated with a raft of adverse mental and physical health outcomes and understanding why victims of childhood sexual abuse are more vulnerable to later sexual assaults has critical implications for their development. In their paper, Noll and Grych noted the hypothesis that sexual abuse in childhood resulted in reduced ability to recognise and/or respond effectively to sexual threats later in life, but, as they reported, studies examining these ideas have produced inconsistent results.[22] Further, this research failed to incorporate the powerful physiological reaction elicited by threats of imminent harm to the self, which has the potential to disrupt cognitive processing and coping behaviour. The authors proposed a model of revictimisation that integrated contemporary theory and research on the biological stress response with cognitive, affective and behavioural factors believed to be involved in adaptive responses to sexual threats. The model provides a conceptual guide to understanding why females with a history of sexual abuse are more vulnerable to revictimisation and offers ideas for improving

[20] J. Woodhams, C.R. Hollin, R. Bull and C. Cooke, *Behaviour displayed by female victims during rapes committed by lone and multiple perpetrators,* Psychology, Public Policy and Law, Vol./is. 18/3 (415–452) (2012).
[21] M.M. Steenkamp, B.D. Dickstein, K. Slaters-Pedneault, S.G. Hofmann, B.D. Dickstein and B.T. Litz, *Trajectories of PTSD symptoms following sexual assault: Is resilience the modal outcome?* Journal of Traumatic Stress, Vol./is. 25/4 (469–474) (2012).
[22] J.G. Noll and J.H. Grych, *Read-react-respond: An integrative model for understanding sexual revictimization,* Psychology of Violence, Vol./is. 1/3 (202–215) (2011).

prevention programmes designed to strengthen females' ability to resist sexual coercion.

Najdowski and Ullman[23] surveyed 555 women twice, with a one-year interval between the two. Path analyses, controlling for baseline coping and depression, revealed that those who were revictimised during the study reported using more maladaptive and adaptive coping strategies than those who were not revictimised. Further, women who were revictimised reported more depression than others. This effect was explained in part by revictimised women's increased maladaptive coping. Results are consistent with other research showing that all traumatic experiences must be taken into consideration to understand fully how sexual assault influences coping and recovery.   23.13E

Other authors have examined social reactions as a predictor of PTSD.[24] Using a longitudinal design, the authors examined the course of PTSD in a group of recent rape survivors. They found four distinct PTSD symptom trajectories that were labelled resilience, recovery, moderate chronicity and high chronicity. Sixty-nine sexual assault survivors completed online questionnaires monthly for the first four months following the assault. These included the Social Reactions Questionnaire,[25] which assesses seven types of positive and negative reactions to sexual assault disclosure (emotional support, treat differently, distraction, take control, informational support, victim blame and egocentric). PTSD symptom severity was assessed using the PTSD Checklist.[26] An analysis of variance indicated that the moderate chronic group reported significantly more negative reactions than both the recovery and resilience groups. Specifically, negative reactions where the person treated the survivor differently or took control of the situation distinguished between the moderate chronic and the recovery/resilience groups. Blaming the victim or making the situation about the person instead of the survivor distinguished between the moderate chronic and the resilience groups. This study therefore confirmed that, consistent with previous studies, negative social reactions to assault disclosure were associated with greater PTSD symptom severity. The study also demonstrated that social reactions after sexual assault predicted distinct PTSD trajectories, with negative reactions predicting a chronic PTSD symptom course. This suggests that reactions of mental health providers, criminal justice workers, friends and family may affect PTSD symptom trajectories in survivors and has implications for improving social reactions to sexual assault disclosure. Thus, in addition to interventions directly targeting survivors'   23.13F

---

[23] C.J. Najdowski and S.E. Ullman, *The effects of revictimization on coping and depression in female sexual assault victims*, Journal of Traumatic Stress, April 2011, Vol./is. 24/2 (218–221) (2011).

[24] L.E. Rosebrock, T.M. Au, B.D. Dickstein, M. Steenkamp, B.T. Litz, *Social reactions as a predictor of PTSD symptom trajectories following sexual assault*, Comprehensive Psychiatry, Vol./is. 52/6 (E13–E14) (2011).

[25] S.E. Ullman, *Social reactions questionnaire* (2000).

[26] F.W. Weathers, B.T. Litz, D.S. Herman, J.A. Huska and T.M. Keane, *PTSD Checklist PCL-C* (1993).

distress and PTSD symptoms after sexual assault, it may be helpful to educate others on the impact of negative social reactions after sexual assault disclosure.

Legal Implications

23.22   There is a growing body of research examining issues relating to the disclosure of sexual assault. Survivors differ in how they disclose, to whom they disclose, and the types of reactions they received during disclosure. A study published in 2010[27] sought to provide a more comprehensive view, identifying patterns of disclosure and how these related to physical and mental health outcomes among a sample of 103 female sexual assault survivors. Results revealed four distinct patterns: non-disclosers, slow starters, crisis disclosers and ongoing disclosers. Assault characteristics and rape acknowledgment distinguished non-disclosers and slow starters from the other two disclosure groups. Slow starters were also less likely to disclose to police and medical personnel, and received fewer negative reactions while non-disclosers experienced more symptoms of depression and PTSD than other groups.

23.22A   The Government's Office for Criminal Justice Reform Consultation paper, *Convicting Rapists and protecting Victims—Justice for Victims of Rape*,[28] aimed to improve the outcome of rape cases through "further strengthening the existing legal framework and improving our care for victims and witnesses". This stemmed from the belief that complainants were being evaluated "without juries appreciating the potential effects of the trauma of serious assault and how it might affect a victim's evidence". As described in the Consultation paper, "we want to ensure that stronger cases are presented to the courts, witnesses are given greater assistance in providing their evidence and courts hear evidence from experts that will better inform juries about the realities of rape and the psychological impact of sexual offences upon victims and address certain myths and stereotypes concerning how a victim might be expected to behave".[29]

23.22B   Given the public misconceptions about the victims of rape and the aftermath of its effects, one has to question the fairness of trials in rape cases. The Crown Court Bench Book (2010), *Directing the Jury*,[30] used by judges as a point of reference when preparing legal directions for summing up, provides particular guidance in this area. It lists the factors which may lead to unjustified stereotyping by juries in rape cases:

---

[27] C.E. Ahrens, J. Stansell, A. Jennings, *To tell or not to tell: the impact of disclosure on sexual assault survivors' recovery*, Violence and victims, Vol./is. 25/5 (631–648) (2010).
[28] Criminal Justice Reform Consultation paper, *Convicting Rapists and protecting Victims—Justice for Victims of Rape* (2006).
[29] Criminal Justice Reform Consultation paper, *Convicting Rapists and protecting Victims—Justice for Victims of Rape* (2006), p.4.
[30] Ch.17, p.353.

- The complainant wore provocative clothing; therefore he/she must have wanted sex.
- The complainant got drunk in male company; therefore he/she must have been prepared for sex.
- An attractive male does not need to have sex without consent.
- A complainant in a relationship with the alleged attacker is likely to have consented.
- Rape takes place between strangers.
- Rape does not take place without physical resistance from the victim.
- If it is rape there must be injuries.
- A person who has been sexually assaulted reports it as soon as possible.
- A person who has been sexually assaulted remembers events consistently.

Over recent years there has been increasing recognition of the vulnerability of **23.22C** many of those reporting rape and serious sexual assaults, making them more likely to be a victim and less likely to report it to the police. The CPS acknowledges that "barriers exist, which mean that some people are less likely to report offences. People with learning difficulties or mental health problems may feel that they will not be believed if they report being raped."[31]

The Stern Review (2010) identified that:

> "[A] pervading theme throughout the evidence was the vulnerability of many of those reporting rape. Their vulnerability means they have less capacity to consent. Many of those who are particularly vulnerable will not be one-off victims, but will experience rape and sexual assault on multiple occasions. Such 'repeat victims' may have mental health problems or learning disabilities which make them vulnerable to being taken advantage of."[32]

Issues relating to victim responsibility and credibility have been further examined in a simulated case.[33] In this study Weiner's attribution model was applied to understand why victim blame impacts credibility and verdict. Weiner's model posits that perceptions of a target's responsibility will lead to less sympathy and therefore reduced willingness to help the target. In line with this model, it was hypothesized that sympathy for a rape victim mediates the relationship between perceptions of victim responsibility, willingness to help the victim, credibility and verdict. Participants read a 1,000-word transcript of a rape trial and made judgments regarding the victim's responsibility for the rape, their sympathy for

---

[31] Crown Prosecution Service, *CPS Policy for prosecuting cases of rape* (2012), which can be found at *http://www.cps.gov.uk/publications/prosecution/rape.html£_07* [accessed January 2, 2014].

[32] The Stern Review, *A report by Baroness Vivien Stern CBE of an independent review into how rape complaints are handled by public authorities in England and Wales* (Government Equalities Office and Home Office, 2010).

[33] K. Sperry and J. T. Siegel, *Victim responsibility, credibility, and verdict in a simulated rape case: Application of Weiner's attribution model*, Legal and Criminological Psychology, Vol./is. 18/1 (16–29) (2013).

the victim, willingness to help the victim, perceived witness credibility and verdict. The statement was manipulated between subjects to give differing impressions of responsibility. The hypotheses were supported that sympathy mediated the relationships between perceived victim responsibility and their willingness to help the victim, credibility and verdict.

CHAPTER 24

DNA, LAW AND STATISTICS

by Victoria Oakes, Barrister

INTRODUCTION

In the main edition of this work, reference is made to the importance of the 24.01
Criminal Procedure Rules 2010 in ensuring that experts approach the legal issues
relating to the admission of DNA evidence appropriately. The Rules currently in
force are the Criminal Procedure Rules 2013, which came into effect on October
7, 2013.[1] Part 33, relating to the requirements for the admissibility of expert
evidence generally, is in the same terms as Pt 33 of the 2010 Rules.

DEVELOPMENTS IN DNA TECHNOLOGY

In December 2010 the Government announced that the Forensic Science Service 24.02
("FSS") was to be wound down by March 2012. On July 1, 2011, the House of
Commons Science and Technology Committee published a report on the FSS,[2]
citing dire financial straits as the reason for closure. Forensic work is now
contracted to the private sector, which has meant that the Forensic Science
Regulator plays an increasingly important role. This post was established in 2008
with the remit "to ensure that the provision of forensic science services across the

[1] The Criminal Procedure (Amendment) Rules (SI 2013/2525) also came into force on October 27,
2013.
[2] The Forensic Science Service, Seventh Report of Session 2010–12, available at *http://www.
publications.parliament.uk/pa/cm201012/cmselect/cmsctech/855/855.pdf* [accessed January 2, 2014].

criminal justice system is subject to an appropriate regime of scientific quality standards". The Regulator is a public appointee, sponsored by the Home Office but operating independently on behalf of the criminal justice system as a whole. The post is currently non-statutory, though at the time of writing the Government is consulting on whether it should be placed on a statutory basis.[3] The Regulator has published a Code of Practice on Forensic Standards and established a number of specialist working groups, including a DNA Analysis Specialist Group. The Group's remit is to review the standards in place as they apply to the National DNA Database (for which see para.24.39, below) and forensic DNA analysis more generally. Alongside the Regulator, the United Kingdom Accreditation Service accredits private providers against the International Organisation for Standardisation, including against the requirements of ISO 17025 (accreditation for laboratory based work), in order to ensure the competency of individuals working within forensic science and the systems and processes being used.

24.03   The SGM Plus system continues to be the dominant technology used in DNA analysis. Efforts continue to be made to develop and improve the technology in this area, as discussed in para.24.42, below.

24.08   The requirements of disclosure within an expert's report are now contained in r.33.3(1)(f) of the Criminal Procedure Rules 2013.

Low Copy Number

24.10   The guidance on the Low Copy Number ("LCN") method given in *Reed and Reed*[4] fell to be interpreted in *R. v C*.[5] The complainant had been raped in the 1980s. Swabs were taken from her vagina at the time, but attempts to retrieve DNA profiles from the swabs had been unsuccessful. Years later, the FSS carried out further analysis using, at first, the SGM Plus system. This produced a major profile and a minor profile. It was ascertained that the major profile came from the complainant, and the minor profile was then compared with DNA profiles held on the national database. There were three possible matches: two were eliminated and the third was the appellant. The sample from the appellant was then subjected to the LCN method in the manner described in *Reed and Reed*. The minor profile was said by the FSS expert to show a match probability of 1 in over 3 million. After the analysis of the further swab taken from the victim and an analysis made

---

[3] *Consultation on new statutory powers for the forensic science regulator* (Home Office, Nov 2013), which is available at *https://www.gov.uk/government/uploads/system/uploads/attachment_data/file/256614/New_statutory_powers_for_the_forensic_science_regulator.pdf* [accessed January 2, 2014]. The consultation closed on January 3, 2014.
[4] [2009] EWCA Crim 2698, referred to in the main work as *Reed and another; Garmston* but frequently referred to by the courts under this name. The observations of the Court in *Reed and Reed* on the admissibility of expert evidence were cited with approval in *Henderson, Butler and Oyediran* [2010] EWCA Crim 1269, at [206].
[5] [2010] EWCA Crim 2578.

combining the SGM Plus and LCN results, the match probability of the minor profile to that of the appellant was 1 in over 50 million. In each of the SGM Plus and LCN processes, more than one run was made. In all runs, the results were compared with one another for stochastic effects and reproducibility.

In accordance with r.33.6 of the Criminal Procedure Rules, a pre-trial meeting took place between the two experts. There were the following areas of disagreement:

    (i) Whether the quantity of the minor profile was such that stochastic variations had been sufficiently taken into account.

    (ii) Whether there were more than two contributors.

    (iii) Whether the way in which the process of analysis was carried out had properly followed the applicable protocols.

    (iv) Whether the samples had been handled, stored and recorded correctly.

    (v) The reproducibility of the runs.

    (vi) The match probability calculation.

    (vii) The applicable statistics.

The appellant's expert was of the view that the cumulative effect of the points of disagreement was such that the DNA evidence was unreliable. On that basis, an application was made to the trial judge for the evidence to be excluded under s.78 of the Police and Criminal Evidence Act 1984. The application was heard at a pre-trial voir dire, in which the Crown's expert was cross-examined for three days, prior to the court hearing legal argument on admissibility. Of particular note in relation to the LCN method was the appellant's submission that if the amount of the minor profile was 50 picograms (as he contended), the profile was inadmissible because it fell below the stochastic threshold set out in *Reed and Reed* of 100–200 picograms. The prosecution submitted that the appellant had misunderstood *Reed and Reed*, and that there could be cases in which the quantities of DNA were below the stochastic threshold but the evidence remained admissible. Furthermore, it was the reliability of the profile that determined admissibility and there was no lower limit below which the DNA evidence was inadmissible. At the conclusion of the hearing the judge gave an ex tempore ruling. He held that the FSS expert had not been undermined in such a way that the DNA evidence should be excluded under s.78 of the 1984 Act. It was the total amount of DNA that mattered, rather than the ratio of the profiles, and it was the quality and reliability of the DNA that mattered rather than the quantity.

The single ground of appeal was that the learned trial judge had wrongly ruled that the DNA evidence was sufficiently reliable to be admitted. The Court of Appeal resoundingly upheld the ruling. It said that its earlier decision in *Broughton*,[6] which had not been available to the judge or the parties at the voir dire, made clear that the submissions advanced by the Crown in this case were

---

[6] [2010] EWCA Crim 549.

entirely correct. In *Broughton,* where the DNA profiles had been derived from unquantified samples of DNA of less than 100 picograms, the Court had said[7]:

> "At these very low levels of DNA, the dangers presented by the possibility of stochastic effects, including allelic drop-out, drop-in and stutter are very real and must be fully appreciated, but they may often be addressed by repeating the process a number of times, as [the Crown's expert] recognised.
>
> There will of course be occasions where profiles generated from less than 200pg are wholly and obviously unreliable. We anticipate that the Crown would never seek to adduce such profiles in evidence. If it put forward such a profile, then the unreliability would be pointed out in the report of the defence expert and, if not accepted by the Crown's expert in the exchange that must take place under Part 34 of the Criminal Procedure Rules, the judge would have to consider the dispute; if they were unreliable, he would exclude them.
>
> There will be other occasions where the probative value of the profiles is more debatable. In such cases the evidence may properly be adduced and it must then be addressed and its weight established by adversarial forensic techniques. But we do not accept that these are reasons for ruling out LTDNA evidence [i.e. LCN DNA evidence] altogether. In our judgment, the science of LTDNA is sufficiently well established to pass the ordinary tests of reliability and relevance and it would be wrong to wholly deprive the justice system of the benefits to be gained from the new techniques and advances which it embodies, in cases where there is clear evidence (adduced in the manner discussed) that the profiles are sufficiently reliable."

On this basis, the Court in *R. v C* held that counsel for the appellant[8]:

> " . . . was wrong in his view that a 'knockout blow' could be achieved if he persuaded the judge that the amount of DNA in the minor male profile was below 100–200 picograms. The sole question was whether, despite the low quantity, a reliable profile could be produced."

It went on to add[9]:

> "Although that is sufficient to affirm that the judge adopted the correct approach, we would add one further observation. In *Reed & Reed* there was no express consideration by the experts who gave evidence in that case as to whether the stochastic threshold of 100–200 picograms related to the amount subject to analysis or, where mixed profiles were obtained, the particular profile. However, it is clear from the whole of that decision that the court was referring to the total quantity of DNA in its reference to the stochastic threshold. Of course if, in the case of a mixed profile, the DNA relating to a particular profile comprises less than 200 picograms, problems may arise. But as was made clear in *Reed & Reed* and in *Broughton,* profiles obtained from less than 200 picograms can be reliable. It is reliability that is the issue, not the quantity, though plainly the quantity is relevant (as has been made clear) to the consideration of stochastic effects."

For an explanation of the approach to mixed samples derived from Low Copy Number DNA, see *Dlugosz, Pickering and MDS,*[10] discussed at para.24.16B, below.

---

[7] At [34]–[37].
[8] Above, fn.5 at [26].
[9] At [27].
[10] [2013] EWCA Crim 2.

CRIMINAL PROCEDURE RULES 2010

For the Criminal Procedure Rules 2010, see now the Criminal Procedure Rules **24.11**
2013.[11] Rule 33.2(1) and 3(1), referred to in the main work, are in the same terms
in both sets of Rules.

It is trite law that an expert has an overriding duty to the court, which overrides **24.11A**
any obligation to the person by whom he is paid. *Cleobury (Dean Charles)*[12]
illustrates the application of this rule in the context of expert evidence provided
in support of an appeal.[13] The case concerned an application for leave to appeal
against a rape conviction. At trial there had been no substantial disagreement
between the two experts in relation to DNA evidence. However, following his
conviction the appellant instructed another expert to compile a report on the
DNA evidence given at trial, for the purpose of informing his decision whether to
appeal. The report was highly critical of the expert who gave evidence at trial, the
conduct of defence counsel and the judge's summing up of the evidence. The
Single Judge refused leave to appeal, but the application was renewed before the
full Court of Appeal. The Court expressed the view that the Single Judge had
been right to refuse leave as "there was strong evidence, quite apart from the DNA
evidence, which made the conviction unarguably safe".[14] Although it was
unnecessary to do so, the Court went on to explain the role of an expert on appeal
in terms that were highly critical of the report placed before it[15]:

> "It has become not uncommon to try to persuade this court to reconsider the DNA
> evidence given at trial by adducing a new report. There are occasions when this is
> justified where there has, for example, been an advance in DNA science; there may be
> other cases where it is in the interests of justice for the court to receive fresh evidence.
> However, as this court has said on many previous occasions, it is for the defence to call
> their expert evidence at trial. It is not the function of this court to permit expert
> evidence to be re-litigated on appeal.
>
> In the present case, there was not a shred of evidence to suggest that [the experts
> at trial] were not competent experts who had set about their task for the Crown and
> the defence in an entirely professional and proper manner. In accordance with Rule 33
> of the Criminal Procedure Rules, the experts had discussed the issues. The evidence
> that they gave was clear; the difference in emphasis that they placed on the issues left
> to the jury reflects two experts acting as experts should in narrowing the issues, giving
> explanations to the jury that were helpful and highlighting their differences of
> opinion.
>
> It may, of course, be the case that after the trial there is some new scientific
> discovery or other matter which, despite the exercise of due diligence by lawyers for
> the defence and the work of a competent expert, make it in the interests of justice for
> this court to consider fresh evidence. That is not the position in this appeal, as would

---

[11] Above, fn.1.

[12] [2012] EWCA Crim 17.

[13] A summary of the other points to note in the case can be found in Roberts, A., *R v Cleobury: fresh
evidence—DNA evidence given by the Crown and defence experts at rape trial* [2012] Crim. L.R. 8, at
[615]–[618].

[14] At [14].

[15] At [15]–[18].

have been apparent if the new expert instructed in this case ... had properly discharged his duty to the court by confining his report to matters within his sphere of expertise, namely the DNA evidence.

When an expert is asked to consider a case after a trial, it is essential that the expert presents his report as evidence within his sphere of expertise and not as an advocate's critique of what happened at the trial. If there are issues properly within the province of an expert, then the expert should write a report in relation to those issues. If the report in this case has been written in such a way ... it would have been readily apparent that the grounds advanced were in fact, as the single judge observed, unarguable."

24.11B *R. v C*[16] illustrates the importance of compliance with the procedure set out in r.33 of the Criminal Procedure Rules if expert evidence is to be admissible. As we saw above, *R. v C* deals with the admissibility of evidence is of LCN DNA. One of the points that arose on the appeal was as to the proper approach to determining the admissibility of DNA evidence. The appellant in that case sought to exclude the evidence under s.78 of the 1984 Act, on the basis that it was so unreliable that it should not be admitted. The Court of Appeal emphasised the importance of strict adherence to Pt 33 of the Criminal Procedure Rules and to the guidance given by the Court in *Reed and Reed*.[17] It said that if the rules and guidance are properly observed, there are likely to be few cases where a voir dire will be necessary to determine whether the Crown's expert evidence in relation to DNA should be excluded under s.78 of the 1984 Act. The Court continued[18]:

> "It is clear that an expert instructed for the defence who disputes the evidence in relation to DNA given by the Crown's expert must set out his reasoning and conclusions in proper detail in a witness statement, duly signed and containing a declaration of truth (r.33.3). The court will then order the opposing experts to prepare a statement for the court of the matters on which they agree and disagree, giving their reasons (r.33.6). If, after such a meeting, the defence expert maintains his view that the overall deficiencies in the way the process has been followed or the conclusions reached are so extensive that the evidence is so unreliable that it should not be admitted, he must make a duly signed and verified statement identifying the shortcomings in the methodology and results of the Crown's expert, and the reasons for asserting that such shortcomings fundamentally undermine the reliability of the Crown's DNA evidence to the point that it should be excluded. It would not be proper for an advocate for a defendant to embark on an application under s.78 of this kind without such a statement from a duly qualified expert which has been provided to the court and to the Crown. At the hearing on admissibility under s.78, the judge will manage the hearing so that it is confined within defined issues and during which both experts would be expected to give evidence. We recognise that sometimes, despite the best efforts of the parties and their experts, points may arise in evidence on a voir dire which have not been foreseen, through non-disclosure or otherwise, but the judge will be astute to manage the hearing so that it does not become the type of protracted hearing that occurred in this case. Furthermore such hearings are not to be used for the ulterior purpose of cross examining experts in advance of the trial; the court must ensure that this does not happen."

[16] [2010] EWCA Crim 2578, discussed in para.24.10.
[17] [2009] EWCA Crim 2698, at [131]–[132].
[18] At [40].

EVALUATING DNA EVIDENCE

It has proved difficult to provide a reliable random match probability ("RMP") in   **24.16**
relation to mixed DNA profiles, i.e. profiles to which there is more than one
contributor. This is due to the increased number of DNA contributors, which
increases the prospect of finding matching DNA components by chance.[19]
Computer software to deal with complex mixed profiles continues to be developed
and practitioners in this area have called for guidance on the topic akin to that
provided in *Reed and Reed*.[20] However, the absence of a statistical basis for a
reliable RMP does not mean that evidence of mixed DNA profiles is a priori
inadmissible. This is at odds with the approach in other countries, such as the
USA and Canada. It is also difficult to square with the emphasis placed in *Doheny
and Adams* on the critical importance of a jury having DNA evidence explained to
them in a manner that enables them to evaluate it properly and to reach a safe
decision on its appropriate weight. How, then, should a jury be directed to
approach DNA evidence in the absence of a reliable RMP?

The courts have begun to move towards the approach used in other areas of
expertise, such as that set out in *Atkins and Atkins*[21] in relation to facial mapping
evidence. Rather than statistical assessment, the court may instead admit an
evaluative opinion based on the judgment and experience of the expert.

In *Ashley Thomas*[22] the appellant had been convicted of possessing a prohibited   **24.16A**
firearm and causing grievous bodily harm with intent following an altercation at a
nightclub. He was arrested, together with two others, after a vehicle chase. A pistol
and a revolver were recovered from a garden adjacent to an alleyway into which his
passengers had run after leaving the appellant's vehicle. A bloodstain was found on
the pistol in which all the components of the appellant's DNA were found to be
present. The interpretation of that evidence was the subject of disagreement
between experts. The Crown's expert considered the results to support the view
that some of the DNA on the gun was from the appellant, whereas the defence
expert said that the evidence could only support the conclusion that the appellant
could not be excluded as a contributor. An application was made at trial to exclude
the DNA results and the opinion of the Crown's expert. The judge rejected this
application and the jury duly convicted.

One of the issues on the appellant's appeal against conviction was whether the
judge had erred in refusing to exclude the DNA evidence. The Court of Appeal
was troubled by the lack of statistical evaluation in a case where the expert felt able
to say the results provided support for the view that the appellant was a
contributor to the DNA. However, it concluded that the absence of such

---

[19] This is sometimes referred to as an "adventitious match".
[20] Bentley, B., and Lownds, P., *DNA—analysis of complex mixed profiles, the new frontier?* Arch. Rev.
2012, 8, 5–8.
[21] [2010] 1 Cr. App. R. 8.
[22] [2011] EWCA Crim 1295. See also *Nicholson* [2012] EWCA Crim 1568, particularly at
[42]–[45].

evaluation was not an automatic bar to the giving of the expert assessment. Since the difference between the experts came down to "almost nothing", and the judge had reminded the jury in clear terms of concessions made by the Crown's expert, the Court considered the summing up to be adequate. It upheld the trial judge's reliance on *Atkins and Atkins* on the basis that an expert assessment based on experience could be admissible even in the absence of a statistical evaluation of likelihood, provided the matter was approached in a suitably cautious manner and the nature and limitations of the assessment were made clear to the jury.

24.16B   Bentley and Lownds have criticised the Court in *Thomas*[23] for omitting to mention the guidance in *Doheny and Adams* and for endorsing an approach that will encourage juries to give inappropriate weight to DNA evidence because of its assumed cogency. They advocate a return to the more traditional approach in which statistical analysis is a prerequisite of admissibility. However, the approach taken by the Court in *Thomas* has since been followed in the case of *Dlugosz, Pickering and MDS*.[24]

That decision concerned conjoined appeals in three cases, in each of which the judge was asked by the Crown to admit Low Copy Number DNA evidence derived from a mixed sample to which at least two or three individuals had contributed. In each case, 19 or 20 of the components of the appellant's DNA had been present in the mixture, but the experts were unable to give a random match probability. Nor were the experts who gave evidence in the case of Dlugosz and Pickering prepared to do so using the sliding scale of expressions used in other areas of expert evidence, such as facial mapping and handwriting, ranging from "lends no support" to "lends powerful support". The judge's decision to admit the evidence was the main issue in each of the appeals.

There was no dispute in Dlugosz and MDS that DNA evidence from a mixed profile could be used simply to establish that the defendant might have been a contributor or could not have been a contributor. It was accepted that it is often useful for a jury simply to know that fact without any further elaboration. What was in issue was what was necessary for an evaluative opinion to be given so that the jury could assess the significance of the DNA findings. The appellants' primary submission was that unless statistical evidence of match probability can be given, then evaluative evidence should not be admitted. That was because, as explained in *Doheny and Adams*, the jury needs to have a firm basis on which they can evaluate the significance of the evidence. In the absence of statistical evidence it was not possible for them to do so. The Court rejected this argument. It said that it is clear from *Atkins and Atkins* and *T (Footwear Mark Evidence)*[25] that the absence of a reliable statistical basis does not mean that a court cannot admit an evaluative opinion, provided there is some other sufficiently reliable basis for its admission. It saw no reason for concluding that evaluative evidence as to whether

---

[23] Above, fn.20.
[24] [2013] EWCA Crim 2. See Brewis, B. and Stockdale, M., *Admissibility of low template DNA evidence*, J. Crim. L. 2013, 77(2), 115–118.
[25] [2010] EWCA Crim 2439, at [92].

the profile can be attributed to a defendant or another person should be placed in a special category and should necessarily be excluded.

The Court went on to dismiss the alternative submission that an evaluative opinion can only be given using a hierarchy or sliding scale of support, like that set out in *Atkins and Atkins*. In the Court's view, an expert is not bound to express an evaluative opinion by reference to the hierarchy; they can use other phrases. The real significance of the expert's inability to use the hierarchy might be that it is indicative of the lack of a proper basis on which to express an opinion. It can be no more than that. It is a matter to be taken into account in an assessment of whether there is a sufficiently reliable scientific basis for such an evaluative opinion to be given.

As to this, the Crown contended that it was not open to the Court to consider whether there was a sufficiently reliable scientific basis for the admission of LCN DNA evidence derived from a mixed sample, as it had determined that question in *Ashley Thomas*. However, the Court said noted in *Thomas* there had been little difference between the experts and the evidence was not central to the safety of the conviction. In the cases of Dluglosz and MDS, by contrast, the DNA evidence was central. The Court therefore considered that it should re-examine whether there was a sufficiently reliable scientific basis in the light of the much fuller material available to it. That material elaborated the experience which it is said enables an evaluative opinion, however qualified, to be given. Having considered it, the Court held that an evaluative opinion based upon the analysis of a mixed profile is admissible in principle, provided it is supported by detailed evidence in the form of a report of the experience relied on, and the particular features of the mixed profile which make it possible to give an evaluative opinion are set out. The Court accepted that there is a risk that a jury could attach a false significance to such an opinion, bearing in mind the substantial trust that is generally placed on DNA evidence. However, it did not consider this to be a reason to exclude such evidence. It was incumbent on the parties and the trial judge to make it clear to the jury that the evaluation had no statistical basis, that the opinion expressed was quite different from the usual DNA evidence based on statistical match probability, and that it was no more than an opinion based on the expert's experience and was thus of more limited assistance.

All three convictions were found to be safe as regards the issue of DNA admissibility, though the conviction of MDS was quashed and a retrial ordered on other grounds.

Adams,[26] considered in the main work, was cited by the Court of Appeal in *Clark* **24.21** *(Sally)*,[27] the well-known case in which the appellant unsuccessfully appealed against her convictions for the murder of her two infant children. In that case the prosecution had invited the jury to accept that the probability of two deaths from

---

[26] [1996] 2 Cr. App. R. 467.
[27] October 2, 2000, Case No.1999/07495/Y3.

Sudden Infant Death Syndrome in the same family was 1 in 73 million. The Court said[28]:

> "[T]he prosecution invited the jury to adopt the figure of 73 million as having a significance in itself when in truth, without reference to the likelihood of a competing possibility, the figure has no relevance or significance at all.
> The competing possibility identified is a double infant murder by a mother. That may be capable of being expressed in terms of a statistical probability, but legally speaking the exercise is not realistic—see *R. v Denis Adams (No.2)* [1998] 1 Cr. App. R. 377, which shows that it is not an exercise the courts would perform."

ADMISSIBILITY OF DNA EVIDENCE

24.24   Before DNA evidence can be admissible in a criminal trial, the scientific approach taken by an expert in attaining the particular results in question must be sufficiently accepted within the scientific community. This is known as "validation". Putting it another way, as the Court of Appeal explained in *Reed and Reed*,[29] expert evidence is inadmissible where "the scientific basis on which it is advanced is insufficiently reliable to be put before a jury".[30]

24.24A   In 2011 the Law Commission reported on the admissibility of expert evidence in criminal trials in England and Wales.[31] It criticised the laissez-faire approach that had developed at common law to the admission of expert opinion evidence without sufficient regard to whether it was sufficiently reliable to be considered by a jury. In the Commission's view, this problem was exacerbated by two factors. First, expert evidence is often technical and complex, and jurors lack the experience to assess its reliability properly. Secondly, there is no clear legal test to safeguard the reliability of expert evidence. The Commission recommended the introduction of a new reliability-based test of admissibility for expert evidence in criminal proceedings, with a view to excluding unreliable evidence. It published a draft Bill alongside the report, but there are no current signs that the Commission's recommendations will be taken forward in full. However, the Forensic Science Regulator recently published a consultation paper on validation,[32] and it is possible that the attention the subject is receiving will lead to changes in due course.

24.24B   Where there is a dispute as to the admissibility of DNA evidence, the parties should ensure that the dispute is dealt with in compliance with the procedure in Pt 33 of the Criminal Procedure Rules 2013. The matter should be raised with the judge at the earliest possible opportunity, and a protracted voir dire of the type that occurred in *R. v C*, discussed in para.24.10, above, should be avoided.

---

[28] At [176].
[29] [2010] 1 Cr. App. R. 23.
[30] At [111].
[31] *Expert Evidence in Criminal Proceedings in England and Wales*, March 22, 2011 (Law Com 325).
[32] Forensic Science Regulator, *Guidance: Validation Consultation Draft*, August 2013, available at *https://www.gov.uk/government/uploads/system/uploads/attachment_data/file/229944/fsr-validation-guidance-consulation-2013.pdf* [accessed January 2, 2014].

SCIENTIFIC BASIS OF DNA EVIDENCE

Section 6C of the Criminal Procedure and Investigations Act 1996,[33] which was 24.26 brought into force on May 1, 2010, requires that, where an accused person intends to call defence witnesses at trial, he must provide advance notice of this to the court and to the prosecution. A failure to do so may lead to comment from any other party to the proceedings or entitle the court or jury to draw such inferences as appear proper in deciding whether the accused person is guilty of the offence. Section 6D of the Criminal Procedure and Investigations Act 1996,[34] which is yet to be brought into force, makes provision for an accused person to provide similar notice when he instructs a person with a view to his providing any expert opinion "for possible use as evidence at the trial of the accused".

In *Weller (Peter)*[35] the Court of Appeal approved the practice whereby a trial 24.31 court, faced with determining whether there is a sufficiently reliable scientific basis for expert evidence to be given, of examining unpublished papers and the experience of experts. The appellant in that case had been convicted of sexual assault by penetration and sentenced to 3 years' imprisonment. He applied for leave to appeal out of time on the basis of fresh evidence relating to the DNA evidence provided at trial, the possibilities of the transfer of DNA material and the ability of experts to evaluate it. In the course of evidence the Court examined a number of scientific papers, one of which remained unpublished. That paper was relied upon by the prosecution expert, Dr Clayton, a highly experienced scientist working on DNA matters at the Forensic Science Service. His interpretation of the paper was contested by the defence expert, Dr Bader, a scholar who lacked practical experience of working with DNA. The Court of Appeal said[36]:

> "The question therefore arises as to whether we are entitled to take into account an unpublished paper and unpublished field experience that Dr Clayton has relied upon. It seems to us there are two clear answers to that question.
> First . . . it is unrealistic to examine a field of science of this kind only by reference to published sources. A court in determining whether there is a sufficiently reliable scientific basis for expert evidence to be given and a jury in evaluating evidence will be entitled to take into account the experience of experts and, if their experience is challenged, to test that. If the evidence upon which they rely for the basis of their experience is challenged, then that can be evaluated by cross-examination.
> Secondly, each of our long experience of dealing with expert witnesses in different fields is that experts often rely of necessity on unpublished papers and on their own experience and experiments. As long ago as 1982 in the case of *R. v Abadom* 76 Cr. App. R., 48, the question arose as to whether an expert could rely on the work of others. Kerr L.J., who had enormous experience of expert evidence in many areas of the law, gave the judgment of the court which included the following passage at page 52:

---

[33] Inserted by s.34 of the CJA 2003.
[34] Inserted by s.35 of the CJA 2003.
[35] [2010] EWCA Crim 1085.
[36] At [36]–[38].

'Once the primary facts on which their opinion is based have been proved by admissible evidence, they are entitled to draw on the work of others as part of the process of arriving at their conclusion. However, where they have done so, they should refer to this material in their evidence so that the cogency and probative value of their conclusion can be tested and evaluated by reference to it.'

What is said by [counsel for the appellant] in this case is that the experience and evidence upon which Dr Clayton relies is not publicly available and was not available to Dr Bader. But the real problem was that Dr Bader was a scholar not a person who had experience of this form of science.

It is clear that there are many competitor providers of expert evidence in DNA science and many individuals of great experience who can draw on their own practical experience. Dr Bader was at the distinct disadvantage that he had none. He therefore could not bring to bear any experience of his own which could challenge the logical cogency and clarity of the evidence given by Dr Clayton.

It therefore seems to us that what this appeal demonstrates is that if one tries to question science purely by reference to published papers and without the practical day-to-day experience upon which others have reached a judgment, that attack is likely to fail, as it did in this case . . .

We accept, of course, the integrity of Dr Bader, but we do hope that the courts will not be troubled in future by attempts to rely on published work by people who have no practical experience in the field and therefore cannot contradict or bring any useful evidence to bear on issues that are not always contained in scientific journals. There are plenty of really experienced experts who are available and it is to those that the courts look for assistance in cases of this kind."

The Hearsay Issue and Section 127 of the Criminal Justice Act 2003

24.32 A party seeking to admit hearsay evidence, whether in the magistrates' court or the Crown Court, must give notice of the intention to introduce such evidence under r.34.2 of the Criminal Procedure Rules 2013. The notice must be served on the court and the parties, and must identify the evidence that is hearsay, the facts on which that party relies to make the evidence admissible, an explanation of how that party will prove those facts if another party disputes them, and an explanation as to why the evidence is admissible. Where the prosecutor wishes to introduce the evidence, notice should be served on the defence not more than 28 days after the defendant pleads not guilty in a magistrates' court or 14 days after the defendant pleads not guilty in the Crown Court. Rule 34.3 sets out the procedure to be followed where the party receiving a hearsay notice objects to the introduction of that evidence.

Weight Of DNA Evidence

24.33 A trial judge should not leave a case to the jury where the only evidence against the accused is from DNA evidence, however strong that evidence may be. In *Ogden*[37] the appellant had been convicted of burglary of a dwelling in which some electrical items had been stolen. Entry had been gained through a smashed window, and in front of the window a scarf had been left which did not belong to

[37] [2013] EWCA Crim 1294.

the occupants. A DNA profile was derived from a small area of blood on the scarf, and this matched the appellant's with a one in a billion probability of it belonging to someone unrelated to him. The DNA could not be dated, so it was possible that another person had carried the scarf to the scene with the appellant's DNA already on it. It was not possible to say how the DNA came to be on the scarf; only one of the two areas of blood on the scarf had been analysed, and there was no other evidence that the burglar had cut himself on the window. Before the trial the scarf had been destroyed, and so the appellant's representatives were unable to pursue the possibility that it might have another person's DNA present on it. The DNA evidence was the only evidence against the appellant, who did not give evidence but had provided answers to questions in interview in which he denied being part of the burglary and stated that he had no idea how the DNA had come to be on the scarf. At the close of the prosecution case, counsel for the defence made a submission of no case to answer. The judge rejected this, stating:

> "It seems to me that the discovery of that scarf in the burgled premises with Mr Ogden's blood on it does in practical terms call for an explanation. Certainly a jury, if no further evidence is given, would be entitled to reach a verdict of guilty. Maybe some juries would, some juries would not but that is entirely within the domain of the jury and so the application is dismissed."

On appeal, it was submitted on behalf of the appellant that the trial judge had been wrong in ruling as he did. Reliance was placed on the cases of *Lashley*[38] and *Grant*[39] in which similar issues were raised on appeal. The Court of Appeal stated that they had "no doubt that in the light of those authorities the judge was wrong in this case not to accede to the half time application".[40]

THE NATIONAL DATABASE

Since October 1, 2012, the National DNA Database ("NDNAD") has been **24.39** controlled and run by the Home Office on behalf of UK police forces. Prior to that, it had been under the control of the National Policing Improvement Agency. The operation of the NDNAD is overseen by a Strategy Board, which publishes annual reports on the operation of the database. As of March 31, 2013, the NDNAD held 6,737,973 DNA profiles from individuals and 428,634 from crime scenes.[41] However, this figure has fallen dramatically because of deletions made pursuant to the Protection of Freedoms Act 2012: by September 2013 a total of 1,766,000 DNA profiles had been destroyed. The Government has dubbed the Act the statutory catalyst for the transformation of the NDNAD from "one that

---

[38] [2000] EWCA Crim 88, where the court had commented that there must be some independence evidence establishing a nexus between the defendant and the crime.
[39] [2008] EWCA Crim 1890, where the argument advanced was identical to that in *Ogden* and the appeal against conviction was successful.
[40] Above, fn.38 at [8].
[41] National DNA Database, Strategy Board Annual Report 2012–2013, Pt 2.2.

infringed the privacy of over a million innocent citizens to one that is proportionate and still effective".[42] In all, 7,753,000 DNA samples have been destroyed under the Protection of Freedoms Act 2012.

24.40   The 2012 Act introduces a new regime for the destruction, retention and use of, amongst other things, DNA profiles taken from the DNA samples of arrested persons. In the main work, reference is made to the amendments that were due to be made to s.64 of the 1984 Act by s.14 of the Crime and Security Act 2010. However, that provision was repealed prior to its commencement and instead ss.1–17 of the Protection of Freedoms Act 2012 have inserted new ss.63D–63U into the 1984 Act. Under these provisions, DNA profiles falling within s.63D of the 1984 Act must be destroyed if it appears to the responsible chief officer of police that the taking of the material from which the DNA profile was derived was unlawful, or the sample was taken as a result of an arrest based on mistaken identity. Otherwise, the material should be destroyed unless it is retained under any of the powers conferred by ss.63E–63O of the 1984 Act or any other power of retention that applies to it.[43] By s.63T of the 1984 Act, where material is required to be destroyed, it must not at any time thereafter be used as evidence against the person from whom it was taken or for the purpose of a criminal investigation, subject to the material being relevant material for the purposes of the Criminal Procedure and Investigations Act 1996.

It should be noted that the retention of DNA samples, as opposed to the profiles derived from those samples, is governed by s.63R of the 1984 Act. A sample taken in the same circumstances as material falling within s.63D must be destroyed as soon as a DNA profile has been derived from it or, if sooner, before the end of the period of six months beginning with the date on which the sample was taken.[44]

24.43   The National DNA Database Strategy Board Annual Report 2012–2013 refers to a project that has been run by the NDNAD Unit in the Home Office to co-ordinate the introduction of an enhanced DNA test to produce DNA profiles. Unlike the SGM Plus system, referred to in the main work, which targets 10 areas of DNA as well as a gender marker, the new tests target an additional 6 areas of DNA. This technology has the potential to allow more complete DNA profiles to be obtained from crime scenes where DNA material may only be present in tiny quantities or where the material has been degraded. It is currently anticipated that the new DNA test technology will be implemented by summer 2014. The NDNAD Unit is currently working with the United Kingdom Accreditation Service in the preparation and assessment processes for forensic laboratories, and on ensuring compliance with the Forensic Science Regulator's Code of Practice.

[42] National DNA Database, Strategy Board Annual Report 2012–2013, Pt 2.2, foreword by Lord Taylor of Holbeach CBE (Parliamentary under Secretary of State for Criminal Information).
[43] Police and Criminal Evidence Act 1984, ss.63D(3)–(4).
[44] Police and Criminal Evidence Act 1984, s.63R(4).

Since DNA evidence should be seen in the context of all the evidence in the case,   **24.47**
it remains appropriate for a jury to consider such evidence even where there is a
dispute about it between expert witnesses. In the conjoined appeals of *Hookway
and Noakes*[45] the appellants sought to argue that their convictions of robbery were
unsafe since experts had disagreed as to their evaluation of DNA found in a stolen
vehicle used in connection with the robbery. The prosecution called an expert who
stated that the DNA evidence provided extremely strong scientific support
connecting the appellants with the vehicle. The defence expert stated that the
evidence provided some support for the assertion that the appellants had
contributed to the sample, but that it was not appropriate to give a statistical
evalution of the evidence. Each expert accepted that the other's interpretation was
accepted within the scientific community. On appeal, it was argued on behalf of
the appellants that, relying on *Cannings (Angela)*,[46] the DNA evidence should
have been withdrawn from the jury because the outcome of the trial had depended
on the resolution of a serious disagreement between experts which the jury could
not have resolved. The Court of Appeal dismissed this argument. The case
differed significantly from *Cannings* in that the prosecution had not depended
exclusively on the disputed DNA evidence. The dispute between the experts
concerned the strength of that evidence, not whether it incriminated the
appellants. The evidence of the prosecution expert had not been criticised as being
unscientific or based on any misconception. Each expert had disagreed with the
other, without stating that the other was wrong. It had therefore been open to the
jury to consider the expert evidence and to place what they considered to be the
appropriate weight on each expert's opinion.

PROSECUTING A DNA CASE

The Court in *Dlugosz, Pickering and MDS*[47] observed that in two of the cases   **24.52**
before it the DNA evidence had been presented at trial through the use of a
written presentation handed to the jury explaining the basic science of DNA. It
noted that this is now general practice and expressed the hope that, unless there
are unusual circumstances, such written material will always be provided to juries.
The Court also saw great advantage in the Forensic Science Regulator, in
conjunction with the Royal Society and the Royal Statistical Society, developing
standardised material for this purpose in a format that is understandable by a jury
and not open to debate.

---

[45] [2011] EWCA Crim 1989.
[46] [2004] EWCA Crim 1.
[47] [2013] EWCA Crim 2, at [29].

CHAPTER 25

DISCLOSURE

By H.H. Judge Johannah Cutts QC

INTRODUCTION

Reference is made in the main work to the plethora of protocols and guidance now   **25.03**
pertaining to third party disclosure. In this climate of ever tighter case management, these protocols have been added to and are to be brought up to date in a
continued effort to eradicate cost and delay caused by misplaced applications and
those made without a proper adherence to the rules. In particular:

- The author of this chapter has long been calling for a national protocol to
  govern third party disclosure. In so far as disclosure is sought by the CPS/
  police, it now exists in the shape of the *2013 Protocol and Good Practice
  Model: Disclosure of information in cases of alleged child abuse and linked
  criminal and care directions hearings.*[1] This is a comprehensive document
  which must be read and followed by all those who make applications of
  third parties and the Family Courts for the disclosure of material. Local
  protocols will continue to exist (indeed, the new Protocol calls for them)
  but will have to comply with this over-arching document.[2] The forms to
  be used for applications made pursuant to the Protocol are contained in the
  annexes thereto.
- New *Attorney General's Guidelines on Disclosure* were published on
  December 3, 2013, replacing the guidelines issued in 2005 and also the

---

[1] See paras 25.38A and 25.96, below. The Protocol was published in October 2013 and came into
force on January 1, 2014. It is available at *http://www.cps.gov.uk/publications/docs/third_party_
protocol_2013.pdf* [accessed December 4, 2013]. All areas are to provide local protocols which will have
input from the family and criminal courts as well as the local authority, police and CPS.
[2] The Protocol also provides for linked Family and Crown Court directions hearings. Disclosure will
be the foremost matter to be dealt with at these hearings.

supplementary guidelines on digital material issued in 2011.[3] The new guidelines should be read together with the revised *Judicial Protocol on the Disclosure of Unused Material in Criminal Cases*, published by the Lord Chief Justice on the same date, which replaces the 2006 disclosure protocol.[4]

- The Crown Prosecution Service has issued relevant guidance concerning the duty of the prosecution in obtaining third party disclosure and the procedure for obtaining it in three useful documents to be found on the CPS website:
  - Chapter 4 of the CPS Disclosure Manual[5];
  - Chapter 15 of the Rape and Sexual Offences Guidance[6]; and
  - Paragraphs 108–118 of the Interim Guidelines on prosecuting cases of child sexual abuse.[7]
- A number of Crown Courts have recently updated their own local protocols for the obtaining of third party material.

The message contained in these protocols and guidance has not changed. The emphasis remains on early identification of issues and potential material held by third parties relevant to that issue. Prosecutors are expected to lead the disclosure process and their own guidance points to the need in allegations of child sexual abuse to seek third party material at an early stage "preferably pre charge".[8] The defence are expected to engage and assist in the early identification of the real issues in the case. The courts will expect disclosure to have been considered from the outset. With the abolition of committals, judges are likely to set a timetable at the preliminary hearing, identifying at that time any likely problems concerning third party material.

25.03A   Early disclosure of third party material will assist the preparation of every case. There may be an even greater argument for it following the announcement in June 2013 by the Ministry of Justice that there is to be a pilot scheme in the Crown Court at Leeds, Liverpool and Kingston-upon-Thames of the implementation of s.28 of the Youth Justice and Criminal Evidence Act 1999, allowing pre-trial cross examination of child witnesses (for which see para.18.34, above). Part of the rationale for this special measure is that the child will not have to wait as long to give evidence. Third party disclosure will have to be obtained early in the trial

---

[3] The guidelines are available at *https://www.gov.uk/government/publications/attorney-generals-guidelines-on-disclosure-2013* [accessed December 7, 2013].

[4] The Protocol is available at *http://www.judiciary.gov.uk/publications-and-reports/protocols/criminal-protocols/protocol-unused-material-criminal-cases* [accessed December 7, 2013].

[5] *http://www.cps.gov.uk/legal/d_to_g/disclosure_manual/* [accessed December 4, 2013].

[6] *http://www.cps.gov.uk/legal/p_to_r/rape_and_sexual_offences/* [accessed December 4, 2013].

[7] *https://www.cps.gov.uk/consultations/csa_consultation.html* [accessed December 4, 2013].

[8] Interim Guidelines on prosecuting cases of child sexual abuse, para.112. This paragraph reminds prosecutors that the material sought may contain information which could enhance and strengthen the prosecution case. This is a welcome recognition which needs to be applied in practice rather than the prosecution seeking only disclosure of that which would strengthen the defence case or undermine their own.

process to allow for effective cross examination of such witnesses potentially weeks or months before any trial.

PROSECUTION DUTY TO DISCLOSE

CRIMINAL PROCEDURE AND INVESTIGATIONS ACT 1996

The procedure for disclosure under the CPIA is now governed by Pt 22 of the **25.08** Criminal Procedure Rules 2013, which came into effect on October 7, 2013. They do not materially alter the procedure in the Criminal Procedure Rules 2010 set out in the main work.

Chapter 4 of the CPS Disclosure Manual, Ch.15 of the CPS Rape and Sexual Offences Guidance and para.10 of the Interim Guidelines on prosecuting cases of child sexual abuse[9] all remind investigators they are under a duty to pursue all reasonable lines of enquiry whether they point towards or away from the suspect. This may include enquiries as to the existence of relevant material in the possession of third parties such as a local authority.

Paragraph 4.7 of the Disclosure Manual states, in accordance with 3.6 of the CPIA Code of Practice, that if the officer in the case, investigator or disclosure officer believes that a third party holds material which may be relevant to the investigation that body should be told of the investigation and alerted to the need to preserve relevant material. Consideration should be given to whether an application should be made to seek access to the material and, if so, steps taken to obtain it. It will be important to do so if the information is material or likely to satisfy the disclosure test. An application should only be made if the statutory conditions of s.2 of the Criminal Procedure (Attendance of Witnesses) Act 1965[10] are met.

The responsibilities imposed by the CPIA and the *Attorney General's Guidelines* **25.11** cannot be sidestepped by not making an enquiry. A police officer who believes that a person may have information which might undermine the case for the prosecution or assist the case for the suspect or defendant cannot decline to make enquiries of that person in order to avoid the need to disclose what the person might say.[11]

The CPIA makes no special provision in relation to material held by individuals or companies overseas or by foreign governmental authorities, or material that may be examined overseas in the course of the investigation. If there is potentially

[9] For which see fnn.5–7, above.
[10] For which see para.25.71 in the main work.
[11] See *Joof* [2012] EWCA Crim 1475. The defendants were charged with murder. The prosecution case relied substantially on the evidence of a witness, T. The police decided not to investigate complaints made by T about an officer as they were concerned that any investigation could undermine his evidence, making it disclosable to the defence.

material held overseas, the duty of disclosure is governed by the third party paragraphs of the *Attorney General's Guidelines*, para.7 of Ch.35 of the CPS disclosure manual and para.3.5 of the Code.[12]

SEXUAL OFFENCES (PROTECTED MATERIAL ACT) 1997

25.26 This Act has still not been brought into force. As stated in the main work, it is designed to ensure that the defendant and others unrelated to the proceedings do not have copies of "protected material" in relation to proceedings for a sexual offence. "Protected material" is defined to include a photograph or pseudo-photograph of a victim of a sexual offence. The Act allows copies of the material to be given to a defendant's legal representative upon undertakings not to leave the defendant alone with it or provide copies to anyone else save in restricted circumstances.

25.26A The problems sought to be addressed in the Act have arisen notwithstanding that it is not yet in force. In *CPS v LR*[13] the defendant was charged with possession of indecent photographs of children. His defence was that in at least some of the photographs the women were over the age of 18. He denied that he was responsible for any of the images, saying that someone else must have used his computer and the relevant credit card. The defence wished copies of the photographs in order to take proper instructions and prepare for the trial. The prosecution refused to supply them, claiming that they would be committing an offence if they copied them in any way at all. Arrangements for the photographs to be viewed only at court with an officer outside the room were unsatisfactory as the conference rooms had glass walls. Discussion could be heard outside. The Judge made orders for service of copies with which the CPS did not comply. The Judge then stayed the indictment. The Court of Appeal lamented the lack of mutual co-operation. It held that the prosecution cannot commit a criminal offence by supplying a copy to the defence pursuant to a judge's order and must propose satisfactory arrangements to enable the defendant to have a sensible and confidential discussion with his lawyers with, in the event of disagreement, the judge deciding whether they are sufficient. In the absence of such proposals, the Court of Appeal could see nothing wrong with the order for a stay. A way forward in these cases was proposed:

> "Lawyers and jurors must be trusted to act in good faith, unless and until there is some reason to suggest that they are deficient in any respect. They are provided with

---

[12] See *Flook* [2009] EWCA Crim 682, in which the Court of Appeal said that although these provisions are expressed in a domestic context they make clear the obligation of the Crown to pursue reasonable lines of enquiry in relation to material that may be held overseas in states outside the EU. The power of the Crown to obtain this information is limited if disclosure is declined. For these reasons there cannot be any absolute obligation on the Crown to disclose relevant material held overseas by entities not subject to the jurisdiction of the English courts. The obligation is to take reasonable steps. The position in such a case should be set out clearly in writing so the court and defence know what the position is.

[13] [2010] EWCA Crim 924.

the material for a very limited and strictly defined purpose. Possession and use outside these limited purposes is unlawful and would put them in peril of prosecution. Thus, at the risk of stating the obvious, no further hard copies or digital copies beyond those necessarily required for the purpose of the conference (or indeed the trial) should be made. All the material must be returned to the custody of the Crown Prosecution Service when the relevant trial has concluded."[14]

The Court observed that with the technology currently available, and its sensible deployment, it should be possible for lawyers to have access to the material without hard copies being made and without any risk that there might be some accidental or inadvertent, let alone deliberate, destruction of the material on which the prosecution relies. In some cases it may be possible for a clean computer to be provided by the police for this purpose.[15]

MATERIAL IN THE HANDS OF THIRD PARTIES

The Court of Appeal has recently highlighted the potential importance of material   **25.33** held by third parties in allegations of historic sexual abuse in *The Queen on the Application of JRP v The Crown Prosecution Service*.[16] The court came to consider this case after a referral by the Criminal Cases Review Commission. P was convicted in 2002 on 15 counts of indecent assault, buggery, incest and rape. The allegations were made by three of his daughters. The central issue for the jury was the credibility of the complainants. Prior to trial, the local authority was asked to review any material held on them. Prosecuting counsel was instructed to look at the files. She identified two and a quarter out of 284 pages that were relevant. The Judge ordered disclosure of those two and a quarter pages. In fact, later perusal of the files by the CCRC revealed significant further material which would, in the view of the Court of Appeal, have had a considerable bearing on the strength of the allegations made and the jury's consideration of the complainants' credibility. In particular:

- There was considerable material to refute the contention made by two of the complainants that they had not wanted to see or live with their father following the period when they claimed to have been abused.
- There was considerable material to support the defence contention (denied by them) that they were taken into care not because of any sexual or physical abuse but because they had been out of control and their father was concerned about them.
- There was material to show that Social Services had investigated the sexual behaviour of two of the complainants that led to proceedings being taken against two other males. They had ample opportunity in the course of that

---

[14] At [22].
[15] At [23].
[16] [2010] EWCA Crim 2438.

investigation to complain about any sexual abuse at the hands of their father but had not done so.

The Court of Appeal said that the Protocol now in existence should mean that the sorry history of this case should not be repeated. Hooper L.J. pointed out:

> "This case undoubtedly provides a salutary lesson to all charged with the responsibility of carrying out this task as to how grave the consequences can be if this task is not carried out diligently."

DOCUMENTS HELD BY THE CIVIL COURT

25.38 Application for obtaining disclosure of information relating to proceedings held in private in the Family Court must now be made in accordance with r.12.75 of the Family Procedure Rules 2010. There has been no change in the wording of this rule from its predecessor, save that it allows in r.12.73(1)(c) that communication of information relating to such proceedings can be made "subject to any direction of the court in accordance with rule 12.75 and practice direction 12G".[17] References to r.11.2 in the main work should be read as references to r.12.73 of the Family Procedure Rules 2010.

2013 PROTOCOL AND GOOD PRACTICE MODEL

25.38A This *2013 Protocol and Good Practice Model*, referred to in para.25.03, above, applies to cases involving criminal investigations into alleged child abuse (child victims who were aged 17 and under at the time of the alleged offending) and/or Family Court proceedings concerning a child (aged 17 and under). It states amongst its aims:

a. Subject to the Family Procedure Rules 2010 (and relevant practice directions),[18] the Criminal Procedure Rules 2013 and the common law duty of confidentiality, to facilitate timely and consistent disclosure of information and documents from the family justice system to the police and/or CPS.

b. To provide a timely, expeditious process for a local authority to respond to a request from the police for material held by the local authority which would assist a criminal investigation.

c. To provide for timely consultation between the CPS and the local authority where local authority material satisfies the test in the CPIA for disclosure to the defence.

d. To provide a streamlined and standard process for applications by the police and/or the CPS for the permission of the Family Court for disclosure of material relating to Family Court proceedings.

---

[17] This relates to communication of information for purposes connected to the proceedings and has no bearing on disclosure for the purposes of criminal proceedings.

[18] In particular Practice Direction 12G.

Part A of the Protocol lays down detailed rules about the procedure for disclosure **25.38B** into the family justice system by the police and/or CPS. Part B is of more direct relevance to criminal practitioners and the courts concerned with trials of sexual offences, as it concerns disclosure from the local authority/family justice system into the criminal justice system.[19] The key provisions of Pt B, in so far as it concerns documents relating to family proceedings, may be summarised as follows.

1. As soon as reasonably practicable, and in any event on issue of proceedings, the local authority will provide notice to the police of the contemplation or existence of Family Court proceedings including, where proceedings have been instituted, the details of all parties and legal representatives. Where criminal proceedings are contemplated or have been instituted, the police will forward this information to the CPS who will give due priority to making charging decisions in cases involving Family Court proceedings.

2. An application by the police and/or CPS to the Family Court for disclosure must be in form C2, must (in the case of the police) contain details of the named officer to whom release is sought, and must specify the purpose and use to which the material is intended to be put. The application should seek leave to disclose the material to the CPS or police (as appropriate) and the defence and (subject to s.98(2) of the Children Act 1989) to use it in evidence in criminal proceedings. The application must be served on all parties to the Family Court proceedings.[20]

3. The application will be determined at a hearing at the Family Court. The police and CPS will not attend unless directed by the Court to do so. Where practicable, the police/CPS should seek prior written consent from all the parties and make a written application for a consent order to the Family Court. Alternatively, and wherever this is possible, the police and/or CPS will ask the local authority allocated lawyer to request that the Family Court considers the issue of disclosure to the police and/or CPS at the next hearing. In this way, the Family Court will be able to make any orders that appear appropriate without the need for an application to the Court. If such a request is made, the local authority must put the other parties to the Family Court proceedings on notice, and provide the Court with details of the officer to whom disclosure is to be made and the purpose for which it is to be made.

4. In rare cases where it considers it appropriate to do so, the Family Court should make orders for disclosure to the police and/or CPS without application having been made.

---

[19] See para.25.96, below.
[20] There is no reference in the Protocol to how the defence should make any application they might wish. This may be because it is envisaged that all necessary disclosure will be applied for by the police/CPS. If this is the rationale, it may be naïve. If the defence do seek disclosure, the same procedure for applications can and probably should be followed.

5. The local authority will forward to the CPS copies of relevant Family Court judgments in their possession. If necessary, these will be appropriately redacted. If not in possession of such a judgment, the local authority will notify the CPS so that the CPS can obtain the judgment directly from the Family Court. In these circumstances no formal application will need to be made. Where it appears to a local authority that a judgment will be relevant to criminal proceedings, the authority will request the Family Court to expedite the preparation of the judgment for release to the CPS. Alternatively, this will be considered at a linked directions hearing.

6. All material obtained from the local authority, including the list of material not disclosed by the authority, will be listed on the sensitive disclosure schedule MG6D. The police will reveal the existence of material obtained in accordance with r.12.73(1)(a)(viii) of the Family Procedure Rules 2010 without describing it on this schedule. As appropriate, the CPS will seek the permission of the Family Court to access the material.

7. Where material has been obtained following an application to the Family Court, the police must indicate to the CPS whether the Court has given permission for the material to be shared with the CPS and defence. Further application may have to be made to the Court by the police/CPS as appropriate.

PARTIES TO WHOM DISCLOSURE CAN BE MADE WITHOUT THE PERMISSION OF THE COURT

(i) A professional legal adviser

25.48   In a recent decision, Bodey J. held that the phrase "professional legal adviser" in r.12.73(1)(a)(iii) covers a solicitor instructed in parallel or subsequent criminal proceedings.[21] No leave of the Family Court is therefore necessary before such disclosure can take place. Bodey J. thus interpreted the rule in completely the opposite way to Sumner J. in the *Reading Borough Council* case, as set out in the main work.

---

[21] See *B (A child: Disclosure of evidence in care proceedings)* [2012] 1 F.L.R 142. In this case the parents had made partial admissions in the family proceedings in respect of failing to protect their baby. The Chief Constable applied for disclosure of the transcripts of their evidence. He sought a delay before such was disclosed to each parent as the police wished to interview each before he or she had sight of what had been said by the other. The Court held that the police should have the disclosure they sought. However, on a proper construction of r.12.73(1)(a)(iii) the application for delayed disclosure to the parents had to fail. The guiding principle was one of fairness and disclosure was to be authorised on such terms as to achieve a proper balance between the competing rights and interests referred to in *C (A Minor)* [1997] 2 W.L.R. 322. Each parent had heard the evidence of the other and had discussed it with their family law teams. Their learning disabilities compounded their difficulty in remembering and telling their criminal defence teams about it. The fairest outcome was for both sets of defence solicitors to have both sets of transcripts with no court imposed delay.

SECTION 2 OF THE CRIMINAL PROCEDURE (ATTENDANCE OF WITNESSES) ACT 1965

PROCEDURE

Applications for third party disclosure made in pursuance of this section are now governed by Pt 28 of the Criminal Procedure Rules 2013, which came into force on October 7, 2013, and the wording of which is the same as its predecessor in the 2010 Rules. **25.74**

PUBLIC INTEREST IMMUNITY

The *2013 Protocol and Good Practice Model*, referred to in para.25.03, above, states that PII applications to withhold local authority material will be rare. This is no longer a "class" of material to which PII applies. The Protocol imposes a duty on the CPS to negotiate with a local authority which does not agree to the disclosure of material to the defence, in order to explore whether disclosure can be made in edited form or by summarising in another document the issues arising in the material. The sensitivity can often be removed in this way. Depending on the sensitivity of the material, the local authority may itself agree that the public interest in the prosecution of crime overrides the interests of confidentiality. In highly exceptional cases, the CPS may need to make disclosure to the defence of the edited/summarised document without the consent of the local authority. **25.92**

If a PII application is appropriate, the CPS should make the application to a criminal court as soon as is reasonably practicable. The CPS should notify the local authority of the date and venue of the application and inform the authority of its right to be represented.

In accordance with the Criminal Procedure Rules,[22] where PII is sought on the basis of lack of consent from the person to whom the document relates, the CPS must notify that person of the date and venue of the PII application and their right to make representations to the court.[23]

THE DUTY TO OBTAIN THIRD PARTY RECORDS IN A CRIMINAL TRIAL

The *2013 Protocol and Good Practice Model*, referred to in paras 25.03 and 25.38A above, deals in Pt B with documents held by local authorities. The key provisions in this regard may be summarised as follows: **25.96**

    1. Following the commencement of a criminal investigation into alleged child abuse, the police will provide to the local authority the form at

---

[22] r.22.3(b)(ii).

[23] The Protocol is still silent as to how that person can be represented if, as is usually the case, he or she cannot afford to privately fund such representation. The author has experience of having to explain to an unrepresented complainant just out of inpatient psychiatric treatment how her records or part of them may be disclosed and the possible use to which they could be put. This is far from satisfactory.

Annex C of the Protocol. This will involve requests for material which must be as prescriptive and detailed as possible and necessary for the pursuit of reasonable lines of enquiry. The form will include reasonable timescales but the presumption will be that the local authority will deal with any request from the police as expeditiously as possible so as not to jeopardise the criminal investigation.

2. Upon receipt of the form at Annex C from the police, the local authority will identify and collate relevant material from Children's Services or other files as appropriate. The local authority SPOC[24] will liaise with relevant departments in the collation of such material for the police to assist the criminal investigation.

3. The local authority will identify for the police the school(s) attended by the child/children subject to the investigation. This will enable the police to approach the school(s) directly. If it is practicable to do so, the local authority will obtain and collate relevant educational files for police examination.

4. Subject to paras 10.4[25] and 10.5[26] of the Protocol, the local authority will ensure that documents relating to Family Court proceedings are not included in the files to be examined by the police. Where there are such documents, the local authority will provide a list (e.g. by providing a redacted copy of the court index) of the material without describing what it is, in order for the police and/or CPS, if appropriate, to apply to the Family Court for disclosure.

5. Where in exceptional circumstances the local authority is not able to include other material (not relating to Family Court proceedings) in the files to be examined by the police, the authority will notify the police in writing of the existence of this material, including the reason why the material is not being made available to them. Such a course should be exceptional because the local authority recognises that the material will be regarded as sensitive by the police and the CPS. It will not be disclosed to the defence without further consultation with the local authority or order of the court.

6. Within the timescales set out in the Annex C request (or otherwise agreed between the police and the local authority), the police will examine and review the material collated by the authority. This will

---

[24] "Single point of contact".

[25] The local authority can disclose to the police documents lodged at court or used in the proceeding which already existed (e.g. pre-existing medical records). The text or summary of a judgment given in the Family Court proceedings can be included in the files to be examined by the police.

[26] The local authority can provide to the police documents or information relating to Family Court proceedings where (a) the police officer to whom disclosure is made is carrying out duties under s.46 of the Children Act 1989 or serving in a child protection or paedophile unit, and (b) disclosure is for the purpose of child protection and not for the purpose of the criminal investigation: r.12.73(1)(a)(viii) of the Family Procedure Rules 2010. Where disclosure is made for these reasons, the police cannot make onward disclosure of any document or information contained therein for the purpose of the investigation or prosecution without the express permission of the Family Court. This will include disclosure to the CPS.

usually take place on local authority premises but may be elsewhere by agreement. The police may make notes and/or take copies of the material. The material will not be disclosed to the defence without further consultation with the local authority or order of the court.

7. The local authority will notify the police and/or CPS if further relevant material comes to light to arrange further examination.

8. Where new issues arise in the criminal case (e.g. following submission of a defence case statement), the police will submit a further Annex C form requesting access to material not previously examined.

9. The CPS will review the material in accordance with its duties under the CPIA and under the Attorney General's Guidelines on Disclosure. Blanket disclosure must not be made to the defence—only material which might undermine the prosecution case or assist the defence case will fall to be disclosed.[27]

10. Where the local authority has not made a document available to the police on the basis of confidentiality (e.g. consent has not been obtained from the person to whom the document relates), the CPS will consider whether it is appropriate to seek access to such material by means of a witness summons under s.2 of the Criminal Procedure (Attendance of Witnesses) Act 1965 in the Crown Court.

11. If application is made by the CPS for such a summons, the CPS will serve the application on the criminal court and the local authority, identifying the local authority SPOC as the person required to produce the documents.[28] In addition, where the Crown Court so directs, the CPS will serve the application on the person to whom the confidential document relates.[29]

12. Where any local authority material falls to be disclosed by the CPS under the CPIA, the CPS will notify the local authority of that decision and the reasons for it within two days of the review, whenever possible. The CPS will provide proposals for editing or summarising material for the purposes of disclosure to the defence. Where no material falls for disclosure, the CPS will inform the local authority that is the case.

13. Within five working days, the local authority will be given an opportunity to make any written representations to the CPS regarding disclosure. Where exceptionally the local authority cannot meet the five working day timetable, the authority will communicate with the CPS to seek an extended timetable.[30]

---

[27] para.13.6.

[28] r.28.5(3)(a) of the Criminal Procedure Rules 2013.

[29] r.28.5(3)(b)(i) of the Criminal Procedure Rules 2013.

[30] Again, there are no provisions for the defence to obtain disclosure. This will have to be done in the way identified in the main work. Local protocols should seek to identify how and when this should be done and whether it is possible to include defence requests in prosecution applications following service of the defence case statement, to avoid the need for the local authority to have to go through the files too many times.

25.96A Local protocols in Crown Court Centres will be amended and updated to comply with the new national Protocol to govern how third party material is to be obtained. However, parties are now expected to consider disclosure from the outset and, as mentioned above, the CPS have identified that third party material should be sought at an early stage, "preferably pre trial".[31] This will be long before any Crown Court protocol is engaged.[32]

25.96B It is now widely recognised, and indeed stated in the new national Protocol, that the prosecution have a duty to obtain third party disclosure and the practice in every case of it being left to the defence should now be a thing of the past.

Attorney General's Guidelines

25.97 As noted in para.25.03, revised *Attorney General's Guidelines on Disclosure* were published on December 3, 2013. The revised Guidelines largely replicate the 2005 Guidelines as regards third party material or information that may be relevant to the prosecution case. Investigators and prosecutors are still expected to take reasonable steps they regard as appropriate to obtain such material. In the event that the third party refuses to disclose, they should still take steps in an appropriate case to acquire it by way of a witness summons issued pursuant to the Criminal Justice (Attendance of Witnesses) Act 1965 and must still consult with the third party before disclosing material obtained from it.

The duties set out in the *Attorney General's Guidelines* are also enshrined in the guidance issued by the CPS in the three documents mentioned in para.25.03 above, all of which deal with the duties of the prosecution in obtaining third party material. In essence they state:

- Investigators are under a duty to pursue all reasonable lines of enquiry whether they point towards or away from a suspect. This may include enquiries as to the existence of relevant material in possession of a third party such as a local authority.[33]
- The investigator and/or prosecutor is not to leave the matter if the third party refuses access to the material sought. If it is reasonable to seek production of it and the requirements of s.2 of the Criminal Procedure (Attendance of Witnesses) Act 1965 are satisfied, the prosecution should apply for a witness summons requiring a representative of the third party to produce the material at court.

---

[31] Above, fn.8.

[32] In practice these protocols will continue to have relevance. The CPS's Interim Guidelines are new and it is likely to be some time before prosecutors appreciate their significance.

[33] Note the material sought is said to be "relevant" in the sense that may point towards and away from the suspect. This is a change in the language and clearly relates to material which may assist either the prosecution or the defence. It is a move away from the previous language which stated that third party material should be sought if it undermined the prosecution or assisted the defence case (the CPIA test).

- Requests should be handled in accordance with local protocols.[34]
- Police will take copies of all relevant local authority material which will be scheduled for the CPS on a sensitive unused material schedule. If it meets the CPIA test for disclosure the prosecution should consult the local authority before disclosure is made. There could be public interest immunity considerations justifying withholding it which would require it to be placed before the court.[35]

HUMAN RIGHTS ACT 1998

ARTICLE 8

The importance of the court taking into account the art.8 rights of the person **25.111** whose records are sought was emphasised by the Court of Appeal in *Niwar Doski v R*.[36] This applies equally to the rare occasion when application is made to the Court of Appeal for disclosure of third party records after conviction. If such an application is made, it must be made in compliance with Pt 28 of the Criminal Procedure Rules 2012.

It is incumbent on the prosecution in possession of a witness's medical or **25.118** counselling notes to disclose only that which falls to be disclosed under the CPIA. If the medical records contain entries of a routine nature irrelevant to the issues in the case they should not be disclosed and the records should be redacted prior to disclosure.[37]

---

[34] In many areas, such as Thames Valley, protocols exist between the police and local authorities for the application for and production of material from third parties.

[35] These provisions are from the Interim Guidance on prosecuting cases of child sexual abuse published in June 2013 (fn.3, above). They are also set out in Ch.4 of the CPS Disclosure Manual and Ch.15 of the CPS Guidance on rape and sexual offences (fnn.5, 6, above).

[36] [2011] EWCA Crim 987.

[37] A recent report on disclosure of medical records and counselling notes following an inspection by HM Crown Prosecution Service Inspectorate identified that in too many cases the CPS were "over disclosing". This was an apparent breach of the complainant's right to private and family life under art.8 of the ECHR as consent to disclosure is generally to material which meets the test under the CPIA.

CHAPTER 26

HISTORIC CASES

INTRODUCTION

Today, in 2013, there are far more sex case prosecutions brought relating to events **26.01** that have occurred years ago.[1] Some involve incidents that are alleged to have taken place several decades ago.[2] There has been a significant increase in these cases being brought to trial during the last few years.[3] An analysis of jury verdicts in all cases between 2006 and 2008 looking at different categories of offence found that sexual offences amounted to the single largest proportion of jury verdicts (31 per cent), and yet they made up 17 per cent of all charges against all defendants.[4] It appears that the trend has continued. In respect of historic cases, whilst many may take matters to their grave without revealing abuse they endured when they were young, in the wake of high profile investigations such as Operation Yewtree[5] there is evidence of greater disclosure. Whilst this is a complex subject and over-

---

[1] See the Joint Statistical Bulletin published by the Ministry of Justice, the Home Office and the Office of National Statistics, *An Overview of Sexual Offending in England and Wales*, January 10, 2013, which is available at *https://www.gov.uk/government/publications/an-overview-of-sexual-offending-in-england-and-wales* [accessed December 31, 2013].

[2] For a recent example see *R. v PS* [2013] EWCA Crim 992, where the allegations related to events that had occurred 34 years before. See also *R. v RD* [2013] EWCA, where the Court of Appeal upheld convictions where the time span in respect of the allegations by four female complainants ranged from 39 to 63 years ago, and *Taylor* [EWCA] Crim 2398 where the Court of Appeal upheld convictions in relation to allegations that the appellant had acted as a sexual predator 33 years ago.

[3] Above, fn.1, p.34. In 2011, 7,061 defendants were tried at the Crown Court for sexual offences, of whom 2,713 (38.4 per cent) pleaded guilty; 1,639 (23.2 per cent) pleaded not guilty and were found guilty; and 2,592 (36.7 per cent) pleaded not guilty and were acquitted. These figures represent an overall 61.6 per cent conviction rate, which is a 7 per cent increase since 2005.

[4] Professor Cheryl Thomas, *Are juries fair?* Ministry of Justice Research series 1/10, p.28, available at *http://www.justice.gov.uk/downloads/publications/research-and-analysis/moj-research/are-juries-fair-research.pdf* [accessed December 31, 2013].

[5] The police investigation into sexual abuse allegations, predominantly the abuse of children, against British media personality Jimmy Savile (who died in 2011) and others: see the joint Metropolitan Police Service and NSPCC report *Giving victims a voice* (January 2013), available at *http://www.nspcc.org.uk/news-and-views/our-news/child-protection-news/13-01-11-yewtree-report/yewtree-report-pdf_wdf93652.pdf* [accessed December 31, 2013].

simplification should be avoided, it is clear that there are a number of reasons for these developments:

> (i) a greater awareness of the psychological harm caused by sexual abuse, and its continuing nature;
>
> (ii) an increase in reporting against the background of a change in social attitudes, reflecting a greater understanding of the scale of historic abuse and the reasons for late reporting; and
>
> (iii) the abolition in 1994 of the law requiring corroboration of the evidence of complainants of sexual offences.[6]

The response of the courts

26.01A The law governing the trial of historic sex cases has developed in a haphazard way, with different constitutions of the Court of Appeal adopting different approaches to both applications to stay for abuse of process on grounds of delay, and sentencing. This left judges and counsel to undertake these trials against the background of contradictory guidance. The period since our last edition in December 2010 has seen welcome intervention in this area by the Court of Appeal, with a powerful lead being given by the last Lord Chief Justice.

First, the five-judge Court of Appeal in *R. v F(S)*[7] gave clear guidance as to the approach to be taken to an application for a stay due to delay. This guidance included assistance as to the appropriate time for such an application, a series of propositions to be followed in determining such applications, and positive discouragement to the courts from trawling through old Court of Appeal authorities when hearing them.

Secondly, the Court of Appeal revisited the sentencing of historic sex cases in *R. v H(J)*.[8] Until that case, in which the then Lord Chief Justice set out the principles underpinning the correct approach, the courts had faced various difficulties when it came to sentencing such cases. In some, the statutory maximum had been increased since the time of the offence. The 2003 Act also introduced some very broad changes in the statutory identification of different forms of sexual crime. In respect of many sexual offences, the Sentencing Guidance Council's Definitive Guideline[9] suggested higher sentences than would have been awarded in the past. In *Millberry*[10] Lord Woolf C.J. had stated that the same starting points should apply to historic cases as to other cases.

In *R. v H(J)* the Lord Chief Justice identified two critical issues where conflicting approaches by the Court of Appeal in its past decisions were discernible and upon which specific guidance was required:

---

[6] By s.32(1)(b) of the Criminal Justice and Public Order Act 1994.
[7] [2011] EWCA Crim 1844, discussed in para.26.25 et seq., below.
[8] [2012] EWCA Crim 2753, discussed in para.26.72, below.
[9] Which, by reason if s.125 of the Coroners and Justice Act 2009, every court, when sentencing an offender, was required to follow unless satisfied that to do so would be contrary to the interests of justice. The guideline applies to the sentencing of offenders convicted of any sexual offences covered by the guideline on or after May 14, 2007.
[10] [2003] 2 Cr. App. R.(S.) 31.

(i) the extent, if any, to which the court passing sentence should reflect the levels of sentence which would have been likely to have been imposed if the defendant had been convicted at a trial shortly after the offences were committed; and

(ii) the extent to which events during the long period between the commission of the crime and the sentencing decision may be relevant.

He then set out the principles to be derived from statute,[11] the authorities which purport to provide guidance, and fact-specific decisions. The Court suggested that with the exception of *Millberry*, and the sentencing guideline (used in a measured way), reference to earlier decisions is unlikely to be helpful and is to be discouraged.

Notwithstanding the important guidance in *R. v H(J)*, judges frequently face difficult sentencing exercises in historic sex cases. There have an increasing number of Attorney General's References in this area. In one of these, *Att Gen's Ref (No.38 of 2013) (R. v Stuart Hall)*,[12] the Court acknowledged that there are public concerns about sexual crimes against children and young victims which for very good reason have been heightened by our increasing understanding of the criminality involved and the serious consequences to the victims, however minor (in the legal sense) the offence may seem to be. Greater awareness of this harm underpins the higher sentences suggested in the new guideline just issued by the Sentencing Council.

THE LAW GOVERNING SEXUAL OFFENCES BEFORE THE SEXUAL OFFENCES ACT 2003

Most commonly charged historic offences (i.e. pre-implementation of Sexual Offences Act 2003)

Attempted rape

The case of one appellant, P, in *R. v H(J)*[13] illustrates the difficulty that arises **26.07** where a court is called upon to sentence for attempted rape committed before September 16, 1985. In January 1978, P had attacked an 18-year-old girl who was waiting for a bus. He told her he had a knife and would kill her. After pushing his erect penis between her legs and ejaculating over her inner thighs and clothing, he forced her to perform oral sex upon him. The effect upon the victim was particularly traumatic. Shortly after the attack she discovered she was pregnant. She was terrified that this could have resulted from P ejaculating over her inner thighs. She went through pregnancy in a state of turmoil, although it later transpired that her husband was the father of her child.

P was arrested after a "cold case review" in 2009. In January 2010 he was convicted by a jury of attempted rape and indecent assault, which reflected the

---

[11] Above, fn.8 at [46]–[47].
[12] [2013] EWCA Crim 1450, for which see para.26.72A, below.
[13] [2011] EWCA Crim 2753, at [116]–[129].

only way in which in 1978 it was possible to indict for oral rape. P had convictions for sexual offences he had committed both before and after the offences of which he was convicted. In February 2010 he was sentenced to life imprisonment for attempted rape and two years' imprisonment concurrent for indecent assault. The minimum specified term was 7 years and 6 months.

The Court of Appeal concluded that if the sentencing court had had the necessary jurisdiction, the sentence would have been entirely appropriate. However, by operation of the Attempted Rape Act 1948 and the Sexual Offences Act 1956, s.37(3) and Sch.II para.(1)(b), the maximum sentence for an offence of attempted rape in 1978 was 7 years' imprisonment. The maximum was increased to life imprisonment for offences committed after September 16, 1985, as a result of ss.3 and 5(5) of the Sexual Offences Act 1985. None of this was affected by the coming into force of the Criminal Attempts Act 1981. The Court therefore quashed the sentence of life imprisonment for the attempted rape and substituted one of 7 years' imprisonment, i.e. the statutory maximum, with the 2-year sentence for indecent assault to run consecutively. It said[14]:

> "This is a most unfortunate case. The sentence imposed, although fully justified, was unlawful. It must be quashed. The reasonable understanding of the victim of the crime, that the life sentence was fully justified, has been dashed. That should not have happened. Without any consideration beyond the aggravating and mitigating features of the individual offence or offences, the sentencing decision in cases like these is never straightforward. It is made more complicated because of the variations in the maximum sentences lawfully available in historic cases . . . Particular care is therefore needed to ensure that before the sentencing hearing begins, the parameters of sentence in force at the time when the offence was committed are identified.
>
> Justice will not appear to the victim to have been done, and for what it is worth, we do not think that the sentence which we must now impose appropriately represents this appellant's criminality. Nevertheless the decision is unavoidable. It is a consequence of the legislation in force at the time, which we are bound to apply. Fortunately that has now been changed, and for such a crime committed today, the sentence imposed on this appellant would have been upheld."

Sentencing powers

26.10A   Sentences are imposed on the basis of the legislative provisions in force at the time of the offence, and it follows that when sentencing historic sex cases, it is important to have two critical dates in mind: (i) May 1, 2004, when the 2003 Act came into force, and (ii) April 4, 2005, when the sentencing provisions of the Criminal Justice Act 2003 ("CJA 2003") came into force. As there were a number of statutes governing the law of sexual offences before the 2003 Act, some of which were themselves amended as to the maximum sentence, it is essential to check what was the maximum sentence at the relevant time, as well as the nature of the sentences then available. The Court should then make the appropriate "measured reference"[15] to the current sentencing guideline.

---

[14] At [124]–[125].
[15] R. v H(J), above, fn.8 at [47(a)].

Sentencing dangerous offenders for offences committed before April 4, 2005

When dealing with a dangerous offender for an offence committed before the   **26.10B**
commencement of the sentencing provisions of the CJA 2003 on April 4, 2005, the
choice now lies between (i) the "old style" discretionary life sentence,[16] applying
the criteria in *Hodgson* and *Whittaker* (for which see the below), (ii) the new style
extended sentence under s.226A of the CJA 2003 (inserted by the Legal Aid,
Sentencing and Punishment of Offenders Act 2012, which is available for
convictions on or after December 3, 2012, irrespective of the date of commission
of the offence, or (iii) the longer than commensurate sentence under s.80(2)(b) of
the Powers of Criminal Courts (Sentencing) Act 2000 ("PCC(S)A 2000").

(i) Life sentence

Notwithstanding the multiple amendments to the law governing the sentencing of   **26.10C**
dangerous offenders during the last 10 years, the law remains unchanged as
regards "old style" discretionary life sentences in respect of offences committed
before April 4, 2005.[17] The criteria for the imposition of such a sentence are set
out in *Hodgson*[18] and *Att Gen's Ref (No.32 of 1996) (R. v Whittaker)*.[19] First, the
offender must have been convicted of a "very serious offence". The meaning of
"very serious offence" was considered in *R. v D*[20] where the Court of Appeal took
the view that the *Hodgson / Whittaker* criteria were satisfied where the offender as
a youth had broken into his grandmother's home and raped her. For fuller
discussion of *R. v D*, see paras 1.42D et seq., above. Secondly, there should be
good grounds for believing that the offender might remain a serious danger to the
public for a period which could not be reliably estimated at the date of sentence.
It was explained in *Whittaker* that by "serious danger" the Court had in mind
particularly serious offences of violence and serious sexual offences.

A good recent illustration of such a sentence is *R. v DP*,[21] in which the appellant
pleaded guilty to a number of sexual offences. One was an offence sexual assault
on a child under 13 by penetration, contrary to s.6(1) of the 2003 Act, committed
between December 2004 and March 2005. It was accepted by the judge and the
Court of Appeal that the appellant should be sentenced by reference to the law
which existed before April 4, 2005, the relevant legislation being the PCC(S)A
2000 and the early release provisions of the Criminal Justice Act 1991. The
complainants were two children of a woman with whom the appellant had formed
a relationship. The appellant had a long record of sexual offences against children.

---

[16] So described by the late Professor David Thomas QC in his commentary on *Saunders* [2013]
Crim. L.R. 935.
[17] *Red Saunders and others* [2013] EWCA Crim 1027. For a fuller discussion of this important case,
see para.1.42A et seq., above.
[18] (1968) 52 Cr. App. R. 113; [1968] Crim. L.R. 46.
[19] [1997] 1 Cr. App. R.(S.) 261; [1996] Crim. L.R. 917.
[20] [2012] EWCA Crim 2370; [2013] 1 Cr. App. R.(S.) 127 (p.674). For fuller discussion of *R. v D*,
see para.1.42D et seq., above.
[21] [2013] EWCA Crim 1143.

He was sentenced to life imprisonment in respect of the s.6 offence with various concurrent determinate sentences for other offences. The Court of Appeal concluded that (i) the offending was of sufficient gravity to warrant a sentence of imprisonment for life, and (ii) the appellant was a serial predatory paedophile, had been so for many years, and at the time of sentence it could not be estimated how long he would remain a danger to younger children.

(ii) Longer than commensurate sentence

26.10E   The operation of the provisions relating to longer than commensurate sentences under s.80(2)(b) of the PCC(S)A 2000 was examined in *R. v S.*[22] Where the threshold for a life sentence has not been crossed, but the court needs to consider whether it is necessary to protect the public from serious harm in the future, then a longer than commensurate sentence can be passed together with an extended licence period. The anticipated harm likely to be produced by the expected future offences may be either physical or psychological, but must be "serious". The offence which is expected to produce the harm must itself be a violent or sexual offence.

(iii) Extended sentence

26.10F   The new-style extended sentence introduced by the Legal Aid, Sentencing and Punishment of Offenders Act 2012 is available for offenders convicted on or after December 3, 2012. It should be borne in mind that this sentence has replaced the old-style extended sentence under s.85 of the PCC(S)A 2000 with retrospective effect.[23] For further discussion in respect of the 'new' extended sentence, see paras 27.08D and 27.60C, below.

Doli incapax

26.11   The rebuttable presumption at common law that a child aged not less than 10 but under 14 years was doli incapax (i.e. incapable of committing a crime) still applies to historic abuse cases relating to events that preceded the presumption's abolition on September 30, 1998.[24] However, since the presumption is rebuttable by evidence that the child knew its actions were "seriously wrong", there may be features in the evidence which will lead the Court of Appeal to conclude, even in the absence of the appropriate direction, that there was no prospect that the jury would not have been convinced that the appellant had known his actions to be seriously wrong.

    Bevan[25] is a good illustration of a case where there was abundant evidence to rebut the presumption. The Court of Appeal was obliged to quash a conviction for

---

[22] [2010] EWCA Crim 1462.
[23] See commentary by the late Professor David Thomas QC on *R. v DP* [2013] Crim. L.R. 862.
[24] *Fethney* [2010] EWCA Crim 3096.
[25] [2011] EWCA Crim 654.

rape alleged to have been committed by the appellant when he may have been aged under 14, thereby engaging the irrebuttable presumption of penetrative incapacity (for which see para.26.12, below). However, the Court of Appeal held that the other convictions, which did not involve penetrative activity, were safe. The evidence was that at no time during the relevant period was the appellant less than 12 years old. His own description of himself as a young teenager was that he was difficult to control, he was streetwise, he truanted from school, and he described himself at the ages of 13 and 14 as "a nasty piece of work". The complainant described how her attacker would threaten her with the consequences if she revealed what she was doing to her: "He would say that mum would get hurt if I said anything and no one would believe me." The activity only happened when both the complainant and the appellant were clothed, so that they could re-adjust themselves if they were interrupted. The appellant would use language towards the complainant about her mother such as "slag" and "whore". The nature of the acts was such as to be inconsistent with the mere sexual curiosity of an immature boy or a game.

Presumption that boys under 14 were incapable of vaginal or anal intercourse

The anomalous common law presumption that a boy under the age of 14 was **26.12** incapable of vaginal or anal intercourse was abolished by s.1 of the Sexual Offences Act 1993, which came into force on September 20, 1993. However, it was not abolished retrospectively. It follows that, whatever the circumstances, a defendant cannot be convicted of rape where the relevant events occurred before September 20, 1993.[26]

THE INDICTMENT

Where an indictment straddles periods covered by the Sexual Offences Act 1956 **26.13** and the 2003 Act, it is important to check that each count is drafted under the right Act.

In *R. v MC*[27] the appellant was charged with sexual offences committed against his natural daughter. The offences were alleged to have occurred some time ago and an additional count of indecent assault, contrary to s.14(1) of the Sexual Offences Act 1956, was added by a late amendment to the indictment. The count was defective as the particulars alleged that the offence had taken place at a time when the Sexual Offences Act 1956 had long since been repealed and replaced by the 2003 Act. On appeal, it was submitted by the Crown that it was open to the Court to substitute for the jury's verdict on the defective count a conviction of

---

[26] *Fethney* [2010] EWCA Crim 3096.
[27] [2012] EWCA Crim 213.

sexual activity with a child, contrary to s.9 of the 2003 Act. The Court of Appeal found a difficulty with this argument because it did not pay sufficient attention to the requirement in s.3 of the Criminal Appeal Act 1968 that the jury could on the indictment have found the appellant guilty of some other offence. The words "on the indictment" were important because in order to find a person guilty of an alternative offence, the allegations in the indictment had to amount to or include an allegation of that other offence.[28] The Court concluded that s.3 of the Criminal Appeal Act 1968 did not allow it to substitute a verdict under s.9 of the 2003 Act.

The situation in *R. v MC* can be contrasted with that in *Stewart*,[29] where it was held in relation to an indictment charging a specimen count of rape by reference to the 2003 Act, that it did not matter that the particulars of the offence specified a period beginning some weeks before, and continuing some weeks beyond, the coming into force of that Act. On the evidence, the jury must have been sure that there had been regular, continuing rapes, and the case was not analogous with those in which there was a single offence which might have been committed before, or after, the coming into force of the Act.

ABUSE OF PROCESS

GUIDANCE DERIVED FROM THE AUTHORITIES

26.25   In what is now the leading case of *R. v F(S)*,[30] the Court of Appeal took the opportunity to carry out a comprehensive review of all the authorities concerning applications for a stay of criminal proceedings on the grounds of delay. The then Lord Chief Justice, Lord Judge, said the review had revealed that the decisions of the Court of Appeal on this issue have not always been consistent, and that some of the jurisprudence about long delays in sexual cases appeared to have become disconnected from the well-known principles in *Galbraith*[31] and to have obscured those principles by eliding the distinct concepts of abuse of process and withdrawal of the case from the jury on evidential grounds. The Lord Chief Justice distilled the principles to be applied in such cases and stressed that applications to stay an indictment for abuse of process must not be elided with submissions of no case to answer.

R. v F(S)—The facts

26.25A   It was alleged that on three occasions in 1992 or 1993, when he was aged about 16, the defendant had abused the complainant, his step-brother, who was aged about

---

[28] *Graham and others* [1997] 1 Cr. App. R.(S.) 302.
[29] *The Times*, May 21, 2012.
[30] [2011] EWCA Crim 1844.
[31] [1981] 73 Cr. App. R. 124; [1981] 1 W.L.R. 1039.

six. It was common ground that at the time the boys shared sleeping accommodation in a caravan in the garden of the family home. No complaint was made until autumn 2008.

At the outset of the trial, the defendant gave notice of an application for a stay of the proceedings on the grounds of abuse of process. The judge, following *Smolinski*,[32] declined to rule on the application at the start of the trial, which then proceeded. During the course of his evidence, the complainant explained why the complaint was delayed and was cross-examined about it. At the conclusion of the prosecution case, the judge considered the application and acceded to it. Since it was a terminating ruling, the prosecution appealed under s.58 of the CJA 2003 with the leave of the Court of Appeal.

Although the application was advanced to the judge as an application to stay, and was granted in those terms, the argument in support of the application ranged widely over what were submitted to be weaknesses in the Crown's case. These included: (i) the fact that the case depended entirely upon the unsupported word of the complainant; (ii) that it concerned events which, if they occurred, had happened some 16 years before any report of them was made and the defendant had any opportunity to deal with them; (iii) that there was no satisfactory explanation for the failure to report the matter, not at the age of six, but when the complainant realised what had happened was seriously wrong, as he clearly had by his mid-teens. He had opportunities to report it when he was receiving counselling for anger management when aged 14, but had failed to do so; (iv) that his initial disclosures, which were partial and limited, were made to his wife in 2008 when he had collapsed apparently suffering from stress; (v) that there was a possibility that what he now said was in part the result of suggestions made by the complainant's mother when, on the following day, he spoke to her; (vi) that the complaint was recorded by way of witness statement rather than by way of ABE interview; (vii) that the explanations offered by the complainant in evidence both as to when he had realised what had happened was wrong, and as to why he had not reported it, were inconsistent and unsatisfactory; (viii) that the notes of the counsellor had been long destroyed; (ix) that if the allegations had been made contemporaneously, the defendant could not have been convicted because as the law then stood the absence of corroboration would have been fatal; and (x) that it had been unfair that the defendant should face trial as an adult rather than as a youth, which he had been when the offences were said to have been committed.

The trial judge approached her decision on the basis of five propositions identified in the then most recent case of *R. v F(TB)*.[33] She quoted in full the fifth of Jackson L.J.'s propositions from that case:

> "That a complainant's delay in coming forward was so unjustified, is relevant to the question whether it is fair to try the defendant so long after the events in issue. In determining whether the complainant's delay is justified, it must be firmly borne in

---

[32] [2004] EWCA Crim 1270. This approach was endorsed by Hooper L.J. in *Burke* [2005] EWCA Crim 29, but did not find favour with the Court of Appeal in *R. v F(S)*.
[33] [2011] EWCA Crim 726.

mind that victims of sexual abuse are often unwilling to reveal or talk about their experiences for some time and for good reason."

The Lord Chief Justice pointed out that this passage suggests that the judge should embark upon a fact-finding decision during the course of the trial in relation to the issue of the credibility of the complainant, which is pre-eminently for the jury's decision.

The judge ruled that a jury properly directed could not safely return a verdict of guilty on the evidence before them. This ruling proceeded on the basis that no specific prejudice had been established other than the fact of potential prejudice inherent in any prolonged delay. However, the judge explained that the absence of justification for the delay was her principal concern, and the basis for her decision was the absence of any "real satisfactory explanation" for the complainant's failure to take advantage of a number of opportunities to report what had happened to him.

The Lord Chief Justice observed that the argument advanced by the defendant, and perhaps in consequence the ruling, represented an amalgam of two distinct questions:

 i) Should the prosecution be stayed for "abuse of process" on the grounds that the defendant could not receive a fair trial?

 ii) Should the case be withdrawn from the jury on the grounds that the evidence was such that a conviction would be unsafe?

The Court of Appeal allowed the prosecution appeal on the ground that the judge had applied the wrong test. She had been led into thinking that the crux of her decision was the presence or absence of justification for the delayed complaint. She had taken into account matters which went to the issue of whether the offences alleged were proved or not. These matters were capable of exploration at trial, and had been explored. They did not provide any reason on abuse of process grounds for preventing the trial from taking place or continuing to its normal end.

R. v F(S)—The Postscript

26.25B The Lord Chief Justice set the governing principles in stone in a postscript to his judgment.[34] He made it clear that when abuse of process submissions on the grounds of delay are advanced, provided the principles articulated in *Galbraith* and *Att Gen's Ref (No.1 of 1990)*[35] are clearly understood, it will no longer be necessary or appropriate for reference to be made to any Court of Appeal decisions except *Stephen Paul S*[36] and the decision in *R. v F(S)*. These four authorities contain all the necessary discussion about the applicable principles. Their application is fact-specific, and, unless the Court of Appeal in any subsequent judgment expressly indicates to the contrary, is to be regarded as a fact-specific

---

[34] At [47]–[49].
[35] [1992] Q.B. 630.
[36] [2006] EWCA Crim 756. See Rose L.J.'s propositions set out in para.26.26 of the main work.

decision rather than an elaboration of or an amendment to the governing principles.

He then drew together the headlines to the Court of Appeal's principal conclusions:

   (i) An application to stay for abuse of process on grounds of delay and a submission of "no case to answer" are two distinct matters. They must receive distinct and separate consideration.

   (ii) An application to stay for abuse of process on grounds of delay must be determined in accordance with *Att Gen's Ref (No.1 of 1990)*. It cannot succeed unless, exceptionally, a fair trial is no longer possible owing to the prejudice occasioned by the delay which cannot fairly be addressed in the normal trial process. The presence or absence of explanation or justification for the delay is relevant only insofar as it bears on that question.

   (iii) An application to stop the case on the grounds that there is no case to answer must be determined in accordance with *Galbraith*. For the reasons there explained, it is dangerous to ask the question in terms of whether a conviction would be safe, or the jury can safely convict, because that invites the judge to evaluate the weight and reliability of the evidence, which is the task of the jury. The question is whether the evidence, viewed overall, is such that the jury could properly convict.

   (iv) There is no different *Galbraith* test for offences which are alleged to have been committed some years ago, whether or not they are sexual offences.

   (v) In general, an application to stay for abuse of process ought ordinarily to be heard and determined at the outset of the case, and before the evidence is heard, unless there is a specific reason to defer it because prejudice and fair trial can better be determined at a later stage. It follows that applications should be preliminary to the trial process unless there is a specific reason for deferment, such as the evaluation of the significance of long-lost evidence, for example institutional records. The practice of deferment that had developed since *Smolinski*[37] will only be appropriate in such cases.

The recent case of *R. v RD*[38] is a highly instructive example in which the **26.25C** principles in *R. v F(S)* were held to have been properly applied. The Court of Appeal there upheld convictions relating to the sexual abuse of four complainants, notwithstanding exceptionally long delay amounting to as much as 63 years in the case of one complainant. The case sheds light on the proper approach to issues arising from the combined effect of delay and missing documents and exhibits. The appellant had argued that the trial judge should have stayed the proceedings

---

[37] Above, fn.32.
[38] [2013] EWCA Crim 1592.

as an abuse of process as the delay had led to him being caused serious prejudice, with the result that a fair trial could not and did not take place.

The allegations, looked at comprehensively, covered the period between 1949 at the outset of the events described by the different complainants and 1973 at their conclusion. The Court of Appeal acknowledged that this level of delay was extreme even by the standards of courts in this jurisdiction, which are used to trying allegations of historical sexual abuse. The first complainant's allegations spanned the years 1949–1956, covering a period when she was aged 8 or 9, up until a time when she was aged about 14. At that stage the appellant was aged between 15 and 22. The offences were alleged to have occurred at the complainant's maternal grandparent's home in South Wales which was also the home address of the appellant. The second complainant's allegations related to the years 1953–1957 when she would have been aged between 10 and 14. It was alleged that sexual abuse occurred when she spent holidays at the home of the appellant's parents. The third complainant was the biological daughter of the appellant. Her complaints related to the period between 1965 and 1971, by which time the appellant had married and was living with his present wife. The final complainant was a niece. Her complaint was confined to a single incident.

Prior to the trial, the judge had rejected an application for a stay on the grounds of abuse of process due to the exceptional delay. On appeal, it was submitted that the cumulative effect of all the missing evidence was that the appellant could not have a fair trial. The judge had wrongly concluded that the trial process could fairly address the issues arising from the delay and the deficits in potential evidence. In particular, it was contended that the judge had wrongly focused on the credibility of the witnesses as a central issue and had failed properly to assess the impact of the missing evidence upon the appellant's ability to mount a defence. It was asserted that the appellant's defence was not merely one of denial, but also raised an alibi which the appellant could not make good. He was prevented from positively attacking the prosecution's case, which he might well have been able to do had the missing evidence been available.

The Court of Appeal accepted that, in summing up, the judge had given appropriate directions about delay and its potential impact upon the ability of the appellant to raise a defence, and had left those issues clearly and fairly to the jury. However, the Court felt that it was right to go on and assess the impact of the missing evidence for itself. The approach it adopted in undertaking this task is instructive.

The Court observed that in considering the question of prejudice to the defence, it was necessary to distinguish between mere speculation about what missing documents or witnesses might show, and missing evidence which represents a significant and demonstrable chance of amounting to decisive or strongly supportive evidence emerging on a specific issue in the case. The Court needed to consider what evidence directly relevant to the appellant's case had been lost by reason of passage of time. It would then need to go on to consider the importance of the missing evidence in the context of the case as a whole and the issues before the jury. The Court would have to identify what prejudice, if any, had been caused to the appellant by the delay and whether judicial directions would be sufficient to compensate for such prejudice as may have been caused or whether in truth a fair trial could not properly be afforded to the appellant.

In carrying out this exercise the Court felt that some of the submissions on behalf of the appellant were overstated, in that it felt unable to accept the assumption that the missing evidence would necessarily have supported his case. Moreover, the complaints were not date specific but were couched in general terms of sexual abuse occurring on very many occasions during visits during school holidays, with wide periods identified in the indictment. Accordingly, an alibi in its true sense was not the issue before the jury. The issue was in reality whether or not the jury could be sure the abuse had taken place. It was not in dispute in relation to each of the premises at which the offences were alleged to have taken place that the appellant was present on occasions so that the opportunity to do what was alleged undoubtedly existed. Fuller evidence about shift patterns at work, or about dates of leave from the army, school holiday records or evidence from family witnesses or military friends would not have taken the matter much further, and was not of a degree of cogency to amount to a finding of serious prejudice in its absence. The question for the jury was to consider whether they were sure the appellant had availed himself of the acknowledged opportunities which existed to commit the offences.

Nonetheless, the Court acknowledged that there was detriment to the appellant's case by reason of delay and that it needed to evaluate the extent and effect of that detriment. The Court accepted that this matter required careful scrutiny because of the very substantial delay in this case. However, having evaluated the impact of substantial delay and missing documents and witnesses for itself, it was satisfied that the judge had been correct in her assessment that the trial process could properly cope with the difficulties faced by the appellant, and that there would be and indeed was no prejudice of a type which would mean he could not and did not get a fair trial. On an analysis of the missing material and the evidence given at trial and the issues before the jury, the Court was satisfied that the appellant received a fair trial, and was not disadvantaged in a way that could properly be described as amounting to serious prejudice to his ability to mount a proper defence to the allegations brought against him.

Previous police investigations and promises not to prosecute

A promise not to prosecute may provide a basis for an abuse argument. We have **26.50A** included a paragraph on recent developments in this area as it is not uncommon for this issue to be raised in abuse applications in respect of historic cases.

To succeed with such an argument, the defence must establish that there has been an unequivocal representation by the CPS upon which the defendant has acted to his detriment.[39] However, even then there may be circumstances in which

---

[39] See *Abu Hamza* [2006] EWCA Crim 2918.

it would not be an abuse of process to proceed. In *Abu Hamza*[40] the Court of Appeal held that if facts come to light which were not known when the representation was made, those facts may justify proceeding despite the representation.

Representations by the CPS must be seen in the context of a victim's right to seek a review of a decision not to prosecute. The procedure is now set out in Victims' Right to Review scheme.[41] In sexual cases it is not unusual for victims to exercise their right to a review. In determining whether in particular circumstances there was an abuse of process, regard must be had to the right of the complainant to have the decision reviewed. The review should be conducted within a reasonable time, but inevitably may contribute to or compound the delay before a case comes to trial.

Once a review is sought, it is then for the independent prosecutor to reach a decision impartially. In reviewing a decision not to prosecute, the CPS is responding appropriately to the rights of complainants in the prosecution process. It is an integral part of the exercise of prosecutorial discretion. The right of a complainant to a review has nothing to do with complaints about the level of service provided by the CPS.

Although the right of a victim to judicially review a decision not to prosecute is well-established, the Court of Appeal in 2011 clarified the position in *Killick*,[42] concluding that as a decision not to prosecute is in reality a final decision for a victim, there must be a right to seek a review of such a decision, particularly as the police have such a right under the charging guidance. As an independent prosecutor, the CPS has a duty to respond to a request made by a complainant for a review of a decision not to prosecute. The Court of Appeal pointed out that it would be disproportionate for a public authority not to have a system of review without recourse to court proceedings. In considering whether to prosecute, the prosecutor has to take into account the interests of the State, the defendant and the victim.[43] The Court of Appeal explained that the complainants in *Killick* were exercising their right to seek a review of the prosecutor's decision. That right under the law and procedure of England and Wales is in essence the same as the right expressed in art.10 of the Draft EU Directive on establishing minimum standards on the rights, support and protection of victims of crime dated May 18, 2011.

26.50B   *Killick* is an instructive case in which the Court of Appeal held that a prosecution brought in 2010 after the CPS reversed their earlier decision taken in 2007 not to prosecute, following a series of complaints and the threat of judicial review, did not amount to an abuse of process.

The three complainants had made serious sexual allegations to the police in 2006. The first allegation dated back to the early 1990s. The complainants all

---

[40] Last note.
[41] See para.3.11A, above.
[42] [2011] EWCA Crim 1608.
[43] cf. *R. v B* [2003] 2 Cr. App. R. 197, at [27] per Lord Woolf C.J.

suffered from cerebral palsy. The appellant also suffered from cerebral palsy, although less severely than that of the complainants. Although the appellant was arrested in April 2006, within a relatively short period of the making of the complaints, the decision on whether to prosecute was not made until June 2007, a year later, when the CPS decided that the appellant should not be prosecuted.

A "complaint"[44] was then made about that decision in accordance with the then CPS complaints procedure. Solicitors acting for the complainants advised that there should be an application for judicial review of the decision not to prosecute and sent a pre-action protocol letter to the CPS in August 2007. This complaint led to a decision to conduct a completely fresh review of the case by one of the CPS Special Casework Lawyers. The review took almost two years, in part because the CPS sought the advice of an independent QC experienced in the prosecution of sexual offences. The QC advised that the decision not to prosecute took into account all the relevant considerations and was wholly reasonable.

The CPS wrote to the complainants' solicitors stating that on the basis of the review, the decision not to prosecute had been correct. This led to the solicitors writing a further pre-action protocol letter indicating their intention to commence judicial review proceedings on the basis that the decision not to prosecute was irrational and on other grounds, including that the decision was arrived at unlawfully by taking into account the complainants' status as disabled persons. The CPS responded to this by initiating a third tier review which was carried out expeditiously by Miss Alison Levitt QC, the Principal Legal Adviser to the Director of Public Prosecutions. She considered the matter afresh. She concluded that the earlier decisions were wrong (though not unreasonable), that there was a realistic prospect of conviction and that it was in the public interest that there should be a prosecution.

It follows that the decision to prosecute was not made until December 9, 2009, three-and-a-half years after the arrest. In the meantime, the appellant had been told he would not be prosecuted in an email to his solicitors in June 2007. The e-mail, which was sent by the police, had not followed the usual CPS practice[45] of including an explanation that the decision was subject to some form of qualification.[46] In November 2007 the appellant's solicitors were informed that, following the request for a further review, the CPS was conducting such a review in accordance with the Code for Crown Prosecutors. In May 2009, an Inspector in the Metropolitan Police wrote to an MP, following his intervention on behalf the appellant, explaining that no further action would be taken. This was a reference to the earlier decision, as the Inspector was unaware of the review then taking place within the CPS. The appellant was subsequently informed following the

---

[44] Thomas L.J. (as he then was) explained (at [23]) that this was not in fact a "complaint" but a request for a review. The use of the term "complaint" can lead to suggestions that the prosecutor is influenced by a complaint, when the CPS is duty bound to carry out an impartial review.

[45] See Phillips L.J. in *R. v Burk*, December 12, 1996, CO/2286/96, Unreported.

[46] In *Killick*, the Court of Appeal concluded (at [22]) that, notwithstanding the absence of the usual qualification, the appellant's solicitor must be taken as having been aware of the usual rights of review.

third tier review that he would be prosecuted when he was summonsed to appear at the magistrates' court in February 2010.

Before the trial, the judge heard an application on behalf of the appellant that the proceedings should be stayed for abuse of process. It was contended that the decision of the Divisional Court in *Croydon Justices Ex p. Dean*[47] made clear that the prosecution of a person to whom it has been represented that he would not be prosecuted would generally amount to an abuse of process. The judge concluded that there was a strong public interest that the case should be tried, particularly as the complainants were very vulnerable, subject to the appellant being able to have a fair trial. In his view, it would have been an affront to justice for the case not to proceed. He dismissed the application, and after the prosecution evidence he affirmed his decision. On appeal, it was submitted that the judge's decision to allow the matter to proceed and to dismiss the application for a stay for abuse of process was wrong. The Court of Appeal held that the trial judge had been correct in his conclusions. There had been no unequivocal representation. Furthermore, whilst accepting there was clear strain upon the appellant, the delay in itself did not amount to an abuse of process or cause prejudice or detriment.

There will be historic cases in which there will have been earlier decisions not to prosecute. To prosecute after such a decision where there has been no manipulation of the process of the court, will not without more amount to an abuse. In any event, often the earlier decision will be understandable in the light of the application of the rules of evidence and/or the landscape of criminal justice at that time.[48]

DIRECTIONS

DELAY

26.58   The courts have decided that even very considerable delays before prosecution can, save exceptionally, be managed within the trial process. The point is often (though not necessarily always) best addressed by a short, self-contained direction that focuses on the defendant rather than one that amalgamates this aspect with other aspects of the relevance of delay, for instance as regards the victim. As with the direction on the burden and standard of proof, the direction regarding delay as it affects the defendant is designed to ensure the trial is fair. Whilst it is appropriate to deal with other aspects of the consequences of delay, such as late reporting by the victim, these should be dealt with separately so as not to dilute the impact of the direction that is designed to protect the defendant from the potential consequences of delay.

---

[47] [1993] Q.B. 769.

[48] See *Taylor* [2013] EWCA Crim 2398, in which Treasury Counsel had advised that the case should not be prosecuted in 1980. The Court of Appeal was satisfied that the trial judge had been correct to reject an application for abuse of process.

In *R. v PS*[49] the Court of Appeal had to consider the adequacy of a judge's   **26.58A**
directions to the jury on the approach they should take to a delay of 34 years before
the alleged events were brought to trial. The complainant V came from a family
of devout Buddhists from Sri Lanka. Every fortnight whilst she was a child her
family travelled from Birmingham to attend services at a temple in West London,
which the appellant had joined as a junior monk in February 1978. The allegation
against the appellant was that in 1978 he committed four sexual assaults upon V
when she was approximately nine, on three occasions in his bedroom and once in
the shrine at the Temple. V told no one at the time, but over the years she told a
friend, a man with whom she had a long term relationship, her sister, her husband
and her mother. V's evidence was that the birth of her child in 2010 provided the
catalyst for informing the police about these offences and her sister confirmed that
V once again started to talk about these events.

The appellant denied the allegations. He stated that he abided by the Buddhist
principle that monks must not touch women. He suggested a nine-year-old child
would not have been in the shrine room on a Saturday or Sunday and that there
were many visitors to the temple (about 400 people during the course of a day).
The appellant did accept that he took sweets to the appellant.

The Court of Appeal rejected the criticism that the judge had erred when he
directed the jury that identity was the issue in the case, as his approach to this
issue reflected the clear reality of the trial and he correctly left identity as the
determinative factor that the jury needed to resolve.

However, it was submitted that the direction on delay regarding identity was
wholly insufficient and that the jury should have been told there was a substantial
need for caution or "conscientious concern", or an expression to like effect. The
judge ought to have focused on the defendant's position alone and he should
not—at that stage—have dealt with other issues linked to the issue of delay. For
instance, whilst it was entirely appropriate for the judge to address delay in the
context of the complainant's evidence, it was contended that wider considerations
of this kind required distinct and separate treatment clearly delineated from the
effect of delay upon the accused's case.

When dealing with the consequences of delay, the judge had described in some
detail the reasons V gave for the delay and suggested some of the questions that
might have influenced V. Whilst the judge had directed the jury that effluxion of
time can affect memory, he did so when reminding the jury that V and the
appellant had been able to remember a substantial amount of the detail of what had
occurred. Thereafter, in suggesting that delay may have acted to the appellant's
disadvantage because "lines of enquiry which might have been open to him have
been closed", particularly as regards the medical evidence for the last of the
allegations (the shrine room incident), the judge then made the observation that if
records had been available they may have assisted the prosecution, and he
commented that this particular contention was in any event dependent upon a

---

[49] [2013] EWCA Crim 992.

nine-year-old girl having made a complaint that would have led to a medical inspection.

The Court of Appeal took the view that, given the facts of this case, the direction to the jury on delay should have included the following elements:

    i) delay can place a defendant at a material disadvantage in challenging allegations arising out of events that occurred many years before, and this was particularly so in this case where the defence was essentially a simple denial;

    ii) the longer the delay, the more difficult meeting the allegation often becomes because of fading memories and evidence that is no longer available—indeed it may be unclear what has been lost;

    iii) when considering the central question whether the prosecution has proved the defendant's guilt, it is necessary to bear in mind the prejudice delay can occasion; and

    iv) a summary of the main elements of prejudice that were identified during the trial.

Whilst the Court accepted that the judge's direction, when considered globally, contained all the essential elements he needed to include when directing the jury on the issue of delay, it did not consider it was structured in the right way given the circumstances of the case. The Court felt that in most cases the correct approach would be a self–contained direction that focuses upon the potential consequences of delay for the accused. Fulford L.J. explained[50]:

> "The risk of combining and interweaving the potential consequences of delay for the accused with other delay-related considerations ('putting the other side of the coin') is that the direction, as the principle means of protecting the defendant, is diluted and its force is diminished."

However, although the Court would have favoured a different approach to this aspect of the summing up, it did not consider what the judge had said amounted to a misdirection. He had addressed all matters relevant to this issue and had made it clear that the problems consequent upon delay were directly related to the burden and standard of proof. This case turned on the central question of the reliability of V's identification of the appellant 34 years after the events in question and it was inconceivable that the jury did not understand the potential difficulties this posed for the defence. The Court was confident that the convictions were safe.

Good Character Since Time of the Allegations

26.64 Where, during the time since which has elapsed since the alleged offence, a defendant has not committed any offence, let alone one involving sexual abuse, the normal propensity direction should be tailored to include this. In *GJB v R.*[51] it was held that such a direction is particularly apt where delay since the date of the

---

[50] At [37].
[51] [2011] EWCA Crim 867.

alleged offence renders it more difficult for a defendant to defend himself. The jury in that case should have been directed that the fact that the appellant had committed no similar offence during the intervening 10 years was an aspect of his character to which they should have had specific regard.

SENTENCING

DISCOUNT FOR DELAY?

In *R. v H(J) and others*[52] the then Lord Chief Justice, Lord Judge, reviewed   26.72
numerous Court of Appeal sentencing decisions in the context of sexual offences committed many years ago but only recently brought to conviction. He found that the Court of Appeal had at different times adopted conflicting approaches to the critical sentencing issues. He identified that specific guidance was required about the extent, if any, to which the court passing sentence should reflect the levels of sentence which would have been likely to have been imposed if the defendant had been convicted at a trial shortly after the offences were committed and, by contrast, the extent to which the events during the long period between the commission of the crime and the sentencing decision may be relevant.

The approach was complicated by the way not only the substantive law and sentencing provisions have changed over the years, but also how over the same period a variety of sentencing regimes have been in force.

In terms of principle, the Lord Chief Justice found it impossible to reconcile all the authorities. However, he summarised as follows the principles to be derived from statute, the authorities which purport to provide guidance, and fact-specific decisions[53]:

> "We suggest that with the exception of *Millberry and others*,[54] and the definitive sentencing guideline (used in the measured way we shall suggest) the following considerations should be treated as guidance. We further suggest that reference to earlier decisions is unlikely to be helpful, and, again dealing with it generally, to be discouraged. Subsequent decisions of this court which do not expressly state they are intended to amend or amplify this guidance should be treated as fact-specific decisions, and therefore unlikely to be of assistance to a court.
>
> (a) Sentence will be imposed at the date of the sentencing hearing, on the basis of the legislative provisions then current, and by measured reference to any definitive sentencing guidelines relevant to the situation revealed by established facts.
>
> (b) Although sentence must be limited to the maximum sentence at the date when the offence was committed, it is wholly unrealistic to attempt an assessment of sentence by seeking to identify in 2011 what the sentence for the individual

---

[52] [2011] EWCA Crim 2753.
[53] At [46]–[47].
[54] [2003] 1 W.L.R. 546.

offence was likely to have been if the offence had come to light at or shortly after the date when it was committed.[55]

(c) As always, the particular circumstances in which the offence was committed and its seriousness must be the main focus. Due allowance for the passage of time may be appropriate. The date may have a considerable bearing on the offender's culpability. If, for example, the offender was very young and immature at the time when the case was committed, that remains a continuing feature of the sentencing decision.[56] Similarly if the allegations had come to light many years earlier, and when confronted with them, the defendant had admitted them, but for whatever reason, the complaint had not been drawn to the attention of, or investigated by, the police, or had been investigated and not then pursued to trial, these too would be relevant features.

(d) In some cases it may be safe to assume that the fact that, notwithstanding the passage of years, the victim has chosen spontaneously to report what happened to him or her in his or her childhood or younger years would be an indication of continuing inner turmoil. However the circumstances in which the facts come to light varies, and careful judgment of the harm done to the victim is always a critical feature of the sentencing decision. Simultaneously, equal care needs to be taken to assess the true extent of the defendant's criminality by reference to what he actually did and the circumstances in which he did it.

(e) The passing of the years may demonstrate aggravating features if, for example, the defendant has continued to commit sexual crime or he represents a continuing risk to the public. On the other hand, mitigation may be found in an unblemished life over the years since the offences were committed, particularly if accompanied by evidence of positive good character.

(f) Early admissions and a guilty plea are of particular importance in historic cases. Just because they relate to facts which are long passed, the defendant will inevitably be tempted to lie his way out of the allegations. It is greatly to his credit if he makes early admissions. Even more powerful mitigation is available to the offender who out of a sense of guilt and remorse reports himself to the authorities. Considerations like these provide the victim with vindication, often a feature of great importance to them."

It follows from (a) above that when passing sentence for an offence committed on or after April 6, 2010, the sentence must follow the relevant guideline unless the court is satisfied that it would be contrary to the interests of justice to do so.[57] To apply a current guideline to an offence committed before it came into force does not offend the rule against retrospectivity as enshrined in art.7 of the ECHR.[58] That article prevents a sentence being imposed which could not have been passed at the time because the maximum was lower. In historic cases, provided sentences fall within or do not exceed the maximum sentence which could lawfully have been

[55] In *R. v S (Paul Martin)* [2012] EWCA Crim 2668, the judge erred in sentencing on the basis of authorities existing at the time of the offence in 2000. However, the sentence under the current regime would not have been significantly different so it was not massively excessive.

[56] It follows that the historic nature of the case is not necessarily irrelevant to the sentencing decision. *R. v O* (CA, December 4, 2012, Unreported) is good example of a case where the appellant's mental age of 8 at the time when he had raped his 17-year-old sister in 1977 was of relevance to the sentencing decision. The offender was 82 at the time of the appeal. The Court of Appeal, in reducing the sentence from 7 to 5-and-a-half years' imprisonment, also took into account the impact of imprisonment upon the appellant's wife who also had mental health difficulties. See also *Robert Clarke* [2012] EWCA Crim 9.

[57] s.125(1) of the Coroners and Justice Act 2009.

[58] *Bao* [2007] EWCA Crim 2781.

imposed at the date when the offence was committed, neither the restrospectivity principle nor art.7 is contravened.[59]

In *Att Gen's Ref (No.38 of 2013) (R. v Stuart Hall)*,[60] the Court of Appeal had 26.72A to consider whether concurrent terms of imprisonment totalling 15 months for 14 counts of indecent assault upon children or teenage girls amounted to an unduly lenient sentence. The offender was aged 83 at the time of sentence. He had no previous convictions. For those with no idea of his criminal activities he was highly regarded. At the time of the offences he had become a well-known television personality, and a popular and successful public figure. The indecent assaults upon 13 female victims took place over a period of almost 20 years between 1967 and 1985–6. The ages of the victims ranged from 9 to 17.

A significant, damaging effect of the offending was that it had caused difficulties between the victims and their parents. For instance, one of the victims, aged 16, had told her parents and grandparents at the time, but the family had decided not to report the matter to the authorities. The victim's initial feelings of shock and humiliation had turned to anger because of her family's decision that she should try and forget about it as there was "no point in reporting it as Mr Hall was rich and famous and we were nobody. After that my anger stayed with me. I had no way to express it and no one I could tell".

Giving the judgment of the Court, the then Lord Chief Justice, Lord Judge, observed[61]:

> "We reject the submission made to the trial judge that somehow the fact that the adults did not report these incidents when the children told their parents or grandparents (or whoever it may have been) provides an indication that they could not have taken the allegations seriously. We know why two families did not formally complain: they could not take on the famous celebrity. The offender's successful career provides no mitigation. On the contrary, it was the career that put him in a position of trust which he was then able to exploit and which contributed to his image as a cheerful, fun-loving, fundamentally decent man. This contributed to the view he could be trusted; and second, if he could not be trusted, effectively he was untouchable. It is true that he had no previous convictions of any kind. It is true that he has behaved decently on occasions and deserves credit for that. But we now know, as the world at large knows, that since the mid-60's he molested children and growing girls and therefore that he lived a lie—a lie for more than half his life; a lie repeated on the steps of the magistrates' court for the benefit of the accompanying media."

The Lord Chief Justice went on to explain that the offender's proclamation of innocence on the steps of the magistrates' court was a seriously aggravating feature. The Court concluded that he was hoping to escape justice and was attempting to manipulate the media for the purpose of possibly influencing jurors. He was traducing 13 adult women who had been sexually assaulted by him in different ways 20–30 years before. Consistent with current sentencing practice, it

---

[59] *R. v H(J) and others*, above, fn.52 at [17] et seq.; *Flynn v HM Advocate* [2004] UKPC D 1; *R. (on the application of Uttley) v Secretary of State for the Home Department* [2004] UKHL 38.
[60] [2013] EWCA Crim 1450.
[61] At [75].

was appropriate to reflect this aggravating feature in the assessment of sentence and then discount from it to allow for the guilty plea.

Taken in isolation, some of the offences would not have required a custodial sentence. Some, as time went by and the offender escaped detection, seemed to the Court to be marked with an increasing degree of thought and premeditation. The result of the offending taken as a whole was that a multiplicity of young girls were sexually molested over an 18-year period, some when they were very young, all when they were in one way or another vulnerable, and all when the offender was in a position to misbehave as he did just because of who he was, which meant he was trusted. All the offences were real assaults, and not just technical assaults because the victims were too young to have consented in law. There was no question of any of the victims consenting to anything.

The Court concluded, making every allowance that could reasonably be made for the matters of mitigation, the sentence was inadequate, and increased it to 30 months' imprisonment. The double jeopardy principle did not apply. The appellant was in custody; he had been sentenced to an immediate custodial term. He had known that the Attorney General proposed to refer the sentence to the Court of Appeal.

DECLINING HEALTH OF THE OFFENDER

26.76 In *Qazi*[62] it was made clear that when passing sentence, the court ought not to concern itself with the adequacy of arrangements for the medical needs of the offender in prison. The medical needs of prisoners are well understood in the administration of prisons. It is only in circumstances where the very fact of imprisonment itself might expose the individual to a real risk of a breach of art.3 of the ECHR that the court will be called upon to enquire into whether sentencing a person to custody will mean a breach of art.3. The Court in *Qazi* was doubtful whether this situation would ever arise. This is not inconsistent with the general position set out by Rose L.J. in *Bernard*,[63] that an offender's serious medical condition may enable a court to impose a lesser sentence as an act of mercy in the exceptional circumstances of a particular case rather than by virtue of any general principle of law.

PRE–CRIMINAL JUSTICE ACT 2003 LICENSING REGIME

26.77 To the discussion in the main work should be added that it is not appropriate to make a reduction in an otherwise appropriate sentence because since the time of the offence the early release provisions have been changed and/or the licensing system made more severe.[64]

---

[62] [2010] EWCA Crim 2579.
[63] [1997] 1 Cr. App. R.(S.) 135.
[64] *Matthews (Alex Joseph)* [2011] EWCA Crim 3110; *Round, Dunn and others* [2009] EWCA Crim 2667; [2010] 2 Cr. App. R.(S.) 45 (p.292), referred in *R. v H(J)*, above, fn.52 at [19].

CHAPTER 27

SENTENCING OF SEX OFFENDERS

by Tim Moloney QC

INTRODUCTION

There have been important changes to sentencing since the publication of our **27.01**
fourth edition in December 2010. The major development is the abolition of
imprisonment for public protection ("IPP"), which remained available only for
that ever diminishing category of offenders convicted before December 3, 2012,
and not yet sentenced. The demise of IPP inevitably limits the options available to
a court concerned to protect the public when an offender fulfils the dangerousness
criteria: these now comprise a "discretionary" life sentence, the new extended
sentence under s.226A of the Criminal Justice Act 2003 ("CJA 2003")[1] or a
determinate sentence accompanied by the appropriate ancillary orders.

The new extended sentence warrants close scrutiny because, despite its
similarity to the old extended sentence, they differ in certain material respects.
Significantly, the new extended sentence is available in respect of historic cases. It
can be expected that wide use will be made of the new sentence to deal with
offenders who pose a continuing risk of serious harm from the commission of

---

[1] As inserted by s.124 of the Legal Aid, Sentencing and Punishment of Offenders Act 2012 as from
December 3, 2012: see SI 2012/2906.

further specified offences, but where the offence(s) committed are not so serious that a life sentence can be justified.

In Ch.26 we deal with sentencing options available in historic cases. As explained there, the judgment of Lord Judge C.J. in *R. v H(J)*[2] is required reading for those dealing with such cases, as it clarifies the approach to be adopted in respect of sentencing guidelines and also how a sentence should take into account the passage of time. The sentencing court should not seek to establish the likely sentence if the offender had been convicted shortly after the date of the offence. Whenever the offence was committed, the sentencing exercise involves having regard to any applicable sentencing guidelines for equivalent offences under the 2003 Act. Given the number of historic cases currently coming before the courts, and the time taken up by Attorney General's references in which the Attorney General argues that a sentence is unduly lenient, we set out briefly below the current sentencing position in respect of such cases. A useful step-by-step guide to the correct approach in sentencing historic cases is set out in Annex B to the new Sexual Offences Definitive Guideline, reproduced in Appendix A to this Supplement.

Finally, as for the new automatic life sentence available under s.224A of the CJA 2003,[3] as we explain below the conditions that must be met for such a sentence to be imposed are expected to be satisfied very rarely.

THE NEW DEFINITIVE GUIDELINE

27.01A   On December 12, 2013, following a thorough consultation process, the Sentencing Council issued a new *Sexual Offences Definitive Guideline* under s.120 of the Coroners and Justice Act 2009 ("2009 Act"). The guideline applies only to offenders aged 18 and older; offenders under 18 will be covered by a separate youth guideline which the Council will begin considering in 2014. For discussion of the reasons for the review of the previous guideline, see para.1.20 et seq., above. In most areas, the sentencing levels in the new guideline have been set to reflect current sentencing practice. However, the Sentencing Council's *Final Resource Assessment: Sexual Offences*[4] estimates that the new guideline for rape will result in a requirement for up to 180 additional prison places due to increased sentences for some offenders. It is important to bear in mind that the guideline is concerned with sentence levels for a single offence.

Section 125(1) of the 2009 Act provides that when sentencing offences committed on or after April 6, 2010:

"Every court—

---

[2] [2011] EWCA Crim 2753.

[3] As inserted by s.122 of the Legal Aid, Sentencing and Punishment of Offenders Act 2012 as from December 3, 2012: see SI 2012/2906.

[4] The Sentencing Council was under a statutory duty (s.127 of the 2009 Act) to produce an assessment which considers the likely effect of its guidelines on the resources required for the provision of prison places, probation and youth justice services.

(a) must, in sentencing an offender, follow any sentencing guideline which is relevant to the offender's case, and

(b) must, in exercising any other function relating to the sentencing of offenders, follow any sentencing guidelines which are relevant to the exercise of the function,

unless the court is satisfied that it would be contrary to the interests of justice to do so."[5]

The new guideline applies to all sentencing decisions in sex cases after its implementation on April 1, 2014, whenever the offence was committed. The old guideline applies to cases sentenced up until then.[6]

We have included the appropriate parts of the new guideline in the chapters of this Supplement dealing with specific offences. In this chapter we simply summarise the main changes, as follows.[7]

Greater focus on harm to the victim whether physical and/or psychological

The new guideline focuses on the extent of the harm to the victim rather than on the nature of the particular physical activity. For instance, in the guideline on sexual assault (s.3 of the 2003 Act), if the victim suffers severe psychological or physical harm this will take the offence into the highest sentencing category. Similarly, vulnerability of the victim is treated as a major indicator of harm. All children are vulnerable, but some are more so because of their very young age or personal circumstances. For instance, in respect of rape of a child under 13 (s.5), where the victim is particularly vulnerable due to extreme youth and/or personal circumstances this will place the offence in a higher category of harm. The circumstances in which a child can be vulnerable have been the subject of research by the Office of the Children's Commissioner and can include situations whether the child has suffered a recent bereavement or is in care.[8]   **27.01B**

Grooming

The guideline reflects greater awareness of the phenomenon of grooming and/or the use of the internet to facilitate sex offending. For example, in respect of rape of a child under 13, grooming behaviour will place the offender in the higher level   **27.01C**

---

[5] But see [2013] Crim. L.R. 998, in which the late Dr David Thomas QC criticises the Court of Appeal in *Karam (Mawawe Ibrahim)* [2013] EWCA Crim 138 for failing to have regard to s.125(3) of the Act, which qualifies the obligation to "follow" the guidelines by making clear that the court is under an obligation to impose a sentence within the offence range but not within the category range. Dr Thomas argues that "the effect of s.125(3) when read as a whole is to preserve the critical discretion of the judge to achieve a just sentence, based upon the detailed facts of the case rather than the increasingly mechanistic application of quasi-statutory guidelines".

[6] *Boakye and others* [2012] EWCA Crim 838.

[7] We are grateful to Michelle Crotty, Head of the Office of the Sentencing Council, for permission to use her summary of the key changes, which we have paraphrased.

[8] See *http://www.childrenscommissioner.gov.uk/content/publications/content*, at 743 [accessed December 22, 2013].

of culpability (and therefore attract a higher starting point) as will the fact that sexual images of the victim have been recorded, retained, solicited or shared.

Ostensible or apparent consent

27.01D   The Sentencing Council agreed with the statement of Pitchford L.J. in *Att Gen's Refs (Nos 11 and 12 of 2012) (Channer and Monteiro)*,[9] that "'[o]stensible consent' and 'willingness' are terms which, in the context of offences against the young in particular, are susceptible to misunderstanding and, even if accurately used, are liable to obscure the true nature of the encounter between the offender and the victim". The new guideline moves away from the language of "ostensible consent" so that the focus in relation to children aged between 13 and 15 is placed not on the behaviour of the victim but on the behaviour and culpability of the offender. Accordingly, harm is determined by the nature of the sexual activity involved, so avoiding the need to consider the child's behaviour or their understanding of their "relationship" with the offender. The guideline places more emphasis on how the offender has persuaded the child to engage in the activity and obtain their apparent consent. Following on from the consideration given to "remote offending" in *Prince*,[10] the guideline confirms that the approach to sentencing and the starting points and ranges apply equally where the offender commits the offence remotely over the internet.

Rape of child under 13

27.01E   The guideline says that the majority of offences of rape of a child under 13 will attract significant custodial sentences, but it acknowledges that the courts may be faced with a wide range of offending behaviour. Exploitative behaviour towards a child should be considered to indicate high culpability even where the child is not subjected to force or fear of force. In wholly exceptional cases, a lengthy community order with a requirement to participate in a sex offender programme may be the best way of changing the offender's behaviour and of protecting the public by preventing any repetition of the offence.

Increase in sentencing levels for some offences of rape

27.01F   The guideline for rape provides two examples where higher sentences will apply than under the previous guideline. Where an offender is convicted of a campaign of rape, against single or multiple victims, the courts are directed that a sentence of 20 years or more should be passed. Additionally, the extreme nature of one or more category 2 harm factors or the extreme impact of a combination of those

---

[9] [2012] EWCA Crim 1119, at [34].
[10] [2013] EWCA Crim 1768.

factors may elevate the offence to category 1 harm. Where this is combined with an increased level of culpability, the starting point for a single offence will be 15 years. The worst cases of assault by penetration (s.2) may receive the same sentences as rape because of the physical harm that will be caused where large or dangerous objects are used by the offender.

Approach to harm and culpability

The new guideline uses a number of models for addressing harm and culpability, **27.01G** each different from the model used in the previous guideline:

(a) *Baseline of inherent harm and culpability*: The model used for the majority of offences, including rape and sexual assault, has a lowest level (a baseline) where inherent harm and culpability are assumed. One or more from an exhaustive list of factors can move the offender to a higher category of harm or culpability with a higher starting point. Factors raising harm and culpability have in certain instances been revised. For instance, the term "abuse of trust" is used rather than the previous "abuse of position of trust" as it is capable of applying even where the offender is not in a formal position of responsibility towards the victim.

(b) *Raised harm and raised culpability*: This model is a variation on the one used by the Sentencing Council in the assault definitive guideline. It identifies factors that indicate raised harm and/or culpability. The highest starting points and ranges, in category 1, are reserved for cases where both raised harm and raised culpability are present; category 2 applies where there is either raised harm or raised culpability and category 3 where there is neither. This model is used for the offences of meeting a child following sexual grooming (s.15); administering a substance with intent (s.61); trespass with intent to commit a sexual offence (s.63); sex with an adult relative (ss.64 and 65); exposure (s.66); and voyeurism (s.67).

(c) *Indecent images of children*: Harm is assessed on the basis of the level of images involved. However, following discussion with experts from the ACPO grading panel, the Sentencing Council reduced the levels from the five set out in *Oliver* to three. Culpability is assessed on the basis of what the offender was doing with the images and is split into three categories: possession, distribution and production. The categories are:
Category A: This broadly coincides with *Oliver* levels 4 and 5 (images involving penetrative sexual activity, sexual activity with an animal and sadism).
Category B: This broadly coincides with *Oliver* level 3 (images involving non-penetrative activity).
Category C: This covers other indecent images not falling within either A or B.

Approach to good character and/or exemplary conduct

27.01H   This factor is retained in the new guideline but is subject to two forms of explanatory wording to provide transparency as to the way in which judges reflect good character in a sentence. Where the offence carries a statutory maximum of under 14 years, the guideline states:

> "Previous good character/exemplary conduct is different from having no previous convictions. The more serious the offence, the less the weight which should normally be attributed to this factor. Where previous good character/exemplary conduct has been used to facilitate the offence, this mitigation should not normally be allowed and such conduct may constitute an aggravating factor."

A classic example of good character being used to facilitate the offence would be the misuse of celebrity status.[11]

Where the offence carries a statutory maximum of 14 years or more, the guideline additionally states:

> "In the context of this offence previous good character/exemplary conduct should not normally be given any significant weight and will not normally justify a reduction in what would otherwise be the appropriate sentence."

A. OFFENCES COMMITTED BEFORE APRIL 4, 2005

SENTENCING THOSE CONVICTED OF SEXUAL OFFENCES COMMITTED BEFORE THE COMMENCEMENT OF THE SEXUAL OFFENCES ACT 2003

27.08A   Sentences are imposed on the basis of the legislative provisions in force at the time of the offence. It follows that when sentencing historic sex cases, it is important to have two critical dates in mind: (i) May 1, 2004, when the 2003 Act came into force, and (ii) April 4, 2005, when the sentencing provisions of the CJA 2003 came into force. There were a number of statutes governing sexual offences before the 2003 Act, some of which were themselves amended as to the maximum sentence, and so it is essential to check the maximum sentence that was available for the offence at the relevant time, as well as the nature of the sentences then available. The Court should then make the appropriate "measured reference"[12] to the current sentencing guideline.

SENTENCING DANGEROUS OFFENDERS FOR OFFENCES COMMITTED BEFORE APRIL 4, 2005

27.08B   The choice of sentence for dealing with a dangerous offender for an offence committed before April 4, 2005, now lies between the "old-style" discretionary

---

[11] See *Att Gen's Ref (No.38 of 2013) (R. v Stuart Hall)* [2013] EWCA Crim 1450.

[12] *R. v H(J)* [2011] EWCA Crim 2753. In *P* (one of the conjoined appeals in *R. v H(J)*) the sentencing court overlooked that the maximum sentence for attempted rape was 7 years at the time: see para.26.07, above.

life sentence;[13] the new extended sentence under s.224A of the CJA 2003; a longer than commensurate sentence under s.80(2)(b) of the Powers of Criminal Courts (Sentencing) Act 2000 ("PCC(S)A 2000"); and a determinate sentence combined with appropriate ancillary orders.

"Old-Style" Discretionary Life Sentence

27.08C

Notwithstanding the multiple amendments made to the law governing the sentencing of dangerous offenders during the last 10 years, the law remains unchanged in respect of discretionary life sentences for offences committed before April 4, 2005.[14] For a good recent illustration, see *R. v DP*[15] which concerned an assault on a child under 13 by digital penetration committed between December 2004 and March 2005 by a predatory paedophile with previous convictions of sexual offences against children.

The criteria for the imposition of a discretionary life sentence in respect of offences committed before April 4, 2005, are set out in *Hodgson*[16] and *Att Gen's Ref (No.32 of 1996) (Whittaker)*.[17] First, the offender must have been convicted of a "very serious offence". The meaning of "very serious offence" was considered in *R. v D*,[18] in which the Court of Appeal upheld a discretionary life sentence in relation to an offender who, as a youth, had broken into his grandmother's home and raped her. Secondly, there must be good grounds for believing that the offender might remain a serious danger to the public for a period which cannot be reliably estimated at the date of sentence. By "serious danger", the Court in *Whittaker* explained that it had in mind particularly serious offences of violence and serious sexual offences. For a recent example in which the Court of Appeal upheld a discretionary life sentence passed in 2012 for a rape committed in 1996, see *Robertsham*.[19] The appellant had subjected a 71-year-old living on her own to a sadistic, violent sexual attack. He had a previous conviction for the rape his own grandmother in 1988. The Court of Appeal held that, nothwithstanding the lack of reports, the judge could not properly be criticised for his assessment that the appellant presented a serious and grave risk to female members of the public of age.

New Extended Sentence

For discussion of the new extended sentence in s.224A of the CJA 2003, see para.27.60C, below. The sentence is available for offenders convicted on or after   **27.08D**

---

[13] So described by the late Dr Thomas QC in his commentary on *Red Saunders and others* [2013] EWCA Crim 1027, at [2013] Crim. L.R. 935.

[14] Lord Judge C.J. in *Red Saunders*, last note. For fuller discussion of this important case, see para.1.42A et seq., above.

[15] [2013] EWCA Crim 1143.

[16] (1968) 52 Cr. App. R. 113; [1968] Crim. L.R. 46.

[17] [1997] 1 Cr. App. R.(S.) 261; [1996] Crim. L.R. 917.

[18] [2012] EWCA Crim 2370 discussed in para.1.42D, above.

[19] [2013] EWCA Crim 635.

December 3, 2012. It has therefore replaced the old extended sentence under s.85 of the PCC(S)A 2000 with retrospective effect from that date.[20]

LONGER THAN COMMENSURATE SENTENCE

27.08E   The operation of s.80(2)(b) of the PCC(S)A 2000 was examined in *R. v S.*[21] Where the threshold for a life sentence has not been crossed, and if necessary to protect the public from serious harm in the future, the court may impose a longer than commensurate sentence under s.80(2)(b) together with an extended licence period. The anticipated harm likely to be produced by the expected future offences may be either physical or psychological, but it must be "serious". The offence which is expected to produce the harm must itself be a violent or sexual offence.

C. OFFENCES COMMITTED ON OR AFTER APRIL 4, 2005

"DISCRETIONARY" LIFE SENTENCE UNDER SECTION 225(1) AND (2) OF THE CRIMINAL JUSTICE ACT 2003

27.60A   A sentence of life imprisonment may be imposed under s.225(1) and (2) of the CJA 2003 if the court is of the opinion that there is "a significant risk to members of the public occasioned by the commission by [the offender] of further specified offences" and concludes that "the seriousness of the offence, or of the offence and one or more offences associated with it, is such as to justify the imposition of a sentence of imprisonment for life". In *Red Saunders and others v R.*[22] Lord Judge C.J., giving the judgment of the Court of Appeal, explained that the sentence of life imprisonment under s.225 continues in force after the changes made to the CJA 2003 by the Legal Aid, Sentencing and Punishment of Offenders Act 2012, and has been frequently described as the "discretionary" life sentence, although once the statutory conditions in s.225(1) and (2) are established it "must" be imposed. His Lordship said[23]:

> "In that broad sense, therefore, this sentence, is also statutory, but it may only be imposed if justified by reference to the seriousness of the offence and the protection of the public in accordance with s.225(1) and (2)."

Life imprisonment remains the sentence of last resort. In *Wilkinson*,[24] the Court of Appeal had said:

> "In our judgment it is clear that as a matter of principle the discretionary life sentence under section 225 should continue to be reserved for offences of the utmost gravity.

---

[20] See commentary by the late Dr David Thomas QC on *R. v DP* [2013] Crim. L.R. 862.
[21] [2010] EWCA Crim 1462.
[22] [2013] EWCA Crim 1027.
[23] At [9].
[24] [2009] EWCA Crim 1925, at [19] per Lord Judge C.J.

Without being prescriptive, we suggest that the sentence should come into contemplation when the judgment of the court is that the seriousness is such that the life
sentence would have ... a 'denunciatory' value, reflective of public abhorrence of the
offence, and where, because of its seriousness, the notional determinate sentence
would be very long, measured in very many years."

However, as explained below, following *Red Saunders* it is no longer necessary for
the seriousness of the offence to be such that the life sentence would have a
denunciatory value reflective of public abhorrence, before such a sentence may be
imposed.

IMPACT OF THE DEMISE OF IMPRISONMENT FOR PUBLIC PROTECTION

The ill-considered sentence of IPP was abolished by the Legal Aid, Sentencing   **27.60B**
and Punishment of Offenders Act 2012, along with detention in a young offender
institution for public protection, with the result that IPP ceased to be available
except for offenders convicted before December 3, 2012 and not yet sentenced.
The demise of the sentence may lead to more sentences of life imprisonment being
passed under s.225 where the sentencer concludes that an extended sentence
under the new s.226A of the CJA 2003 would not afford sufficient public
protection. In the past, in the overwhelming majority of cases, the relatively minor
distinctions between life imprisonment and IPP were irrelevant, and so IPP was
normally sufficient to address the protection of the public from a dangerous
offender who would, if made subject to the order, continue to be detained until the
Parole Board was satisfied that he no longer represented a risk to the public. Now,
where a dangerous offender is convicted of rape, the sentencing options will be a
sentence of life imprisonment under s.225(1) and (2) of the CJA 2003, the new
extended sentence under s.226A of the CJA 2003 (inserted in place of s.227 by the
Legal Aid, Sentencing and Punishment of Offenders Act 2012 ("LASPO")) or a
determinate sentence.

In *Red Saunders*, Lord Judge C.J. explained the impact of the removal of IPP as
a sentencing option as follows[25]:

"The new statutory life sentence[26] has not replaced the IPP. Many offenders who
represent a danger to the public may not 'qualify' for the statutory life sentence. Yet,
for some offenders, the imperative of public protection continues undiminished, and
is not wholly met by the 'new' extended sentence. Very long term public protection
must therefore be provided by the imposition of a discretionary life sentence. That is
consequent on s.225(1) and (2) which, in the context of the discretionary life sentence
for serious offences continue, as we have explained, in full force."

His Lordship noted that under the new extended sentence the offender will not be
released during the custodial term until at least the two-thirds point of it has been
reached. Where the custodial term is 10 years or more, or the offences for which
the sentence was imposed included one in Sch.15B to the CJA 2003 (for which see

---

[25] Above, fn.22 at [15].
[26] Under s.224A of the CJA 2003, inserted by s.122 of the Legal Aid, Sentencing and Punishment
of Offenders Act 2012.

para.27.60D below), he will not be released until the Parole Board has directed his release on the ground that his continued incarceration is no longer necessary for public protection. Under the old form of extended sentence, release was automatic half way through the custodial term. In relation to public protection as it arises under the new extended sentence, having assessed the appropriate custodial term, the extension period during which the offender would be subject to licence is limited, in the context of a specified sexual offence, to 8 years. Further, in relation to some of the specified sexual offences, the maximum available term is 10 or 14 years' imprisonment, and that term may not be exceeded. His Lordship said that it is therefore clear that in relation to the offender who will continue to represent a significant risk to the safety of the public for an indefinite period, the new extended sentence cannot be treated as a direct replacement for the old IPP. He continued[27]:

> "Accordingly, in cases in which, prior to the enactment of LASPO, the court would have been driven to the conclusion that an IPP was required for public protection (on the basis on a judgment made on the particular facts rather than one to which the court was driven by some of the more troublesome assumptions required by the legislation in its original form) the discretionary life sentence will arise for considera-tion, and where appropriate, if the necessary level of public protection cannot be achieved by the new extended sentence, ordered. The 'denunciatory' ingredient identified to distinguish between the circumstances in which the discretionary life sentence rather than the IPP should be imposed is no longer apposite. By that we mean that although the 'denunciatory' element of the sentencing decision may continue to justify the discretionary life sentence, its absence does not preclude such an order. As every judge appreciates, however, the life sentence remains the sentence of last resort."

NEW EXTENDED SENTENCE

27.60C   Section 226A of the CJA 2003, inserted in place of s.227 by s.124 of the Legal Aid, Sentencing and Punishment of Offenders Act 2012, provides for extended sentences of imprisonment. The power to pass an extended sentence applies where an offender aged 18 or over is convicted of a specified offence, whether the offence was committed before or after the section came into force on December 3, 2012 (see para.27.88 of the main work). The pre-condition that the dangerousness criteria must be satisfied is retained, as are the criteria themselves. In this respect the new extended sentence is similar to the old one. The reference in s.227 to Sch.15A is replaced by a reference in s.226A to the new Sch.15B (for which see para.27.60D, below). There are, however, differences between the old and new extended sentences. The most significant relates to release on licence. Under the old system, release was ordinarily at the half-way point of the custodial term. Now, release will ordinarily be when two-thirds of the custodial term has been served, unless that term is at least 10 years *or* the extended sentence was imposed for an offence or offences listed in Pt 1 of Sch.15B. In the latter circumstances, the case is referred to the Parole Board at the two-thirds point for it to consider whether

---

[27] Above, fn.22 at [18].

or not the offender should be released. Under s.246A(6)(b) of the CJA 2003, the Parole Board must not direct the release of the offender unless it is satisfied that it is no longer necessary for the protection of the public that the offender should be confined. If an offender subject to an extended sentence is not released on the direction of the Parole Board, he must be released when he has served the whole of the custodial term unless he has already been released on licence and recalled.

The provisions of the CJA 2003 dealing with extended sentences are now as follows:

"**226A Extended sentence for certain violent or sexual offences: persons 18 or over**

(1) This section applies where—
  (a) a person aged 18 or over is convicted of a specified offence (whether the offence was committed before or after this section comes into force),
  (b) the court considers that there is a significant risk to members of the public of serious harm occasioned by the commission by the offender of further specified offences,
  (c) the court is not required by section 224A or 225(2) to impose a sentence of imprisonment for life, and
  (d) condition A or B is met.

(2) Condition A is that, at the time the offence was committed, the offender had been convicted of an offence listed in Schedule 15B.

(3) Condition B is that, if the court were to impose an extended sentence of imprisonment, the term that it would specify as the appropriate custodial term would be at least 4 years.

(4) The court may impose an extended sentence of imprisonment on the offender.

(5) An extended sentence of imprisonment is a sentence of imprisonment the term of which is equal to the aggregate of—
  (a) the appropriate custodial term, and
  (b) a further period (the "extension period") for which the offender is to be subject to a licence.

(6) The appropriate custodial term is the term of imprisonment that would (apart from this section) be imposed in compliance with section 153(2).

(7) The extension period must be a period of such length as the court considers necessary for the purpose of protecting members of the public from serious harm occasioned by the commission by the offender of further specified offences, subject to subsections (8) and (9).

(8) The extension period must not exceed—
  (a) 5 years in the case of a specified violent offence, and
  (b) 8 years in the case of a specified sexual offence.

(9) The term of an extended sentence of imprisonment imposed under this section in respect of an offence must not exceed the term that, at the time the offence was committed, was the maximum term permitted for the offence.

(10) In subsections (1)(a) and (8), references to a specified offence, a specified violent offence and a specified sexual offence include an offence that—
  (a) was abolished before 4 April 2005, and
  (b) would have constituted such an offence if committed on the day on which the offender was convicted of the offence.

(11) Where the offence mentioned in subsection (1)(a) was committed before 4 April 2005—

(a) subsection (1)(c) has effect as if the words "by section 224A or 225(2)" were omitted, and

(b) subsection (6) has effect as if the words "in compliance with section 153(2)" were omitted.

226B Extended sentence for certain violent or sexual offences: persons under 18

(1) This section applies where—

(a) a person aged under 18 is convicted of a specified offence (whether the offence was committed before or after this section comes into force),

(b) the court considers that there is a significant risk to members of the public of serious harm occasioned by the commission by the offender of further specified offences,

(c) the court is not required by section 226(2) to impose a sentence of detention for life under section 91 of the Sentencing Act, and

(d) if the court were to impose an extended sentence of detention, the term that it would specify as the appropriate custodial term would be at least 4 years.

(2) The court may impose an extended sentence of detention on the offender.

(3) An extended sentence of detention is a sentence of detention the term of which is equal to the aggregate of—

(a) the appropriate custodial term, and

(b) a further period (the "extension period") for which the offender is to be subject to a licence.

(4) The appropriate custodial term is the term of detention that would (apart from this section) be imposed in compliance with section 153(2).

(5) The extension period must be a period of such length as the court considers necessary for the purpose of protecting members of the public from serious harm occasioned by the commission by the offender of further specified offences, subject to subsections (6) and (7).

(6) The extension period must not exceed—

(a) 5 years in the case of a specified violent offence, and

(b) 8 years in the case of a specified sexual offence.

(7) The term of an extended sentence of detention imposed under this section in respect of an offence may not exceed the term that, at the time the offence was committed, was the maximum term of imprisonment permitted for the offence in the case of a person aged 18 or over.

(8) In subsections (1)(a) and (6), references to a specified offence, a specified violent offence and a specified sexual offence include an offence that—

(a) was abolished before 4 April 2005, and

(b) would have constituted such an offence if committed on the day on which the offender was convicted of the offence.

(9) Where the offence mentioned in subsection (1)(a) was committed before 4 April 2005—

(a) subsection (1) has effect as if paragraph (c) were omitted, and

(b) subsection (4) has effect as if the words "in compliance with section 153(2)" were omitted."

. . .

246A Release on licence of prisoners serving extended sentence under section 226A or 226B

(1) This section applies to a prisoner ("P") who is serving an extended sentence imposed under section 226A or 226B.

(2) It is the duty of the Secretary of State to release P on licence under this section as soon as P has served the requisite custodial period for the purposes of this section unless either or both of the following conditions are met—

(a) the appropriate custodial term is 10 years or more;

(b) the sentence was imposed in respect of an offence listed in Parts 1 to 3 of Schedule 15B or in respect of offences that include one or more offences listed in those Parts of that Schedule.

(3) If either or both of those conditions are met, it is the duty of the Secretary of State to release P on licence in accordance with subsections (4) to (7).

(4) The Secretary of State must refer P's case to the Board—

(a) as soon as P has served the requisite custodial period, and

(b) where there has been a previous reference of P's case to the Board under this subsection and the Board did not direct P's release, not later than the second anniversary of the disposal of that reference.

(5) It is the duty of the Secretary of State to release P on licence under this section as soon as—

(a) P has served the requisite custodial period, and

(b) the Board has directed P's release under this section.

(6) The Board must not give a direction under subsection (5) unless—

(a) the Secretary of State has referred P's case to the Board, and

(b) the Board is satisfied that it is no longer necessary for the protection of the public that P should be confined.

(7) It is the duty of the Secretary of State to release P on licence under this section as soon as P has served the appropriate custodial term, unless P has previously been released on licence under this section and recalled under section 254 (provision for the release of such persons being made by section 255C).

(8) For the purposes of this section—

"appropriate custodial term" means the term determined as such by the court under section 226A or 226B (as appropriate);

"the requisite custodial period" means—

(a) in relation to a person serving one sentence, two-thirds of the appropriate custodial term, and

(b) in relation to a person serving two or more concurrent or consecutive sentences, the period determined under sections 263(2) and 264(2)."

New Automatic Life Sentence—Statutory Life Under Section 224A of the CJA Following Conviction for a Second Listed Offence

Section 224A of the CJA 2003, inserted by s.122 of the Legal Aid, Sentencing and **27.60D** Punishment of Offenders Act 2012, provides for the new "life sentence for a second listed offence". The sentence is available where:

(i) a person aged 18 or over is convicted of an offence listed in Pt 1 of the new Sch.15B to the CJA 2003 (for which see below);

(ii) the offence is such that the court would have imposed a determinate sentence of 10 years or more (including an extended sentence where the *custodial* term would have been 10 years or more) after taking into account all relevant considerations, including the offender's plea ("the sentence condition"); and

(iii) the offender has a previous conviction for an offence listed in Sch.15B (Pt 1 or Pt 2) for which he received a "life sentence" with a minimum term of at least 5 years or a determinate sentence of 10 years or more (including an extended sentence where the *custodial* term was 10 years or more) ("the previous offence" condition).

The restrictions inherent in the "sentence" and "previous offence" conditions mean that this sentence will have limited application. Where the conditions are satisfied, it is likely that the offence will, in any event, attract a life sentence. See further para.1.42E, above.

Section 224A(10) specifically incorporates the definition of "life sentence" found in s.34 of the Crime (Sentences) Act 1997, which includes a sentence of IPP. Therefore, a previous conviction that was dealt with by way of IPP with a minimum term of 5 years or more will be sufficient to bring the offender within the "life sentence for a second listed offence" scheme.

The new offence must be listed in Pt 1 of Sch.15B, while the previous offence can be listed anywhere in the Schedule. Accordingly, the previous offence can be an offence of murder or one of a number of offences that have now been repealed. Of particular relevance for present purposes are the repealed sexual offences formerly contained in the Sexual Offences Act 1956.

Even if the specified conditions are met, a court need not pass a s.224A life sentence if there are "particular circumstances" relating to either the current offence or the past offence, or to the offender, which would make it "unjust to do so in all the circumstances". This formulation has the effect of conferring a wider discretion on the sentencing court than the reference to "exceptional circumstances" in s.109(2) of the PCC(S)A 2000 (for which see para.27.48 et seq. in the main work).

Section 224A and Sch.15B provide as follows:

"224A Life sentence for second listed offence

    (1) This section applies where—
        (a) a person aged 18 or over is convicted of an offence listed in Part 1 of Schedule 15B,
        (b) the offence was committed after this section comes into force, and
        (c) the sentence condition and the previous offence condition are met.
    (2) The court must impose a sentence of imprisonment for life unless the court is of the opinion that there are particular circumstances which—
        (a) relate to the offence, to the previous offence referred to in subsection (4) or to the offender, and
        (b) would make it unjust to do so in all the circumstances.
    (3) The sentence condition is that, but for this section, the court would, in compliance with sections 152(2) and 153(2), impose a sentence of imprisonment for 10 years or more, disregarding any extension period imposed under section 226A.
    (4) The previous offence condition is that —
        (a) at the time the offence was committed, the offender had been convicted of an offence listed in Schedule 15B ("the previous offence"), and
        (b) a relevant life sentence or a relevant sentence of imprisonment or detention for a determinate period was imposed on the offender for the previous offence.
    (5) A life sentence is relevant for the purposes of subsection (4)(b) if—

(a) the offender was not eligible for release during the first 5 years of the sentence, or

(b) the offender would not have been eligible for release during that period but for the reduction of the period of ineligibility to take account of a relevant pre-sentence period.

(6) An extended sentence imposed under this Act . . . is relevant for the purposes of subsection (4)(b) if the appropriate custodial term imposed was 10 years or more.

(7) Any other extended sentence is relevant for the purposes of subsection (4)(b) if the custodial term imposed was 10 years or more.

(8) Any other sentence of imprisonment or detention for a determinate period is relevant for the purposes of subsection (4)(b) if it was for a period of 10 years or more.

(9) An extended sentence or other sentence of imprisonment or detention is also relevant if it would have been relevant under subsection (7) or (8) but for the reduction of the sentence, or any part of the sentence, to take account of a relevant pre-sentence period.

(10) For the purposes of subsections (4) to (9)—
"extended sentence" means—
(a) a sentence imposed under section 85 of the Sentencing Act or under section 226A, 226B, 227 or 228 of this Act . . . ;
"life sentence" means –
(a) a life sentence as defined in section 34 of the Crime (Sentences) Act 1997 . . .

. . .

SCHEDULE 15B

OFFENCES LISTED FOR THE PURPOSES OF SECTIONS 224A, 226A AND 246A

PART 1

OFFENCES UNDER THE LAW OF ENGLAND AND WALES LISTED FOR THE PURPOSES OF SECTIONS 224A(1), 224A(4), 226A AND 246A

The following offences to the extent that they are offences under the law of England and Wales—

1 Manslaughter.

2 An offence under section 4 of the Offences against the Person Act 1861 (soliciting murder).

3 An offence under section 18 of that Act (wounding with intent to cause grievous bodily harm).

4 An offence under section 16 of the Firearms Act 1968 (possession of a firearm with intent to endanger life).

5 An offence under section 17(1) of that Act (use of a firearm to resist arrest).

6 An offence under section 18 of that Act (carrying a firearm with criminal intent).

7 An offence of robbery under section 8 of the Theft Act 1968 where, at some time during the commission of the offence, the offender had in his possession a firearm or an imitation firearm within the meaning of the Firearms Act 1968.

8 An offence under section 1 of the Protection of Children Act 1978 (indecent images of children).

9 An offence under section 56 of the Terrorism Act 2000 (directing terrorist organisation).

10 An offence under section 57 of that Act (possession of article for terrorist purposes).

11 An offence under section 59 of that Act (inciting terrorism overseas) if the offender is liable on conviction on indictment to imprisonment for life.

12 An offence under section 47 of the Anti-terrorism, Crime and Security Act 2001 (use etc of nuclear weapons).

13 An offence under section 50 of that Act (assisting or inducing certain weapons-related acts overseas).

14 An offence under section 113 of that Act (use of noxious substance or thing to cause harm or intimidate).

15 An offence under section 1 of the Sexual Offences Act 2003 (rape).

16 An offence under section 2 of that Act (assault by penetration).

17 An offence under section 4 of that Act (causing a person to engage in sexual activity without consent) if the offender is liable on conviction on indictment to imprisonment for life.

18 An offence under section 5 of that Act (rape of a child under 13).

19 An offence under section 6 of that Act (assault of a child under 13 by penetration).

20 An offence under section 7 of that Act (sexual assault of a child under 13).

21 An offence under section 8 of that Act (causing or inciting a child under 13 to engage in sexual activity).

22 An offence under section 9 of that Act (sexual activity with a child).

23 An offence under section 10 of that Act (causing or inciting a child to engage in sexual activity).

24 An offence under section 11 of that Act (engaging in sexual activity in the presence of a child).

25 An offence under section 12 of that Act (causing a child to watch a sexual act).

26 An offence under section 14 of that Act (arranging or facilitating commission of a child sex offence).

27 An offence under section 15 of that Act (meeting a child following sexual grooming etc).

28 An offence under section 25 of that Act (sexual activity with a child family member) if the offender is aged 18 or over at the time of the offence.

29 An offence under section 26 of that Act (inciting a child family member to engage in sexual activity) if the offender is aged 18 or over at the time of the offence.

30 An offence under section 30 of that Act (sexual activity with a person with a mental disorder impeding choice) if the offender is liable on conviction on indictment to imprisonment for life.

31 An offence under section 31 of that Act (causing or inciting a person with a mental disorder to engage in sexual activity) if the offender is liable on conviction on indictment to imprisonment for life.

32 An offence under section 34 of that Act (inducement, threat or deception to procure sexual activity with a person with a mental disorder) if the offender is liable on conviction on indictment to imprisonment for life.

33 An offence under section 35 of that Act (causing a person with a mental disorder to engage in or agree to engage in sexual activity by inducement etc)

if the offender is liable on conviction on indictment to imprisonment for life.

34 An offence under section 47 of that Act (paying for sexual services of a child) against a person aged under 16.

35 An offence under section 48 of that Act (causing or inciting child prostitution or pornography).

36 An offence under section 49 of that Act (controlling a child prostitute or a child involved in pornography).

37 An offence under section 50 of that Act (arranging or facilitating child prostitution or pornography).

38 An offence under section 62 of that Act (committing an offence with intent to commit a sexual offence) if the offender is liable on conviction on indictment to imprisonment for life.

39 An offence under section 5 of the Domestic Violence, Crime and Victims Act 2004 (causing or allowing the death of a child or vulnerable adult).

40 An offence under section 5 of the Terrorism Act 2006 (preparation of terrorist acts).

41 An offence under section 9 of that Act (making or possession of radioactive device or materials).

42 An offence under section 10 of that Act (misuse of radioactive devices or material and misuse and damage of facilities).

43 An offence under section 11 of that Act (terrorist threats relating to radioactive devices, materials or facilities).

44(1) An attempt to commit an offence specified in the preceding paragraphs of this Part of this Schedule ("a listed offence") or murder.

(2) Conspiracy to commit a listed offence or murder.

(3) Incitement to commit a listed offence or murder.

(4) An offence under Part 2 of the Serious Crime Act 2007 in relation to which a listed offence or murder is the offence (or one of the offences) which the person intended or believed would be committed.

(5) Aiding, abetting, counselling or procuring the commission of a listed offence.

PART 2

FURTHER OFFENCES UNDER THE LAW OF ENGLAND AND WALES LISTED FOR THE PURPOSES OF SECTIONS 224A(4), 226A AND 246A

The following offences to the extent that they are offences under the law of England and Wales—

45 Murder.

46 (1) Any offence that—

(a) was abolished (with or without savings) before the coming into force of this Schedule, and

(b) would, if committed on the relevant day, have constituted an offence specified in Part 1 of this Schedule.

(2) "Relevant day", in relation to an offence, means—

(a) for the purposes of this paragraph as it applies for the purposes of section 246A(2), the day on which the offender was convicted of that offence, and

(b) for the purposes of this paragraph as it applies for the purposes of sections 224A(4) and 226A(2), the day on which the offender was convicted of the offence referred to in section 224A(1)(a) or 226A(1)(a) (as appropriate)."

D. SENTENCING FOR MURDER IN A SEXUAL CONTEXT

27.106   In *Att Gen's Ref (No.73 of 2012) (Christopher John Halliwell)*[28] the Court of Appeal rejected the proposition that, once it is established there was a sexual context to the murder, the lowest minimum term must be 30 years before aggravating and mitigating features are brought into account. In that case, the Attorney General sought leave to refer as unduly lenient a sentence of life imprisonment with a minimum term of 25 years imposed on the offender following a plea of guilty to murder. He was a taxi driver who had picked up the 22-year-old victim, who was extremely drunk, in the early hours of the morning. He drove for 30 minutes in the opposite direction to the victim's home until he reached a forest, where he sexually assaulted and stabbed her. The sentencing judge found that the offender had been driving around looking for a female victim; that his motivation was sexual; that he drove deliberately in a direction opposite to the address which he had been given; that the victim would quickly have realised that she was in grave danger and would have been terrified, and for that reason her ordeal was prolonged; that there was a sexual assault; that there was severe violence, during which the offender intended to kill; and that he moved the body in an unsuccessful attempt to avoid detection. The judge, having selected a provisional starting point of 30 years in accordance with para.5 of Sch.21 to the 2003 Act, said after taking into account all the relevant aggravating factors that the ultimate starting point would be 30 years. She then gave a discount of one-sixth to reflect credit due for the late guilty plea. The Attorney General submitted that the aggravating factors, viewed cumulatively, should have attracted a significant uplift in the starting point from the 30 years provided for in Sch.21 para.5, in the absence of any significant mitigating factors. The Court refused the application. The Attorney General's submission rested upon an assumption that once it was established that there was a sexual context in a murder, the lowest minimum term must be 30 years before aggravating and mitigating features were brought into account. That proposition could not be accepted. The judge had not overlooked the relevant factors, nor had she misapplied Sch.21. Under Sch.21 para.5, it was the judge's responsibility to make an assessment of whether the seriousness of the offence was particularly high, and if so what minimum term should reflect that seriousness. Schedule 21 was not a sentencing grid, and para.5 did not set a non-reducible starting point. It was a guide which the sentencing judge should follow. The judge in this case had been entitled to conclude that the limited sexual component of the offence, important though it was in the context of the murder, taken together with the other aggravating factors, comprised the particularly high seriousness of the offence, which would properly be reflected in a minimum term of 30 years after a trial, and before discount for the plea of guilty. She had been entitled to conclude that the relevant aggravating factors which she had identified

---

[28] [2012] EWCA Crim 2924, [2013] Crim. L.R. 440.

did not require any further uplift. The minimum term imposed was not unduly lenient.

DISQUALIFICATION FROM WORKING WITH CHILDREN AND VULNERABLE ADULTS

The Independent Barring Board was renamed the Independent Safeguarding 27.113 Authority by virtue of s.81 of the Policing and Crime Act 2009. The functions of the Independent Safeguarding Authority under the Safeguarding Vulnerable Groups Act 2006 have since been transferred to the Disclosure and Barring Service, established under s.87(1) of the Protection of Freedoms Act 2012.[29]

---

[29] Which came into force on December 1, 2012 by virtue of SI 2012/3006.

CHAPTER 28

NOTIFICATION AND NOTIFICATION ORDERS*

INTRODUCTION

The Sexual Offences Act 2003 (Notification Requirements) (England and Wales)   **28.01**
Regulations 2012[1] introduced measures to extend and strengthen the system of
notification requirements placed on registered sex offenders (commonly referred
to as the sex offenders' register). The new measures came into force on August 13,
2012, and require offenders subject to the notification requirements under the
2003 Act to notify to the police:

- any intended travel outside the UK (not just travel of three days or more
  as previously);
- where they have no sole or main residence, the address or location where
  they can regularly be found, on a weekly basis (rather than yearly as
  before);
- any residence or stay of at least 12 hours in a household containing a
  person aged under 18; and
- any bank account, credit or debit card, passport or other identity document
  (so that sex offenders can no longer seek to avoid being on the register by
  changing their name: see further para.28.25, below).

---

* The authors are indebted to William Hotham, Barrister, of Six Pump Court, for his enormous
assistance in updating this chapter.
[1] SI 2012/1876.

Qualifying Offenders

28.06   In *R. v M, B and H*[2] the Court of Appeal held that the notification requirements did not apply to three appellants variously aged 15 and 16 who were sentenced to detention and training orders ("DTOs") for offences of sexual activity with a child, contrary to s.13 of the 2003 Act. H was sentenced to a DTO of 18 months' duration and M and B to DTOs of 12 months' duration. The judge also purported to make orders requiring the appellants to comply with the notification requirements, for 10 years in the case of H and 7 years in the cases of B and M. The Court of Appeal, citing *Longworth* (discussed in the main work), quashed the purported notification orders on the ground that the notification requirements apply, if at all, by operation of law and not by order of the court. It went on to consider whether the requirements applied in this case. It noted the stipulation in the 2003 Act[3] that an offence under s.13 attracts notification only if the offender is sentenced to imprisonment for a term of at least 12 months. Although none of the appellants was sentenced to imprisonment, s.131(a) of the 2003 Act provides that the notification provisions apply to a period of detention which a person is liable to serve under a DTO as it applies to an equivalent sentence of imprisonment. The question was therefore what period of detention the appellants were liable to serve under their DTOs. Section 102(2) of the Powers of Criminal Courts (Sentencing) Act 2000 ("PCC(S)A 2000") provides that "the period of detention and training under a detention and training order shall be one-half of the term of the order". The Court noted that this provision was considered in *Slocombe*,[4] the effect of which was that in interpreting the relevant provisions of the 2003 Act, the relevant period is the period of time which will actually be served in detention. This was 9 months in the case of H and 6 months in the cases of B and M, and accordingly, none of the appellants was sentenced to a period of detention sufficient to trigger the notification requirements.

28.06A   What is the appropriate period of notification when a suspended sentence is passed? Section 82 of the 2003 Act sets the notification period for an offender who is sentenced to a term of imprisonment by reference to the length of the term. A person who receives a suspended sentence is not in fact imprisoned, and it may be arguable whether they are "A person of any other description" within the rubric at the end of s.82. However, s.189(6) of the Criminal Justice Act 2003 ("CJA 2003") provides that a suspended sentence is to be treated as a sentence of imprisonment for all purposes. This has the result that the notification periods set out in s.82 of the 2003 Act apply to all sentences of imprisonment, whether or not they are suspended.

---

[2] [2010] EWCA Crim 42.
[3] Sch.3 para.22.
[4] [2006] 1 Cr. App. R. 33, discussed in para.28.23 of the main work.

THE NOTIFICATION PERIOD

In *Alary (Bruno)*[5] it was held that a sexual offences prevention order ("SOPO")   **28.16**
may properly be imposed for a greater length of time than the period fixed by the
statutory notification requirements, if this is justified by the facts.

REVIEW OF INDEFINITE NOTIFICATION

Sections 91A–91F were inserted in the 2003 Act by the Sexual Offences Act 2003   **28.17**
(Remedial) Order 2012[6] following the decision of the Supreme Court in *F and
another, R. (on the application of) v Secretary of State for the Home Department.*[7]
They provide a mechanism by which indefinite notification requirements may be
reviewed. In short, the offender may apply to the chief officer of police for the area
in which the offender lives, or has lived for the most days in the previous 12
months, for a determination that the offender is no longer subject to the indefinite
notification requirements (s.91A). An application must be in writing (s.91B). For
offenders who were made the subject of the indefinite notification requirements
when aged 18 or over, the earliest they may apply under s.91B is 15 years after they
first made a required notification. For those who were under 18 at the relevant
time, the first date on which they may apply is 8 years after they first made a
required notification. For the purposes of the determination of an application
under s.91B, the offender must satisfy the relevant chief officer of police that it is
not necessary for the purpose of protecting the public or any particular members
of the public from sexual harm for him to remain subject to the indefinite
notification requirements (s.91C). If the chief officer of police determines that the
offender should remain subject to the indefinite notification requirements, the
offender may not re-apply under s.91B for a period of 8 years from the date of the
determination, or such longer period, up to a maximum of 15 years, as the chief
officer considers to be justified by the risk of sexual harm posed by the offender.
Section 91D sets out the factors to be taken into account by a chief officer of police
in considering an application under s.91B. These include the seriousness of the
offence which gave rise to the indefinite notification requirements to which the
offender is subject; any assessment of the risk posed by the offender prepared by
any responsible authority; and evidence or submission from a victim of the offence
which gave rise to the indefinite notification requirements; and any conviction or
other finding made by a court in relation to the subsequent commission of an
offence under Sch.3 to the 2003 Act by the offender. There is a right of appeal
against a determination by a chief officer of police that an offender must remain
subject to the indefinite notification requirements (s.91E). An appeal may be made
to a magistrates' court by complaint within 21 days of receipt of the notice of

---

[5] [2012] EWCA Crim 1534.
[6] SI 2012/1883.
[7] [2010] UKSC 17.

determination. The Secretary of State is under a statutory duty to issue guidance to chief officers of police in relation to the determination of applications under s.91B (s.91F).[8]

Sections 91A–F provide:

"91A. Review of indefinite notification requirements: qualifying relevant offender

(1) A qualifying relevant offender may apply to the relevant chief officer of police for a determination that the qualifying relevant offender is no longer subject to the indefinite notification requirements ("an application for review").

(2) A qualifying relevant offender means a relevant offender who, on the date on which he makes an application for review, is—

    (a) subject to the indefinite notification requirements; and

    (b) not subject to a sexual offences prevention order under section 104(1) or an interim sexual offences prevention order under section 109(3).

(3) The "indefinite notification requirements" mean the notification requirements of this Part for an indefinite period by virtue of—

    (a) section 80(1);

    (b) section 81(1); or

    (c) a notification order made under section 97(5).

(4) In this Part, the "relevant chief officer of police" means, subject to subsection (5), the chief officer of police for the police area in which a qualifying relevant offender is recorded as residing or staying in the most recent notification given by him under section 84(1) or 85(1).

(5) Subsection (6) applies if a qualifying relevant offender is recorded as residing or staying at more than one address in the most recent notification given by him under section 84(1) or 85(1).

(6) If this subsection applies, the "relevant chief officer of police" means the chief officer of police for the police area in which, during the relevant period, the qualifying relevant offender has resided or stayed on a number of days which equals or exceeds the number of days on which he has resided or stayed in any other police area.

(7) In subsection (6), "the relevant period" means the period of 12 months ending on the day on which the qualifying relevant offender makes an application for review.

91B. Review of indefinite notification requirements: application for review and qualifying dates

(1) An application for review must be in writing and may be made on or after the qualifying date or, as the case may be, the further qualifying date.

(2) Subject to subsection (7), the qualifying date is—

    (a) where the qualifying relevant offender was 18 or over on the relevant date, the day after the end of the 15 year period beginning with the day on which the qualifying relevant offender gives the relevant notification; or

---

[8] See the Home Office's *Guidance on Review of Indefinite Notification Requirements issued under section 91F of the Sexual Offences Act 2003*, available at *https://www.gov.uk/government/uploads/system/uploads/attachment_data/file/98378/review-notification-requirements.pdf* [accessed October 8, 2013].

(b) where the qualifying relevant offender was under 18 on the relevant date, the day after the end of the 8 year period beginning with the day on which the qualifying relevant offender gives the relevant notification.

(3) Subject to subsections (4) to (6), the further qualifying date is the day after the end of the 8 year period beginning with the day on which the relevant chief officer of police makes a determination under section 91C to require a qualifying relevant offender to remain subject to the indefinite notification requirements.

(4) Subsection (5) applies if the relevant chief officer of police, when making a determination under section 91C to require a qualifying relevant offender to remain subject to the indefinite notification requirements, considers that the risk of sexual harm posed by a qualifying relevant offender is sufficient to justify a continuation of those requirements after the end of the 8 year period beginning with the day on which the determination is made.

(5) If this subsection applies, the relevant chief officer of police may make a determination to require a qualifying relevant offender to remain subject to the indefinite notification requirements for a period which may be no longer than the 15 year period beginning with the day on which the determination is made.

(6) If subsection (5) applies, the further qualifying date is the day after the end of the period determined under that subsection.

(7) The qualifying date must not be earlier than the expiry of the fixed period specified in a notification continuation order made in relation to a qualifying relevant offender in accordance with sections 88A to 88I.

(8) The relevant chief officer of police within 14 days of receipt of an application for review—
 (a) must give an acknowledgment of receipt of the application to the qualifying relevant offender, and
 (b) may notify a responsible body that the application has been made.

(9) Where a responsible body is notified of the application for review under subsection (8)(b) and holds information which it considers to be relevant to the application, the responsible body must give such information to the relevant chief officer of police within 28 days of receipt of the notification.

(10) In this section "the relevant notification" means the first notification which the relevant offender gives under section 83, 84 or 85 when he is first released after—
 (a) being remanded in or committed to custody by an order of a court in relation to the conviction for the offence giving rise to the indefinite notification requirements;
 (b) serving a sentence of imprisonment or a term of service detention in relation to that conviction;
 (c) being detained in hospital in relation to that conviction.

(11) For the purposes of this Part—
 (a) "responsible body" means—
  (i) the probation trust for any area that includes any part of the police area concerned,
  (ii) in relation to any part of the police area concerned for which there is no probation trust, each provider of probation services which has been identified as a relevant provider of probation services for the purposes of section 325 of the Criminal Justice Act 2003 by arrangements under section 3 of the Offender Management Act 2007,
  (iii) the Minister of the Crown exercising functions in relation to prisons (and for this purpose "prison" has the same meaning as in the Prison Act 1952), and

(iv) each body mentioned in section 325(6) of the Criminal Justice Act 2003, but as if the references in that subsection to the relevant area were references to the police area concerned;

(b) "risk of sexual harm" means a risk of physical or psychological harm to the public in the United Kingdom or any particular members of the public caused by the qualifying relevant offender committing one or more of the offences listed in Schedule 3.

91C. Review of indefinite notification requirements: determination of application for review

(1) The relevant chief officer of police must, within 6 weeks of the latest date on which any body to which a notification has been given under section 91B(8)(b) may give information under section 91B(9)—
   (a) determine the application for review, and
   (b) give notice of the determination to the qualifying relevant offender.

(2) For the purposes of the determination of an application for review under this section, a qualifying relevant offender must satisfy the relevant chief officer of police that it is not necessary for the purpose of protecting the public or any particular members of the public from sexual harm for the qualifying relevant offender to remain subject to the indefinite notification requirements.

(3) If the relevant chief officer of police determines under this section that the qualifying relevant offender should remain subject to the indefinite notification requirements, the notice of the determination must—
   (a) contain a statement of reasons for the determination, and
   (b) inform the qualifying relevant offender that he may appeal the determination in accordance with section 91E.

(4) If the relevant chief officer of police determines under this section that a qualifying relevant offender should not remain subject to the indefinite notification requirements, the qualifying relevant offender ceases to be subject to the indefinite notification requirements on the date of receipt of the notice of determination.

(5) The Secretary of State may by order amend the period in subsection (1).

91D. Review of indefinite notification requirements: factors applying to determination under section 91C

(1) In determining an application for review under section 91C, the relevant chief officer of police must—
   (a) have regard to information (if any) received from a responsible body;
   (b) consider the risk of sexual harm posed by the qualifying relevant offender and the effect of a continuation of the indefinite notification requirements on the offender; and
   (c) take into account the matters listed in subsection (2).

(2) The matters are—
   (a) the seriousness of the offence in relation to which the qualifying relevant offender became subject to the indefinite notification requirements;
   (b) the period of time which has elapsed since the qualifying relevant offender committed the offence (or other offences);
   (c) where the qualifying relevant offender falls within section 81(1), whether the qualifying relevant offender committed any offence under section 3 of the Sex Offenders Act 1997;
   (d) whether the qualifying relevant offender has committed any offence under section 91;

(e) the age of the qualifying relevant offender at the qualifying date or further qualifying date;

(f) the age of the qualifying relevant offender at the time the offence referred to in paragraph (a) was committed;

(g) the age of any person who was a victim of any such offence (where applicable) and the difference in age between the victim and the qualifying relevant offender at the time the offence was committed;

(h) any assessment of the risk posed by the qualifying relevant offender which has been made by a responsible body under the arrangements for managing and assessing risk established under section 325 of the Criminal Justice Act 2003;

(i) any submission or evidence from a victim of the offence giving rise to the indefinite notification requirements;

(j) any convictions or findings made by a court (including by a court in Scotland, Northern Ireland or countries outside the United Kingdom) in respect of the qualifying relevant offender for any offence listed in Schedule 3 other than the one referred to in paragraph (a);

(k) any caution which the qualifying relevant offender has received for an offence (including for an offence in Northern Ireland or countries outside the United Kingdom) which is listed in Schedule 3;

(l) any convictions or findings made by a court in Scotland, Northern Ireland or countries outside the United Kingdom in respect of the qualifying relevant offender for any offence listed in Schedule 5 where the behaviour of the qualifying relevant offender since the date of such conviction or finding indicates a risk of sexual harm;

(m) any other submission or evidence of the risk of sexual harm posed by the qualifying relevant offender;

(n) any evidence presented by or on behalf of the qualifying relevant offender which demonstrates that the qualifying relevant offender does not pose a risk of sexual harm; and

(o) any other matter which the relevant chief officer of police considers to be appropriate.

(3) In this section, a reference to a conviction, finding or caution for an offence committed in a country outside the United Kingdom means a conviction, finding or caution for an act which—

(a) constituted an offence under the law in force in the country concerned, and

(b) would have constituted an offence listed in Schedule 3 or Schedule 5 if it had been done in any part of the United Kingdom.

91E. Review of indefinite notification requirements: appeals

(1) A qualifying relevant offender may appeal against a determination of the relevant chief officer of police under section 91C.

(2) An appeal under this section may be made by complaint to a magistrates' court within the period of 21 days beginning with the day of receipt of the notice of determination.

(3) A qualifying relevant offender may appeal under this section to any magistrates' court in a local justice area which includes any part of the police area for which the chief officer is the relevant chief officer of police.

(4) If the court makes an order that a qualifying relevant offender should not remain subject to the indefinite notification requirements, the qualifying relevant offender ceases to be subject to the indefinite notification requirements on the date of the order.

91F. Review of indefinite notification requirements: guidance

(1) The Secretary of State must issue guidance to relevant chief officers of police in relation to the determination by them of applications made under section 91B.

(2) The Secretary of State may, from time to time, revise the guidance issued under subsection (1).

(3) The Secretary of State must arrange for any guidance issued or revised under this section to be published in such manner as the Secretary of State considers appropriate."

28.22   In *R. (Minter) v Chief Constable of Hampshire Constabulary*[9] the Court of Appeal (Civil Division) confirmed (in accordance with *Wiles*[10]) that the whole term of an extended sentence imposed under s.85 of the Powers of Criminal Courts (Sentencing) Act 2000 constitutes the term for which a person is "sentenced to imprisonment" for the purpose of determining the length of the appropriate notification period under s.82(1) of the 2003 Act. The Court held there was nothing arbitrary or disproportionate about the imposition of an indefinite notification period given the statutory purpose and the existence of review provisions in ss.91A–F of the 2003 Act.

Notification Requirements

28.25   A requirement has been introduced for offenders to disclose banking details, in order to enhance the ability of the police to trace quickly an individual who fails to comply with notification requirements. Regulations 12 and 13 of the Sexual Offences Act 2003 (Notification Requirements) (England and Wales) Regulations 2012[11] require offenders subject to the notification requirements to notify information about their bank accounts and debit and credit cards. Regulation 12(1) requires relevant offenders to notify the police about whether they hold an account with a banking institution (defined as a bank, building society or any other institution providing banking services), a debit card in relation to such an account, a credit card account or a credit card. If relevant offenders hold an account or card, they are required to notify the information specified in reg.12(2)–(7). In respect of bank accounts, the information is the name of the institution, its address, the number of the account and the sort code. In respect of debit and credit cards, it is the card number, the validation date, the expiry date and, if the card is held jointly with another person or in the name of a business, the name of that person or business. Regulation 13 provides for provision of information where circumstances changed. It applies where an account is opened or closed, a debit or credit card is obtained, no longer held or has expired, and information previously notified by the offender has altered or become inaccurate or incomplete.

[9] [2013] EWCA Civ 697.
[10] [2004] 2 Cr. App. R. 88.
[11] SI 2012/1876.

Regulation 12 was held to be compatible with art.8 of the ECHR in *R. (Prothero)* **28.25A**
v Secretary of State for the Home Department.[12] The Court noted that the
information is securely recorded and that possession of it does not entitle the
police to examine the details of bank account or credit card transactions: to do so
they would ordinarily have to obtain an order from a judge. Accordingly, the
interference with art.8, although material, is not nearly as significant as the
interference already brought about by the other notification requirements. As to
the justification for that interference, the Court was in no doubt that it had a
legitimate policy objective, namely enabling the police to trace an offender quickly,
to guard against the risk of an offender using another identity or to obtain quick
access to a credit card account to investigate offences in relation to indecent
images. Further, evidence before the Court as to the use of similar powers in
Scotland showed that the objective can be achieved.

Accordingly, the Court considered the requirements imposed by reg.12 to be a
necessary, practical and proportionate means of preventing other persons becoming potential victims of sex offenders[13]:

> "The materials before the court and other matters well within the knowledge of any
> court provide sufficient evidence that the means are both appropriate and propor-
> tionate. Apart from the specific evidence from Scotland it is, in our view, self-evident
> that if such details are not provided by an offender, then the only course open to the
> police to identify the bank or institution at which the offender has a bank or credit card
> account would be to use their statutory powers to make applications in respect of the
> many banks and other institutions operating in England and Wales to see which bank
> or institution held an account in the name of the offender as that name was set out on
> the Sexual Offenders Register or otherwise known. The process of making such
> applications would be time consuming and expensive. Moreover, if the offender had
> changed the name under which he operated the account, the difficulties facing the
> police would be more considerable. By having details of the bank or other institution
> at which the offender held an account, the police would quickly be able to trace, by
> seeking appropriate orders. Any subsequent change of identity could be discovered by
> the well tested route of 'following the money'."

For the 2010 Regulations, see now the Sexual Offences Act 2003 (Prescribed Police **28.29**
Stations) Regulations 2013.[14] For Northern Ireland, see the Sexual Offences Act
2003 (Prescribed Police Stations) Regulations (Northern Ireland) 2012.[15]

CHANGES TO THE NOTIFIED PARTICULARS

Regulations 10 and 11 of the Sexual Offences Act 2003 (Notification Require- **28.30**
ments) (England and Wales) Regulations 2012[16] require offenders to notify the
police when they reside, or stay for at least 12 hours, at a relevant household. A
"relevant household" is a household or other place at which a child (defined as a

---

[12] [2013] EWHC 2830 (Admin).
[13] At [27].
[14] SI 2013/300.
[15] SI 2012/325.
[16] SI 2012/1876.

person aged under 18 years) resides or stays (whether with its parent, guardian or carer, with another child or alone) and to which the public do not have access. The information must include the date on which the offender begins to reside or stay at the relevant household, its address and the period for which the offender intends to reside or stay at that place.

Annual Re-Notification

28.33 Regulation 9 of the Sexual Offences Act 2003 (Notification Requirements) (England and Wales) Regulations 2012[17] has the effect of requiring offenders who have no sole or main residence to notify every seven days the address or location of a place in the UK where they can regularly be found. Previously, Pt 2 of the 2003 Act required such an offender to give notification once every year.

28.34 Section 85 of the 2003 Act as amended (in relation to England, Wales and Northern Ireland)[18] reads as follows:

> "**85 Notification requirements: periodic notification**
>
> (1) A relevant offender must, within the applicable period after each event within subsection (2), notify to the police the information set out in section 83(5), unless within that period he has given a notification under section 84(1).
> (2) The events are—
>   (a) the commencement of this Part (but only in the case of a person who is a relevant offender from that commencement);
>   (b) any notification given by the relevant offender under section 83(1) or 84(1); and
>   (c) any notification given by him under subsection (1).
> (3) Where the applicable period would (apart from this subsection) end whilst subsection (4) applies to the relevant offender, that period is to be treated as continuing until the end of the period of 3 days beginning when subsection (4) first ceases to apply to him.
> (4) This subsection applies to the relevant offender if he is—
>   (a) remanded in or committed to custody by an order of a court or kept in service custody,
>   (b) serving a sentence of imprisonment or a term of service detention,
>   (c) detained in a hospital, or
>   (d) outside the United Kingdom.
> (5) In this section, "the applicable period" means—
>   (a) in any case where subsection (6) applies to the relevant offender, such period as may be prescribed by regulations made by the Secretary of State, and
>   (b) in any other case, the period of one year.
> (6) This subsection applies to the relevant offender if the last home address notified by him under section 83(1) or 84(1) or subsection (1) was the address or location of such a place as is mentioned in section 83(7)(b)."

---

[17] SI 2012/1876.
[18] By the Criminal Justice and Immigration Act 2008, ss.73, 142(7)–(9), 148(1), 153(7) and Sch.26 para.55; SI 2008/1586, art.2 and Sch.1 para.45 (subject to Sch.2); SI 2009/2606, art.3(i).

CHECKING THE NOTIFIED INFORMATION

In *M v Chief Constable of Hampshire*[19] the Divisional Court held that the power of   **28.35**
the police to obtain a search warrant to enter a sex offender's home without notice
under s.96B of the 2003 Act is compatible with the ECHR.

The claimant (M) was a repeat child sex offender and subject to the notification
requirements. In 2005 and 2006 he received police visits for the purpose of
assessing the risk he posed. Section 96B was enacted in 2007. The visits
continued. M found them intrusive and, on the last, he refused to answer
questions and told the police officers to leave. M sought a declaration that s.96B
was to be interpreted so as not to allow a senior police officer to apply for a search
warrant to enter his home without notice; alternatively, he sought a declaration
that the section is incompatible with the ECHR. M argued that the visits since the
enactment of s.96B had been unlawful as they had not been consensual, as the
police could threaten to obtain a warrant if he did not comply. He also argued that
he should be given advance notification of any application for a search warrant
under s.96B and that no application should be made unless there were reasonable
grounds to believe that there was material in his home to demonstrate that he had
offended or was about to offend.

The Court dismissed these arguments. It held that a notification and monitoring regime for sex offenders was necessary in order to protect potential victims of
sexual offences, and the issue was as to the proportionality of the regime. In
relation to M, regular police visits were the only way of providing protection to the
children with whom he might come into contact. Such visits might throw up a risk
which would otherwise go unnoticed, and unannounced visits were a sensible
precaution. The combination of consensual visits coupled with the possibility of
searches under compulsion, if necessary and approved by the court, was
appropriate. The Court rejected the suggestion that the visits to M's home had not
been consensual. M had had the right to refuse the police entry and on the one
occasion that he had insisted that the police officers leave, they had. He could then
have made representations to the chief constable as to why he believed the visits
were overly intrusive. The chief constable's response might have been to agree or
to authorise a senior officer to seek a warrant, which a magistrate might or might
not have granted. The senior officer would have to persuade the court that a
warrant was necessary to assess the risk, and not merely desirable. What was
necessary depended on all the circumstances, and there would therefore be focus
on the individual offender's circumstances. If there was no urgency and no need
for the application to be without notice, the magistrate could, if he considered it
appropriate, call for representations from the individual. Should the warrant be
granted, there was the possibility of oversight by the Divisional Court. There was
therefore considerable judicial oversight of the operation of s.96B. Further, the
principle of rehabilitation was catered for in that, if the offender could establish,
after what Parliament had deemed to be a reasonable time, that he no longer posed

[19] [2012] EWHC 4034 (Admin).

a risk, he could apply to come off the register and he would no longer be subject to the s.96B regime. On the Court's reading, the words of s.96B were clear, Parliament had not intended to import into the section the additional requirements suggested by M, and there was no need to read down the section to make it compatible with the Convention.

Advance Notification of Foreign Travel

28.36   Regulation 5 of the Sexual Offences Act 2003 (Notification Requirements) (England and Wales) Regulations 2012[20] provides that offenders who are required to notify their personal details to the police under Pt 2 of the 2003 Act (including those subject to a foreign travel order) must notify the police of any intended travel outside the UK (regardless of the length of the trip). Previously, the 2004 Regulations only required offenders to notify the police of intended travel outside the UK for three or more days. Regulation 5 also provides that offenders are required to notify their intended travel not less than seven days before departure, or exceptionally not less than 12 hours before departure. Previously, the 2004 Regulations only permitted offenders exceptionally to notify the intended travel not less than 24 hours before departure. Regulation 6 provides that relevant offenders must notify additional information about their intended travel. Regulations 7 and 8 make consequential amendments to the 2004 Regulations, including provision for offenders exceptionally to notify a change to information previously notified by them less than 12 hours before departure.

Notification Offences

28.43   In Carnell[21] the appellant had originally pleaded guilty to an offence of voyeurism and was sentenced to a community order with supervision and required to comply with the notification requirements. On two occasions he complied with the notification requirements by notifying the police of his intention to travel to Sweden, where his brother lived. However, on another occasion he travelled there without notifying them. He returned voluntarily to the UK when he learned that the police had been enquiring as to his whereabouts. The appellant pleaded guilty at the first opportunity to failing to comply with the notification requirements and was sentenced to 26 weeks' imprisonment. On appeal, his counsel drew attention to his early guilty plea and the absence of any antecedents apart from the voyeurism conviction itself. It was submitted that there were no aggravating features because, whilst the appellant had left the jurisdiction, which would normally be a serious aggravating matter, he had been to Sweden before with permission and he came back voluntarily on learning of the police enquiries. Finally, there was personal mitigation in that as a result of his conviction the appellant had lost his job and experienced emotional turmoil. The Court of

---

[20] [2012] EWHC 4034 (Admin).
[21] [2012] EWCA Crim 248.

Appeal had regard to *Grosvenor*,[22] which suggests that the sentencing range following conviction for failing to notify a change of address for periods up to three months or so is in the range of 4–6 months where there are no aggravating factors. The present case fell to be dealt with on the basis of plea, not conviction. The Court noted the importance of the notification requirements being complied with, but on the facts, taking particular account of the appellant's voluntary return, and applying the guidance in *Grosvenor*, it considered that on an early plea the appropriate sentence was 3 months' imprisonment, and it therefore allowed the appeal and substituted that sentence.

In *Petraitis*[23] the appellant had originally been convicted for sexual assault on a 28.43A
13-year-old girl. He was later released on licence and required to comply with notification requirements for 10 years. The appellant did not comply with the requirements: he gave the police a false address, did not comply with the reporting requirements and was arrested whilst attempting to leave the UK. He pleaded guilty to failing to comply with the notification requirements and was sentenced to 9 months' imprisonment, i.e. a starting point of 12 months and a 25 per cent credit for the guilty plea. His appeal against sentence was allowed, the Court of Appeal holding that the starting point of 12 months was too high. The case was less serious than *Grosvenor*, in which a starting point of 12 months was correct. However, the appellant could not expect to be treated favourably when he had made it clear from the outset that he was not going to comply with the notification requirements, and any sentence imposed for a breach had to reflect that. A starting point of 8 months was appropriate. When the 25 per cent discount was applied, that resulted in a sentence of 6 months' imprisonment.

In *R. v P and E*[24] the applicants applied for leave to appeal against sentences 28.43B
imposed following guilty pleas to offences of failing to comply with notification requirements. P had been convicted in 2005 of indecent assault on his 9-year-old niece and his 11-year-old nephew. He was sentenced to 3 years' imprisonment and was released on licence in 2006. He initially complied with the notification requirements, but left the UK in 2007 and went to Europe. He was arrested in 2011. He pleaded guilty to failing to comply with the notification requirements on the basis that he thought that all he had to do was tell the police that he intended to leave the country on a permanent basis. There was a *Newton* hearing in which the sentencing judge rejected P's account and concluded that he knew what the notification requirements were and that he had not complied with them. Some credit was due for guilty plea, but it was reduced because of the unsuccessful *Newton* hearing. P was sentenced to 22 months' imprisonment. E had been convicted in 2005 of four offences of indecent assault on two young girls. He was sentenced to 3 years' imprisonment and was subject to the notification requirements. He was released on licence in 2006 and initially complied with the

---

[22] [2010] 2 Cr. App. R(S.) 100.
[23] [2013] EWCA Crim 997.
[24] [2011] EWCA Crim 2496.

requirements. He became friends with another man (M) who lived with a woman with a 9-year-old daughter. E stayed with M on a number of occasions, but did not notify the police or tell M about his history. E also met a woman (L) who had two young children. He later moved in with her and she became pregnant with his child. He failed to tell police about his change of address. L had no idea about E's previous convictions. E claimed that he did not appreciate that he had to notify the police if he stayed at an address for a cumulative total of 7 days in a 12-month period. There was a *Newton* hearing in which the sentencing judge rejected E's account and he was sentenced to 3 years' imprisonment. P and E argued that the authorities suggested that the sentencing range should have been lower, and that the judge gave insufficient credit for plea. The Court of Appeal noted the importance of the provisions of the 2003 Act requiring notification, which were included principally for the safety of the public. There was great and understandable public concern about what offenders might do on release if not monitored. That was particularly important where others, for example mothers of young children, did not know of an offender's sexual offending and came to trust a released offender. Offenders on release had to be made to realise that those requirements were important. In P's case, the period of non-compliance was a very long one, namely 4 years. The mitigation of the plea was diminished by the rejection of the evidence at the *Newton* hearing. Taking all matters into consideration, the sentence of 22 months' imprisonment was well merited and P's application for leave to appeal was therefore refused. In E's case, there was deception of M and, more importantly, of L. E's offences were persistent and devious and spanned many months. They enabled E to come into contact with young children without the police and social services having the opportunity to intervene. Although there were pleas of guilty, much of that mitigation was dissipated by the evidence at the *Newton* hearing. Nonetheless, a sentence of 3 years' imprisonment on a guilty plea was very substantial, and the Court substituted a sentence of 2 years and 3 months' imprisonment.

CHAPTER 29

SEXUAL OFFENCES PREVENTION ORDERS, FOREIGN TRAVEL ORDERS AND RISK OF SEXUAL HARM ORDERS

by H.H. Judge Martin Picton

INTRODUCTION

Preventative orders imposed by the courts have proved problematic in a number   29.01
of fields, but rarely more so than in respect of those designed to guard against the
potential for sexual offending. Of the three types of order covered in the main
work, the most frequently made and also the most frequently appealed are sexual
offences prevention orders ("SOPOs") imposed under s.104 of the 2003 Act. In
Collard,[1] the Court of Appeal set out a high test that had to be satisfied before a
court could legitimately impose a SOPO, which, if applied appropriately, should
result in prohibitions (where required at all) that are necessary, reasonable,
proportionate and capable of being both understood and sensibly enforced. It
would appear incontrovertible by reference to the number of successful appeals
against SOPOs, imposed often without opposition at the point of sentence, that
the "*Collard* test" is often not in fact applied with any, or sufficient, rigour.

The "*Collard* test" can be stated thus:
   1. A prohibition may be imposed only if it is necessary for the purpose of
      protecting the public or any particular members of the public from
      serious sexual harm[2] from the defendant. That is a high threshold. That
      it may be considered desirable to impose such a prohibition is not
      sufficient. There must be material before the judge on the basis of which
      he can reasonably conclude that a prohibition is necessary for that
      purpose.

---

[1] [2004] EWCA Crim 1664.
[2] s.106(3): "serious physical or psychological harm caused by the defendant committing one or more
offences listed in Schedule 3".

2. The court must consider the number of offences, their duration, the nature of the material, the extent of publication and the use to which the material was put.
3. The court must have regard to the offender's antecedents, his personal circumstances and the risk of his re-offending.
4. Where the court makes a sexual offences prevention order, its terms must be tailored to meet the danger that this offender presents.
5. The order must be proportionate to the danger presented. In this respect the judge must have regard in particular to the provisions of the European Convention on Human Rights and the Human Rights Act and in particular the right to private life under Article 8 of the Convention.

29.01A The above test is consistent with the statutory requirement that the only prohibitions that may be included in a SOPO are those that are "necessary for the purpose of protecting the public or any particular members of the public from serious sexual harm".[3] In the case of *Smith and Ors*,[4] which is essential reading for anyone considering SOPOs, the Vice President (as he then was) attempted to address the issues identified as being responsible for the multiplicity of appeals with which the Court of Appeal has for years been plagued by reason of the imposition of inappropriate SOPOs. The degree to which that has been achieved, in the sense of stemming the flow of appeals, is open to question. The continuing failure of prosecutors to comply with Pt 50 of the Criminal Procedure Rules, dealing with civil behaviour orders after verdict or finding, must be a significant factor. The Criminal Procedure Rules have now been amended so as to make specific reference to SOPOs and the observations in *Smith* as to the giving of notice of the application have been adopted.[5] Overly inventive drafting certainly has played a part in the past, but *Smith* should have discouraged that tendency, at least for the moment.

29.01B Particular issues that frequently arise in the framing of SOPO terms, and that are discussed below, relate to access to computers, non-contact prohibitions and prohibitions that amount to compulsions. The imposition of SOPOs calls for the application of drafting discipline of a kind more normally required in the civil sphere. Regrettably, the case law demonstrates that such discipline has often been conspicuous by its absence.

All change! Anti-Social Behaviour, Crime and Policing Bill

29.01C The Anti-Social Behaviour and Policing Bill currently before Parliament will, if enacted in its present form, make major changes to the scheme of the protective orders considered in this chapter. SOPOs and Foreign Travel Orders ("FTOs")

---

[3] s.107(2).
[4] [2011] EWCA Crim 1772.
[5] CPR 2013 r.50.3(1)(b) and (5).

will be combined in a single order entitled a Sexual Harm Prevention Order ("SHPO"). Risk of Sexual Harm Orders ("RHSOs") and FTOs will also be combined in a Sexual Risk Order ("SRO"). A more detailed analysis of the proposed changes can be found in para.29.46 et seq., below. In terms of the drafting of prohibitions, it is not expected that the Bill materially will affect the current position. So far as eligibility for an order is concerned, it should be noted that a defendant will be eligible for a SHPO if there is a risk of "sexual harm", whereas under the present scheme the contemplated risk has to be of "serious sexual harm".

SEXUAL OFFENCES PREVENTION ORDERS

SOPO MADE AT TIME OF DEALING WITH OFFENDER FOR AN OFFENCE

The making of a SOPO in respect of an offender who falls within s.104(3) of the **29.08** 2003 Act would seem to engage similar issues to those that can arise where an Anti Social Behaviour Order[6] is made against someone suffering from a mental disorder.[7] Accordingly, a SOPO should not be made where the offender's mental impairment is such that he is incapable of understanding or complying with its terms. In such circumstances a SOPO is incapable of protecting the public and so cannot be said to be necessary to protect them within the terms of s.104. Moreover, for a court to make a SOPO knowing that the offender is incapable of complying with it would amount to an improper exercise of the court's discretion. However, although an offender who suffers from a personality disorder might be liable to disobey a SOPO, that is not a sufficient reason for holding that an order which is otherwise necessary to protect the public from serious sexual harm is not necessary for that purpose, or that the court should not exercise its discretion to make such an order. The position will be less problematic if the insanity or other disability to which the offender was subject at the time of the commission of the offence was temporary, is capable of being treated or is otherwise of a nature that does not make it unreasonable to impose prohibitions.

Applications made under s.104(5) in the magistrates' court are initiated by way of **29.08A** summons. Post-conviction applications should be notified in advance of the application being made in court so as to comply with r.50.3 of the CPR. This was emphasised by Maddison J. in *Lawrence*[8]:

> "It is necessary that the prosecution should consider in every case whether it is reasonably arguable that it is necessary for such an order to be made. The prosecution should also consider carefully the evidence upon which they seek to rely in support of

---

[6] s.1C of the Crime and Disorder Act 1998, discussed in para.12.65 et seq. of the main work.
[7] cf. *R. (Cooke) v DPP* [2008] EWHC 2703 (Admin) and *Fairweather v The Commissioner of Police for the Metropolis* [2008] EWHC 3073 (Admin).
[8] [2011] EWCA Crim 3185.

any such application. Should it then be decided, as it should be decided well in advance of the sentencing hearing, that an application for such an order should be made, then care should be taken to ensure compliance with the procedural and evidential provisions of Part 50 of the Criminal Procedure Rules, which are in place for the specific purpose of avoiding the difficulties of the kind that arose in this case and avoiding the possibility that a Sexual Offences Prevention Order might be made without proper consideration of the relevant statutory provisions."

29.08B   The need for the court and the defence to be informed of the fact of a proposed application for a SOPO and the terms of any order sought was a point also made forcefully in *Smith*[9]:

"Arrangements for the provision of a draft order will necessarily vary from court to court. We say no more than that it is essential that there is a written draft, properly considered in advance of the sentencing hearing. The normal requirement should be that it is served on the court and the defendant before the sentencing hearing—we suggest not less than two clear days before but in any event not at the hearing. This will usually be possible because sentencing in such cases only occasionally follows immediately on conviction. Because the draft is likely to require amendment before it is issued by the court staff, it is sensible for it to be available in electronic as well as paper form. If a judge finds that insufficient time for consideration has been given, he has ample power to put the issue back to another hearing, but this is wasteful and the occasion for it ought to be avoided by prior service of the draft."

SOPO Made by a Magistrates' Court on Application by a Chief Officer of Police

29.09   SOPOs arising from a prosecution for a sexual or other offence listed in Schs 3 or 5 are most usually made at the point of sentence, but the provision in s.104(5) does allow a SOPO to be imposed upon a "qualifying offender" even at a later date, on application by a chief officer to a magistrates' court, if there has been subsequent behaviour of a kind that gives "reasonable cause to believe that it is necessary for such an order to be made".[10]

29.09A   The Magistrates' Courts (Sexual Offences Prevention Orders) Rules 2004[11] were amended by the Magistrates' Courts (Sexual Offences Act 2003) (Miscellaneous Amendments) Rules 2012[12] with effect from September 3, 2012 so as to remove the requirement for a summons in respect of a SOPO or interim SOPO to be in a prescribed form.

29.10   The definition of "qualifying offender" in s.106 of the Act covers both domestic and relevant foreign convictions, but by virtue of s.106(3) a SOPO may only be imposed to protect the public within the UK. As noted in the main work, on an application to a magistrates' court both the fact that the subject of the application

[9] At [26].
[10] s.104(5)(b).
[11] SI 2004/1054.
[12] SI 2012/2018.

is a "qualifying offender" and that he has behaved in a relevant manner have to be "proved" to the criminal standard.[13] That is so despite the fact that the proceedings are civil in their nature. Hearsay evidence is admissible, as in any other civil proceedings, but the court must be "sure" on the evidence before it that the qualifying conditions are met.

Necessity and Proportionality

At Appendix B of the main work are some examples of the types of clause that may **29.12** properly feature in SOPOs, depending upon the particular circumstances of the case in question. The examples should be approached with care. The fact that a prohibition may be capable of being formulated in a way that compliance with it might be regarded as being socially beneficial does not mean that it will be either necessary or proportionate in the particular case. What might be termed "shopping list SOPOs" are unlikely to find favour if subject to review on appeal. The greater the number of SOPO terms and the more complex the provisions, the more likely it is that they will be the subject of successful challenge.

In *Jackson*[14] the Court of Appeal said that it is the responsibility of the prosecution **29.12A** to put before the judge in a proposed SOPO provisions which are necessary and proportionate. The Court said it is essential that prosecuting counsel appreciates that he is responsible for putting before the judge an appropriate SOPO which meets the individual case and provides the necessary protection for the future. It is a dereliction of counsel's duty if he fails to consider what is proportionate and what the judge should impose. Furthermore, if there is a question of what are the appropriate provisions that should be included in a particular SOPO, or argument as to the extent to which the prohibitions should be imposed, it is essential that the judge is referred to the leading authorities, so that he or she is able to decide what is appropriate.

SOPOs and computers

Offenders who download indecent images of children ("browsers"), distribute **29.14** such images or otherwise make use of computers when committing scheduled offences are frequently the subject of SOPO applications. Orders made in respect of such offenders have given rise to numerous appeals.

As explained in the main work, the courts quickly recognised the impracticability **29.14A** of imposing a ban on the ownership and/or use of computers. The nature of permissible prohibitions that might be imposed to address the potential for further offending by the medium of the internet have gone through a variety of

---

[13] *Cleveland Police v Haggas* [2009] EWHC 3231 (Admin), applying *B v Chief Constable of Avon and Somerset Constabulary* [2001] 1 All E.R. 562.
[14] [2012] EWCA Crim 2602.

permutations (see, e.g. *Hemsley*[15] and *Mortimer*[16]), but since *Smith and others*[17] the older decisions should be regarded as being of academic interest only. The wording of a SOPO relevant to a "browser", or other cases in which the internet is a relevant issue, as settled upon in *Smith* is:

> *The defendant is prohibited from:*
> 1. *Using any device capable of accessing the internet unless:*
>   (i) *it has the capacity to retain and display the history of internet use, and*
>   (ii) *he makes the device available on request for inspection by a police officer;*
> 2. *Deleting such history;*
> 3. *Possessing any device capable of storing digital images unless he makes it available on request for inspection by a police officer.*

29.14B   The use of social networking sites is a common feature of the type of offending that might properly attract the imposition of a SOPO. *Filor*[18] is an example of a case with a *Smith*-type prohibition tailored to address that issue. In that case there was, in addition to the *Smith* retention and inspection clause, a separate prohibition against the offender "accessing social networking sites (chatrooms)". Cases not infrequently feature offenders making contact via Facebook and other mediums of Internet communication. The use of file sharing sites, which provide ready access to indecent images of children, is also commonplace and the use of those could legitimately be worthy of inclusion in a prohibition if the evidence demonstrates such a potential.

29.14C   There are limitations to the *Smith* formulation. In *Warbutton*[19] the Court addressed the potential for a computer to be set to automatically delete the history of internet usage at the end of each session. Set up in that way, the computer would still have the "capacity to retain and display the history of internet use", it just would not do so. The Court suggested that the addition of the words "and is at all times set to do so" could meet that potential difficulty. Even worded in this way, however, the prohibition does not cater for the fact that the default setting of most computers is to retain the record of the history internet usage for a relatively short period (three to four weeks being typical). With "smart" phones, the history retention period may be shorter still. The frequency of visits by monitoring police officers, even in the case of offenders perceived to be "high risk", varies between different forces, but as little twice a year is not unknown. Even if a browsing history is available to be reviewed, there is a question mark as to how enlightening such a process will be not least because of the volume of data produced by someone who makes significant use of the internet. Periods in which the offender

---

[15] [2010] EWCA Crim 225.
[16] [2010] EWCA Crim 1303.
[17] [2011] EWCA Crim 1772.
[18] [2012] EWCA Crim 850.
[19] [2012] EWCA Crim 3146.

did not have the device set to retain the history of internet use are unlikely to be detected by a review of usage carried out by a monitoring officer, as opposed to a full forensic examination of the computer. Further, the *Smith* formula, even with the *Warbutton* variation, is potentially and very easily rendered effectively worthless by an offender utilising the "in private" browsing setting with the result, it would appear, that no "history" recoverable by the police is created at all. All web browsers have the capacity to operate in that mode as standard.

There was for a time a fashion for imposing upon an offender a prohibition against **29.14D** the possession of a computer or other device capable of accessing the internet without notifying the police of that fact. The potential advantage of such a clause is that if an offender is found in possession of such a device without having given notice then a breach of the SOPO is easily established. Further, an inference could, in appropriate circumstances, be drawn that the reason for the offender's failure to give due notice was the product of the use to which the computer was being put. In *Smith*, however, the Court disapproved of clauses of that nature save in occasional situations where such a prohibition could be regarded as being the only way to prevent offending. The reason given was that such a prohibition places too onerous burden on both the offender and the police. Given the limitations of the *Smith* computer prohibition, there may be an argument in favour of revisiting that position at least where the court is dealing with what might be termed a committed offender.

In some cases there is the potential for a prohibition which requires the installation **29.14E** of either filtering or monitoring software. This is sometimes described as software that is "designed to prevent access to child pornography"[20] or "monitoring software (e.g. Securus, Net Nanny) that is approved and monitored by [X] Police or any other police force area in which he resides".[21] The Court in *Smith* suggested that such a prohibition might be appropriate but pointed out that there may be uncertainty as to what is required and that the policing of the provision might be attended by some difficulty.[22] There is considerable doubt attaching to the effectiveness of software that might be said to be designed to prevent access to indecent images of children. Given the prevalence of tablet devices and "smart" phones capable of accessing the internet, in respect of which there may be no capacity to install such software, it might be thought necessary for there to be very clear evidence that such software exists and can be installed on relevant devices prior to the imposition of such a prohibition. Not all police forces have approved and/or make use of monitoring software such as that developed by Securus.[23] If an offender can only use a computer that has such software installed upon it and which is approved and monitored by the police force in whose area he resides, then that could effectively be converted into a total ban on computer use should he

---

[20] *Morris* [2011] EWCA Crim 2639.
[21] *Turnbull* [2010] EWCA Crim 3149.
[22] Above, fn.17 at [20(iv)], and see *Cilla* [2013] EWCA Crim 1810.
[23] Currently 16 out of 49, but 5 other forces are awaiting funding.

move to an area where such software is not approved and monitored. Any clause of this kind should be the subject of evidence in support and very careful scrutiny and drafting.

29.14F See further on this topic Ian Walden and Martin Wasik, *The Internet: Access Denied Controlled!* [2011] Crim. L.R. 377.

SOPO prohibitions on denying entry to premises

29.17 As noted in the main work, there have been a number of cases in which the courts have disapproved of SOPO clauses creating what amounts to an open-ended search warrant executable at the whim of the police. In *Thompson*[24] the offender was held to be insufficiently "dangerous or recusant" to justify a clause prohibiting him from refusing the police access to his home in order to examine computer equipment that might be on the premises. There is, however, an element of compulsion in the drafting of the prohibition settled upon by the then Vice President in *Smith*.[25] The subject of the prohibition is required to make the "device available on request for inspection", and with a desktop computer it is perhaps difficult to imagine how in practical terms that is to be achieved without granting a police officer access to the place where the computer is being used. The justification, adverted to in *Thompson* and confirmed by the approach in *Smith*, is that "the power of the court to impose prohibitions . . . must include the power to impose prohibitions subject to exceptions or conditions".[26]

29.17A In *M. v Chief Constable of Hampshire Police*[27] s.96B of the 2003 Act (referred to in fn.38 of the main work), which provides for the police to have power to enter and search a notified person's home address, was found to be compatible with art.8 of the ECHR. The Divisional Court held that the powers conferred by the section are proportionate, sensible and necessary and that the safeguards are sufficient given that there is provision for judicial oversight prior to the issue of a warrant and such issue would be open to judicial review. The Court rejected an argument that art.8 requires the offender to be given notice of an application under the section and the opportunity to make representations, on the ground that this would defeat the purpose of the application. It also rejected an argument that s.96B offends against art.7 of the ECHR (prohibition on retroactive penalties), holding that it is a preventative measure and not a punitive one.

Non-contact prohibitions

29.18 Non-contact prohibitions are frequently included in SOPOs, but there have been many cases in which such a prohibition has had to be amended due to the absence

---

[24] [2009] EWCA Crim 3258; see also *Christopher Smith* [2009] EWCA Crim 785.
[25] Above, fn.17.
[26] *Thompson*, above, fn.24 at [16].
[27] [2012] EWHC 4034 (Admin).

of a saving for incidental contact. This was an issue addressed in *Smith* and the suggested formulation settled upon was:

> *The defendant is prohibited from:*
> 1. *living in the same household as any female under the age of 16 unless with the express approval of Social Services for the area;*
> 2. *having any unsupervised contact or communication of any kind with any female under the age of 16, other than*
>   (i) *such as is inadvertent and not reasonably avoidable in the course of lawful daily life, or*
>   (ii) *with the consent of the child's parent or guardian (who has knowledge of his convictions)* <u>and</u> *with the express approval of Social Services for the area.*

The age specified in the prohibition should be 16 unless the trigger or potential **29.18A** offences for which the prohibition is designed to cater are offences contrary to ss.16–19, 25 or 26 of the 2003 Act.[28] Where what might be termed the offender's "target gender" is apparent, there will be no justification for a clause that prohibits contact with a different gender.[29] The Court in *Smith*[30] emphasised the need to take account of the offender's family circumstances and the risk, if any, that the offender might pose to members of the family, balancing against that the entitlement of, for example, the offender's own children to family life. As the balance may change over time, the inclusion of a reference to the approval of the Social Services is critical to cater for the unforeseeable.

The imposition of a non-contact prohibition is unlikely to be challenged in the **29.18B** context of an offender who engages in contact offending. The justification for such a clause in respect of "browsers" is more problematic, but may still exist if there are grounds upon which the court can conclude that there is a significant risk of the offender progressing to contact offending. In one of the conjoined appeals in *Smith*, a non-contact prohibition was upheld in relation to an offender who had been convicted of downloading offences.[31] There are many other examples of non-contact prohibitions being overturned in what might be termed pure "browsing" situations.[32] However, the case of *Turner*[33] may indicate a growing realisation that those who "browse" may legitimately be assessed as having the potential to go on to commit contact offences. In that case, a non-contact prohibition was imposed on a man convicted of possession of indecent images of children. His ex-partner had made a statement describing examples of what she considered to be inappropriate behaviour by the appellant with, and demonstrated sexual interest in, female children. The Court of Appeal upheld the prohibition, stating that

---

[28] Above, fn.17 at [21].
[29] *Morris* [2013] EWCA Crim 467, at [33]–[36].
[30] Above, fn.17.
[31] *Hall*, above, fn.17 at [34]–[43].
[32] See, e.g. *Turnbull* [2010] EWCA Crim 3149; *Lea* [2011] EWCA Crim 487; *Fung* [2012] EWCA Crim 761; *James* [2012] EWCA Crim 81.
[33] Unreported, January 30, 2013 (CACD).

whilst it is not acceptable to include such a prohibition "just in case", one may be imposed if the court finds there is a risk of contact offences, and there does not have to be a finding of certainty. In this case, the finding of risk was justified by the combined force of the ex-partner's evidence as to her concerns about the appellant's sexual interest in real young girls, the subsequent discovery of the indecent images, and the appellant's continuing denial of any sexual interest in young girls.

29.18C   It is beholden on a court imposing a non-contact prohibition in such circumstances to explain why it considers it necessary so to do.

29.18D   A form of non-contact prohibition that features not infrequently is one which bars an offender from going to parks or swimming pools or hanging around outside schools. Such clauses must be expressed with sufficient clarity that the offender knows where he can and cannot go and also to enable the prohibition to be sensibly policed.

29.18E   In *R. (on the application of Paul Richards) v Teesside Magistrates' Court and the Chief Constable of Cleveland*,[34] the use of an electronic tagging device as a method of monitoring and thus enforcing a non-contact prohibition was approved. Such a measure is only likely to be justified in an extreme case.

RELATIONSHIP BETWEEN SOPOS AND OTHER SENTENCES

29.19   A prohibition in a SOPO will not be "necessary" if its effect is merely to duplicate another relevant regime. In *Smith*[35] the Court of Appeal compared and contrasted the variety of other sentences, orders and conditions to which a sex offender may be expected to be subject as a result of a conviction and identified the type of overlap that should be avoided. It said that SOPOs should not be expressed in the same terms and/or in a way that has the same effect as a disqualification from working with children imposed under s.26 of the Criminal Justice and Court Services Act 2000 (now repealed) or the "barred list" maintained by the Disclosure and Barring Service (which was established in succession to the Independent Safeguarding Authority by the Protection of Freedoms Act 2012). It was also held in *Smith* that it would almost never be necessary to impose a SOPO at the same time as a sentence of imprisonment for public protection, but that the same does not apply to determinate or extended sentences. The reason is that whilst conditions may be attached to the licence, that licence will have a defined and limited life. The SOPO by contrast can extend beyond it and this may be necessary to protect the public from further offences and serious sexual harm as a result.[36]

---

[34] [2013] EWHC 2208.
[35] Above, fn.17 at [9]–[17].
[36] Above, fn.17 at [14]–[15].

Since the decision in *Smith*, the position with regard to the potential interaction **29.19A**
of SOPOs to other sentences has changed somewhat. Disqualification orders
under the Criminal Justice and Court Services Act 2000 have been abolished, and
inclusion in a barred list is automatic and not potentially subject to the making of
representations only where the offender has committed one of the more serious
sexual offences.[37] These changes mean that a court could be justified in imposing
a SOPO prohibition couched in much the same language as disqualifications under
the Criminal Justice and Court Services Act 2000 were previously expressed in a
case where the offender has committed a relatively low level offence (such as
making indecent photographs of children) but it would be legitimate to seek to
prohibit contact in a work or other situation.

EFFECT OF A SOPO

If the court makes a SOPO in respect of an offender who is already subject to such **29.20**
an order, the earlier order "ceases to have effect".[38] Accordingly, when a "new"
SOPO is made, any terms from a pre-existing SOPO that are still relevant and
appropriate will have to be included in the new order or they will otherwise no
longer apply. In *Pelletier*[39] the Court of Appeal underlined the need to check that
the SOPO as drawn up by the court clerk actually reflects that which the
sentencing judge imposed. In that case, there were differences between the order
as enunciated by the judge in court and as drawn up. The Court held that the
former was determinative and quashed the appellant's conviction for breaching
the order as drawn.

VARIATION, RENEWAL OR DISCHARGE OF A SOPO

In *Hoath and Standage*[40] the Court of Appeal had occasion to examine the **29.23**
relationship between s.108 of the 2003 Act, which provides for applications to vary
SOPOs, and s.110, which provides a right of appeal to the Crown Court in respect
of SOPOs and interim SOPOs imposed in the magistrates' court, and to the Court
of Appeal in respect of SOPOs imposed in the Crown Court. The Court in *Hoath*
held that there is a right of appeal to the Court of Appeal under s.110(3)(a) against
the refusal of the Crown Court to vary a SOPO.[41] Further, the Court said that
such a refusal in the context of an application under s.108 was, by reference to
s.11(3) of the Criminal Appeal Act 1968, a "sentence", thus permitting the Court
to quash the order of the Crown Court and to make "another appropriate
order".

---

[37] See the Safeguarding Vulnerable Groups Act 2006, s.2 and Sch.3, and the Safeguarding
Vulnerable Groups Act (Prescribed Criteria and Miscellaneous Provisions) Regulations 2009 (SI
2009/37).
[38] s.107(6).
[39] [2012] EWCA Crim 1060.
[40] [2011] EWCA Crim 274.
[41] The point was considered in *Warbutton*, above, fn.19.

The Court expressed the view that the Crown Court was not the venue in which to address the issue of a SOPO being non-compliant with *Smith*.[42] Simon J. suggested that applications to the Crown Court should be for more limited purposes:

"10. Although minor but necessary adjustments to the order may be required, in which case application should be made to the Crown Court to vary the order, in circumstances where a defendant has not appealed to the Court of Appeal, we would not expect the Crown Court to make other than minor adjustments to the term of the order, at least in the short term.

11. Usually the defendant will need to rely on a change of circumstances. In such a case, the Crown Court will need to be satisfied that the order in its original form is no longer necessary for the statutory purpose of protecting the public (or particular members of the public) from serious sexual harm from the defendant, or that those objectives can properly and sufficiently be secured by the proposed variation."

This is potentially a somewhat inconvenient position, in terms of what might be thought to be the most expedient and cost effective way of dealing with pre-*Smith* SOPOs, but it was confirmed in *Aldridge and Eaton*.[43] *Beeden*[44] is an example of an order being varied in the Crown Court in order to remove a non-*Smith* compliant term.

RIGHT OF APPEAL AGAINST IMPOSITION OF A SOPO

29.25   See the discussion in para.29.23, above. In *Instone and others*[45] the Court of Appeal was faced with appeals sought to be advanced out of time against SOPOs imposed at the same time as a sentence of Imprisonment for Public Protection ("IPP"), the basis for the applications being the decision in *Smith*.[46] The Court set out the position thus:

"19. However, the fresh guidance given by *Smith* does not provide the basis for a successful appeal against a SOPO imposed long before *Smith* was decided and which, but for the licensing conditions which will be imposed on release, was made with every justification. Sentence is imposed on the basis of the relevant legislation, the principles, practice and guidance, whether from this court or the Sentencing Council, which are current at the date when sentence is imposed. An existing sentence should not be varied on appeal because of subsequent changes to them."

In *James*[47] the court dismissed an appeal against the imposition of a sentence of IPP imposed prior to *Smith* but declined to remove the SOPO notwithstanding the guidance provided therein. *Neish* and *M*,[48] however, are examples of the court adjusting SOPOs that were not complaint with *Smith* in order to make them so.

---

[42] Above, fn.17.
[43] [2012] EWCA Crim 1456.
[44] [2013] EWCA Crim 63.
[45] [2012] EWCA Crim 1792.
[46] Above, fn.17.
[47] [2013] EWCA Crim 847.
[48] [2012] EWCA Crim 62 and [2012] EWCA Crim 852.

BREACH OF A SOPO

There is no power to impose a SOPO for a breach offence.[49] If a SOPO as **29.26** originally imposed was clearly invalid then it is suggested that in an extreme case it could be regarded as unenforceable.[50]

There is no current sentencing guideline for breaching a SOPO but the passage **29.26A** from the judgment of Leveson J. (as he then was) in *Fenton*,[51] set out in the main work, is frequently cited. In *Brown*[52] it was suggested that the quality of the acts constituting the breach are not the only consideration; the protection of children is the foremost issue. In *Moore*[53] it was said that the sentencing judge is entitled to treat an offender as dangerous and as deliberately breaching the order for a sinister purpose, even if no overtly sexual activity has been established.

The Court of Appeal in *Morris*[54] reviewed a range of cases dealing with breach of **29.26B** a SOPO and reduced a sentence of 16 months' imprisonment to one of 10 months' in respect of an offender who had created a situation whereby there was an obvious risk that he might offend by committing a contact offence, albeit he had not in fact done so. The Court observed:

> "The breaches here created real and obvious risks which it is unnecessary to spell out. SOPOs are designed to protect children from such risks. Those who breach such orders must expect to be dealt with severely but proportionately. It is clear that the applicant recognised the purpose of the SOPO in his case but that, nevertheless, he took chances and flouted the order on two separate dates. Accordingly, the sentence of imprisonment was, in our judgment, not wrong in principle."

In *Beeden*[55] the offender, who had a history of offending against children and in **29.26C** respect of indecent images, was made subject to a SOPO one term of which prohibited him from "owning or having personal possession of any piece of equipment or device that is capable of connecting to the internet". He breached this prohibition on two occasions, but by the time the case came to be sentenced the prohibition had been removed in the light of the guidance in *Smith*.[56] Despite the fact that, as the SOPO stood by the time sentence was imposed, his conduct would not have constituted any offence at all, the Court of Appeal still upheld the sentence of immediate custody imposed at first instance.

As a matter of practice, sentences for SOPO breaches tend to range from 9 **29.26D** months' to 3 years' imprisonment, depending on the facts of the breach and the nature of the offender's antecedents.

---

[49] *Hadley* [2012] EWCA Crim 1997.
[50] *R.(W.) v DPP* [2005] EWHC 1333, but see *Proctor* [2014] EWCA Crim 162.
[51] [2007] 1 Cr. App. R.(S.) 97, at [25].
[52] (2002) 1 Cr. App. R.(S.) 1.
[53] (2005) Cr. App. R.(S.) 101.
[54] [2013] EWCA Crim 350.
[55] [2013] EWCA 63.
[56] Above, fn.17.

FOREIGN TRAVEL ORDERS

29.29 The Magistrates' Courts (Foreign Travel Orders) Rules 2004[57] were amended by the Magistrates' Courts (Foreign Travel Orders) (Amendment) Rules 2010[58] which substituted new forms of summons and of FTO. The amendments were consequential upon the changes made to the FTO regime by the Policing and Crime Act 2009, as explained in the main work.

The Rules were further amended with effect from 3 September 2012 by the Magistrates' Courts (Sexual Offences Act 2003) (Miscellaneous Amendments) Rules 2012,[59] which delete the prescribed forms of summons and FTO and substitute a list of the information that must be included in an FTO.

RISK OF SEXUAL HARM ORDERS

29.38 The Magistrates' Courts (Risk of Sexual Harm Orders) Rules 2004[60] were amended with effect from September 3, 2012 by the Magistrates' Courts (Sexual Offences Act 2003) (Miscellaneous Amendments) Rules 2012,[61] which delete the prescribed forms of summons and RSHO and substitute a list of the information that must be included in an RSHO.

29.40 The standard of proof on an application for a RSHO under s.123(4) of the 2003 Act is the criminal standard.[62]

ANTI-SOCIAL BEHAVIOUR, CRIME AND POLICING BILL

29.46 As noted in the Introduction to this chapter, the Anti-Social Behaviour and Policing Bill currently before Parliament[63] will, if enacted in its present form, make major changes to the scheme of the protective orders considered in this chapter. SOPOs and Foreign Travel Orders FTOs will in effect be combined in a single order entitled a SHPO, and RHSOs and FTOs will be combined in a SRO. This will be achieved by amending the 2003 Act by inserting new provisions relating to SHPOs (ss.103A–J) and SROs (ss.122A–J) to replace the provisions

[57] SI 2004/1051.
[58] SI 2010/605.
[59] SI 2012/2018.
[60] SI 2004/1053.
[61] SI 2012/2018.
[62] *Commissioner of Police of the Metropolis v Ebanks* [2012] EWHC 2368 (Admin).
[63] Royal Assent anticipated March 2014.

relating to SOPOs, FTOs and RSHOs which will be repealed. Existing orders will remain in force and be dealt with as at present, although the Bill provides (cl.105(5)) that after a period of five years from the commencement date, existing SOPOs, etc, will "have effect, with any necessary modifications . . . as if the provisions of the order were provisions of a new order".

The drafting of the new provisions is very similar, at least in their effect, to those   **29.47** in the 2003 Act that they will replace.[64] Perhaps the most significant difference relates to the threshold test for making a SHPO, whereby a defendant will be eligible for a SHPO if there is a risk of "sexual harm", whereas under the present scheme the contemplated risk has to be of "serious sexual harm". Also, the new SHPO will seek to protect children and vulnerable adults "outside the United Kingdom", i.e. in effect including what was previously a FTO within the scope of a SHPO. In this way FTOs will fall within the jurisdiction of the Crown Court. SROs, as RHSOs before them, will be made as appropriate by the magistrates' court on application by a chief officer of police or the Director General of the National Crime Agency. SROs may encompass a "prohibition on foreign travel". Breach of an SHPO or SRO will be an either way offence with a maximum penalty of 5 years' imprisonment on conviction on indictment. There is a scheme for interim orders, as at present.

---

[64] See Terry Thomas and David Thompson, *New Civil Orders to Contain Sexual Offending—A Matter of "Purposive Logic"?* 177 C.L. & J. 703, questioning the application of the civil standard of proof to consideration of the need for a SHPO or SRO.

CHAPTER 30

THE ASSESSMENT AND TREATMENT OF SEX OFFENDERS AFTER SENTENCING

There have been no updates to this chapter since the fourth edition published. Please refer to the main work at p.1,127 onwards for commentary on this area.

CHAPTER 31

SEXUAL OFFENCES IN THE YOUTH COURT*

INTRODUCTION

To update the figures given in the main work, sexual offences continue to form   **31.02**
only a very small proportion of youth court cases: in 2011–12, 1,888 sexual
offences were proven against young people, less than 2 per cent of all offences dealt
with in that court.[1]

PRELIMINARY MATTERS

THE DECISION TO PROSECUTE YOUTHS

Code for Crown Prosecutors

Paragraph 4.12(d) of the *Code for Crown Prosecutors* (as revised in February 2013)[2]   **31.10**
identifies the age of the suspect as a factor to be considered when assessing if the
case passes the public interest stage. It states that:

> "The criminal justice system treats children and young people differently from adults
> and significant weight must be attached to the age of the suspect if they are a child or
> young person under 18. The best interests of the child or young person must be
> considered including whether a prosecution is likely to have an adverse impact on his

---

* The authors are indebted to Gillian Jones, Barrister, and Naomi Parsons, Barrister, both of Red
Lion Chambers, who were the principal drafters of the update of this chapter.
[1] Youth Justice Statistics 2011/12, England and Wales.
[2] The *Code* is available at *http://www.cps.gov.uk/publications/docs/code_2013_accessible_english.pdf*
[accessed January 2, 2014].

or her future prospects that is disproportionate to the seriousness of the offending. Prosecutors must have regard to the principal aim of the youth justice system which is to prevent offending by children and young people . . . "

It appears that particular consideration should be given to the suitability of an out-of-court disposal, as the Code continues:

"However, there may be circumstances which mean that notwithstanding the fact that the suspect is under 18, a prosecution is in the public interest. These include . . . where the absence of an admission means that out-of-court disposals which might have addressed the offending behaviour are not available."

Legal Guidance: Youth Offenders and *Legal Guidance: Sexual Offences Act 2003*

31.14 Note also the CPS's *Legal Guidance: Youth Offenders*[3] which provides:

"Prosecutors are reminded of the need to consider all the circumstances surrounding the offence and the circumstances of the youth before reaching a decision to prosecute and to apply all relevant CPS policies and documents. Failure to do so may result in proceedings for judicial review: *R v Chief Constable of Kent ex parte L, R v DPP ex parte B* [1991] 93 Cr App R 416."

The Guidance then sets out additional factors to consider, including a set of aggravating and mitigating factors. One aggravating feature is that the offence is a sexual offence.

Rape and offences against children under 13 (ss.5–8 of the Sexual Offences Act 2003)

31.15 The CPS's *Legal Guidance: Youth Offenders* provides that when reviewing a case in which a youth under 18 is alleged to have committed an offence contrary to ss.5–8 of the 2003 Act, prosecutors should obtain and consider:

- the views of local authority Children's and Young Peoples Service;
- any risk assessment or report conducted by the local authority or youth offending service in respect of sexually harmful behaviour (such as AIM (Assessment, Intervention and Moving On));
- background information and history of the parties; and
- the views of the families of all parties.

And careful regard should be paid to the following factors:

- the relative ages of the parties;
- the existence of and nature of any relationship;
- the sexual and emotional maturity of the parties and any emotional or physical effects as a result of the conduct;
- whether the child under 13 in fact freely consented (even though in law this is not a defence) or a genuine mistake as to age was in fact made;

---

[3] Available at *http://www.cps.gov.uk/legal/v_to_z/youth_offenders/* [accessed January 2, 2014].

- whether any element of seduction, breach of any duty of responsibility to the child or other exploitation is disclosed by the evidence; and
- the impact of a prosecution on each child involved.

REPRIMANDS, WARNINGS AND YOUTH CONDITIONAL CAUTIONS

Reprimands and warnings (known as the "final warning scheme") were abolished[4]   **31.22**
and a new form of disposal, the youth caution, was introduced with effect from April 8, 2013, by s.135 of the Legal Aid, Sentencing and Punishment of Offenders Act 2012. The new scheme comprises youth cautions (ss.66ZA of the Crime and Disorder Act 1998 ("1998 Act")) and youth conditional cautions (s.66A). Youth cautions and youth conditional cautions are not court orders. However, familiarity with these pre-court disposal schemes are important in the youth court: not only are they relevant to considerations of bail and sentence, but representations can sometimes be made to adjourn proceedings if a case is one which may suitable for an alternative disposal.[5] CPS decisions on case disposal are judicially reviewable.[6]

By s.66ZA(1)(a)–(c) of the 1998 Act, a youth caution can be given if there is sufficient evidence to charge, the offence is admitted, and the constable does not consider that the offender should be prosecuted or given a youth conditional caution. Guidance on such disposals can be found in *Youth Cautions – Guidance for Police and Youth Offending Teams*, issued by the Ministry of Justice and the Youth Justice Board in April 2013.[7] By virtue of ss.80(1)(d) and 113(1) of the 1998 Act, youth cautions trigger notification requirements in relation to the same set of offences that trigger notification where a person is convicted at court.

Youth conditional cautions

Guidance on the use of youth conditional cautions is to be found in *The Director's*   **31.27**
Guidance on Youth Conditional Cautions[8] and the *Code of Practice for Youth Conditional Cautions*[9] (both revised April 2013). The Director's Guidance states that conditional cautions can be used for all offences classified (in the case of adults) as summary only or triable either way. Cases which are triable only on indictment in the case of adults must be referred to a prosecutor before a youth conditional caution is given.

---

[4] By the repeal of ss.65 and 66 of the 1998 Act.
[5] *F v CPS* (2004) 168 J.P. 93.
[6] See, e.g. *S. v DPP* [2006] EWHC 2231 (Admin) where the court scrutinised the CPS's decision to prosecute a 15-year-old for an offence under ss.9 and 13 of the 2003 Act in light of the CPS guidance *Legal Guidance: Youth Offenders* and *Legal Guidance: Sexual Offences*.
[7] Available at *http://www.justice.gov.uk/downloads/oocd/youth-cautions-guidance-police-yots-oocd.pdf* [accessed January 2, 2014].
[8] *http://www.cps.gov.uk/publications/directors_guidance/youth_conditional_cautions.html* [accessed January 2, 2014].
[9] *http://www.justice.gov.uk/downloads/oocd/code-practice-youth-conditional-cautions-oocd.pdf* [accessed January 2, 2014].

Mode of Trial

31.29 The *Code for Crown Prosecutors*,[10] updated in January 2013, includes a new section on mode of trial of youths. It states (para.8.3) that prosecutors should try youths in the youth court wherever possible, as that is the court best designed to meet their specific needs. It states that a trial in the Crown Court should be reserved for the most serious offences or where the interests of justice require that the youth is tried jointly with an adult.

Bail

31.31 Sections 91–102 of the Legal Aid, Sentencing and Punishment of Offenders Act 2012 replace the bail provisions in s.23 of the Children and Young Persons Act 1969. Under the new provisions, if the court refuses bail, there are two options for those under 18:

- Remand to local authority accommodation, with or without conditions (ss.92–97). If certain conditions are met, the court may consider imposing electronic monitoring as a condition where the child has been charged with a sexual offence (ss.93(2) and 94).
- Remand to youth detention accommodation (s.102). If the youth is charged with a sexual offence, the court can only remand if the child has reached the age of 12, and such detention is the only adequate way to protect the public from death or serious personal injury or to prevent the commission of imprisonable offences by the child (s.98).

TRIAL IN THE YOUTH COURT

Constitution and Operation of a Youth Court

31.34 In *R. v Birmingham Justices, Ex p. F (A Juvenile)*[11] it was held that the court should consider representations before proceeding with a single-sex Bench.

Disclosure

31.44 Disclosure is now governed by Pt 22 of the Criminal Procedure Rules 2013, which came into force on October 7, 2013.[12]

---

[10] Above, fn.2.
[11] [2000] Crim. L.R. 588.
[12] The Rules, with amendments, are available at *http://www.justice.gov.uk/courts/procedure-rules/criminal/rulesmenu* [accessed January 2, 2014].

OATHS

The words "I promise" are used in place of "I swear" in any oath administered   **31.57**
to and taken by any person before a youth court and any child or young person
before any other court.[13]

SPECIAL MEASURES

Persons eligible for special measures

Footnote 66: Section 98 of the Coroners and Justice Act 2009, which amends   **31.60**
s.16(1)(a) of the Youth Justice and Criminal Evidence Act 1999 so as to extend
automatic eligibility for special measures from those under 17 to those under 18,
came into force on June 27, 2011.[14]

Types of special measures

Footnote 71: Section 28 of the Youth Justice and Criminal Evidence Act 1999,   **31.61**
which provides for pre-recorded cross-examination where a special measures
direction provides for video-recorded examination-in-chief under s.27 of the Act,
is not in force as of the date of writing (January 3, 2014). However, the Ministry
of Justice has announced a six-month pilot of the provision for child victims and
witnesses and vulnerable adults, to be run from the end of 2013 in the Crown
Court at Leeds, Liverpool and Kingston-upon-Thames: see para.18.34, above.

Procedure

Footnote 74: For rr.29.3 and 29.10 of the Criminal Procedure Rules 2010, see now   **31.63**
rr.29.3 and 29.10 of the Criminal Procedure Rules 2013.

MODE OF TRIAL

The procedure for determining the mode of trial of youths was modified on the   **31.70**
coming into force of ss.24A–24D of the Magistrates' Courts Act 1980 on June 18,
2012. The effect of those provisions, which were enacted in the Criminal Justice
Act 2003 ("CJA 2003"), is to introduce a mode of trial procedure similar to that
for adults. Thus, where there is a possibility that the youth may be tried in the
Crown Court (in one of the limited circumstances explained in the main work), the
youth will be invited to plead guilty or not guilty. If a guilty plea is entered, the
youth court can proceed to the sentencing stage. If the offence is one to which s.91

---

[13] Children and Young Persons Act 1968, s.28.
[14] Children and Young Persons Act 1968, s.28.

of the Powers of Criminal Courts (Sentencing) Act 2000 ("PCC(S)A 2000") applies, then the youth court may commit to the Crown Court for sentence under s.3B of the Act. If a not-guilty plea is entered, the youth court will determine mode of trial in accordance with the procedure set out in the main work.

The bringing into force of the provisions of the Magistrates' Courts Act 1980 referred to above was accompanied by the repeal of s.24(1)(a) of the Act, in which the term "grave crime" appeared. Accordingly, references in the main work to "grave crimes" in this and subsequent paragraphs should be read as a reference to offences under s.91(1) of the PCC(S)A 2000.

31.71   The *Code for Crown Prosecutors*[15] states (in para.8.3) that prosecutors should try youths in the youth court wherever possible, as that is the court best designed to meet their specific needs. It goes on to state that a trial in the Crown Court should be reserved for the most serious of offences or where the interests of justice require that the youth is tried jointly with an adult.

SECTION 91 PCC(S)A 2000: GRAVE CRIMES

31.72   Section 24(1) of the Magistrates' Court Act 1980 as amended by Sch.3 para.9 of the CJA 2003 (brought into force in relation to specified local justice areas by SI 2012/1320 and SI 2012/2574) provides:

> "(1) Where a person under the age of 18 years appears or is brought before a magistrates' court on an information charging him with an indictable offence he shall, subject to section 51 and 51A of the Crime and Disorder Act 1998 and subject to sections 24A and 24B below, be tried summarily".

Section 51(7)(b) of the 1998 Act as amended by Sch.3 para.18 of the CJA 2003 (brought into force in relation to specified local justice areas by SI 2012/1320 and SI 2012/2574) provides that where:

> " . . . a child or young person appears or is brought before the court on the same or a subsequent occasion jointly charged with A [i.e. an adult] with an indictable offence for which A is sent to trial . . . or an indictable offence which appears to be related to that offence, the court shall, if it considers it necessary in the interests of justice to do so, send the child or young person forthwith to the Crown Court for trial for the indictable offence."

Section 51A(3) of the 1998 Act as amended by Sch.3 para.18 of the CJA 2003 (brought into force in relation to specified local justice areas by SI 2012/1320 and SI 2012/2574) sets out the conditions on the basis of which the court shall send the child or young person forthwith to the Crown Court for trial. They are as follows:

> (a) the offence falls within s.51A(12), i.e. it is an offence of homicide that attracts a minimum sentence under s.51A of the Firearms Act 1968 or s.29(3) of the Violent Crime Reduction Act 2006;

---

[15] Above, fn.2.

(b) the offence is mentioned in s.91(1) of the PCC(S)A 2000 (other than an offence mentioned in s.51A(3)(d) of the 1998 Act, below, in relation to which it appears to the court as mentioned there) and the court considers that if the child or young person is found guilty of the offence it ought to be possible to sentence him in pursuance of s.91(3) of that Act);

(c) notice is given to the court under s.51B or s.51C of the 1998 Act, which concern respectively serious or complex fraud cases and cases involving an alleged offence under inter alia the Sexual Offences Act 1956, the Protection of Children Act 1978 or the 2003 Act, where the welfare of a child witness requires the case to proceed without delay to the Crown Court; or

(d) the offence is a specified offence (within the meaning of s.224 of the CJA 2003) and it appears to the court that if the child or young person is found guilty the criteria for the imposition of a sentence under s.226B of that Act would be met (under which young persons convicted on indictment of certain grave crimes may be sentenced to be detained for long periods).

It follows from the provisions mentioned in the last paragraph that the reference **31.73** in the main work to s.91(1) or (2) of the PCC(S)A 2000 should now be read as a reference to s.91(1) alone. The offences mentioned in s.91(1) and (2) were known as "grave crimes", a phrase taken from s.24(1)(a) of the Magistrates' Court Act 1980. As noted above, that provision is now repealed and so it is no longer appropriate to use the term "grave crime" in this context; reference should be made instead to offences mentioned in s.91(1) of the PCC(S)A 2000.

The application of the "grave crimes" exception

As noted above, following the repeal of s.24(1)(a) of the Magistrates' Courts Act **31.81** 1980, in which the term "grave crime" appeared, the reference in the heading to "grave crimes" should be read as a reference to s.91 of the PCC(S)A 2000.

Grave crimes: rape and other sexual offences in the youth court

As noted above, following the repeal of s.24(1)(a) of the Magistrates' Courts Act **31.86** 1980, in which the term "grave crime" appeared, the reference in the heading to "grave crimes" should be read as a reference to s.91 of the PCC(S)A 2000.

"Specified" Offences: Dangerous Offenders

Section 51A(3) of the 1998 Act was amended by the Legal Aid, Sentencing and **31.92** Punishment of Offenders Act 2012[16] with effect from December 3, 2012, to reflect changes made by that Act to the sentencing provisions of the Criminal Justice Act

---

[16] s.126 and Sch.21 para.6.

2003, namely the abolition of detention for public protection and the enactment of a replacement provision governing extended sentences in relation to persons under 18. Section 51A(3)(d) as amended reads as follows:

"(d) the offence is a specified offence (within the meaning of section 224 of the Criminal Justice Act 2003) and it appears to the court that if he is found guilty of the offence the criteria for the imposition of a sentence under section 226B [*extended sentence for certain violent sexual offences: persons under 18*] of that Act would be met."

Grave crimes and specified offences

31.99   As noted above, following the repeal of s.24(1)(a) of the Magistrates' Courts Act 1980, in which the term "grave crime" appeared, the reference in the heading and body of this paragraph to "grave crimes" should be read as a reference to s.91 of the PCC(S)A 2000.

Prospective Changes To Mode of Trial Procedure For Youths

31.102   Sections 24A–24D of the Magistrates' Courts Act 1980 are now in force: see para.31.70, above.

SENTENCING YOUTHS FOR SEXUAL OFFENCES

Sentencing Guidelines

Sexual Offences Act 2003: Definitive Guideline

31.126   As noted in para.1.20 et seq., above, this Guideline, published in 2007 by the Sentencing Guidelines Council, has been superseded by a new Definitive Guideline issued by the Sentencing Council. The new guideline applies to offenders aged 18 and older sentenced on or after April 1, 2014.[17] The Council is proposing to undertake a review of the youth sentencing guidelines in Autumn 2014. In its consultation on the draft guideline,[18] the Council noted that child sexual offences committed by young offenders can be very different in nature to those committed by adults, not least because of the use of social media. It was also concerned that producing guidelines for this narrow range of youth offending, without considering the wider approach that should be adopted to the sentencing of those under 18, could cause problems when it came to review youth sentencing generally. Accordingly, the Council decided not to cover youth offending in the

---

[17] Although the new guideline was published in December 2013, the previous guideline continued to apply to all sexual offences sentenced before April 1, 2014: cf. *Boakye and others* [2012] EWCA Crim 838. From that date the new guideline applies to all such offences, whenever committed.

[18] *Sexual Offences Guideline: Consultation* (December 6, 2012).

new guideline. But in order to minimise the risk of sentencers continuing to follow the SGC guideline, or of creating a sentencing "gap", it included the following narrative guidance designed to mitigate the risk of its decision causing confusion:

> "When sentencing offenders under 18, a court must in particular:
> - follow the definitive guideline **Overarching Principles—Sentencing Youths**; and have regard to:
> - the principal aim of the youth justice system (to prevent offending by children and young people); [19] and
> - the welfare of the young offender." [20]

Magistrates' Court Sentencing Guidelines: Definitive Guideline

This Guideline was updated in October 2009.[21] It covers a range of sexual offences **31.128** more commonly dealt with in the magistrates' court. It is based on the *Sexual Offences Act 2003: Definitive Guideline*, although it goes into greater detail and thereby provide more guidance by way of sentencing. The offences covered are:

- sexual assault (ss.3 and 7 of the 2003 Act),
- child prostitution or pornography offences (ss.48–50),
- exploitation of prostitution (ss.52 and 53),
- keeping a brothel for use in prostitution (s.55),
- exposure (s.66),
- voyeurism (s.67),
- sexual activity in a public lavatory (s.71),
- indecent photographs of children (s.1 of the Protection of Children Act 1978 and s.160 of the Criminal Justice Act 1960), and
- failure to comply with notification requirements or supply of false information for the sex offender register (s.91 of the 2003 Act).

DANGEROUSNESS PROVISIONS

For recent amendments to the provisions of the CJA 2003 relating to the **31.131** sentencing of dangerous offenders, see Ch.27, above.

NOTIFICATION

Reprimands and warnings were abolished[22] and a new form of disposal, the youth **31.145** caution, was introduced with effect from April 8, 2013, by the Legal Aid, Sentencing and Punishment of Offenders Act 2012: see para.31.22, above. The

---

[19] s.37 of the 1998 Act.
[20] s.44 of the Children and Young Persons Act 1933.
[21] Available at *http://sentencingcouncil.judiciary.gov.uk/guidelines/guidelines-to-download.htm* [accessed January 2, 2014].
[22] By the repeal of ss.65 and 66 of the 1998 Act and the insertion into the Act of s.66ZA.

notification requirements apply to those who have been cautioned in respect of an offence mentioned in para.31.144 of the main work. Thus, a child or young person will be required to register on the sex offenders' register in the event that they accept a youth caution for such an offence. This requirement should be explained to the youth, or to the appropriate adult, before a caution is accepted.[23]

---

[23] *Youth Cautions—Guidance for Police and Youth Offending Teams* (Ministry of Justice/Youth Justice Board, 2013), above, fn.7 para.11.10.

CHAPTER 32

SEXUAL OFFENCES IN NORTHERN IRELAND

by H.H. Judge David McFarland

INTRODUCTION

On February 12, 2010 policing and justice powers were devolved to the Northern **32.01** Ireland Assembly by the Northern Ireland Act 1998 (Devolution of Policing and Justice Functions) Order 2010.[1]

The Court of Appeal in *Wilkinson*[2] stated that when dealing with the common law **32.02** offence of rape, and recklessness as to the defendant's state of mind as to whether the victim was consenting, the form of words approved by the English Court of Appeal in *Adkins*[3] was acceptable, i.e. "a man is reckless as to whether the woman consented to sexual intercourse if you are sure that he neither knew nor cared whether she was consenting or not. In other words his state of mind was that he could not have cared less."

In relation to the offence of unlawful carnal knowledge (contrary to ss.4 and 5 of the Criminal Law Amendment Act 1885[4]) the Court of Appeal in *Hamilton*[5]

---

[1] SI 2010/976. See also Department of Justice Act (Northern Ireland) 2010 c.3 (NI).
[2] [2011] NICA 29.
[3] [2000] 2 All E.R. 185.
[4] Ch.69 48 & 49 Vict.
[5] [2011] NICA 46.

decided that the removal of the "young man's defence"[6] did not contravene any ECHR rights of the defendant. A further argument as to the requirement on the prosecution to prove knowledge of the girl's age was also rejected in *Brown*.[7] This argument was based on a submission that the removal of the defences in the 1885 Act by the Criminal Law Amendment Act (Northern Ireland) 1923[8] resulted in the legislation being silent on the question of *mens rea* and therefore required its importation.[9]

32.03 The abolition of the presumption that a boy under the age of 14 was incapable of sexual intercourse came into operation on July 28, 2003.[10] Doli incapax (the rebuttable presumption that a child of 10 or over but less than 14 is incapable of committing a criminal offence) was abolished on December 1, 1998.[11]

Sexual Offences (Northern Ireland) Order 2008

32.05 The provisions of ss.57–59 of the 2003 Act were applied to Northern Ireland under art.11 of the Sexual Offences (NI Consequential Amendments) Order 2008.[12] Section 109 of the Protection of Freedoms Act 2012[13] (which repealed ss.57–59 and introduced an extended new s.59A) did not apply to Northern Ireland. Section 6 of the Criminal Justice Act (Northern Ireland) 2013[14] (not yet in force) introduces a new offence (s.58A of the 2003 Act) of trafficking outside the UK for sexual exploitation. As a consequence, all forms of trafficking for sexual exploitation will now be offences in Northern Ireland—into the UK (s.57), within the UK (s.58), outside the UK (s.58A) and out of the UK (s.59). This mirrors the position in England & Wales, although the offences applicable there are contained entirely within s.59A of the 2003 Act.

Application of 2003 Act to Northern Ireland

32.07 To address the decision of the Supreme Court in *F. and Thompson*,[15] s.1 of the Criminal Justice Act (Northern Ireland) 2013 inserted a new s.82(7) and Sch.3A in the 2003 Act[16] which, when brought into force, will provide for a review of an

---

[6] Established in England & Wales for men aged 23 and under by s.2 of the Criminal Law Amendment Act 1922 (c.56).

[7] [2011] NICA 47 and [2013] UKSC 43.

[8] c.8.

[9] See, e.g. *B. v DPP* [2000] 2 A.C. 428 and *R. v K* [2001] UKHL 41. However, this argument was regarded as contrived by the Supreme Court, see [2013] UKSC 43 at [36].

[10] Criminal Justice (2003 Order) (Commencement No.2) Order (NI) 2003 SR 2003/352 (c.27).

[11] Articles 1(2) and 3 of the Criminal Justice (Northern Ireland) Order 1998/2839 (NI 20). For a correct direction in relation to doli incapax, see *R. v ML* [2013] NICA 23.

[12] 2008/1779.

[13] c.9.

[14] c.7.

[15] [2010] UKSC 17.

[16] Equivalent to the new s.91F(1) of the 2003 Act introduced in England & Wales by the Sexual Offences Act 2003 (Remedial) Order 2012 (No.1883).

indefinite notification requirement after 15 years (8 years in the case of an offender who was under 18 at the time of the offence).

Section 2 of the Criminal Justice Act (Northern Ireland) 2013, when brought into force, will require an offender to notify police of any intended absence of more than three days from his home address.

SENTENCING

In *R. v ML*[17] the Court of Appeal gave guidance to judges on the approach to   **32.11**
sentencing in historic cases. Morgan L.C.J. set out the factors that should be taken into account[18]:

  (i) the statutory framework applicable at the time of the commission of the offences;
 (ii) the sentencing guidelines at the time at which the sentence is imposed;
 (iii) the primary considerations are the culpability of the offender, the harm to the victim and the risk of harm in the future;
 (iv) the youth of the offender will be material to the issue of culpability;
  (v) the court should not seek to establish what sentence would have been imposed had the offender been detected shortly after the commission of the offences;
 (vi) the passage of time may often assist the understanding of the long term effects of the offences on the victim;
(vii) the passage of time may also be relevant to the assessment of risk; and
(viii) the attitude of the offender (when he is of full age) at the time of disclosure/interview is significant and admission will attract significant discount in the sentence.

In *R. v ML* a man of 35 at the time of sentencing had abused his younger sister when he was 13 and 14 years of age. The sentence was reduced from a custody probation order of 1-and-a-half years' custody and a 3-year probation order (a commensurate sentence of 4-and-a-half years) to 1 year's custody, with a suggestion that had he faced up to his responsibilities at an earlier stage a non-custodial outcome may have been possible. However, the Court emphasised in *DPP's Ref (No.4 of 2012)*[19] that in cases of higher culpability, a suspended sentence could be justified only in the most exceptional circumstances.[20]

OFFENCES COMMITTED ON OR AFTER APRIL 1, 2009

Determinate custodial sentences   **32.21**

When considering a determinate custodial sentence under art.8 of the Criminal Justice (Northern Ireland) Order 2008, and in particular the licence period and the

---

[17] [2013] NICA 27.
[18] At [20].
[19] [2013] NICA 10.
[20] See also *DPP's Ref (No.1 of 2012)* [2012] NICA 36.

resulting custodial period, a judge should give brief reasons for a decision should he or she determine that the licence period is more than half of the determinate term.[21] This may be of particular relevance should a judge be considering the suitability of an offender undergoing the Probation Board's sex offenders' programme, which usually has a duration of three years.

Offender levy

A levy is now imposed on offenders convicted of offences occurring on or after June 6, 2012, although the current arrangements (£15 in the event of a fine, £25 in the event of immediate imprisonment/detention of 2 years or less, and £50 in the event of an indeterminate sentence or immediate imprisonment/detention of more than 2 years) are transitional.[22]

Dangerous Offenders

32.26 The judgment in *Owens* is now reported at [2011] NICA 48. In *R. v EB*[23] the Court of Appeal approved the approach to assessment of dangerousness set out in the English case of *Lang*.[24]

Sentencing Generally

32.31 In *R. v SG*[25] the Court of Appeal stated that there is assistance to be derived from the final report of the Sentencing Guidelines Council in England & Wales on similar offences under the 2003 Act. The same will no doubt apply to the new sentencing guideline introduced by the Sentencing Council, discussed in para.1.20 et seq., above.

Sexual Offences Prevention Orders

32.33 In *R. v EB*[26] and *Jones*[27] it was again emphasised by the Court of Appeal that when SOPOs are being considered there is a need, first, to establish whether or not the necessity for an order is established through risk of recurrence, and, if so, whether it is necessary and proportionate to make an order beyond the statutory minimum period of five years.

32.33A Section 5 of the Criminal Justice Act (Northern Ireland) 2013, when brought into force, will permit a court to include a requirement, in addition to a prohibition, in a SOPO.

[21] *McKeown, DPP's Ref (No.2 of 2013)* [2013] NICA 28 at [31].
[22] Ch.1 of Pt 1 of the Justice Act (Northern Ireland) 2011 (c.24) and the Justice (2011 Act) (Commencement No.4 and Transitory Provision) Order (Northern Ireland) 2012/214 (c.18).
[23] [2010] NICA 40.
[24] [2005] EWCA Crim 2864.
[25] [2010] NICA 32.
[26] [2010] NICA 40.
[27] [2011] NICA 62.

EVIDENCE

In relation to recent complaint, it was held in *Greene*[28] that the evidence of   **32.34**
disclosure by a complainant (born in 1983) to her mother in 2000, her boyfriend
in 2002 and her doctor in 2004 of alleged events from 1991–1993, was rightly
admitted as evidence, and that the trial judge's directions covering whether the
disclosures had been made, the lapse of time from the alleged incidents, the
circumstances of the disclosures, and the fact that they were not independent
evidence were correct.[29] The Court of Appeal suggested that the trial judge could
have gone beyond the agreed position of both prosecution and defence that the
jury should only consider the evidence on the issue of the complainant's
credibility, as the evidence was also admissible for the purpose of proving the truth
of what had been said. The Court of Appeal approved such a dual-purpose
direction given in *R. v JSK*.[30]

Section 9 of the Justice Act (Northern Ireland) 2011[31] inserted a new art.10A in   **32.35**
the Criminal Evidence (Northern Ireland) Order 1999, providing that adult
complainants alleging sexual offences are entitled to give video-recorded evidence
in chief.

Section 12 of the Justice Act (Northern Ireland) 2011 introduced a new special   **32.35A**
measure extending the use of intermediaries to defendants. The new art.21BA,
combined with art.17 of the Criminal Evidence (Northern Ireland) Order 1999,
now enables intermediaries to assist all witnesses if their use is likely to improve
the quality of the witness's evidence, in terms of its completeness, coherence and
accuracy.[32]

DELAY

The difficulties in trials involving substantial delay between the date of the alleged   **32.40**
incidents and the hearing have been highlighted in recent cases. The Judicial
Studies Board for Northern Ireland direction mentioned in the main work is
currently under review in light of the judgments of the Court of Appeal in *R. v*

---

[28] [2010] NICA 47. For further examples of an approved direction to a jury and relevance of
demeanour during a disclosure, see *R. v WM* [2012] NICA 33 at [19]–[20] and [22], and of a criticism
due to a lack of directions on both issues see *Chakwane* [2013] NICA 24. For demeanour of
complainant when in the company of the defendant, see *Warnock* [2013] NICA 34.
[29] As to the importance of a specific direction as to a disclosure not providing independent
corroboration, see *R. v AG* [2010] NICA 20 and *R. v JSK* [2011] NICA 44.
[30] [2011] NICA 44.
[31] c.24.
[32] A pilot scheme began on May 13, 2013 for cases relating to offences alleged to have been
committed within the Belfast City Council boundary was extended to all of Northern Ireland from
November 11, 2013: see the Criminal Evidence (Northern Ireland) Order 1999 (Commencement No.8)
Order 2013/126 (c.8).

W [33] and *R. v McK.*[34] Previously, the more generalised direction was considered acceptable and no adverse comment was expressed about it in *Greene,*[35] *R. v JSK*[36] or even in *R. v DS,*[37] where no direction on delay was given at all.[38]

Girvan L.J. in *R. v W* emphasised that the counter-balance to the lack of any limitation period in the criminal justice system has to be the requirement for scrupulous care by the court in ensuring the jury appreciates the potential for unfairness to the defendant. He concluded by stating that counsel for the parties should make submissions to the judge as to the content of the judge's direction to the jury and in particular how the defendant may be prejudiced by the delay, and how the defendant may be prejudiced in relation to particular allegations in the specific context of the charges. Morgan L.C.J. in *R. v McK* reinforced the comments made in *R. v W* by emphasising that the jury needs to be fully aware of any prejudice, both general and specific, that the defendant may have in defending himself. Judges should also desist from suggesting that the delay, and the absence of witnesses or evidence, could have equally impacted on the prosecution case.

32.40A   The Court of Appeal in *R. v SR*[39] held that in cases where there has been delay in the trial process, as opposed to delay between the alleged incident and the complaint, due regard should be given to the complexity of the case when considering the period of delay, and further that complexity is not confined to legal and factual issues but could include the non-availability for genuine reasons of a central witness. In that case where the reasons for delay were university examinations and then psychiatric factors which impacted on the complainant's availability to give evidence, the Court allowed a prosecution appeal against an order staying proceedings as an abuse of process.

Third Party Disclosure

32.42A   The need for the defence to take an appropriate and timely approach to the third party disclosure procedure was emphasised by the Court of Appeal in *R. v FN.*[40] In that case, the judge refused a defence application for further consideration of disclosure that was made after the jury had been sworn and on the day the evidence was due to be heard. The Court of Appeal was critical of the casual approach taken to the issue by the defence, particularly as the focus of the late application had not been raised in the Defence Statement. The Court said that there is, however, an obligation on the trial judge to review disclosure as a trial progresses and new issues emerge, although such issues should be raised by way of an amended Defence Statement.

---

[33] [2013] NICA 6.
[34] [2013] NICA 11.
[35] [2010] NICA 47.
[36] [2011] NICA 44.
[37] [2010] NICA 18.
[38] For an example of an approved direction, see *Joshi* [2012] NICA 56.
[39] [2011] NICA 49. See also *Dyer v Watson* [2004] 1 AC 379 and *Konig v Germany* (1978) 2 EHRR 170.
[40] [2012] NICA 38.

APPENDIX A

SEXUAL OFFENCES: DEFINITIVE GUIDELINE

APPLICABILITY OF GUIDELINE

In accordance with section 120 of the Coroners and Justice Act 2009, the Sentencing Council issues this definitive guideline. It applies to all offenders aged 18 and older, who are sentenced on or after 1 April 2014.

Section 125(1) of the Coroners and Justice Act 2009 provides that when sentencing offences committed on or after 6 April 2010:

"Every court—
  (a) must, in sentencing an offender, follow any sentencing guideline which is relevant to the offender's case, and
  (b) must, in exercising any other function relating to the sentencing of offenders, follow any sentencing guidelines which are relevant to the exercise of the function, unless the court is satisfied that it would be contrary to the interests of justice to do so."

This guideline applies only to offenders aged 18 and older. General principles to be considered in the sentencing of youths are in the Sentencing Guidelines Council's definitive guideline, *Overarching Principles—Sentencing Youths.*

Structure, ranges and starting points

For the purposes of section 125(3)–(4) of the Coroners and Justice Act 2009, the guideline specifies offence ranges—the range of sentences appropriate for each type of offence. Within each offence, the Council has specified different categories which reflect varying degrees of seriousness. The offence range is split into category ranges—sentences appropriate for each level of seriousness. The Council has also identified a starting point within each category.

Starting points define the position within a category range from which to start calculating the provisional sentence. **Starting points apply to all offences within the corresponding category and are applicable to all offenders, in all cases.** Once the starting point is established, the court should consider further

665

aggravating and mitigating factors and previous convictions so as to adjust the sentence within the range. Starting points and ranges apply to all offenders, whether they have pleaded guilty or been convicted after trial. Credit for a guilty plea is taken into consideration only at step four in the decision making process, after the appropriate sentence has been identified.

Information on ancillary orders is set out at Annex A. Information on historic offences is set out at Annexes B and C.

Information on community orders and fine bands is set out at Annex D.

RAPE

Sexual Offences Act 2003 (section 1)

Triable only on indictment
Maximum: Life imprisonment

Offence range: 4–19 years' custody

This is a serious specified offence for the purposes of sections 224 and 225(2) (life sentence for serious offences) of the Criminal Justice Act 2003.

For offences committed on or after 3 December 2012, this is an offence listed in Part 1 of Schedule 15B for the purposes of sections 224A (life sentence for second listed offence) of the Criminal Justice Act 2003.

For convictions on or after 3 December 2012 (irrespective of the date of commission of the offence), this is a specified offence for the purposes of section 226A (extended sentence for certain violent or sexual offences) of the Criminal Justice Act 2003.

STEP ONE
Determining the offence category

The court should determine which categories of harm and culpability the offence falls into by reference only to the tables below.

Offences may be of such severity, for example involving a campaign of rape, that sentences of 20 years and above may be appropriate.

Harm	Culpability
Category 1 The extreme nature of one or more category 2 factors or the extreme impact caused by a combination of category 2 factors may elevate to category 1	**A** Significant degree of planning Offender acts together with others to commit the offence Use of alcohol/drugs on victim to facilitate the offence
Category 2 • Severe psychological or physical harm • Pregnancy or STI as a consequence of offence • Additional degradation/humiliation • Abduction • Prolonged detention/sustained incident • Violence or threats of violence (beyond that which is inherent in the offence) • Forced/uninvited entry into victim's home • Victim is particularly vulnerable due to personal circumstances* * for children under 13 please refer to the guideline on page 27	Abuse of trust Previous violence against victim Offence committed in course of burglary Recording of the offence Commercial exploitation and/or motivation Offence racially or religiously aggravated Offence motivated by, or demonstrating, hostility to the victim based on his or her sexual orientation (or presumed sexual orientation) or transgender identity (or presumed transgender identity) Offence motivated by, or demonstrating, hostility to the victim based on his or her disability (or presumed disability) **B** Factor(s) in category A not present
Category 3 Factor(s) in categories 1 and 2 not present	

STEP TWO
Starting point and category range

Having determined the category, the court should use the corresponding starting points to reach a sentence within the category range on the next page. The starting point applies to all offenders irrespective of plea or previous convictions. Having determined the starting point, step two allows further adjustment for aggravating or mitigating features set out on the next page.

A case of particular gravity, reflected by multiple features of culpability or harm in step one, could merit upward adjustment from the starting point before further adjustment for aggravating or mitigating features, set out on the next page.

	A	B
Category 1	**Starting point** 15 years' custody	**Starting point** 12 years' custody
	Category range 13–19 years' custody	**Category range** 10–15 years' custody
Category 2	**Starting point** 10 years' custody	**Starting point** 8 years' custody
	Category range 9–13 years' custody	**Category range** 7–9 years' custody
Category 3	**Starting point** 7 years' custody	**Starting point** 5 years' custody
	Category range 6–9 years' custody	**Category range** 4–7 years' custody

The table below contains a **non-exhaustive** list of additional factual elements providing the context of the offence and factors relating to the offender. Identify whether any combination of these, or other relevant factors, should result in an upward or downward adjustment from the starting point. **In particular, relevant recent convictions are likely to result in an upward adjustment.** In some cases, having considered these factors, it may be appropriate to move outside the identified category range.

Aggravating factors	Mitigating factors
Statutory aggravating factors	No previous convictions **or** no relevant/recent convictions
Previous convictions, having regard to a) the nature of the offence to which the conviction relates and its relevance to the current offence; and b) the time that has elapsed since the conviction	Remorse
	Previous good character and/or exemplary conduct*
	Age and/or lack of maturity where it affects the responsibility of the offender
Offence committed whilst on bail	Mental disorder or learning disability, particularly where linked to the commission of the offence
Other aggravating factors	
Specific targeting of a particularly vulnerable victim	* Previous good character/exemplary conduct is different from having no previous convictions. The more serious the offence, the less the weight which should normally be attributed to this factor. Where previous good character/exemplary conduct has been used to facilitate the offence, this mitigation should not normally be allowed and such conduct may constitute an aggravating factor.
Ejaculation (where not taken into account at step one)	
Blackmail or other threats made (where not taken into account at step one)	
Location of offence	
Timing of offence	In the context of this offence, previous good character/exemplary conduct should not normally be given any significant weight and will not normally justify a reduction in what would otherwise be the appropriate sentence.
Use of weapon or other item to frighten or injure	
Victim compelled to leave their home (including victims of domestic violence)	
Failure to comply with current court orders	
Offence committed whilst on licence	
Exploiting contact arrangements with a child to commit an offence	
Presence of others, especially children	
Any steps taken to prevent the victim reporting an incident, obtaining assistance and/or from assisting or supporting the prosecution	
Attempts to dispose of or conceal evidence	
Commission of offence whilst under the influence of alcohol or drugs	

STEP THREE
Consider any factors which indicate a reduction, such as assistance to the prosecution
The court should take into account sections 73 and 74 of the Serious Organised Crime and Police Act 2005 (assistance by defendants: reduction or review of sentence) and any other rule of law by virtue of which an offender may receive a discounted sentence in consequence of assistance given (or offered) to the prosecutor or investigator.

STEP FOUR
Reduction for guilty pleas
The court should take account of any potential reduction for a guilty plea in accordance with section 144 of the Criminal Justice Act 2003 and the Guilty Plea guideline.

STEP FIVE
Dangerousness
The court should consider whether having regard to the criteria contained in Chapter 5 of Part 12 of the Criminal Justice Act 2003 it would be appropriate to award a life sentence (section 224A or section 225(2)) or an extended sentence (section 226A). When sentencing offenders to a life sentence under these provisions, the notional determinate sentence should be used as the basis for the setting of a minimum term.

STEP SIX
Totality principle
If sentencing an offender for more than one offence, or where the offender is already serving a sentence, consider whether the total sentence is just and proportionate to the offending behaviour.

STEP SEVEN
Ancillary orders
The court must consider whether to make any ancillary orders. The court must also consider what other requirements or provisions may automatically apply. Further information is included at Annex A on page 153.

STEP EIGHT
Reasons
Section 174 of the Criminal Justice Act 2003 imposes a duty to give reasons for, and explain the effect of, the sentence.

> **STEP NINE**
> Consideration for time spent on bail
> The court must consider whether to give credit for time spent on bail in accordance with section 240A of the Criminal Justice Act 2003.

ASSAULT BY PENETRATION

Sexual Offences Act 2003 (section 2)

Triable only on indictment
Maximum: Life imprisonment

Offence range: Community order – 19 years' custody

This is a serious specified offence for the purposes of sections 224 and 225(2) (life sentence for serious offences) of the Criminal Justice Act 2003.

For offences committed on or after 3 December 2012, this is an offence listed in Part 1 of Schedule 15B for the purposes of sections 224A (life sentence for second listed offence) of the Criminal Justice Act 2003.

For convictions on or after 3 December 2012 (irrespective of the date of commission of the offence), this is a specified offence for the purposes of section 226A (extended sentence for certain violent or sexual offences) of the Criminal Justice Act 2003.

> **STEP ONE**
> Determining the offence category

The court should determine which categories of harm and culpability the offence falls into by reference only to the tables below.

Harm		Culpability	
Category 1	The extreme nature of one or more category 2 factors or the extreme impact caused by a combination of category 2 factors may elevate to category 1	**A**	
		Significant degree of planning	
		Offender acts together with others to commit the offence	
		Use of alcohol/drugs on victim to facilitate the offence	
Category 2	• Severe psychological or physical harm	Abuse of trust	
	• Penetration using large or dangerous object(s)	Previous violence against victim	
		Offence committed in course of burglary	
	• Additional degradation/humiliation	Recording of the offence	
	• Abduction	Commercial exploitation and/or motivation	
	• Prolonged detention/sustained incident	Offence racially or religiously aggravated	
	• Violence or threats of violence (beyond that which is inherent in the offence)	Offence motivated by, or demonstrating, hostility to the victim based on his or her sexual orientation (or presumed sexual orientation) or transgender identity (or presumed transgender identity)	
	• Forced/uninvited entry into victim's home		
	• Victim is particularly vulnerable due to personal circumstances*	Offence motivated by, or demonstrating, hostility to the victim based on his or her disability (or presumed disability)	
	* for children under 13 please refer to the guideline on page 33	**B**	
		Factor(s) in category A not present	
Category 3	Factor(s) in categories 1 and 2 not present		

> **STEP TWO**
> **Starting point and category range**

Having determined the category, the court should use the corresponding starting points to reach a sentence within the category range on the next page. The starting point applies to all offenders irrespective of plea or previous convictions.

Having determined the starting point, step two allows further adjustment for aggravating or mitigating features, set out on the next page.

A case of particular gravity, reflected by multiple features of culpability or harm in step one, could merit upward adjustment from the starting point before further adjustment for aggravating or mitigating features, set out on the next page.

Where there is a sufficient prospect of rehabilitation, a community order with a sex offender treatment programme requirement under section 202 of the Criminal Justice Act 2003 can be a proper alternative to a short or moderate length custodial sentence.

	A	B
Category 1	Starting point 15 years' custody	Starting point 12 years' custody
	Category range 13–19 years' custody	Category range 10–15 years' custody
Category 2	Starting point 8 years' custody	Starting point 6 years' custody
	Category range 5–13 years' custody	Category range 4–9 years' custody
Category 3	Starting point 4 years' custody	Starting point 2 years' custody
	Category range 2–6 years' custody	Category range High level community order – 4 years' custody

The table below contains a **non-exhaustive** list of additional factual elements providing the context of the offence and factors relating to the offender. Identify whether any combination of these, or other relevant factors, should result in an upward or downward adjustment from the starting point. **In particular, relevant recent convictions are likely to result in an upward adjustment.** In some cases, having considered these factors, it may be appropriate to move outside the identified category range.

When sentencing appropriate **category 3 offences**, the court should also consider the custody threshold as follows:

- has the custody threshold been passed?
- if so, is it unavoidable that a custodial sentence be imposed?
- if so, can that sentence be suspended?

Aggravating factors	Mitigating factors
Statutory aggravating factors	No previous convictions **or** no relevant/recent convictions

Aggravating factors

Statutory aggravating factors

Previous convictions, having regard to a) the nature of the offence to which the conviction relates and its relevance to the current offence; and b) the time that has elapsed since the conviction

Offence committed whilst on bail

Other aggravating factors

Specific targeting of a particularly vulnerable victim

Ejaculation (where not taken into account at step one)

Blackmail or other threats made (where not taken into account at step one)

Location of offence

Timing of offence

Use of weapon or other item to frighten or injure

Victim compelled to leave their home (including victims of domestic violence)

Failure to comply with current court orders

Offence committed whilst on licence

Exploiting contact arrangements with a child to commit an offence

Presence of others, especially children

Any steps taken to prevent the victim reporting an incident, obtaining assistance and/or from assisting or supporting the prosecution

Attempts to dispose of or conceal evidence

Commission of offence whilst under the influence of alcohol or drugs

Mitigating factors

No previous convictions **or** no relevant/recent convictions

Remorse

Previous good character and/or exemplary conduct*

Age and/or lack of maturity where it affects the responsibility of the offender

Mental disorder or learning disability, particularly where linked to the commission of the offence

---

* Previous good character/exemplary conduct is different from having no previous convictions. The more serious the offence, the less the weight which should normally be attributed to this factor. Where previous good character/exemplary conduct has been used to facilitate the offence, this mitigation should not normally be allowed and such conduct may constitute an aggravating factor.

In the context of this offence, previous good character/exemplary conduct should not normally be given any significant weight and will not normally justify a reduction in what would otherwise be the appropriate sentence.

STEP THREE
Consider any factors which indicate a reduction, such as assistance to the prosecution
The court should take into account sections 73 and 74 of the Serious Organised Crime and Police Act 2005 (assistance by defendants: reduction or review of sentence) and any other rule of law by virtue of which an offender may receive a discounted sentence in consequence of assistance given (or offered) to the prosecutor or investigator.

STEP FOUR
Reduction for guilty pleas
The court should take account of any potential reduction for a guilty plea in accordance with section 144 of the Criminal Justice Act 2003 and the Guilty Plea guideline.

STEP FIVE
Dangerousness
The court should consider whether having regard to the criteria contained in Chapter 5 of Part 12 of the Criminal Justice Act 2003 it would be appropriate to award a life sentence (section 224A or section 225(2)) or an extended sentence (section 226A). When sentencing offenders to a life sentence under these provisions, the notional determinate sentence should be used as the basis for the setting of a minimum term.

STEP SIX
Totality principle
If sentencing an offender for more than one offence, or where the offender is already serving a sentence, consider whether the total sentence is just and proportionate to the offending behaviour.

STEP SEVEN
Ancillary orders
The court must consider whether to make any ancillary orders. The court must also consider what other requirements or provisions may automatically apply. Further information is included at Annex A on page 153.

STEP EIGHT
Reasons
Section 174 of the Criminal Justice Act 2003 imposes a duty to give reasons for, and explain the effect of, the sentence.

> **STEP NINE**
> **Consideration for time spent on bail**
> The court must consider whether to give credit for time spent on bail in accordance with section 240A of the Criminal Justice Act 2003.

Sexual Assault

Sexual Offences Act 2003 (section 3)

Triable either way
Maximum: 10 years' custody

Offence range: Community order – 7 years' custody

For convictions on or after 3 December 2012 (irrespective of the date of commission of the offence), this is a specified offence for the purposes of section 226A (extended sentence for certain violent or sexual offences) of the Criminal Justice Act 2003.

> **STEP ONE**
> **Determining the offence category**

The court should determine which categories of harm and culpability the offence falls into by reference **only** to the tables below.

Harm	Culpability
Category 1 • Severe psychological or physical harm • Abduction • Violence or threats of violence • Forced/uninvited entry into victim's home	**A** Significant degree of planning Offender acts together with others to commit the offence Use of alcohol/drugs on victim to facilitate the offence Abuse of trust
Category 2 • Touching of naked genitalia or naked breasts • Prolonged detention/ sustained incident • Additional degrada- tion/humiliation • Victim is particularly vulnerable due to per- sonal circumstances* * for children under 13 please refer to the guide- line on page 37	Previous violence against victim Offence committed in course of burglary Recording of offence Commercial exploitation and/or motivation Offence racially or religiously aggravated Offence motivated by, or demonstrating, hostility to the victim based on his or her sexual orientation (or presumed sexual orientation) or transgender identity (or presumed transgender identity) Offence motivated by, or demonstrating, hostility to the victim based on his or her disability (or presumed disability)
Category 3 Factor(s) in categories 1 and 2 not present	**B** Factor(s) in category A not present

---

STEP TWO
Starting point and category range

Having determined the category, the court should use the corresponding starting points to reach a sentence within the category range on the next page. The starting point applies to all offenders irrespective of plea or previous convictions. Having determined the starting point, step two allows further adjustment for aggravating or mitigating features, set out on the next page.

677

A case of particular gravity, reflected by multiple features of culpability or harm in step one, could merit upward adjustment from the starting point before further adjustment for aggravating or mitigating features, set out on the next page.

Where there is a sufficient prospect of rehabilitation, a community order with a sex offender treatment programme requirement under section 202 of the Criminal Justice Act 2003 can be a proper alternative to a short or moderate length custodial sentence.

	A	B
Category 1	**Starting point** 4 years' custody **Category range** 3–7 years' custody	**Starting point** 2 years 6 months' custody **Category range** 2–4 years' custody
Category 2	**Starting point** 2 years' custody **Category range** 1–4 years' custody	**Starting point** 1 years' custody **Category range** High level community order – 2 years' custody
Category 3	**Starting point** 26 weeks' custody **Category range** High level community order – 1 year's custody	**Starting point** High level community order **Category range** Medium level community order – 26 weeks' custody

The table below contains a **non-exhaustive** list of additional factual elements providing the context of the offence and factors relating to the offender. Identify whether any combination of these, or other relevant factors, should result in an upward or downward adjustment from the starting point. **In particular, relevant recent convictions are likely to result in an upward adjustment.** In some cases, having considered these factors, it may be appropriate to move outside the identified category range.

When sentencing appropriate **category 2 or 3 offences**, the court should also consider the custody threshold as follows:

- has the custody threshold been passed?
- if so, is it unavoidable that a custodial sentence be imposed?
- if so, can that sentence be suspended?

Aggravating factors	Mitigating factors
Statutory aggravating factors	No previous convictions **or** no relevant/recent convictions
Previous convictions, having regard to a) the nature of the offence to which the conviction relates and its relevance to the current offence; and b) the time that has elapsed since the conviction	Remorse
	Previous good character and/or exemplary conduct*
	Age and/or lack of maturity where it affects the responsibility of the offender
Offence committed whilst on bail	Mental disorder or learning disability, particularly where linked to the commission of the offence
Other aggravating factors	Demonstration of steps taken to address offending behaviour
Specific targeting of a particularly vulnerable victim	
Blackmail or other threats made (where not taken into account at step one)	* Previous good character/exemplary conduct is different from having no previous convictions. The more serious the offence, the less the weight which should normally be attributed to this factor. Where previous good character/exemplary conduct has been used to facilitate the offence, this mitigation should not normally be allowed and such conduct may constitute an aggravating factor.
Location of offence	
Timing of offence	
Use of weapon or other item to frighten or injure	
Victim compelled to leave their home (including victims of domestic violence)	
Failure to comply with current court orders	
Offence committed whilst on licence	
Exploiting contact arrangements with a child to commit an offence	
Presence of others, especially children	
Any steps taken to prevent the victim reporting an incident, obtaining assistance and/or from assisting or supporting the prosecutionAttempts to dispose of or conceal evidence	
Commission of offence whilst under the influence of alcohol or drugs	

STEP THREE
Consider any factors which indicate a reduction, such as assistance to the prosecution
The court should take into account sections 73 and 74 of the Serious Organised Crime and Police Act 2005 (assistance by defendants: reduction or review of sentence) and any other rule of law by virtue of which an offender may receive a discounted sentence in consequence of assistance given (or offered) to the prosecutor or investigator.

STEP FOUR
Reduction for guilty pleas
The court should take account of any potential reduction for a guilty plea in accordance with section 144 of the Criminal Justice Act 2003 and the Guilty Plea guideline.

STEP FIVE
Dangerousness
The court should consider whether having regard to the criteria contained in Chapter 5 of Part 12 of the Criminal Justice Act 2003 it would be appropriate to award an extended sentence (section 226A).

STEP SIX
Totality principle
If sentencing an offender for more than one offence, or where the offender is already serving a sentence, consider whether the total sentence is just and proportionate to the offending behaviour.

STEP SEVEN
Ancillary orders
The court must consider whether to make any ancillary orders. The court must also consider what other requirements or provisions may automatically apply. Further information is included at Annex A on page 153.

STEP EIGHT
Reasons
Section 174 of the Criminal Justice Act 2003 imposes a duty to give reasons for, and explain the effect of, the sentence.

STEP NINE
Consideration for time spent on bail
The court must consider whether to give credit for time spent on bail in accordance with section 240A of the Criminal Justice Act 2003.

Causing a Person to Engage in Sexual Activity Without Consent

Sexual Offences Act 2003 (section 4)

Triable only on indictment (if penetration involved)
—otherwise, triable either way

Maximum: Life imprisonment (if penetration involved)
—otherwise, 10 years

Offence range: Community order – 7 years' custody (if no penetration involved) / 19 years' custody (if penetration involved)

This is a serious specified offence for the purposes of section 224 and, where the offence involved penetration, section 225(2) (life sentence for serious offences) of the Criminal Justice Act 2003.

For offences involving penetration, committed on or after 3 December 2012, this is an offence listed in Part 1 of Schedule 15B for the purposes of sections 224A (life sentence for second listed offence) of the Criminal Justice Act 2003.

For convictions on or after 3 December 2012 (irrespective of the date of commission of the offence), this is a specified offence for the purposes of section 226A (extended sentence for certain violent or sexual offences) of the Criminal Justice Act 2003.

STEP ONE
Determining the offence category

The court should determine which categories of harm and culpability the offence falls into by reference only to the tables below.

Harm	Culpability
Category 1 The extreme nature of one or more category 2 factors or the extreme impact caused by a combination of category 2 factors **may** elevate to category 1	**A** Significant degree of planning Offender acts together with others to commit the offence Use of alcohol/drugs on victim to facilitate the offence
Category 2 • Severe psychological or physical harm • Penetration using large or dangerous object(s) • Pregnancy or STI as a consequence of offence • Additional degradation/humiliation • Abduction • Prolonged detention/sustained incident • Violence or threats of violence • Forced/uninvited entry into victim's home • Victim is particularly vulnerable due to personal circumstances* * for children under 13 please refer to the guideline on page 41	Abuse of trust Previous violence against victim Offence committed in course of burglary Recording of the offence Commercial exploitation and/or motivation Offence racially or religiously aggravated Offence motivated by, or demonstrating, hostility to the victim based on his or her sexual orientation (or presumed sexual orientation) or transgender identity (or presumed transgender identity) Offence motivated by, or demonstrating, hostility to the victim based on his or her disability (or presumed disability) **B** Factor(s) in category A not present
Category 3 Factor(s) in categories 1 and 2 not present	

STEP TWO
Starting point and category range

Having determined the category, the court should use the corresponding starting points to reach a sentence within the category range on the next page. The starting point applies to all offenders irrespective of plea or previous convictions. Having determined the starting point, step two allows further adjustment for aggravating or mitigating features, set out on the next page.

A case of particular gravity, reflected by multiple features of culpability or harm in step one, could merit upward adjustment from the starting point before further adjustment for aggravating or mitigating features, set out on the next page.

Where there is a sufficient prospect of rehabilitation, a community order with a sex offender treatment programme requirement under section 202 of the Criminal Justice Act 2003 can be a proper alternative to a short or moderate length custodial sentence.

Where offence involved penetration

	A	B
Category 1	Starting point 15 years' custody	Starting point 12 years' custody
	Category range 13–19 years' custody	Category range 10–15 years' custody
Category 2	Starting point 8 years' custody	Starting point 6 years' custody
	Category range 5–13 years' custody	Category range 4–9 years' custody
Category 3	Starting point 4 years' custody	Starting point 2 years' custody
	Category range 2–6 years' custody	Category range High level community order – 4 years' custody

Where offence did not involve penetration

	A	B
Category 1	Starting point 4 years' custody	Starting point 2 years 6 months' custody
	Category range 3–7 years' custody	Category range 2–4 years' custody

	A	B
Category 2	**Starting point** 2 years' custody	**Starting point** 1 years' custody
	Category range 1–4 years' custody	**Category range** High level community order – 2 years' custody
Category 3	**Starting point** 26 weeks' custody	**Starting point** High level community order
	Category range High level community order – 1 year's custody	**Category range** Medium level community order – 26 weeks' custody

The table below contains a **non-exhaustive** list of additional factual elements providing the context of the offence and factors relating to the offender. Identify whether any combination of these, or other relevant factors, should result in an upward or downward adjustment from the starting point. **In particular, relevant recent convictions are likely to result in an upward adjustment.** In some cases, having considered these factors, it may be appropriate to move outside the identified category range.

When sentencing appropriate **category 2 or 3** offences, the court should also consider the custody threshold as follows:

- has the custody threshold been passed?
- if so, is it unavoidable that a custodial sentence be imposed?
- if so, can that sentence be suspended?

Aggravating factors	Mitigating factors
Statutory aggravating factors	No previous convictions **or** no relevant/recent convictions
Previous convictions, having regard to a) the nature of the offence to which the conviction relates and its relevance to the current offence; and b) the time that has elapsed since the conviction	Remorse
	Previous good character and/or exemplary conduct*
	Age and/or lack of maturity where it affects the responsibility of the offender
Offence committed whilst on bail	Mental disorder or learning disability, particularly where linked to the commission of the offence
Other aggravating factors	
Specific targeting of a particularly vulnerable victim	
Ejaculation (where not taken into account at step one)	
Blackmail or other threats made (where not taken into account at step one)	
Location of offence	
Timing of offence	
Use of weapon or other item to frighten or injure	
Victim compelled to leave their home (including victims of domestic violence)	
Failure to comply with current court orders	
Offence committed whilst on licence	
Exploiting contact arrangements with a child to commit an offence	
Presence of others, especially children	
Any steps taken to prevent the victim reporting an incident, obtaining assistance and/or from assisting or supporting the prosecution	
Attempts to dispose of or conceal evidence	
Commission of offence whilst under the influence of alcohol or drugs	

* Previous good character/exemplary conduct is different from having no previous convictions. The more serious the offence, the less the weight which should normally be attributed to this factor. Where previous good character/exemplary conduct has been used to facilitate the offence, this mitigation should not normally be allowed and such conduct may constitute an aggravating factor.

In the context of this offence, previous good character/exemplary conduct should not normally be given any significant weight and will not normally justify a reduction in what would otherwise be the appropriate sentence.

STEP THREE
Consider any factors which indicate a reduction, such as assistance to the prosecution
The court should take into account sections 73 and 74 of the Serious Organised Crime and Police Act 2005 (assistance by defendants: reduction or review of sentence) and any other rule of law by virtue of which an offender may receive a discounted sentence in consequence of assistance given (or offered) to the prosecutor or investigator.

STEP FOUR
Reduction for guilty pleas
The court should take account of any potential reduction for a guilty plea in accordance with section 144 of the Criminal Justice Act 2003 and the Guilty Plea guideline.

STEP FIVE
Dangerousness
The court should consider whether having regard to the criteria contained in Chapter 5 of Part 12 of the Criminal Justice Act 2003 it would be appropriate to award a life sentence (section 224A or section 225(2)) or an extended sentence (section 226A). When sentencing offenders to a life sentence under these provisions, the notional determinate sentence should be used as the basis for the setting of a minimum term.

STEP SIX
Totality principle
If sentencing an offender for more than one offence, or where the offender is already serving a sentence, consider whether the total sentence is just and proportionate to the offending behaviour.

STEP SEVEN
Ancillary orders
The court must consider whether to make any ancillary orders. The court must also consider what other requirements or provisions may automatically apply. Further information is included at Annex A on page 153.

STEP EIGHT
Reasons
Section 174 of the Criminal Justice Act 2003 imposes a duty to give reasons for, and explain the effect of, the sentence.

> **STEP NINE**
> Consideration for time spent on bail
> The court must consider whether to give credit for time spent on bail in accordance with section 240A of the Criminal Justice Act 2003.

RAPE OF A CHILD UNDER 13

Sexual Offences Act 2003 (section 5)

Triable only on indictment
Maximum: Life imprisonment

Offence range: 6–19 years' custody

This is a serious specified offence for the purposes of sections 224 and 225(2) (life sentence for serious offences) of the Criminal Justice Act 2003.

For offences committed on or after 3 December 2012, this is an offence listed in Part 1 of Schedule 15B for the purposes of section 224A (life sentence for second listed offence) of the Criminal Justice Act 2003.

For convictions on or after 3 December 2012 (irrespective of the date of commission of the offence), this is a specified offence for the purposes of section 226A (extended sentence for certain violent or sexual offences) of the Criminal Justice Act 2003.

> **STEP ONE**
> Determining the offence category

The court should determine which categories of harm and culpability the offence falls into by reference only to the tables on the next page.

Offences may be of such severity, for example involving a campaign of rape, that sentences of 20 years and above may be appropriate.

When dealing with the statutory offence of rape of a child under 13, the court may be faced with a wide range of offending behaviour.

Sentencers should have particular regard to the fact that these offences are not only committed through force or fear of force but may include exploitative behaviour towards a child which should be considered to indicate high culpability.

This guideline is designed to deal with the majority of offending behaviour which deserves a significant custodial sentence; the starting points and ranges reflect the fact that such offending merits such an approach. There may also be **exceptional** cases, where a lengthy community order with a requirement to participate in a sex offender treatment programme may be the best way of changing the offender's behaviour and of protecting the public by preventing any repetition of the offence. This guideline may not be appropriate where the sentencer is satisfied that on the available evidence, and in the absence of exploitation, a young or particularly immature defendant genuinely believed, on reasonable grounds, that the victim was aged 16 or over and that they were engaging in lawful sexual activity.

Sentencers are reminded that if sentencing outside the guideline they must be satisfied that it would be contrary to the interests of justice to follow the guideline.

Harm		Culpability
Category 1	The extreme nature of one or more category 2 factors or the extreme impact caused by a combination of category 2 factors may elevate to category 1	**A** Significant degree of planning Offender acts together with others to commit the offence Use of alcohol/drugs on victim to facilitate the offence
Category 2	• Severe psychological or physical harm • Pregnancy or STI as a consequence of offence • Additional degradation/humiliation • Abduction • Prolonged detention/sustained incident • Violence or threats of violenc • Forced/uninvited entry into victim's home • Child is particularly vulnerable due to extreme youth and/or personal circumstances	Grooming behaviour used against victim Abuse of trust Previous violence against victim Offence committed in course of burglary Sexual images of victim recorded, retained, solicited or shared Deliberate isolation of victim Commercial exploitation and/or motivation Offence racially or religiously aggravated Offence motivated by, or demonstrating, hostility to the victim based on his or her sexual orientation (or presumed sexual orientation) or transgender identity (or presumed transgender identity)

Harm	Culpability
Category 3 Factor(s) in categories 1 and 2 not present	**A**
	Offence motivated by, or demonstrating, hostility to the victim based on his or her disability (or presumed disability)
	B
	Factor(s) in category A not present

STEP TWO
Starting point and category range

Having determined the category, the court should use the corresponding starting points to reach a sentence within the category range below. The starting point applies to all offenders irrespective of plea or previous convictions. Having determined the starting point, step two allows further adjustment for aggravating or mitigating features, set out on the next page.

A case of particular gravity, reflected by multiple features of culpability or harm in step one, could merit upward adjustment from the starting point before further adjustment for aggravating or mitigating features, set out on the next page.

Sentencers should also note the wording set out at step one which may be applicable in exceptional cases.

	A	B
Category 1	**Starting point** 16 years' custody	**Starting point** 13 years' custody
	Category range 13–19 years' custody	**Category range** 11–17 years' custody
Category 2	**Starting point** 13 years' custody	**Starting point** 10 years' custody
	Category range 11–17 years' custody	**Category range** 8–13 years' custody

	A	B
Category 3	**Starting point** 10 years' custody	**Starting point** 8 years' custody
	Category range 8–13 years' custody	**Category range** 6–11 years' custody

The table below contains a non-exhaustive list of additional factual elements providing the context of the offence and factors relating to the offender. Identify whether any combination of these, or other relevant factors, should result in an upward or downward adjustment from the starting point. In particular, relevant recent convictions are likely to result in an upward adjustment. In some cases, having considered these factors, it may be appropriate to move outside the identified category range.

Aggravating factors	Mitigating factors
Statutory aggravating factors	No previous convictions or no relevant/recent convictions
Previous convictions, having regard to a) the nature of the offence to which the conviction relates and its relevance to the current offence; and b) the time that has elapsed since the conviction	Remorse
	Previous good character and/or exemplary conduct*
	Age and/or lack of maturity where it affects the responsibility of the offender
Offence committed whilst on bail	
Other aggravating factors	Mental disorder or learning disability, particularly where linked to the commission of the offence
Specific targeting of a particularly vulnerable victim	

* Previous good character/exemplary conduct is different from having no previous convictions. The more serious the offence, the less the weight which should normally be attributed to this factor. Where previous good character/exemplary conduct has been used to facilitate the offence, this mitigation should not normally be allowed and such conduct may constitute an aggravating factor.

In the context of this offence, previous good character/exemplary conduct should not normally be given any significant weight and will not normally justify a reduction in what would otherwise be the appropriate sentence

Ejaculation (where not taken into account at step one)

Blackmail or other threats made (where not taken into account at step one)

Location of offence

Timing of offence

Use of weapon or other item to frighten or injure

Victim compelled to leave their home, school, etc

Failure to comply with current court orders

Aggravating factors

Offence committed whilst on licence

Exploiting contact arrangements with a child to commit an offence

Presence of others, especially other children

Any steps taken to prevent the victim reporting an incident, obtaining assistance and/or from assisting or supporting the prosecution

Attempts to dispose of or conceal evidence

Commission of offence whilst offender under the influence of alcohol or drugs

Victim encouraged to recruit others

STEP THREE

Consider any factors which indicate a reduction, such as assistance to the prosecution

The court should take into account sections 73 and 74 of the Serious Organised Crime and Police Act 2005 (assistance by defendants: reduction or review of sentence) and any other rule of law by virtue of which an offender may receive a discounted sentence in consequence of assistance given (or offered) to the prosecutor or investigator.

STEP FOUR

Reduction for guilty pleas

The court should take account of any potential reduction for a guilty plea in accordance with section 144 of the Criminal Justice Act 2003 and the Guilty Plea guideline.

STEP FIVE

Dangerousness

The court should consider whether having regard to the criteria contained in Chapter 5 of Part 12 of the Criminal Justice Act 2003 it would be appropriate to award a life sentence (section 224A or section 225(2)) or an extended sentence (section 226A). When sentencing offenders to a life sentence under these provisions, the notional determinate sentence should be used as the basis for the setting of a minimum term.

691

STEP SIX

Totality principle

If sentencing an offender for more than one offence, or where the offender is already serving a sentence, consider whether the total sentence is just and proportionate to the offending behaviour.

STEP SEVEN

Ancillary orders

The court must consider whether to make any ancillary orders. The court must also consider what other requirements or provisions may automatically apply. Further information is included at Annex A on page 153.

STEP EIGHT

Reasons

Section 174 of the Criminal Justice Act 2003 imposes a duty to give reasons for, and explain the effect of, the sentence.

STEP NINE

Consideration for time spent on bail

The court must consider whether to give credit for time spent on bail in accordance with section 240A of the Criminal Justice Act 2003.

ASSAULT OF A CHILD UNDER 13 BY PENETRATION

Sexual Offences Act 2003 (section 6)

Triable only on indictment
Maximum: Life imprisonment

Offence range: 2–19 years' custody

This is a serious specified offence for the purposes of sections 224 and 225(2) (life sentence for serious offences) of the Criminal Justice Act 2003.

For offences committed on or after 3 December 2012, this is an offence listed in Part 1 of Schedule 15B for the purposes of section 224A (life sentence for second listed offence) of the Criminal Justice Act 2003.

For convictions on or after 3 December 2012 (irrespective of the date of commission of the offence), this is a specified offence for the purposes of section 226A (extended sentence for certain violent or sexual offences) of the Criminal Justice Act 2003.

STEP ONE
Determining the offence category

The court should determine which categories of harm and culpability the offence falls into by reference **only** to the tables below.

Harm	Culpability
Category 1 The extreme nature of one or more category 2 factors or the extreme impact caused by a combination of category 2 factors **may** elevate to category 1	**A**
	Significant degree of planning
	Offender acts together with others to commit the offence
	Use of alcohol/drugs on victim to facilitate the offence
Category 2 • Severe psychological or physical harm	Grooming behaviour used against victim
• Penetration using large or dangerous object(s)	Abuse of trust
	Previous violence against victim
• Additional degrada-tion/humiliation	Offence committed in course of burglary
• Abduction	Sexual images of victim recorded, retained, solicited or shared
• Prolonged detention/sustained incident	Deliberate isolation of victim
• Violence or threats of violence	Commercial exploitation and/or motivation
• Forced/uninvited entry into victim's home	Offence racially or religiously aggravated
• Child is particularly vulnerable due to extreme youth and/or personal circum-stances	Offence motivated by, or demonstrating, hostility to the victim based on his or her sexual orientation (or presumed sexual orientation) or transgender identity (or presumed transgender identity)
Category 3 Factor(s) in categories 1 and 2 not present	Offence motivated by, or demonstrating, hostility to the victim based on his or her disability (or presumed disability)
	B
	Factor(s) in category A not present

693

> **STEP TWO**
> Starting point and category range

Having determined the category, the court should use the corresponding starting points to reach a sentence within the category range on the next page. The starting point applies to all offenders irrespective of plea or previous convictions. Having determined the starting point, step two allows further adjustment for aggravating or mitigating features, set out on the next page.

A case of particular gravity, reflected by multiple features of culpability or harm in step one, could merit upward adjustment from the starting point before further adjustment for aggravating or mitigating features, set out on the next page.

	A	B
Category 1	**Starting point** 16 years' custody	**Starting point** 13 years' custody
	Category range 13–19 years' custody	**Category range** 11–17 years' custody
Category 2	**Starting point** 11 years' custody	**Starting point** 8 years' custody
	Category range 7–15 years' custody	**Category range** 5–13 years' custody
Category 3	**Starting point** 6 years' custody	**Starting point** 4 years' custody
	Category range 4–9 years' custody	**Category range** 2–6 years' custody

The table below contains a **non-exhaustive** list of additional factual elements providing the context of the offence and factors relating to the offender. Identify whether any combination of these, or other relevant factors, should result in an upward or downward adjustment from the starting point. **In particular, relevant recent convictions are likely to result in an upward adjustment.** In some cases, having considered these factors, it may be appropriate to move outside the identified category range.

Aggravating factors	Mitigating factors
Statutory aggravating factors	No previous convictions or no relevant/recent convictions
Previous convictions, having regard to a) the nature of the offence to which the conviction relates and its relevance to the current offence; and b) the time that has elapsed since the conviction	Remorse
	Previous good character and/or exemplary conduct*
	Age and/or lack of maturity where it affects the responsibility of the offender
Offence committed whilst on bail	Mental disorder or learning disability, particularly where linked to the commission of the offence
Other aggravating factors	
Specific targeting of a particularly vulnerable victim	
Blackmail or other threats made (where not taken into account at step one)	
Location of offence	
Timing of offence	
Use of weapon or other item to frighten or injure	
Victim compelled to leave their home, school etc	
Failure to comply with current court orders	
Offence committed whilst on licence	
Exploiting contact arrangements with a child to commit an offence	
Presence of others, especially other children	
Any steps taken to prevent the victim reporting an incident, obtaining assistance and/or from assisting or supporting the prosecution	
Attempts to dispose of or conceal evidence	
Commission of offence whilst under the influence of alcohol or drugs	
Victim encouraged to recruit others	

* Previous good character/exemplary conduct is different from having no previous convictions. The more serious the offence, the less the weight which should normally be attributed to this factor. Where previous good character/exemplary conduct has been used to facilitate the offence, this mitigation should not normally be allowed and such conduct may constitute an aggravating factor.

In the context of this offence, previous good character/exemplary conduct should not normally be given any significant weight and will not normally justify a reduction in what would otherwise be the appropriate sentence.

STEP THREE
Consider any factors which indicate a reduction, such as assistance to the prosecution
The court should take into account sections 73 and 74 of the Serious Organised Crime and Police Act 2005 (assistance by defendants: reduction or review of sentence) and any other rule of law by virtue of which an offender may receive a discounted sentence in consequence of assistance given (or offered) to the prosecutor or investigator.

STEP FOUR
Reduction for guilty pleas
The court should take account of any potential reduction for a guilty plea in accordance with section 144 of the Criminal Justice Act 2003 and the Guilty Plea guideline.

STEP FIVE
Dangerousness
The court should consider whether having regard to the criteria contained in Chapter 5 of Part 12 of the Criminal Justice Act 2003 it would be appropriate to award a life sentence (section 224A or section 225(2)) or an extended sentence (section 226A). When sentencing offenders to a life sentence under these provisions, the notional determinate sentence should be used as the basis for the setting of a minimum term.

STEP SIX
Totality principle
If sentencing an offender for more than one offence, or where the offender is already serving a sentence, consider whether the total sentence is just and proportionate to the offending behaviour.

STEP SEVEN
Ancillary orders
The court must consider whether to make any ancillary orders. The court must also consider what other requirements or provisions may automatically apply. Further information is included at Annex A on page 153.

STEP EIGHT
Reasons
Section 174 of the Criminal Justice Act 2003 imposes a duty to give reasons for, and explain the effect of, the sentence.

> **STEP NINE**
> **Consideration for time spent on bail**
> The court must consider whether to give credit for time spent on bail in
> accordance with section 240A of the Criminal Justice Act 2003.

SEXUAL ASSAULT OF A CHILD UNDER 13

Sexual Offences Act 2003 (section 7)

Triable either way
Maximum: 14 years' custody

Offence range: Community order – 9 years' custody

For offences committed on or after 3 December 2012, this is an offence
listed in Part 1 of Schedule 15B for the purposes of section 224A (life
sentence for second listed offence) of the Criminal Justice Act 2003.

For convictions on or after 3 December 2012 (irrespective of the date of
commission of the offence), this is a specified offence for the purposes of
section 226A (extended sentence for certain violent or sexual offences) of
the Criminal Justice Act 2003.

> **STEP ONE**
> **Determining the offence category**

The court should determine which categories of harm and culpability the offence
falls into by reference only to the tables below.

Harm	Culpability
Category 1 • Severe psychological or physical harm • Abduction • Violence or threats of violence • Forced/uninvited entry into victim's home	**A** Significant degree of planning Offender acts together with others to commit the offence Use of alcohol/drugs on victim to facilitate the offence Grooming behaviour used against victim Abuse of trust
Category 2 • Touching of naked genitalia or naked breast area • Prolonged detention/ sustained incident • Additional degrada-tion/humiliation • Child is particularly vulnerable due to extreme youth and/or personal circum-stances	Previous violence against victim Offence committed in course of burglary Sexual images of victim recorded, retained, solicited or shared Deliberate isolation of victim Commercial exploitation and/or motivation Offence racially or religiously aggravated
Category 3 Factor(s) in categories 1 and 2 not present	Offence motivated by, or demonstrating, hostility to the victim based on his or her sexual orientation (or presumed sexual orientation) or transgender identity (or presumed transgender identity) Offence motivated by, or demonstrating, hostility to the victim based on his or her disability (or presumed disability)
	B Factor(s) in category A not present

STEP TWO
Starting point and category range

Having determined the category, the court should use the corresponding starting points to reach a sentence within the category range on the next page. The starting point applies to all offenders irrespective of plea or previous convictions. Having determined the starting point, step two allows further adjustment for aggravating or mitigating features, set out on the next page.

A case of particular gravity, reflected by multiple features of culpability or harm in step one, could merit upward adjustment from the starting point before further adjustment for aggravating or mitigating features, set out on the next page.

Where there is a sufficient prospect of rehabilitation, a community order with a sex offender treatment programme requirement under section 202 of the Criminal Justice Act 2003 can be a proper alternative to a short or moderate length custodial sentence.

	A	B
Category 1	**Starting point** 6 years' custody	**Starting point** 4 years' custody
	Category range 4–9 years' custody	**Category range** 3–7 years' custody
Category 2	**Starting point** 4 years' custody	**Starting point** 2 years' custody
	Category range 3–7 years' custody	**Category range** 1–4 years' custody
Category 3	**Starting point** 1 year's custody	**Starting point** 26 weeks' custody
	Category range 26 weeks' – 2 years' custody	**Category range** High level community order – 1 year's custody

The table below contains a **non-exhaustive** list of additional factual elements providing the context of the offence and factors relating to the offender. Identify whether any combination of these, or other relevant factors, should result in an upward or downward adjustment from the starting point. **In particular, relevant recent convictions are likely to result in an upward adjustment.** In some cases, having considered these factors, it may be appropriate to move outside the identified category range.

Aggravating factors	Mitigating factors
Statutory aggravating factors	No previous convictions or no relevant/recent convictions
Previous convictions, having regard to a) the nature of the offence to which the conviction relates and its relevance to the current offence; and b) the time that has elapsed since the conviction	Remorse
	Previous good character and/or exemplary conduct*
	Age and/or lack of maturity where it affects the responsibility of the offender
Offence committed whilst on bail	Mental disorder or learning disability, particularly where linked to the commission of the offence
Other aggravating factors	
Specific targeting of a particularly vulnerable victim	

* Previous good character/exemplary conduct is different from having no previous convictions. The more serious the offence, the less the weight which should normally be attributed to this factor. Where previous good character/exemplary conduct has been used to facilitate the offence, this mitigation should not normally be allowed and such conduct may constitute an aggravating factor.

In the context of this offence, previous good character/exemplary conduct should not normally be given any significant weight and will not normally justify a reduction in what would otherwise be the appropriate sentence.

Blackmail or other threats made (where not taken into account at step one)

Location of offence

Timing of offence

Use of weapon or other item to frighten or injure

Victim compelled to leave their home, school etc

Failure to comply with current court orders

Offence committed whilst on licence

Exploiting contact arrangements with a child to commit an offence

Presence of others, especially other children

Any steps taken to prevent the victim reporting an incident, obtaining assistance and/or from assisting or supporting the prosecution

Attempts to dispose of or conceal evidence

Commission of offence whilst under the influence of alcohol or drugs

Victim encouraged to recruit others

STEP THREE

Consider any factors which indicate a reduction, such as assistance to the prosecution

The court should take into account sections 73 and 74 of the Serious Organised Crime and Police Act 2005 (assistance by defendants: reduction or review of sentence) and any other rule of law by virtue of which an offender may receive a discounted sentence in consequence of assistance given (or offered) to the prosecutor or investigator.

STEP FOUR

Reduction for guilty pleas

The court should take account of any potential reduction for a guilty plea in accordance with section 144 of the Criminal Justice Act 2003 and the Guilty Plea guideline.

STEP FIVE

Dangerousness

The court should consider whether having regard to the criteria contained in Chapter 5 of Part 12 of the Criminal Justice Act 2003 it would be appropriate to award a life sentence (section 224A) or an extended sentence (section 226A). When sentencing offenders to a life sentence under these provisions, the notional determinate sentence should be used as the basis for the setting of a minimum term.

STEP SIX

Totality principle

If sentencing an offender for more than one offence, or where the offender is already serving a sentence, consider whether the total sentence is just and proportionate to the offending behaviour.

STEP SEVEN

Ancillary orders

The court must consider whether to make any ancillary orders. The court must also consider what other requirements or provisions may automatically apply. Further information is included at Annex A on page 153.

STEP EIGHT

Reasons

Section 174 of the Criminal Justice Act 2003 imposes a duty to give reasons for, and explain the effect of, the sentence.

> **STEP NINE**
> Consideration for time spent on bail
> The court must consider whether to give credit for time spent on bail in accordance with section 240A of the Criminal Justice Act 2003.

CAUSING OR INCITING A CHILD UNDER 13 TO ENGAGE IN SEXUAL ACTIVITY

Sexual Offences Act 2003 (section 8)

Triable only on indictment (if penetration involved)
—otherwise, triable either way

Maximum: Life imprisonment (if penetration involved)
—otherwise, 14 years' custody

Offence range: 1–17 years' custody

This is a serious specified offence for the purposes of sections 224 and, where the offence involved penetration, 225(2) (life sentence for serious offences) of the Criminal Justice Act 2003.

For offences committed on or after 3 December 2012, this is an offence listed in Part 1 of Schedule 15B for the purposes of section 224A (life sentence for second listed offence) of the Criminal Justice Act 2003.

For convictions on or after 3 December 2012 (irrespective of the date of commission of the offence), this is a specified offence for the purposes of section 226A (extended sentence for certain violent or sexual offences) of the Criminal Justice Act 2003.

> **STEP ONE**
> Determining the offence category

The court should determine which categories of harm and culpability the offence falls into by reference only to the tables below.

Harm		Culpability
Category 1	The extreme nature of one or more category 2 factors or the extreme impact caused by a combination of category 2 factors may elevate to category 1	**A** Significant degree of planning Offender acts together with others to commit the offence Use of alcohol/drugs on victim to facilitate the offence Grooming behaviour used against victim Abuse of trust Previous violence against victim Offence committed in course of burglary Sexual images of victim recorded, retained, solicited or shared Deliberate isolation of victim Commercial exploitation and/or motivation Offence racially or religiously aggravated Offence motivated by, or demonstrating hostility to the victim based on his or her sexual orientation (or presumed sexual orientation) or transgender identity (or presumed transgender identity) Offence motivated by, or demonstrating, hostility to the victim based on his or her disability (or presumed disability)
Category 2	• Severe psychological or physical harm • Penetration of vagina or anus (using body or object) by, or of, the victim • Penile penetration of mouth by, or of, the victim • Additional degradation/humiliation • Abduction • Prolonged detention/sustained incident • Violence or threats of violence • Forced/uninvited entry into victim's home • Child is particularly vulnerable due to extreme youth and/or personal circumstances	
Category 3	Factor(s) in categories 1 and 2 not present	**B** Factor(s) in category A not present

---

STEP TWO
Starting point and category range

Having determined the category, the court should use the corresponding starting points to reach a sentence within the category range on the next page. The starting point applies to all offenders irrespective of plea or previous convictions. Having determined the starting point, step two allows further adjustment for aggravating or mitigating features, set out on the next page.

A case of particular gravity, reflected by multiple features of culpability or harm in step one, could merit upward adjustment from the starting point before further adjustment for aggravating or mitigating features, set out on the next page.

	A	B
Category 1	**Starting point** 13 years' custody	**Starting point** 11 years' custody
	Category range 11–17 years' custody	**Category range** 10–15 years' custody
Category 2	**Starting point** 8 years' custody	**Starting point** 6 years' custody
	Category range 5–10 years' custody	**Category range** 3–9 years' custody
Category 3	**Starting point** 5 year's custody	**Starting point** 2 years' custody
	Category range 3–8 years' custody custody	**Category range** 1–4 years' custody

The table below contains a **non–exhaustive** list of additional factual elements providing the context of the offence and factors relating to the offender. Identify whether any combination of these, or other relevant factors, should result in an upward or downward adjustment from the starting point. **In particular, relevant recent convictions are likely to result in an upward adjustment.** In some cases, having considered these factors, it may be appropriate to move outside the identified category range.

Aggravating factors	Mitigating factors
Statutory aggravating factors	No previous convictions **or** no relevant/recent convictions
Previous convictions, having regard to a) the nature of the offence to which the conviction relates and its relevance to the current offence; and b) the time that has elapsed since the conviction	Remorse
	Previous good character and/or exemplary conduct*
Offence committed whilst on bail	Age and/or lack of maturity where it affects the responsibility of the offender
Other aggravating factors	Mental disorder or learning disability, particularly where linked to the commission of the offence
Specific targeting of a particularly vulnerable child	Sexual activity was incited but no activity took place because the offender voluntarily desisted or intervened to prevent it
Ejaculation (where not taken into account at step one)	
Blackmail or other threats made (where not taken into account at step one)	

Aggravating factors (continued):

Pregnancy or STI as a consequence of offence

Location of offence

Timing of offence

Use of weapon or other item to frighten or injure

Victim compelled to leave their home, school, etc

Failure to comply with current court orders

Offence committed whilst on licence

Exploiting contact arrangements with a child to commit an offence

Presence of others, especially other children

Any steps taken to prevent the victim reporting an incident, obtaining assistance and/or from assisting or supporting the prosecution

Attempts to dispose of or conceal evidence

Commission of offence whilst offender under the influence of alcohol or drugs

Victim encouraged to recruit others

Mitigating factors footnote:

* Previous good character/exemplary conduct is different from having no previous convictions. The more serious the offence, the less the weight which should normally be attributed to this factor. Where previous good character/exemplary conduct has been used to facilitate the offence, this mitigation should not normally be allowed and such conduct may constitute an aggravating factor.

In the context of this offence, previous good character/exemplary conduct should not normally be given any significant weight and will not normally justify a reduction in what would otherwise be the appropriate sentence.

STEP THREE
Consider any factors which indicate a reduction, such as assistance to the prosecution
The court should take into account sections 73 and 74 of the Serious Organised Crime and Police Act 2005 (assistance by defendants: reduction or review of sentence) and any other rule of law by virtue of which an offender may receive a discounted sentence in consequence of assistance given (or offered) to the prosecutor or investigator.

STEP FOUR
Reduction for guilty pleas
The court should take account of any potential reduction for a guilty plea in accordance with section 144 of the Criminal Justice Act 2003 and the Guilty Plea guideline.

STEP FIVE
Dangerousness
The court should consider whether having regard to the criteria contained in Chapter 5 of Part 12 of the Criminal Justice Act 2003 it would be appropriate to award a life sentence (section 224A or section 225(2)) or an extended sentence (section 226A). When sentencing offenders to a life sentence under these provisions, the notional determinate sentence should be used as the basis for the setting of a minimum term.

STEP SIX
Totality principle
If sentencing an offender for more than one offence, or where the offender is already serving a sentence, consider whether the total sentence is just and proportionate to the offending behaviour.

STEP SEVEN
Ancillary orders
The court must consider whether to make any ancillary orders. The court must also consider what other requirements or provisions may automatically apply. Further information is included at Annex A on page 153.

STEP EIGHT
Reasons
Section 174 of the Criminal Justice Act 2003 imposes a duty to give reasons for, and explain the effect of, the sentence.

> **STEP NINE**
> **Consideration for time spent on bail**
> The court must consider whether to give credit for time spent on bail in accordance with section 240A of the Criminal Justice Act 2003.

SEXUAL ACTIVITY WITH A CHILD

Sexual Offences Act 2003 (section 9)

CAUSING OR INCITING A CHILD TO ENGAGE IN SEXUAL ACTIVITY

Sexual Offences Act 2003 (section 10)

Triable only on indictment (if penetration involved)
—otherwise, triable either way

Maximum: 14 years' custody

Offence range: Community order – 10 years' custody

For offences committed on or after 3 December 2012, these are offences listed in Part 1 of Schedule 15B for the purposes of section 224A (life sentence for second listed offence) of the Criminal Justice Act 2003.

For convictions on or after 3 December 2012 (irrespective of the date of commission of the offence), these are specified offences for the purposes of section 226A (extended sentence for certain violent or sexual offences) of the Criminal Justice Act 2003.

> **Arranging or facilitating the commission of a child offence (section 14 of the Sexual Offences Act 2003 – page 61)**
>
> The starting points and ranges in this guideline are also applicable to offences of arranging or facilitating the commission of a child offence. In such cases, the level of harm should be determined by reference to the type of activity arranged or facilitated. Sentences commensurate with the applicable starting point and range will ordinarily be appropriate. For offences involving significant commercial exploitation and/or an international element, it may, in the interests of justice, be appropriate to increase a sentence to a point above the category range. In exceptional cases, such as where a vulnerable offender performed a limited role, having been coerced or exploited by others, sentences below the starting point and range may be appropriate.

> **STEP ONE**
> Determining the offence category

The court should determine which categories of harm and culpability the offence falls into by reference **only** to the tables below.

This guideline also applies to offences committed remotely/online.

Harm	Culpability
Category 1 • Penetration of vagina or anus (using body or object) • Penile penetration of mouth In either case by, or of, the victim	**A** Significant degree of planning Offender acts together with others to commit the offence Use of alcohol/drugs on victim to facilitate the offence Grooming behaviour used against victim Abuse of trust Use of threats (including blackmail)
Category 2 • Touching, or exposure, of naked genitalia or naked breasts by, or of, the victim	Sexual images of victim recorded, retained, solicited or shared Specific targeting of a particularly vulnerable child Offender lied about age Significant disparity in age
Category 3 Other sexual activity	Commercial exploitation and/or motivation Offence racially or religiously aggravated Offence motivated by, or demonstrating, hostility to the victim based on his or her sexual orientation (or presumed sexual orientation) or transgender identity (or presumed transgender identity) Offence motivated by, or demonstrating, hostility to the victim based on his or her disability (or presumed disability)
	B Factor(s) in category A not present

STEP TWO
Starting point and category range

Having determined the category, the court should use the corresponding starting points to reach a sentence within the category range below. The starting point applies to all offenders irrespective of plea or previous convictions. Having determined the starting point, step two allows further adjustment for aggravating or mitigating features, set out on the next page.

A case of particular gravity, reflected by multiple features of culpability or harm in step one, could merit upward adjustment from the starting point before further adjustment for aggravating or mitigating features, set out on the next page.

Where there is a sufficient prospect of rehabilitation, a community order with a sex offender treatment programme requirement under section 202 of the Criminal Justice Act 2003 can be a proper alternative to a short or moderate length custodial sentence.

	A	**B**
Category 1	**Starting point** 5 years' custody	**Starting point** 1 years' custody
	Category range 4–10 years' custody	**Category range** High level community order – 2 years' custody
Category 2	**Starting point** 3 years' custody	**Starting point** 26 years' custody
	Category range 2–6 years' custody	**Category range** High level community order – 1 year's custody
Category 3	**Starting point** 26 weeks' custody	**Starting point** Medium level community order
	Category range High level community order – 3 years' custody custody	**Category range** Low level community order – High level community order

The table below contains a **non-exhaustive** list of additional factual elements providing the context of the offence and factors relating to the offender. Identify whether any combination of these, or other relevant factors, should result in an upward or downward adjustment from the starting point. **In particular, relevant recent convictions are likely to result in an upward adjustment.** In some cases, having considered these factors, it may be appropriate to move outside the identified category range.

When sentencing appropriate category 2 or 3 offences, the court should also consider the custody threshold as follows:

- has the custody threshold been passed?
- if so, is it unavoidable that a custodial sentence be imposed?
- if so, can that sentence be suspended?

Aggravating factors	Mitigating factors
Statutory aggravating factors	No previous convictions **or no** relevant/recent convictions
Previous convictions, having regard to a) the nature of the offence to which the conviction relates and its relevance to the current offence; and b) the time that has elapsed since the conviction	Remorse
	Previous good character and/or exemplary conduct*
	Age and/or lack of maturity where it affects the responsibility of the offender
Offence committed whilst on bail	
Other aggravating factors	Mental disorder or learning disability, particularly where linked to the commission of the offence
Severe psychological or physical harm	
Ejaculation	Sexual activity was incited but no activity took place because the offender voluntarily desisted or intervened to prevent it
Pregnancy or STI as a consequence of offence	
Location of offence	
Timing of offence	* Previous good character/exemplary conduct is different from having no previous convictions. The more serious the offence, the less the weight which should normally be attributed to this factor. Where previous good character/exemplary conduct has been used to facilitate the offence, this mitigation should not normally be allowed and such conduct may constitute an aggravating factor.
Victim compelled to leave their home, school, etc	
Failure to comply with current court orders	
Offence committed whilst on licence	
Exploiting contact arrangements with a child to commit an offence	In the context of this offence, previous good character/exemplary conduct should not normally be given any significant weight and will not normally justify a reduction in what would otherwise be the appropriate sentence.
Presence of others, especially other children	
Any steps taken to prevent the victim reporting an incident, obtaining assistance and/or from assisting or supporting the prosecution	

Aggravating factors

Attempts to dispose of or conceal
evidence

Failure of offender to respond to
previous warnings

Commission of offence whilst under
the influence of alcohol or drugs

Victim encouraged to recruit others

Period over which offence committed

STEP THREE

Consider any factors which indicate a reduction, such as assistance to the prosecution

The court should take into account sections 73 and 74 of the Serious Organised Crime and Police Act 2005 (assistance by defendants: reduction or review of sentence) and any other rule of law by virtue of which an offender may receive a discounted sentence in consequence of assistance given (or offered) to the prosecutor or investigator.

STEP FOUR

Reduction for guilty pleas

The court should take account of any potential reduction for a guilty plea in accordance with section 144 of the Criminal Justice Act 2003 and the Guilty Plea guideline.

STEP FIVE

Dangerousness

The court should consider whether having regard to the criteria contained in Chapter 5 of Part 12 of the Criminal Justice Act 2003 it would be appropriate to award a life sentence (section 224A) or an extended sentence (section 226A). When sentencing offenders to a life sentence under these provisions, the notional determinate sentence should be used as the basis for the setting of a minimum term.

STEP SIX

Totality principle

If sentencing an offender for more than one offence, or where the offender is already serving a sentence, consider whether the total sentence is just and proportionate to the offending behaviour.

> **STEP SEVEN**
> Ancillary orders
> The court must consider whether to make any ancillary orders. The court must also consider what other requirements or provisions may automatically apply. Further information is included at Annex A on page 153.

> **STEP EIGHT**
> Reasons
> Section 174 of the Criminal Justice Act 2003 imposes a duty to give reasons for, and explain the effect of, the sentence.

> **STEP NINE**
> Consideration for time spent on bail
> The court must consider whether to give credit for time spent on bail in accordance with section 240A of the Criminal Justice Act 2003.

Sexual Activity with a Child Family Member

Sexual Offences Act 2003

Inciting a Child Family Member to Engage in Sexual Activity

Sexual Offences Act 2003 (section 26)

Triable only on indictment (if penetration involved)
—otherwise, triable either way

Maximum: 14 years' custody

Offence range: Community order – 10 years' custody

For offences committed on or after 3 December 2012, these are offences listed in Part 1 of Schedule 15B for the purposes of section 224A (life sentence for second listed offence) of the Criminal Justice Act 2003.

For convictions on or after 3 December 2012 (irrespective of the date of commission of the offence), these are specified offences for the purposes of section 226A (extended sentence for certain violent or sexual offences) of the Criminal Justice Act 2003.

> **STEP ONE**
> Determining the offence category

The court should determine which categories of harm and culpability the offence falls into by reference **only** to the tables below. This offence involves those who have a family relationship with the victim and it should be assumed that the greater the abuse of trust within this relationship the more grave the offence.

Harm	Culpability
Category 1 • Penetration of vagina or anus (using body or object) • Penile penetration of mouth In either case by, or of, the victim	**A** Significant degree of planning Offender acts together with others to commit the offence Use of alcohol/drugs on victim to facilitate the offence Grooming behaviour used against victim
Category 2 • Touching of naked genitalia or naked breasts by, or of, the victim	Use of threats (including blackmail) Sexual images of victim recorded, retained, solicited or shared
Category 3 Other sexual activity	Specific targeting of a particularly vulnerable child Significant disparity in age Commercial exploitation and/or motivation Offence racially or religiously aggravated Offence motivated by, or demonstrating, hostility to the victim based on his or her sexual orientation (or presumed sexual orientation) or transgender identity (or presumed transgender identity) Offence motivated by, or demonstrating, hostility to the victim based on his or her disability (or presumed disability)
	B Factor(s) in category A not present

STEP TWO
Starting point and category range

Having determined the category, the court should use the corresponding starting points to reach a sentence within the category range below. The starting point applies to all offenders irrespective of plea or previous convictions. Having determined the starting point, step two allows further adjustment for aggravating or mitigating features, set out on the next page.

A case of particular gravity, reflected by multiple features of culpability or harm in step one, could merit upward adjustment from the starting point before further adjustment for aggravating or mitigating features, set out on the next page.

Where there is a sufficient prospect of rehabilitation, a community order with a sex offender treatment programme requirement under section 202 of the Criminal Justice Act 2003 can be a proper alternative to a short or moderate length custodial sentence.

	A	B
Category 1	**Starting point** 6 years' custody	**Starting point** 3 years 6 months' custody
	Category range 4–10 years' custody	**Category range** 2 years 6 months' – 5 years' custody
Category 2	**Starting point** 4 years' custody	**Starting point** 18 months' custody
	Category range 2–6 years' custody	**Category range** 26 weeks' – 2 years 6 months' custody
Category 3	**Starting point** 1 year's custody	**Starting point** Medium level community order
	Category range High level community order – 3 years' custody custody	**Category range** Low level community order – High level community order

The table below contains a **non-exhaustive** list of additional factual elements providing the context of the offence and factors relating to the offender. Identify whether any combination of these, or other relevant factors, should result in an upward or downward adjustment from the starting point. **In particular, relevant recent convictions are likely to result in an upward adjustment.** In some cases, having considered these factors, it may be appropriate to move outside the identified category range.

When sentencing appropriate **category 3 offences,** the court should also consider the custody threshold as follows:

- has the custody threshold been passed?
- if so, is it unavoidable that a custodial sentence be imposed?
- if so, can that sentence be suspended?

Aggravating factors	Mitigating factors
Statutory aggravating factors	No previous convictions **or** no relevant/recent convictions
Previous convictions, having regard to a) the nature of the offence to which the conviction relates and its relevance to the current offence; and b) the time that has elapsed since the conviction	Remorse
	Previous good character and/or exemplary conduct*
Offence committed whilst on bail	Age and/or lack of maturity where it affects the responsibility of the offender
Other aggravating factors	Mental disorder or learning disability, particularly where linked to the commission of the offence
Severe psychological or physical harm	Sexual activity was incited but no activity took place because the offender voluntarily desisted or intervened to prevent it
Ejaculation	
Pregnancy or STI as a consequence of offence	
Location of offence	* Previous good character/exemplary conduct is different from having no previous convictions. The more serious the offence, the less the weight which should normally be attributed to this factor. Where previous good character/exemplary conduct has been used to facilitate the offence, this mitigation should not normally be allowed and such conduct may constitute an aggravating factor.
Timing of offence	
Victim compelled to leave their home, school, etc	
Failure to comply with current court orders	
Offence committed whilst on licence	
Exploiting contact arrangements with a child to commit an offence	In the context of this offence, previous good character/exemplary conduct should not normally be given any significant weight and will not normally justify a reduction in what would otherwise be the appropriate sentence.
Presence of others, especially other children	
Any steps taken to prevent the victim reporting an incident, obtaining assistance and/or from assisting or supporting the prosecution	

Aggravating factors

Attempts to dispose of or conceal
evidence

Failure of offender to respond to
previous warnings

Commission of offence whilst under
the influence of alcohol or drugs

Victim encouraged to recruit others

Period over which offence committed

STEP THREE

Consider any factors which indicate a reduction, such as assistance to the prosecution

The court should take into account sections 73 and 74 of the Serious Organised Crime and Police Act 2005 (assistance by defendants: reduction or review of sentence) and any other rule of law by virtue of which an offender may receive a discounted sentence in consequence of assistance given (or offered) to the prosecutor or investigator.

STEP FOUR

Reduction for guilty pleas

The court should take account of any potential reduction for a guilty plea in accordance with section 144 of the Criminal Justice Act 2003 and the Guilty Plea guideline.

STEP FIVE

Dangerousness

The court should consider whether having regard to the criteria contained in Chapter 5 of Part 12 of the Criminal Justice Act 2003 it would be appropriate to award a life sentence (section 224A) or an extended sentence (section 226A). When sentencing offenders to a life sentence under these provisions, the notional determinate sentence should be used as the basis for the setting of a minimum term.

STEP SIX

Totality principle

If sentencing an offender for more than one offence, or where the offender is already serving a sentence, consider whether the total sentence is just and proportionate to the offending behaviour.

STEP SEVEN
Ancillary orders
The court must consider whether to make any ancillary orders. The court must also consider what other requirements or provisions may automatically apply. Further information is included at Annex A on page 153.

STEP EIGHT
Reasons
Section 174 of the Criminal Justice Act 2003 imposes a duty to give reasons for, and explain the effect of, the sentence.

STEP NINE
Consideration for time spent on bail
The court must consider whether to give credit for time spent on bail in accordance with section 240A of the Criminal Justice Act 2003.

ENGAGING IN SEXUAL ACTIVITY IN THE PRESENCE OF A CHILD

Sexual Offences Act 2003 (section 11)

CAUSING A CHILD TO WATCH A SEXUAL ACT

Sexual Offences Act 2003 (section 12)

Triable either way
Maximum: 10 years' custody

Offence range: Community order – 6 years' custody

For offences committed on or after 3 December 2012, these are offences listed in Part 1 of Schedule 15B for the purposes of section 224A (life sentence for second listed offence) of the Criminal Justice Act 2003.

For convictions on or after 3 December 2012 (irrespective of the date of commission of the offence), these are specified offences for the purposes of section 226A (extended sentence for certain violent or sexual offences) of the Criminal Justice Act 2003.

Arranging or facilitating the commission of a child offence (section 14 of the Sexual Offences Act 2003 – guidance on page 61)

The starting points and ranges in this guideline are also applicable to offences of arranging or facilitating the commission of a child offence. In such cases, the level of harm should be determined by reference to the type of activity arranged or facilitated. Sentences commensurate with the applicable starting point and range will ordinarily be appropriate. For offences involving significant commercial exploitation and/or an international element, it may, in the interests of justice, be appropriate to increase a sentence to a point above the category range. In exceptional cases, such as where a vulnerable offender performed a limited role, having been coerced or exploited by others, sentences below the starting point and range may be appropriate.

STEP ONE
Determining the offence category

The court should determine which categories of harm and culpability the offence falls into by reference only to the tables below.

Harm	Culpability
Category 1 • Causing victim to view extreme pornography • Causing victim to view indecent/prohibited images of children • Engaging in, or causing a victim to view live, sexual activity involving sadism/ violence/sexual activity with an animal/a child	**A** Significant degree of planning Offender acts together with others in order to commit the offence Use of alcohol/drugs on victim to facilitate the offence Grooming behaviour used against victim Abuse of trust Use of threats (including blackmail) Specific targeting of a particularly vulnerable child Significant disparity in age
Category 2 Engaging in, or causing a victim to view images of or view live, sexual activity involving: • penetration of vagina or anus (using body or object)	Commercial exploitation and/or motivation Offence racially or religiously aggravated Offence motivated by, or demonstrating, hostility to the victim based on his or her sexual

Harm		Culpability
	• penile penetration of the mouth • masturbation	**A**
Category 3	Factor(s) in categories 1 and 2 not present	orientation (or presumed sexual orientation) or transgender identity (or presumed transgender identity) Offence motivated by, or demonstrating, hostility to the victim based on his or her disability (or presumed disability)
		B
		Factor(s) in category A not present

STEP TWO
Starting point and category range

Having determined the category, the court should use the corresponding starting points to reach a sentence within the category range on the next page. The starting point applies to all offenders irrespective of plea or previous convictions. Having determined the starting point, step two allows further adjustment for aggravating or mitigating features, set out on the next page.

A case of particular gravity, reflected by multiple features of culpability or harm in step one, could merit upward adjustment from the starting point before further adjustment for aggravating or mitigating features, set out on the next page.

Where there is a sufficient prospect of rehabilitation, a community order with a sex offender treatment programme requirement under section 202 of the Criminal Justice Act 2003 can be a proper alternative to a short or moderate length custodial sentence.

	A	B
Category 1	**Starting point** 4 years' custody	**Starting point** 2 years' custody
	Category range 3–6 years' custody	**Category range** 1–3 years' custody

	A	B
Category 2	**Starting point** 2 years' custody	**Starting point** 1 year's custody
	Category range 1–3 years' custody	**Category range** High level community order – 18 months' custody
Category 3	**Starting point** 26 weeks' custody	**Starting point** Medium level community order
	Category range High level community order – 1 year's custody	**Category range** Low level community order – High level community order

The table below contains a **non-exhaustive** list of additional factual elements providing the context of the offence and factors relating to the offender. Identify whether any combination of these, or other relevant factors, should result in an upward or downward adjustment from the starting point. **In particular, relevant recent convictions are likely to result in an upward adjustment.** In some cases, having considered these factors, it may be appropriate to move outside the identified category range.

When sentencing appropriate **category 2 or 3 offences**, the court should also consider the custody threshold as follows:

- has the custody threshold been passed?
- if so, is it unavoidable that a custodial sentence be imposed?
- if so, can that sentence be suspended?

Aggravating factors	Mitigating factors
Statutory aggravating factors	No previous convictions **or** no relevant/recent convictions
Previous convictions, having regard to a) the nature of the offence to which the conviction relates and its relevance to the current offence; and b) the time that has elapsed since the conviction	Remorse
	Previous good character and/or exemplary conduct*
	Age and/or lack of maturity where it affects the responsibility of the offender
Offence committed whilst on bail	Mental disorder or learning disability, particularly where linked to the commission of the offence
Other aggravating factors	
Location of offence	Demonstration of steps taken to address offending behaviour
Timing of offence	
Victim compelled to leave their home, school, etc	
Failure to comply with current court orders	* Previous good character/exemplary conduct is different from having no previous convictions. The more serious the offence, the less the weight which should normally be attributed to this factor. Where previous good character/exemplary conduct has been used to facilitate the offence, this mitigation should not normally be allowed and such conduct may constitute an aggravating factor.
Offence committed whilst on licence	
Exploiting contact arrangements with a child to commit an offence	
Presence of others, especially other children	
Any steps taken to prevent the victim reporting an incident, obtaining assistance and/or from assisting or supporting the prosecution	
Attempts to dispose of or conceal evidence	
Failure of offender to respond to previous warnings	
Commission of offence whilst offender under the influence of alcohol or drugs	
Victim encouraged to recruit others	

STEP THREE
Consider any factors which indicate a reduction, such as assistance to the prosecution
The court should take into account sections 73 and 74 of the Serious Organised Crime and Police Act 2005 (assistance by defendants: reduction or review of sentence) and any other rule of law by virtue of which an offender may receive a discounted sentence in consequence of assistance given (or offered) to the prosecutor or investigator.

STEP FOUR
Reduction for guilty pleas
The court should take account of any potential reduction for a guilty plea in accordance with section 144 of the Criminal Justice Act 2003 and the Guilty Plea guideline.

STEP FIVE
Dangerousness
The court should consider whether having regard to the criteria contained in Chapter 5 of Part 12 of the Criminal Justice Act 2003 it would be appropriate to award a life sentence (section 224A) or an extended sentence (section 226A). When sentencing offenders to a life sentence under these provisions, the notional determinate sentence should be used as the basis for the setting of a minimum term.

STEP SIX
Totality principle
If sentencing an offender for more than one offence, or where the offender is already serving a sentence, consider whether the total sentence is just and proportionate to the offending behaviour.

STEP SEVEN
Ancillary orders
The court must consider whether to make any ancillary orders. The court must also consider what other requirements or provisions may automatically apply. Further information is included at Annex A on page 153.

STEP EIGHT
Reasons
Section 174 of the Criminal Justice Act 2003 imposes a duty to give reasons for, and explain the effect of, the sentence.

STEP NINE
Consideration for time spent on bail
The court must consider whether to give credit for time spent on bail in accordance with section 240A of the Criminal Justice Act 2003.

ARRANGING OR FACILITATING THE COMMISSION OF A CHILD SEX OFFENCE

Sexual Offences Act 2003 (section 14)

Triable either way
Maximum: 14 years' custody

For offences committed on or after 3 December 2012, these are offences listed in Part 1 of Schedule 15B for the purposes of section 224A (life sentence for second listed offence) of the Criminal Justice Act 2003.

For convictions on or after 3 December 2012 (irrespective of the date of commission of the offence), these are specified offences for the purposes of section 226A (extended sentence for certain violent or sexual offences) of the Criminal Justice Act 2003.

Sentencers should refer to the guideline for the applicable, substantive offence of arranging or facilitating under sections 9 to 12. See pages 45 to 49 and 57 to 60. The level of harm should be determined by reference to the type of activity arranged or facilitated. Sentences commensurate with the applicable starting point and range will ordinarily be appropriate. For offences involving significant commercial exploitation and/or an international element, it may, in the interests of justice, be appropriate to increase a sentence to a point above the category range. In exceptional cases, such as where a vulnerable offender performed a limited role, having been coerced or exploited by others, sentences below the starting point and range may be appropriate.

MEETING A CHILD FOLLOWING SEXUAL GROOMING

Sexual Offences Act 2003 (section 15)

Triable either way
Maximum: 10 years' custody

Offence range: 1–7 years' custody

For offences committed on or after 3 December 2012, this is an offence listed in Part 1 of Schedule 15B for the purposes of section 224A (life sentence for second listed offence) of the Criminal Justice Act 2003.

For convictions on or after 3 December 2012 (irrespective of the date of commission of the offence), this is a specified offence for the purposes of section 226A (extended sentence for certain violent or sexual offences) of the Criminal Justice Act 2003.

STEP ONE
Determining the offence category

The court should determine the offence category using the table below.

Category 1	Raised harm and raised culpability
Category 2	Raised harm or raised culpability
Category 3	Grooming without raised harm or culpability factors present

The court should determine culpability and harm caused or intended, by reference only to the factors below, which comprise the principal factual elements of the offence. Where an offence does not fall squarely into a category, individual factors may require a degree of weighting before making an overall assessment and determining the appropriate offence category.

Factors indicating raised harm	Factors indicating raised culpability
Continued contact despite victim's attempts to terminate contact	Offender acts together with others to commit the offence
Sexual images exchanged	Communication indicates penetrative sexual activity is intended
Victim exposed to extreme sexual content (for example, extreme pornography)	Offender lied about age/persona
Child is particularly vulnerable due to personal circumstances	Use of threats (including blackmail), gifts or bribes
	Abuse of trust
	Specific targeting of a particularly vulnerable child
	Abduction/detention
	Commercial exploitation and/or motivation
	Offence racially or religiously aggravated

	Factors indicating raised culpability
	Offence motivated by, or demonstrating, hostility to the victim based on his or her sexual orientation (or presumed sexual orientation) or transgender identity (or presumed transgender identity)
	Offence motivated by, or demonstrating, hostility to the victim based on his or her disability (or presumed disability)

STEP TWO
Starting point and category range

Having determined the category, the court should use the corresponding starting points to reach a sentence within the category range below. The starting point applies to all offenders irrespective of plea or previous convictions. Having determined the starting point, step two allows further adjustment for aggravating or mitigating features, set out below.

A case of particular gravity, reflected by multiple features of culpability or harm in step one, could merit upward adjustment from the starting point before further adjustment for aggravating or mitigating features, set out below.

Category 1	Starting point
	4 years' custody
	Category range
	3–7 years' custody
Category 2	Starting point
	2 years' custody
	Category range
	1–4 years' custody
Category 3	Starting point
	18 months' custody
	Category range
	1 year – 2 years 6 months' custody

The table below contains a **non-exhaustive** list of additional factual elements providing the context of the offence and factors relating to the offender. Identify whether any combination of these, or other relevant factors, should result in an upward or downward adjustment from the starting point. **In particular, relevant recent convictions are likely to result in an upward adjustment.** In some cases, having considered these factors, it may be appropriate to move outside the identified category range.

Aggravating factors	Mitigating factors
Statutory aggravating factors	No previous convictions or no relevant/recent convictions
Previous convictions, having regard to a) the nature of the offence to which the conviction relates and its relevance to the current offence; and b) the time that has elapsed since the conviction	Remorse
	Previous good character and/or exemplary conduct*
	Age and/or lack of maturity where it affects the responsibility of the offender
Offence committed whilst on bail	Mental disorder or learning disability, particularly where linked to the commission of the offence
Other aggravating factors	
Failure to comply with current court orders	
Offence committed whilst on licence	Demonstration of steps taken to address offending behaviour
Any steps taken to prevent the victim reporting an incident, obtaining assistance and/or from assisting or supporting the prosecution	
Attempts to dispose of or conceal evidence	
Victim encouraged to recruit others	

* Previous good character/exemplary conduct is different from having no previous convictions. The more serious the offence, the less the weight which should normally be attributed to this factor. Where previous good character/exemplary conduct has been used to facilitate the offence, this mitigation should not normally be allowed and such conduct may constitute an aggravating factor.

STEP THREE
Consider any factors which indicate a reduction, such as assistance to the prosecution
The court should take into account sections 73 and 74 of the Serious Organised Crime and Police Act 2005 (assistance by defendants: reduction or review of sentence) and any other rule of law by virtue of which an offender may receive a discounted sentence in consequence of assistance given (or offered) to the prosecutor or investigator.

STEP FOUR
Reduction for guilty pleas
The court should take account of any potential reduction for a guilty plea in accordance with section 144 of the Criminal Justice Act 2003 and the Guilty Plea guideline.

STEP FIVE
Dangerousness
The court should consider whether having regard to the criteria contained in Chapter 5 of Part 12 of the Criminal Justice Act 2003 it would be appropriate to award a life sentence (section 224A) or an extended sentence (section 226A). When sentencing offenders to a life sentence under these provisions, the notional determinate sentence should be used as the basis for the setting of a minimum term.

STEP SIX
Totality principle
If sentencing an offender for more than one offence, or where the offender is already serving a sentence, consider whether the total sentence is just and proportionate to the offending behaviour.

STEP SEVEN
Ancillary orders
The court must consider whether to make any ancillary orders. The court must also consider what other requirements or provisions may automatically apply. Further information is included at Annex A on page 153.

STEP EIGHT
Reasons
Section 174 of the Criminal Justice Act 2003 imposes a duty to give reasons for, and explain the effect of, the sentence.

STEP NINE
Consideration for time spent on bail
The court must consider whether to give credit for time spent on bail in accordance with section 240A of the Criminal Justice Act 2003.

ABUSE OF POSITION OF TRUST: SEXUAL ACTIVITY WITH A CHILD

Sexual Offences Act 2003 (section 16)

ABUSE OF POSITION OF TRUST: CAUSING OR INCITING A CHILD TO ENGAGE IN SEXUAL ACTIVITY

Sexual Offences Act 2003 (section 17)

Triable either way
Maximum: 5 years' custody

Offence range: Community order – 2 years' custody

For convictions on or after 3 December 2012 (irrespective of the date of commission of the offence), these are specified offences for the purposes of section 226A (extended sentence for certain violent or sexual offences) of the Criminal Justice Act 2003.

STEP ONE
Determining the offence category

The court should determine which categories of harm and culpability the offence falls into by reference only to the tables below.

This guideline also applies to offences committed remotely/online.

Harm		Culpability
Category 1	• Penetration of vagina or anus (using body or object) • Penile penetration of mouth In either case by, or of, the victim	**A** Significant degree of planning Offender acts together with others to commit the offence Use of alcohol/drugs on victim to facilitate the offence Grooming behaviour used against victim Use of threats (including blackmail) Sexual images of victim recorded, retained, solicited or shared
Category 2	• Touching, or exposure, of naked genitalia or naked breasts by, or of, the victim	

Harm	Culpability
Category 3 Factor(s) in categories 1 and 2 not present	**A**
	Specific targeting of a particularly vulnerable child
	Commercial exploitation and/or motivation
	Offence racially or religiously aggravated
	Offence motivated by, or demonstrating, hostility to the victim based on his or her sexual orientation (or presumed sexual orientation) or transgender identity (or presumed transgender identity)
	Offence motivated by, or demonstrating, hostility to the victim based on his or her disability (or presumed disability)
	B
	Factor(s) in category A not present

STEP TWO
Starting point and category range

Having determined the category, the court should use the corresponding starting points to reach a sentence within the category range on the next page. The starting point applies to all offenders irrespective of plea or previous convictions. Having determined the starting point, step two allows further adjustment for aggravating or mitigating features, set out on the next page.

A case of particular gravity, reflected by multiple features of culpability or harm in step one, could merit upward adjustment from the starting point before further adjustment for aggravating or mitigating features, set out on the next page.

Where there is a sufficient prospect of rehabilitation, a community order with a sex offender treatment programme requirement under section 202 of the Criminal Justice Act 2003 can be a proper alternative to a short or moderate length custodial sentence.

	A	B
Category 1	**Starting point** 18 months' custody	**Starting point** 1 year's custody
	Category range 1–2 years' custody	**Category range** 26 weeks' – 18 months' custody
Category 2	**Starting point** 1 year's custody	**Starting point** 26 weeks' custody
	Category range 26 weeks' – 18 months' custody	**Category range** High level community order – 1 year's custody
Category 3	**Starting point** 26 weeks' custody	**Starting point** Medium level community order **Category range**
	Category range High level community order – 1 year's custody	**Category range** Low level community order – High level community order

The table below contains a **non-exhaustive** list of additional factual elements providing the context of the offence and factors relating to the offender. Identify whether any combination of these, or other relevant factors, should result in an upward or downward adjustment from the starting point. **In particular, relevant recent convictions are likely to result in an upward adjustment.** In some cases, having considered these factors, it may be appropriate to move outside the identified category range.

When sentencing appropriate **category 2 or 3 offences**, the court should also consider the custody threshold as follows:

- has the custody threshold been passed?
- if so, is it unavoidable that a custodial sentence be imposed?
- if so, can that sentence be suspended?

730

Aggravating factors	Mitigating factors
Statutory aggravating factors	No previous convictions or no relevant/recent convictions
Previous convictions, having regard to a) the nature of the offence to which the conviction relates and its relevance to the current offence; and b) the time that has elapsed since the conviction	Remorse
	Previous good character and/or exemplary conduct*
	Age and/or lack of maturity where it affects the responsibility of the offender
Offence committed whilst on bail	Mental disorder or learning disability, particularly where linked to the commission of the offence
Other aggravating factors	
Ejaculation	Sexual activity was incited but no activity took place because the offender voluntarily desisted or intervened to prevent it
Pregnancy or STI as a consequence of offence	
Location of offence	
Timing of offence	
Victim compelled to leave their home, school, etc	Demonstration of steps taken to address offending behaviour
Failure to comply with current court orders	
Offence committed whilst on licence	
Presence of others, especially other children	
Any steps taken to prevent the victim reporting an incident, obtaining assistance and/or from assisting or supporting the prosecution	
Attempts to dispose of or conceal evidence	
Failure of offender to respond to previous warnings	
Commission of offence whilst under the influence of alcohol or drugs	
Victim encouraged to recruit others	

* Previous good character/exemplary conduct is different from having no previous convictions. The more serious the offence, the less the weight which should normally be attributed to this factor. Where previous good character/exemplary conduct has been used to facilitate the offence, this mitigation should not normally be allowed and such conduct may constitute an aggravating factor.

STEP THREE
Consider any factors which indicate a reduction, such as assistance to the prosecution
The court should take into account sections 73 and 74 of the Serious Organised Crime and Police Act 2005 (assistance by defendants: reduction or review of sentence) and any other rule of law by virtue of which an offender may receive a discounted sentence in consequence of assistance given (or offered) to the prosecutor or investigator.

STEP FOUR
Reduction for guilty pleas
The court should take account of any potential reduction for a guilty plea in accordance with section 144 of the Criminal Justice Act 2003 and the Guilty Plea guideline.

STEP FIVE
Dangerousness
The court should consider whether having regard to the criteria contained in Chapter 5 of Part 12 of the Criminal Justice Act 2003 it would be appropriate to award an extended sentence (section 226A).

STEP SIX
Totality principle
If sentencing an offender for more than one offence, or where the offender is already serving a sentence, consider whether the total sentence is just and proportionate to the offending behaviour.

STEP SEVEN
Ancillary orders
The court must consider whether to make any ancillary orders. The court must also consider what other requirements or provisions may automatically apply. Further information is included at Annex A on page 153.

STEP EIGHT
Reasons
Section 174 of the Criminal Justice Act 2003 imposes a duty to give reasons for, and explain the effect of, the sentence.

STEP NINE
Consideration for time spent on bail
The court must consider whether to give credit for time spent on bail in accordance with section 240A of the Criminal Justice Act 2003.

ABUSE OF POSITION OF TRUST: SEXUAL ACTIVITY IN THE PRESENCE OF A CHILD

Sexual Offences Act 2003 (section 18)

ABUSE OF POSITION OF TRUST: CAUSING A CHILD TO WATCH A SEXUAL ACT

Sexual Offences Act 2003 (section 19)

Triable either way
Maximum: 5 years' custody

Offence range: Community order – 2 years' custody

For convictions on or after 3 December 2012 (irrespective of the date of commission of the offence), these are specified offences for the purposes of section 226A (extended sentence for certain violent or sexual offences) of the Criminal Justice Act 2003.

STEP ONE
Determining the offence category

The court should determine which categories of harm and culpability the offence falls into by reference only to the tables below.

Harm	Culpability
Category 1 • Causing victim to view extreme pornography • Causing victim to view indecent/prohibited images of children • Engaging in, or causing a victim to view live, sexual activity involving sadism/violence/sexual activity with an animal/a child	**A** Significant degree of planning Offender acts together with others to commit the offence Use of alcohol/drugs on victim to facilitate the offence Grooming behaviour used against victim Use of threats (including blackmail) Specific targeting of a particularly vulnerable child Commercial exploitation and/or motivation

Harm	Culpability
Category 2 Engaging in, or causing a victim to view images of or view live, sexual activity involving: • penetration of vagina or anus (using body or object) • penile penetration of the mouth • masturbation	**A** Offence racially or religiously aggravated Offence motivated by, or demonstrating, hostility to the victim based on his or her sexual orientation (or presumed sexual orientation) or transgender identity (or presumed transgender identity)
Category 3 Factor(s) in categories 1 and 2 not present	Offence motivated by, or demonstrating, hostility to the victim based on his or her disability (or presumed disability)
	B Factor(s) in category A not present

> **STEP TWO**
> **Starting point and category range**

Having determined the category, the court should use the corresponding starting points to reach a sentence within the category range on the next page. The starting point applies to all offenders irrespective of plea or previous convictions. Having determined the starting point, step two allows further adjustment for aggravating or mitigating features, set out on the next page.

A case of particular gravity, reflected by multiple features of culpability or harm in step one, could merit upward adjustment from the starting point before further adjustment for aggravating or mitigating features, set out on the next page.

Where there is a sufficient prospect of rehabilitation, a community order with a sex offender treatment programme requirement under section 202 of the Criminal Justice Act 2003 can be a proper alternative to a short or moderate length custodial sentence.

	A	B
Category 1	**Starting point** 18 months' custody	**Starting point** 1 year's custody
	Category range 1–2 years' custody	**Category range** 26 weeks' – 18 months' custody
Category 2	**Starting point** 1 year's custody	**Starting point** 26 weeks' custody
	Category range 26 weeks' – 18 months' custody	**Category range** High level community order – 1 year's custody
Category 3	**Starting point** 26 weeks' custody	**Starting point** Medium level community order
	Category range High level community order – 1 year's custody	**Category range** Low level community order – High level community order

The table below contains a **non-exhaustive** list of additional factual elements providing the context of the offence and factors relating to the offender. Identify whether any combination of these, or other relevant factors, should result in an upward or downward adjustment from the starting point. **In particular, relevant recent convictions are likely to result in an upward adjustment.** In some cases, having considered these factors, it may be appropriate to move outside the identified category range.

When sentencing appropriate category 2 or 3 offences, the court should also consider the custody threshold as follows:

- has the custody threshold been passed?
- if so, is it unavoidable that a custodial sentence be imposed?
- if so, can that sentence be suspended?

Aggravating factors	Mitigating factors
Statutory aggravating factors	No previous convictions or no relevant/recent convictions
Previous convictions, having regard to a) the nature of the offence to which the conviction relates and its relevance to the current offence; and b) the time that has elapsed since the conviction	Remorse
	Previous good character and/or exemplary conduct*
	Age and/or lack of maturity where it affects the responsibility of the offender
Offence committed whilst on bail	Mental disorder or learning disability, particularly where linked to the commission of the offence
Other aggravating factors	
Location of offence	Demonstration of steps taken to address offending behaviour
Timing of offence	
Victim compelled to leave their home, school, etc	* Previous good character/exemplary conduct is different from having no previous convictions. The more serious the offence, the less the weight which should normally be attributed to this factor. Where previous good character/exemplary conduct has been used to facilitate the offence, this mitigation should not normally be allowed and such conduct may constitute an aggravating factor.
Failure to comply with current court orders	
Offence committed whilst on licence	
Presence of others, especially other children	
Any steps taken to prevent the victim reporting an incident, obtaining assistance and/or from assisting or supporting the prosecution	
Attempts to dispose of or conceal evidence	
Failure of offender to respond to previous warnings	
Commission of offence whilst under the influence of alcohol or drugs	
Victim encouraged to recruit others	

STEP THREE

Consider any factors which indicate a reduction, such as assistance to the prosecution

The court should take into account sections 73 and 74 of the Serious Organised Crime and Police Act 2005 (assistance by defendants: reduction or review of sentence) and any other rule of law by virtue of which an offender may receive a discounted sentence in consequence of assistance given (or offered) to the prosecutor or investigator.

STEP FOUR
Reduction for guilty pleas
The court should take account of any potential reduction for a guilty plea in accordance with section 144 of the Criminal Justice Act 2003 and the Guilty Plea guideline.

STEP FIVE
Dangerousness
The court should consider whether having regard to the criteria contained in Chapter 5 of Part 12 of the Criminal Justice Act 2003 it would be appropriate to award an extended sentence (section 226A).

STEP SIX
Totality principle
If sentencing an offender for more than one offence, or where the offender is already serving a sentence, consider whether the total sentence is just and proportionate to the offending behaviour.

STEP SEVEN
Ancillary orders
The court must consider whether to make any ancillary orders. The court must also consider what other requirements or provisions may automatically apply. Further information is included at Annex A on page 153.

STEP EIGHT
Reasons
Section 174 of the Criminal Justice Act 2003 imposes a duty to give reasons for, and explain the effect of, the sentence.

STEP NINE
Consideration for time spent on bail
The court must consider whether to give credit for time spent on bail in accordance with section 240A of the Criminal Justice Act 2003.

POSSESSION OF INDECENT PHOTOGRAPH OF CHILD

Criminal Justice Act 1988 (section 160)

Triable either way
Maximum: 5 years' custody

Offence range: Community order – 3 years' custody

INDECENT PHOTOGRAPHS OF CHILDREN

Protection of Children Act 1978 (section 1)

Triable either way
Maximum: 10 years' custody

Offence range: Community order – 9 years' custody

For section 1 offences committed on or after 3 December 2012, this is an offence listed in Part 1 of Schedule 15B for the purposes of section 224A (life sentence for second listed offence) of the Criminal Justice Act 2003.

For convictions on or after 3 December 2012 (irrespective of the date of commission of the offence), these are specified offences for the purposes of section 226A (extended sentence for certain violent or sexual offences) of the Criminal Justice Act 2003.

STEP ONE
Determining the offence category

The court should determine the offence category using the table below.

	Possession	Distribution*	Production**
Category A	Possession of images involving penetrative sexual activity	Sharing images involving penetrative sexual activity	Creating images involving penentrative sexual activity
	Possession of images involving sexual activity with an animal or sadism	Sharing images involving sexual activity with an animal or sadism	Creating images involving sexual activity with an animal or sadism
Category B	Possession of images involving non-penetrative sexual activity	Sharing of images involving non-penetrative sexual activity	Creating images involving non-penetrative sexual activity

	Possession	Distribution*	Production**
Category C	Possession of other indecent images not falling within categories A or B	Sharing of other indecent images not falling within categories A or B	Creating other indecent images not falling within categories A or B

* Distribution includes possession with a view to distributing or sharing images.
** Production includes the taking or making of any image at source, for instance the original image.
Making an image by simple downloading should be treated as possession for the purposes of sentencing.

In most cases the intrinsic character of the most serious of the offending images will initially determine the appropriate category. If, however, the most serious images are unrepresentative of the offender's conduct a lower category may be appropriate. A lower category will not, however, be appropriate if the offender has produced or taken (for example photographed) images of a higher category.

STEP TWO
Starting point and category range

Having determined the category, the court should use the corresponding starting points to reach a sentence within the category range below. The starting point applies to all offenders irrespective of plea or previous convictions. Having determined the starting point, step two allows further adjustment for aggravating or mitigating features, set out on the next page.

Where there is a sufficient prospect of rehabilitation, a community order with a sex offender treatment programme requirement under section 202 of the Criminal Justice Act 2003 can be a proper alternative to a short or moderate length custodial sentence.

	Possession	Distribution	Production
Category A	**Starting point** 1 year's custody	**Starting point** 3 years' custody	**Starting point** 6 years' custody
	Category range 26 weeks' – 3 years' custody	**Category range** 2–5 years' custody	**Category range** 4–9 years' custody

	Possession	Distribution	Production
Category B	**Starting point** 26 weeks' custody	**Starting point** 1 year's custody	**Starting point** 2 years' custody
	Category range High level community order – 18 months' custody	**Category range** 26 weeks' – 2 years' custody	**Category range** 1–4 years' custody
Category C	**Starting point** High level community order	**Starting point** 13 weeks' custody	**Starting point** 18 months' custody
	Category range Medium level community order – 26 weeks' custody	**Category range** High level community order – 26 weeks' custody	**Category range** 1–3 years' custody

The table below contains a **non-exhaustive** list of additional factual elements providing the context of the offence and factors relating to the offender. Identify whether any combination of these, or other relevant factors, should result in an upward or downward adjustment from the starting point. **In particular, relevant recent convictions are likely to result in an upward adjustment.** In some cases, having considered these factors, it may be appropriate to move outside the identified category range.

When sentencing appropriate **category 2 or 3 offences,** the court should also consider the custody threshold as follows:

- has the custody threshold been passed?
- if so, is it unavoidable that a custodial sentence be imposed?
- if so, can that sentence be suspended?

Aggravating factors	Mitigating factors
Statutory aggravating factors	No previous convictions **or** no relevant/recent convictions
Previous convictions, having regard to a) the nature of the offence to which the conviction relates and its relevance to the current offence; and b) the time that has elapsed since the conviction	Remorse
	Previous good character and/or exemplary conduct*
	Age and/or lack of maturity where it affects the responsibility of the offender
Offence committed whilst on bail	Mental disorder or learning disability, particularly where linked to the commission of the offence
Other aggravating factors	Demonstration of steps taken to address offending behaviour
Failure to comply with current court orders	
Offence committed whilst on licence	

Age and/or vulnerability of the child depicted†

Discernable pain or distress suffered by child depicted

Period over which images were possessed, distributed or produced

High volume of images possessed, distributed or produced

Placing images where there is the potential for a high volume of viewers

Collection includes moving images

Attempts to dispose of or conceal evidence

Abuse of trust

Child depicted known to the offender

Active involvement in a network or process that facilitates or commissions the creation or sharing of indecent images of children

Commercial exploitation and/or motivation

* Previous good character/exemplary conduct is different from having no previous convictions. The more serious the offence, the less the weight which should normally be attributed to this factor. Where previous good character/exemplary conduct has been used to facilitate the offence, this mitigation should not normally be allowed and such conduct may constitute an aggravating factor.

Aggravating factors
Deliberate or systematic searching for images portraying young children, category A images or the portrayal of familial sexual abuse
Large number of different victims
Child depicted intoxicated or drugged

‡ Age and/or vulnerability of the child should be given significant weight. In cases where the actual age of the victim is difficult to determine sentencers should consider the development of the child (infant, pre-pubescent, post-pubescent).

STEP THREE

Consider any factors which indicate a reduction, such as assistance to the prosecution

The court should take into account sections 73 and 74 of the Serious Organised Crime and Police Act 2005 (assistance by defendants: reduction or review of sentence) and any other rule of law by virtue of which an offender may receive a discounted sentence in consequence of assistance given (or offered) to the prosecutor or investigator.

STEP FOUR

Reduction for guilty pleas

The court should take account of any potential reduction for a guilty plea in accordance with section 144 of the Criminal Justice Act 2003 and the Guilty Plea guideline.

STEP FIVE

Dangerousness

The court should consider whether having regard to the criteria contained in Chapter 5 of Part 12 of the Criminal Justice Act 2003 it would be appropriate to award a life sentence (section 224A) or an extended sentence (section 226A). When sentencing offenders to a life sentence under these provisions, the notional determinate sentence should be used as the basis for the setting of a minimum term.

STEP SIX

Totality principle

If sentencing an offender for more than one offence, or where the offender is already serving a sentence, consider whether the total sentence is just and proportionate to the offending behaviour.

STEP SEVEN
Ancillary orders
The court must consider whether to make any ancillary orders. The court must also consider what other requirements or provisions may automatically apply. Further information is included at Annex A on page 153.

STEP EIGHT
Reasons
Section 174 of the Criminal Justice Act 2003 imposes a duty to give reasons for, and explain the effect of, the sentence.

STEP NINE
Consideration for time spent on bail
The court must consider whether to give credit for time spent on bail in accordance with section 240A of the Criminal Justice Act 2003.

Causing or Inciting Prostitution for Gain

Sexual Offences Act 2003 (section 52)

Controlling Prostitution for Gain

Sexual Offences Act 2003 (section 53)

Triable either way
Maximum: 7 years' custody

Offence range: Community order – 6 years' custody

For convictions on or after 3 December 2012 (irrespective of the date of commission of the offence), these are specified offences for the purposes of section 226A (extended sentence for certain violent or sexual offences) of the Criminal Justice Act 2003.

The terms "prostitute" and "prostitution" are used in this guideline in accordance with the statutory language contained in the Sexual Offences Act 2003.

STEP ONE
Determining the offence category

The court should determine which categories of harm and culpability the offence falls into by reference only to the tables below.

Harm	Culpability
Category 1 • Abduction/detention • Violence or threats of violence • Sustained and systematic psychological abuse • Individual(s) forced or coerced to participate in unsafe/degrading sexual activity • Individual(s) forced or coerced into seeing many "customers" • Individual(s) forced/coerced/deceived into prostitution	**A** Causing, inciting or controlling prostitution on significant commercial basis Expectation of significant financial or other gain Abuse of trust Exploitation of those known to be trafficked Significant involvement in limiting the freedom of prostitute(s) Grooming of individual(s) to enter prostitution including through cultivation of a dependency on drugs or alcohol
Category 2 Factor(s) in category 1 not present	**B** Close involvement with prostitute(s), for example control of finances, choice of clients, working conditions, etc (where offender's involvement is not as a result of coercion)
	C Performs limited function under direction Close involvement but engaged by coercion/intimidation/ exploitation

---

STEP TWO
Starting point and category range

Having determined the category, the court should use the corresponding starting points to reach a sentence within the category range on the next page. The starting point applies to all offenders irrespective of plea or previous convictions. Having determined the starting point, step two allows further adjustment for aggravating or mitigating features, set out on the next page.

A case of particular gravity, reflected by multiple features of culpability or harm in step one, could merit upward adjustment from the starting point before further adjustment for aggravating or mitigating features, set out on the next page.

Where there is a sufficient prospect of rehabilitation, a community order with a sex offender treatment programme requirement under section 202 of the Criminal Justice Act 2003 can be a proper alternative to a short or moderate length custodial sentence.

	A	B	C
Category 1	**Starting point** 4 years' custody	**Starting point** 2 years' 6 month's custody	**Starting point** 1 years' custody
	Category range 3–6 years' custody	**Category range** 2–4 years' custody	**Category range** 26 weeks' – 2 years' custody
Category 2	**Starting point** 2 years' 6 month's custody	**Starting point** 1 year's custody	**Starting point** Medium level community order
	Category range 2–5 years' custody	**Category range** High level community order – 2 years' custody	**Category range** Low level community order – High level community order

The table below contains a **non-exhaustive** list of additional factual elements providing the context of the offence and factors relating to the offender. Identify whether any combination of these, or other relevant factors, should result in an upward or downward adjustment from the starting point. **In particular, relevant recent convictions are likely to result in an upward adjustment.** In some cases, having considered these factors, it may be appropriate to move outside the identified category range.

When sentencing appropriate **category 2 offences**, the court should also consider the custody threshold as follows:

- has the custody threshold been passed?
- if so, is it unavoidable that a custodial sentence be imposed?
- if so, can that sentence be suspended?

Aggravating factors	Mitigating factors
Statutory aggravating factors	No previous convictions **or** no relevant/recent convictions
Previous convictions, having regard to a) the nature of the offence to which the conviction relates and its relevance to the current offence; and b) the time that has elapsed since the conviction	Remorse
	Previous good character and/or exemplary conduct*
Offence committed whilst on bail	Age and/or lack of maturity where it affects the responsibility of the offender
Other aggravating factors	Mental disorder or learning disability, particularly where linked to the commission of the offence
Failure to comply with current court orders	Demonstration of steps taken to address offending behaviour
Offence committed whilst on licence	
Deliberate isolation of prostitute(s)	
Threats made to expose prostitute(s) to the authorities (for example, immigration or police), family/friends or others	
Harm threatened against the family/friends of prostitute(s)	
Passport/identity documents removed	
Prostitute(s) prevented from seeking medical treatment	
Food withheld	
Earnings withheld/kept by offender or evidence of excessive wage reduction or debt bondage, inflated travel or living expenses or unreasonable interest rates	
Any steps taken to prevent the reporting of an incident, obtaining assistance and/or from assisting or supporting the prosecution	
Attempts to dispose of or conceal evidence	
Prostitute(s) forced or coerced into pornography	
Timescale over which operation has been run	

* Previous good character/exemplary conduct is different from having no previous convictions. The more serious the offence, the less the weight which should normally be attributed to this factor. Where previous good character/exemplary conduct has been used to facilitate the offence, this mitigation should not normally be allowed and such conduct may constitute an aggravating factor.

STEP THREE
Consider any factors which indicate a reduction, such as assistance to the prosecution
The court should take into account sections 73 and 74 of the Serious Organised Crime and Police Act 2005 (assistance by defendants: reduction or review of sentence) and any other rule of law by virtue of which an offender may receive a discounted sentence in consequence of assistance given (or offered) to the prosecutor or investigator.

STEP FOUR
Reduction for guilty pleas
The court should take account of any potential reduction for a guilty plea in accordance with section 144 of the Criminal Justice Act 2003 and the Guilty Plea guideline.

STEP FIVE
Dangerousness
The court should consider whether having regard to the criteria contained in Chapter 5 of Part 12 of the Criminal Justice Act 2003 it would be appropriate to award an extended sentence (section 226A).

STEP SIX
Totality principle
If sentencing an offender for more than one offence, or where the offender is already serving a sentence, consider whether the total sentence is just and proportionate to the offending behaviour.

STEP SEVEN
Ancillary orders
The court must consider whether to make any ancillary orders. The court must also consider what other requirements or provisions may automatically apply. Further information is included at Annex A on page 153.

STEP EIGHT
Reasons
Section 174 of the Criminal Justice Act 2003 imposes a duty to give reasons for, and explain the effect of, the sentence.

STEP NINE
Consideration for time spent on bail
The court must consider whether to give credit for time spent on bail in accordance with section 240A of the Criminal Justice Act 2003.

KEEPING A BROTHEL USED FOR PROSTITUTION

Sexual Offences Act 1956 (section 33A)

Triable either way
Maximum: 7 years' custody

Offence range: Community order – 6 years' custody

The terms "prostitute" and "prostitution" are used in this guideline in accordance with the statutory language contained in the Sexual Offences Act 2003.

STEP ONE
Determining the offence category

The court should determine which categories of harm and culpability the offence falls into by reference only to the tables below.

Harm	Culpability
Category 1 • Under 18 year olds working in brothel	**A**
• Abduction/detention	Keeping brothel on significant commercial basis
• Violence or threats of violence	Involvement in keeping a number of brothels
• Sustained and systematic psychological abuse	Expectation of significant financial or other gain
• Those working in brothel forced or coerced to participate in unsafe/degrading sexual activity	Abuse of trust
	Exploitation of those known to be trafficked
• Those working in brothel forced or coerced into seeing many "customers"	Significant involvement in limiting freedom of those working in brothel
• Those working in brothel forced/coerced/deceived into prostitution	Grooming of a person to work in the brothel including through cultivation of a dependency on drugs or alcohol
• Established evidence of community impact	

Harm	Culpability
Category 2 Factor(s) in category 1 not present	**B**
	Keeping/managing premises
	Close involvement with those working in brothel, for example control of finances, choice of clients, working conditions, etc (where offender's involvement is not as a result of coercion)
	C
	Performs limited function under direction
	Close involvement but engaged by coercion/intimidation/exploitation

> **STEP TWO**
> **Starting point and category range**

Having determined the category, the court should use the corresponding starting points to reach a sentence within the category range on the next page. The starting point applies to all offenders irrespective of plea or previous convictions. Having determined the starting point, step two allows further adjustment for aggravating or mitigating features, set out on the next page.

A case of particular gravity, reflected by multiple features of culpability or harm in step one, could merit upward adjustment from the starting point before further adjustment for aggravating or mitigating features, set out on the next page.

Where there is a sufficient prospect of rehabilitation, a community order with a sex offender treatment programme requirement under section 202 of the Criminal Justice Act 2003 can be a proper alternative to a short or moderate length custodial sentence.

	A	B	C
Category 1	**Starting point** 5 year's custody	**Starting point** 3 years' custody	**Starting point** 1 year's custody
	Category range 3–6 years' custody	**Category range** 2–5 years' custody	**Category range** High level community order – 18 months' custody
Category 2	**Starting point** 3 years' custody	**Starting point** 12 months' custody	**Starting point** Medium level community order
	Category range 2–5 years' custody	**Category range** 26 weeks' – 2 years' custody	**Category range** Low level community order – High level community order

The table below contains a **non-exhaustive** list of additional factual elements providing the context of the offence and factors relating to the offender. Identify whether any combination of these, or other relevant factors, should result in an upward or downward adjustment from the starting point. **In particular, relevant recent convictions are likely to result in an upward adjustment.** In some cases, having considered these factors, it may be appropriate to move outside the identified category range.

When sentencing appropriate **category 1 offences**, the court should also consider the custody threshold as follows:

- has the custody threshold been passed?
- if so, is it unavoidable that a custodial sentence be imposed?
- if so, can that sentence be suspended?

Aggravating factors	Mitigating factors
Statutory aggravating factors	No previous convictions or no relevant/recent convictions
Previous convictions, having regard to a) the nature of the offence to which the conviction relates and its relevance to the current offence; and b) the time that has elapsed since the conviction	Remorse
	Previous good character and/or exemplary conduct*
	Age and/or lack of maturity where it affects the responsibility of the offender
Offence committed whilst on bail	Mental disorder or learning disability, particularly where linked to the commission of the offence
Other aggravating factors	Demonstration of steps taken to address offending behaviour
Failure to comply with current court orders	

Offence committed whilst on licence

Deliberate isolation of those working in brothel

Threats made to expose those working in brothel to the authorities (for example, immigration or police), family/friends or others

Harm threatened against the family/ friends of those working in brothel

Passport/identity documents removed

Those working in brothel prevented from seeking medical treatment

Food withheld

Those working in brothel passed around by offender and moved to other brothels

Earnings of those working in brothel withheld/kept by offender or evidence of excessive wage reduction or debt bondage, inflated travel or living expenses or unreasonable interest rates

Any steps taken to prevent those working in brothel reporting an incident, obtaining assistance and/or from assisting or supporting the prosecution

* Previous good character/exemplary conduct is different from having no previous convictions. The more serious the offence, the less the weight which should normally be attributed to this factor. Where previous good character/exemplary conduct has been used to facilitate the offence, this mitigation should not normally be allowed and such conduct may constitute an aggravating factor.

Aggravating factors

Attempts to dispose of or conceal evidence

Those working in brothel forced or coerced into pornography

Timescale over which operation has been run

STEP THREE

Consider any factors which indicate a reduction, such as assistance to the prosecution

The court should take into account sections 73 and 74 of the Serious Organised Crime and Police Act 2005 (assistance by defendants: reduction or review of sentence) and any other rule of law by virtue of which an offender may receive a discounted sentence in consequence of assistance given (or offered) to the prosecutor or investigator.

STEP FOUR

Reduction for guilty pleas

The court should take account of any potential reduction for a guilty plea in accordance with section 144 of the Criminal Justice Act 2003 and the Guilty Plea guideline.

STEP FIVE

Totality principle

If sentencing an offender for more than one offence, or where the offender is already serving a sentence, consider whether the total sentence is just and proportionate to the offending behaviour.

STEP SIX

Ancillary orders

The court must consider whether to make any ancillary orders. The court must also consider what other requirements or provisions may automatically apply. Further information is included at Annex A on page 153.

STEP SEVEN

Reasons

Section 174 of the Criminal Justice Act 2003 imposes a duty to give reasons for, and explain the effect of, the sentence.

STEP EIGHT
Consideration for time spent on bail
The court must consider whether to give credit for time spent on bail in
accordance with section 240A of the Criminal Justice Act 2003.

CAUSING OR INCITING CHILD PROSTITUTION OR PORNOGRAPHY

Sexual Offences Act 2003 (section 48)

CONTROLLING A CHILD PROSTITUTE OR CHILD INVOLVED IN PORNOGRAPHY

Sexual Offences Act 2003 (section 49)

ARRANGING OR FACILITATING CHILD PROSTITUTION OR PORNOGRAPHY

Sexual Offences Act 2003 (section 50)

Triable either way
Maximum: 14 years' custody

Offence range: Victim aged under 13   1–13 years' custody
                Victim aged 13–15   26 weeks' – 11 years' custody
                Victim aged 16–17   Community order – 7 years'
                                       custody

For offences committed on or after 3 December 2012, these are offences
listed in Part 1 of Schedule 15B for the purposes of sections 224A (life
sentence for second listed offence) of the Criminal Justice Act 2003.

For convictions on or after 3 December 2012 (irrespective of the date of
commission of the offence), these are specified offences for the purposes
of section 226A (extended sentence for certain violent or sexual offences)
of the Criminal Justice Act 2003.

The terms "child prostitute", "child prostitution" and "child involved in pornography" are used in this guideline in accordance with the statutory language
contained in the Sexual Offences Act 2003.

STEP ONE
Determining the offence category

The court should determine which categories of harm and culpability the offence falls into by reference only to the tables below.

For offences that involve wide scale commercial and/or international activity sentences above the category range may be appropriate.

Harm	Culpability
Category 1 • Victims involved in penetrative sexual activity • Abduction/detention • Violence or threats of violence • Sustained and systematic psychological abuse • Victim(s) participated in unsafe/ degrading sexual activity beyond that which is inherent in the offence • Victim(s) passed around by the offender to other "customers" and/or moved to other brothels	**A** Directing or organising child prostitution or pornography on significant commercial basis Expectation of significant financial or other gain Abuse of trust Exploitation of victim(s) known to be trafficked Significant involvement in limiting the freedom of the victim(s) Grooming of a victim to enter prostitution or pornography including through cultivation of a dependency on drugs or alcohol
Category 2 Factor(s) in category 1 not present	**B** Close involvement with inciting, controlling, arranging or facilitating child prostitution or pornography (where offender's involvement is not as a result of coercion)
	C Performs limited function under direction Close involvement but engaged by coercion/intimidation/exploitation

---

STEP TWO
Starting point and category range

Having determined the category, the court should use the corresponding starting points to reach a sentence within the category range below. The starting point applies to all offenders irrespective of plea or previous convictions. Having determined the starting point, step two allows further adjustment for aggravating or mitigating features, set out on the next page.

A case of particular gravity, reflected by multiple features of culpability or harm in step one, could merit upward adjustment from the starting point before further adjustment for aggravating or mitigating features, set out on the next page.

Where there is a sufficient prospect of rehabilitation, a community order with a sex offender treatment programme requirement under section 202 of the Criminal Justice Act 2003 can be a proper alternative to a short or moderate length custodial sentence.

		A	B	C
Category 1	U13	Starting point 10 years' custody	Starting point 8 years' custody	Starting point 5 years' custody
		Category range 8–13 years' custody	Category range 6–11 years' custody	Category range 2–6 years' custody
	13–15	Starting point 8 years' custody	Starting point 5 years' custody	Starting point 2 years 6 months' custody
		Category range 6–11 years' custody	Category range 4–8 years' custody	Category range 1–4 years' custody
	16–17	Starting point 4 years' custody	Starting point 2 years' custody	Starting point 1 year's custody
		Category range 3–7 years' custody	Category range 1–4 years' custody	Category range 26 weeks' – 2 years' custody
Category 2	U13	Starting point 8 years' custody	Starting point 6 years' custody	Starting point 2 years' custody
		Category range 6–11 years' custody	Category range 4–9 years' custody	Category range 1–4 years' custody
	13–15	Starting point 6 years' custody	Starting point 3 years' custody	Starting point 1 year's custody
		Category range 4–9 years' custody	Category range 2–5 years' custody	Category range 26 weeks' – 2 years' custody

	A	B	C
16–17	**Starting point** 3 years' custody	**Starting point** 1 year's custody	**Starting point** 26 weeks' custody
	Category range 2–5 years' custody	**Category range** 26 weeks' – 2 years' custody	**Category range** High level community order – 1 year's custody

The table below contains a **non-exhaustive** list of additional factual elements providing the context of the offence and factors relating to the offender. Identify whether any combination of these, or other relevant factors, should result in an upward or downward adjustment from the starting point. **In particular, relevant recent convictions are likely to result in an upward adjustment.** In some cases, having considered these factors, it may be appropriate to move outside the identified category range.

When sentencing appropriate **category 2 offences**, the court should also consider the custody threshold as follows:

- has the custody threshold been passed?
- if so, is it unavoidable that a custodial sentence be imposed?
- if so, can that sentence be suspended?

Aggravating factors	Mitigating factors
Statutory aggravating factors	No previous convictions **or** no relevant/recent convictions
Previous convictions, having regard to a) the nature of the offence to which the conviction relates and its relevance to the current offence; and b) the time that has elapsed since the conviction	Remorse
	Previous good character and/or exemplary conduct*
	Age and/or lack of maturity where it affects the responsibility of the offender
Offence committed whilst on bail	
Other aggravating factors	Mental disorder or learning disability, particularly where linked to the commission of the offence
Failure to comply with current court orders	
Offence committed whilst on licence	* Previous good character/exemplary conduct is different from having no previous convictions. The more serious the offence, the less the weight which should normally be attributed to this factor. Where previous good character/ exemplary conduct has been used to facilitate the offence, this mitigation should not normally be allowed and such conduct may constitute an aggravating factor.
Deliberate isolation of victim(s)	
Vulnerability of victim(s)	

Aggravating factors	Mitigating factors
Threats made to expose victim(s) to the authorities (for example, immigration or police), family/friends or others	In the context of this offence, previous good character/exemplary conduct should not normally be given any significant weight and will not normally justify a reduction in what would otherwise be the appropriate sentence.
Harm threatened against the family/ friends of victim(s)	
Passport/identity documents removed	
Victim(s) prevented from seeking medical treatment	
Victim(s) prevented from attending school	
Food withheld	
Earnings withheld/kept by offender or evidence of excessive wage reduction or debt bondage, inflated travel or living expenses or unreasonable interest rates	
Any steps taken to prevent the victim reporting an incident, obtaining assistance and/or from assisting or supporting the prosecution	
Attempts to dispose of or conceal evidence	
Timescale over which the operation has been run	

STEP THREE

Consider any factors which indicate a reduction, such as assistance to the prosecution

The court should take into account sections 73 and 74 of the Serious Organised Crime and Police Act 2005 (assistance by defendants: reduction or review of sentence) and any other rule of law by virtue of which an offender may receive a discounted sentence in consequence of assistance given (or offered) to the prosecutor or investigator.

STEP FOUR
Reduction for guilty pleas
The court should take account of any potential reduction for a guilty plea in accordance with section 144 of the Criminal Justice Act 2003 and the Guilty Plea guideline.

STEP FIVE
Dangerousness
The court should consider whether having regard to the criteria contained in Chapter 5 of Part 12 of the Criminal Justice Act 2003 it would be appropriate to award a life sentence (section 224A) or an extended sentence (section 226A). When sentencing offenders to a life sentence under these provisions, the notional determinate sentence should be used as the basis for the setting of a minimum term.

STEP SIX
Totality principle
If sentencing an offender for more than one offence, or where the offender is already serving a sentence, consider whether the total sentence is just and proportionate to the offending behaviour.

STEP SEVEN
Ancillary orders
The court must consider whether to make any ancillary orders. The court must also consider what other requirements or provisions may automatically apply. Further information is included at Annex A on page 153.

STEP EIGHT
Reasons
Section 174 of the Criminal Justice Act 2003 imposes a duty to give reasons for, and explain the effect of, the sentence.

STEP NINE
Consideration for time spent on bail
The court must consider whether to give credit for time spent on bail in accordance with section 240A of the Criminal Justice Act 2003.

Paying for the Sexual Services of a Child

Sexual Offences Act 2003 (section 47)

Triable only on indictment (if involving penetration against victim under 16)
—otherwise triable either way

Maximum:	Victim under 13 (penetrative)	Life imprisonment
	Victim under 13 (non-penetrative)	14 years' custody
	Victim aged 13–15	14 years' custody
	Victim aged 16–17	7 years' custody
Offence range:	Victim aged 16–17	Community order – 5 years' custody

This guideline should only be used where the victim is aged 16 or 17 years old. If the victim is under 13 please refer to the guidelines for rape of a child under 13, assault by penetration of a child under 13, sexual assault of a child under 13 or causing or inciting a child under 13 to engage in sexual activity, depending on the activity involved in the offence.

If the victim is aged 13–15 please refer to the sexual activity with a child guideline.

Where the victim is 16 or 17 years old—for convictions on or after 3 December 2012 (irrespective of the date of commission of the offence), this is a specified offence for the purposes of section 226A (extended sentence for certain violent or sexual offences) of the Criminal Justice Act 2003.

STEP ONE
Determining the offence category

The court should determine which categories of harm and culpability the offence falls into by reference only to the tables below.

Harm	Culpability
Category 1 • Penetration of vagina or anus (using body or object) by, or of, the victim • Penile penetration of mouth by, or of, the victim • Violence or threats of violence • Victim subjected to unsafe/degrading sexual activity (beyond that which is inherent in the offence)	**A** Abduction/detention Sexual images of victim recorded, retained, solicited or shared Offender acts together with others to commit the offence Use of alcohol/drugs on victim Abuse of trust Previous violence against victim Sexual images of victim recorded, retained, solicited or shared Blackmail or other threats made (including to expose victim to the authorities, family/friends or others) Offender aware that he has a sexually transmitted disease Offender aware victim has been trafficked
Category 2 Touching of naked genitalia or naked breasts by, or of, the victim	
Category 3 Other sexual activity	
	B Factor(s) in category A not present

STEP TWO
Starting point and category range

Having determined the category, the court should use the corresponding starting points to reach a sentence within the category range on the next page for victims aged 16 or 17. The starting point applies to all offenders irrespective of plea or previous convictions. Having determined the starting point, step two allows further adjustment for aggravating or mitigating features, set out on the next page.

A case of particular gravity, reflected by multiple features of culpability in step one, could merit upward adjustment from the starting point before further adjustment for aggravating or mitigating features, set out on the next page.

Where there is a sufficient prospect of rehabilitation, a community order with a sex offender treatment programme requirement under section 202 of the Criminal

Justice Act 2003 can be a proper alternative to a short or moderate length custodial sentence.

	A	**B**
Category 1	**Starting point** 4 years' custody	**Starting point** 2 years' custody
	Category range 2–5 years' custody	**Category range** 1–4 years' custody
Category 2	**Starting point** 3 years' custody	**Starting point** 1 year's custody
	Category range 1–4 years' custody	**Category range** 26 weeks' – 2 years' custody
Category 3	**Starting point** 1 year's custody	**Starting point** 26 weeks' custody
	Category range 26 weeks' – 2 years' custody	**Category range** High level community order – 1 year's custody

The table below contains a **non-exhaustive** list of additional factual elements providing the context of the offence and factors relating to the offender. Identify whether any combination of these, or other relevant factors, should result in an upward or downward adjustment from the starting point. **In particular, relevant recent convictions are likely to result in an upward adjustment.** In some cases, having considered these factors, it may be appropriate to move outside the identified category range.

When sentencing appropriate **category 3 offences,** the court should also consider the custody threshold as follows:

- has the custody threshold been passed?
- if so, is it unavoidable that a custodial sentence be imposed?
- if so, can that sentence be suspended?

Aggravating factors	Mitigating factors
Statutory aggravating factors	No previous convictions **or** no relevant/recent convictions
Previous convictions, having regard to a) the nature of the offence to which the conviction relates and its relevance to the current offence; and b) the time that has elapsed since the conviction	Remorse
	Previous good character and/or exemplary conduct*
	Age and/or lack of maturity where it affects the responsibility of the offender
Offence committed whilst on bail	
Other aggravating factors	Mental disorder or learning disability, particularly where linked to the commission of the offence
Ejaculation	
Failure to comply with current court orders	Demonstration of steps taken to address offending behaviour
Offence committed whilst on licence	
Any steps taken to prevent the victim reporting an incident, obtaining assistance and/or from assisting or supporting the prosecution	* Previous good character/exemplary conduct is different from having no previous convictions. The more serious the offence, the less the weight which should normally be attributed to this factor. Where previous good character/exemplary conduct has been used to facilitate the offence, this mitigation should not normally be allowed and such conduct may constitute an aggravating factor.
Attempts to dispose of or conceal evidence	

STEP THREE
Consider any factors which indicate a reduction, such as assistance to the prosecution
The court should take into account sections 73 and 74 of the Serious Organised Crime and Police Act 2005 (assistance by defendants: reduction or review of sentence) and any other rule of law by virtue of which an offender may receive a discounted sentence in consequence of assistance given (or offered) to the prosecutor or investigator.

STEP FOUR
Reduction for guilty pleas
The court should take account of any potential reduction for a guilty plea in accordance with section 144 of the Criminal Justice Act 2003 and the Guilty Plea guideline.

STEP FIVE
Dangerousness
The court should consider whether having regard to the criteria contained in Chapter 5 of Part 12 of the Criminal Justice Act 2003 it would be appropriate to award an extended sentence (section 226A).

STEP SIX
Totality principle
If sentencing an offender for more than one offence, or where the offender is already serving a sentence, consider whether the total sentence is just and proportionate to the offending behaviour.

STEP SEVEN
Ancillary orders
The court must consider whether to make any ancillary orders. The court must also consider what other requirements or provisions may automatically apply. Further information is included at Annex A on page 153.

STEP EIGHT
Reasons
Section 174 of the Criminal Justice Act 2003 imposes a duty to give reasons for, and explain the effect of, the sentence.

STEP NINE
Consideration for time spent on bail
The court must consider whether to give credit for time spent on bail in accordance with section 240A of the Criminal Justice Act 2003.

TRAFFICKING PEOPLE FOR SEXUAL EXPLOITATION

Sexual Offences Act 2003 (sections 59A)

(This guideline also applies to offences, committed before 6 April 2013, of trafficking into/within/out of the UK for sexual exploitation contrary to sections 57 to 59 of the Sexual Offences Act 2003)

Triable either way
Maximum: 14 years' custody

Offence range: Community order – 12 years' custody

For convictions on or after 3 December 2012 (irrespective of the date of commission of the offence), this is a specified offence for the purposes of section 226A (extended sentence for certain violent or sexual offences) of the Criminal Justice Act 2003.

The term "prostitution" is used in this guideline in accordance with the statutory language contained in the Sexual Offences Act 2003.

STEP ONE
Determining the offence category

The court should determine which categories of harm and culpability the offence falls into by reference only to the tables below.

Harm	Culpability
Category 1 • Abduction/detention • Violence or threats of violence • Sustained and systematic psychological abuse • Victim(s) under 18 • Victim(s) forced or coerced to participate in unsafe/degrading sexual activity • Victim(s) forced/coerced into prostitution • Victim(s) tricked/deceived as to purpose of visit	**A** Directing or organising trafficking on significant commercial basis Expectation of significant financial or other gain Significant influence over others in trafficking organisation/hierarchy Abuse of trust
	B Operational or management function within hierarchy Involves others in operation whether by coercion/ intimidation/ exploitation or reward (and offender's involvement is not as a result of coercion)
Category 2 Factor(s) in category 1 not present	
	C Performs limited function under direction Close involvement but engaged by coercion/ intimidation/ exploitation

---

STEP TWO
Starting point and category range

Having determined the category of harm and culpability, the court should use the corresponding starting points to reach a sentence within the category range on the next page. The starting point applies to all offenders irrespective of plea or previous convictions. Having determined the starting point, step two allows further adjustment for aggravating or mitigating features, set out on the next page.

A case of particular gravity, reflected by multiple features of culpability or harm in step one, could merit upward adjustment from the starting point before further adjustment for aggravating or mitigating features, set out on the next page.

Where there is a sufficient prospect of rehabilitation, a community order with a sex offender treatment programme requirement under section 202 of the Criminal Justice Act 2003 can be a proper alternative to a short or moderate length custodial sentence.

	A	B	C
Category 1	Starting point 8 years' custody	Starting point 6 years' custody	Starting point 18 months' custody
	Category range 6–12 years' custody	Category range 4–8 years' custody	Category range 26 weeks' – 2 years' custody
Category 2	Starting point 6 years' custody	Starting point 4 year's custody	Starting point 26 weeks' custody
	Category range 4–8 years' custody	Category range 2–6 years' custody	Category range High level community order – 18 months' custody

The table below contains a **non-exhaustive** list of additional factual elements providing the context of the offence and factors relating to the offender. Identify whether any combination of these, or other relevant factors, should result in an upward or downward adjustment from the starting point. **In particular, relevant recent convictions are likely to result in an upward adjustment.** In some cases, having considered these factors, it may be appropriate to move outside the identified category range.

When sentencing appropriate **category 2 offences**, the court should also consider the custody threshold as follows:

- has the custody threshold been passed?

765

- if so, is it unavoidable that a custodial sentence be imposed?
- if so, can that sentence be suspended?

Aggravating factors	Mitigating factors
Statutory aggravating factors	No previous convictions **or** no relevant/recent convictions
Previous convictions, having regard to a) the nature of the offence to which the conviction relates and its relevance to the current offence; and b) the time that has elapsed since the conviction	Remorse
	Previous good character and/or exemplary conduct*
	Age and/or lack of maturity where it affects the responsibility of the offender
Offence committed whilst on bail	Mental disorder or learning disability, particularly where linked to the commission of the offence
Other aggravating factors	
Failure to comply with current court orders	

* Previous good character/exemplary conduct is different from having no previous convictions. The more serious the offence, the less the weight which should normally be attributed to this factor. Where previous good character/exemplary conduct has been used to facilitate the offence, this mitigation should not normally be allowed and such conduct may constitute an aggravating factor.

In the context of this offence, previous good character/exemplary conduct should not normally be given any significant weight and will not normally justify a reduction in what would otherwise be the appropriate sentence.

Offence committed whilst on licence

Deliberate isolation of victim(s)

Children of victim(s) left in home country due to trafficking

Threats made to expose victim(s) to the authorities (for example, immigration or police), family/friends or others

Harm threatened against the family/ friends of victim

Exploitation of victim(s) from particularly vulnerable backgrounds

Victim(s) previously trafficked/sold/ passed around

Passport/identity documents removed

Victim(s) prevented from seeking medical treatment

Food withheld

Use of drugs/alcohol or other substance to secure victim's compliance

Earnings of victim(s) withheld/kept by offender or evidence of excessive wage reduction, debt bondage, inflated travel or living expenses, unreasonable interest rates

---

Aggravating factors

Any steps taken to prevent the victim reporting an incident, obtaining assistance and/or from assisting or supporting the prosecution

Attempts to dispose of or conceal evidence

Timescale over which operation has been run

STEP THREE

Consider any factors which indicate a reduction, such as assistance to the prosecution

The court should take into account sections 73 and 74 of the Serious Organised Crime and Police Act 2005 (assistance by defendants: reduction or review of sentence) and any other rule of law by virtue of which an offender may receive a discounted sentence in consequence of assistance given (or offered) to the prosecutor or investigator.

STEP FOUR

Reduction for guilty pleas

The court should take account of any potential reduction for a guilty plea in accordance with section 144 of the Criminal Justice Act 2003 and the Guilty Plea guideline.

STEP FIVE

Dangerousness

The court should consider whether having regard to the criteria contained in Chapter 5 of Part 12 of the Criminal Justice Act 2003 it would be appropriate to award an extended sentence (section 226A).

STEP SIX

Totality principle

If sentencing an offender for more than one offence, or where the offender is already serving a sentence, consider whether the total sentence is just and proportionate to the offending behaviour.

> **STEP SEVEN**
> Ancillary orders
> The court must consider whether to make any ancillary orders. The court must also consider what other requirements or provisions may automatically apply. Further information is included at Annex A on page 153.

> **STEP EIGHT**
> Reasons
> Section 174 of the Criminal Justice Act 2003 imposes a duty to give reasons for, and explain the effect of, the sentence.

> **STEP NINE**
> Consideration for time spent on bail
> The court must consider whether to give credit for time spent on bail in accordance with section 240A of the Criminal Justice Act 2003.

Sexual Activity With a Person With a Mental Disorder Impeding Choice

Sexual Offences Act 2003 (section 30)

Causing or Inciting a Person, With a Mental Disorder Impeding Choice, to Engage in Sexual Activity

Sexual Offences Act 2003 (section 31)

Triable only on indictment (if penetration involved)
—otherwise, triable either way

Maximum: Life imprisonment (if penetration involved)
—otherwise 14 years' custody

Offence range: Community order – 19 years' custody

These are serious specified offences for the purposes of section 224 and, where the offence involved penetration, section 225(2) (life sentence for serious offences) of the Criminal Justice Act 2003.

For offences involving penetration, committed on or after 3 December 2012, these are offences listed in Part 1 of Schedule 15B for the purposes of section 224A (life sentence for second listed offence) of the Criminal Justice Act 2003.

For convictions on or after 3 December 2012 (irrespective of the date of commission of the offence), these are specified offences for the purposes of section 226A (extended sentence for certain violent or sexual offences) of the Criminal Justice Act 2003.

STEP ONE
Determining the offence category

The court should determine which categories of harm and culpability the offence falls into by reference only to the tables below.

Harm	Culpability
Category 1 The extreme nature of one or more category 2 factors or the extreme impact caused by a combination of category 2 factors may elevate to category 1	**A** Significant degree of planning Offender acts together with others to commit the offence Use of alcohol/drugs on victim to facilitate the offence
Category 2 • Severe psychological or physical harm • Pregnancy or STI as a consequence of offence • Additional degradation/humiliation • Abduction • Prolonged detention/sustained incident • Violence or threats of violence • Forced/uninvited entry into victim's home or residence	Grooming behaviour used against victim Abuse of trust Previous violence against victim Offence committed in course of burglary Sexual images of victim recorded, retained, solicited or shared Deliberate isolation of victim Commercial exploitation and/or motivation Offence racially or religiously aggravated
Category 3 Factor(s) in categories 1 and 2 not present	Offence motivated by, or demonstrating, hostility to the victim based on his or her sexual orientation (or presumed sexual orientation) or transgender identity (or presumed transgender identity)

Culpability
Offence motivated by, or demonstrating, hostility to the victim based on his or her disability (or presumed disability)
B
Factor(s) in category A not present

STEP TWO
Starting point and category range

Having determined the category of harm and culpability, the court should use the corresponding starting points to reach a sentence within the category range below. The starting point applies to all offenders irrespective of plea or previous convictions. Having determined the starting point, step two allows further adjustment for aggravating or mitigating features, set out on the next page.

A case of particular gravity, reflected by multiple features of culpability or harm in step one, could merit upward adjustment from the starting point before further adjustment for aggravating or mitigating features, set out on the next page.

Where there is a sufficient prospect of rehabilitation, a community order with a sex offender treatment programme requirement under section 202 of the Criminal Justice Act 2003 can be a proper alternative to a short or moderate length custodial sentence.

Where offence involved penetration		
	A	**B**
Category 1	**Starting point** 16 years' custody	**Starting point** 13 years' custody
	Category range 13–19 years' custody	**Category range** 11–17 years' custody
Category 2	**Starting point** 13 years' custody	**Starting point** 10 years' custody
	Category range 11–17 years' custody	**Category range** 8–13 years' custody

Category 3	Starting point 10 years' custody	Starting point 8 years' custody
	Category range 8–13 years' custody	Category range 6–11 years' custody

Where offence did not involve penetration

	A	B
Category 1	Starting point 6 years' custody	Starting point 4 years custody
	Category range 4–9 years' custody	Category range 3–7 years' custody
Category 2	Starting point 4 years' custody	Starting point 2 years' custody
	Category range 3–7 years' custody	Category range 1–4 years' custody

Where offence did not involve penetration

	A	B
Category 3	Starting point 1 years' custody	Starting point High level community order
	Category range 26 weeks' – 2 years' custody	Category range High level community order – 1 year's custody

The table below contains a **non-exhaustive** list of additional factual elements providing the context of the offence and factors relating to the offender. Identify whether any combination of these, or other relevant factors, should result in an upward or downward adjustment from the starting point. **In particular, relevant recent convictions are likely to result in an upward adjustment.** In some cases, having considered these factors, it may be appropriate to move outside the identified category range.

When appropriate, the court should also consider the custody threshold as follows:

- has the custody threshold been passed?
- if so, is it unavoidable that a custodial sentence be imposed?
- if so, can that sentence be suspended?

Aggravating factors	Mitigating factors
Statutory aggravating factors	No previous convictions **or** no relevant/recent convictions
Previous convictions, having regard to a) the nature of the offence to which the conviction relates and its relevance to the current offence; and b) the time that has elapsed since the conviction	Remorse
	Previous good character and/or exemplary conduct*
Offence committed whilst on bail	Age and/or lack of maturity where it affects the responsibility of the offender
Other aggravating factors	Mental disorder or learning disability, particularly where linked to the commission of the offence
Ejaculation (where not taken into account at step one)	Sexual activity was incited but no activity took place because the offender voluntarily desisted or intervened to prevent it
Blackmail or other threats made (where not taken into account at step one)	
Location of offence	
Timing of offence	
Use of weapon or other item to frighten or injure	
Victim compelled to leave their home or institution (including victims of domestic violence)	
Failure to comply with current court orders	
Offence committed whilst on licence	
Presence of others, especially children	
Any steps taken to prevent the victim reporting an incident, obtaining assistance and/or from assisting or supporting the prosecution	
Attempts to dispose of or conceal evidence	
Commission of offence whilst under the influence of alcohol or drugs	

* Previous good character/exemplary conduct is different from having no previous convictions. The more serious the offence, the less the weight which should normally be attributed to this factor. Where previous good character/exemplary conduct has been used to facilitate the offence, this mitigation should not normally be allowed and such conduct may constitute an aggravating factor.

In the context of this offence, previous good character/exemplary conduct should not normally be given any significant weight and will not normally justify a reduction in what would otherwise be the appropriate sentence.

STEP THREE
Consider any factors which indicate a reduction, such as assistance to the prosecution
The court should take into account sections 73 and 74 of the Serious Organised Crime and Police Act 2005 (assistance by defendants: reduction or review of sentence) and any other rule of law by virtue of which an offender may receive a discounted sentence in consequence of assistance given (or offered) to the prosecutor or investigator.

STEP FOUR
Reduction for guilty pleas
The court should take account of any potential reduction for a guilty plea in accordance with section 144 of the Criminal Justice Act 2003 and the Guilty Plea guideline.

STEP FIVE
Dangerousness
The court should consider whether having regard to the criteria contained in Chapter 5 of Part 12 of the Criminal Justice Act 2003 it would be appropriate to award a life sentence (section 224A or section 225(2)) or an extended sentence (section 226A). When sentencing offenders to a life sentence under these provisions, the notional determinate sentence should be used as the basis for the setting of a minimum term.

STEP SIX
Totality principle
If sentencing an offender for more than one offence, or where the offender is already serving a sentence, consider whether the total sentence is just and proportionate to the offending behaviour.

STEP SEVEN
Ancillary orders
The court must consider whether to make any ancillary orders. The court must also consider what other requirements or provisions may automatically apply. Further information is included at Annex A on page 153.

STEP EIGHT
Reasons
Section 174 of the Criminal Justice Act 2003 imposes a duty to give reasons for, and explain the effect of, the sentence.

> **STEP NINE**
> Consideration for time spent on bail
> The court must consider whether to give credit for time spent on bail in accordance with section 240A of the Criminal Justice Act 2003.

Engaging in Sexual Activity in the Presence of a Person With Mental Disorder Impeding Choice

Sexual Offences Act 2003 (section 32)

Causing a Person, With Mental Disorder Impeding Choice, To Watch a Sexual Act

Sexual Offences Act 2003 (section 33)

Triable either way
Maximum: 10 years' custody

Offence range: Community order – 6 years' custody

For convictions on or after 3 December 2012 (irrespective of the date of commission of the offence), these are specified offences for the purposes of section 226A (extended sentence for certain violent or sexual offences) of the Criminal Justice Act 2003.

> **STEP ONE**
> Determining the offence category

The court should determine which categories of harm and culpability the offence falls into by reference only to the tables below.

Harm	Culpability
Category 1 • Causing victim to view extreme pornography • Causing victim to view indecent/prohibited images of children • Engaging in, or causing a victim to view live, sexual activity involving sadism/violence/sexual activity with an animal/a child	**A** Significant degree of planning Offender acts together with others in order to commit the offence Use of alcohol/drugs on victim to facilitate the offence Grooming behaviour used against victim Abuse of trust Use of threats (including blackmail) Commercial exploitation and/or motivation Offence racially or religiously aggravated
Category 2 Engaging in, or causing a victim to view images of or view live, sexual activity involving: • penetration of vagina or anus (using body or object) • penile penetration of mouth • masturbation	Offence motivated by, or demonstrating, hostility to the victim based on his or her sexual orientation (or presumed sexual orientation) or transgender identity (or presumed transgender identity) Offence motivated by, or demonstrating, hostility to the victim based on his or her disability (or presumed disability)
Category 3 Factor(s) in categories 1 and 2 not present	**B** Factor(s) in category A not present

---

STEP TWO
Starting point and category range

Having determined the category of harm and culpability, the court should use the corresponding starting points to reach a sentence within the category range on the next page. The starting point applies to all offenders irrespective of plea or previous convictions. Having determined the starting point, step two allows further adjustment for aggravating or mitigating features, set out on the next page.

A case of particular gravity, reflected by multiple features of culpability or harm in step one, could merit upward adjustment from the starting point before further adjustment for aggravating or mitigating features, set out on the next page.

Where there is a sufficient prospect of rehabilitation, a community order with a sex offender treatment programme requirement under section 202 of the Criminal Justice Act 2003 can be a proper alternative to a short or moderate length custodial sentence.

	A	B
Category 1	Starting point 4 year's custody	Starting point 2 year's custody
	Category range 3–6 years' custody	Category range 1–3 years' custody
Category 2	Starting point 2 year's custody	Starting point 1 years' custody
	Category range 1–3 years' custody	Category range High level community order – 18 months' custody
Category 3	Starting point 26 weeks' custody	Starting point Medium level community order
	Category range High level community order – 1 year's custody	Category range Low level community order – High level community order

The table below contains a **non-exhaustive** list of additional factual elements providing the context of the offence and factors relating to the offender. Identify whether any combination of these, or other relevant factors, should result in an upward or downward adjustment from the starting point. **In particular, relevant recent convictions are likely to result in an upward adjustment.** In some cases, having considered these factors, it may be appropriate to move outside the identified category range.

When sentencing appropriate **category 2 or 3 offences**, the court should also consider the custody threshold as follows:

- has the custody threshold been passed?

- if so, is it unavoidable that a custodial sentence be imposed?
- if so, can that sentence be suspended?

Aggravating factors	Mitigating factors
Statutory aggravating factors	No previous convictions **or** no relevant/recent convictions
Previous convictions, having regard to a) the nature of the offence to which the conviction relates and its relevance to the current offence; and b) the time that has elapsed since the conviction	Remorse
	Previous good character and/or exemplary conduct*
	Age and/or lack of maturity where it affects the responsibility of the offender
Offence committed whilst on bail	Mental disorder or learning disability, particularly where linked to the commission of the offence
Other aggravating factors	
Location of offence	Demonstration of steps taken to address offending behaviour
Timing of offence	
Failure to comply with current court orders	
Offence committed whilst on licence	* Previous good character/exemplary conduct is different from having no previous convictions. The more serious the offence, the less the weight which should normally be attributed to this factor. Where previous good character/exemplary conduct has been used to facilitate the offence, this mitigation should not normally be allowed and such conduct may constitute an aggravating factor.
Any steps taken to prevent the victim reporting an incident, obtaining assistance and/or from assisting or supporting the prosecution	
Attempts to dispose of or conceal evidence	
Commission of offence whilst under the influence of alcohol or drugs	

STEP THREE
Consider any factors which indicate a reduction, such as assistance to the prosecution
The court should take into account sections 73 and 74 of the Serious Organised Crime and Police Act 2005 (assistance by defendants: reduction or review of sentence) and any other rule of law by virtue of which an offender may receive a discounted sentence in consequence of assistance given (or offered) to the prosecutor or investigator.

STEP FOUR

Reduction for guilty pleas

The court should take account of any potential reduction for a guilty plea in accordance with section 144 of the Criminal Justice Act 2003 and the Guilty Plea guideline.

STEP FIVE

Dangerousness

The court should consider whether having regard to the criteria contained in Chapter 5 of Part 12 of the Criminal Justice Act 2003 it would be appropriate to award an extended sentence (section 226A).

STEP SIX

Totality principle

If sentencing an offender for more than one offence, or where the offender is already serving a sentence, consider whether the total sentence is just and proportionate to the offending behaviour.

STEP SEVEN

Ancillary orders

The court must consider whether to make any ancillary orders. The court must also consider what other requirements or provisions may automatically apply. Further information is included at Annex A on page 153.

STEP EIGHT

Reasons

Section 174 of the Criminal Justice Act 2003 imposes a duty to give reasons for, and explain the effect of, the sentence.

STEP NINE

Consideration for time spent on bail

The court must consider whether to give credit for time spent on bail in accordance with section 240A of the Criminal Justice Act 2003.

INDUCEMENT, THREAT OR DECEPTION TO PROCURE SEXUAL ACTIVITY WITH A PERSON WITH A MENTAL DISORDER

Sexual Offences Act 2003 (section 34)

CAUSING A PERSON WITH A MENTAL DISORDER TO ENGAGE IN OR AGREE TO ENGAGE IN SEXUAL ACTIVITY BY INDUCEMENT, THREAT OR DECEPTION

Sexual Offences Act 2003 (section 35)

Triable only on indictment (if penetration involved)
—otherwise triable either way

Maximum: Life imprisonment (if penetration involved)
—otherwise 14 years' custody

Offence range: Community order – 10 years' custody

These are serious specified offences for the purposes of section 224 and, where the offence involved penetration, section 225(2) (life sentence for serious offences) of the Criminal Justice Act 2003.

For offences involving penetration, committed on or after 3 December 2012, these are offences listed in Part 1 of Schedule 15B for the purposes of section 224A (life sentence for second listed offence) of the Criminal Justice Act 2003.

For convictions on or after 3 December 2012 (irrespective of the date of commission of the offence), these are specified offences for the purposes of section 226A (extended sentence for certain violent or sexual offences) of the Criminal Justice Act 2003.

STEP ONE
Determining the offence category

The court should determine which categories of harm and culpability the offence falls into by reference only to the tables below.

This guideline also applies to offences committed remotely/online.

Harm	Culpability
Category 1 • Penetration of vagina or anus (using body or object) • Penile penetration of mouth In either case by, or of, the victim	**A** Significant degree of planning Offender acts together with others to commit the offence Use of alcohol/drugs on victim to facilitate the offence Abuse of trust
Category 2 • Touching, or exposure, of naked genitalia or naked breasts by, or of, the victim	Sexual images of victim recorded, retained, solicited or shared Commercial exploitation and/or motivation
Category 3 Other sexual activity	Offence racially or religiously aggravated Offence motivated by, or demonstrating, hostility to the victim based on his or her sexual orientation (or presumed sexual orientation) or transgender identity (or presumed transgender identity) Offence motivated by, or demonstrating, hostility to the victim based on his or her disability (or presumed disability)
	B Factor(s) in category A not present

STEP TWO
Starting point and category range

Having determined the category of harm and culpability, the court should use the corresponding starting points to reach a sentence within the category range on the next page. The starting point applies to all offenders irrespective of plea or previous convictions. Having determined the starting point, step two allows further adjustment for aggravating or mitigating features, set out on the next page.

A case of particular gravity, reflected by multiple features of culpability or harm in step one, could merit upward adjustment from the starting point before further adjustment for aggravating or mitigating features, set out on the next page.

Where there is a sufficient prospect of rehabilitation, a community order with a sex offender treatment programme requirement under section 202 of the Criminal Justice Act 2003 can be a proper alternative to a short or moderate length custodial sentence.

	A	B
Category 1	**Starting point** 5 year's custody	**Starting point** 1 year's custody
	Category range 4–10 years' custody	**Category range** High level community order – 2 year's custody
Category 2	**Starting point** 3 year's custody	**Starting point** 26 weeks' custody
	Category range 2–6 years' custody	**Category range** High level community order – 1 year's custody
Category 3	**Starting point** 26 weeks' custody	**Starting point** Medium level community order
	Category range High level community order – 3 year's custody	**Category range** Low level community order – High level community order

The table below contains a **non-exhaustive** list of additional factual elements providing the context of the offence and factors relating to the offender. Identify whether any combination of these, or other relevant factors, should result in an upward or downward adjustment from the starting point. **In particular, relevant recent convictions are likely to result in an upward adjustment.** In some cases, having considered these factors, it may be appropriate to move outside the identified category range.

When sentencing appropriate **category 2 or 3 offences**, the court should also consider the custody threshold as follows:

- has the custody threshold been passed?
- if so, is it unavoidable that a custodial sentence be imposed?
- if so, can that sentence be suspended?

Aggravating factors	Mitigating factors
Statutory aggravating factors	No previous convictions **or** no relevant/recent convictions
Previous convictions, having regard to a) the nature of the offence to which the conviction relates and its relevance to the current offence; and b) the time that has elapsed since the conviction	Remorse
	Previous good character and/or exemplary conduct*
	Age and/or lack of maturity where it affects the responsibility of the offender
Offence committed whilst on bail	
Other aggravating factors	Mental disorder or learning disability, particularly where linked to the commission of the offence
Severe psychological or physical harm	
Ejaculation	
Pregnancy or STI as a consequence of offence	
Location of offence	
Timing of offence	
Victim compelled to leave their home or institution (including victims of domestic violence)	
Failure to comply with current court orders	
Offence committed whilst on licence	
Any steps taken to prevent the victim reporting an incident, obtaining assistance and/or from assisting or supporting the prosecution	
Attempts to dispose of or conceal evidence	
Commission of offence whilst under the influence of alcohol or drugs	

* Previous good character/exemplary conduct is different from having no previous convictions. The more serious the offence, the less the weight which should normally be attributed to this factor. Where previous good character/exemplary conduct has been used to facilitate the offence, this mitigation should not normally be allowed and such conduct may constitute an aggravating factor.

In the context of this offence, previous good character/exemplary conduct should not normally be given any significant weight and will not normally justify a reduction in what would otherwise be the appropriate sentence.

STEP THREE
Consider any factors which indicate a reduction, such as assistance to the prosecution
The court should take into account sections 73 and 74 of the Serious Organised Crime and Police Act 2005 (assistance by defendants: reduction or review of sentence) and any other rule of law by virtue of which an offender may receive a discounted sentence in consequence of assistance given (or offered) to the prosecutor or investigator.

STEP FOUR
Reduction for guilty pleas
The court should take account of any potential reduction for a guilty plea in accordance with section 144 of the Criminal Justice Act 2003 and the Guilty Plea guideline.

STEP FIVE
Dangerousness
The court should consider whether having regard to the criteria contained in Chapter 5 of Part 12 of the Criminal Justice Act 2003 it would be appropriate to award a life sentence (section 224A or section 225(2)) or an extended sentence (section 226A). When sentencing offenders to a life sentence under these provisions, the notional determinate sentence should be used as the basis for the setting of a minimum term.

STEP SIX
Totality principle
If sentencing an offender for more than one offence, or where the offender is already serving a sentence, consider whether the total sentence is just and proportionate to the offending behaviour.

STEP SEVEN
Ancillary orders
The court must consider whether to make any ancillary orders. The court must also consider what other requirements or provisions may automatically apply. Further information is included at Annex A on page 153.

STEP EIGHT
Reasons
Section 174 of the Criminal Justice Act 2003 imposes a duty to give reasons for, and explain the effect of, the sentence.

> **STEP NINE**
> Consideration for time spent on bail
> The court must consider whether to give credit for time spent on bail in accordance with section 240A of the Criminal Justice Act 2003.

ENGAGING IN SEXUAL ACTIVITY IN THE PRESENCE, PROCURED BY INDUCEMENT, THREAT OR DECEPTION, OF A PERSON WITH A MENTAL DISORDER

Sexual Offences Act 2003 (section 36)

CAUSING A PERSON WITH A MENTAL DISORDER TO WATCH A SEXUAL ACT BY INDUCEMENT, THREAT OR DECEPTION

Sexual Offences Act 2003 (section 37)

Triable either way
Maximum: 10 years' custody

Offence range: Community order – 6 years' custody

For convictions on or after 3 December 2012 (irrespective of the date of commission of the offence), these are specified offences for the purposes of section 226A (extended sentence for certain violent or sexual offences) of the Criminal Justice Act 2003.

> **STEP ONE**
> Determining the offence category

The court should determine which categories of harm and culpability the offence falls into by reference only to the tables below.

Harm	Culpability
Category 1 • Causing victim to view extreme pornography • Causing victim to view indecent/prohibited images of children • Engaging in, or causing a victim to view live, sexual activity involving sadism/violence/sexual activity with an animal/a child	**A** Significant degree of planning Offender acts together with others in order to commit the offence Use of alcohol/drugs on victim to facilitate the offence Abuse of trust Commercial exploitation and/or motivation Offence racially or religiously aggravated Offence motivated by, or demonstrating, hostility to the victim based on his or her sexual orientation (or presumed sexual orientation) or transgender identity (or presumed transgender identity) Offence motivated by, or demonstrating, hostility to the victim based on his or her disability (or presumed disability)
Category 2 Engaging in, or causing a victim to view images of or view live, sexual activity involving: • penetration of vagina or anus (using body or object) • penile penetration of mouth • masturbation	
	B Factor(s) in category A not present
Category 3 Factor(s) in categories 1 and 2 not present	

STEP TWO
Starting point and category range

Having determined the category of harm and culpability, the court should use the corresponding starting points to reach a sentence within the category range on the next page. The starting point applies to all offenders irrespective of plea or previous convictions. Having determined the starting point, step two allows further adjustment for aggravating or mitigating features, set out on the next page.

A case of particular gravity, reflected by multiple features of culpability or harm in step one, could merit upward adjustment from the starting point before further adjustment for aggravating or mitigating features, set out on the next page.

Where there is a sufficient prospect of rehabilitation, a community order with a sex offender treatment programme requirement under section 202 of the Criminal Justice Act 2003 can be a proper alternative to a short or moderate length custodial sentence.

	A	B
Category 1	Starting point 4 year's custody	Starting point 2 year's custody
	Category range 3–6 years' custody	Category range 1–3 year's custody
Category 2	Starting point 2 year's custody	Starting point 1 year's custody
	Category range 1–3 year's custody	Category range High level community order – 18 months' custody
Category 3	Starting point 26 weeks' custody	Starting point Medium level community order
	Category range High level community order – 1 year's custody	Category range Low level community order – High level community order

The table below contains a **non-exhaustive** list of additional factual elements providing the context of the offence and factors relating to the offender. Identify whether any combination of these, or other relevant factors, should result in an upward or downward adjustment from the starting point. **In particular, relevant recent convictions are likely to result in an upward adjustment.** In some cases, having considered these factors, it may be appropriate to move outside the identified category range.

When sentencing appropriate **category 2 or 3 offences**, the court should also consider the custody threshold as follows:

- has the custody threshold been passed?
- if so, is it unavoidable that a custodial sentence be imposed?
- if so, can that sentence be suspended?

Aggravating factors	Mitigating factors
Statutory aggravating factors	No previous convictions or no relevant/recent convictions
Previous convictions, having regard to a) the nature of the offence to which the conviction relates and its relevance to the current offence; and b) the time that has elapsed since the conviction	Remorse
	Previous good character and/or exemplary conduct*
	Age and/or lack of maturity where it affects the responsibility of the offender
Offence committed whilst on bail	Mental disorder or learning disability, particularly where linked to the commission of the offence
Other aggravating factors	
Location of offence	Demonstration of steps taken to address offending behaviour
Timing of offence	
Failure to comply with current court orders	
Offence committed whilst on licence	* Previous good character/exemplary conduct is different from having no previous convictions. The more serious the offence, the less the weight which should normally be attributed to this factor. Where previous good character/exemplary conduct has been used to facilitate the offence, this mitigation should not normally be allowed and such conduct may constitute an aggravating factor.
Any steps taken to prevent the victim reporting an incident, obtaining assistance and/or from assisting or supporting the prosecution	
Attempts to dispose of or conceal evidence	
Commission of offence whilst under the influence of alcohol or drugs	

STEP THREE
Consider any factors which indicate a reduction, such as assistance to the prosecution
The court should take into account sections 73 and 74 of the Serious Organised Crime and Police Act 2005 (assistance by defendants: reduction or review of sentence) and any other rule of law by virtue of which an offender may receive a discounted sentence in consequence of assistance given (or offered) to the prosecutor or investigator.

STEP FOUR
Reduction for guilty pleas
The court should take account of any potential reduction for a guilty plea in accordance with section 144 of the Criminal Justice Act 2003 and the Guilty Plea guideline.

STEP FIVE
Dangerousness
The court should consider whether having regard to the criteria contained in Chapter 5 of Part 12 of the Criminal Justice Act 2003 it would be appropriate to award an extended sentence (section 226A)..

STEP SIX
Totality principle
If sentencing an offender for more than one offence, or where the offender is already serving a sentence, consider whether the total sentence is just and proportionate to the offending behaviour.

STEP SEVEN
Ancillary orders
The court must consider whether to make any ancillary orders. The court must also consider what other requirements or provisions may automatically apply. Further information is included at Annex A on page 153.

STEP EIGHT
Reasons
Section 174 of the Criminal Justice Act 2003 imposes a duty to give reasons for, and explain the effect of, the sentence.

STEP NINE
Consideration for time spent on bail
The court must consider whether to give credit for time spent on bail in accordance with section 240A of the Criminal Justice Act 2003.

CARE WORKERS: SEXUAL ACTIVITY WITH A PERSON WITH A MENTAL DISORDER

Sexual Offences Act 2003 (section 38)

CARE WORKERS: CAUSING OR INCITING SEXUAL ACTIVITY

Sexual Offences Act 2003 (section 39)

Triable only on indictment (if penetration involved)
—otherwise triable either way

Maximum: 14 years' custody (if penetration involved)
—otherwise 10 years' custody

Offence range: Community order – 10 years' custody

For convictions on or after 3 December 2012 (irrespective of the date of commission of the offence), these are specified offences for the purposes of section 226A (extended sentence for certain violent or sexual offences) of the Criminal Justice Act 2003.

STEP ONE
Determining the offence category

The court should determine which categories of harm and culpability the offence falls into by reference only to the tables below.

This guideline also applies to offences committed remotely/online.

Harm	Culpability
Category 1 • Penetration of vagina or anus (using body or object) • Penile penetration of mouth In either case by, or of, the victim	**A** Significant degree of planning Offender acts together with others to commit the offence Use of alcohol/drugs on victim to facilitate the offence Grooming behaviour used against victim Use of threats (including blackmail) Sexual images of victim recorded, retained, solicited or shared Commercial exploitation and/or motivation Offence racially or religiously aggravated Offence motivated by, or demonstrating, hostility to the victim based on his or her sexual orientation (or presumed sexual orientation) or transgender identity (or presumed transgender identity) Offence motivated by, or demonstrating, hostility to the victim based on his or her disability (or presumed disability)
Category 2 • Touching, or exposure, of naked genitalia or naked breasts by, or of, the victim	
Category 3 Factor(s) in categories 1 and 2 not present	

789

Culpability
B
Factor(s) in category A not present

STEP TWO
Starting point and category range

Having determined the category of harm and culpability, the court should use the corresponding starting points to reach a sentence within the category range on the next page. The starting point applies to all offenders irrespective of plea or previous convictions. Having determined the starting point, step two allows further adjustment for aggravating or mitigating features, set out on the next page.

A case of particular gravity, reflected by multiple features of culpability or harm in step one, could merit upward adjustment from the starting point before further adjustment for aggravating or mitigating features, set out on the next page.

Where there is a sufficient prospect of rehabilitation, a community order with a sex offender treatment programme requirement under section 202 of the Criminal Justice Act 2003 can be a proper alternative to a short or moderate length custodial sentence.

	A	**B**
Category 1	**Starting point** 5 year's custody	**Starting point** 18 months' custody
	Category range 4–10 years' custody	**Category range** 1–2 years' custody
Category 2	**Starting point** 3 year's custody	**Starting point** 26 weeks' custody
	Category range 2–6 years' custody	**Category range** Medium level community order – 1 year's custody

	A	B
Category 3	**Starting point** 26 weeks' custody	**Starting point** Medium level community order
	Category range High level community order – 3 year's custody	**Category range** Low level community order – High level community order

The table below contains a **non-exhaustive** list of additional factual elements providing the context of the offence and factors relating to the offender. Identify whether any combination of these, or other relevant factors, should result in an upward or downward adjustment from the starting point. **In particular, relevant recent convictions are likely to result in an upward adjustment.** In some cases, having considered these factors, it may be appropriate to move outside the identified category range.

When sentencing appropriate category 2 or 3 offences, the court should also consider the custody threshold as follows:

- has the custody threshold been passed?
- if so, is it unavoidable that a custodial sentence be imposed?
- if so, can that sentence be suspended?

Aggravating factors	Mitigating factors
Statutory aggravating factors	No previous convictions **or** no relevant/recent convictions
Previous convictions, having regard to a) the nature of the offence to which the conviction relates and its relevance to the current offence; and b) the time that has elapsed since the conviction	Remorse
	Previous good character and/or exemplary conduct*
	Age and/or lack of maturity where it affects the responsibility of the offender
Offence committed whilst on bail	
Other aggravating factors	Mental disorder or learning disability, particularly where linked to the commission of the offence
Ejaculation	
Pregnancy or STI as a consequence of offence	

791

Aggravating factors	Mitigating factors
Location of offence	Sexual activity was incited but no activity took place because the offender voluntarily desisted or intervened to prevent it
Timing of offence	
Victim compelled to leave their home or institution (including victims of domestic violence)	
Failure to comply with current court orders	* Previous good character/exemplary conduct is different from having no previous convictions. The more serious the offence, the less the weight which should normally be attributed to this factor. Where previous good character/exemplary conduct has been used to facilitate the offence, this mitigation should not normally be allowed and such conduct may constitute an aggravating factor.
Offence committed whilst on licence	
Any steps taken to prevent the victim reporting an incident, obtaining assistance and/or from assisting or supporting the prosecution	
Attempts to dispose of or conceal evidences	In the context of this offence, previous good character/exemplary conduct should not normally be given any significant weight and will not normally justify a reduction in what would otherwise be the appropriate sentence.
Failure of offender to respond to previous warnings	
Commission of offence whilst under the influence of alcohol or drugs	

STEP THREE

Consider any factors which indicate a reduction, such as assistance to the prosecution

The court should take into account sections 73 and 74 of the Serious Organised Crime and Police Act 2005 (assistance by defendants: reduction or review of sentence) and any other rule of law by virtue of which an offender may receive a discounted sentence in consequence of assistance given (or offered) to the prosecutor or investigator.

STEP FOUR

Reduction for guilty pleas

The court should take account of any potential reduction for a guilty plea in accordance with section 144 of the Criminal Justice Act 2003 and the Guilty Plea guideline.

STEP FIVE

Dangerousness

The court should consider whether having regard to the criteria contained in Chapter 5 of Part 12 of the Criminal Justice Act 2003 it would be appropriate to award an extended sentence (section 226A).

STEP SIX
Totality principle
If sentencing an offender for more than one offence, or where the offender is already serving a sentence, consider whether the total sentence is just and proportionate to the offending behaviour.

STEP SEVEN
Ancillary orders
The court must consider whether to make any ancillary orders. The court must also consider what other requirements or provisions may automatically apply. Further information is included at Annex A on page 153.

STEP EIGHT
Reasons
Section 174 of the Criminal Justice Act 2003 imposes a duty to give reasons for, and explain the effect of, the sentence.

STEP NINE
Consideration for time spent on bail
The court must consider whether to give credit for time spent on bail in accordance with section 240A of the Criminal Justice Act 2003.

CARE WORKERS: SEXUAL ACTIVITY IN THE PRESENCE OF A PERSON WITH A MENTAL DISORDER

Sexual Offences Act 2003 (section 40)

CARE WORKERS: CAUSING A PERSON WITH A MENTAL DISORDER TO WATCH A SEXUAL ACT

Sexual Offences Act 2003 (section 41)

Triable either way
Maximum: 7 years' custody

Offence range: Community order – 2 years' custody

For convictions on or after 3 December 2012 (irrespective of the date of commission of the offence), these are specified offences for the purposes of section 226A (extended sentence for certain violent or sexual offences) of the Criminal Justice Act 2003.

STEP ONE
Determining the offence category

The court should determine which categories of harm and culpability the offence falls into by reference only to the tables below.

Harm	Culpability
Category 1 • Causing victim to view extreme pornography • Causing victim to view indecent/prohibited images of children • Engaging in, or causing a victim to view live, sexual activity involving sadism/violence/sexual activity with an animal/a child	**A** Significant degree of planning Offender acts together with others to commit the offence Use of alcohol/drugs on victim to facilitate the offence Grooming behaviour used against victim Use of threats (including blackmail) Commercial exploitation and/or motivation Offence racially or religiously aggravated Offence motivated by, or demonstrating, hostility to the victim based on his or her sexual orientation (or presumed sexual orientation) or transgender identity (or presumed transgender identity) Offence motivated by, or demonstrating, hostility to the victim based on his or her disability (or presumed disability)
Category 2 Engaging in, or causing a victim to view images of or view live, sexual activity involving: • penetration of vagina or anus (using body or object) • penile penetration of mouth • masturbation	
Category 3 Factor(s) in categories 1 and 2 not present	**B** Factor(s) in category A not present

---

STEP TWO
Starting point and category range

Having determined the category of harm and culpability, the court should use the corresponding starting points to reach a sentence within the category range on the next page. The starting point applies to all offenders irrespective of plea or previous convictions. Having determined the starting point, step two allows further adjustment for aggravating or mitigating features, set out on the next page.

A case of particular gravity, reflected by multiple features of culpability or harm in step one, could merit upward adjustment from the starting point before further adjustment for aggravating or mitigating features, set out on the next page.

Where there is a sufficient prospect of rehabilitation, a community order with a sex offender treatment programme requirement under section 202 of the Criminal Justice Act 2003 can be a proper alternative to a short or moderate length custodial sentence.

	A	B
Category 1	**Starting point** 18 years' custody	**Starting point** 1 year's custody
	Category range 1–2 years' custody	**Category range** 26 weeks' – 18 months' custody
Category 2	**Starting point** 1 year's custody	**Starting point** 26 weeks' custody
	Category range 26 weeks' – 18 months' custody	**Category range** High level community order – 1 year's custody
Category 3	**Starting point** 26 weeks' custody	**Starting point** Medium level community order
	Category range High level community order – 1 year's custody	**Category range** Low level community order – High level community order

The table below contains a **non-exhaustive** list of additional factual elements providing the context of the offence and factors relating to the offender. Identify whether any combination of these, or other relevant factors, should result in an upward or downward adjustment from the starting point. **In particular, relevant recent convictions are likely to result in an upward adjustment.** In some cases, having considered these factors, it may be appropriate to move outside the identified category range.

When sentencing appropriate **category 2 or 3 offences**, the court should also consider the custody threshold as follows:

- has the custody threshold been passed?
- if so, is it unavoidable that a custodial sentence be imposed?
- if so, can that sentence be suspended?

Aggravating factors	Mitigating factors
Statutory aggravating factors	No previous convictions **or** no relevant/recent convictions
Previous convictions, having regard to a) the nature of the offence to which the conviction relates and its relevance to the current offence; and b) the time that has elapsed since the conviction	Remorse
	Previous good character and/or exemplary conduct*
Offence committed whilst on bail	Age and/or lack of maturity where it affects the responsibility of the offender
Other aggravating factors	Mental disorder or learning disability, particularly where linked to the commission of the offence
Location of offence	
Timing of offence	Demonstration of steps taken to address offending behaviour
Failure to comply with current court orders	
Offence committed whilst on licence	* Previous good character/exemplary conduct is different from having no previous convictions. The more serious the offence, the less the weight which should normally be attributed to this factor. Where previous good character/exemplary conduct has been used to facilitate the offence, this mitigation should not normally be allowed and such conduct may constitute an aggravating factor.
Any steps taken to prevent the victim reporting an incident, obtaining assistance and/or from assisting or supporting the prosecution	
Attempts to dispose of or conceal evidence	
Failure of offender to respond to previous warnings	
Commission of offence whilst under the influence of alcohol or drugs	

STEP THREE

Consider any factors which indicate a reduction, such as assistance to the prosecution

The court should take into account sections 73 and 74 of the Serious Organised Crime and Police Act 2005 (assistance by defendants: reduction or review of sentence) and any other rule of law by virtue of which an offender may receive a discounted sentence in consequence of assistance given (or offered) to the prosecutor or investigator.

STEP FOUR
Reduction for guilty pleas
The court should take account of any potential reduction for a guilty plea in accordance with section 144 of the Criminal Justice Act 2003 and the Guilty Plea guideline.

STEP FIVE
Dangerousness
The court should consider whether having regard to the criteria contained in Chapter 5 of Part 12 of the Criminal Justice Act 2003 it would be appropriate to award an extended sentence (section 226A).

STEP SIX
Totality principle
If sentencing an offender for more than one offence, or where the offender is already serving a sentence, consider whether the total sentence is just and proportionate to the offending behaviour.

STEP SEVEN
Ancillary orders
The court must consider whether to make any ancillary orders. The court must also consider what other requirements or provisions may automatically apply. Further information is included at Annex A on page 153.

STEP EIGHT
Reasons
Section 174 of the Criminal Justice Act 2003 imposes a duty to give reasons for, and explain the effect of, the sentence.

STEP NINE
Consideration for time spent on bail
The court must consider whether to give credit for time spent on bail in accordance with section 240A of the Criminal Justice Act 2003.

EXPOSURE

Sexual Offences Act 2003 (section 66)

Triable either way
Maximum: 2 years' custody

Offence range: Fine – 1 year's custody

For convictions on or after 3 December 2012 (irrespective of the date of commission of the offence), this is a specified offence for the purposes of section 226A (extended sentence for certain violent or sexual offences) of the Criminal Justice Act 2003.

STEP ONE
Determining the offence category

The court should determine the offence category using the table below.

Category 1	Raised harm and raised culpability
Category 2	Raised harm or raised culpability
Category 3	Grooming without raised harm or culpability factors present

The court should determine culpability and harm caused or intended, by reference only to the factors below, which comprise the principal factual elements of the offence. Where an offence does not fall squarely into a category, individual factors may require a degree of weighting before making an overall assessment and determining the appropriate offence category.

Factors indicating raised harm	Factors indicating raised culpability
Victim followed/pursued	
Offender masturbated	Specific or previous targeting of a particularly vulnerable victim
	Abuse of trust
	Use of threats (including blackmail)
	Offence racially or religiously aggravated
	Offence motivated by, or demonstrating, hostility to the victim based on his or her sexual orientation (or presumed sexual orientation) or transgender identity (or presumed transgender identity)
	Offence motivated by, or demonstrating, hostility to the victim based on his or her disability (or presumed disability)

STEP TWO
Starting point and category range

Having determined the category, the court should use the corresponding starting points to reach a sentence within the category range on the next page. The starting point applies to all offenders irrespective of plea or previous convictions. Having determined the starting point, step two allows further adjustment for aggravating or mitigating features, set out on the next page.

A case of particular gravity, reflected by multiple features of culpability or harm in step one, could merit upward adjustment from the starting point before further adjustment for aggravating or mitigating features, set out on the next page.

Where there is a sufficient prospect of rehabilitation, a community order with a sex offender treatment programme requirement under section 202 of the Criminal Justice Act 2003 can be a proper alternative to a short or moderate length custodial sentence.

Category 1	**Starting point**
	26 week' custody
	Category range
	12 weeks' – 1 years' custody
Category 2	**Starting point**
	High level community order
	Category range
	Medium level community order – 26 weeks' custody
Category 3	**Starting point**
	Medium level community order
	Category range
	Band A fine – High level community order

The table below contains a **non-exhaustive** list of additional factual elements providing the context of the offence and factors relating to the offender. Identify whether any combination of these, or other relevant factors, should result in an upward or downward adjustment from the starting point. In particular, relevant recent convictions are likely to result in an upward adjustment. In some cases, having considered these factors, it may be appropriate to move outside the identified category range.

When sentencing **category 2 offences**, the court should also consider the custody threshold as follows:

- has the custody threshold been passed?
- if so, is it unavoidable that a custodial sentence be imposed?
- if so, can that sentence be suspended?

When sentencing **category 3 offences**, the court should also consider the community order threshold as follows:

- has the community order threshold been passed?

Aggravating factors	Mitigating factors
Statutory aggravating factors	No previous convictions **or** no relevant/recent convictions
Previous convictions, having regard to a) the nature of the offence to which the conviction relates and its relevance to the current offence; and b) the time that has elapsed since the conviction	Remorse
	Previous good character and/or exemplary conduct*
	Age and/or lack of maturity where it affects the responsibility of the offender
Offence committed whilst on bail	
Other aggravating factors	Mental disorder or learning disability, particularly where linked to the commission of the offence
Location of offence	
Timing of offence	Demonstration of steps taken to address offending behaviour
Any steps taken to prevent the victim reporting an incident, obtaining assistance and/or from assisting or supporting the prosecution	* Previous good character/exemplary conduct is different from having no previous convictions. The more serious the offence, the less the weight which should normally be attributed to this factor. Where previous good character/exemplary conduct has been used to facilitate the offence, this mitigation should not normally be allowed and such conduct may constitute an aggravating factor.
Failure to comply with current court orders	
Offence committed whilst on licence	
Commission of offence whilst under the influence of alcohol or drugs	
Presence of others, especially children	

STEP THREE
Consider any factors which indicate a reduction, such as assistance to the prosecution
The court should take into account sections 73 and 74 of the Serious Organised Crime and Police Act 2005 (assistance by defendants: reduction or review of sentence) and any other rule of law by virtue of which an offender may receive a discounted sentence in consequence of assistance given (or offered) to the prosecutor or investigator.

STEP FOUR
Reduction for guilty pleas
The court should take account of any potential reduction for a guilty plea in accordance with section 144 of the Criminal Justice Act 2003 and the Guilty Plea guideline.

STEP FIVE
Dangerousness
The court should consider whether having regard to the criteria contained in Chapter 5 of Part 12 of the Criminal Justice Act 2003 it would be appropriate to award an extended sentence (section 226A).

STEP SIX
Totality principle
If sentencing an offender for more than one offence, or where the offender is already serving a sentence, consider whether the total sentence is just and proportionate to the offending behaviour.

STEP SEVEN
Ancillary orders
The court must consider whether to make any ancillary orders. The court must also consider what other requirements or provisions may automatically apply. Further information is included at Annex A on page 153.

STEP EIGHT
Reasons
Section 174 of the Criminal Justice Act 2003 imposes a duty to give reasons for, and explain the effect of, the sentence.

STEP NINE
Consideration for time spent on bail
The court must consider whether to give credit for time spent on bail in accordance with section 240A of the Criminal Justice Act 2003.

VOYEURISM

Sexual Offences Act 2003 (section 67)

Triable either way
Maximum: 2 years' custody

Offence range: Fine – 18 months' custody

For convictions on or after such date (irrespective of the date of commission of the offence), these are specified offences for the purposes of section 226A (extended sentence for certain violent or sexual offences) of the Criminal Justice Act 2003.

STEP ONE
Determining the offence category

The court should determine the offence category using the table below.

Category 1	Raised harm and raised culpability
Category 2	Raised harm or raised culpability
Category 3	Voyeurism without raised harm or culpability factors present

The court should determine culpability and harm caused or intended, by reference only to the factors below, which comprise the principal factual elements of the offence. Where an offence does not fall squarely into a category, individual factors may require a degree of weighting before making an overall assessment and determining the appropriate offence category.

Factors indicating raised harm	Factors indicating raised culpability
Image(s) available to be viewed by others	Significant degree of planning
Victim observed or recorded in their own home or residence	Image(s) recorded
	Abuse of trust
	Specific or previous targeting of a particularly vulnerable victim
	Commercial exploitation and/or motivation
	Offence racially or religiously aggravated
	Offence motivated by, or demonstrating, hostility to the victim based on his or her sexual orientation (or presumed sexual orientation) or transgender identity (or presumed transgender identity)
	Offence motivated by, or demonstrating, hostility to the victim based on his or her disability (or presumed disability)

> **STEP TWO**
> **Starting point and category range**

Having determined the category, the court should use the corresponding starting points to reach a sentence within the category range on the next page. The starting point applies to all offenders irrespective of plea or previous convictions. Having determined the starting point, step two allows further adjustment for aggravating or mitigating features, set out on the next page.

A case of particular gravity, reflected by multiple features of culpability or harm in step one, could merit upward adjustment from the starting point before further adjustment for aggravating or mitigating features, set out on the next page.

Where there is a sufficient prospect of rehabilitation, a community order with a sex offender treatment programme requirement under section 202 of the Criminal Justice Act 2003 can be a proper alternative to a short or moderate length custodial sentence.

Category 1	**Starting point** 26 week' custody
	Category range 12 weeks' – 18 months' custody
Category 2	**Starting point** High level community order
	Category range Medium level community order – 26 weeks' custody
Category 3	**Starting point** Medium level community order
	Category range Band A fine – High level community order

The table below contains a **non-exhaustive** list of additional factual elements providing the context of the offence and factors relating to the offender. Identify whether any combination of these, or other relevant factors, should result in an upward or downward adjustment from the starting point. **In particular, relevant recent convictions are likely to result in an upward adjustment.** In some cases, having considered these factors, it may be appropriate to move outside the identified category range.

When sentencing **category 2 offences**, the court should also consider the custody threshold as follows:

- has the custody threshold been passed?
- if so, is it unavoidable that a custodial sentence be imposed?
- if so, can that sentence be suspended?

When sentencing **category 3 offences**, the court should also consider the community order threshold as follows:

- has the community order threshold been passed?

Aggravating factors	Mitigating factors
Statutory aggravating factors	No previous convictions **or** no relevant/recent convictions
Previous convictions, having regard to a) the nature of the offence to which the conviction relates and its relevance to the current offence; and b) the time that has elapsed since the conviction	Remorse
	Previous good character and/or exemplary conduct*
	Age and/or lack of maturity where it affects the responsibility of the offender
Offence committed whilst on bail	
Other aggravating factors	Mental disorder or learning disability, particularly where linked to the commission of the offence
Location of offence	Demonstration of steps taken to address offending behaviour
Timing of offence	
Failure to comply with current court orders	
Offence committed whilst on licence	* Previous good character/exemplary conduct is different from having no previous convictions. The more serious the offence, the less the weight which should normally be attributed to this factor. Where previous good character/exemplary conduct has been used to facilitate the offence, this mitigation should not normally be allowed and such conduct may constitute an aggravating factor.
Distribution of images, whether or not for gain	
Placing images where there is the potential for a high volume of viewers	
Period over which victim observed	
Period over which images were made or distributed	
Any steps taken to prevent victim reporting an incident, obtaining assistance and/or from assisting or supporting the prosecution	
Attempts to dispose of or conceal evidence	

STEP THREE
Consider any factors which indicate a reduction, such as assistance to the prosecution
The court should take into account sections 73 and 74 of the Serious Organised Crime and Police Act 2005 (assistance by defendants: reduction or review of sentence) and any other rule of law by virtue of which an offender may receive a discounted sentence in consequence of assistance given (or offered) to the prosecutor or investigator.

STEP FOUR
Reduction for guilty pleas
The court should take account of any potential reduction for a guilty plea in accordance with section 144 of the Criminal Justice Act 2003 and the Guilty Plea guideline.

STEP FIVE
Dangerousness
The court should consider whether having regard to the criteria contained in Chapter 5 of Part 12 of the Criminal Justice Act 2003 it would be appropriate to award an extended sentence (section 226A).

STEP SIX
Totality principle
If sentencing an offender for more than one offence, or where the offender is already serving a sentence, consider whether the total sentence is just and proportionate to the offending behaviour.

STEP SEVEN
Ancillary orders
The court must consider whether to make any ancillary orders. The court must also consider what other requirements or provisions may automatically apply. Further information is included at Annex A on page 153.

STEP EIGHT
Reasons
Section 174 of the Criminal Justice Act 2003 imposes a duty to give reasons for, and explain the effect of, the sentence.

STEP NINE
Consideration for time spent on bail
The court must consider whether to give credit for time spent on bail in accordance with section 240A of the Criminal Justice Act 2003.

SEX WITH AN ADULT RELATIVE: PENETRATION

Sexual Offences Act 2003 (section 64)

SEX WITH AN ADULT RELATIVE: CONSENTING TO PENETRATION

Sexual Offences Act 2003 (section 65)

Triable either way
Maximum: 2 years' custody

Offence range: Fine – 2 years' custody

For convictions on or after 3 December 2012 (irrespective of the date of commission of the offence), these are specified offences for the purposes of section 226A (extended sentence for certain violent or sexual offences) of the Criminal Justice Act 2003.

STEP ONE
Determining the offence category

The court should determine the offence category using the table below.

Category 1	Raised harm **and** raised culpability
Category 2	Raised harm **or** raised culpability
Category 3	Sex with an adult relative **without** raised harm or culpability factors present

The court should determine culpability and harm caused or intended, by reference only to the factors below, which comprise the principal factual elements of the offence. Where an offence does not fall squarely into a category, individual factors may require a degree of weighting before making an overall assessment and determining the appropriate offence category.

Factors indicating raised harm	Factors indicating raised culpability
Victim is particularly vulnerable due to personal circumstances	Grooming behaviour used against victim
Child conceived	Use of threats (including blackmail)

STEP TWO
Starting point and category range

Having determined the category, the court should use the corresponding starting points to reach a sentence within the category range on the next page. The starting point applies to all offenders irrespective of plea or previous convictions. Having determined the starting point, step two allows further adjustment for aggravating or mitigating features, set out on the next page.

A case of particular gravity, reflected by multiple features of culpability or harm in step one, could merit upward adjustment from the starting point before further adjustment for aggravating or mitigating features, set out on the next page.

Where there is a sufficient prospect of rehabilitation, a community order with a sex offender treatment programme requirement under section 202 of the Criminal Justice Act 2003 can be a proper alternative to a short or moderate length custodial sentence.

Category 1	Starting point 1 year's custody
	Category range 26 weeks' – 2 years' custody
Category 2	Starting point High level community order
	Category range Medium level community order – 1 year's custody
Category 3	Starting point Medium level community order
	Category range Band A fine – High level community order

The table below contains a **non-exhaustive** list of additional factual elements providing the context of the offence and factors relating to the offender. Identify whether any combination of these, or other relevant factors, should result in an upward or downward adjustment from the starting point. **In particular, relevant recent convictions are likely to result in an upward adjustment.** In some cases, having considered these factors, it may be appropriate to move outside the identified category range.

When sentencing **category 2 offences**, the court should also consider the custody threshold as follows:

- has the custody threshold been passed?
- if so, is it unavoidable that a custodial sentence be imposed?
- if so, can that sentence be suspended?

When sentencing **category 3 offences**, the court should also consider the community order threshold as follows:

- has the community order threshold been passed?

Aggravating factors	Mitigating factors
Statutory aggravating factors	No previous convictions or no relevant/recent convictions
Previous convictions, having regard to a) the nature of the offence to which the conviction relates and its relevance to the current offence; and b) the time that has elapsed since the conviction	Remorse
	Previous good character and/or exemplary conduct*
	Age and/or lack of maturity where it affects the responsibility of the offender
Offence committed whilst on bail	
Other aggravating factors	Mental disorder or learning disability, particularly where linked to the commission of the offence
Failure to comply with current court orders	Demonstration of steps taken to address offending behaviour
Offence committed whilst on licence	
Failure of offender to respond to previous warnings	* Previous good character/exemplary conduct is different from having no previous convictions. The more serious the offence, the less the weight which should normally be attributed to this factor. Where previous good character/exemplary conduct has been used to facilitate the offence, this mitigation should not normally be allowed and such conduct may constitute an aggravating factor.
Any steps taken to prevent reporting an incident, obtaining assistance and/or from assisting or supporting the prosecution	
Attempts to dispose of or conceal evidence	

STEP THREE
Consider any factors which indicate a reduction, such as assistance to the prosecution
The court should take into account sections 73 and 74 of the Serious Organised Crime and Police Act 2005 (assistance by defendants: reduction or review of sentence) and any other rule of law by virtue of which an offender may receive a discounted sentence in consequence of assistance given (or offered) to the prosecutor or investigator.

STEP FOUR
Reduction for guilty pleas
The court should take account of any potential reduction for a guilty plea in accordance with section 144 of the Criminal Justice Act 2003 and the Guilty Plea guideline.

STEP FIVE
Dangerousness
The court should consider whether having regard to the criteria contained in Chapter 5 of Part 12 of the Criminal Justice Act 2003 it would be appropriate to award an extended sentence (section 226A).

STEP SIX
Totality principle
If sentencing an offender for more than one offence, or where the offender is already serving a sentence, consider whether the total sentence is just and proportionate to the offending behaviour.

STEP SEVEN
Ancillary orders
The court must consider whether to make any ancillary orders. The court must also consider what other requirements or provisions may automatically apply. Further information is included at Annex A on page 153.

STEP EIGHT
Reasons
Section 174 of the Criminal Justice Act 2003 imposes a duty to give reasons for, and explain the effect of, the sentence.

STEP NINE
Consideration for time spent on bail
The court must consider whether to give credit for time spent on bail in accordance with section 240A of the Criminal Justice Act 2003.

ADMINISTERING A SUBSTANCE WITH INTENT

Sexual Offences Act 2003 (section 61)

Triable either way
Maximum: 10 years' custody

Offence range: 1–9 years' custody

For convictions on or after 3 December 2012 (irrespective of the date of commission of the offence), this is a specified offence for the purposes of section 226A (extended sentence for certain violent or sexual offences) of the Criminal Justice Act 2003.

STEP ONE
Determining the offence category

The court should determine the offence category using the table below.

Category 1	Raised harm and raised culpability
Category 2	Raised harm or raised culpability
Category 3	Administering a substance with intent without raised harm or culpability factors present

The court should determine culpability and harm caused or intended, by reference only to the factors below, which comprise the principal factual elements of the offence. Where an offence does not fall squarely into a category, individual factors may require a degree of weighting before making an overall assessment and determining the appropriate offence category. Where no substantive sexual offence has been committed the main consideration for the court will be the offender's conduct as a whole including, but not exclusively, the offender's intention.

Factors indicating raised harm	Factors indicating raised culpability
Severe psychological or physical harm	Significant degree of planning
Prolonged detention /sustained incident	Specific targeting of a particularly vulnerable victim
Additional degradation/humiliation	Intended sexual offence carries a statutory maximum of life
	Abuse of trust
	Recording of offence
	Offender acts together with others to commit the offence
	Commercial exploitation and/or motivation
	Offence racially or religiously aggravated
	Offence motivated by, or demonstrating, hostility to the victim based on his or her sexual orientation

Factors indicating raised culpability

(or presumed sexual orientation) or transgender identity (or presumed transgender identity)

Offence motivated by, or demonstrating, hostility to the victim based on his or her disability (or presumed disability)

STEP TWO
Starting point and category range

Having determined the category, the court should use the corresponding starting points to reach a sentence within the category range below. The starting point applies to all offenders irrespective of plea or previous convictions. Having determined the starting point, step two allows further adjustment for aggravating or mitigating features, set out below.

A case of particular gravity, reflected by multiple features of culpability or harm in step one, could merit upward adjustment from the starting point before further adjustment for aggravating or mitigating features, set out below.

Category 1	**Starting point**
	6 years' custody
	Category range
	4–9 years' custody
Category 2	**Starting point**
	4 years' custody
	Category range
	3–7 years' custody
Category 3	**Starting point**
	2 years' custody
	Category range
	1–5 years' custody

The table below contains a **non-exhaustive** list of additional factual elements providing the context of the offence and factors relating to the offender. Identify whether any combination of these, or other relevant factors, should result in an upward or downward adjustment from the starting point. **In particular, relevant recent convictions are likely to result in an upward adjustment.** In some cases, having considered these factors, it may be appropriate to move outside the identified category range.

Aggravating factors	Mitigating factors
Statutory aggravating factors	No previous convictions **or** no relevant/recent convictions
Previous convictions, having regard to a) the nature of the offence to which the conviction relates and its relevance to the current offence; and b) the time that has elapsed since the conviction	Remorse
	Previous good character and/or exemplary conduct*
	Age and/or lack of maturity where it affects the responsibility of the offender
Offence committed whilst on bail	
Other aggravating factors	Mental disorder or learning disability, particularly where linked to the commission of the offence
Location of offence	
Timing of offence	Demonstration of steps taken to address offending behaviour
Any steps taken to prevent reporting an incident, obtaining assistance and/or from assisting or supporting the prosecution	
Attempts to dispose of or conceal evidence	
Failure to comply with current court orders	
Offence committed whilst on licence	

* Previous good character/exemplary conduct is different from having no previous convictions. The more serious the offence, the less the weight which should normally be attributed to this factor. Where previous good character/exemplary conduct has been used to facilitate the offence, this mitigation should not normally be allowed and such conduct may constitute an aggravating factor.

STEP THREE
Consider any factors which indicate a reduction, such as assistance to the prosecution
The court should take into account sections 73 and 74 of the Serious Organised Crime and Police Act 2005 (assistance by defendants: reduction or review of sentence) and any other rule of law by virtue of which an offender may receive a discounted sentence in consequence of assistance given (or offered) to the prosecutor or investigator.

STEP FOUR
Reduction for guilty pleas
The court should take account of any potential reduction for a guilty plea in accordance with section 144 of the Criminal Justice Act 2003 and the Guilty Plea guideline.

STEP FIVE
Dangerousness
The court should consider whether having regard to the criteria contained in Chapter 5 of Part 12 of the Criminal Justice Act 2003 it would be appropriate to award an extended sentence (section 226A).

STEP SIX
Totality principle
If sentencing an offender for more than one offence, or where the offender is already serving a sentence, consider whether the total sentence is just and proportionate to the offending behaviour.

STEP SEVEN
Ancillary orders
The court must consider whether to make any ancillary orders. The court must also consider what other requirements or provisions may automatically apply. Further information is included at Annex A on page 153.

STEP EIGHT
Reasons
Section 174 of the Criminal Justice Act 2003 imposes a duty to give reasons for, and explain the effect of, the sentence.

STEP NINE
Consideration for time spent on bail
The court must consider whether to give credit for time spent on bail in accordance with section 240A of the Criminal Justice Act 2003.

COMMITTING AN OFFENCE WITH INTENT TO COMMIT A SEXUAL OFFENCE

Sexual Offences Act 2003 (section 62)

Triable only on indictment (if kidnapping or false imprisonment committed)
—otherwise, triable either way

Maximum: Life imprisonment (if kidnapping or false imprisonment committed)
—otherwise, 10 years

This is a serious specified offence for the purposes of section 224 and, where kidnapping or false imprisonment was committed, section 225(2) (life sentence for serious offences) of the Criminal Justice Act 2003.

For offences committed by kidnapping or false imprisonment, on or after 3 December 2012, this is an offence listed in Part 1 of Schedule 15B for the purposes of sections 224A (life sentence for second listed offence) of the Criminal Justice Act 2003.

For convictions on or after 3 December 2012 (irrespective of the date of commission of the offence), this is a specified offence for the purposes of section 226A (extended sentence for certain violent or sexual offences) of the Criminal Justice Act 2003.

The starting point and range should be commensurate with that for the preliminary offence actually committed, but with an enhancement to reflect the intention to commit a sexual offence.

The enhancement will vary depending on the nature and seriousness of the intended sexual offence, but 2 years is suggested as a suitable enhancement where the intent was to commit rape or assault by penetration.

TRESPASS WITH INTENT TO COMMIT A SEXUAL OFFENCE

Sexual Offences Act 2003 (section 63)

Triable either way
Maximum: 10 years' custody

Offence range: 1–9 years' custody

For convictions on or after 3 December 2012 (irrespective of the date of commission of the offence), this is a specified offence for the purposes of section 226A (extended sentence for certain violent or sexual offences) of the Criminal Justice Act 2003.

STEP ONE
Determining the offence category

The court should determine the offence category using the table below.

Category 1	Raised harm **and** raised culpability
Category 2	Raised harm **or** raised culpability
Category 3	Trespass with intent to commit a sexual offence **without** raised harm or culpability factors present

The court should determine culpability and harm caused or intended, by reference only to the factors below, which comprise the principal factual elements of the offence. Where an offence does not fall squarely into a category, individual factors may require a degree of weighting before making an overall assessment and determining the appropriate offence category. Where no substantive sexual offence has been committed the main consideration for the court will be the offender's conduct as a whole including, but not exclusively, the offender's intention.

Factors indicating raised harm	**Factors indicating raised culpability**
Prolonged detention/sustained incident	Significant degree of planning
Additional degradation/humiliation	Specific targeting of a particularly vulnerable victim
Offence committed in victim's home	Intended sexual offence attracts a statutory maximum of life imprisonment
	Possession of weapon or other item to frighten or injure
	Abuse of trust
	Offender acts together with others to commit the offence
	Commercial exploitation and/or motivation
	Offence racially or religiously aggravated
	Offence motivated by, or demonstrating, hostility to the victim based on his or her sexual orientation (or presumed sexual orientation) or transgender identity (or presumed transgender identity)
	Offence motivated by, or demonstrating, hostility to the victim based on his or her disability (or presumed disability)

> **STEP TWO**
> Starting point and category range

Having determined the category, the court should use the corresponding starting points to reach a sentence within the category range below. The starting point applies to all offenders irrespective of plea or previous convictions. Having determined the starting point, step two allows further adjustment for aggravating or mitigating features, set out below.

A case of particular gravity, reflected by multiple features of culpability or harm in step one, could merit upward adjustment from the starting point before further adjustment for aggravating or mitigating features, set out below.

Category 1	**Starting point**
	6 years' custody
	Category range
	4–9 years' custody
Category 2	**Starting point**
	4 years' custody
	Category range
	3–7 years' custody
Category 3	**Starting point**
	2 years' custody
	Category range
	1–5 years' custody

The table below contains a **non-exhaustive** list of additional factual elements providing the context of the offence and factors relating to the offender. Identify whether any combination of these, or other relevant factors, should result in an upward or downward adjustment from the starting point. **In particular, relevant recent convictions are likely to result in an upward adjustment.** In some cases, having considered these factors, it may be appropriate to move outside the identified category range.

Aggravating factors	Mitigating factors
Statutory aggravating factors	No previous convictions **or** no relevant/recent convictions
Previous convictions, having regard to a) the nature of the offence to which the conviction relates and its relevance to the current offence; and b) the time that has elapsed since the conviction	Remorse
	Previous good character and/or exemplary conduct*
	Age and/or lack of maturity where it affects the responsibility of the offender
Offence committed whilst on bail	Mental disorder or learning disability, particularly where linked to the commission of the offence
Other aggravating factors	
Location of offence	
Timing of offence	Demonstration of steps taken to address offending behaviour
Any steps taken to prevent reporting an incident, obtaining assistance and/ or from assisting or supporting the prosecution	* Previous good character/exemplary conduct is different from having no previous convictions. The more serious the offence, the less the weight which should normally be attributed to this factor. Where previous good character/exemplary conduct has been used to facilitate the offence, this mitigation should not normally be allowed and such conduct may constitute an aggravating factor.
Attempts to dispose of or conceal evidence	
Failure to comply with current court orders	
Offence committed whilst on licence	

STEP THREE
Consider any factors which indicate a reduction, such as assistance to the prosecution
The court should take into account sections 73 and 74 of the Serious Organised Crime and Police Act 2005 (assistance by defendants: reduction or review of sentence) and any other rule of law by virtue of which an offender may receive a discounted sentence in consequence of assistance given (or offered) to the prosecutor or investigator.

STEP FOUR
Reduction for guilty pleas
The court should take account of any potential reduction for a guilty plea in accordance with section 144 of the Criminal Justice Act 2003 and the Guilty Plea guideline.

> **STEP FIVE**
> **Dangerousness**
> The court should consider whether having regard to the criteria contained in Chapter 5 of Part 12 of the Criminal Justice Act 2003 it would be appropriate to award an extended sentence (section 226A).

> **STEP SIX**
> **Totality principle**
> If sentencing an offender for more than one offence, or where the offender is already serving a sentence, consider whether the total sentence is just and proportionate to the offending behaviour.

> **STEP SEVEN**
> **Ancillary orders**
> The court must consider whether to make any ancillary orders. The court must also consider what other requirements or provisions may automatically apply. Further information is included at Annex A on page 153.

> **STEP EIGHT**
> **Reasons**
> Section 174 of the Criminal Justice Act 2003 imposes a duty to give reasons for, and explain the effect of, the sentence.

> **STEP NINE**
> **Consideration for time spent on bail**
> The court must consider whether to give credit for time spent on bail in accordance with section 240A of the Criminal Justice Act 2003.

CHILD SEX OFFENCES COMMITTED BY CHILDREN OR YOUNG PERSONS (SECTIONS 9–12) (OFFENDER UNDER 18)

Sexual Offences Act 2003 (section 13)

SEXUAL ACTIVITY WITH A CHILD FAMILY MEMBER (OFFENDER UNDER 18)

Sexual Offences Act 2003 (section 25)

INCITING A CHILD FAMILY MEMBER TO ENGAGE IN SEXUAL ACTIVITY (OFFENDER UNDER 18)

Sexual Offences Act 2003 (section 26)

Triable either way
Maximum: 5 years' custody

These are 'grave crimes' for the purposes of section 91 of the Powers of Criminal Courts (Sentencing) Act 2000.

For convictions on or after 3 December 2012 (irrespective of the date of commission of the offence), these are specified offences for the purposes of section 226B (extended sentence for certain violent or sexual offences: persons under 18) of the Criminal Justice Act 2003.

Definitive guidelines for the sentencing of offenders under 18 years old are not included.

When sentencing offenders under 18, a court must in particular:
- follow the definitive guideline Overarching Principles – Sentencing Youths;

and have regard to:
- the principal aim of the youth justice system (to prevent offending by children and young people); and
- the welfare of the young offender.

Annex A

Ancillary orders

This summary of the key provisions is correct as at the date of publication but will be subject to subsequent changes in law. If necessary, seek legal advice.

ANCILLARY ORDER	STATUTORY REFERENCE
Compensation The court must consider making a compensation order in any case in which personal injury, loss or damage has resulted from the offence. The court must give reasons if it decides not to make an order in such cases.	Section 130 of the Powers of Criminal Courts (Sentencing) Act 2000
Confiscation A confiscation order may be made by the Crown Court in circumstances in which the offender has obtained a financial benefit as a result of, or in connection with, his criminal conduct.	Section 6 and Schedule 2 of the Proceeds of Crime Act 2002
Deprivation of property The court may order the offender is deprived of property used for the purpose of committing, or facilitating the commission of, any offence, or intended for that purpose.	Section 143 of the Powers of Criminal Courts (Sentencing) Act 2000
Disqualification from working with children From 17 June 2013 courts **no longer** have the power to disqualify offenders from working with children pursuant to the Criminal Justice and Court Services Act 2000.	Schedule 10 of the Safeguarding Vulnerable Groups Act 2006 Safeguarding Vulnerable Groups Act 2006 (Commencement No. 8 and Saving) Order 2012 (SI 2012/2231) Protection of Freedoms Act 2012 (Commencement No. 6) Order 2013 (SI 2013/1180)

ANCILLARY ORDER	STATUTORY REFERENCE
Restraining order Following a conviction or an acquittal, a court may make a restraining order for the purpose of protecting the victim or another person from harassment or a fear of violence.	Sections 5 and 5A of the Protection from Harassment Act 1997
Serious crime prevention order (SCPO) An SCPO may be made by the Crown Court in respect of qualifying offenders, if the court is satisfied such an order would protect the public by preventing, restricting or disrupting the involvement of the offender in serious crime.	Section 19 and Schedule 1 of the Serious Crime Act 2007
Sexual offences prevention order (SOPO) A SOPO may be made against qualifying offenders if the court is satisfied such an order is necessary to protect the public or any particular member of the public from serious sexual harm from the offender. The terms of the SOPO must be proportionate to the objective of protecting the public and consistent with the sentence and other ancillary orders, conditions and requirements to which the offender is subject.	Section 104 and Schedules 3 and 5 of the Seuxal Offences Act 2003

AUTOMATIC ORDERS ON CONVICTION

The following requirements or provisions are **not** part of the sentence imposed by the court but apply automatically by operation of law. The role of the court is to inform the offender of the applicable requirements and/or prohibition.

REQUIREMENT OR PROVISION	STATUTORY REFERENCE
Notification requirements A relevant offender automatically becomes subject to notification requirements, obliging him to notify the police of specified information for a specified period. The court should inform the offender accordingly. *The operation of the notification requirement is not a relevant consideration in determining the sentence for the offence.*	Sections 80 to 88 and Schedule 3 of the Sexual Offences Act 2003
Protection for children and vulnerable adults A statutory scheme pursuant to which offenders *will* or *may* be barred from regulated activity relating to children or vulnerable adults, with or without the right to make representations, depending on the offence. The court should inform the offender accordingly.	Section 2 and Schedule 3 of the Safeguarding Vulnerable Groups Act 2006 Safeguarding Vulnerable Groups Act 2006 (Prescribed Criteria and Miscellaneous Provisions) Regulations 2009 (SI 2009/37) (as amended)

ANNEX B

Approach to sentencing historic sexual offences

Details of the principal offences are set out in the table at Annex C.

When sentencing sexual offences under the Sexual Offences Act 1956, or other legislation pre-dating the 2003 Act, the court should apply the following principles[1]:

1. The offender must be sentenced in accordance with the sentencing regime applicable at the *date of sentence*. Under the Criminal Justice Act 2003[2] the court must have regard to the statutory purposes of sentencing and must base the sentencing exercise on its assessment of the seriousness of the offence.

2. The sentence is limited to the maximum sentence available at the *date of the commission of the offence*. If the maximum sentence has been reduced, the lower maximum will be applicable.

3. The court should have regard to any applicable sentencing guidelines for equivalent offences under the Sexual Offences Act 2003.

4. The seriousness of the offence, assessed by the culpability of the offender and the harm caused or intended, is the main consideration for the court. The court should not seek to establish the likely sentence had the offender been convicted shortly after the date of the offence.

5. When assessing the culpability of the offender, the court should have regard to relevant culpability factors set out in any applicable guideline.

6. The court must assess carefully the harm done to the victim based on the facts available to it, having regard to relevant harm factors set out in any applicable guideline. Consideration of the circumstances which brought the offence to light will be of importance.

7. The court must consider the relevance of the passage of time carefully as it has the potential to aggravate or mitigate the seriousness of the offence. It will be an aggravating factor where the offender has continued to commit sexual offences against the victim or others or has continued to prevent the victim reporting the offence.

8. Where there is an absence of further offending over a long period of time, especially combined with evidence of good character, this may be treated by the court as a mitigating factor. However, as with offences dealt with under the Sexual Offences Act 2003, previous good character/

---

[1] *R v H and others* [2011] EWCA Crim 2753.
[2] Section 143.

exemplary conduct is different from having no previous convictions. The more serious the offence, the less the weight which should normally be attributed to this factor. Where previous good character/exemplary conduct has been used to facilitate the offence, this mitigation should not normally be allowed and such conduct may constitute an aggravating factor.

9. If the offender was very young and immature at the time of the offence, depending on the circumstances of the offence, this may be regarded as personal mitigation.

10. If the offender made admissions at the time of the offence that were not investigated this is likely to be regarded as personal mitigation. Even greater mitigation is available to the offender who reported himself to the police and/or made early admissions.

11. A reduction for an early guilty plea should be made in the usual manner.

ANNEX C

Historic offences

OFFENCE (Sexual Offences Act 1956 unless stated otherwise)	EFFECTIVE DATES	MAXIMUM
Rape and assault offences Rape (section 1)	1 January 1957 – 30 April 2004	Life
Buggery with a person or animal (section 12)	1 January 1957 – 30 April 2004 (from 3 November 1994 non-consensual acts of buggery were defined as rape)	Life 1 January 1957 – 31 December 1960: 2 years
Indecent assault on a woman (section 14)	1 January 1957 – 30 April 2004	1 January 1961 – 15 September 1985: 2 years or 5 years if victim under 13 and age stated on indictment 16 September 1985 onwards: 10 years
Indecent assault upon a man (section 15)	1 January 1957 – 30 April 2004	10 years
Offences against children Sexual intercourse with a girl under 13 (section 5) Life	1 January 1957 – 30 April 2004	
Incest by a male person (section 10)	1 January 1957 – 30 April 2004	Life if victim under 13; otherwise 7 years
Incest by a female person (section 11)	1 January 1957 – 30 April 2004	7 years

OFFENCE (Sexual Offences Act 1956 unless stated otherwise)	EFFECTIVE DATES	MAXIMUM
Gross indecency (section 13)	1 January 1957 – 30 April 2004	Male offender over 21 with male under age of consent: 5 years Otherwise: 2 years 1 January 1961 – 30 September 1997: 2 years
Indecency with a child (section 1 of the Indecency with Children Act 1960)	1 January 1961 – 30 April 2004	1 October 1997 onwards: 10 years *Note: on 11 January 2001 the age definition of a child increased from 14 to 16.*
Incitement of a girl under 16 to commit incest (section 54 of the Criminal Law Act 1977)	8 September 1977 – 30 April 2004	2 years
Abuse of position of trust (section 3 of the Sexual Offences (Amendment) Act 2000)	8 January 2001 – 30 April 2004	5 years
Indecent images Taking indecent photographs of a child (section 1 of the Protection of Children Act 1978)	20 August 1978 – present	20 August 1978 – 10 January 2001: 3 years 11 January 2001 onwards: 10 years
Possession of indecent photographs of a child (section 160 of the Criminal Justice Act 1988)	11 January 1988 – present	11 January 1988 – 10 January 2001: 6 months 11 January 2001 onwards: 5 years

OFFENCE (Sexual Offences Act 1956 unless stated otherwise)	EFFECTIVE DATES	MAXIMUM
Exploitation offences Procurement of woman by threats (section 2)	1 January 1957 – 30 April 2004	2 years
Procurement by false pretences (section 3)	1 January 1957 – 30 April 2004	2 years
Causing prostitution of women (section 22)	1 January 1957 – 30 April 2004	2 years
Procuration of girl under 21 for unlawful sexual intercourse in any part of the world (section 23)	1 January 1957 – 30 April 2004	2 years
Detention in a brothel (section 24)	1 January 1957 – 30 April 2004	2 years
Permitting a defective to use premises for intercourse (section 27)	1 January 1957 – 30 April 2004	2 years
Causing or encouraging prostitution (etc) of a girl under 16 (section 28)	1 January 1957 – 30 April 2004	2 years
Causing or encouraging prostitution of a defective (section 29)	1 January 1957 – 30 April 2004	2 years
Living on earnings of prostitution (section 30)	1 January 1957 – 30 April 2004	7 years
Controlling a prostitute (section 31)	1 January 1957 – 30 April 2004	7 years

OFFENCE (Sexual Offences Act 1956 unless stated otherwise)	EFFECTIVE DATES	MAXIMUM
Trafficking into/ within/out of the UK for sexual exploitation (sections 57 – 59 of the Sexual Offences Act 2003)	1 May 2005 – 5 April 2013	14 years
Offences against those with a mental disorder Intercourse with a defective (section 7) 2 years	1 January 1957 – 30 April 2004	
Procurement of a defective (section 9)	1 January 1957 – 30 April 2004	2 years
Sexual intercourse with patients (section 128 of the Mental Health Act 1956)	1 November 1960 – 30 April 2004	2 years
Other offences Administering drugs to obtain or facilitate intercourse (section 4)	1 January 1957 – 30 April 2004	2 years
Burglary with intent to commit rape (section 9 of the Theft Act 1968)	1 January 1969 – 30 April 2004	14 years if dwelling; otherwise 10 years

ANNEX D

Fine bands and community orders

FINE BANDS

In this guideline, fines are expressed as one of three fine bands (A, B or C).

Fine Band	Starting Point *(Applicable to all offenders)*	Category Range *(Applicable to all offenders)*
Band A	50% of relevant weekly income	25–75% of relevant weekly income
Band B	100% of relevant weekly income	75–125% of relevant weekly income
Band C	150% of relevant weekly income	125–175% of relevant weekly income

COMMUNITY ORDERS

In this guideline, community orders are expressed as one of three levels (low, medium and high).

An illustrative description of examples of requirements that might be appropriate for each level is provided below. Where two or more requirements are ordered, they must be compatible with each other.

LOW	MEDIUM	HIGH
In general, only one requirement will be appropriate and the length may be curtailed if additional requirements are necessary		More intensive sentences which combine two or more requirements may be appropriate

LOW	MEDIUM	HIGH
Suitable requirements might include:	Suitable requirements might include:	Suitable requirements might include:
• 40–80 hours unpaid work;	• appropriate treatment programme;	• appropriate treatment programme;
• curfew requirement within the lowest range (for example, up to 12 hours per day for a few weeks);	• greater number of hours of unpaid work (for example, 80–150 hours);	• 150–300 hours unpaid work;
• exclusion requirement, without electronic monitoring, for a few months;	• an activity requirement in the middle range (20–30 days);	• activity requirement up to the maximum of 60 days;
• prohibited activity requirement;	• curfew requirement within the middle range (for example, up to 12 hours for 2–3 months);	• curfew requirement up to 12 hours per day for 4–6 months;
• attendance centre requirement (where available).	• exclusion requirement, lasting in the region of 6 months;	• exclusion order lasting in the region of 12 months.
	• prohibited activity requirement.	

The *Magistrates' Court Sentencing Guidelines* includes further guidance on fines and community orders.

APPENDIX I

GUIDELINES ON PROSECUTING CASES OF CHILD SEXUAL ABUSE

Issued by the Director of Public Prosecutions on October 17, 2013

Introduction

1. These guidelines are designed to set out the approach that prosecutors should take when dealing with child sexual abuse cases. Experience has shown that these cases bring with them particular issues that differentiate them from other types of case particularly in terms of, for example, a victim's response both to the sexual abuse and the subsequent intervention by the police. These guidelines are intended to cover the range of child sexual abuse, including the abuse referred to as 'child sexual exploitation' and which featured for example in the cases of *R v Safi, Aziz, Hassan and others* ('Operation Span') and *R v Jamil, Dogar, Dogar, Hussain, Karrar, Karrar and Ahmed* ('Operation Bullfinch'). The guidelines are intended to be inclusive and should be applied to cases where a sexual offence has been committed against a child or young person, unless there are good reasons why not in a particular case and these reasons are noted clearly by the prosecutor. The guidelines also include cases of adult victims of sexual abuse in childhood. These guidelines replace the interim guidelines issued on 11 June 2013 and come into immediate effect.

2. The guidelines will on occasion refer to victims as 'she' or 'her'. However, we fully recognise that boys as well as girls can be victims of child sexual abuse and the principles stated below, where relevant, will apply equally to boys as well as girls. Similarly offenders are known to be female as well as male, although it is recognised that the majority of offenders are male.

3. The guidelines should be read in conjunction with other relevant guidance, including the CPS Rape and Sexual Offences (RASO) Legal Guidance which sets out the approach to be taken in cases involving allegations of rape and sexual assault. Of particular relevance are:

- Chapter 2, RASO Legal Guidance, which sets out the principal offences of the Sexual Offences Act 2003;
- Chapter 3, RASO Legal Guidance, which deals with the issue of consent;
- Chapter 21, RASO Legal Guidance, which discusses some of the myths and stereotypes around rape and sexual violence;
- CPS Youth Offenders Legal Guidance, section Sexual Offences and Child Abuse by Young Offenders; and
- Human Trafficking and Smuggling Legal Guidance, which sets out detailed advice on trafficking related issues.

Early consultation between the police and CPS

4. In large or complex child sexual abuse cases there should be early consultation between the police and the CPS. The CPS should be consulted on and informed of the investigation strategy so that early advice can be provided to the police if necessary. The decision to involve the CPS at an early stage is a matter for the police but experience has shown that early CPS involvement can help address some of the evidential or presentational issues that may arise at a later stage of a case.

5. It is important that the police and CPS work closely together and, in more complex cases, joint case review meetings should take place periodically so that progress can be checked and advice on case matters can be given. The frequency and timing of the meetings will be dictated by the size and scale of the investigation and prosecution. However, it is important that these take place so that a strong prosecution case can be built.

How cases will be managed within the CPS

6. The relevant CPS point of contact for the police is the Rape and Serious Sexual Offences (RASSO) Unit in each CPS Area. The RASSO Unit is a specialist prosecutor unit which provides a central point of expertise in the CPS Area and conducts the prosecution of all rape and serious sexual offences cases locally, including child sexual abuse cases.

7. In particular, the local police should be aware of the identity and contact details of the CPS Area Child Sexual Abuse (CSA) lead. The Area CSA lead is based in the Area RASSO Unit. They have an important role as they are specialist rape prosecutors who provide particular expertise, guidance and good practice in child sexual abuse cases. The police are encouraged to use the Area CSA lead as the single CPS point of contact in these cases, at least initially until case ownership is allocated within the RASSO Unit.

8. The Area CSA leads are also part of a national CPS network established to ensure that best practice is shared and overseen by the National CSA lead. The

roles and responsibilities of the National and Area CSA leads can be found at Annex A. The national CPS network will support and play an important role in raising the level of expertise within the CPS to prosecute child sexual abuse cases and support training initiatives in this area. In addition, the DPP has extended the remit of rape advocates on the Advocates Panel to include other sexual offences involving children. This means that advocates prosecuting in court in all child sexual abuse cases will now be specialists and will have had appropriate training.

Context and circumstances of child sexual abuse

9. Child sexual abuse covers a range of offending behaviour and types of offenders (which is defined in more detail in Annex B). It is therefore important that prosecutors have regard to the context and circumstances in which the offending is alleged to have taken place, as this will determine how the evidential case should be built and what are relevant lines of enquiry.

10. There is no one model of child sexual abuse. Sexual abuse of children and young people can be perpetrated by family members, family friends, girlfriends and boyfriends, gangs, 'peer on peer', strangers, adults via the internet and people in positions of trust such as teachers or carers. Institutional sexual abuse may occur in any care, health, religious, or academic setting and may be carried out by an individual or group of individuals. Children who are very young or with special needs may be particularly vulnerable to abuse.

11. Online grooming and abuse can take place through chat rooms and social networking sites and gaming devices which have the ability to connect to the internet. Offenders may target hundreds of children at a time and once initial contact with a child is made this can escalate into threats and intimidation. The online abuse can be an end in itself without any contact offences taking place, but in other cases contact offences can occur.

12. Coercion and manipulation often feature in abusive situations so that the perception of what is happening is sometimes difficult for the child or young person to understand. Offenders may groom not only the child or young person but also their family which can mean that the parent or guardian trusts the offender as a friend of the family or potential boyfriend. Conversely, an offender might make threats to the child or young person or members of their family in order to keep them in an abusive situation.

13. Child sexual abuse comes in a number of different forms. Sexual abuse by coordinated networks is a form of child sexual abuse that has become more prominent recently and is referred to as child sexual exploitation (which is defined in more detail in Annex B). These networks may be informal clusters of people linked through a set of victims or 'friendship' groups or they can be more organised criminal groups or gangs. Children and young people may be groomed

into 'party' lifestyles where they go to houses, flats, hotels and bed and breakfast accommodation with numerous men and other child victims. Sometimes a single relationship may be formed, but in some cases, there is no single relationship and instead a general network exists. The 'parties' are usually organised by adults with young people sometimes being coerced into bringing friends along.

14. Offenders may avoid suspicion by taking victims to be abused only for a short time, or during school hours or returning them home before anyone considers them to be missing or absent. The fact that a victim of abuse is maintaining a seemingly normal routine does not mean that they cannot have been the victim of sexual abuse.

15. Prosecutors should also be aware that offenders may use various control elements as a tool to stop a victim reporting the sexual abuse. For example the control might take the form of threatening to publish photographs or recordings of them, including images of them naked or being abused or threatening harm to the victim and/or their family. The exertion of control could sometimes be through the offender implicating the victim in other criminal activity (e.g. possession of illegal drugs or shoplifting).

16. Another example of the offender exerting control over the victim, which might be particularly relevant to some Black and Minority Ethnic (BME) communities, is that the offender may claim the victim has brought shame on their family and use this as a means of controlling them. In this regard, prosecutors should be aware of the additional cultural barriers that some BME victims might face in coming forward and reporting abuse, as there may be pressure on the victim about what damage such allegations might do to the standing or 'honour' of their family.

Supporting victims and witnesses

17. Victims and witnesses should be made aware from the outset of the investigation exactly what is expected of them, particularly in terms of attending court and giving evidence, and they should be offered support to help them in the process. Support for victims and witnesses can be provided in a number of ways before, during, and after criminal proceedings. It is important that the need for support is identified early and kept under close review during the progress of the case. Prosecutors should proactively raise this matter in case discussions with the police and other relevant agencies so that victims and witnesses are given the best possible support. Where appropriate, parents and guardians should also be made aware from the outset what is expected and the support that can be offered. (It would be inappropriate if a parent or guardian was at the centre of the allegations).

18. It is also important to recognise that since many of the victims and witnesses will be children or young people, the support available before, during and after

trial in court should be explained to them in age appropriate terms (or developmentally appropriate terms) so that they understand what is being discussed and, where possible and appropriate, the parents or guardians are involved and the support available is also discussed with them. It should be noted that this support is distinct and separate from counselling (which is dealt with in paragraphs 32 to 34 below).

19. Some police forces may appoint Family Liaison Officers or officers with a similar role to support victims of child sexual abuse.

Before the court case

20. Children and young people who have been the subject of sexual abuse are likely to require a very high level of support. The police will be responsible primarily for facilitating this, although they will not be responsible for delivering emotional or psychological support. Achieving Best Evidence in Criminal Proceedings - Guidance on interviewing victims and witnesses, and guidance on using special measures (ABE) provides guidelines for pre-trial preparation of young victims and witnesses and should be followed closely. The guidance (re-published in 2011) provides assistance for those responsible for conducting video-recorded interviews with vulnerable and intimidated witnesses as well as those tasked with preparing and supporting witnesses during the criminal justice process.

21. The prosecutor has an important part to play in ensuring that the requisite support is provided and should be asking questions about this from the outset of their involvement in the case. Prosecutors should be aware of the type of support available and, if necessary, should be able to signpost this support to the child or young person (or their parent/carer) via the police officer in the case or the Witness Care Unit, as appropriate.

22. Specialised support is provided by a range of organisations and such support is likely to be essential in ensuring that the child or young person (and where appropriate, their parents or guardian) maintains their engagement with the criminal justice process. Support can be provided by a wide range of agencies both local and national, e.g. Rape Crisis England and Wales, the Survivor's Trust, National Society for the Prevention of Cruelty to Children, and Barnardo's. In some areas, the Witness Service/Victim Support provides a specialist Young Witness Service, and there are also other specialist support services such as Independent Sexual Violence Advisors (ISVAs) that play an important role and should be considered as a vital source of support.

Independent Sexual Violence Advisers

23. ISVAs support victims of rape and sexual violence, including victims of child sexual abuse. They are victim-focused advocates who work with people who have experienced sexual violence, helping them to access the support services that they

may need. They are independent from the police and are distinct from therapists, counsellors and Registered Intermediaries.

24. The support provided by an ISVA will vary from case to case, depending on the requirements of the victim and their particular circumstances. However, the main role of an ISVA includes making sure that victims of sexual abuse have the best possible practical advice on:

- the counselling and other services available to them;
- the process involved in reporting a crime to the police; and
- taking their case through the criminal justice process, should they choose to do so.

25. Prosecutors should know whether ISVAs operate in their area and whether they specifically provide support to victims of child sexual abuse.

Attending court

26. Attendance at court for trial should be discussed in advance with the victim or witnesses (and where appropriate, their parents/guardian) in order that any fears can be addressed, such as being cross examined or being seen entering the court building by the defendants and their associates. Wherever possible, practical arrangements should be made to address the concern, e.g. visits to court to take place in advance of the trial so that the victim can familiarise themselves with the venue and processes involved; and by using entrances and/or using vehicles at the trial itself that facilitate discreet arrival and departure from court. This discussion should take place more than once as the victim or witness may change their mind, or have new concerns, the nearer it gets to the date of the trial.

27. With the approval of the court, a victim or witness can have a supporter present when being cross examined in a live link room for the purposes of providing emotional support to reduce anxiety and distress and improve the accuracy of their recall. The Youth Justice and Criminal Evidence Act 1999, as amended by the Coroners and Justice Act 2009, provides that, when making a live links direction and after taking into account the views of the witness, the court may also direct that a person specified by the court can accompany the person when giving evidence by live link. This person could be, for example, a volunteer from Victim Support or the Witness Service or from a more specialised support service such as the NSPCC or an ISVA. There are also a number of smaller local support services who can also provide effective support and should be considered. Where the trial is taking place in a court some distance away from where the victim or witness usually reside, active consideration should be given as to whether the victim or witness in these circumstances can give evidence by live link from a location nearer to their home.

28. The role of the supporter in the live link room is to provide emotional support and they must have received appropriate training. Victim Support and other support organisations locally may provide this service. The supporter should have a relationship of trust with the witness, should not be a party to, or a witness in, the case and must only have basic information about the case.

29. Supporting and engaging with victims (and where appropriate, their parents/guardian) should continue after the court process has concluded, regardless of the outcome, and is often provided by the relevant support organisations. There may also still be risks to the victim that need to be reduced and managed by the police and other agencies including social services; the victim may still be at risk of further exploitation by others.

Keeping victims and witnesses informed

30. The Code of Practice for Victims of Crime (the Victims' Code) sets out the minimum standard of service and aims to ensure that victims of crime are provided with timely, accurate information about their case at all stages of the criminal justice process. Prosecutors should be aware of these minimum obligations.

31. The nature and sensitivity of child sexual abuse cases will inevitably mean that prosecutors (and the police) should go beyond the minimum requirements of the Victims' Code where appropriate to do so, and this should be agreed, recorded and actioned by the prosecutor and the police in the case.

Counselling and therapy

32. The CPS guidance Provision of Therapy for Child Witnesses Prior to a Criminal Trial is clear that the best interests of the victim or witness are the paramount consideration in decisions about therapy. There is no bar to a victim seeking pre-trial therapy or counselling and neither the police nor the CPS should prevent therapy from taking place prior to a trial. Prosecutors should be familiar with the content of the CPS guidance on pre-trial therapy so that they can advise police and witnesses on the correct approach.

33. Providers of counselling or therapy should ensure that records are kept and that the child or young person (and if relevant, parents or guardian) is advised at the start of the process that there may be a requirement to disclose the fact that counselling has taken place, particularly if detail of the alleged offending is raised. Experience over a number of years has shown that properly conducted and recorded counselling or therapy has not caused problems with the criminal trial process. Where the therapist or counsellor is known to the investigation, they should be briefed at an early stage to inform them about the court process and their disclosure obligations.

34. Prosecutors have a duty to disclose the fact that a victim has undergone therapy or counselling and to disclose any other matter which is determined by the usual tests as to whether it is relevant to an issue in the case. This is part of the continuing duty on the CPS to disclose.

The statement taking stage

35. Particular care should be given when deciding how to take the victim's statement. A video recorded interview (and subsequent use of the live link in court) is often the most appropriate means but may not always be so. For example, if the abuse of the victim has been filmed and the victim does not want to be videoed as a consequence.

36. Practical matters to consider when visually recording a victim's interview include ensuring that there is a close shot of the head and shoulders of the witness, even if slightly side on, rather than from a distance where facial characteristics are too remote. Consideration should also be given, if possible, to a second camera showing the witness's more general body language.

37. The assistance of a Registered Intermediary should be considered at this stage. They can help the victim give their account in the interview and understand what is being asked of them. The earlier the intervention the more likely it is that successful rapport building will take place and the child or young person will be able to give their best evidence. Even if the victim appears to understand, they are unlikely to be familiar with the terms sometimes used in questions posed in interviews, or may not understand a term in the same way as the interviewer, and an Intermediary can ensure that age appropriate language (or developmentally appropriate language) is used and terms are explained.

38. A victim of child sexual abuse may not give their best and fullest account during their first recorded (ABE) interview or statement. This may be for a variety of reasons: they could have been threatened; they might be fearful for themselves or their family; the offending may have been reported by others and they may be reluctant to cooperate at that stage. They might not have identified themselves as a victim or they could be fearful that the police will not believe their allegations. They may initially distrust the police and could well use the interview to test the credibility of the police.

39. The account given may take a number of interviews, with the child or young person giving their account piecemeal, sometimes saving the 'worst' till last, having satisfied themselves that they can trust the person to whom they are giving their account.

40. Carefully thought out patient intervention by the police and other agencies can ultimately disrupt and break the link to the offender(s). A seemingly contradictory initial account is therefore not a reason in itself to disbelieve subsequent accounts

given by the victim and these contradictory accounts should instead be seen as at least potentially symptomatic of the abuse.

41. The police must inform the victim of their right to make a Victim Personal Statement (VPS) and it would be appropriate to do this at the statement taking stage. Whether and when to make a VPS is a decision for the victim, and it is therefore important that police clearly explain the purpose of the VPS and the way in which it will be used (i.e. that it will be disclosed to the defence, may be read out or played in court and could be reported on in the media). It should also be made clear that if the victim does not wish to make a VPS at the time they give their evidential statement, they may make a VPS later. Careful consideration should be given to when and how to take the VPS, taking into account the issues highlighted in paragraphs above, including talking to the parents or guardian if appropriate.

Telling a victim about other allegations

42. There is no rule which prevents victims being told that they are not the only ones to have made a complaint of abuse. If such a rule existed, and it was taken to its logical conclusion, it would mean that any victim who came forward having learned about offences committed against others could never pursue his or her own complaint.

43. In terms of enabling a child or young person to give an account of what has occurred to them, they can be told, in very general terms, that the suspect has been the subject of complaints by others. Doing so may strengthen their resolve to continue their engagement with the criminal justice process.

44. In most circumstances this should only be done after the victim's statement has been given or a video interview has taken place. However, in exceptional circumstances, and with the authorisation of a police officer of at least Super-intendent rank, this may take place before the statement has been given or a video interview has taken place if it is considered to be necessary in all the circumstances of the case.

45. However, the details of the other allegations should not be disclosed and a careful record should be kept of what the child or young person has been told.

46. Informing a victim of the existence of other allegations of a similar nature or proactively contacting a potential victim based on a clear intelligence assessment (e.g. they are known to associate with the suspect) is very different to what is sometimes referred to as 'trawling'.

47. The term 'trawling' is used in this context to describe the process whereby the police contact potential victims even though they have not been named in any of the statements given in the course of the investigation and there is little if any

intelligence to suggest the individual might be a potential victim. Such a process should be avoided because of the risk that it may give rise to false allegations. For example, in some cases involving allegations of abuse in a care home, it had been police practice years ago to contact all, or a significant proportion of, those who had been resident in the institution at the time that the offences were alleged to have taken place, rather than taking an intelligence-led approach towards identifying potential victims. This practice of "trawling" was criticised heavily in court and led to a number of cases collapsing, but contacting potential victims on a firm intelligence or evidence led basis is not prevented.

The credibility or reliability of a child or young person

48. When assessing the credibility of a child or young person, police and prosecutors should focus on the credibility of the allegation, rather than focussing solely on the victim.

49. A number of factors have previously militated against some children and young people being regarded as credible victims of sexual abuse. These include:

- the offence was not reported immediately after its commission;
- the account given was inconsistent;
- the victim 'voluntarily' returned to the alleged abuser;
- the victim has a learning disability or mental illness;
- the victim is perceived as consenting to sexual activity;
- the victim has previously told untruths about other matters; and,
- the victim has been, or is, abusing drink or drugs.

50. These factors have tended to be seen as undermining the credibility of the victim's account. However, these factors may, in fact, point the other way and could be seen as supporting the allegations of sexual abuse, not least because the behaviour set out above are often seen in victims of abuse. Police and prosecutors should therefore look to build a case which looks more widely at the credibility of the overall allegation rather than focusing primarily on the credibility and/or reliability of the child or young person.

51. A victim's circumstances or experiences will often influence their actions and it is important that prosecutors have an understanding of these issues. Victims of sexual abuse may have a chaotic background or lifestyle and they may not display the 'usual' behaviours that one might expect from a victim of a sexual offence. They may crave love and affection and wrongly attribute such feelings to their abuser. They may develop an allegiance to their abuser as a consequence and not consider themselves to be the victim of any type of sexual abuse. They might initially refuse to identify as a 'victim' of abuse, believing that they were in a genuine, loving and non-abusive relationship.

52. The victim may be reluctant to co-operate with those in authority or to participate in the criminal justice process. Inconsistent accounts are not uncommon in victims of child sexual abuse, especially during initial interviews, possibly because of an 'allegiance' to their abuser. The length of time between an alleged incident of sexual abuse and giving the account to the authorities is not a reliable indication of credibility.

53. Children or young people who have been in the care of, or have come to the attention of, social services will inevitably have a great deal of information about them contained within social services records compared to other children or young people. Every episode of 'bad' behaviour, even of the most minor nature, is likely to be a matter of record. Most children misbehave; but not every child has their misbehaviour recorded. Victims who are, or have been, in the care of the social services should not be disadvantaged in the criminal process by this fact, and prosecutors should be prepared to address this issue as part of the presentation of the prosecution case.

54. All of these factors must be taken into account and understood by prosecutors when reviewing allegations of child sexual abuse. Prosecutors must also have an understanding of the consequences faced by a child if they say 'no' to their abuser and this should form part of the prosecution strategy to address perceived weaknesses or anomalies in the victim's account.

55. Prosecutors should also have regard to whether there is any credible third party evidence to suggest that the complainant has malicious intent to make a false allegation. However, prosecutors should guard against looking for 'corroboration' of the victim's account or using the lack of 'corroboration' as a reason not to proceed with a case.

56. Prosecutors must check with the police and the CPS Case Management System (CMS) to see whether there are any pending allegations involving the same victim or suspect(s). A note that this has been done should form part of the formal review. If there are pending allegations then the details should be obtained to see if there are any links or similarities to the on-going case.

Identifying children who may be at risk of sexual exploitation

57. In 2012, the Office of the Children's Commissioner in England (OCCE) began an enquiry into child sexual exploitation in gangs and groups. The interim report of this enquiry (I thought I was the only one, the only one in the world) outlines a list of vulnerabilities which may be present in children prior to abuse and a further list of signs and behaviours generally seen in children who are already being sexually exploited. Prosecutors should consider whether the victim whose evidence they are considering demonstrates any of these factors. Whilst the absence of any of these characteristics does not mean that an allegation of exploitation is unlikely to be true, their presence may assist the prosecutor in

forming an overall view in the case. The OCCE listed the following (pages 51-52 in the interim report, November 2012):

Typical vulnerabilities in children prior to abuse

- living in a chaotic or dysfunctional household (including parental substance use, domestic violence, parental mental health issues, parental criminality);
- history of abuse (including familial child sexual abuse, risk of forced marriage, risk of 'honour' based violence, physical and emotional abuse and neglect);
- recent bereavement or loss;
- gang association either through relatives, peers or intimate relationships (in cases of gang associated child sexual exploitation only);
- attending school with young people who are sexually exploited;
- learning disabilities;
- unsure about their sexual orientation or unable to disclose sexual orientation to their families;
- friends with young people who are sexually exploited;
- homeless;
- lacking friends from the same age group;
- living in a gang neighbourhood;
- living in residential care;
- living in hostel, bed and breakfast accommodation or a foyer;
- low self-esteem or self-confidence;
- young carer.

The following signs and behaviour are generally seen in children who are already being sexually exploited

- missing from home or care;
- physical injuries;
- drug or alcohol misuse;
- involvement in offending;
- repeat sexually-transmitted infections, pregnancy and terminations;
- absent from school;
- change in physical appearance;
- evidence of sexual bullying and/or vulnerability through the internet and/or social networking sites;
- estranged from their family;
- receipt of gifts from unknown sources;
- recruiting others into exploitative situations;
- poor mental health;
- self-harm;
- thoughts of or attempts at suicide.

Merits-based approach

58. As in all cases you must apply the test prescribed by the Code for Crown Prosecutors, namely that there is sufficient evidence to provide a realistic prospect of conviction and a prosecution is required in the public interest. The 'merits-based approach' reminds prosecutors of how to approach the evidential stage of the Code test in that even though past experience might tell a prosecutor that juries can be unwilling to convict in cases where, for example, there has been a lengthy delay in reporting the offence, or the complainant had been drinking at the time the rape was committed. These sorts of prejudices against complainants should not be regarded as determinative for the purposes of deciding whether or not there is a realistic prospect of conviction.

59. In other words, the prosecutor should proceed on the basis of a notional jury which is wholly unaffected by any myths such as, for example, were an allegation really true it would have been reported at the time. The prosecutor must further assume that the jury will faithfully apply directions from the judge, such as the fact that they can still convict even where it is one person's word against another's without any supporting evidence.

Previous convictions of the child/young witness

60. Some victims of child sexual abuse may have previous convictions which, on the face of it, may cast doubt upon their reliability as a witness of truth. Robust enquiries should be made of the police about the circumstances of the offending before coming to any conclusion about the truthfulness or otherwise of the witness testimony.

61. Prosecutors are encouraged to look beyond the previous offending by the victim and consider the drivers and circumstances of the offending behaviour. Victims may sometimes commit what is called 'survival crime',

i.e. committing crime to find safety or committing crime to ensure justice. An example of this is damaging property belonging to the offender or an associate. Offending might also be a reaction to the abuse which a child or young person is suffering, i.e. externally expressing their internal trauma. The victim may also have committed an offence whilst under the influence of the abuser and this may be used by the abuser as a means of controlling the victim and deterring them from making a complaint about the abuse they are experiencing.

62. Full details of a victim's previous convictions will be required from the police including:

- type of offence;
- location of offence;
- who they were with, e.g. other young people or adults significantly older than them;

- what explanation they gave to the police at the time of arrest or in interview; and
- any other relevant circumstances.

63. A child or young person may even have played a role in procuring others who are then abused. In past cases there is evidence that this may have been as a direct consequence of violence, threats or coercion or because they were in a vulnerable situation and put in considerable fear. In such circumstances, careful thought must be given as to the role, if any, that child or young person plays in any potential prosecution.

64. It will be an essential part of the prosecution case to provide an explanation to the jury about the circumstances of any relevant offending by the witness, rather than it being put to the witness in the course of any cross examination.

Assessing the credibility of child abuse allegations: circumstances of the suspect

65. In child sexual abuse cases, the circumstances of the suspect need to be considered as intensely as the reliability of the complainant. Prosecutors should have regard to the following non-exhaustive list of evidential considerations:

- are there any relevant antecedents in respect of the suspect
- is there relevant police intelligence about the suspect in their local area or elsewhere;
- has the suspect been the recipient of a child abduction warning notice (formerly known as the 'harbourer's warning') in relation to the victim in this case or any other child and young person;
- is it likely that the suspect will have come into contact with the victim through the position or employment held by the suspect or the victim's lifestyle;
- has the suspect been the subject of any other allegations of sexual abuse whether these have resulted in a conviction or not. In many abuse cases, there is often more than one victim and inquiries should be made as to whether there are further victims;
- are there credible third party accounts supporting the allegations against the suspect or any other allegations made against the suspect;
- is there any credible evidence showing the suspect in contact with the victim (e.g. CCTV, texts, social media);
- does the suspect associate with others suspected of committing similar offences;
- does the suspect have indecent images of children (e.g. on personal computer, mobile phone etc).

66. It is important that the prosecutor checks that the suspect's account has been investigated by the police in interview or through gathering further evidence. The

questioning should ascertain whether the suspect deliberately targeted a victim's vulnerability and should disclose what their motivation was. If the suspect confirms that they know the victim, the prosecutor should ensure that the nature of the suspect's relationship with the victim is investigated by the police. This should include assessing whether the suspect is able to give a credible account of how and why they know the victim.

67. An early account should be taken from the suspect and the possibility of having to wait a significant period of time for comprehensive expert medical statements should not prevent an arrest taking place and an early explanation from the suspect.

Other case building issues

68. In some cases, the first complaint may not be from the victim but from a concerned individual. The case may need to be built against the suspect before an account is obtained from the child or young person.

69. Child sexual abuse can involve certain patterns of behaviour; a police officer may be presented with an apparently minor issue which in isolation may not cause concern but which is actually a pattern of abuse. It is also possible that concerns about individual children that on the face of it are unconnected are in reality part of a pattern of abuse by either the same offender or different but connected offenders. Concerns about one child or young person may also raise concerns about other children or young people with whom the suspect has contact. Identifying such patterns depends upon careful, accurate and co-ordinated record keeping by the police and other agencies and also upon prosecutors being alert to the issue and asking the right questions.

70. Partner agencies (e.g. social services, voluntary sector and other local support services) and, if appropriate, parents or carers, should be encouraged to involve the police as early as possible to ensure that information critical to a prosecution case is not lost. It is vital that information is gathered and collated even in cases where the child or young person has not made a formal complaint. In many cases, the process of supporting a child or young person to recognise the exploitative nature of their relationship with the offender will be lengthy. By the time the child's account is given, crucial information could be lost or destroyed unless there is a strategy of evidence gathering from the outset.

71. Other types of evidence that should be gathered to help build a case before the child or young person gives a statement include: obtaining DNA evidence, including from clothing seized; obtaining mobile phone evidence; CCTV footage; car number plate recognition; house searches; and early consideration of directed or intrusive surveillance. The possibility of information coming from house to house enquiries should not be overlooked. Neighbours may well not have seen anything first hand but they could be a useful source of other information about

the wider context. Other useful information could be obtained from friends of the victims and their peer group especially about the wider context.

72. In cases where the victim makes an initial allegation and then becomes uncooperative, a conventional investigation may be difficult. However, a review of the intelligence held by the police on any suspect(s) may be sufficient for a proactive operation to be commenced.

Offending patterns/behaviour of the offender

73. People who abuse are not bound by geographic boundaries. Offenders may move victims from one place to another to be sexually exploited. The young victim may not know where they are when the abuse takes place. They may agree to travel between different locations and there may not be any coercion for them to do so.

74. Moving children and young people around may be part of a deliberate strategy by offenders to prevent any single police force from obtaining a complete picture of the offending behaviour. The fact that a child or a young person is taken to an unfamiliar location can also make it harder for them to identify the time, date and location of the abuse.

75. Young people under 18 cannot consent to being moved for the commission of a relevant offence under the Sexual Offences Act 2003. The fact of the movement and the intent are sufficient for the offence to be proved. In these circumstances, as well as relevant 'contact offences', prosecutors should consider charges under section 58 of the Sexual Offences Act 2003. Fuller guidance on human trafficking and the associated set of issues is set out in the Legal Guidance on Human Trafficking and Smuggling.

Case presentation in court

76. For the reasons outlined above, the ABE interview process may be lengthy and the account by the victim may be given over a number of interviews, with the fullest account not being given until the final interview. The ABE interview is primarily an investigative tool but is also required for evidential purposes, but sometimes this dual purpose can cause presentational difficulties at court. Prosecutors should be familiar with police ABE procedures and mindful of the need for a clear and focused ABE interview to be presented at the trial. This will often mean that careful editing is required, and this should be done by the police and prosecutor as soon as is reasonably practical. (An unedited version of the videoed interview is disclosed to the defence unless Public Interest Immunity considerations apply).

Myths and stereotypes raised in court

77. It is very important that prosecutors use their best endeavours to ensure that 'myths and stereotypes' about child sexual abuse are challenged in court. For

example, by ensuring that they are addressed in Counsel's opening speech to the jury, by challenging Defence Counsel, by adducing expert evidence where appropriate, or by asking the judge to give specific directions to the jury.

78. The Crown Court Bench Book sets out specimen directions for use by judges in the Crown Court. Chapter 17 The Trial of Sexual Offences addresses myths, stereotypes and generalisations that may influence jury members in their deliberations. Trial advocates should take the lead in suggesting to the judge appropriate directions from the Bench Book for inclusion in his or her summing up.

79. At Annex C, a number of common myths and stereotypes surrounding this type of offending have been set out including the basis for rebutting them.

Defence case statement

80. Following service of initial disclosure by the prosecution, the time limit for service of a defence statement and service of the details of any defence witnesses is 14 days in the magistrates' court and 28 days in the Crown Court, unless that period has been extended by the court.

81. The defence statement gives a valuable opportunity for the prosecution to confirm or rebut defence allegations and it is likely to point the prosecution to other lines of inquiry, for example, the investigation of an alibi, or where forensic expert evidence is involved.

82. Where there is no defence statement, or it is considered inadequate, the prosecutor should contact the defence indicating that further disclosure will not take place or will be limited (as appropriate) and inviting them to specify or clarify the defence case. Where the defence fails to respond, or refuses to clarify the defence case, the prosecutor should consider raising the issue at a pre-trial hearing to invite the court to give a statutory warning under section 6E(2) of the Criminal Procedure and Investigation Act 1996.

Special measures

83. There is separate CPS Legal Guidance on Special Measures which sets out the full range of measures that can be applied for to the court. By virtue of their age, children are automatically eligible for special measures, although the measures will not automatically be available at trial. An application for special measures needs to be made by the party calling the witness. The decision as to whether the special measure applied for is granted is a matter for the court.

84. Prosecutors should discuss with the police, and consider carefully, which, if any, of the special measures should be used. The views of the victim (and where appropriate, their parents/guardian) should be taken into account as well as the type of offending alleged. Prosecutors should actively raise the issue of special

measures with the police if there is not a note of a discussion with the victim (and where appropriate, their parents/guardian) and also ensure that the measures requested are kept under close review as the date of the trial approaches.

85. We have referred to Registered Intermediaries in paragraph 37 above in respect of being involved at the interview stage with the victim. Intermediaries should be considered in all cases of child sexual abuse, not just those involving very young witnesses, and if not involved earlier in the case, they should still be actively considered in advance of the trial as a means of supporting the victim giving evidence in court. Children and young people do not approach communication in the same way as adults and ability across all age ranges can vary considerably.

86. Registered Intermediaries can be crucial in enabling witnesses to give their best evidence both at statement taking/interview stage and during the court process. If an Intermediary has not been used at the interview stage but communication needs are identified at the review stage this does not mean that they cannot be instructed for the court process. However, it is preferable for the need for a Registered Intermediary to be identified early in the process so that there is sufficient time for rapport building to take place.

> "The use of intermediaries has introduced fresh insights into the criminal justice process. There was some opposition. It was said, for example, that intermediaries would interfere with the process of cross examination. Others suggested that they were expert witnesses or supporters of the witness. They are not. They are independent and neutral. They are properly registered. Their responsibility is to the court . . . their use is a step which improved the administration of justice and it has done so without a diminution in the entitlement of the defendant to a fair trial."

> The Rt. Hon. The Lord Judge, Lord Chief Justice of England and Wales, 7 September 2012, speaking at the 17th Australian Institute of Judicial Administration Conference on 'Vulnerable Witnesses in the Administration of Criminal Justice'.

87. Registered Intermediaries fulfil a different role and purpose to that of a witness 'supporter' and the two roles should not be conflated.

88. Further, more detailed, information can be found in the CPS Special Measures: Intermediaries (including their engagement) Legal Guidance.

Support given to victims and witnesses in court

89. Comprehensive advice can be found on all aspects of case management and preparation for vulnerable victims and witnesses in the Advocates' Gateway and prosecutors should read and be familiar with its content, along with the Judicial College Bench Checklist for Young Witness Cases.

90. Prosecutors should assist the courts to ensure that effective timetabling and case progression of child sexual abuse cases takes place. Cases involving children

or young people should be heard as soon as possible, with delay for child victims kept to 'an irreducible minimum' (Part 3D General Matters of the Criminal Practice Directions 2013). Young witnesses should not be kept waiting at court and should know that the time given to attend court is when they give evidence so that they are not kept waiting around.

91. Trial dates should not be vacated unless this is absolutely unavoidable. This includes avoiding any last minute changes in Prosecution Counsel because of the disruption it can cause to victims and witnesses. If a change of Counsel does happen, it should only take place where it is unavoidable (for example, illness).

92. Ground rules hearings about cross examination in court are recommended in any young witness trial but required in any intermediary cases. This includes the defence agreeing who will be the lead counsel to put questions to the victim in cases with more than one defendant and the length of time given to the cross examination. The ground rules hearings should take place in advance of the day of the trial so that everyone, particularly the victim, is aware of what to expect and how long the proceedings in court should take. Prosecutors are reminded of rule 3.10 of the Criminal Procedure Rules that states:

Conduct of a trial

3.10—In order to manage a trial or appeal the court —

a) must establish, with active assistance of the parties, what are the disputed issues
b) must consider setting a timetable that—
    i) takes account of those issues, and of any timetable proposed by a party, and
    ii) may limit the duration of any stage of the hearing
c) may require a party to identify—
    i) which witness that party wants to give evidence in person
    ii) the order in which that party wants those witnesses to give their evidence
    iii) whether the party requires an order compelling the attendance of a witness
    iv) what arrangements are desirable to facilitate the giving of evidence by a witness
    v) what arrangements are desirable to facilitate the participation of any other person including the defendant
    vi) what written evidence that parties intend to introduce
    vii) what other material, if any, that person intends to make available to the court in the presentation of the case, and
    viii) whether the party intends to raise any point of law that could effect the conduct of the trial or appeal; and
d) may limit—

    i) the examination, cross-examination or re-examination of a wit-
ness, and

    ii) the duration of any stage of the hearing.

Prosecutors should also assist the court in dealing with questioning of the victim or witness.

93. The Court of Appeal has addressed restrictions on cross examination:

- where there is a risk of a child acquiescing to leading questions (*R v B* [2010] EWCA Crim 4); and
- on 'putting your case' to a child (*R v Wills* [2011] EWCA Crim 1938 and *R v E* [2011] EWCA Crim 2028).

As the Court of Appeal observed in Wills:

> "Some of the most effective cross-examination is conducted without long and complicated questions being posed in a leading or 'tagged' manner."

94. Where limits are 'necessary and appropriate', the Court of Appeal in Wills stated that:

- limitations on questioning must be clearly defined;
- the judge has a duty to ensure that limitations are complied with;
- the judge should explain limitations to the jury and reasons for them;
- if the advocate fails to comply with limitations, the judge should give relevant directions to the jury when that occurs; and
- instead of commenting on inconsistencies during cross-examination, the advocate/judge may point out important inconsistencies after (instead of during) the witness's evidence, following discussion with the advocates. The judge should be alert to alleged inconsistencies that are not in fact inconsistent, or are trivial.

95. As set out in paragraphs 92 to 94 above, in multiple defendant cases the judge should be asked to consider whether repeat cross examination on similar points should be restricted. Being accused of lying, particularly if repeated, may cause the witness to give inaccurate answers or to agree simply to bring questioning to an end. It may also have a longer term damaging impact on the child or young person. If such a challenge is essential, it should be addressed separately, in simple language, at the end of cross examination.

Adult victims of childhood sexual abuse

96. Some victims of sexual abuse may not feel confident or strong enough to report until many years after the abuse has taken place, and often not until they are adults. This delay in reporting can be for a wide range of reasons, but many of the same considerations for child victims will also apply to adults who were victims of

sexual abuse in their childhood, particularly around assessing the credibility of the overall allegation and the need for effective and proactive case-building.

97. Prosecutors should be mindful of the potential for severe re-traumatisation faced by some victims. The process of giving an account of the abuse may cause flashbacks where an adult finds themself in the same emotional state as when the sexual abuse took place and with the resilience and understanding of a child of that age. Consistent and effective support should be provided including keeping under constant review whether there is a need for counselling and special measures.

98. It is recognised that some adult victims of childhood sexual abuse may suffer severe mental health problems as a result of their experience and may never be able to give evidence in court. However, it should not be overlooked that they may have important information which might be of assistance in supporting the account given by other victim(s) against the same offender(s).

Witnesses who withdraw support for the prosecution or indicate that they are no longer willing to give evidence

99. Chapter 5 of the CPS Rape and Sexual Offences Legal Guidance deals with this issue in detail. In child sexual abuse cases, prosecutors must ensure that the reason for a victim's ostensible retraction is thoroughly investigated by the police before a decision about how to proceed is made. Prosecutors must be sure that the victim (and where appropriate, their parents/guardian) has had special measures and reporting restrictions (see the CPS Legal Guidance Contempt of Court and Reporting Restrictions) explained to them thoroughly and in an age-appropriate way (or developmentally appropriate), as this may influence their decision to continue with the process.

100. Particular regard should be had to the highly organised nature of some offenders who will go to great lengths to ensure that if witness intimidation takes place it is several steps removed from them.

Criminal and family proceedings

101. Cases which involve criminal proceedings and family proceedings, together with their respective investigations, taking place either simultaneously or with some degree of overlap, can present challenges for the different agencies concerned. See Annex D for further information.

102. Proceedings in the Family Courts begin when a statutory body, usually the Local Authority, initiate care proceedings in relation to one or more children within a family unit. Such an application is usually based on the belief that the child or children have or are likely to suffer significant harm as a result of child abuse in one or more of the following: physical abuse; sexual abuse; emotional abuse; or neglect.

103. In any of the above circumstances, a child or children can be removed from the family under emergency powers conferred by either section 44 or 46 of the Children Act 1989.

104. In cases relating to the use of section 44 and 46, it is then the responsibility of the Local Authority under section 47 of the Children Act to make, or cause to be made, such enquiries as they consider necessary to enable them to decide what action they should take to safeguard or promote the child's welfare. This action is commonly known as a 'section 47 investigation' and in the majority of cases, will take the form of a joint enquiry conducted by both police and social workers from the Local Authority Children's Services, with police concentrating on the criminal aspect of the enquiry.

105. If a child is removed into police protection under section 46, then a maximum period of 72 hours is permitted before they must be returned to the family or an application is made to the Family Court for an 'emergency protection order' (EPO) under section 44 in order that further enquiries can be carried out as above. The EPO has effect for a period not exceeding 8 days, including any time already spent under police protection; although it can be extended once for a maximum of 7 days.

106. On expiration of this period, an application can be made to the Family Court for a care order under section 31. Once care proceedings are issued, a first hearing will take place within three days at which the court may make an interim care order. It is then the responsibility of the court to draw up a timetable with a view to disposing of the application for a care order without delay.

Role of the police and CPS in Family Proceedings

107. When family proceedings are instituted to decide on the most appropriate care plan for any child or children subject to the proceedings, a number of preliminary hearings take place, followed in the latter stages by a fact finding hearing and a final determination hearing. It is likely that each 'party' to the proceedings will be represented.

108. Parties to family proceedings are those who have an immediate claim to the care of the child, usually each parent and the Local Authority who have placed the child in care. A children's guardian, appointed by the court to represent a child's best interests, is also a party to the proceedings. Others can, on application to the court, become parties to the proceedings, or an 'intervener', such as potential carers or grandparents. However it is important to note that alleged perpetrators of sexual abuse are sometimes joined as parties or interveners and that where findings are sought in family proceedings against an alleged perpetrator that person is invited routinely by the family court to be so joined. They can be non-family members but are commonly also family members or partners of family members.

109. The focus in the Family Courts is on establishing the facts and achieving the most appropriate outcome for the child, not on the prosecution of the alleged abuser.

110. Therefore, despite the fact that police might be conducting a parallel criminal investigation into the actions of one or more of the parties against a child (or a sibling) who is the subject of the family proceedings, neither the police nor the CPS are parties to the family proceedings.

111. It would neither be appropriate nor desirable for the police or CPS to be present throughout family proceedings. Many aspects of the hearings would be irrelevant to the criminal investigation and contempt issues may arise if the police or CPS make use in the criminal proceedings of material arising in the Family Court proceedings without the permission of the Family Court.

112. If an alleged abuser were to incriminate himself/herself during the course of the family proceedings they would have the benefit of protection from prosecution by virtue of section 98(2) of the Children Act 1989, whereby a statement or admission made in such proceedings is not admissible against the person making it or his spouse in criminal proceedings (other than for an offence of perjury).

113. Prosecutors should note that the protection in section 98(2) does not extend to the criminal investigation. The police may put relevant statements and admissions to a suspect in interview. If adopted by the suspect, the statements/admissions are admissible in criminal proceedings (subject to the usual provisions of sections 76 and 78 of the Police and Criminal Evidence Act 1984). Similarly, putting inconsistent statements made in Family Court proceedings to a defendant in cross examination in the criminal case should not be contrary to section 98 of the Children Act 1989.

Third party material

114. Chapter 4 of the Disclosure Manual sets out the procedure to be adopted with reference to third party material. It is highly likely that many child sexual abuse cases will involve and require access to third party material when building the evidential case.

115. The following are examples of third party material which may be relevant: medical notes; social services/Children's Services material; education notes; counselling/therapy notes; information or evidence arising in parallel family/civil proceedings; or information kept by voluntary sector organisations.

116. Investigators are under a duty to pursue all reasonable lines of enquiry, whether these point towards or away from a suspect. Reasonable lines of enquiry may include enquiries as to the existence of relevant material in the possession of a third party, for example, the Local Authority.

117. If the third party declines or refuses to allow access to it, the matter should not be left. If, despite any reasons put forward by the third party, it is reasonable to seek production of the material or information and the requirements of section 2 of the Criminal Procedure (Attendance of Witnesses) Act 1965 are satisfied, then prosecutors should apply for a witness summons requiring a representative of the third party to produce the material to the court.

118. Third party material should be sought at an early stage, preferably pre charge, and sufficient time should be set aside to receive and process third party material, especially in particularly large or complex cases. The material may contain information that could enhance and strengthen the prosecution case.

Protocol with the Local Authority

119. Prosecutors and investigators should handle requests for Local Authority material in accordance with any applicable local or national protocol. The protocol will ensure that the Local Authority makes disclosure to the police and CPS to the full extent permitted by law (taking into account the common law of confidentiality, the Data Protection Act 1998 and the Family Procedure Rules 2010, see Annex E). The Local Authority will make all relevant material available to the police at the earliest opportunity, or provide reasons why certain material (listed but not described) is not being made available, for example because it is related to Family Court proceedings.

120. The police will take copies of all relevant Local Authority material which will then be scheduled for the CPS on the schedule of sensitive unused material. Where any of the material meets the Criminal Procedure and Investigations Act test for disclosure to the defence, the prosecutor should consult with the Local Authority before disclosure is made. There may be public interest reasons which justify withholding disclosure to the defence and which would require the issue of disclosure of the information to be placed before the court. However, following the decision of the House of Lords in *R v H & C* [2004] 2 AC 134, applications for public interest immunity will be rare. Prosecutors should make disclosure in summarised or redacted form where this is possible.

Obtaining material relating to Family Court proceedings

121. Relevant material might include statements and admissions made in the Family Court proceedings by defendants and witnesses in the criminal case, or might include expert testimony in the Family Court proceedings. There are a number of ways in which prosecutors will become aware of the existence of relevant material relating to Family Court proceedings. For example:

- The police may have obtained the material from the Local Authority (or elsewhere) in line with their duties of child protection. Note that, in these circumstances, the police cannot share the material with the CPS (nor can they share with the CPS the information on which documentation is based) without the permission of the Family Court. The police have to simply alert the CPS to the fact that relevant Family Court material exists.

- In accordance with the terms of a local or national protocol, the Local Authority may have alerted the CPS to the existence of relevant material relating to Family Court proceedings.

122. Prosecutors and investigators will determine whether to apply to the Family Court for permission to access such relevant material. Protocols may provide a streamlined process for making the application to the court; and may provide for the Local Authority to make the application on behalf of the police and CPS; or for the Family Court to make an order for disclosure without the need for an application. Any application to the Family Court should make it clear that the material might need to be shared with the defence and (subject to section 98 of the Children Act 1989) used in evidence.

123. The Family Procedure Rules 2010 provide that the text of summary of a judgment in Family Court proceedings can be disclosed to the police and CPS without the permission of the court. The Local Authority (or others) can disclose to the police and CPS documents which are lodged at the Family Court, or used in the proceedings which already existed.

124. A local or national protocol may provide for linked directions hearings at which directions in concurrent criminal and Family Court proceedings can be made jointly by the same judge. Directions will include disclosure of material between the two jurisdictions, timetabling of the respective proceedings and the coordination of the use of expert witnesses.

Information sharing between agencies

125. Working Together to Safeguard Children—A guide to inter-agency working to safeguard and promote the welfare of children (2013) provides guidance about sharing information about children in England (and there is separate similar guidance applicable in Wales). In deciding whether there is a need to share information, professionals need to consider their legal obligations, including whether they have a duty of confidentiality. Where there is such a duty, the professional may lawfully share information if consent is obtained or if there is a public interest of sufficient weight. Where there is a clear risk of significant harm to a child, the public interest test will almost certainly be satisfied. Lack of consent to share information is irrelevant where there is a clear concern about a risk of harm to the child or young person.

126. Prosecutors must be proactive in highlighting to police officers information which is of concern to them. If it is not possible to prosecute a case, but information available causes concern to the prosecutor, they should ensure that

this is brought to the attention of the relevant investigating police officers, so that they can in turn share this with the relevant agencies including Local Authorities.

127. Prosecutors who receive relevant cases from the police should check with the police that they have complied with their statutory duties to share information with Local Authorities and any other relevant bodies. CPS case files should not be closed until this confirmation is received.

128. In addition to applying the above information sharing principles, prosecutors and investigators will need to ensure that disclosure does not prejudice the criminal investigation and prosecution. Material disclosed to the Local Authority will be shared with all parties to the Family Court proceedings and the parties are likely to include the defendant(s) and witnesses in the criminal case. The Local Authority may be able to secure a Family Court order prohibiting onward disclosure to named individuals, i.e. defendants and witnesses in the criminal case. Alternatively, it may be possible to delay disclosure of prosecution material to the Local Authority until a later date (although, other than in exceptional circumstances, the existence of criminal proceedings is not reason to adjourn Family Court proceedings). Prosecutors should consult with the police where the request for disclosure of prosecution material is made to the police.

Crown Prosecution Service
17 October 2013

ANNEX A

National Child Sexual Abuse lead

The National Child Sexual Abuse (CSA) lead will:

- oversee the national CSA Network drawing on their expertise in high profile CSA casework;
- encourage good practice and offer best practice guidance in CSA cases via the CSA Network;
- develop close relations with partner agencies, in particular with ACPO;
- liaise and work closely with CPS Headquarters to develop and disseminate good practice and identify aspects for improvement and issues for concern; and
- attend and play a leading part in the CSA review panel.

Area Child Sexual Abuse lead

The Area CSA lead will:

- meet the criteria set out in the standard for rape specialist prosecutors;
- act as an Area source of expertise, guidance and good practice for colleagues both locally and nationally dealing with child sexual abuse cases;
- be an initial single point of contact for police forces and other relevant agencies in their Area providing general advice and guidance in CSA cases;
- establish liaison with police CSA lead officers in order to review and develop local investigative practice;
- attend local partnership CSA strategic meetings to develop criminal justice improvements for victims and witnesses;
- maintain a CSA caseload;
- liaise and work closely with CPS Headquarters to develop and disseminate good practice and identify aspects for improvement and issues for concern;
- produce brief six monthly reports for the Director as part of the bi-annual VAWG Assurance collated through VAWG Coordinators;
- ensure that an Area overview of CSA investigations and prosecutions is maintained to include information about ethnicity, age, gender and offences where practicable;

- work closely with, and assist in training, the police and relevant voluntary sector agencies in relation to general good practice and procedure in relation to CSA cases;
- be a member of the national CPS CSA network, attending training events and seminars as required and maintaining regular dialogue with other CSA leads; and
- attend the CSA review panel when invited.

ANNEX B

Child / Children / Young Person

Anyone who has not yet reached their 18th birthday. The fact that a child has reached 16 years of age, is living independently or is in further education, is a member of the armed forces, is in hospital or in custody in the secure estate, does not change his/her status or entitlement to services or protection.

Abuse

A form of maltreatment of a child. Somebody may abuse or neglect a child by inflicting harm, or by failing to prevent harm. Children may be abused in a family or in an institutional or community setting by those known to them or, more rarely, by others (e.g. via the internet). They may be abused by an adult or adults, or another child or children.

Child sexual abuse

Involves forcing or enticing a child or young person to take part in sexual activities, not necessarily involving a high level of violence, whether or not the child is aware of what is happening. The activities may involve physical contact, including assault by penetration (for example, rape or oral sex) or non-penetrative acts such as masturbation, kissing, rubbing and touching outside of clothing. They may also include non-contact activities, such as involving children in looking at, or in the production of, sexual images, watching sexual activities, encouraging children to behave in sexually inappropriate ways, or grooming a child in preparation for abuse (including via the internet). Sexual abuse is not solely perpetrated by adult males. Women can also commit acts of sexual abuse, as can other children.

Child sexual exploitation

There is no specific offence of child sexual exploitation (CSE); it is defined in government guidance and policy in this way:

> 'The sexual exploitation of children and young people under 18 involves exploitative situations, contexts and friendships where young people (or a third person or persons) receive 'something' (e.g. food, accommodation, drugs, alcohol, cigarettes, affection, gifts, money) as a result of performing, and/or others performing on them, sexual activities.

'Child sexual exploitation can occur through the use of technology without the child's immediate recognition, for example the persuasion to post sexual images on the internet/mobile phones with no immediate payment or gain. In all cases those exploiting the child/young person have power over them by virtue of their age, gender, intellect, physical strength and/or economic or other resources.

'Violence, coercion and intimidation are common, involvement in exploitative relationships being characterised in the main by the child or young person's limited availability of choice resulting from their social/economic and/or emotional vulnerability.'

CSE can involve a broad range of exploitative activity, from seemingly 'consensual' relationships and informal exchanges of sex for attention, accommodation, gifts or cigarettes, through to very serious organised crime. Young people do not always receive something tangible in return for sexual activities; the promise of something or apparent love and affection may be all that they receive.

The police should know the nature, extent and type of offending they are investigating and will be expected to indicate whether they consider a case involves CSE. However, prosecutors also have a duty to identify potential CSE cases even if the police have omitted to do so. For example, often a case starts with one suspect and one victim in one location but if properly investigated may grow to meet the CSE criteria.

Grooming

'Grooming' is not a specific form of child sexual exploitation but should be seen as a way in which perpetrators target children and manipulate their environments. It is an approach to exploitation and may be the beginning of a complex process adopted by abusers. Grooming can be defined as developing the trust of a young person or his or her family in order to engage in illegal sexual activity or for others to engage in illegal sexual activity with that child or young person.

ANNEX C

Myths and Stereotypes

It is very important that prosecutors use their best endeavours to ensure that 'myths and stereotypes' about child sexual abuse are challenged in court. If they are left unchallenged, it may lead to members of the jury approaching the victim's evidence with unwarranted scepticism.

This Annex lists some of the more common myths and stereotypes and the basis for why they should be challenged. It should be stressed that the list below is non-exhaustive.

(a) The victim invited sex by the way they dressed or acted

This is an attempt to excuse the rape or sexual assault and blame the victim. It assumes that a child or young person who attracts attention by their dress or manner is looking for sex and excuses the behaviour of the abuser. A child or young person under 16 can never consent to sex whatever the circumstances.

(b) The victim drank alcohol or used drugs and she was therefore available sexually

This is an attempt to excuse the abuser of rape or sexual assault and blame the victim. It assumes that as the child or young person was drunk or under the influence of drugs they were willing sexual partners. An adult is unable to consent to sex if they are drunk, drugged or unconscious, and a child or young person under 16 can never consent to sex whatever the circumstances.

(c) The victim didn't scream, fight or protest and so it can't be sexual assault

It implies the victim is not telling the truth and invalidates the experience of the victim. Also, a child may experience a 'freeze' response to trauma meaning they become incapable of responding in an active way. It does not take account of how the victim's behaviour may have been influenced by threats whether real or perceived, or how manipulative techniques might have been used by the abuser to intimidate or control the victim. A child or young person under 16 can never consent to sex whatever the circumstances.

(d) If the victim didn't complain immediately it wasn't sexual assault

It implies the victim is not telling the truth and invalidates the experience of the victim. It does not take account of how the victim's behaviour may have been influenced by threats whether real or perceived, or how manipulative techniques might have been used by the abuser to intimidate or control the victim. A child or young person under 16 can never consent to sex whatever the circumstances.

In addition, the trauma can cause feelings of shame and guilt which might inhibit a victim from making a complaint. This was recognised by the Court of Appeal in *R v D (JA)* [2008] EWCA Crim 2557, where it was held that judges are entitled to direct juries that due to shame and shock, victims of rape might not complain for some time, and that "a late complaint does not necessarily mean it is a false complaint".

(e) A victim in a relationship with the alleged offender is a willing sexual partner

A child or young person under 16 can never consent to sex whatever the circumstances. It invalidates the experience of the victim and it does not take account of how the victim's relationship may have been influenced by threats whether real or perceived, or how manipulative techniques might have been used by the abuser to intimidate or control the victim. The grooming process can actively distort understanding of consent and is often used for that purpose. Feelings of powerlessness and fatalism are common amongst victims.

(f) A victim who has been sexually assaulted will remember events consistently

It implies the victim is not telling the truth and invalidates the experience of the victim. It also fails to take account of how children and young people do not have the same standards of logic, understanding and consistency as adults do. They will not have the same experience of life as adults and are less sophisticated in their understanding of what has happened. A child may not fully understand the significance of activity which is sexual and this may be reflected in how they remember or describe it. A child is very likely to have a different perception of time to that of an adult. Also the process by which memories are laid down during a traumatic event may impact on issues such as consistency. A child's memory can fade and their recall of when and in what order events took place may not be accurate. A child may not be able to speak of the context in which the events took place, and this may include having particular difficulty with conceptual questions as to how they felt some time ago, or why they did or did not take a particular course of action.

(g) Parents should know what is happening to the victim and be able to stop it

This is an attempt to excuse the abuser of rape or sexual assault and place the blame on the victim's parents. Parents may be unable to identify what is happening. Even if they suspect that something is not right, they may not be in a position to stop it due to the control over the victim exercised by the abuser. There can also be risks to parents when seeking to protect their child and they can need support as well as the child.

(h) Children and young people can consent to their own sexual exploitation

This is an attempt to excuse the abuser of rape or sexual assault and blame the victim. A child or young person under 16 can never consent to sex whatever the circumstances. A child or young person under 18 cannot consent to being trafficked for purposes of their own exploitation. Regardless of age, a person is unable to consent to sex if they are drunk, drugged or unconscious.

(i) Sexual exploitation only happens in large towns and cities

Sexual exploitation is a form of child sexual abuse and can happen anywhere and it is not confined to particular towns or cities. Children and young people can be trafficked between different areas of the country for the purpose of exploitation.

(j) It only happens to teenage girls by adult men

Sexual abuse and exploitation is not limited to teenage girls by adult men. The victims may be either boys or girls and victims are not limited to any particular age and can include very young children. The abusers can include peers the same age of the victim, and sometimes peers, even if not directly perpetrating rape or sexual assault, can be used to 'recruit' other children and young people to take them to locations where they are introduced to adult abusers.

(k) The victim is usually living in a care home away from their family

There are different types of child sexual abuse and exploitation and victims come from all parts of society. The victim could be living in a care home, but often the victim is living at home with their parents and family. Many children are living at home when their abuse begins. Children who grow up in loving and secure homes may also be vulnerable to child sexual exploitation if they live in a gang-affected neighbourhood, have a friend who is being sexually exploited, or go to a school where other children have been sexually exploited.

(l) Sexual exploitation is only perpetrated by certain ethnic/cultural communities

Perpetrators of sexual exploitation come from a range of different backgrounds and it is not restricted to one ethnic or cultural community. There is more than one type of perpetrator, model and approach to child sexual exploitation by gangs and groups. It invalidates the experience of victims abused by perpetrators from other backgrounds and risks such abuse being overlooked. What all perpetrators have in common, regardless of the differences in age, ethnicity, or social background, is their abuse of power in relation to their victims.

(m) It only happens to girls and young women

Boys and young men are also at risk of sexual abuse and exploitation. It implies the boy or young man is not telling the truth and invalidates the experience of the victim. A child or young person under 16 can never consent to sex whatever the circumstances.

(n) Sexual abuse and exploitation does not happen to children and young people from Black and Minority Ethnic (BME) backgrounds

Victims of child sexual abuse and exploitation come from a range of ethnic backgrounds and are not restricted to just one ethnicity. What is common to all victims is their powerlessness and vulnerability, not their age, ethnicity, disability or sexual orientation. It implies that children and young people from BME backgrounds are not telling the truth and invalidates their experience. It also risks such abuse being overlooked.

(o) Children who are being abused will show physical evidence of abuse

Research shows that genital injuries are the exception even in cases where the abuse has been proven. Even where an injury is sustained it may heal very quickly.

Child Protection systems in England and Wales

Child Protection in England is the overall responsibility of the Department for Education which issues guidance to local authorities. The most recent guidance, issued in March 2013, is Working Together to Safeguard Children. Local Safeguarding Children's Boards (LSCBs) use this guidance to produce their own procedures that should be followed by practitioners and professionals who come into contact with children and their families in their local authority area. Wales has the All Wales Child Protection Procedures which provides Local Safeguarding Children Boards with a single set of procedures and a range of protocols from which they all work.

In many cases of child sexual abuse, there will be social services involvement, often prior to any police involvement. In brief this will involve one, or all, of the following steps:

1 A referral to local authority children's social care, which can come from the child themselves, teachers, a GP, the police, health visitors, family members and members of the public.

2 An assessment taking place to establish whether the child requires immediate protection and urgent action is required; or, the child is in need and should be assessed under section 17 of the Children Act 1989; or, there is reasonable cause to suspect that the child is suffering, or likely to suffer, significant harm, and whether enquiries must be made and the child assessed under section 47 of the Children Act.

3 If there is a risk to the life of a child or a likelihood of serious immediate harm, local authority social workers, the police or NSPCC must use their statutory child protection powers to act immediately to secure the safety of the child. If the child is identified as being in need, a social worker should lead a multi-agency assessment under section 17. Where information gathered during an assessment results in the social worker suspecting that the child is suffering or likely to suffer significant harm, the local authority should hold a strategy discussion to enable it to decide, with other agencies, whether to initiate enquiries under section 47.

For the purposes of the multi-agency assessments, the police should assist other agencies to carry out their responsibilities where there are concerns about the child's welfare, whether or not a crime has been committed. If a crime has been committed, the police should be informed by the local authority children's social care.

For the purposes of the strategy discussion, the police must discuss the basis for any criminal investigation and any relevant processes that other agencies might need to know about, including the timing and methods of evidence gathering; and lead the criminal investigation where joint enquiries take place. The local authority children's social care has the lead for the section 47 enquiries and assessment of the child's welfare.

Social services involvement will potentially generate a great deal of information which police and prosecutors should make enquiries about. The enquiry should not be from the standpoint of looking for material to undermine the child or young person. There may be material which could enhance and strengthen the prosecution case.

All prosecutors who review child sexual abuse cases should have a good working knowledge of the legislative requirements and expectations on individual services to safeguard and promote the welfare of children. Prosecutors should also be aware of the 2013 Protocol and Good Practice Model in respect of Disclosure of information in cases of alleged child abuse and linked criminal care directions hearings.

Annex E

Family Procedure Rules Part 12

Practice Direction 12A is a key piece of guidance for prosecutors. It sets out the Public Law Proceedings Guide to Case Management: April 2010, incorporating the Public Law Outline 2010 (PLO). Where there are parallel criminal and care proceedings, it is vital that prosecutors understand the timetables and processes of the Family Court.

The Practice Direction sets out the stages (Issue and First Appointment; Advocates' Meeting and Case Management Conference; Advocates' Meeting and Issues Resolution Meeting; Final Hearing) and the timescales involved. The PLO forms to be used include information of relevance to prosecutors, such as the Local Authority Case Summary, Draft Case Management Order, Timetable for the Child/Children, Standard Directions, disclosure etc.

Practice Direction 12A states at paragraph 3.9: 'Where there are parallel care proceedings and criminal proceedings against a person connected with the child for a serious offence against the child, linked directions hearings should where practicable take place as the case progresses. The timing of the proceedings in a linked care and criminal case should appear in the Timetable for the Child.'

PLO Form 4 makes specific reference to parallel criminal proceedings.

The Timetable for the Child

The Timetable for the Child includes not only legal steps but also social care, health and education steps. Due regard is paid to the Timetable to ensure that the court remains child focussed throughout the progress of the proceedings and that any procedural steps proposed under the PLO are considered in the context of significant events in the child's life.

The expectations are that the proceedings should be finally determined within the timetable fixed by the court in accordance with the Timetable for the Child. The timescales in the PLO being adhered to and being taken as the maximum permissible time for the taking of the step referred to in the Outline, unless the Timetable for the Child demands otherwise.

Prosecutors should ensure that they are aware of the Timetable. They will need to provide information regarding criminal proceedings dates/events and, equally, they should take the contents of the Timetable into account when contributing to their own case management procedures in the criminal proceedings. For example, where a trial appears likely it should not simply be a matter of witness availability, but information should be obtained concerning significant steps in the child's life that are likely to take place during the proceedings (such as exams, revision, special events, Family Court proceedings, etc) and efforts should be made to fix the trial date accordingly.

Such an approach should help both the family court and the criminal court to work in synchronisation in the interests of justice and the welfare of the child.

Other matters of relevance to prosecutors

Case Management Orders will include orders relating to the disclosure of documents into the proceedings held by third parties, including medical records, police records and the disclosure of documents and information relating to the proceedings to non-parties.

The court may give directions without a hearing.

Where facilities are available to the court and the parties, the court will consider making full use of technology including electronic information exchange and video or telephone conferencing.

Communication of Information Practice Direction 12G

Practice Direction 12G sets out what information can be communicated to third parties -including the police and CPS. The tables from the old rules (Part X, Rules 11.2 -11.9 of the Family Proceedings [Amendment] [No. 2] Rules 2009, which include the Family Proceedings Rules 1991) are restated.

In essence, a party in family proceedings or any person lawfully in receipt of information can give 'the text or summary of the whole or part of a judgment given in the proceedings' to a police officer for the purposes of a criminal investigation or to a member of the CPS 'to enable the Crown Prosecution Service to discharge its functions under any enactment.'

Apart from the judgment, there may also be information contained in family court case papers that would be relevant to the criminal case, such as: previous consistent or inconsistent statements of witnesses or defendants; evidence of similar incidents; material for bad character applications; or medical reports/ medical expert evidence. Disclosure and use of such documents is restricted.

The Rules permit the communication of information relating to the proceedings (whether or not contained in a document filed with the court) not only where the court gives permission, but also where communication is to (amongst others) 'a professional acting in furtherance of the protection of children', which is defined as including a police officer who is exercising powers under section 46 of the Children Act 1989 (removal and accommodation of children in an emergency) or is serving in a child protection unit or a paedophile unit of a police force, or a professional person attending a child protection conference or review in relation to a child who is the subject of proceedings to which the information relates.

Information or documentation communicated as above 'in furtherance of the protection of children' cannot be communicated to CPS without the express permission of the Family Court.

APPENDIX J

R. v CED

No.2012/02824 B4

Court Of Appeal (Criminal Division)

November 15, 2012

[2012] EWCA Crim 2593

Before: Lord Judge Chief Justice, Mr Justice Simon and Mr Justice Wilkie,
November 15, 2012

Representation

Miss K Scrivener appeared on behalf of the Applicant.

Mr K Barker appeared on behalf of the Crown.

Judgment

The Lord Chief Justice:

1 On 13 April 2012 in the Crown Court at Exeter before His Honour Judge
Cottle and a jury the applicant was convicted of offences involving sexual
activity with a child: on counts 1 to 6, gross indecency; and on count 7 indecent
assault. He was sentenced to a term of seven and a half years' imprisonment.
Appropriate further orders were made which have no bearing on the present
proceedings. His application for leave to appeal against conviction has been
referred to the full court by the Registrar.

2 The complainant was the applicant's adopted daughter. She was adopted at
the age of 7. The prosecution case was that he sexually abused her from the age
of 7 until she was about 14. The abuse generally took the form of making the
girl masturbate him or perform oral sex on him, although there was one specific

incident when she awoke to find him performing oral sex on her. Such activity occurred frequently during trips in his lorry when he would take the complainant along with him to accompany him. She reported the abuse to the police in 2010 in the context of an unrelated investigation.

3 The defence case was that the allegations were untrue; there had never been any occasion when the child had been sexually abused by the applicant. The evidence of other witnesses who testified in support of her complaint was also and equally untrue.

4 The question for the jury was clear: were the allegations, or may they have been, fabricated? We need not recite the evidence further.

5 The issue which arises in this application relates to the jury. The jurors were sworn in the usual way. We assume that they were given the standard directions about the way in which they should face up to their responsibilities.

6 Shortly after the prosecution began to open its case, a juror passed a note to the usher who handed it on to the judge. The note read:

> "I was raped at 20 years old, but not reported it. I'm not sure if I can be totally biased."

The juror plainly meant "unbiased". We need not record the name of the juror who sent the note.

7 Having had his attention drawn to the note, the judge stopped the case and invited the jury to leave court. The juror who had written the note was separated from the others and a discussion then took place with counsel. Having listened to counsel briefly, the judge said that he could not make any assumptions about the thought processes of the juror; all he had was the note in front of him which "obviously raised an important question" for him to resolve one way or another. His inclination was to see whether the juror could give him a complete assurance that she could address the issues in the case in an unbiased way. After further discussion with counsel, the juror was invited into court. By that stage the court had been cleared of everybody who had no professional interest in the proceedings.

8 We have studied the transcript of what then happened. The judge made it clear that there would be no investigation whatever by him into the first part of the note (the reference to the juror having been raped). He focused on the second part of the note. First, he explained that the issue was whether or not the accusation made against the defendant was true. Then he said to the juror:

> "What I require from you, if you are able to give it to me, is your complete assurance that you would be able to address that issue in an unbiased way. .... That is the question to which I need an answer before I make a decision." (our emphasis)

Although the transcript records the juror's response as "inaudible", it is clear from the rest of the transcript that she said "I believe I can". She must have said that in a very low voice because it is not only the transcript that records "inaudible", but Judge Cottle responded by saying "You believe you?" She then responded—and again, although the transcript records her answer as inaudible, it is common ground, and derived from the transcript later—"I believe I can". The judge said:

> "You have been thinking about it since you have been out of the room, I expect. I do need your complete assurance that you can approach this case in an open-minded way and make a decision that is conscientiously based on the evidence that you will hear in the course of this case. That is what I require.
>
> THE JUROR: I will.
>
> JUDGE COTTLE: You will. All right."

The judge then commented that she had given him a complete assurance. That was as much as he could ask, but certainly what he required. The juror left court and the judge said:

> "The impression that I gained from even a short discussion with this juror is that she strikes me as being an extremely conscientious, reflective, thoughtful individual whose immediate response to hearing what this case was about was to write this note expressing her concern. She has had a little time in which to think about it. She has grasped what I require from her by way of an assurance and has given me that."

There was then a short discussion with counsel during which the judge said:

> " . . . if I was in any doubt about her ability to be completely open-minded I would not have her continue on this jury."

Accordingly the juror returned to join the remaining jurors and the jury returned to court in its original constitution and the case proceeded. Evidence was given in the usual way and, following the judge's directions to the jury and his summing-up, the applicant was convicted.

9 The application for leave to appeal against conviction is based on a single ground. Miss Scrivener submits that the juror should have been discharged; there was at least a risk that she would be biased, whether consciously or unconsciously, against the applicant, and any reasonable, fair-minded observer sitting in court would have concluded that there was a real possibility of bias. It is, of course, trite law that an impartial tribunal—and a tribunal from which the perception of bias is excluded are essential concomitants of a fair trial. The principle applies to each juror as well as to any judge sitting on his or her own.

10 It is for the judge to control the proceedings at trial. Among the other matters for which he is responsible, there is the supervision and, if necessary, control of the jury, which entitles him as a matter of judgment in an appropriate case to discharge the whole jury or, indeed, an individual juror, and to do so on the basis of actual bias, or perceived bias, or the possibility that the reasonable, fair-minded observer would conclude that there was such a real possibility. At the same time a judge is entitled to reflect on the anxieties of a troubled juror; and he is entitled, where necessary, to give advice, reassurance and encouragement to such a juror. It is legitimate for him to do so. There are balancing considerations when he has to decide whether a juror should or should not be discharged.

11 But what are the facts here? This juror chose to write a note to the judge rather than, as she may very well have done without any danger of her sensitive predicament becoming known, to remain silent. It is clear that she approached her responsibilities, and her anxiety to do unbiased justice to the defendant, with the utmost seriousness. That is the only conclusion that can be drawn from the very fact that she wrote the note about something as sensitive as the fact that she had been a victim of rape when she was 20 years old. The judge examined the information. He satisfied himself that the juror would and could approach the issues in a fair, unbiased way. There was, therefore, no reason to discharge her.

12 We do not agree with the submission that the juror was, in effect, led into expressing something that did not truly reflect her actual state of mind. There was no need to discharge the juror because she had been a victim of crime, even if the crime was of a similar, if not identical, sexual nature. That is not a requirement of the principle of a fair trial. We must not, and do not, assume that a victim of crime will somehow be less committed to the principles which govern trial by jury than any other of its potential or actual individual members.

13 This application fails on both grounds. Our system permits someone who has been the victim of a crime to sit on a jury. The judge made the necessary enquiries to satisfy himself that the juror could deal with her responsibilities in the fair, unbiased way which is required.

14 Accordingly, the application is refused.

INDEX

(All references are to paragraph number)